Louis H. Rappaport, a retired partner of Lybrand, Ross Bros. & Montgomery, served as his firm's National Director of Accounting, Auditing, and SEC Services, and specialized in the SEC aspects of the firm's practice for over three decades. Mr. Rappaport is a Certified Public Accountant in New York, Pennsylvania, Illinois, Louisiana, Michigan, Ohio, Missouri, and West Virginia. Mr. Rappaport's column on the SEC and accounting practice was long a regular feature of the *New York Certified Public Accountant*.

S E C
ACCOUNTING PRACTICE
AND PROCEDURE

LOUIS H. RAPPAPORT, C.P.A.

LYBRAND, ROSS BROS. & MONTGOMERY

THIRD EDITION

THE RONALD PRESS COMPANY · NEW YORK

Library of Congress Catalog Card Number: 78–183439
PRINTED IN THE UNITED STATES OF AMERICA

To
M.C.R.

PREFACE

Like its predecessors, this Third Edition is designed as a guide to the financial reporting requirements—both formal and informal—of the Securities and Exchange Commission. These requirements have a direct bearing on the day-to-day activities of public accountants, corporate officials, investment bankers, and brokers and dealers in securities. Investment analysts and lawyers practicing in the SEC field also have a vital interest in the SEC's requirements relating to financial reporting.

The past nine years have seen unprecedented and far-reaching changes in SEC practice. The changes are the outgrowth of new legislation, new and revised rules and regulations promulgated by the SEC, litigation growing out of the securities laws, new interpretations and rulings by the Commission's staff, and the increasing activity of the Accounting Principles Board and Committee on Auditing Procedure of the American Institute of Certified Public Accountants.

Of these many changes, the revisions in Regulation S–X governing the form and content of financial statements to be filed with the SEC, are of paramount importance. One key revision has eliminated the provision that financial statements of banks need not be audited by independent public accountants. Another has made it mandatory that financial statements filed with the SEC include a statement of the source and application of funds. More important, however, was the major revision in 1972 of the Regulation—the first such revision in twenty years. This will result in public disclosure of a material amount of additional critical information, such as the amount of a company's advertising expenses and its expenditures for research and development, which have been closely guarded by many corporations in the past.

Probably the most significant of the new SEC requirements are those relating to disclosure of the operating results of each of the principal lines of business in which publicly-owned companies are engaged—an eventuality that most companies have resisted for years. Line-of-business reporting is not required within the financial statements, per se, and does not have to be certified by independent auditors. Accountants should be thoroughly familiar with the requirements, however, since their advice and help will be sought in preparing the needed information.

Few developments have had as profound an effect on accountants practicing in the SEC field as the issues and implications inherent in the growing volume of litigation. These have been so many and so consequential—

resulting in the issuance by the AICPA Committee on Auditing Procedure of new Statements concerning after-acquired information and comfort letters for underwriters—that two chapters have been necessary to deal with accountants' liabilities.

As in earlier editions, this book makes use of numerous illustrative examples demonstrating how the myriad requirements for SEC filings have been complied with in actual practice. The sources drawn on in the preparation of the book include all of the published SEC decisions, reports, and releases, and the Commission's annual reports to Congress, as well as important informal unpublished sources, chief among which are the deficiency letters resulting from the staff's review of registration statements and reports.

In addition to my own three decades of experience in this field, I have also benefited from the experience of my partners and associates. My firm's research staff have been most helpful in bringing to my attention unusual treatments of financial items resulting from their continuing review of current prospectuses. Thus this book reflects the suggestions of many individuals. Nevertheless, the responsibility for the views expressed is mine alone.

LOUIS H. RAPPAPORT

Ridgefield, Conn.
June, 1972

ACKNOWLEDGMENTS

One of the pleasures in writing a book of this kind is to acknowledge the assistance I have received from my partners, associates, and others. In this respect I have been most fortunate, for although the book indicates that I am the sole author, I am deeply indebted to many people for their assistance in many capacities.

Extensive portions of the manuscript were critically reviewed by Dr. Leopold A. Bernstein, by my partners, Donald F. Moran, Samuel A. Sakol, and Glenn O. Petty, and by Marshall W. Samuels, of my firm's research staff. Their views and comments were most helpful. In addition, Messrs. Moran, Sakol, and Petty participated in the research and in the drafting of portions of the text—particularly in the areas of the problems of foreign issuers, litigation, accounting changes, accountants' independence, pro forma financial statements, and business combinations.

Several sections of the manuscript were also reviewed by my partners, James J. Quinn and Fred S. Spindel, and by Paul M. Foster, consultant to my firm's SEC Review Board. Each of them had many constructive comments and suggestions, to most of which I have given effect. Mr. Quinn has done a considerable amount of writing in the SEC field, and I have borrowed liberally from his writings in the areas of comfort letters and review of proxy materials.

In writing this book, I also received many suggestions from my partners, William J. McHugh, Marvin L. Baris, Louis C. Moscarello, Victor F. St. Thomas, Robert W. Davis, Edmund A. Staub, and James D. McMenamin. Also, Ernest C. Janson, Jr., Alvin J. Mentzel, John R. Berthoud, George H. Kern, John K. S. Arthur, Edward J. Premo, Robert W. Egner, Thomas W. McKibben, Lloyd A. Schwartz, William R. Richards, John J. Mulcare, Glenn E. Wabel, John E. Hart, John W. Kennedy, Jr., David V. Burgett, Richard W. Russell, William P. Tellini, Peter R. Scanlon, and Frederick J. Wonsetler.

In addition, I have had the benefit of consulting with other partners, including Philip L. Defliese, Kenneth P. Johnson, and Norman E. Auerbach.

The portions of the book dealing with the programs for review of unaudited financial statements for the purpose of underwriters' comfort letters were reviewed and updated by my partners, Reed L. Colegrove, Eugene M. Freedman, and Bradley H. Green, who were assisted by Clark L. Bernard and Jay S. Kamen, of my firm's staff.

Various sections of the manuscript involving accountants' legal responsibilities were reviewed by Harris J. Amhowitz, Marvin Schwartz, Victor M. Earle, and E. Henry Shappiro, members of the New York Bar. I also consulted with other members of the New York bar, including John F. Byrne and John A. Garrity. The advice and suggestions received from all of these men were most helpful.

The portions of the book involving listing on the New York Stock Exchange and the American Stock Exchange were reviewed by Merle S. Wick and Vincent W. Plaza of the New York exchange and Bernard H. Maas of the American exchange. If the discussion in this book involving these exchanges is accurate, it is largely because of their efforts.

I have also consulted on many occasions with Carl J. Simon, Irving H. Worden, Greville C. B. Gidley-Kitchin, Harold Cohen, James B. Fish, and Michael R. Fielding, all of whom gave me information, advice, and suggestions which I know have made this a better book than it otherwise would have been. Over the years, since this book was first published in 1956, Mr. Simon has been very helpful, and has never hesitated to make a suggestion that he thought would make for improvement.

A large part of the editorial effort in writing this Third Edition was the review of relevant material published since 1963 when the previous edition was printed. For the purpose of this review, an exhaustive bibliography was compiled by Miss Dorothy Kasman, Chief Librarian of my firm. Miss Kasman and Miss Kathleen B. McGovern, Assistant Librarian, willingly produced any book, article, magazine, annual report, or prospectus that I requested.

To a considerable extent, the initial review of published material relating to developments in the SEC field was made by Samuel J. Chasky, James D. O'Neill, and Ronald E. Wasserman, of my firm's staff, and by Robert H. Kaiser. Miss Rosemarie C. Bool, of my firm's staff, reviewed much of the published material involving litigation.

With respect to the SEC problems of foreign issuers, I have been fortunate in being able to consult with Walter J. Gruber of Smith, Barney and Company, and William J. Williams, of the New York bar. I have also had the benefit of consulting with Marshall S. Armstrong regarding the displacement of small CPA firms when their clients go public, and with Professor Maurice Moonitz, of the University of California, regarding the investment credit.

I have also consulted with several present and former members of the SEC organization. All of them have crowded calendars, and so I appreciate all the more the time they gave me. They include: Commissioner James J. Needham and former Commissioners William L. Cary, Manuel F. Cohen and Byron D. Woodside. Also, Andrew Barr, Charles F. Burhenne, Ralph

C. Hocker, Howard P. Hodges, Jr., Robert R. Love, Walter Mickelsen, Lindsey J. Millard, and A. Clarence Sampson, Jr.

It is also a pleasure to acknowledge the cooperation and assistance I have received from Curtis C. Munn, Jr.; Melvin S. Fishman; James B. Alfano; my secretary, Mrs. Alice Hennelly; and from many others in my firm's organization.

L.H.R.

CONTENTS

THE SEC AND THE LAWS IT ADMINISTERS

CONTENTS

The Securities and Exchange Commission

The Securities and Exchange Commission (often referred to in this book as "the SEC" or "the Commission") is an independent regulatory agency of the United States government. It was created by an act of Congress in 1934 and exercises a vital, quasi-judicial role in controlling the business of distributing and trading in securities.

The Commission is composed of five members appointed by the President with the consent of the Senate. One member is designated by the President to serve as chairman. Not more than three of the commissioners may be members of the same political party, thus assuring the bi-partisan make-up of the Commission. In general, commissioners are appointed for a term of five years.

The importance of the SEC's role is indicated by the following list of statutes which it administers:

Securities Act of 1933
Securities Exchange Act of 1934
Public Utility Holding Company Act of 1935
Trust Indenture Act of 1939

Investment Company Act of 1940
Investment Advisers Act of 1940

The Commission's duties and responsibilities are set forth in the laws which it administers. It also has important functions under the Securities Investor Protection Act of 1970, which amended the Securities Exchange Act of 1934.

The SEC also serves as adviser to federal courts in reorganization proceedings under Chapter X of the National Bankruptcy Act, and has certain duties under Section 851 of the Internal Revenue Code of 1954 (relating to investment companies furnishing capital to development corporations), and with respect to Section 15(a) of the Bretton Woods Agreements Act (relating to the International Bank for Reconstruction and Development).

Originally, the Securities Act of 1933 was administered by the Federal Trade Commission. The Securities Exchange Act of 1934, however, created the Securities and Exchange Commission, and in September, 1934, the duty of administering the 1933 Act was transferred to the SEC.

For a discussion of recent proposals to reorganize the Commission which, among other things, would replace the five-man Commission with a single administrator, see "Proposals to Restructure the SEC: the Ash Report" in this chapter.

The Securities Act of 1933

Principal Provisions.—The Securities Act of 1933 is one of the earliest of the "New Deal" laws following the stock market crash of 1929. The Act was the first in a series of laws designed to protect the public from misrepresentation, manipulation, and other fraudulent practices in the buying and selling of securities. The law provides for the registration of securities with the Commission before they may be sold to the public. The Act gives the Commission the power to exempt from registration small offerings; that is, where the aggregate amount of the offering does not exceed $500,000. Under this provision the SEC has promulgated Regulations A and E, relating to offerings of less than $500,000. Also exempt from the registration requirements are the securities of the United States government, states, municipalities, and other governmental units, and the securities of certain common carriers (such as interstate railroads).

The law exempts from the registration provisions transactions not involving a *public* offering. Thus, for example, if an entire issue of securities is sold to an insurance company which acquires the securities for investment and not with a view to distributing them, the transaction is a private one and does not involve an offering to the public. In other instances, however, the determination of what constitutes a "public" offering is one of the most difficult questions with which experienced lawyers have to deal. The Commission has said that whether a transaction is one not involving any public offering is a question of fact and necessitates a consideration of all the surrounding circumstances, including such factors as the relationship between the offerees and the issuer, the nature, scope, size, type, and manner of the offering. As in all matters involving legal interpretations, a public account-ant, as such, is not qualified to advise whether or not a proposed transaction involves an offering to the "public," or whether registration under the 1933 Act is required. In this situation the best advice the accountant can give is to suggest that a lawyer be consulted.

The 1933 Act is a *disclosure* statute. The disclosure is provided by means of a registration statement and a prospectus, each of which contains specified financial and other information. A copy of the prospectus must be furnished to the buyer of the registered security. Except as stated in Chapter 7 under "Confidential Treatment," the registration statement is a public document available for inspection by any person, and photocopies of any portion of the document may be obtained from the SEC at nominal cost.

The preparation of a registration statement is a complicated, technical process. The SEC's job is to examine the registration statement to see that full and accurate disclosure is made of all pertinent information relating, among other things, to the company's business, its securities, its financial position and earnings, its officers and directors, and the underwriting ar-rangements, so that the prospective investor may have a basis for deciding whether to purchase its securities. Under the law it is the seller (not the buyer) who must beware, because the Commission's responsibility is to protect the public—not the issuer or the underwriters of the securities.

The Act does not prohibit the sale of low grade or speculative securities. In fact, the prospectus relating to an offering of such securities will recite in detail all the negative aspects of the offering. On reading such a prospec-tus, one doubts whether the offering can be successfully concluded. The suc-cess of such offerings, however, leads one to question whether prospective investors take the trouble to read the selling literature which the Act and the SEC have caused to be placed before them.

It is unlawful for anyone to represent that, because a registration state-ment is in effect with respect to a security, the statement is true and correct. The outside front cover of every prospectus—whether the securities offered are speculative or investment grade—contains a required legend in capital letters and bold face type reading as follows:

THESE SECURITIES HAVE NOT BEEN APPROVED OR DISAPPROVED BY THE SECURITIES AND EXCHANGE COMMISSION NOR HAS THE COMMISSION PASSED UPON THE ACCURACY OR ADEQUACY OF THIS PROSPECTUS. ANY REPRESENTATION TO THE CONTRARY IS A CRIM-INAL OFFENSE.

The aforementioned mandatory statement may give the impression that the SEC does not pass on the merits of any security registered with it, but it would be a mistake to conclude that this is always the position of the Commission. In some cases, the SEC may demand that a speculative offering be so characterized and the speculative features of the offering be prominently set forth under the heading "Introductory Statement" in the forepart of the prospectus. In extreme cases, where the staff has strong feelings that the offering should not be permitted, it has been known to exhaust the patience of the prospective registrant with interminable delaying tactics with the result that management frequently withdraws or abandons the registration statement. Sometimes, in fact, the staff suggests that the registration statement be withdrawn because of the many deficiencies in it. In one case with which the author is familiar, the staff suggested that a registration statement be withdrawn, but counsel for the registrant refused to do so and contended that the staff was making "value judgments" which was not their proper function. The prospective issuer was in dire financial straits and its prospects were very poor—even with the hoped-for infusion of new money from the public. After a long series of delays, counsel concluded that the registrant had no choice but to withdraw the registration statement.

The staff of the Commission endeavors to see that all the material facts with respect to a security and its issuer are adequately disclosed and that no material information is withheld, but, in the last analysis, it is up to the investor to decide whether or not to buy the security. The Commission strives to prevent fraudulent practices in the offering and sale of securities but does not guarantee the investor against loss.

A former chairman of the SEC has said that a basic intent of the securities laws is that "the Government should not take the responsibility for determining the investor's choice among investment opportunities but should make certain that the investor has an opportunity to make such choice on the basis of full disclosure of the pertinent facts and in the absence of fraud." [1]

If all the facts regarding a security are not adequately disclosed in the registration statement, or if important information is omitted, the Commission may require the registration statement to be corrected or amplified, as required, by means of an appropriate amendment. If the amendment does not cure the deficiencies, the Commission may exercise its "stop-order" or "refusal-order" powers to prevent the registration statement from becoming effective and the securities from being sold until the deficiencies are cured. Sometimes the stop-order is issued after the registration statement has

---

[1] Hamer H. Budge, Statement before Subcommittee on Antitrust and Monopoly of Senate Committee on the Judiciary, Feb. 18, 1970.

become effective and the securities have been sold, in which event the order prevents further sales of the securities by the issuer or the underwriter.

The staff of the Commission frequently furnishes advice and assistance on an informal basis to prospective registrants, their counsel and accountants, and others. This includes the issuance of so-called "no-action" letters. These are letters written by members of the SEC staff in answer to inquiries as to whether in a given set of circumstances a proposed issuance of securities has to be registered with the Commission under the Act. In the letter the staff member would say that based on the facts set forth, the staff would not recommend that the Commission take any action, such as enjoining the proposed transaction—hence the term "no-action" letter. If the staff member were of the opinion that the securities had to be registered, he would advise the interested persons to that effect.

The Act provides for the civil liability of the issuer, underwriter, and experts (including accountants) where there have been materially false or inadequate representations. The law also imposes criminal penalties for fraudulent acts and practices in the sale of securities in interstate commerce whether the securities are registered with the SEC or not.

From the foregoing it will be apparent that the 1933 Act is concerned primarily with the distribution of securities rather than with trading in securities. The matter of trading in securities is the province of the Securities Exchange Act of 1934.

Accountant's Function.—The registration statement and prospectus filed with the SEC under the 1933 Act—whether by privately owned companies or by publicly owned companies—must contain financial statements, certain supporting schedules, and, in most cases, summaries of earnings. These are among the most important elements of a registration statement and prospectus. Chapter **9** sets forth the financial requirements of those registration forms which are most commonly in use. As will be seen, most of the financial data must be certified by an independent public accountant or an independent certified public accountant. The certifying accountant must manually sign his certificate in the registration statement, and he must consent in writing to the inclusion of his certificate in the registration document.

When the 1933 Act was under consideration by the Congress, some thought was given to the idea of having the required financial statements reviewed by government auditors. A representative of the accounting profession, Colonel Arthur Carter, urged that independent public accountants were capable of performing this function. Because of their familiarity with their clients' affairs, he said that public accountants would be able to make the required examinations more quickly and more economically than an army of government auditors. His suggestion was adopted in the 1933 Act which gave the SEC authority to require certification of financial statements filed pursuant to the Act, and the Commission has availed itself of that authority. (Speaking of the consideration that had been given to the alternative of having the financial statements filed under the 1933 Act verified by government auditors or by independent accountants, Commissioner Hugh F. Owens said, "I believe we can all agree that independent certification was, and is, the better choice." This factor, he said, has insured that there would be a close relationship between the SEC and the accounting profession in view of the importance of the financial statements in most filings.)[2]

Similar certification provisions were included in other statutes as Congress added to the structure of Federal legislation dealing with the securities markets and those who do business in them.

The Securities Exchange Act of 1934

Principal Provisions.—The Securities Exchange Act of 1934 is also a "New Deal" measure. It provides for the registration of national securities exchanges, securities listed on exchanges, and brokers and dealers trading in the over-the-counter securities markets. As a result of the 1964 amendments to the Act, certain publicly-owned, unlisted companies are also required to register with the SEC if they meet the requirements as to size (measured by amount of assets and number of shareholders). In a very broad sense, this provision (Section 12(g) of the Act) requires a company to register with the Commission when its assets exceed $1,000,000 and it has a class of equity securities (other than an exempted security) held of record by 500 or more persons.

Certain brokers and dealers are required by law to file annual reports of their financial condition and their income and expenses. As in the case of the 1933 Act, the Commission's responsibility is to protect the public—not the issuer of securities, or brokers, or dealers. The law prohibits market manipulations by means of wash sales or matched orders (effected to give a false or misleading appearance of active trading) or by any other deceptive devices or fraudulent practice, and it provides for the regulation of certain manipulative activities, such as stabilizing of prices and short sales. The Commission, under the law, also regulates the hypothecation of customers' securities, the business of specialists and odd-lot dealers, and the solicitation of proxies from the stockholders of registered companies.

Corporate insiders—that is, directors and officers of registered corporations and principal owners of their equity securities—are required to file statements of their holdings of the equity securities of their company and

[2] Hugh F. Owens, speech before Accounting and Auditing Symposium of Texas CPAs, May 25, 1971.

also to file monthly reports of changes in such holdings. If such corporate insiders realize profits on any sale and purchase, or purchase and sale, of the company's equity securities within a six-month period, the profits inure to, and are recoverable by, the company.

The law provides for the filing of a registration statement by any company which desires to have its securities listed for exchange trading and by certain publicly-owned unlisted issuers referred to above. This registration contains much of the same information regarding the company and its business as is contained in a registration under the 1933 Act. The information in the registration is kept reasonably up-to-date by means of annual, quarterly, and certain other periodic reports. The registration and reports filed by companies affected, and the reports of holdings and changes in holdings filed by officers, directors, and principal holders of the company's securities, are public information and are available for inspection at the SEC and at the securities exchanges on which the company's securities are listed. Photocopies of such information may be obtained from the SEC at nominal cost. The registration and the reports are intended to assist a person in reaching an informed opinion as to whether he should buy the company's securities, or, if he already owns them, whether to sell them.

Securities which are not listed for trading on a national securities exchange are not subject to the provisions relating to insider-trading, proxy solicitation, and registration, except for those publicly-owned companies which, as a result of the Securities Acts Amendments of 1964 (referred to above) became subject to these provisions.

The law also provides for controlling the use of the nation's credit resources in securities speculation by regulating margin requirements and borrowing by brokers and dealers. The power to regulate the use of credit for the purchase of securities or for carrying securities is in the hands of the Federal Reserve Board and is enforced by the SEC.

After a privately owned company has "gone public" by means of a registration statement filed under the 1933 Act, the management may or may not make application to have the securities listed for trading on a national securities exchange. Some of the advantages and disadvantages in such listing are discussed in Chapter **29**. If the company meets the requirements for listing and decides to proceed with the application therefor, much of the information in the 1933 Act registration will also be useful for purposes of the listing.

See also the discussion below regarding the Securities Investor Protection Act of 1970 which amended the 1934 Act.

Accountant's Function.—As in the case of a filing under the 1933 Act, a registration statement filed under the 1934 Act by an issuer of securities must contain financial statements and certain supporting schedules.

Chapter **15** sets forth the requirements as to financial statements in Forms 10 and 10–K, which are, respectively, the registration and annual report forms most commonly used. As will be seen, practically all of the financial statements and schedules in Forms 10 and 10–K must be accompanied by a certificate of an independent public accountant or independent certified public accountant.

Recent revisions in the registration and annual report forms require the inclusion in such forms of five-year summaries of operations and, in certain cases, comprehensive disclosures with respect to an issuer's principal lines of business. Although the SEC does not require this information to be certified, there is no doubt that in many cases the officers and directors of companies registered with the SEC will request their auditors to certify the summaries of operations when that is practicable and feasible. In many cases, also, they will ask their auditors at least to assist in the preparation of the information regarding the principal lines of business.

Chapter **22** of this book deals with proxy solicitations. If a solicitation is subject to SEC rules, a proxy statement has to be prepared and filed with the SEC before it can be used. Depending on the purpose for which the proxy is solicited, the proxy statement may have to contain financial statements. More often than not, such financial statements must be certified by independent public accountants or independent certified public accountants.

In Chapter **14** reference is made to the reports filed with the SEC by certain brokers and dealers who extend credit to the public. Not only must the financial statements in these reports be certified, but also in this connection the SEC has prescribed certain audit requirements. Among other things, the accountant must comment in his certificate upon any material inadequacies found to exist in the accounting system, the internal accounting control, and procedures for safeguarding securities, and any corrective action taken or proposed. If an accountant is to certify the financial statements of a broker-dealer, he should be familiar with the audit requirements which are set forth in Chapter **5**; a suggested form of accountant's certificate is set forth in Chapter **25**.

Securities Investor Protection Act of 1970

Because of the sizable losses suffered by investors in recent years growing out of the failures and financial difficulties of brokers and dealers in securities, the Congress enacted the Securities Investor Protection Act of 1970, as an amendment to the Securities Exchange Act of 1934.

The 1970 Act created the Securities Investor Protection Corporation (SIPC), a non-profit, membership corporation, the members of which are brokers and dealers registered under Section 15(b) of the 1934 Act, and, with certain exceptions, members of national securities exchanges. Although SIPC is not an agency of the United States Government, its Board of Directors, consisting of seven persons, is appointed: five by the President of the United States, and one each by the Secretary of the Treasury, and the Federal Reserve Board. Two of the President's appointees may not be associated with the securities industry.

The Act gives SIPC authority to assess its members for the purpose of creating a fund (SIPC Fund) to be used for the protection of customers of brokers and dealers to a limit of $50,000 for each account, including a maximum of $20,000 for cash claims in each account.

The SEC has important functions under the 1970 Act. It has broad authority with respect to the by-laws and rules of SIPC. Through the SEC, SIPC may receive financial assistance from the United States Treasury. If SIPC refuses to act to protect the customers of any member of SIPC, the SEC may apply to a United States District Court for an order compelling SIPC to discharge its obligations. The SEC is authorized to make inspections and examinations of SIPC, and may require SIPC to file reports with it. SIPC is required to file annual reports, including certified financial statements, with the SEC—such reports to deal with SIPC's business and the exercise of its rights and powers under the 1970 Act.

The Public Utility Holding Company Act of 1935

Principal Provisions.—The Public Utility Holding Company Act of 1935 provides for the registration of holding companies in holding company systems engaged in the electric utility business or in the retail gas business. As in the case of the 1933 and 1934 Acts, the Holding Company Act employs the registration device. Registration with the SEC under the Holding Company Act is designed to furnish information regarding the company's capital structure and the nature of its business. The information in the registration is kept reasonably up-to-date by annual reports.

The Act contains the so-called "death sentence" which makes it the duty of the SEC to require such companies to integrate their properties geographically and to simplify their capital structures with the aim of restricting each holding company to a single system having a simple capitalization. Under the law the Commission has considerable control over the security transactions of holding companies and their subsidiaries, the acquisition or disposition of assets by such companies, intercompany loans, capital contributions, dividend payments, proxy solicitations, service and construction contracts, and accounting practices. This is the only statute administered by the SEC which is concerned with the interests of the consumer and is not designed solely to protect investors in securities although it is clear that investors have benefited from SEC regulation by the improvement in financial strength and stability of public utility companies. The Act is regulatory in nature, but the Commission has no power to set rates which utilities may charge for service.

Under the Act, corporate insiders—that is, officers and directors of registered holding companies—are required to report their holdings of, and transactions in, the company's securities. Profits of corporate insiders on sales and purchases, or purchases and sales, of securities of the holding company or its subsidiaries within a period of six months are recoverable by the holding company or the subsidiary.

Accountant's Function.—The financial statements contained in the registration statements and annual reports of holding companies subject to the Act must be certified by independent public accountants or certified public accountants. Because of the limited interest in this Act, the requirements of such registration statements and annual reports are not set forth in this book. The forms and instructions can be obtained by writing to the SEC in Washington, D. C., or by reference to the looseleaf services containing this information.

Two matters, however, in connection with this Act deserve the attention of accountants: one is the Uniform System of Accounts for Public Utility Holding Companies; the other is the Uniform System of Accounts for Mutual Service Companies and Subsidiary Service Companies. These systems, promulgated by the SEC, represent the only instances in which the Commission has dictated the detailed manner in which accounts shall be kept. These uniform systems are limited, as their titles imply, to the small number of companies to which the Act applies.

The Trust Indenture Act of 1939

Principal Provisions.—The Trust Indenture Act of 1939 provides that bonds, debentures, and other evidences of indebtedness (with certain exceptions) may not be offered to the public unless they are issued under a trust indenture which has been qualified with the Commission. The law was passed because some issuers of debt securities had failed in the past to provide independent trustees to protect the rights of investors or because of the inadequate power given to such trustees when they were appointed.

As in the case of the 1933, 1934, and 1935 Acts, this law also employs the registration device. The documents filed must contain an analysis of the indenture provisions and other information which will enable the Commission to pass upon the eligibility of the trustee. To be eligible to serve as a trustee under an indenture, a person must satisfy the requirements as to independence and may not have conflicting interests. There must at all times be one or more trustees, at least one of which must be a corporation having trust powers and subject to examination by governmental authority and having capital and surplus of at least $150,000.

Annual reports are required of the trustee and may be required of the obligor (the issuer of the security). Civil liability is imposed for false or misleading statements made in reports or applications filed with the Commission and for omissions of material facts.

Accountant's Function.—The public accountant has no part in the preparation of the registration statement or annual reports required to be filed under this Act. In Chapter **11**, however, the reader's attention is directed to the desirability of having the accountant review the indenture before it becomes final. The indenture often contains restrictions and covenants that the independent public accountant must be able to understand and apply.

The Investment Company Act of 1940

Principal Provisions.—The Investment Company Act of 1940 was passed after a comprehensive four-year investigation by the SEC of the practices of investment trusts in the 1920's. Intended to remedy a number of abuses associated with investment trusts, the law represents a compromise measure worked out by industry representatives and the SEC.

The Act controls the composition of boards of directors of investment companies and prohibits investment bankers and brokers from constituting more than a minority of the directors of such companies. Under the law contracts to manage investment companies must be approved by security holders, and the custody of the companies' security investments is regulated by the SEC. Transactions between the companies and their officers and directors and affiliates are subject to approval by the SEC. Investment policies may not be changed unless the change is approved by shareholders.

The Investment Company Act also employs the registration device, and investment companies subject to the Act must register with the SEC. In the registration statement, the investment company is required to set forth its investment and trading policies and to file almost the same financial and other information as would be required in a registration under the 1933 and 1934 Acts. The information in the registration statement is kept reasonably current by means of annual and other reports.

Accountant's Function.—The registration statements and reports of regulated investment companies contain financial statements and schedules in great detail. These statements and schedules must be certified by an independent public accountant or independent certified public accountant, who must be elected by stockholders or whose appointment by the management or directors must be ratified by the stockholders. If the securities and investments owned by the investment company are in the custody of the company or in the custody of a member of a national securities exchange, an accountant is required to make periodic examinations of the securities— some of these examinations must be without advance notice to the custodian

—and must report his findings to the SEC. (Suggested forms of accountants' reports for this purpose appear in Chapter **25**.)

Annual reports to the Commission are filed on Form N–1R by all management investment companies except those which issue periodic payment plan certificates and small business investment companies licensed as such under the Small Business Investment Act of 1958 which file annual reports on Form N–5R. The annual report form N–1R consists of two parts: Part I consists of 39 "items" of information plus financial statements, all of which become public information when filed; Part II consists of 32 items of information and the investment company may request that it not be publicly disclosed. In addition to a certificate covering the financial statements, the registrant is required to furnish an accountant's opinion covering many of the items in the form, and giving "negative assurance" with respect to some of the items. These matters are discussed in Chapter **25**.

Because of the specialized nature of investment companies, the registration and report forms filed by such companies under the Investment Company Act are omitted from this book. These forms and the applicable instructions may be obtained from the SEC or by reference to the looseleaf services.

The Investment Advisers Act of 1940

The Investment Advisers Act of 1940 requires the registration with the Commission of certain persons engaged in the business of advising others with respect to trading in securities and prohibits fraudulent practices by such persons. A companion measure to the Investment Company Act of 1940, this Act also employs the registration device. The application for registration must set forth information about the investment adviser, his background and business affiliations, his authority with respect to clients' funds and accounts, and the basis for his compensation. Under the law, investment advisory contracts may not provide for compensation to the investment adviser based on sharing capital gains of clients' funds or capital appreciation of clients' funds. Such contracts must provide that they may not be assigned by the investment adviser without the consent of the client.

Under the law, the SEC adopted Rule 204–2 which contains a comprehensive listing of the books, records, papers, and memoranda which investment advisers subject to the Act must keep and preserve.

Rule 206(4)–2 under the Act sets forth the conditions under which an investment adviser may take action with respect to any funds or securities in the custody of the investment adviser in which any of his clients has a beneficial interest. Included among such conditions is the requirement that all such funds and securities of clients be verified by actual examination at least once during each calendar year by an independent public accountant at a time which shall be chosen by the accountant without prior notice to the investment adviser. The accountant's certificate stating that he has made an examination has to be filed with the Commission promptly after each such examination. The scope of examination required for this purpose is set forth in Chapter **25**.

Chapter X of the Bankruptcy Act

Chapter X of the Bankruptcy Act provides a procedure for corporate reorganization, and the SEC has certain duties under that chapter. Depending on the circumstances, the judge may or may not submit to the SEC for its examination any reorganization plan which he thinks is worth considering. The SEC's job is to be a disinterested adviser to the court and investors on the various legal and financial questions that arise in the bankruptcy proceeding and to prepare advisory reports on reorganization plans. Generally, the Commission participates only in proceedings in which there is a substantial public investor interest. The Commission has no authority to veto a reorganization plan, or to require the adoption of a plan, or to render a decision on any other issue in the proceedings.

The independent public accountant has no function in a reorganization proceeding except to the extent that he may be the accountant either for the debtor, the trustee, or another interested party.

Internal Organization of the SEC

The main office of the SEC is in Washington. It has regional offices in New York, Boston, Atlanta, Chicago, Fort Worth, Denver, San Francisco, Seattle, and Arlington, Va., and branch offices in Cleveland, Detroit, Houston, Miami, St. Louis, Salt Lake City, and Los Angeles. The public may obtain opinions and interpretations from any office of the Commission, including the regional offices. Filings under Regulations A and A–M are processed in the regional offices, which also perform some of the investigative and enforcement work of the Commission. The regional offices also examine the reports filed with them by exchange members and registered brokers and dealers.

The Commission is assisted by a professional staff consisting of lawyers, accountants, engineers, securities analysts, and examiners. The staff is organized into the following divisions and offices which are directly responsible to the Commission:

Division of Corporation Finance
Division of Trading and Markets
Division of Corporate Regulation
Regional Offices
Office of General Counsel
Office of Chief Accountant

Office of Opinion Writing
Office of the Secretary
Office of Hearing Examiners

The public accountant who has clients subject to the various SEC-administered Acts is concerned primarily with the workings of the Division of Corporation Finance and the Office of Chief Accountant. To a lesser extent the public accountant is concerned with the work of the Division of Trading and Markets and the Division of Corporate Regulation. All four will be briefly discussed to show what they attempt to do and how they do it.

Division of Corporation Finance.—The Division of Corporation Finance has duties in connection with most of the statutes administered by the SEC. The Division's principal responsibility is the prevention of fraudulent offerings of securities to the public and dissemination of false or misleading information in relation to securities. The Division establishes standards of economic and financial and non-financial information to be included in registration statements, reports, and other documents filed with the Commission, and enforces adherence to such standards by issuers, underwriters, trustees, and others with respect to securities offered for sale to the public or listed for trading on securities exchanges or traded in the over-the-counter market. The Division prescribes the kinds of information to be included in proxies, proxy statements, and other proxy-soliciting material, and is responsible for enforcing compliance with such standards. The Division is responsible for court actions to enjoin violations of the registration and reporting provisions of Sections 12, 13, and 15(d) of the 1934 Act.

A director supervises the work of the Division. He is assisted by assistant directors, branch chiefs, and a number of examining "branches," the Office of General Counsel, and the Office of Chief Accountant. Each examining branch is headed by a securities analyst and is responsible to an Assistant Director of the Division. In addition to a branch chief each branch contains accountants, lawyers, and examiners. When necessary, the various branches have recourse to engineers, geologists, valuation experts, statisticians, and other experts for consultation on technical problems in their respective fields. Each branch usually handles all matters relating to each company whose affairs are assigned to it. Thus, a company filing under various Acts administered by the Commission will ordinarily be subject to review by the same group of persons under all the Acts. The accounting work in the Division is coordinated and supervised by the Chief Accountant of the Division who consults with the Chief Accountant of the Commission regarding new or important accounting and auditing problems.

The Division examines all registration statements (including the financial statements), prospectuses, appraisals, engineering reports, certificates of incorporation and other documents, annual and periodic reports, and amendments to all of the foregoing that are filed with SEC with respect to securities offered for sale to the public or registered under the 1934 Act. The Division also examines forms of proxies, proxy statements, and proxy-soliciting material filed with it. The prospectuses and oil and gas offering sheets filed in accordance with the Commission's regulations providing for exemption from registration under the 1933 Act are reviewed by this Division. The Division also reviews the reports of trading in equity securities by officers and directors of registered corporations and principal holders of such securities. Upon completion of these examinations, "letters of comment" are often prepared for issuance to registrants. The staff of the Division makes field investigations, and conducts hearings in stop-order proceedings for the development of facts and the verification of data submitted in registration statements and applications.

The Division is in charge of the drafting of rules, regulations, and registration, report, and other forms, and gives advice and responds to inquiries regarding application and interpretation of the statutes and the rules, regulations, and forms.

Office of Chief Accountant.—The Chief Accountant is the principal staff adviser to the Commission on all matters relating to accounting and auditing. He brings particularly difficult or controversial questions before the Commission, and is responsible for the execution of Commission policy with respect to accounting principles, auditing practices, the form and content of financial statements filed with the Commission, uniform systems of accounts, and the interpretation and application thereof in unusual situations.

The Chief Accountant initiates and supervises studies relating to accounting and auditing. In connection with the drafting and interpretation of accounting and auditing rules and regulations, he confers with accounting authorities, such as professional organizations, public accountants, and officials of the federal and state governments. He answers questions received from registrants or their public accountants dealing with accounting and auditing. Some of his opinions are published by the SEC as "Accounting Series Releases."

The Chief Accountant is responsible for the consideration of all cases dealing with the independence and qualifications of public accountants who practice before the Commission. He supervises and makes recommendations concerning disciplinary proceedings involving public accountants under Rule 2(e) of the Commission's Rules of Practice which are discussed in Chapter **27**. He also participates in administrative or court proceedings involving accounting and auditing matters and is responsible for investigations having to do with these matters.

Division of Trading and Markets.—The Division of Trading and Markets is responsible for policing the securities markets. Accordingly, the Division watches closely trading activities on securities exchanges and in the over-the-counter markets, including the activities of brokers and dealers. The Division attempts to prevent fraudulent trading practices and market manipulations, and investigates unusual trading activities and unlawful practices, such as wash sales, matched orders, pool operations, the dissemination of false and misleading information concerning securities, and other manipulative or deceptive devices. The rules relating to stabilization of prices of securities are administered by this Division.

The Division supervises the broker-dealer inspection program and reviews the applications and reports filed by securities exchanges, brokers, dealers, and investment advisers. The Division also reviews the disciplinary actions taken by exchanges and by the National Association of Securities Dealers. It also has duties and responsibilities with respect to investment advisers under the Investment Advisers Act.

Division of Corporate Regulation.—The Division of Corporate Regulation is the vehicle through which the SEC administers the Public Utility Holding Company Act of 1935, the regulatory provisions of the Investment Company Act of 1940 (including review of all filings by investment companies), and its function as adviser to federal courts in reorganization proceedings under the Bankruptcy Act.

Inquiries as to the Requirements; Prefiling Conferences

The staff of the Commission devotes a large part of its time to answering inquiries and requests for information. The staff is available for consultation both before and after a registration statement, report, or other document is filed with the SEC. The Commission urges all persons having questions concerning its requirements to discuss their problems freely with the staff. This can be done by letter, by telephone, or in person at the main office in Washington or at a regional office, depending on the nature of the question to be raised.

As far as accountants are concerned, the author strongly recommends the prefiling conference whenever there are important accounting or auditing problems that need to be resolved in advance of filing. This conference not only enables the issuer and his accountant to obtain the SEC's views at an early date with regard to the problem, but also affords the staff an opportunity to ask questions and thereby elicit more background information than is usually available from the financial statements or accountant's report. Accountants who are not familiar with SEC requirements make frequent use of the prefiling conference. Experienced practitioners also make use of this procedure; they find it not only saves expense in the long run, but—what may be more important—it saves time. Especially where the time schedule for a security flotation is "tight," the factor of time can be an important consideration. Many years ago the Commission said:

. . . All members of the Commission's accounting staff are available to advise prospective registrants and their accountants in conference or by correspondence, prior to filing. Experienced practitioners who recognize unique problems regularly follow this procedure and save valuable time for themselves and their clients. The public accountant without experience with the Commission should not hesitate to do likewise. [14 SEC Ann. Rep. 106 (1948).]

More recently, in its "Guides for Preparation and Filing of Registration Statements" (Release No. 33–4936, Dec. 9, 1968) the Commission reiterated its policy:

The Commission has a long established policy of holding its staff available for conferences with prospective registrants or their representatives in advance of filing a registration statement. These conferences may be held for the purpose of discussing generally the problems confronting a registrant in effecting registration or to resolve specific problems of an unusual nature which are sometimes presented by involved or complicated financial transactions.

Arrangements for a conference on accounting or auditing matters should be made with the Chief Accountant of the Division having jurisdiction. If a new or controversial problem is involved, conference arrangements may be made directly with the Chief Accountant of the Commission. Requests for a review of interpretations made in the Divisions may also be presented to the Chief Accountant of the Commission. If the results of the conferences at the Division level or with the Office of the Chief Accountant do not resolve the accounting or auditing problems to the registrant's satisfaction, the registrant and its advisers have one further appeal route within the Commission: they can ask for a meeting with the members of the Commission. This does not happen very often, but it can be done and has been done when the issue is important and the registrant wants to leave no stone unturned to be sure that the matter is carefully considered at every level in the Commission. When a conference on accounting or auditing matters is held with the members of the Commission, the Chief Accountant (or one of his associates) is normally asked to attend in the event that his views might be sought, but this should not discourage anyone from discussing his problems with the Commission members since they have not always been completely in agreement with the views of their accounting advisers.

Some thought should also be given to the question of who should attend the prefiling conference with the SEC's staff. As a minimum, there should be representatives of the registrant and the independent public accountants, usually a senior financial or accounting officer of the former and a partner of the latter. If the discussion will be confined to accounting or auditing matters, there is ordinarily no need for persons other than the aforementioned to be present unless they have information, expertise, or points of view that will be helpful at the meeting. The underwriters and lawyers often indicate that, for various reasons, they would also like to attend the conference. The author has sometimes found it advisable in these circumstances to advise such persons that there is no objection to their being present at the meeting, and they may feel free to participate when necessary, but they should understand that they are not to lead the discussion. This is due to the fact that the conference, being on accounting or auditing matters, will be with representatives of the Commission's accounting staff, although in some cases there may also be other persons present representing the Commission. Some lawyers especially, being advocates, have a tendency to be excessively zealous at such meetings in their desire to serve their clients. Capable lawyers with experience in the SEC field do not have to be told what to do at accounting-auditing conferences. They do not usually speak the accountants' language and have found it desirable to let the auditors and the company's financial or accounting officials lead the discussion, and to participate only when they can make a real contribution to the solution of the problem at hand.

The prefiling conference should be arranged far enough in advance of the proposed filing date so that, if a decision is not reached at the meeting, the SEC's staff may have enough time to study and research the problem if that is needed in order to reach a decision. Time should also be allotted for the possibility that the staff's decision may not be acceptable to the company and its auditors, in which event there may have to be another meeting with the staff or with the Commission itself, in those rare instances in which it appears to be necessary.

It seems almost unnecessary to have to point out that the persons who will attend the prefiling conference must have done their homework before the meeting. The representatives of the registrant and the independent public accountants should be thoroughly familiar with the accounting or auditing problem to be discussed as well as those aspects of the registrant's business or of the auditors' examination involved in the problem. It is important also that they have at least some tentative thoughts about the solution of the problem. If they have been thinking about it for weeks or months, they ought not to go to Washington without at least some ideas about the solution. At the very least they should know how they would like to solve the problem, even though that might not be the best solution. Experience has shown that the SEC's staff are more likely to agree with a reasonable solution that is proposed to them than if they have to research the problem and reach a decision entirely on their own. Also, if the conferees are presented with a tentative solution that is a reasonable one, it may take less time to reach a final decision. On the other hand, it should be clearly understood that if the proposed solution is not satisfactory to the SEC's representatives, they will not hesitate to let that fact be known.

It is also desirable that the representatives of the company and the auditors who attend the prefiling conference have with them a prepared memorandum of the facts concerning the problem and the proposed solution. This can be left with the SEC's staff at the conclusion of the meeting if that appears desirable. In addition, if agreement on a solution to the problem is reached at the meeting, it is desirable to confirm the understanding in a letter to the Commission. This is helpful to all persons at the meeting in making sure that there was agreement as to the facts, the problem, and the solution.

Opinions received from members of the SEC staff are not official opinions of the Commission and are not binding on the Commission. Certain members of the SEC staff are in a better position than others to be familiar with SEC policy; for example, the Director and Assistant Directors of the divisions, the Chief Accountant of the Commission, the General Counsel, and the Chief Accountant and Chief Counsel of a division. Because of the experience acquired in their day-to-day activities, any opinion obtained from them serves as a reasonable basis for reliance that the opinion also reflects SEC opinion. Such, at least, has been the author's experience. Furthermore, it is no secret that members of the staff in upper echelons check with the Commissioners on borderline questions.

Availability of Information on File with SEC.—Except for information and documents to which the Commission has granted confidential treatment, all of the information in registration statements and reports filed with the SEC pursuant to the statutes administered by it are available for public inspection. At its main office in Washington, D. C., the Commission maintains a public reference room where all such documents and information may be inspected by any interested person. It is only necessary to identify the name of the company and the particular document in which the reader is interested; he is not asked why he wants to see the document. Copying machines are also available in case an interested reader wishes a photocopy of something in the Commission's files.

The Commission also furnishes at a small charge photocopies of information on file with it. Experience with this service indicates, however, that it is apt to be quite slow depending on the volume of requests from the public and from other government agencies.

In addition the Commission has recently made available so-called "microfiche" copies of certain of the documents filed with it. A microfiche is a small, plastic file card containing photographic impressions of up to 60 standard size pages. A single microfiche card will therefore contain a complete average annual report on Form 10–K. A reading machine is required to enlarge the images on the card so that they can be read. The Commission has executed a contract with a private company under which Form 10–K reports are made available on a subscription basis in microfiche form. Subscribers to the service receive their microfiche copies of the 10–Ks by mail within a few days after the documents have been filed with the SEC. The microfiche service has been extended to include quarterly reports of investment companies and Form 8–K, and, in all likelihood, will be extended to other documents in the future.

Proposals to Restructure the SEC: the Ash Report.—The SEC, together with several of the other so-called "independent" agencies, was the subject of a study by a group called The President's Advisory Council on Executive Organization, appointed by President Nixon. The Council's report, issued in January 1971, is entitled "Report on Selected Independent Regulatory Agencies"—often referred to as the Ash Report, after its chairman, Roy L. Ash.

The independent agencies studied have long been considered an anomaly in the structure of the United States Government. Housed in the executive branch of the government, they carry out legislative functions, and behave like courts. In the past quarter century, the growth of the regulated industries and the national economy has outdistanced the commissions' ability to cope constructively with regulatory problems.

The Ash Report asserted that inadequacies in regulatory structure have adversely affected the implementation of Congressional mandates, the interests of the public generally, and the ability of the regulated industries to operate their businesses profitably or to plan for the future with some degree of assurance of what regulatory policy will be.

The report was critical, in general, of the commission form for structuring a governmental agency. Under this arrangement, an agency is headed by several colleagues, each having equal authority. As a consequence, when action is called for, the commissioners are likely to be involved in debating among themselves what the action should be, with consequent delay in reaching a prompt decision.

The report observed that some of the deficiencies in the performance of the regulatory commissions are due to the difficulty of attracting and retaining commissioners and staff having administrative skill and broad perspective largely because of the procedures and traditions associated with the commissions. Even able administrators have difficulty in serving as coequals on regulatory commissions. Given these traditions and the shared responsibility of the collegial form, it is not likely, said the report, that there will be greater interest in the future in commission positions.

According to the Ash Report the SEC is regarded as one of the ablest of the independent regulatory commissions. The SEC has, for the most part, carried out its Congressional mandate and has earned a measure of investor confidence. The need for restructuring the SEC arises less from past failures than from the necessity for assuring its ability to respond to the ever-increasing pace and complexity of the securities industry.

The SEC has not been able in the past to obtain adequate support and additional legislative authority largely because of its independence from Congress and the President. Although the SEC has done well with the resources at its disposal, accelerating securities distributions and voluminous trading have impeded its ability to respond to problems. As an example, the report referred to the increasing demands on the Division of Corporation Finance, where the workload increased dramatically in the past seven years. Filings of registration statements more than tripled, while the number of personnel assigned to the Division actually was reduced, with the result that the time for processing registration statements nearly doubled, and backlogs reached unprecedented levels. Yet the SEC's budget remained almost constant since 1965, and personnel levels for the SEC as a whole declined. Various studies have recommended increasing the funding of the SEC and its manpower, but neither the President nor Congress has given full support to these proposals.

Radical changes in the securities industry have raised questions about the ability of a multi-headed commission to provide adequate protection for investors. At the peak of market activity in December 1968, the brokerage industry "failed to deliver" $4.1 billion of securities by the required settlement date. In 1962 it was estimated that trading volume on the New York Stock Exchange would double by 1975; by 1968 that volume had already quadrupled. In 1970 a record 2.937 billion shares were traded on the New York Stock Exchange, a daily average of 11.7 million shares. Exchanges found it necessary to curtail their operations to keep abreast with the pace of trading.

The increase in trading volume is only one aspect of the changes in the nation's financial structure that needs attention. Financial instability was a principal factor in explaining why, since the beginning of 1969, 110 brokerage houses either failed or merged; during 1970 the fifth largest stock brokerage firm, faced with economic adversity, merged with the largest house. These and related pressures resulted in the enactment in 1970 of the Securities Investor Protection Act to guard against investor losses of cash and securities held by brokers.

Institutional investors now dominate market trading, representing 62% of the volume on the New York Stock Exchange. Registered investment companies have grown from $2.5 billion in assets and 400,000 shareholders in 1940 to $70 billion in assets and 8 million shareholders in 1969. And yet, despite this phenomenal growth, some of the SEC's activities, such as inspections of investment companies, for example, have been declining.

As a collegial body, the SEC at times finds itself debating what needs to be done while problems in the investment community continue to mount. The collegial form also conflicts with comprehensive policy-making and planning. Protracted proceedings and deliberations prevent it from keeping pace with the changes in the investment community.

The Ash Report proposed the creation of a new Securities and Exchange Agency to take over the job done by the SEC. The new agency would be headed by a single administrator, to be appointed by the President, confirmed by the Senate, and subject to removal by the President. The administrator would be responsible for all executive functions of the agency, including internal management, policy-making within Congressional and Presidential mandates, summary actions not requiring notice and hearing, promulgation of rules and regulations, granting exemptions, analyzing securities problems, making legislative recommendations, and initiating cases to enforce the securities statutes and the agency's rules and regulations.

The SEC presently exercises judicial functions to a certain extent when it reviews agency proceedings. These review functions, according to the Ash Report, conflict with the SEC's responsibilities to formulate and prosecute policy. The report contended that it is important to change this posture and recommended that the single administrator have 30 days for a limited review to assure that examiners' decisions are consistent with agency policy; thereafter, appeals would be heard by a newly created Administrative Court of the United States (which was another of the proposals in the Ash Report).

The report also recommended that regulation of public utility holding companies be transferred to a newly created Federal Power Agency (which the report recommended to take over the functions of the Federal Power Commission).

Frederick R. Kappel, a member of the Advisory Council, dissented from the recommendations of the Council's report. He pointed out that the reasoning in the report is supported in its references, quotes, and documentation by inclusion of views and writings from numerous sources. In connection with the conclusions it reached, the Council's staff had had more than 200 interviews, but there were almost no references or views from the regulated entities. Anyone who accepted the report on its face value, Mr. Kappel said, must recognize that "it is almost totally lacking in this very important respect."

Mr. Kappel did not share the views of his associates in recommending a single administrator and a separate administrative court. There was no certainty, he said, that these proposals would result in more effective administration. In his view, more careful attention to the selection of commissioners and key personnel was as likely to improve the administrative process as was the single administrator and the administrative court.

Speaking in Chicago on April 1, 1971, Commissioner James J. Needham referred to the Ash Report and its criticisms of the collegial form and said, "The Ash Report is right." He also agreed with the report's principal recommendation: the replacement of the multi-member commission by a single administrator.

In the area of administrative review proceedings within the SEC, Mr. Needham concurred in the recommendations of the Ash Report but said that they did not go far enough. He thought that the function of the SEC's hearing examiners should be removed from the Commission's control and established in a lower level court system. He also proposed that a seven man Board of Directors be created to make all policy decisions and to evaluate the daily operations of the Commission from a broad, practical perspective. He said, "The recommendation of the Ash Report for a single administrator when coupled with my recommendation for a Board of Directors should overcome the fears of those who otherwise recognize the need for reorganizing the Commission." Under Commissioner Needham's proposal, the Board would be chaired by the Administrator of the Commission and would be composed of members who would be from each of the following groups: the accounting, economic and legal professions; the mutual fund industry; the broker-dealer community; and a consumer-investor oriented individual.

As part of a program of returning government to the people, Commissioner Needham stated that the federal government in Washington should be dismantled and regionalized wherever possible. "Regionalizing the government to the greatest extent possible should help to convince the nation that their government is not only in touch with reality but is actively responding to their needs." He concluded by saying that the Ash Report proposals, together with his, "will result in a structure which is more capable of accomplishing those goals."

SEC Orders Are Subject to Judicial Review

The rulings and orders of the SEC are subject to judicial review when they are not in accordance with the standards adopted by the SEC. Experience indicates, however, that the courts will not substitute their discretion for the SEC's unless the administrative view is "so entirely at odds with fundamental principles of correct accounting . . . as to be the expression of a whim rather than an exercise of judgment." [3]

---

[3] Loss, *Securities Regulation,* 2d ed. (1961), p. 350.

SEC's Economic Reports: the "R" Forms

The Commission issues the following periodic reports relating to certain aspects of the United States economy:

(a) Securities Traded on Exchanges.
   An annual directory of securities traded on exchanges, with quarterly supplements.
(b) Plant and Equipment Expenditures.
   Quarterly report of plant and equipment expenditures—both actual and anticipated. (Joint study with Department of Commerce)
(c) Net Working Capital.
   Information on current assets and liabilities of United States corporations.
(d) Quarterly Financial Report.
   Quarterly balance sheet and income statement information of United States manufacturing corporations. (Joint study with Federal Trade Commission)
(e) New Securities Offerings.
   Quarterly information on new securities offerings in United States.
(f) Private Non-Insured Pension Funds.
   Annual estimates of private non-insured pension fund assets and their make-up, and information on receipts, expenditures, and common stock transactions.

The information in the above reports is based on data obtained from a series of forms that are designated "R" forms. These forms are sent by the SEC to some corporations which on a voluntary basis supply the information requested by the forms. The SEC reviews the information supplied in the forms and releases the information only in the form of industry aggregates and in such a way that the amounts with respect to any one corporation can not be identified. The "R" reports are confidential and for the use of the Commission only to prepare the above-named reports on the economy.

Following is a list of the "R" reports presently in use and a brief indication of their scope:

Form R–1. Sent to corporations that file annual financial reports with the SEC. Calls for condensed balance sheet and income and surplus information for three month period. Information in Form R–1 reports is used to prepare the "Quarterly Financial Report" (Item d above).

Form R–2. Calls for information on current assets, current liabilities, and long-term debt. Used to prepare the "Net Working Capital" report (Item c above).

Form R–3. A report on actual and anticipated expenditures for plant and equipment. Used to prepare "Plant and Equipment Expenditures" report (Item b above).

Form R–4. Information regarding pension and retirement funds and profit-sharing plans with retirement benefits. Used to˙ prepare "Private Non-Insured Pension Funds" report (Item f above).

Form R–4a. A condensed version of Form R–4. Used in connection with some of the foregoing reports (Items a, d, e, and f above).

Form R–5. Reports of stock transactions by property and casualty insurance companies. Used in connection with preparation of report on "Private Non-Insured Pension Funds" (Item f above).

Form R–8. Information regarding securities issued but not registered under 1933 Act. Used to prepare "New Securities Offerings" report (Item e above).

Form R–8a. A condensed version of Form R–8.

CHAPTER 2

ACCOUNTING REGULATION BY THE SEC

Statutory Bases; Accounting Series Releases; General Observations Affecting CPAs' Practice

CONTENTS

Many of the reports or documents required to be filed with the Commission contain financial data, mostly in the form of financial statements, earnings summaries, and related schedules. These are always a vital, often the most significant, element of the information upon which the investor bases his investment decisions. Because Congress recognized that accounting and accountants performed such an important role in achieving the statutory purpose of disclosure, the statutes administered by the Commission deal extensively with accounting. Activities of the Commission in the field of accounting are necessarily significant.

Statutory Basis of Accounting Regulation

1933 Act.—The Securities Act of 1933 gives the Commission broad powers to make, amend, and rescind any rules and regulations that may be necessary to carry out the provisions of the law. The Commission is authorized to define accounting, technical, and trade terms used in the law and has the power to prescribe the form in which required information shall be set forth and the items or details to be shown in the financial statements. The Commission may prescribe the methods to be followed in the preparation of accounts, in the appraisal or valuation of the assets and liabilities, in the determination of depreciation and depletion, in the differentiation of recurring and non-recurring income, in the differentiation of investment and operating income, and in the preparation of consolidated financial statements of companies controlling or controlled by the issuer or under common control with the issuer. Insofar as the Commission's rules relate to any common carrier subject to Section 20 of the Interstate Commerce Act, the Commission's rules with respect to accounts may not be inconsistent with the requirements imposed by the Interstate Commerce Commission (Section 19(a) of the 1933 Act).

1934 Act.—Under the Securities Exchange Act of 1934, the Commission has broad powers to prescribe the form in which the information required by the law shall be set forth, and the items or details to be shown in the financial statements. The Commission has authority to prescribe the methods to be followed in the preparation of reports, in the appraisal or valuation of assets and liabilities, in the determination of depreciation and depletion, in the differentiation of recurring and non-recurring income, in the differentiation of investment and operating income, and in the preparation (where the Commission deems it necessary or desirable) of separate and/or consolidated financial statements of any person controlling or controlled by the issuer or any person under common control with the issuer. In the case, however, of reports of any company whose methods of accounting are prescribed under the provisions of any federal law or regulation, the Commission's rules with respect to reports may not be inconsistent with the requirements imposed by such law or regulation in respect of the same subject matter (Section 13(b) of the 1934 Act).

1935 Act.—The Commission has even broader powers under the Holding Company Act of 1935. Registered holding companies and their subsidiaries must keep such accounts and records as the Commission deems necessary or appropriate in the public interest or for the protection of investors or consumers. Affiliates of registered holding companies and their subsidiaries must also keep such accounts and records as may be prescribed by the SEC. Every mutual service company and affiliates of mutual service companies must keep such accounts and records as may be prescribed by the SEC, and this requirement is also applicable to every person whose principal business is the performance of service, sales, or construction contracts for public utility or holding companies. The Commission is authorized to prescribe the form and manner of keeping accounts and records, and SEC representatives may examine these accounts and records. The Commission may prescribe the accounts in which receipts, disbursements, and transactions of regulated companies shall be entered and may require entries to be modified or supplemented. Under its authority the Commission has promulgated two uniform systems of accounts: one for public utility holding companies and one for mutual service companies and subsidiary service companies.

Under the Holding Company Act of 1935, the Commission has authority to make, issue, amend, and rescind any rules and regulations which it may deem necessary or appropriate to carry out the provisions of the law, including rules and regulations defining accounting, technical, and trade terms used in the law. The Commission is authorized to prescribe the form in which information required in any document filed with the Commission shall be set forth, and the items or details to be shown in balance sheets and in income and surplus statements. The Commission has the power to prescribe the manner in which the cost of all assets, whenever determinable, shall be shown in regard to documents filed with the Commission or accounts required to be kept by Commission orders, and the methods to be followed in the keeping of accounts and preparation of reports. The Commission may prescribe the methods used in the segregation and allocation of costs, in the determination of liabilities, in the determination of depreciation and depletion, in the differentiation of recurring and non-recurring income, in the differentiation of investment and operating income, and in the preparation of separate or consolidated financial statements for any companies in the same holding company system.

The SEC has adopted several important accounting rules under this Act, among which are the following.

RULE 250.27.—Registered holding companies and subsidiaries whose account-keeping is not prescribed by either the Federal Power Commission or a state commission, insofar as they are electric utilities must keep their accounts in the manner prescribed for electric companies by the Federal Power Commission, and insofar as they are gas utilities, in the manner recommended by the National Association of Railroad and Utilities Commissioners. There are provisions in the Rule under which exceptions may be made for companies whose public utility business is a minor part of their total business.

RULE 250.28.—This Rule is intended to prevent inconsistent financial statements. It provides that no registered holding company or subsidiary shall distribute to its security holders or publish financial statements which are inconsistent with the books of account or financial statements filed with the SEC. This Rule, however, is not to be deemed to prevent the distribution or publication of financial statements on a cash or other basis pursuant to the requirements of an indenture, or mortgage given to secure bonds, or similar instruments, or of appropriate financial statements of a receiver or trustee appointed by a United States court.

1940 Act.—Under the Investment Company Act of 1940, registered investment companies must maintain such accounts and documents as constitute the record forming the basis for financial statements required to be filed with the Commission. Under its statutory authority, the Commission has issued detailed rules governing the form of journals and other books of original entry, ledgers, and other records that must be maintained by registered investment companies. The rules also contain provisions with respect to the length of time that investment companies must maintain such records. Such accounts and records are subject to examination by the Commission representatives. The Commission is authorized to issue rules and regulations providing for a reasonable degree of uniformity in the accounting policies and principles to be followed by registered investment companies in maintaining their accounting records and in preparing financial statements required by the law. The Commission has authority to make, issue, amend, and rescind any rules and regulations defining accounting, technical, and trade terms used in the law. The Commission may prescribe the form in which there is to be set forth the information required in registration statements, applications, and reports to the Commission. The law requires the filing of reports with the SEC and the transmission of other reports to stockholders, and provides that the latter shall not be misleading in the light of the former.

Investment Advisers Act of 1940.—Investment advisers subject to the Investment Advisers Act of 1940 are required to maintain and keep accounts, books, records, journals, correspondence, memoranda, and other records. These are subject to periodic and other types of examinations by the SEC and, to a certain extent, by independent public accountants.

Regulation S–X

Under the authority of the various Acts which it administers, the SEC in 1940 promulgated Regulation S–X and has amended it several times since that date. This is the principal accounting regulation of the SEC and, together with the Accounting Series Releases (referred to below), governs the form and content of most financial statements required to be filed under the Securities Act of 1933, the Securities Exchange Act of 1934, the Public Utility Holding Company Act of 1935, and the Investment Company Act of 1940. The regulation is considered at length in Chapters **16** through **20** and **24** through **26**.

Accounting Series Releases

From time to time the rules and regulations of the SEC are amended and new ones issued. Notices of new and amending rules and regulations, and other information, are given in so-called "releases." The SEC from time to time also publishes (in the form of "releases") opinions of the Commission and/or its Chief Accountant relating to major accounting and auditing questions or to administrative policy with respect to financial statements and certain other material of importance to accountants. Releases of the Commission on accounting matters do not necessarily reflect the views of its Chief Accountant. Public accountants should familiarize themselves with these releases which are published as the Accounting Series. They may be obtained by writing to the Commission and asking to be put on the mailing list for them.

While the releases in the SEC's Accounting Series are not physically part of Regulation S–X, in effect they are a part of that Regulation. Rule 1–01 of Regulation S–X provides that the Regulation "(together with the Accounting Series Releases)" states the requirements applicable to the form and content of all financial statements required to be filed as part of filings with the Commission under the 1933, 1934, 1935, and 1940 Acts.

The first release in the Accounting Series appeared in 1937. Since that time and to the date of this writing there have been 126 releases in the Accounting Series. Some of these releases are mere announcements of proposals to adopt amendments to Regulation S–X; others are announcements of the adoption of amendments. Several of the releases announce the results of disciplinary proceedings involving accountants under the Commission's Rules of Practice; these are discussed in Chapter **27**. A list of the releases in the Accounting Series appears in Appendix A.

Considering the period during which the Accounting Series Releases have been issued, their number is surprisingly small. This may be due to the fact that the SEC has, for the most part as a matter of policy, not wished to impose its views on the accounting profession. Whenever possible, the SEC prefers to have pronouncements relating to accounting and auditing originate with the accounting profession and accordingly it works closely with the profession. The over-all result, in the opinion of one highly qualified observer, "has been an immeasurable improvement in American accounting standards since 1933." [1] Occasionally, however, the SEC finds it desirable to issue an opinion on an accounting or auditing matter. Before doing so, however, copies of the proposed opinion are submitted to the various professional and other interested groups for their criticisms and suggestions.[2] At the same time other interested persons are also invited to

---

[1] Arthur H. Dean, "Twenty-Five Years of Federal Securities Regulation by the Securities and Exchange Commission," 59 *Colum. L. Rev.* 746 (1959).

[2] An exception to the usual procedure occurred in connection with the issuance of ASR No. 90 (1962) relating to accountants' certificates in "first time" examinations. See the discussion regarding this release in Chapter **24**.

Also, when the Commission announced the issuance of Form 7–K (a quarterly financial report to be filed by certain real estate investment companies which has been superseded by Form 7–Q) there was no attempt to obtain the views of the companies

submit their views regarding the proposed opinion. Experience indicates that not only does the SEC invite these comments regarding its proposed opinions, but it also considers them carefully and in some cases modifies the original proposal accordingly.

It is important to understand, however, that some of the Commission's views with regard to accounting and auditing do not appear either in Regulation S–X or in the Accounting Series Releases. Some of the Commission's requirements are informal and are adopted administratively. Although they may have general applicability, they are often not publicized, and the practitioner is apt to learn about them via a deficiency letter. (This matter is discussed further in this chapter.) The SEC's opinion on a specific accounting question may be included in a stop order decision. See, for example, the discussion in Chapter **17** regarding the failure by Atlantic Research Corporation to deal with a company as a controlled subsidiary and to consolidate the financial statements of the subsidiary with those of the parent company. This is not calculated to make more difficult the job of the person interested in learning the SEC's views on accounting matters, but it certainly has that result.

Accounting Series Release No. 4.—In 1938 the Commission issued, in ASR No. 4, the following statement of its administrative policy with respect to financial statements filed under the 1933 and 1934 Acts:

In cases where financial statements filed with this Commission pursuant to its rules and regulations under the Securities Act of 1933 or the Securities Exchange Act of 1934 are prepared in accordance with accounting principles for which there is no substantial authoritative support, such financial statements will be presumed to be misleading or inaccurate despite disclosures contained in the certificate of the accountant or in footnotes to the statements provided the matters involved are material. In cases where there is a difference of opinion between the Commission and the registrant as to the proper principles of accounting to be followed, disclosure will be accepted in lieu of correction of the financial statements themselves only if the points involved are such that there is substantial authoritative support for the practices followed by the registrant and the position of the Commission has not previously been expressed in rules, regulations or other official releases of the Commission, including the published opinions of its Chief Accountant.

The importance of the release to public accountants should be apparent. It means that an accountant whose clients file financial statements with the SEC must be familiar not only with the rules and regulations of the SEC, but also with its accounting opinions, whether in the form of releases in the Accounting Series or in official decisions and reports. If a company files

affected by the new form or of public accountants regarding the requirements of the form. In this case also, the form and the rules requiring it to be filed were effective on issuance.

financial statements with the SEC, and the statements reflect an accounting principle which has been formally disapproved by the SEC, *the financial statements will be presumed to be misleading even though there is full disclosure of the accounting principle in question.*

If a company's financial statements are based on unsupportable accounting practice, the accountant attempts to persuade his client to change the statements; if this fails, and if the matters involved are material, he qualifies his opinion with respect to the statements. The SEC is in a much stronger position to enforce its requirements than the accountant. The SEC requires correction of statements based on (1) accounting principles having no substantial authoritative support, or (2) accounting principles which have been formally disapproved by the Commission. See, for example, the discussion on page **3·**32 regarding two companies that filed statements with the SEC in which depreciation was based not on historical cost but on replacement values.

BACKGROUND OF ACCOUNTING SERIES RELEASE No. 4.—The Securities Act has been called the "Truth in Securities Law." It has also been referred to as a "disclosure" statute. Both terms suggest that the Commission's function is to see that full disclosure is made of all material facts so that an informed investor can make up his mind as to the merits of the security which is offered to him. Regardless of how speculative the security may be, the SEC would be powerless (in theory at least, if not in practice) to prevent it from being offered and sold *provided* all the essential facts were adequately disclosed. Since the 1933 Act is a disclosure statute, ASR No. 4 is somewhat anomalous.

Members of the Commission had apparently been concerned about their conflicting attitude in respect of the material contained in different parts of documents filed with the Commission. Where the matter in question related to the so-called "narrative" section of the document, the Commission was willing to rely on disclosure. Where the matter in question, however, related to the financial section of the document, some members of the Commission believed that disclosure was not a cure if the financial statements were prepared in accordance with unsupportable accounting principles.

The matter came to a head in 1934 when the Commission issued a release in the matter of *Northern States Power Company* (Securities Act Release No. 254). At the time the Commission said that when this company's registration statement was filed with it, there was a difference of opinion among the Commissioners as to the disclosure attending, and the treatment accorded, certain items in the registration statement. The accounting question involved concerned the write-up of fixed capital and investment accounts by $15,000,000 in 1924. Of this amount, $8,000,000 had been credited to capital surplus. In 1924 and 1925 the company wrote off substantially all of its unamortized bond discount and expense (totaling $8,000,000) to the aforementioned capital surplus. In subsequent years there were no charges made against earnings or retained earnings for amortizing such discount and expense.

Three of the Commissioners thought that the circumstances were sufficiently disclosed in the registration statement; two of the Commissioners thought that adequate disclosure and treatment required that the financial statements should be restated and should be accompanied by a statement of the company's past accounting practices. Also, at that time the Commission said that a more detailed expression of the circumstances and of the views of the majority and minority would be made public at an early date.

The "more detailed expression of the circumstances and of the views of the majority and minority," promised in 1934, was never issued. Instead, ASR No. 4 was issued in 1938. Since 1938 the rule followed by the Commission has been based on Release No. 4. If transactions have been improperly recorded and reflected in the financial statements, disclosure of the impropriety will be of no avail; the statements have to be changed. (See page **25**·3 for a discussion of the effect of this policy in practice.)

"SUBSTANTIAL AUTHORITATIVE SUPPORT."—ASR No. 4 (quoted in the previous section) refers to accounting principles and practices having "substantial authoritative support." The Commission has not elaborated on the meaning of these words, nor does the author know of any interpretation thereof by anyone connected with the Commission. In some circumstances it may be important to know what is meant by the words in question.

In this connection it is worth noting the recommendations adopted by the Council of the AICPA in October 1964. The Council issued a special bulletin "Disclosure of Departures from Opinions of the Accounting Principles Board" which recommended that departures from the Opinions of the APB be disclosed either in footnotes to financial statements or in the report of independent auditors. Among other things, the Council stated that:

(a) "Generally accepted accounting principles" are those principles which have substantial authoritative support.

(b) Opinions of the APB constitute "substantial authoritative support."

(c) "Substantial authoritative support" can exist for accounting principles that differ from Opinions of the APB.

It seems to the author that "substantial authoritative support" includes at least the following:

Pronouncements by the American Institute of Certified Public Accountants, including the Accounting Principles Board (and its predecessor, the Committee on Accounting Procedure) and senior technical committees of the Institute, such as the Committee on Auditing Procedure

Pronouncements by the American Accounting Association

Pronouncements by the Financial Executives Institute

Uniform systems of accounts, regulations, and rulings of federal and state regulatory authorities in the fields, for example, of communication, transportation, public utilities (electric, gas, and water), natural gas, and insurance

Uniform systems of accounts recommended by certain major trade associations for members of an industry (such as the petroleum industry)

In the absence of any of the above, predominant practice within an industry or of business enterprises in general

Many of the Commission's decisions relating to accounting and auditing matters contain citations to authors of well-known works in their respective fields. Presumably the citations are intended, in part at least, to back up the Commission's views and therefore constitute "support." Certainly an author would not be cited if the SEC did not believe he was an "authority." It would appear therefore that standard texts by authors whose works are widely read and highly regarded may, in certain areas, represent "substantial authoritative support."

In this respect, however, mention should be made of the SEC's decision in *Interstate Hosiery Mills,* discussed on page **5·46**. In that case the Commission said that the testimony of qualified expert accountants engaged in public practice was relevant and helpful "although the Commission must in the end weigh the value of all expert testimony *against its own judgment of what is sound accounting practice."* (Emphasis supplied.) [4 SEC 715 (1939). Similar views were also expressed in ASR No. 73, p. 11 (1952).]

In a given case an issuer and its accountants may be faced with a situation in which the staff of the SEC has raised a question regarding an accounting principle reflected in the financial statements. The principle is one, let us assume, which is in agreement with a specific pronouncement of the APB. Thus, the principle has "substantial authoritative support." Assume also that the SEC has not publicly stated that its views differ from those of the APB. Would the SEC set aside such support and exercise "its own judgment of what is sound accounting practice?" Under ASR No. 4, it appears that the SEC would be bound to accept the financial statements. If the SEC disagreed with the principle in question, it would have to make its position known formally, and *thereafter* it could reject financial statements filed with it which reflected the principle.

The issuer and its accountants would be in a much more difficult situation if the only support to be found for the principle reflected in the statements is, say, a magazine article by an individual CPA—particularly if the position taken in the article is challenged (as frequently happens) by other CPAs of equal standing and ability.

In between these two extremes there can be infinite variation of the circumstances. It is impossible to predict what the Commission's position under ASR No. 4 would be in a particular case without knowledge of the circumstances in the case.

The preceding discussion has included mention of the fact that departures from Opinions of the APB have to be disclosed either in footnotes to financial statements or in the independent auditor's report. Presumably the same disclosure rule would apply to pronouncements of the Financial Accounting Standards Board (FASB). The FASB is a newly created Board of seven full time salaried members appointed by Financial Accounting Foundation. During their term of office, Board members may have no other business affiliations. The Foundation is separate from all existing professional bodies and is governed by nine trustees (four CPAs in public practice, two financial executives, one financial analyst, one accounting educator, and the AICPA president serving ex officio), whose principal duties will be to appoint the members of the FASB and to raise funds for its operations. The FASB will replace the 18-member, voluntary APB and is expected to begin functioning in 1973. The creation of the Foundation and the FASB was recommended by the Study on Establishment of Accounting Principles whose report was approved by the AICPA Council in May 1972.[3]

Some ASRs Need to Be Revised or Withdrawn.—As previously noted, the SEC has adopted an accounting regulation—designated Regulation S–X—which is applicable to the form and content of financial statements filed with the Commission. At its very outset, the regulation states that, *together with the Accounting Series Releases,* it applies to all financial statements filed under the 1933, 1934, 1935, and 1940 Acts which are administered by the Commission. Accordingly, it is important that the ASRs be reviewed by the SEC from time to time and revised if necessary or withdrawn when they no longer represent the Commission's current thinking. Although the regulation has been revised from time to time—most recently in 1972, when it was extensively revised—the ASRs have never been amended, nor have any of them been withdrawn.

Many of the ASRs are mere announcements of rules which the SEC proposes to adopt or amend, and they are followed in many instances by

[3] Readers interested in the report are referred to "Establishing Financial Accounting Standards," AICPA, March 1972.

other ASRs which announce that the proposed rules have been adopted or amended. As such they furnish no guidance for persons interested in knowing what the SEC's present rules are. The Commission recognized this fact in 1968 when it published a compilation of the ASRs but omitted many that had no current value.

There are other releases which also have no continuing value or relevance, such as those which announce the results of disciplinary proceedings affecting accountants which do not set forth any of the facts on which the Commission's action was based.

More important, however, are the ASRs which do not reflect the Commission's present views in the accounting or auditing areas. ASR No. 53 is a good example.

ASR No. 53 was issued by the Commission in 1945. It is a long and thoughtful discussion by the Commission's then Chief Accountant on the subject of accounting for income taxes, and it dealt with tax reductions and charges in lieu of taxes. As such it dealt not only with taxes payable currently, but also with taxes applicable to current income payable in subsequent years because of provisions in the income tax statutes. It dealt also with reductions in taxes brought about by unusual circumstances in the current year which had a distorting effect on income of the year. It pointed up a significant difference of opinion which existed *at that time* between the Chief Accountant and the staff of the SEC on the one hand and, on the other hand, certain members of the accounting profession. (It should be borne in mind that this incident occurred in 1945—long before the APB and its predecessor committee issued their pronouncements on accounting for income taxes. The most recent of such pronouncements was APB Opinion No. 11, "Accounting for Income Taxes," issued in 1967.)

The SEC's views in ASR No. 53 were presented in relation to the facts surrounding a specific registration statement, which was chosen because it was typical of most cases in which the problem of accounting for income taxes arose. Readers interested in the specific matters dealt with in the release are referred to the release. The Commission's views concerning the treatment of tax savings in financial statements were summarized in the release, and included the statement that *the amount shown as provision for taxes should reflect only actual taxes believed to be payable under the applicable tax laws.*

The Commission's views as stated in ASR No. 53 were somewhat modified by the subsequent issuance of ASR Nos. 85 and 86. In the latter releases the SEC recognized the propriety of the tax allocation principle with specific reference to fixed assets which are depreciated for tax purposes at a faster rate than for financial statement purposes. These releases, however, did not rationalize the difference in viewpoint expressed in the releases as compared with Release No. 53, and there has not been a more recent expression of the Commission's views regarding accounting for income taxes than those contained in ASR Nos. 85 and 86.

As matters now stand, the record shows that the SEC took exception to matters which have become generally accepted accounting practice as most recently exemplified in APB Opinion No. 11. What is more important, however, is that the SEC's staff currently supports the principles set forth in Opinion No. 11 and does not support the main views expressed in Release No. 53, especially as they relate to interperiod tax allocations arising out of timing differences. In fact, it is no exaggeration to say that, if financial statements were filed with the SEC which conformed with the accounting philosophy stated in ASR No. 53, the statements in all likelihood would be challenged by the SEC's staff as not being in conformity with generally accepted accounting principles and might also be the target of a stop-order proceeding or other litigation.

For many years members of the SEC's staff have conceded informally that Release No. 53 had eroded with the passage of time, and, for all practical purposes, many of its provisions were not followed by most registrants or accountants or enforced by the staff. With the revision of Regulation S–X in 1972, it is apparent more than ever that the release is obsolete. In the revised regulation, the rules relating to the general notes to financial statements provide for the showing of the components of income tax expense in a way that recognizes clearly the comprehensive tax allocation theory enunciated in APB Opinion No. 11, which contradicts some of the principal conclusions of Release No. 53. (The revised requirements are included in Chapter **16**.)

It might be said that, since it is generally understood that ASR No. 53 is dead, why does anything have to be done about it? The fact that the release is dead is reason enough to withdraw it since it contradicts current Commission policy in a significant area.

There is also the matter of the auditor's conformity letter (or compliance letter) referred to in Chapter **11**, in which the auditor states, in effect, that the financial statements included in the registration statement and covered by his report comply as to form with the Commission's regulations— including Regulation S–X of which the ASRs are a part. There is no doubt that many compliance letters are issued with respect to financial statements that contravene what the Commission said in ASR No. 53. In this respect the auditor may derive some comfort from the fact that the 1972 revision of the general notes to financial statements of Regulation S–X (referred to above) reflects many of the provisions of APB Opinion No. 11 and, to that extent, may be said to supersede Release No. 53.

ASR No. 50 is another example of a release that needs to be amended. This release deals with the propriety of writing down goodwill arising from the acquisition of a business by means of charges to capital surplus. While the release states that a write-off of such goodwill to capital surplus is contrary to sound accounting principles, it goes on to say:

It is clear that if the goodwill here involved is, or were to become worthless, it would be necessary to write it off. Preferably such write-off should have been accomplished through timely charges to income . . .

From this statement it might be inferred that the SEC has a more liberal position regarding the amortization of goodwill than is expressed in APB Opinion No. 17. In fact, the SEC fully supports the mandatory amortization provisions in Opinion No. 17 with respect to intangible assets acquired after its effective date.

The Commission is aware of the fact that some of the Accounting Series Releases may be obsolete. In ASR No. 125 (June 1972), announcing the revision of Regulation S–X, the SEC said that a study of the Accounting Series Releases was being made "to determine whether certain of the releases should be rescinded."

SEC Decisions on Accounting and Auditing Matters

The decisions and reports of the SEC, issued currently in the form of releases, are periodically printed as bound volumes and sold by the Superintendent of Documents, U. S. Government Printing Office, Washington, D. C. They contain the SEC decisions and reports through May 31, 1964. For decisions and reports subsequent to that date, recourse must be had to the current releases.

Many of the Commission's opinions on accounting and auditing matters were issued before the Accounting Series Releases were instituted. In order to learn the Commission's views on these matters, one must read a large number of decided cases. For the purpose of this book all reported cases under the 1933 and 1934 Acts have been reviewed. The cases under the Holding Company Act of 1935 and Investment Company Act of 1940, with a few exceptions, have not been similarly reviewed since they are based largely on regulatory considerations.

The SEC is one of the "independent agencies" and makes an annual report of its activities to Congress. These reports frequently comment on accounting and auditing matters and the Commission's activities in these areas. These reports have also been reviewed for the purpose of this volume.

Index of SEC Opinions Not Available.—The SEC's opinions on accounting are not necessarily synonymous with generally accepted principles of accounting (see, for example, the discussion of the investment credit on page **3·14**). It is clear, however, that opinions of the SEC on accounting and auditing matters carry considerable authority. Practitioners, teachers, and students read with great interest all SEC pronouncements dealing with such matters. In addition to Regulation S–X, the media through which the Commission makes known its views in the fields of accounting and auditing are its decisions and reports and the Accounting Series Releases.

Each of the volumes of SEC decisions and reports contains a so-called index-digest of the cases contained in that volume. This index-digest consists, for the most part, of a reprint of the headnotes preceding each decision and report. Although these headnotes are a skillful condensation of the matter discussed in the decision or report, as a reference source they leave much to be desired. The SEC has not published an index covering all of its decisions and reports, nor does the author know of one issued by any other organization. The SEC's Annual Reports contain neither an index nor an index-digest, and there is no index of the Accounting Series Releases. In the opinion of the author, there is a real need for such an all-inclusive index so that the SEC's views on accounting and auditing matters may be readily available. It is hoped that this book will, in some degree, answer that need.

In the chapters which follow, frequent reference is made to SEC decisions, reports, and opinions relating to specific accounting and auditing matters. In this chapter and in the following chapters, consideration is given to those SEC views of a more general nature.

SEC's Informal Rulings Not Publicized.—The SEC's formal rulings as expressed in its decisions, reports, and Accounting Series Releases are discussed in the preceding pages. Even though the SEC has not published an index of these rulings (which would make them more accessible), the fact is that the rulings have been published and are available. On the other hand, there is a considerable number of SEC *informal* rulings bearing on accounting and auditing which the Commission has not publicized but which are important not only to accountants but also to all persons and organizations having business with the Commission.

What happens is this: the accounting staff of the Commission may be faced with a problem in a particular filing, and, after discussing the matter, will take a position with respect to it. The decision reached in that case often becomes a precedent as far as the SEC's staff is concerned for similar problems in other cases when, and if, they occur. Unfortunately, the public is not aware of these informal administrative decisions and learns about them only as the result of encountering them in specific instances. The following is an example taken from an actual case which illustrates the problem.

A publicly owned company which had been located in New York City for many years, moved its headquarters to another city. Expenses were incurred in connection with the move, with respect to which it was not expected that there would be a future benefit. In conjunction with its independent accountants, the company considered the nature and amount of these costs, and concluded that they should be shown in the income statement in the company's published annual report as an "extraordinary item," that is, it would be shown as an expense of the year but after the items of income and expense relating to normal operations.

Some time thereafter the company filed its Form 10–K report with the SEC. The income statement included in this document treated the moving expense consistent with the treatment in the published annual report, that is, as an extraordinary item. Subsequently a letter of comments was received from the SEC. Insofar as the financial statements were concerned, there was only one comment: the letter stated that the moving expenses should be included in normal operating expenses—not shown as an extraordinary item.

The company's independent auditors discussed the accounting matter with the SEC's staff. The staff said that it had previously taken the position that, where a future benefit was expected to be derived from a move, the attendant expenses should be capitalized and amortized over some future period by charges to ordinary income, rather than charging such expenses to income in the year incurred as an extraordinary item. By implication, based upon the letter of comments, a decision not to capitalize moving costs would require a charge against ordinary income notwithstanding the extraordinary nature of the item. Under the circumstances of this case, the SEC conceded the point and withdrew its comment.

If there had been any likelihood of a future benefit arising from the move, and the SEC had insisted on its position, a significant effect on the make-up of the net income as between ordinary income and extraordinary items would have resulted. Had the Commission's position been publicized in an Accounting Series Release, the company and its auditors would have complied initially whether or not they agreed with it. But it is annoying (and sometimes embarrassing) to learn of these informal SEC decisions which have general applicability by means of a deficiency letter on a specific filing.

Sometimes these informal rulings do get publicized even though they are not published as an Accounting Series Release. They may be included in a speech delivered by a member of the SEC's accounting staff, or included in an article in an accounting publication. Sometimes the rulings are referred to when members of the SEC staff participate in professional development courses sponsored by the AICPA and the state societies of CPAs, such as one entitled "Filings with the SEC," in which several members of the SEC's staff have participated.

Sometimes also the Commission's informal opinions on accounting and auditing matters may be publicized as the result of articles written in professional publications. An excellent example is the discussion which appears frequently in "SEC Commentary," a department in *CPA Journal,* the monthly magazine of the New York State Society of CPAs.

In 1970 the SEC announced a program for publicizing the decisions taken by its staff with respect to requests for so-called "no action" and interpretative letters (Release No. 33–5098, October 29, 1970). (In a "no action" letter, the SEC staff advises the person soliciting its views that, under a described set of facts, the staff would not recommend that the Commission take any action, such as enjoining a proposed transaction, if the transaction described were carried out.) At the date of this writing, the author understands that the program of publicizing interpretative letters will not include interpretations of the Commission's accounting and auditing requirements.

Precedents May Not Always Be Precedents.—Sometimes an accountant is faced with a knotty accounting or auditing problem, and, as part of his research on the subject, may review a number of recent prospectuses to see whether a similar or identical problem has arisen before. If any of the prospectuses indicate how the problem was previously dealt with, the accountant may conclude that he has an indication of the SEC's position on the subject since prospectuses are reviewed by the SEC's staff. In the author's opinion, however, it is unwise to rely completely on such "precedents"—particularly if one disagrees with the solution to the problem indicated by the prospectus.

There are several reasons for not jumping at the conclusion that "if you see it in a prospectus—especially a recent prospectus—it reflects the SEC's views."

In the first place, the SEC and its staff make no claim of infallibility. As the result of the staff's review of financial statements filed with the SEC, the Commission often furnishes the registrant with a memorandum of comments setting forth those areas in which the statements appear to need revision. These comments are often discussed by representatives of the registrant and its auditors with the SEC's staff, and the comments are frequently withdrawn.

Sometimes, however, a prospectus may reflect an accounting treatment which the reader may believe does represent a precedent for a problem confronting him. He may not be certain that the fact patterns are similar and decides to discuss his problem and the precedent with the SEC's staff. The author has known of instances of this kind in which the staff agreed that the fact patterns were substantially similar but that the accounting reflected in the prospectus was improper and that the SEC's concurrence in the accounting was an error. As such, it could not serve as a valid precedent.

In July 1971, for instance, the SEC's staff took exception to the computation of the ratio of earnings to fixed charges in a prospectus filed with it relating to an offering of debentures. The effect of the method of computation which the staff insisted had to be followed was very significant, and the issuer decided to discuss the matter with the staff. In the discussion the staff admitted that it had not publicized its views with respect to the computation of the ratio, but said that it had enforced the new method administratively and informally since late in 1970. The registrant had in its possession, however, a prospectus of one of the world's largest industrial enterprises dated in March 1971 and relating to a debenture offering, in which the ratio had not been computed in accordance with the method insisted upon by the staff. The staff was unable to account for the treatment in the earlier prospectus, and conceded that the presentation in the prospectus was contrary to its views at that time and must have slipped by the examiners.

In the second place, as a result of the cursory examination contemplated by the curtailed review procedures adopted by the Commission (discussed in Chapter **7**), it is not to be expected that the staff will have fully considered every accounting problem and its solution as reflected in a prospectus. In the brief examination resulting from the curtailed procedures, it is not reasonable to expect that in every case the staff will know whether all the relevant facts have been properly reflected in the prospectus.

Third, although the facts with respect to a matter reflected in a prospectus may appear to be similar to those in a problem facing the accountant, the similarity is often superficial. In his search for precedents, the author has often come across prospectuses that included a problem apparently similar to one facing him, only to find, after further inquiry, that there were significant undisclosed differences in the underlying facts, so that reliance could not be placed on the "precedent" as being representative of the thinking that might be appropriate to the facts in the problem at hand.

Not long ago, for example, the author was considering the question of the appropriateness of equity accounting in a case where Company A owned 40% of Company B. Both companies were listed for trading on a securities exchange, and the remaining ownership of B was widely dispersed. Not only did A have the *power* to control B, but it had demonstrated its control by using it. The entire Board of Directors of B consisted of persons designated by A. In the circumstances, A considered it appropriate to employ equity accounting for the investment in B, but understood that the SEC opposed the use of the method unless the holding was 50% or more. (This was before the APB issued its Opinion No. 18 in March 1971 making it possible to employ the equity method where the investment represented as little as 20% of the voting power.) In the course of reviewing prospectuses, the author came across a June 1970 prospectus of the EGF Company (not its real name). EGF owned 36% of the outstanding stock of AGT Company (not its real name). EGF accounted for the investment in AGT on the equity basis beginning in 1969, with the approval of its independent auditors, and apparently without objection by the SEC. On further inquiry, however, it developed that AGT was a joint venture in corporate form, and so the case had no value as a precedent to Company A since it was well known that equity accounting for corporate joint ventures had been an accepted accounting method for many years.

Fourth, the problem involved may be in a developing area, and what may have been acceptable a year ago, may not be acceptable today. For a multitude of examples, one need only cite the accounting for business combinations in the period before the issuance of APB Opinion No. 16 (1970) in which the AICPA re-defined the guidelines for determining the accounting for business combinations. The original concept of pooling of interests as a fusion of equity interests was modified in practice as the use of the method expanded. The method was first applied in accounting for combinations of affiliated corporations. It was then extended to some combinations of unrelated corporate ownership interests of comparable size. Ultimately the factor of the relative size of the constituents was, in practice, virtually ignored. In promulgating the new Opinion, the APB carefully and explicitly considered the criterion of relative size, but, in the end, abandoned it. Consequently, although the relative size of the constituent companies of the combination may have been a factor to be considered in the past, it no longer is.

In 1963, the SEC's Chief Accountant referred to the fact that any marginal practice appearing in a prospectus or annual report which has not been challenged by the SEC's staff "whether from oversight, lack of materiality or other cause" is often cited back to the Commission as proof that it is generally accepted practice. "This," he said, "seems to conform to the operation of Gresham's Law." [4]

Whose Statements Are They?

It has been made abundantly clear that financial statements are the representations of management—not the representations of the certifying accountants. In *Montgomery's Auditing* the authors stated:

> It should be clearly understood that owners or management are responsible for the financial statements; the auditor is responsible for his report and opinion. The auditor may assist, advise, and persuade management with respect to form and content of financial statements, but he cannot compel management to accept his recommendations. The auditor can, and should, state in his report

[4] Andrew Barr, "Financial Statements—How Reliable?", *NAA Bulletin,* Sept. 1963, p. 7.

wherein he disagrees with the fairness of presentation of financial statements if he cannot persuade management to make changes he believes necessary.[5]

The AICPA Committee on Auditing Procedure has said:

Management has the responsibility for adopting sound accounting policies, for maintaining an adequate and effective system of accounts, for the safeguarding of assets, and for devising a system of internal control that will, among other things, help assure the production of proper financial statements. The transactions which should be reflected in the accounts and in the financial statements are matters within the direct knowledge and control of management. The auditor's knowledge of such transactions is limited to that acquired through his examination. Accordingly, the fairness of the representations made through financial statements is an implicit and integral part of management's responsibility. The independent auditor may make suggestions as to the form or content of financial statements or he may draft them in whole or in part, based on the management's accounts and records. However, his responsibility for the statements he has examined is confined to the expression of his opinion on them. The financial statements remain the representations of the management.[6]

A few large corporations authorize their chief financial officer to sign the financial statements in their published reports, which are sometimes accompanied by a short report of this officer. This practice is recommended by the New York Stock Exchange. It emphasizes the responsibility of management for published financial statements and, by contrast, the responsibility of the independent public accountant for his opinion. It stresses that the accountant's function is to check on management's discharge of its responsibility.

In a clear statement of its views on this question, the SEC has said that the fundamental and primary responsibility for the accuracy of information filed with the Commission and disseminated among investors rests upon management. [*Interstate Hosiery Mills, Inc.,* 4 SEC 721 (1939)]. Management does not discharge its obligations in this respect by the employment of independent public accountants, however reputable. Accountants' certificates are required not as a substitute for management's accounting of its stewardship, but as a check upon that accounting.

Emphasizing the primary responsibility of management for financial statements, the SEC in an earlier case said:

Responsibility for the non-disclosure of these matters . . . must lie with its officers. Accurate and complete information was not furnished the accountants. Representatives of [the certifying accountants] testified that if they had known of the facts in this case which we have discussed, the registrant's financial statements would have been prepared in a form which would fully have disclosed them. [*Breeze Corporations, Inc.,* 3 SEC 729 (1938)].

---

[5] Lenhart and Defliese, *Montgomery's Auditing* (8th ed., 1957), p. 95.

[6] Statement on Auditing Procedure No. 33 (1963, p. 9). See also Accounting Research Bulletin No. 43 (1953), p. 10.

In ASR No. 62 (1947), the Chief Accountant of the SEC said, "Financial statements filed for the registrant and its subsidiaries have been recognized by this Commission and by public accountants generally as representations of management upon whom rests the primary responsibility for their propriety and accuracy."

An SEC decision in 1948 stressed management's responsibility not only for financial statements but also for an examination of those statements meeting SEC requirements. [*Arleen W. Hughes,* 27 SEC 629 (1948)]. The Commission had instituted a proceeding to determine whether the registration of a broker-dealer under the 1934 Act should be suspended or revoked. The order for hearing alleged, among other things, that the broker-dealer had violated the law and Rule 17a–5 adopted thereunder by filing reports of financial condition which did not meet the minimum audit requirements prescribed by the rule. The broker-dealer testified that she had relied upon her accountants to prepare the reports and believed that they were being prepared in accordance with Commission requirements. The SEC said, "a broker-dealer is not relieved of the responsibility of complying with Rule 17a–5 merely by relying on accountants for the preparation of the reports required by the rule." [*Arleen W. Hughes,* 27 SEC 631 (1948)].

A former chairman of the SEC stated very clearly that the primary responsibility for financial statements rested on management, which, in turn, depended on the financial officers, and that independent auditors operated as a check on management. He said:

> As we see it, financial statements under the Acts are, first and foremost, the responsibility of management—which, of course, in large measure must depend upon the financial officers. Independent accountants lend authority by their opinions as experts and operate as a check in assuring that generally accepted accounting principles are used and that figures are fairly determined in accordance with accepted auditing standards. But it is the financial executive who furnishes these figures. His key position is underscored by the Securities Act of 1933 which requires that a registration statement be signed by "its principal financial officer, its comptroller or principal accounting officer . . ."[7]

Employment and Training of Staff

In *Interstate Hosiery* [4 SEC 706 (1939)] one of the principal issues was whether the certifying accountants had exercised due care in employing Raymond Marien, the author of the falsifications in the financial statements. Marien filed an application for employment with the accounting firm as a result of an advertisement by the firm in a New York newspaper. He was interviewed by a partner of the firm in May, 1928. The application stated that Marien was a graduate of the University of Montreal, with several degrees, and that he had eight years' public accounting experience, including

---

[7] William L. Cary, address before Financial Executives Institute, Oct. 8, 1963.

industrial, mercantile, banking, and brokerage assignments. A letter addressed to a former employer whom Marien had given for reference elicited the reply that Marien had worked for that firm for about eight years until February, 1928, and that he was considered by them "a thoroughly competent senior accountant," highly recommended "for his keen analytical ability, his sound mental training, his tact, his loyalty, and the thoroughness of his work." Marien was thereupon hired with no further investigation. Press reports at the time Interstate's stock was suspended from dealings indicated that Marien had been convicted of forgery in 1924, but this, if it was a fact, was not known to the partner of the accounting firm when he hired Marien. In commenting on this matter, however, the SEC said that, "any possible deficiency in the investigation of Marien's background at the time of his employment loses significance in view of the favorable experience which [the certifying accountants] had with Marien in the succeeding five years before the irregularities commenced."

The SEC also commented on the matter of staff training, development, and supervision in its report on the *McKesson & Robbins* case. A partner of the certifying accountants in that case had written that an important responsibility of the firm and of the profession is to provide adequate facilities for the training of the staff in order to equip the members thereof for meeting the demands of accountancy work. The firm attempted to meet their responsibility in this regard by means of classes during the fall months and by encouraging the staff to keep abreast of current literature in the field and to attend meetings of the professional societies. In the practical application of accounting knowledge, supervision while on the engagement was considered perhaps the most essential phase of the training, and success in the training program was measured by results obtained in the field. The top echelons of the staff reported currently on the qualifications and personalities of the men working under them. These reports were analyzed to form the basis for a periodic review of the status and salary of each member of the organization. Concerning these arrangements the SEC said:

We have found that there is great similarity among accounting firms in the organization of the staff and assignments to engagements. We deplore, as do accounting firms, the necessity for recruiting large numbers of temporary employees during a very short busy season. This condition and the lack of training in the firm's methods which it ordinarily entails are inimical to attaining the best results from the auditors' services. A major improvement in this condition could be made by the general adoption by corporations of the natural business year for accounting purposes. The recruiting of temporary employees was more aggravated in [the certifying accountants] than in other comparable firms whose representatives testified as experts. This situation, coupled with the fact that [the certifying accountants] had a higher ratio of both permanent and peak staff per partner than other firms, leads us to the conclusion that [the certifying accountants'] partners could not have given adequate attention to the training, development, and supervision of their staff. [ASR No. 19 (1940)]

In its report on investigation of McKesson & Robbins, Inc., the SEC included a chart showing the size of the staffs of various firms as compared with the number of partners. The chart also indicated the seasonal nature of public accounting work and the responsibilities devolving upon partners. With the names of the firms deleted, the chart follows:

Firm	Number of Partners	Number of Staff Per Partner		Peak Season Increase —Per Cent of Permanent
		Permanent	Peak	
McKesson's auditors	24	31.3	61.0	95
National firm A	25	*	*	*
National firm B	11	11.4	15.9	39
National firm C	17	8.8	13.5	54
National firm D	57	12.6	19.7	56
National firm E	32	18.4	25.5	39
National firm F	17	15.3	20.6	35
National firm G	27	24.1	35.2	46
National firm H	15	*	*	54
Local firm 1	4	10.0	10.0	0
Local firm 2	4	6.3	6.3	0
Local firm 3	6	8.3	16.7	100

* Information sufficiently accurate for this purpose not supplied.

The table showed, the SEC pointed out, that McKesson's auditors expanded their staff in the peak season to a much greater extent than the other firms represented in the table, with the exception of one much smaller firm. Furthermore, this expansion was added to a staff which in the slack season was much larger in relation to the number of partners than was the case for any of the other firms listed. "It seems inevitable," the SEC said, "that the burden on the partners, managers, and permanent staff seniors must have been greater with an increase of 95% in the staff during the peak season (over 60% of these serving for the first time) than with the increase of 56% or less shown for the other large firms." [8]

Investigation of New Clients

An important aspect of the SEC's report in the *McKesson & Robbins* case was the manner and extent of the investigation of new clients by the certifying accountants. It was especially important in this case because of the criminal background of the principal architect of the fraud who was a twice-convicted swindler.

A partner of the accounting firm which served as McKesson's independent auditors testified as to the manner in which his firm first became con-

[8] *In the Matter of McKesson & Robbins, Inc., Report on Investigation* (1940), p. 371.

nected with Coster (Musica), the president of McKesson. The partner said that a corporation official had met another partner of the accounting firm one day and said that an acquaintance of his, named Coster, wanted some accounting work done, and that the corporation official had given Coster the name of the accounting firm. The official thought that the firm might hear from Coster in a few days. This single personal contact seems to have been the only information obtained by the accounting firm about the prospective client except what came to them in the correspondence with the client. Entire reliance for information about the client was placed upon an examination of the books after taking the engagement.

The SEC commented:

While there is no indication that an investigation by an independent agency would have, in this case, disclosed the fraud we feel that for the future the small expense involved in making some check of the reputation of the management of the client would be well warranted, for even if such reports on their face do not disclose clear irregularities, they may condition the approach to certain phases of the work or the acceptance of explanations given by officers of the client.[9]

The SEC also said, "Such inquiry should provide a valuable background for interpreting conditions revealed during the audit or, in extreme cases, might lead to a refusal of the engagement." [10]

Because of the importance of the case and the SEC's association with it, the case is discussed at greater length in Chapter 5.

Natural Business Year

The benefits not only to public accountants but also to business that would result from the widespread adoption of a natural business year are well known. The SEC also has spoken strongly in favor of the natural business year. In ASR No. 17 (1940), the SEC's Chief Accountant said:

. . . The advantages to be obtained from the adoption of a fiscal-year-end date which coincides with the lowest point in the annual cycle of operations are clear and to my mind have never been shown to be outweighed by related disadvantages. Among the more important advantages there may be mentioned the probability of obtaining more complete and reliable financial statements since at the close of the natural business year incomplete transactions, and such items as inventories, would ordinarily be at a minimum. Mention may also be made of the fact that the general adoption of the natural business year would facilitate the work of public accountants by permitting them to spread much of their work throughout the calendar year, and thus aid them in rendering the most effective service to their clients.

Also in the *McKesson* case, the SEC deplored the necessity for accounting firms to recruit large numbers of temporary employees during a very short busy season; see the quotation from the SEC's opinion on page 2·21.

[9] *In the Matter of McKesson & Robbins, Inc., Report on Investigation*, p. 378.
[10] *Ibid.,* at 6.

Audit Committees Composed of Outside Directors

Following its investigation of the *McKesson & Robbins* case, the SEC recommended the adoption of a program for: (1) current election of auditors at the annual meeting of stockholders; (2) nomination of auditors and arranging the details of the audit by a committee of nonofficer members of the board of directors; (3) addressing of the auditors' report to the stockholders; (4) mandatory attendance by the auditors at annual meetings of stockholders; and (5) mandatory submission by auditors of a report on the amount of work done and of the reasons for noncompletion in situations where audit engagements are not completed.

In 1967 the AICPA Executive Committee recommended that standing audit committees of outside directors should nominate auditors for the annual audits of publicly-owned companies and should discuss the audit work with the auditors appointed to perform the audit. The AICPA considered that such committees ". . . can be a constructive force in the overall review of internal controls and financial structure, and give added assurance to stockholders as to the objectivity of corporate financial statements." (*The Journal of Accountancy*, Sept. 1967, p. 10).

The SEC recently reaffirmed its support of the proposal for standing audit committees composed of outside directors. The Commission said it endorsed the establishment of such committees and urged the business and financial communities and all shareholders of publicly-owned companies to support the proposal in order to assist in affording the greatest possible protection to investors. (Accounting Series Release No. 123, March 23, 1972).

CHAPTER 3

SEC VIEWS ON ACCOUNTING PRINCIPLES

Part 1

CONTENTS

Accounting Principles Not Prescribed by the SEC.—Although the SEC has the authority to prescribe the accounting principles to be followed in financial statements filed with it, the Commission has not, with certain exceptions, invoked its authority to dictate how financial statements shall be prepared. In Regulation S–X (see Chapters **16** through **20**) it has set forth its requirements as to the *form and content* of financial statements filed under the several laws administered by it. In its decisions and in the Accounting Series Releases it has stated its opinion concerning a limited number of accounting principles and practices. Under the Holding Company Act it has promulgated two uniform systems of accounts which are applicable to a small number of companies. Under the Investment Advisers Act it has specified the books, records, and other information which must be maintained by investment advisers subject to the Act. As to the large body of accounting principles underlying the preparation of financial statements, however, the SEC has for the most part been content to rely on generally accepted principles of accounting as they exist or develop with the passage of time. (But see page **5·3** regarding the SEC's statement reserving the right to determine what is "sound accounting practice.") It would be regrettable if the SEC were to prescribe one set of accounting principles and to have business generally follow different principles for purposes other than filing with the SEC. In fact, it would be more than regrettable; it would be virtually impossible as will be seen from the discussion of the SEC's proxy regulation in Chapter **22**.

The authority over the development of accounting given to the SEC in the 1933 Act was applauded by a few and deplored by many. In the latter group was George O. May, one of the outstanding accountants of his day, whose contributions to his profession were enormous. In 1943 he pointed out that the grant of authority to the SEC to prescribe accounting rules was at variance with English concepts.[1] In England, he said, the view prevailed which was expressed by the Greene Committee in 1916: "The matter of accounts is one in which we are satisfied upon the evidence before us that within reasonable limits companies should be left a free hand."

May wrote that experience under the 1933 Act during the decade ending in 1943 had served only to strengthen his conviction "that the grant of powers to prescribe accounting procedure, was as unwise and unnecessary as it was inadequately considered." He continued: "It struck a wanton and unjustified blow at the development of a profession which, despite lapses, had made remarkable progress in the forty years of its existence."

If audits were required under the 1933 Act and a heavy liability placed on the profession for the proper discharge of the duty thus imposed upon it, May said there could be no reason for striking at its professional character by taking the responsibility for accounting rules and principles out of its hands and placing it in those of a policy-making body that was not expert. "The provisions were manifestly written into the law by people who had no adequate understanding of the nature of accounting."

The Commission's underlying philosophy regarding the responsibility for the development of proper accounting methods was expressed by a member of the Commission in 1937. Speaking before the Wisconsin Society of CPAs, Commissioner George C. Mathews said that a "governmental agency should frame rules to govern the exercise of professional functions only when the need for such rules has been shown to be of real public importance. Mere preference of the administrative agency for one form or one method is not sufficient reason for taking the formulation of principles and practices out of the hands of the members of a profession, and where the profession gives evidence of its capacity and willingness to develop and apply proper methods without evasion or undue delay, it should be encouraged to take on the responsibility."

More recently, William L. Cary, a former chairman of the SEC, testi-

[1] George O. May, *Financial Accounting,* The Macmillan Co. (1943), pp. 61–62.

fied before the Subcommittee on Commerce and Finance of the Committee on Interstate and Foreign Commerce, House of Representatives. He spoke of the alternatives existing in generally accepted accounting principles and the efforts and progress being made by the accountancy profession and the SEC in eliminating or reducing the alternatives. He said that the Commission had encouraged the accountancy profession to exercise leadership in accounting and auditing matters but, at the same time, "has not hesitated to criticize and prod, to take exception to accounting presentations, and to discipline members of the profession when circumstances warranted." [2]

Mr. Cary said that the Commission was working with the AICPA and other organizations in their efforts to narrow the areas of differences in accounting, and that "such efforts are clearly in the interest of investors." He observed that this is an unending process for as uniformity of practice is achieved in some areas, new problems arise in others because of changing economic conditions and business practices. Continuing, he said:

> . . . Much improvement in financial reporting practices has occurred since the enactment of the first Federal securities law in 1933. The Commission believes that its policy of working with and supporting the accounting profession in the development of accounting principles has directly influenced this progress and is the best means of assuring continuing improvement of accounting practice.

Mr. Cary furnished the Congressional committee with a list of some of the areas of accounting where alternative practices could produce materially different results under generally accepted accounting principles. Broadly speaking, the areas were as follows: (1) valuation of inventories, (2) depreciation and depletion practices, (3) allocation of income taxes, (4) accounting for pensions, (5) research and development costs, (6) goodwill, (7) the timing of income realization, and (8) presentation in income statements of extraordinary and special items. [*Author's Note*: The SEC's Chief Accountant acknowledged in a speech in November 1969 that virtually every one of the areas included in the 1964 list had since been the subject of an APB Opinion, or was under consideration by the Board, or was being researched by the Accounting Research Division of the AICPA in anticipation of APB action. (*The Journal of Accountancy*, Jan. 1970, p. 16)]

One of the outstanding accountants who approved the SEC's decision to rely on the profession for the development and promulgation of accounting principles was Robert M. Trueblood. He said, "In my judgement, the most important single event affecting the profession during my professional career has been the SEC's decision that the profession should assume pri-

---

[2] "Uniformity in Accounting," *The Journal of Accountancy*, June 1964, pp. 56–61.

mary responsibility for establishing accounting principles." [3] With few exceptions, he continued, the SEC had adhered to that policy, in consequence of which the organized practicing profession had had immense opportunity and concomitant responsibility, but had not fully realized its potential.

From time to time there have been indications that some members of the Commission have been less than enthusiastic about relying on the accountancy profession to develop generally accepted accounting principles. In 1963 a former member of the Commission said:

> . . . The Commission has exercised [its] sweeping powers [under Section 19 of the Securities Act] with considerable restraint. The Commission's philosophy in this regard was set forth in its Accounting [Series] Release No. 4, dated April 25, 1938, and it has not changed in 25 years. A reliance upon "generally accepted accounting principles," as developed by the accounting profession, has left a great deal of room for variation in the accounting practices and principles observed by companies, whether or not they are subject to the requirements of the Commission. The unanswered question presented by this history, . . . is whether the Commission's restraint has been and continues to be in the public interest and in the interest of investors. Do the disclosures of accounting principles followed, as contained in the prospectus, really make it possible for an analyst to make a side by side comparison of two competing companies' earnings statements? I doubt it. I do not suggest that unvarying application of uniform accounting principles is a desirable end in itself. I don't like strait jackets. However, we may not have gone as far in that direction as we should.[4]

One writer who was highly dissatisfied with the status quo was Professor Robert N. Anthony. Like others before him, he wrote in 1963 that if the APB did not take the initiative in formulating accounting principles, the SEC would surely step in and do the job (*Harvard Business Review*, May–June 1963). He discussed the need for establishing accounting principles and the fact that the SEC has the authority and the will to meet this need.

In Anthony's view the task of establishing a comprehensive statement of principles is neither difficult nor time-consuming. The SEC's chairman has only to instruct the SEC's Chief Accountant of what is desired, and a tentative statement of principles would be ready in six months. Allow three or four months for exposure and hearings, according to Anthony, and the SEC would have a revised document on which it could take action.

When he wrote his article in 1963, Anthony was pessimistic of the APB's efforts to meet the need for a coherent statement of accounting principles and itemized what he regarded as the Board's puny accomplishments to that date. Although he did not like the idea of government stepping in to fill the vacuum, "we must admit that SEC action is preferable to no action at all."

[3] Address before American Accounting Association, August 27, 1969.

[4] Jack M. Whitney II, Address before Washington Society of Investment Analysts, Feb. 5, 1963.

The then chairman of the SEC, William L. Cary, commented on Anthony's article as follows:

> . . . Anthony says we (SEC) should set the rules. We have the power, and perhaps should lend more concrete rule-making support to decisions reached by a body such as the Accounting Principles Board. But Government should not be called upon to do everything, and actually we do not want to . . . We are, therefore, not prepared to accept the mantle which Professor Anthony has cast over us. (*The Journal of Accountancy,* December 1963, p. 49)

Robert E. Witschey, a former president of the AICPA, in a reply to Professor Anthony, said that the Institute's effort in defining accounting standards was very much alive. If the SEC preferred to rely on the profession to define those standards, it was because the SEC understood how tough the problems were. If the SEC should take the initiative away from the profession, it would encounter the same difficulties, he said, in resolving complex problems which now confront the profession. He conceded that the SEC would be able to move with greater speed only by imposing arbitrary decisions upon the accounting profession and the business community, which might not prove to be in the best interests of investors. (*Harvard Business Review,* September–October 1963)

Byron D. Woodside, a former commissioner of the SEC, commented on the SEC's reluctance to dictate the accounting rules to be followed by issuers and their accountants. He said:

> . . . I know from personal experience that at times there have been some in the legal and accounting professions who found it easy to respond to comment or suggestion with a demand for a rule. But by and large this has not been so, and the accountants in particular have asked for the opportunity to grow and develop free of rules.
>
> The Commission has employed a number of techniques to inform issuers and accountants as to its views in accounting matters without resorting to rule-making procedures. Speeches by members of the Commission, its chief accountants or division directors, participations in panel discussions and briefing sessions have served a useful purpose. I think that progress in the development of auditing standards and notions as to the independence of accountants . . . was accelerated by some pointed critical public observations on these subjects by responsible members of the accounting profession as well as by Commission personnel.
>
> Through the years, we have continued as a matter of policy our case-by-case approach. In general, we have avoided rule-making in the accounting area; we have tried in our day-to-day work and, in particular, through the efforts of our chief accountants, to encourage the acceptance by the profession of the difficult task of defining and refining accounting principles.
>
> . . . We have recognized, however, that, as between different issuers which may or may not be otherwise comparable, alternative accounting procedures with respect to a particular accounting presentation might be employed if there was, to quote Release No. 4 again, substantial authoritative support for the practice followed. I think it is fair to say that we have not sought to insure as

an end in itself that the financial statements of Company A compare in all material respects with those of Company B.[5]

The Commission's preference for the accountancy profession to have the primary responsibility for the development of accounting principles and auditing procedures should not be interpreted as a hands-off policy on the part of the Commission. It is a fact that the SEC is very much involved in these developments. The professional groups charged with the responsibility for developing accounting principles and improving auditing practices consult frequently with representatives of the Commission's staff before issuing their APB Opinions and Statements on Auditing Procedure. The involvement by SEC representatives is very much in keeping with a statement by William J. Casey, chairman of the SEC, who quoted Clemenceau as having said that "accounting is too important to be left entirely to the accountants." [6]

Manuel F. Cohen, a former chairman of the SEC, has often stressed the need for comparability of financial statements and the corresponding need to narrow the choice of acceptable but alternative principles of accounting and managements' freedom to choose among them. The existence of these alternatives constitutes the main obstacle to achieving comparability. Mr. Cohen noted in 1966 that "Although the Commission has the authority under the securities laws to impose uniform systems of accounts on issuers registering securities under the 1933 or 1934 Act, we have not done so." [7] Instead, the statutory authority had been used only to require that financial statements be accompanied by the opinion of an independent accountant to the effect that the statements conform with generally accepted accounting principles and to promulgate Regulation S-X, "and we have looked primarily to the accounting profession for formulation of those principles." The Commission's principal activity in recent years in the accounting area had centered for the most part on particular cases rather than on the development of overall principles of general applicability.

Mr. Cohen noted the debate that raged over the relative mertis of flexibility on the one hand and uniformity on the other as a guide to the preparation of financial statements. There were those, he acknowledged, who argued that comparability was such a desirable goal that a uniform system of accounts was a practical necessity, but there were others who insisted that the need for judgment in the preparation of financial statements precluded

---

[5] Byron D. Woodside, "A Review of the Commission's Administrative Policies Relating to Financial Reporting Under the Securities Acts," Hayden, Stone and Company, Inc., Fourth Annual Accounting Forum, New York University Graduate School, Nov. 18, 1965.

[6] William J. Casey, "The Public Interest in our Securities Markets," address before Institutional Trading Conference, New York, N. Y., June 17, 1971.

[7] Address before Financial Analysts Federation, May 24, 1966. Printed in *The Journal of Accountancy,* August 1966.

the establishment of hard and fast lines of the kind contemplated by the advocates of uniformity. He agreed that comparability was a desirable goal, but it was not at all certain that even in the best of all possible accounting worlds, it would be possible to develop a system of absolute comparability of financial statements. "I believe," he said, "that the arguments would be less heated, and more productive, if both sides would emphasize the common goal of eliminating unjustified variances in financial reporting, and thereby achieve a maximum degree of comparability of financial statements of similar companies."

Saying he had "no intention to criticize," he proceeded to be highly critical of the accounting profession, noting that the profession had "been unable to reduce significantly, if not eliminate, the variety of accounting principles deemed permissible in the reporting of similar financial conditions and results." He continued:

> The result has, of course, been questionable diversity in accounting treatment of similar matters. It is possible to have two companies, whose financial condition and experience are substantially identical, presenting their balance sheets and income statements in very different ways. It may be argued that each form of presentation, standing alone, is permissible, in that the form of presentation is logical, internally consistent, and appropriate to an understanding of the financial condition of the company once the premises of the particular accounting system are fully explained. But direct comparison between the financial statements of the two companies is impossible, certainly without the most sophisticated analyses based upon assumptions which may or may not be justified. As long as different accounting principles are permitted to be applied to substantially the same facts, however logical those principles may be, true comparability is impaired, and an important purpose of financial reporting is thwarted.[8]

One avenue being followed toward the goal of uniformity, according to Mr. Cohen, was stronger leadership by the SEC. An example of this, he said, was the issuance of ASR No. 102 in December 1965 dealing with the balance sheet classification of deferred income taxes arising from instalment sales. Before the release was issued, at least four different reporting methods were in use by companies for which the item was important, but in each case the statements were accompanied by conventional, unqualified accountants' certificates.

Mr. Cohen acknowledged that the AICPA had not ignored the deferred tax problem, but had not been able to resolve it. (The position taken by the SEC in its ASR No. 102 was later affirmed by the APB as a miniscule part of its very comprehensive Opinion No. 11 dealing with the accounting for income taxes, issued in December 1967.) There were also other reasons for the SEC to take action. One was a formal "petition" by a leading accounting firm which requested that the SEC issue a release requiring consistency

[8] *Ibid.*

in treatment of deferred taxes. Another reason was the belief that some companies, put at a disadvantage when compared with the reporting method followed by other companies, were about to change their methods of reporting deferred taxes, and the SEC wanted to ensure that change, if any, would be for the better.

(In ASR No. 102 the Commission determined that the most appropriate treatment of deferred taxes in balance sheets was to require classification as between current and non-current consistent with that of the related instalment receivables.)

The evolution of ASR No. 102, according to Mr. Cohen, was an interesting illustration of one of the principal hindrances to achievement of uniformity, that is, the inability of the financial world to agree on the most appropriate method of presentation, even though there was general agreement on the desirability of a uniform method. Unless there developed a willingness to concede that the goal of uniformity was more important than any particular accounting treatment, he thought that progress toward uniformity would continue to be painfully slow. He conceded that in ASR No. 102 the Commission was dealing with a subject especially appropriate for uniform treatment. The essential operative facts had been agreed upon; all that was lacking was the determination of the most appropriate method of accounting presentation. He acknowledged that there were other areas, however, where judgment plays a much greater role and which were more difficult to resolve.

Mr. Cohen emphasized that the elimination, wherever possible, of unjustified differences in financial statements of similar companies had to be a goal of the highest rank. Although ASR No. 102 was used to resolve one problem of uniformity, he did not believe it would be necessary for the SEC to use that device with great frequency although the option was always open. The extent to which action on the SEC's part was required would depend, he said, in large measure "on the vigor and determination of the [APB] which has the principal responsibility of defining accounting principles to be used in financial reporting."

In a Los Angeles speech in 1969, Commissioner James J. Needham referred to the papers and talks presented at the Seaview (N. J.) Symposium at which the topic was "Corporate Financial Reporting: Conflicts and Challenges." He said that many people on many occasions had found much to criticize about the APB and its predecessor committee. "As for me," Mr. Needham said, "I came here to praise Caesar, not to bury him." Referring to a prediction made by one of the contributors to the Symposium that the SEC would usurp the authority of the APB, he said, "nothing in the record supports that opinion." He added that the SEC "will look to the APB to play the major role in the development of accounting principles and disclosure requirements so as to improve corporate financial reporting."

Commissioner Needham observed that the SEC might find it necessary from time to time to spur the profession on or to suggest priorities for subjects different from those established by the profession. Though the order of scheduled accomplishments is important, he said, it is secondary. "The main thrust is—is the Board . . . committed to a course of action for the development and improvement of accounting principles and reporting techniques?" He said that the APB is dedicated to the advancement of knowledge in these areas, and that the profession is now doing all within its power to produce the solutions to the many problems confronting those involved in corporate financial reporting. He also acknowledged the outstanding contribution of the Financial Executives Institute toward the development of the Commission's release on product line reporting.

Impatient with the alleged slow pace of the Accounting Principles Board in formulating accounting principles and reducing the number of acceptable alternatives, several voices have been raised in recent years to the effect that the job could be done better and faster by the SEC, and that the Commission should assume that responsibility. Commissioner Needham however, thought that the APB was doing a good job and the results would be no different if it were being done by the SEC. He said:

> The Accounting Principles Board is the acknowledged body responsible for reducing the number of alternative ways of reporting seemingly identical events. Their efforts appear to be torturous to many of you—but, then, so is the subject matter they must consider. The problems confronting the Board are complex and of great significance. Furthermore, the many diverse interests of the business community further complicate their efforts. All of these factors tend to slow the rule making process. Hopefully, the pace will accelerate; but, I must inform you that, in my opinion, were the responsibility for rule making lodged elsewhere, for example, at the SEC, the results would not be any different. Private industry will serve its own best interests by supporting the Board's activities.[9]

Since financial statements are the representations of management, the accountant's opinion of those statements is customarily expressed in his report. Occasionally the accountant does not agree with the accounting principles followed in the financial statements and so states in his report. Before taking exception, the accountant, it may be assumed, has tried to persuade management to revise the statements so that he can issue an unqualified report. Although the accountant may not have been successful in having the statements appropriately revised, the SEC is usually in a position to be more persuasive and insists on compliance with generally accepted accounting principles. See, for example, the discussion on page **25·3** where accountants qualified their reports in respect of the accounting principles followed by their clients, and the action taken by SEC.

[9] Commissioner James J. Needham, Address before The National Industrial Conference Board, Los Angeles, Calif., Apr. 29, 1970.

Elimination of Differences Between SEC Requirements and Those of Good Practice Generally.—Even where there are differences between the requirements of the SEC and those of generally accepted accounting practice, the differences tend to disappear with the passage of time largely because the Commission's requirements often become formal requirements of the profession generally as the result of their inclusion in the pronouncements or opinions of the APB. A few examples come to mind.

BALANCE SHEET CLASSIFICATION OF DEFERRED TAXES ON INSTALMENT SALES.—The SEC had been concerned for some time by the fact that deferred taxes were shown in balance sheets as noncurrent liabilities whereas the instalment receivables to which the taxes related were shown as current assets. Accordingly, in 1965, the Commission took the position in ASR No. 102 that where instalment receivables are classified as current assets in conformity with the operating cycle theory, the related liabilities or credit items maturing or expiring in the time period of the operating cycle, including the deferred income taxes, should be classified as current liabilities. (The circumstances surrounding the issuance of this release have previously been referred to in this chapter.)

The SEC's position was subsequently affirmed by the APB which, in 1967, issued its Opinion No. 11 dealing with accounting for income taxes. This opinion provides, in paragraph 57, that if instalment receivables are classified as a current asset, the deferred credits representing the tax effects of uncollected instalment sales should also be a current item.

BALANCE SHEET TREATMENT OF CREDIT EQUIVALENT TO REDUCTION IN INCOME TAXES.—The accounting followed by companies in their income tax returns sometimes differs in material respects from the accounting employed in the preparation of financial statements included in their reports to shareholders. In their income tax returns, for example, companies may use one of the accelerated depreciation methods permitted by the Internal Revenue Code, whereas their published financial statements may be based on other appropriate methods. Also, provisions may be made in the income statement for possible losses which are not yet realized but which require recognition under generally accepted accounting principles, such losses, however, being deductible for tax purposes only when they are actually incurred. On the other hand, deductions may be taken in the tax return which are not included in the income statement, such as charges against an estimated liability account created in a prior year. Also, credits in the income statement may not be includible in taxable income, as when an unneeded past provision for an estimated liability is restored to income.

In the case of depreciation, where an accelerated method is used for tax purposes and another appropriate method is used for financial statement purposes, accounting recognition is given to deferred income taxes if the amounts are material, except in those rare cases where special circumstances make the procedure inappropriate. Where, for example, charges for deferred income taxes are not allowed for rate-making purposes by regulatory authorities, accounting recognition need not be given to the deferment of taxes if it may reasonably be expected that increased future income taxes (resulting from the earlier deduction of accelerated depreciation for tax purposes only) will be allowed in future rate determinations.

A common practice of some companies—particularly utility companies—that followed such tax effect accounting was to credit the deferred taxes to an account included in the equity section of their balance sheets, such as, "Earned surplus—restricted" or "Earned surplus—appropriated." The Commission disapproved including the deferred tax account in the equity section of balance sheets, and, in 1960, set forth its views to that effect in ASR No. 85. In that release the Commission said that:

> . . . any financial statement filed with this Commission which designates as earned surplus (or its equivalent) or in any manner as a part of equity capital (even though accompanied by words of limitation such as "restricted" or "appropriated") the accumulated credit arising from accounting for reductions in income taxes resulting from deducting costs for income tax purposes at a more rapid rate than for financial statement purposes will be presumed by the Commission to be misleading or inaccurate despite disclosure contained in the certificate of the accountant or in footnotes to the statements, provided the amounts involved are material.

In this case also the Commission's position was later affirmed by the APB. In its Opinion No. 11, issued in 1967, the APB said that deferred taxes represent tax effects recognized in the determination of income tax expense in current and prior periods, and they should, therefore, "be excluded from retained earnings or from any other account in the stockholders' equity section of the balance sheet."

CLASSIFICATION AND DISCLOSURE OF ALLOWANCES.—For many years it has been a requirement of Regulation S-X that valuation and allowance accounts shall be shown separately in the financial statements as deductions from the specific assets to which they apply. While this has conformed to practice generally, there have been instances—particularly in the case of public utility companies—where the allowances have been shown among liabilities or elsewhere on the credit side of the balance sheet. Utility companies that showed their depreciation reserves on the credit side of their published balance sheets pointed to the requirements of the applicable public service commission as justifying such treatment. Nonetheless, in their filings with the SEC such companies were required to deduct the depreciation reserves from the related asset accounts. Although this had no effect on stockholders' equity, it did have a material effect on the amount shown as total assets.

In 1967, the APB issued its Opinion No. 12 which provided, among other things, that the allowance accounts should be deducted from the assets to which they relate with appropriate disclosure.

DISCLOSURE OF DEPRECIABLE ASSETS AND DEPRECIATION METHODS.—It had been general practice for many years to disclose the amount of depreciation expense provided during the period covered by income statements when the amount thereof is material. It had not been general practice, however, to disclose the amounts of the major classes of fixed assets or the methods of depreciation or depletion followed with respect thereto, although the disclosure of these matters has been a requirement of Regulation S-X for many years.

In 1967 the APB provided in its Opinion No. 12 that these matters should be disclosed in financial statements or in notes thereto.

BREAK-DOWN OF INCOME TAXES IN FINANCIAL STATEMENTS.—Balance sheets customarily show the break-down of the provision for income taxes as between taxes currently payable, and taxes deferred. As far as the income statement is concerned, this analysis has not customarily been furnished on the premise that it is not the function of the income statement to disclose the maturities of expenses that have been provided for—that being the function of the balance sheet. It had been an informal administrative requirement of the SEC for many years to disclose in the income statement the amounts of income taxes (1) currently payable, and (2) deferred.

With the adoption of Opinion No. 11 by the APB in 1967, the method of disclosure preferred by that staff of the SEC has become a requirement of practice generally. That opinion provides for showing the components of income tax expense of the period as follows: (a) Taxes estimated to be payable; (b) Tax effects of timing differencees; and (c) Tax effects of operating losses. In the 1972 revision of Regulation S–X, provision was made for an even more detailed break-down of income taxes in the income statement; see page **16·**39.

DISCLOSURE OF PENSION INFORMATION.—For many years it had been a requirement of Regulation S-X to disclose information with respect to pension and retirement plans in notes to the financial statements filed with the SEC, although this information was not required by good accounting practice generally.

In 1966 the APB issued its Opinion No. 8 dealing with accounting for the cost of pension plans. With one important exception, this opinion adopted all of the SEC's then existing disclosure requirements and even went beyond them. The exception concerned the unfunded past service cost of a pension plan. Under Regulation S–X, this amount must be disclosed; under the APB Opinion, it need not be disclosed. It is reasonable to assume that the Board was aware of this difference between its disclosure requirements and those of the SEC, and concluded that the information was not significant and need not be given.

ACQUISITION OF COMPANY WHICH HAS LOSS CARRY-FORWARD.—When Corporation A acquires Corporation B in a purchase transaction (as opposed to a pooling of interests transaction) one of the accounting problems involved is dealing with the difference between the cost of the investment in B and the amount of B's net assets. An authoritative statement on this subject was issued by the APB in August 1970 (Opinion No. 16, "Business Combinations").

When A pays more for B than the book amount of the latter's net assets, the excess cost is assigned to the assets acquired in the manner indicated in the aforementioned APB Opinion. Frequently a substantial portion of the excess cost is assigned to intangible assets, such as goodwill. B may have a substantial amount of operating loss carry-forwards for tax purposes, which, pursuant to good accounting practice, is not reflected in the figures in its balance sheet, but exists nonetheless. The loss carry-forward also can not be set up as an asset in a balance sheet which consolidates (or combines) A and B. It is one of the anomalies of good accounting practice, that this potentially very valuable asset can ordinarily not be shown in money amounts among the assets of a balance sheet, although it can be disclosed in notes to the balance sheet.

After the acquisition, if benefits are derived from the use of the loss carry-forwards, how should they be accounted for? Should the benefit be allowed to flow through the income statement, or is some other treatment indicated?

The SEC's accounting staff has held for many years that the benefits in these circumstances should not be permitted to rest in income, but should be used to reduce the intangible created on the acquisition, with an appropriate charge to the income statement.

In August 1970, when the APB issued its Opinion No. 16 on "Business Combinations", it made similar provision (in paragraph 88) for the treatment of the benefits derived from purchased loss carry-forwards.

BENEFITS FROM LOSS CARRY-FORWARDS AFTER A QUASI-REORGANIZATION.—When a corporation decides to make a fresh start and to eliminate the deficit in its retained earnings, it often has a substantial operating loss carry-forward which, pursuant to good accounting practice, ordinarily is not recorded as an asset on its balance sheet either before or after the quasi-reorganization. Potentially this loss carry-forward may prove to be extremely valuable if the corporation can begin to operate profitably.

If, after the quasi-reorganization, the corporation does begin making money and is able to utilize its loss carry-forwards, how should the tax benefits so derived be accounted for?

For many years it has been the position of the SEC's accounting staff that the tax benefits resulting from the utilization of such loss carry-forwards that existed on the date of the quasi-reorganization should be credited to capital surplus with an appropriate charge to income.[10] In December 1967, when the APB issued its Opinion No. 11 on "Accounting for Income Taxes", it adopted a rule (in paragraph 50) similar to the SEC's with respect to the benefits after a quasi-reorganization from loss carry-forwards that existed on the date of the quasi-reorganization.

ACCOUNTING FOR THE "INVESTMENT CREDIT".—One of the most important examples showing the influence of the SEC on the development of accounting in the United States occurred in connection with accounting for the "investment credit." As will be seen, in the view of this author, the entire matter does not reflect favorably on the SEC; in fact, it is the author's opinion that in this instance the SEC rendered a distinct disservice to investors, industry, and the accountancy profession.

As an inducement to business to expand and modernize its facilities, Congress created a new tax concept in the Revenue Act of 1962. The Act provided for an "investment credit" which represented a percentage of the cost of certain depreciable assets acquired and placed in service after 1961. The amount of the credit available in any year was used to reduce the amount of income tax payable for that year. For income tax purposes the full amount of the investment credit under the 1962 Act was to be treated as a reduction in the basis of the property, but the Revenue Act of 1964 eliminated this requirement. The investment credit was repealed by the Tax Reform Act of 1969, although in July 1971 President Richard M. Nixon recommended that it be reinstated as part of a comprehensive economic program. The discussion that follows is, therefore, partly of historical interest, and, in any case, is intended to illustrate the Commission's influence on the development of accounting principles.

The APB considered the appropriate method of accounting for the investment credit, and issued its opinion (APB Opinion No. 2) in December 1962. Fourteen members of the Board voted in favor of the opinion; six members dissented and stated the basis for their dissent. In that opinion, the APB concluded that the investment credit should be reflected in in-

---

[10] Walter Mickelsen, "Recent Developments in the SEC Accounting Field," May 24, 1966.

come over the productive life of acquired property and not in the year in which it was placed in service. The Board's conclusion, in effect, rejected a contrary position that the credit—either in full or after considering possible future tax effect—should be accounted for as a reduction of Federal income tax expense of the year in which it is obtained. The Board indicated that it found no significant disagreement with the view that the investment credit was a factor influencing the determination of net income and that therefore the only issue which required decision involved a question of timing, viz., the accounting period(s) in which the credit should be reflected in income.

The Board considered and rejected two other concepts as to the substance of the investment credit:

1. That it was a subsidy by way of a contribution to capital.
2. That it was in substance a selective reduction in taxes related to the taxable income of the year in which the credit arose—in other words, that the purchase of property created income by reducing tax expense. (It was the Board's view that earnings arise from the *use* of facilities—not from their *acquisition.*)

The Board acknowledged that its opinions might not be applicable in the case of regulated companies (such as public utilities) where the authorities having jurisdiction might require the use of different methods of accounting for the investment credit.

Shortly thereafter, the SEC also stated its views regarding the accounting for the investment credit. These were contained in ASR No. 96 (January, 1963) and were materially different in some respects from those of the APB. The SEC stated that in recognition of the substantial diversity of opinion which existed among responsible persons in the matter of accounting for the investment credit, it would accept either of the following methods:[11]

1. A method which reflected the investment credit in income over the productive life of the acquired property (this was the method recommended in APB Opinion No. 2) ; *or*
2. A partial flow-through method which reflected 48 per cent of the investment credit in income as a reduction of the tax expense of the year in which the credit arose and deferred the balance of 52 per cent to subsequent accounting periods. (This "48–52" method, which assumed an income tax rate of 52 per cent, was considered and rejected by the APB. The method had merit only when the tax law

[11] Customarily, opinions on accounting or auditing matters published by the SEC in its ASR series, represent opinions of its Chief Accountant. In the case of ASR No. 96, however, it is noteworthy that the views expressed in that release were those of the Commission.

provided that the credit was to be treated as a reduction in the basis of the property. With the change in the law in 1964, this method lost its supporters.)

In view of the position taken by the SEC, what followed was not entirely unexpected, but represents a regrettable (to say the least) episode in the development of accounting principles in the United States. The accounting recommended by the majority of the APB was not followed by a significant number of American corporations. Their financial statements—which conformed for the most part with the SEC views—were certified nevertheless without qualification by their independent public accountants.

The APB was aware that the conclusions expressed in its Opinion No. 2 had not attained the degree of acceptability which was necessary to make the opinion effective, and understood that the authority of its opinions rested upon their general acceptability. Taking cognizance of the situation that had developed (including the position taken by the SEC in its Release No. 96 and the change in the Revenue Act of 1964), the APB issued a new opinion (No. 4, March, 1964) substantially amending its earlier opinion. In the new opinion the APB said that the method of accounting for the investment credit recommended in its earlier opinion should be considered to be *preferable,* that is, reflection in income over the productive life of acquired property. The Board said, however, that the alternative method of treating the credit as a reduction of Federal income taxes of the year in which the credit arose (which it had previously rejected) was also acceptable. (This alternative method is sometimes referred to as the "full flow-through" method.) Although both methods were acceptable, obviously they were significantly different, and, depending on which method was employed, the effect on net income could be material. The accounting recommended in APB Opinion No. 4 was accepted by the SEC in substance with minor changes in the requirements as to presentation.

The accountancy profession in the United States has been criticized with justification by the SEC and others for permitting too many alternative but equally acceptable accounting principles. One result of the action taken by the SEC in issuing its ASR No. 96 was to create additional accounting alternatives that had not existed previously, and thereby aggravate a situation that was already bad enough. Furthermore, it involved an area of accounting where the choice of methods had a material effect on income statements—unlike the issuance of ASR No. 102 relating to the showing of deferred taxes on instalment receivables, which affected only the balance sheet.

In the case of the investment credit, there was a once-in-a-generation opportunity to prescribe a uniform method of accounting in an area where theory had not crystallized and practice had not yet developed, and accordingly no one had the burden of promoting or defending one position as against another. (The investment credit was a new concept in United States taxation, but similar tax incentives had existed for many years in foreign countries. The Netherlands, for example, had an "investment allowance," which was similar in many ways to the United States investment credit; the United Kingdom and Belgium had similar investment allowances. Although the Board was apprised of the corresponding situations in foreign countries, there is no indication that the accounting employed in these countries with respect to these tax incentives was influential in determining the principles adopted in the United States.)

Furthermore, the problem of the investment credit was purely one of accounting theory where all the facts were known. There were no complications arising out of practical considerations involving judgmental matters, such as the estimate of units of production of a machine or the estimate of its useful life. The only question that had to be resolved was the nature of the credit which would determine the method of accounting for it. There was no disagreement among the members of the APB that the credit increased net income; the Board's problem centered on the accounting period(s) during which it should be reflected in income.

In view of the criticism voiced by some members of the Commission with respect to the accountancy profession's painfully slow progress in reducing or eliminating alternatives, the question might well be asked: Why did the SEC issue ASR No. 96 and thereby undermine the APB's decision as to the accounting for the investment credit?

Professor Maurice Moonitz, writing in *Journal of Accounting Research* (Vol. 4, No. 1, Spring 1966, pp. 47–61), has thrown some light on the subject. (At the time APB Opinion No. 2 was issued, Moonitz was staff assistant to the APB, but was a member of the APB at the time the Board issued its Opinion No. 4, and he dissented from that Opinion.) He wrote that the SEC had little or nothing to do with the promulgation of the APB's first Opinion (No. 2) on the subject of the investment credit. The members of the APB did receive copies of a letter from the SEC's Chief Accountant, but not until the morning of the meeting of December 10, 1962, the meeting at which the APB adopted Opinion No. 2. The Chief Accountant's letter was in response to the exposure draft (dated November 1, 1962) of the APB's proposed opinion, and was received too late to be of much influence. At any rate, according to Moonitz, the APB clearly did not vote the way of the SEC.

The Commission delayed its own release on the subject (ASR No. 96) until January 10, 1963.

A group representing the AICPA and the APB (including Professor Moonitz) met informally with the SEC in Washington, D. C., the Friday before Christmas 1962. The group included two members of the APB representing the two principal views on the investment credit. The SEC group consisted of four commissioners (Cary, chairman; Cohen; Whitney; and Woodside; the fifth commissioner, Mr. Frear, was ill) and members of their staff. (All of these commissioners have since resigned or retired.)

Moonitz wrote that the commissioners seemed reluctant to issue a release on the investment credit, and were reminded by their Chief Accountant that, if they did not, their hand would be forced by some registrant who would file financial statements using a method not endorsed by the APB. The commissioners were "genuinely relieved" to hear that the APB was seriously concerned with only two methods of accounting for the credit; they had been led to believe that six or seven different methods were in the offing. (The Commission's own release permitted three methods, but the third method was the "100% flow-through" method which they would accept only if it was ordered by a regulatory commission.)

Moonitz continued with this significant passage:

. . . Finally, and most important, the commissioners made clear their own inability under the law to select one method of accounting and to insist on it to the exclusion of all others. If the SEC should, in fact, support a single method (e.g., as reflected in Opinion No. 2 of the APB), they would certainly be challenged by some registrant who wished to use a different method. The ultimate weapon under the law at the SEC's disposal is the "stop order," the suspending of trading in the registrant's securities. Were the SEC to go that far, they would no doubt be subject to a court order requiring them to show cause for their action. To support their action, they would have to demonstrate that there was no substantial authoritative support for the registrant's method of accounting, and they felt this would be impossible in the face of the strongly-held opinions backing several available methods in accounting for the investment credit. The implication was clear—the SEC would not support the APB because the commissioners were convinced they could not sustain the SEC position in court. In fact, ASR No. 96 expressly states that several methods are approved "in recognition of the substantial diversity of opinion which exists among responsible persons in the matter of accounting for the investment credit . . ."

In short, said Moonitz, the SEC apparently was sympathetic to the APB's effort to impose a single method of accounting for the investment credit, *but felt that it did not have the power to sustain such a position in a court of law.*

If Moonitz correctly set forth the rationale for the SEC's action in issuing ASR No. 96, it is difficult to reconcile the SEC's reasoning with its actions in other situations. In the case of ASR No. 102, for example, the SEC was faced with a similar problem when it laid down a rule for presenting deferred taxes on instalment receivables in balance sheets. Nonetheless the Commission laid down a rule and said that the deferred taxes had to be shown on the same basis as the related instalment receivables, notwithstanding that there was considerable support for alternative methods. In this instance may one assume that the SEC was not concerned about being subject to a court order requiring the Commission to show cause for its action in the face of other strongly-held opinions backing other methods of presenting the deferred taxes in question?

Even more importantly, consider the Commission's action in promulgating Rule 14a–3 which, in effect, says that a company's financial statements in its published annual report to stockholders should not be inconsistent in any material way with the financial statements filed with the Commission. (The rule is discussed in Chapter **22**.) Assume, for example, that a company in its published report consolidates a subsidiary which, pursuant to Regulation S–X, may not be consolidated in statements filed with the SEC. Assume also that the statements in the published report are certified without qualification by an independent public accountant and that the subsidiary is significant, as a consequence of which the statements are materially different from those filed, or to be filed, with the SEC. In promulgating Rule 14a–3, may one assume that the SEC was not concerned about being subject to a court order requiring it to show cause for its action in the face of the fact that the statements in the published report were based on accounting principles for which there was substantial authoritative support?

The author does not question the accuracy of Moonitz's reporting of the meeting with the former SEC commissioners, but finds it difficult to accept as being a complete statement of the rationale for the SEC's action in issuing ASR No. 96.

The chairman of the SEC during the period in which the investment credit was an issue was William L. Cary. In an article entitled "The SEC and Accounting," Mr. Cary referred very briefly to the fact that the Commission had been criticized for not supporting the Accounting Principles Board on the investment credit (*The Journal of Accountancy,* December 1963, p. 49). His sole comment on this important matter was "I shall not labor that question." He continued, however, saying—somewhat paradoxically—that the Commission's interest over the years had been to support the accounting profession in narrowing areas of difference in financial reporting and that "This is still our view."

Jack M. Whitney II was also a Commissioner when the accounting for the investment credit was under consideration, and he participated in the SEC's decision in this matter. On October 15, 1964, when he was no longer a Commissioner, Mr. Whitney addressed the Corporate Counsel Institute and referred briefly to that episode. He said that in issuing ASR No. 96 the Commission may have been correct in the conclusion it reached *tested by disclosure standards,* but, he added, "I have regretfully concluded, however, with the benefit of hindsight, that the Commission did not quite rise to the occasion handed to it on a platter to restate forcefully the need that reporting corporations observe the consensus reached voluntarily in the private sector as to the content of a substantive accounting rule." [12]

Byron D. Woodside was also a Commissioner at the time of the investment credit episode. He thought that the dismay surrounding the reaction to the episode was "most unfortunate." The SEC, he said, had "intended no rebuff to the profession or the Accounting Principles Board." On the contrary, he said, "we have encouraged and continue to encourage them in their work." Mr. Woodside appeared to be dubious of the profession's efforts to narrow the alternatives and achieve conformity. He said: [13]

. . . The task you set yourselves to force conformity on matters of accounting principle when there is not in fact acceptance of conformity, I think, is an impossible one. In any event, such a step calls for full exploration of problems and procedures. But this view in no sense reflects upon the efforts of those dedicated, highly intelligent and articulate public-minded members of the profession who vigorously urge more, and more penetrating, research and who constantly seek to narrow differences and, where possible, broaden the scope of that which is truly "the acceptable" of the profession. We salute them and their efforts.

The Commission's performance in the investment credit fiasco has been severely and justifiably criticized, and there were some who said that it marked the end of leadership by the accountancy profession in the development of accounting principles. Manuel F. Cohen, a Commissioner at the time who later became chairman of the SEC, in a speech in 1964, denied that the SEC had withdrawn its support of the profession. He said:

. . . This episode [involving the investment credit] has been discussed so vehemently that many persons seem to feel we have withdrawn our support of the profession's efforts to narrow the areas of differences in accounting principles and have abandoned the policy announced in 1937 of issuing "opinions on accounting principles for the purpose of contributing to the development of uniform standards and practice in major accounting questions." This is not the case. (*The Journal of Accountancy,* October 1964)

Accounting for Deferred Compensation Contracts.—Deferred compensation arrangements ordinarily provide for compensation to be paid to an employee (generally an officer) beginning with his retirement and for a stipulated number of years thereafter. Payments are usually contingent upon the employee's being available for consultation and refraining from competitive activities. These arrangements are ordinarily made apart from, or in addition to, formal retirement plans instituted on behalf of all or

---

[12] "Corporate Responsibilities under the Developing Federal Securities Laws," *Proceedings of the Third Annual Corporate Counsel Institute,* p. 137.

[13] Byron D. Woodside, address before National Association of Accountants, June 23, 1964, quoted in *The Journal of Accountancy,* Sept. 1964, p. 68.

substantial groups of employees and which provide for lifetime pensions upon retirement.

These arrangements are usually entered into primarily in consideration of services rendered by an employee during his active service life, and in most instances are essentially supplementary compensation for services during that period. However, since payments are subject to conditions such as those referred to in the preceding paragraph and, further, to continuance of employment until retirement age and continued life during the period of payment, the accruing obligation has frequently been considered to be sufficiently contingent to justify omission of accruals, with recognition of expense only as payments are made. (See the discussion below, however, regarding the change in accounting growing out of APB Opinion No. 12.)

Some of these agreements, however, include provisions under which payments (sometimes reduced) are to be made to an employee in the event of disability or to designated beneficiaries in the event of his death. These provisions reduce the contingent aspect of the payments and raise the possibility of significant amounts of vested rights arising in the event of disability or death. Consequently, it may be that under such circumstances the contingent aspect of these agreements is no longer sufficient to justify omission of provision for supplementary compensation during the active service lives of the covered employees.

There may be cases where the agreements in fact contemplate the rendering of substantial service by an employee subsequent to formal retirement. To the extent that such services are contemplated, provision for them during the post-retirement period is appropriate. This construction of the purpose of an agreement, however, would appear to be negated to the extent of the existence of substantial death or disability clauses.

In 1956, when the AICPA Committee on Accounting Procedure issued Bulletin No. 47 setting forth its views as to the accounting for the costs of pension plans, the Committee made it clear that it was not dealing with deferred compensation contracts with individuals. When the Committee's successor, the APB, issued its Opinion No. 8 (1966) dealing with accounting for the cost of pension plans, it said that the opinion applied to deferred compensation contracts with individuals "if such contracts, taken together, are equivalent to a pension plan."

The SEC, on the other hand, has had strong views on this subject. In several deficiency letters and in speeches by its Chief Accountant, the SEC has made it clear that provision for deferred compensation should ordinarily be made during the period in which the individuals render services and before their retirement. The Chief Accountant has said:

As a matter of principle it appears to us that in most cases deferred compensation should be provided for prior to the individuals' retirement and assumption of a status as consultants and advisors. The amounts involved are not material in most cases, perhaps, but this should not be used as a reason for omitting proper accruals.[14]

In 1967 the APB issued its Opinion No. 12 which deals, in part, with deferred compensation contracts. The APB's views on this subject are in harmony with those of the SEC, that is, the estimated amounts to be paid under a contract should be accrued in a systematic and rational manner over the period of active employment, unless it is evident that future services expected to be received by the employer are commensurate with the payments or a portion of the payments to be made. If elements of both current and future services are present, only the portion applicable to current service should be accrued.

Good Accounting Practice: Judged by Present-Day Standards or Those at Time of Transaction?—A problem which frequently confronts the practicing public accountant who attempts to reconstruct accounts retroactively is this: Shall the revision be on the basis of good accounting practice as it existed at the time of the transactions or events, or on the basis of good accounting practice as we know it today? Suppose, for example, a corporation has only one surplus account and it contains several different types of surplus, and it is desired to restate the account so as to show the various kinds of surplus. Suppose also that there occurred in the past a transaction or event which, according to good practice, would have been treated one way at the time of the transaction or event but would be treated a different way today. The SEC issued an opinion (ASR No. 56) in 1946 which, although not concerned primarily with this question, did contain a relevant observation.

The opinion was in answer to a question confronting management investment companies which were faced with the problem of allocating past dividends so as to arrive at (1) the balance of undistributed net income (excluding gain or loss on investments); and (2) accumulated net realized gain or loss on investments. The problem arose out of the requirements of Section 19 of the Investment Company Act which provides that dividend payments made by a registered investment company must be accompanied by written statements adequately disclosing the source of the dividend if it is paid wholly or partly from any source other than:

1. The company's accumulated undistributed net income, determined in accordance with good accounting practice and not including profits or loss realized upon the sale of securities or other properties; or
2. The company's net income so determined for the current or preceding fiscal year.

[14] Andrew Barr, "Disclosure in Theory and Practise," *The New York CPA,* Sept. 1959, p. 639.

After suggesting how past dividends should be allocated, the opinion makes the following suggestion:

> . . . In examining the past to make the necessary determination of available balances now, transactions must be reviewed in the light of "good accounting practice," the standard set up in Section 19. Your problem is whether that standard is the good accounting practice of the present day or that of the date of any particular transaction. In my opinion, it is the latter.

The principle enunciated by the SEC makes sense and, in the opinion of the author, has a much broader application than the particular question to which it was addressed. It is also consistent with the position taken by the AICPA in ARB No. 1 (1939) which said:

> No pronouncement issued by the committee [on accounting procedure] is intended to have a retroactive effect unless it contains a statement of such intention. Thus a pronouncement will ordinarily have no application to any transaction arising prior to its publication, nor to transactions uncompleted at the time of publication. But, while the committee considers it inexpedient to make its general statements retroactive, it does not wish to discourage the revision of past accounts in an individual case if the accountants think it desirable in the circumstances.

See also the discussion under "Restatement of Previously Reported Statements," beginning on page **13·16**.

Tax Accounting Not Necessarily Good Accounting.—It seems almost needless to point out that tax accounting is not the same as generally accepted principles of accounting. Because of the divergences between them, Congress attempted in 1954 to bring them more nearly into agreement by amendment of the Internal Revenue Code. (The legislation was later reversed when it developed that the drain on federal revenues would be much greater than had been estimated.) And yet, one of the chief difficulties encountered by the SEC results from the inclusion in registration statements (and in offering circulars relating to exempt offerings) of financial statements prepared on a tax basis but certified by public accountants as being in conformity with generally accepted principles of accounting. This may seem ridiculous, but it represents a serious problem to the Commission's staff. A former Chief Accountant of the SEC had this situation in mind when he said:

> Another common characteristic of new filings and a frequent cause for delay is the tendency on the part of agents of new registrants, and their accountants alike, to insist that accounting, including tax accounting, which has served adequately for a successful business enterprise is equally good when the company "goes public." This is a mistake. Hours spent on insisting that our staff must accept the statements as presented not only delay the subject filing but take reviewers' valuable time from other cases. Some of the recurring subjects for debate are that all overhead, and sometimes even direct labor, may be omitted

from inventory; that cash basis accounting is generally acceptable when inventories of goods for sale are not a factor; that dubious deferred charges must be retained in the balance sheet and amortized over excessively long periods in the future; and that since the company has never prepared consolidated statements before, it need not do so now.[15]

Financial statements have been filed with the SEC in which life insurance premiums were charged to surplus for the sole reason that they were not deductible for tax purposes. Other statements have been filed in which the current provision for federal income taxes was also charged to surplus, presumably on the basis that it represented a sharing of profits with the government. Financial statements have also been filed in which losses inherent in the realization or liquidation of certain assets had not been reflected in the accounts or statements because of the belief that losses should be booked in the year of realization. This may be the tax rule, but it is contrary to the requirements of generally accepted accounting principles.

See the discussion under "Restatement by Closely-Held Companies When Going Public" on page **13·21**.

Accounting for Property and Appraisals.—It is perhaps not surprising that most of the SEC decisions relating to accounting matters deal with newly formed corporations that issued large amounts of stock for assets having little, if any, value. The promoters, however, often have not hesitated to set up the assets at amounts having no relation to the cost or value of the assets acquired or the value of the stock issued. The Commission prevented many of these corporations from proceeding with the sale of their securities to the public and issued many decisions on accounting for property acquired for stock, property under option, promotional services, appraisals, and the like. These and other cases are summarized below as an indication of the SEC's thinking in this important area of accounting.

PROPERTY ACCOUNTS.—In the case of property acquired for stock, it is improper to set up the acquired assets at a valuation based on the par value of the stock when other sales of the same stock are made at about the same time at prices considerably below par or when the stock is worth less than par. *Automatic Telephone Dialer, Inc.,* 10 SEC 698 (1941); *Canusa Gold Mines, Ltd.,* 2 SEC 549 (1937); *Continental Distillers and Importers Corp.,* 1 SEC 54 (1935); *National Boston Montana Mines Corp.,* 2 SEC 228 (1937); *Poulin Mining Co., Ltd.,* 8 SEC 116 (1940); *Queensboro Gold Mines Ltd.,* 2 SEC 860 (1937); *Unity Gold Corp.,* 1 SEC 33 (1934); *Virginia City Gold Mining Co.,* 2 SEC 855 (1937); *Yumuri Jute Mills Co.,* 2 SEC 86 (1937).

---

[15] Andrew Barr, "Current Practice with the SEC; Duties and Responsibilities of the CPA," address before California Society of CPAs, June 26, 1961.

Financial statements in an offering circular under Regulation A were held to be misleading because they listed assets acquired in exchange for stock at the par value of the stock rather than at an amount not in excess of the identifiable cash cost of such assets to the transferors. *Edsco Manufacturing Co.,* Sec. Act Release No. 4413, Sept. 20, 1961.

When assets (particularly property, tangible or intangible) are acquired for stock, it is improper to include in the cost of the assets the shares concurrently donated back to the company. *Automatic Telephone Dialer, Inc.,* 10 SEC 698 (1941); *Bering Straits Tin Mines, Inc.,* 2 SEC 486 (1937); *Consolidated Grain Corp.,* 6 SEC 597 (1940); *Finger Canadian Lumber Co., Ltd.,* 5 SEC 543 (1939); *Thomas Bond, Inc.,* 5 SEC 60 (1939); *Thomascolor, Inc.,* 27 SEC 151 (1947); *Unity Gold Corp.,* 1 SEC 30 (1934); *Virginia City Gold Mining Co.,* 2 SEC 855 (1937); *Yumuri Jute Mills Co.,* 2 SEC 81 (1937). In one case, however, about two months after the original issue of stock, a director agreed to donate 15,000 shares to the company to raise capital. The SEC held that this transaction would seem to be a donation to the corporation, and not a cancellation or readjustment of the initial purchase price. *Franco Mining Corp.,* 1 SEC 288 (1936).

A corporation's fixed assets were held to be overstated by the inclusion therein of survey costs for a new paper mill—a project that had been abandoned by the corporation. *Dixie Land and Timber Corp.,* ___ SEC ___ (1966).

Promotional services may not be included in the cost of capital assets. *Automatic Telephone Dialer, Inc.,* 10 SEC 698 (1941); *MacDonald Mines, Ltd.,* 7 SEC 223 (1940); *National Boston Montana Mines Corp.,* 2 SEC 228 (1937); *Paper Sales Company of Detroit, Inc.,* 2 SEC 748 (1937); *Platoro Gold Mines, Inc.,* 3 SEC 873 (1938); *Poulin Mining Co., Ltd.,* 8 SEC 116 (1940); *Rickard Ramore Gold Mines, Ltd.,* 2 SEC 377 (1937); *Thomas Bond, Inc.,* 5 SEC 60 (1939); *Thomascolor, Inc.,* 27 SEC 151 (1947); *Unity Gold Corp.,* 1 SEC 30 (1934); *Yumuri Jute Mills Co.,* 2 SEC 81 (1937).

It is misleading to include in a balance sheet property that does not represent either cost or value arrived at by accepted methods, without disclosure that the basis used is arbitrary. *Bering Straits Tin Mines, Inc.,* 2 SEC 486 (1937); *Breeze Corporations, Inc.,* 3 SEC 709 (1938); *MacDonald Mines, Ltd.,* 7 SEC 223 (1940); *Thomas Bond, Inc.,* 5 SEC 60 (1939); *Thomascolor, Inc.,* 27 SEC 151 (1947).

Although an accountant is not expected to place valuations upon assets such as patents or real property, he should at least indicate that the dollar values assigned to them upon the balance sheet are purely arbitrary figures. *Lewis American Airways, Inc.,* 1 SEC 330 (1936).

Where stock is issued for a consideration far less than its par value and is shown as outstanding, it is misleading to omit this fact. *Great Dike Gold Mines, Inc.,* 1 SEC 621 (1936).

In transactions between the registrant on the one hand and, on the other, persons in control of the registrant or the principal promoter or management of the registrant, the absence of arm's-length bargaining must be disclosed. *Automatic Telephone Dialer, Inc.,* 10 SEC 698 (1941); *Breeze Corporations, Inc.,* 3 SEC 725 (1938); *MacDonald Mines, Ltd.,* 7 SEC 223 (1940); *Petersen Engine Co., Inc.,* 2 SEC 893 (1937); *Platoro Gold Mines, Inc.,* 3 SEC 873 (1938); *Red Bank Oil Co.,* 21 SEC 695 (1946); *Reiter-Foster Oil Corp.,* 6 SEC 1028 (1940); *Resources Corporation International,* 7 SEC 689 (1940); *Rickard Ramore Gold Mines, Ltd.,* 2 SEC 377 (1937); *Thomas Bond, Inc.,* 5 SEC 60 (1939); *Thomascolor, Inc.,* 27 SEC 151 (1947).

Where the balance sheet of the registrant based value of unpatented mining claims on par value of own stock issued (pursuant to contract) to another company in return for those mining claims and the stock was returned shortly thereafter to the registrant as liquidated damages for termination of the contract, SEC held the balance sheet false and misleading in that the cost of the mining claims (which were retained by the registrant upon termination of the contract) was materially overstated. *Condor Gold Mining Co.,* 11 SEC 190 (1942).

Inclusion in the balance sheet of a figure representing property "at cost," equal to the par value of shares issued to promoters for a promise to expend that sum of money in improving the property or to be sold to provide a fund for that purpose, renders the balance sheet untrue and misleading. *Continental Distillers and Importers Corp.,* 1 SEC 54 (1935).

Where the balance sheet indicated the "cost to promoter" was $359,000 as compared with carrying value of $9,000,000, SEC held this was misleading when the promoter spent none of his own money. *Resources Corporation International,* 7 SEC 689 (1940).

A corporation sold its notes at a discount. The debt discount was included in the cost of the asset purchased with the proceeds of the notes. The SEC said this was an untrue statement of the cost of the asset. *American Terminals and Transit Co.,* 1 SEC 701 (1936).

A balance sheet showing a substantial portion of registrant's assets as "prospective value" of exposed ore body was held to be materially misleading where such value is shown to have represented gross value, arrived at by calculations from estimates in an engineer's report, and making no allowance for extraction cost and other pertinent cost factors. *Comstock-Dexter Mines, Inc.,* 10 SEC 358 (1941).

Property account and capital surplus of a mining corporation were held to be misleading where they were based upon a figure for value of mining property determined by multiplying estimated recoverable ore by estimated gold content per ton less mining cost but without adjustment to determine the "present worth" of that sum. *La Luz Mining Corp.,* 1 SEC 217 (1935) ; *Emporia Gold Mines, Inc.,* 2 SEC 210 (1937) ; *Mining and Development Corp.,* 1 SEC 786 (1936).

"Corporate franchise" (represented by a lease and option) included in a balance sheet was held to be misleading since it was of no potential or actual value. *Great Dike Gold Mines, Inc.,* 1 SEC 621 (1936).

Setting up as an asset the full value of property upon which the company has merely an option is not in accord with accepted accounting procedure even though payments have been made under the option. *Paper Sales Company of Detroit, Inc.,* 2 SEC 748 (1937) ; *Poulin Mining Co., Ltd.,* 8 SEC 116 (1940).

The failure to disclose the amount of assets which would be lost to the company if the remaining payments were not made was held to be a material deficiency. *Canusa Gold Mines, Ltd.,* 2 SEC 549 (1937).

Properties held under lease-and-option-to-purchase, upon which a substantial amount remained unpaid, were merged with fee properties in a balance sheet. It is improper to include such property held on lease and showing the value of properties held in fee, even though the notes to the balance sheet reveal the inclusion of property in which less than a fee interest is held. *Canusa Gold Mines, Ltd.,* 2 SEC 549 (1937) ; *Finger Canadian Lumber Co., Ltd.,* 5 SEC 543 (1939) ; *Franco Mining Corp.,* 1 SEC 289 (1936).

A company held property appraised at $47,400 on a five-year lease with an option to purchase at any time during the lease term upon payment of $18,000. Even where the appraisal is not questioned, the SEC held that setting out the appraised fee value of the leased property as an asset is untrue, since the fee is the asset of the lessor, not of the lessee. Furthermore, showing the property as an asset "real estate, $47,400" is misleading since it does not indicate that the interest in the property is less than fee. *American Terminals and Transit Co.,* 1 SEC 701 (1936).

ASSET WRITE-UPS.—The SEC's opposition to write-ups of assets is well known as the result of numerous decisions, some of which are referred to later in this chapter. As will be seen from those decisions, the write-ups in many cases were unconscionable and based on the flimsiest support.

Even in cases where there are ample indications of value, the SEC, as a matter of policy, disapproves the writing-up of assets above their cost. Take, for example, the case of a group of investors in real estate who decide to pool their holdings in a tax-free transaction in one new corporation, and then offer securities of the new corporation to the public. Under present SEC practice, the properties must be carried by the new company at the costs to the predecessor owners. The staff of the Commission appear to believe that while relative fair market value should be considered in apportioning securities to the investors, it should be disregarded in accounting for the assets of the new company (unless the transaction be a taxable one). A's property may be worth twice as much as B's, but there is probably no good way to determine whether the properties of A and B should be carried at \$200,000 and \$100,000, respectively, or at \$300,000 and \$150,000, respectively. On the other hand, if the transaction is *taxable,* there is a presumption that a fair market value has been arrived at, and the properties may be carried at amounts in excess of cost.

In one case with which the author is familiar, the management of a real estate company disagreed with the SEC's "no write-up" policy. Even if the policy had merit in the usual case, the company believed that the facts in its case distinguished it from others and merited a departure from the general prohibition against write-ups.

The company had issued 43,450 shares of its \$10 par value stock to two unrelated partnership groups in exchange for the partnership interests (represented by real estate) and other real property. The securities were issued on the basis of the net fair market value of the properties acquired as determined by independent, formal appraisal of the properties. It was agreed by the issuer and the two partnership groups that fair market value, rather than the historical cost to the predecessors, would be the most equitable basis for determining the number of shares to be issued. The issuance of the stock was recorded by crediting \$10 per share (the par value) to the capital stock account, and \$10 per share (the excess of appraisal over par value) to capital surplus. In the following three months, the company sold 2,050 additional shares for cash at \$20 per share—virtually all of it to persons not previously connected with the company or its predecessors. The company believed that the consideration received for the shares sold for cash supported its view that the fair market value of the stock was \$20 per share at a time near the exchange of the shares for the real property. The company proposed to file a registration statement covering additional shares to be sold to the public at \$20 per share.

The company took the matter up with the Commission, and said that, in this case, it was proper to state the acquired properties at the appraised values, which were the same as the values indicated by the subsequent sales of the shares to outsiders for cash. The company proposed to disclose in a note to the balance sheet the difference between such book amounts and the historical tax basis. The company argued that:

1. Generally accepted accounting principles require the company to state investment properties acquired in exchange for stock at the fair value of the consideration given or at the fair value of the property acquired, whichever is the more clearly evident.

2. It would be misleading to prospective investors to state the properties at the predecessors' cost. The anticipated yield from the properties would bear no relationship to such cost. If the properties were recorded at such amounts, the investor would have no way of measuring the value of the company's assets as against the offering price of the stock.

The Commission disagreed with the views expressed by the company. In view of the limited sales of the company's shares at $20 per share, the SEC believed that such amount could not be considered as the fair value of the shares issued, and therefore the company must look to the fair value of the property as the basis for recording the transaction. In view of the "non-arm's-length" aspects of the exchange transactions and the Commission's position to disregard as a matter of policy appraised values as a basis for recording property, the SEC believed that predecessors' cost represented the only "objective" basis for recording the assets acquired in the exchange transactions. The SEC requested that this procedure be followed in any filing with the Commission. With respect to the company's second argument, the SEC said that the recording of the properties at predecessors' cost was necessary in this case "in order that the financial statements will not be misleading," but, unlike the company, did not give the rationale to support its conclusion.

An industrial company, in its promotional stages with no record of business or earning capacity, wrote up fixed assets from cost of $200,000 to appraised value of $720,042, the excess being credited to "Surplus arising from revaluation of property." SEC required the company to restate the fixed assets to their cost amount. [ASR No. 8 (1938)].

A write-up of assets was disapproved where appreciation figures were arrived at through use of haphazard and erroneous estimates of ore blocked out, of mining costs, and of mining and milling capacity, and where the original representation of value antedated the facts which were supposed to have been its basis. *Consolidated Mines Syndicate,* 2 SEC 316 (1937).

A write-up of assets based on improvement in potential value from improved transportation facilities was held to be misleading where no account was taken of the necessity for material expenditures for a road or tramway before such facilities could be used. *Consolidated Mines Syndicate,* 2 SEC 316 (1937).

A write-up of assets based on the ground that their value has been increased by the driving of a tunnel was held to be without possible reasonable basis where the registrant knows nothing more about the existence of ore bodies than before the tunnel was driven. *Consolidated Mines Syndicate,* 2 SEC 316 (1937).

A write-up in the valuation of the deferred development of a mining company which is still in the development stage, which has no blocked-out ore, and which has not shown a net profit in over two years of operation is misleading where such unrealized appreciation is based solely on an appraisal of the cost of reproducing such assets new. *Unity Gold Corp.,* 3 SEC 620 (1938).

APPRAISALS.—Where the appraiser is not independent, that fact must be disclosed. *Associated Gas and Electric Co.,* 11 SEC 975 (1942).

An implication that directors made an independent valuation of property was held to be misleading where the directors did no more than accept, without investigation, the statements of a promoter as to previous contributions of syndicate members and were not in fact informed of profits to promoters. *Resources Corporation International,* 7 SEC 689 (1940).

Accepted bases for appraisal of a patent are: (1) the amount of a bona fide cash sale or offer for the patent; (2) a capitalization of the royalties derived from the patents; or (3) a capitalization of the earnings strictly attributable to the ownership of a patent. The assignment of value to a patent application also involves the further contingency that letters patent may never be granted. In the absence of information upon which one of the foregoing criteria of value can be applied, any value given to a patent or patent application would not constitute an appraisal but would be a guess. In such case only a nominal value can be attributed to a patent or patent application. *Petersen Engine Co., Inc.,* 2 SEC 893 (1937).

If an appraisal or a representation of value purportedly based thereon is not to be misleading, the appraisal must meet two tests: first, it must be based on scientific methods; second, there must be a fair and accurate application of the methods purported to be followed. *Breeze Corporations, Inc.,* 3 SEC 717 (1938); *Winnebago Distilling Co.,* 6 SEC 926 (1940).

Valuations contained in an appraisal purporting to follow certain norms, even though in the final analysis they merely represent informed judgments, nevertheless are representations that these norms have been accurately and fairly followed. Where evidence disclosed that such norms were not followed, it was held that the valuations arrived at were in essence misrepresentations of fact because they describe untruthfully the basis upon which judgment concerning the valuations had been exercised. *Haddam Distillers Corp.,* 1 SEC 37 (1934); *Continental Distillers and Importers Corp.,* 1 SEC 54 (1935).

Where a mining engineer's report used techniques proper in an operating report but improper in an appraisal report and bore no indication that the engineer intended it as an appraisal, SEC ruled that it is improper to use such figures and the ore reserve valuations therein as appraisal figures. *Mining and Development Corp.,* 1 SEC 786 (1936).

Appraisal value which failed to take into account the cost to promoters and disregarded assessed value, prior sales of the property, and the local real estate market is misleading. *Continental Distillers and Importers Corp.,* 1 SEC 54 (1935) ; *Winnebago Distilling Co.,* 6 SEC 926 (1940).

Where the presence of a stream and other water rights were considered in determining the appraisal value of land, it is misleading to appraise the water rights separately. *Continental Distillers and Importers Corp.,* 1 SEC 54 (1935).

It is a misrepresentation to file an appraisal, knowing that it included buildings and equipment no longer in existence or destined for the junk heap, without full disclosure of the facts. *Continental Distillers and Importers Corp.,* 1 SEC 54 (1935).

The inclusion in an appraisal of the cost of development work which is of no present value is a misrepresentation. *Marquette Mines, Inc.,* 8 SEC 172 (1940).

Going concern value is not a proper basis for an appraisal of properties which have not been successfully operated for a number of years. *Marquette Mines, Inc.,* 8 SEC 172 (1940).

It is misleading to assign, without explanation, cost value to underground and surface development, having small present or potential value and, at the same time, assign replacement value to the buildings and equipment. *Marquette Mines, Inc.,* 8 SEC 172 (1940).

Properties of a corporation were appraised on the basis of reproduction cost which included an allowance for indirect overhead costs. In lieu of the overhead so computed, the registrant substituted an allowance arbitrarily computed at 45.2 per cent on the ground that this percentage was allowed by a Federal court in an unrelated case [*Brooklyn Borough Gas Co. v. Prendergast,* 16 F.(2d) 615 (1926)]. SEC said this practice was unjustifiable and caused the balance sheet to be misleading. *Associated Gas and Electric Co.,* 11 SEC 1012 (1942).

Where a registration statement properly contains an appraisal of mining properties based on future returns, a risk rate of 7 per cent, employed to capitalize estimated future returns of a speculative enterprise, is unjustifiably low and the resulting figure purporting to be appraised present value of such property is unjustifiably high and misleading. *Monitor Gold Mining Co.,* 4 SEC 347 (1939).

Where volume and stated net value of ore are accepted, it is necessary to apply a suitable formula for reduction of value of such ore to present worth if the extraction will cover any considerable period of time. *Sunset Gold Fields, Inc.,* 2 SEC 329 (1937).

An estimate of value of property by an attorney or an accountant without experience as an appraiser or with no knowledge of appraisal methods renders the balance sheet misleading. *Breeze Corporations, Inc.,* 3 SEC 717 (1938) ; *Great Dike Gold Mines, Inc.,* 1 SEC 621 (1936).

Substitution of "estimate" for "appraisal" does not lessen the misrepresentation inherent in an erroneous valuation. *Mining and Development Corp.,* 1 SEC 786 (1936).

Depreciation Based on Current or Replacement Value.—In recent years, with the increase in price levels, there has been some advocacy of a theory that depreciation should be based not on historical cost but on current or replacement cost. It has been argued that depreciation charges are inadequate unless they provide for the replacement of the applicable assets at the time they are retired from service. It has also been said that there is not a fair matching of costs and revenues if depreciation based on costs of fixed assets acquired at one price level is deducted from sales made at a materially different level. Others maintain that regardless of the matching theory, costs are not correctly stated unless they reflect current values of capital consumed in the business. Holders of these views would, in effect, abandon historical costs by adjusting such costs in financial statements to reflect changes in the purchasing power of the dollar.

The SEC has made it clear that it would require adherence to historical costs[16] in statements filed with it, but has permitted deviation from this rule by foreign companies, as referred to in Chapter **31**. The Commission in fact denied a formal application to adopt a requirement that "economic" depreciation (based on replacement at current prices) be reflected either in the accounts or by other appropriate disclosures.

Two companies filed statements with the SEC with depreciation based on current price levels, only to have them rejected by the Commission.[17]

Case 1

Iowa-Illinois Gas and Electric Company deducted price-level depreciation as an operating expense in computing net income for 1958. The following explanation appeared among the notes to financial statements:

A 1957 decision of the Iowa Supreme Court in the case of the *City of Fort Dodge* vs. *Iowa-Illinois Gas and Electric Company* gave recognition to the inadequacies of cost depreciation and permitted the recovery, through rates charged customers, of the fair value of the property used to serve customers. Rate increases which include an allowance for fair value depreciation have subsequently been obtained in certain Iowa districts.

In June 1958, the Company began charging fair value depreciation to operating expenses based on the fair value of the property in those districts where such depreciation had been allowed in the determination of rates. An amount equivalent to revenues collected to provide fair value depreciation ($420,000), after reduction for the estimated income tax on such increased revenues, or a net amount of $198,000, has been credited to an account for capital maintained by recovery of fair value depreciation.

[16] 18 SEC Ann. Rep. 182 (1952) ; 20 SEC Ann. Rep. 107 (1954).
[17] Source: *The Journal of Accountancy,* September, 1959.

The middle paragraph of the auditors' certificate read as follows:

In 1958, the Company commenced collecting increased revenues in certain of its operating areas in recognition of depreciation allowed in rate proceedings on the fair value of related property. To the extent recovered in increased rates, fair value depreciation has been recorded by the Company as set forth in the notes to the financial statements. Although generally accepted accounting principles presently provide that depreciation shall be based upon cost, it is our opinion that these principles should be changed with respect to depreciation to recognize increased price levels. We approve of the practice adopted by the Company, since it results, in our opinion, in a fairer statement of income for the year than that resulting from the application of generally accepted accounting principles. In all other respects, the financial statements were prepared in conformity with generally accepted accounting principles applied on a basis consistent with that of the preceding year.

Iowa-Illinois filed its 1958 statements as part of a registration statement. Subsequently, the company amended the statement and showed the fair value depreciation of $198,000 after the amount designated as "Net income." The financial statement notes included the following:

The provision for fair value depreciation represents an amount equivalent to revenues collected to provide fair value depreciation ($420,000) after reduction for the estimated income tax on such increased revenues, and has been credited to an account for capital maintained by recovery of fair value depreciation. The Company believes that such a provision should be reflected as an operating expense and, hence, deducted before arriving at operating income. *However, the Company is informed that such treatment will not be acceptable to the Securities and Exchange Commission.* Therefore, the provision for fair value depreciation is shown in the accompanying statement of income as an appropriation of net income. (Emphasis supplied.)

The auditors' report covering the amended financial statements was a conventional, short-form report (see Chapter **24**).

Case 2

Ayrshire Collieries Corporation filed an annual report on Form 10–K with the SEC for the fiscal year ended June 30, 1958. The statement of earnings concluded as follows:

Net income for the year	$2,884,256
Provision for price-level depreciation (see note)	195,429
Balance of net income	2,688,827
Equity in undistributed net income of affiliated companies....	311,226
Net earnings, including equity in undistributed net income of affiliated companies	$3,000,053

Note: The provision for price-level depreciation represents the excess of depreciation cost measured by the current purchasing power of the dollar over depreciation cost measured by the purchasing power of the dollar at the dates of acquisition or construction of the companies' depreciable property.

The auditors gave an unqualified opinion on the Ayrshire statements in which the first two paragraphs were equivalent to a standard short-form certificate; the third paragraph read as follows:

In our opinion, however, the net income for the year is more fairly presented after deducting the provision for price-level depreciation, since current price levels have been recognized in determining the current cost of property consumed in operations. Generally accepted principles of accounting for cost of property do not reflect the effect of price-level changes since dates of acquisition or construction of the companies' depreciable property.

An amended statement was later submitted to the SEC. The amended statement concluded as follows:

Income after federal income taxes	$2,884,256
Equity in undistributed net income of nonconsolidated affiliates	311,226
Net income	3,195,482
Appropriation for price-level depreciation (see note)	195,429
Balance of net income transferred to earned surplus	$3,000,053

Note: . . . The Company believes such appropriations of net income should be deducted before arriving at net income for the year, but is informed that such treatment is not in accordance with generally accepted accounting principles and *will not be accepted by the Securities and Exchange Commission.* (Emphasis supplied.)

The amended auditors' certificate was the same as the original except for the first sentence in the third paragraph which was revised as follows:

In our opinion, however, the net income of the companies for the year is more fairly presented by the amounts reported as "balance of net income transferred to earned surplus" since, in arriving at such amounts, current price levels have been recognized in determining the current cost of property consumed in operations.

For a discussion of this subject in relation to foreign companies, see Chapter **31**.

Accounting for Intangible Assets and Deferred Costs.—In 1970 the Accounting Principles Board issued Opinion No. 17 on the subject of "Intangible Assets" which made it a requirement to amortize intangible assets, including goodwill, over the period benefited—not exceeding 40 years. The Opinion is applicable to intangible assets acquired after October 31, 1970. Prior to the issuance of that Opinion, there was no mandatory requirement to amortize goodwill when it was apparent that there had been no decrease in its value, and this was also the SEC's position.

The SEC, however, has informal administrative rules regarding the accounting for intangible assets (other than goodwill) and other deferred items as well as their amortization. These were never published as part of the SEC's Accounting Series Releases, but experienced practitioners have known of their existence as a result of discussions with members of the

SEC's staff and comments received from the staff on material filed with the Commission. It was known that the Commission's accounting staff had strong views regarding the capitalization and amortization of start-up costs, research and development costs, opening expenses of stores, finance offices, and bowling alleys, and unusually large advertising programs. It was known also that the method and amortization rates of intangibles and deferred costs capitalized had to be set forth in the notes to financial statements.

The Commission's views with respect to the foregoing were expressed by Walter Mickelsen, Chief Accountant of the SEC's Division of Corporation Finance, in 1966 as part of the AICPA's course on "Filings with the SEC." The comments which follow are taken from Mr. Mickelsen's prepared remarks.

In the case of purchases of small loan finance paper, the SEC has limited amortization of the excess purchase price to three years.

Three years is also deemed by the Commission's staff to be an appropriate amortization period applicable to costs of opening new bowling alleys and stores.

In general, the SEC's staff consider that deferred advertising and special promotional costs have a very short life and should be amortized over periods ranging from three to six months.

When plant moving and relocation costs are deferred, the SEC in a few instances accepted amortization over a maximum period of up to six years, although three years is considered realistic in most cases.

In addition to determination of the amortization periods, questions often arise as to the kind of expense items that may be included in the deferred costs, i.e., direct costs, overhead costs, and sometimes items of dubious validity. The SEC takes the position in general that a policy of limiting deferrals to direct costs and related overhead on conservative and realistic bases should be followed. The deferred income taxes related to deferred expenses should not be netted against them, but rather included with other deferred income tax amounts on the balance sheet.

Mr. Mickelsen conceded that some of the Commission's staff look upon many deferrals "with a jaundiced eye, inasmuch as the practice of expense deferrals may be used not only by profitable companies but also by companies whose long term earnings prospects are poor." In some instances, he said, the practice of deferring expenses may mask a deteriorating situation in a company that had previously been profitable.

Two areas in which the Commission's staff has required amortization of excess purchase prices paid over book value of businesses acquired have been in the case of small loan finance businesses and mortgage servicing companies. For some years, the Commission has permitted an upper limit of six years for premiums paid to acquire a small loan business. In a few instances, where it has been clearly established that some of the premium represents a price paid for the inherent value of a State-granted license to operate an office, the SEC has permitted an appropriate portion of the premium to be treated as a permanent license cost. (Under APB Opinion No. 17, "Intangible Assets," however, despite its permanence, it would have to be amortized over a period not exceeding 40 years.) Mr. Mickelsen said, "This area presumably needs further study in instances where a manufacturing or industrial company in a widespread diversification program acquires at a large premium a successful small loan or finance company along with . . . other unrelated types of businesses."

During the last decade the Commission has, with very few exceptions, required that goodwill or excess purchase price paid on the purchase of mortgage servicing companies acquired by other such companies, or companies in related fields (such as real estate), be amortized over a period not exceeding eight or nine years, on the basis that the then currently held portfolio of mortgages being serviced had an approximate life of such duration. In one recent case the amortization was limited to the Federal income tax benefits that were derived from the addition of the mortgage servicing company to the acquiring company.

Where a balance sheet filed with the Commission reflects a material amount of "Research and Development Cost," or similar items, the staff has requested an analysis of this account to be included in the notes to the financial statements showing the following:

(a) Additions to, amortization, and charge-offs for a minimum of three years;

(b) Policy of amortization;

(c) A representation that such amounts relate to items being commercially produced or are deemed to be commercially feasible;

(d) Upon determination that any amounts capitalized cannot be recovered by future sales, a representation as to immediate write-off to income; and

(e) The Federal income tax treatment accorded the deferred costs.

As to amortization of research and development costs, the SEC's staff feels that five years is usually the maximum period, "this coinciding with the maximum allowed if deferral and later amortization is chosen for both financial reporting and Federal income tax purposes." The amortization should be on a unit of production or sale basis which could amortize the deferrals over considerably less than five years, with a minimum floor of, say, 20%, in a five year time period, for each year.

One of the SEC Annual Reports discusses a case in which the proper classification of, and accounting for, intangible assets presented a serious problem.

The consolidated balance sheets included an item designated "Contracts and goodwill" in the amount of $7,332,389 which was represented as consisting principally of the excess of cost of acquisition over the cost of inventories and allocated cost of assets acquired at the inception of the corporation. The footnotes to the financial statements disclosed that during the year 1953 the corporation reached a settlement with the Internal Revenue Service with respect to the 1946 to 1948 federal income tax returns, in which deductions had been claimed for amortization of contracts. Under the terms of this settlement, the amount at which "Contracts and goodwill" was stated ($7,332,389) was construed for federal income tax purposes to be made up of $2,931,729 subject to amortization on an agreed basis, and $4,400,660 was considered to be goodwill and not subject to amortization.

The registrant was advised by the SEC that the basis of settlement with the Internal Revenue Service in this case was likewise appropriate for financial accounting purposes, that segregation of the item covering both contracts and goodwill should be made, and that retroactive effect should be given to amortization of the contract portion. The financial statements were amended accordingly. (21 SEC Ann. Rep. 19 (1955)).

As previously noted, goodwill acquired after October 31, 1970, must be amortized over a period not exceeding 40 years. (APB Opinion No. 17, "Intangible Assets," (August 1970)).

CHAPTER 4

SEC VIEWS ON ACCOUNTING PRINCIPLES

Part 2

CONTENTS

Accounting for Transactions Involving Real Estate (Including Sales and Leasebacks).—Some real estate development companies, in order to show profits, have entered into transactions which give the appearance of profits but which, as a matter of fact, do not actually result in profits at the time of the transaction. Some of these transactions have come before the SEC in connection with registration statements or reports filed with that agency. After investigating the facts, the SEC in some cases caused the "profits" to be eliminated in the documents filed with it. Having had a number of such experiences involving transactions in real estate, the SEC issued ASR No. 95 in December, 1962, for the purpose of setting forth its views regarding the recognition of profits in such transactions.

According to the release, a number of cases had come to the SEC's attention in which the profits on certain real estate transactions were taken into income under circumstances which indicated that the profits were not actually realized in the period in which the transactions were recorded. The recognition of profit at the time of sale, in accordance with generally accepted accounting principles, is appropriate, the Commission said, "if it is reasonable to conclude, in the light of all the circumstances, that a profit has been realized." The release quoted AICPA Accounting Research Bulletin No. 43 to the effect that a profit is deemed to be realized when a sale in the ordinary course of business is effected, unless the circumstances are such that the collection of the sales price is not reasonably assured. Thus, said the SEC, recognition of profit is appropriate only when a bona fide sales transaction has taken place, and then only to the extent that the consideration received in the transaction can be reasonably evaluated.

In some of the cases coming before the SEC, it appeared, according to the Commission, that the sale of property was "a mere fiction designed to create the illusion of profits or value as a basis for the sale of securities." Moreover, even in bona fide transactions the degree of uncertainty as to ultimate realization of profit may be so great that "business prudence, as well as generally accepted accounting principles, would preclude the recognition of gain at the time of sale."

The Commission said that circumstances such as the following tend to raise a question as to the propriety of current recognition of profit:

1. Evidence of financial weakness of the purchaser
2. Substantial uncertainty as to amount of costs and expenses to be incurred
3. Substantial uncertainty as to amount of proceeds to be realized because of form of consideration or method of settlement; e.g., non-recourse notes, non-interest-bearing notes, purchaser's stock, and notes with optional settlement provisions, all of indeterminable value
4. Retention of effective control of the property by the seller
5. Limitations and restrictions on the purchaser's profits and on the development or disposition of the property
6. Simultaneous sale and repurchase by the same or affiliated interests
7. Concurrent loans to purchasers
8. Small or no down payment
9. Simultaneous sale and leaseback of property

Any of the foregoing circumstances, taken alone, the Commission conceded, might not preclude the recognition of profit in appropriate amount, but the degree of uncertainty "may be accentuated by the presence of a combination of the foregoing factors."

Appended to the release were seven illustrative cases taken from filings with the SEC (with the names of the companies omitted) in which the Commission deemed it inappropriate to recognize the recorded gross profit as having been realized at the time of sale. Because of space limitations, only two of the cases are reproduced below—Case 1 and Case 7. Case 1 is presented because it contains several of the "circumstances" specified by the SEC which created uncertainty as to the realization of profit. Case 7 is presented for another reason as will be seen from the comments which follow it.

Case 1

On the last day of its fiscal year, a registrant engaged principally in the development of real estate sold a block of 1,000 lots to a non-affiliated construction company for $1,100,000, receiving a cash payment of $100,000 and an nonrecourse note of $1,000,000 due in one year, secured only by the lots transferred. Interest was limited to 6% for one year or $120 per house. A profit of $500,000 before taxes was recorded on the transaction.

The transaction was subject to, among others, the following conditions and arrangements:

    a. Each lot was to be released upon payment of $1,000 plus interest at the time of closing the sale of a house and lot.

    b. The registrant was to make the determination of when the houses were to be constructed and to arrange the construction loans.

    c. The registrant was to be exclusive sales agent for the construction company, arrange financing and conduct closings with the home buyers.

    d. The construction company was to be paid a maximum of $500 profit and an additional $100 to cover overhead expenses on each house sold. Profits to be received by the construction company were to be applied against the note owed to the registrant.

*   *   *

Case 7

In early 1960 a registrant sold to an unaffiliated purchaser a manufacturing plant and another building used in its operations for a total consideration of $1,500,000 reflecting a profit of $600,000 after taxes. The consideration was realized in the form of cash and assumption of an existing mortgage. The seller simultaneously leased these same properties back at an annual rental of $160,000 for a period of 25 years. The registration statement as effective reported the profit as deferred and to be amortized against rental payments over the life of the leases.

On page **4·7** of this book is a discussion of a case in which the SEC had objected to the recognition of profit in a transaction involving the sale and leaseback of personal property, namely, a fleet of trucks. The company subsequently reversed the gain retroactively in its next published report to shareholders and indicated it would amortize the gain over the period of the lease as a reduction of the lease rentals. Case 7 (.eproduced above) indicates that the SEC may also challenge the recognition of profit in transactions involving the sale and leaseback of real estate.

There may be instances in which a sale and leaseback, in essence, is nothing more or less than a financing arrangement (that is, a loan secured by real or personal property), and in which, consequently, there is no real gain—there is merely a loan which must be repaid with interest over the life of the lease. In these circumstances it may be misleading to report a profit at the time of the sale which will be offset by increased rental expense in the future; the realities of the transaction would suggest that the profit be deferred and amortized against future rent expense.

On the other hand, there may be situations where a profit has, in fact, been realized on the sale-leaseback. Take the case, for example, of a company which is in the business of constructing and operating large office buildings. Shortly after a building is completed and fully occupied, the company sells the building to an insurance company. The insurance company makes its own appraisal and investigation of the property to ascertain whether it represents the kind of asset in which it should invest its policy-holders' funds. The insurance company buys the property and, at the same time, leases it back to the builder who will continue to operate it. On a sale of $33,000,000 the builder recorded a profit of $3,000,000 at the time of the transaction. The builder is now in a more liquid position and able to proceed with other construction. He has realized a profit on the sale of his investment for cash and will be in a position to show future earnings from operating the property. The insurance company would prefer not to operate the building but knows that if anything should happen to the operator, the insurance company will continue to own a valuable asset, namely, a new building, fully occupied by responsible tenants having long-term leases. In these circumstances most accountants would have no hesitation in acknowledging that the builder has earned the profit of $3,000,000, and the author believes that the staff of the SEC would also share this view. As noted on page **4·7** the APB stated in its Opinion No. 5 (1964) that ordinarily gain should not be recognized on a sale and leaseback of property, but that in certain exceptional circumstances (such as those assumed above), it would be appropriate to recognize the gain.

Despite the issuance of ASR No. 95, the Chief Accountant of the SEC's Division of Corporation Finance stated that "We still run into cases where we feel that profits are recorded prematurely and prior to the time they were really earned."[1] As an example he cited a company which in 1964 recorded a profit of about $600,000 on a sale of about $800,000, of which $75,000 had been received in cash and the balance in the form of an interest-bearing note secured by a first deed of trust. One year later the company had foreclosed on the property and was again its owner, and proposed to

[1] Walter Mickelsen, "Recent Developments in the SEC Accounting Field," May 24, 1966.

reverse the previously recorded profit. The Chief Accountant of the Division said that the very unsatisfactory operating results of some real estate organizations in recent years indicate that more care and conservatism should have been used in recording real estate profits.

There are also other examples. For instance, the SEC announced on April 8, 1971 (Release No. 34–9137) that it had ordered Major Realty Corporation to revise its annual reports for the fiscal years ended May 31, 1968 and 1969 after determining that the company had accounted improperly for a transaction involving a parcel of land. The Commission had instituted a proceeding under the 1934 Act to determine whether Major had failed to comply with the Act by filing reports for the years indicated which included untrue statements or material omissions.

The SEC took exception to the accounting treatment of an agreement regarding a parcel of land. According to the Commission, Major had entered into a contract in fiscal 1968 to sell the land which provided that Major had the right to rescind the sale if the buyer failed to commence construction of a shopping mall by June 1, 1969, but that if prior to that date, the buyer furnished evidence of a lease or letter of intent to lease from a major department store, the date for beginning of construction would be extended to June 1, 1970.

The buyer assigned its obligations under the contract to a wholly-owned subsidiary to which title to the land was transferred in April 1968, and Major received a $25,000 cash down payment and a promissory note of the subsidiary in the amount of $3,475,000 secured by a first mortgage lien on the property. The note bore interest at 6% per annum commencing February 1, 1970 and the principal was payable in three equal annual instalments beginning February 1, 1971.

Major's financial statements included in its 1968 10–K reflected a recognition of income of $3,152,170 from the transaction, and a reduction of the deficit in Retained Earnings by the same amount, and the note of $3,475,000 was included in the asset account "Mortgage Notes Receivable." The SEC said that Major improperly treated the land transaction as a reportable sale and thereby overstated its income and understated the deficit in Retained Earnings in view of these facts:

1. Major received a down payment representing less than 1% of the purchase price;

2. Major retained the right, under certain conditions, to rescind the sale subsequent to closing, and no interest or principal payments were to be made until such right to rescind no longer existed; and

3. The buyer's subsidiary, which had assumed the buyer's obligation with respect to the transaction, had assets of only a nominal amount, and the note given Major by such subsidiary was a non-recourse note.

The SEC asserted that the transaction had to be accounted for based on its substance rather than its legal form. Major had obtained, the SEC charged, "nothing more from the buyer than a deposit in exchange for an option to purchase the property if it was able to fulfill certain conditions." The purchaser at the date of signing the agreement, and for a long period thereafter, had "so little economic interest in the property that the transaction could not be deemed a sale for accounting purposes."

The defects in the 1968 10–K carried over into the 1969 report. On or about June 30, 1969, three months before filing the 1969 10–K, in response to a request by the buyer for a twelve month extension of the terms of the contract relating to the start of construction, Major notified the buyer of its willingness to grant an extension only until October 1, 1969, and further stated that it (Major) had elected to exercise its right to rescission unless the buyer agreed in writing by August 15, 1969 to accept the extension. No written agreement was ever given by the buyer.

(In fiscal 1970 Major reported that it had rescinded the sale and returned the $25,000 cash down payment and the note, and the buyer had reconveyed the land to Major.)

Major offered to settle the SEC matter, and, for the purpose of the proceeding, agreed that the annual reports were misleading. The company also offered to correct the reports and to send its shareholders a copy of the SEC's findings and opinion before the next annual meeting. The SEC accepted the offer of settlement.

Profit on Sale and Leaseback of Personal Property.—There have been several instances in which the SEC has taken a dim view of the reality of so-called "profits" on the sale and leaseback of personal property. This is not to say that the SEC prohibits the recognition of gain on sale-and-leaseback transactions; on the contrary, there have been numerous cases where gain in such transactions has been accepted by the staff of the Commission. On the other hand, the SEC has questioned enough transactions of this kind so that registrants and their independent public accountants should be prepared to defend the accounting in connection with such transactions. This is particularly true where the subject of the sale-and-leaseback is personal property—such as trucks and machinery. See also the discussion on page **4·3** regarding sale and leaseback of real property.

Especially in the case of a buy-(or build)-sale-leaseback transaction, the staff of the Commission is apt to suggest that there may have been no real gain; that the transaction in effect is a financing arrangement, that is, it is a loan transaction in which the property serves merely as collateral. If this is a correct analysis of the transaction, then there is no real gain, and the so-called gain should be treated as a deferred credit to be amortized against future rentals.

The annual report of one company[2] for 1961 indicated that the SEC may have required the company to revise its accounting in connection with a sale of trucks and automobiles and concurrent leaseback of the equipment. A note to the financial statements in the report read as follows:

> Adjustment has been made in the consolidated financial statements to give effect to a change in accounting method as recommended by the Securities and Exchange Commission, requiring that the gain, net of income taxes, amounting to $103,688, from the sale made August 1, 1960 of certain trucks and automobiles subject to concurrent leaseback contracts with the purchaser thereof be amortized over the four-year term of the leases expiring July 31, 1964. In accordance with the revised accounting method, net gain amortization of $10,800 for the period August 1 to December 31, 1960 and $33,422 for the year 1961 has been recorded in the accounts.

As previously noted, the SEC's position denying recognition of gain in some transactions involving the sale and leaseback of personal property was subsequently supported by the APB. The Board issued Opinion No. 5 (Sept. 1964) on "Reporting of Leases in Financial Statements of Lessee." It stated that its Opinion made no distinction between leases of real property and those of personal property. The Board's position is that material gains or losses resulting from the sale of properties which are the subject of sale and leaseback transactions, together with the related tax effect, should be amortized over the life of the lease as an adjustment of the rental cost (or, if the lease property is capitalized, as an adjustment of depreciation). This is the general rule, and exceptions are expected to be rare. In cases where the use of the leased property changes with the sale and leaseback and the sale price falls within the limits which could reasonably be set by independent transactions (for example, companies engaged in both constructing and operating office buildings or other commercial investment property may sell a property after construction and lease it back for operation) the exceptional circumstances surrounding a particular sale and leaseback transaction may clearly justify recognition of all or part of the gain or loss at the time of the sale.

Preparation of Consolidated Financial Statements.—There have been a number of SEC decisions—informal as well as formal—having to do with the preparation of consolidated financial statements. For convenience, all of these are included and discussed in Chapter **17** which also includes the rules in Regulation S–X relating to consolidated and combined statements.

Accounting for Stock or Warrants Distributed to Shareholders. —Chapter **18** of this book contains a discussion of the SEC's attitude con-

[2] Pepsi-Cola Bottling Company of Long Island, Inc.

cerning the accounting for stock dividends and for warrants distributed to shareholders. It also contains a discussion of a proposed rule which, if adopted, would preclude an issuer whose stock is publicly offered or traded from misrepresenting the results of its operations by distributing stock dividends unless the issuer has retained earnings in sufficient amount to cover the fair value of the shares distributed.

Accounting for Investment Securities (Other than Restricted Securities) by Investment Companies.—In 1970 the SEC published ASR No. 118 concerning the accounting by registered investment companies for investment securities in financial statements and in computations of net asset value for pricing their shares. The release also discussed related auditing procedures for the guidance of independent accountants who examine such statements. The special considerations that apply to restricted securities are also discussed in the following pages.

The financial statements of investment companies registered under the Investment Company Act of 1940 are governed by the Act, the rules thereunder, and by Regulation S–X.

INCLUSION OF SECURITIES IN THE PORTFOLIO.—The statement of assets and liabilities of an investment company includes not only investments on hand or held by a custodian, but also securities which have been purchased but have not been received. Securities that have been sold are excluded from the statement. In the ordinary transaction through a broker, the trade date—rather than the settlement date—is the established and acceptable practice in investment company accounting for determining when securities have been bought or sold.

In the case of transactions through channels other than the usual brokerage route, the date as of which the transaction should be recorded, in the SEC's view, is the date on which the investment company obtains an enforceable right to demand the securities in the case of a purchase, or payment in the case of a sale. If a question arises as to when an enforceable right is obtained, a written opinion of legal counsel should be obtained by the company. A copy of the opinion should be made available to, and retained by, the company's independent auditors.

When the propriety or validity of an investment is questionable because of provisions of the Act, or state law, or the company's investment policy, or any other reason, the company should also obtain a written legal opinion. A copy of the opinion should be made available to, and retained by, the independent auditors. If the questions as to propriety or validity are not satisfactorily resolved, the circumstances of the investment should be disclosed in the financial statements.

Auditing the Physical Existence of the Portfolio.—Securities held by the company or its custodian should be substantiated by the independent auditors by inspection of the securities or by obtaining confirmation from a custodian which holds the securities pursuant to Section 17(f)(1) of the Act. (See the discussion on page **5·52**.) Securities purchased but not received should be confirmed with the broker or other person responsible for delivering the securities. Where satisfactory confirmation has been received, audit procedures normally need not include evidence of subsequent receipt of the securities unless, under the circumstances, additional substantiation is considered necessary by the auditors. Where satisfactory confirmation has not been received, subsequent receipt of the securities should be substantiated by other appropriate procedures.

Under Section 30(e) of the Act, the auditors' certificate should include a brief statement concerning the substantiation of securities owned. Except for securities bought but not received, the certificate should state that the securities were either inspected by the auditors or, where the securities were held by a custodian pursuant to Section 17(f)(1) of the Act, were confirmed to him by the custodian. As to securities bought but not received, the certificate should refer to confirmations received or to alternative procedures employed.

Valuation of Securities.—Under Regulation S–X, the statement of assets and liabilities of *open-end investment companies* must reflect all assets at value, showing cost parenthetically; *closed-end companies* may use either this basis or the cost basis, showing value parenthetically.

"Value" is defined in Section 2(a)(39) of the Act as: "(i) with respect to securities for which market quotations are readily available, the market value of such securities; and (ii) with respect to other securities and assets, fair value as determined in good faith by the board of directors . . ." This definition is also used in Rule 2a–4 as the required basis for computing the current net asset value of redeemable securities of investment companies for the purpose of pricing their shares.

The SEC's release sets forth standards for determining valuation policies which investment companies should follow. Variations from the standards should be disclosed in the financial statements even though the variation conforms with the company's stated valuation policy. Any deviation from a stated valuation policy, whether or not in conformity with the standards, should also be disclosed.

Securities Traded on Exchanges.—If a security was traded on the valuation date, the last sale price is used. In the case of a security listed on more than one exchange, the last sale, up to the time of valuation, on the exchange on which the security is principally traded should be used; if there were no sales on that exchange on the valuation date, the last sale, up to the time of valuation, on the other exchange should be used.

With respect to the time of valuation, Rule 22c–1 requires that current net asset value be computed at least once daily as of the close of trading on the New York Stock Exchange.

If there was no sale on the valuation date but published closing bid and asked prices are available, the valuation should be within the range of these prices. Some companies use the bid price, others use the mean of the bid and asked prices, and others use a valuation within the range considered best to represent value in the circumstances; each of these policies is acceptable if consistently applied. It is not normally acceptable to use the asked price alone.

If, on the valuation date, only a bid price or an asked price is quoted or the spread between the bid and asked price is substantial, quotations for several days should be reviewed. If sales have been infrequent or there is a thin market in the security, consideration should be given to whether "market quotations are readily available." If it is decided that they are not readily available, the alternative valuation method prescribed by Section 2(a)(39)—"fair value as determined in good faith by the board of directors"—should be used.

Over-the-Counter Securities.—Because of the multiple sources of prices for securities traded over-the-counter, a company often has more options open to it in valuing such securities than it does for listed securities. A company may adopt a policy of using a mean of the bid prices from several sources, or of the bid and asked prices, or of the prices of a representative selection of broker-dealers quoting on a security; or it may use a valuation within the range of bid and asked prices considered best to represent value in the circumstances. Any of these policies is acceptable if consistently applied. The use of the asked price alone is normally not acceptable.

Ordinarily, quotations for a security should be obtained from more than one broker-dealer, particularly if quotations are available only from broker-dealers not known to be market-makers for that security, and quotations for several days should be reviewed. If the quotations appear to be questionable, or if the number of quotations indicates a thin market, consideration should be given to whether "market quotations are readily available." If the decision is negative, the security should be valued by the board of directors.

Securities Valued "in Good Faith."—To comply with Section 2(a) (39) and Rule 2a–4, the company's board of directors must satisfy themselves that all appropriate factors relevant to the value of securities for which market quotations are not readily available have been considered, and determine the method of arriving at the fair value of each such security. The board may appoint persons to assist them in the determination of such value, and to make the actual calculations. The board must also continuously review the appropriateness of the method used in valuing each security. Whenever technical assistance is received from non-directors, the board must review their findings to satisfy themselves that the resulting valuations are fair.

No single standard for determining "fair value . . . in good faith" can be laid down, since fair value depends upon the circumstances of each case. In general, the current fair value of a security is the amount which the owner might reasonably expect to receive in a current sale. Methods conforming to this principle may, for example, be based on a multiple of earnings, or a discount from market of a similar freely traded security, or on yield to maturity with respect to debt issues, or on a combination of these and other methods.

Some of the general factors which should be considered in valuing a security include: (1) the fundamental analytical data relating to the investment; (2) the nature and duration of restrictions on disposition of the securities; and (3) an evaluation of the forces influencing the market in which these securities are traded. Among the more specific factors to be considered are: type of security, financial statements, cost, size of holding, discount from market of unrestricted securities of the same class at time of purchase, special reports prepared by analysts, information as to transactions or offers with respect to the security, existence of merger proposals or tender offers affecting the security, price and extent of public trading in similar securities of the issuer or comparable companies, and other relevant matters. ASR No. 118 does not purport to delineate all the factors the directors must consider in valuing securities.

The information considered by the directors and the judgmental factors applied should be documented in the board's minutes and the supporting data retained for inspection by the independent auditors.

AUDITING SECURITY VALUATIONS.—In the case of securities for which market quotations are readily available, the independent auditor should verify the quotations and satisfy himself that they may properly be used under the standards in ASR No. 118.

In the case of "fair value" as determined by the directors, the accountant is not an appraiser and is not expected to substitute his judgment for that of the directors; rather, he should review all information considered by the board or by analysts reporting to it, read relevant minutes of directors' meetings, and ascertain the procedures followed by the directors. If the accountant is unable to express an unqualified opinion because of the uncertainty inherent in the valuations of the securities based on the directors' subjective judgment, he should nevertheless state in his certificate whether in the circumstances the procedures appear to be reasonable and the underlying documentation appropriate. The accountant may have to furnish a "subject to" certificate. This matter is discussed in Chapter **25**.

When considering security values, the auditor should consider any limitations or conditions on acquiring or holding such securities which may be imposed by the Investment Company Act, by the charter or bylaws, by contract, or by its filings with the SEC. If such restrictions are met by a narrow margin, the auditor may need to exercise extra care to satisfy himself that the valuations were not biased to meet those restrictions.

INVESTMENTS IN AFFILIATES OR AFFILIATED PERSONS.—Regulation S–X requires that the financial statements of an investment company state separately investments in, investment income from, gain or loss on sales of securities of, and management or other service fees payable to, (a)· controlled companies and (b) other "affiliates." The terms "affiliate" and "control" are defined in the Act and in the regulation. The term "affiliated person" includes one in whom there is ownership of 5% or more of the outstanding voting securities, and certain persons connected with the issuer, investment company, investment adviser, or member of an advisory board thereof.

In ascertaining the existence of such affiliations, the independent auditor should consider the facts obtained during the audit, and should make inquiries of the company's management. As evidence of his inquiries, he should obtain and retain written representations from management which should be in the form of a statement that the company, except to the extent indicated,

   (i) does not own any securities either of persons who are directly affiliated, or, to the best information and belief of management, of persons who are indirectly affiliated,

  (ii) has not received income from or realized gain or loss on sales of investments in or indebtedness of such persons,

 (iii) has not incurred expenses for management or other service fees payable to such persons, and

 (iv) has not otherwise engaged in transactions with such persons.

Where there is a question as to the existence of an affiliation, a written legal opinion should be obtained by the company's management, and a copy made available to, and retained by, the independent accountant.

Valuation of Investments in Restricted Securities.—"Restricted securities" in the discussion which follows are securities which may not be offered for sale to the public without first being registered under the 1933 Act. Such securities are often acquired from an issuer or its controlling stockholder in a transaction in which the buyer furnishes a letter to the seller stating, in effect, that he is acquiring the securities for investment and not with a view to distribution, as a consequence of which the securities are sometimes referred to as "letter securities" or "investment letter securities." The letter provides a record of the buyer's intent in order to substantiate a claim that the transaction is exempt from registration under the 1933 Act since it did not involve a public offering. The letter is not a guarantee, however, that the exemption is available. The letter is only one of the facts to be considered in determining whether the transaction is a non-public offering and therefore exempt.

Investment companies have been among the principal purchasers of restricted securities in recent years. For the year 1968 annual reports filed by registered investment companies indicated that they held more than $4.2 billion of restricted equity securities. Because these companies are registered under the Investment Company Act, the acquisition of restricted securities has created a regulatory problem for the SEC.

Open-end investment companies are those which stand ready at all times to sell additional shares to the public and to redeem their outstanding shares. Accordingly, they must be prepared at all times to dispose of securities in their portfolios in order to meet the demand for redemptions. But whether the investment company is open-end or closed-end, it must be in a position to sell portfolio securities (including restricted securities) when good business judgment indicates that they should be sold.

Since the fund may find it difficult to dispose of a restricted security, the obvious question is: Why did the fund buy the security? According to SEC Commissioner Hugh F. Owens, in an address before the Midwest Securities Commissioners Association on July 16, 1969, the answer "is simply the great and unprecedented emphasis on performance," and he pointed to several indications of such emphasis by all institutions—industrial companies, pension funds, universities, and life insurance companies—not merely investment companies. The portfolio turnover rates of investment companies have increased in recent years, indicating the accent on performance. For the quarter ending September 1968, at least 14 open-end companies had a portfolio turnover of 100%.

Restricted securities may be attractive to an investment company or any other investor whose objective is performance. Such securities are usually acquired at a discount from the market price for the issuer's unrestricted securities of the same class. Furthermore—and this is the attraction for an investment company—the buyer frequently acquires a position in a growth situation where there is a relatively small number of the issuer's securities publicly available, or before the public is given an opportunity to buy the issuer's securities.

When an investment company acquires restricted securities, it is faced with the problem of the proper valuation of such securities. The solution of the problem is important since any distortion in valuation will affect the price at which the company sells and redeems its shares. A distortion may also affect the fee paid to the fund managers if their compensation is based on net asset value or performance.

A secondary problem is: *When* should the transaction first be reflected in the company's accounts? ASR No. 113 (1969) states that restricted securities should be included in the portfolio and valued to determine net asset value on the date that the investment company has an enforceable right to demand the securities from the seller.

Under the Investment Company Act and rules, in determining net asset value, securities for which market quotations are readily available must be valued at current market value. Other securities and assets must be valued at "fair value in good faith" by the board of directors. Although there is a limited *private* market for restricted securities, there can be no *public* transactions in such securities, and they must be valued by the directors since market quotations are not readily available for them. This obligation continues so long as these securities are retained in the portfolio.

The purchase of restricted securities at a discount from the market price of similar unrestricted securities is a reflection of the fact that securities which cannot be publicly sold are less valuable than securities which can be freely sold, and also the fact that, by direct sale of such restricted securities, the sellers avoid the expense, time, and disclosures that would be entailed if registration were necessary.

In general, the fair value of restricted securities would appear to be the amount which the owner might reasonably expect to receive for them upon their current sale. This depends upon their inherent worth, without regard to the restriction, adjusted for any diminution in value resulting from the restriction. Consequently, the valuation of restricted securities at the market quotations for unrestricted securities of the same class would, except for most unusual situations, be improper. Further, the continued valuation of such securities at cost would also be improper if, as a result of the issuer's operations, change in general market conditions, or for other reasons, cost has ceased to represent fair value.

Some investment companies have valued their holdings of restricted securities by applying either a constant percentage discount or an absolute dollar discount to the market quotation for unrestricted securities of the same class. The SEC said that this method would also not appear to satisfy the requirement of the Act that each security, for which a market quotation is not readily available, be valued at fair value by the directors in good faith. Consideration has to be given to other relevant factors such as, for example, the extent to which the inherent value of the securities may have changed.

Furthermore, the valuation of restricted securities by reference to the market for unrestricted securities of the same class assumes that the market price for the latter is representative of the fair value of the securities. The SEC pointed out that this may not be the case when only a limited volume of unrestricted shares is available for trading. In a thin market, the news of the investment company's purchase of the restricted securities may, by itself, have the effect of stimulating a demand for the unrestricted securities, the supply of which has not been increased, and thus lead to a spiraling increase in the valuation of both the restricted and unrestricted securities.

Moreover, if in valuing restricted securities, the decrease in value attributable to the restriction is itself affected by factors subject to change, such as the length of time which must elapse before the investment company may require the issuer to register the securities for public sale, the valuation should reflect any such changes.

Some companies have valued restricted securities acquired at a discount by amortizing the discount over some chosen period on the assumption that it will be possible to sell them at the market price for unrestricted securities at the end of the period. It cannot always be determined either that the securities will be effectively registered at the end of that period or that their public sale will be possible. The issuer, for example, may be unable or unwilling to register at the end of the period, and public sale at that time without registration may not be lawful. Consequently, the practice of automatically amortizing the discount over an arbitrarily chosen period creates the appearance of appreciation in the value of the securities which has not, in fact, occurred, and, accordingly, is improper.

An undertaking by the issuer to register the securities within a specified period would not yield a different result. In view of the many factors that may affect the date of the proposed public offering, it is speculative to use such an undertaking alone as the basis for amortizing the discount.

In summary, there is no automatic formula by which a company can value restricted securities to comply with the Act and the rules thereunder. It is the directors' responsibility to determine the fair value of restricted securities in good faith, and the information considered and the analysis thereof should be retained for inspection by the independent auditors. While the board may, consistent with this responsibility, determine the method of valuing each issue of restricted security in the company's portfolio, it must continuously review the appropriateness of any method. The actual calculations may be made by persons acting pursuant to the board's direction.

Subsequent to the issuance of the above-mentioned release, the SEC issued another release (No. 118) on accounting for securities other than restricted securities by investment companies. This release is discussed in the preceding pages of this chapter and is relevant to the above comments on restricted securities because of the observations regarding steps to be taken by the independent public accountant and the content of his certificate when he is unable to form an opinion as to the fairness of the values of certain securities determined by the directors.

Accounting for Moving Expenses.—The reader is referred to the discussion of moving expenses on page **2·14** in which the SEC challenged and then accepted the classification of such expenses as an extraordinary item. The author is familiar with another case in which the SEC argued for capitalization of such costs and subsequent amortization. In the latter case the registrant and its independent auditors also maintained that under APB No. 9, such costs were properly classified as extraordinary items in the determination of net income. The accountants in this case contended that the SEC's indicated preference was based on a policy adopted in the early 1960s when many companies treated moving expenses as "special items" in their Form 10–K reports and as direct charges to retained earnings in their reports to stockholders. During that period, the financial services, in reporting earnings, gave priority to the earnings per share *before moving expenses,* and often ignored charges to retained earnings and "special items."

The company and its auditors asserted that, as a result of the issuance of APB No. 9, circumstances had changed. "Special items" are no longer used, and the services reported earnings per share before and after extraordinary items. Furthermore, because of Rule 14a–3 (discussed in Chapter **22** relating to proxy statements) the financial statements in published reports to shareholders are comparable to the statements filed with the SEC. As a consequence, when a company decides not to capitalize moving expenses, it becomes a deduction in the determination of net income—not a charge to retained earnings—in the period in which the cost is incurred. This accomplishes not only the inclusion of the cost in net income, but also the separate identification of the amount which, under the SEC's policy of capitalization and amortization, is obscured.

On this basis the SEC's representatives determined that the treatment of moving expenses as an extraordinary item is the preferred treatment notwithstanding any future benefits resulting from the move.

Accounting for Non-Interest-Bearing Obligations.—For reasons which are not pertinent to this book, there has been a noticeable increase in recent years in the number and variety of transactions in which all or part of the consideration is represented by long-term non-interest-bearing notes or other evidences of indebtedness. Where the discount of such obligations to their "present value" is not material, the general practice has been to record such obligations at their principal amount and to ignore the discount. If the discount is material, however, the best practice is to record the notes initially at their discounted amount, increasing the book amount on a systematic and reasonable basis to the face amount at the maturity of the notes.

The SEC's staff has challenged the accounting in a number of cases involving non-interest-bearing notes which were recorded initially at their face amount. Accordingly, it appears that this is a matter which registrants and their accountants should consider carefully before deciding on the accounting to be followed in connection with a transaction involving non-interest-bearing obligations.

To give background to the discussion which follows, it may be well to disclose the facts in an actual case which were set forth in a registration statement filed under the 1933 Act. Because of the importance of the transaction, it was described in some detail in the text of the company's prospectus. Eliminating details which are not relevant for the present purpose, the transaction consisted of the sale of one of the company's major assets. The consideration received was a substantial sum in cash plus a non-interest-bearing note maturing in 15 years for the balance. The company recorded the long-term note at the principal amount thereof and accrued the full amount of the profit on the transaction after making provision for taxes.

The SEC took exception to recording the note receivable at its principal amount, and said that it should be discounted to its present value at a 6 per cent rate to maturity. In discussing the matter, the SEC representatives asked whether the debtor would have to pay the full amount of the note if it chose to prepay it. The company acknowledged that in event of prepayment the debtor would be entitled to a discount. Even though the note, by its terms, was non-interest-bearing, the SEC staff said it would be unrealistic to assume that an interest factor was not included. Obviously, a non-interest-bearing note maturing in 15 years is not worth its face amount. There may have been good tax reasons for casting the transaction in the form used, but the SEC contended it would be improper to set up as an asset the full face amount of the note at the date it was acquired, knowing that its value was substantially less than that amount. The SEC insisted that the financial statements be amended to reduce the book amount of the note (and the profit on the transaction) by the factor of imputed interest, which interest would be taken into income over the life of the note.

The SEC has raised the question of imputed interest not only in relation to receivables but also in relation to non-interest-bearing liabilities. Here again it may be well to state the circumstances in an actual case together with the decision, particularly in view of the fact that the SEC, having raised an objection, subsequently withdrew it.

A listed company filed a preliminary proxy statement in connection with a proposal to acquire the business and assets of another company, subject to the liabilities. The proxy statement was prepared in connection with the solicitation of stockholders' proxies approving the acquisition. Financial statements were furnished for the listed company (the purchaser) and for the company to be acquired (the seller). In addition, a pro forma balance sheet was furnished giving effect to the transaction which, for accounting purposes, was on the basis of a purchase—not a pooling of interests. A pro forma statement of income was also submitted for the latest fiscal year showing what the results of operations might have been had the businesses been combined at the beginning of the period.

The consideration to be given for the business was as follows: (1) two-thirds of the total cost was to be paid in cash and securities of the listed company, and (2) one-third was to be paid out of a portion of the future profits of the acquired business. The total consideration was substantially more than the net assets shown by the seller's books. In the pro forma balance sheet the excess cost was allocated to inventories, fixed assets, and goodwill. The company also stated that it intended to retain the portion of the excess cost allocated to goodwill in view of the seller's history of earnings. Consequently, no provision was made in the pro forma income statement for amortization of goodwill. (In view of the changed requirements governing the accounting for intangible assets growing out of the issuance of APB No. 17 (Aug. 1970), goodwill acquired after October 31, 1970 has to be amortized.)

In its letter of comment the SEC noted that the company had not provided for amortization of intangibles or for imputed interest upon the liability for payments out of future profits. The SEC said that a question was raised as to the accounting propriety of not making at least one or the other of the two provisions.

The company maintained that under generally accepted accounting principles existing at that time (which, as noted above, have been changed), it was not required to amortize goodwill. As to imputing interest on the liability for payment out of profits, the company insisted that the liability did not include a hidden interest factor. In fact, the company maintained, after the price had been agreed upon, the seller had urged that it was entitled to interest on the payments out of future profits. The buyer, however, had refused to make this concession, and the matter of interest was dropped. To impute interest to the liability was therefore contrary to the intent and understanding of the parties. Furthermore, if interest were imputed, over what period should it apply? The company had no way of estimating the period of time required to liquidate the liability since this would involve a forecast of future profits of the acquired business. Upon reconsideration the SEC waived both the amortization of intangibles and imputing of interest.

In connection with the question of whether to impute interest to a non-interest-bearing obligation, a related question might well be: What should the rate of interest be? The author believes that the SEC's staff is less concerned with the specific rate used than it is in knowing that interest has been imputed, and that the rate used is not unreasonable.

Among the factors that might be considered in determining the interest rate would be:

1. The credit standing of the maker of the note
2. The period of the note, since short-term loans ordinarily carry a lower rate than long-term loans
3. Whether or not the note is secured
4. Whether the maker of the note is restricted in any way during the period of the note, and the nature of the restrictions.

The APB issued an opinion (No. 21) in August 1971 on the subject of "Interest on Receivables and Payables" which sets forth the accounting to be followed with respect to obligations that are non-interest bearing or have a stated interest rate which is different from the rate of interest appropriate for the debt at the date of the transaction.

Overstatement of Interim Earnings Due to Overstatement of Inventory: The Clinton Engines Case.—Clinton Engines Corporation filed a registration statement under the 1933 Act covering an offering of common stock. The registration statement became effective on February 25, 1960, and the underwritten portion of the offering was sold on that day. On September 28, 1964, more than four and a half years later, the SEC issued a stop order suspending the effectiveness of the registration statement.[3]

The statement of operations in the registration statement included audited figures for the five fiscal years ended February 28, 1959, which showed that operations for the latest fiscal year had shown some improvement over the preceding year, as follows:

	(In thousands) Years Ended Feb. 28	
	1958	1959
Gross receipts	$29,697	$35,067
Net earnings	131	295

[3] In the Matter of Clinton Engines Corporation, Sec. Act. Rel. No. 4724, Sept. 28, 1964.

The registration statement also contained unaudited figures for the eight months ended October 31, 1959 that indicated an even more favorable trend. In that eight months period the company earned $336,000, which was more than it had earned in the entire fiscal year ended February 28, 1959 and was in sharp contrast with the loss of $35,000 sustained in the eight months ended October 31, 1958.

The favorable unaudited earnings for the interim 1959 period resulted largely from a substantial overstatement of the book amount of inventories at the end of that period, which, in turn, caused a material understatement of cost of goods sold. The certified balance sheet of February 28, 1959 showed inventories of $4,478,117, a figure based on a physical count. The unaudited balance sheet of October 31, 1959 showed inventories by that date had risen to $5,348,141, which amount was not based on a physical count; according to the prospectus, it was a book amount "computed in accordance with the Corporation's regular method of inventory accounting."

The company made a careful physical inventory count as of December 31, 1959 in the presence of its independent auditors, who approved the procedures followed. As in prior years, this count was intended to serve as the basis for the inventory data in the audited statements to be prepared for the full fiscal year after its close on February 29, 1960. In mid-March, three weeks after the registration statement became effective, processing of the December 1959 inventory was almost complete, and it became apparent to the company's officers that the actual December 31, 1959 inventory was about $1,500,000 less than the book inventory at that date.

The independent auditors were requested to ascertain the precise extent of the shortage in the physical inventory, and, after an investigation, they concluded that the February 29, 1960 inventory was overstated in its books of account in a net amount of $1,444,334. After adjustment of the company's accounts in accordance with the independent auditors' findings, the $336,321 net profit shown by the unaudited statement in the prospectus for the eight months ended October 31, 1959 was reduced to $13,108 (after a federal income tax recovery of $97,000 for the full year ended February 29, 1960).

Although the record in the stop-order proceedings did not show the precise amount of the inventory shortage as of December 31, 1959, it did make it clear that it did not differ substantially from the $1,444,334 shortage that admittedly existed on February 29, 1960. The inventory amount in the audited balance sheet at February 28, 1959 was based on a physical count and had not been questioned, and accordingly the large inventory shortage at the end of 1959, said the SEC, "must have come into being during the period beginning March 1, 1959." The Commission's decision said that the record further supported the conclusion that the unaudited statements of October 31, 1959 materially overstated its inventory on that date, and materially understated the cost of goods sold during the eight-month period ended on that date. The company offered no evidence to show, and did not suggest, that the large discrepancy at December 31, 1959 between its books and the physical inventory was the result of factors that did not begin to operate until November 1, 1959. The evidence indicated, on the contrary, that various factors present from March 1, 1959 until the end of that year (principally a departure in March 1959 from the company's prior inventory valuation practices) operated to inflate substantially the book inventory and to understate cost of goods sold during that period.

The company had followed a practice of using estimated standard costs to compute its cost of production which, prior to 1959, were adjusted from time to time in the light of experience with respect to actual costs. At or about the beginning of each new fiscal year prior to 1959, the company had revised the standard costs of all types of engines on the basis of the previous year's experience. The system seemed to have functioned satisfactorily prior to 1959, and adjustments from book to physical amounts were minor in amount. In March 1959, however, only a partial revision of standard costs was made.

New standard costs were determined for each of the company's 40 basic engine models, but no study or computation was made of the costs applicable to approximately 2,000 "variations" to those models as had been done in former years, the standard costs of the variations being fixed on the basis of arbitrarily chosen averages. Those averages were in fact much below the actual costs of the variations, so that whenever the company sold a variation during the period after March 31, 1959, it relieved its inventory account and charged cost of goods sold with an amount that was below actual cost. This continuous undercosting of variations sold led to a substantial overstatement of the book inventory. (The overstatement attributable to this factor alone was estimated by the independent auditors to be $652,000 at December 31, 1959.)

The registration statement made no reference to this material change in the company's cost accounting procedures. The prospectus represented that the October 31, 1959 inventory had been "computed in accordance with the Corporation's regular method of inventory accounting." The SEC held that this representation was materially false and misleading.

The inadequate and defective standard costs adopted on March 1, 1959, coupled with insufficient and poorly trained record-keeping personnel, led to what one accountant on the staff of the independent auditors described as "almost a complete breakdown" in the cost accounting system and to a growing gap between the book inventory and the inventory actually on hand. By July 1959 persons in charge of the company's Maquoketa operations suspected that a shortage existed, and a physical count was made of most of the inventory on hand in that Division, which count indicated, as suspected, a substantial overstatement of the book inventory.

The SEC concluded that the unaudited financial statements as of October 31, 1959 and for the interim period then ended in the prospectus were materially distorted because of the inventory overstatement, which rendered the statements false and misleading. For these and other reasons, the Commission issued a stop-order.

The company objected to the entry of the stop-order, and pointed to two earlier SEC cases which involved inventory misstatements (see the *Londontown Manufacturing Company* and *Miami Window Corporation* cases discussed in this book) in registration statements and in which stop-orders were not issued. The SEC said these cases were clearly distinguishable. Among other things, said the SEC, Clinton Engines Corporation had "never taken adequate steps to bring the deficiencies in its registration statement to the attention of its stockholders and to investors." Instead, those in control of the company "kept the large and important inventory overstatement obscured." In June 1960 the company distributed an annual report to stockholders containing references to the subject that "were so cryptic and so cursory as to suggest that its purpose was to confuse rather than to enlighten"; it said:

As a result of an extended review of the records, initiated by your present management, substantial adjustments including inventory reevaluations, were made at the year end, and the profits were thereby lower than those anticipated earlier in the year.

The notes to the financial statements made no specific reference to the $1,444,334 inventory write-off, the subject of inventory merely being discussed in the following manner:

The Corporation has refined certain of its policies with respect to inventory valuation at February 29, 1960, which increased the amount stated for inventories at that date by approximately $210,000. Allowances for receivables at February 29, 1960, have been adjusted to give effect to estimated income tax reductions. These changes increased net income for the year, after income taxes, by approximately $145,000.

The Commission pointed out that not until after the record in the stop-order proceedings had been closed and oral argument before the SEC had been scheduled—three and three-quarters years after the discovery of the overstatement—did the company offer to inform its own stockholders of the deficiencies in the registration statement.

Contingent Payments Based on Profits Following an Acquisition. —Assets are generally recorded at their cost, whether in cash or stock. Where the purchase price of the asset is fixed or determinable, there is no problem in recording the cost. Sometimes, however, the cost may be based, in part, on the operating results of the assets acquired. For example, Company A may acquire an investment in a subsidiary, paying a fixed amount in cash ($1,000,000) and agreeing to pay a contingent amount (not to exceed $500,000) based on 10 per cent of the subsidiary's net income in each of the succeeding five years. Ordinarily the investment account will be charged with the original fixed cost ($1,000,000) plus any additional payments subsequently required under the formula (not to exceed $500,000).

In *Faradyne Electronics Corporation* [40 SEC 1053 (1962)] the SEC ruled that, in the circumstances of that case, the contingent payments based on the subsidiary's profits represented a sharing of profits with the seller and were not includible in the cost of assets acquired.

Faradyne, through a subsidiary, had acquired the business and assets of a predecessor partnership in March, 1960, for $1,550,000, of which $150,000 was paid in cash and the balance of $1,400,000 was to be paid on specified dates. In addition the purchaser agreed to a maximum contingent payment of $2,500,000 payable in annual instalments representing 50 per cent of the subsidiary's net profits (after taxes) beginning with fiscal 1961. All of the obligations of the subsidiary had been guaranteed by Faradyne, the registrant. In its prospectus filed in April, 1961, an accrual of $150,000 (subsequently determined to be $134,696) had been made on account of the annual instalment due at the end of the year. The purchase agreement provided that the obligation to make contingent payments would terminate in 1980 but if the subsidiary should incur losses for any fiscal year ended in 1966 or thereafter, the 20-year period ended in 1980 would be extended one year for each such loss year.

The assets acquired by the subsidiary had been carried on the books of the transferor partnership at $364,000. Initially these assets—consisting of machinery, inventories, and written technical information—were recorded at the fixed contract price of $1,550,000. No part of the purchase price was allocated to goodwill, although the SEC said there was no evidence in the record of the SEC's stop-order proceedings to support the allocation of the entire $1,550,000 to fixed assets. Furthermore, said the SEC, the registrant "proposes to increase the carrying value of plant assets by the whole amount of the contingent payments or accruals based on [the subsidiary's] earnings and to give no recognition to goodwill."

The SEC pointed out that the total of the fixed ($1,550,000) and contingent ($2,500,000) payments, aggregating $4,050,000 was more than eleven times the book value of the assets at the date of acquisition. The amount of $4,050,000 was based on the agreement of the parties that the formula for determining the purchase price should be ten times earnings as defined in the agreement.

Since there was no evidence that the physical assets acquired had a value of more than the initial non-contingent payments—if they had even that much value—"it is clearly improper to allocate the additional contingent payments exclusively to plant." The SEC continued:

The foregoing discussion respecting the asset account to which contingent payments should be allocated rests on the premise that such payments represent an application of income received by Faradyne to the cost of assets. However, we believe the premise itself is totally unsound in the circumstances of this case. The transaction is actually a profit-sharing or division-of-earnings arrangement —or to put it another way—it provides for the receipt of net earnings after 50% reserved to the sellers. Indeed, no contingent payments can ever be said in any realistic sense to become the property of the registrant.

Since Faradyne obtained for an indefinite period in the future only 50% of the net income of the business, we conclude that it is improper to inflate the carrying value of total assets by setting up the payments on the contract either as goodwill or plant; or to report as net income the earnings before deducting the payments under the contract. The payments should be shown as a deduction before arriving at net income. We conclude that registrant's failure to deduct from earnings the $134,696 accrued on the contract for acquisition of the [predecessor partnership's] assets resulted in a misleading overstatement of earnings by that amount for the year ended January 31, 1961.

The SEC's conclusion was that the contingent payments based on earnings in this case should be accounted for on a division-of-earnings arrangement, rather than as additional cost of assets. The reader should not conclude from the decision, however, that the accounting preferred by the SEC in this case is to be followed in all instances involving contingent additional costs based on earnings. Where such payments do, in fact, represent additional costs of acquisition, the SEC concurs in the accounting ordinarily followed in such cases, which is summarized briefly at the beginning of this section.

Quasi-Reorganizations.—The term *quasi-reorganization* in accounting means the procedure in the course of which a corporation, without creating a new corporate entity and without resort to formal court proceedings, is enabled to eliminate a deficit in earned surplus and to establish a new earned surplus account for the accumulation of earnings subsequent to the effective date of the quasi-reorganization. The SEC's views regarding quasi-reorganizations are stated in ASR Nos. 15 (1940), 16 (1940), and 25 (1941).

A quasi-reorganization is not considered by the SEC to have been effected unless all of the following conditions exist:

1. Earned surplus as of the date selected is exhausted.
2. Upon consummation of the quasi-reorganization no deficit exists in any surplus account.
3. The entire procedure is made known to all persons entitled to vote

on matters of general corporate policy and the appropriate consents to the particular transactions are obtained in advance in accordance with the law and charter provisions (see, however, page **4·26**).

4. The procedure accomplishes with respect to the accounts substantially what might be accomplished in a reorganization by legal proceedings—namely, the restatement of assets in terms of present conditions, as well as appropriate modifications of capital and capital surplus, in order to obviate so far as possible the necessity of future reorganizations of like nature.

Reductions in the carrying value of assets at the effective date may not be made beyond a point which gives appropriate recognition to conditions that appear to have resulted in relatively permanent reductions in asset values; as for example, complete or partial obsolescence, lessened utility value, reduction in investment value due to changed economic conditions, or, in the case of current assets, declines in indicated realization value. A procedure of this kind should not be employed recurrently but only under circumstances that would justify an actual reorganization or formation of a new company, particularly if the principal purpose of the quasi-reorganization is the elimination of a deficit in earned surplus.

A clear report should be made to the stockholders of the proposed restatement and their consent obtained when necessary.

Full disclosure of the quasi-reorganization should be made in the financial statements for the fiscal year involved, and all subsequent statements of surplus should designate the point of time from which the new earned surplus dates. The SEC also states:

. . . Until such time as the results of operations of the company on the new basis are available for an appropriate period of years (at least three) any statement or showing of earned surplus should, in order to provide additional disclosure of the occurrence and the significance of the quasi-reorganization, indicate the total amount of the deficit and any charges that were made to capital surplus in the course of the quasi-reorganization which would otherwise have been required to be made against income or earned surplus.

In February, 1956, the AICPA Committee on Accounting Procedure issued ARB No. 46 in which it stated that the dating of earned surplus following a quasi-reorganization would rarely, if ever, be of significance after a period of ten years. The Committee further stated that there may be exceptional circumstances in which the discontinuance of the dating of earned surplus could be justified at the conclusion of a period less than ten years. The author understands that the views expressed in that bulletin are, in general, shared by the SEC, although the Commission reserves the right to consider other periods of time as appropriate with respect to discontinuance of dating of surplus in the light of specific circumstances. The author does not view the SEC's position as constituting a qualified assent of the AICPA bulletin, since the bulletin itself seems to deal with ordinary cases in which the dating disclosure has no significance. (See also Regulation S–X, Rule 5–02, caption 39(c).)

When the transfer of a deficit to capital surplus is effected by resolution of the board of directors but without approval of the stockholders, the SEC has additional requirements. In that situation it is necessary to make a complete disclosure of all the attendant facts and circumstances and their effect on the company's financial position in each balance sheet and surplus statement filed with the SEC thereafter. To effect the minimum appropriate disclosure in the surplus accounts, information should be given in respect of subsequent earned surplus in approximately the following fashion :

Total deficit to December 31, 19__	$700,000	
Less deficit at January 1, 19__, charged to capital surplus by resolution of the Board of Directors and without approval of stockholders, such action being permissible under the applicable state law	800,000	
Earned surplus since January 1, 19__		$100,000

As an additional disclosure in cases where the write-off of deficit has not been approved by stockholders, the SEC requires, in the registration statement or other filing containing financial statements first reflecting the directors' action, that there be included an explanation of the action taken and an indication of its possible effect on the character of future dividends. For example :

It should be noted that on (date) by action of the Board of Directors, without action by the stockholders, the company charged off a $————— deficit in earned surplus against its capital surplus. This procedure will permit the company in the future to reflect undistributed earnings subsequent to (date) as earned surplus, instead of as a reduction of the deficit charged off to capital surplus. One result of this procedure is to permit the distribution, as ordinary dividends, of earned surplus accruing subsequent to (date), without regard to the deficit charged off to capital surplus. Furthermore, if earnings subsequent to (date) are less than the deficit written off, distributions thereof may in effect represent distributions of capital or capital surplus.

In the case of the quasi-reorganization of a parent company, the SEC holds that it is implicit in the procedure that the effective date should be recognized as having the significance of a date of acquisition of control of subsidiaries. Hence, dividends subsequently received from subsidiaries should be treated as income only to the extent that they are declared by subsidiaries out of earnings subsequent to the effective date. Likewise, in consolidated financial statements, earned surplus of subsidiaries at the effective date should be excluded from consolidated earned surplus.

Recapitalization in the Form of a Merger.—In connection with a forthcoming special meeting of stockholders, a corporation filed preliminary proxy-soliciting material with the SEC. The meeting was called for the purpose of effecting a plan of recapitalization of the company in order to eliminate accumulated and unpaid dividends of approximately $8,600,000 on the preferred stock of the company. The proposed recapitalization was to be effected through a statutory merger of the company with its wholly owned subsidiary. The plan contemplated the issuance by the surviving parent company of debentures and new common stock primarily to the preferred stockholders in exchange for their preferred stock and in satisfaction of the unpaid dividends on this stock. The preliminary proxy material included a pro forma balance sheet giving effect to the proposed recapitalization of the company. In this balance sheet the earned surplus of the parent company in the amount of $578,000 was brought forward in the merger as earned surplus of the surviving company rather than as capital surplus. In its letter of comment the SEC said that because of the substantial accumulated and unpaid dividends on the preferred stock, which far exceeded the amount of earned surplus, the latter amount should be brought forward as capital surplus rather than as earned surplus in the merger and that subsequently accumulated earned surplus should be dated from the date of reorganization. The pro forma balance sheet in the definitive proxy material as sent to stockholders was changed accordingly to reflect the earned surplus of the company as capital surplus after the merger [18 SEC Ann. Rep. 60 (1952)].

Accounting for Production Payments.—Many companies that own natural resources make use of a financing device called a "production payment," or a "carved-out production payment." Oil and gas producers are the most frequent sellers of such payments.

A company that had sold carved-out gas production payments to an institutional purchaser filed a registration statement with the SEC under the 1933 Act. In its financial statements the company recognized the gain from the sale on the "current income" method, treating the proceeds of the sale as income when received after making provision for future lifting costs, depreciation, depletion, and amortization. The company had followed this accounting method in previous registration statements, and the method was used by a few other companies in the industry. On this occasion, however, the SEC's staff challenged the accounting and argued for the "deferral method," under which the proceeds from the sale would be deferred and taken into income as the gas was actually produced.

The then chairman of the SEC, William L. Cary, discussed this incident in an article entitled "The SEC and Accounting" (*The Journal of Accountancy,* December 1963, p. 49). The Commission accepted a compromise under which the past accounting would not be disturbed, but in the future similar sales would be reported on the deferral method. According to Mr. Cary, even the accountant involved recognized that the deferral method was preferable and a survey of practices in the area showed that substantially all companies filing with the SEC followed this method. In this case, as it has done in the past, said Mr. Cary, the Commission exercised its authority to support the use of an accounting principle which is almost universally recognized as the most appropriate.

Release from Obligation Upon Payment of Consideration by a Principal Shareholder.—In June, 1960, Hazel Bishop, Inc., a company then engaged in the cosmetics business, filed a registration statement (SEC File No. 2–16761) with the SEC under the 1933 Act. The registration statement related to outstanding shares which might be offered to the public by the shareholders. In October, 1960, the registration statement was amended, and shortly thereafter the Commission began proceedings to determine whether a stop-order should be issued suspending the effectiveness of the registration statement and preventing the sale of the securities to the public. After the stop-order proceedings were started, the company filed further amendments to its registration statement on March 6, April 3, and April 17, 1961.

One of the principal issues in the stop-order proceedings related to the financial statements, including the summary of earnings. The SEC alleged that the summary of earnings was "deceptive and misleading" in several respects. In at least one respect the facts (and the SEC's interpretation of the financial and accounting implications in those facts) will be read with interest by accountants and others interested in accounting [40 SEC 718 (1961)].

In May, 1958, Raymond Spector, who owned 542,000 shares of Hazel Bishop's common stock (about half of the shares then outstanding) and 98,000 shares of convertible preferred stock (the entire issue) sold all of his stock to Television Industries, Inc. ("TVI"). The contract of sale provided that TVI was to pay for the shares purchased over a period of ten years.

At about the same time Hazel Bishop agreed to purchase television spot advertising time from TVI and to make monthly cash payments therefor. By October, 1959, Hazel Bishop owed TVI $1,110,000 under this agreement.

About that same time, Hazel Bishop was in urgent need of additional working capital, and a complicated series of transactions was effected which, within the space of a few months, resulted in the company's receiving $2,400,000 in cash and a release, without any payment by the company, of its entire obligation to TVI. The pertinent transactions were these:

1. Spector and TVI rescinded their 1958 agreement, TVI returning to Spector the common and preferred stocks of Hazel Bishop formerly owned by Spector, and Spector repaying or agreeing to repay all sums which TVI had paid on account of the purchase price of such shares;
2. TVI waived payment of its claims against Hazel Bishop for advertising *without any payment by Hazel Bishop;* and
3. Spector agreed *to transfer to TVI 150,000 shares of Hazel Bishop common stock owned by Spector.*

Hazel Bishop's indebtedness to TVI for advertising was $1,110,000. Of this amount, $935,000 was applicable to the fiscal year ended October 31, 1959 and $175,000 to the preceding fiscal year. In the summary of earnings as originally filed, advertising expenses for fiscal 1958 and 1959 were reduced in the aggregate by $1,110,000, representing the amount owed to TVI for advertising which was forgiven without payment of any consideration by Hazel Bishop. The SEC said this presentation was deceptive and misleading because "operating costs for 1958 and 1959 had been relieved of material amounts of advertising expenses incurred by registrant and presumably necessary to produce the sales volume shown."

Spector, it will be recalled, transferred 150,000 shares of his common stock to TVI in settlement of Hazel Bishop's entire obligation to TVI. A value of $675,000 was attributed to the stock so transferred. The financial statements were amended to reflect this amount ($675,000) as a capital contribution by Spector. The difference between $675,000 and the amount of the claim ($1,110,000), that is, $435,000, was treated as a reduction in advertising costs for 1958 and 1959. These and other adjustments had the effect of transforming a profit of $102,000 as originally reported for 1959 into a loss of $707,000.

In short, the view taken by the company in its revised financial statements, and concurred in by the SEC, was that consideration had been given for the release of TVI's claims. The consideration was felt to be the fair value of the 150,000 shares of stock. This amount represented an indirect capital contribution by a principal shareholder rather than a reduction of advertising expense.

On the basis of the revised financial statements, the stop-order was subsequently lifted and the registration statement permitted to become effective.

Dividends from Pre-Acquisition Surplus.—A registrant acquired during its fiscal year over 50 per cent of the stock of another company. According to a periodic report filed with the SEC, the acquisition was for investment and not for resale. During the same year the acquired company paid a dividend which was more than its entire earnings for that year. In its annual report for that year, the registrant reported its investment as a current asset and the entire dividend received as income.

When the staff of the Commission objected to these procedures, the registrant sought to justify the accounting on the basis that, between the time its fiscal year ended and its annual report to shareholders was completed, the registrant had abandoned its original plan to acquire additional shares of the company and eventually to merge it. On this basis, it was urged that the shares held, being listed securities, could properly be classified as a current asset and the dividends received on the shares should be treated as income from marketable securities without regard to the fact that those dividends exceeded the registrant's proportionate share in the earnings since the date of acquisition.

The SEC staff noted, however, that the abandonment of the original plan was only temporary, and that the plan was carried out substantially in its original form. The financial statements were thereupon amended to exclude the investment from current assets in the balance sheet, and to reduce that investment and the registrant's previously reported income by the amount of dividends paid out of earnings accumulated prior to the date of acquisition by the registrant [21 SEC Ann. Rep. 28 (1955)].

SEC Opposition to "Cash Flow" Statements.—In recent years there has been increasing emphasis on the "cash flow" concept. Along with this development has been an attempt to downgrade the significance of earnings as customarily presented in income statements based on generally accepted accounting principles. The "cash flow" terminology is widely used by security analysts and is also used by some companies in their published reports to security holders. The term "cash flow" does not have a precise meaning, however, and it is clear that it means different things to different people. There are many variations of the term "cash flow" currently in use, such as "cash income," "cash throw-off," "cash flow income," and so on.

The SEC's Chief Accountant commented on the cash flow concept in a 1963 speech on the subject of "Financial Statements—How Reliable?" In his view, the most common meaning of "cash flow," that is, net income plus depreciation, "is, strictly speaking, neither cash nor flow," and the use of the variations of the term tends to create confusion since they seem to be outright misnomers. He stated that the use of "cash flow" or similar terminology seemed to suggest to the stockholder that his interest in the company should be evaluated in those terms rather than in terms of earnings computed on a conventional basis.

The Chief Accountant acknowledged that information regarding the funds or the financial resources of a business, in addition to that presented in the conventional financial statements, can be meaningful and helpful to the investor if properly presented, but "cash flow" is often miscalculated, misunderstood, and even misused.

The SEC has opposed the usage of the "cash flow" concept in statements filed with it. According to the Chief Accountant, one company, for example, arranged its statements of earnings so that the last caption stated that net income *plus depreciation and amortization* amounted to the amounts shown, and then gave the amounts, year by year. The Commission insisted that the caption and the amounts be omitted and that depreciation and amortization included in costs and expenses be disclosed as supplemental information (which is required in any case).

More recently the SEC has made it a requirement in several of its registration and report forms to include a statement of the source and application of funds for the same period as the related income statement. Also, Regulation S–X was amended to include requirements with respect to the form and content of the funds statement.

In 1963 the APB recommended the wider use of the funds statement (APB Opinion No. 3), and in 1971 the Board made the use of such statements mandatory (APB Opinion No. 19), but recommended that they be called "Statements of Changes in Financial Position."

CHAPTER **5**

SEC VIEWS ON AUDITING PRACTICES

CONTENTS

Audit Procedures Not Prescribed by SEC.—With a few exceptions indicated below, the SEC does not prescribe the procedures to be followed by the independent public accountant in his examination for the purpose of certifying financial statements to be filed with the Commission. Under the various acts that it administers, the Commission has broad powers, and these may extend to prescribing the detailed steps to be followed by accountants in certifying statements for filing with the Commission. The Commission is aware of this authority and its responsibility thereunder. In its report on the McKesson and Robbins investigation the Commission stated that one of the purposes of the investigation was to inquire into generally accepted audit procedures with a view to determining their adequacy in assuring accurate and reliable financial statements. Largely as a result of the action taken by the accountancy profession in adopting the Extensions of Auditing

Procedure,[1] the SEC decided, for the time being, not to prescribe specific auditing procedures. The Commission said:

> We have carefully considered the desirability of specific rules and regulations governing the auditing steps to be performed by accountants in certifying financial statements to be filed with us. Action has already been taken by the accounting profession adopting certain of the auditing procedures considered in this case. We have no reason to believe at this time that these extensions will not be maintained or that further extensions of auditing procedures along the lines suggested in this report will not be made. Further, the adoption of the specific recommendations made in this report as to the type of disclosure to be made in the accountant's certificate and as to the election of accountants by stockholders should insure that acceptable standards of auditing procedure will be observed, that specific deviations therefrom may be considered in the particular instances in which they arise, and that accountants will be more independent of management. Until experience should prove the contrary, we feel that this program is preferable to its alternative—the detailed prescription of the scope of and procedures to be followed in the audit for the various types of issuers of securities who file statements with us—and will allow for further consideration of varying audit procedures and for the development of different treatment for specific types of issuers [ASR No. 19 (1940)].

In an accountant's certificate filed pursuant to Regulation S–X (which is the Commission's basic accounting regulation and is considered at length in Chapters **16** through **20**, and **24** through **26**) the SEC does require the certifying accountant to make certain representations regarding his audit. The regulation requires the accountant in his certificate to:

1. State whether the audit was made in accordance with generally accepted auditing standards; and
2. Designate any auditing procedures deemed necessary by the accountant under the circumstances of the particular case, which have been omitted, and the reasons for their omission.

The Commission's rule further provides that nothing in the rule shall be construed to imply authority for the omission of any procedure which independent accountants would ordinarily employ in the course of an audit made for the purpose of expressing the opinions which are required to be expressed. The requirements of Regulation S–X relating to certificates appear in Chapter **24**.

The first exception to the general rule that SEC does not prescribe audit procedures relates to reports of financial condition filed by certain members of national securities exchanges, brokers, and dealers in securities. This report is designated Form X–17A–5 and recites in some detail the audit requirements applicable to the independent public accountant's examination. These audit requirements begin on page **5·54**.

---

[1] Originally issued as SAP No. 1 (1939). Now included in SAP No. 43 (1970).

The second exception referred to above relates to investment companies registered with SEC under the Investment Company Act of 1940. When the securities of such investment companies are in the custody of the company itself or are held by members of national securities exchanges, there are certain requirements as to the examination of such securities by independent public accountants. The requirements and suggested forms of accountant's certificates are set forth on page **5·**52 and on page **25·**34.

Another exception relates to the audit of financial statements of registered investment companies. In ASR Nos. 113 and 118, the SEC set forth the procedures to be followed by independent public accountants in connection with their examinations of the investments of such companies, and the valuation of such investments—including restricted securities. These matters are discussed beginning on page **4·**8.

The SEC has been critical of the reports issued by certifying accountants in a number of cases, because, in the SEC's view, the reports were based on inadequate examinations. A summary of these reports begins on page **5·**11.

Generally Accepted Practice Not Necessarily Binding on SEC. —The SEC has, for the most part, been satisfied to let the public accounting profession lead the way in accounting and auditing progress. The Commission, on the other hand, has not hesitated to criticize any practice that may be generally accepted within the profession but is, in the Commission's view, faulty. In *Interstate Hosiery Mills, Inc.* [4 SEC 706 (1939)], for example, the SEC conducted an investigation following the discovery that the company's financial statements had been materially falsified. The company objected to the introduction of expert testimony by the certifying accountants. The Commission said, "We think the testimony of qualified expert accountants engaged in public practice was relevant and helpful although the Commission must in the end weigh the value of all expert testimony against *its own judgment of what is sound accounting practice.*" (Emphasis supplied.) [4 SEC 715]. Similar views were also expressed in ASR No. 73 (1952).

McKesson and Robbins Case.—Beyond any doubt the SEC case which had the greatest impact on the public accounting profession was that involving McKesson and Robbins, Incorporated.[2] Because of the magnitude of the fraud, the manner in which it was accomplished, and the sensational developments following the exposure, the facts in the case were widely publicized in 1938–39. Accountants, however, are concerned prin-

---

[2] *In the Matter of McKesson & Robbins, Inc., Report on Investigation* (1940). The summary of the report constitutes ASR No. 19 (1940).

cipally with the SEC's investigation of the fraud and the report which followed.

The case is considered at this point because many of the SEC's views relating to auditing and the public accountancy profession were contained in the Commission's report on its investigation of the case referred to below.

Following is a brief summary of the principal facts disclosed by the SEC. The securities of McKesson were listed on the New York Stock Exchange and registered under the 1934 Act. The company's financial statements, certified by independent public accountants, were filed with the SEC and the Exchange. The statements for 1937 (the last before the disclosure of the fraud) reported total assets of more than $87,000,000, approximately $19,000,000 of which was subsequently shown to have been fictitious. The fictitious items consisted almost entirely of inventories ($10,000,000) and accounts receivable ($9,000,000) and arose out of the operation at the offices in Bridgeport, Connecticut, of a wholly fictitious foreign crude drug business shown on the books of McKesson's Connecticut Division and a Canadian subsidiary. For the year 1937, fictitious sales in these units amounted to $18,247,000, on which fictitious gross profit of $1,801,000 was recorded. At the time of the exposure of the fraud in December, 1938, the fictitious assets had increased to approximately $21,000,000.

The fraud was engineered by the president of the company with the assistance of his three brothers. All four were masquerading under assumed names. The president, Frank Donald Coster, was in reality Philip M. Musica and, under the latter name, was a twice-convicted swindler. George E. Dietrich, assistant treasurer of the corporation, was in reality George Musica. Robert J. Dietrich, head of the shipping, receiving, and warehousing department at Bridgeport, was actually Robert Musica. George Vernard was Arthur Musica and managed the offices, mailing addresses, bank accounts, and other activities of the dummy concerns with which the McKesson companies supposedly conducted the fictitious business.

To accomplish the deception, purchases were pretended to have been made by the McKesson companies from five Canadian vendors, who thereafter purportedly retained the merchandise at their warehouses for the account of McKesson. Sales were pretended to have been made for McKesson's account by W. W. Smith and Company, Inc., and the goods shipped directly by the latter to the customers. Payments for goods purchased and collections from customers for goods sold were pretended to have been made by the Montreal banking firm of Manning and Company, also for the account of McKesson. W. W. Smith and Company, Inc., Manning and Company, and the five Canadian vendors were subsequently discovered to have been either entirely fictitious or merely blinds used by Coster for the purpose of supporting the fictitious transactions.

Invoices, advices, and other documents prepared on printed forms in the names of these firms were used to give an appearance of reality to the fictitious transactions. In addition to this manufacture of documents, a series of contracts and guarantees with Smith and with Manning and forged credit reports on Smith were also utilized. The foreign firms to whom the goods were supposed to have been sold were real but had done no business of the type indicated with McKesson.

The fictitious transactions originated early in the life of Girard and Company, Inc., Coster's predecessor concern, which was incorporated in 1923 and merged with McKesson in 1926. The manner of handling the transactions described above was the one used since the middle of 1935. Prior to that time, the fictitious goods were supposed to have been physically received at and reshipped from the Bridgeport plant of McKesson. And prior to 1931 McKesson made actual cash payments directly for the fictitious purchases, which at that time were supposed to have been made from a group of domestic vendors, but recovered a large part of this cash purportedly as collections on the fictitious sales. The change from using actual cash to the supposed clearance through Manning and Company was not effected abruptly but for some time after 1931 both systems were used. The Canadian vendors, however, were used only in connection with the Manning clearance system. From the report of the accountant for the trustee in reorganization of McKesson and Robbins, Incorporated, it appeared that out of an actual cash outgo from the McKesson companies in connection with these fictitious transactions of $24,777,000, all but $2,869,-000 came back to the McKesson companies in collection of fictitious receivables or as cash transfers from the pretended bank of Manning and Company.

The SEC instituted an investigation under Section 21(a) of the 1934 Act, based on information that financial statements filed by McKeeson with the Commission were false and misleading. The principal purpose of the investigation was to determine:

1. The character and scope of the audit made by the certifying accountants;
2. Whether the audit by the accountants conformed to generally accepted standards; and
3. Whether generally accepted auditing standards were adequate to assure the reliability of financial statements.

This was the most searching investigation ever conducted by a governmental organization of an audit made by a public accounting firm and the practices of the profession in general. The accountants who had certified the McKesson financial statements testified at the hearings as to the scope of their examinations and the detailed steps and procedures followed. They also testified with respect to a wide variety of other matters, such as the make-up of their firm, their investigation of new clients, organization and training of staff accountants, review of client's system of internal control, review of work of subordinates, and many other matters. In addition, a number of expert witnesses representing other public accounting firms and educators testified as to what, in their opinions, constituted generally accepted auditing standards and procedures at that time. The testimony of the expert witnesses established that there was wide disagreement in material respects as to the procedures to be employed in the examination of inventories and receivables.

The Commission summarized its report regarding the examination of inventories by McKesson's independent auditors as follows:

[The certifying accountants'] audit program for the verification of inventories was essentially that which was prescribed by generally accepted auditing practice for the period. However, we find that a substantial difference of opinion existed among accountants during this time as to the extent of the auditors' duties and responsibilities in connection with physical verification of quantities, quality, and condition. [The certifying accountants], in common with a substantial portion of the profession, took the position that the verification of quantities, quality, and condition of inventories should be confined to the records. There was, however, a substantial body of equally authoritative opinion which supported the view, which we endorse, that auditors should gain physical contact with the inventory either by test counts, by observation of the inventory taking, or by a combination of these methods. Meticulous verification of the inventory was not needed in this case to discover the fraud. We are not satisfied, therefore, that even under [the certifying accountants'] views other accountants would condone their failure to make inquiries of the employees who actually took the inventory and to determine by inspection whether there was an inventory as represented by the client. We commend the action of the profession in subsequently adopting, as normal, procedures requiring physical contact with clients' inventories.

From the testimony of the expert witnesses at the hearings, it was clear a marked difference of opinion existed as to the auditor's duties and responsibilities in connection with physical verification of quantities, quality, and condition. At one extreme was the view of one witness that the accountant was not concerned with physical quantities, quality, or condition of the inventories; representations of management were accepted and that fact reported in the balance sheet. At the other extreme was the view that accountants are obliged to do such work as they consider necessary to establish to their own satisfaction that the inventories are as represented, and this includes physical contact with inventories. The SEC recommended:

In our opinion, the time has come when auditors must, as part of their examination whenever reasonable and practicable, make physical contact with the inventory and assume reasonable responsibility therefor as had already become the practice in many cases before the present hearings. By this we do not mean that auditors should be, or by making such tests become, the guarantors of inventories any more than of any of the other items in the financial statements but we do mean that they should make all reasonable tests and inquiries, and not merely those limited to the books, in order to state their professional opinion, as auditors, as to the truthfulness of that item in the same way as they do for the other items in the statements.

Concerning the examination of receivables by McKesson's independent auditors, the Commission summarized its report as follows:

Viewed as a whole the audit program for accounts receivable as used by [the certifying accountants] conformed to then generally accepted procedures for an examination of financial statements although confirmation of the accounts was not included in the program. The facts of this case, however, demonstrate the utility of circularization and the wisdom of the profession in subsequently adopting confirmation of accounts and notes receivable as a required procedure ". . . wherever practicable and reasonable, and where the aggregate amount of notes and accounts receivable represents a significant proportion of the current assets or of the total assets of a concern. . . ."

With respect to receivables, the majority of authoritative opinion at the time supported the view that confirmation was not essential in cases in which substantial collection of the accounts prior to the conclusion of the audit is proved. The SEC recommended:

A judicious confirmation of customers' accounts, while it has not been considered mandatory in all cases, is good practice and in our opinion should be a normal audit procedure.

Even before the SEC made known the results of its investigation in the McKesson affair, the accountancy profession began to put its house in order. The American Institute of Certified Public Accountants, the national organization of professional accountants, was especially concerned about the impact of the McKesson fraud on the public's confidence in certificates of independent public accountants. A special Institute committee on auditing procedure prepared a report entitled "Extensions of Auditing Procedure" and submitted it to the council of the Institute. The report set forth the additional procedures regarding inventories and accounts receivable which the committee believed should be regarded as generally accepted practice. In May, 1939, the council adopted the report, and it was anticipated that the committee would make a supplemental report for submission to the membership of the Institute at its annual meeting in September, 1939. The council also adopted the supplemental report of the committee which, after discussion at the annual meeting of the Institute in September, 1939, was approved. The executive committee of the Institute was authorized and instructed by the council to coordinate the two reports into one document and to distribute it to the membership. The document constitutes SAP No. 1 (October, 1939) and is entitled "Extensions of Auditing Procedure." The statement made important recommendations with respect to the examination of inventories and receivables. As subsequently amended and revised, the statement now constitutes SAP No. 43, issued by the AICPA Committee on Auditing Procedure in September 1970. As every public accountant should know, the extended procedures require observation of inventories and confirmation of receivables where either of these assets represents a significant proportion of the current assets or of the total assets of a concern. Failure to apply them, where they are practicable and reasonable, generally precludes expression of an opinion on the fairness of the financial statements taken as a whole. (If no physical inventory is or can be taken by the company involved, or if the auditor can not be present at the inventory-taking, the auditor may or may not be able to form an opinion as to the reasonableness of inventory quantities by the application of alternative procedures.)

The SEC's report of its investigation in the McKesson matter was published in 1940—some months after the Institute had adopted the extended procedures relating to inventories and receivables. The Institute's SAP No. 1 prescribing the extended procedures, in fact, constituted a part of Appendix A of the Commission's report.

Detection of Concealed Overstatement of Assets or Profits.—Mc-Kesson and Robbins Case.—The SEC's report in the McKesson and Robbins case has been previously referred to. It will be conceded that the fraud perpetrated by the president of the company in collusion with his three brothers was of truly significant proportions. The Commission acknowledged that the audits by the accountants who had certified the Mc-Kesson financial statements conformed, in form, as to the scope and procedures employed, to what was generally considered mandatory at the time. The failure of the accountants to discover the fraud was attributable, the Commission said, to the manner in which the audit work was done. The accountants, according to the SEC, "failed to employ that degree of vigilance, inquisitiveness, and analysis of the evidence available that is necessary in a professional undertaking and is recommended in all well-known and authoritative works on auditing." Speaking generally the SEC said:

Moreover, we believe that, even in balance sheet examinations for corporations whose securities are held by the public, accountants can be expected to detect gross overstatements of assets and profits whether resulting from collusive fraud or otherwise. We believe that alertness on the part of the entire staff, coupled with intelligent analysis by experienced accountants of the manner of doing business, should detect overstatements in the accounts, regardless of their cause, long before they assume the magnitude reached in this case. Furthermore, an examination of this kind should not, in our opinion, exclude the highest officers of the corporation from its appraisal of the manner in which the business under review is conducted. Without underestimating the important service rendered by independent public accountants in their review of the accounting principles employed in the preparation of financial statements filed with us and issued to stockholders, we feel that the discovery of gross over-statements in the accounts is a major purpose of such an audit even though it be conceded that it might not disclose every minor defalcation. [ASR No. 19 (1940)].

Many accountants will disagree with the SEC's general statement regarding the accountants' responsibility for detection of fraud. The viewpoint of the profession is stated in the following excerpt from SAP No. 33:

5. In making the ordinary examination, the independent auditor is aware of the possibility that fraud may exist. Financial statements may be misstated as the result of defalcations and similar irregularities, or deliberate misrepresentation by management, or both. The auditor recognizes that fraud, if sufficiently material, may affect his opinion on the financial statements, and his examination, made in accordance with generally accepted auditing standards, gives consideration to this possibility. However, the ordinary examination directed to the expression of an opinion on financial statements is not primarily or specifically designed, and cannot be relied upon, to disclose defalcations and other similar irregularities, although their discovery may result. Similarly, although the discovery of deliberate misrepresentation by management is usually more closely associated with the objective of the ordinary examination, such examination cannot be relied upon to assure its discovery. The responsibility of the independent auditor for failure to detect fraud (which responsibility differs as to clients and others) arises only when such failure clearly results from failure to comply with generally accepted auditing standards.

6. Reliance for the prevention and detection of fraud should be placed principally upon an adequate accounting system with appropriate internal control. The well-established practice of the independent auditor of evaluating the adequacy and effectiveness of the system of internal control by testing the accounting records and related data and by relying on such evaluation for the selection and timing of his other auditing procedures has generally proved sufficient for making an adequate examination. If an objective of an independent auditor's examination were the discovery of all fraud, he would have to extend his work to a point where its cost would be prohibitive. Even then he could not give assurance that all types of fraud had been detected, or that none existed, because items such as unrecorded transactions, forgeries, and collusive fraud would not necessarily be uncovered. Accordingly, it is generally recognized that good internal control and fidelity bonds provide protection more economically and effectively. In the case of fidelity bonds, protection is afforded not only by the indemnification for discovered defalcations but also by the possible deterrent effect upon employees; the presence of fidelity bonds, however, should not affect the scope of the auditor's examination.

7. When an independent auditor's examination leading to an opinion on financial statements discloses specific circumstances that make him suspect that fraud may exist, he should decide whether the fraud, if in fact it should exist, might be of such magnitude as to affect his opinion on the financial statements. If the independent auditor believes that fraud so material as to affect his opinion may have occurred, he should reach an understanding with the proper representatives of the client as to whether the auditor or the client, subject to the auditor's review, is to make the investigation necessary to determine whether

fraud has in fact occurred, and, if so, the amount thereof. If, on the other hand, the independent auditor concludes that any such fraud could not be so material as to affect his opinion, he should refer the matter to the proper representatives of the client with the recommendation that it be pursued to a conclusion. For example, frauds involving "lapping" accounts receivable collections, or frauds involving overstatements of inventory, could be material, while those involving peculations from a small imprest fund would normally be of little significance because the operation and size of the fund tends to establish a limitation.

8. The subsequent discovery that fraud existed during the period covered by the independent auditor's examination does not of itself indicate negligence on his part. He is not an insurer or guarantor; if his examination was made with due professional skill and care in accordance with generally accepted auditing standards, he has fulfilled all of the obligations implicit in his undertaking. [SAP No. 33 (1963), pp. 10–12.]

In making arrangements for an examination of financial statements, some accounting firms make it a practice to reach a written understanding with their clients as to the accountant's responsibility for detection of fraud and other irregularities. The understanding frequently takes the form of an exchange of letters between the accountant and his client which, in effect, incorporates the views expressed in the foregoing quotation from the Institute's Statement on Auditing Procedure.

THE OLEN COMPANY CASE.—The *Olen Company* case involved a gross overstatement of net income and net assets which was not detected by the company's auditors. The overstatement was accomplished by falsification of inventories, liabilities, and fixed assets. The company had gone public on the basis of false financial statements included in a registration statement under the 1933 Act.

Shortly thereafter, the company merged into H. L. Green Company on the basis of a proxy statement which also included false financial statements of Olen Company. Maurice Olen became president of Green after the merger.

When the falsity of the Olen financial statements was discovered, Olen resigned as president of Green and paid $1,600,000 to Green as partial restitution.

The SEC brought proceedings under Rule 2(e) of its Rules of Practice to determine whether Olen's auditors should be permitted to practice before the SEC. The case is discussed at greater length later in this chapter, together with excerpts from the report of the SEC's investigation.

YALE EXPRESS CASE.—The *Yale Express* case (*Fischer et al. v. Kletz et al.*) also involved a material overstatement of net income and net assets. The overstatement was subsequently discovered by the independent auditors in the course of a "non-audit" engagement. The case is discussed in this chapter under "Auditor's Duty to Disclose After-Acquired Information" and in Chapter **28**.

THE LONDONTOWN MANUFACTURING COMPANY CASE.—The *Londontown Manufacturing* case involved a material overstatement of net income in the latest fiscal year included in an income statement in a registration statement when the company went public. The overstatement was the result of inventory understatements in prior years which were taken into income in the most recent year when the inventory situation was corrected. The case is discussed in more detail later in this chapter.

SEC Decisions Relating to Inadequate Examinations

There have been a number of SEC decisions involving the adequacy of the examination made by independent public accountants. In one early case [*Big Wedge Gold Mining Co.*, 1 SEC 108 (1935)], the Commission said it was doubtful whether the accountant examined anything more than the papers and documents filed with, or as a part of, the registration statement. The Commission said: "The accountant certainly made no such examination as should underlie a certification of a balance sheet and as is required by the Commission's regulations. The resultant balance sheet even omits to set forth the current liabilities of the company. Our conclusion is that the accountant did not make a reasonable investigation of the matters to which he certified in the balance sheet."

In another, more recent, case [ASR No. 48 (1944)] the SEC stated that it had permanently disqualified a certified public accountant from practicing before the Commission. The accountant had certified financial statements in a registration statement although he had made no audit of the registrant, had not examined its books, but had accepted without question the financial statements prepared by an employee of the registrant. The accountant had a practice of splitting fees in other matters with this employee and certified other statements likewise without audit.

In the criminal action involving the accountants in the Continental Vending Machine Company case there was no decision or opinion by the SEC which would otherwise be included in this chapter. It should be noted, however, that two employees of the SEC testified for the government in that litigation; the case is discussed in Chapter **28**.

McKesson and Robbins Case.—This case has been previously referred to in this chapter. The SEC's report on its investigation commented, among other things, as to the adequacy of the examinations which had been made by the certifying accountants. The Commission concluded that the examinations substantially conformed, in form, as to the scope and procedures employed, to what was generally considered mandatory at the time.

The failure to discover the overstatement of assets and of earnings, the SEC said, was attributable to the manner in which the audit work was done.

As to accounts receivable, the SEC said the program used by the accountants followed generally accepted practice at the time, and the failure of the program to warn the auditors resulted from lack of proper observation and appreciation of the evidence in hand. As to inventories, the SEC said, "In our opinion the complete omission of any attempt at physical contact with the inventory while it was supposed to have been at Bridgeport cannot be justified even on the theory of nonassumption of responsibility by the auditors for inventory quantities." (At the time of the fraud there was a difference of opinion among auditors as to their responsibility for inventory quantities; this difference was eliminated with the adoption in 1939 by the AICPA of "Extensions of Auditing Procedure" after the disclosure of the McKesson fraud.) The mechanics of review procedure followed by the certifying accountants was in accord with the practice of other accounting firms at the time. In this case, however, the SEC said, ". . . the review of the work did not result in a searching analysis of the ultimate facts developed in the course of the actual audit, because, although performed by a partner of many years' experience, it was not done by a person sufficiently familiar with the business practices of the client's industry, or with a sufficient interest in the basic questions of internal check and control to comprehend the significance of the facts reported."

The Londontown Manufacturing Company Case.—The Londontown Manufacturing Company, a Baltimore manufacturer of raincoats and golf jackets, was organized in 1946. In October, 1961, the president of the company, who owned all of the company's stock, sold 150,000 shares (representing 40 per cent of his holdings) to the public through underwriters. The price to the public was $14 per share. The stock was quickly sold and went to a premium in the over-the-counter market, selling as high as $35 a share.

The company's fiscal year ended February 28. The summary of earnings in the prospectus covered the five fiscal years ended February 28, 1961 and the three months ended May 31, 1961. This entire period was covered by the report of independent public accountants. In addition, "capsule" information was furnished following the summary, that is, sales and net earnings, on an unaudited basis, for the following quarter ended August 31, 1961. Figures for the corresponding three-month periods of the previous fiscal year were omitted, apparently on the basis of the following statement in the text of the prospectus:

The Company does not maintain perpetual inventory records or cost records integrated with its general accounting system and reliable operating results necessitate the taking of physical inventories. Since physical inventories were not taken at May 31, 1960 and August 31, 1960, figures for the three month periods ended on those dates have not been included.

The earnings tabulation showed sales increasing each year: from $1,757,000 in 1957 to $5,361,000 in 1961. Net earnings also increased each year: from $43,000 in 1957 to $525,000 in 1961. Per share earnings were 12 cents in 1957, 23 cents in 1958, 32 cents in 1959, 76 cents in 1960, and $1.40 in 1961. In the next quarter (ended May 31, 1961) per share earnings were 41 cents, and in the following quarter 27 cents.

The gross profit ratio, which was 23 per cent in 1957, was 30 per cent in 1960 and almost 39 per cent in 1961. (There was no explanation in the prospectus of this increase.) From the beginning of 1959 to the end of fiscal 1961 sales went up about 60 per cent, but inventories, as reported, increased 350 per cent. (This disproportionate increase was also not explained.)

The accountants' report covered the balance sheet at May 31, 1961, and the summary of earnings for the five years and three months then ended. The report was as follows:

We have examined the balance sheet of The Londontown Manufacturing Company as of May 31, 1961 and the related statement of earnings and retained earnings for the five years and three months then ended which is included under the caption "Summary of Earnings" in this Prospectus. Except as indicated in the succeeding paragraph, our examination was made in accordance with generally accepted auditing standards and included such tests of the accounting records and such other auditing procedures as we considered necessary in the circumstances.

Since we were first engaged to examine the financial statements of The Londontown Manufacturing Company in May, 1961, we were not present to observe the taking of physical inventories at February 28, 1956, 1957, 1958, 1959, 1960 and 1961 nor were we able to apply alternative auditing procedures with respect to the inventory quantities at those dates. However, based on the procedures which we were able to apply such inventories appear to be reasonable although there may be variations which would affect the reporting of earnings as between the respective periods.

In our opinion, such financial statements present fairly the financial position of The Londontown Manufacturing Company at May 31, 1961 and, with the explanation in the preceding paragraph as to the limitation with respect to the examination of inventories, the results of operations for the five years and three months then ended, in conformity with generally accepted accounting principles applied each year on a basis consistent with that of the preceding year.

(*Author's Note:* The reader's attention is directed to the discussion of ASR No. 90 in Chapter **24** from which it will be seen that certificates such as the foregoing—"with an explanation"—are no longer acceptable to the SEC.)

Another firm of independent public accountants had previously examined Londontown's books as of February 29, 1960 for a prospective purchaser, but the purchase had not been consummated. These accountants had not issued an opinion or formal report covering their examination. They obtained a copy of the Londontown prospectus and noted a material discrepancy in the 1960 inventory. According to their information, the inventory at that date was materially understated in the prospectus, which fact, if true, would have the effect of materially overstating the earnings of the following fiscal year (1961). These accountants thereupon informed the accountants who had certified Londontown's financial statements included in the offering prospectus of the discrepancy.

The certifying accountants and the underwriters of the public offering confronted the president of Londontown with the information concerning the 1960 inventory. The president acknowledged that he had been responsible for removing from the company's files the original inventory tabulations at the end of the fiscal years February 1956–1960 and substituting therefor revised tabulations with greatly reduced quantities. The quantities of some items were omitted from the revised tabulation and the quantities of some other items were reduced by exactly 60%. Nearly all of the previously unreported inventory was included in the closing inventory of the fiscal year ended February 28, 1961. The original inventory tabulations were held in a special file—during part of the period they were kept in the president's home—and were not made available to the certifying accountants until the above-mentioned confrontation. The quantities in the inventory as of May 31, 1961, which had been observed by the certifying accountants, had been correctly stated.

The president agreed to indemnify and hold the company harmless as a result of inclusion of erroneous figures in the original registration statement.

Londontown filed a post-effective amendment with the SEC which included a revised prospectus showing financial statements with significantly different figures. Substantial corrections were made in inventories for fiscal years ended in 1957 through 1960. The inventory at February 29, 1960, originally reported as $291,000, was increased to $710,000. The February 28, 1961 inventory was increased $65,000. Per share earnings were revised as follows:

| | Per Share Earnings | |
	As Originally Reported	As Revised
Fiscal years ended Feb. 28:		
1957	$ .12	$.13
1958	.23	.30
1959	.32	.53
1960	.76	.77
1961	1.40	.93
Three months ended May 31, 1961	.41	.32

The post-effective amendment included a prospectus dated January 31, 1962, containing a "Preliminary Statement," in which it was stated in part as follows:

This Amended Prospectus is part of a Post-Effective Amendment to the Registration Statement filed in order to correct certain inventory and earnings figures set forth in the Prospectus dated October 4, 1961, and to bring the Registration Statement up to date in other respects. For a period of time prior to May 31, 1961, the Company's inventory was greater than that shown in its financial statements since quantities were reported at less than the quantities actually on hand. Between March 1, 1960, and May 31, 1961, this condition was corrected and the latest inventory shown in the Prospectus dated October 4, 1961, that of May 31, 1961, was fairly stated in the opinion of [the independent public accountants] who observed the taking of such inventory. However, management's decision to include in the year ended February 28, 1961, nearly all of the previously unreported inventory caused the earnings for that year to appear greater than actual earnings. Correspondingly, actual earnings for the affected years prior to March 1, 1960, were considerably higher than reported earnings. The independent certified public accountants, who examined the financial statements included in the Prospectus dated October 4, 1961, were not engaged until May 1961, and since management did not then furnish them with the correct inventory listings for periods during which they had not been associated with the company, they were not aware of these inaccuracies. The correct inventory listings have now been supplied to [the independent auditors] and the company has now corrected the figures in the Summary of Earnings and has set forth the retroactive adjustments in Note (1) of the notes to the Financial Statements included in this Amended Prospectus. [Name of president], as the Selling Stockholder and as the chief executive and financial officer of the Company at the time the Prospectus dated October 4, 1961, was filed has agreed to indemnify and hold the Company harmless to the extent of any and all liabilities which may be asserted against the Company predicated upon the inclusion of the erroneous figures in the Prospectus dated October 4, 1961.

Note (1) to the financial statements included in the post-effective amendment set forth the following information:

Retroactive adjustments:
Since the issuance of a previous prospectus on October 4, 1961, management has revised the quantities relating to all inventories prior to May 31, 1961, used in the determination of cost of sales. The following tabulation shows the inventories, net earnings and earnings per share originally disclosed and as now revised:

[Tabulation omitted here]

The revision in the inventory at February 28, 1956, the beginning of the period covered in the Summary of Earnings shown elsewhere in this Amended Prospectus, resulted in shifting $73,399 of net earnings to periods prior to the fiscal year ended February 28, 1957.
The use in the Prospectus dated October 4, 1961, of the original figures and of the resulting original net earnings figures, now revised as shown above, may

give rise to certain contingent liabilities on the part of the Company, the extent of which cannot be determined at this time. No provision for such contingent liabilities has been made in above balance sheet, however, since [name of president], as the Selling Stockholder, has agreed to indemnify and hold the Company harmless to the extent of any and all liabilities which may be asserted against the Company predicated upon the inclusion of the aforementioned figures in the Prospectus dated October 4, 1961 . . .

Londontown also disclosed to the Internal Revenue Service the situation with respect to its inventories. In March 1962, a settlement was made with the IRS in which adjustments were agreed upon for the fiscal years ended February 29, 1956–1961, resulting in a penalty assessment of $117,-000 by reason of understatements of taxable income in some years. This amount was paid by Londontown and immediately reimbursed to Londontown in full by its president.

Before permitting the amendment to become effective, the SEC held hearings to consider the case and to determine whether a stop-order should issue against the registration statement and whether the post-effective amendment should be declared effective. The certifying accountants were permitted to participate in the proceedings. The Commission's decision was issued on October 31, 1963 (41 SEC 676–688).

The facts in the case were included in a lengthy (314 pages) stipulation filed with the SEC on September 26, 1963. The stipulation detailed the various computations made by the certifying accountants in connection with their investigation of the inventories for all of the fiscal years included in the summary of earnings in the prospectus. These computations were reflected in the various inventory and cost studies made by the certifying accountants prior to the issuance of their opinion, both before the initial filing of the registration statement and after receiving the SEC's comment letter following the staff's review of the filing. These studies had been undertaken to obtain reasons for the substantial indicated variations in the gross profit margin as between years.

The certifying accountants had discussed the practicability of reconciling inventory quantities backwards from May 31, 1961, the date as of which they had observed the taking of physical inventories. In view of the variations in the cost of types of items in inventory, the accountants considered that such a reconciliation, in order to be meaningful, should account for individual models in work-in-process and finished goods, and for individual items of raw materials. Such a reconciliation was not deemed practicable to make where the necessary records are not maintained in sufficient detail and are not integrated with the general accounting records. Based on their experience, the accountants were of the view that the results of any attempted reconciliation were almost invariably unsatisfactory, and they decided not to undertake the reconciliation unless other avenues of inquiry failed to provide reasonable explanations for the variations in gross profit margins.

When their studies were completed, the results were not considered by the accountants to be altogether conclusive, but they believed that reasonable explanations had been obtained and that the procedures followed were in accordance with generally accepted auditing standards and were adequate in the circumstances. They did not consider that they had any basis to doubt the president's assurances that inventory quantities were properly stated, having in mind also that another firm of CPAs (not the firm which made the 1960 examination) had examined and reported without qualification on the Londontown financial statements for several years including the years ended February 1957–1961.

Subsequent to the president's admission of the inventory manipulations in prior years, additional tabulations and reconciliations were made, especially by reference to available inventory, production, and shipment records. These tabulations and reconciliations suggested errors in quantities shown in certain prior period inventories.

The stipulation referred to procedures which were not utilized by the certifying accountants in connection with their audit. Some of these matters are listed below:

> No inquiries were made of subordinate employees who took the inventory of piece goods (raw materials) or other inventories as of February 29, 1960.
>
> No inquiries were made concerning the quantities of piece goods on inventory cards maintained by the purchasing agent as of February 29, 1960 (when a substantial number of items in the inventory reflected in the original prospectus were 40% of the quantities on the cards).
>
> No tabulation was made of quantities of piece goods included in the inventories.
>
> No tabulation or schedule was prepared to work back the quantity of finished garments in the May 31, 1961 inventory to the February 29, 1960 inventory by reference to records of weekly production and shipping maintained by the plant or production manager and to the summaries of shipments net of returns, prepared by a service bureau.
>
> No computation was made to compare the average selling price per garment sold during the year ended February 28, 1961, with the average cost per garment finished during the year, to determine the average gross profit percentage for the year. (This computation revealed an average gross profit per garment of 32.28% which approximated the gross profit ratio of 31.99% finally determined by using the correct inventories, as contrasted with 38.59% computed from the inventories in the original prospectus.)

No examination was made of receiving reports for the purpose of checking whether the inventories at the end of the fiscal years 1957–1960 included piece goods recorded as having been received on the inventory dates.

On the basis of the stipulation, counsel for Londontown submitted an offer of settlement pursuant to Rule 8(a) of the Commission's Rules of Practice, and counsel for the certifying accountants raised no objection. Because of the widespread publicity given to the facts in the case, the settlement offer was accepted, the stop-order proceedings were dismissed, and the post-effective amendment was permitted to become effective. While the SEC's decision contains no criticism whatever of the independent accountants, the case became the basis for ASR No. 90 (discussed in Chapter 24).

Seaboard Commercial Corporation Case.—Seaboard Commercial Corporation began business in 1934 at which time it was engaged in the automobile financing business. Over the years the financing nature of its business had changed drastically, so that by the end of 1947 its assets consisted principally of investments in and advances to six companies. As of December 31, 1947, such investments and advances aggregated $5,238,000 out of its stated total assets of $7,987,000. The company's principal liabilities consisted of loans payable to banks which, at December 31, 1947, aggregated $4,600,000. All of these financial facts were shown in the company's annual report on Form 10–K for 1947 filed by the company with the Commission as required by the 1934 Act.

The facts shown by the report were so alarming that the banks in 1948 terminated their credits to Seaboard, which resulted in its liquidation in 1949.

In 1952 the SEC instituted proceedings against the certifying accountants under Rule 2(e) of the Commission's Rules of Practice alleging that the 1947 financial statements of Seaboard certified by them were materially misleading and that the accountants failed to comply with generally accepted auditing standards and disregarded generally accepted accounting principles and the rules and regulations of the Commission. In 1957—five years after the commencement of the proceedings—the SEC announced its decision in ASR No. 78 (1957). The Commission determined that the firm of accountants and two of its partners had engaged in improper professional conduct in connection with the firm's certification of the 1947 Seaboard financial statements, and suspended the firm and the two partners from practice before the Commission for a period of 15 days.

When the accountants commenced their examination of the 1947 financial statements, Seaboard's reserve for losses on investments in and advances to the six companies was $119,000. Management argued that this amount was all that was needed, but the accountants said it was clearly inadequate.

The companies had all incurred operating losses and had continually required further advances from Seaboard during 1947. The aggregate excess of liabilities over assets of three of the companies exceeded $1,200,000 as of the end of 1947. The senior in charge of the field work (which included supplementary procedures undertaken because of the accountants' awareness of the seriousness of the situation) had estimated, at the conclusion of his work, that a reserve of $1,453,000 (not including Coastal referred to below) was required. After a conference with management, the partner in charge of the audit had arrived at an estimated reserve of $1,345,000. A draft of a certificate used by the accountants after several meetings with management referred to the need for a reserve of about $1,350,000. After further conferences with management, the accountants agreed to a reserve of $857,000. With the liquidation of Seaboard in 1949, its losses far exceeded the reserve provided at the end of 1947 for investments in, and advances to, its debtors.

The SEC said that the reserve for losses of $857,000 was materially inadequate, and that the accountants, in certifying the statements including this reserve, had failed to follow generally accepted accounting and auditing standards and ·failed to exercise an independent and informed judgment. The Commission conceded that the question of the adequacy of the reserve should be determined in the light of the circumstances at the time of the accountants' examination, although the hearings were commenced in 1952 —long after the liquidation of Seaboard. In its decision the Commission stated that it had ignored facts not in existence or not available at the time of the audit, and that to the exent that it had referred to events that took place after the audit "such reference has been only for informational purposes."

The accountants argued that the earlier estimates of the reserve required were tentative only, but the SEC maintained that the information furnished by management subsequent to such determinations was not of a character which would warrant a retreat from such earlier estimates.

In connection with their examination, the accountants received recent financial information on some of the six companies, but not on others. The SEC was critical of the accountants in this respect and said that proper auditing procedures required the obtaining of the latest financial information available prior to the completion of their audit in order to give them a basis on which to assess the reasonableness of the representations regarding the companies by Seaboard's management. The accountants asserted that Seaboard's close contact with the debtor companies made its judgment and intentions more significant than more current statements of the companies since the companies were not in good financial condition and "in the course of rehabilitation financing of this type it was not unusual for there to be deficits from operations, low current ratios, and other unfavorable financial conditions." The SEC said the argument was not persuasive, and that it was an unwarranted premise to say that Seaboard was of its own accord engaged in rehabilitation financing, since Seaboard's normal business was that of a regular commercial finance company. Seaboard's loans to its major accounts started as ordinary finance loans, without any intention or expectation on Seaboard's part of financing companies needing rehabilitation.

The SEC said that the accountants' failure to request more current financial statements or to communicate with or inspect any of the underlying companies indicated that they deferred to the judgment of Seaboard's management in reducing their original estimate of the needed reserve.

The Commission also found that the accountants failed to make independent inquiries to determine whether inventories pledged as collateral were properly stated. In one instance, where Seaboard's advances of about $1,500,000 were primarily secured by inventories, it developed that the inventories were overstated $635,000.

In finding the reserve inadequate, the SEC noted that no reserve was provided for Seaboard's investment of $512,000 in Coastal Machine Works, Inc., a wholly owned subsidiary, notwithstanding that Coastal had suffered a "permanent decline in value and earning power" and that its net assets (stated at slightly more than Seaboard's investment) improperly reflected an appraisal write-up of about $439,000 which the accountants (who were also Coastal's accountants) had questioned.

The SEC said that the accountants improperly deferred to management's wishes in deleting from their certificate language indicating the condition of Seaboard's major accounts. The Commission also held that the accountants should have taken exception to a note to the reserve figure which was materially misleading in indicating that the reserve was set up "to provide for future losses that might result from uncertain general business conditions," rather than in recognition of the specific deterioration of Seaboard's accounts.

The Commission also found Seaboard's income statement to be misleading. The addition of $750,000 to the reserve (which the SEC found to be inadequate) was charged to earned surplus rather than to income, "notwithstanding that an addition to the reserve was necessitated by developments during 1947." If the increase in the reserve had been charged to income, Seaboard's reported net income of almost $250,000 would have been converted into a loss of $500,000. An adequate provision for losses on uncollectible accounts, said the SEC, would have produced a loss of more than $1,000,000. The SEC also observed that while the reserve increase had been charged to earned surplus, the company credited to income $542,000 realized on the disposition of an investment in a subsidiary.

Because of the poor financial condition of its debtors, the accountants had originally estimated that $1,374,000 or $1,500,000 of Seaboard's advances to companies other than Coastal should be excluded from current assets. The certified balance sheet, however, excluded from current assets only $641,000 of such advances which the SEC stated was materially inadequate in the light of the available information.

Of the indebtedness from Coastal, $300,000 was classified as current. The SEC said this did not conform to good accounting practice since Coastal was not in a position to liquidate its indebtedness currently, and Coastal's net current asset position did not justify such classification. Coastal's balance sheet (also certified by the same accountants) overstated net current assets by improperly excluding from current liabilities a reserve for renegotiation claims.

Noting that Seaboard owned the stock of two of its debtors, and exercised complete control over others, the SEC said that the balance sheet was further misleading in listing amounts owed by these companies as due from customers rather than from subsidiaries.

The Commission acknowledged that the accountants had insisted upon certain disclosures and an increase over the reserve figure originally proposed by Seaboard. The SEC concluded, however, that the financial statements and the certificate as a whole improperly minimized adverse disclosures and failed to portray realistically the financial condition of Seaboard. The SEC emphasized that the responsibility of an independent public accountant is not only to the client who pays his fee, but also to investors, creditors, and others who may rely on the financial statements which he certifies, and that he must report fairly on the facts as he finds them.

The Olen Company Case.—Early in 1958 Olen Company, Inc. made a public sale of common stock pursuant to a registration statement filed under the 1933 Act. As of October 31, 1958 Olen Company and its subsidiaries were merged into H. L. Green Company, Inc. and became the Olen Division of Green. Maurice E. Olen, who had been president and a principal stockholder of Olen Company, became president of Green. The Olen Division retained its separate offices, warehouse, and accounting records.

Financial statements of Olen Company for its fiscal year ended January 31, 1958, certified by its public accountants, were included in the registration statement in connection with the public sale of stock and were also included in the proxy statement of Green and Olen filed with the SEC in connection with the merger. These statements showed Olen Company as having at that time:

Current assets	$4,400,000 (including $3,850,000 in inventories)
Stockholders' equity	1,200,000
Net income for the year	450,000

The proxy statement also included unaudited Olen Company financial statements for the six months period ended July 31, 1958 prepared (but not certified) by Olen's public accountants. Before the merger was consummated, the accountants furnished certified statements to Green for the same period which differed only slightly from the unaudited statements.

After the merger, Olen's accountants continued to serve the Olen Division whereas another accounting firm audited the balance of the Green operations. Olen's accountants prepared and certified financial statements of the Olen Division for the year ended January 31, 1959 which were to be included in Green's annual report to be filed with the SEC. Before that report was filed, however, Green discovered that the Olen Division inventories were substantially overstated and that its accounts payable were substantially understated. Following a reaudit by Green Co.'s accountants, it was determined that there was an overstatement of Olen Division's net assets as of January 31, 1959 of about $4,700,000. This deficiency resulted from inventory shortages of more than $2,800,000 and unrecorded accounts payable of about $2,700,000, the aggregate thereof being reduced by an understatement of almost $800,000 in fixed assets which had been charged improperly to expenses instead of being capitalized.

On February 20, 1959, Mr. Olen admitted that the accounts of the Olen Division had been falsified and that the inventories, fixed assets, and liabilities were materially misstated. He resigned as president and director of Green.

The financial statements of January 31 and July 31, 1958 had also been false. Olen Co. at those dates had in fact been insolvent and had been operating at a loss. Accordingly, shares of Olen Company had been sold to the public on the basis of a false and misleading registration statement, the approval of the merger by Green Co.'s stockholders had been solicited on the basis of a false and misleading proxy statement, and Green Co. had been led to consummate the merger on the basis of false and misleading financial statements. Green Co. collected $1,600,000 from Mr. Olen as partial restitution.

The SEC instituted proceedings pursuant to Rule 2(e) of its Rules of Practice to determine whether Olen's accountants, its senior partner, and a junior partner should be denied the privilege of practicing before the Commission because of alleged unethical or improper professional conduct in connection with the preparation and certification of financial statements of the Olen Company, Inc. and its successor, the Olen Division of H. L. Green Co., Inc.

After the SEC proceedings had been started, the senior partner of the accounting firm died. Previously the partnership had been dissolved. The junior partner, without admitting the allegations against him, tendered his withdrawal from practice and agreed not to practice before the SEC, with the understanding that the proceedings would be discontinued and that the Commission could issue a statement with respect to its action.

The SEC dismissed the proceedings and made public a report of its staff investigation with respect to the preparation and certification of financial statements by Olen's public accountants. The report constitutes part of ASR No. 105 (July 29, 1966).

According to the staff report, the accounts of Olen Co. and of the Olen Division had been grossly misstated at the direction of Mr. Olen for a number of years prior to January 31, 1959. The principal methods of falsifying the accounts were (1) the failure to record invoices covering large quantities of merchandise in the accounting period in which the related merchandise was received, thereby materially understating merchandise purchases, cost of sales, and liabilities; (2) the manipulation and falsification of the retail inventory records in such a manner as substantially to overstate the retail store inventories, gross profits, net income, and earned surplus; and (3) the charging to expense of capital improvements, thereby reducing the net income for income tax purposes. (The company seems to have been torn in opposite directions, and had paid over $200,000 in income taxes for the fiscal year ended January 31, 1958 on income which had not in fact been earned.)

The methods followed by the Olen management to falsify its books and financial statements are set forth in the aforementioned Release No. 105 and will not be repeated or summarized here. Of more immediate concern are the observations in the SEC's staff report bearing on the nature of the examination made by Olen's auditors.

Olen Co.'s records were in such condition that "even a cursory examination of the merchandise voucher records, the disbursing records, the merchandise receiving records, the accounts payable records, or the merchandise inventory records, would have disclosed the inaccuracy and falsity of the merchandise and accounts payable figures." The invoice numbers and dates were reflected on the vouchers and usually on the voucher checks and voucher purchase journal. Each invoice usually bore the number of the related receiving report and of the voucher on which the invoice was recorded, the latter number indicating the month in which the voucher was prepared. "Any review of these records would have disclosed the delay in vouchering invoices." For example, only a very few of the first 500 vouchers in the month of February 1958 covered invoices dated in that month. "Any examination would have disclosed the existence of material amounts of unrecorded purchases and accounts payable at the end of any month."

Each receiving report bore the date on which the merchandise was received by the store, and the related invoice and month-keyed voucher numbers. "Thus it would have been immediately apparent to an auditor examining the retail inventory records and the supporting merchandise receiving reports that there were wide discrepancies between the dates merchandise was received and the dates on which related invoices had been vouchered, and that the accounts payable, therefore, could not have been correctly stated."

The auditors' representatives observed the taking of the inventory in the Mobile warehouse; "they could hardly have been unaware of the obvious inaccuracy of the reported warehouse inventory figure of $112,210." A check of the retail inventory records and the underlying documents "would have readily disclosed the falsity of such records and the composition of 'merchandise in transit' as actually representing unrecorded invoices for merchandise."

In connection with their audit as at January 31, 1958, the auditors' employees observed the taking of physical inventories in about one-third of the retail stores in addition to the warehouse. Also, the physical inventory records of the retail stores were reconciled with the related book inventories shown by the respective retail inventory records. In any verification of the inventory records, "it would have been necessary to account for all of the receiving reports issued, which were pre-numbered in bound books." Such a review "would have disclosed the nature of the 'merchandise in transit,' the large amounts of unrecorded invoices at all times, and the discrepancies arising from the manipulation of the inventory records and the extensive vouchering after January 31, 1958, of invoices for merchandise received prior thereto."

The SEC staff said that appropriate testing of accounts payable by direct confirmation with principal suppliers would have disclosed the failure to record purchases in the fiscal year in which the goods and services were received and the existence of large amounts of unrecorded purchases and liabilities. "Proper confirmation procedures most certainly would have brought to light discrepancies in accounts payable of the magnitude of $2,900,000."

During the course of the January 31, 1958 audit, an employee of the auditors observed that certain items which should have been charged to fixed assets were charged to expense. He reported this fact to the junior partner of the audit firm, but the misstatements were not corrected.

During the July 31, 1958 audit the same employee found in a file separate from the paid-invoice file a number of invoices for non-merchandise items received prior to the audit date (in some instances several months prior thereto) which had not been recorded at that date. A sampling of such invoices totaled about $80,000. The next day he attempted to ascertain the extent of such unrecorded items, but was told by Olen's office manager that the requested files were being used, that he could not see them at that time, and that in the future, when the auditors wished to see any files, they should ask her or one of Olen Co.'s clerks for them. The accountant made a list of the unrecorded vouchers or invoices he had seen and asked the office manager for them. When the file folders were given to him, the unrecorded items had been removed and he was told that they had never been in the folders. He reported these events to the junior partner of the audit firm.

Concerned that the same situation might exist in connection with merchandise purchases, the accountant then examined the voucher register for dates on and after August 1, 1958 and found recorded in it invoices dated prior to that date, many of which were several months old, representing more than $700,000 worth of merchandise purchases which had been omitted from the accounts as of July 31, 1958. He also reported this discovery to the junior partner of the audit firm. Thereafter, upon learning that the financial statements were being certified without exception—despite the omission of material amounts of liabilities and purchases—he protested and resigned from the firm.

Although the physical inventory in the warehouse actually aggregated about $1,138,000, Olen employees raised the quantities on many of the inventory count tickets so as to show $2,640,000, and even that figure was "arbitrarily" raised another $603,000 to approximately the book figure. Although the auditors' representatives observed the taking of the warehouse inventory and made test counts, they did not retain the inventory count tickets prepared by Olen employees and such tickets were falsified before they were turned over to the firm. (The SEC staff report does not say whether the auditors kept a list of the tickets with respect to which they had made test counts, but the presumption is that they did not.) However, the auditing firm and its predecessors had been examining the financial statements of Olen Division and its predecessors for several years and were familiar with its affairs, and "could not fail to question the incredible increase in the warehouse inventory from $112,210 to $2,640,137 in one year, let alone the higher figure of $3,243,000 actually used by the firm."

The auditors apparently confirmed amounts due to trade creditors, but the SEC staff said that the procedures employed were grossly defective. These amounts at January 31, 1959 were understated on the books by about $2,700,000. Confirmations were sent to suppliers named on two lists prepared by Olen's personnel which omitted several of the largest regular suppliers of merchandise to the Olen Division, to six of whom about $740,000 was owed at January 31, 1959 and from whom the receiving records showed that large shipments were received during the latter part of January and the first ten days of February 1959.

The SEC investigators observed:

Where as here requests are made for confirmation of merchandise accounts payable, it is customary to request confirmation from major suppliers during the period under audit regardless of whether or not the records show amounts due to them. It is also a basic auditing procedure to check the receiving records for a short time prior and subsequent to the balance sheet date to determine that all merchandise received prior to the balance sheet date or in transit at that date has been included in the accounts. The firm either did not employ these basic procedures although they were certified public accountants of many years experience to whom such procedures should have been well known, or they disregarded the results of such procedures.

The SEC staff said that within the procedures followed by the auditors, there were numerous circumstances which, if investigated adequately, must have revealed the gross inaccuracies in the financial statements. The direct physical contact with inventories that the auditors had through their representatives (who observed the inventory taking in the warehouse and in many of the stores and made test counts) should have precluded the use of the completely unrealistic inventory figures reflected in the financial statements. The discrepancies were of such a gross and extensive nature "that they could not have been overlooked." The SEC investigators said that it was "unbelievable" that, under the circumstances, the auditors did not know that the inventories were grossly misstated.

The same situation, said the SEC, prevailed with respect to accounts payable. "Any reasonable review of the system of internal check and control would have disclosed that the system of recording purchases was not operating as it was supposed to." The failure to record purchases extended back at least to 1954. The juggling of the payable records was so clumsy and open that "any review of the accounting procedures and controls would have disclosed numerous unrecorded invoices of material amount." A scanning of transactions recorded in voucher and disbursement records the first few days after the balance sheet date (a customary auditing procedure) would have disclosed numerous instances of unrecorded liabilities and purchases as of that date.

According to the SEC investigators, ordinary tests of the accounts and records would have disclosed an inordinate number of errors and omissions. This would have called for further testing and employment of extended auditing procedures, which would have revealed that recording invoices concurrently with the receipt of merchandise was the exception rather than the rule. "It is not conceivable that so many gross misstatements over so extended a period of time could have remained undiscovered by anyone following accepted auditing procedures. The discovery of gross misstatements in the accounts is certainly one of the major purposes of an independent audit."

Miami Window Corporation Case.—In the Miami Window Corporation case [41 SEC 68 (1962)] the independent auditors had observed the taking of the physical inventories. After the amount of the inventory had been computed, however, the company, by various means, arbitrarily inflated the dollar value thereof. After the company's securities had been sold, the SEC instituted stop-order proceedings, and, in its decision, the SEC disclosed the methods employed by the company in overstating the inventory. The Commission was also critical of the independent auditors and said that the procedures they followed were inadequate in the circumstances.

The company and its subsidiaries manufactured windows and other products. Its fiscal year ended in February. The financial statements challenged were the balance sheet at November 30, 1958, and the operating statements for the nine months then ended. The statements showed total inventories at November 30, 1958, of $3,043,000 and net income of $371,000 for the nine months then ended.

A. FINISHED WINDOWS.—Finished windows were overstated $189,000. This was accomplished by considering as finished windows items that had been inventoried as empty containers. Inventory tickets for "boxes" and "cartons" were altered to "boxed" and "cartoned" to make them appear as finished windows in boxes and cartons. This change was made after the inventory had been priced and summarized and a copy given to the independent auditors. Miami's cost accountant (who of all the witnesses was most familiar with the designation of inventory items) testified that he had never had any doubt that the tickets represented empty cartons. When he asked the auditors to return the inventory tickets in their possession, he said he wanted to review them—that as the result of errors in interpretation certain tickets in the finished window category had been erroneously priced as cartons. The auditor said not to erase any figures that needed to be changed, but to cross out the original figures so as to leave them legible and to write in the revised figures in another color. When the tickets were later returned to him, they included 51 tickets on which the item designation had been changed and from which the lower part reflecting the original pricing had been cut off, and were accompanied by schedules prepared by Miami's cost accountant reflecting the increases resulting from altering the tickets. The auditor asked to see the windows involved and was taken to the area where finished windows were stored. There he and the cost accountant spent from 15 to 30 minutes. On the basis of this superficial examination and because a partner of the CPA firm thought that the original window inventory figure seemed too low in view of the volume of business, the auditors accepted the adjustment.

The SEC said that the auditors' verification procedures were inadequate. Their instruction to leave the original figures on the inventory tickets had been violated by the cutting off of parts of the tickets. The new designations "boxed" and "cartoned" had not been used on any of the tickets originally designated as windows. The irregularities of which they were on notice required that they take all possible steps to make certain that the large number of finished windows after the ticket alteration actually existed. This included appropriate inquiries of the person whose initials appeared on the altered tickets and a careful inspection of the stock of finished windows. Without such steps, it was not proper to certify the financial statements.

In the course of their work, the auditors had found in the cost accountant's possession an inventory sheet reflecting non-existent items. The cost accountant admitted this and said he was acting pursuant to the comptroller's specific instructions. The partners of the CPA firm and their staff auditor expressed their serious concern over the false inventory sheet to Miami's cost accountant, but received no satisfactory explanation. Also, on the same day that the auditor discovered the false sheet, he learned that the comptroller had prepared a consolidating balance sheet showing an inventory figure of $2,651,000 for the company (unconsolidated) although at that time the corresponding figure computed by the auditors was $2,286,000 (exclusive of engineering work in process referred to below). The appearance of this larger figure, the comptroller's resistance to inventory reductions considered proper by the auditors, remarks by Miami's president and the comptroller indicating that an effort was being made to reach a predetermined profit figure likely to make the proposed securities offering successful—all caused the auditors concern as to the reliability of Miami's figures, and made it clear that they had to extend their inventory audit procedures.

B. WINDOWS IN TRANSIT.—A Puerto Rican subsidiary made windows that were shipped to the company. In the preliminary inventory summary, such windows in transit were shown at $118,000 (reduced later to $108,-000). The cost accountant arrived at this amount by selecting invoices from the subsidiary bearing dates subsequent to November 4, 1958. This procedure was based on prior experience indicating that it took three to four weeks from the invoice date for a shipment to reach Miami's plant. There were no receiving reports, however, covering the invoices selected, no proof whether the windows in such invoices had been received, and no records to match invoices against windows received.

The comptroller said the in-transit figure was too low and instructed the cost accountant to select additional invoices dated in October and November, 1958, for inclusion in this item. The latter accordingly selected additional invoices ranging back to October 10, 1958, and totaling $108,000, making a new total of $216,000 for windows in transit.

The auditor told the cost accountant he was unable to verify the increase from the files in the purchasing department. The auditor said he would accept it if Mr. H (who was in charge of the department) would mark the dates of receipt on the invoices and gave them to Mr. H for that purpose. The comptroller and the cost accountant instructed Mr. H to place receipt dates later than November 30 on the invoices and assured him that the auditors could not check them since there were no records reflecting dates of receipt. Mr. H thereupon put dates ranging from December 1 to December 19, 1958, on the invoices without any basis for believing that they reflected actual dates of receipt. Some of the windows had been received before November 30, and the company had no basis for adjusting the preliminary in-transit figures.

As far as the auditors were concerned, a key question was the date placed on the invoices by Mr. H, and this, the Commission said, was "the subject of only very limited verification efforts by the auditors." They matched some dates against purchase orders most of which, however, had no notation of the dates of receipt of the windows, and one of which bore a date different from that placed on the invoice by Mr. H. A partner of the CPA firm said he had made his own spot check of documents relating to a few of the invoices. Among such documents were sheets which he described as "informal receiving reports." These sheets did not contain any indication that they related to receipt of deliveries nor did they refer to invoice numbers, but merely listed quantities of windows of various sizes and contained dates which coincided in almost all cases with the arbitrary dates placed by Mr. H on invoices relating to windows of like size and quantity as those listed on the sheets. (The SEC's decision does not explain the function or the purpose of these sheets, which is regrettable since the auditors placed some reliance on them.)

The SEC said that, despite the doubts the auditors had regarding the in-transit figures, they relied greatly on Mr. H "and either failed to make an adequate check of the available records, or disregarded inconsistencies disclosed by such records." Thus, notations on copies of purchase orders in the files showed that the items covered by three of the invoices in question were received by the company on November 19, 1958. Also, copies of certain invoices bore notations indicating that they had been sent to the accounting department prior to November 30, 1958. This fact is significant because, under the system in use, such transmittal was made only after the items covered by the invoices had been received and payment for them was to be made.

C. WORK IN PROCESS ENGINEERING.—The company produced so-called engineered, or custom-made, windows in addition to its regular line. The inventory figure in the financial statements included $154,000 designated "work in process engineering," the purpose of which was to defer the costs applicable to windows the income from which had not been realized.

The company did not have a job cost system which would enable it to identify costs applicable to: (1) contracts on which income had been realized, and (2) contracts on which income would be realized in the future.

The determination of the expenses to be deferred was made on the basis of a formula evolved jointly by the comptroller and the CPA firm. The formula resulted in allocating to future periods certain expenses having no relation to engineered windows. Detailed time records were not available which would support an allocation of the time spent by the engineering department on the company's regular line and on the custom-made line. The formula did not take into account that expenses in connection with the preparation of unsuccessful bids should not have been deferred. The SEC concluded that the work in process amount was based on unreliable calculations and included expenses not attributable to engineering work, which made the statements misleading.

D. SCROLL AND STERLING INVENTORIES.—The company had two subsidiaries, one of which was referred to as Scroll and the other as Sterling. After Scroll's inventory of $95,000 had been submitted to Miami's comptroller, he instructed Scroll's bookkeeper to raise it to $163,000. Scroll's bookkeeper thereafter altered many inventory tickets.

The auditor either failed to notice the alterations or was satisfied with the bookkeeper's explanation. Among other things, the bookkeeper had increased the conversion rate for aluminum bars, thereby increasing the total weight and valuation of the bars. The auditor did not verify the conversion rate although the engineering specifications, which contained the correct conversion rate, were available to him. The bookkeeper doubled the labor factor on some inventory tickets and increased the overhead based on the increased amount for labor. The auditor did nothing to verify the labor factor although the tickets carried a warning of the impropriety.

Sterling's inventory totaled $49,000. Miami's comptroller instructed that it be raised to $96,000. The job cost records were two months in arrears, and the pricing of work in process was based on engineering estimates of degree of completion of various jobs. Lacking up-to-date job cost information, the auditors relied on a gross profit test. For the nine months in question the gross profit percentage was 17% as compared with 21% in the preceding fiscal year. The SEC said this comparison could not take the place of verification—the job cost records could have been brought up to date and the pricing thus verified.

E. CONCLUSION.—The SEC concluded that the financial statements were materially false and misleading. The SEC also concluded that the auditors failed to comply with generally accepted auditing standards, and that their certificate was materially false and misleading in representing: (1) that there had been such compliance, and (2) that the financial statements fairly presented the company's financial position and results of operations.

Keller Brothers Securities Co., Inc. Case.—This company was a registered broker-dealer whose financial statements were filed with the SEC on Form X–17A–5 and were certified by a certified public accountant. The accountant represented, in his certificate, that his examination was made in accordance with generally accepted auditing standards, and included tests of accounting records and other auditing procedures considered necessary in the circumstances. He had made four examinations, and the SEC said that he had omitted in each of them many of the Commission's specific audit requirements, and had failed to comply with generally accepted auditing standards followed by independent accountants in audits of broker-dealers.

The SEC said that the accountant did not properly obtain confirmations of customers' accounts or of closed accounts. Although he requested all customers whose accounts showed money balances at the audit date to report any discrepancies in such balances ("negative confirmation"), he did not request any confirmation as to the securities shown in these accounts. In addition, no requests for confirmation were sent to customers whose accounts showed a zero money balance, even though such accounts contained securities, or whose accounts had been closed since the previous audit.

According to the Commission, the audit procedures followed by the accountant in his examination of Keller's securities record were also inadequate in that he failed to balance properly the securities positions. He prepared a list of securities quantities from the short positions of the securities record showing items in physical possession, safekeeping and transfer, and purchased but not yet received from sellers. His verification consisted of physically counting securities in Keller's office and requesting positive written confirmation of the purchased but unreceived items. He did not prepare a comparable list of the long securities positions of the securities record or compare the short and long securities positions with the securities reflected in the customers' accounts.

In addition, the SEC said, the accountant failed adequately to verify securities in transfer in that he did not obtain written confirmation of securities in the hands of transfer agents at the audit date. He asserted that items in transfer had been verified by examination at a later date during the course of the audit after they had been received at Keller's office, but the circumstances did not indicate that the application of this procedure of verifying securities in transfer was an acceptable alternative to written confirmations.

The SEC concluded that the audit omitted many specifically required and basic procedures. [ASR No. 97 (1963)].

Associated Gas and Electric Co.—The Commission said that the certificate of the independent auditors in this case [11 SEC 1046 (1942)] did not comply with SEC requirements in that: (1) the audits made by the accountants were inadequate in scope to place them in a position to form a conclusive opinion in respect of the financial statements of, and the accounting principles and practices followed by, the company and its subsidiaries; (2) the accountants' opinions were not clearly stated as required; and (3) the exceptions and explanations were so pervasive in character as, in the SEC's opinion, to render nugatory the expression of their general opinion that the statements fairly presented the position of the companies and the results of their operations.

Specifically the SEC was critical of the scope of the accountants' examination for the following reasons:

1. The accountants' failure to determine the effect of the company's practice in entering items in capital surplus rather than in earned surplus.
2. Failure to determine the amounts which were included in consolidated fixed asset amounts which should have been charged against the consolidated depreciation reserve.

A partner of the accounting firm who testified had difficulty on the stand in pointing out which comments in his firm's certificates were intended to be exceptions, and which comments were designed to show that the company followed certain principles for which there was authoritative support at the time, but which he did not prefer. He conceded that his firms' certificates did not state the firm's opinion in respect of the principles which he did not prefer. In addition, said the SEC, the certifying accountants did not take exception to or explain the use of various other accounting practices which the SEC believed to be faulty. The Commission observed:

One of the basic faults, we believe, in [the certifying accountants'] approach to the problem of certifying these statements lay in their assumption that a modicum of disclosure of variations would compensate for failure to adhere to acceptable norms. We need not now consider whether complete disclosure may ever have the effect contended for, but used to the extent and in the manner relied on in this case, we are clear that such disclosure as a substitute for adherence to accounting principles leaves the financial statements at best meaningless and at worst deceptive. Indeed, the disclosure in this case seemed designed less to convey full information than to protect against criticism or liability. . . .

. . . We are left with the feeling that the principal purpose of the company was not to disclose frankly, but to mystify, baffle, mislead and conceal and that the audits and certificates of the accountants did nothing to prevent the accomplishment of that purpose. . . . We should have hesitated to criticize the accountants on individual items had we not been unequivocally satisfied that the financial statements, looked at as a whole, were not truthfully informative and should never have been certified.

Drayer-Hanson, Inc.—The Commission issued an opinion in this case[3] following an investigation under the 1933 Act. A principal issue in the investigation was the financial statements. The Commission found that the representation in the auditors' certificate to the effect that they had no reason to believe that the inventories were unfairly stated was without justification. The financial statements in the registration statement were in error in overstating inventory of work in process at April 30, 1946, and pre-tax profits for the period then ended by $97,000. The error arose through the failure to relieve the work-in-process account of costs applicable to partial shipments.

On March 31, 1946, a physical count of all inventories except work in process had been taken by the registrant and observed by the auditors. As to work in process, a list showing the accumulated cost of each job in process was prepared by the registrant. This list totaled $219,501 and was $54,189 less than the work-in-process account in the general ledger. The latter account was adjusted to bring it into agreement with the list. With respect to inventories, the accountants' report stated:

We were present only during the taking of a physical inventory, which did not include work in process, as at March 31, 1946, and satisfied ourselves as to the procedures followed in the determination of inventory quantities as of that date. We were not in attendance at the physical count of the inventories taken at the close of each of the years 1942, 1943, and 1944, and we were informed that such procedures were not performed by any other independent public accountants. In the absence of a physical inventory of work in process at March 31, 1946, we subsequently made test inspections of selected items to assure ourselves as to the existence of the inventory and the adequacy of the related accounting data. The inventories at the close of each of the years 1942 and 1944 were reviewed by us as to the basis of pricing and clerical accuracy and we inquired into the methods used by the corporation employees in determining physical quantities to ascertain that methods were employed which would assure reasonable accuracy. We were informed that an inventory was taken as at December 31, 1943, but we were advised that such inventory was lost and therefore was not available for our inspection. We were informed that no physical inventory was taken as of June 30, 1945. On the basis of the examinations and tests made by us, we have no reason to believe that the inventories as set forth in the accompanying statements are unfairly stated.

Although an inventory of work in process had not been taken since December 31, 1944, the auditors did not object to the company's decision also to omit such inventory at March 31, 1946. It subsequently developed that the accountants were aware of several shortcomings in the system of internal control. These are discussed on page **5·45**.

The Commission was also critical of the manner in which the accountants employed alternative auditing procedures in the absence of a physical

[3] 27 SEC 838 (1948). Also issued as ASR No. 64 (1948). See also ASR No. 67 (1949).

inventory. The accountants had doubts as to the dependability of the company's cost system, particularly with respect to the accounting for partial shipments, but they failed to check, even by test, any of the individual job cost sheets from which the list purported to represent work in process at March 31, 1946, was prepared, to determine that costs applicable to partial shipments had been eliminated. The auditors knew of the company's practice of making partial shipments, for they inquired regarding the method of removing such shipments. The Commission said it would not have been an involved procedure to test-check job cost sheets to determine that partial shipments had been accounted for properly. It meant merely the scrutiny of production orders to determine whether partial shipments were indicated and the examination of the applicable job cost sheets to see that they were relieved of costs applicable to partial shipments. No such procedure was followed.

The Commission concluded:

It is our conclusion that here again as we stated with reference to the auditing procedures followed in another case ". . . [the accountants'] failure to discover the gross overstatement of assets and of earnings is attributable to the manner in which the audit work was done. In carrying out the work they failed to employ the degree of vigilance, inquisitiveness, and analysis of the evidence available that is necessary in the professional undertaking and is recommended in all well-known and authoritative works on auditing." [4]

The SEC subsequently instituted proceedings under Rule 2(e) of its Rules of Practice to determine whether the privilage of practicing before the Commission should be denied to the accounting firm and two of its employees. [ASR No. 67 (1949)]. The Commission found: that the firm had failed to supervise the audit in the manner required by existing circumstances; that the senior accountant was negligent because of the inadequate manner in which he had employed alternative procedures; and that the office manager of the firm was negligent because the procedures followed under his supervision were not employed with due professional care.

Monroe Loan Society.—This case [3 SEC 407 (1938)] involved a stop-order proceeding under the 1933 Act following the disclosure of a defalcation at the registrant's Philadelphia branch. The manager of that branch had embezzled approximately half a million dollars, representing 25 per cent of the registrant's total assets and over 83 per cent of the Philadelphia branch assets.

Prior to the discovery of the defalcation in 1938 the accountants had uniformly confined their examination to the home office accounts in Newark, N. J., although they had been auditing the registrant's accounts reg-

[4] *In the Matter of McKesson & Robbins, Inc., Report on Investigation,* p. 443.

ularly since 1927. So far as the branches were concerned, the records at Newark consisted only of duplicate loan cards, daily reports, bank statements, canceled checks, and expense vouchers. Prior to 1938 no representative of the accountants had visited any branch office of the registrant for audit purposes, no notes or loan applications held at branch offices had been examined by the accountants, and no branch office loans were verified by confirmation with the borrower by the accountant.

The accountants reflected the extent of their investigation in their certificate as follows:

This examination did not include a verification of the records maintained at the branch offices of the corporation, but was confined to the records kept at the main office [street address], Newark, New Jersey, which included duplicate records of the several branch offices. The duplicate records are written up from daily reports submitted by the respective branch offices and were in agreement with monthly statements of the subsidiary companies. The branch bank accounts are controlled by the main office and were reconciled with independent confirmations from the various depositaries. *Our examination in respect to the branch office records was sufficient in scope to satisfy ourselves as to the correctness of those accounts.* [Emphasis added.]

A partner of the accounting firm testified that his firm did not examine the original records at registrant's branch offices because the arrangements with the registrant called for an audit of the home office accounts only. He considered the examination of the branch office accounts both desirable and necessary and had so informed officers of the registrant on numerous occasions, but had not insisted on such examination because he was "reasonably satisfied" that the registrant's system of internal check was adequate.

The Commission said there was some doubt that the accountants were actually familiar with the system of branch audit and control followed by the registrant. Had the accountants attempted fully to satisfy themselves concerning the internal controls, said the Commission, they would have discovered at least two areas in which the branch office supervisor was not following prescribed procedures; that is, he was not personally mailing to borrowers the confirmation of their accounts, and he was not insisting upon the verification by investigators employed for that purpose of the applications pertaining to a large majority of the loans made at the branch. Compliance with either of these requirements, said the SEC, undoubtedly would have disclosed the defalcations at an early date. The SEC held that the accountants had omitted procedures recognized as the essentials of an audit of a financial company such as the registrant. "The omission of an adequate examination constituted so complete a disregard of recognized accounting practice as to invalidate the accountant's original audit certificate and to impugn the integrity of the financial statements contained in the registration statement. . . ."

Metropolitan Personal Loan Co.—The evidence in this proceeding [2 SEC 812 (1937)] showed that during part of the period covered by the accountants' report they had not visited any of the registrant's branches outside of Allentown, Pa., and had not examined loan collateral. At the balance sheet date the accountants examined loans receivable and supporting documents of the Allentown branch—constituting about 15 per cent of the total outstanding loans. The Commission held that the following statement in the accountants' certificate was false and misleading:

> During all years the borrowers' ledger cards in the home office have been examined and totaled and supporting collateral examined, consisting of lease agreements, judgment notes, chattel mortgages, etc.

The accountant testified that at the balance sheet date no verification had been made of cash in banks, cash on hand, or loans payable. The Commission said:

> The certification by an independent accountant of the balance sheet of a small loan company, most of the assets of which, by their nature, are readily convertible into cash or are pledgable, is of little or no value without the actual examination or verification of such assets.

Coastal Finance Corporation.—This case [35 SEC 706 (1957)] involved the suspension of an exemption under Regulation A because of false and misleading statements in the offering circular and because the scope of audit made by the certifying accountant was inadequate. The company was engaged in the consumer finance business and operated twelve loan offices.

The independent accountants conducted surprise audits of each of the loan offices at least once a year. During the year 1954 it conducted these audits between May 17 and December 15. In 1955, however, the firm did not begin its schedule of annual examinations until August 16, and it was on this occasion that they discovered irregularities in the accounts.

The accountants' certification of the financial statements in the offering circular covered statements for June 30, 1955, and the six months then ended. Their certificate was dated August 3, 1955. Between January 1 and August 3, 1955, the accountants made no field examination of any offices. During this period its work was limited to bookkeeping activities at the home office. The SEC held that the representation in the accountants' certificate, with respect to the June 30, 1955 financial statements, that their examination was made in accordance with generally accepted auditing standards and accordingly included such tests of the accounting records and such other auditing procedures as were considered necessary, was inaccurate and misleading.

Illinois Zinc Company.—This case [6 SEC 851 (1940)] related to an inventory shortage which was concealed in the accounts and not detected by the certifying accountants. In the milling process employed by the company, dust losses were unavoidable. The normal dust loss throughout the industry was 2 per cent, and the company purported to follow the norm although its losses ran as high as 6 per cent of the ore milled. Failure to make adequate provision for dust losses resulted in inflation of the inventory accounts. On September 30, 1937 (the close of the registrant's fiscal year), the inventory on the company's books was 1,454 tons of concentrates when actually only 253 tons were on hand. The accountants relied on inventory certificates obtained from registrant's employees without independent verification of quantities.

To eliminate the shortage, it was decided to record no production at the company's mine and mill for the month of November, 1937, and to capitalize the actual cost of production of that month as development. The scheme worked as planned, with the result that in the financial statements for the quarter ended December 31, 1937, the shortage in the inventory account had been shifted to the development account, again without detection by the certifying accountants. In the balance sheet filed with the registration statement the development account was overstated by about $30,000; profits of an indeterminate period were similarly overstated.

The SEC said if the accountants had been more thorough and careful in their audit, the shortage and the method used to conceal it would have been discovered. The development account for the month of November, 1937, included about $2,000 for freight charges on ore shipments from mine to mill, which should have put the accountants on notice that the company was engaged in normal production during a period when it was supposed to have been engaged solely in development. The accountants, said the SEC, were derelict in not discovering the freight items.

The Commission also believed that the audit should have included an examination of the books at the plants and should not have been confined to the main office in Chicago, because of the decentralized accounting system in use. It stated:

In cases such as this, we believe that the requirements of a thorough audit are not met by a review of books and records at a point so far removed from the scene of operations that personal contact with employees engaged in the operations and those directly responsible for the bookkeeping entries is not possible.

Also, the SEC said, the accountants should have inspected the plants and products, and should have made "an appropriate verification of the inventory quantities." (As in the McKesson and Robbins case, generally accepted auditing standards at that time did not require the auditor to make a physical test of inventories; that procedure was adopted by the accounting profession at a later date.) The SEC was also critical of the company's accounting for depreciation, depletion, and amortization of development, and said that the accountants should have expressed in their certificate, in a definite and forthright manner, their disagreement with that policy.

Interstate Hosiery Mills, Inc.—In this case there was a material overstatement of assets and profits, the instigator of which was an accountant employed by the certifying accountants. A principal issue in the case was the review of the work of the staff accountant. A discussion of the case and a summary of the Commission's recommendations as to the review of the work of subordinates, begins on page **5·46**.

National Electric Signal Co.—The accountant who prepared the statements in this case [8 SEC 165 (1940)] testified that he had been employed "to try to straighten out the mess the books were in . . ."; that he had not made an audit; that the financial statements merely reflected the facts shown by the books and had been prepared without adequate verification; that certain items in the balance sheet had been improperly classified; that the bank account had not been reconciled for some time; and that he had been unable to reconcile it. The accountant's certificates were entirely silent as to these matters. The Commission commented that this was "a substantial deficiency, particularly in view of the concededly poor state of the books."

Franco Mining Corp.—The company's certifying accountant had seen neither books nor vouchers, nor had he seen evidence of them. He said that he had relied upon affidavits submitted to him by the officers of the company. The Commission said:

The apparent omission of any examination of the minute book of the corporation raises some doubt as to whether the accountant has in fact made a reasonable examination, but this we need not now decide. If an accountant submits a balance sheet without having access to the minute book and to proper disbursement vouchers, he should most certainly qualify his certificate by stating the basis upon which he made his audit, and the reasons why such investigation is deemed by him to be reasonable. [1 SEC 289 (1936)].

American Tung Grove Developments, Inc.—The certifying accountant in this case had failed to make any inquiry as to the existence of contingent liabilities and apparently made no attempt to determine the collectibility of the accounts receivable other than to accept the statement of an officer that the accounts were all good. These and other circumstances, said the SEC, "constitute a severe indictment of the value of his report." [8 SEC 62 (1940)].

National Boston Montana Mines Corp.—The facts in this case [2 SEC 249 (1937)] are set forth on page **26·47**. The SEC was critical of certain aspects of the examination made by the certifying accountant, since the accountant had not audited certain records, did not have access to other records, and to a large extent had relied on unverified information furnished to him by the chairman of the board of directors. These facts not only raised a question as to the accountant's independence, but also caused the SEC to find that the certificate was false and misleading in stating that the balance sheet was based upon the books and records of the corporation.

The Republic Co.—A question involved in this case [6 SEC 1076 (1940)] was the inclusion among the company's assets of notes received on the sale of the company's stock. The evidence showed that the notes were not only doubtful of collection, but that the company had no intention of pressing their collection. No investigation had been made of the financial integrity of the makers of the notes. At the time of filing, payments on 425 of 545 of such notes were delinquent. Despite the defaults, no serious efforts were made to collect the notes. "It is clear," the Commission said, "that the notes were at least doubtful of collection and some probably worthless."

In the SEC's view the preferable method of showing the notes would be as a deduction from capital, but it conceded that it may be proper to carry them among the assets. (Regulation S–X requires that receivables from subscriptions to capital stock be shown on the balance sheet as a deduction in the stockholders' equity section.) Under no circumstances, however, should the asset be carried at more than realizable value. The Commission found the accountant's certificate faulty in not taking exception to the company's financial statements.

Mining and Development Corp.—The SEC ruled on the inclusion in a balance sheet of property under a lease-purchase contract which was in default and subject to foreclosure. The balance sheet was dated April 30, 1936—the day before the default. The audit by independent public accountants took place in the latter part of May and the early part of June, 1936, so that the default existed at the time the audit was made. The balance sheet did not disclose the default. The accountant in charge of the examination testified that he was not aware of the default. He had accepted signed certificates from the board chairman's personal auditor and from registrant's treasurer to the effect that there were no contingent liabilities other than those shown on the books, and that this had foreclosed for him any inquiry as to default on the contract. The SEC said:

It is clear that an adequate audit would have disclosed that, under the terms of the (contract), registrant's interest . . . was in jeopardy as an asset of the corporation at the time the audit was made, and hence that, in the absence of disclosure of this fact, the balance sheet figure became highly misleading the day after the date of the balance sheet, and continued to be misleading at the time the audit was made and at the time the registration statement was filed. [1 SEC 793 (1936)].

Reiter-Foster Oil Corp.—The SEC considered an unusual transaction between this corporation and persons connected with the management. The corporation transferred practically all of its producing properties on December 22, 1934, to Mr. A, who had no official connection with the company but had been designated to procure financing for it. He in turn executed an instrument of trust which provided that the properties would secure various claims against the company asserted by him and persons connected with the management. The claims were based on services previously rendered by the beneficiaries of the trust. The trust agreement provided that if the claims secured thereby were not paid within six months from the date of the instrument, absolute title should vest in Mr. A for the benefit of the claimants.

The debts were not paid at the end of the six-month period. The original cost of the properties was $191,839. They had a book value of $145,593. In 1935 the company gave full effect to the literal terms of the trust instrument, and wrote off the properties and eliminated the debts secured thereby. The book loss of $132,008 on this transaction was included in an item of $136,349 designated as loss from "sale of capital assets" in the income statement.

There seems to have been some doubt as to whether the trust was, in effect, an absolute conveyance or merely a mortgage. As late as May, 1937, one of the persons whose claim was secured by the trust believed that the properties should be returned to the company on payment of the debt. Furthermore, in July, 1936, the company executed what was in effect a second mortgage on the properties in the A trust to secure another debt, thereby indicating that it believed it still had an equity in the trust properties. The SEC did not decide whether the trust instruments constituted a mortgage or a conveyance. If a mortgage, the pledged assets should have been carried in the balance sheet together with the debts secured thereby. If a conveyance, said the Commission, there should have been a clear disclosure of the nature of the transaction resulting in a book loss of $132,008. "It was misleading," the SEC said, "to lump a loss of such proportions and so unusual in nature along with other losses in an item designated 'sale of capital assets.'" The Commission further stated:

If [the registrant's accounting firm] exercised reasonable care in the conduct of its audit, it should have noted the unusual nature of the transaction and, accordingly, should have insisted that appropriate disclosure be made in the financial statements. Absent such disclosure in the financial statements, it was incumbent upon the firm to point out the facts in its certificate. The requisite disclosure not appearing in either the financial statements or the accountant's certificate, we must hold both materially deficient. [6 SEC 1051 (1940)].

Adolf Gobel, Inc.—This case [*In the Matter of Adolf Gobel, Inc. and Anthony DeAngelis,* 35 SEC 535–539 (1954)] involved a substantial overstatement of assets which, for a time, escaped detection by the company's independent public accountants. The securities of Adolf Gobel, Incorporated, a corporation engaged in the meat packing business, were listed for trading on a national securities exchange. The company mailed an annual report to its stockholders, covering the fiscal year ended November 1, 1952. The report, certified by Gobel's independent accountant, showed a loss of $437,000. After the report was mailed and before any statements had been filed with the SEC or the exchange, it came to the accountant's attention that the loss was understated by approximately $213,000. This was on the basis of information that the accountant obtained after he had completed his audit. The accountant brought the matter to the attention of the SEC which suspended exchange trading in Gobel's stock and instituted an investigation. The suspension was continued for almost a year. On February 18, 1954, the suspension was lifted and exchange trading in the Gobel stock was permitted to be resumed. In the meantime the company was in reorganization under Chapter X of the Bankruptcy Act and filed financial statements with the SEC, accompanied by a report of a different firm of public accountants. The new accountants reported that they were unable to give an over-all opinion on the statements because: (1) they were not present to supervise the taking of a physical inventory, which represented approximately one-third of the total assets; (2) the lack of internal controls made it impossible to ascertain ownership of the physical inventory; (3) the books and records were not kept in conformity with generally accepted accounting principles; and (4) they did not verify by direct correspondence any of the assets or liabilities.

(Readers may be interested to learn that the perpetrator of the deception in the Adolf Gobel case, Anthony DeAngelis, went on to far greater hoaxes and deceptions. DeAngelis was the owner of Allied Crude Vegetable Oil Refining Corporation which perpetrated the incredible "salad oil" swindle of the 1960's and caused losses running into more than $100 million to issuers of warehouse receipts against purportedly vast quantities of edible oils that were virtually non-existent.)

Tucker Corp.—The SEC's decision in this case [26 SEC 261 (1947)] noted that the auditors' certificate, as originally filed, failed to reflect adequate information as to the extent of the verification made by the auditors of certain transactions with promoters, particularly an item of $100,000 paid for claims representing amounts asserted to have been expended on behalf of the company. As to this, the *amended* certificate of the auditors stated: "We cannot of our own knowledge state that the sum referred to was expended for the benefit of Tucker Corporation."

The amended certificate also pointed out that the auditors had received no information showing that a sum borrowed by a promoter personally and repaid by the corporation to the lender had been expended for the benefit of the corporation. The auditors also stated, in their amended certificate, that they were unable to ascertain the cost to the promoter of assets transferred by him to a corporation owned by his mother and of which he was general manager, and eventually to Tucker Corporation.

This case is also discussed on page **24·53**.

Platoro Gold Mines.—This decision related to an accountant's certificate based on an inadequate examination, and is discussed on page **24·54**.

Health Institute, Inc. (NSL).—The Commission's decision in this case [ASR No. 68 (1949)] resulted from proceedings under Rule 2(e) of the Commission's Rules of Practice to determine whether an accountant's privilege of practicing before the Commission should be withdrawn. The case resulted from a registration statement filed by Health Institute, Inc. (NSL). The registrant's balance sheet included, among other things, amounts for construction work in progress and organization expense, the total of which was offset by an amount due the president and principal promoter of the company. It appeared that the accountant had examined vouchers in support of only a small portion of the amount due the president. The accountant had relied on a written statement by the president that the company owed him the amount shown in the balance sheet. The accountant's working papers showed that he participated with the president in drafting the written statement which was later typed and signed by the president. Such procedure, said the SEC, does not constitute adequate verification, and the statement in the accountant's certificate that his "examination was made in accordance with generally accepted auditing standards applicable in the circumstances" was manifestly false. The president later disclaimed the purported indebtedness and admitted that he had not made expenditures for the account of the corporation in the amounts shown in the balance sheet. In a subsequent amendment to the registration statement, the amounts in question were omitted from the balance sheet.

Thomascolor, Inc.—Following the Commission's decision in the Thomascolor case, the SEC instituted a proceeding under Rule 2(e) of its Rules of Practice to determine whether the accountant's privilege of practicing before the Commission should be suspended or withdrawn [ASR No. 73 (1952)]. In that case, the principal issues involved dealt with the accounting for intangible assets acquired for capital stock. In the balance sheet filed in respect of one of the Thomascolor predecessors, an amount had been assigned to "license agreement" which the SEC maintained represented promotion services. The accountants conceded that when stock is issued for promotion services, the consideration received therefor should be shown in the balance sheet as promotion services and not included in property accounts. The accountants maintained that in this case promotion services were not involved and that the evidence available to them in connection with their audit so indicated. The SEC disagreed, saying:

We cannot agree with respondents' position that the evidence that no promotional services were involved was so clear that they were justified in accepting it as a fact without further inquiry. It was evident that the stock in question had been issued in connection with the promotion of the company, particularly in view of the facts that it had been treated as "promotional shares" by the California Division of Corporations and had been referred to as "promotion stock" by various persons associated with the enterprise. In such circumstances and in the light of the many cases in which problems had arisen with respect to the description of promotional items, there was an affirmative duty on respondents as accountants practicing before this Commission to make certain that the stock was not issued for promotion services. In our opinion respondents unjustifiably placed too much weight on the language of the permit as indicating that the license was the sole consideration for the issuance of the stock. Adequate inquiry into the background of the issuance of the permit was not made.

Review of Client's System of Internal Control.—In the standard short form of accountant's report (see Chapter **24**), the "scope" paragraph refers to compliance with "generally accepted auditing standards." These standards include, among other things, a proper study and evaluation of the existing internal control as a basis for reliance thereon and for the determination of the resultant extent of the tests to which auditing procedures are to be restricted. [SAP No. 33 (1963), p. 16.] While the study and evaluation represent the requirements of good practice generally, they also represent SEC requirements.

The SEC has said that the examination of the client's system of internal control is "a most important step on balance sheet audits or examinations" and has a twofold purpose:

A correct appraisal of the client's system is needed not only to ascertain the proportion of transactions necessary to be examined but also the type of tests necessary to be made in order to determine the reliability of the records specifically examined and by inference (though not conclusive) of those not specifically examined. In other words, to reach his conclusion as to the reliability of the figures contained on the financial statements, the auditor will examine certain records and will make various tests not only based on the company's records but independent of them. The proportion of the records to be examined and the type of the tests to be made will depend upon how much confidence as to reliability of the records can, in the first instance, be placed in the company's own system—whether because of internal check and control arising automatically from division of functions of personnel or from physical and mechanical checks, or as the result of internal audits. . . . Finally it seems to us that an examination of the system of internal check is not to be limited to particular accounting functions but should lead to a full knowledge of the manner in which, persons by whom, and place where the transactions are handled. . . .[5]

In the McKesson case, the certifying auditors employed the questionnaire method in developing information in respect of the company's system of internal control. The SEC said that, on paper, the procedures employed by such accountants would appear to be designed to produce a comprehensive review of the client's accounting procedures and the relationship of the various members of the office staff affected by the audit. The results obtained, however, were weakened by the failure to carry out the item of the questionnaire which called for an outline of the company's organization showing each department and to whom it is responsible. This failure, said the Commission, left undisclosed, at least in writing, that George Dietrich (alias George Musica), the assistant treasurer, who, according to the 1932 questionnaire, controlled the cashiers, signed checks, supervised the cashiers who reconciled the bank accounts, held the petty cash fund, opened the mail, held unclaimed wages, mailed regular monthly statements to customers, passed on credits, held securities, authorized capital expenditures, signed notes payable and acceptances, and authorized loans to officials and employees, *also*, under Coster (alias Philip Musica), ran the foreign crude drug business (which comprised over 65 per cent of all business done at Bridgeport) at least to the extent that his initials or verbal clearance furnished the internal authority respecting all foreign crude drug purchase and sales transactions.

. . . Alert observation of the system in operation, whether weak or strong, affords one of the best opportunities for the detection of fraud. Nor can this requirement for observation of the procedures be satisfied without a full knowledge and careful testing of the procedures and this in turn cannot be accomplished by a mere interrogation of officials without independent observation of the basic facts.[6]

In summarizing this aspect of the McKesson matter, the SEC said:

We are convinced by the record that the review of the system of internal check and control at the Bridgeport offices of McKesson & Robbins was carried out in an unsatisfactory manner. The testimony of the experts leads us to the further conclusion that this vital and basic problem of all audits for the purpose of certifying financial statements has been treated in entirely too casual a manner by many accountants. Since in examinations of financial statements of corporations whose securities are publicly owned the procedures of testing and sampling are employed in most cases, it appears to us that the necessity for a comprehensive knowledge of the client's system of internal check and control cannot be overemphasized.[7]

[5] *In the Matter of McKesson & Robbins, Inc., Report on Investigation* (1940), p. 378.
[6] *Ibid.*, p. 383.
[7] *Ibid.*, p. 6.

In *Drayer-Hanson* [ASR No. 64 (1948)] there was an overstatement of inventories and surplus arising from the company's failure to relieve the inventory accounts for partial shipments. The certifying accountants did not insist on a physical inventory of work in process and did not discover the overstatement of inventory in a balance sheet which they certified. At the SEC hearings following the disclosure of the error in the inventory, the senior accountant in charge of the examination for the certifying firm testified that one of his first steps in the examination was to make a review of the system and controls over a fairly long period, as a result of which he found a number of deficiencies, including (1) there was no tie-in between units in the plant and the dollar amounts of inventories; (2) the raw material account was not supported by a detailed stores record in dollars; (3) the segregation of material in the plant was not entirely adequate; (4) requisitions were not being prepared for all material withdrawn from stores, and frequent retroactive requisitions necessary to bring the costs up to the proper material consumption were noted; (5) no record was kept in the accounting department or the cost department of the units manufactured to date; (6) while a job was still open, the applicable job cost sheet in the cost department would not show how many units had been produced, or shipped, applicable to that job to any particular date; (7) no record was kept on the job cost sheets of units and dollars transferred to finished goods either for partially or entirely completed jobs; and (8) many instances were noted where no record was made on the job cost sheets of partial shipments, either to customers or stock. The accountant concluded that while a revision of the cost system appeared to be in order, he, nevertheless, would be able to use alternative procedures to assure himself with respect to work in process "that the inventory was there."

The SEC concluded:

It seems clear also that the representatives of the auditors should have made a more thorough examination of the registrant's system of internal control and its cost system, and should have determined that they were being operated effectively before acquiescing in the omission of a physical inventory of work in process as at March 31, 1946. And once they found, as they did in the course of their examination, that there was, in fact, no effective system of internal control and the alleged job cost system existed more in theory than in fact, they should have insisted that a work-in-process inventory be taken as at April 30, 1946. Notwithstanding these conditions, the company represented that there was in operation a controlled job cost system and the auditors represented in their certificate that they satisfied themselves as to the adequacy of such system and the dependability of the company's system of internal control. We find these misrepresentations to be misleading. It seems to us, however, that the auditors' dereliction in these respects is overshadowed by the inadequate manner in which they employed alternative auditing procedures in the absence of a physical inventory.

This case is also discussed on page **5**·33.

The Monroe Loan Society case [3 SEC 407 (1938)] involved a defalcation at a branch office of the company which was concealed in the accounts and not discovered by the certifying accountants. The accountants had not examined the original records of the branch in question because they were reasonably satisfied that the company's system of internal check was adequate. The SEC said there was some doubt that the accountants were actually familiar with the system of branch audit and control followed by the company. This aspect of the case is discussed on page **5**·34.

In *Illinois Zinc Company* [6 SEC 851 (1940)] there was also a purposeful overstatement of assets which was not detected by the certifying accountants. The company's accounting system was decentralized. All operating and fixed asset accounts, inventory controls, cost ledgers, and related journals and vouchers were located at the plants and were sent to the company's main office where the audit was conducted. "In our opinion," said the SEC, "the audit should have been conducted at the plants."

In cases such as this, we believe that the requirements of a thorough audit are not met by a review of books and records at a point so far removed from the scene of operations that personal contact with employees engaged in the operations and those directly responsible for the bookkeeping entries is not possible.

If the audit had been conducted at the plants, the accountants would have been able to familiarize themselves with the plant layout, the operating methods, the nature of the products, the personnel of the accounting department, and the methods of internal check and control. Leading accountants are of the opinion that accountants should familiarize themselves with these matters. Plainly, familiarity with these matters could not have been obtained in the instant case without visiting the plants. Yet, [the certifying accountants] made only one such visit; they visited the Peru, Illinois, plant in January, 1935.

Additional information concerning this case appears on page **5**·36.

Review of Work of Subordinates.—From the viewpoint of the day-to-day practice of public accountants, the decision in *Interstate Hosiery Mills, Inc.* [4 SEC 706 (1939)] is one of the most important of the Commission's decisions. The company had filed false financial statements with the SEC and the exchange on which the company's securities were listed for trading. The financial statements overstated substantially the company's assets and earnings. The author of the falsifications was Raymond Marien, an employee of the certifying firm of accountants. Exposure came in 1938 on the accidental discovery that Marien had forged several checks on the company's bank account. Representatives of the company and the accounting firm called on Marien in an effort to obtain an explanation of what he had done. He said only that he must have been crazy, that he received nothing for what he had done, and that he did not know why he had done it.

The exchange suspended trading in the company's securities, and the SEC instituted an investigation to determine whether the company's securities should be delisted. One of the principal issues at the hearing was whether the accountants had exercised due care in reviewing Marien's work.

The testimony at the hearing did not show that the accounting firm's review of Marien's work was less extensive than that ordinarily made by accounting firms. Expert witnesses testified as to the usual review procedure followed by independent public accountants. The SEC said:

. . . If we accept the views of these expert witnesses as to the usual practice followed by independent public accountants in reviewing the work of those responsible for the actual carrying out of audit procedures, in our opinion the practice requires thorough revision.

The review upon which an accounting firm assumes responsibility for work done by subordinates, said the SEC, must be more than a series of perfunctory questions as to the performance of particular items in an audit program; explanations of unusual items should not be accepted by a reviewer without detailed support in the working papers. The review should be designed, in the SEC's view, with two objectives in mind: first, to insure the integration of the original work papers with the financial statements; second, to analyze in a searching manner the ultimate facts developed in the course of the actual audit. The Commission said:

. . . An adequate review with the first purpose in mind should serve not only to disclose intentional or accidental misstatements, but should also serve as a method of internal check and control on the work of the firm's subordinates. This branch of the review, it seems to us, need not necessarily be carried out by a partner, but should at least be done by one well versed in the procedures adopted by the firm and in the general principles and terminology of auditing and accounting. If not a partner of the firm, such review should, in our opinion, be made by persons who are independent of those actually performing or supervising the audit work as well as of those who prepared the draft of the financial statements. The second branch of the review is designed to enable the accounting firm to interpret intelligently the figures it has obtained and to which it is to certify. This part of the review should, it seems to us, be made by a person, preferably a partner, qualified by his knowledge of sound accounting principles and his familiarity with the accounting phases of the industry and the more important problems of the particular company. In this manner the facts ascertained by competent employees can be subjected to the independent and broader judgment of a more experienced person who can by searching inquiry of the supervisor or senior and by examination of significant items in the work papers and schedules, reach an informed judgment both as to the adequacy of the audit work done and as to the integrity and clarity of the financial statements themselves. . . .

The reader's attention is directed to the sentence in the foregoing extract reading as follows: "If not a partner of the firm, such review should, in our opinion, be made by persons who are independent of those actually performing or supervising the audit work as well as those who prepared the draft of the financial statements." The author does not construe this sentence as restricting the reviewer to a review function only. In some accounting firms, for example, the review with the "first purpose" that the SEC had in mind is made by so-called "managers" which is the highest classification on the firm's audit staff. Below the manager classification are "supervisors," who, as the name implies, supervise the day-to-day conduct of the audit engagement under the over-all direction of a manager, who, in turn, is responsible to a partner (or partners) in charge of the engagement.

Red Bank Oil Company also involved the failure of the head of an accounting firm to make an adequate review of the work of a subordinate. It appeared that the latter had not made the critical and objective examination which is the obligation of an independent public accountant. The case is discussed at length in Chapters **24** and **26**.

In *McKesson and Robbins* the SEC inquired, among other things, as to the review procedure employed by the certifying accountants. The SEC said:

> . . . It seems to us that such figures as were set forth concerning particulars of the foreign crude drug business and indicating its remarkable growth with all profits going back into increased inventories and receivables should have suggested the desirability of independent inquiry to a person with some knowledge of the drug trade. If review by a partner is to prevent less experienced staff men from being too easily satisfied by explanations of clients and to keep them from erroneous conclusions as to the satisfactory state of the clients' affairs, it would appear necessary that the partner have had experience with other companies in the same line of business or else undertake to inform himself in respect to the industry as a basis for a sound judgment.
> . . . The review of the work did not result in a searching analysis of the ultimate facts developed in the course of the actual audit, because, although performed by a partner of many years' experience, it was not done by a person sufficiently familiar with the business practices of the client's industry, or with a sufficient interest in the basic questions of internal check and control to comprehend the significance of the facts reported.[8]

In September 1967 the AICPA Committee on Auditing Procedure issued its SAP No. 39 dealing with the subject of "Working Papers." These are the records kept by the independent auditor of the procedures he followed, the tests he performed, the information he obtained, and the conclusions he reached pertinent to his examination. The Statement, among other things, sets forth guidelines with respect to the quantity, type, and content of working papers, although it recognizes that these factors will vary with the circumstances. Generally, however, the working papers

[8] *In the Matter of McKesson & Robbins, Inc., Report on Investigation,* pp. 427–28.

should include, or show, that the work of any assistants had been supervised and reviewed, thereby indicating observance of one of the generally accepted auditing standards which is to the effect that the work is to be adequately planned and assistants, if any, are to be properly supervised.

Auditor's Duty to Disclose After-Acquired Information.—In Chapter **28** of this book there is a discussion of certain aspects of the Yale Express case (cited *Fischer et al. v. Kletz et al.*). One aspect of the case involves the discovery by the auditors that Yale's 1963 financial statements, certified by them, were materially incorrect in that they overstated net income and net assets.

The discovery of the error was made in the course of a "non-audit" engagement which the accountants performed for Yale. Thus the accountants' relationship to Yale was changed from that of an independent public accountant with responsibilities under the 1934 Act (to which Yale, as a listed company, was subject) to that of a management consultant.

There was a factual dispute as to when the auditors learned about the error and when it was disclosed to public agencies. Inasmuch as the case was settled without a trial, the resolution of the dispute is not a matter of public record.

The plaintiffs contended that disclosure of the error in the statements was not made until about a year later when Yale's annual report for 1964 was issued. (The author has been informed, however, that disclosure was made to the SEC and the New York Stock Exchange in February 1965.) The 1964 report also included the figures for 1963 on a restated basis. A note to the financial statements in the report discussed the restatement and indicated the nature and amount of the revisions.

A number of suits were brought against various persons (including the auditors) alleging that the error in the 1963 financial statements should have been disclosed, as far as the auditors were concerned, as soon as they learned about it. The auditors moved to dismiss this portion of the complaint. They contended that no legal or ethical duty existed which imposed on an auditor the obligation to voluntarily reveal (other than to his client) confidential information which he receives after he has certified financial statements which contradicts those statements. In their view the ethical considerations pointed the other way since the auditor is bound to treat such information—acquired in the course of a non-audit engagement—in confidence.

The SEC, as *amicus curiae*, filed a memorandum with the court having jurisdiction in opposition to the auditors' motion. The Commission took no position as to the factual validity of the allegations in the complaint, but assumed for the purpose of its memorandum that the facts as pleaded were true, and limited its participation to the issue of an accountant's duty under the SEC statutes to disclose his subsequently acquired knowledge that the financial statements he has certified are false.

The SEC said that the auditors' contention referred to above (namely, that no legal or ethical duty existed to disclose after-acquired information) represented neither good law nor sound accounting practice. The Commission contended that an accountant may not be silent if he knows that financial statements filed with the Commission and stock exchanges, which bear his certificate, are false. In evaluating the securities of a listed company, the SEC maintained, public investors have a right to rely on the accountant's certificate "as a continuing representation on the part of the accountant, that the statements which bear his certificate present fairly the financial position of the registrant as of the date of the financial statements". The SEC said also that failure by an accountant to disclose that financial statements of a company that he has certified are false, when he has become aware of that fact, is, under SEC Rule 10b-5, "an act or course of business which operates as a fraud on persons in connection with the purchase or sale of securities of that company."

Part of the Commission's argument was based on the requirements under Section 11 of the 1933 Act when a registration statement becomes effective without the accountant's knowledge and the statement contains an important error or omission. In such circumstances, subsection (b) of Section 11 enumerates the steps that the accountant should take. The independent accountants for Yale, in their reply memorandum, pointed out that Section 11, relied on by the SEC, did not apply to the case at bar since a registration statement under the 1933 Act had not been filed. They also said that it was significant that the 1934 Act (which was applicable to Yale and the accountants) did not contain a provision similar to Section 11 of the 1933 Act.

The accountants also observed in their reply memorandum that neither the plaintiffs nor the SEC faced up to certain questions that were relevant if indeed the accountants had the duty to disclose what was alleged by the plaintiffs and the SEC. Such questions included the following:

> For how long a period of time would the purported duty to disclose exist?
> To whom would the duty run?
> In what manner should the notification be accomplished?
> Does liability exist if the after-acquired knowledge is obtained in connection with the examination of a different client?
> Does liability exist if the after-acquired knowledge is obtained by a different auditor?

Commenting on the SEC's *amicus curiae* memorandum, a prominent lawyer wrote: ". . . The SEC brief had little statutory grounds to support it. A number of lawyers regarded it as more of an emotional than a legal plea." [9]

As indicated in the discussion of this case in Chapter **28**, the judge filed an opinion which appeared to adopt the SEC's conclusions if not its reasoning.

The SEC's memorandum was dated November 9, 1966. In October 1969, the AICPA's Committee on Auditing Procedure issued an authoritative statement on the same subject. It is designated SAP No. 41 and is entitled "Subsequent Discovery of Facts Existing at the Date of the Auditor's Report." Prior to the issuance of this Statement, there was no authoritative professional pronouncement dealing with the obligation of the auditor to disclose information that comes to his attention after he has certified financial statements, which information convinces him that the statements were materially erroneous when they were issued. It seems clear that the AICPA Statement grew partially out of the SEC memorandum, the judge's opinion, and the profession's recognition of the vacuum which existed with respect to the point involved.

Under SAP No. 41, if such after-acquired information comes to the attention of the auditor, it is clear that something has to be done. The AICPA Statement lists in detail what needs to be done by way of verifying the information, discussing the matter with the client, and advising him of the disclosures that need to be made. If the client refuses to make the required disclosures, the Statement recites the steps which the auditor should take.

Familiarity with Client's Business.—Most accountants would probably contend that an auditor cannot do a thoroughly professional job unless he is familiar with the client's products, methods, and business. Without exception, all of the expert witnesses who appeared in the McKesson and Robbins hearings testified generally that they expected their staffs to become familiar with the trade or industry of the client before going on the job or, at least, before finishing it the first time. The SEC stated its views on this question as follows:

. . . While the evidence before us is not conclusive that most other accountants would have done more, it does not seem unreasonable to us to expect an accountant to have sufficient interest in his client's business to learn enough independently about that trade or industry to give him a background for his work and a basis for appraising the operations of his client. Failure to do this in this case was an omission of the first magnitude.[10]

See also the comment regarding this case under "Review of Work of Subordinates."

[9] Walter J. Coakley, "Accountants' Legal Liability," *The Ohio CPA,* Winter 1968, p. 41.

[10] *In the Matter of McKesson & Robbins, Inc., Report on Investigation,* p. 376.

Examination of Securities of Investment Companies.—The custody of securities of regulated investment companies is subject to SEC rules. Where the securities are held by a member of a national securities exchange, the arrangement must be pursuant to a written contract meeting the requirements of Rule 270.17f–1. Among other things, this rule provides as follows:

(4) Such securities and investments shall be verified by actual examination at the end of each annual and semiannual fiscal period by an independent public accountant retained by the registered management investment company, and shall be examined by such accountant at least one other time, chosen by him, during the fiscal year. Certificates of such independent public accountant stating that he has made an examination of such securities and investments, and describing the nature of the examination, shall be transmitted to the Commission promptly after each such examination.

The securities of a regulated investment company may be maintained in its custody only in accordance with the provisions of Rule 270.17f–2. Investments maintained by such company with a bank or other company whose functions and physical facilities are supervised by federal or state authority under any arrangement whereunder the directors, officers, employees, or agents of the investment company are authorized or permitted to withdraw investments upon their mere receipt, are deemed to be in the custody of the investment company. The rule provides, among other things, as follows:

(f) Such securities and similar investments shall be verified by complete examination by an independent public accountant retained by the investment company at least three times during each fiscal year, at least two of which shall be chosen by such accountant without prior notice to such company. A certificate of such accountant, stating that he has made an examination of such securities and investments and describing the nature and extent of the examination shall be transmitted to the Commission by the accountant promptly after each such examination.

The SEC has issued an opinion of its Chief Accountant concerning the nature and scope of examination by independent public accountants required by the foregoing rules [ASR No. 27 (1941)]. The examination and the accountants' certificate under Rule 270.17f–2 should include: (a) securities on deposit in a vault or other depository maintained by a bank or other company whose function and physical facilities are supervised by federal or state authority; (b) securities which are collateralized to the extent of their full market value; (c) securities hypothecated, pledged, or placed in escrow for the account of such registered company; and (d) securities in transit. The SEC's Chief Accountant stated:

In order to make a complete examination of the securities, it is, in my opinion, necessary for the accountant not only to make a physical examination of the securities themselves, or in certain cases to obtain confirmation, but also to reconcile the physical count or confirmation with the book records. Furthermore, in my opinion it is a necessary prerequisite to such a reconciliation that there have been made an appropriate examination of the investment accounts and supporting records, including an adequate check or analysis of the security transactions since the last examination and the entries pertaining thereto. While the certificate filed must describe the nature and extent of the examination made, it is not necessary that each step taken be set out; instead, there should be included in the certificate in general terms an appropriate description of the scope of the examination of the accounts and the physical examination or confirmation of the securities.

Finally, in order to meet the requirements of . . . [Rule 270.17f–2] the certificate should comply with the usual technical requirements as to dating, salutation and manual signature and, in addition to the description of the examination made, should set forth:

(a) the date of the physical count and verification, and the period for which the investment accounts and transactions were examined;
(b) a clear designation of the depository;
(c) whether the examination was made without prior notice to the company; and
(d) the results of the examination.

With respect to Rule 270.17f–1, the Chief Accountant said that paragraph (4) of that rule involves substantially the same considerations as those of paragraph (f) of Rule 270.17f–2, and the discussion quoted above is therefore also applicable to the examination and certificate required by such paragraph (4).

The SEC also set forth its views regarding the accounting for investment securities owned by registered investment companies in ASR No. 113 (1969) and ASR No. 118 (1970). The former relates to "restricted securities" and the latter to securities other than "restricted securities".

The releases discuss the date as of which purchase and sale transactions should be reflected in the financial statements of the investment company and the valuation of securities and other assets of the company for the purpose of preparing financial statements and computing the net asset value and pricing the company's shares. The releases set forth the procedures to be followed by the company's independent public accountants in substantiating the existence of the portfolio and in verifying the valuation of the individual securities. All of the foregoing are discussed in Chapter **4**.

Release No. 118 also recognizes that, in certain circumstances, the independent accountant may not be in a position to furnish a conventional unqualified certificate with respect to an investment company's portfolio. This matter and the form of certificate appropriate in the circumstances are discussed in Chapter **25**.

Audit Requirements for Form X–17A–5.—Under the 1934 Act reports of financial condition must be filed by certain members of national securities exchanges, and brokers and dealers in securities. The reports are filed on Form X–17A–5, and its content is described on page **15·39**. The report is principally of a financial nature and must be accompanied by a certificate of an independent public accountant. A suggested form of accountants' certificate appears in Chapter **25**.

An examination made for the purpose of certifying the financial statements in Form X–17A–5 must comply with certain audit requirements prescribed by the SEC. These are as follows:

The audit shall be made in accordance with generally accepted auditing standards and shall include a review of the accounting system, the internal accounting control and procedures for safeguarding securities including appropriate tests thereof for the period since the prior examination date. It shall include all procedures necessary under the circumstances to substantiate the assets and liabilities and securities and commodities positions as of the date of the responses to the financial questionnaire and to permit the expression of an opinion by the independent public accountant as to the financial condition of the respondent at that date. Based upon such audit, the accountant shall comment upon any material inadequacies found to exist in: (a) the accounting system; (b) the internal accounting control; (c) procedures for safeguarding securities; (d) the practices and procedures employed in complying with Rule 17a–13 and in the resolution of securities differences; and shall indicate any corrective action taken or proposed.

The scope of the audit shall include the following procedures, but nothing herein shall be construed as limiting the audit or permitting the omission of any additional audit procedure which an independent public accountant would deem necessary under the circumstances. As of the audit date the independent public accountant shall:

(1) Compare ledger accounts with the trial balances obtained from the general and private ledgers and prove the aggregates of subsidiary ledgers with their respective controlling accounts.

(2) Account for by physical examination and comparison with the books and records: all securities, including those held in segregation and safekeeping; material amounts of currency and tax stamps; warehouse receipts; and other assets on hand, in vault, in box or otherwise in physical possession. Control shall be maintained over such assets during the course of the physical examination and comparison.

(3) Verify securities in transfer or in transit between offices of respondent.

(4) Balance positions in all securities and spot and future commodities as shown by the books and records at the audit date.

(5) Reconcile balances shown by bank statements with cash accounts. After giving ample time for clearance of outstanding checks and transfers of funds, the independent public accountant shall obtain from depositaries bank statements and cancelled checks of the accounts and by appropriate audit procedures substantiate the reconciliation as of the audit date.

(6) Obtain written confirmations with respect to the following (see Note):
(a) Bank balances and other deposits.

(b) Open contractual positions and deposits of funds with clearing corporations and associations.

(c) Money borrowed and detail of collateral.

(d) Accounts, securities, commodities and commitments carried for the respondent by others.

(e) Details of:
  (i) Securities borowed
  (ii) Securities loaned
  (iii) Securities failed to deliver
  (iv) Securities failed to receive
  (v) Contractual commitments (see General Instruction B.11 for Form X–17A–5).

(f) Customers', partners', officers', directors', and respondents' accounts. Confirmation of these accounts may be in the form of a written acknowledgment of the accuracy of the statement of money balances, securities and/or commodities positions, and open contractual commitments (other than uncleared "regular way" purchases and sales of securities) accompanying the first request for confirmation mailed by the independent public accountant. Customers' accounts without balances, position or commitments, and accounts closed since the last prior audit shall be confirmed on a test basis.

(g) Borrowings and accounts covered by "satisfactory subordination agreements."

(h) Guarantees in cases where required to protect accounts guaranteed as of audit date.

(i) All other accounts which in the opinion of the independent public accountant should be confirmed.

Note: Compliance with requirements for obtaining written confirmation with respect to the above accounts shall be deemed to have been made if requests for confirmation have been mailed by the independent public accountant in an envelope bearing his own return address and second requests are similarly mailed to those not replying to the first requests, together with such auditing procedures as may be necessary; provided, however, that with respect to customers' accounts closed since the last prior audit the accountant may use either positive or negative confirmation requests; and it is further provided that with respect to periodic investment plans sponsored by member firms of a national securities exchange, whose members are exempted from Rule 15c3–1 by paragraph (b)(2) thereof, the independent public accountant examining the financial statements of the originating member firm may omit direct written confirmation of such plan accounts with customers when, in his judgment, such procedures are not necessary, if (1) the originating member firm does not receive or hold securities belonging to such plan accounts and does not receive or hold funds for such accounts, except the initial payment which is promptly transmitted to the custodian; (2) the custodian is a member firm of such national securities exchange and files certified reports complying with Rule 17a–5 in connection with which the customers' accounts are confirmed by an independent public accountant; and (3) funds and securities held by the custodian for each such customer's account are reconciled with the records of the originating member firm as of the date of the most recent audit of the custodian.

(7) Obtain a written statement from the proprietor, partner (if a partnership) or officer (if a corporation) as to the assets, liabilities, and accountabilities, contingent or otherwise, not recorded on the books of the respondent.

(8) Verify the computation of the ratio of aggregate indebtedness to net capital at the audit date and review the procedures followed in making the periodic computations required under the provisions of Rule 17a–3(a) (11).

(9) Review the practices and procedures employed for the making of the securities examinations, counts, verifications, comparisons and the recordation of differences required by Rule 17a–13, and the methods employed in the resolution of the differences uncovered.

Note: Provisions of Rule 17a–5 require that the reports of certain brokers and dealers be audited by a certified public accountant or public accountant who shall be in fact independent. With respect to qualifications of accountants, accountant's certificate, opinions to be expressed, and exceptions, please refer to Rule 17a–5.

Form X–17A–5 was extensively revised in 1967. In its release announcing the revised form, the SEC said:

In the audit of a broker or dealer in securities it has long been recognized that for full effectiveness the audit should be commenced at a time unannounced to anyone associated with the broker-dealer. This procedure is now widely followed in the audit of larger broker-dealers. It is recommended that the independent public accountant have an arrangement with his client under which the examination and audit can be made on such an unannounced basis.

Commenting on the foregoing recommendation, John J. Mulcare, the then chairman of the AICPA committee on stock brokerage accounting and auditing, said that it is expected that accountants will follow the SEC's recommendations, although they are not required to do so. (*The Journal of Accountancy,* January 1968, p. 55) He said that there are a few cases where this might be deemed to be unduly burdensome, as, for example, where the broker-dealer organization is also required to file another annual report, such as 10–K, with the SEC. In these cases, an unannounced visit during an interim period to perform some audit procedures and make tests in the more sensitive areas of the operations probably would be deemed to be in keeping with the spirit of the SEC's recommendations.

Several of the SEC's Accounting Series Releases deal with proceedings under Rule 2(e) of its Rules of Practice in which the Commission had serious questions as to whether the accountants involved had violated the audit requirements applicable to financial statements in Form X–17A–5. The releases are: No. 51, 59, 97, 108, 109, and 110. The cases are discussed briefly in Chapter **27**.

For an authoritative guide to examination of the financial statements of brokers or dealers in securities or commodities, the reader is referred to "Audits of Brokers or Dealers in Securities by Independent Certified Public Accountants," published in 1956 by the AICPA Committee on Auditing Procedure. The booklet was prepared by an advisory subcommittee of specialists in examinations of such brokers and dealers in consultation with representatives of the SEC and the New York Stock Exchange. (At the date of this writing, a proposed new audit guide had been released for comment by interested persons. The 218-page document has been two years in preparation by a committee of the AICPA.)

Examination of Clients' Funds and Securities Held by Investment Advisers.—When an investment adviser has in his custody or possession the funds or securities of his clients, all such funds and securities have to be verified by actual examination at least once during each calendar year by an independent public accountant at a time which shall be chosen by such accountant without prior notice to the investment adviser (Rule 206 (4)–2 under the Investment Advisers Act of 1940; the rule is not applicable to certain broker-dealers as provided in the rule).

Rule 204–2 under the Act requires that an investment adviser who has custody or possession of funds or securities of any client must record all transactions for such clients in a journal and in separate ledger accounts for each client and must maintain copies of confirmations of all transactions in such accounts and a position record for each security in which a client has an interest.

Rule 206(4)–2 is to the effect that it shall constitute a fraudulent, deceptive or manipulative act or practice for any investment adviser who has custody or possession of funds or securities of clients to do any act or to take any action with respect to any such funds or securities unless (1) all such securities are segregated, marked for identification, and held in safe keeping in a reasonably safe place; (2) the funds are deposited in one or more bank accounts, in the name of the investment adviser as agent or trustee for clients, which contain only clients' funds and certain appropriate records with respect thereto are maintained; (3) immediately after accepting such funds and securities the investment adviser notifies the client in writing of the place and manner in which they will be maintained; (4) not less frequently than once every three-month period each client is sent an itemized statement showing the debits, credits, and transactions in his account during the period and the funds and securities held at the end of the period; and the funds and securities are verified by an independent accountant as stated above, whose certificate is filed with the Commission. (The complete text of the rule appears in Chapter **25**.)

The SEC stated in ASR No. 103 (1966) its views regarding the nature of the examination to be made by the independent accountant and the content of his certificate. The SEC said: In order to make an appropriate examination the independent public accountant, at a date chosen by him and without prior notice to the investment adviser, should make a physical examination of securities and obtain confirmation as appropriate; should obtain confirmation of funds on deposit in banks; and should reconcile the physical count and confirmations to the books and records. These books and records should be verified by adequate examination of the security records and transactions since the last examination and by obtaining from clients written confirmation of the funds and securities in the clients' accounts as of the date of the physical examination. If clients' accounts have been closed or securities or funds of such clients have been returned since the last examination, these should be confirmed on a test basis. Such additional audit procedures as the accountant deems necessary under the circumstances should, of course, also be performed.

The Commission's views with respect to the content of the accountant's certificate in these circumstances are set forth in Chapter **25**.

CHAPTER 6

"GOING PUBLIC"; DISPLACEMENT OF SMALL ACCOUNTING FIRMS BY BIG FIRMS

———

CONTENTS

———

"Going Public": A Recent Phenomenon.—Securities offered for sale to the public may be classified as (1) securities of companies that are publicly owned, and (2) securities of companies that were previously privately owned. A phenomenon of recent years is the increase in offerings of securities of privately owned companies the owners of which have decided to "go public."

WHAT IS MEANT BY "GOING PUBLIC."—The phrase "going public" denotes the process by which the securities of a privately owned company are sold to the public, as a result of which the company becomes publicly owned. The securities sold may be those belonging to the owners of the company, in which event the owners receive the proceeds; this is a "secondary distribution." On the other hand, the company itself may sell additional shares to raise additional capital, in which case the company will receive the proceeds. Sometimes the offering may be a combination, that is, partly for the account of shareholders and partly for the account of the company.

INCREASE IN OFFERINGS BY FIRST-TIME REGISTRANTS.—In the fiscal year ended June 30, 1958, securities totaling $17 billion were registered with the SEC in 913 filings, of which 28 per cent were by companies that had had no previous filing experience with the SEC. In the fiscal year ended June 30, 1962, securities totaling $21.6 billion were registered in 2,307 filings, of which 60 per cent were first-time filings. The year 1962 was the peak year as far as the percentage of first-time filings was concerned. In the year ended June 30, 1970, securities totaling $67 billion were registered in 4,314 filings, of which 48 per cent were first-time filings.

The record of filings in the thirteen fiscal years ended June 30, 1970, discloses the following :[1]

Fiscal Year Ended June 30	Number of Filings	Dollar Amount (billions)	Per Cent of Filings Represented by Companies with No Previous Filing
1958	913	$16.9	28
1959	1,226	16.6	39
1960	1,628	15.8	47
1961	1,830	20.6	52
1962	2,307	21.6	60
1963	1,159	14.7	31
1964	1,192	18.6	27
1965	1,376	19.1	33
1966	1,697	31.1	25
1967	1,836	36.2	24
1968	2,906	54.0	34
1969	4,706	86.9	50
1970	4,314	67.0	48

The growth in number of first-time registrants from 28 per cent in 1958 to a peak of 60 per cent in 1962 (especially in the face of a decline in the dollar amount from 1958 to 1960) and more recently to 48 per cent is certainly an indication of the interest in "going public."

Following the *BarChris* decision (discussed in Chapter **28**) some writers observed that one of its primary effects would be to make accountants and lawyers who are not thoroughly familiar with the registration and issuance of securities hesitate to undertake engagements in this field. A member of the SEC has observed that this has not been the case:

I have been told this has not been borne out by a review of the number of first filings the Commission received during the past year (about 50% of all filings) many of which were prepared by professionals trying their hand for the first time at preparing a registration statement. It is my opinion that a competent professional who prepares adequately should be able to serve his client in matters involving the Commission; however, as was indicated in *BarChris,* the professional has special responsibilities when dealing with the Commission's disclosure statutes; therefore, he, the professional, should proceed prudently.[2]

REASONS FOR "GOING PUBLIC."—In view of the large number of companies that have "gone public" in recent years, it is obvious that there must be good reasons for so doing. Some of these reasons follow.

[1] Data from SEC Annual Reports.

[2] James J. Needham, address before Securities Law Committee, The Federal Bar Association, Washington, D.C., Dec. 2, 1970. (Mr. Needham, a CPA, is the first *practicing* CPA to serve as a Commissioner.)

1. If, as frequently happens, the owner of a business has all or most of his wealth invested in his business, "going public" is one means by which he can sell part of his holdings and diversify. Often he will sell only a portion of his holdings and retain enough to keep control of the business.

2. The owner of a business may be well along in years and consequently be facing estate-planning problems. In the event of death, shares in the company may have to be disposed of by executors in order to provide funds for estate taxes. Or the owner may want to dispose of a portion of his holdings during his lifetime in order to be in a more liquid position. This is easier when there is an established market for the securities of his company. Also, when a company's shares are widely owned by the public, the problem of setting a value for estate tax purposes is minimized. If, in addition to being publicly owned, the company lists its securities for trading on an exchange, the market value of the securities is even less open to challenge. (From the viewpoint of the tax consequences, this can also be an important disadvantage if the public evaluation of the stock is too high in relation to earnings or book values.)

3. While it is privately owned, a company may be severely restricted in its sources of capital. For the most part, the company expands by plowing back its undistributed earnings or by looking to its owners for additional capital funds. The company can also look to banks and institutional lenders. For long-term or permanent capital, however, the company may decide its interests are best served by the sale of its securities to the public through underwriters. If the offering is attractive enough, the company will have access to a tremendous capital market. Furthermore, once the company and its securities are known to the investing public, succeeding issues of the company—assuming no adverse change in its affairs—become easier to market. Lending institutions in fact prefer borrowers that are publicly-owned, since the market represents a potential source of additional equity capital. In the long run this may have a beneficial effect on the company's credit position.

4. When the company's securities have an established market, it is easier to negotiate mergers or acquisitions with other companies without using the company's cash resources. When privately owned or closely held companies want to merge, there is little they can do to demonstrate the value of the company except to exhibit their financial statements. With publicly-held shares there is less room for argument about the value of those shares—the newspaper listings of quotations show the value that the investing public places on the shares. All other things being equal, the owners of a private company are ordinarily more interested in merging with a public company than with another private company because the shareholders usually prefer to exchange their holdings for a marketable security. Often the share-

holders of the private company will not accept securities of another private company under any condition.

5. When a company is publicly owned, it is possible to establish restricted stock option plans which will serve as an inducement to attract and keep key personnel. Stock option plans may be more attractive to officers and other key personnel than generous salary arrangements. For one thing, the income on gains from stock option plans is, hopefully, taxed at capital gain rates rather than at rates applicable to ordinary income. Apart from the tax advantage, however, is the fact that stock option plans are a potent means of rewarding people by giving them "a piece of the action." Also, they do not require the outlay of current funds.

6. It is easier for the owner of the business or any other shareholder to borrow money with collateral consisting of marketable securities than with securities having no market.

7. Every shareholder is a potential customer. Especially if the company sells something that the public buys—whether it be automobiles or coffee or toothpaste—the company often benefits when its shares are owned by the public. The more widespread the distribution of shares, the greater the benefits.

8. Ordinarily a sale to the public of a substantial block of securities by the owner of a business has to be run through the SEC machinery. The securities generally must be registered under the Securities Act of 1933 before they may be offered to the public. Once the company and its securities have gone through the SEC's registration procedure, succeeding issues will ordinarily be processed by the same group in the Commission. This usually results in a reduction of the time required before the securities actually reach the market.

DISADVANTAGES OF "GOING PUBLIC."—The reasons for "going public" are not one-sided by any means. There are some significant disadvantages associated with the process, and the owner of a business should consider them before making his decision.

1. Prior to "going public," the owner of the business can run it to suit himself. He can take whatever risks he wishes to take, secure in the knowledge that it is only his own money that is at stake. Once the company becomes publicly owned, he acquires as many partners as he has shareholders, and he will be accountable to them. This may have a bearing on the risks that the business should take. A man is often willing to risk his own capital—but not his partners'—in a new venture. Furthermore, the ability to act quickly may be lost if the venture is one that requires a vote of shareholders.

2. The registration statement and subsequent reports to shareholders

will require disclosure of many facets of the company's business, operations, and finances which may never before have been known outside the company. Some particularly sensitive areas of disclosure as far as the registration statement is concerned will be the remuneration of officers and directors; the interests of insiders in certain transactions; the security holdings of officers, directors, and controlling stockholders; details regarding option plans and deferred compensation plans; and complete financial information, including sales, cost of sales, gross profits, and net income. Not only is important financial information revealed as to the business *as a whole,* but in recent years the disclosure requirements have expanded materially, so that now it is often necessary to disclose significant financial information concerning the principal *segments* of the business. One well-informed authority wrote, "Owners of a privately held business often fear that disclosure of such information as sales and profits would place them at a severe competitive disadvantage, although in my experience there are rarely the significant adverse consequences which were envisioned." [3]

3. The process of "going public" is expensive and time-consuming. The preparation of the registration document is a complicated process that occupies the time of many important people within the organization and several outside experts. Ordinarily the document must pass critical review by two sets of lawyers, and some of the financial statements must be certified by an independent public accountant. The printing bill alone in an undertaking of this kind is sometimes surprisingly high.

4. After "going public," the company usually becomes subject to the SEC's reporting requirements which are designed to keep the information in the registration statement up-to-date; see the comments beginning on page **14·12**. If the registration was painful, the reporting requirements may be equally painful.

5. As a privately owned company, the owner of a business may have declared dividends sporadically, depending on his needs and with one eye on the sections of the Internal Revenue Code dealing with unreasonable accumulations of earnings. As a publicly owned company, however, the company may have to adopt a more regular dividend policy.

As investors in the enterprise, the public is entitled to look for a return on its investment. A dividend omission is apt to have a significant effect not only on that return but also on the market value of the investment itself. Thus there is a pressure on the directors of publicly owned companies to declare dividends; this does not occur in a privately owned company.

6. After the public offering, the officers, directors, and principal holders of the company's equity securities will, in all probability, become subject to

[3] Carl W. Schneider, "Going Public," *The Legal Intelligencer,* July 24–25, 1962.

the insider trading provisions in Section 16(b) of the 1934 Act. Under this section, officers, directors, and principal shareholders must report monthly on all transactions in, and holdings of, the company's equity securities, and these reports are open to the public. Furthermore, such persons (officers, directors, and principal shareholders) must exercise caution in trading in the company's equity securities. If an officer, for example, buys shares of the company and then sells them within six months at a profit, that profit inures to, and is recoverable by, the company. Also, on a sale and a purchase within six months, the gain, if any, may have to be turned over to the company.

7. As a result of the Securities Acts Amendments of 1964, the SEC's proxy requirements, which previously were applicable only to listed and SEC-regulated companies, are now applicable to many publicly-owned but unlisted companies.

SEC Regulation 14A deals with the solicitation of proxies. If proxies are solicited, shareholders must be furnished certain information in the form of a "proxy statement." The proxy and the proxy statement must be reviewed by the SEC before they can be used. Even if proxies are not solicited, the SEC requires companies to furnish to shareholders information substantially equivalent to what would be required if proxies were solicited; see the discussion in Chapter **22**.

8. After the sale of the securities, the company may want to list on an exchange. Listing is not cheap. The fee arrangements vary among different exchanges. Some make an initial charge only; others charge an initial and then an annual fee.

Displacement of Small Accounting Firms by Big Firms.—When a small firm of public accountants or an individual practitioner has been doing satisfactory work for a client for many years, it comes as an understandable blow when the firm (or the individual) is displaced because the client has decided to "go public." The displacement is usually caused by the underwriter of the securities, although occasionally it is counsel for the proposed registrant who recommends that the company retain a larger, better-known firm or a so-called "national" firm of public accountants for SEC registration purposes.

This is not because the underwriter or the lawyer lacks confidence in the small firm. Usually he does not even know the firm. What is more important, however, is that he thinks the investing public also does not know the firm. Experienced practitioners know that the big firms do not, by any means, have a monopoly on accounting talent.

One of the most highly qualified lawyers in the securities field considered the question of Big Firm v. Small Firm in an article dealing with the BarChris case (which is discussed in Chapter **28** of this book). He asked whether selection "with reasonable care" of an auditing firm was difficult to establish when the choice went outside of the so-called "Big Eight" national firms of auditors. He said:

I don't see why it should be and I don't think it is. What you are looking for is integrity, skill and top professional standing in the community in which the accountants practice; and where the company functions in more than one locality, a firm which has the necessary branch offices or correspondent relationships to do a proper job on the observation of inventory. It may not be easy to find this outside of the ambit of the larger firms but it can and will continue to be found if the search is diligent enough, and with it you will probably also find enough familiarity with Regulation S–X to handle any but the most esoteric of accounting problems.[4]

It is probably true that the larger firms, by virtue of their greater involvement in the SEC area, are more familiar than the smaller firms with the accounting and auditing requirements of the SEC. Underwriters, however, often point out that the presence of a big firm's certificate in a prospectus helps in the marketing of the securities—a point of view with which the author does not agree. One representative of a small firm took the trouble to make a survey of about 75 clients and friends (other than accountants) who were interested in the stock market. He asked them if they looked to see who the accountants were in the prospectuses they received from their brokers, and if they could tell him the name of the accountant in the prospectus of the last stock they purchased. Of the 75, only two said they occasionally looked to see who the accounting firm was, and only one could tell him the name of the firm.[5]

There are thousands of thoroughly qualified and competent small firms and individual practitioners, and many of them have certified the financial statements in registration statements filed with the SEC. The Chief Accountant of the SEC demonstrated convincingly the participation of small firms in SEC work when he said:

In the flood of registration statements of the last two and a half years we have seen many names of accountants we never heard of before. . . . I do not have any more recent statistics than those I used at the [AICPA] meeting in 1957 when I reported that in a list of 3,072 filings on Form 10–K for 1955 and 1956 there were 558 different accounting firms of which 384 each certified to only one statement, 77 firms each certified to two statements, and only the top ten firms each certified to more than 25 statements, as had been the case ten years earlier. While it is undoubtedly true that the big get bigger, there is plenty of evidence that with the growth of small companies into public companies, small accounting firms in substantial numbers do follow their clients into the new area of practice.[6]

[4] Carlos L. Israels, "Preparation of Registration Statement: Issuer's Counsel—Advice to My Client," *The Business Lawyer,* Jan. 1969, p. 101.

[5] Mel Marvin, letter to the editor, *The Journal of Accountancy,* May 1971, p. 80.

[6] Andrew Barr, "Accounting and Auditing Problems with Particular Reference to New Registrants with the SEC," *The New York CPA,* Jan. 1961, p. 29.

A glance at a representative number of prospectuses will convince anyone who has any doubt on this score that small firms of accountants and individual practitioners do indeed have a role in public offerings.

The American Institute of CPA's (including its members who are partners in large CPA firms) is concerned about the displacement problem, would like to do something about it, and has set up a special committee to survey the problem and make recommendations as to what can be done about it. The committee's first task was to find out how serious is the problem.

To that end, the AICPA sent questionnaires to approximately 2,400 CPA firms represented in the Accounting Research Association, and received responses from 30% of the addressees. With respect to those who replied, 77% stated that they had not participated in SEC filings; 23% had participated in SEC filings. ("Participation" in this sense included filings under all SEC-administered statutes—not merely the 1933 Act. In other words, if a CPA firm certified financial statements included in a Form 10–K filing under the 1934 Act, it participated in an SEC filing.)

The most significant finding of the survey was this: of the 23% of the firms that had participated in SEC filings, 62% were displaced when their clients filed registration statements under the 1933 Act.

The foregoing statistics regarding displacement were taken from an article by Marshall S. Armstrong written when he was president of the AICPA.[7] He observed that fewer than 4% of the accounting firms represented in the membership of the AICPA did any registration work in 1969. In his view, the main hope of the CPA firms interested in opening up SEC work to a larger number of practice units lies in a comprehensive program of education involving CPA firms and their personnel, underwriting houses and their syndicate managers, clients and their financial officers, and the SEC itself. With regard to what the CPA firms should do, Mr. Armstrong said:

> CPA firms must prepare themselves for SEC work by *acquiring* or *hiring* the expertise they need; by meeting and maintaining a standard of independence satisfactory to the underwriters, the SEC and the profession; by building a staff adequate to the task of registration; by establishing financial responsibility, including adequate liability coverage; by sharpening the focus of their client relations radar to such acuity that they are immediately aware of a client's changing financial requirements and are at his side when he goes to the market place seeking capital.

The 62% figure used above represents, in absolute terms, 103 displacements of CPA firms. Commenting on this matter, Charles G. Carpenter and Robert H. Strawser have written that 98 out of the 103 were displacements by nationally known CPA firms. Where efforts to retain the client

---

[7] *The CPA,* March 1971, p. 2.

were successful, they said that strong client support and the excellence of the firm's reputation were the primary considerations. Where the displacement occurred, however, they said, it was possible that the client may have decided to use the occasion of going public as an appropriate point to sever a relationship when otherwise he might have been reluctant to do so. Client needs may have grown to the point where the displaced firm was less able to provide the needed services; "indeed, in 26 of the 103 cases of displacement reported, the firm withdrew in recognition of its professional inabilities." [8]

Carpenter and Strawser concluded that efforts by the profession to assist small firms in reducing displacements from clients going public must succeed in the following respects: (1) improve practitioner technical abilities; (2) improve existing intraprofessional referral activities for areas where smaller firms might not be reasonably expected to have such expertise; (3) educate clients of firm capabilities, or the firm's ability to obtain expert assistance should the need arise; and (4) persuade underwriters that the success of a security issuance is not dependent upon the national reputation of the auditing firm.

As previously stated, the AICPA appointed a special committee to study the displacement problem. The chairman of the committee, John W. Hoyt, reported on the results of the committee's investigation of the circumstances surrounding the displacement of accountants when their clients go public. The Committee found that some CPA firms have avoided displacement when the client insists on the firm's retention and the firm demonstrates the qualities looked for by underwriters and the SEC. In studying these firms, the committee found the following recognizable pattern that may be emulated by almost any firm:

The firm has prepared itself to meet the strict demands of underwriters for integrity, independence, SEC competence, sufficient staff and adequate financial responsibility.

If lacking in some of these important requirements, the firm has arranged with an experienced firm to serve as a consultant on the SEC engagement. Under such an agreement the inexperienced firm learns by doing and, by issuing opinions on financial statements contained in the prospectuses, becomes better known to underwriters.

The firm has developed a bond of mutual respect and loyalty with the client. In such an atmosphere candid discussion of problems of going public are possible and result in a forthright decision in favor of the incumbent auditor. [9]

It would be ridiculous to deny that the larger firms do not like new business, but it is also reasonable to believe that they are not anxious to get it at someone else's expense, especially where the client has been

---

[8] "Displacement of Auditors When Clients Go Public", *The Journal of Accountancy,* June 1971, pp. 55–58.

[9] *The CPA,* June 1971, p. 16.

capably served by the small firm. It is a fact of life, however, that when companies "go public," small firms of accountants and individual practitioners are often displaced by larger or national firms of accountants. What can the small practitioner do to prevent this displacement and the resulting erosion of his practice?

SMALL ACCOUNTANT NEED NOT CAPITULATE.—As the SEC's Chief Accountant has said, "My suggestion . . . is to get acquainted with the rules that may affect you before they deprive you of the client you have raised from infancy." [10] With a knowledge of the SEC's rules and regulations, the accountant can demonstrate to the underwriter that he is a competent practitioner, that not only is he qualified in the practice of public accounting generally, but he has also "done his homework" as far as SEC registration is concerned. If he has worked on an SEC registration previously, he can show the offering prospectus to the underwriter; the printed word is often effective and is sometimes able to put across a thought which modesty prevents.

If, in the earlier registration, the accountant worked closely with the underwriter or the lawyers, it might be in order to suggest that they put in a good word for the accountant with the present or proposed underwriter or counsel. Sometimes a recommendation from another underwriter or a knowledgeable lawyer is all that is needed to tip the scales in favor of the individual practitioner.

SMALL ACCOUNTANT CAN DO PART OF THE JOB.—With a little effort, the small accountant may be able to minimize the big firm's participation in the registration project. He can suggest to his client and the underwriter that the big firm certify the balance sheet and the income statement for the latest interim period or the latest year, with the small firm reporting on all previous years in the prospectus. This is not an uncommon arrangement, and a glance at a representative group of prospectuses will be convincing proof of how often it occurs in practice. This arrangement appeals to clients because it is less costly than having the big firm examine and report upon all of the earlier years. It also has some appeal both to the client and to the underwriter because there is a saving in time, and, in a public offering, time is important. If the accountant is successful in remaining in the picture for the registration even to this limited extent, he will have some contact with the underwriter and will get to know him. If there is a second registration for the same company, the accountant may be able to do the whole job.

---

[10] Andrew Barr, "Accounting and Auditing Problems with Particular Reference to New Registrants with the SEC," *The New York CPA,* Jan. 1961, p. 29.

FAULT SOMETIMES LIES WITH CLIENTS.—One of the reasons for the displacement of small firms is that loyalty on the part of a client is almost non-existent when the client has made up his mind to "go public." In his desire to cooperate with and accommodate the underwriter, he is apt to give little thought to his accountant. A satisfactory relationship of many years is often scrapped because it does not occur to the client that if he insisted on retaining his accountant for registration purposes, the underwriter might not insist on a big firm.

The author knows of a case which is directly in point. One of the national firms of accountants was employed to examine and report upon the financial statements of a company which had never registered previously with the SEC. The company's statements had been audited for many years by a small firm which the big firm knew to be both reputable and competent. A partner of the big firm talked to the underwriter about the possibility of using the small firm's certificate covering the earlier years of the earnings summary. The underwriter refused, and the reason he gave was interesting, to say the least. He said, "I haven't a thing against Mr. Small Accountant, but when I suggested using a national firm, Mr. Registrant made absolutely no effort to keep his accountant in the picture. If he had made an effort, I would not have insisted on a big firm for registration purposes." This case may or may not be typical, but the author believes that if clients extended themselves and spoke up for their accountants, there would be fewer displacements of small firms.

SMALL FIRMS CAN WORK WITH BIG FIRMS.—Sometimes the underwriter suggests that a national firm not only should certify the financial statements in the registration statement, but that the firm should also be retained for all future reports to the SEC and to shareholders. In that case, if the small firm has been doing monthly or quarterly audits and the registrant's tax work, the firm should make every effort to continue to be retained for that work. There are many cases where large and small firms work together under this kind of an arrangement, that is, the interim work and the tax work are done by the small firm, and the big firm makes the annual examination and reviews the tax returns or consults on tax matters. In connection with the annual examination, the small firm may be able to furnish staff assistants to work directly under the supervision and control of the big firm, which will have over-all responsibility for the engagement. This arrangement, the author knows, can be satisfactory to both firms.[11]

[11] For an interesting and informative article, based on the actual experience of a small accounting firm working with a large firm, see Robert S. Lehmann, "A Case History in Co-operation," *The Journal of Accountancy,* April 1965, pp. 43–45. Also, Mel Marvin, letters to the editor, *The Journal of Accountancy,* May 1971, p. 80.

RETENTION OF BIG FIRMS AS CONSULTANTS.—Sometimes the small accountant can stay in the SEC picture if he personally retains a large firm on a consulting basis to back him up and help him do the job. This sometimes—but not always—helps the small firm to continue with the client for the SEC engagement, because under this arrangement the big firm's name cannot be used in the registration statement or prospectus, and such omission would defeat the very thing the underwriter had hoped to accomplish. This has been done often enough, however, so that it is perfectly in order for the small accountant to suggest it. If the underwriter is less interested in a name than he is in making sure that the work is done properly, he ought to be willing to entertain the idea.

CHAPTER 7

PROCESSING OF REGISTRATION
STATEMENTS UNDER THE 1933 ACT

CONTENTS

The preparation of a registration statement for filing under the Securities Act of 1933 is almost invariably a combined operation. Representatives of the management of the registering company, the underwriters, the independent public accountants, counsel for the company, counsel for the underwriters, and, occasionally, engineers or appraisers—all have important roles in preparing the registration document. When the registration statement has been completed, an executed copy together with conformed copies and exhibits will be taken or mailed to the principal office of the SEC in Washington, D. C., for "filing" with the Commission. If the registration is filed by a company which has previously filed with the SEC, the statement will usually be assigned to the section which previously handled the affairs of this company. If, however, the company has not previously filed with the SEC, the registration will be assigned to a new section.

Processing of Registration Statement.—The registration statement will be processed in the Division of Corporation Finance which will review the document to see whether it contains untrue statements of material facts, or whether there are omissions of material facts which make misleading the statements that are made; in short, whether there has been full and fair disclosure. In the processing, the registration statement will be reviewed by a group working under the supervision of an Assistant Director of the Division. The group will include a lawyer, an accountant, and a financial analyst, and a copy of the registration statement will be furnished to each of them. If necessary or desirable, the group will consult with other experts (such as mining engineers or petroleum engineers) or with other departments of the government. The group, working individually and collectively, will review the registration statement and will prepare memoranda of their findings. (See, however, the discussion which follows regarding the staff's limited or deferred review when the backlog of filings is heavy.) In some cases they will send a copy of the document to other government agencies if it appears the agency may have an interest in the document.

As one very knowledgeable writer put it:

. . . This examination does not guarantee accuracy nor absolve the company from liability. Obviously the staff cannot be in possession of all of the facts known to the company. At most the staff can depend only on the material in the registration statement, other material concerning the company on file with the Commission, and its general knowledge of industry and knowledge of the particular industry to aid it in its analysis. It cannot be emphasized too strongly that the accuracy and adequacy of the registration statement is ultimately the responsibility of the company and its directors, officers, underwriters and the independent public accountants whose audit and certificate in respect of financial statements is required by the statute . . .[1]

Some of the questions that might otherwise have been raised by the examining group may have been disposed of in advance by means of the prefiling conference (referred to on page 1·16) or in prefiling correspondence. In other cases where such a conference is not held or there has been no correspondence, registrants that file frequently with the SEC make it their practice to review with the SEC's staff on the day of the filing those features in the new registration statement which are new or unusual, or which might be misunderstood.

In order to be assured that the registration statement, as filed, will comply with the requirements of the 1933 Act and the Commission's rules thereunder, a procedure which has suggested itself to many registrants is to have the complete registration document reviewed informally by the SEC's staff *before* it is officially filed with the Commission. Requests for such prefiling reviews are uniformly rejected by the Commission and its staff. The Commission, in fact, stated its policy in this respect in a 1968 release entitled "Guides for the Preparation and Filing of Registration Statements" as follows:

Occasionally a registrant will request a prefiling review of a registration statement, but such a review has been refused since it would delay the examination of material which has already been filed and would favor certain issuers at the expense of others. Registrants or their representatives also occasionally request the staff to draft a paragraph or other statement which will comply with some requirement or request for disclosure. The staff cannot undertake to prepare material for filing but limits itself to stating the kind of disclosure

[1] Harry Heller, "Disclosure Requirements Under Federal Securities Regulation," *The Business Lawyer*, Jan. 1961, p. 301.

required, leaving the actual drafting to the registrant and its representatives. (Release No. 33–4936, Dec. 9, 1968).

To the author's knowledge there have been a few exceptions to the SEC's policy regarding prefiling reviews, but their number has been minute.

As far as the accounting review is concerned, the SEC staff accountant (who is a professionally trained accountant) will read the entire prospectus and relevant portions of the remainder of the registration statement so that he (or she) may become familiar with the company and its business. He may also refer to published annual and interim reports and newspaper articles for information regarding the company and its industry. As for the financial statements and the accountants' certificate, the SEC accountant-reviewer will be concerned first of all that the statements appear to comply with the requirements of the Commission's Regulation S–X and the instructions of the applicable form, the Accounting Series Releases, and any other SEC decisions and precedents bearing on accounting and auditing matters. He will also be concerned whether the financial statements and certificate appear to comply with the pronouncements of the AICPA and the unwritten and informal SEC staff policies which usually agree with such pronouncements.

A frequent source of annoyance to "first time" registrants are the challenges from the SEC's staff with respect to some of the assertions in a registration statement. The management of a company may know, for example, that the company is, say, the third largest company in the industry. They may know this so well and be so certain of it, that it would never occur to them that the authority for the statement might be challenged. They should be prepared, accordingly, to document or prove any statement the truth of which might not be self-evident to the SEC's examiners.

Another source of irritation is the prohibition against the use of forecasts in registration statements. Management may feel that based on its intimate knowledge of the company, the industry, and the economic climate, it is in a good position to talk about the company's prospects for at least several months ahead. Since this involves a forecast, it would not ordinarily be permitted in a registration statement filed under the Act.

There is one significant exception to the SEC's general prohibition against the use of forecasts. It occurs in connection with registration statements filed by companies organized to acquire and hold for investment a specific property or group of properties. In that case what is required is not the historical income of the property in the hands of the prior owner, but a projection of income based on the results of a recent period. (This subject is discussed in Chapter **10**.)

The SEC's position with respect to the use of forecasts is in interesting contrast with the practice in the United Kingdom, where it is taken for granted that the offeror will of course be expected to discuss the concern's prospects.

There are indications, however that the SEC may be having a change of heart regarding its prohibition against the use of forecasts. In a speech, for example, on April 21, 1972 before the Association of the Bar of the City of New York, the Chairman of the SEC, William J. Casey, said:

. . . I have spoken on a number of occasions about the fact that a backward looking prospectus only tells half of the story. Investors do not put up their money solely on the basis of past history. They are always partly sold, and particularly in the new issue area, by verbal assurances about the prospects of the company. Such projections are at least as valuable, if not more so, than the past three years' financial record, particularly if the company is just starting up. We recognize there is a legal problem for a company to predict its future earnings. We believe, however, that it is possible for companies to make good faith projections of future prospects; after all, analysts make such projections and make research reports on that basis, management estimates do circulate, and trading values do relate to earnings estimates more than anything else. The Division of Corporation Finance is studying the liability and reliability aspects of earning projections and seeking the advice of accountants, financial executives, analysts, and lawyers. We hope to have an opinion crystallized before cold weather returns. We might start by *permitting* projections on a limited scale, then, on the basis of experience, consider later the notion of *requiring* them as the British do.

Curtailed or Limited SEC Review When Backlog Is Heavy.—The preceding pages of this chapter have described the SEC's normal or customary review of registration statements. In 1968, however, due to a substantial increase in the volume of filings under the 1933 Act, coupled with a reduction of personnel because of budgetary cuts, the SEC announced a change in its review procedure in order to cope with the increase in its backlog (Release No. 33–4934). The SEC pointed out what was apparent to all, namely, that "the statutory standards remain unchanged," but that, under the circumstances, there would be a change in processing procedures at the SEC until such time as normal procedures may be resumed. In some cases, the SEC said, the staff's review would be merely a "cursory review." If it appeared that the registration statement was poorly prepared or otherwise presented serious problems, no further review would be made. In either event, the staff would not provide oral or written comments. (For a discussion of the SEC's right to withhold the comments of its staff, see the comments in this chapter concerning the Boruski case.)

Among the innovations contemplated by the cursory review procedure, was a requirement for letters to be sent to the SEC, as supplemental information, from the issuer's chief executive officer, the independent auditors, and the managing underwriter. These letters were to include representations from the respective persons along the lines described below under "Cursory Review."

On February 3, 1972, because of another bulge in registration activity without a corresponding increase in its staff, the SEC reaffirmed the 1968 announcement (Release No. 33–5231). The Commission stated that its Division of Corporation Finance employs four different review procedures, and that the Division—not the registrant—decides which type of review a registration statement will receive. These were classified by the SEC as follows: (1) deferred review; (2) cursory review; (3) summary review; and (4) customary review. (The SEC's release also directed attention to the BarChris case which is discussed in Chapter **28**.) The scope of the different review procedures is described below.

DEFERRED REVIEW.—The deferred review procedure is invoked when a supervisory staff official of the SEC decides that the registration document is so poorly prepared or otherwise presents problems so serious that review will be deferred since further staff time would not be justified. Detailed staff comments will not be prepared or issued. The registrant will be notified accordingly, and it will have to consider whether to go forward or to withdraw or amend the registration statement. If the registrant decides to go forward without taking corrective steps, the staff will then make recommendations to the Commission for appropriate action.

CURSORY REVIEW.—Under the cursory review procedure, the registrant is advised that the staff has made only a cursory review of the registration statement, and that no written or oral comments will be provided. Registrants will be requested to furnish, as supplemental information, letters from the chief executive officer of the issuer, the independent auditors, and the managing underwriter on behalf of all underwriters. These letters are to include representations that the respective persons are aware that the staff has made only a cursory rather than a detailed review of the registration statement, and that they are also aware of their statutory responsibilities under the 1933 Act. (For a suggested form of letter to be written by the independent auditors to the SEC in this connection, see Chapter **25**.)

Registrants will be advised that, upon receipt of such letters, the staff will recommend that the registration statement be declared effective.

SUMMARY REVIEW.—The summary review procedure involves a variation of the cursory treatment described above. Under the summary review, the registrant is notified that only a limited review of the registration material has been made, and only such staff comments as may arise from such review will be furnished to the registrant. The registrant will be requested to provide supplemental letters from the same persons mentioned under

"Cursory Review" and containing similar representations. Registration statements reviewed in this manner will be declared effective upon receipt of the aforementioned letters and upon satisfactory compliance with the staff's limited comments.

CUSTOMARY REVIEW.—In the final review category, registration statements will receive the more complete accounting, financial, and legal review described previously in this chapter under "Processing of Registration Statement."

Letters of Comment; Deficiency Letters.—The 1933 Act did not set up a specified procedure to be followed by the Commission in processing registration statements filed under the Act. Manuel F. Cohen, a former chairman of the SEC, said in a 1964 speech that the statute seems to offer only a choice between automatic effectiveness upon the lapse (or acceleration) of the statutory period or the institution of formal proceedings looking to a stop order banning the sale of the securities involved. In those cases where revision of the registration statement seemed required, if resort could only be had to formal proceedings, serious delays would be caused and securities flotation would be hampered. Since this appeared to be contrary to the Congressional intent, and since the Commission's staff was, in any event, required to review the registration statement as a basis for Commission action, an informal procedure was devised which would make available to registrants the benefit of the comments resulting from the SEC's staff review and permit appropriate revision or modification of the registration statement without formal proceedings. This informal comment technique has proved to be an effective method of clearing up defects and permitting the registration statement to become effective. The manner in which the technique is employed is described in the following pages.

In the case of a "customary review" described above, the SEC's branch chief, in collaboration with his group, drafts a "letter of comments" to be sent to the registrant, setting forth those respects in which it appears that the registration statement fails to comply with the specific rules, regulations, and instructions, and the requirements as to completeness demanded by the law. A letter of comment may not be sent out, however, where the circumstances are such that an investigatory or stop-order proceeding is deemed more appropriate. The draft of the letter is reviewed by the Assistant Director of the Division in charge of the case. The draft is frequently (but not always) reviewed as to accounting matters by the Chief Accountant of the Division. When the Assistant Director and the Chief Accountant have completed their reviews, the letter is prepared for mailing.

The letter of comment will be signed by the Assistant Director and will be mailed to the "Agent for Service" (the person designated in the registration statement to receive notices from the Commission). The letter will contain all the comments, criticisms, and suggestions resulting from the SEC's review of the registration statement. For some time such letters were known as "deficiency letters," but because of the unintended stigma attaching to this term, they came to be known as "letters of comment," which is much more descriptive of their character. "Letters of comment," however, are still commonly known as "deficiency letters." These letters are not a matter of public record.

Despite the great amount of care which goes into the preparation of a registration statement, it frequently happens that some obscure instruction has been overlooked, or some information may have been omitted or inadequately stressed. Sometimes there are errors in the financial statements or the notes thereto because of carelessness or the time pressures which exist in almost all registration engagements. In one case, for example, a note to the financial statements in a registration statement stated that the registrant sold substantially all of its receivables to a factor without recourse. The balance sheet, however, showed trade receivables aggregating about $332,000, which certainly was inconsistent with the note and had to be corrected by amendment.

When the registration document has not been carefully prepared, the letter of comment may prove to be extremely troublesome. In that event it will list in detail all those instructions which have been overlooked and will point out those respects in which it appears there is an important omission or inaccuracy. In the case of a carefully prepared document, however, the SEC's comments are few in number and minor in character. Whether the comments are few or many, however, they cannot be ignored; they must be taken care of. If the SEC's comments are well founded and material, the registration statement must be appropriately amended. Otherwise, the comments may form the basis of stop-order proceedings under the Act, or the Commission may refuse to "accelerate" the effective date (see p. **7**·12).

In recent years, as a result of the explosive increase in number of registration statements filed with the Commission with no commensurate increase in the staff required to process the statements, the SEC has been under tremendous pressure to keep pace with the flood of new registrations. One of the measures adopted to conserve the time of the staff is to telephone the staff's comments on its review of the statement to the agent for service in lieu of writing a letter. This innovation was warmly welcomed especially by underwriters.

There was a period in the SEC's history when all of the staff's comments relating to the financial statements in registration statements under the 1933 Act were screened by the Chief Accountant of the Division of Corporation Finance. One additional result of the enormous increase in the number of filings under that Act was that it became impossible for the

Division's Chief Accountant to review all of the staff's comments on financial statement matters. This was unfortunate, because it deprived registrants of the Chief Accountant's expertise and ability to sift out and discard what is trivial or inconsequential. Because of the change in procedure within the Division, there have been many so-called "comments" that never should have been raised; they simply represent an excess of zeal on the part of the examiner who may think that the value of his review is in direct proportion to the number of comments that he writes.

For example, the author has the SEC's letter of comments on a 1933 Act registration statement. One of the comments is as follows: "The first sentence of Note 2 on page 25 is grammatically incorrect." The examiner was, of course, correct, but it seems to the author that this is something that ought to concern the registrant and its auditors a little—but the Commission's staff not at all.

Another example involved a company that had filed a registration statement under the 1933 Act. The company had par value shares outstanding. In its balance sheet, the company included in its capital stock account the total consideration received for its shares—including the amount in excess of par value. A note to the financial statements disclosed this fact and indicated for each of three years the amounts in excess of par value credited to capital stock. This was admittedly an unusual presentation, but certainly not a pioneering one. The SEC commented with respect to this matter as follows:

. . . [I]t is our position that the carrying value of par value stock represents the dollar equivalent of the number of shares issued and outstanding multiplied by the par value per share. Any capital contributions in excess of such par value per share are required to be credited to capital surplus.

The company was not inclined to yield on the point involved. The company knew that its position was supported by authoritative works on accounting and the Commission's "position" as stated in the comment letter had never been set forth in an Accounting Series Release of the SEC. The presentation followed in the SEC filing was also the one used by the company in its published report to shareholders. The matter was discussed with the Chief Accountant of the Division of Corporation who, after very little discussion, withdrew the comment.

It would be a simple matter to add examples to the list of asserted deficiencies that should never have been raised, but the author will cite only one more. A company had included in a note to its financial statements the information that would normally be included in a statement of capital surplus. This was done in the interest of brevity, since the information was neither extensive nor significant. The Commission's letter of comment said:

"The information in Note (8) should be furnished as a separate statement and the accountants' opinion should explicitly cover such statement."

It would have been a simple matter to comply with the asserted "deficiency," but the registrant was not inclined to do so. An officer of the registrant telephoned the Chief Accountant of the Division of Corporation Finance to discuss the matter, and said:

1. The rules of Regulation S–X contained flexibility provisions so that the information called for by any statement or schedule could be furnished in a note as long as that presentation did not result in a confusing or misleading presentation. Just as the information called for by Schedule XVI, Supplementary Income Statement Information, can be (and often is) presented in a note, so the capital surplus statement can be presented in the form of a note.

2. Regarding the certification suggestion, the notes to the financial statements were an integral part of the financial statements, and there was no necessity to single out one of the notes for special certification treatment.

The Chief Accountant of the Division withdrew the deficiency with no further discussion.

Lawyers as well as accountants have complained of the SEC staff's practice in issuing letters of comment on matters of general applicability which are not called for either in the registration forms *or* in the Commission's published guidelines. Two very knowledgeable lawyers, for example, made these observations:

The Commission has recently and most properly asked for industry cooperation in its efforts to simplify and improve disclosure. Unfortunately, at the same time, staff members continue to use the letter of comment as a vehicle for imposing disclosure requirements of general applicability that are not to be found in the disclosure forms or published guidelines.

This administrative practice may well introduce poor or insufficiently considered materials into already overlong disclosure documents. It certainly does nothing to promote the desired cooperative spirit between the SEC and its clientele. More advance warning and uniformity of application is needed in connection with comments on recurring matters of general significance.[2] (Footnotes omitted.)

For an example of a comment on financial statements having general applicability, see the discussion in Chapters **8** and **10** regarding the ratio of earnings to fixed charges and the ratio of earnings to fixed charges and preferred dividends combined.

[2] Carl W. Schneider and Joseph M. Manko, "The Comment Letter Practice," *The Review of Securities Regulation,* May 6, 1971, p. 929.

Correcting Deficiencies.—After the registration statement has been filed with the SEC, those who prepared it will look forward with interest to seeing what the SEC's examiners have to say about the document. Time is so important to the underwriter and the issuer that, when a reasonable period of time has passed since the filing date, one of them (or his counsel) may telephone the SEC and have the staff's comments read over the telephone if they are ready.

When the SEC's comments have been received, they are carefully considered by everyone concerned with the registration statement. Matters having to do with financial statements and schedules and the summaries of earnings are usually delegated to the issuer's financial and accounting personnel and the certifying accountants. Between them they usually agree on what, if anything, to do about the SEC's comments that are of immediate concern to them.

If it is decided to comply with the SEC's comments, the question remains: How to do it? Usually this can be disposed of by a telephone call to inform the Commission how the matter in question is to be dealt with.

If, however, it is decided to resist the SEC's suggestions or comments, or if the suggestions or comments are not clear, a more difficult problem arises. Time is important, and the issuer and underwriter are often not in favor of opposing the SEC's suggestions where the matters involved are, in their view, not vital. All too often issuers comply with those SEC suggestions which they believe are without merit for the sole purpose of having the registration become effective so that the securities can be sold. There have been cases, too, where issuers, under the pressure of financing, have agreed to filing amendments which committed them to policies to which they would never agree under other circumstances. There was a period, for example, when the SEC was conducting something in the nature of a campaign to eliminate goodwill from all balance sheets filed with it. (This was long before the APB issued its Opinion No. 17 (1970) which made mandatory the amortization of goodwill acquired after October 31, 1970.) As a condition to having their registration statements become effective promptly, several corporations agreed to amortize or write off goodwill appearing in their balance sheets. By these means the SEC was instrumental in eliminating large amounts of intangibles from the balance sheets of American corporations. (The Commission's policy with respect to the amortization of intangible assets is now parallel with that of the accountancy profession as set forth in APB Opinion No. 17.) The author refers to these cases not with a view to reflecting on the value of the comments resulting from the SEC's review of the registration material but, rather, to point up the pressures which exist to a greater or lesser degree in many registration engagements.

The truth of the matter is that the great majority of the SEC's comments and suggestions are very worth while indeed. It would be surprising, if they were otherwise, because they represent the comments and suggestions of a battery of experts: lawyers, accountants, analysts, engineers, and others. Sometimes, being human, they are wrong, or their suggestions are impractical. Sometimes their comments may be based on a misunderstanding of the facts because of inadequate information. When that happens, they should be told why they are wrong, or in what respect their suggestions are impractical or based on insufficient information.

If the matter in question relates to the financial data (including earnings summaries) rather than the textual matter, it is advisable to have the accounting people (the comptroller of the company or the certifying accountant, for example) take the question up with the Chief Accountant of the Division of Corporation Finance. It is not advisable for lawyers to consult with the SEC regarding accounting matters, just as independent public accountants should not take up legal matters with the SEC. Matters relating to the narrative section, on the other hand, should be handled by the issuer's representatives, by lawyers, or by other qualified persons.

If it is decided to discuss with the SEC the comments or suggestions on accounting matters, the problem is: How? The least desirable method is by writing a letter. This is time consuming, and time is usually important. What is more to the point, however, is that it is almost impossible to anticipate all the questions that may arise in the course of discussing a controversial matter. A letter is the least effective way of dealing with a difficult question.

A better plan is to telephone. This overcomes the time disadvantage of a letter. It permits the exposition of the facts and explanation of the circumstances which may not have been known to the SEC people when they drafted their deficiency letter. It also affords the SEC an opportunity to explore the problem, ask questions, and learn the answers.

The best plan, if time permits, is to go to Washington. This has all the advantages of telephoning plus a face-to-face meeting. Considerations of time and distance frequently prevent dealing with a problem in this way. Whenever the accountant is faced with an important problem involving the SEC and time permits, the author strongly urges: Go to Washington and talk it over with the SEC people. It is not unusual for them to modify or withdraw a deficiency when they have learned firsthand some of the facts they did not know before. Because of its heavy workload, the SEC staff discourages conferences in Washington except on important or complicated matters. They prefer to dispose of questions they have raised either by letter or by telephone.

When there is a meeting of the minds as to what, if anything, needs to be done to the registration statement as a result of the Commission's comments, the next step is the preparation of the amendment. If the amendment includes matter covered by the accountant's certificate, a new consent (manually signed) must be included in the amendment. If the certificate is also amended, the amended certificate must also be manually signed. For the forms of such consents and certificates, see Chapters **11** and **24**, respectively.

All amendments to the registration statement are examined by the SEC in the same manner as the original registration. If it appears that the registration as amended still needs work, a further letter of comment will be sent to the registrant.

The "Waiting" Period.—A major premise of the Securities Act is the provision that a registration statement shall become effective 20 days after it has been filed or at such earlier date as the Commission may determine. In making such determination, the SEC considers, among other things, the adequacy of the information concerning the issuer previously available to the public, the nature of the securities being offered, and the ease with which the rights of holders of the securities can be understood. Normally the "waiting" period (sometimes also called the "cooling" or "incubation" period) is about 20 days, but, as stated above, the Commission may accelerate the effective date, upon request.

In recent years, with the tremendous increase in number of registration statements filed—particularly in the number of registration statements filed by companies with no previous SEC experience (see the discussion on page **6·1**)—there has been no such thing as a "normal" waiting period. In early 1962, when there was a large number of "first time" registrants, it was not unusual for three months to pass between the filing date and the receipt of the staff's comments. In 1965, the interval was as short as ten days.

Everyone who has a part in the preparation of the registration document is concerned with doing as good a job as he knows how to do so that the waiting period will be no longer than is necessary. Especially in a period of rapidly changing securities markets, the issuer and the underwriter, having financial stakes in the proposed offering, are anxious to have the registration become effective and the securities sold as soon as possible.

Effect of Filing an Amendment; Acceleration.—Whenever an amendment to a registration statement is filed, it has the effect of starting the waiting period all over again, unless the Commission consents to the registrant's request to consider that the amendment is filed "now as of then." This is referred to as granting "acceleration" to an amendment. (See also the discussion regarding the filing date on page **9·2**.) Rule 461 provides that a request for acceleration shall be made in writing by the issuer, the managing underwriter, and the selling security holders, if any. The granting of acceleration is discretionary with the SEC. The power to deny acceleration is a potent means by which the SEC can impose its will in a situation where it might not otherwise be able to do so.

The Commission's policy with respect to granting acceleration is set forth in Rule 460. This rule provides, among other things, that the Commission will not accelerate the effective date of a registration statement unless the preliminary prospectus contained in the registration statement is distributed to underwriters and dealers who it is reasonably anticipated will be invited to participate in the distribution of the security to be offered or sold. The purpose of this requirement is to afford all persons effecting the distribution a means of being informed with respect to the offering so that they can advise their customers of the investment merits of the security.

A note to Rule 460 refers to five situations which are among those in which the SEC "may refuse to accelerate the effective date" of the registration statement:

(1) Where by reason of any charter provision, by-law or otherwise, provision is made for indemnification by the registrant of a director, officer or a controlling person of the registrant against liabilities arising under the Act unless (a) such indemnification is waived, or (b) there is included in the registration statement a brief description of the indemnification provision and a statement to the effect that, in the opinion of the SEC, the indemnification is against public policy and unenforceable, and that it will not be honored (except to the extent of the expenses in a successful defense) without a judicial test.

(2) Where the underwriting agreement contains provisions by which indemnification against liabilities arising under the Act are given by the registrant to the underwriter or controlling persons of the underwriter and a director, officer or controlling person of the registrant is such an underwriter or a controlling person thereof or member of any firm which is such an underwriter unless a waiver or a statement similar to that referred to in (1) above is included in the registration statement.

(3) Where the Commission is currently investigating the issuer, a person controlling the issuer, or one of the underwriters, pursuant to any of the acts administered by the Commission.

(4) Where one or more of the underwriters, although firmly committed, are subject to and do not meet the financial responsibility requirements of Rule 15c3–1 under the 1934 Act.

(5) Where the market price of the security being offered has been manipulated by persons connected with the offering.

The SEC has also invoked its policy refusing to accelerate in another situation. When a company has had a pooling of interests with another company, financial statements of the combined businesses for periods prior to the pooling customarily are retroactively restated to give effect to the pooling. Companies usually restate their formal financial statements in this respect, but some companies do not give similar treatment to the combination in the "highlights" or "up front" section of their published annual reports, or in similar tabulations of operating statistics. In Release No.

4910 under the 1933 Act, the SEC stated that where companies did not restate for poolings, the Commission would refuse to grant acceleration to the registration statement of the company involved. The author understands that the staff of the Commission has recently gone even further than the aforementioned release indicates; the staff has stated that in applicable situations it would refuse to process any filings by the company involved unless the company agreed to revise the "highlights" section or statistical tables appearing in future annual reports to shareholders along the lines indicated in the Commission's release.

Formerly there were two additional situations in which the SEC also denied acceleration, but these were withdrawn when the present acceleration policy set forth in the note to Rule 460 was adopted:

(1) Where there was no fair sharing of expenses in a secondary distribution, that is, a sale for the account of a shareholder; and

(2) Where the liquidating preference of preferred stock was materially in excess of its par value.

The Commission's former policy on payment of expenses by controlling stockholders in "secondary offerings" is supported at the present time by the securities administrators of ten states, namely, Illinois, Ohio, Michigan, Texas, Colorado, Nebraska, Arkansas, Wisconsin, Minnesota, and Indiana. In connection with applications to qualify or register securities for sale to the public under the "blue-sky" laws[3] of these states, the administrators adopted the following statement of policy: "It is also the consensus that in the case of sale of stock by stockholders, such stockholders shall pay their equitable proportion of the expense incident to the offering." [4] The above statement of policy by ten administrators was approved in 1946 by the National Association of Securities Administrators (name changed in 1957 to North American Securities Administrators).

The SEC's acceleration policy has been the subject of a great deal of controversy. Many people believe that the SEC is without authority to deny acceleration in some situations in which it exercises that authority. A Hoover Commission task force, in fact, cited the SEC's policy to support its conclusion that the SEC "is using this important authority to achieve purposes which have not been declared by Congress and are not within the general statutory objective of full disclosure." [5]

Delaying and Substantive Amendments.—If the registrant has not disposed of the Commission's comments before the effective date, the registration statement may become effective in deficient form. To prevent the

---

[3] These are discussed briefly on p. 11·14.

[4] CCH *Blue Sky Law Reporter*, p. 493.

[5] *Task Force Report on Regulatory Commissions Prepared for the Commission on Organization of the Executive Branch of the Government* (1949), pp. 148–49.

registration from becoming effective in that form, it was the practice of the SEC, in its letter of comments, to suggest that an amendment delaying the proposed offering date be filed on or before a specified date. This was a simple document which did nothing more than postpone the proposed public offering date and was called a "delaying amendment."

In order to avoid the red tape involved in filing delaying amendments, the Commission adopted Rule 473 pursuant to which the following legend appears on most, if not all, registration statements filed with the SEC:

> The registrant hereby amends this registration statement on such date or dates as may be necessary to delay its effective date until the registrant shall file a further amendment which specifically states that this registration statement shall thereafter become effective in accordance with Section 8(a) of the Securities Act of 1933 or until the registration statement shall become effective on such date as the Commission, acting pursuant to said Section 8(a), may determine.

Ordinarily, if the SEC's comments are not serious or if they do not have far-reaching implications, the company will want to file a "substantive" amendment as soon as possible. As its name suggests, a "substantive" amendment is one containing matters of substance. A substantive amendment is filed to correct the deficiencies in the initial filing subsequently discovered by the company and its experts as well as to comply with the SEC's comments and suggestions. The amendment is also filed whenever necessary to bring the information in the registration statement up to date, as may be necessary to give effect to changed conditions since the original filing.

The Price Amendment.—When a registration statement is filed, usually there is a meeting of minds between the issuer and the underwriter as to the type of security to be sold; that is, whether the offering will consist of common stock or preferred stock or bonds or, perhaps, a combination of them. In almost all cases, however, the issuer and the underwriter have not agreed on the price at which the securities are to be offered to the public, the underwriter's discount or commission, and the net proceeds to the issuer. Similarly, if the registration statement relates to preferred stock or bonds, there is usually no agreement at the time of the initial filing as to the precise terms, or the interest or dividend rate. These matters usually are still undecided at the time of filing the amendment which cures the SEC deficiencies, if any. This state of indecision is understandable in view of the fact that much depends on the situation then existing in the securities markets and the prices of similar securities of companies in similar industries.

While the registration statement and the amendment curing the SEC's deficiencies are in process of preparation, negotiations are conducted leading up to the final underwriting agreement. At the appropriate time the blank spaces in the underwriting agreement will be filled in, and the agreement will be signed by authorized representatives of the issuer and the underwriters. At this time another amendment to the registration statement will be prepared. This amendment will fill in the blank spaces in previous SEC filings relating to the interest rate, the dividend rate, the public offering price, the underwriter's discount or commission, and the net proceeds to the company (or selling stockholders). This is called the "price amendment," and at the time of its filing the issuer (or selling stockholder) and the underwriter customarily request acceleration so that the proposed offering to the public may be made promptly. The result of this procedure is that the waiting period, in effect, becomes the negotiating period. That is, in the interval between the initial filing and the day before the offering, the issuer (or selling stockholder) negotiates with the underwriter regarding the price to be paid for the securities to be sold.

If Required Amendments Are Not Filed.—If it appears to the SEC's examining group that the registrant has not complied with all the suggestions in its letter of comments, the group may nonetheless recommend that the registration statement be permitted to become effective in deficient form but without acceleration. This will be permitted, however, only if the matters involved are not material. On the other hand, if the matters in question are material, the group may recommend that the Commission begin proceedings under Section 8(b), refusing to permit the registration statement to become effective. Before or after the effective date, the Commission is also authorized to institute stop-order proceedings under Section 8(d), or it may begin an investigation under Section 8(e) to determine whether a stop-order should issue. Such proceedings are primarily the concern of lawyers and are outside the scope of this book.

SEC Declares Registration Statement Effective.—When the staff of the Commission inform the Commissioners that they have no important reservations with respect to the registration statement, that all the deficiencies have been properly disposed of, and the Commissioners are satisfied, the Commission declares the registration statement effective. The issuer and the underwriter are then in a position to proceed with the proposed sale.

The Commission may permit the registration statement to become effective in deficient form. This is a legal technicality into which it is not the purpose of this book to inquire. The managements of most companies, however, would not permit their registration statements to become effective in deficient form. On the contrary, they would insist that all deficiencies be taken care of to the satisfaction of all concerned, including the staff of the SEC.

Withdrawal of Registration Statement.—After a registration statement is filed with the Commission, the issuer, for various reasons, may wish to withdraw the registration statement. There may be changes in the securities market which make the proposed offering inadvisable. Even though the market may be favorable, the issuer (or selling stockholder) may not have been able to conclude a satisfactory agreement with the underwriter. In other cases, companies have successfully concluded private financing arrangements while a registration statement was incubating, and consequently the need for public financing no longer exists. In these and other circumstances, the registrant may wish to withdraw the registration statement.

The rules of the SEC provide that a registration statement or amendment may be withdrawn upon application to the Commission if the Commission finds such withdrawal consistent with the public interest and the protection of investors and consents to the withdrawal. Under Rule 477 the withdrawal application must be signed and must state fully the grounds on which it is made. If the Commission consents to the withdrawal, the fee paid to the SEC upon the original filing will not be refunded. If the Commission consents to withdrawal of the registration statement or amendment, the papers constituting the registration or amendment will not be removed from the SEC files, but will be marked "Withdrawn upon the request of the registrant, the Commission consenting thereto."

If the request for withdrawal is filed before the registration becomes effective, it is now the Commission's practice to consent to such withdrawal. Prior to the Jones case, [*Jones v. SEC*, 298 U. S. 1 (1936)] the SEC held that a registration statement, whether effective or pending, could be withdrawn only with its consent. In the Jones case, however, the Supreme Court of the United States held that a registrant had the unqualified right to withdraw a registration statement that had not yet become effective. The Commission, however, has never regarded the Jones case as binding when it appeared that the registrant had actually sold any of the registered securities or had previously sold other securities of the same class.[6]

Confidential Treatment.—A question frequently asked is whether any of the information required to be filed with the SEC under the 1933 Act may be filed in confidence and not disclosed to the public. In general, anything contained in a registration statement filed with the Commission becomes a public record available for public inspection at the time it is filed. The Commission, however, has promulgated Rule 485 under which the provisions of certain contracts will not be publicly disclosed if the Commission determines that such disclosure would impair the value of the contract and is not necessary for the protection of investors. The rule prescribes the

[6] Loss, *Securities Regulation,* 2d ed. (1961), p. 314.

procedure to be followed by registrants who request the SEC to accord confidential treatment to a contract or a portion of a contract. In an application for such confidential treatment, the applicant should state among other things whether or not the applicant is willing to permit the disclosure of the contract to other governmental bodies, since such permission is one factor which will be considered by the SEC in ruling on the application (Release No. 33–4936, Dec. 9, 1968).

General Instruction E of Form S–1 provides that information required by any item or other requirement of that form with respect to a foreign subsidiary may be omitted to the extent that the required disclosure would be detrimental to the registrant, provided a statement is made that such information has been omitted. In such case, a statement of the names of the subsidiaries omitted shall be separately furnished. The Commission may, in its discretion, call for justification that the required disclosure would be detrimental.

Rule 25 of the Commission's Rules of Practice sets forth the procedure to be followed in connection with a request for confidential treatment of information. The text of the rule follows:

Rule 25. Confidential Treatment of Certain Matters

(a) *Requests for Confidential Treatment.* Confidential treatment of material listed in [Rule 25(a)] may be requested for good cause where authorized by statute. Request for confidential treatment may be made pursuant to the provisions of Clause 30 of Schedule A of the [1933] Act [which deals with material contracts] and [Rule 485] thereunder [which also deals with material contracts], Section 24(b) of the [1934] Act [relating to nondisclosure of information] and [Rule 24b-2] thereunder [also relating to nondisclosure of information], Section 22(b) of the Public Utility Holding Company Act of 1935 and [Rule 104] thereunder, Section 45(a) of the Investment Company Act of 1940 and [Rule 45a-1] thereunder. . . . In any case where a hearing for the purpose of taking testimony relating to whether confidential treatment should be granted or continued is to be held, the Commission may in its discretion, prior to the hearing, require the person desiring the confidential treatment to furnish in writing additional information in respect of its grounds of objection to public disclosure. Failure to supply the information so requested within 15 days from the date of receipt by the registrant of a notice of the information required, shall be deemed a waiver of the objections to public disclosure of that portion of the information filed confidentially with respect to which the additional information required by the Commission relates, unless the Commission shall otherwise order for good cause shown at or before the expiration of such 15-day period.

(b) *Procedure in Confidential Treatment Cases.* (1) All papers containing data as to which confidential treatment is sought, together with any application making objection to the disclosure thereof, or other papers relating in any way to such application, shall be made available to the public only in accordance with orders of the Commission and/or the applicable provisions of [Rule 485 under the 1933 Act, Rule 24b-2 under the 1934 Act, Rule 104 under the Holding

Company Act], section 45 of the Investment Company Act of 1940 and [Rule 45a-1 thereunder]. . . .

(2) Proposed findings and conclusions and briefs in support of such proposed findings and conclusions, an initial decision, any petition for Commission review thereof, and any briefs pursuant to Commission order for review which are filed in connection with any proceeding concerning confidential treatment shall, unless otherwise ordered by the Commission, be for the confidential use only of the hearing officer, the Commission, the parties and counsel. The initial page of copies of such an initial decision will contain a statement that such decision is nonpublic. The order of the Commission sustaining or denying the application for confidential treatment shall be made available to the public. Any findings or opinion issued by a hearing officer or by the Commission in any proceeding relating to confidential treatment shall be made public at such time as the material filed confidentially is made available to the public.

[Paragraph (c) of the rule was repealed in 1964.]

(d) *Purchase of Transcripts of Private Hearings.* Transcripts of private hearings will be supplied to the parties at the prescribed rates.

Rule 171 under the 1933 Act provides, in part: "Any requirement to the contrary notwithstanding, no registration statement, prospectus, or other document filed with the Commission or used in connection with the offering or sale of any securities shall contain any document or information that has been classified or determined by an appropriate department or agency of the United States to require protection in the interests of national defense."

Except as stated above, there is no provision for confidential treatment of matter filed as part of a registration statement (including the financial statements). In a particular case, a registrant may apply for confidential treatment of a portion of the financial statements. In the opinion of the author, the application has little possibility of being granted unless the reasons for the request are compelling.

The Boruski Case.—In January 1971 there was a decision in the U.S. District Court (S. D. N. Y.) which considered, among other things, the question of whether the SEC was within its rights in refusing to furnish a registrant under the 1933 Act with the comments and criticisms of the SEC's staff concerning a registration statement. Particularly since the inception of the cursory review procedure discussed previously in this chapter, the SEC has not hesitated to suggest that a registration statement be withdrawn when it seemed to be poorly and carelessly prepared rather than furnishing the registrant with a detailed list of deficiencies. The Court decision referred to above was in the case of *Boruski, et al. v. Division of Corporation Finance of the SEC* (CCH Fed. Sec. Law Rep., p. 90461–4).

The plaintiff submitted two registration statements early in 1970 under the 1933 Act. The checks in payment of the SEC registration fees had not been certified, however, and the documents had not been properly signed. The documents were returned to the plaintiff who, at the same time, was advised that a cursory review of each registration statement indicated it was so poorly prepared and presented such serious disclosure problems that, even if properly filed, no further staff review would be made; also that no oral or written comments would be provided, for to do so would delay the review of other registration statements which did not contain substantial disclosure deficiencies. The SEC staff recommended to the plaintiff that, prior to resubmission of the registration statements, they be revised to set forth properly all the required information to comply with statutory requirements.

The plaintiff resubmitted the registration statements in substantially the original form. This time, however, the checks were certified and the statements were properly signed.

The SEC wrote the plaintiff calling his attention to its previous comments and informed him that unless withdrawn, the resubmitted statements would become effective by operation of law. To avoid the statements becoming effective in deficient form, the SEC recommended that the statements be withdrawn. The SEC also informed him that any offers or sales of securities covered by the registration statements "may constitute serious violations of the securities laws." He was asked to inform the Commission of his intentions. Upon his failure to do so, he was notified that the SEC had authorized an examination and private investigation into the adequacy and accuracy of the disclosures in the registration statements pursuant to the SEC statutes. He was also informed again that any offerings or sales of securities of the companies would constitute a violation of the federal securities laws.

Thereafter the plaintiff replied, and, in the words of the judge, "rather blithely ignoring the substance of the Commission's earlier communications," he wrote to the Commission as follows:

. . . We are indeed pleased to learn that the registration for [names of registrants] became effective . . . We accept this registration, and we are proceeding to act upon it.

We are also pleased to note that you have not specified any deficiency in your prior letters . . . nor in your telegram . . . nor in your current letter . . .

We have examined [sections of the 1933 and 1934 Acts] and we fail to find any violations on our part, any deficiencies, or any inaccuracies. Any claims by you to the contrary are wilful, wrongful and malicious lies (termed 'perjury' in polite legalese) . . .

In connection with its investigation, the SEC subpoenaed the plaintiff as a witness and also served a subpoena duces tecum for the production of specified books, records, etc. The plaintiff testified, but did not produce any books or records, and said that there were none.

The Court said that it had examined the registration statements in question as well as the testimony, and that the Commission's staff was fully justified in its position with respect to the inadequacies of the registration statements. The Court said:

. . . A mere reading of them indicates they include a number of matters that in fact are incomprehensible, and their incomprehensibility is underscored by plaintiff's purported explanation when he testified at the hearing. Some of the matters contained in the statement are so unilluminating as to foreclose meaningful comment thereon. Moreover, each registration statement sets forth that plaintiff had '36 years investing experience and 19 years in investment brokerage', but failed to disclose that orders had been entered by the Commission, revoking his broker-dealer registration, expelling him from the National Association of Securities Dealers and denying him registration as an investment adviser. . . . With the registration statements so palpably deficient, the Commission was not required to . . . specify their shortcomings.

The Court observed that the responsibility for submitting an adequate registration statement complying with the law is upon the issuer and cannot be shifted to the Commission or its staff by requiring them to pinpoint each inadequacy, misstatement, or failure to disclose a material fact. The Court found "entirely reasonable" the Commission's refusal to furnish comment letters in cases when the deficiencies appear to stem from careless disregard of the statutes and rules or a deliberate attempt to conceal or mislead.

Based on the facts presented, the Court asserted that the Commission's staff had acted "properly and in accordance with the Commission's usual and reasonable procedure applicable to the processing of registration statements." With respect to the registration statements in question, the Court said there was not "the slightest basis for any charge of improper conduct against the Commission or any of its staff."

All of the plaintiff's claims were accordingly denied.

CHAPTER 8

1933 ACT REGISTRATION AND NOTIFICATION FORMS

CONTENTS

Section 7 and Schedules A and B of the 1933 Act

The statutory foundation for the contents of a registration statement filed pursuant to the Securities Act of 1933 is in Section 7 of the Act, which sets forth the information required in a registration statement. This section provides that a registration statement relating to a security other than that of a foreign government or a political subdivision thereof shall contain the information, and be accompanied by the documents, specified in Schedule A of the Act. When the registration relates to a security issued by a foreign government, or a political subdivision thereof, the registration statement has to contain the information, and be accompanied by the documents, specified in Schedule B of the Act. The Commission, however, has authority to provide that any of the information or documents specified in Schedules A and B need not be included in respect of any class of issuers or securities if it finds that the requirement for such information or documents is not applicable to such class and that adequate disclosure for the protection of investors is otherwise required to be included in the registration statement. In addition, Section 7 provides that registration statements shall contain such other information as the Commission may require as being necessary or appropriate in the public interest or for the protection of investors.

Schedule A of the 1933 Act sets forth 32 items of information for inclusion in registration statements of issuers other than foreign governments. Item 25 sets forth the requirements for balance sheets, Item 26 the requirements for profit and loss statements, and Item 27 the requirements with regard to profit and loss statements of businesses to be acquired with the proceeds of the security being registered. As indicated in Section 7 of the Act discussed in the preceding paragraph, the Commission has considerable discretion in determining what should be in a registration statement, and so Schedule A is not necessarily controlling. Schedule A, for example, calls for a balance sheet of the issuer as of a date within 90 days of filing the registration. As will be seen from the discussion of the requirements for financial statements of various forms that follows, in many cases a balance sheet may be filed as of a date within six months.

In addition, the financial requirements are often stated in general terms. Item 25, for example, states that the balance sheet of the issuer shall include all the liabilities of the issuer "in such detail and such form as the Commission shall prescribe." The Commission's requirements as to form and content of financial statements are set forth in its Regulation S–X.

Consequently, as far as the financial statements are concerned, the registrant and the independent public accountant are primarily concerned with the SEC's requirements as set forth in the applicable registration form and in the regulations—principally Regulation S–X.

Registration Statement Forms Under 1933 Act

The SEC has promulgated several "forms" applicable to different types of issuers filing registration statements under the 1933 Act. These are not blank forms intended to be filled in like a tax return form. They serve merely as a guide setting forth the "items" of information required to be furnished and the instructions relating thereto. An issuer may have a choice of forms depending on the type of securities being registered.

The decision as to which form to use for registration in a specific case is usually made by the company in consultation with its counsel. Since the question of which form to use is primarily a legal one, the certifying accountant should not make the decision, although he can often help in determining whether a company fulfills the requirements of a particular form, as for example, in the case of Form S–9, the use of which depends in part on compliance with stated ratios of earnings to fixed charges. A wrong decision as to the form to be used is apt to have serious or embarrassing consequences.

SEC Rule 401 provides that, "A registration statement shall be prepared in accordance with the form prescribed therefor by the Commission as in effect on the date of filing. Any registration statement shall be deemed to be filed on the proper form unless objection to the form is made by the Commission prior to the effective date of the statement."

A complete listing of all registration statement forms under the Securities Act of 1933 currently in use follows.

Form S–1, General Form.—Form S–1 is used for registration of securities of all issuers for which no other form is authorized or prescribed, except that this form shall not be used for securities of foreign governments or political subdivisions thereof. This is the form most commonly used to register securities under the 1933 Act. A brief indication of the scope and content of a registration statement on Form S–1 is indicated by the following listing of the items of information required to be included in the form.

Part I.   Information required in the prospectus:

Item 1.   Offering price information and distribution spread

Item 2.   Plan of distribution, names of underwriters and their participations, and nature of the underwriters' obligation

Item 3.   Use of proceeds to registrant

Item 4.   Sales of securities otherwise than for cash

Item 5.   Capital structure

Item 6.   Summary of earnings (see Chapter **10**)

Item 7.   State and date of incorporation and type of organization of the registrant

Item 8.   Parents of the registrant and basis of control

Item 9.   Description of the business and its development during the past five years. This is the item which requires disclosure in certain cases of information with respect to principal lines of business, and is commented upon in Chapter **23**.

Item 10.   Description and location of principal plants, mines, and other physical properties

Item 11.   If organized within five years, names of and transactions with promoters

Item 12.   Pending legal proceedings other than routine litigation

Items 13, 14, and 15.   Information as to capital stock, funded debt, or other securities being registered

Item 16.   Names of directors and executive officers and the principal occupations of the latter during the past five years

Item 17.   Remuneration paid by the affiliated group during latest fiscal year to (1) each director, and each of the three highest paid officers, of the registrant who received more than $30,000, and (2) all directors and officers as a group

Item 18.   Outstanding options to purchase securities from the registrant or subsidiaries

Item 19.   Principal holders of registrant's securities

Item 20.   Interest of directors, officers, and certain other persons in certain material transactions during last three years or in any proposed transaction

Item 21.   Financial statements (see Chapter **9**)

Part II.   Information not required in the prospectus:

Item 22.   Arrangements limiting, restricting, or stabilizing the market for securities being offered

Item 23.   Expenses of the issue

Item 24.   Relationship with registrant of experts named in the registration statement (including accountants—see Chapter **26**)

Item 25.   Sales of securities to special parties

Item 26.   Recent sales of unregistered securities

Item 27.   List of subsidiaries of the registrant

Item 28.   Franchises or concessions held by the registrant and subsidiaries

Item 29.   Indemnification arrangements for officers and directors

Item 30.   Accounting for proceeds from sale of capital stock being registered

Item 31.   List of financial statements (see Chapter **9**) and exhibits

Form S–2, for Commercial and Industrial Companies in the Development Stage.—This form may be used for registration of shares of stock of any corporation which are to be sold to the public for cash if such corporation:

(a) Is not an insurance, investment or mining company;

(b) Has not had any substantial gross returns from the sale of products or services, or any substantial net income from any source, for any fiscal year ended during the past five years;

(c) Has not succeeded and does not intend to succeed to any business which has had any substantial gross returns from the sale of products or services, or any substantial net income from any source, for any fiscal year ended during the past five years; and

(d) Does not have and does not intend to have any subsidiaries other than inactive subsidiaries with no more than nominal assets.

The scope and content of a registration statement on Form S–2 are indicated by the following list of items of information that must be included in the form.

Part I. Information required in the prospectus:

Item 1. Offering price information and distribution spread

Item 2. Plan of distribution, names of underwriters, their participations, and nature of their obligation

Item 3. Use of proceeds to the registrant

Item 4. Year and state of incorporation of registrant, and kind of business done or intended to be done

Item 5. Location and description of principal plants and physical properties

Item 6. Material pending litigation

Item 7. Title and description of shares being registered

Item 8. Names and addresses of promoters

Item 9. Remuneration paid by the registrant during latest fiscal year to (1) each director, and each of the three highest paid officers, of the registrant who received more than $20,000, and (2) all directors and officers as a group

Item 10. Options to purchase securities of the registrant

Item 11. Securities of the registrant held by directors and officers as a group, and by persons holding more than 10% of any class of such securities

Item 12. Interest of directors, officers, and certain other persons in certain material transactions during the last five years or in any material proposed transactions

Item 13. Financial statements (see Chapter **9**)

Part II. Information not required in the prospectus:

Item 14. Expenses of the issue

Item 15. Relationship with registrant of experts named in the registration statement (including accountants—see Chapter **26**)

Item 16. Recent sales of unregistered securities

Item 17. Indemnification arrangements for officers and directors

Item 18. List of exhibits

Form S–3, for Shares of Mining Corporations in the Promotional Stage.—This form is to be used for registration of shares of any corporation engaged or intending to engage primarily in the exploration, development, or exploitation of mineral deposits other than oil or gas deposits, if the securities being registered are to be sold to the public for cash and if the following conditions are met:

(a) The aggregate gross receipts of the registrant from the sale of its products during the past five years have not exceeded the aggregate amount of its exploration, development and operating expenses for that period, exclusive of expenditures and liabilities incurred for plants and major equipment;

(b) The registrant has not succeeded and does not intend to succeed to any business the aggregate gross receipts of which from the sale of its products during the past five years have exceeded the aggregate amount of its exploration, development and operating expenses for that period, exclusive of expenditures and liabilities incurred for plants or major equipment; and

(c) The registrant does not have and does not intend to have any subsidiaries other than inactive subsidiaries with no more than nominal assets.

The scope and content of a registration statement on Form S–3 are indicated by the following listing of items of information that must be furnished:

Part I.   Information required in the prospectus:

Item 1.   Offering price information and distribution spread

Item 2.   Names of underwriters, their participations, and nature of their obligation

Item 3.   Use of proceeds to registrant

Item 4.   Year and state of incorporation and kind of business done or intended to be done

Item 5.   Material pending legal proceedings

Item 6.   Title and description of shares being registered

Item 7.   Names and addresses of promoters

Item 8.   Remuneration paid by the registrant during latest fiscal year to (1) each director, and each of the three highest paid officers, of the registrant who received more than $20,000, and (2) all officers and directors as a group

Item 9.   Options to purchase securities of the registrant

Item 10.   Securities of the registrant held by directors and officers as a group, and by persons holding more than 10% of any class of such securities

Item 11.   Interest of directors, officers, and certain other persons in certain material transactions during the last five years or in any material proposed transactions

Item 12.   Financial statements (see Chapter **9**)

Part II.   Information not required in the prospectus:

Item 13.   Expenses of the issue

Item 14.   Relationship with registrant of experts named in the registration statement (including accountants—see Chapter **26**)

Item 15.   Recent sales of unregistered securities

Item 16.   Indemnification arrangements for directors and officers of the registrant

Item 17.   List of exhibits

Form S–4, for Closed-End Management Investment Companies Registered on Form N–8B–1.—This form is to be used for registration under the 1933 Act of securities of any *closed-end* management investment company registered under the Investment Company Act of 1940 on Form N–8B–1.

The scope and content of a registration statement on Form S–4 are indicated by the following list of items of information that must be furnished in such a registration statement:

Part I.   Information required in the prospectus:

Item 1.   Offering price and distribution spread

Item 2.   Names of underwriters, their participations, and nature of their obligation

Item 3.   Use of proceeds to registrant

Item 4.   Purpose of the distribution if securities are to be offered otherwise than for cash

Item 5.   Information that would be required by the following items of Form N–8B–1 if a registration statement on that form were currently being filed under the Investment Company Act:

1. Form of organization, state and date of incorporation
2. Nature of any business other than that of investment company during past five years; material interests of affiliated persons during past three years in transactions with registrant
3. Classification of registrant (diversified or non-diversified)
4. Fundamental policies of registrant (issuance of senior securities, borrowing money, concentration in certain industries, real estate transactions, commodity transactions, loans to others, etc.)
5. Policies with respect to security investments
8. Compliance with Supplement Q of Internal Revenue Code
9. Material pending legal proceedings
10. Capitalization table
11. Defaults and arrears on senior securities
12. Condensed financial information for the last ten years plus the stub period to the date of the most recent balance sheet filed, setting forth per share income and capital changes
13. Persons controlling the registrant
14. Ownership of equity securities of the registrant by officers, directors, and certain other persons

16. Names and addresses of directors and executive officers
17. Names and addresses of members of advisory board, if any
18. Remuneration of each director, each of the three highest paid officers, and each member of the advisory board, of the registrant who received more than $30,000, and of all directors, officers, and advisory board members as a group
21(a). Name and address of custodian of securities if other than a commercial bank or trust company
22. Name and address of investment advisers
25. Remuneration of certain affiliated persons
26. If capital stock is being registered, the title of the issue and a description thereof
27. If long-term debt is being registered, the title of the issue and a description thereof
28. If securities other than capital stock or long-term debt are being registered, the title of the issue and a description thereof

Item 6.   Financial statements (see Chapter **9**)

Part II.   Information not required in prospectus:

Item 7.   Marketing arrangements
Item 8.   Expenses of the issue
Item 9.   Indemnification arrangements for directors and officers
Item 10.   List of financial statements (see Chapter **9**) and exhibits

Form S–5, for Open-End Management Investment Companies Registered on Form N–8B–1.—This form is used for registration under the 1933 Act of securities of any *open-end* management investment company registered under the Investment Company Act of 1940 on Form N–8B–1.

A prospectus for securities registered on Form S–5 has to include the financial statements listed in Chapter **9** and the information that would be required by the following items of Form N–8B–1 if a registration statement on that form were being currently filed under the Investment Company Act:

1. Form of organization, state and date of incorporation
2. Nature of any business other than that of an investment company during past five years; material interests of affiliated persons during past three years in transactions with registrant
3. Classification of registrant (diversified or non-diversified)
4. Fundamental policies of registrant (issuance of senior securities, borrowing money, investing in real estate and commodities, lending money, etc.)
5. Policies with respect to security investments
8. Compliance with Supplement Q of Internal Revenue Code

9. Material pending legal proceedings

12. Condensed financial information for the last ten years plus the stub period to the date of the most recent balance sheet filed, setting forth per share income and capital changes

13. Persons controlling the registrant

14. Ownership of equity securities of the registrant by officers, directors, and certain other persons

16. Names and addresses of directors and executive officers

17. Names and addresses of members of advisory board, if any

18. Remuneration of each director, each of the three highest paid officers, and each member of the advisory board, of the registrant who received more than $30,000, and of all directors, officers, and advisory board members as a group

21(a). Name and address of custodian of securities if other than a commercial bank or trust company

22. Name and address of investment adviser

25. Remuneration of certain affiliated persons

26. If capital stock is being registered, the title of the issue and a description thereof

30. Method followed in pricing registrant's securities for sale, redemption, or repurchase

31(a). Names and addresses of principal underwriters and nature of any material relationship with registrant

32. Relationship between persons affiliated with underwriters and persons affiliated with registrant

33. Compensation of underwriters affiliated with registrant

The prospectus in a Form S–5 registration statement must also contain the financial statements set forth in Chapter **9**.

Form S–6, for Unit Investment Trusts Registered on Form N–8B–2.—This form may be used for registration under the Securities Act of 1933 of securities of any unit investment trust registered under the Investment Company Act of 1940 on Form N–8B–2. Inasmuch as this form is seldom used, its scope and content are not described here.

Form S–7, for Registration of Securities of Certain Issuers to Be Offered for Cash.—This is a short form for registration under the 1933 Act of securities which are to be offered for cash provided the registrant meets the following conditions:

(a) The registrant (1) has a class of equity securities registered pursuant to Section 12(b) of the 1934 Act; or (2) is organized under the laws of the United States or any state or territory or the District of Columbia, has its principal business operations in the United States or its territories, and has a class of equity securities registered pursuant to Section 12(g) of the 1934 Act.

(b) The registrant has been subject to and has complied in all respects, including timeliness, with the requirements of Sections 13 and 14 of the 1934 Act for a period of at least three fiscal years immediately preceding the filing of the registration statement on Form S–7.

(c) A majority of the existing Board of Directors of the registrant have been directors thereof or a predecessor from the beginning of the registrant's last three fiscal years to the date of filing the registration statement on Form S–7.

(d) The registrant and its subsidiaries have not during the past ten years defaulted in the payment of any dividend or sinking fund instalment on preferred stock, or in the payment of any principal, interest, or sinking fund instalment on any indebtedness for borrowed money, or in the payment of rentals under long-term leases.

(e) The registrant and its consolidated subsidiaries had net income, after taxes but before extraordinary items net of tax effect, of at least $500,000 for each of the last five fiscal years.

(f) If the securities to be registered are common stock or securities convertible into common stock, the registrant earned in each of the last five fiscal years any dividends, including the fair market value of any stock dividends, paid in each such year on all classes of securities. If the registrant paid a stock dividend in any of such fiscal years, the aggregate amount transferred from additional capital to capital in respect of each such dividend was charged only to retained earnings account and was equal to the aggregate fair market value of the stocks issued as such dividend.

The Commission has, on occasion, been liberal in its interpretations of its rules for the use of Form S–7 and has permitted it to be used in circumstances not strictly complying with the rules. For example, one of the world's largest manufacturing enterprises did not earn in one year the dividends it paid to shareholders in that year because of a strike by employees, and hence did not comply with the conditions in paragraph (f) above. Nonetheless, the Commission permitted the company to use Form S–7 since it complied in all other respects.

Also, the rules for the use of Form S–7 state that it is to be used only in connection with offerings of securities for cash. The Commission has waived this requirement, however, and permitted the form to be used for the registration of securities to be issued upon conversion of Eurobonds by companies which, in all other respects, met the requirements for use of the form. In a particular case, however, if it appears to the staff of the Commission that Form S–7 would not be appropriate, it may not be permitted.

On the other hand, the Commission has occasionally insisted on strict compliance with some of the conditions for the use of Form S–7. For example, in the second of the conditions listed above, one of the requirements refers to "timeliness" of filings. The SEC prohibited a registrant from using Form S–7 because, in the three most recent years, the company had been two to three days late in filing two Form 8–K's and one Form 9–K (formerly a semi-annual report which has been replaced by Form 10–Q, a quarterly report form).

Like several of the other registration forms, Form S–7 consists of two parts—Part I consisting of information to be included in the prospectus, and Part II consisting of information that may be omitted from the prospectus. Part I consists of the following items of information:

Item 1. Offering price and distribution spread

Item 2. Names of underwriters, if any, amount of their participations, and nature of their underwriting obligation

Item 3. Use of proceeds to the registrant

Item 4. Sales by security holders and their holdings (as a percentage of the class) after the offering

Item 5. Description of the business of the registrant and subsidiaries. This is the item which requires disclosure in certain cases of information with respect to principal lines of business, and is commented upon in Chapter **23**

Item 6. Statement of income; see Chapter **9**

Item 7. If capital stock is being registered, the title and a description thereof

Item 8. If debt securities are being registered, the title and a description thereof

Item 9. If other securities are being registered, an outline of the rights thereof

Item 10. Other financial statements; see Chapter **9**

Item 11. Statement of availability of other information pursuant to requirements of 1934 Act

Part II consists of the following items of information that need not be included in the prospectus:

Item 12. Other expenses of issuance and distribution

Item 13. Relationship with registrant and subsidiaries of any expert named in the registration statement (including accountants—see Chapter **26**)

Item 14. Indemnification arrangements for directors and officers

Form S–8, for Registration of Securities to Be Offered to Employees Pursuant to Certain Plans.—Any issuer which, at the time of filing a registration statement on Form S–8, is required to file reports pursuant to Section 13 or 15(d) of the 1934 Act may use Form S–8 for registration under the 1933 Act of the following securities:

(a) Securities of such issuer to be offered to its employees, or to employees of its subsidiaries, pursuant to a stock purchase, savings, or similar plan which meets the following conditions:

(1) Periodic cash payments are made, or periodic payroll deductions are authorized, by participating employees in an amount not to exceed a specified percentage of the employee's compensation or a specified maximum annual amount;

(2) Contributions are made by the employer in cash, securities of the issuer, or other substantial benefits, including the offering of securities at a discount from the market value thereof or the payment of expenses of the plan, in accordance with a specified formula or arrangement;

(3) Securities purchased with funds of the plan are acquired in amounts which, at the time of the payment of the purchase price, do not exceed the funds deposited or otherwise available for such payment; provided, that such purchases are made periodically, or from time to time, upon a reasonably current basis, and at prices not in excess of the current market price at the time of purchase;

(4) Prior to the time the employee becomes entitled to withdraw all funds or securities allocable to his account, he may withdraw at least that portion of the cash and securities in his account representing his contributions.

(b) Interests in the above plan, if such interests constitute securities and are required to be registered under the 1933 Act.

(c) Stock to be offered pursuant to "qualified," or "employee stock purchase plan" stock options as those terms are defined in Section 422 and 423 of the Internal Revenue Code of 1954, as amended, or "restricted stock options" as defined in Section 424(b) thereof, provided however, that for the purposes of this paragraph an option which meets all of the conditions of that Section other than the date of issuance shall be deemed to be "restricted stock options."

Except as to certain exhibits, all of the required information in a Form S–8 registration statement has to be included in the prospectus. The scope and content of the prospectus are indicated by the following listing of required items of information:

Note: Items 1 to 11, inclusive, apply only to plans other than qualified or restricted stock option plans, and need not be answered with respect to such plans.

Item 1. General information regarding the plan

Item 2. Who may participate

Item 3. Contributions under the plan

Item 4. Withdrawal provisions

Item 5. Default provisions

Item 6. Administration of the plan

Item 7. Investment and disposition of funds

Item 8. Creation of liens on assets of the plan

Item 9. Termination and extension of the plan

Item 10. Other charges and deductions against participants or property of the plan

Item 11. Financial statements of the plan (see Chapter **9**)

Note: Items 12 to 18, inclusive, apply only to qualified or restricted stock option plans, and need not be answered with respect to other plans.

Item 12. Issuer and who may participate

Item 13. Nature, purpose, and duration of the plan, and tax aspects thereof

Item 14. Securities subject to the plan

Item 15. Eligibility and extent of participation

Item 16. Exercise of options

Item 17. Provisions regarding death of employee, termination of employment, and assignment of options

Item 18. Information regarding outstanding options

Item 19. Summary of earnings (see Chapter **10**)

Item 20. Range of market prices of issuer's securities

Item 21. Certain significant developments in last five years involving the issuer

Item 22. Information regarding capital stock being registered

Item 23. Information regarding other securities being registered

Item 24. Principal holders of equity securities

Item 25. Financial statements (see Chapter **9**)

Form S–9, for Registration of Nonconvertible Fixed Interest Debt Securities.—This form may be used for registration under the 1933 Act of nonconvertible, fixed interest, debt securities of an issuer which files reports pursuant to Section 13 or 15(d) of the 1934 Act if the following conditions are met:

(1) The issuer is organized under the laws of the United States, any State or Territory or the District of Columbia, or under the laws of Canada or any political subdivision thereof, and has its principal business operations in the United States, its Territories, or Canada;

(2) The issuer has been engaged in business of substantially the same general character for at least the last ten years;

(3) The issuer has had a net income during each of its last five fiscal years and has not during that period defaulted in the payment of principal, interest, or sinking fund on any indebtedness for borrowed money or in the payment of rentals under long-term leases;

(4) If the issuer has had fixed charges during any of its last five fiscal years or any more recently-ended twelve-month period reported in the registration statement, then (i) the earnings of the issuer (after all operating and income deductions, except fixed charges and taxes based on income or profits and after eliminating undistributed income of unconsolidated companies, have been at least three times its fixed charges in the case of utilities, or ten times its fixed charges in the case of any other issuer, for each such fiscal year and twelve-month period; and (ii) for the last fiscal year or twelve-month period so reported, such earnings have been at least three times its fixed charges in the case of utilities, or six times its fixed charges in the case of any other issuer, for such period, adjusted to give effect to (A) the issuance of securities to be registered, (B) any issuance or retirement of securities during or after such period, or (C) any presently proposed issuance, retirement or redemption of securities;

(5) If the issuer has had no fixed charges since the beginning of its last three fiscal years, then the earnings of the issuer, computed as in (4) above, have been three times its fixed charges with respect to the securities being registered in the case of utilities, or six times such fixed charges in the case of any other issuer, for each of such fiscal years and any more recently-ended twelve-month period reported, adjusted to give effect to the securities being registered and to any presently proposed issuance of securities;

(6) The securities being registered amount to not less than $1,000,000 principal amount, and are to be offered for cash in units of not less than $500 principal amount on terms intended to provide reasonable assurance that, if any of such securities are sold, all will be sold; and

(7) The securities being registered are not expressly subordinated, as to payment of principal or interest, to the prior payment of any outstanding securities of the issuer and the indenture does not permit such subordination without the consent of the holders of at least a majority in principal amount of the outstanding securities of the class being registered.

The term "fixed charges" has a special meaning; see the discussion of "Ratio of earnings to fixed charges" on page **8·19**.

If the registration statement includes consolidated financial statements, satisfaction of the conditions specified in (2) through (5) above must be determined on a consolidated basis for the periods covered by such statements. The term "issuer" as used above will include predecessors of the issuer if the registrant so elects; and in such event the earnings and fixed charges of the issuer and its predecessors for the same period are to be combined for the purpose of determining compliance with the above conditions. In the case of utilities, interest credit charged to construction, where applicable, shall for the purposes of these computations be added to gross income and not deducted from interest.

Form S–9 reduces the prospectus informational requirements (Part I of the registration statement) essentially to five items as follows:

Item 1.   Offering price and distribution spread

Item 2.   Use of proceeds to registrant

Item 3(a).   Summary of earnings and surplus (see Chapters **9** and **10**)

Item 3(b).   Principal products or services, information as to reserves of extractive industries, gross property additions and retirements in last five years

Item 4.   Securities being registered

Item 5.   Other financial statements (See Chapter **9**)

Part II of the registration statement on Form S–9 includes the following items of information:

Item 6.   List of underwriters and their participations, and nature of their affiliations with the registrant

Item 7.   Expenses of the issue

Item 8.   Relationship with registrant or its affiliates of experts named in the registration statement (including accountants—see Chapter **26**)

Item 9.   List of financial statements and exhibits

Form S–10, for Oil and Gas Interests or Rights.—Form S–10 is used for registration of landowners' royalty interests, overriding royalty interests, participating interests, working interests, oil or gas payments, oil or gas fee interests, oil or gas leasehold interests, and other producing or non-producing oil or gas interests or rights.

Form S–11, for Securities of Certain Real Estate Companies.— Form S–11 is used for registration of (i) securities issued by real estate investment trusts, as defined in Section 856 of the Internal Revenue Code, or (ii) securities issued by other issuers whose business is primarily that of acquiring and holding for investment real estate, or interests in real estate, or interests in other issuers whose business is primarily that of acquiring and holding real estate or interests in real estate for investment. This form is not used by investment companies subject to the Investment Company Act of 1940. In recent years real estate investment trusts have become an increasingly widespread form of investment.

The scope and content of registration statements on Form S–11 are set forth below:

Part I.   Information required in prospectus

Item 1.   Offering price and distribution spread
Item 2.   List of underwriters, their participations, and nature of their obligation
Item 3.   Use of proceeds to registrant
Item 4.   Sales of securities otherwise than for cash
Item 5.   Capitalization table
Item 6.   Summary of earnings (see Chapter **10**)
Item 7.   General information regarding registrant
Item 8.   Policy with respect to certain activities
Item 9.   Investment policies
Item 10.   Description of real estate
Item 11.   Operating data with respect to each material improved property
Item 12.   Tax treatment of registrant and security holders
Item 13.   Description of shares being registered
Item 14.   Description of long-term debt being registered
Item 15.   Other securities being registered
Item 16.   Material pending legal proceedings
Item 17.   Parents of the registrant
Item 18.   Equity securities of the registrant owned by directors and officers and "principal holders"
Item 19.   Names of directors and principal executive officers, and their principal occupations during past five years
Item 20.   Remuneration of each director, and each of the three highest paid officers, of the registrant who received more than $30,000 in latest fiscal year, and remuneration of all directors and officers as a group
Item 21.   Description of outstanding options to purchase securities of the registrant
Item 22.   Selection of management and registrant's investments
Item 23.   Provisions of governing instruments with respect to certain transactions
Item 24.   Interest of certain persons in transactions with registrant
Item 25.   Limitations of liability
Item 26.   Financial statements (see Chapter **9**)

Part II.   Information not required in prospectus

Item 27.   Expenses of issue and distribution
Item 28.   Relationship with registrant and its affiliates of experts

named in the registration statement (including accountants—Chapter **26**)

Item 29. Sales to special parties

Item 30. Recent sales of unregistered securities

Item 31. List of subsidiaries of registrant

Item 32. Indemnification arrangements for directors and officers

Item 33. Accounting treatment of proceeds from stock being registered

Item 34. List of financial statements (see Chapter **9**) and exhibits

Form S–12, for American Depository Receipts Issued Against Outstanding Foreign Securities.—Form S–12 is used for registration of American Depository Receipts issued against securities of foreign issuers deposited or to be deposited with an American depository (whether physically held by such depository in America or abroad) provided: (i) that the holder of the receipts may withdraw the deposited securities at any time, subject only to certain specified conditions, and (ii) that the deposited securities, if sold in the United States or its territories, would not be subject to the registration provisions of the 1933 Act.

Form S–13, for Voting Trust Certificates.—Form S–13 is used for the registration under the 1933 Act of voting trust certificates. The form is seldom encountered in practice and its content is therefore omitted here.

Form S–14, for Securities Issued Under Rule 133(a) Transactions.—Form S–14 may be used for registration of securities issued in a transaction specified in paragraph (a) of Rule 133 and which may be offered to the public by underwriters as defined in paragraphs (b) and (c) of such rule, if the registrant was subject to and solicited proxies from its stockholders with respect to such transaction in accordance with the provisions of the proxy regulation under the 1934 Act. Issuers that do not meet these conditions must use the form otherwise appropriate for registration. In a registration on Form S–14, the proxy statement becomes the basis for the prospectus to which a small amount of additional information is added to become the complete registration statement.

Form S–16, for Registration of Certain Securities of Issuers Entitled to Use Form S–7.—Form S–16 is a recently adopted registration form, having become effective on January 29, 1971. As will be seen from the discussion of Item 6 below and in Chapter **9**, a large part of a registration statement on this form consists of a mandatory incorporation by reference of all the statements and reports filed by the registrant under a different SEC statute, namely, the 1934 Act. In addition, a statement must be made in response to Item 6 that similar material subsequently filed under the 1934 Act is also deemed to be incorporated by reference.

Form S–16 is the first form under the 1933 Act to have been adopted by the Commission in which the prospectus simply incorporates by reference other materials as major portions of the normal disclosure requirements. Because of this tie-in with material filed under the 1934 Act, the adoption of Form S–16 represents an important first step in the integration of the Federal securities laws. In adopting the form, the SEC announced that it was in the nature of an experiment, and that the form would be amended or rescinded if experience with its use indicates that such action is necessary or desirable (Release No. 33–5117, Dec. 23, 1970).

Form S–16 may be used for registration under the 1933 Act of the following securities of any issuer which at the time of filing the registration statement meets the requirements applicable to the use of Form S–7:

(1) Securities to be offered on behalf of persons, other than the registrant, in the regular way on a national securities exchange if securities of the same class are listed and registered on an exchange at the time of filing the registration statement on this form.

(2) Securities to be offered to the holders of convertible securities of an affiliate of the registrant and the registered securities are the securities such holders are entitled to receive upon conversion, provided no commission or other remuneration is paid for solicitation of the conversion of such securities; or

(3) Securities of an issuer to be offered to the holders of outstanding warrants upon the exercise thereof provided no commission or other remuneration is paid for soliciting the exercise of such warrants.

Part I of the form consists of the following items of information that must be included in the prospectus:

Item 1.   Identity of the issuer of securities to be registered.

Item 2.   Title and amount of securities to be registered.

Item 3.   Names of selling stockholders, amounts held, to be sold, and to be held after the sale.

Item 4.   Securities to be offered upon conversion of other securities.

Item 5.   Securities to be offered upon exercise of warrants.

Item 6.   A mandatory incorporation by reference of documents and information filed and to be filed under the 1934 Act, such as, annual reports, proxy statements, information statements, and also recent prospectuses. (The requirements of Item 6 are discussed at greater length in Chapter **9**.)

Item 7.   Additional information—particularly with respect to material adverse changes in registrant's affairs subsequent to the date of the latest fiscal year for which certified financial statements were included in the material incorporated by reference in Item 6.

Part II of the registration statement consists of two items:

Item 8.   Required undertaking.
Item 9.   List of exhibits.

Form N–5, for Registration of Small Business Investment Company under the Securities Act of 1933 and the Investment Company Act of 1940.—This form is used for registration under the 1933 Act of securities issued by any small business investment company which is registered under the Investment Company Act of 1940, and which is licensed under the Small Business Investment Company Act of 1958 or which has received the preliminary approval of the Small Business Administration and has been notified by the Administration that it may submit a license application. This form may also be used for the registration statement of such company pursuant to section 8(b) of the Investment Company Act of 1940.

Because of the limited interest in SBIC's, the scope of Form N–5 is not set forth in this volume.

Miscellaneous Forms.—There are also other forms for registration under the 1933 Act. They are not discussed here since they do not require the inclusion of financial statements. A list of the forms follows:

Form C–2, for certain types of certificates of interest in securities
Form C–3, for American certificates against foreign issues and for the underlying securities
Form D–1, for certificates of deposit
Form D–1A, for certificates of deposit issued by issuer of securities called for deposit

Ratio of Earnings to Fixed Charges

Requirements of Various SEC Forms.—From the discussion regarding Form S–9 it will be apparent that the form was designed for the registration of high grade debt securities. As such, the form is available only to companies which comply with certain prescribed ratios of earnings to fixed charges set forth in the instructions for the use of the form, in addition to complying with other specified conditions. The minimum ratios are relatively low for utilities in recognition of the stability of their earnings, and higher for other issuers. Since the ratios are an important consideration in determining the eligibility of an issuer to use the form, and since the information is important to investors in such securities, it is not surprising that the ratios must appear on the face of the income statement included in the prospectus. Furthermore there must also be shown on the income statement the pro forma ratio giving effect to the issuance of the securities to be registered and other changes in securities—effected or proposed.

Several of the other registration and report forms under the 1933 and 1934 Acts contain instructions relating to showing the ratio of earnings to fixed charges—some of them on a voluntary basis, others on a mandatory basis if the document to be filed with the SEC relates to a debt offering. In some instances, the instructions are in relation to the summary of earnings; in other instances (in S–9, for example) the instructions with respect to the ratio appear in connection with the income statement. Following is a tabulation of the principal registration and report forms under the 1933 and 1934 Acts summarizing briefly the SEC's *published* requirements with respect to furnishing the ratio of earnings to fixed charges:

| | *Is disclosure of ratio of earnings to fixed charges required* | |
	In summary of earnings (or summary of operations)?	*In statement of income?*
SEC registration or report form		
1933 Act:		
S–1	Optional, even when debt securities are registered	No provision
S–2, S–3, S–4, S–5	No provision	No provision
S–7	No summary included	Mandatory if debt securities are being registered
S–8	No provision	No provision
S–9	No summary included	Mandatory
S–11	Mandatory if debt securities are being registered	No provision
S–14	No provision	No provision
S–16	No provision	No provision
1934 Act:		
10	Optional when debt securities are to be registered	No provision
10–K	Optional when debt securities are registered	No provision

From the foregoing tabulation it will appear that, in a Form S–1 registration statement, it is optional with the registrant whether or not to show the ratio of earnings to fixed charges—even when the offering relates to debt securities. The SEC, however, has unpublished administrative requirements pursuant to which such ratio information *must* be furnished when the offering relates to *debt securities.*

Ratio Calculation and Presentation.—While the instructions for calculating the ratio of earnings to fixed charges and the definition of "fixed charges" are similar as between the various registration and report forms, they are not identical. Since there are variations in language, there are also variations in interpretation. Inasmuch as the intent is the same in all the forms, it would seem logical that the instructions and definitions should be uniform. (At the time of this writing, in fact, the term "fixed charges" has two different definitions in Form S–9—one in the instructions for the use of the form, and a slightly different one in the instructions for Item 3 relating to the income statement.)

The discussion that follows will relate principally to the calculation of the ratio as applied to the income statement in Form S–9 since the instructions for calculating the ratio and the definition of "fixed charges" in that connection appear to represent the present views of the Commission.

With regard to the income statement in Form S–9, the registrant is required to show for each fiscal year or other period of the statement, the ratio of earnings to fixed charges. A pro forma ratio of earnings to fixed charges, adjusted to give effect to the issuance of the securities to be registered, any issuance or retirement of securities during or after such period, or any presently proposed issuance, retirement or redemption of securities must also be shown for the latest fiscal year or twelve-month period.

For the purpose of the ratio, earnings are computed after all operating and income deductions except fixed charges and taxes based on income or profits and after eliminating undistributed income of unconsolidated companies. (In Forms S–1 and S–11, however, earnings for ratio purposes are "computed in accordance with generally accepted accounting principles after all operating and income deductions, except taxes based on income or profits and fixed charges." Note the absence of instructions regarding undistributed income of unconsolidated companies.)

In the case of utilities, interest credits charged to construction have to be added to gross income and not deducted from interest. This is ordinarily not a significant item in the case of companies other than utilities, although it could be in the case of a company involved in a long-term construction program financed with borrowed funds.

For the purpose of the ratio, "fixed charges" in Form S–9 means (i) interest and amortization of debt discount and expense and premium on all indebtedness; (ii) one-third of all rentals reported in Schedule XVI of Regulation S–X (supplementary income statement information), or such portion as can be demonstrated to be representative of the interest factor in the particular case; and (iii) in case consolidated figures are used, preferred stock dividend requirements of consolidated subsidiaries, excluding in all cases items eliminated in consolidation. (In Form S–1, the reference to rentals in clause (ii) reads "an appropriate portion of rentals under long-term leases.")

The "interest factor" [1] mentioned in the preceeding paragraph represents the owner's profit on his investment plus his interest charges, and this is the portion of the rent that is considered to be a "fixed charge" if the registrant elects not to use the arbitrary "one-third of all rentals reported in Schedule XVI."

"Delay rentals" paid on leaseholds to retain mineral rights before development of leased acreage are not in the nature of ordinary rental for the use of property. Delay rentals or other items included in rentals in Schedule XVI that can be shown to contain little or no interest factor may properly be excluded under the alternate treatment. (Release No. 33–4245, June 30, 1960.)

The registrant has to file as an exhibit to the registration statement a statement setting forth in reasonable detail the computations of the ratios of earnings to fixed charges. For the purpose of this exhibit and the pro forma ratio referred to above, an assumed maximum interest rate may be used on securities as to which the interest rate has not yet been fixed, which assumed rate has to be shown.

In Form S–9, the information regarding ratios is required to be certified to the same extent as the income statement to which it relates. In some of the other forms, (S–1, for example, or Forms 10 and 10–K) since the summary of earnings is not required to be certified, the ratio information also need not be certified when it is furnished as part of the summary.

For an example showing how the ratio of earnings to fixed charges is reported and explained, it is instructive to refer to the prospectus dated February 9, 1971 of American Telephone and Telegraph Company. This prospectus included a consolidated income statement for the calendar years 1965–1969 and for the nine-month interim periods ended September 30, 1969 and 1970; there was no separate summary of earnings. In accordance with the company's long-standing practice, the statement consolidated the company's telephone subsidiaries but not Western Electric Company, the principal manufacturing and supply unit of the Bell system. The company's interest in the earnings of Western, however, was included in the consolidated income statement and disclosed in a note to the statement analyzed as between dividends received from Western and the interest in Western's undistributed earnings. Interest charged to construction was shown as a

---

[1] For background information concerning this provision, see *Security Analysis*, 4th ed., by Graham, Dodd and Cottle, p. 370. Copyright, 1962. McGraw-Hill Book Company, Inc.

separate item in the income statement and was not included in interest deductions; in other words, interest deductions were not reduced for interest charged to construction.

Following the caption "Net Income," was the ratio of earnings to fixed charges with a reference to an explanatory note. The note explained "earnings" and "fixed charges" as follows:

For the purpose of this ratio: (i) Earnings have been calculated by adding to Income Before Interest Deductions the amount of related taxes on income, minority interests in net income of subsidiaries and one-third of rentals paid to others than subsidiaries (see Item ___ on page ___) and by deducting therefrom the interest of the companies consolidated in the income in excess of dividends of subsidiaries not consolidated; (ii) Fixed Charges comprise Total Interest Deductions, one-third of rentals paid as described in (i) and dividends on preferred shares of a subsidiary consolidated held by minority interests.

The pro forma ratio was furnished for the most recent full year (1969) and for the two interim periods and the underlying assumptions explained in a paragraph as follows:

Pro forma ratios for the nine months ended September 30, 1970, for the nine months ended September 30, 1969 and for the year 1969, giving effect to all external financing completed from January 1, 1969 through the date of receipt of proceeds from the Debentures offered hereby and to all further financing authorized by the Company and its subsidiaries consolidated (including the Debentures offered hereby), would be 3.74, 3.92 and 3.92, respectively. For the purpose of these ratios an assumed interest rate of $7\frac{1}{8}\%$ has been used for such further financing authorized by subsidiaries consolidated. For each $\frac{1}{4}\%$ change in the assumed interest rate the ratios would change by about .01.

A schedule showing the computation of the pro forma ratio was included in the registration statement as Exhibit 5. The exhibit is included in Appendix C of this book.

Treatment of Unconsolidated Subsidiaries in Ratios.—A question is sometimes raised as to the computation of the ratio of earnings to fixed charges in the case of a registrant that has unconsolidated subsidiaries. The question may be significant when the unconsolidated subsidiaries are finance subsidiaries that have fixed charges of their own. This question involves an area in which the SEC's requirements have been in the process of crystallizing as will be seen from illustrations that follow.

A prospectus of J. C. Penney Company, Inc. (July 7, 1970) showed that Penney had finance subsidiaries that were not consolidated in the usual manner, but the income of the subsidiaries was included in the consolidated income statement as a "one line" item. A note to the income statement described the computation of the ratio of available income to fixed charges.

For this purpose, the income of the finance subsidiaries was deducted from consolidated pre-tax income. Fixed charges of the finance subsidiaries were also not included in computing the ratio, and the note disclosed the fixed charges of the subsidiaries, year by year for five years, as follows:

> The fixed charges of the Company's unconsolidated finance subsidiaries have not been included in computing the ratios of earnings to fixed charges. The fixed charges of these subsidiaries, consisting of interest expense and one-third of rental expense, were as follows (in millions of dollars): 1970—$311.7; 1969 —$229.8; 1968—$141.8; 1967—$97.3; and 1966—$85.1.

A more recent prospectus of General Electric Company (dated March 3, 1971) relating to an offering of its debentures due 1996 contained less information with respect to the ratio of earnings to fixed charges than the Penney prospectus, although the GE prospectus was dated months later. GE had several finance subsidiaries which were not consolidated in the consolidated financial statements of GE. Because of their materiality, separate financial statements of the finance subsidiaries were included in the prospectus. The income statement of GE and its consolidated affiliates was followed by a single line of information giving the ratio of earnings to fixed charges for each of the years 1966–1970. A note to the statement explained how the ratio was computed; the note was as follows:

> For the purpose of this ratio, earnings consist of earnings before income taxes, undistributed earnings of unconsolidated affiliates and associated companies, and fixed charges. Fixed charges consist of interest and other financial charges, one-third of rentals, and preferred stock dividend requirements of a consolidated affiliate. The pro-forma ratio of earnings to fixed charges for 1970 after giving effect to the issuance of the Debentures, the retirement of short-term borrowings in an equivalent amount, and transfer to a subsidiary of Honeywell Inc. of approximately $220 million of indebtedness at October 1, 1970, is 6.08.

There was no indication at this point of the prospectus of the fixed charges of the finance subsidiaries or the effect on the ratio if the fixed charges of the subsidiaries were included in the computation. According to the income statement of the finance subsidiaries, the expense of interest and discount for 1970 was $116.7 million.

In the case of Ford Motor Company, it appeared that the SEC insisted on a different computation and presentation. The company's prospectus (July 22, 1971) relating to an offering of Notes due 1977 included the customary information with respect to the ratio of earnings to fixed charges beneath the statement of income and retained earnings. A note to the statement explained "earnings" and "fixed charges." The second paragraph of the note was as follows:

A combined ratio of earnings to fixed charges for the Company and its consolidated subsidiaries, together with unconsolidated financing subsidiaries as if consolidated, has been included below at the direction of the Staff of the Securities and Exchange Commission. Such ratio, computed as indicated above, was as follows: [ratios omitted here]. The pro forma ratio for the year 1970 is 3.2, after giving effect, etc. . . . The Company questions the significance of this combined ratio because it considers the ratio of earnings to fixed charges for the Company and its consolidated subsidiaries, shown above in the summary of earnings, to be of primary relevance to purchasers of the Notes. (Emphasis supplied)

In August 1971 the SEC issued a release in which it stated that the fixed charges of unconsolidated subsidiaries had to be taken into consideration in furnishing the ratio of earnings to fixed charges. In addition to furnishing such information in the customary manner, supplemental information must be supplied including the fixed charges of unconsolidated subsidiaries as if consolidated. In addition, if the registrant guarantees the debt of another company (such as a supplier) or agrees to service the debt of such a company, the fixed charges of such companies should be included in the supplementary ratio data. Also, the Commission's release stated, the supplemental ratios should be shown as a line item in the same manner as the ratios computed in the customary manner. (ASR No. 122, August 10, 1971).

Improper Computation of Ratio of Earnings to Fixed Charges.— On June 15, 1971 the SEC issued a release (ASR No. 119) commenting on the improper computation of the ratio of earnings to fixed charges. The Commission said that some registrants, in computing the ratio, had deducted from fixed charges amounts comprising (1) interest income or investment income earned on funds in excess of the requirements for working capital, and (2) gains on retirement of debt at less than its principal amount. Some registrants, in computing the pro forma ratio, had imputed interest or investment income on amounts of funds to be obtained from the registered offering which is in excess of the immediate requirements for debt retirement or capital expenditures, and had deducted such imputed income from the pro forma fixed charges in computing the pro forma ratio.

The Commission said it had considered the propriety of reducing fixed charges by amounts representing interest or investment income or gains on retirement of debt. In the light of the purposes for which the ratios are used, the Commission said it had determined that the reduction of fixed charges by the amount of either actual or imputed interest or investment income or debt retirement gains for the purpose of computing fixed charge ratios results in incorrect ratios and is therefore inappropriate. Accordingly, such reductions will no longer be deemed acceptable in registration statements or reports filed with the SEC.

Ratio of Earnings to Fixed Charges and Preferred Dividends Combined

The preceeding discussion has been concerned with the computation and presentation of the ratio of earnings to fixed charges which is required to be included in some SEC filings pursuant to the Commission's requirements, some of which are formal, published requirements, and some of which are informal and unpublished.

There are no formal, published requirements with respect to furnishing the ratio of earnings to *fixed charges and preferred dividends combined,* but they exist nonetheless. Since April 1971 the staff of the Commission has required such ratio information to be included in prospectuses used in connection with offerings of preferred stock or preference stock, but has not publicized its requirements.[2] Having previously taken the position that the conventional ratio of earnings to fixed charges was essential information in all prospectuses relating to *debt* offerings, the Commission's staff has now taken the position that somewhat similar information is desirable in the case of offerings of *preferred or preference stock.*

The ratio of earnings to fixed charges and preferred dividends combined must be furnished for all periods covered by the summary of earnings during which preferred stock was outstanding. In addition, a pro forma ratio must be furnished for the latest year of the summary and for the interim periods, if any. The historical ratios must appear as a line item after net income in the same manner as the conventional ratio of earnings to fixed charges. The pro forma ratios may also appear as a line item or they can be included in a note to the summary. In either case, the ratios should be keyed to a note which explains the method of calculation.

Following is an example of a note which explains the components of the historical ratios and the computation of the pro forma ratios:

For purposes of this ratio, earnings represent income before income taxes and fixed charges. Fixed charges represent interest charges plus one-third of annual rentals shown in Note ___ to the financial statements. Preferred dividends represent preferred dividend requirements multiplied by the ratio that pre-tax income bears to net income. The pro forma ratio for the (period), giving effect to the annual interest requirements and annual preferred dividend requirements on debt and preferred stock to be outstanding after the sale of the preferred stock offered thereby (assuming a dividend rate of ___%) and the application of the net proceeds therefrom to retire short-term debt would be (ratio). A change of (fraction) of 1% in the assumed dividend rate on the

---

[2] The source of much of this information is an article by C. E. Youngdahl which appeared in "SEC Commentary" (a department), *The New York CPA,* July 1971, pp. 517–521.

new preferred stock would result in a change of approximately (amount) in this ratio.

Registration Statement Usually Consists of Two Parts

A registration statement under the 1933 Act filed on most of the forms discussed above usually (but not always) consists of two parts. Part I consists of the items of information that must be included in the prospectus. Part II consists of the information that must be included in the registration statement but need not be included in the prospectus. Customarily, a copy of the prospectus is submitted in full satisfaction of the requirements of Part I. (As used here, the term "prospectus" means a general prospectus, as distinguished from a summary prospectus [see page **11·26**] or a prospectus in the form of a newspaper advertisement.)

The registration requirements vary depending on which registration form is used. The requirements applicable to a filing on Form S–1 are briefly set forth in the preceeding pages of this chapter. A prospectus in an S–1 filing contains the information specified in Items 1 through 21. Part II of a registration statement on Form S–1 contains the information required by Items 22 through 31, the supporting schedules to financial statements, the exhibits, and consents of experts. Included among the exhibits are copies of the charter, by-laws, certain franchises, indentures and contracts, and an opinion of counsel as to legality of the securities being registered.

Form S–9, on the other hand, is a much more abbreviated form than S–1 and is available only to registrants meeting the requirements (see page **8·13**). In Form S–9 information need not be furnished as to remuneration of officers and directors. Also, S–9 contains no items equal to those in S–1 calling for information as to the kind of business being conducted and recent developments in the business, although S–9 does call for a statement of the products or services that constitute the principal sources of sales or revenues, or both, and information regarding reserves (in the case of extractive industries), property additions, and retirements. Because of the conditions restricting the use of Form S–9, information regarding remuneration, kind of business, and developments in the business is publicly available as to companies using the form. The fact that some of this information need not be included in a Form S–9 prospectus makes that form a desirable one to use whenever possible.

Exemptive Regulations and Notification Forms

The 1933 Act contains provisions exempting certain securities, such as securities of the United States, any state of the United States, or any political subdivision of any state. Also exempt are the securities issued by any national bank or by any bank organized under the laws of any state or territory or the District of Columbia, the business of which is supervised by a banking commission. Notes, drafts, bills of exchange, and bankers' acceptances that have a maturity at the time of issuance of nine months or less are likewise exempt, as are certain securities of building and loan associations, farmers' cooperative associations, securities of common or contract carriers subject to Section 20a of the Interstate Commerce Act, and insurance policies and annuity contracts. The foregoing list is not a complete listing of exempt securities; it is intended to give the reader an indication of the scope of exemptions available in Section 3(a) of the 1933 Act.

In addition, the Commission has the authority under Section 3(b) of the Act to make rules and regulations exempting additional classes of securities, provided the aggregate amount at which the securities are offered to the public is not more than $500,000. Under this authority the Commission has promulgated regulations and rules dealing with exemptions.

Regulation A.—Regulation A provides a general exemption from the registration requirements for certain securities of domestic and Canadian issuers, the aggregate offering price of which (together with other exempt offerings within a two-year period) is not over $500,000. The exemption is limited to $100,000 in the case of an offering on behalf of a person other than the issuer, but this limitation does not apply if the securities are to be offered on behalf of the estate of a deceased person within two years after the death of such person. In certain cases, in computing the aggregate offering price of securities having a determinable market value, the higher of the offering price or market value is used. The regulation also excludes from the exemption provisions certain types of securities or interests and the securities of certain issuers. Canadian issuers are treated the same as domestic issuers, but Canadian companies must qualify their securities under provincial laws.

Regulation A requires the use of offering circulars containing certain information (including financial data) in the distribution of securities, but such circulars need not be used in connection with an offering not in excess of $50,000 by a company with earnings in one of the last two years. The circular must be filed with the Commission at least ten days before it is proposed to be used. It must contain information that will inform the prospective investor as to the nature of the enterprise and the essential facts concerning its securities. The circulars are filed in the appropriate regional office of the Commission where they are examined to see whether there has been adequate disclosure and whether there is any indication of the existence of fraud. This is important because, although securities may be exempt from the registration requirements of the Act, they are not exempt from the antifraud provisions of the Act.

Form 1–A is for use in notifying the Commission of an offering of securities to be made pursuant to Regulation A. The offering circular referred to in the preceeding paragraph is filed with, and is deemed a part of, this notification.

Regulation E.—Regulation E provides a conditional exemption for securities of small business investment companies which are registered under the Investment Company Act of 1940 and licensed (or received preliminary licensing approval) under the Small Business Investment Company Act of 1958. The amount of securities exempted is limited to $500,000.

Under Regulation E an offering circular must be prepared and filed with the appropriate regional office of the Commission and given to each person to whom the securities are offered, but such circulars need not be used in connection with offerings not exceeding $50,000. The offering circular must contain information (including financial statements) regarding the issuer's business and the securities being proposed to be offered for sale, and must be filed with the SEC at least ten days before being used.

Form 1–E is used to notify the Commission of an offering under Regulation E. The offering circular is filed with, and is a part of, the notification.

Regulation F.—Regulation F provides an exemption for assessments on assessable stock and for assessable stock offered or sold to realize the amount of an assessment levied thereon or re-offered to the public by an underwriter or dealer. The aggregate amount of all assessments levied on assessable stock plus the aggregate price of all securities of the issuer offered under the regulation or any other rule or regulation under Section 3(b) of the Act may not exceed $300,000 in any calendar year. Form 1–F is the form used to notify the Commission of an offering under the regulation, but there is no requirement for financial statements.

Other Exemptions.—In addition to the foregoing, the Commission has promulgated other regulations and rules exempting different types of securities as follows :

> *Regulation B* exempts certain fractional undivided interests in oil or gas rights.
>
> *Rule 234* provides a special exemption for promissory notes directly secured by a first lien on real estate where the public offering does not exceed $100,000 and certain other conditions are complied with.
>
> *Rule 235* provides a special exemption for securities of cooperative housing corporations where the public offering does not exceed $300,000 and there is compliance with certain other conditions.
>
> *Rule 236* provides a special exemption for securities sold to provide not

more than $100,000 for distribution to shareholders in lieu of issuing fractional shares, scrip certificates or order forms following a stock dividend, stock split, reverse split, merger, etc.

Public Offerings by Brokers and Dealers

Registration statements under the 1933 Act have been filed by a few brokers and dealers in securities relating to proposed public offerings of their securities. Generally, broker-dealers have used Form S–1 for this purpose. In view of the Commission's limited experience with this kind of offering, the Commission said that it had determined not to propose a form for such registration statements or to propose guidelines for disclosures (Release No. 33–5222, January 3, 1972).

In order to minimize delays in the reviews of such registration statements, the SEC published in the aforementioned release the comments and suggestions of its staff to assist all persons concerned with the preparation of such registration statements. Because of the limited number of such offerings, the contents of that release are not included here. (In the case of public offerings by nonmember broker-dealers, the reader is also referred to Release No. 34–9555, April 12, 1972.)

CHAPTER 9

FINANCIAL STATEMENTS REQUIRED BY PRINCIPAL 1933 ACT REGISTRATION FORMS

CONTENTS

Statutory Basis for Financial Requirements

The Securities Act of 1933 provides that a registration statement (when relating to a security other than a security issued by a foreign government or political subdivision thereof) shall contain the information specified in Schedule A of the law. The Commission, however, is authorized to provide by rule or regulation for the omission of any such information if the Commission finds that the requirement of such information is not applicable to any class of issuers or securities and that disclosure fully adequate for the protection of investors is otherwise required to be included in the registration statement. In addition to the items listed in Schedule A of the statute, the Commission has authority to require the inclusion in registration statements of such other information as the Commission may, by rules or regulations, require as being necessary or appropriate in the public interest or for the protection of investors.

Because of the flexibility that the law gives to the Commission, practitioners are concerned less with Schedule A of the law than with the requirements for financial statements contained in the registration forms. The requirements for financial statements in Forms S–1, S–2, S–3, S–4, S–5, S–7, S–8, S–9, S–11, S–16, and in the notification forms relating to exemptions are set forth in this chapter, since these are the forms most commonly used.

The "Filing Date"

In the instructions for financial statements contained in the various registration forms there are requirements to the effect that the statements must be furnished as of a date within a specified period prior to the date of filing the registration statement.[1] Each amendment to the registration statement, however, creates a new date of filing of the registration statement itself, unless the amendment is filed with the consent of the Commission (see page **7·12**). The SEC stated its opinion on this question in a 1936 decision. In that case the balance sheet filed with the registration statement was dated November 30, 1934, which was not within 90 days prior to the date of filing of the last amendment on March 20, 1935. The Commission said: "Under Section 8(a) of the Securities Act, each amendment filed prior to the effective date of a registration statement creates a new filing date, unless the consent of the Commission to the filing of the amendment is obtained. The consent of the Commission not having been obtained, the registrant's balance sheet is not as of a date within the required period." [2]

Commission Policy on Need for Updating Financial Statements

All too often, because of the time involved in preparing and auditing financial statements, a registration statement is filed just in time to beat the 90-day deadline requirement. Because of the substantive and price amendments which almost invariably follow, does this mean that the financial statements must also be brought up to a more recent date in the amendments? The question is not one which is the exclusive concern of the SEC. If, after the original filing, there has been a material and radical change in the registrant's financial picture, its management will need to consider carefully whether information as to its changed financial status should be furnished even though not requested by the staff of the SEC (see the discussion beginning on page **12·7**).

The age of the financial statements in every registration statement is a matter that is carefully considered by the staff of the Commission before the registration statement is allowed to become effective. Whether or not to insist on the filing of financial statements more recent than those in the original registration statement will depend on a number of factors, such as the company, its financial position and earnings, the nature of the industry, and similar considerations.

As a guide for determining the need for updating financial statements

---

[1] Rule 417 provides that whenever financial statements are required to be furnished as of a date within a specified period prior to the date of filing the registration statement and the last day of such period falls on a Saturday, Sunday or holiday, such registration statement may be filed on the first business day following the last day of the specified period.

[2] *Mutual Industrial Bankers, Inc.,* 1 SEC 272 (1936). Affirmed in *Old Diamond Gold Mines, Ltd.,* 2 SEC 788 (1937).

and related data in registration statements filed under the 1933 Act, the Commission issued the following statement (Release No. 33–4936, Dec. 9, 1968):

(a) *Financial Statements*

(1) *Form S–1:* Registrants presently subject to the reporting requirements of the Securities Exchange Act of 1934 and other companies with a substantial record of earnings which publish financial information on a regular basis, should be prepared to add later information as to sales and net income on a current and comparable basis in a paragraph following the summary of earnings when such later information has been published or is to be published in an interim report prior to the effective date of the registration statement. Whether or not such a report is published, later sales and net income information on current and comparable prior year bases should be included in such a paragraph when an adverse trend is shown. Such disclosure is necessary regardless of the certified or noncertified status of the financial statements in the prospectus. It should be understood that when a fiscal year ends within 90 days prior to the date of filing and certified financial statements for the year are available for publication before the proposed effective date, such statements should be substituted for the interim statements in the registration statement as originally filed.

Companies registering for the first time with no previous record of publishing information, but with an established record of earnings and in a sound financial condition, should be prepared to furnish the above data compared with a similar period of the preceding year, if the amendment when effective would otherwise include data over four months old.

New registrants with no established record of earnings and old registrants currently showing losses or a weak financial condition should not only furnish the above data but be prepared to bring the financial statements up to the latest practicable date not more than 90 days prior to filing the amendment upon which it is expected the filing will become effective. If delay carries the date beyond the close of the fiscal year and by applying due diligence the registrant and its independent accountant can have an audit completed prior to the planned effective date, certified statements for the fiscal year should be substituted for interim statements whether or not the interim financial statements have been certified.

When later interim financial statements are to be furnished to supplement either fiscal year or interim statements which have been certified, the later statements would in the usual case be unaudited. However, when numerous or involved financial transactions have been effected since the date of the financial statements furnished or it is recognized that unusual conditions affect the determination of earnings, the Commission has indicated that later financial statements may be requested on a certified basis as a condition to acceleration under Section 8(a) of the Act.

(2) *Forms S–2 and S–3:* All financial statements on these forms are required to be certified. In all cases of extended delay later statements should be prepared so that at the expected effective date the statements are not over four months old.

(3) *Forms S–7, S–8 and S–9:* In cases of unusual delay of effectiveness of the registration statement, consideration should be given to presenting such later

financial data, including interim earnings, when such information has been published or issued to stockholders.

(4) *Form S–11:* Principles set forth above for Form S–1 should be applied to filings on this form as appropriate.

(b) *Financial Data*

Volume statistics, loss experience in insurance companies, bad debt and collection experience in finance, real estate and small loan companies, backlog and similar data should be brought up to date when later financial information is furnished.

Financial Statements Required by Form S–1

Form S–1 is the principal registration statement form under the Securities Act of 1933 and is used whenever no other form is authorized or prescribed. The content of the form is described briefly in Chapter **8**. The SEC's instructions as to financial statements to be filed as part of Form S–1 are set forth and discussed in the following pages and relate to:

Financial statements of the registrant
Consolidated financial statements
Financial statements of unconsolidated subsidiaries and 50 per cent owned companies
Financial statements of affiliates whose securities are pledged as collateral
Special provisions in connection with:
(a) Reorganization of the registrant
(b) Succession to other businesses
(c) Acquisition of other businesses
Filing of other financial statements in certain cases
Historical financial information
Summary of earnings

In reading these instructions, the SEC's policy on the need for updating financial statements (see page **9·3**) in certain circumstances should be borne in mind.

The requirements for "line of business" information in Item 9 of the registration statement are discussed in Chapter **23**.

Financial Statements of the Registrant.—A balance sheet of the registrant (unconsolidated) is required to be filed as of a date within 90 days prior to the date of filing the registration statement. In lieu of this 90-day statement, however, the balance sheet may be as of a date within six months prior to the filing date if *all* of the following conditions exist:

1. The registrant files annual and other reports (Form 10–K, for example) pursuant to Section 13 or 15(d) of the Securities Exchange Act of 1934;
2. The total assets of the registrant and its subsidiaries, as shown by the latest consolidated balance sheet filed, amount to $5,000,000 or more, exclusive of intangibles; and
3. No long-term debt of the registrant is in default as to principal, interest, or sinking fund provisions.

See also page **9·47** regarding possible waiver of the requirement for 90-day statements in other cases.

The balance sheet referred to in the preceding paragraph—whether within 90 days or six months—need not be certified. If it is not certified, there must be filed in addition a certified balance sheet as of a date within one year prior to the filing date unless the fiscal year of the registrant has ended within 90 days prior to such filing, in which case the certified balance sheet may be as of the end of the preceding fiscal year.

The registrant must file its income statement (unconsolidated) for each of the three· fiscal years preceding the date of the latest balance sheet filed, and for the period, if any, between the close of the latest of such fiscal years and the date of the latest balance sheet filed. Unconsolidated statements of retained earnings, other additional capital, and source and application of funds must be filed for the registrant for the same period as the related income statement. The statement of retained earnings may be a separate statement or a continuation of the income statement. The statements of income, retained earnings, other additional capital, and source and application of funds must be certified up to the date of the latest certified balance sheet filed. (See page **10·10** regarding the practice of presenting the income statement under "Summary of Earnings" or a similar caption in the prospectus.)

Notwithstanding what has been said in the preceding paragraphs, however, the individual (unconsolidated) financial statements of the registrant may be omitted if (1) consolidated statements of the registrant and one or more of its subsidiaries are filed, (2) the conditions specified in *either* of the following paragraphs are met, and (3) the Commission is advised as to the reasons for such omission:

(a) The registrant is primarily an operating company and all subsidiaries included in the consolidated financial statements filed are "totally-held subsidiaries" (see definition on page **16·8**) ; *or*

(b) The registrant's total assets, exclusive of investments in and advances to the consolidated subsidiaries, constitute 85 per cent or more of the total assets shown by the consolidated balance sheets filed *and* the registrant's total gross sales or revenues for the period for which its income statements would be filed, exclusive of interest and dividends received from the consolidated subsidiaries, constitute 85 per cent or more of the total gross sales or revenues shown by the consolidated income statement filed.

(See page **9·48** regarding possible omission of parent company statements in cases not complying strictly with the rules for omission quoted above.)

The reference in (3) above on advising the Commission may raise a question: How is this accomplished? Form S–1, it will be recalled, consists of two parts. Part I contains those items of information which must be included in the prospectus. Part II contains those items of information which must be filed with the Commission but need not be included in the prospectus. Item 31 in Part II is a listing of all the financial statements and exhibits which are filed as part of the registration statement—including those in the prospectus.

Item 31(a) is the listing of financial statements, Item 31(b) the listing of exhibits. In the former, the registrant will list all those financial statements and supporting schedules which are furnished as well as those which are omitted together with the reasons for such omission. If, pursuant to the instructions for financial statements in Form S–1, the individual statements of the registrant are omitted, the registrant will make a statement in Item 31(a) somewhat as follows:

Individual financial statements of (name of company) are omitted from this registration statement inasmuch as the Company is primarily an operating company, consolidated financial statements of the Company and its subsidiaries are filed, and the subsidiaries included in such consolidated statements are totally-held subsidiaries.

In other circumstances (when, for example, the consolidated subsidiaries are not totally-held), the form of declaration suggested above may be modified as follows:

Individual financial statements of (name of company) are omitted from this registration statement inasmuch as consolidated financial statements of the Company and its subsidiaries are filed, and the Company's total assets, exclusive of investments in and advances to the consolidated subsidiaries, exceed 85 per cent of the assets shown by the consolidated balance sheet filed, and the Company's gross sales (or revenues), exclusive of interest and dividends from consolidated subsidiaries, exceed 85 per cent of the consolidated sales (or revenues) shown by the consolidated income statement filed.

Consolidated Financial Statements.—The registration statement must contain a consolidated balance sheet of the registrant and its subsidiaries as of the same date as each balance sheet of the registrant filed pursuant to the instructions set forth above. The consolidated balance sheet must be certified if the registrant's balance sheet as of the same date is certified. If the registrant's individual balance sheets are not filed as permitted by the instructions, the consolidated balance sheets filed must be as of the same dates as the balance sheet of the registrant which would otherwise be required; the consolidated balance sheet must be certified if the corresponding balance sheet of the registrant would be required to be certified.

The registration statement must include a consolidated income statement of the registrant and its subsidiaries for each of the three fiscal years preceding the date of the latest consolidated balance sheet filed, and for the period, if any, between the close of the latest of such fiscal years and the date of the latest consolidated balance sheet filed. Consolidated statements of retained earnings, other additional capital, and source and application of funds must be filed for the same period as the related income statement. The statement of retained earnings may be a separate statement or a continuation of the income statement. The statements of income, retained earnings, other additional capital, and source and application of funds must be certified up to the date of the latest related certified consolidated balance sheet filed. (See page **10**·10 regarding the practice of presenting the income statement under "Summary of Earnings" or a similar caption in the prospectus.)

Financial Statements of Unconsolidated Subsidiaries and 50 Per Cent Owned Companies.—Financial statements must be filed for each majority-owned subsidiary of the registrant not consolidated which would be required if the subsidiary were itself a registrant. Insofar as practicable, these statements must be as of the same dates and for the same periods as those of the registrant. See the discussion on page **17**·18 regarding Rule 4–03 of Regulation S–X which permits the registrant to consolidate or combine the financial statements of unconsolidated majority-owned subsidiaries.

If it is impracticable to file a balance sheet of any unconsolidated subsidiary as of a date within 90 days prior to the date of filing the registration statement, there may be filed in lieu thereof a certified balance sheet of the subsidiary as of the end of its latest annual or semiannual fiscal period preceding the date of filing the registration statement for which it is practicable to do so.

If the registrant owns, directly or indirectly, approximately 50 per cent of the voting securities of any company and the remaining 50 per cent is owned, directly or indirectly, by another single interest, there must be filed for each such company the financial statements which would be required if it were a registrant. The statements filed for each such company must identify the other single interest which owns the remaining 50 per cent of the voting securities.

Notwithstanding the instructions referred to in the preceding paragraphs, there may be omitted from the registration statement all financial statements of any one or more unconsolidated subsidiaries or 50 per cent owned companies, if all such subsidiaries and 50 per cent owned companies for which statements are so omitted, considered in the aggregate as a single subsidiary, would not constitute a "significant subsidiary" (see definition on page **16**· 8).   For an interpretation of the instructions as to omission of statements of unconsolidated subsidiaries and 50 per cent owned companies, see page **9**· 5 5).

The instructions relating to unconsolidated subsidiaries and 50 per cent owned companies assume that such subsidiaries and companies had that relationship to the registrant during the entire three-year period that would normally be covered by the required income statement. What would be the situation, however, if an unconsolidated subsidiary, for example, had been owned by its present parent (the registrant) for only one year, having been purchased from a third party? In this connection, see the discussion on page **9**·12 concerning Release No. 4950, dealing with the financial statements of acquired companies or companies to be acquired.

In the unconsolidated statements of a parent company it is becoming increasingly customary to adjust the investments in subsidiaries to reflect the parent company's share of the earnings and losses of subsidiaries since acquisition. In the case of parent company financial statements prepared for issuance to shareholders as the financial statements of the primary reporting entity, this method (sometimes referred to as the "equity method") was made mandatory by APB Opinion No. 18 (1971) entitled "The Equity Method of Accounting for Investments in Common Stock." In its earlier Opinion No. 10 (1966), the APB had recommended the equity method of accounting for investments in common stock of unconsolidated *domestic* subsidiaries in consolidated financial statements. The Board extended this recommendation in Opinion No. 18 to investments in common stock of *all* unconsolidated subsidiaries (foreign as well as domestic) in consolidated financial statements. An exception to this general rule would apply where a subsidiary is excluded from consolidation because of exchange restrictions or other reasons which raise the question of whether the increase in equity has actually accrued to the credit of the group. The practice of reflecting equities was extended in APB Opinion No. 18 to corporate joint ventures and certain other investments in voting common stock where the investor's holding is as little as 20 per cent of the total outstanding.

When the investments in unconsolidated subsidiaries and 50 per cent owned companies are adjusted to reflect equities, the question is raised whether it is necessary to furnish financial statements of such subsidiaries and companies. In the opinion of the author, if such subsidiaries and companies are significant as measured by the SEC's rules, there is no relief from the requirement to furnish their statements based merely on the fact that the consolidated statements reflect the equity in such companies. The underlying statements must be furnished in order that the investor-reader may know what is represented by the investment.

Financial Statements of Affiliates Whose Securities Are Pledged as Collateral.—For each affiliate, securities of which constitute or are to constitute a substantial portion of the collateral securing any class of securities being registered, there must be filed the financial statements that would be required if the affiliate were a registrant. For the purpose of this instruction, securities of a company shall be deemed to constitute a substantial portion of collateral if the aggregate principal amount, par value, or book value, as shown by the books of the registrant, or market value, whichever is the greatest, of such securities equals 20 per cent or more of the principal amount of the class secured thereby.

Reorganization of Registrant.—If, during the period for which its income statements are required, the registrant has emerged from a reorganization in which substantial changes occurred in its asset, liability, capital stock, surplus, or reserve accounts, a brief explanation of such changes must be set forth in a note or supporting schedule to the balance sheets filed.

If the registrant is about to emerge from such a reorganization, there shall be filed, in addition to the balance sheets of the registrant otherwise required, a balance sheet giving effect to the plan of reorganization. These balance sheets must be set forth in such form (preferably columnar) as will show in related manner (1) the balance sheet of the registrant prior to the reorganization, (2) the changes to be effected in the reorganization, and (3) the balance sheet of the registrant after giving effect to the plan of reorganization. By a footnote, or otherwise, a brief explanation of the changes must be given.

Succession to Other Businesses.—If, during the period for which its income statement is required, the registrant has by merger, consolidation, or otherwise succeeded to one or more businesses, the additions, eliminations, and other changes effected in the succession must be appropriately set forth in a note or supporting schedule to the balance sheets filed. In addition, statements of income, retained earnings, and other additional capital for each constituent business shall be filed for such period prior to the succession as may be necessary when added to the time, if any, for which such statements after the succession are filed to cover the equivalent of the three-year period. If appropriate, combined statements of the constituent businesses may be furnished in lieu of individual statements.

If the registrant, by merger, consolidation, or otherwise, is *about* to succeed to one or more businesses, financial statements must be filed for each of the constituent businesses as would be required if they were registering securities under the 1933 Act. If appropriate, combined (pro forma) statements of such constituent businesses may be filed in lieu of individual statements for each constituent business. In addition, there must be filed a balance sheet (pro forma) of the registrant giving effect to the plan of succession. These balance sheets are to be set forth in such form (preferably columnar) as will show in related manner (1) the balance sheets of the constituent businesses, (2) the changes to be effected in the succession, and (3) the balance sheet (pro forma) of the registrant after giving effect to the plan of succession. A brief explanation of the changes must be given by footnote or otherwise.

The two paragraphs immediately preceding do not apply to the registrant's succession to the business of any "totally-held subsidiary" or to any acquisition of a business by purchase.

Financial Statements of a Predecessor Partnership.—Occasionally the owners of a business which is conducted as a partnership or a sole proprietorship desire to sell a portion of their holdings. Frequently the most feasible way of accomplishing this objective is to transfer the business to a corporation and then have the owners sell a portion of their stock holdings. If the corporation were recently formed, a registration statement in these circumstances would probably contain financial information of the predecessor partnership or sole proprietorship. Inasmuch as the financial statements of a partnership or a sole proprietorship would not reflect the expenses which would apply if the business were operated as a corporation, the SEC has in most cases requested that the financial statements of the predecessor partnership or sole proprietorship be adjusted to reflect the results of operations which would have appeared had the business been operated as a corporation. Compliance with the SEC's request in this situation might result in the presentation of a pro forma statement of income rather than an actual statement of income. (For a discussion of pro forma statements, see Chapter **21**.)

Acquisition of Other Businesses.—Financial statements must be filed for any business directly or indirectly acquired by the registrant *after* the date of the latest balance sheet filed pursuant to the instructions relating to financial statements of the registrant (page **9·5**) and the consolidation (page **9·7**). Financial statements must also be furnished in respect of any business *to be directly or indirectly acquired* by the registrant. The financial statements to be submitted in respect of such business acquired or to be acquired are those which would be furnished if such business were a registrant. These instructions would make it appear that financial statements are not required in respect of a business acquired *before* the date of the latest balance sheet of the registrant and/or consolidated group, but this is not the case; see the comment below relating to the SEC's release on this subject.

The acquisition of securities is deemed to be the acquisition of a business if such securities (combined with securities already held) give control of the business. In addition, the acquisition of securities which will extend the registrant's control of a business is deemed to be the acquisition of the business if any of the securities being registered are to be offered in exchange for the securities to be acquired. (See the discussion of pro forma statements in Chapter **21**.)

Financial statements need not be filed, however, for any business acquired or to be acquired from a "totally-held subsidiary." In addition, the statements of any one or more businesses may be omitted if such businesses, considered in the aggregate as a single subsidiary, would not constitute a significant subsidiary, provided, however, that the statements of any business may not be omitted where any of the securities being registered are to be offered in exchange for securities representing such business.

RELEASE No. 4950: FINANCIAL STATEMENTS OF COMPANIES ACQUIRED OR TO BE ACQUIRED.—As indicated above there has been some ambiguity in the SEC's instructions relating to financial statements of acquired businesses. Those instructions seem to indicate that such statements are not required for businesses acquired *before* the date of the latest balance sheet filed for the registrant and/or consolidated group. Obviously this would not make sense where Company A (the registrant) acquires Company B shortly before the date of A's balance sheet, and B is ten times the size of A. B would ordinarily be included in A's consolidated balance sheet and in its income statement since the date of acquisition (in the case of a purchase). But what about B's operating results before its acquisition by A? In view of its size, is not B the real registrant? It may well be that the changes brought about as a result of the acquisition (changes in depreciation charges, interest expense, and income taxes, for example) might minimize the significance of B's historical operating results before the acquisition, but, in many cases, the pre-acquisition results are likely to be material to the investor.

With the increase in the number of mergers and acquisitions in the late 1960's, this became a matter of some importance, and the staff of the SEC began demanding that financial statements of acquired businesses be included in registration statements in circumstances where the instructions did not specifically call for them. Sometimes the statements of the acquired business were certified, but, in other cases, they were included on an unaudited basis. The problem grew in importance not only because there were no clear SEC guidelines as to when financial statements of an acquired business had to be furnished and the inconsistent staff positions as to whether the statements had to be certified, but also because registrants often found it impossible to have the statements certified. All too often a registrant had acquired a company or a business whose financial statements either were not certified or were certified with qualifications that rendered them unacceptable to the SEC. One result of this situation was that the Commission received many requests for relief from the staff's certification requirements and concluded that the time had come to set forth clearly its requirements in this area. Accordingly, the Commission issued Release No. 4950 on February 20, 1969 under the 1933 Act dealing with certified financial statements of businesses acquired or to be acquired. The release follows:

GENERAL REQUIREMENTS FOR CERTIFIED FINANCIAL STATEMENTS OF COMPANIES ACQUIRED OR TO BE ACQUIRED

The increasing number of business acquisitions has led to numerous requests for relief from the requirements for certification of financial statements of the acquired businesses on the representation that it is impossible to obtain certification. When an acquiring company plans to register securities under the Securities Act the necessity for furnishing financial statements for the new business must be considered by it. Item 27 of Schedule A of the Securities Act of 1933 and Instructions 11 and 12 to Form S-1 for registration under the Act require certified financial statements for a company acquired or to be acquired. Instruction 13 of Form S-1 permits the Commission to grant relief from this requirement of certification where such relief is consistent with the protection of investors. Generally, relief has been requested because no independent certified public accountant has observed the taking of inventory of the acquired company necessary for certification of financial statements for three years and alternative methods of verification were not available.

When a representation is made that certification of financial statements of acquired companies for a full three year period cannot be obtained and compelling and satisfactory evidence in support of such representation is furnished, the Commission considers the relationship of the following items of the acquired companies to those of the registrant (on a consolidated basis without inclusion of such companies) in determining whether relief from the three-year certification requirement should be granted:

1. gross sales and operating revenues;
2. net income;
3. total assets;
4. total stockholder equity; and
5. total purchase price compared to total assets of registrant.

The above items will be evaluated as follows:

    A. If none of the items exceed 10 per cent, certified statements will not be required;

    B. If any of the items exceed 10 per cent but none exceed 25 per cent, certification of the balance sheet and the income statement for not less than six months will be required;

    C. If any of the items exceed 25 per cent but none exceed 45 per cent, certification of the balance sheet and the income statement for at least twelve months will be required.

    D. If any of the items exceed 45 per cent, certification of the balance sheet and the income statement for three years will be required, consistent with similar requirements as to the registrant.

In connection with any request for relief from the three year certification requirement the items of information mentioned above should be furnished in tabular form, comparing the five items set forth therein of the acquired companies (individually and in the aggregate) with the registrant on a consolidated basis (without the acquired companies), with dates of acquisition and other pertinent data. To the extent any of the data is not based on audit reports, the basis or lack of basis for reliance on the data should be fully stated (including the nature and method of checking the accuracy of the underlying figures).

Income statements for periods not certified shall not be combined with the certified statements if to do so would result in a qualification by the auditors on grounds of materiality.

NOTE. This release does not apply to the financial statements of a company to be acquired where the securities to be registered are to be offered to the security holders of that company in exchange for their securities. In such a case certified financial statements of that company shall be furnished in accordance with the requirements of the applicable registration form.

Filing of Other Financial Statements in Certain Cases.—The Commission may, upon the request of the registrant, and where consistent with the protection of investors, permit the omission of one or more of the required statements as set forth above, or the filing in substitution therefor of appropriate statements of comparable character. The Commission may also require the filing of other statements in addition to, or in substitution for, the statements required by the instructions for Form S–1 in any case where such statements are necessary or appropriate for an adequate presentation of the financial condition of any company whose financial statements are required, or whose statements are otherwise necessary for the protection of investors. Although the preceding sentence states that other statements may be required where necessary to present fairly the *"financial condition"* of a company, the author believes the SEC would not hesitate to require additional statements when they are necessary for a fair presentation of *results of operations* (as distinct from financial condition).

The provisions in the foregoing paragraph are frequently invoked in relation to a requirement for pro forma financial statements (see the discussion of this subject in Chapter **21**). For examples showing how the foregoing provisions were availed of by registrants, see "Omission of Parent Company Financial Statements" on page **9·48**. The foregoing provisions are also invoked in connection with other special situations, particularly where the data required to be furnished are so bulky as to destroy the usefulness of the prospectus.

An example from actual practice will illustrate how this provision in the instructions for financial statements is applied by the staff in a specific situation. A land development company filed a registration statement on Form S–1 in 1967. The company was in the business of selling land to prospective home builders on the basis of $10 down with the balance of the selling price payable at the rate of $10 a month over a period of several years. The company undertook to make certain improvements to the property before title passed to the buyer. Profit on the transaction was recognized by the company when it received the third payment, since the company's experience indicated that the great majority of buyers who made three payments completed their contracts. Along with the recognition of gain, the company provided for the cost of the contemplated improvements and for the possibility of noncollection from customers who might not complete their contracts. Because of the stretched out period in which the receivables would be collected, a constantly increasing volume of sales, and the need for cash to make the agreed improvements, the company was forced to borrow substantial sums of money and accordingly incurred substantial interest costs. The result of this situation was that the company reported substantial earnings on the accrual basis but was constantly pressed for cash.

In due course, the company received the SEC's comments on its registration statement. One of the comments relating to the financial statements was as follows:

Because of the company's high interest costs and its unique cash problems which are obscured by the method used to record income from sales of lots, it is requested that the income statement be followed by a certified statement of the source and application of funds for each period covered by the summary of earnings.

The company and its independent auditors agreed that the SEC's request was appropriate, and the statement in question was furnished by amendment to the registration statement. (In 1971 the SEC amended the instructions for financial statements in several of its forms to provide for the furnishing of statements of source and application of funds by all registrants using those forms.)

As another example: Form S–2 is the form intended to be used by certain registrants in the development stage, but its use is circumscribed by conditions which sometimes have the effect of prohibiting use of the form in a situation where it would be most appropriate. Form S–2 may not be used, for instance, if the registrant has, or intends to acquire, a subsidiary other than an inactive subsidiary with no more than nominal assets. There have been cases where the existence of active subsidiaries has ruled out the use of Form S–2, but the circumstances were such that the financial instructions of that form were believed to be appropriate. The author has discussed situations of this kind with the Commission's staff who have always welcomed the suggestion that the financial statements be furnished in the format appropriate to Form S–2 notwithstanding that they would be included in a Form S–1 registration statement.

The important thing to remember is this: if any SEC rule involves a real hardship, or if it results in a form of financial statement that is less informative than an alternative statement, it is highly desirable to discuss the problem with the staff of the SEC. The Commission's rules provide a certain amount of flexibility. It may be found that the problem is one the Commission has had to consider many times and has decided along lines that may be agreeable to all concerned. Sometimes the registration involves a unique problem which was not contemplated by the formal requirements. The SEC frequently waives the formal rules in favor of a more logical or understandable statement or presentation.

Historical Financial Information.—The information required by the instructions set forth below must be submitted in respect of each company or group of companies whose balance sheet is filed as part of the registration statement. The information is to cover the seven-year period preceding the three-year period for which the related income statements are filed. The information must be given as to all of the accounts specified below whether or not they are presently carried on the books of account. The information required by these instructions does not call for an audit, but only for a survey or review of the accounts specified. (For a form of report covering this type of information, see Chapter **24**.) The information should not be detailed beyond a point material to an investor. What is more important, however, is that the information may be entirely omitted as to any company for which equivalent information for the period has previously been filed with the SEC pursuant to the 1933 or 1934 Acts.

It will be noted that the instructions require certain information to be filed for a period of seven years preceding the income statements *which are filed*. Note that the instruction does not speak of a seven-year period preceding the income statements *required to be filed*. If, instead of a three-year income statement, a company files a ten-year income statement, does this mean that Historical Financial Information must cover the period of seven years preceding the ten-year statement? In the author's opinion, the applicable SEC instructions are not to be interpreted literally. The information is intended to cover a period which, combined with the *required* income statement, will aggregate ten years.

REVALUATION OF PROPERTY.—If there were any material increases or decreases in investments, in property, plant, and equipment, or in intangible assets, resulting from revaluing such assets, a statement is required as to (1) in what year or years such revaluations were made; (2) the amounts of such increases or decreases, and the accounts affected, including all related entries; and (3) if in connection with such revaluation any related adjustments were made in reserve accounts, the accounts and amounts must be disclosed with explanations. Information is not required as to adjustments made in the ordinary course of business, but only as to major revaluations made for the purpose of entering in the books of account current values, reproduction cost, or any values other than original cost. Information need not be furnished with respect to any revaluation entry which was subsequently reversed or with respect to the reversal of a revaluation entry recorded prior to the period if a statement as to the reversal is made.

Some corporations—principally public utility holding corporations—follow the practice, in their consolidated balance sheets, of including the uneliminated balance of investments in subsidiaries in consolidated fixed assets without further designation or disclosure. If the fixed assets of subsidiaries are written up, the uneliminated investment amount is correspondingly reduced, with the result that the consolidated fixed assets are not affected. Question sometimes arises whether this is the type of revaluation which must be reported under Historical Financial Information.

In *Associated Gas and Electric Co.* [11 SEC 1002 (1942)] properties of subsidiaries were written up on the basis of reproduction cost appraisals. This caused a reduction in the uneliminated balance of the parent company investments, but did not affect the balance sheet item designated "property, plant and equipment, and intangibles." The company did not report the revaluations of properties by subsidiaries or the related effect on the uneliminated investment amount. The company contended that these matters did not have to be disclosed since there was no effect on consolidated fixed assets. SEC ruled that this position was untenable. Since the subsidiary property had been written up on the basis of a reproduction cost appraisal, the uneliminated amount represented, in effect, an intangible asset. For the purpose of reporting revaluations, property accounts may not be combined with intangibles—both items must be reported. This is especially so when, as in the case cited, the appraiser could not be considered an independent person.

CAPITAL SHARES.—If there were any material restatements of capital shares which resulted in transfers from capital share liability to surplus or reserve accounts, a statement must be made of the amount of each such restatement and all related entries. Information is not required as to restatements resulting from the declaration of stock dividends.

If there was an original issue of capital shares, any part of the proceeds of which was credited to accounts other than capital share accounts, a statement must be made as to the title of the class, the accounts, and the respective amounts credited thereto.

DEBT DISCOUNT AND EXPENSE WRITTEN OFF.—If any material amount of debt discount and expense, on long-term debt still outstanding, was written off earlier than as required under any periodic amortization plan, the following information must be given: (1) title of the securities, (2) date of the write-off, (3) amount written off, and (4) to what account charged.

PREMIUMS AND DISCOUNT AND EXPENSE ON SECURITIES RETIRED.—If any material amount of long-term debt or preferred shares was retired, and if either the retirement was made at a premium or there remained, at the time of retirement, a material amount of unamortized discount and expense applicable to the securities retired, a statement must be made for each class giving: (1) title of the securities retired, (2) date of retirement, (3) amount of premium paid and of unamortized discount and expense, (4) to what account charged, and (5) whether being amortized and, if so, the plan of amortization.

OTHER CHANGES IN SURPLUS.—If there were any material increases or decreases in surplus, other than those resulting from transactions specified above, the closing of the income statement, or the declaration or payment of dividends, the following information must be furnished: (1) the year or years in which such increases or decreases were made, (2) the nature and amounts thereof, and (3) the accounts affected, including all material related entries. Information, however, need not be furnished with respect to any revaluation entry which was subsequently reversed or with respect to the reversal of a revaluation entry recorded prior to the period, if a statement as to the reversal is made.

PREDECESSORS.—Historical Financial Information shall be furnished, to the extent it is material, concerning any predecessor of the registrant from the beginning of the period to the date of succession, not only as to the entries made respectively in the books of the predecessor or the successor, but also as to the changes effected in the transfer of the assets from the predecessor. However, no information need be furnished as to any one or more predecessors which, considered in the aggregate, would not constitute a significant predecessor.

OMISSION OF CERTAIN INFORMATION.—No information need be furnished as to any subsidiary, whether consolidated or unconsolidated, for the period prior to the date on which it became a majority-owned subsidiary of the registrant or of a predecessor for which information is required above.

No information need be furnished as to any one or more unconsolidated subsidiaries for which separate financial statements are filed if all subsidiaries for which the information is so omitted, considered in the aggregate as a single subsidiary, would not constitute a "significant subsidiary" (see definition on page **16·8**).

Only the information specified under "Revaluation of Property" above needs to be given as to any predecessor or any subsidiary thereof if, immediately prior to the date of succession thereto by a company for which information is required, the predecessor or subsidiary was in insolvency proceedings.

Supporting Schedules.—In addition to the financial statements indicated above, a registration statement on Form S–1 must include certain supplemental schedules. These schedules, insofar as they relate to a commercial and industrial company, are described in Chapter **20** together with the related instructions and the requirements as to the form and content of such schedules. (See also page **9·58** concerning the possibility of incorporating these schedules by reference to information already on file with the SEC.)

Financial Statements Included in Prospectus.—A prospectus prepared for filing as part of a registration on Form S–1 must include all the financial statements required by the "Instructions as to Financial Statements" except those specified below:

1. All schedules to balance sheets and income statements may be omitted from the prospectus except those containing "Supplementary Income Statement Information" (Schedule XVI) and "Investments in Securities of Affiliates— Banks" (for bank holding companies only) and "Summary of Investments in Securities—Other than Securities of Affiliates" (for insurance companies other than life and title insurance companies). All "Historical Financial Information" (see page **9·16**) may also be omitted from the prospectus.

2. If the income and earned surplus statements required are included in their entirety in the summary of earnings, they need not be otherwise included in the prospectus or elsewhere in the registration statement.

As to the ordinary industrial company, the prospectus will contain the prime financial statements (that is, balance sheets and statements of income, retained earnings, other additional capital, source and application of funds, and earnings summaries) plus the information contained in "Supplementary Income Statement Information" either in a separate schedule or in notes to the financial statements. All supporting schedules (except "Supplementary Income Statement Information") and "Historical Financial Information" are included in Part II of the registration statement.

For the SEC's requirements applicable to a "summary prospectus," see the discussion beginning on page **11·26**.

Application of Regulation S–X.—Regulation S–X applies to all the financial statements and schedules included in a registration statement on Form S–1. For the requirements as to financial statements of commercial and industrial companies, see Chapters **16** through **20** and **24** through **26**.

Summary of Earnings.—Item 6 of Form S–1 calls for the inclusion in the prospectus of a summary of earnings. This subject is discussed in Chapter **10**.

Ratio Information in Form S–1.—If the registration statement relates to an offering of *debt securities,* there must be furnished information regarding the ratio of earnings to fixed charges for each period of the summary of earnings. A pro forma ratio must also be furnished for the latest year of the summary and interim periods, if any.

If the registration statement relates to an offering of *preferred stock,* there must be furnished information regarding the ratio of earnings to fixed charges and preferred dividends combined for each period of the summary in which preferred stock was outstanding. A corresponding pro forma ratio must be given for the latest year and interim periods, if any.

The registrant must file an exhibit to the registration statement setting forth the computations of the aforesaid ratios.

For further information regarding the ratios, their computation and presentation, see the discussion in Chapter **8**.

Financial Statements Required by Form S–2

The kinds of business to which Form S–2 is restricted and the limitations on its use are set forth in Chapter **8**. The following financial statements must be filed as part of a registration statement on Form S–2:

Statement of assets and unrecovered promotional, exploratory, and
  development costs
Statement of liabilities

Statement of capital shares
Statement of other securities
Statement of cash receipts and disbursements

An important feature of the financial instructions applicable to Form S–2 is that *all the financial statements which are required to be furnished must be certified*. This seems rather harsh when it is considered that the form is intended to be used by recently organized companies in the early stages of development. Often because of delays in processing by the staff of the SEC, the financial statements have to be brought up to a more recent date. In addition to all the other expenses involved in updating the financial statements, the registrant must also submit to the additional cost of updating the audit.

See page **9**·3 for a statement of the Commission's policy regarding the need for updating the financial statements in certain circumstances.

On page **9**·14 there is a discussion of the possibilities of furnishing other financial statements in substitution for, or in addition to, those required by the specific instructions of Form S–1. Similar instructions also apply to Form S–2.

Statement of Assets and Unrecovered Promotional, Exploratory, and Development Costs.—There must be filed for the registrant a certified statement of assets and unrecovered promotional, exploratory, and development costs as of a date within 90 days prior to the date of filing the registration statement.

Statement of Liabilities.—There must be filed a certified statement of liabilities as of the same date as the statement of assets and unrecovered promotional, exploratory, and development costs.

Statement of Capital Shares.—A certified statement of capital shares must be filed for the registrant as of the same date as the statement of assets and unrecovered promotional, exploratory, and development costs.

Statement of Other Securities.—If the registrant has any securities with respect to which information is not called for in the statements of liabilities or capital shares, information must be furnished as to such securities corresponding to that required in those statements.

Statement of Cash Receipts and Disbursements.—The registrant must file a certified statement of its cash receipts and disbursements for each of its last three fiscal years (or for the life of the registrant, if less) and for the period from the close of the most recent of such fiscal years to the date as of which the statement of assets and unrecovered promotional, exploratory, and development costs is filed.

Regulation S–X.—Regulation S–X contains the requirements as to the form and content of the financial statements required to be included in a registration statement on Form S–2. (See Chapters **16** through **20** and **24** through **26** as to the form and content of such financial statements and certification by independent public accountants.)

Consolidated Statements and Statements of Unconsolidated Subsidiaries.—Since Form S–2 may not be used by companies having active subsidiaries, there are no requirements for consolidated statements or for statements of unconsolidated subsidiaries.

Supporting Schedules.—There are no requirements for supporting schedules to financial statements in Form S–2, and none need be furnished.

Summary of Earnings.—Since Form S–2 does not call for information as to income or loss, there is also no requirement to furnish a summary of earnings.

Financial Statements Included in Prospectus.—The financial statements required to be included in a registration statement on Form S–2 are set forth above. All of these financial statements must appear in the related prospectus.

Financial Statements Required by Form S–3

The kinds of business for which Form S–3 was designed and the limitations on its use are set forth in Chapter **8**. Following is a list of the financial statements of the registrant that must be included in a Form S–3 registration statement:

> Statement of assets and unrecovered promotional, exploratory, and development costs
> Statement of liabilities
> Statement of capital shares
> Statement of other securities
> Statement of cash receipts and disbursements

All of the foregoing statements must be certified by independent public accountants in accordance with the applicable provisions of Regulation S–X; see Chapters **24** and **25**. Unlike the instructions in some of the other registration forms (such as Form S–1), there is no provision in Form S–3 for the submission of interim financial data on an unaudited basis.

See the discussion on page **9·3** regarding the Commission's policy as to the necessity of updating financial statements in certain circumstances.

See also the discussion on page **9·14** regarding the possibilities of furnishing other financial statements in substitution for, or in addition to, those required by the specific instructions of Form S–1. Similar instructions also apply to Form S–3.

Statement of Assets and Unrecovered Promotional, Exploratory, and Development Costs.—There must be filed for the registrant a certified statement of assets and unrecovered promotional, exploratory, and development costs as of a date within 90 days prior to the date of filing the registration statement.

Statement of Liabilities.—There must be filed for the registrant a certified statement of liabilities as of the same date as the aforementioned statement of assets and unrecovered promotional, exploratory, and development costs.

Statement of Capital Shares.—A certified statement of capital shares of the registrant must be furnished as of the same date as the aforementioned statement of assets and unrecovered promotional, exploratory, and development costs.

Statement of Other Securities.—A certified statement of other securities of the registrant must be filed as of the same date as the aforementioned statement of assets and unrecovered promotional, exploratory, and development costs.

Statement of Cash Receipts and Disbursements.—The registration statement must include a certified statement of cash receipts and disbursements of the registrant for each of its last three fiscal years, or for the life of the registrant if less, and for the period from the close of the most recent of such fiscal years to the date of the statement of assets and unrecovered promotional, exploratory, and development costs.

Regulation S–X.—Regulation S–X contains the requirements as to the form and content of the aforementioned statements that have to be included in a Form S–3 registration statement. See Chapters **16** through **20** and **24** through **26** as to the form and content of such financial statements and certification by independent public accountants.

Consolidated Statements and Statements of Unconsolidated Subsidiaries.—Since Form S–3 may not be used by companies having active subsidiaries, there are no requirements for consolidated statements or for statements of unconsolidated subsidiaries.

Supporting Schedules.—There are no requirements in Form S–3 for supporting schedules for financial statements, and none need be furnished.

Summary of Earnings.—Inasmuch as Form S–3 does not call for an income statement, there is also no requirement to furnish a summary of earnings.

Financial Statements Included in Prospectus.—The financial statements that must be included in a Form S–3 registration statement are set forth above. All of these statements must be included in the prospectus.

Financial Statements Required by Form S–4

Form S–4 is used for filing registration statements under the 1933 Act by *closed-end* management investment companies registered under the Investment Company Act of 1940. A brief indication of the contents of a Form S–4 registration statement is given in Chapter **8**.

The financial statements that must be included in a registration statement on Form S–4 relate to the following :

Financial statements of the registrant (unconsolidated)
Consolidated financial statements
Financial statements of unconsolidated subsidiaries
Special provisions in connection with :
    (a) Reorganization of the registrant
    (b) Succession to other business
Historical financial information

Financial Statements of the Registrant.—The following financial statements have to be furnished in respect of the registrant (unconsolidated) :

1. Balance sheets (or statements of assets and liabilities) :
    (a) A certified balance sheet (or statement of assets and liabilities) as of the close of its latest fiscal year unless such fiscal year has ended within 90 days prior to the date of filing the registration statement, in which case the statements may be as of the close of the preceding fiscal year.
    (b) If the latest fiscal year of the registrant has ended within 90 days prior to the date of filing and the statement required by

the preceding paragraph is filed as of the end of the preceding fiscal year, there has to be filed as an amendment to the registration statement, within 120 days after the date of filing, a certified statement of the registrant as of the end of its latest fiscal year.

2. The statements specified in Rules 6–04 (statement of income and expense), 6–05 (statement of realized gain or loss on investments), and 6–06 (statement of unrealized appreciation or depreciation of investments) of Regulation S–X have to be filed for the registrant for each of its last three fiscal years preceding the date of the statement required by 1(a) above, and, by amendment to the registration statement, for the fiscal year immediately preceding the date of each statement filed pursuant to 1(b) above. These statements must be certified.

If, at the date of filing the registration statement, the financial statements are not as of a date within 90 days prior to the date of filing, see "If Statements Not Within 90 Days of Filing" below.

Consolidated Financial Statements.—The following consolidated financial statements must be included in the registration statement:

1. Consolidated balance sheets (or statements of assets and liabilities) :
    (a) A certified consolidated balance sheet (or statement of assets and liabilities) of the registrant and its subsidiaries as of the close of the latest fiscal year of the registrant, unless such fiscal year has ended within 90 days prior to the date of filing, in which case the statements may be as of the close of the preceding fiscal year.
    (b) If the latest fiscal year of the registrant has ended within 90 days prior to the date of filing and the statement required by the preceding paragraph is filed as of the end of the preceding fiscal year, there has to be filed as an amendment to the registration statement, within 120 days after the date of filing, a certified consolidated balance sheet (or statement of assets and liabilities) of the registrant and its subsidiaries as of the end of the latest fiscal year.

2. The statements specified in Rules 6–04 (statement of income and expense), 6–05 (statement of realized gain or loss on investments), and 6–06 (statement of unrealized appreciation or depreciation of investments) of Regulation S–X have to be filed for the registrant and its subsidiaries consolidated for each of the last three fiscal years preceding the date of the consolidated statement required by 1(a) above, and, by amendment to the registration statement, for the fiscal

year immediately preceding the date of each consolidated statement filed pursuant to 1(b) above. These statements must be certified.

If, at the date of filing the registration statement, the consolidated financial statements are not as of a date within 90 days prior to the date of filing, see "If Statements Not Within 90 Days of Filing" below.

Financial Statements of Unconsolidated Subsidiaries.—Subject to Rules 4–03 (see page **17**· 18) and 6–02–3 (see page **19**· 10) of Regulation S–X regarding group statements of unconsolidated subsidiaries, there has to be filed for each subsidiary of the registrant not consolidated, the financial statements which would be required if the subsidiary were itself a registrant. However, the profit and loss statements or statements of income and expense, realized and unrealized gain or loss on investments, filed for any subsidiary which is less than majority-owned need cover only the last fiscal year immediately preceding the date of the balance sheet or statement of assets and liabilities filed for such subsidiary.

If the fiscal year of any unconsolidated subsidiary ends within 90 days before the date of filing the registration statement, or ends after the date of filing, the subsidiary's financial statements may be filed as an amendment to the registration statement within 120 days after the end of the subsidiary's fiscal year.

All financial statements of any one or more unconsolidated subsidiaries may be omitted if all such subsidiaries for which statements are so omitted, considered in the aggregate as a single subsidiary, would not constitute a "significant subsidiary."

If Statements Not Within 90 Days of Filing.—If any balance sheet (or statement of assets and liabilities) filed pursuant to the foregoing requirements of Form S–4 is not as of a date within 90 days prior to the date of filing the registration statement, there must also be included in the prospectus a corresponding balance sheet (or statement of assets and liabilities) as of a date within 90 days prior to the filing date. In addition, the related statements prescribed by Article 6 (see page **19**· 10) of Regulation S–X have to be included from the close of the latest fiscal year for which such statements are furnished up to the date of the balance sheet (or statement of assets and liabilities) referred to in the preceding sentence. The statements required by this paragraph do not have to be certified; if they are certified, however, the balance sheet (or statement of assets and liabilities) as of the end of the last fiscal year may be omitted.

Reorganization of the Registrant.—If, during the period for which statements of income and expense, realized and unrealized gain or loss on investments are required to be filed with the registration statement, the registrant has emerged from a reorganization in which substantial changes occurred in its asset, liability, capital share, surplus, or reserve accounts, a brief explanation of such changes has to be set forth in a note or supporting schedule to the balance sheets (or statements of assets and liabilities) filed.

Succession to Other Businesses.—If, during the period for which statements of income and expense, realized and unrealized gain or loss on investments are required to be filed with the registration statement, the registrant has acquired by merger, consolidation or other succession one or more businesses representing, in the aggregate, assets valued in excess of 15 per cent of the value of the registrant's assets at the time of filing, the additions, eliminations, and other changes effected in the succession have to be appropriately set forth in a note or supporting schedule to the balance sheets (or statements of assets and liabilities) filed. In addition, profit and loss or income statements for each business so acquired, or combined statements if appropriate, have to be filed for such period prior to the succession as may be necessary when added to the time, if any, for which profit and loss or income statements after the succession are filed to cover the equivalent of three full fiscal years.

Filing of Other Financial Statements in Certain Cases.—The instructions for financial statements in Form S–4 contain a flexibility provision similar to the one in Form S–1. See the discussion of the latter beginning on page **9·**14.

Historical Financial Information.—A registration statement on Form S–4 has to contain certain historical financial information similar to that in a registration statement on Form S–1. The following portions of the S–4 requirements are almost identical with the corresponding S–1 requirements set forth beginning on page **9·**16 and are therefore not repeated here:

Revaluation of assets
Capital shares
Debt discount and expense written off
Other changes in surplus
Predecessors
Omission of certain information

Form S–4, however, contains two requirements with respect to historical financial information that are different from those in S–1. They are as follows:

SEC Instruction No. 13

Premiums and discount and expense on securities retired:

(a) If any material amount of long-term debt or preferred shares was retired and if either the retirement was made at a premium or there remained, at the time of retirement, a material amount of unamortized discount and expense applicable to the securities retired, state for each class (1) title of the securities retired, (2) date of retirement, (3) amount of premium paid and of unamortized discount and expense, (4) to what account charged, and (5) whether being amortized and, if so, the plan of amortization.

(b) In the case of preferred shares, the premium or discount shall be measured by the difference between the price paid and the involuntary liquidating preference of the shares.

SEC Instruction No. 14

Discount on securities retired.

If any material amount of long-term debt or preferred shares was retired and if such retirement was made at a discount, state for each year and with respect to each such class of securities (1) the title of the class retired, (2) the amount of discount, and (3) to what account credited. Instruction 13(b) above also applies here.

Supporting Schedules.—In addition to the financial statements and information indicated above, a Form S–4 registration statement must contain the supporting schedules prescribed by Rule 6–10 (see page **19·23**) of Regulation S–X.

Financial Statements Included in Prospectus.—A registration statement prepared for filing on Form S–4 must contain the financial statements and information referred to above, except that the following may be omitted from the prospectus:

(1) The statements of any subsidiary that is not a majority-owned subsidiary;

(2) All schedules in support of the most recent balance sheet (or statement of assets and liabilities) filed except the following:
Schedule I (Investments in securities of unaffiliated issuers)
Columns A, E, F, and G of Schedule II (Investments—Other than securities)
Columns A, B, C, and D of Schedule III (Investments in affiliates), omitting the information called for by paragraph (b) of footnote 1 to Column A

(3) Historical financial information

If the registrant has only one class of outstanding capital securities, it may, at its option, furnish all the financial statements and information referred to in the preceding pages in Part II of the registration statement and include only the following statements in the prospectus:

(1) A statement of assets and liabilities in which the details of Schedules I, II, and III prescribed above may be substituted for the summaries of these items as prescribed by Rule 6–03 (see page **19**·13) of Regulation S–X. If this option is elected, the statement required by Rule 6–09 (see page **19**·23) may be omitted from the prospectus.

(2) An income statement for the latest fiscal year in the form specified in Rule 6–04 (see page **19**·17) of Regulation S–X, including, on the same page, (i) the items specified in caption 5 of Rule 6–05 (see page **19**·19) and caption 2 of Rule 6–06 (see page **19**·20), and (ii) the ratio of total operating and management expenses to total investment income. "Total operating and management expenses" means the aggregate of the expenses described in captions 2 and 3 of Rule 6–04 of Regulation S–X. "Total investment income" does not include equalization adjustments.

(3) Statement of changes in net assets for the three full fiscal years prior to the date of filing (or for the life of the registrant, if less) as prescribed by Rule 6–08 (see page **19**·21) of Regulation S–X.

Except that the statement prescribed by (2) above is required for only one fiscal year plus an interim period, if any, to within 90 days of filing, the instructions as to dates and certification referred to in the preceding pages of the S–4 requirements are applicable to the optional statements discussed above.

Application of Regulation S–X.—Regulation S–X applies to all of the financial statements and schedules included in a Form S–4 registration statement.

Summary of Earnings.—There is no requirement for a summary of earnings as such in a Form S–4 registration statement. Item 5 of the registration statement, however, includes a requirement for condensed financial information for a period of ten years plus the interim period to the date of the most recent balance sheet, setting forth per share income and capital changes.

Financial Statements Required by Form S–5

Form S–5 is used for filing registration statements under the 1933 Act by all *open-end* management investment companies registered under the Investment Company Act of 1940. A brief indication of the scope of a Form S–5 registration statement is given in Chapter **8**.

The instructions for the financial statements to be included in Form S–5 are virtually identical with those for Form S–4 which are described beginning on page **9**·24 of this book, and therefore are not repeated here. The only significant exception in S–5 is with respect to the optional statements for the prospectus in an S–4 registration statement which are described on page **9·28**. With respect to Instruction 1 of such optional statements, Form S–5 includes the following additional instruction:

The specimen price make-up sheet required by Item 30(a) may be furnished as a continuation of this statement [that is, as a continuation of the statement of assets and liabilities].

The instructions with respect to the supporting schedules in Form S–5 are the same as in S–4, and the same is true as to the financial statements to be included in the prospectus. For these S–4 requirements, see the preceding pages of this chapter.

The discussion of the applicability of Regulation S–X and the summary of earnings in the preceding pages dealing with Form S–4 is also applicable to Form S–5.

Financial Statements Required by Form S–7

A brief indication of the scope of Form S–7 is given in Chapter **8**, together with the conditions under which the form may be used. From a reading of these conditions, it will be apparent that the form is available only to substantial companies with respect to which much information is publicly available, whose business has not changed materially in the last five years, and whose earnings have exceeded the dividends (including stock dividends) declared in that period. The company must be one that has a class of equity securities registered pursuant to Section 12 of the 1934 Act, and must have complied in all respects with the requirements of Section 13 (periodical and other reports) and Section 14 (proxies) of that Act.

The requirements for financial statements in Form S–7 are set forth in Items 6 and 10 of the form. These contain the instructions with respect to the following:

> Item 6:
>> Statements of income
>> Statements of retained earnings
>> Statements of other additional capital
>> Statements of source and application of funds
> Item 10:
>> Balance sheets, schedules, and other financial statements

The requirements with respect to principal lines of business are in Item 5 of Form S–7; these are discussed in Chapter **23**.

Balance Sheets and Other Financial Statements.—Balance sheets of the registrant (unconsolidated) and of the consolidated group have to be furnished as of a date within six months prior to the date of filing the registration statement. These balance sheets need not be certified by independent public accountants, but if they are not certified, there have to be furnished in addition certified balance sheets as of a date within one year, unless the fiscal year of the registrant ended within 90 days prior to the filing date, in which case the certified balance sheets may be as of the end of the preceding fiscal year. These balance sheets have to be prepared in compliance with the applicable balance sheet requirements of Regulation S–X.

The unconsolidated balance sheets of the registrant may be omitted if (i) consolidated balance sheets of the registrant and one or more of its subsidiaries are furnished, (ii) either one of the following conditions is met, and (iii) the SEC is advised as to the reasons for such omission:

(1) The registrant is primarily an operating company and all subsidiaries included in the consolidated balance sheets furnished are wholly-owned subsidiaries and are not indebted to any person other than the parent or the consolidated subsidiaries in an amount which is material in relation to the total consolidated assets at the date of the latest balance sheet filed, except indebtedness incurred in the ordinary course of business which is not overdue and which matures within one year from the date of its creation, whether evidenced by securities or not. Indebtedness of a subsidiary which is guaranteed by, or secured by leases of, its parent or the parent's consolidated subsidiaries is to be excluded for the purpose of this determination.

(2) The registrant's total assets, exclusive of investments in and advances to the consolidated subsidiaries, constitute 75% or more of the total assets shown by the latest consolidated balance sheet filed, and the registrant's total gross revenues for the latest period for which its income statements would be filed, exclusive of interest and dividends received, or equity in income, from the consolidated subsidiaries, constitute 75% or more of the total gross revenue shown by the consolidated income statements filed.

Subject to Rule 4–03 of Regulation S–X, regarding group statements of unconsolidated subsidiaries, there has to be furnished for each majority-owned subsidiary of the registrant not included in the consolidated statements, the balance sheets that would be required if the subsidiary were itself a registrant.

If the registrant owns, directly or indirectly, approximately 50% of the voting securities of a company and approximately 50% of the voting securities of such company is owned, directly or indirectly, by another single interest, or if the registrant takes up the equity in undistributed earnings of any other unconsolidated company, there has to be filed for each such company the balance sheets which would be required if it were a registrant. The statements filed for each such company have to identify the other single interest or other interests in any company operated jointly. Where appropriate, group statements may be filed for such companies.

Insofar as practicable, the balance sheets of unconsolidated subsidiaries, 50% owned and jointly operated companies (referred to in the two preceding paragraphs) have to be as of the same dates as those of the registrant.

All balance sheets of any one or more unconsolidated subsidiaries, 50% owned companies, and other companies may be omitted:

(a) if all such subsidiaries and companies whose balance sheets are so omitted, considered in the aggregate as a single subsidiary, would not constitute a significant subsidiary, or

(b) if the investments in and advances to such companies by the parent and the parent's other subsidiaries, and the parent's and the other subsidiaries' equity in the net income of the companies, does not exceed 10% of the total consolidated assets at the date of the latest balance sheet filed or the consolidated net income for the latest fiscal year for which income statements are filed, respectively.

For any business directly or indirectly acquired by the registrant *after* the date of the latest balance sheet filed for the registrant or the affiliated group, there has to be filed the financial statements that would be required if such business were a registrant. Similar statements are required with respect to a business *to be* directly or indirectly acquired by the registrant. The acquisition of securities is deemed to be the acquisition of a business if such securities give control of the business or, combined with securities already held, give such control. No financial statements need be filed, however, for any business acquired or to be acquired from a totally-held subsidiary. Also, the statements of any one or more businesses may be omitted if such businesses, considered in the aggregate as a single subsidiary, would not constitute a significant subsidiary.

If during the period for which its income statements are required, the registrant has by merger, consolidation, or otherwise, succeeded to one or more businesses, the additions, eliminations, and other changes effected in the succession must be appropriately set forth in a note or supporting schedule to the balance sheets filed. In addition, income statements for each constituent business, or combined statements if appropriate, have to be filed for such period prior to the succession as may be necessary when added to the time, if any, for which income statements after the succession are filed to cover the equivalent of the period specified in Item 6, relating to required income statements. These instructions do not apply in the case of the registrant's succession to the business of a totally-held subsidiary or to the acquisition of one or more businesses by purchase if such businesses, considered in the aggregate as a single subsidiary, would not constitute a significant subsidiary.

If the registrant is *about to succeed* to one or more businesses by merger, consolidation, or otherwise, there needs to be filed for the constituent businesses financial statements, combined if appropriate, which would be required if they were registering securities under the 1933 Act. In addition, a balance sheet of the registrant has to be filed giving effect to the plan of succession. These balance sheets have to be set forth in such form, preferably columnar, as will show in related manner the balance sheets of the constituent businesses, the changes to be effected in the succession, and the balance sheet after giving effect to the plan of succession. A brief explanation of the changes has to be given by a footnote or otherwise. These instructions do not apply with respect to the registrant's succession to the business of any totally-held subsidiary, or to the acquisition of one or more businesses by purchase if such businesses, considered in the aggregate as a single subsidiary, would not constitute a significant subsidiary.

With respect to the discussion in the three preceding paragraphs concerning financial statements of acquired businesses, it is important to refer to the SEC's policy statement dealing with this subject and the certification requirements, which are discussed on page **9·**12.

Statements of Income.—Form S–7 contains no provisions for a summary of earnings. Instead there is required to be included a statement of income for the registrant, or for the registrant and its subsidiaries consolidated, or both, as appropriate, in comparative columnar form. The period to be covered by such statements is the last five fiscal years of the registrant and for any interim period between the end of the latest of such fiscal years and the date of the latest balance sheet furnished pursuant to Item 10(a) referred to above, and for the corresponding interim period of the preceding fiscal year. Comparable data for additional fiscal years must be included where necessary to keep the statements from being misleading. Also, where necessary, information and explanations of material significance to investors in appraising the results shown must be included.

It will be noted that the instructions call for an income statement for the registrant, or for the consolidated group, *or both, as appropriate.* It may be observed that these instructions follow very closely the instructions applicable to a summary of earnings in Form S–1. See the discussion of this matter on page **10·**5 where it is stated that when a consolidated summary of earnings is furnished, a summary for the registrant (unconsolidated) is seldom required or furnished or called for by the SEC's staff in its comment letter. The same may be said with respect to income statements in Form S–7: if a consolidated income statement is furnished, there is seldom a need to furnish an unconsolidated income statement of the registrant. (See also the discussion on page 9·48 regarding omission of parent company financial statements.)

Statements of income must also be submitted for unconsolidated subsidiaries, 50% owned companies, and other companies in respect of which balance sheets have to be furnished pursuant to Item 10(b). Income statements may also be required for businesses acquired, or to be acquired; see the discussion below concerning balance sheets and other financial statements.

Regulation S–X is applicable to all income statements furnished, and the statements have to be certified to the date of the respective certified balance sheets included in the prospectus.

In lieu of the statements for the interim period referred to above, certain companies in the electric, gas, and telephone business may furnish income statements for the period of 12 months ended on the interim date.

If a period or periods reported on include operations of a business prior to the date of acquisition (for example, when there has been a pooling of interests), or for other causes differ from reports previously issued for any period, the statement has to be reconciled as to sales (or revenues) and net income with the amounts previously reported. This reconciliation may be made either in the statement itself or in a footnote thereto.

If appropriate, the income statement must show earnings applicable to common stock. Per share earnings and dividends declared for each period of the statement must also be stated, together with the basis of the computation and the number of shares used in the computation. The registrant must file as an exhibit to the registration statement a statement setting forth the computation of per share earnings, unless the computation is clearly set forth on the income statement or in a note thereto.

The information with respect to the computation of per share earnings on both primary and fully diluted bases, presented in the exhibit or otherwise, must be furnished even though the amounts of per share earnings on the fully diluted basis are not required to be stated under the provisions of APB Opinion No. 15. That Opinion provides that any reduction of less than 3% need not be considered as dilution (footnote to paragraph 14 of the Opinion) and that a computation on the fully diluted basis which results in improvement of earnings per share need not be taken into account (paragraph 40 of the Opinion). (Release No. 33–5133, Feb. 18, 1971).

If preferred stock is to be registered, the annual dividend requirements on such preferred stock must be shown. To the extent that an issue represents refinancing, only the additional dividend requirements, if any, need be stated.

If *debt securities* are to be registered, the ratio of earnings to fixed charges must be shown for each fiscal year or other period of the statement, and a pro forma ratio must also be shown for the latest fiscal year or 12-month period. If *preferred stock* is to be registered, the ratio of earnings to *fixed charges and preferred dividends combined* is to be shown for each year or period of the statement in which preferred stock was outstanding, together with a pro forma ratio for the latest year or 12-month period. The computations of the ratios must be shown in an exhibit to the registration. For a discussion of this subject, see Chapter **8**.

In connection with any unaudited statement for an interim period, a statement has to be made that all adjustments necessary to a fair statement of the results for such interim period have been included. If all such adjustments are of a normal recurring nature, a statement to that effect has to be made; otherwise, a letter must be furnished (as supplemental information but not as part of the registration statement) describing in detail the nature and amount of any adjustments, other than normal recurring adjustments, entering into the determination of the results shown.

See the discussion beginning on page **9**·3 regarding the need for updating the financial data in Form S–7 in certain circumstances.

Statements of Retained Earnings.—A statement of retained earnings has to be furnished for each fiscal year or other period for which an income statement is required to be furnished. This may be a separate statement or a continuation of the income statement. The statement must be certified for the same period as the income statement and has to be prepared in conformity with the provisions of Regulation S–X. If income statements are required in respect of unconsolidated subsidiaries and 50% owned companies, then statements of retained earnings must likewise be submitted.

Statements of Other Additional Capital.—A statement of other additional capital accounts must be submitted for the period covered by the income statements and certified to the same extent. Such statements must also be furnished for unconsolidated subsidiaries and 50% owned companies with respect to which income statements are required and certified to the same extent. Regulation S–X is applicable to the statements outlined in this paragraph.

Statements of Source and Application of Funds.—Statements of the source and application of funds, conforming with the requirements of Regulation S–X, must be furnished in respect of each entity for which income statements are furnished pursuant to the instructions and for the same period. The statements must also be certified for the same period as the related income statements.

Supporting Schedules.—No supporting schedules are required to be furnished except those prepared in accordance with the following rules of Regulation S–X:

Rule 12–16.   Supplementary income statement information

Rule 12–27.   Summary of investments in securities—Other than securities of affiliates (for insurance companies)

Rule 12–32.   Investments in securities of affiliates—Banks (for bank holding companies only).

The schedule of supplementary income statement information would be furnished for the same period as the income statement to which it relates, namely, five years plus in some cases an interim period. The other two schedules are furnished as of the date of the latest balance sheet to which they relate. In addition, if an unconsolidated income statement as well as a consolidated income statement is furnished, then the schedule of supplementary income statement information must be furnished on both an unconsolidated and a consolidated basis.

Financial Statements Included in Prospectus.—All of the financial statements referred to above are included in a prospectus forming part of a registration statement on Form S–7. In the case of a "summary prospectus," see the discussion in Chapter **11**.

Application of Regulation S–X.—The financial statements included in Form S–7 must be prepared in conformity with the applicable requirements of Regulation S–X. The requirements of that regulation are discussed hereinafter.

Financial Statements of Businesses Acquired or to be Acquired.— See the discussion beginning on page **9·12** with respect to the SEC's requirements applicable to businesses acquired or to be acquired and the certification requirements.

Financial Statements Required by Form S–8

As indicated in Chapter **8**, Form S–8 is used in connection with employee stock purchase, savings, or similar plans, and qualified and restricted stock option plans by registrants which meet the requirements.

One of the important conditions underlying the use of Form S–8 is that the issuer must be one that files reports with the SEC pursuant to Section 13 or 15(d) of the 1934 Act. Because of this prerequisite, registrations on this form invariably relate to companies with respect to which there is a great deal of information available—including financial information.

Another condition governing the use of Form S–8 is that a copy of the issuer's annual report to stockholders for the last fiscal year must be delivered with the prospectus to each eligible employee who does not otherwise receive a copy of such report as a stockholder of the issuer. If the issuer's last fiscal year has ended within 90 days prior to the use of the prospectus, the annual report for the preceding year may be delivered provided the annual report for the last fiscal year is furnished to each such employee when available.

Inasmuch as the persons to whom an offering on Form S–8 is made are familiar to some degree with the affairs of the issuer, the requirements relating to financial statements are relatively simple.

Financial Statements.—Item 11 of Form S–8 contains the requirements for financial statements for any plans other than qualified or restricted stock option plans. For employee stock purchase, savings, and similar plans (other than qualified or restricted stock option plans) financial statements of the plan are required as follows:

1. A certified statement of financial condition of the plan as of the end of the latest fiscal year.
2. A certified statement of income of the plan and changes in plan equity for the latest fiscal year.

If certified financial statements substantially meeting the above requirements have been furnished to all employees who receive a copy of the prospectus, such statements may be incorporated by reference in the prospectus. The required statements must be prepared and certified in accordance with the applicable provisions of Regulation S–X and must be accompanied by the schedules specified in the regulation. The form contains the usual provision permitting the omission of certain statements or the filing of other statements in substitution therefor upon informal written request of the registrant, and also provides that the Commission may require other statements in addition to, or in substitution for, those specified in the form.

Item 19 contains the requirements for the summary of earnings of the issuer, and Item 25 the requirements for financial statements of the issuer, both of which must be included in the prospectus, whether it relates to a savings, stock purchase and investment plan or to a stock option plan.

Item 25 calls for inclusion in the prospectus of the certified financial statements of the issuer required to be included in the annual report which the issuer has filed, or is required to file, for its last fiscal year pursuant to Section 13 or 15(d) of the 1934 Act—Form 10–K, for example. If the annual report includes certified consolidated financial statements of the issuer and its subsidiaries, the latter must be furnished in lieu of the unconsolidated statements of the issuer. No supporting schedules of any kind need be included in the prospectus or in the registration statement.

If the published annual report of the issuer to its security holders for its last fiscal year includes certified financial statements "substantially meeting the above requirements," such statements may be incorporated by reference in the prospectus and not duplicated. In practice this provision is usually availed of. (When the financial statements in the annual report are incorporated by reference, the accountants' certificate in one copy of the report must be manually signed by the accountants.)

The SEC staff interpret liberally the words "substantially meeting the above requirements." Published financial statements ordinarily do not contain many of the compliance notes required by Regulation S–X, but ordinarily this is no bar to using the published report in complete satisfaction of the requirements for financial statements in Form S–8.

This is not to suggest, however, that the SEC accepts without question the financial statements in a published annual report in satisfaction of the requirements of Item 25 of Form S–8. The SEC staff do, in fact, review the annual report to determine the degree of divergence between the statements in the report and the requirements of Regulation S–X. The author had a case in which this very point was involved. The registrant was a public utility company operating under a Uniform System of Accounts. In conformity with the requirements of the system, the company's published reports showed the reserve for depreciation on the liability side of the balance sheet and not deducted from utility plant as required by Regulation S–X. The company filed a registration statement on Form S–8 in connection with an employees' stock purchase plan. In lieu of furnishing the statements required by Item 25 of the form, the company incorporated the financial statements in its published annual report.

After examining the registration statement, the SEC said:

Item [25] of Form S–8 provides that if the annual report of the issuer to its security holders for its last fiscal year includes certified financial statements substantially meeting the requirements of Regulation S–X, such statements may be incorporated by reference in the prospectus. In this connection, it is noted that the annual report to shareholders includes the reserves for depreciation and amortization under the caption "Reserves and other credits" rather than as a *deduction* from utility plant contrary to the specific requirements of Regulation S–X and therefore would not meet the concept of "substantially meeting the requirements." However, this Division will raise no objection to the use of the annual report to shareholders provided the first paragraph under "Financial Statements and Summary of Earnings" on page _____ is expanded to include a discussion of the difference in accounting presentation of the above referred to item.

Accordingly, the company included the following paragraph in its prospectus to comply with the request in the Commission's letter:

The Company's annual report to its stockholders for the [period], a copy of which is filed as Exhibit No. 5 to the Registration Statement, contains on pages _____ through _____ the balance sheet as at [date], related statements of income and earned surplus for the year then ended, notes to financial statements, and the auditor's certificate. The "Reserves for Depreciation and Amortization of Utility Plant" is included under the caption "Reserves and Other Credits" in the balance sheet and has not been deducted from "Utility Plant" as required by regulations of the Securities and Exchange Commission. If such reserves were deducted from "Utility Plant" in accordance with such regulations, the net utility plant at the end of [year] would be [amount].

The published reports to stockholders of many publicly-owned companies do not include a statement of the source and application of funds, whereas that statement is required to be included in Form 10–K and in Form S–8. In a Form S–8 registration statement, if the financial statements in a published report are incorporated by reference, and the source and application of funds statement is lacking, the registration statement will have to be supplemented accordingly.

See page **9·3** for a statement of the Commission's policy regarding the need to update financial statements in certain circumstances.

Summary of Earnings.—The requirements applicable to a summary of earnings in Form S–8 are set forth in Chapter **10**.

Financial Statements Required by Form S–9

Form S–9 is the form used to register under the Securities Act of 1933 high-grade nonconvertible debt securities when the issuer meets certain requirements, among others, as to "fixed charges," which term is discussed on page **8·21**. The conditions relating to the use of the form are set forth in Chapter **8**.

The instructions for financial statements in Form S–9 are included in Items 3(a) and 5 of the form. These items contain the instructions with respect to the following:

Item 3(a) :
Statements of income
Statements of retained earnings
Statements of other additional capital
Statements of source and application of funds
Item 5:
Balance sheets and schedules

The instructions for financial statements in S–9 are similar to those in S–7, the principal differences arising from the fact that the use of S–9 is limited to the registration of high-grade, straight debt securities, whereas S–7 may be used for other kinds of securities. In addition, S–9 contains no requirements for furnishing financial statements of 50% owned companies, whereas in S–7 there is such a requirement.

See page **9**·3 for a statement of the SEC's policy regarding the need to update financial statements in a registration statement in certain circumstances.

Balance Sheets.—A balance sheet of the registrant (unconsolidated) is required to be filed as of a date within six months prior to the date of filing the registration statement. This balance sheet need not be certified. If it is not certified, there must also be furnished a certified balance sheet of the registrant as of a date within one year of the filing date unless the fiscal year of the registrant has ended within 90 days prior to the filing date, in which case the certified balance sheet may be as of the end of the preceding fiscal year.

The individual (unconsolidated) balance sheets of the registrant may be omitted if (1) consolidated balance sheets of the registrant and one or more of its subsidiaries are furnished, (2) the conditions specified in *either* of the following paragraphs are met, and (3) the Commission is advised as to the reasons for such omission:

(a) The registrant is primarily an operating company and all subsidiaries included in the consolidated balance sheets which are filed are totally-held subsidiaries; or

(b) The registrant's total assets, exclusive of investments in and advances to the consolidated subsidiaries, constitute 85 per cent or more of the total assets shown by the consolidated balance sheets which are furnished.

It will be noted that the tests for omission of the registrant's (unconsolidated) balance sheets listed above are different from those in S–1 and S–7.

See page **9**·48 regarding the possibility of omitting the unconsolidated statements of a parent company in cases not complying entirely with the rule for omission given above.   See also page **9**·7 for a discussion, which is also applicable to Form S–9, of the means by which the Commission is advised as to the reasons for omission of financial statements of the registrant from a registration statement on Form S–1; in Form S–9 the listing of financial statements appears in Item 9 in Part II.

The registration statement must contain a consolidated balance sheet of the registrant and its subsidiaries as of a date within six months prior to the date of filing the registration statement. This balance sheet need not be certified. If it is not certified, there must also be furnished a certified consolidated balance sheet as of a date within one year of the filing date unless the fiscal year of the registrant has ended within 90 days prior to the filing date, in which case the certified balance sheet may be as of the end of the preceding fiscal year.

There must be furnished for each majority-owned subsidiary of the registrant not included in the consolidated statements the balance sheets which would be required if the subsidiary were itself a registrant. Insofar as practicable, these balance sheets shall be as of the same dates as those of the registrant. All balance sheets of any one or more unconsolidated subsidiaries may be omitted if all such subsidiaries whose balance sheets are so omitted, considered in the aggregate as a single subsidiary, would not constitute a "significant subsidiary" (see definition on page **16· 8**). For a discussion of this requirement, see page **9·55**.   See also Rule 4–03 in Chapter **17** regarding the filing of group statements for unconsolidated subsidiaries.

Statements of Income.—Form S–9 contains no requirements for a summary of earnings. Instead there are requirements for statements of income prepared in compliance with the applicable requirements of Regulation S–X.

The instructions call for a statement of income in comparative columnar form for the registrant, or for the registrant and its subsidiaries consolidated, or both, as appropriate. The income statement must cover each of the last five fiscal years of the registrant and any interim period between the end of the latest of such fiscal years and the date of the latest balance sheet furnished pursuant to the requirements discussed above, and the corresponding interim period of the preceding fiscal year. Comparable data for additional fiscal years must be included if necessary to keep the statement from being misleading. Also, where necessary, information and explanations of material significance to investors in appraising the results shown must be included, or reference may be made to such information or explanation set forth elsewhere in the prospectus.

It will be noted from the above discussion that the instructions call for an income statement for the registrant, or for the consolidated group, *or both, as appropriate.* It may be observed that these instructions follow very closely the instructions applicable to a summary of earnings in Form S–1. See the discussion of this matter on page **10·5** where it is stated that when a consolidated summary of earnings is furnished, a summary for the registrant (unconsolidated) is seldom required or furnished or called for by the SEC's staff in its comment letter. The same may be said with respect to income statements in Form S–9: if a consolidated income statement is furnished, there is seldom a need to furnish an unconsolidated income statement of the registrant. (See also the discussion on page **9·48** regarding omission of parent company financial statements.)

The income statement has to be certified to the date of the respective certified balance sheet included in the prospectus.

In lieu of the statements for the interim period referred to above, certain companies in the electric, gas, and telephone business may furnish income statements for the period of 12 months ended on the interim date.

If a period or periods reported on include operations of a business prior to the date of acquisition (for example, when there has been a pooling of interests), or for other causes differ from reports previously issued for any period, the statement has to be reconciled as to sales (or revenues) and net income with the amounts previously reported. This reconciliation may be made either in the statement itself or in a footnote thereto.

The ratio of earnings to fixed charges must be shown in tabular form for each fiscal year or other period, and a pro forma ratio must also be shown for the latest fiscal year or 12-month period. The ratio of earnings to fixed charges and the definition of "fixed charges" are discussed in Chapter **8**. An exhibit to the registration statement must set forth the computations of the required ratios.

Since the registration statement on Form S–9 relates to fixed interest non-convertible debt securities, there is no requirement to show earnings or dividends per share. The information as to earnings per share is, however, required to be disclosed by APB Opinion No. 15 (1969). Nonetheless some companies filing on Form S–9 have omitted earnings per share information on the basis that it was not relevant to the purpose of the offering. The prospectus of R. J. Reynolds Company in 1969 omitted this information and the following note appeared immediately after the statement of earnings:

Earnings per share are customarily shown by the Company in accordance with generally accepted accounting principles. Such data have been omitted in the foregoing statement of earnings since such presentation would not be of primary concern to the prospective purchasers of the Debentures and the Notes offered hereby.

In connection with any unaudited statement for an interim period, a statement has to be made that all adjustments necessary to a fair statement of the results for such interim period have been included. If all such adjustments are of a normal recurring nature, a statement to that effect has to be made; otherwise, a letter must be furnished (as supplemental information but not as part of the registration statement) describing in detail the nature and amount of any adjustments, other than normal recurring adjustments, entering into the determination of the results shown.

Statements of income conforming to the requirements discussed above must be furnished for each majority-owned subsidiary, or group of such subsidiaries, whose balance sheets are required to be furnished as referred to in the discussion of required balance sheets. There is no requirement in Form S–9, however, for income statements in respect of 50% owned companies as in Forms S–1 or S–7.

Statements of Retained Earnings.—A statement of retained earnings has to be furnished for each fiscal year or other period for which an income statement is required to be furnished. The statement may be submitted as a separate statement or as a continuation of the income statement. The statement has to be certified to the date of the respective certified balance sheet included in the prospectus.

Statements of Other Additional Capital.—A statement of other additional capital has to be furnished for each fiscal year or other period for which an income statement is required to be furnished. The statement has to be certified to the date of the respective certified balance sheet included in the prospectus.

Statements of Source and Application of Funds.—A statement of source and application of funds has to be furnished for each fiscal year or other period for which an income statement is required to be furnished, and must be certified to the date of the respective certified balance sheet included in the prospectus.

Supporting Schedules and the Prospectus.—No supporting schedules need be filed either in the prospectus or in Part II of the registration statement, except the data called for by the schedule of supplementary income statement information (maintenance and repairs, depreciation, etc.) which must be included in the prospectus.

All the financial statements called for by Items 3(a) and 5 of Form S–9 (discussed above) must be included in the prospectus.

Application of Regulation S–X.—The financial statements included in Form S–9 must be prepared pursuant to the provisions of Regulation S–X. For the requirements of that Regulation see Chapters **16** through **20** and **24** through **26**.

Financial Statements of Businesses Acquired or to be Acquired. —See the discussion beginning on page **9·12** with respect to the SEC's requirements relating to businesses acquired or to be acquired and the certification requirements.

The Summary Prospectus.—A "summary prospectus" is permitted to be used in connection with securities registered on Form S–9; see the discussion of this subject on page **11·26**.

Financial Statements Required by Form S–11

As indicated in Chapter **8**, Form S–11 is the form of registration statement designated for filing by certain real estate companies. The SEC's instructions for financial statements in this registration form are divided as between (a) general provisions and (b) special provision as to real estate investment trusts. Experience with this form has indicated that, in complicated cases, it is especially desirable to have a conference with the SEC staff regarding the financial statements before filing them with the SEC. See page **9**·3 regarding the need to update in certain cases.

General Provisions.—Except for the summary of earnings, the financial statements filed as part of Form S–11 must be in accordance with the requirements of Form S–1. The financial requirements of the latter form are discussed beginning on page **9**·5.

Special Provision for Real Estate Investment Trusts.—In lieu of the income statements required by Rule 5.03 of Regulation S–X (page **18**·22), there must be filed statements of income and expense and statements of realized capital gain or loss on investments which generally conform with the requirements of Rules 6.04 and 6.05 of Regulation S–X (page **19**·17). In place of the balance sheet caption prescribed by Rule 5.02.39(a)(3) of Regulation S–X, there shall be shown separately (1) the balance of undistributed net income and (2) accumulated net realized gain or loss on investments, and the statements of surplus shall generally conform to the requirements of Rule 6.07 of Regulation S–X.

The trust's status as a "real estate investment trust" under applicable provisions of the Internal Revenue Code as amended must be stated in a note referred to in the appropriate statements. The note must also indicate briefly the principal present assumptions on which the trust has relied in making or not making provisions for taxes.

Special Provisions as to Schedules.—Except as provided in A through D below, the schedules specified by Rule 5.04 of Regulation S–X (see page **18**·39) are to be filed as part of the registration statement.

A. *Marketable Securities—Other Security Investments (Schedule I).*
  In lieu of the schedule of Marketable Securities—Other Security Investments prescribed by Rule 12.02 required as Schedule I, there must be filed a schedule in accordance with that prescribed by Rule 12.19.

B. *Real Estate and Accumulated Depreciation (Schedule XVIII).*
  Investments in real estate and the related reserve for depreciation are to be reported on the schedule prescribed by Rule 12.42. (Real estate, furniture and fixtures, and the related reserve for depreciation and amortization, which are used in the business and are not considered as investments must be included on Schedules V and VI.) This schedule is designated Schedule XVIII and is in addition to the stated requirements of Rule 5–04. (At the date of this writing, the instructions for financial statements of Form S–11 call for the registrant to furnish the information required by Rule 12–38 with certain

changes; however, the Commission's release (ASR No. 125) announcing the revision of Regulation S–X stated that the information called for by Rule 12–42 (real estate and accumulated depreciation) was to be substituted for the Rule 12–38 schedule, and that the instructions as to financial statements of Form S–11 would be amended in the near future to conform the instructions to the announced changes.

C. *Mortgage Loans on Real Estate (Schedule XIX).*

A schedule of investments in mortgage loans on real estate as prescribed by Rule 12.43 must be furnished. This schedule is designated Schedule XIX and is in addition to the stated requirements of Rule 5–04. (At the date of this writing, the instructions for financial statements of Form S–11 call for the registrant to furnish the information required by Rule 12–37 rather than 12.43 as noted; however, the Commission's release (ASR No. 125) announcing the revision of Regulation S–X stated that the information called for by Rule 12.43 (mortgage loans on real estate) was to be substituted for the Rule 12–37 schedule, and that the instructions as to financial statements of Form S–11 would be amended in the near future to conform the instructions to the announced changes.

D. *Other Investments (Schedule XX).*

If there are any other investments not included in the schedules required, there must be set forth in a separate schedule information concerning such investments corresponding to that included in the prescribed schedules. This schedule is in addition to the stated requirements of Rule 5.04 and is designated Schedule XX.

Financial Statements Included in Prospectus.—All financial statements called for by the "Instructions as to Financial Statements" for Form S–11 must be included in the prospectus except as set forth below:

(a) All schedules to balance sheets and income statements may be omitted from the prospectus except those prepared in accordance with A through D above and Rule 12.16 of Regulation S–X (Supplementary income statement information) which are applicable to balance sheets included in the prospectus. All "Historical Financial Information" required by Part E of the Form S–1 financial instructions may also be omitted from the prospectus.

(b) If the statements of income and expenses and realized capital gain or loss on investments or the related statement of surplus are included in their entirety in lieu of the summary financial data required by Item 6, the statements so included need not be otherwise included in the prospectus or elsewhere in the registration statement.

Application of Regulation S–X.—Regulation S–X governs the certification, consolidation, and form and content of financial statements filed as part of a registration statement on Form S–11. The financial statements, including the statements of surplus and schedules to be filed in support thereof, are to be in accordance with the requirements of Article 5 of Regulation S–X except as specified in "Special Provisions as to Schedules" above.

Filing of Other Statements in Certain Cases.—The comment under "Filing of Other Financial Statements in Certain Cases" on page **9·14** is also applicable to a filing on Form S–11.

Summary of Earnings.—The requirements applicable to a summary of earnings included in Form S–11 are discussed in Chapter **10**.

Financial Statements Required by Form S–16

As indicated in Chapter **8**, Form S–16 is an optional short form that may be used to register certain securities under the 1933 Act if the issuer of the securities meets the requirements for the use of Form S–7.

There are no requirements for inclusion of financial statements as such in a Form S–16 registration statement. The form provides, however, in Item 6, that the registrant shall incorporate the following documents in the prospectus by reference and shall state that all reports subsequently filed pursuant to Section 13 of the 1934 Act prior to the termination of the offering of the securities shall be deemed to be incorporated by reference in the prospectus and to be a part thereof:

(a) Its latest annual report filed pursuant to Section 13 of the 1934 Act or the latest prospectus filed pursuant to Rule 424(b) or (c) under the 1933 Act, which contains certified financial statements for the registrant's latest fiscal year for which such statements have been filed.

(b) All other reports filed pursuant to Section 13 of the 1934 Act since the end of the fiscal year covered by the annual report or prospectus referred to in (a) above. (This would include reports on Forms 8–K, 10–Q, and 7–Q.)

(c) The registrant's definitive proxy statement or information statement filed pursuant to Section 14 of the 1934 Act in connection with the latest annual meeting of its stockholders, and any definitive proxy or information statements so filed in connection with any subsequent special meetings of such stockholders.

In addition, Item 7 of the Form S–16 registration statement calls for a description of any material adverse changes in the registrant's affairs which have occurred since the end of the latest fiscal year for which certified financial statements were included in an annual report or prospectus incorporated by reference in response to the provisions of Item 6.

Accountant's Consent Required.—As indicated above, the prospectus in a Form S–16 registration statement consists for the most part of the incorporation by reference to other documents on file with the SEC. The prospectus must also tell the reader where such data can be inspected and copies obtained. When the information incorporated by reference consists of certified financial statements, it presumably includes not only the statements themselves, but also the auditor's certificate relating to such statements. The auditor must consent in writing to the incorporation by reference of his certificate, and his consent has to be included in the documents that comprise the registration statement.

It goes without saying that the auditor's consent should not be given automatically; on the contrary, the auditor should carefully consider the matter before giving his consent. He may have certified the financial statements of a company for inclusion in a Form 10–K annual report that was filed under the 1934 Act with the SEC several months before the registration statement on Form S–16 is filed under the 1933 Act. As will be seen later in this book, the two acts have far different statutory liabilities. If the auditor has had no significant contact with the financial affairs of his client since he signed his certificate in Form 10–K, he should take some steps to assure himself that he would be willing to sign again his certificate if it were physically included in a 1933 Act registration statement.

Waiver of Requirement for Statements as of Date Within 90 Days of Filing

The instructions for financial statements in Form S–1 are described earlier in this chapter. As stated there, balance sheets must be submitted as of a date within 90 days of filing the registration statement, except that in certain cases, the balance sheets may be as of a date within six months of filing. The exceptions are intended, generally, to cover large, publicly owned companies that are not in default on long-term debt, and file annual and other reports under Section 13 or 15(d) of the 1934 Act. In the case of a large, *privately* owned company registering for the first time, the rule requiring 90-day statements may work a hardship, particularly if the registrant desires to have such 90-day statements certified by independent public accountants.

Where conditions warrant, the SEC may permit a registrant to take advantage of the six-month provision even though the company does not meet all the applicable requirements. The 90-day rule was waived in the case of a company, for example, that:

1. Had consolidated assets totaling $80,000,000;
2. Had consolidated sales in the year preceding registration of $110,000,000;

3. Did a world-wide business;
4. Had no funded debt in default; and
5. Was privately owned, and accordingly filed no reports under the 1934 Act.

Since the company met all the requirements except that it was privately owned, SEC allowed the company to take advantage of the six-month rule.

The Commission also waived strict compliance with the 90-day rule in the case of a publicly owned, foreign corporation whose securities were actively traded over the counter in the United States. The company was based in The Netherlands but was engaged in business on a world-wide scale. The consolidated assets (in United States currency) were $1,736,-000,000 and sales for the latest fiscal year were $1,370,000,000. The companies were highly successful judged by any standards and had no funded debt in default.

Another case involved a filing by a privately owned company that planned to "go public." The company's fiscal year ended September 30. The company planned to file its registration statement on April 8, 1960. The registration would contain certified statements as of September 30, 1959 and for the three years then ended plus unaudited interim statements as of December 31, 1959, and for the first quarter then ended. The registration, therefore, would not comply with the SEC's instructions.

The company had total assets of about $71,000,000 and sales for the latest full year of $60,000,000. For various reasons it was impracticable to furnish statements as of a date other than a calendar quarter. Accordingly, the company proposed to file an amendment to its registration statement about the end of April, 1960, in which financial statements as of March 31, 1960, and for the six months then ended would be substituted for those at December 31, 1959, and for the quarter then ended. Because of the then existing backlog of registrations at the SEC, the company believed that under its plan the amendment would be filed before the SEC's comments would be received.

The SEC agreed with the company's proposal and raised no objection regarding the date of the statements in the original filing.

Omission of Parent Company Financial Statements

The custom of reporting on a consolidated basis for a parent company and its subsidiaries has become so widespread that it sometimes comes as a surprise to management and its independent CPAs to learn that a registration statement being prepared for filing with the SEC must sometimes contain unconsolidated statements of the parent company (the registrant or issuer) as well as consolidated statements.

From time to time the Commission invites suggestions from accountants, lawyers, investment bankers, financial analysts, and other interested persons for condensing and improving the content of prospectuses and registration statements. One of the suggestions most frequently made is the elimination of parent company (unconsolidated) financial statements in all cases where consolidated statements are furnished. The author is one of the many who have made that suggestion. In 1969, in connection with a request for comments on proposed revisions of Forms 10 and 10–K, the AICPA wrote to the SEC as follows:

We note that Forms 10 and 10–K would continue to require the inclusion of parent-company financial statements in addition to consolidated statements. The presumption that consolidated statements are usually more meaningful than separate statements is widely recognized. Furthermore, the Commission will now be requiring information as to lines of business and classes of products, as well as separate financial statements for certain unconsolidated subsidiaries and other partially-owned companies. We believe that the Commission should revise its policy regarding the requirement of parent-company statements, giving effect to a principle that such statements should not be required if consolidated statements, together with the other information being presented, are sufficient for a fair presentation of financial position and results of operations.

The published annual reports of almost every large company in the United States that has subsidiaries contain consolidated statements only— supplemented in some cases by statements of important unconsolidated subsidiaries and jointly-owned companies. The author is not aware of any ground swell of demand from investors, analysts, stock exchanges, investment bankers, or others demanding the inclusion in such reports of parent company statements. On the contrary, a few important holding companies that formerly included such statements as well as consolidated statements, decided to omit the unconsolidated statements because they were apt to be more confusing than enlightening. The omission of such statements caused no adverse reaction from shareholders, analysts, or anyone else.

Some of the leading publishers of financial manuals disclose in their publications that the information is taken from SEC files. It has been noted that the manuals include only consolidated financial data even in cases where the SEC files also contain unconsolidated data.

With the increasing adoption of equity accounting, there is even less to be said in favor of furnishing unconsolidated statements than formerly. Under the equity method, for example, net income is usually the same both for the parent company and the affiliated group.

The Commission has resisted suggestions for omission of parent company statements saying that some financial analysts find such statements "useful." Since they contain information that is not revealed in consolidated statements, they are obviously "useful" to some extent. They show the amount of the parent company's cash, for example, and some readers might find that information "useful." The logical extension of the "useful" argument would require the inclusion of *consolidating* statements; in that way, analysts (and competitors) could see the financial picture of each company in the affiliated group—not merely the parent company and the consolidation. In the case of an enterprise with hundreds of subsidiaries, that would result in a staggering presentation.

The question that needs to be answered is whether the statements of a parent company alone contribute enough to warrant their inclusion in a document that is often so oversize and forbidding that there is serious cause for concern that it will not be read at all.

If condensation of the prospectus will result in a document that investors are more likely to read, then the omission of parent company statements is one step in that direction. (Another step would be the elimination of the requirement for including in the prospectus Schedule XVI, supplementary income statement information.)

The only concession the SEC has made to repeated suggestions to eliminate parent company statements is to relax slightly the conditions under which such statements may be omitted. One of the tests of long standing for omission of such statements in Form S–1, for example, is to the general effect that the parent has to represent, in effect, 85% of the consolidated group (the actual requirements are set forth on page **9·6**).   In a recent revision of Forms 10 and 10–K which previously had similar requirements, the test was reduced to 75% (the requirements applicable to those forms are set forth in Chapter **15**).   In short, the Commission from time to time has chipped away at the conditions under which the statements of a parent company may be omitted, but has been reluctant to take the step which will contribute to condensation of the prospectus in many cases, namely, the omission of parent company statements in all instances where consolidated statements are furnished.

Each of the registration forms sets forth the instructions for financial statements applicable to that form. When parent company statements are required to be furnished, the instructions also set forth the conditions under which they may be omitted. It is important to know at the outset that the conditions for omission of such statements are different—sometimes materially different—as between the various registration forms. Form S–1, for example, contains specified conditions for omission of such statements, and these are significantly different from those in S–7 which, in turn, are different from those in S–8, and these, in turn, are different from those in S–9. Consequently the practitioner must refer to the instructions for financial statements in the applicable form to see whether parent company statements can be omitted in the circumstances of a particular company in view of the requirements of the particular form.

The conditions for omission of parent company statements in the most important of the registration forms under the 1933 Act are discussed in the preceding pages of this chapter. The specific provisions of some of these conditions are discussed in the following pages with special emphasis on how the SEC's staff interprets the requirements.

Subsidiary with Insignificant Minority Interest or Publicly-Held Debt.—One of the tests for omission of parent company financial statements in Forms S–1 and S–9 involves a determination of whether a subsidiary that is included in consolidated statements is a "totally-held subsidiary" as that term is defined in Regulation S–X. In interpreting the term, the SEC's staff have not insisted on a literal reading of the definition where an insignificant minority interest exists or where the publicly-held debt of the subsidiary is not material in relation to the consolidated group.

When the minority interest shown in the most recent consolidated balance sheet is not more than 2½% of total assets in that balance sheet, the staff have agreed that this circumstance, by itself, should not cause a company to file statements of the parent company, and have waived the requirement for such statements.

Another test used by the staff to determine whether a consolidated subsidiary is "totally-held" is this: if the parent company is an operating company and the long-term debt of consolidated subsidiaries included in the consolidated balance sheet (and not guaranteed by the parent company) is not more than 3¾% of total assets as shown by the consolidated balance sheet, the SEC's staff will waive the requirement for separate statements of the parent company unless there are compelling reasons to insist on their inclusion in the registration. For the purpose of the foregoing test, the minority interest in net assets of consolidated subsidiaries is treated as debt.

The interpretations in the two preceding paragraphs apply to all filings with the SEC—not merely to registration statements under the 1933 Act.

Subsidiary's Publicly-Held Debt Not Material in Relation to Consolidated Stockholders' Equity.—A United States corporation that had securities listed for trading on the New York Stock Exchange had a number of subsidiaries operating in European countries. Five of the European subsidiaries had obtained long-term bank loans from European banks in the aggregate amount of $4 million. This amount was material in relation to the subsidiaries, and it was conceded that the subsidiaries were not "totally-held" subsidiaries as defined in Regulation S–X. The United States parent company did not guarantee the principal or interest on the debt.

The parent company did not come within the instructions pursuant to which its unconsolidated statements could be omitted from its 10–K, but the company nonetheless discussed with the SEC's staff the possibility of omitting such statements, and pointed out:

1. Consolidated retained earnings of the affiliated group were 14 times the debt in question.
2. Under the terms of the loan agreement, the United States parent agreed to furnish up to $2.5 million in the event that the current ratio of the European subsidiaries fell below a specified ratio.
3. The proceeds of these loans made possible the repayment of approximately $2 million to the United States parent and therefore affected favorably the nation's balance of payments.

The SEC granted the company's request to omit parent company statements from the 10–K report.

"Primarily an Operating Company."—One of the conditions in Form S–1 and in some other forms for omitting statements of the registrant (unconsolidated) depends on whether or not the registrant is "primarily an operating company." There is nothing in the instructions, rules, or in any official SEC literature that defines or explains what is meant by "primarily an operating company."

There is no mathematical test to determine whether a registrant is primarily an operating company. It is not always possible therefore to determine solely from the parent company's financial statements whether it qualifies as being primarily an operating company. The test seems to be this: Is the parent primarily a *holding* company, or does it conduct a significant portion of the operations of the affiliated group of companies? If a parent has significant investments in subsidiaries, but is also an operating company, and half of the consolidated sales to the public are those of the parent company, it would seem that the parent would qualify as being principally an operating company.

Insofar as this particular matter is involved, the staff of the SEC interpret the instructions liberally. The author knows, for example, of a parent company with a large number of subsidiaries in the retail business. The sales to the public are made entirely by the subsidiaries; the parent does no business with the public. The parent company, however, conducts a central buying service for the subsidiaries, and receives and warehouses all merchandise that is not shipped directly to the subsidiaries' stores. The parent company finances the subsidiaries by guaranteeing their loans, purchasing their receivables, and making advances to them to meet their seasonal needs. The parent company furnishes merchandising and advertising counsel on a centralized basis. The registration stated that the company "conducted a retail merchandising business operating through subsidiaries." The balance sheet of the parent company showed that a preponderance of its assets was represented by investments in its operating subsidiaries.

Nonetheless, the SEC agreed with the registrant's contention that it was "primarily an operating company."

Guarantee of Subsidiary Debt.—Sometimes the only reason for not being able to omit parent company statements in a Form S–1 registration statement is that a consolidated subsidiary has debt outstanding that is held by the public, and hence the subsidiary is not "totally held" as defined in Regulation S–X. If the parent company will guarantee the debt of the subsidiary, the SEC will overlook the fact that all or part of the subsidiary's debt is publicly-held, and parent company (unconsolidated) statements may be omitted from the registration statement or other report filed with the SEC.

For this purpose it is immaterial whether the guarantee is evidenced by a specific instrument or by an arrangement that has that effect. The author, for example, had a case involving a company that directly and through subsidiaries operated a chain of retail "discount" stores. The fixtures in the stores were owned by a subsidiary which leased the fixtures to the operating companies, including the parent company. The fixtures and the long-term debt incurred in connection with the acquisition of the fixtures were reflected on the books of the leasing subsidiary. The fixture rentals payable by the various subsidiaries to the leasing subsidiary were guaranteed by the parent company. In the event of a default by a subsidiary, the parent would be obligated to make the rental payments to the leasing company. Since the rental payments were used by the leasing company to make the required payments on its indebtedness, the guarantee of the subsidiaries' rental obligations was, in effect, the guarantee of the underlying fixture indebtedness. In the circumstances the staff of the SEC agreed that unconsolidated statements of the parent company could be omitted from the registration statement.

Registrant Not Primarily an Operating Company and Subsidiaries Not Totally Held.—The author participated in the preparation of a registration statement involving a company whose subsidiaries were included in the consolidated statements. The subsidiaries had a substantial amount of debt outstanding in the hands of the public. Hence, the subsidiaries were not "totally held subsidiaries" as defined.

The company was approximately one-half an operating company and one-half a holding company. Hence, there was some doubt as to whether the company was "primarily an operating company."

The holding company aspects of the operations arose basically due to the provisions of the Internal Revenue Code relating to Western Hemisphere Trade Corporations. The subsidiaries' income was wholly in United States dollars and freely transferable to the parent company.

Two of the company's subsidiaries became divisions of the parent company shortly before the registration statement was filed. If the subsidiaries had been divisions for all of the preceding year, the parent company's sales would have represented more than one-half of consolidated sales in that year.

Practically all of the publicly held subsidiary debt was guaranteed by the parent company.

The company technically did not comply with the provisions under which statements of the parent company (unconsolidated) could be omitted from the registration statement. Nevertheless, in view of the circumstances, the SEC granted the company's request to dispense with such parent company statements.

Parent Company Statements Omitted Because Meaningless.—The author participated in a registration statement filed by a company that had a significant subsidiary that was engaged in a business complementary to that of the parent company. The production of the subsidiary was sold principally to the parent company for further processing; the parent's production was sold to the consuming public.

The construction of the subsidiary's plant had been financed principally by bonds sold privately to institutional investors. The indenture securing the bonds provided for a pricing formula of the subsidiary's products that was calculated to provide the subsidiary with funds to service its long-term debt. The statements of the parent company alone and of the subsidiary alone were meaningless in that they reflected operations under an arbitrary pricing arrangement. The only significant statements were those of the consolidated group.

The registration statement referred to above was to be filed by the parent company, and the proceeds were to be used, among other things, to redeem the subsidiary's debt. After the registration became effective, the only debt to be outstanding would be that of the parent company. The pricing formula under the old indenture would be eliminated when the related bonds were redeemed. In the circumstances, it appeared that no good purpose would be served by filing unconsolidated statements of the parent company despite the fact that a literal reading of the instructions for financial statements in Form S–1 called for such statements to be furnished. In view of other provisions in the instructions as to financial statements (see page **9·14**), the question of omitting parent company statements from the proposed registration was discussed with SEC representatives. They agreed that, in the circumstances of this case, unconsolidated financial statements of the parent company should be omitted from the proposed filing. Item 31(a) of the Form S–1 registration statement (which lists the financial statements that are filed, those that are omitted, and the reasons for omission) stated that "Statements of the parent company, alone, are omitted pursuant to permission granted by the Securities and Exchange Commission pursuant to its rules and regulations."

Statements of Unconsolidated Subsidiaries and 50 Per Cent Owned Companies

The SEC's instructions as to financial statements in Form S–1 and other forms are set forth in this chapter. Among other things, the instructions specify the financial statements that must be furnished for the registrant's unconsolidated subsidiaries and for companies 50 per cent owned by the registrant where another single interest owns the other 50 per cent. At this point it is pertinent to consider the requirements relating to statements of unconsolidated subsidiaries and 50 per cent owned companies. For simplicity, however, this discussion will be confined to unconsolidated subsidiaries, although it is equally applicable to 50 per cent owned companies.

The SEC instructions relating to the filing of statements for a majority owned, unconsolidated subsidiary are generally to the effect that the same financial statements shall be filed for such subsidiary that would be required if the subsidiary were itself a registrant. (The term "majority owned subsidiary" is defined on page **16·7**.)

The SEC instructions also provide that, notwithstanding the requirement to file financial statements of unconsolidated subsidiaries, all such statements may be omitted if all subsidiaries whose statements are so omitted, considered in the aggregate as a single subsidiary, would not constitute a "significant subsidiary." In order to understand the following discussion, it is important to see the definition of "significant subsidiary" on page **16·8** and its application in relation to a registrant that has a number of unconsolidated subsidiaries which are not significant individually but which, in the aggregate, constitute a "significant subsidiary." Assume, for example, a group of companies which, on the basis of their customary consolidation practice, has assets aggregating $100,000, and that such assets include investments in ten unconsolidated, *wholly owned* subsidiaries. These subsidiaries, in turn, have assets aggregating $25,000 as follows:

Subsidiary No. 1	$ 6,000
Subsidiary No. 2	5,000
Subsidiary No. 3	4,000
Subsidiary No. 4	3,000
Subsidiaries Nos. 5 to 10, inclusive	7,000
	$25,000

It is apparent that financial statements will have to be submitted for some of the unconsolidated subsidiaries. The question is: How far down the line will the registrant have to go?

In measuring the significance of unconsolidated subsidiaries for this purpose, some accountants have been under the mistaken impression that it is necessary to prepare a consolidated balance sheet that consolidates all subsidiaries whether normally included in consolidated statements or not. The SEC, however, measures significance in relation to the most recent annual consolidated financial statements being filed.

Referring again to the example given above, if the registrant were to furnish consolidated statements only and omit statements for all of its unconsolidated subsidiaries, the assets of companies omitted would aggregate $25,000, which is 25/100, or 25 per cent of the assets of the consolidated group for which statements would be filed. If the registrant files the statements of Subsidiary No. 1 (whose assets are $6,000), the ratio of what is omitted to the consolidation becomes 19/100, or 19 per cent, which means that additional statements must be furnished for some other members of the unconsolidated group.

If, in addition to Subsidiary No. 1, statements of Subsidiary No. 2 (whose assets are $5,000) are furnished, the ratio of what is omitted to the consolidation becomes 14/100, or 14 per cent, which means that the remaining subsidiaries constitute a significant subsidiary and additional statements will have to be furnished.

In this case the registrant therefore will have to file statements on at least one more subsidiary, presumably Subsidiary No. 3 (whose assets are $4,000). That would bring the ratio down to 10/100, or 10 per cent, and statements of Subsidiaries No. 4 through No. 10 need not be filed.

It should be remembered, however, that it is permissible to combine the statements of unconsolidated subsidiaries in the interest of a streamlined presentation, provided the combination clearly reflects the financial condition and results of operations of the combined group.

In determining what is a "significant subsidiary," the measure of materiality is not only in relation to assets but also to sales or revenues. For simplicity, this discussion has dealt with assets only, but the same reasoning would apply to sales or revenues.

It should also be remembered that the significance of an unconsolidated subsidiary is not determined solely on the basis of relative assets and sales (or revenues). If the parent's investment in and advances to the subsidiary are more than 10 per cent of the consolidated assets, the subsidiary is significant.

This discussion also assumed that there is no question as to the propriety of omitting the subsidiaries from the consolidated statements. The registrant must be prepared to justify the omission of any majority owned subsidiary from the consolidation. See the discussion of Rule 4.02 in Chapter **17**.

The preceding discussion also assumed that the unconsolidated subsidiaries were *wholly owned*. If the subsidiaries are majority-owned, but not wholly owned, see the comments that follow.

Unconsolidated Subsidiaries with Different Percentages of Voting Control or Equity in Assets.—The computations underlying the discussion in the preceding section were based on the assumption that the unconsolidated subsidiaries were *wholly owned*. The question is sometimes asked: For this purpose shall the same weight be given to a wholly owned subsidiary as to one in which the registrant has a bare majority of voting control?

If an unconsolidated subsidiary is majority-owned, but less than wholly owned, the measure of its significance is based on the parent's and the parent's other subsidiaries' *proportionate share* of the assets and sales (or revenues) of the subsidiary. Thus, if the parent and the parent's other subsidiaries own 75% of the unconsolidated subsidiary, it would compute 75% of the subsidiary's assets and sales (or revenues) and relate such computed amounts to the consolidated assets and sales (or revenues) shown in the most recent annual consolidated financial statements of the registrant being filed.

It should also be remembered that an unconsolidated subsidiary may be significant because of the materiality of the investment in and advances to the subsidiary.

Domestic Subsidiaries vs. Foreign Subsidiaries.—The question is also raised as to whether distinction should be made between domestic subsidiaries and foreign subsidiaries. Whatever their reasons, investors certainly do not give the same weight to two subsidiaries that are equal in all respects except that one is a domestic corporation and the other is a foreign corporation.

For the purpose of determining whether statements should be furnished for unconsolidated subsidiaries, the Commission has made no distinction between domestic and foreign subsidiaries. As a practical matter it is probably impossible for the SEC to do otherwise.

Significance Based on What Date or Period.—In determining whether an unconsolidated subsidiary (or group of such subsidiaries) is a "significant subsidiary," the measure of significance (as stated on page **9·55**) is determined generally by the relation of the subsidiary's assets and sales (or revenues) to consolidated assets and sales (or revenues). These questions may arise:

1. Assets as of what date?

2. Sales (or revenues) for what period?

According to the definition of a significant subsidiary in Regulation S–X, materiality for this purpose is determined by comparing the most recent annual financial statements of the subsidiary with the most recent annual consolidated financial statements being filed. If the subsidiary, in turn, also has subsidiaries, the statements of the subsidiary would have to be on a consolidated basis.

Incorporation by Reference

Two rules under the 1933 Act relate to the incorporation of certain information in a registration statement by reference to other sources.

Rule 411 provides as follows:

Rule 411.   Incorporation of Certain Information by Reference.

(a) Where an item calls for information not required to be included in the prospectus, matter contained in any part of the registration statement, other than exhibits, may be incorporated by reference in answer, or partial answer, to such item. Matter contained in an exhibit may be so incorporated to the extent specified in Rule 422.

(b) Any financial statement or part thereof filed with the Commission pursuant to any Act administered by the Commission may be incorporated by reference in any registration statement if it substantially conforms to the requirements of the appropriate form and is not required to be included in the prospectus. However, a financial schedule incorporated by reference to an annual report filed with the Commission pursuant to any Act administered by it need not be certified, if such schedule was not required to be certified in connection with the filing of the annual report, any requirement of any registration form to the contrary notwithstanding.

This is how the rule works. Assume that a company has been filing annual reports on Form 10–K for many years. The company files a registration statement on Form S–1. The registration statement must include certain supporting schedules for the three-year period covered by the income statement which is included in the prospectus. Inasmuch as the information in the three-year schedules is already on file with SEC in the applicable annual reports on Form 10–K, Rule 411 quoted above makes it clear that the schedules need not be physically reproduced in the Form S–1 registration but may be included by making reference to the applicable Form 10–K reports.

Note that Rule 411 relates to incorporation by reference in a registration statement of information not required to be included in the prospectus. From this it would appear that incorporation by reference is not permitted with respect to matter that has to be included in the prospectus. This is understandable since the prospectus must be furnished to the prospective buyer of the securities being registered, and he should be furnished with the prime financial statements and not told where they are officially on file if he wants to see them. (This observation would seem to fly in the face of the rationale underlying Form S–16, a recently adopted short-form of registration in which the prospectus consists almost entirely of a statement incorporating by reference documents filed and to be filed with the SEC. In Form S–16, however, there are no requirements for financial statements to be physically included in the prospectus.)

Rule 412 relates to the form of, and limitation upon, incorporation by reference. The rule follows:

Rule 412. Form of and Limitation Upon Incorporation by Reference.

Material incorporated by reference shall be subject to the limitations of Rule 24 of the Commission's Rules of Practice and shall be clearly identified in the reference. An express statement that the specified matter is incorporated by reference shall be made at the particular place in the registration statement where the information is required. Matter shall not be incorporated by reference in any case where such incorporation would render the statement incomplete, unclear or confusing.

(Rule 24 of the Rules of Practice is quoted below.)

Thus, where the supporting schedules for the three-year period are incorporated by reference, the "express statement" required by Rule 412 quoted above should be made in Item 31(a) of the Form S–1 registration statement (Item 9 in Form S–9), since this is the "particular place in the registration statement where the information is required."

Although the supporting schedules may be incorporated by reference to documents previously filed with SEC, the schedules usually must be certified by independent accountants. This certification may be accomplished in different ways: (1) the accountant's certificates in the Form 10–K reports may also be incorporated by reference, in which case the certifying accountant must consent to the incorporation by reference of his certificates, or (2) the accountant must certify the supporting schedules listed in Item 31(a) of the registration statement. For the form of consent applicable in the former case, see page **14·23**; for the form of certificate applicable in the latter situation, see page **24·9**.

In view of the reference in Rule 412 to Rule 24 of the Commission's Rules of Practice, the provisions of the latter rule are pertinent. It also deals with incorporation by reference and provides as follows:

Rule 24 of the Rules of Practice.

(a) *Requirements.* Where rules, regulations, or instructions to forms permit incorporation by reference, a document may be so incorporated only by reference to the specific document and to the prior filing in which it was physically filed, not to another file which incorporates it by reference. No document which has been on file with the Commission for a period of more than 10 years may be incorporated by reference in a current filing except basic documents as designated under paragraph (b) of this section.

(b) *Basic Documents.* The Commission, on its own initiative or upon request, may classify as basic documents certain documents filed under the various Acts administered by the Commission, which appear to the Commission to possess such administrative, legal, historical or other values as to warrant being retained and considered available for incorporation by reference for an indefinite period. Requests for such classification shall be submitted to the Commission in duplicate and shall contain (1) a precise description of the document and of the filing in which it is physically filed and (2) the reasons for the request. A request will be considered to have been granted if notification of denial is not given within 60 days of the receipt of the request. If the Commission grants a request pursuant to this paragraph, it may subsequently dispose of any basic document the retention of which would in its opinion no longer serve a substantial purpose, after giving the person who made the request notice of the proposed disposition and an opportunity to object thereto.

Confidential Treatment of Financial Statements

The possibility of filing information with the SEC with the request that it be treated confidentially is discussed on page **7·17**. Normally any financial statement included in a registration statement filed with the Commission pursuant to the 1933 Act becomes a public record and is available for inspection by anyone immediately on filing.

Financial Statements Required by Regulations A and E

As stated in Chapter **8**, the SEC is authorized to exempt new issues of securities from the registration requirements of the Securities Act of 1933 provided the aggregate public offering price does not exceed $500,000. The SEC has promulgated Regulations A and E which set forth the requirements applicable to certain exempt issues. Under these regulations, at least ten days before an exempt offering of securities is to be made, the SEC must be notified on Form 1–A or Form 1–E, respectively. If the offering relates to an issue in excess of $50,000, Forms 1–A and 1–E must contain a written offering circular containing certain specified information, including financial statements.

Financial Statements Required by Form 1–A.—The offering circular in Form 1–A must contain financial statements of the issuer, or of the issuer and its predecessors, as indicated below. The statements have to be prepared in accordance with generally accepted accounting principles and practices. Although Regulation S–X is not applicable to financial statements in a Regulation A filing, in practice the SEC examiners interpret "generally accepted accounting principles" as requiring substantial compliance with Regulation S–X.

The statements required for the issuer's latest fiscal year have to be certified by an independent public accountant if the issuer has filed or is required to file with the SEC certified statements for that year; statements filed for periods preceding such latest year need not be certified.

COMPANIES NOT IN THE DEVELOPMENT STAGE.—If the issuer is not a commercial, industrial, or extractive company in the promotional, exploratory, or development stage, the following statements are to be furnished:

1. A balance sheet as of a date within 90 days prior to the filing of the notification, or such longer period of time, not exceeding six months, as the Commission may permit at the written request of the issuer upon a showing of good cause therefor.
2. Income and surplus statements for at least the two full fiscal years preceding the balance sheet specified above, and for the period, if any, between the close of the last full fiscal year and the date of the balance sheet, or for the period of the issuer's existence if that is less than the period specified above.

COMPANIES IN THE DEVELOPMENT STAGE.—If the issuer is a commercial, industrial, or extractive company in the promotional, exploratory, or development stage, the following statements are required:

1. Separate statements of (i) assets, (ii) liabilities, and (iii) capital shares, as of a date within 90 days prior to the filing of the notification, or such longer period of time, not exceeding six months, as the Commission may permit at the written request of the issuer upon a showing of good cause therefor. (A balance sheet in conventional form may nevertheless be furnished in lieu of the statements specified if the assets reflected therein which were acquired in exchange for capital stock are not carried at an amount in excess of identifiable cash cost to promoters, predecessor companies or other transferors.)
2. A statement of cash receipts and disbursements for each of at least two full fiscal years prior to the date of the statements furnished pursuant to (1) above, and for the period, if any, between the close of the last full fiscal year and the date of such statements, or for the period of the issuer's existence if less than the period specified above.

In the above statements, dollar amounts are to be extended only for cash transactions and transactions involving amounts receivable or payable in cash. If, for example, property was acquired for capital stock, the property may not be shown in money amounts. Amounts due to or from, or paid to or received from, underwriters, promoters, directors, officers, employees, and principal stockholders, must be stated separately for each such class of persons, if significant in amount. The statement of assets should include as a separate item unrecovered promotional, exploratory, and development costs. The statement of cash receipts and disbursements should be itemized as appropriate to the nature of the enterprise.

STATEMENTS ON A CONSOLIDATED OR UNCONSOLIDATED BASIS?—The SEC's instructions for Form 1–A relating both to companies in the development stage and those not in that stage are silent as to whether financial statements should be furnished (1) for the issuer alone, (2) for the issuer and its subsidiaries consolidated, or (3) for both. The author understands that if proper consolidated statements are furnished for an affiliated group, the statements will be accepted in complete fulfillment of the requirements for financial statements.

Financial Statements Required by Form 1–E.—The requirements for financial statements in the offering circular which is part of Form 1–E are set forth in Rule 610a. The financial statements that must be furnished are as follows:

(a) A balance sheet as of a date within 90 days prior to the date of filing the notification with the Commission.

(b) An income statement for each of the last three fiscal years and for any subsequent period up to the date of the balance sheet furnished pursuant to (a) above.

The statements must be prepared in accordance with generally accepted accounting principles and practices but need not be certified by independent public accountants. If the statements are certified, the certifying accountant must comply with the SEC's requirements with respect to independence; see the discussion of this subject in Chapter **26**.

CHAPTER **10**

THE SUMMARY OF EARNINGS (OR OPERATIONS)

CONTENTS

Increasing Use of Earnings Summaries

Several of the registration statement forms under the 1933 Act call for a "summary of earnings" to be included in the prospectus as a basic element of information relating to the enterprise whose securities are proposed to be offered to investors. Form S–1, for example, requires the registrant to furnish an earnings summary covering at least five years in the offering prospectus. Form S–8 (used in connection with certain employee stock purchase and savings plans) also requires the issuer of the securities to furnish a summary for at least five years. Form S–11 (applicable to certain real estate companies) includes a five-year summary among the financial requirements. Depending on the issuer and the circumstances, Form S–14 may also require the submission of a summary of earnings.

Prior to 1970, there were no requirements for a summary of earnings to be included in Form 10 or Form 10–K, which are, respectively, the principal forms for registration and annual reports under the 1934 Act. In connection with extensive revisions of those forms in 1970, there was inserted in each a new requirement for a "summary of operations" covering a minimum period of five years. As far as their content is concerned, however, these summaries of operations are undistinguishable from summaries of earnings.

Proxy statements used in connection with proposed mergers, consolidations, and similar acquisitions require financial statements of the business to be merged, consolidated, or acquired. Although the SEC's formal instructions for proxy statements do not call for summaries of earnings of the companies whose businesses are proposed to be combined, it has become standard practice to furnish not only earnings summaries of the constituent companies but also pro forma summaries in many cases. The pro forma summaries are intended to portray the combined operations of the companies in order to indicate what the combined results might have been had the constituent companies operated during the entire period on a pooled basis, or, in the case of a purchase (as opposed to a pooling), what the combined results might have been had the company been acquired, say, one or two years previously.

Importance of the Summary of Earnings

The summary of earnings is, without a doubt, the most important single financial statement in a prospectus prepared for filing with the SEC. The reader of the prospectus may give little attention to a company's balance sheet and even less to the notes to its financial statements. More often than not, however, he will be interested in the trend of the company's sales and earnings shown in the summary. This is the most significant source of information in answer to the investor's key question: To buy, or not to buy?

One of the most highly qualified professionals ever to have worked for the SEC, Sydney C. Orbach, who was for many years Chief Accountant of the Commission's Division of Corporation Finance, has said, "In my opinion, [the summary of earnings] probably represents the most significant item in Form S–1 insofar as the company, the public investors and the underwriters are concerned . . . Because of the importance of the summary, particular attention is given to this item by both the group accountant and the group analyst." [1]

In a conversation with the author, a former SEC Commissioner said that, in the interest of brevity, serious consideration might well be given to the possibility of eliminating from the prospectus the accountants' certificate and all financial statements *except the summary of earnings and*

---

[1] "Accounting Problems of First-Time Registration Statements," address before Georgia Society of CPAs, March 6, 1962.

the capitalization table. (The author does not agree with this suggestion but would support the idea of omitting other information—such as unconsolidated statements of a registrant when consolidated statements are furnished).

Especially in relation to a prospectus, the earnings summary enables the investor to determine quickly whether the offering price for the securities is reasonable. Also, if the offering relates to debt securities, the summary indicates clearly and quickly whether the company is likely to be in a position to earn the interest requirements on the debt. In view of the overriding importance of the summary, it is difficult to believe that there was a time when it was not required by the SEC. The Commission's requirements have always included an income statement for a minimum of three years (or a shorter period if the company has been in business for less than three years), but not a summary of earnings for at least the most recent five fiscal years as is now required.

As an indication of the importance which the SEC attaches to the summary of earnings, it is fair to say that the number of deficiencies cited by the SEC in relation to such summaries exceeds those relating to all other financial statements combined. This does not mean that summaries are carelessly prepared by registrants or inadequately reviewed by their certifying accountants. It simply reflects the importance which the SEC examiners attach to the summary. For this reason, it is a statement that deserves the utmost care in its preparation. In practice, it is the financial statement upon which the greatest attention is focused by the draftsmen of the registration statement—officers and directors of the registrant, the independent accountants, underwriters, and lawyers—as well as the Commission's staff.

Title of the Statement

Since the instructions in the various registration forms under the 1933 Act call for a "summary of earnings," it is customary to furnish the statement under that or a similar title. If the summary is furnished in complete fulfillment of the requirements for the formal income statement, it is frequently captioned "Statement of Income."

When, however, the summary shows a preponderance of losses, the inclusion of the word "earnings" in the title is contradictory and may be misleading to one who runs as he reads. As a consequence, the staff of the SEC often suggest that the title of the statement in these circumstances be changed to "Summary of Losses," or "Statement of Operations," or "Summary of Loss and Deficit."

In those instances when the summary of earnings is furnished in sufficient detail so as to make it unnecessary to furnish a separate income statement, the staff of the Commission has occasionally requested that the statement be called an income statement (or a profit and loss statment)—

rather than a summary of earnings—and be so referred to in the headnote and the accountant's certificate.

As previously stated, in connection with comprehensive revisions in 1970 of Forms 10 and 10–K under the 1934 Act, the SEC inserted in each form a new requirement for a "summary of operations," which, as far as its content is concerned, is the same as a summary of earnings. It is probable, however, that the caption "summary of operations" represents the terminology preferred by the SEC for the reason that it is appropriate regardless of whether the statement shows earnings or losses.

Form S–1

In this section there will be considered the requirements applicable to a summary of earnings for inclusion in Form S–1, the most commonly used form of registration statement under the Securities Act of 1933. From a reading of this section it will be apparent that many of the comments in relation to Form S–1 are equally applicable to summaries of earnings (or summaries of operations) appearing in other registration and report forms, and in proxy statements and information statements—both under the 1933 Act as well as under the 1934 Act. For convenience, however, much of the comment that follows will be in relation to Form S–1 summaries, but the reader should bear in mind that *many of these comments apply equally to summaries in any document intended for SEC filing.*

The Headnote.—In most prospectuses the earnings summary is placed in the forepart whereas the remainder of the financial statements are placed in the back of the prospectus. If the income statement serves the dual purpose of the summary as well as the required income statement, it is usually placed where the summary would be. In most cases, this means that the summary is separated by several pages of text material from the auditors' certificate as well as the main portion of the financial statements and notes.

The architects of the prospectus want the reader of the summary (or income statement) to know the extent to which the summary is "expertized" (certified). Accordingly, the summary is usually preceded by a headnote informing the reader of the extent to which the summary is certified and by whom, and that their certificate appears later in the prospectus. If the certificate is qualified, the nature of the qualification should be disclosed at this point. If the principal accountant has relied on other accountants for examination of certain portions of the enterprise, that fact should also be indicated in the headnote.

If the summary includes unaudited interim periods, it is customary to state that fact in the headnote together with the required representation on the part of the company that the unaudited figures include all adjustments necessary for a statement of the results for the periods. See the discussion of this subject under the caption "Unaudited Interim Periods."

In its simplest form the headnote would read somewhat as follows:

The following summary of earnings of (name of company) and its subsidiaries, insofar as it relates to the five years ended (date) has been examined by (name of independent accountants), independent public accountants, whose opinion thereon appears elsewhere in this prospectus. The information for the (interim periods) has not been examined by independent public accountants; in the opinion of (name of company) all adjustments (consisting only of normal recurring adjustments) necessary for a fair statement of the results of operations for the (interim periods) have been included. This summary should be read in conjunction with the consolidated financial statements and related notes included elsewhere in this prospectus.

Sometimes the seasonal nature of the interim figures is disclosed in the headnote, although this disclosure is made just as frequently in footnotes to the summary.

The headnote sometimes also discloses that certain of the figures differ from amounts previously reported for the years or periods in question, but this kind of information is more often furnished in footnotes.

For Whom Furnished.—The instructions for Form S–1 call for the submission of a summary of earnings for the registrant, or for the registrant and its subsidiaries consolidated, or both, as appropriate.

The SEC's instructions are silent as to when it is "appropriate" to furnish the summary for the parent company, or for the consolidation, or for both. It is pertinent to consider what needs to be done in order to make certain that the registration statement, as originally filed, is as free as possible of errors of omission.

In some circumstances, by the addition of a few more details, the summary can be submitted in complete satisfaction of the requirements for the summary as well as those for the income statements; see the discussion on page **10·**10. It is clear that if this is done, the instructions applicable to both the summary and the income statement must be complied with. In other words, if the instructions for financial statements clearly call for income statements for both the registrant and the consolidation, and the summary of earnings is intended to fulfill these requirements, then two summaries must be furnished: one for the parent company, and one for the consolidated group.

Assume, however, that a summary is furnished *in addition to* formal income statements. As stated above, the SEC's instructions do not help one to decide whether it is "appropriate" to furnish a summary for the parent, or for the affiliated group, or for both. Except for holding companies in utility holding company systems (electric, gas, water, telephone, etc.), it is not customary to furnish more than one summary; the summary furnished is almost invariably for the consolidated group. Holding companies frequently furnish two summaries, because, being closely regulated, they wish to show how the parent company's earnings compare with the dividends paid. Such companies do not have the same freedom of operation with respect to subsidiaries which an industrial company might have. Utility holding companies are also restricted in their accounting for investments in subsidiaries, as a consequence of which there are—or may be—significant differences between net income of the parent company and net income of the consolidated group.

As far as practice is concerned, the author does not know of a single instance in which the SEC demanded that a summary be furnished for the parent company if the registration statement contained a summary for the consolidated group. In this respect it might be said that the SEC's requirements are more nearly in line with those of published reports to shareholders which—except for public utility holding companies—are customarily limited to consolidated statements.

A presentation frequently met in practice is this: A summary on a consolidated basis is furnished for the required five-year period (see the discussion that follows) and a parent company income statement is furnished for the required three-year period—plus, in each case, interim periods when necessary. This presentation is acceptable to the SEC examiners.

It is worth noting, however, that the disparity between income on a parent company only basis and that on a consolidated basis has been progressively narrowed. A first step in that direction was the result of APB Opinion No. 10 which required that in consolidated statements, the accounts of all subsidiaries whose principal business activity is leasing property or other facilities to their parent or other affiliates should be consolidated, and that if any other domestic subsidiary was not included in the consolidation, the appropriate share of its income or loss must nevertheless be included. The disparity was narrowed even more by APB Opinion No. 18 under which the above requirement as to inclusion in income was made applicable to all unconsolidated subsidiaries—foreign as well as domestic. The Opinion further requires inclusion of the share of income or loss of corporate joint ventures and of investments in which voting stock ownership (even if under 50%) gives significant influence over operating and financial policies—any holding or 20% or more being presumed to create such influence. (Opinion No. 18 is effective for fiscal periods beginning after December 31, 1971 and is to be applied retroactively for any period for which results from operations are shown.)

Although the SEC's instructions specifically call for formal financial statements in certain circumstances with respect to majority-owned subsidiaries and 50% owned companies (see the discussion of this subject in

Chapter **9**), there are no comparable requirements for furnishing a summary of earnings for such companies. Where the operations of such companies are truly significant as compared with the operations of the consolidated group, the desirability of furnishing summaries for such companies should be considered.

Period Covered.—The summary (or summaries) must be furnished for each of at least the last five fiscal years of the company (or for the life of the company and its immediate predecessors, if less) and for any period between the end of the latest of such fiscal years and the date of the latest balance sheet furnished, and for the corresponding period of the preceding fiscal year. The instructions calling for the information for the corresponding interim period of the preceding year are for the purpose of furnishing a basis with which to compare the current interim period. This is especially important in the case of a company whose operations are subject to significant seasonal fluctuations, as in the case of a retail department store. It is interesting to note, however, that while the SEC's instructions call for the data for the corresponding interim period of the preceding year in connection with the earnings summary, there are no similar instructions applicable to the formal income statements.

Although the summary must cover at least the last five fiscal years, the instructions provide that comparable data shall be included for any additional fiscal years that may be necessary to keep the summary from being misleading. This instruction is repeated in a release published in 1968 by the SEC entitled "Guides for Preparation and Filing of Registration Statements." In connection with the summary of earnings, the release pointed out that the necessity for the inclusion of an additional previous period should be considered (Release No. 33–4936, Dec. 9, 1968). What this probably means is this: If the company's business during the required five-year minimum period was unduly influenced by extraordinary or non-recurring conditions (such as war production), the summary should be extended into a more distant period so as to include a number of years that are more nearly representative of the company's operations under normal conditions. Similarly, in the case of a company whose business is subject to extreme cyclical fluctuations, if the five-year period was all good and the preceding three years were all bad, presumably the five-year period would not be representative and might be misleading. In that case it would be desirable to include some of the earlier years in order to show that the company's operations have not always been in the black.

The author participated in a registration engagement for a very large, privately-owned company that filed under the 1933 Act in connection with the distribution of its shares by controlling shareholders. During the required five-year period covered by the summary of earnings, the picture was that of a healthy, growing, profitable company. The company decided, however, to expand the summary to cover a period of ten years. At the due diligence meeting of the underwriters with representatives of the company and its experts, the president of the company commented on this fact. He pointed out that the company had voluntarily expanded the period covered by the summary with the objective of going back far enough in time to show a loss. In the first year of the ten-year period, there had been extensive changes in the company's product, which caused the company to show a loss in that year. The president added, "We wanted all of you to know that this is not a uranium mine—this company has been known to lose money!"

Would the SEC insist on an earnings summary if the company were no longer in the kind of business in which it had been engaged during the period required to be covered by the summary? The likelihood is that the SEC would consent to the omission of the summary from the prospectus. In some circumstances the SEC might insist that it be excluded from the prospectus; in other circumstances it might demand that it be included in Part II of the registration statement. Exclusion from the prospectus would probably be based on the belief that the summary applicable to the old business would not be useful to the investor in appraising the results apt to be achieved in the future because of the drastic change in the nature of the business. It is wise not to proceed blindly, however, in the belief that the Commission's staff will agree to the omission of the summary from the prospectus or from Part II. Because of its importance, the matter should be discussed with the staff of the Commission and a formal waiver obtained. See also the discussion beginning on page **13·2**.

In some circumstances, where there are compelling reasons, it is possible to omit the information for the interim period of the preceding year. This was done, for example, in the 1961 prospectus of Londontown Manufacturing Company. The summary of earnings in that case contained information for the five fiscal years ended February 28, 1961. Information was also furnished for the three months ended May 31, 1961, and the three months ended August 31, 1961, but not for the corresponding quarters of the preceding fiscal year. With respect to the omission of such interim data of the prior year, the prospectus commented as follows:

> The company does not maintain perpetual inventory records or cost records integrated with its general accounting system, and reliable operating results necessitate the taking of physical inventories. Since physical inventories were not taken at May 31, 1960 and August 31, 1960, figures for the three-month periods ended on those dates have not been included.

A registrant that is a company engaged primarily (1) in the generation, transmission, or distribution of electricity; the manufacture, mixing, transmission, or distribution of gas; the supplying or distribution of water; or in furnishing telephone or telegraph service, or (2) in holding securities in such companies may, at its option, include a summary for a twelve-month period to the date of the latest balance sheet furnished, in lieu of both the summary for the interim period between the end of the last fiscal year and such balance sheet date and the summary for the corresponding period of the preceding fiscal year. If a company takes advantage of this option and submits its earnings summary in sufficient detail so that it meets the requirements of an income statement, the author understands that the short interim period required by the instructions for the latter statement need not be furnished. The instructions do not support that interpretation, but the author understands that was the SEC's intent.

Is Regulation S–X Applicable?—The requirements with respect to the form and content of the summary of earnings in Form S–1 are set forth in Item 6 of the registration statement and the applicable instructions. The provisions of Regulation S–X do not apply to Item 6.

On the other hand, when it is intended that the summary shall be furnished not only to comply with Item 6 but also with the instructions applicable to an income statement (to which the Regulation does apply) obviously the summary must comply with the Regulation.

Items of Information.—Subject to appropriate variation to conform to the nature of the business or the purpose of the offering, the following items of information must be included in the summary of earnings: net sales or operating revenues; cost of goods sold or operating expenses (or gross profit); interest charges; income taxes; income before extraordinary items; extraordinary items; and net income.

At the date of this writing (May 1972) the foregoing represent the *informal,* administrative requirements of the SEC and they conform with the present formal requirements for summaries in Forms 10 and 10–K. The instructions in the last two named forms represent the Commission's most recent formal expression of its views regarding the items of information that must be shown in summaries. At the date of this writing, the SEC's *formal* instructions for S–1 summaries call for a showing of net sales or operating revenues; cost of goods sold or operating expenses (or gross profit); interest charges; income taxes; net income; special items; and net income and special items. These were the SEC's requirements before the APB issued its Opinion No. 9 (Reporting the Results of Operations) in December 1966 which, for the first time, set forth the standards for determining and reporting extraordinary items in income statements. The SEC concurred in the views expressed in Opinion No. 9, and scrapped its long-standing requirements for the showing of "special items." Although the Commission changed its administrative procedures to conform with the views expressed in Opinion No. 9, it has not yet revised the Form S–1 summary to reflect its present requirements.

As used in the instructions for Item 6, the term "operating expenses" means expenses applicable to operating revenues—as in the case, for example, of a public utility company. In the case of the ordinary manufacturing or merchandising organization whose principal source of income is from the sale of a tangible product, the summary would begin with "net sales" although it might also have operating revenues from rental income or service income.

The foregoing discussion of the items of information that must be included in a Form S–1 earnings summary represent minimum requirements. The SEC has pointed out publicly that the necessity of disclosing items in addition to those specified in the instructions of the form will depend on the circumstances. The instructions in the SEC's forms "cannot, of course, cover all situations which may arise nor is it practicable to set forth a statement of policy dealing specifically with all possible situations. The existence of any unusual conditions affecting the propriety of the presentation . . . should be considered." (Release No. 33–4936, Dec. 9, 1968)

In the case of public utilities, for example, charges for maintenance, repairs, and depreciation are significant items of information. As a consequence, in conformity with the SEC's instructions and industry practice, such items are usually set out separately in the summary of earnings (or in the income statement) or in a footnote to the summary.

See the comment on page **18·25** regarding the practice of some companies in stating cost of goods sold exclusive of depreciation and showing depreciation as a separate item which includes not only the portion applicable to cost of goods sold but also to other profit and loss accounts.

If the provision for income taxes includes a substantial amount for deferred taxes, see the requirements of Regulation S–X on page **16·39**.

If the summary of earnings furnishes substantially all the information that would be contained in the formal income statement, the latter statement may be omitted. The tendency is in that direction. In many cases, by the addition of a few details, the summary of earnings can be made to comply with the requirements for an income statement. In the author's opinion, this development should be encouraged since it contributes in a constructive way to simplifying the prospectus and eliminating duplication. In this connection, it should be noted that although the SEC has not revised the requirements for an earnings summary in Form S–1, it has revised the requirements for formal income statements; see the requirements of Rule 5–03 of Regulation S–X in Chapter **18**.

If the S–1 registration statement registers common stock, the summary must present earnings applicable to common stock. Per share earnings and dividends declared for each period of the summary also have to be included "unless inappropriate" according to the instructions. As far as a showing of earnings per share is concerned, the words "unless inappropriate" may be disregarded inasmuch as APB Opinion No. 15 makes it mandatory to furnish such information on the face of all income statements and summaries of earnings. Beginning on page **10·44** are some comments on the SEC's views regarding the reporting of earnings per share.

Where per share earnings are disclosed, the information with respect to the computation of per share earnings on both primary and fully diluted bases, presented by exhibit or otherwise, must be furnished even though the amounts of per share earnings on the fully diluted basis are not required to be stated under the provisions of APB Opinion No. 15. That Opinion provides that any reduction of less than 3% need not be considered as dilution (footnote to paragraph 14 of the Opinion) and that a computation on the fully diluted basis which results in improvement of earnings per share not be taken into account (paragraph 40 of the Opinion). (Release No. 33–5133, Feb. 18, 1971.)

If the registration statement relates to long-term debt or preferred stock, there must be shown the annual interest requirements on such long-term debt or the annual dividend requirements on such preferred stock. To the extent that an issue represents refunding or refinancing, only the *additional* interest or dividend requirements shall be stated. It is true that the interest and dividend requirements may be calculated from the capitalization table which must be included in the prospectus; the SEC instruction eliminates the necessity of the investor having to make the computation.

Retroactive Adjustments May Be Required.—The summary must reflect the retroactive adjustment of any material items affecting the comparability of the results. See, for example, the discussion of the London-town Manufacturing case in Chapter **5**. Before going public late in 1961, the company's inventories had been substantially understated. Almost all of the understatement was restored in the income statement for the fiscal year ended February 28, 1961 and in the balance sheet at that date. The effect of the inventory manipulation was to understate income of the earlier years and to overstate income of the year in which the inventory was correctly stated. When the inventory situation was brought to light, the company disclosed the effect of the incorrect figures, including a restatement of earnings—year by year—on the basis of the correct inventory amounts. The corrected figures were set forth in a post-effective amendment to the company's registration statement, inasmuch as the original registration statement (including the erroneous figures) had become effective and the securities had been sold.

Ordinarily there is no problem in interpreting the SEC's instructions regarding retroactive adjustments. The SEC's policy is sometimes applied in a way and in circumstances that are puzzling. The following example, which is taken from an actual case, will illustrate the point. Eliminating the captions and interim periods which are of no particular interest for the present purpose, the summary of earnings as initially filed by Company X with the SEC was as shown below.

	(in thousands of dollars)				
	1960	*1961*	*1962*	*1963*	*1964*
Sales	$11,121	$10,785	$10,901	$12,147	$16,809
Gross profit	2,224	2,363	2,426	2,545	3,836
Income (loss) after taxes but before nonrecurring items	(43)	128	129	196	577
Nonrecurring credits (charges):					
Deferred development expenses charged off, net of deferred Federal income taxes (see note)					(155)
Other items not pertinent to this discussion	115				
Net earnings	72	128	129	196	422

A note to the summary explained the write-off of the deferred development expenses in 1964 as follows:

The company deferred all expenses, net of deferred Federal income taxes, incurred to December 31, 1963 ($53,000 in 1962 and $102,000 in 1963) relating to the development of [a new process]. In 1964, the company began a policy of amortization over thirty-six months which amounted to $27,000 for the first quarter of 1964. It became apparent before the end of the year that little or no benefit would be obtained from these development expenses, and accordingly the entire amount, net of the related tax effect, was written off as a nonrecurring charge.

The SEC took exception to the write-off in 1964 of the deferred development expenses. The Commission's memorandum of comments had this to say about the matter:

Reference is made to the item of deferred development expenses charged off in 1964 which has been treated as a nonrecurring charge in the summary of earnings. In view of the circumstances described in the note to that summary, it is our opinion that these expenses should be applied retroactively to the year in which incurred in a manner similar to that contemplated by Instruction 1 [referred to above]. . . . This suggested revision is consistent with the policy of this division in these circumstances.

The certifying accountant was convinced that the presentation in the original filing was correct, but the SEC's staff insisted on the position taken in its letter of comments. The company and the underwriter were, of course, delighted to comply with the SEC's request.

The company revised the summary in accordance with the SEC's wishes, charging the development costs to the periods in which the expenditures were made instead of the period when the development costs were determined to have little or no benefit. The rationale in support of the SEC's position appeared to be this: In 1965, when the earnings summary was prepared, and with the benefit of hindsight, it was known that the amounts deferred in 1962 and 1963 were not recoverable, and in the SEC's view that is when the loss occurred—not when the company concluded that the development costs were a total loss.

In connection with the subject of retroactive adjustments, the reader should refer to the discussion beginning on page **13·16** under "Restatement of Previously Reported Financial Statements," including the effect of APB Opinion No. 20 (1971) on "Accounting Changes."

Reconciliation with Previously Reported Amounts.—When amounts previously reported have been materially revised as the result of retroactive restatements for poolings of interest or for any other reason, it is necessary to reconcile the new figures with the corresponding amounts previously reported. This subject is discussed in Chapter **13**, and the discussion is equally applicable to summaries of earnings.

Unaudited Interim Periods.—In connection with any unaudited summary for an interim period or periods between the end of the last fiscal year and the balance sheet date, and any comparable unaudited prior periods, a statement has to be made that all adjustments necessary to a fair statement of the results for such interim period or periods have been included. In addition there should be furnished in such cases, as supplemental information but not as a part of the registration statement, a letter from the registrant to the SEC describing in detail the nature and amount of any adjustments, other than normal recurring items, entering into the determination of the results shown. The precise SEC instructions, as a matter of fact, refer to "other than normal recurring accruals." In the author's opinion, this is probably unintentional error, since it seems clear that the SEC is not concerned here with ordinary accruals *or* deferrals. It is more appropriate therefore to refer to "normal recurring adjustments" rather than "normal recurring accruals." In Form S–11 (which is a more recent expression of the SEC's requirements than S–1) the SEC uses the phrase "other than normal recurring adjustments" in setting forth the instructions applicable to the summary of earnings.

As to the reason for this requirement and what may be contemplated by "adjustments other than normal recurring items," see the discussion of the Kaiser-Frazer case and the Heller Committee report in Chapter **13**. In practice the following form of representation has been found to be acceptable:

The summary of earnings for the (periods) ended (date) and (date) has been prepared from the records of the Company without audit by independent public accountants, and, in the opinion of the Company, reflects all adjustments necessary to present fairly the results of operations for the periods.

If the adjustments reflected in the statement were ordinary and recurring, the supplemental letter to the SEC can be dispensed with by modifying the suggested form of representation above to read as follows:

. . . reflects all adjustments (none of which were other than normal, recurring adjustments) necessary to present fairly, etc. . . .

It should be understood that this form of representation is appropriate only if the adjustments were of a normal, recurring nature. If the adjustments were extraordinary in nature, the language should be appropriately modified; in some circumstances, the statements may have to be appropriately revised depending on the nature and amount of the adjustments.

For suggested forms of a letter to SEC setting forth the adjustments reflected in unaudited figures, and the SEC's views as to the importance of this requirement, see page **12·59**.

Following is an example showing how the disclosure can be made when the adjustments reflected in the interim figures are other than normal recurring items; it is taken from a 1963 prospectus of Celanese Corporation of America. The summary of earnings included unaudited figures for the 34 weeks ended August 25, 1962 in respect of which the company represented that all adjustments necessary for a fair statement of the results of operations for such period were included, and that such adjustments consisted of normal recurring items "and the provision referred to in Note B." In the statement itself, under "Income from foreign operations," was an item captioned "Exchange losses and in 1962 provision for other asset revaluations" with a reference to Note B. Note B, following the summary, was as follows: "Exchange losses and provision for other asset revaluations in 1962 included $2,320,000 representing anticipated losses from financial reorganization and disposition of certain assets of subsidiary companies in Venezuela of which $1,700,000 is included in the period ended August 25, 1962."

It is probably worth emphasizing that the representation regarding the inclusion of adjustments necessary for a fair statement of results is required only in relation to statements or summaries for unaudited *interim* periods. If the interim period is covered by a certificate of an independent public accountant, the representation does not have to be made. When the first two years of a five year summary are not certified (which is often the case when a company goes public), the representation is also not required with respect to those two years.

In the past some registrants have made representations regarding unaudited interim periods using a negative form, as, for example, the following:

The summary for the (periods) ended (date) and (date) has not been examined by independent public accountants; the Company does not know of any adjustment necessary for a fair statement of the results for such periods.

The negative form of representation is not acceptable to the SEC; the SEC staff insists on a positive form of representation as required by its instructions.

In releasing interim financial data to the public and security holders, some companies indicate that the information is "subject to year-end audit adjustments," or they use other language with the purpose of emphasizing the tentative nature of the reported financial information. The phrase "subject to year-end audit adjustment," standing by itself, is not acceptable to the staff of the Commission. The company must be in a position to stand behind the figures and represent that they include all adjustments necessary for a fair statement of the results.

On the other hand, the "subject to" phrase is acceptable in certain cases where the reason therefor is explained. As an example, the following statement appeared in the November 24, 1969 prospectus of Stokely-Van Camp, Inc., after the capsule information for the three-month periods ended August 30, 1969 and August 31, 1968:

The financial information set forth in the preceding paragraph is based upon certain estimates and will be subject to and will be affected by year-end audit and adjustments. Seasonal products, that is fruit and vegetable items which are packed in a relatively short growing period and then warehoused for sale throughout the balance of the year, account for approximately 54% of the Company's sales on a consolidated basis. The rate at which the products are moved and the prices which they will bring vary from year to year and from month to month. In order to develop the estimated financial information set forth in the preceding paragraph, many major expenses were tentatively charged to income on the basis of an estimate of dollar volume of sales for the entire year. If actual dollar volume of sales declines or increases during the last nine months of the year due either to a decline or an increase in the number of cases sold or a decline or an increase in the prices at which products are sold or due to a combination of both factors, then the estimated financial information for the first three months will not have reflected the absorption of the appropriate amount of interim expenses with the result that such financial information may overstate or understate the profits resulting from the operation during the period. Subject to the foregoing, all adjustments necessary to a fair statement of the results for such interim periods have been included.

"CAPSULE INFORMATION."—In many prospectuses and proxy statements the information shown in the summary of earnings (or income statement) is supplemented by unaudited information concerning subsequent sales and earnings—commonly called "capsule information." This later information is often shown in a paragraph following the summary, either in narrative or in tabular form, for a period in the current year and for the corresponding period of the preceding year. Capsule information is also subject to the SEC's requirements discussed above regarding the inclusion in the amounts shown of all adjustments necessary for a fair statement of results for the periods.

Following are examples taken from recent prospectuses showing how this information has been furnished in actual cases:

Example 1

For the three months ended (date) and (date), net sales were $
and $, respectively, and net income was $ ($
per share) and $ ($ per share), respectively. Net income for the three months ended (date) includes an extraordinary gain of $
(after deducting $ of tax), equivalent to $ per share, resulting from the discontinuance of a small product line. All adjustments (consisting only of normal recurring adjustments) which are considered necessary to present a fair statement of the results for such interim periods have been made.

Example 2

In the first six months of (year) the Company's consolidated sales, service and rental income amounted to $ consolidated income before taxes was $, and consolidated net income was $, ($
per share), as compared with $, $, and $ ($
per share), respectively, in the corresponding period last year. The amounts set forth in this paragraph are unaudited but, in the opinion of the Company, include all adjustments (which comprise only normal recurring adjustments) necessary for a fair presentation of the consolidated results of operations for the interim periods. The results of operations for the six months of (year) should not be regarded as necessarily indicative of the results that may be expected for the entire year.

Example 3
(An electric utility company reporting for twelve
months ended on an interim date)

For the twelve months ended June 30, 19—, electric revenues were $ and net income was $; these amounts are unaudited but, in the opinion of the Company, include all adjustments (consisting only of normal recurring adjustments) necessary for a fair presentation of the results of operations. The decline in net income for the twelve months ended June 30, 19— is largely attributable to increased costs, particularly to substantial increases in the cost of fossil fuels and in the cost of capital. These factors are continuing to affect net income adversely.

OVERSTATEMENT OF INTERIM EARNINGS DUE TO OVERSTATEMENT OF SHIPMENTS: THE BURGMASTER CASE.—It is of the utmost importance that the statements for interim periods be consistent, not only with each other, but also with those for full fiscal years. If they are inconsistent due to changes in accounting principles or practices, the changes should be disclosed if they are material.

What can happen if inconsistencies are not discovered is illustrated by a filing by Burgmaster Corporation in 1961. The company is a leader in the application of electronic numerical controls to multiple spindle turret drilling machines. The company manufactures the machines and has the electronic controls manufactured to its specifications by others. The company's prospectus as originally filed included certified statements for a first quarter compared with an unaudited first quarter of the preceding year as to which the required representation as to adjustments was made. The comparisons showed a substantial drop in volume of sales and earnings in the current period, so the staff made a customary request for later information. This was furnished for two more months on an unaudited basis and also was covered by the required representations as to adjustments.

On May 15, 1961, the registration statement became effective. The shares were fully subscribed for on that same day and began trading on a "when issued" basis. The closing (when the company and the selling stockholders were to deliver the securities against payment by the underwriters) was scheduled for May 24, 1961.

Between May 15 and May 24, 1961, however, it was learned that there was an accounting inconsistency between the method of preparation of the unaudited interim figures for the two months ended March 31, 1961, as compared with the certified figures in the prospectus. For internal monthly accounting purposes, the company recorded its sales as of invoice dates, determined on the basis of substantial completion, whereas sales reflected in the certified statements were based on shipment dates. Shipments normally occurred on or within a day or so after a sale was invoiced. The May 15, 1961, prospectus contained the statement, "Based on unaudited interim figures, net sales, gross profits and net income during the two months ended March 31, 1961 amounted to $699,037, $306,356 and $66,481, respectively, . . ." These figures were based on invoices whereas the certified figures included in the summary of earnings were based on shipments. On a shipment basis, the figures would have been $578,450, $248,817, and

$41,742, respectively. On March 31, 1961, (a Friday), the company invoiced $120,587 of machines, which were not actually shipped until the following Monday, April 3, 1961.

Due to this inconsistency, the closing did not occur. The registration statement containing the May 15, 1961 prospectus was withdrawn, and all initial subscriptions and subsequent transactions in the stock were cancelled. The shares were re-registered and re-offered in a new prospectus dated June 19, 1961. The only material change in the new prospectus as compared with the old was the correction and updating of the unaudited financial information.

Necessary Information and Explanations.—In connection with the summary the instructions provide that "whenever necessary," information or explanations "of material significance to investors in appraising the results shown" shall be reflected; if the information or explanations are set forth elsewhere in the prospectus, cross-reference is permitted. *This is the only place in the entire financial section of the S–1 registration statement where an instruction of this kind appears.*

The SEC has commented upon the investor's need for explanatory information in connection with the proper use of earning summaries. The Commission said, "If, for example, the reported earnings reflect the results of unusual conditions, or in certain years include significant nonrecurring items of income or expenses, an appropriate disclosure of such conditions or items is made either in the summary or in footnotes thereto." [ASR No. 62, (1947)].

In the same release (ASR No. 62) the SEC pointed out that where the summary reflected operations of a predecessor, or where there had been violent or radical changes in the enterprise, appropriate disclosures or adjustments may be required; or the summary may, in fact, be entirely deleted. The release said:

Ordinarily, the summary earnings table will reflect the operations of the registrant, or of the registrant and its subsidiaries, during the period covered. However, under special circumstances, as where the registrant has succeeded to the business of one or more predecessors, it may be necessary for the summary to be specially constructed so as to reflect as far as possible for the period covered the earnings applicable to the enterprise now represented by the registrant. Where, for example, a predecessor operated as a partnership it is ordinarily necessary to indicate in an appropriate manner the adjustments required to place the partnership income on a corporate basis. In other unusual cases there may have been such violent and radical changes in the business of the registrant that a long summary of past earnings might be of very little or no value and might well be misleading. In several such cases, the registrant has been requested either to delete the summary entirely or to furnish only a brief statement of the over-all, aggregate results, without a breakdown as between the several years. In any case, where special and unusual circumstances exist, a decision as to the content of the summary and as to whether or not a summary should be furnished at all can only be reached after careful appraisal of the particular facts of each case.

The reader is also referred to the discussion in Chapter **13**, "Full Disclosure: Some Suggestions," and under the heading on page **21·9**, "Predecessor Business Operated as a Partnership or Sole Proprietorship."

In some cases, it may appear that certain gains or losses, although properly included in the determination of net income for the period or periods of the summary, are non-recurring items, and failure to disclose the extraordinary nature of these items may result in misleading inferences. In this situation, disclosure of the amounts (total and per share) would ordinarily be required.

When a company shows an erratic sales or net income picture for the period covered by the summary, or where the gross profit percentages show an abnormal relationship from year to year, the SEC customarily requires a brief explanation of the factors that contributed to these results. A simple example showing compliance with this requirement is furnished by a 1970 prospectus of ESL Incorporated. Its summary of earnings (in the form of an income statement) showed sales of $4.7 million in 1967 and $4.5 million in 1968. In the same years net income dropped from $202,000 to $160,000. Following the notes to the statement, the text of the prospectus furnished this explanation of the decline:

> The decline in sales and profits in 1968 is attributable primarily to the dilution of the Company's customary marketing efforts necessitated by the preparation, submission and follow-up in late 1967 and early 1968 of a proposal for a three-year Government contract in excess of $60,000,000. The Company was not awarded this contract and considerable time was expended thereafter in identifying and pursuing other opportunities for 1968 business.

Ramada Inns, Inc. is engaged chiefly in the operation of motor hotels for its own account. The company also operates a system under which independent motor hotel operators are franchised to use the Ramada name. In a 1968 prospectus the company thought it advisable to disclose the amounts and the nonrecurring nature of the fees from the sale of franchises, although such fees had increased during the five year period covered by the summary of earnings. The company said:

> For 1967 the Company's fees from the sale of motor hotel franchises amounted to $1,004,000 as compared to $818,000, $866,000, $564,000, and $372,000 in the years 1966 through 1963. These fees constitute non-recurring revenue in the sense that such revenue depends on continuing sales of franchises, and the amounts of such revenues in such years are not necessarily indicative of the amounts which may be realized from this source in the future. The contribution of such revenues to net income before taxes is, of course, reduced by expenses incurred in connection with making franchise sales, by the cost of Company services provided to franchisees and by certain general expenses of

the franchise division. See "Motor Hotel Franchise Operations" under "Business".

The income of Denny's Restaurants, Inc. also derived to a large extent from the sale of franchises. The company's 1970 prospectus included a summary of earnings, which disclosed, on the face of the statement, the revenues from the sale of franchises, which increased from $561,000 in fiscal 1965 to $1,757,000 in fiscal 1969, and to $3,275,000 in the nine months ended March 27, 1970. A note to the summary dealt further with this matter:

Income from the sales of franchises of individual restaurant units is taken into income at the time the restaurant is opened by the franchisee. Sales of area franchises included in sale of franchises for the year ended June 27, 1969 and the nine months ended March 28, 1969 are $290,124 and $164,800, respectively. This program has been discontinued and no area franchises have been sold subsequent to June 27, 1969. Reference is made to Note 4 to financial statements and "Business—Franchising and Operating Agreements—Area Restaurant Franchises", regarding the Company's franchising policies and information concerning the Company's subsequent acquisition of a controlling interest in one of the area franchises and termination of certain of the other area franchises.

A 1970 prospectus of American Airlines included a summary of earnings (in the form of an income statement) in which revenues were broken down as between: (1) passenger, (2) freight, (3) mail, (4) express, and (5) other. The last-named category, namely, "other," fluctuated widely during the period of the summary as follows (amounts in thousands): 1965 $4,229; 1966 ($22,971); 1967 $3,449; 1968 $3,897; 1969 $24,652; 1st 1/4 1969 $20,168; 1st 1/4 1970 $936. The company explained in a note to the summary that payments to other airlines under mutual aid agreements and amounts received from other airlines under such agreements are, for the most part, included in "Revenues—Other." The note was as follows:

(b) Under a mutual aid agreement with several other airlines, revenues from added traffic to member carriers not on strike, less the expenses of handling this added traffic, are paid to the member carriers on strike. Additional contributions by non-struck member carriers are required under this agreement when such net revenues from added traffic of non-struck member carriers are not sufficient to cover certain minimum percentages of the normal operating expenses of the struck carriers. In 1966, the Company, under this agreement, made payments totaling $29,000,000 to four airlines. Such payments were charged to "Revenues—Other" ($26,000,000) in respect of net revenues from added traffic and to "Other income (deductions)—Miscellaneous—net" ($3,000,000) in respect of the remaining payments. As a result of a 21-day strike, the Company, under this agreement, received approximately $19,800,000 and $20,300,000 from other airlines for the three months ended March 31, 1969 and the year 1969, respectively, and such payments were credited to "Revenues

—Other." For the three months ended March 31, 1970 the Company accrued payments to another carrier totaling approximately $1,416,000. Such anticipated payments were charged to "Revenues—Other" ($182,000) in respect of net revenues from added traffic and to "Other income (deductions)—Miscellaneous —net" ($1,234,000) in respect of the remaining payments to cover certain minimum percentages of the normal operating expenses of the struck carrier. (See "Business—General" for recent amendments to the mutual aid agreement.)

The following additional disclosures were made in the narrative portion of the prospectus immediately after the notes to the summary of earnings:

Net earnings for 1966 reflect the increase in traffic carried by American during a 43-day strike in July and August against five other trunk airlines as well as the payments to four of such airlines under the Mutual Aid Agreement (see Note (b) above).

Net earnings for 1969 were adversely affected by a 21-day strike in February and March, during which all operations were suspended, by increased costs, new capacity added by American and its competitors which exceeded increases in traffic and reduction in earnings from Military Airlift Command operations. Offsetting factors were payments received from other airlines under the Mutual Aid Agreement and passenger fare increases of approximately 3.6% and 7.5%, which became effective in February 1969 and October 1969, respectively.

The business of Ford Motor Credit Company is primarily that of providing wholesale financing to Ford-franchised dealers and purchasing retail instalment sales paper from such dealers. The company's 1970 prospectus showed a substantial increase in operating income attributable to commercial and industrial financing, and this source provided the major contribution to net income in 1969 and the first two months of 1970. The company commented on this factor in a paragraph following the summary of earnings as follows:

The Company's commercial and industrial financing made the major contribution to net income during 1969 and the first two months of 1970. Because of a general shortage of funds available to customers from traditional sources for such financing, the Company had the opportunity to increase substantially its lending in this area. In addition, this activity benefitted from the receipt of a substantial amount of commitment fee income with respect to commitments to make real estate loans in the future. The volume of business and the profitability of commercial and industrial financing may be affected by future changes in the general supply of lendable funds, interest rates or other factors.

Mack Financial Corporation is a wholly owned subsidiary of Mack Trucks, Inc., which in turn is a wholly owned subsidiary of The Signal Companies, Inc. Mack Financial Corporation sold an issue of senior debentures through underwriters, and the summary of earnings included in the prospectus used in connection with the offering contained a number of significant explanations. The summary covered the calendar years 1965–1969. During the five-year period, net income increased from $1,436,000 to $2,561,000. In the 1969 year (and only in that year) there was a credit amount of $939,000 included in income and described as "Adjustment paid by Mack (parent company)." There was also a reference to a footnote which read as follows:

(b) In an agreement dated as of April 28, 1960, as amended, Mack [Trucks, Inc.] agreed to pay to the Company with respect to receivables purchased in each fiscal quarter an amount which, when added to net earnings available for fixed charges for the period from the beginning of the fiscal year to the end of such fiscal quarter, shall increase such net earnings to an amount not less than one and one-half times fixed charges for such period.

Also there was a sharp dip in the provision for losses on collections of receivables in 1968 as compared with the preceding year (1967) or the following year (1969). This was explained in a note to the summary which was as follows:

(a) During 1968, the Company received $401,000 from Mack [Trucks, Inc.] related to a specific customer's account and credited such amount to the provision for losses on collections of receivables.

The prospectus of Lithium Corporation of America, Inc. (1960) is an excellent example of an explanation of material significance to investors. During the period covered by the summary of earnings, substantial changes took place in the company's operations and earnings. The following abstract from the prospectus indicates the significance of the changes and the explanation which was presented.

| | | Thousands of Dollars | |
| | | Pre-tax Earnings | Net Earnings |
Period	Sales	(loss)	(loss)
1955	$ 6,381	$ 269	$ 182
1956	12,151	1,532	865
1957	12,239	709	465
1958	11,186	1,378	763
1959	10,841	(1,202)	(599)*
Six months 1959	5,720	827	442
" " 1960	2,314	(22)	(13)

* After loss carry-back credit of $603 and after deducting extraordinary item of $2,780. See Note 1.

Note 1 to the summary follows:

The data for the six months ended June 30, 1960 are not necessarily indicative of the operations and earnings that may be expected for the full year ending December 31, 1960; nor are they comparable with the data for any prior period, for the following reasons:
(a)   Over 50 % of the annual sales volume for the four years ended December 31, 1959 was represented by sales to the Atomic Energy Commission. Deliveries under this sales contract were completed by December 31, 1959.

(b) During 1959, the Company terminated its contract with Quebec Lithium Corporation for the purchase of lithium concentrates, claiming material breach of certain provisions of the purchase contract. Ensuing litigation was settled on December 29, 1959 at a cost to the Company of $1,955,000.

(c) Also during 1959 the Company determined to relocate its facilities in St. Louis Park, Minnesota, and to consolidate all of its chemical operations at a single site near Bessemer City, North Carolina. Losses, writedowns and other costs relating to moving and consolidating the chemical facilities and research laboratories amounted to $825,000.

Earnings for 1959 thus include total special items of $2,780,000, representing charges under items (b) and (c) above. The nature of these special charges is such that it is not practicable to make any allocation thereof to other periods or years.

The prospectus of H. M. Harper Company (1959) included a summary of earnings which covered the ten-year period 1949–58 and, in addition, the nine months ended September 30, 1958 and 1959. In the ten-year period, net earnings applicable to common (in thousands of dollars) were as follows: 1949, $34; 1950, $414; 1951, $569; 1952, $455; 1953, $319; 1954, $188 (loss) ; 1955, $44; 1956, $259; 1957, $218; 1958, $413; in the nine months 1958 and 1959, the corresponding amounts were $318 and $540. A note to the summary explained the poor results in the period 1954–57 as follows:

Net earnings of the company were adversely affected during the years 1954 to 1957 primarily by the substantial losses incurred by the Metals Division in developing the extrusion process (see The Company's Business) and by the Aero Division due to contract changes and cancellations. The following tabulation of gross profits (losses) of the three divisions is based upon data from the Company's accounting records without audit. . . .

	Bolt Division	Metals Division	Aero Division	Total
Year ended December 31:		($000 omitted)		
1953	$2,880	($136)	$ 175	$2,919
1954	2,414	(619)	(150)	1,645
1955	2,977	(491)	(175)	2,311
1956	3,507	(395)	(116)	2,996
1957	3,240	(210)	(66)	2,964
1958	3,027	117	98	3,242
Nine months ended September 30:				
1958	2,226	165	55	2,446
1959	2,554	473	58	3,085

A 1963 prospectus of the SONY Company contained an explanation of the increase in selling, general and administrative expenses in a note to the summary (which was in the form of an income statement) reading as follows:

(A) As a result of a change in the commodity tax law in 1959, certain of the Company's previously exempt products became subject to this tax and, effective April 1, 1961, the tax on tape recorders was increased from 5% to 10%. Selling, general and administrative expenses include commodity taxes as follows:

	1958	1959	1960	1961	1962
In millions of yen	¥ 8	¥ 94	¥279	¥ 505	¥ 797
In thousands of dollars	$23	$262	$776	$1,403	$2,214

Ryder System, Inc. is primarily in the business of leasing and renting trucks. The company issued a prospectus in 1970 in connection with an issue of debentures. A summary of earnings included in the prospectus covered the calendar years 1965–1969, and the first quarters of 1969 and 1970. In the five year period, revenues increased from $72 million to $156 million, and net income from $2,795,000 to $8,647,000. First quarter revenues increased from $33 million in 1969 to $47 million in 1970; net income increased from $1,669,000 to $1,993,000. A note to the summary disclosed the effect on operations of companies purchased in 1968–1970 as follows:

(c)   The effect on operating revenues and net income of companies acquired in 1968, 1969 and 1970 and accounted for as purchases (see Note 1 of "Notes to Financial Statements" of the Company) is summarized below. Several companies acquired prior to 1968 and accounted for as purchases are, in the aggregate, not considered material.

	Years		3 months ended 3/31	
	1968	1969	1969	1970
	(In thousands of dollars)			
Operating revenues:				
Companies acquired in 1968	$8,745	$17,619	$4,124	$ 3,552
" " " 1969	—	5,728	875	1,716
" " " 1970	—	—	—	5,907
	$8,745	$23,347	$5,000	$11,175
Net income:				
Companies acquired in 1968	$330	$475	$113	$135
" " " 1969	—	140	20	131
" " " 1970	—	—	—	300
	$330	$615	$132	$566

Privately owned companies are in a position to control their expenses and hence their profits to some extent by varying the amounts of compensation which the owners and operators of the business pay to themselves. This factor may require disclosure when the company "goes public." An example of the kind of explanation that would be made in these circumstances appeared in the prospectus of Bin-Dicator Company (1961). Selling and administrative expenses and net income were as follows:

(in thousands of dollars)

	1956	1957	1958	1959	1960	Five Months Ended 5/31		Nine Months Ended 9/30	
						1960	1961	1960	1961
Selling and administrative expenses	$204	$249	$275	$246	$285	$113	$118	$199	$210
Net income	31	44	51	136	170	75	77	139	151

A note to the summary disclosed the variation in amounts paid to the owners of the business as follows :

Compensation of the two principal selling stockholders included in selling and administrative expenses for the respective periods was as follows: 1956— $107,471 ; 1957—$135,148; 1958—$146,786; 1959—$84,000; 1960—$79,000; five-month periods ended May 31, 1960 and 1961—$33,500 and $32,500, respectively; nine-month periods ended September 30, 1960 and 1961—$59,500 and $58,500, respectively.

On the other hand, the prospectus of Brad Ragan, Inc., dated November 17, 1970, indicated in a note to the summary of earnings that "Effective with the date of the offering of stock to the public, the principal shareholder's salary will be reduced from an annual rate of $160,000 to $90,000."

MATERIAL CHANGES IN COST OF SALES PERCENTAGE.—As previously indicated the SEC customarily requires an explanation in the prospectus of abnormal relationships from year to year in the gross profit expressed as a percentage of sales. This is especially important when the latest period or periods show a marked improvement in gross profit over earlier periods, and the narrative section of the prospectus furnishes no clue regarding the reason for the improvement.

In the Londontown Manufacturing Company case (which is discussed in Chapter **5**), the gross profit percentage was a matter of some consequence. The Londontown prospectus disclosed an increase in gross profit percentage from 23 per cent in fiscal 1957 to almost 39 per cent in fiscal 1961. In the last three years covered by the summary of earnings, the gross profit percentages were 25 per cent, 30 per cent, and almost 39 per cent, respectively. In that same period, sales increased from $3,236,000 to $5,361,000—an increase of 66 per cent. Inventories, however, as disclosed by the prospectus, increased from $221,000 at the beginning of the three-year period to $757,000 at the end of that period—an increase of 243 per cent. The prospectus contained no comment or explanation of these facts, and the reader of the prospectus might wonder whether the matter was inadvertently overlooked or whether the SEC's staff did not believe that an explanation was essential.

As indicated in the discussion of the Londontown case, the SEC made an investigation after it was brought out that the company's inventories prior to May 31, 1961 (as of which date they had been observed by the certifying accountants) had been falsified. Nearly all of the previously unreported inventory was included in the earnings of the fiscal year ended February 28, 1961. The investigation was ended and the case was settled on the basis of a stipulation of the facts.

The stipulation indicated that the SEC's staff had, in fact, raised a question in its letter of comment concerning the gross profit percentage. The staff's comment was as follows:

In view of the material variations in the gross margin percentage, and the substantial increase in inventories at February 28, 1961, it is requested that this Division be furnished, prior to amendment, with a letter from the independent accountants detailing the auditing procedures which they were able to apply with regard to the inventories and the basis for the statement in their report that "such inventories do not appear to be unreasonable." Upon receipt of such information, we will have further comment upon the language used in the certificate. (Stipulation, p. 148.)

Representatives of the certifying accountants met with members of the SEC's staff to discuss the accountants' draft of a proposed reply to the above comment. The proposed reply (which, as it will be noted, was subsequently modified before being sent to the SEC) was as follows:

In your letter of comments dated September 25, 1961 relating to the registration statement of Londontown Manufacturing Company, File No. 2-18654, you have requested that we advise you as to the audit procedures which we were able to apply with respect to inventories and the basis of the statement in our report dated August 2, 1961 to the effect that "such inventories do not appear to be unreasonable."

The company maintains no cost system which is integrated into the general accounting system. We satisfied ourselves as to cost of raw materials included in inventories by reference to purchase invoices. Costs of finished goods and work-in-process are determined by the company by pricing direct labor and materials used in each of the various styles and sizes of garments by reference to piece rates paid for various production operations, by pricing materials included therein by reference to bills of material, by applying burden based on labor costs and by giving effect to the factor of style obsolescence. We tested piece work rates and material costs used in developing the pricing formula, applied certain tests to establish the reliability of the method used to allocate burden costs and satisfied ourselves as to the reasonableness of the factor applied to reflect style obsolescence. Based on the aforementioned audit operations, we were satisfied as to the reasonableness of the inventory pricing for each of the audited periods covered in the summary of earnings.

As a further test of the reasonableness of the aggregate inventory valuations we applied gross profit tests and inquired into the reasons for fluctuations in the gross profit ratios as between the various audited periods covered by the summary of earnings. We satisfied ourselves that the variations were due primarily to causes such as price changes, style changes, volume changes, etc. During the fiscal year ended February 28, 1959 some portion of the variation was attributed to the operation of a theft ring within the plant. While the company recovered admitted theft losses from its insurance carrier, it was impossible to ascertain the full extent of the theft loss.

On the basis of our tests of inventories as outlined above, we were satisfied as to the reasonableness of the inventory valuation. * * * The substantial increase in inventories at February 28, 1961 is explained by the fact that the move to the new plant in January, 1961 provided more storage facilities and permitted the company to build up its inventories to a level which management deemed necessary to maintain efficient production schedules. (Stipulation, pp. 148–149.)

The SEC representatives questioned the portion of the auditors' certificate reading ". . . based on the procedures which we were able to apply, such inventories do not appear to be unreasonable . . ." The SEC suggested that it be changed to read ". . . based on the procedures which we were able to apply, such inventories appear to be reasonable . . ." The auditors said there did not seem to be an essential difference between the two phrases and accepted the suggestion. The auditors' reply to the SEC's letter of comment was revised accordingly. The auditors asked whether their reply satisfactorily answered the questions to which it was addressed, and the SEC representative responded that he had no further question (Stipulation, p. 148).

The prospectus of a company that manufactured television picture tubes contained this explanation of an increase in the cost of sales percentage:

The increase in the ratio of cost of sales to net sales for the (period), as compared to the (period), was primarily the result of two factors. One factor was high initial production costs on a new laminated safety glass picture tube which was introduced in (period). This new line of picture tubes is now in volume production, and manufacturing costs have been reduced to a level comparable to that for other types of tubes. The other factor was lower selling prices of tubes which became effective in (period) and prevailed until the latter part of (period) and, when prices of tubes were increased to levels equal to, or greater than, those in effect prior to such price reductions.

The foregoing appeared in the narrative section following the summary of earnings and was not part of the summary itself.

The prospectus of a company that manufactured high fidelity sound equipment furnished an example of an explanation of a decline in the gross profit percentage. In two of the years included in the summary, sales increased from $1,406,000 to $1,614,000. Cost of goods sold, however, increased from $903,000 to $1,134,000, with the result that the gross profit declined from $502,000 to $479,000. A note to the summary (keyed to cost of goods sold) disclosed the reason for the declining gross profit as follows:

In the fiscal year ended (date), the company incurred substantial non-recurring retooling costs due to its conversion to stereophonic production.

A manufacturing company furnished the following explanation, in the narrative section of its prospectus, of the improvement in profit ratios and increase in inventories:

The increase in the ratio of operating profit to net sales for the (period) is in the opinion of management due to reduction in cost prices attributable, among other reasons, to an increase in the use of joint purchasing procedures and to increases in the size of orders by the Company for fastenings resulting from the Company's packaging many types of fastenings under its own labels rather than purchasing them already packaged. Accordingly, the Company's inventory increased substantially during (year) and particularly during (year) and has continued to increase during the (period). As a result, it has been possible to supply a greater portion of the requirements of the customers from the Company's warehouses.

The author had an experience in connection with a registration statement which raises some doubt as to what the SEC expects by way of explanation of changes in gross profit percentage—particularly when the percentage figures are at their best in the most recent periods. In the case involved, the gross profit increased from about 21 per cent in the first year of the summary to about 26 per cent in the fifth year. Following the summary of earnings, the company inserted a short paragraph in the narrative section calling attention to the increase in gross profit percentage, and said it was attributable primarily to the benefits accruing from volume purchasing and the institution of more effective pricing policies, and no assurance could be given that the trend would continue. The company's sales had shown a healthy growth and selling, general, and administrative expenses had increased proportionately as might be expected. Inasmuch as the company had not explained the increase in selling, general, and administrative expenses, the SEC suggested that the company delete the explanation of the increase in gross profit percentage, which, of course, the company complied with.

It seems to this author that the SEC's indicated requirement to explain material changes in gross profit percentages is a sensible one, but, as indicated above, it apparently does not represent an invariable requirement.

Explanations of the changes in the percentage of gross profit do not have to be too detailed. A simple explanation will usually suffice, as in the case of The American Welding & Manufacturing Company prospectus dated March 24, 1966. The summary of earnings showed sales ranging between $20 million and $24 million in the first four years of the summary. During that four-year period the percentage of gross profit (a computed figure not shown on the face of the summary) declined from 17.2% in the first year to 15.7% in the fourth year. In the fifth (and most recent) year, however, sales increased to almost $32 million and the percentage of gross profit rose to 19.6%. In explanation of the increase, the company furnished the following explanation:

Sales for the year ended November 30, 1965 were favorably affected by an increased use of jet aircraft engines both for military and commercial purposes. Improved manufacturing methods, as well as increased volume, contributed to the improvement in the gross profit margin for 1965.

DECLINING TREND.—It is self-evident that if a declining trend has set in which affects the issuer's sales or net income, *this is a fact of prime importance which must be brought to the investor's attention.* Ordinarily, this situation is apparent from the figures appearing in the summary of earnings. For example, RCA Corporation issued a proxy statement in 1971 in connection with a special meeting of shareholders to consider a proposal to increase the authorized common stock. (The fact that it was a proxy statement rather than a prospectus is irrelevant for the purpose of the present discussion.) The proxy statement included a summary of earnings for the years 1965–1969 (audited) and the nine months ended Sept. 30, 1970 and 1969 (unaudited). The results for the interim periods showed a sharp decline in earnings from $1.60 per share in 1969 to $.74 in 1970. Following the summary was a paragraph explaining the decline as follows:

The results of operations for the nine months ended September 30, 1970 reflected the strike referred to under "Employees" beginning at page   of this Proxy Statement, and the general slowdown of the national economy and the pressures of increasing costs and expenses on profit, which are continuing. Sales were down approximately 4% from the comparable 1969 period; net profit was down 51%. The profit impact was most severe in color television and other durable home products, with lesser effect in broadcasting, vehicle and equipment renting and commercial electronic equipment. These declines were partially offset by the improved sales and net profit of RCA's communications and publishing activities . . . . . and by increased earnings, despite lower sales, of RCA's service activities. . . . .

In some cases, however, the decline may not be apparent from the face of the summary—usually because the decline set in following the period covered by the summary. For a more complete coverage of this matter, the reader is referred to the discussion beginning on page **13·22**.

Occasionally the narrative or text portion of a prospectus will include a discussion of factors indicating an adverse change in operating results subsequent to the latest period included in the summary. When such a downtrend has occurred and the factors that caused it are important enough to warrant discussion in the prospectus, it is also important that the discussion be brought to the attention of persons reading the summary. In these circumstances, in fact, the SEC has said that the summary should call attention to the adverse change, in a headnote or in a footnote, and should refer to the place in the prospectus where it is discussed (Release No. 33–4936, Dec. 9, 1968). This is a matter which will concern everyone involved with the registration statement—including the independent auditors, if for no other reason than the customary requirement for a comfort letter.

NON-RECURRING GROSS PROFITS.—When one company buys another company at a substantial discount from the book amounts of the underlying net assets, one of the accounting problems will be the allocation of the discount. In some cases a portion of the discount will be found to be allocable to inventories. When the inventories are sold in the normal course of business soon after their acquisition, an unusual non-recurring profit may be realized. A former Chief Accountant of the SEC said that there have been several cases in which this was so significant that the non-recurring gain was removed from gross profit and reported below with a clear explanation of the source of the gain.[2] In one case the matter was disclosed by a footnote as follows:

The gross profit of $_____ for the (period) includes approximate $_____ of higher than normal mark-up attributable to a special purchase of inventories.

DECLINE IN EARNINGS IN FACE OF INCREASE IN SALES.—The operations of companies in some industries are subject to widely fluctuating raw material costs. For competitive or other reasons, companies in such industries may be unable to adjust their selling prices in order to maintain their profit margins, or they may not be able to adjust their selling prices promptly to keep pace with their increased costs. In these circumstances, it is possible for a company, despite an increase in sales, to suffer a decline in net income. It would appear that this is precisely the kind of situation that calls for "information or explanation" in order that investors may be able to appraise the results shown in the earnings summary. In one case where the information was not furnished in the initial filing, the SEC, in its letter of comment, said:

Some indication should be given as to the reason for the sharply decreased earnings in (year) as compared with (year) despite an increase in sales. If the factors which contributed to this reduction in earnings may be expected to continue throughout the next few years, appropriate disclosure should be made. Consideration might also be given to adding a discussion of any factors, characteristic of the industry in which [name of company] operates, which may tend to cause wide fluctuations in sales and earnings from year to year.

Representative prospectuses contain numerous examples of disclosures which explain declining net income in the face of increasing sales.

[2] Andrew Barr, "Disclosure in Theory and Practice," *The New York CPA*, Sept. 1959, p. 640.

A 1970 prospectus of Copper Range Company included a summary of earnings covering the calendar years 1965–1969. Except for 1967, the summary disclosed constantly increasing sales volume. Net income, however, fluctuated widely. The significant figures are summarized below:

	1969	1968	1967	1966	1965
	(Millions of dollars)				
Net sales	102	82	60	74	67
Income before income taxes and extraordinary item	19.6	12.4	1.1	10.9	11.3
Income before extraordinary item	15.8	9.7	.6	8.4	8.5
Net income	15.8	9.7	.6	6.4	8.5

In explanation of the above, the following appeared in the text portion of the prospectus "under the bar" which usually separates the notes to the summary from the text of the prospectus:

Earnings were adversely affected in 1967 primarily due to a strike which interrupted all mining and smelting operations during a portion of the year, with a strike also interrupting fabricating operations in 1968. Although net sales increased in 1966, income before federal income taxes decreased, largely due to the mining of lower-grade ores with resultant lowering of copper production, to the costs incurred in the preparation for expanded White Pine production necessitated by the hiring and training of new personnel and the completion of development work in advance of normal schedule and to increased costs occasioned by the operation of the smelter at White Pine beyond its physical capacity and by some difficult conditions at the White Pine mine.

The prospectus of Lamb-Weston, Inc., dated October 1, 1969, included a statement of earnings (in lieu of a summary of earnings) for five fiscal years ended April 30, 1969 together with the three months ended July 31, 1968 and 1969. In fiscal 1967 sales were $24.8 million, an increase of almost $5 million from the volume of $20 million in fiscal 1966. Before taking into account the results of discontinued operations, the consolidated earnings were $291 thousand in fiscal 1967, a decline of almost $1 million from the earnings of $1,172 thousand in fiscal 1966.

In the narrative section of the prospectus, after the notes to the income statement, the company explained the poor results in fiscal 1967 as compared with fiscal 1966 in the face of the increase in sales. The explanation was as follows:

During the 1966 harvest, freezing weather damaged the Idaho potato crop. In order to obtain raw potatoes meeting its standards of quality, the Company purchased undamaged potatoes at high prices. Processable potatoes were available in greater quantity than the Company had anticipated, and other processors were able to purchase potatoes at lower prices. Market prices for finished potato products fell, and the Company was unable to recover the cost of its relatively high-priced potatoes. In the opinion of management, these factors were the primary cause of the decline in net earnings in fiscal 1967, and, together with a poor 1967 pea crop, also adversely affected fiscal 1968 earnings.

Philips Industries Inc. (not to be confused with the Dutch company of a similar name) is a major supplier to the mobile home and recreational vehicle industry and to the conventional home construction industry. Philips issued a prospectus in 1970 which contained a summary of earnings covering the five fiscal years ended March 31, 1970. During this period consolidated net sales (in millions) increased as follows: $66, $72, $85, $123, and $137. Net income increased during the first four years, but declined sharply in the most recent year, despite a substantial increase in sales. Net income in fiscal 1969 was $5,995,000, and $4,642,000 in fiscal 1970. The decline in net income was explained in a paragraph following the notes to the summary of earnings as follows:

Net income for fiscal 1970 was affected by the prevailing economic climate and by several internal operating problems. The Company, having prepared itself through a $19,400,000 capital expenditure program during the fiscal years ended March 31, 1969 and 1970 for a strong increase in mobile home and recreational vehicle production and for some stabilization in conventional home building, was faced with heavy fixed charges (including interest at higher rates) and new plant start-up costs that resulted in reduced earnings. Production of mobile homes and recreational vehicles in the last five months of fiscal 1970 did not meet expectations. In addition, the continued low level of conventional housing starts and the high cost of lumber seriously reduced the profit contribution from several of the subsidiaries directly serving the conventional housing market. Other factors that had a negative effect on net income during the past year included operating problems in the Company's Cucamonga, California plant and a six-week strike in the Dayton window plant. The Company was also faced throughout the year with higher material costs not fully covered by increases in selling prices of products.

Similarly, Inland Steel Company explained the drop in net income from $81 million in 1968 to $60 million in 1969, despite an increase in sales from $1,129 million in 1968 to $1,216 million in 1969. The company's 1970 prospectus furnished the following explanation: "The decrease in net income of the Company for 1969 as compared with 1968 is attributable to higher employment costs, work stoppages in certain iron ore and coal operations, increased costs of materials and services, shortages of production personnel, major maintenance problems, and increased provisions for depreciation and state and local taxes."

A prospectus of Apache Corporation dated August 27, 1970 contained capsule information for the first half of 1969 and 1970. This showed that revenues had increased from $33.5 million in 1969 to $45.9 in 1970. Income before extraordinary items, however, declined from $2,169,000 in 1969 to $1,828,000 in 1970. In explanation of the foregoing, the narrative section of the prospectus contained this information:

Total revenue increased in the first half of 1970 as a result of purchase acquisitions, notwithstanding significant revenue declines in several areas of business, particularly in the segment of the industrial division supplying the computer and aerospace industries and in the oil and gas division. Apache, like many other businesses, has been adversely affected by the economic slowdown as well as by higher interest rates. In addition, net income declined in the first half of 1970 as a result of the merger of NACC into a subsidiary of Continental Telephone Corporation, the Continental dividends received by Apache in 1970 being approximately $.06 per Apache share less than its portion of NACC's income included in the first half of 1969. The slowdown of automobile production and competitive conditions have also reduced profit margins in the metal service centers of Apache's industrial operations.

The prospectus of Clarkson Industries, Inc., dated March 28, 1968, included capsule information for the ten months ended February 29, 1968 and for the corresponding period of the preceding fiscal year. This information indicated that sales increased from $7.8 million to $8.5 million, but that net income declined from $448 thousand to $354 thousand. The company not only furnished an explanation for the decline in net income, but, for most of the items causing the decline, put a price tag on the causes. The company's explanation (in the narrative portion of the prospectus) follows:

The decline in consolidated net income for the ten months ended February 29, 1968, as compared to the ten months ended February 28, 1967, was attributable to increased labor and material costs, the costs of starting up a systems installation division (approximately $40,000 before income taxes), the costs of phasing in improvements to present product lines (approximately $70,000 before income taxes) and the start-up costs (approximately $75,000 before income taxes) incurred in the manufacture of newly developed filtration equipment.

INCREASE IN EARNINGS BUT DECLINE IN EARNINGS AS A PER CENT OF SALES.—Occasionally a company will report an increase in the amount of net income in the current period as compared with a previous period, but, *stated as a per cent of sales,* net income may have declined. A question may arise as to whether this is a situation that should be called to the investor's attention together with an explanation of the factors or circumstances which contributed to the increase in the absolute amount of net earnings in the face of a decrease in earnings stated as a per cent of sales. One explanation for this situation could be the "mix" of sales: in the current period there may have been an increase in the sales of products which are relatively less profitable, accompanied possibly by a decrease in sales of more profitable items.

There are no specific SEC requirements with respect to disclosing circumstances of this kind, and the author is not aware of any authoritative pronouncements in this area. To some extent, however, they may be brought to light in connection with the disclosures of "line of business" information in the narrative section of the registration statement (Item 9 of Form S–1, for example). The SEC's "line of business" requirements are discussed in Chapter **23**.

RECENT OR PROSPECTIVE COST INCREASES.—When a privately owned company "goes public," it is quite common to enter into new salary arrangements with management or to set up new profit sharing arrangements or pension plans. In that event, the additional costs to be incurred in the future are not reflected in the summary of earnings. These additional costs may be material and should be brought to the attention of the prospective investor. Complete information relating to the new arrangements is included elsewhere in the prospectus, and a cross-reference to this information in a note to the summary will ordinarily suffice to put the investor on notice.

If there has been a material wage increase in the latter part of the last year covered by the summary of earnings, and the wage increase has not been compensated by a corresponding increase in the selling price of the company's product or a decrease in other costs, a disclosure is frequently made of the wage increase. Usually this can be done by a cross-reference to the narrative portion of the prospectus that discloses recent wage increases. Even where there has been an increase in selling prices that appears to offset cost increases, a point to bear in mind is possible consumer resistance to increased selling prices, as well as the fact that a company may be pricing itself out of the market by raising the sales price of its product. Unless the company's competitors also raise their prices, the company may have to rescind the increase in its selling prices. In the 1956 prospectus of the Ford Motor Company the financial statements were as of September 30, 1955, and for the nine months then ended. The summary of earnings was followed by this paragraph:

> During 1955, there were increases in wages, salaries and other employee benefits and in prices for certain materials and components purchased by the company. The selling prices of the company's products were also increased during the year.

More recently, the prospectus of Uniroyal, Inc., dated April 3, 1971, commented on the continuing cost-price squeeze. The summary of earnings included the interim period of 39 weeks ended September 28, 1969 and September 27, 1970. Sales and operating revenues were about even in the two periods, but net income declined from $38 million in 1969 to $27 million in 1970. In the text of the prospectus, the company had this to say about the decline:

> Profits for the thirty-nine weeks ended September 27, 1970 were adversely affected by the continuing escalation of interest charges as well as sharply higher employment costs, transportation and other costs which were not absorbed completely through price increases or productivity improvements. In

addition, the General Motors Corporation strike, which started in mid-September, resulted in lower sales and forced production cutbacks in plants manufacturing tires and related products, industrial products and chemicals. General softness in the economy also adversely affected operations.

In the case of Jim Walter Corporation, the decline in earnings in 1970 as compared with 1969 was attributed largely to an increase in interest rates. The company's prospectus dated January 26, 1971 showed that sales and revenues had increased from $626 million in 1969 to $679 million in 1970. Despite this increase in sales and revenues, income before extraordinary items declined from $23.8 million in 1969 to $21.5 in 1970. Interest expense was $21.5 million in 1969 and $29.2 million in 1970. In the text of the prospectus, the company said that the decline in net income from 1969 to 1970 was due principally to higher effective interest rates and the general effects of reduced construction activity with resulting impairment of prices of certain company products.

If a wage increase is reflected for a full year (or almost a full year) in the summary of earnings, in the opinion of this author a disclosure of the increase need not be made. Depending on the circumstances, it also may not be necessary to refer to a wage increase that is reflected in full during all of the most recent interim period of the summary. This would seem to apply in the case of a company whose business is not subject to marked seasonal fluctuations, as, for example, many public utility companies.

The foregoing paragraphs relate largely to wage and interest increases, but the principle involved would be equally applicable to any other cost increases not compensated by corresponding increases in selling price or rates, or by a decrease in other costs. In the Potrero Sugar and Central Specialty cases discussed in Chapter 13, the SEC held that the failure to make similar disclosures of the type here discussed did not render the income statements misleading. It should be borne in mind, however, that these are old cases and there were then no SEC requirements applicable to summaries of earnings such as now exist in Form S–1.

One of the items of financial information that the SEC examiners watch carefully is selling, general, and administrative expenses—not only as an absolute amount but also as a relative amount based on net sales. In one case where there had been a continuous increase in the ratio of these expenses to sales and the registration statement contained no explanation or other information on the subject, the SEC said in its deficiency letter:

. . . The continuous increase in the ratio of selling, general and administrative expenses to net sales that has occurred during the past three years should receive appropriate comment.

Public utility companies frequently combine the disclosure of recent increases in operating costs with a disclosure of recent increases in their rates for service. A typical disclosure along these lines follows: "See page —— as to increased costs of operation and recent wage increases and page —— as to rates."

In *Faradyne Electronics Corporation* [40 SEC 1053 (1962)] (summarized on page **4·23**), a registration statement had been filed covering a proposed offering of convertible subordinated debentures at a total public offering price of $2,000,000. Of the proceeds, $1,200,000 was to be used to pay a non-interest bearing obligation. The replacement of the interest-free debt by interest-bearing obligations would result in additional costs of $78,000 per year plus amortization of the expenses of the offering. The SEC was not merely critical of the registrant for having failed to disclose the effect on income of the refinancing of its debt, but said: "Also making the summary of earnings materially misleading [was] the failure to present a pro forma earnings statement to reflect debenture interest chargeable to the replacement of the $1,200,000 interest-free obligation . . . with an interest-bearing obligation. . . ."

In one case with which the author is familiar, it was apparent from a note to the financial statements that the impact of federal income taxes on the earnings of the registrant would be much greater in the future than it had been in the past. The note in question indicated that several of the company's subsidiaries had been merged into the registrant subsequent to the date of the balance sheet, and the capital stock of another company had been contributed to the registrant by the owners thereof (who also owned all the stock of the registrant) and had thereby become a subsidiary. In its deficiency letter the SEC referred to this note and said:

It is assumed that the provision for income taxes shown on the summary of earnings represents the actual taxes for the five separate companies. If this is the case, it would appear that a note should be included to discuss the computation of the taxes on the basis of the new parent and subsidiary structure discussed in [note to the financial statements] and earnings per share recomputed on such basis and appropriately explained.

The summary of earnings was amended by adding a note indicating what net income and earnings per share would have been assuming the new structure had been in effect during the period of the summary.

RECENT REDUCTIONS IN SELLING PRICES OR RATES.—The preceding paragraphs give the requirements that, in the opinion of this author, are applicable where there has been a recent material increase in costs. There remains to be considered the related question where there have been material reductions in selling prices or rates that are not compensated by corresponding reductions in costs or expenses. The principle enunciated in the preceding paragraphs is also applicable here: If such reductions in selling prices or rates are material, are not reflected for approximately a year in the income statement or summary of earnings (or, as some suggest, for all of an interim period), and are not compensated by corresponding reductions in costs or expenses, that fact should be disclosed, either in a note to the summary or income statement or by cross-reference to the narrative section, if any, of the prospectus that deals with the matter.

UNUSUAL RELATIONSHIP OF TAXES TO PRE-TAX INCOME.—In some cases, the percentage relationship of income taxes to income before taxes may be so unusual as to require explanation or comment either in a note to the summary or in the text of the prospectus. This may be due to circumstances peculiar to a specific industry or because of a multiple corporation set-up with surtax benefits for each corporation, or a company whose income is based in large measure upon the lower capital gains rates.

In the case of a multi-corporate organization, if, upon the completion of the public offering, the corporation proposes to file subsequent tax returns upon a consolidated basis and thus lose valuable individual surtax benefits, according to the Chief Accountant of the SEC's Division of Corporation Finance, "this is required to be disclosed in an income statement note." [3]

An unusual relationship of taxes to pre-tax income could also exist in a consolidated income statement that includes foreign subsidiaries that enjoy tax relief over a limited period of years and which statement does not provide for federal income taxes if the income is distributed. In the last named situation, disclosure of the circumstances and the amounts of income involved would be required.

APB Opinion No. 11 recommends (in Paragraph 63) that disclosure be made of the reasons for significant variations in the customary relationships between income tax expense and pre-tax accounting income, if they are not otherwise apparent from the financial statements or from the nature of the entity's business.

The following is an example of a note dealing with income of a Puerto Rican subsidiary.

Under the Industrial Tax Exemption Act of 1948 of Puerto Rico and the Industrial Incentive Act of 1954 of Puerto Rico, (subsidiary) has been granted an exemption from income taxes for the period from (date) to (date). If the net income of (subsidiary) included in combined net income (periods and amounts) had been fully subject to income taxes in Puerto Rico, the resultant income taxes would have been approximately: (periods and amounts) and correspondingly the earnings per share would have been approximately: (periods and amounts).

A similar disclosure was furnished in the prospectus of Bzura Chemical Company, Inc. (1960). For the year 1959 the pre-tax earnings were

[3] Walter Mickelsen, "Recent Developments in the SEC Accounting Field", May 24, 1966.

$435,000 and the tax provision was $55,000. For the six months ended June 30, 1960 pre-tax earnings were $506,000, and the tax provision was only $600. The summary included a Bahamian affiliate organized in August, 1959, the income of which "is not considered to be taxable until distributed to its U. S. Shareholders," and no income tax was provided on the affiliate's income of $144,000 for 1959 and $434,000 for the first half of 1960. The company stated that it "intends to invest such earnings in foreign facilities and operations for the foreseeable future" and added that the company's sales arrangements with its affiliates are subject to review by the Internal Revenue Service.

Tenneco Corporation and its subsidiaries are engaged to a large extent in all phases of the petroleum industry; the companies are also engaged in other industries as well. A 1970 prospectus of Tenneco showed a very low relationship of income taxes to pre-tax earnings. In calendar year 1969, for example, the provision for Federal income taxes charged to income consisted of:

	Millions
Current provision before investment tax credit	$11.6
Investment tax credit (flow-through method)	(4.2)
Deferred provision	5.2
Total	$12.6

Pre-tax income in 1969 (before equity in undistributed earnings of 50% owned companies, outside stockholders' interest, and extraordinary items) was approximately $103 million. A note to the income statement included in the prospectus (in lieu of a summary of earnings) stated that Federal income taxes had been substantially reduced due to statutory depletion and deductions for exploration and development costs which were capitalized for financial statement purposes.

A 1970 prospectus of El Paso Natural Gas Company contained a similar note reading as follows: "Provision for federal income taxes has been substantially reduced during each of the periods because of certain deductions for tax purposes, principally intangible development costs capitalized on the books, and the excess of tax charges for depreciation over book charges on the regulated portion of El Paso's properties."

A 1970 prospectus of Denny's Restaurants, Inc. included a summary of earnings from which it appeared that the provision for Federal income taxes was low in relation to pre-tax income. The company explained in a note to the summary that this was due in part to multiple surtax exemptions arising out of the fact that the companies in the affiliated group filed separate tax returns, and in part to the availability of investment tax credits. The note follows:

The Company and each of its subsidiaries file separate income tax returns. The multiple surtax exemptions have resulted in provisions for federal income tax which were less than those which would have resulted had returns been filed on a consolidated basis. Federal income tax was reduced as a result of investment tax credits in the year realized, approximately as follows: $107,000 ($.02 per share) in 1965, $155,000 ($.02 per share) in 1966, $203,000 ($.03 per share) in 1967, $207,000 ($.03 per share) in 1968 and $231,000 ($.03 per share) in 1969. At June 27, 1969 various of the companies had unused investment tax credits aggregating approximately $353,000 (before consolidation of Imperial) which may be used to offset future federal income tax and which expire in different years for different companies through 1976. At March 31, 1969 Imperial had a tax net operating loss carryover of approximately $186,000 which may be used to offset future taxable income. Recently enacted tax legislation restricts investment credit carryforwards and eliminates in steps over the next six years, multiple surtax exemptions . . .

A 1970 prospectus of Ryder System, Inc. included a summary of earnings for the calendar years 1965–1969 and for the first quarters of 1969 and 1970. The company's accounting for investment tax credits had a material effect on the provision for taxes shown in the summary. Income taxes stated as a percentage of pre-tax income increased from about 34% in 1965 to about 40% in the first quarter of 1970. A note to the summary disclosed that the company recorded investment tax credits as reductions of the provision for Federal taxes (current and deferred) "to the extent that such credits are available and could have been utilized on the tax return if the taxes being deferred were paid currently." The note continued by showing the amounts by which the provisions for Federal income taxes have been so reduced, and stated that substantially all investment tax credits had been utilized as of March 31, 1970. In addition, a paragraph following the summary stated:

Prior to March 31, 1970, the Company's Federal income taxes were substantially reduced by application of investment tax credits . . . The investment tax credit was repealed in 1969, and as of March 31, 1970 the Company had used substantially all remaining investment tax credits. Therefore, assuming no change in the Federal tax laws or in the Company's operations, the effective Federal income tax rate applicable to the Company for the balance of 1970 and thereafter will be materially increased from that prevailing in prior periods.

DISCONTINUED OPERATIONS.—The matter of operations which have been discontinued will have to be considered in connection with the preparation of the summary of earnings. This subject is discussed in Chapter 13 and is equally applicable to summaries of earnings.

EFFECTS OF SEASONAL BUSINESS.—It was pointed out earlier in this chapter that where the summary of earnings includes data for a recent interim period, there must also be furnished the data for the corresponding interim period of the preceding fiscal year. (Special provisions are available for certain utility companies under which they may furnish statements for twelve months ending on an interim date.)

The operating results of many businesses depend, in some degree, on the time of the year. In department stores, for example, the period preceding Christmas is normally the most profitable of the entire fiscal year. In the months following the holiday season, the stores may operate on a break-even basis or even at a loss. For companies selling fans and air conditioners, the hot summer months give rise to the maximum sales activity and profits. For companies that sell home-heating oils, on the other hand, the cold winter months are the most profitable months. Most businesses are affected in some degree by seasonal factors. Even for automobile manufacturers and dealers, the sales volume in the last quarter of the calendar year (following the introduction of new models) is normally better than the volume in the succeeding quarter.

Many investors take the operating results for, say, six months and multiply them by two, thus arriving at their estimate of the results for a full year. They annualize the results of a three-month period by multiplying them by four. The result of this process is apt to be misleading in many cases and especially where the business is subject to seasonal influences. To guard against this tendency, it is important to consider whether the seasonal aspects of a business need to be disclosed or highlighted in any way in relation to financial statements of an interim period.

When the summary of earnings contains only full fiscal years, no particular emphasis is necessary as to the seasonal aspects of the operations. Some filings, however, have been made based on financial statements prior to the close of the fiscal year and generally after the peak season. In these cases the interim data are accompanied by data for the corresponding interim period of the preceding fiscal year. Referring to this kind of situation, a former Chief Accountant of the SEC's Division of Corporation Finance has said:

Although it may be argued that comparable interim periods highlight the seasonal trend, I am not sure that such a conclusion is obvious. As a result, when prior historical results show that the balance of the year . . . is normally a break-even or loss period, a specific statement to that effect is required.[4]

The author participated in the registration of an oil company. The company's fiscal year ended September 30, that being its natural business year since the company had a large business in light fuel oil for home heating. Interim statements for the most recent six months ended March

[4] Sydney C. Orbach, "Accounting Problems of First-Time Registration Statements," address before Georgia Society of CPAs, March 6, 1962.

31 were furnished together with corresponding interim figures for the preceding fiscal year. These amounts were referenced to a note which read as follows:

Because the company does a large volume of business in light fuel oil for home heating, the six month periods ended March 31 are normally the period of greatest sales volume. For this reason the results for such periods may not be indicative of the results of operations for an entire year.

In another case involving a company engaged in the business of making and selling fans and air conditioners, the following note was appended to the summary of earnings:

Owing to the seasonal nature of the fan and room air conditioner business, substantially all earnings historically have been earned during the first half of the fiscal year. Accordingly, the results for three month periods ended February 28 should not be taken as indicative of results for the balance of the year.

An example of the kind of disclosure that should be made occurred in the prospectus of a candy company. The summary of earnings covered five fiscal years ended January 31, and, in addition, the four month periods ended May 31, of the current and preceding fiscal years. A note to the summary was as follows:

Owing to the seasonal nature of the candy business, the results for the four months ended May 31, [year] are not necessarily indicative of the results for the balance of the fiscal year. Losses historically have occurred during the summer months.

The opposite picture was presented in the prospectus of a pharmaceutical manufacturer. The company's fiscal year is a calendar year. The summary of earnings covered five calendar years and, in addition, the first quarters of the current and preceding years. A note to the summary disclosed that the first quarter's sales normally were lower than those for the balance of the year, as follows:

Net sales are normally higher in October and November and reflect increased shipments (on extended payment terms—see "Borrowings" under "Business") to avoid freezing weather which damages the Company's main product. For the same reason, net sales in the first quarter of a year are usually lower than in the latter part of the year. Net sales by quarters for the years 1969 and 1970 and for the first quarter of 1971 were:

	1971	1970	1969
1st Quarter	$2,567,187	$2,106,428	$1,625,134
2nd Quarter	—	2,588,922	2,082,576
3rd Quarter	—	2,609,996	2,027,730
4th Quarter	—	4,089,076	3,289,151

The prospectus of a text book publisher contained the following note to its summary of earnings discussing the seasonal effect of its business:

The text book industry is highly seasonal. Considerably larger sales and earnings normally occur in the four months of June through September than in any other period of the year. The relationship of net earnings for the period ended August 31, 1969 to net earnings for the year ended December 31, 1969 will not necessarily be indicative of the relationship of net earnings for the corresponding interim 1970 period, as compared with a full fiscal year. See page _____ with respect to a comparison of sales for the two months ended October 31, 1970 with the two months ended October 31, 1969. Due to the seasonal nature of the company's business, net earnings for the full year of 1970 may not exceed those for the period ended August 31, 1970.

(The company's fiscal year was a calendar year and the period ended August 31 referred to above represented eight months.)

When figures are submitted for corresponding interim periods of two consecutive years, a point to bear in mind is that the periods may lack comparability for reasons other than seasonal influences. There may have been major differences in operations of the two periods that are not discernible from the figures themselves, but which should be disclosed in order to understand the significance of the amounts reported. An example is a note which appeared in the prospectus of an automobile manufacturer. The summary of earnings in the prospectus covered the nine-month periods ended September 30, of the current and preceding years. Referenced to such periods was the following note:

The change-over to new models occurred in different periods of 1965 and 1964. The costs and losses in production related to model change-over were incurred principally in the third quarter of 1965 and principally in the fourth quarter of 1964.

EFFECTS OF CASUALTY.—The prospectus of Keystone Alloys Company (1960) disclosed a decline in net sales in fiscal 1958 and fiscal 1959. Following the summary and as part of the text was the following paragraph:

Net sales as reported above for fiscal years ended February 1958 and 1959 were adversely affected by the total destruction by fire in October, 1957 of the company's facilities for the manufacture of aluminum siding, sales of which had previously accounted for approximately 33 per cent of net sales. Aluminum siding operations were not resumed on a full scale until the company's present modern plant was completed in November, 1958. It is impossible to determine the precise amount of the reduction in net income for fiscal 1958 and 1959 by reason of the fire, but it is the company's opinion that its net income for such years was substantially and adversely affected.

In a similar vein, the prospectus of an electric utility company contained a note to the summary of earnings disclosing the effects of a flood loss as follows:

Operation and maintenance expenses include approximately $_____ for costs of cleanup, repairs to property and restoration of service resulting from floods of [year].

Ratio of Earnings to Fixed Charges.—Form S–1 does not contain a mandatory requirement for showing the ratio of earnings to fixed charges. A registrant may, however, at its option, furnish such information in tabular form for each fiscal year or other period of the earnings summary (or income statement, if such statement is furnished in satisfaction of the requirements of the summary and formal income statement). (In some of the other registration forms—S–9, for instance—the showing of such ratio information is mandatory.) When Form S–1 is used, however, in connection with an offering of *debt securities,* the SEC's staff insists that the ratio information be disclosed at the bottom of the earnings summary or income statement.

If the ratio is shown, the pro forma ratio of earnings to fixed charges adjusted to give effect to the issuance of securities being registered and to any presently proposed issuance, retirement, or redemption of securities should be furnished for the latest fiscal year and interim periods, if any. The calculation of the ratio of earnings to fixed charges and the definition of "fixed charges" are discussed in Chapter **8**.

Any registrant electing to show the ratio of earnings to fixed charges must file as an exhibit to the registration statement a statement showing in reasonable detail the computations of such ratios.

In addition, if the prospectus is used in connection with an offering of *preferred stock or preference stock,* the SEC's staff further insists that there be shown at the bottom of the earnings summary or income statement the ratio of earnings to *fixed charges and preferred dividends combined* for each year or period of the summary in which preferred stock was outstanding. There are no formal requirements in any of the SEC forms for ratio data of this kind; the fact that it is called for nonetheless represents another example of the SEC's unpublished administrative requirements that have general application which registrants and their independent auditors learn about the hard way, that is, via the deficiency letter route. Chapter **8** also contains a discussion of the computation of this ratio. This ratio should also be furnished on a pro forma basis for the latest fiscal year and for the interim periods of the summary, if any. Also, an exhibit to the registration statement must show, in reasonable detail, the computation of the ratios.

Certification by Independent Public Accountants.—The SEC does not require earnings summaries in Form S–1 to be certified by independent public accountants. In practice, however, underwriters usually require that the summary of earnings be certified at least for that period (usually three years) which must be certified in the more detailed income statements required by SEC.

Where an accountant's name is used in connection with the summary

—to the effect that he has "reviewed" or "examined" the summary—the accountant's certificate must be furnished. ASR No. 62 provides, in substance, that if an accountant's name is used in connection with a summary, the accountant's certificate must be furnished. The release also provides that the accountant may not certify the summary of earnings unless the scope of his examination conformed to generally accepted auditing standards. For the form of certificate applicable to a summary of earnings, see the discussion in Chapter **24**.

Earnings summaries are frequently preceded by a headnote or other introductory material, the purpose of which is to inform the reader that the summary is certified or not certified by independent public accountants. For a discussion of this matter—particularly where the accountant qualifies his opinion as to the summary—see the discussion beginning on page **10·**4.

In a stop order proceeding involving American Trailer Rentals Company, a "summary of operations" had apparently been furnished to comply with the requirements for an income statement. The independent accountants reported that, because of the inadequacy of the company's records, they were unable to furnish an over-all opinion with respect to the "summary." For this reason, the Commission ruled that the "summary" did not meet its requirements. [41 SEC 544 (1963)].

Pro Forma Summaries.—The matter of pro forma summaries and pro forma adjustments to actual (or historical) summaries is considered in Chapter **21**.

Foreign Issuers.—For a discussion of the accounting problems of foreign issuers registering with the SEC under the 1933 Act, see Chapter **31**.

Earnings and Dividends Per Share of Common Stock.—The SEC's instructions for the earnings summary provide:

(a) If common stock is being registered, the summary must show the net income applicable to common stock; and

(b) In addition, the earnings per share of common stock and dividends declared per share for each period of the summary "unless inappropriate."

In May 1969 the APB issued its Opinion No. 15 on "Earnings per Share." One of the provisions of the Opinion is that earnings per share information must appear on the face of the income statement or summary of earnings, except in the case of those companies to which the Opinion, by its terms, does not apply (such as parent company statements when accompanied by consolidated statements, statements of wholly owned subsidiaries, special purpose statements, registered investment companies, mutual companies having no common stock outstanding, government corporations, and non-profit corporations). Accordingly, this information must be furnished in connection with earnings summaries to conform with APB pronouncements even though not required by the instructions for Form S-1 and regardless of whether common stock is being registered.

APB Opinion No. 15 is a long, complicated discussion of a difficult subject, made more complicated by the wide variety of unorthodox securities created during the 1960's. It is not the purpose of this book to repeat or summarize the provisions of that Opinion. Although the SEC concurs in the conclusions expressed in the Opinion, in its day-to-day work the SEC has indicated its views in a few areas that are not covered by the Opinion, and these are discussed below.

DILUTIVE EFFECT OF "CHEAP STOCK."—For the purpose of the following discussion, assume that The ABC Corporation has 700,000 shares of its common stock outstanding and is proposing to sell 100,000 additional shares. The corporation has no other senior securities outstanding, nor are there any options or warrants or any other agreements evidencing a present or future call on common stock. The public offering will be made through underwriters who will pay the corporation $9.50 per share for the additional shares and will reoffer such shares to the public at $10.00 per share. The underwriting discount or commission is 50 cents per share. However, as an additional inducement to the underwriters to enter into the transaction, the corporation agrees to sell the underwriters 10,000 additional shares at 25 cents a share. Stock sold under this kind of an arrangement is frequently called "cheap stock." For the block of 10,000 shares it is apparent that the proceeds to the corporation will be nominal as compared with the proceeds from the block of 100,000 shares.

In computing earnings per share, it is customary to base the calculation on the weighted average number of common shares and common share equivalents outstanding during the period (APB Opinion No. 15, paragraph 47). It is not customary to base the computation on the weighted average of common shares and common share equivalents outstanding *plus* the shares proposed to be issued. To do so would be manifestly incorrect for the reason that the reported earnings did not benefit from the proceeds of the shares proposed to be issued. There is also the justifiable presumption that the proceeds of the new shares will be profitably employed by the company, or there would be no useful purpose in proceeding with the proposed offering of such shares.

In the example cited, if there were no changes in capitalization during the period covered by the summary of earnings, the earnings per share would be computed for each period by dividing the earnings of the period by 700,000—not by 800,000.

The SEC, however, takes a different view with respect to "cheap stock" to be sold to the underwriters by the company. The proceeds of such stock would be nominal and on issuance there would be an immediate dilution of per share earnings. In cases of this kind, the SEC has requested that earnings per share be computed taking into account the dilution arising from the issuance of "cheap stock." In a typical case, the SEC's comment was: "Since the company sold shares to the underwriter at a nominal price, it appears that these shares should be included in the base (710,000) to determine earnings per share."

In these circumstances, in the opinion of the author, the primary earnings per share data should be furnished in the customary manner, and should be supplemented by additional earnings per share data based on the weighted average of shares actually outstanding during the period *plus* the shares issued to underwriters for nominal consideration.

One possible way of avoiding this problem is this: instead of buying the "cheap stock" from the company, the underwriter can arrange to buy such shares directly from a principal shareholder. In that case there would be no dilution in earnings per share and no need to make the supplementary representation referred to above.

DILUTIVE EFFECT OF STOCK TO BE ISSUED TO RETIRE DEBT.—Under "Application of Proceeds" or a similar caption, a prospectus may disclose that the entire proceeds from the issuance of capital stock will be used to retire outstanding debt of the company. In that event the company's operating results will be improved to the extent of the reduction or elimination of interest expense less the related tax effect. On the other hand, because of the increase in shares to be outstanding, the improvement in operating results may be accompanied by a decline in earnings *per share.*

In one case with which the author is familiar, the entire proceeds from the sale of common stock were to be used to reduce non-interest-bearing debt owing to the sole stockholder of the issuer. In that case the reduction of the debt would result in no improvement in net income, and the *per share* earnings would necessarily decline. In its letter of comment the SEC said, "In view of the fact that the entire proceeds from the offering will be used to reduce the advances from [sole stockholder], it is the opinion of this Division that an additional line showing pro forma earnings per share based on the dilutive effect resulting from the total of [number] shares of Common Stock to be outstanding should be included."

In cases such as the foregoing, in addition to showing the actual earnings per share, it is often desirable to supplement this information to show earnings per share adjusted for the dilution arising from the offering—in other words, what the earnings per share would have been for the latest fiscal year and any subsequent interim period presented if the retirement had taken place at the beginning of the respective periods. The number of shares of common stock whose proceeds are to be used to retire the debt should be included in the computation, and the bases of the supplementary computations should be disclosed.

STOCK SPLIT IN THE FORM OF A SALE OF SHARES HAVING NO RELATION TO MARKET VALUE.—APB Opinion No. 15 discusses the situation involving a stock split, a stock dividend, or a reverse split. If the number of shares of common stock outstanding increases as the result of a stock split or stock dividend, or decreases as the result of a reverse split, the computation of earnings per share should give retroactive recognition to an appropriate equivalent change in capital structure for all periods presented in the summary of earnings.

An interesting variation of the split-up problem is presented in the case of companies that sell common stock to their shareholders at a price which bears no relation to the market value of the shares. Especially in the case of foreign issuers, it is not unusual to sell new shares at their par value even though the market value may be many times the par value. In essence, the transaction has all the earmarks of a split-up accompanied by the raising of some additional capital. This situation was considered in a prospectus of Sony Corporation (1963). A note following the summary of earnings explained the computation of earnings per share as follows:

(C) The Company, in keeping with customary practice in Japan, has made several issues of common stock through subscription offerings to existing stockholders at par value which has always been less than the market price at the time of issuance. For purposes of computing the above amounts per share, a portion of the shares issued pursuant to each subscription offering has been considered as a stock split. The portion of the shares issued not considered as a stock split is the number of shares that the Company would have had to issue at an estimated normal public offering price, at the time each subscription offering was announced, to raise a comparable amount of new equity capital; in estimating the normal public offering price, no effect has been given to changes in market price from the date of announcement to the date of issuance. The computation of the above amounts per share has been based on the average number of shares outstanding during each period, appropriately adjusted for the stock split portion of the subscription offerings consummated in 1958, 1959 and 1961, the latter including the concurrent free distribution, all as described under "Common Stock Distributions" elsewhere in this Prospectus. The above per share amounts do not reflect the one-for-five free distribution of shares proposed to be made to stockholders of record on April 30, 1963, including the holders of the shares of Common Stock offered hereby. Net income and cash dividends per American Depositary Share (each representing ten shares of

Common Stock) for the year ended October 31, 1962, if such free distribution were reflected, would be ¥222.8 (*61.9¢*) and ¥104.2 (*28.9¢*), respectively.

"EQUATED" EARNINGS PER SHARE.—When it is proposed to combine the businesses of two or more publicly-owned companies—whether in the form of a merger, consolidation, acquisition, or otherwise—the companies often ask their respective security holders to approve the transaction. In that connection, proxies are solicited, and if the proxy solicitations are subject to SEC rules, proxy statements are prepared as discussed in Chapter **22**.

For the purpose of the discussion which follows, assume that Company A proposes to acquire the business of Company X. The proposal contemplates that A will issue a block of its common shares to X which will liquidate and distribute to its shareholders the shares of A. If the transaction is consummated, one share of X will become five shares of A; this is the "exchange ratio." Assume also that the transaction qualifies for "pooling of interests" treatment as discussed in Chapter **21**.

Ordinarily in these circumstances the proxy statement of each company will contain historical financial statements (including income statements and/or earnings summaries) of each constituent, and, in addition, pro forma combined statements prepared on the assumption that the combination had been in effect for several years—usually five years. The earnings summaries (or income statements) will show earnings per share for each company and, on a pro forma basis, for the combined enterprise.

In the case of a shareholder of X, it may not be enough to show the earnings applicable to one share of X and to one share of the combined enterprise. His one share of X will become five shares of the combined enterprise. Consequently, in addition to showing the historical earnings applicable to one share of X, the SEC requires that there be shown the earnings per share "equated to a common basis," which, in this case, represents the earnings applicable to five shares of the combined enterprise. In that way, the shareholder of X will be able to compare the earnings applicable to his present holdings as against the earnings applicable to his future holdings if the proposed transaction is consummated.

There are several ways of presenting equated earnings per share. One way of presenting the information is in a tabulation in the narrative section of the proxy statement along the following lines:

The following table reflects the historical earnings per share of Company X for the periods indicated. The table also sets forth the pro forma combined earnings applicable to five shares of Company A common stock to be exchanged for each share of capital stock of Company X upon liquidation of Company X after consummation of the transactions contemplated by the merger agreement.

Comparative Historical and Pro Forma Earnings per Share:

	19—	19—	19—	19—	19—
Company X (historical)	$	$	$	$	$
Pro forma combined earnings applicable to five shares of Company A	$	$	$	$	$

Another way of presenting equated earnings per share is to state the earnings of both companies involved and the pro forma combined results in terms of the *same unit of measure*. To accomplish this, the earnings of each of the companies being pooled are stated in terms of the number of shares of the *surviving* company which are issued to acquire the earnings of each such company. To illustrate, assume that Company P has outstanding 100,000 shares and that Company P is going to issue 50,000 shares to acquire Company Q making a total of 150,000 shares of Company P outstanding after the pooling. Earnings per share of the two companies would be presented for comparative purposes as follows:

Comparative Historical and Pro Forma Earnings per Share:

	19—	19—	19—	19—	19—
Earnings of Company P (based on 100,000 shares outstanding)	$	$	$	$	$
Earnings of Company Q (based on 50,000 shares of Company P to be issued therefor)	$	$	$	$	$
Pro forma combined earnings (based on 150,000 shares to be outstanding)	$	$	$	$	$

In the above tabulation, the earnings of each of the constituents are stated in terms of shares of Company P as a common unit of measurement. Thus, stockholders of Company P can readily see what they are contributing to the pooled enterprise in relation to what the stockholders of Company Q are contributing. Similarly, the stockholders of Company Q can readily evaluate their contribution of earnings to the combined enterprise in relation to the earnings being contributed by Company P. And the stockholders of both companies can compare what they have before the pooling with what they will have after the pooling.

Either of the two foregoing presentations appears to be acceptable to the SEC in proxy statements covering most mergers. The first illustration (Company X and Company A) is probably more widely used where only one of the two companies being pooled is required to solicit proxies for stockholder approval. On the other hand, the latter of the two presentations would appear to have greater merit where the stockholders of both companies being pooled are called upon to approve the transaction by means of a proxy statement.

Form S–8

The requirements for a summary of earnings in a registration statement on Form S–8 are contained in Item 19 of the form.

The summary must be in comparative columnar form and must cover a representative period but at least each of the last five fiscal years of the issuer (or the life of the issuer and its immediate predecessor if the issuer has been in business less than five years).

If the issuer's annual report to the SEC (Form 10–K, for example) contains an income statement on a consolidated basis, then the summary of earnings in Form S–8 must also be on a consolidated basis.

The summary must be certified by independent public accountants for at least the last three fiscal years included in the summary.

The items of information to be included in a Form S–8 summary are the same as those in a Form S–1 summary; see page **10·9**. The instructions applicable to the Form S–8 summary are similar to those applicable to Form S–1 insofar as they relate to retroactive adjustments, necessary information and explanations, and earnings and dividends per share; see the discussion earlier in this chapter concerning Form S–1 summaries.

When earnings per share information is furnished pursuant to the requirements of APB Opinion No. 15, the information with respect to the computation of per share earnings on both primary and fully diluted bases must be furnished to the SEC by exhibit or otherwise even though the amounts of per share earnings on the fully diluted basis are not required to be stated under APB Opinion No. 15. That Opinion provides that any reduction of less than 3% need not be considered as dilution (footnote to paragraph 14 of the Opinion) and that a computation on the fully diluted basis which results in an improvement of earnings per share not be taken into account (paragraph 40 of the Opinion) (Release No. 33–5133, Feb. 18, 1971).

If the published annual report to stockholders which must accompany the prospectus contains a summary of earnings which substantially meets the SEC's requirements, such summary may be incorporated by reference in the prospectus.

See page **9·3** for a statement of the Commission's policy regarding the need to update financial statements (including the summary of earnings) in certain circumstances.

Form S–11

Form S–11 is used for the registration of securities issued by real estate investment trusts or by other issuers whose business is primarily investing, directly or indirectly, in real estate. The requirements for the summary of earnings are set forth in Item 6 of the form.

The summary is to be furnished in comparative columnar form for the registrant, or for the registrant and its subsidiaries consolidated, or both, as appropriate. See the discussion of this requirement in relation to Form S–1 on page **10·5** where it is stated that, if a consolidated summary of earnings is furnished, it is rarely necessary to supply also a summary for the parent company.

The summary must be furnished for each of the last five fiscal years of the registrant (or for the life of the registrant if less) and for any interim period between the end of the latest of such fiscal years and the date of the latest balance sheet furnished, and for the corresponding interim period of the preceding fiscal year. Comparable data must also be included for any additional fiscal years of the registrant or its immediate predecessors necessary to keep the summary from being misleading or to cover the total period specified.

Subject to appropriate variation to conform to the nature of the business or the purpose of the offering, the summary must include: rental income, mortgage interest income, management fees, operating expenses, real estate taxes, depreciation, interest expenses, other income, income taxes, and net income. Realized gain or loss on investments must be shown as a separate item after net operating income.

The summary does not have to be certified. If, however, the summary is furnished in sufficient detail so that it meets the requirements for the statements of income and realized capital gain or loss on investments, and the latter statements are therefore omitted from the registration statement, then the summary must be certified for that portion of the over-all period to which the certification requirements are applicable. See the discussion below if the registrant was organized to acquire property for investment.

The instructions provide that any unaudited summary for an interim period shall be prepared on a basis consistent with the summary for annual periods. In connection with any unaudited summary for an interim period, a statement must be made that all adjustments necessary to a fair presentation of the results for such period have been made. If all such adjustments are of a normal recurring nature, a statement to that effect must be made; otherwise, there must be furnished as supplemental information, but not as a part of the registration statement, a letter describing in detail the nature and amount of any adjustments, other than normal recurring adjustments, entering into the determination of the results shown.

If common stock is being registered, the summary must show earnings applicable to common stock. Per share earnings and distributions for each period of the summary must also be shown and the basis of computation and the status for federal income tax purposes stated.

When per share earnings are disclosed, the information with respect to the computation of per share earnings on both primary and fully diluted bases must be furnished to the SEC by exhibit or otherwise even though the amounts of per share earnings on the fully diluted basis are not required to be stated under the provisions of APB Opinion No. 15. That Opinion provides that any reduction of less than 3% need not be considered as dilution (footnote to paragraph 14 of the Opinion) and that a computation on the fully diluted basis which results in improvement of earnings per share not be taken into account (paragraph 40 of the Opinion) (Release No. 33–5133, Feb. 18, 1971).

If debt securities are being registered, the registrant must show for each year or period, the ratio of earnings to fixed charges. The computation of the ratio and the definition of "fixed charges" are discussed in Chapter **8**. The pro forma ratio of earnings to fixed charges adjusted to give effect to the issuance of securities being registered and to any presently proposed issuance, retirement, or redemption of securities must also be shown for the latest fiscal year and for the interim periods, if any. An exhibit to the registration statement must be filed setting forth in reasonable detail the computation of such ratios.

If preferred stock is being registered, the annual dividend requirements on such stock must be stated. In addition, there must be shown for each year or period of the summary the ratio of earnings to *fixed charges and preferred dividends combined* for each year or period of the summary in which preferred stock was outstanding. The ratio should also be furnished on a pro forma basis for the latest fiscal year and for the interim periods, if any. The computation of these ratios is discussed in Chapter **8**. An exhibit to the registration must show the computation of the ratios in reasonable detail.

The SEC's instructions applicable to the Form S–11 summary are similar to those in Form S–1 insofar as they relate to retroactive adjustments, and necessary information and explanations: much of the discussion beginning on page **10·11** is also applicable here.

If the registrant was organized to acquire and hold primarily for investment one specific property or group of properties, the following must be furnished in lieu of the summary of earnings requirements set forth above:

(1) An historical summary of operations for the period specified above (that is, a minimum of five years plus an interim period) which will exclude items not comparable to the proposed future operation of the property, such as mortgage interest, leasehold rental, depreciation, corporate expenses, and federal and state income taxes. Earnings per unit must not be given in this summary. The three most recent fiscal years of this summary must be certified.

With respect to this certification requirement, the Chief Accountant of the SEC's Division of Corporation Finance observed in a speech in 1966 that ". . . we are besieged with requests for waivers of this requirement." [4] He said that these circumstances result in delays which could be avoided if arrangements for certified statements were made at the time of acquisition.

(2) If the property is to be operated by the registrant, a statement must be submitted showing the estimated taxable operating results of the registrant based on the most recent twelve-month period including such adjustments as can be factually supported. If the property is to be acquired subject to a net lease, the estimated taxable operating results must be based on the rent to be paid for the first year of the lease. In either case the estimated amount of cash to be made available by operations must be shown. The principal assumptions which have been made in preparing the statements of estimated taxable operating results and cash to be made available by operations must be stated in an introductory paragraph.

(3) If appropriate under the circumstances, there must be given in tabular form for a limited number of years the estimated cash distribution per unit showing the portion thereof reportable as taxable income and the portion representing a return of capital together with an explanation of annual variations, if any. If taxable net income per unit will become greater than the cash available for distribution per unit, that fact and the approximate year of occurrence must be stated if significant.

Form S–14

When a company registered under the Securities Exchange Act of 1934 solicits proxies in connection with a proposed merger, it must comply with the SEC's Regulation 14A (the proxy regulation) under the 1934 Act. In most mergers the transaction is exempt from registration under the 1933 Act because of Rule 133 [5] under that Act. In some cases, however, persons

[4] Walter Mickelsen, "Recent Developments in the SEC Accounting Field," May 24, 1966.

[5] Paragraph (a) of Rule 133 follows:

(a) For purposes only of section 5 of the Act, no "sale," "offer," "offer to sell," or "offer for sale" shall be deemed to be involved so far as the stockholders of a corporation are concerned where, pursuant to statutory provisions in the State of incorporation or provisions contained in the certificate of incorporation, there is submitted to the vote of such stockholders a plan or agreement for a statutory merger or consolidation or reclassification of securities, or a proposal for the transfer of assets of such corporation to another person in consideration of the issuance of securities of such other person or securities of a corporation which owns stock possessing at least 80 percent of the total combined voting power of all classes of stock entitled to vote and at least 80 percent of the total number of shares of all other classes of stock of such other person, under such circumstances that the vote of a required favorable majority (1) will operate to authorize the proposed transaction as far as concerns the corporation whose stockholders are voting (except for the taking of action by the directors of the corporation involved and for compliance with such statutory provisions as the filing of the plan or agreement with the appropriate State authority), and (2) will bind all stockholders of such cor-

who later participate in the distribution of the securities may be "underwriters." Registration is then necessary because the "underwriter" must be in a position to furnish a statutory prospectus. Form S–14 is an optional form that was designed to simplify registration in such circumstances. The form is restricted to securities issued in a Rule 133 transaction which may be offered to the public by "underwriters" as defined in the rule.

In practice, the registration usually consists of little more than a wrapper surrounding a proxy statement. Form S–14 does not call for a summary of earnings. If the proxy statement, however, contained a summary, the Form S–14 registration will, of necessity, also contain a summary. The information (including financial statements) in the proxy statement must be current in terms of the requirements of the appropriate registration form, other than Form S–14, at the time the registration statement is filed. The financial statements included in the proxy statement must include statements of each constituent corporation meeting the requirements of such appropriate registration form at the time of filing the registration statement, unless and to the extent that the SEC determines in a particular case that the furnishing of other financial statements "would not be inappropriate."

Forms 10 and 10–K

One of the recommendations made in the 1969 report entitled "Disclosure to Investors—A Reappraisal of Federal Administrative Policies under the '33 and '34 Acts" (often referred to as "The Wheat Report") was the elimination of the requirement in Form 10 for a three-year income statement and the substitution therefore of a five-year summary of earnings similar to the summaries contained in 1933 Act registration statements. The Commission accepted part of the recommendation in the Wheat Report and rejected the other part: it revised Form 10 in 1970 by including a new requirement for a five-year "summary of operations," but retained the requirement for a three-year income statement. The Commission used the title "summary of operations" in the revised Form 10, but, as will be seen, the content of the summary is the same as in a summary of earnings.

The Wheat Report also recommended that Form 10–K annual reports be revised to include each year a five-year summary of earnings. This recommendation was also adopted, and in 1970 the Commission revised Form 10–K to include a new requirement for a "summary of operations" covering a five-year period.

As a consequence of the actions taken by the Commission, a running

poration except to the extent that dissenting stockholders may be entitled, under statutory provisions or provisions contained in the certificate of incorporation, to receive the appraised or fair value of their holdings.

five-year summary of operations will be publicly available at all times with respect to every company that is registered on Form 10 or that reports annually on Form 10–K.

In Form 10 the requirements for the summary are set forth in Item 2; in Form 10–K the requirements for the summary are also set forth in Item 2. The requirements are identical in both forms except as indicated in the paragraph following and except for minor variations in language caused by the fact that in Form 10 the instructions necessarily refer to "registration statement," whereas in Form 10–K the corresponding instructions refer to "report." Since the requirements are, for all practical purposes, identical, this discussion will concern itself primarily with Form 10, but the reader will understand that it applies equally to Form 10–K.

In relation to a summary in Form 10–K, there are special SEC instructions which are quoted below:

Describe any change in accounting principles or practices followed by the registrant, or any change in the method of applying any such accounting principles or practices, which will materially affect the financial statements filed or to be filed for the current year with the Commission and which had not been previously reported hereunder. State the date of the change and the reasons therefor. A letter from the registrant's independent accountants, approving or otherwise commenting on the change, shall be filed as an exhibit.

(The above instruction reflects a revision in Form 10–K made in 1971. Similar revisions were also made at the same time in Forms 7–Q and 10–Q.)

The Form 10 instructions call for a summary of operations in comparative columnar form "for the registrant, or for the registrant and its subsidiaries consolidated, or both, as appropriate." This is the same as the SEC's requirements applicable to Form S–1. As indicated in this chapter in connection with the discussion of Form S–1, if a consolidated summary is furnished, seldom—if ever—does the Commission request that a summary also be furnished for the registrant alone.

The period to be covered by the Form 10 summary is:

(a) Each of the last five fiscal years of the registrant (or for the life of the registrant and its predecessors, if less), and

(b) Any additional fiscal years necessary to keep the summary from being misleading.

As compared with the corresponding requirements in Form S–1, it will be noted that in Form 10 there is no requirement for "stub" periods, that is, interim periods from the close of the latest fiscal year to a recent date. This is due to the fact that whereas S–1 calls for balance sheets as of a date within 90 days of filing (as of a date within six months of filing in the case of certain large companies), there is no similar requirement in Form 10.

The minimum period to be covered by the summary is five years. If the summary is limited to five years and gives a misleading picture, additional fiscal years have to be added so that it will not be misleading. This subject is discussed in this chapter in relation to Form S–1.

Where necessary, the summary must include information or explanation of material significance to investors in appraising the results shown in the summary, or reference may be made to such information or explanation set forth elsewhere in the registration statement.

An analysis of retained earnings and other additional capital accounts has to be furnished for each fiscal year covered by the summary. The author understands that the words "other additional capital accounts" is intended to be limited to capital surplus accounts and not to include capital stock accounts. (In APB Opinion No. 12, paragraph 10, however, it is stated that changes in the separate accounts comprising stockholders' equity and changes in the number of shares of equity securities during at least the most recent annual fiscal period and any subsequent interim period presented is required to be disclosed when both financial position and results of operations are shown.)

Subject to appropriate variation to conform to the nature of the business, the following items of information have to be included in the summary: net sales or operating revenues; cost of goods sold or operating expenses (or gross profit); interest charges; income taxes; income before extraordinary items; extraordinary items; and net income. This subject is also commented upon in connection with the discussion of the S–1 summary requirements.

If either the income statement or the retained earnings statement called for by the instructions for financial statements in Form 10 are included in their entirety in the summary of operations, the statements so included need not be included elsewhere in the Form 10 registration statement.

If a period or periods reported on in the summary include operations of a business prior to the date of acquisition (in the case of poolings of interest, for instance) or for other causes differ from reports previously issued for any period, the summary has to be reconciled as to sales or revenues and net income in the summary or by footnote with the amounts previously reported.

Following is an example showing how one company reconciled the reported sales and net income in a summary of earnings with the amounts previously reported. In this case the changes in the previously reported figures were due entirely to the acquisition of companies during the period covered by the summary in transactions that were accounted for as poolings of interest:

	Year 1	Year 2	Year 3	Year 4	Year 5
Net sales:					
The ABC Corp. and subsidiaries as previously reported	$	$	$	$	$
Businesses acquired in poolings of interest—sales prior to year first included	$	$	$	$	$
As revised	$	$	$	$	$
Net income:					
The ABC Corp. and subsidiaries as previously reported	$	$	$	$	$
Businesses acquired in poolings of interest—net income prior to year first included	$	$	$	$	$
As revised	$	$	$	$	$

The question may be raised as to whether such reconciliations, once included in a document filed with the SEC, need to be repeated in subsequent filings. The author understands that the SEC's staff has taken the position that reconciliations relating to restatements resulting from poolings of interest will have to be repeated in all filings until the years restated are no longer required in the summary; reconciliations relating to restatements arising from other causes will not have to be repeated. The reasoning underlying this distinction is not clear to the author.

The SEC's instructions provide that if appropriate, the summary is to show earnings applicable to common stock. Per share earnings and dividends declared for each period of the summary is to be included and the basis of the computation stated together with the number of shares used in the computation. In addition, the registrant has to file as an exhibit a statement setting forth in reasonable detail the computation of per share earnings.

Where per share earnings are disclosed, the information with respect to the computation of per share earnings on both primary and fully diluted bases, presented by exhibit or otherwise, must be furnished even though the amounts of per share earnings on the fully diluted basis are not required to be stated under the provisions of APB Opinion No. 15. That Opinion provides that any reduction of less than 3% need not be considered as dilution (footnote to paragraph 14 of the Opinion) and that a computation on the fully diluted basis which results in improvement of earnings per share not be taken into account (paragraph 40 of the Opinion). (Release No. 34–9083, Feb. 18, 1971.)

If the Form 10 registration statement covers debt securities, the registrant may, at its option, show in tabular form for each fiscal year the ratio of earnings to fixed charges. The calculation of the ratio of earnings to fixed charges and the definition of "fixed charges" are discussed in Chapter

8. If a registrant elects to show the ratio of earnings to fixed charges, it must file as an exhibit to Form 10 a statement setting forth in reasonable detail the computations of the ratios shown.

The SEC does not require the summary of operations to be certified by independent public accountants. If the summary is furnished in sufficient detail so that it satisfies the requirement for the three-year income statement (which does have to be certified) called for by Form 10 and the latter statement is consequently omitted, it (the summary) has to be certified for a minimum of three years. In the case of such a detailed summary included in Form 10–K in satisfaction of the requirements for the required certified two-year income statement, the summary has to be certified for a minimum of two years.

Proxy Statements

The subject of proxy statements is considered in Chapter **22**. As stated in that chapter, proxy statements—particularly those relating to proposed merger transactions—often contain summaries of earnings. For a discussion of such summaries in proxy statements, see the discussion of Item 14 of Schedule 14A on page **22**·13.

CHAPTER 11

REGISTRATION PROCEDURE UNDER THE 1933 ACT

Part 1. Preliminary Considerations

CONTENTS

At the beginning of an engagement involving the filing of a registration statement under the 1933 Act, a number of matters deserve consideration by the independent public accountant.

Independence of the Certifying Accountants.—The independence of the certifying accountants is discussed at length in Chapter **26**. This matter is one which should receive attention early in the engagement. In several registration statements filed with the SEC it developed that the certifying accountants were not independent as required by the Commission's rules. In one case [18 SEC Ann. Rep. 15 (1952)] the certifying accountant was also treasurer, director, and a stockholder of the registrant. Any one of these relationships is sufficient to disqualify an accountant under the Commission's definition of an independent accountant. The disqualification of the accountant resulted in needless expense because of having to engage other auditors and the consequent delay in the effective date.

Pre-Filing Check Lists

Review of SEC Requirements.—The accountant should review with his client the SEC requirements relating to the financial section of the registration statement. The accountant should show his client the amount of information that must be included in the financial statements, and the period that must be covered by the financial statements. Some companies are reluctant to disclose their sales and cost of sales. They may have no objection to giving this information privately to the SEC but would be distressed at the thought of having the information fall into the hands of competitors or customers. This is understandable, but the prospective registrant ought to know at the outset that the information *must be furnished in the registration statement*—not privately to the SEC—and that the registration statement is a public document. When it is filed, it is possible that competitors will obtain a copy of the document and will read every word in it even though prospective investors may not. This fact alone may have an important bearing on the client's decision whether or not to go ahead with the project.

The company may have limited the scope of the auditor's examination in the past because there was no need for fully certified statements. If the auditor points out to the prospective registrant that he must now furnish fully certified statements because they are required by the SEC, the client may decide that the cost of the project is out of proportion to the benefits. See also the comment in Chapter **9** regarding the need for furnishing certified financial statements of acquired businesses in certain circumstances for periods prior to their acquisition, and the comment on page **10·52**—concerning registration statements on Form S–11 where certified financial information may have to be furnished in respect of the operations by prior owners of real properties acquired or to be acquired.

The client may have been borrowing substantial sums from his own business rather than paying out the funds in the form of dividends. He may be thinking of repaying his loans, thereby dressing up his company's balance sheet. He may be under the impression that there will be no need to disclose that he has been using the company as a private bank. The auditor should point out to him that the repayment of the loan will not result in concealing either the borrowing or the repayment. One of the supporting schedules called for by Regulation S–X (Schedule II) calls for information of this kind year by year for a minimum of three years even though there is no balance due at the end of the period.

Review of Accounting Principles.—The CPA should also review with his client, or the client's controller, the accounting principles followed by the company. It is no secret that the accounting principles followed by many privately owned companies are based on the legitimate desire to minimize taxes. This does not include deliberate understatements of inventories, which are tantamount to fraud. The author refers rather to those things which a business can legitimately do which have the immediate effect of reducing taxes. Many of these devices merely postpone the taxes but, at least for the period of the postponement, the company in effect has an interest-free loan from the government.

The company may have been following in its accounts one of the accelerated depreciation methods permitted by the Internal Revenue Code. For the purposes of the prospectus there is no necessity that the same depreciation methods be followed.

On the other hand, the company may have been following an accounting practice which has never been challenged by the tax authorities, but which is not acceptable for published statement purposes. For example, the company, with the knowledge of the tax authorities, may have been omitting all overhead from its inventories. Ordinarily, if inventories are relatively stable from year to year, the omission of overhead may have no material effect on the income statement, and it may also have no material effect on the balance sheet. On the other hand, if it does have an important effect on either financial statement, it will not suffice merely to disclose in the prospectus that overhead has been omitted, since the omission is wrong in principle. It is a fundamental rule in SEC work that disclosure of an improper accounting practice will not obviate the need for correcting the statement if the matter involved is material; the statements will have to be appropriately corrected. (See the discussion in Chapter **2** regarding ASR No. 4.) To adjust the statement may be time-consuming and costly. Furthermore, the management may feel that the adjustment of inventories to include overhead may create serious tax consequences. There can be no better reason why the accountant and his client should know about these problems before the SEC engagement gets under way.

The Timetable.—Before the detailed work in connection with the preparation of a registration statement is begun, a timetable is often prepared (usually by counsel) for the guidance of all concerned with the registration. Sometimes in great detail, sometimes in less detail, the timetable shows the steps which are to be taken to consummate the proposed offering. The timetable also shows the dates on which it is planned to accomplish each of the steps listed.

The independent public accountant who certifies the financial statements included in the registration document has an important part in accomplishing the desired objective. A copy of the timetable is usually given to him and should be obtained by him in all cases. The accountant should review the timetable, noting carefully those dates which are of immediate concern to him, such as the date on which it is proposed to file the registration statement, the date on which the SEC's deficiency letter is expected to be received, the date on which it is planned to file the substantive amendment (curing the SEC's deficiencies and bringing the registration statement up to date because of changed conditions since the original filing date), the date of the due diligence meeting, and the date on which it is expected that the registration statement will become effective. All of these dates are important to the accountant in planning his work relating to the engagement.

Frequently the timetable is prepared in collaboration with the certifying accountant. If, however, the accountant did not help prepare it, he should make it a point to see whether, as far as he is concerned, the dates listed are within his ability to meet them. The author has known cases where the timetable had to be revised because those who prepared it were not adequately informed as to the time required to make an audit.

In a typical case the timetable would resemble the one appearing in Appendix B. This timetable was prepared by a corporation which proposed (1) to solicit proxies from stockholders approving an increase in the amount of authorized common stock; and (2) to offer its common stockholders the right to subscribe to additional shares of common stock, the unsubscribed shares being taken up by underwriters.

Importance of Reading the Registration Statement.—The accountant who participates in the preparation of a registration statement is concerned primarily with the examination of the financial data to which his certificate relates. He should make it a rule, however, to read carefully the entire registration statement—not merely the financial data. There are several reasons for this.

1. The accountant is interested in making sure that the representations in the so-called "narrative" section of the registration do not conflict with the representations in the financial section. If there are such conflicts, obviously they must be resolved. The conflicts are not always resolved before the registration statement is filed and, because of this, "it is frequently necessary to request supplemental information reconciling disclosures in various sections of the prospectus." [1] As an example, Item 12 in a Form S–1 registration statement calls for information in respect of material pending legal proceedings to which the registrant or any of its subsidiaries is a party or of which any of their property is the subject. This is a matter concerning which the auditor inquires in the course of his examination.

---

[1] Andrew Barr, "Current Practice with the SEC; Duties and Responsibilities of the CPA," address before California Society of CPAs, June 26, 1961.

Obviously, the response to Item 12 should confirm the results of the auditor's independent inquiry.

Another example: Item 13 of Form S–1 calls for certain information regarding capital stock being registered, including dividend rights, liquidation rights, conversion rights, redemption provisions, and sinking fund provisions. The response to Item 13 should confirm the information obtained by the auditor in the course of his examination.

Item 19 of Form S–1 requires information as to principal holders of *voting* securities of the registrant, specifically persons owning of record or beneficially more than 10 per cent of any class of such securities. Several of the detailed instructions in Regulation S–X pertaining to form and content of financial statements make reference to "principal holders of *equity* securities." The term is defined on page **16·7**.   Also Schedule II required by Rule 5–04 of Regulation S–X may, in some circumstances, call for information regarding transactions with principal holders of equity securities. The information in Item 19 should be reconcilable with the information and representations contained in the financial statements.

A minor matter concerns the sequence of years in financial statements (including earnings summaries) and in tabular material appearing in the narrative section of a prospectus. Should the most recent year be presented in the first column or in the last column of the table or financial statement? This is admittedly not important, but the SEC staff seldom fails to call the registrant's attention to the fact that one sequence (or different sequences) is used in tables in the narrative whereas another is used in the statements. The staff ordinarily requires that the inconsistencies be eliminated by amendment. The staff has not, to the author's knowledge, expressed a strong preference for any one method, but have insisted that, whichever method is adopted, it be followed consistently throughout the entire prospectus, including the financial statements. The staff apparently feels that it places too much of a burden on the reader if he has to shift gears each time he looks at a table or statement covering a period of years. The accountant participating in a registration engagement should see to it that the financial statements are consistently presented in this respect, and if the tables in the text are on a different basis, he should call this matter to the attention of counsel for the company or the underwriter.

2. In the usual case, except for the management representatives, there are few persons connected with the project who are as familiar with the company and its affairs as the independent public accountant. In the course of auditing the company's financial statements over the years, the accountant could not help but acquire much information about the company, its plants, its products, its manufacturing processes and problems, its labor situation, its distribution problems, capital needs, and similar matters. Since these

matters run to the very heart of the prospectus, the accountant is often in a position to make important and constructive suggestions in drafting the prospectus.

Not only does the accountant have an extensive background in the company's affairs but, what may be equally important, he has an independent and objective point of view. The author is not referring now to the need for independence in order for the accountant to be in a position to certify for SEC purposes. He is referring rather to the essential difference in the point of view between the owners of the business or the management on the one hand and the accountant on the other hand. The owners and management are often inclined to be overly optimistic and to minimize their problems, and this is apt to be especially true when they are preparing a prospectus as the basis for a public offering of their company's securities.

Often the lawyer who is drafting the prospectus will seek the accountant's advice or opinion on a matter which has nothing whatever to do with the financial statements. The lawyer knows that the accountant is more likely to have an objective, disinterested view of the problem than the owner of the business or an officer of the company.

One of the commissioners of the SEC must have had something like the foregoing in mind when he said in 1969:

> I recently read a proposed description of the financial condition of a company and frankly was amazed at its complexity. In fact, I believe it was misleading. When I asked our staff which accounting firm had been consulted when the description was being prepared, I was told that it had been prepared by the company's attorneys, without consulting the accountants. Now I am not here to drum up business for the accounting profession, but I would like to point out that it may be helpful for an attorney when preparing the financial description of a company to obtain suggestions from the accountants. Too often the lawyer is over-zealous in trying to protect his client at the cost of a meaningful presentation. His basic objective is fine when done in moderation, but when carried too far may in fact be harmful, as in this case, to the average investor.[2]

3. There may be material in the narrative section of the registration which should be cross-referenced in the financial section, or vice versa. For example, if the narrative section discloses a recent material increase in wages or other costs which are not reflected in the financial statements or have been reflected for only a short period, it may be desirable to disclose in the financial section these recent increases in costs and expenses. The most practicable way of making this disclosure is by a simple cross-reference to that section of the narrative which contains the information in question. Similarly, if the narrative section discloses a recent substantial increase in rates for service or changes in selling price of products, and these increases or changes have not been reflected in the financial statements, a

---

[2] James J. Needham, address before Securities Law Committee of The Federal Bar Association, Washington, D. C., Dec. 2, 1969.

disclosure in the financial section may be in order—either by a cross-reference to the appropriate narrative section of the registration or by repeating the information in question in the financial section.

Another example: if the registrant's commitments under long-term leases are material, that fact will have to be disclosed in the financial statements as required by Rule 3–16(i) of Regulation S–X (see page **16·29**). On the other hand, the table containing information regarding a company's capital structure which must appear in a Form S–1 prospectus must also contain a cross-reference to the note in the financial statements setting forth information concerning the extent of obligations under leases on real property.

The notes to financial statements must set forth some of the provisions of the company's pension plan if it has one, including a brief description of the plan together with a statement of the annual cost thereof and the unfunded cost of credits for service rendered prior to the adoption of the plan. The matter of pensions is often described in the section of the prospectus dealing with employee relations or under a similar heading. Rather than repeat all this information in the financial statements, it is desirable to make a cross-reference in the statement notes to that section of the prospectus which sets forth the material otherwise required to be included in the financials. Sometimes as originally drafted (usually by counsel) the discussion of pensions does not give all the information that would be required in the financial section. Everyone concerned with the preparation of the registration document is desirous of making the document—especially the prospectus—as condensed as is consistent with the responsibilities assumed under the 1933 Act. If, therefore, the accountant suggests that by adding a sentence or two to the section of the narrative dealing with pensions, he will be able to omit a lengthy discussion regarding pensions from the financial statements, he can be reasonably sure that his suggestion will be carefully considered.

Furthermore, one of the general instructions of Form S–1 (one of the principal registration forms under the 1933 Act) provides that cross-references of the kind referred to above shall be made to avoid duplication:

Unless clearly indicated otherwise, information set forth in any part of the prospectus need not be duplicated elsewhere in the prospectus. Where it is deemed necessary or desirable to call attention to such information in more than one part of the prospectus, this may be accomplished by appropriate cross-references. *In lieu of restating information in the form of notes to financial statements, references should be made to other parts of the prospectus where such information is set forth.* (Emphasis supplied.)

An objective of the foregoing instructions was also the objective of a 1968 release by the SEC entitled "Guides for Preparation and Filing of Registration Statements." The SEC said: "When the text of the prospectus contains a discussion of factors indicating an adverse change in operating results subsequent to the latest period included in the summary of earnings, the summary should call attention to the change, in a headnote or in a footnote, and refer to the place in the prospectus where it is discussed." (Release No. 33–4936, Dec. 9, 1968)

See also the discussion below, "When Cross-Reference Is Made to the Text, Is It Thereby Certified?"

4. An AICPA Committee on Auditing Procedure issued a bulletin[3] which dealt with events subsequent to the date of financial statements. In one section of this bulletin the Committee sets forth its views as to the special requirements in connection with registration statements filed under the Securities Act of 1933. The Committee said that, in its opinion, a reasonable investigation in this connection would include the reading of the entire prospectus and review of other pertinent portions of the registration statement.

5. By reading the sections of the prospectus describing the underwriting arrangements and the compensation to be paid to the underwriters, the accountant may learn that, in addition to the shares to which the prospectus relates, a block of securities is to be sold to the underwriters at a nominal price: so-called "cheap stock." Depending on the circumstances, this may have a dilutive effect on earnings per share and may have to be considered in connection with the presentation of the summary of earnings. See the applicable discussion on page **10·45**.

6. The prospectus will disclose the uses to which the registrant intends to apply the proceeds of the public offering. The accountant should read this section and consider its effect on, or relevancy to, the financial statements (including the summary of earnings). In *Faradyne Electronics Corporation* [40 SEC 1053 (1962)] (summarized on page **4·23**), for example, a registration statement was filed covering a proposed offering of convertible subordinated debentures at a total public offering price of $2,000,000. Of this amount, $1,200,000 was to be used to discharge a non-interest-bearing debt. The replacement of the interest-free debt by interest-bearing obligations would result in a substantial increase in expenses. The SEC was highly critical of the registrant for failing to present a pro forma earnings statement showing the impact on earnings of the replacement of the interest-free debt with interest-bearing debentures.

When Cross-Reference Is Made to the Text, Is It Thereby Certified?—There has been a reluctance on the part of some independent accountants to make a cross-reference in financial statements certified by them to matter in the narrative or text portion of the registration statement that is

---

[3] SAP No. 47 (1971).

not covered by their certificate. They have based their opposition to such cross-reference on the belief that when such a cross-reference is made, it might be claimed that the information in the text is made a part of the financial statements and is therefore covered by the accountants' certificate to the same extent as the notes to the certified financial statements.

The author concedes that there may have been a basis for this belief, and, in fact, this constituted one of the claims of the plaintiffs in *BarChris* which is discussed in Chapter **28**. The plaintiffs in *BarChris* claimed that the independent accountants were responsible for a portion of the text of the prospectus pertaining to "Methods of Operation," because a reference to it was made in Note 9 to the balance sheet. The judge ruled against the plaintiffs on this point and said:

. . . The cross reference in footnote 9 to the "Methods of Operation" passage in the prospectus was inserted merely for the convenience of the reader. It is not a fair construction to say that it thereby imported into the balance sheet everything in that portion of the text, much of which had nothing to do with the figures in the balance sheet.

Importance of Reading the Underwriting Agreement.—As soon as he can conveniently do so, the accountant who participates in the preparation of a registration statement should read the underwriting agreement. At the time of the initial filing with the SEC, the agreement is usually tentative and unsigned. The underwriting agreement ordinarily becomes final and is executed shortly before the public offering date of the securities to which the registration statement relates. *The accountant, however, should not wait until the underwriting agreement is signed; he should read the agreement as soon as he can obtain a draft.* At that time there is usually agreement in principle as to what is expected of all the parties in the agreement. The principal omissions relate to price, interest or dividend rate, redemption prices, etc., all of which do not concern the accountant. There are a number of reasons why the accountant should read the draft of the underwriting agreement before it is final.

1. The underwriting agreement frequently contains provisions that affect the accountant in one way or another. For example, the agreement often provides that on or before the "closing date" (that is, the date on which the securities are delivered to the underwriters and paid for by them), the certifying accountant is to issue a letter or report in which he states that the financial statements, supporting schedules, and summary of earnings covered by his certificate comply as to form with the requirements of the Securities Act. Also, the accountant may be required to report concerning a review of any unaudited financial statements or summary of earnings included in the registration statement. Frequently the underwriting agree-

ment also contains a provision to the effect that the accountant is to issue a letter concerning recent changes in the company's capital structure or in its financial condition, or material decreases in sales or net income, otherwise than as disclosed in the registration statement or prospectus. Some underwriting agreements also contain a provision that the accountant is to issue a separate letter or report to the underwriters concerning the income tax situation of the company and its subsidiaries.

2. Underwriting agreements sometimes contain provisions requiring an accountant's opinion covering such matters as the amounts of additions to, and retirements of, fixed assets during the last five years. Where the matter in question is as simple as this, the accountant may be able to comply with this provision of the underwriting agreement without much, if any, additional work.

Underwriters and their counsel are sometimes under the impression that the accountant who certifies the financial statements is also in a position to certify almost any figure appearing in the registration document. As a result, their agreements may require the accountant to review and report on matters that he does not ordinarily go into in the course of his annual examination. These and similar provisions in underwriting agreements are not the result of any SEC requirements; they serve to supplement the investigation made by an underwriter before offering securities of an issuer to the public. The underwriting agreement may provide, for example, that the accountant is to certify to the underwriters the remuneration paid to officers and directors, or an analysis of sales by products, by customers, or by models. These are matters with which the accountant may be familiar but which he may not be in a position to certify without undertaking some additional work.

Accountants are glad to assist in the preparation of the registration statement in any way compatible with their position as independent experts. Thus, some of these provisions in underwriting agreements, while outside the scope of the usual audit engagement, can be complied with; but it is important to find out about them before the agreement is executed, not at the closing when the securities are delivered and paid for. Also, if the provisions of the agreement involve a considerable amount of work on the part of the accountant, this may have a bearing on the client's willingness to have the work done. If the cost of the additional work is disproportionate to its value, the underwriter may be willing to waive the particular provision of the agreement.

The author is familiar with a case involving a registration statement of a company that was a major supplier of electronic military equipment as a prime contractor to the United States government. In the narrative section of the prospectus that discussed the company's business, there was presented a table showing for the last two years, by quarters, the company's sales, net income, and net income per share. The table was apparently furnished with two purposes in mind: (1) to indicate that most recent earnings were on the uptrend, and (2) to indicate that a fluctuation in sales produced a disproportionate fluctuation in net income and net income per share. Profits were dependent in large measure on the "mix" of sales, and so sales alone were not a useful indication of the company's progress. A draft of the underwriting agreement provided that the accountants were to review this table and give "negative assurance" to the underwriters in the comfort letter that was to follow. The accountants immediately pointed out to the company that a substantial amount of work would have to be done by them in order to put themselves in a position to cover the table in question. The matter was discussed with the underwriters, including an estimate of the cost of doing the work. The company thought that the cost was out of proportion to the value or importance of having the independent auditors review the table and so informed the underwriters. The underwriters agreed, and the provision in the underwriting agreement was withdrawn.

The author also knows of a case involving a real estate development company where the underwriting agreement contained the usual provisions requiring the certifying accountant to represent that he was independent, and that the statements covered by his certificate complied with the SEC's requirements. In addition, the agreement provided that the accountants were to represent to the underwriters that the answers to the following items in the registration statement were "to the best of their knowledge correct statements":

Item 5 (This sets forth the capital structure of the registrant as of a recent specified date, but not necessarily the audit date.)

Item 18 (This deals with options to purchase securities from the registrant which are outstanding as of a specified date within 30 days prior to the date of filing the registration statement. This information is therefore not necessarily related to the information shown in the certified financial statements. In addition, it calls for data regarding options held by each director and each officer named in Item 17(a)(1) of the registration statement, and all directors and officers as a group. The response to Item 18 is almost invariably prepared by counsel or is covered by counsel's compliance letter.)

Item 25 (This covers sales to special parties to whom securities have been sold within the past six months, or are to be sold, by the registrant or selling stockholder, at a price varying from that at which securities of the same class "are to be offered to the general public pursuant to this registration," etc. The response to this item is ordinarily prepared or reviewed by counsel.)

Item 26 (This includes information regarding recent sales of securities not registered under the 1933 Act. Detailed information is required together with an indication of the section of the law or SEC rule under which exemption from registration is claimed and a statement of the fact relied upon to make the exemption available. The response to this item is usually prepared or reviewed by counsel.)

The accountants' comfort letter was also to cover all the figures and percentages appearing in the narrative section of the prospectus as follows:

The statistical data under "Homesite Sales"
The statistical data under "Utility Operations"
The amounts in the sections dealing with an insurance company note agreement and warrant to purchase the registrant's stock
The following information in the prospectus under "Properties":
   Amounts of outstanding mortgages and purchase money mortgages
   Number of homesite lots sold, for x years
   Number of houses for which sale had been closed, for x years
   Estimated costs of improvements for homesite lots sold
   Amounts of principal payments received with respect to homesite lots sold
   Amounts spent on improvements

The independent accountants promptly called their client's attention to the fact that they had not checked the foregoing information in connection with their examination for the purpose of certifying the company's financial statements, and that compliance with the provisions of the underwriting agreement relating to the accountants would be difficult, time consuming, and costly. The company, however, stated that it had agreed in principle with all the provisions of the agreement. Accordingly, the accountants were requested to do whatever was necessary to comply with the agreement. The work was highly unusual in nature, and it was important for all concerned to know that an accountant cannot automatically check a number or a percentage merely because he has made an audit. In this case, the work was done, and the accountants' letter, properly hedged, was furnished to the underwriters.

3. When the underwriting agreement provides that the accountant is to furnish letters as to compliance, capital changes, etc., it is advisable to clear with the interested parties in advance the form of such letters and opinions proposed to be issued in satisfaction of the underwriting provision. The objective is to have agreement in principle at an early date as to the form that it is expected these letters will take. If, for some reason, the independent auditor finds it necessary to qualify his report called for by the underwriting agreement, that fact may have an important bearing on the underwriter's willingness to proceed with the offering, or it may put the underwriter on notice of an area that he should investigate further in his exercise of "due diligence." At the closing there is no time to resolve differences between the accountant and the underwriter regarding the content of the accountant's report. (See the discussion of the Burgmaster case on page 10·17 where an important accounting inconsistency in unaudited interim figures was discovered after the effective date of a registration statement but before the closing date.)

Importance of Reading the Indenture or Charter Provisions.—If the registration statement relates to a new issue of funded debt, the probabilities are that a new indenture is in process of being drafted at the same time. This indenture will recite at length and in detail certain agreements (called "covenants") to which the borrowing company agrees as a condition to borrowing the money. In other cases the financing may relate to a new issue of preferred stock the terms of which may be governed by an amendment to the company's certificate of incorporation. Regardless of the form of the governing instrument—whether it be an indenture or an amendment to the certificate of incorporation—it is important that the certifying accountant read it while it is in draft form and before it becomes final.

Primarily it is important for the accountant to read the underlying instrument because if he is to continue to serve the company in the future, the instrument is something that he will have to live with. Indentures and charters frequently contain provisions relating to the payment of dividends on junior securities, such as preferred and common stocks. These dividends may be geared to earnings accumulated subsequent to a stated date; dividends may also be limited by such considerations as available working capital. Frequently the governing instrument may limit distributions in the form of property other than cash and may contain restrictions as to the reacquisition by a corporation of its own securities. In other cases the indenture may contain sinking fund provisions that require payments into a fund for the repurchase or redemption of a corporation's own securities. The amount of the fund may be governed by the amount of net income available for that purpose as defined in the indenture.

Often the indenture provides that a certificate of an independent accountant is to be obtained that will certify as to the amount of surplus available for dividends based on earnings, distributions, and working capital. The indenture may also provide that the accountant is to certify the amount to be paid into the sinking fund. The indenture may also provide for certification in the future by the accountant concerning his knowledge of defaults by the company in indenture provisions. These provisions are not unusual, and, if they will require an accountant's opinion, his views regarding them should be sought in advance—preferably while the indenture or charter amendment is being drafted.

Experience has shown that the certifying accountant can be helpful in eliminating ambiguities in the indenture or other governing instrument. Everyone involved in the financing is anxious that ambiguities be eliminated so that future misunderstandings will be kept to a minimum. These instruments are ordinarily drawn up by lawyers or investment bankers with a great deal of experience in this kind of work. They cannot, however, anticipate all the problems which may arise in the operations of a company as they relate to a particular indenture. Because of the accountant's familiarity with the company, the industry, and the manner in which the financial statements are prepared from the accounts, he can frequently make suggestions that will be welcomed by all concerned.

Since the indenture or other governing instrument is often drafted by lawyers or investment bankers, it frequently happens that the language used in the instrument has a meaning that is different from that of the same words used by public accountants. For example, the term "net income" as used in the indenture may have a meaning quite different from what it is understood to mean in accounting. In the indenture, the term "net income" may be (and frequently is) exclusive of gains or losses from the sale or retirement of fixed assets. In the financial statements of an unregulated company (that is to say, not a public utility or similarly regulated company) capital gains and losses are usually included in the income statement and enter into the determination of net income. If the indenture defines "net income" so that it cannot be misunderstood, it can have any meaning the draftsmen choose to give it. If, however, the term is not defined, the accountant will interpret it in its usual accounting sense; and this may be quite different from what is contemplated by the lender and the borrower. Wherever possible, it is desirable that the language and the terms used in the indenture conform to their ordinary accounting meaning. This will not only narrow the field of uncertainty as to the meaning of terms in the future, but what is more important, it will expedite the preparation at a later date of statements showing compliance or non-compliance with charter or indenture provisions.

Importance of Checking the "Blue-Sky" Requirements.—Long before the SEC and the Securities Act were thought of, most of the states had laws governing the sale of securities within those states. These laws are called "blue-sky" laws and vary considerably among the various states.

Loss wrote that credit for the first comprehensive laws providing for the registration of securities and securities salesmen goes to Kansas for its statute of 1911. It was there, apparently, that the term "blue-sky law" first came into general use to describe legislation aimed at promoters who "would sell building lots in the blue sky in fee simple." The fashion set by Kansas soon spread. Today there are blue-sky laws in every state except Delaware.[4]

The "blue-sky" laws differ in detail but they may be classified into four groups:

1. The so-called "fraud type" laws provide the least amount of regulation. They provide penalties for the fraudulent sale of securities.

---

[4] Loss, *Securities Regulation,* Supplement to 2d ed. (1969), p. 2209.

2. Certain states have laws that regulate the securities dealers or brokers and their salesmen and agents only.
3. Some states have laws providing for the registration of securities that are to be sold in the state but do not provide for the licensing of dealers or brokers.
4. The majority of states provide for the licensing of dealers and salesmen and the registration of securities. In some states registration is by qualification; in others, by notification. More often, however, qualification and notification are required. Registration by notification is generally limited to securities issued by a corporation that has been in operation and has a favorable earning record for a number of years, or issues secured by designated collateral. Registration by qualification requires the filing of a prescribed form.

Many states exempt from the operation of their securities laws securities of regulated public utilities and securities that are listed on designated stock exchanges and/or securities that are senior to those so listed. Such exchanges usually include the New York Stock Exchange, the American Stock Exchange, and the Midwest Stock Exchange. Some states provide that if the securities in question are registered with the SEC, they are exempt from registration with the state commission. In other states the filing with the state commission of a copy of the registration statement and prospectus filed with the SEC fulfills the state registration requirements. A few states exempt securities of companies that are listed in recognized securities manuals, such *Standard and Poor's, Moody's,* and *Fitch.*

As previously noted, the Federal securities laws are not concerned primarily with the quality of securities registered with the SEC by the companies issuing them. The state securities laws, on the other hand, are often concerned with the quality of the securities offered to their residents or the fairness of the offering. Under the Ohio law, for example, that state's Division of Securities may suspend the registration of securities if it finds that such securities are being sold on "grossly unfair terms."

When making arrangements for an engagement under the Securities Act, it is desirable to inquire of counsel for the company and the underwriter as to whether the "blue-skying" of the securities will require any additional work on the part of the public accountant. In some states the prospectus and registration statement filed with the federal authorities is not enough; additional information may be necessary.

New York's "blue-sky" law requires registration by dealers and the filing of "dealers' statements" in certain cases. The Attorney General of New York may grant exemptions, however, to seasoned corporations that comply with specified requirements as to past payments of principal or interest and dividends. The exemption is available for common stock "upon which dividends have been paid annually for a continuous immediately preceding period of six years at the rate of not less than 3 per cent of the book value of such common stock as shown by its balance sheet at the date of the close of the fiscal year in which such dividends were paid, *as certified by an independent certified public accountant.*" [5] (Emphasis added.)

Counsel for the underwriters usually furnishes members of the underwriting group with a memorandum of those states in which the proposed issue of securities may be sold. The certifying accountant is frequently asked to assist in making the computations which lead up to this memorandum. In Colorado, for example, sales of securities (except exempt securities or securities sold in exempt transactions) are unlawful unless the securities have been registered for sale within the state. Registration may be by "notification," "coordination," or by "qualification." Section 125–1–7 of the Colorado Blue Sky Law describes the securities eligible for registration by notification, and provides, in part, as follows:

(b)(1) Any securities whose issuer and any predecessors have been in continuous operation for at least five years if there has been no default during the current fiscal year or within the three preceding fiscal years in the payment of principal, interest, or dividends on any securities of the issuer or any predecessor with a fixed maturity or a fixed interest or dividend provision, and if the issuer and any predecessors during the past three years have had average net earnings, determined in accordance with generally accepted accounting practices, (ii) which are applicable to all securities without a fixed maturity or a fixed interest or dividend provision outstanding at the date the registration statement is filed and equal [to] at least five percent of the amount of such outstanding securities (as measured by the maximum offering price or the market price on a day, selected by the registrant, within thirty days before the date of filing the registration statement, whichever is higher, or book value on a day, selected by the registrant, within ninety days of the date of filing the registration statement to the extent that there is neither a readily determinable market price nor a cash offering price), or (iii) which, if the issuer and any predecessors have not had any security of the type specified in subparagraph (ii) of this subsection (1) outstanding for three full fiscal years equal at least to five percent of the amount as measured in subparagraph (ii) of this subsection (1), of all securities which will be outstanding if all the securities being offered or proposed to be offered (whether or not they are proposed to be registered or offered in this state) are issued.

The accountant is often asked to make the computations contemplated by the section of the law quoted above.

The accounting terms used in the "blue-sky" laws are sometimes not defined, and as a result the accountant may find it difficult, if not impossible, to understand and interpret the statutes. Since the accountant does not qualify as an expert in interpreting law, when these difficulties arise, he should seek competent legal advice.

[5] New York Fraudulent Practices Act, Sec. 359-f(2)(a).

Legal Investments.—The states have laws regulating the securities in which savings banks, insurance companies, and fiduciaries may invest. Securities eligible for purchase by such investors are called "legal investments." Often the question of whether or not a security qualifies as a legal investment in a particular state will be determined by whether or not the issuer of the security meets certain earnings tests prescribed by the laws of that state.

Counsel for the company or the underwriter may ask the certifying accountant to assist in making the computations necessary to determine whether the securities proposed to be offered are legal investments in certain states and to furnish a letter setting forth the accountant's findings.

LETTER AS TO COMPLIANCE WITH LEGAL INVESTMENT PROVISIONS. —Below is a typical letter written by an accountant regarding compliance with legal investment provisions. It is reproduced here in order to illustrate the problems with which the accountant may be faced in this kind of work.

We have your letter of (date) with which you enclosed extracts from the statutes of certain states outlining the earnings and capitalization tests relating to investments by insurance companies in such states. You requested that we make the required computations and comparisons in order to notify you of those states in which the proposed issue of debentures of the XYZ Corporation would meet such tests.

Upon the basis of the statutory excerpts enclosed with your letter, our understanding of the accounting terms used in the statutes, and certain assumptions outlined below, we have complied with your request. Without holding ourselves out as qualified to interpret the statutes involved and subject to the comments set forth below as to certain requirements of the states of Minnesota and Missouri, our computations and comparisons indicate that the Company's debentures meet the requirements in Indiana, Iowa, Massachusetts, Minnesota, Missouri, Nebraska, New York, Pennsylvania, Virginia, and Wisconsin.

In performance of our work we have assumed the following:

1. That the face amount of the debentures to be issued and outstanding will be $_____, that the interest rate will be ___ per cent per annum, and that the debentures are to be sold by the Company at their principal amount.
2. That the financial data called for by the various statutes relate to those of the Company and its subsidiaries *consolidated* and not to the Company alone.
3. Where the statutes referred to "net earnings" we have taken this to mean *consolidated net income* as shown by the Company's consolidated financial statements for the (period) which we have examined.
4. Where the statutes referred to "net earnings (or income) after allowance for operating and maintenance expenses, depreciation, and taxes, other than federal and state income taxes, but excluding extraordinary nonrecurring items of income and expense," we have used the amounts reflected in the aforementioned consolidated financial statements as in-

come before provision for taxes on income and before extraordinary items.

5. Where the statutes define "fixed charges" as "including" certain elements of cost and expense, it has been assumed that the word "including" (or "include") is intended to exclude from fixed charges elements not specifically mentioned as being included.

6. Where the statutes call for interest on indebtedness as computed at date of acquisition or date of investment (presumably referring to acquisition or investment by the prospective investor) we have computed such interest on the basis of the companies' indebtedness on (date) as stated to us by Mr. _____, Treasurer of the Company.

With respect to the excerpts from the Missouri statutes which contain requirements that the net earnings be in excess of "annual fixed charges" by a stated ratio, you have informed us that the statute does not define "annual fixed charges." The statutes of Minnesota contain a somewhat similar ratio provision and do not define "fixed charges." In these cases, pursuant to your instructions, we have taken "fixed charges" to consist of interest charges on outstanding notes, mortgages, bank loans, and the proposed debentures plus appropriate amounts for amortization of the estimated expenses of issuing the debentures. On this basis the Company's debentures meet the tests applicable to these states. As mentioned in our discussions with you over the telephone, the term "fixed charges" frequently includes property taxes, depreciation, rents for leased property, etc.; however, pursuant to your instructions and in reliance thereon, we have excluded all such charges in making the computations with respect to the requirements of Minnesota and Missouri.

The Consent.—The 1933 Act provides that "if any accountant . . . or any person whose profession gives authority to a statement made by him, is named as having prepared or certified any part of the registration statement, or is named as having prepared or certified a report . . . for use in connection with the registration statement, the written consent of such person shall be filed with the registration statement." (Sec. 7 of the Act.) The consent must be dated and signed manually.

FORM OF CONSENT.—Below is a suggested form of consent which, with appropriate modifications, may be used by the certifying accountant:

We consent to the inclusion of the following reports in the registration statement to be used in registering, under the Securities Act of 1933, (title of issue) of the (name of company): (1) our report dated _____ accompanying the financial statements of (name of company) and of that company and its subsidiaries consolidated, and the summary of earnings, which are included in the prospectus; (2) our report dated _____ accompanying the supporting schedules listed in Item 31 of the registration statement; and (3) our report dated _____ accompanying the historical financial information listed in Item 31 of the registration statement.

(City)   (Signature of certifying accountant)
(Date of signing)

If, as frequently happens, the accountant is named as having reviewed financial data in the registration statement, or if it is stated that any financial data are set forth in the registration upon the authority of, or in reliance upon, the accountant as an expert, the accountant must also consent in writing to the making of such statement (see page **11·22**). This may be accomplished by adding to the form suggested above the following additional paragraph: "We also consent to the references to our firm under the captions 'Summary of Earnings' and 'Experts' in the prospectus." If the accountant has confidence in those responsible for the preparation of the registration document and feels that he is being kept currently informed with respect to all important developments bearing on the document, he may be disposed to word this portion of his consent as follows: "We also consent to all references to our firm in the prospectus."

In the case of an amendment of financial data covered by the accountant's certificate, his consent to the use of his certificate in connection with the amended information must be filed as part of the amendment. This may be accomplished by repeating in the amendment and re-signing the consent that appeared in the original filing, except that the new consent will bear a current date.

It has been the policy of the SEC to require consent of independent accountants to the use of their certificate in a "bring-up" prospectus (see page **11·28**). A suggested form of consent to be used for this special purpose follows:

We consent to the inclusion of our report dated _____ accompanying the financial statements and summary of earnings of _____ _____ Company appearing in its prospectus dated _____, relating to its (title of issue), to be filed with the Securities and Exchange Commission under the provisions of the Securities Act of 1933.

This consent must also be dated and must be manually signed.

CAN REGISTRANT FILE UNSIGNED CONSENT?—Sometimes in their anxiety to get the registration statement filed and the "waiting period" started, the company officials feel they cannot wait for the certifying accountant to complete his audit. In that somewhat unusual situation the company may attempt to file the registration statement without a manual signature of the accountant on his certificate and consent. As a general rule the SEC will not accept for filing a registration statement that is not fully executed, including the manually signed certificate and consent of the independent public accountants. The SEC's position is substantially this: Until the registration statement is signed by all responsible parties—including the accountants—the statement is an uncompleted document.

APPLICATION TO DISPENSE WITH CONSENT.—In some cases the obtaining of a consent of experts involves undue hardship or is impracticable for a number of reasons. The accountant who certified the earliest years in an earnings summary or financial statements, included in the registration statement, of a predecessor company, may have retired from practice, or he may have died, or he may be disqualified from serving for reasons bearing on lack of independence. Rule 437 provides that the SEC may dispense with any written consent in certain circumstances. The rule reads as follows:

An application to the Commission to dispense with any written consent of an expert pursuant to Section 7 of the Act shall be made by the registrant and shall be supported by an affidavit or affidavits establishing that the obtaining of such consent is impracticable or involves undue hardship on the registrant. Such application shall be filed and the consent of the Commission shall be obtained prior to the effective date of the registration statement.

WITHDRAWAL OF CONSENT.—In October 1969, the AICPA Committee on Auditing Procedure issued its SAP No. 41 dealing with the discovery, after the auditor's certification, of facts which existed at the date of his report but which were not known to him at that time. If the information is found to have existed at the date of his report, the auditor should advise his client to make appropriate disclosure of the newly discovered facts to persons who are known to be relying, or who are likely to rely, on the financial statements. If the client refuses to make the disclosures, the auditor should take steps as outlined in the Statement to prevent future reliance upon his report. This includes notification to persons known to be relying on the statements. Notification to a regulatory agency having jurisdiction over the client will usually be the only practicable way for the auditor to provide appropriate disclosure. The SEC is one of the appropriate agencies for this purpose as to corporations within its jurisdiction.

When the independent public accountant concludes that his certificate can not be relied upon and takes steps to withdraw it, additional steps may be necessary if the certificate was included, with his consent, in a registration statement filed with the SEC. Hopefully this situation will seldom occur, but when it does, the auditor should promptly inform the SEC that the certificate and his consent have been withdrawn and the reason therefor. A suggested form of letter to accomplish this withdrawal follows:

Securities and Exchange Commission
500 North Capitol St.
Washington, D. C. 20549.

Re: (Name of registrant)

Dear Sirs:

The following reports of our firm have, with our consent, been included in a registration statement filed by (name of company) (the registrant) pursuant to the Securities Act of 1933:

1. Our report dated (date) relating to the financial statements of the registrant as of (date) and for the (period) then ended, and the summary of earnings for the (period) then ended.
2. Our report dated (date) relating to the supporting schedules as of (date) and for the (period) then ended included in Part II of the registration statement.

We have recently acquired additional information of a material nature which raises serious questions as to the fairness of presentation of the financial position and results of operations of the registrant as of the date and for the periods covered by the reports of our firm listed above. Accordingly, no further reliance should be placed upon these reports. We have advised the registrant that our consent to the use of these reports has been withdrawn.

Very truly yours,

(Signature of independent auditors)

If the auditors' reports were also included in other documents filed with the SEC, e.g., an annual report on Form 10–K, it would be well also to withdraw the auditors' report relating to the financial statements in that document.

The Conformity (or Compliance) Letter.—In most registration engagements there are at least two experts employed by the company—lawyers and accountants. Lawyers frequently participate in the drafting of the so-called "narrative" section of the registration statement, or they review the statement prepared by others. Accountants may help with the preparation of the financial statements and supporting schedules, but primarily they are employed to furnish an independent opinion concerning such statements and schedules.

At some point in the proceedings (at least in underwritten issues), the attorneys are usually asked to give their legal opinion as to the compliance of the registration statement, except the financial statements and schedules and earnings summary (as to which they are not in a position to express an opinion), with the requirements of the Securities Act of 1933 and the rules and regulations thereunder.

To complete the compliance picture, a "conformity" letter (sometimes called a "compliance" letter) is customarily furnished by the certifying accountant. Sometimes the request for this conformity letter springs from a provision to that effect in the underwriting agreement; at other times, where no underwriting is involved, it will be requested for the benefit of the directors of the corporation who sign the registration statement. But whatever the source, the accountant will usually be requested to report whether, in his opinion, the financial statements, summary of earnings, and supporting schedules covered by his certificates in the registration statement comply as to form with the Commission's rules and regulations thereunder.

A typical form of such a conformity letter follows:

(Name of client)
(Address)

We previously submitted our reports dated _____ upon our examination of the financial statements and supporting schedules of (name of company) and the consolidated financial statements and supporting schedules of that company and its subsidiaries as of _____ and for the years _____, _____, and _____, and the summary of earnings for the years _____ to _____, inclusive. The afore-mentioned statements, supporting schedules and summary of earnings together with the said reports appear in registration statement No. _____ filed by (name of company) with the Securities and Exchange Commission.

In our opinion, the financial statements, supporting schedules, and summary of earnings covered by our reports comply as to form in all material respects with the applicable accounting requirements of the Securities Act of 1933 and the published rules and regulations thereunder.

The conformity letter (such as the foregoing specimen) is ordinarily addressed to the accountant's client, but there is no objection to furnishing copies to other interested parties, such as underwriters, if the accountant is authorized to do so by his client.

The date of the conformity letter is usually the effective date of the registration statement, or, in the case of a letter addressed to underwriters, the date of delivery of and payment for the securities (the "closing date").

The conformity letter is often furnished as part of a comfort letter; see the discussion in Chapter **12**.

"Upon the Authority of an Expert."—The Securities Act of 1933 imposes possible liability for false or misleading statements, but provides that this liability may not exist, except as to the issuer of the securities, as regards any part of the registration statement purporting to be made "upon the authority of an expert." [6] Because of the protection afforded by this provision to officers, directors, and underwriters with respect to any statement made upon the authority of an expert, lawyers for the company and the underwriters usually request the insertion in the prospectus and registration statement of language specifically bringing within the scope of this provision certified financial statements, summaries of earnings, supporting schedules, and other data.

Financial statements are primarily the statements and representations of the company. This fact has been frequently enunciated by the AICPA and acknowledged by the SEC; see page **2**·18. The language used in registration statements and prospectuses to identify the financial representations contained therein should be equally clear in characterizing the account-

---

[6] For a more detailed discussion of this subject, see SAP No. 33 (1963), p. 14.

ant's relationship to those representations. The view of accountants is that, since the financial statements and earnings summaries are representations by the company, the "expertizing declaration" should be so phrased as to make it clear that the certificate or report of the accountants, rather than the financial statements or summaries, is the information given upon their authority as experts. Accountants therefore prefer that the reference to them in such declarations (when relating to financial statements and earnings summaries in the prospectus) be substantially in the following form:

The financial statements on pages _____ to _____ of this prospectus and the summary of earnings on page _____ have been examined by (name of accountants), independent public accountants, and are included in the prospectus in reliance upon the accompanying report of said firm which report is given upon their authority as experts in accounting and auditing.

However, many lawyers insist that the "expertizing declaration" conform to the language in Section 11 of the Act. In that event, the final clause in the above paragraph may be revised along the following lines: ". . . and are included in the prospectus in reliance upon the accompanying report of said firm and upon their authority as experts in accounting and auditing." Similar language, appropriately modified, should be used with respect to schedules and other certified financial data included in the registration statement but omitted from the prospectus.

The language to be used should avoid such phrases as *"has been prepared* by (name of accountants), independent certified public accountants," for they may be interpreted as imputing to the accountant greater responsibility with respect to the financial statements than he intended to assume.

When the prospectus includes unaudited as well as audited financial statements, the expertizing declaration should be limited to that portion of the financial presentation which is covered by the accountant's certificate.

When a prospective investor reads the expertizing declaration, he is apt to assume—unless he is informed to the contrary—that the accountants' report is unqualified. For this reason, when the accountants' report is qualified in an important respect, the declaration should be appropriately modified to disclose that fact. Following is an example showing how the disclosure was made in one case:

The following summary of earnings of the Company has been reviewed by (name of accountants), independent certified public accountants, whose opinion with respect thereto accompanies the financial statements in this prospectus. It is the policy of the Company to record in its accounts amortization of facilities covered by certificates of necessity in the same amounts as are claimed for tax purposes, rather than to spread the cost over the estimated useful economic lives of the facilities. For the years _____ and _____, the accountants' opinion is qualified with respect to the effect of this policy on earnings . . .

In another case the accountants' report was qualified in respect of deferred product development costs. The headnote to the summary of earnings was as follows:

The following summary of earnings has been examined by (name of accountants), independent public accountants, whose report with respect thereto (which contains a qualification with respect to such adjustment, if any, of deferred product development costs as might be required as a result of future developments) appears elsewhere in this prospectus. . . .

The "Due Diligence" Meeting.—After the registration statement is filed but before it becomes effective, a meeting (called the "due diligence" meeting or an "underwriters' information" meeting) is usually held under the auspices of the principal underwriters. Among those attending are representatives of the company whose securities are proposed to be offered, counsel for the company, the underwriters and their counsel, independent public accountants, and engineers, if any. At this meeting the members of the underwriting group are afforded an opportunity to exercise "due diligence" as to the proposed offering of securities in that they may ask any questions which may have occurred to them concerning the company, its business, products, competitive position, recent financial and other developments, and prospects. These questions may have arisen as a result of having read the prospectus or the registration statement, or they may have arisen as a result of developments in the news of the day. Questions are invited with respect to anything in the registration document, including the financial statements. If questions are asked concerning any matter as to which the certifying accountant may be expected to know the answer, the accountant is frequently requested to furnish the answer.

These meetings run from a few minutes to several hours depending on a number of considerations. If the company has registered several times previously and its securities have been sold to the public, then the meeting may be somewhat perfunctory since the company, its earnings, products, and prospects are reasonably well known, and the members of the underwriting group may have all the background information they need. If, on the other hand, the company's securities are being offered to the public for the first time, then it may be expected that the members of the underwriting group will have a large number of varied questions to ask, and these questions frequently are of a searching variety.

The accountant is almost invariably requested to attend the "due diligence" meeting. Some accountants consider this to be a burden, but, in the opinion of this author, they should welcome the opportunity of attending. The questioning sometimes elicits answers from high-ranking officers of the corporation which frequently confirm information which the auditor has obtained in the course of making his examination. In any case, the accountant will want to consider whether the information learned at the "due diligence" meeting is of a character that has a bearing on the financial data included in the registration statement. This is a matter which, it is true, will also concern the company, its counsel, the underwriters, and counsel for the underwriters.

The "Red Herring" Prospectus.—A preliminary prospectus may be sent to interested persons prior to the effective date of the registration statement. Rule 433 of the SEC contains the provisions relating to such preliminary prospectuses. This rule, among other things, requires that the outside front cover page of the prospectus shall bear, *in red ink,* the caption "Preliminary Prospectus" and the following statement printed in type as large as that generally in the body of the prospectus:

A registration statement relating to these securities has been filed with the Securities and Exchange Commission but has not yet become effective. Information contained herein is subject to completion or amendment. These securities may not be sold nor may offers to buy be accepted prior to the time the registration statement becomes effective. This prospectus shall not constitute an offer to sell or the solicitation of an offer to buy nor shall there be any sale of these securities in any State in which such offer, solicitation or sale would be unlawful prior to registration or qualification under the securities laws of any such State.

Because the required legend quoted above must appear in red ink, prospectuses containing this legend are referred to as "red herring" prospectuses. The rule is intended to facilitate the dissemination of information in Securities Act registrations.

"Tombstone Ads."—The 1933 Act provides that "a notice, circular, advertisement, letter, or communication in respect of a security shall not be deemed to be a prospectus if it states from whom a written prospectus meeting the requirements of Section 10 may be obtained and, in addition, does no more than identify the security, state the price thereof, state by whom orders will be executed, and contains such other information as the Commission, by rules or regulations deemed necessary or appropriate in the public interest and for the protection of investors, and subject to such terms and conditions as may be prescribed therein, may permit." (Sec. 2(10) of the Act.)

Because of the form that advertisements take when prepared under this clause, they are usually referred to as "tombstone ads." A typical "tombstone ad" would be somewhat as follows:

This advertisement is neither an offer to sell nor a solicitation of offers to buy any of these securities. The offering is made only by the Prospectus.

Not a New Issue

———— Shares

—————————— **Gas Corporation**

Common Stock
(Par Value $1 Per Share)

————

Price $—— Per Share

————

Copies of the Prospectus may be obtained from such of the under-signed as are Registered Dealers in this State.

(Names of underwriters)

The "tombstone ad" is not intended to be a selling document. Its purpose is to assist in locating potential buyers who might be sufficiently interested in the security being advertised to make an effort to obtain a statutory prospectus. "Tombstone ads" may be used during the waiting period or after the effective date.

The Summary Prospectus.—For many years there existed a special rule providing for the publication of condensed information in newspapers of general circulation; these were called "newspaper prospectuses." The rule was seldom availed of because the cost of the space needed to publish the required amount of information was prohibitive. The rule was repealed and, in its stead, the SEC promulgated new rules dealing with "summary prospectuses." Summary prospectuses are of two kinds: one is provided for by Rule 434 of the Commission and is prepared, not by the issuer of the securities, but by independent organizations primarily engaged in publishing statistical and financial manuals with respect to securities generally; the other is provided for by SEC Rule 434A, and is prepared by the registrant and filed as part of the registration statement. The Rule 434 summary prospectus is used only during the waiting period of the registration process; the Rule 434A summary prospectus may be used either during the waiting period or after the registration statement becomes effective. The balance of the discussion below is concerned only with the Rule 434A prospectus since this is the one prepared for the registration statement.

Summary prospectuses may be used only by certain registrants who comply with the instructions contained in Rule 434A. The summary prospectus contains only a small portion of the information contained in the official, statutory prospectus, and the buyer of the securities must in any case be furnished with a copy of the statutory prospectus. As a consequence, summary prospectuses are seldom used. The Wheat Report pointed out, in fact, that "only a handful have been filed within the past five years." [7] They are used often enough so that the reader should be familiar with them and their contents.

A summary prospectus may be used only if the form used for registration of the securities to be offered provides for the use of a summary prospectus and if *either* of the following conditions is met:

(1) the registrant is subject to the reporting requirements of Section 13 or 15(d) of the 1934 Act (which includes companies listed on exchanges, many publicly-owned unlisted companies, and certain 1933 Act registrants subject to the undertaking discussed on page **14·13**); *or*

(2) the registrant (i) has net assets of at least $5,000,000; (ii) has filed income statements with the registration statement for at least three full fiscal years and has been engaged in substantially the same business during that period; (iii) has had net income of at least $500,000 for each of the last three years; and (iv) has distributed to its stockholders and made available to the public generally an informative annual report for each of the last three years which included a balance sheet at the end of the year and income and surplus statements for the year then ended, all prepared in accordance with generally accepted accounting principles and certified in accordance with generally accepted auditing standards. The amounts in clauses (i) and (iii) shall be based on consolidated statements if such statements are filed. The Commission may, upon a showing of good cause, waive the requirement in clause (iv).

At the present time, summary prospectuses may be used only in connection with registration statements on Forms S–1, S–5, S–7, and S–9, by registrants who comply with all the other requirements in the rule.

Following are the requirements with respect to the financial statements that may be included in summary prospectuses in connection with Forms S–1, S–7, and S–9; *no other financial statements may be included:*

Form S–1:
  The summary of earnings required by Item 6.
Form S–7:
  The statements of income, retained earnings, other additional capital, and source and application of funds called for by Item 6.

[7] "Disclosure to Investors: A Reappraisal of Federal Administrative Policies under the '33 and '34 Acts" (The Wheat Report). Commerce Clearing House, Inc. 1969, p. 110.

A tabular presentation of notes payable, long-term debt, deferred credits, minority interests, if material, and the equity section of the latest balance sheet filed for the registrant, or the latest consolidated balance sheet filed, as appropriate.

Form S–9:

The statements of income, retained earnings, other additional capital, and source and application of funds called for by Item 3(a).

Summary prospectuses may be used in certain circumstances in connection with Form S–5. No financial statements or lists of investments are required to be included in such summary prospectuses.

If the summary prospectus is used during the waiting period, it must be captioned "Preliminary Summary Prospectus." The summary prospectus, regardless of when it is used, must contain a statement to the following effect: "Copies of a more complete prospectus may be obtained from (insert name)."

Prospectuses Used More Than Nine Months After Effective Date. —Shortly after the registration statement becomes effective, in most cases the securities are sold and the distribution is completed promptly. In some situations, however, because of market or other conditions, the public offering date may be delayed or the process of making the public distribution may take a considerable period of time. In still other cases, at the time the registration statement was filed it may have been contemplated that the process of distribution would take a considerable length of time. For example, an issue of preferred stock may have been registered with warrants attached entitling the holders at some future date to purchase common stock of the registrant; or convertible debentures may have been registered, which debentures are convertible into common stock at some future date by surrendering the debentures plus a certain amount in cash for common stock. In these and similar situations the issuer must be in a position to furnish an up-to-date prospectus. The 1933 Act and the Commission's rules contain provisions relating to prospectuses used more than nine months after the effective date of the registration statement.

Section 10(a)(3) of the 1933 Act relates to a prospectus used more than nine months after the effective date of the registration statement to which it relates. The section provides as follows:

Notwithstanding the provisions of paragraphs (1) and (2) of this subsection (a) when a prospectus is used more than nine months after the effective date of the registration statement, the information contained therein shall be as of a date not more than 16 months prior to such use, so far as such information is known to the user of such prospectus or can be furnished by such user without unreasonable effort or expense.

Rule 427 under the 1933 Act provides as follows:

Rule 427. Contents of Prospectus Used After Nine Months.

(a) There may be omitted from any prospectus used more than nine months after the effective date of the registration statement any information previously required to be contained in the prospectus insofar as later information covering the same subjects, including the latest available certified financial statement, as of a date not more than 16 months prior to the use of the prospectus is contained therein.

(b) Notwithstanding the foregoing, a prospectus filed as a part of an amendment to an effective registration statement on any form may be prepared in accordance with the requirements of any other form which would then be appropriate for the registration of the securities to which the prospectus relates, provided all of the requirements of such other form (including the filing of any required undertakings) are met. The amendment shall be deemed to relate to the proper form if the Commission declares it effective.

The following example illustrates how the above SEC rule works. Corporation A filed a registration statement which became effective March 15, 1971. The financial statements included in the registration statement and in the prospectus were as of December 31, 1970, and for the period then ended. Under Rule 427 prospectuses used after December 15, 1971, must contain certified financial statements as of a date within 16 months of its use —presumably the certified financial statements as of December 31, 1970— and these financial statements may be used without further supplement until April 30, 1972. After April 30, 1972, certified financial statements as of a date more recent than December 31, 1970, must be substituted; presumably by such date certified financial statements as of December 31, 1971, will be available and may be included in the prospectus.

The effect of Rule 427 is that, under some circumstances, the *certified* financial statements in a registration statement may be quite "stale" before there is a need to substitute more recent *certified* statements. This will be demonstrated by the following example. Assume a company whose fiscal year is a calendar year. The company files a registration statement in September, 1971, which includes certified financial statements as of December 31, 1970, and for the three years then ended, and unaudited statements as of August 31, 1971, and for the eight months then ended. The registration statement becomes effective on October 25, 1971. The prospectus may be used for nine months after the effective date, which means that the prospectus in the form in which it became effective may be used until July 25, 1972. On July 25, 1972, the *certified* financial statements (as of December 31, 1970) are almost nineteen months old, although they are accompanied by more recent (as of August 31, 1971) unaudited data. In a prospectus used *after* July 25, 1972, presumably audited statements as of December 31, 1971, would be used, and this prospectus could be used without further change until April 30, 1973.

Out of Date Prospectuses Involving Employee Stock Purchase and Similar Plans.—When securities are registered under the 1933 Act pursuant to an employee stock purchase, savings, or similar plan, the interests in the plan are usually registered on Form S–8., as indicated in Chapter **8**. Appropriate financial statements of the plan must be included in the prospectus, as indicated in Chapter **9**. In a number of cases, the fiscal year of the plan ends on a date different from that of the employer company, so that information regarding the plan may become out of date for the purpose of Section 10(a)(3) of the 1933 Act prior to that relating to the company, or vice versa. The question is sometimes raised whether the prospectus may continue to be used until up-to-date financial statements and other information is available for both the plan and the company.

The SEC has stated that, in such a case, after information with respect to the plan or the employer company becomes out of date, it is not permissible to continue using a prospectus which does not contain the required up-to-date information. However, a registrant may file a post-effective amendment to the registration statement containing the required information and, after the amendment becomes effective, may continue to use the old prospectus with the up-to-date financial statements and other information attached, until the prospectus must be revised to include up-to-date financial statements and other information with respect to the plan or the employer company, as the case may be. A copy of the prospectus with up-to-date information attached need not be furnished to existing participants in the plan who have previously received a copy of the prospectus and who are otherwise furnished with a copy of such up-to-date information, provided the prospectus contains a statement to the effect that such financial statements are to be deemed to be incorporated therein by reference for all purposes of the Act and the rules and regulations thereunder (Release No. 33–4936, Dec. 9, 1968).

CHAPTER 12

REGISTRATION PROCEDURE UNDER THE 1933 ACT, CONTINUED

Part 2. Post-Statement Events; "Keeping Current" Review; Comfort Letters

CONTENTS

Events Subsequent to the Statement Date

One of the most troublesome aspects of a public accountant's practice is the treatment and/or disclosure of events which occur subsequent to the date of the financial statements upon which he is reporting. An authoritative statement on the subject—designated Statement on Auditing Procedure No. 47—was issued in September 1971 by the AICPA Committee on Auditing Procedure.

The Committee pointed out that events or transactions sometimes occur subsequent to the date of a balance sheet, but prior to the issuance of the financial statements and the auditor's report, that have a material effect on the financial statements and therefore require adjustment or disclosure in the statements. Two types of subsequent events and transactions require consideration by management and evaluation by the independent auditor:

a. The first type consists of those events that provide additional evidence with respect to conditions that existed at the date of the balance sheet and affect the estimates inherent in the process of preparing financial statements. All information that becomes available prior to the issuance of the financial statements should be used in evaluating the conditions on which the estimates were based. The financial statements should be adjusted for any changes in estimates resulting from the use of such evidence. As the Committee pointed out, identifying events that require adjustment of the statements calls for the exercise of judgment and knowledge of the facts. For example, a loss on an uncollectible receivable as a result of a customer's deteriorating financial condition leading to bankruptcy subsequent to the balance sheet date would be indicative of conditions existing at the balance sheet date, thereby calling for adjustment of the statements before their issuance. On the other hand, a similar loss resulting from a customer's major casualty such as a fire or flood subsequent to the balance sheet date would not be indicative of conditions existing at the balance sheet, and adjustment would not be called for.

b. The second type consists of events that provide evidence with respect to conditions that did not exist at the balance sheet date but arose subsequent to that date. These events should not result in adjustment of the statements, although there is no intention to preclude giving effect, with appropriate disclosure, to stock dividends, stock splits, or reverse splits consummated after the date of the balance sheet but before its issuance. Some of these events, however, may be of such a nature that the omission of their disclosure may result in misleading statements. Occasionally such an event may be so significant that disclosure can best be made by supplementing the historical financial statements with pro forma financial data giving effect to the event as if it had occurred on the balance sheet date. Examples of this type of event (which should not result in adjustment) are: sale of a bond or stock issue, purchase of a business, and loss from fire or flood.

In SAP No. 47 the Committee discussed the general and specific auditing procedures that extend into the subsequent period, such as, the examination of data to assure that proper cutoffs have been made, and the examination of data which aid in the evaluation of assets and liabilities at the date of the balance sheet. In addition, the auditor should perform other auditing procedures in the subsequent period for the purpose of ascertaining whether subsequent events or transactions have occurred which require adjustment or disclosure. These procedures—to be performed at or near the completion of the field work—include:

    a. Reading the latest available interim statements, comparing them with the audited statements, and making any other appropriate comparisons.

    b. Inquiring concerning contingent liabilities and commitments, changes in capital stock, long-term debt, or working capital, unusual subsequent adjustments, and the status of items that had been accounted for on the basis of tentative or inconclusive information.

    c. Reading available minutes and inquiring concerning meetings for which minutes are not available.

    d. Obtaining a letter from legal counsel concerning litigation, claims, and contingent liabilities.

    e. Obtaining written representations from responsible officers concerning subsequent events.

An independent auditor may have to reissue his report in connection with financial statements included in annual reports filed with the SEC (Form 10-K, for example) or other regulatory agencies. Use of the original report date in a reissued report removes any implication that records, events, or transactions have been examined after that date. In such cases, the independent auditor has no obligation to make further investigation or inquiry as to events which may have occurred during the period between the original report date and the date of the release of additional reports. When the reissued report is included in a registration statement filed under the 1933 Securities Act, however, the auditor has additional responsibilities as discussed beginning on page **12·11**.

SEC Decisions Involving Subsequent Transactions and Events. —The foregoing discussion has been based principally on Statement on Auditing Procedure No. 47, issued in September 1971 by the AICPA Committee on Auditing Procedure. Prior to that statement (and its predecessor, SAP No. 33, chapter 11), the SEC had stated its views in a number of cases on the matter of disclosure of events and transactions subsequent to the statement date.

In *Potrero Sugar Company* (5 SEC 982 (1939)) the Commission held that a financial statement was not misleading if it failed to disclose subsequent cost increases in connection with settlement of a strike. Substantially the same issue was discussed in *Central Specialty Company*. (10 SEC 1102 (1942)) These cases are discussed on pages **13**·29 and **13**·30.

In *Oklahoma Hotel Building Company* (4 SEC 584 (1939)) the registrant had defaulted in the payment of interest after the date of the balance sheet but before the date of the accountant's certificate. The SEC held that the failure to disclose the default was a material omission. The duty to disclose the default, said the SEC, rested both on accepted accounting standards and on the requirements of full disclosure under the Securities Act.

Colorado Milling and Elevator Company (15 SEC 20 (1943)) dealt with extraordinary transactions and events before and after the statement date. The case is discussed on page **13**·5.

In March, 1951, a utility company filed its registration statement for an offer of common stock. The income statements for 1949 and 1950 included approximately $125,000 and $415,000 ($75,000 and $228,000 after taxes), respectively, and the balance sheet included a deferred credit for contingent revenues of approximately $412,000 (equivalent to $227,000 after taxes) for revenues billed by the registrant pursuant to a rate increase granted by the local regulatory commission. At the time of filing the United States Court of Appeals had affirmed the action of the United States District Court in vacating the regulatory commission's order and had ordered amounts collected after a certain date impounded. The Court had ordered that the registrant refund to its customers all monies collected under the increased rates but had granted a stay of its judgment pending appeal to the Supreme Court. The above situation was fully disclosed in the financial statements, and matters requiring amendment had been corrected to put the statement in final form. However, at about the time the registration statement was to become effective, the Supreme Court refused to review the Appellate Court's findings that the order of the local regulatory commission be vacated. The registrant and its accountants then proposed to expand the footnote describing the litigation to explain the effect of the Supreme Court's action but without eliminating from the income statements the revenues then to be refunded or correcting the balance sheet to show the liability for the ordered refund. The registrant was requested by the SEC's staff, however, *to adjust the income statements and balance sheet* in respect of the refundable amounts, since under the circumstances no accounting justification then existed for including in the income statements amounts which clearly were not proper revenue items and for failing to show the proper current liabilities. The statements were amended as requested by the SEC. [17 SEC Ann. Rep. 16 (1951)].

In one case discussed by the SEC the subsequent event was the payment of a substantial amount of cash to officers of the registrant. In a note to the financial statements contained in a registration statement it was stated that payments on certain obligations to affiliated persons, reported as non-current liabilities in the balance sheet, had been accelerated subsequent to the balance sheet date. Since the acceleration resulted in a substantial reduction in the working capital indicated in the balance sheet, the registrant was requested to include in the captions Total Current Assets and Total Current Liabilities a cross-reference to the aforementioned note, which was expanded to disclose the source of the funds used in the acceleration. The disclosure indicated a reduction in working capital of more than $500,000 in the two months after the balance sheet date when working capital amounted to approximately $750,000. [21 SEC Ann. Rep. 18 (1955)].

A registrant engaged in the liquor business included in its annual report to the SEC, as a note to the financial statements, a disclosure that, within the month subsequent to the balance sheet date, settlement in a substantial amount had been made in respect of claims against it relating to its sale several years before of investments in certain companies. The accountants' opinion covering the financial statement was signed approximately seven weeks after the settlement date. On the basis that the accountants had knowledge of the final status of the claims prior to the signing of their opinion, the Division of Corporation Finance requested and obtained the filing of revised financial statements reflecting the settlement. [18 SEC Ann. Rep. 33 (1952)].

The preceding paragraph relates to an annual report filed with the SEC. Presumably the point involved would be even more applicable in the case of a filing of a registration statement.

Method of Disclosing Subsequent Transactions and Events.—As previously noted, as a part of their examination, independent public accountants are concerned with events and transactions subsequent to the date of the financial statements they certify. While many accountants incorporate such events and transactions in the statements or the footnotes, other accountants go to great lengths to distinguish between those events and transactions occurring between the date of the balance sheet and the date of their certificate, and those subsequent to the date of their certificate. The following note appearing in the financial statements in a prospectus filed with the SEC shows how one accountant disclosed events and transactions subsequent to the statement date.

NOTE 15. EVENTS SUBSEQUENT TO DECEMBER 31, 19__:

To Date of Opinion of Independent Public Accountants
February 23, 19__

The Corporation acquired on January 3, 19__, pursuant to an exchange offer agreement of November 23, 19__, certain shares of preferred and common stocks of (Company A) by the issuance of _____ shares of a new series of Cumulative Preferred Stock, entitled $5 Dividend Series B 19___, having a stated value of $100 per share, and _____ shares of Common Stock. Subsequent to consummation of said agreement, or on or about January 26, 19___, additional shares of (Company A) common stock were acquired by a cash payment of $ _____ , so that at February 23, 19___ the minority interest in (Company A) amounted to approximately ___ %. (See comment (i) below.)

On February 23, 19___, an exchange offer agreement was entered into with the stockholders and certain noteholders of (Company B) by which the Corporation would acquire (a) all of the outstanding stock of that company by the subsequent issuance of _____ shares of Common Stock, and (b) $ _____ principal amount of the 4% promissory notes of that company by the subsequent issuance of _____ shares of a new series of Cumulative Preferred stock, entitled $5 Dividend Series A 19___, having a stated value of $100 per share. (See comment (ii) below.)

AFTER DATE OF OPINION OF INDEPENDENT PUBLIC ACCOUNTANTS

(i) After February 23, 19___, and on or about March 3 and April 1, 19___, additional shares of preferred stock and common stock of (Company A) were acquired by the Corporation, resulting in the issuance by the Corporation of _____ shares of Cumulative Preferred Stock, $5 Dividend Series B 19___, and _____ shares of Common Stock. The aggregate value of the investment of the Corporation in (Company A), as determined by the Board of Directors for all shares of stock of the Corporation issued and cash paid, amounted to $ _____

(ii) The issuance and delivery of (a) the _____ shares of Common Stock in exchange for all of the outstanding stock of (Company B) and (b) the _____ shares of Cumulative Preferred Stock, $5 Dividend Series A 19___, having a stated value of $100 per share, in exchange for the above mentioned promissory notes of said company, was made on March 7, 19___. The aggregate value of this investment and the notes receivable acquired, as determined by the Board of Directors of the Corporation for shares of stock issued, was $ _____

(iii) At the annual stockholders' meeting on April 26, 19___, the stockholders approved:

(a) An increase in the authorized number of shares of Preferred Stock, without par value, from _____ to _____

(b) The stock option agreements, dated December 29, 19___ (referred to in the last paragraph of Note ___ above.)

(c) The employees' stock option or purchase plan previously approved by the stockholders in 19___, under which additional stock options may be granted.

(iv) The exchange was made on April 28, 19___, of the remaining retained shares of (Company C) (referred to in the second paragraph of Note ___ above) by the issuance of _____ shares of Common Stock of the Corporation.

(v) Events subsequent to February 23, 19___, referred to in various sections of the Prospectus:

(a) Offer to stockholders of various series of outstanding Preferred Stocks to exchange such Stocks for shares of a new series of Cumulative Preferred Stock, the expected redemption of remaining Preferred Stocks not exchanged, and the borrowing restrictions effected by, and the sinking fund benefits of, the new series—refer to "Exchange Offer" and "Description of Preferred Stock" in the Prospectus.

(b) Arrangements for new long-term borrowing by the Corporation involving further or different restrictions from those described in Note ___ above on dividends and other distributions on and purchases and other acquisitions of capital stock and certain investments—refer to "Purpose of Financing," and "Dividend Rights and Restrictions" under "Description of Preferred Stock" in the Prospectus.

Other accountants believe that there is little to be said in favor of classifying footnote information along the lines indicated in the preceding example. These accountants believe that, since the financial statements are management's representations, the information in footnotes should be in the form that would be used by management, and, accordingly, there should be no distinction as to events and transactions which occurred before or after the date of the accountants' report.

These accountants prefer to retain as the date of their report the date on which they originally formed their opinion on the financial statements. They may be troubled, however, by the fact that while the report is dated, say February 15, the information in the footnotes may speak as of a later date, say April 10. They overcome this difficulty by dating their certificate in the registration statement as follows: "February 15, 19___, except as to the matter referred to in Note___ of the Notes to Financial Statements as to which the date is April 10, 19___." (This subject is discussed at greater length under "Date of Certificate" in Chapter **24**.)

Registration Statement Speaks as of Effective Date

When a registration statement is filed under the Securities Act of 1933, there are several dates which are important to the certifying accountant:

1. The date of the balance sheet
2. The date of the accountant's certificate, i.e., the date on which he formed his opinion of the balance sheet
3. The filing date of the registration statement, i.e., the date on which the registration document is filed with the Securities and Exchange Commission
4. The effective date of the registration statement, after which the securities may be offered to the public.

Section 11 of the 1933 Act provides, in part, as follows:

In case any part of the registration statement, *when such part became effective,* contained an untrue statement of a material fact or omitted to state a material fact required to be stated therein or necessary to make the statements therein not misleading, any person acquiring such security . . . may . . . sue . . . every accountant . . . who has with his consent been named as having

. . . certified any part of the registration statement . . . with respect to the statement in such registration statement . . . which purports to have been . . . certified by him. (Emphasis added.)

The law provides, however, that the accountant may avoid liability if he can prove that, after reasonable investigation, he had reasonable ground to believe and did believe in the truth and completeness of the statements made on his authority; see Chapter **27**.

The BarChris Decision.—It has long been the opinion of many accountants (including the author) that, based on the section of the law quoted above, the *registration statement speaks as of its effective date.* This means that, *when it becomes effective* the registration statement must be true and there must be no material omissions. The opinions of laymen, however, are not convincing in an area involving legal interpretations of the 1933 Act. The judge's decision in the *BarChris* case (discussed in Chapter **28**) made it clear that the responsibility of all concerned will be viewed in the light of the situation existing on the effective date of the registration statement.

In *BarChris,* the accountants' certificate covered a balance sheet as of December 31, 1960 and the period then ended. The accountants' certificate was dated February 23, 1961, and was included in a registration statement under the 1933 Act that became effective on May 16, 1961. The judge's opinion observed that the part of the registration statement made upon the authority of the accountants as experts was the 1960 figures. But because the statute required the court to determine the accountants' belief, and the grounds thereof, "at the time such part of the registration statement became effective," the judge said, *"for the purposes of this affirmative defense the matter must be viewed as of May 16, 1961,* and the question is whether *at that time* [the independent accountants,] after reasonable investigation, had reasonable ground to believe and did believe that the 1960 figures were true and that no material fact had been omitted from the registration statement which should have been included in order to make the 1960 figures not misleading." (Emphasis added.)

SEC Decisions Emphasizing Importance of Effective Date.— One of the earliest decisions of the SEC discussed the time as of which the truth of a statement will be tested [*Charles A. Howard,* 1 SEC 9 (1934)]. The case involved a registration statement under the Securities Act of 1933. The registration form called for a statement of legal proceedings known to the registrant which might be pending or might be threatened and which might materially affect the securities to be called for deposit. The registration also asked for a brief description of their nature and a statement of the names of the parties to the actions. To this item the registrant replied

"None known." The evidence showed that a suit was pending in the Pennsylvania courts for the appointment of a receiver for the successor in interest of the original issuer of the bonds sought to be called for deposit. The Commission conceded that registrants had no actual knowledge of this pending litigation and that consequently the statement made by them in the registration statement was true as of the time of the making of that statement.

. . . But if, prior to the time that the registration statement became effective, registrants learned of the pendency of such litigation, they would be required to amend that statement in their registration statement in order for the registration statement to be free from deficiencies, *since under Section 11 the truth of the statements in the registration statement is to be tested as of the time that they become effective.* This does not, of course, mean that a statement in the registration statement purporting obviously to state a fact as of some time in the past, as for example, statements in a dated balance sheet, must speak as of the date of the effectiveness of the registration statement; but, in order to be certain to avoid the possibility of liability arising under Section 11, it becomes necessary for registrants in answer to a question, such as that embodied in Item 11, which calls merely for such facts as are within their actual knowledge, to state those facts as of the time that the registration statement becomes effective. In other words, if the state of the registrant's knowledge changes between the time that the registration statement is actually signed and the time that it becomes effective, the registration statement should reflect that change. (Emphasis supplied.)

In *Globe Aircraft Corporation* [26 SEC 48(1947)] the prospectus filed as part of the registration statement included a table showing the company's capital securities as of February 23, 1946. Subsequent to that date and the effective date of the registration statement, the amount of the company's outstanding notes payable increased substantially, but this fact was not disclosed. The instructions for the form of registration statement used by the company provided that there should be indicated any material changes since the date as of which the information given with reference to capital securities (which include notes) is furnished.

The SEC said that *"the adequacy of the disclosure must be judged as of the effective date,* and as of that date it is clear that the data in the prospectus . . . was materially misleading" (emphasis supplied).

A former associate general counsel of the SEC, however, expressed some doubt concerning the date as of which the registration speaks. On this fundamental question, he said, the statute is not too clear on its face. "At any rate," he wrote, "it has been the consistent administrative construction . . . that the registration statement is required to be true and adequate only as of its effective date." [1] Referring to the *Charles A. Howard* decision (quoted, in part, above) he continued:

[1] Loss, *Securities Regulation,* 2d ed., (1961), p. 290.

Nor does it mean that it suffices if the registration statement is true, and adequate as of the date of its *filing;* if the state of the registrant's knowledge or the facts change between the filing and effective dates, the registration statement must be corrected by amendment. But it does mean that the registration statement need not be amended *after* its effective date to reflect post-effective developments.[2]

See also page **12·**59, especially as the quoted matter refers to transactions and events subsequent to the statement date.

Necessity for Auditor to Keep in Touch with Client's Financial Affairs Afer Filing Date.—From what has been said in the preceding pages, it should be apparent that the law imposes a duty on all concerned with a registration statement which does not end with the filing of the registration statement with the SEC in Washington, D. C. As far as the independent public accountant is concerned, when he has signed his certificate covering the financial statements and his consent to the inclusion of his certificate in the registration document, his job is also not finished.

After the filing date and up to the effective date, the accountant must take reasonable steps to ascertain whether anything has happened in the interim which materially affects the statements he certifies. This is a responsibility which, it is true, he shares with others, but it is not a complete defense to say that his responsibility is only secondary and that the primary responsibility is the registrant's. Suppose, for example, that on the date of the statements and on the filing date an important lawsuit was pending, as to which no provision had been or could be made for an adverse decision. Shortly after the filing date a decision is handed down against the registrant. Under the law, unless this information is included in the registration statement, it might be construed as an omission of a material fact which would subject those participating in the registration to the liabilities provided in the statute.

It seems clear that the obligation of the certifying accountant does not end with the filing of the registration statement. The accountant may not relax his vigilance after the filing and simply sit back and wait for the SEC's memorandum of comments, and, ultimately, the effective date. On the other hand, the independent accountant as a practical matter cannot be expected to keep his audit going continuously until the effective date; this may take weeks or even months. The delay may be occasioned by administrative procedures; it may be caused by postponement by the issuer or underwriter of the proposed offering as a result of market or other conditions.

The author has not interpreted the clause "at the time such part of the registration statement became effective" as requiring the accountant to

---

[2] *Author's note*: The quoted section apparently is not intended to relate to prospectuses used more than nine months after the effective date of the registration statement. See the applicable discussion on page **11·**28.

continue his examination of the books and records to the effective date. It should be his practice, however, to keep in touch with the financial affairs of his client in some manner.

Section 11 of the 1933 Act provides in effect that no independent auditor shall be liable, as provided therein, if such auditor shall sustain the burden of proof that as to the part of the registration statement purporting to be made on his authority as an expert,

. . . he had, *after reasonable investigation,* reasonable ground to believe and did believe, *at the time such part of the registration statement became effective,* that the statements therein were true and that there was no omission to state a material fact required to be stated therein or necessary to make the statements therein not misleading . . . (Emphasis added.)

To sustain the burden of proof that he has made a "reasonable investigation," the independent public accountant should supplement his audit procedures by performing certain additional procedures with respect to subsequent events up to, or reasonably close to, the effective date of the registration statement to the extent reasonable and practicable in the circumstances. The additional procedures recommended by the AICPA Committee on Auditing Procedure are set forth below.

Requirements as to "Keeping Current" Review.—SAP No. 47 states what the independent auditor must do with respect to subsequent events from the date of his report up to the effective date of the registration statement filed under the 1933 Act, or as close thereto as is reasonable and practicable in the circumstances. First of all, the auditor should arrange to be kept advised by his client of the progress of the registration proceedings so that his review of subsequent events can be completed by the effective date. The likelihood of the auditor discovering subsequent events must necessarily decrease following the completion of the field work and, as a practical matter, subsequent to that time the independent auditor may rely, for the most part, on inquiries of responsible officers and employees.

At or near the effective date, the auditor should repeat those procedures which he performed in connection with the original issuance of his report for the purpose of ascertaining the occurrence of subsequent events that may require adjustment of, or disclosure in, the financial statements:

a. Read the latest available interim financial statements; compare them with the financial statements being reported upon; and make any other comparisons considered appropriate in the circumstances. In order to make these procedures as meaningful as possible for the purpose expressed above, the auditor should inquire of officers and other executives having responsibility for financial and accounting matters as to whether the interim statements have been prepared on the same basis as that used for the statements under examination.

    b. Inquire of and discuss with officers and other executives having responsibility for financial and accounting matters (limited where appropriate to major locations) as to:

        (i) Whether any substantial contingent liabilities or commitments existed at the date of the balance sheet being reported on or at the date of inquiry.

       (ii) Whether there was any significant change in the capital stock, long-term debt, or working capital to the date of inquiry.

      (iii) The current status of items, in the financial statements being reported on, that were accounted for on the basis of tentative, preliminary, or inconclusive data.

      (iv) Whether any unusual adjustments had been made during the period from the balance sheet date to the date of inquiry.

    c. Read the available minutes of meetings of stockholders, directors and appropriate committees; as to meetings for which minutes are not available, inquire about matters dealt with at such meetings.

    d. Obtain from legal counsel a description and evaluation of any litigation, impending litigation, claims and contingent liabilities of which he has knowledge that existed at the date of the balance sheet being reported on, together with a description and evaluation of any additional matters of such nature coming to his attention up to the date the information is furnished.

    e. Obtain a letter of representations, dated as of the date of the auditor's report, from appropriate officials, generally the chief executive officer and chief financial officer, as to whether any events occurred subsequent to the date of the financial statements being reported on by the independent auditor that in the officers' opinion would require adjustment or disclosure in these statements. The auditor may elect to have the client include representations as to significant matters disclosed to the auditor in his performance of the procedures in subparagraphs (a) to (d) above and (f) below.

    f. Make such additional inquiries or perform such procedures as he considers necessary and appropriate to dispose of questions that arise in carrying out the foregoing procedures, inquiries and discussions.

In addition to the procedures described above, SAP No. 47 states that, at or near the effective date of the registration statement, the auditor generally should do the following:

    a. Read the entire prospectus and other pertinent portions of the registration statement.

    b. Inquire of and obtain written confirmation from officers and other executives having responsibility for financial and accounting matters (limited where appropriate to major locations) as to whether there have occurred any events other than those reflected or disclosed in the registration statement which, in the officers' opinion, have a material effect on the audited financial statements included therein or which should be disclosed in order to keep those statements from being misleading.

With respect to unaudited financial statements that may be included in the registration, because he has not audited them, the independent public accountant can not be expected to have an opinion as to whether such statements have been prepared in conformity with generally accepted accounting principles. If, however, on the basis of facts known to him, the auditor concludes that the unaudited statements are *not* in conformity with generally accepted accounting principles, SAP No. 47 states that the auditor has to do something:

a. He should insist upon appropriate revision of the unaudited statements;

b. Failing that, he should add a comment in his report calling attention to the departure from generally accepted accounting principles;

c. Further, he should consider—probably with the advice of legal counsel—withholding his consent to the use of his report on the audited financial statements in the registration statement. (As indicated in SAP No. 38, paragraph 7, dealing with unaudited financial statements, the auditor may have to consider withdrawing from the engagement.)

It will be noted that the procedures recommended in SAP No. 47 (which are listed above) include, among other things, reading the latest available interim financial statements (whether or not they are included in the registration document), obtaining a representation letter from management, and making inquiries of appropriate responsible officials concerning the preparation of the interim financial statements and subsequent transactions and events. These are required procedures whether or not the auditor is requested to furnish a comfort letter for the benefit of the underwriters. The subject of comfort letters is considered in subsequent pages of this chapter. It should be understood, however, that any additional procedures performed by the auditor at the request of the underwriter for his benefit in connection with the issuance by the auditor of a comfort letter are not required for the purpose of the "keeping current" review contemplated by SAP No. 47.

If the registration statement contains the reports of two or more auditors covering different periods, see the discussion under "Keeping Current When Registrant Has Changed Auditors."

Keeping Current and the BarChris Case.—In Chapter **28** of this book is a discussion of *Escott v. BarChris Construction Corporation*[3]—commonly known as the BarChris case. It is without a doubt the most important

[3] 283 F. Supp. 643 (S. D. N. Y. 1968).

decision to date involving the civil liabilities of issuers, officers, directors, underwriters, and independent auditors under the 1933 Act. As will be seen from the discussion in Chapter **28**, the independent auditors who certified the BarChris financial statements included in a registration statement filed under the Act were held to have been negligent, and not to have established the defense of due diligence provided in the Act. The decision established clearly that the liability of all concerned (including the accountants) is determined by the situation existing on the effective date of a registration statement filed under the Act, and considered carefully the procedures employed by the auditors to make certain that, as of that date, there were no material misstatements or omissions.

The decision in the BarChris case was rendered by a Federal court judge, and much of his decision, insofar as it relates to the auditors, turned on the quality of the review made by the auditors with a view to "keeping current" with respect to the company's financial affairs down to approximately the effective date of the registration statement. BarChris' independent auditors were aware of their responsibilities in this respect, and had a written program for what they called the "S-1 review." (The designation "S-1 review," in the opinion of the author, is a poor choice of words, since the scope of the review is the same regardless of the registration form used —whether S-1, S-7, S-9, or any of the other registration forms under the 1933 Act. In this book the term "keeping current review" is used, but in the BarChris decision the judge employed the term "S-1 review" because that was what the auditors called it.)

The judge said that the auditors' written S-1 review program conformed to generally accepted auditing standards, but he was critical of the auditors for the manner in which the work was done, the small amount of time that was devoted to this task, and the omission of procedures set forth in their own written review program. These matters are summarized at some length in Chapter **28** in connection with consideration of the entire case, and will not be repeated here.

As will be seen from the discussion in the aforementioned chapter, the judge who decided the BarChris case said that accountants "should not be held to a standard higher than that recognized in their profession." Lest any public accountant derive too much comfort from this statement, it is worth noting that at least one authority takes strong exception to it. A professor of law said that this dictum is "a gross overstatement, since the relevance of professional standards in establishing the legal duty of care should always remain open to the reviewing court." [4] He also stated that making the standards of private groups conclusive of the legal requirements of care and diligence "would delegate authority without statutory authoriza-

[4] Ernest L. Folk, III, "Civil Liabilities Under the Federal Securities Acts: The *BarChris* Case," *Virginia Law Review*, Feb. 1969, p. 62.

tion and could conceivably afford incentives to ease potential liabilities by lowering professional standards." Furthermore, he said, it would be bad policy to make the AICPA standards conclusive:

". . . First, they apparently contemplate internal procedures only without investigation outside the organization being audited, although in some situations updating the audited statements may well demand outside inquiry to be effective. Thus, in *BarChris* it would have been proper and not burdensome for the S-1 reviewer to check out BarChris' then current status with its factor; this would likely have uncovered many facts misstated in the prospectus. Second, the AICPA standards call only for reading the "available" minutes of meetings of directors, committees, or shareholders, although *BarChris* demonstrates how such a rule could block access to needed current information. [Auditors] can reasonably demand all minutes necessary to update their statements, or at least obtain a clear and convincing explanation of why such material is unavailable." [5]

(The writer's comments were based on the then requirements of SAP No. 33, chapter 11, which were superseded by SAP No. 47 in September 1971. The revised requirements call for the auditor to "Read the available minutes of meetings of stockholders, directors and appropriate committees; as to meetings for which minutes are not available, inquire about matters dealt with at such meetings.")

Despite the professor's comments, it is the opinion of this author that compliance with professional standards is both a must and an absolute minimum. The professor reached the same conclusion when he said: ". . . However, *BarChris'* endorsment of the AICPA standards makes it an indispensable minimum for accountants to adhere strictly to their professional canons for conducting the critical S-1 review . . ." [6]

Writing about the BarChris case, A. A. Sommer, Jr. observed that the judge placed some responsibility upon the accountants with regard to post-balance sheet date events by his determination with regard to the responsibility of accountants subsequent to the date of their opinion or the date of the balance sheet. Sommer wrote that "the Court made clear that the responsibility with respect to post-balance sheet events existed only to the extent that such events renderd the financial statements as to which they rendered an opinion misleading." [7]

Keeping Current When Registrant Has Changed Auditors.—Companies do not, as a rule, change auditors frequently. When a change has occurred, however, a company's registration statement may contain the reports of two (or more) auditors covering different parts of the total period of the earnings summary. A question may arise as to the responsibility of

[5] Ibid. (footnotes omitted).
[6] Ibid., p. 82.
[7] A. A. Sommer, Jr., "Accountant's Counsel—Advice to My Client," *The Business Lawyer*, Jan. 1969, p. 595.

the auditor who certifies the earlier periods with regard to transactions and events subsequent to the date of his report and the scope of the current review required of him.

A change of auditors occurs most often when Company A is acquired by Company B, and the auditor of the latter company becomes the auditor for the combined enterprise. When certified statements are required for periods preceding the combination and if it was accounted for as a pooling of interests, A's auditor will often be asked to report on that portion of the pooled figures represented by A; B's auditor will report on B's figures prior to the pooling. B will also report on the combined figures and, if he has audited the post-combination figures, the statements on the enterprise after the pooling.

The AICPA Committee on Auditing Procedure considered the problem which occurs when there has been a change of auditors, and what has to be done by the auditor who, having been replaced, is requested to report on periods which he previously examined for inclusion in a registration statement under the 1933 Act. In SAP No. 47 (paragraph 24) the Committee said that an auditor who has not examined the financial statements for the most recent audited period included in the registration statement has a responsibility relating to events subsequent to the date of the financial statements on which he is reporting which continues to the effective date, and he generally should:

a. Read pertinent portions of the prospectus and of the registration statement.
b. Obtain a letter of representations from the successor independent auditor as to whether his examination (including his procedures with respect to subsequent events) revealed any matters which, in his opinion, might have a material effect on the financial statements reported on by the predecessor auditor or would require disclosure in the notes thereto.

For a form of letter of representation from the successor auditor to the predecessor auditor, as suggested in the preceding paragraph, see the recommended forms beginning on page **24**·35.

If the predecessor auditor becomes aware of any events or transactions which require adjustment of, or disclosure in, the financial statements examined by him, the statements should be adjusted or the subsequent event should be disclosed or the auditor should qualify his report. (In some cases, rather than a qualification of the report, a disclaimer of opinion or an adverse opinion may be appropriate.)

The Shonts Case.—Prior to the BarChris case, according to the author's information, there was only one case in which the court had to consider the question of the accountant's responsibility under the Securities Act of 1933 for events occurring after the statement date but before the effective date. The case was *Shonts v. Hirliman* [28 F. Supp. 478 (S. D. Cal. 1939)], and the court in effect held the accountant not liable for events occurring subsequent to the date of his certificate. The decision was in the District Court for the Southern District of California and was not appealed to a higher court.

THE FACTS IN THE SHONTS CASE.—A motion picture company was organized as successor to several predecessors and filed a registration statement on December 30, 1936, under the 1933 Act. The certificate of the certifying accountants and their consent were dated December 28, 1936. The company had no material amount of fixed assets and did not own a studio in which to "shoot" motion pictures.

A "delaying" amendment was filed on January 15, 1937, and was followed by a second amendment on January 23, 1937. In this second amendment changes were made in the narrative section as well as in the financial section of the registration, and accordingly a new certificate dated January 19, 1937, and a consent were signed by the certifying accountants. A third amendment was filed on February 1, 1937, but apparently no changes were made in the financial statements because a new accountants' consent was not filed. The SEC declared the registration effective on February 3, 1937, as of January 19, 1937. After the effective date, more amendments were filed. Some of the stock had been sold when the SEC instituted stop-order proceedings. On May 11, 1937, the Commission issued a stop-order suspending the effectiveness of the registration statement (2 SEC 292) and preventing further sales of the stock.

Some of the people who purchased the shares brought suit against certain officials of the corporation and the certifying accountants. The actions were to recover damages (the price paid for the stock) under Section 11 of the 1933 Act, alleging falsity in the registration statement. The falsity relied on by the plaintiffs related to misrepresentations and omissions concerning a lease between the motion picture company and the owner of a studio, and the failure to set forth in the amendments to the registration statement that the motion picture company was obligated under the lease to use the studio a minimum of 100 days a year at a total rental of $35,000.

The evidence showed that a formal lease was not entered into until March 9, 1937. However, a telegram signed by the studio president, dated January 31, 1937, committed the company to a rental arrangement to be followed by a formal leasing. This telegram indicated that the studios were rented for $350 per shooting day but did not refer to a minimum guarantee. The formal agreement of March 9, 1937, committed the motion picture company to shoot at least 100 days a year at a rental charge of $350 per day while in the studio and $175 per day while on location. The judge said he was satisfied that the omission from the statement of the minimum requirements in the lease, which obligated the picture company to shoot at least 100 days a year, was material. The judge continued:

> It is not of any great significance that the lease was not actually entered into until later. For that reason, I am of the view that there is no falsity in the statement that they had certain rental arrangements with a particular company. I think the oral negotiations and the telegram of January 31, 1937, showed a commitment which the parties themselves considered binding, and which was to be later embodied in a more formal instrument. The effect of these conclusions is this: No misstatement or omission appears in the registration statement until after the last certificate of [the certifying accountants], dated January 19, 1937. Prior to January 31, 1937, there were merely discussions of rental, and no definite undertaking by either side or guarantee of a minimum which was binding on the company. The failure of the certificate of [the certifying accountants] to set up the rental undertaking and the minimum guarantee of $35,000 as a contingent liability is not the omission of anything which existed then. The rental arrangement was not called to their attention. There was no entry on the books at their disposal, from which, by further inquiry, they might have discovered that there was such an undertaking. Absent these, they cannot be charged with a misrepresentation which was made later—long after their certification.

As to the accountants the judge concluded:

> In sum, we cannot as to [the certifying accountants], take the subsequent omissions and retroject them to the date of January 19, 1937, so as to "tie" them to a certificate, which they made on the basis of facts as they then existed and which showed no rental arrangement of any kind.

If the telegram confirming the lease arrangement had been dated prior to the date of the accountants' last certificate, would the judge have upheld the plaintiffs as against the accountants? Is there any significance in the fact that the registration statement was declared effective on February 3, 1937, as of January 19, 1937? These are interesting questions, the answers to which will have to await judicial interpretation.

An article which appeared in the *Yale Law Journal* in 1940 commented on this case as follows:

> The court in this case thus set out as reasonable an investigatory standard far below that which is customary in the profession and necessary for the detection of possible contingent liabilities, which must be listed in the registration statement. The usual investigation, it appears, would include securing information from the responsible corporate officials as to the extent of any contingent expenditures, legal opinions on the possibility of damages being assessed against the company as a consequence of any pending litigation, and the inspection of the minutes of stockholders' and directors' meetings. It is true that the discovery of such contingent liabilities is among the most difficult problems facing the accountant, but the accountant, alone, will be able to bring to light these items of potential importance to security buyers, and he should therefore be fully liable for any failure to take whatever means are available and customary in discovering any such concealed obligations.

A law professor who was formerly associate general counsel of the SEC wrote critically of the Shonts decision and referred to the "surprisingly low accounting standards which seemed to satisfy the court." He also made this observation:

The fact is that the District Court set a standard of care far below that which is customary for the profession and necessary for the detection of possible contingent liabilities to be listed in the registration statement. Few reputable accounting firms would be satisfied with a mere perusal of matters coming to their attention through inspection of the "books at their disposal." [8]

More recently, A. A. Sommer, Jr., attacked the Shonts decision saying that it was a clear distortion of the language of Section 11 of the 1933 Act:

The Court exonerated the accountants on the ground that at the date they gave their opinion a lease obligation was not in existence and hence liability could not be based on their failure to disclose it. The Court did not discuss the significance of the statement in Section 11 . . . that an accountant had a responsibility with respect to his portion of the registration statement related to "the time such part of the registration statement became effective." *In effect the Court said that the responsibility of the accountant terminated when he rendered his opinion. This is patently contrary to the language of the statute.*[9] (Emphasis supplied.)

The Shonts decision is an unsatisfactory one, and it raises almost as many questions as it answers. Because of the many attacks on the decision, prudence requires the independent auditor to be guided by the decision in the BarChris case and to keep in touch with the financial affairs of his client up to the effective date of the registration statement.

Comfort Letters

The agreements between issuers of securities (or selling stockholders) and investment bankers providing for the offering and sale of securities to the public usually are conditioned upon the receipt by the investment bankers (the underwriters) of a letter from the issuer's independent public accountants. In a typical case, the accountants will be asked to comment in their letter on the following matters:

a. The independence of the certifying accountants
b. The compliance of the audited financial statements with the requirements of the 1933 Act and the SEC's rules
c. Unaudited financial statements included in the registration statement
d. Subsequent changes in the companies' capitalization, long-term debt, and in certain financial statement items
e. Tables, statistics, and other designated financial information in the registration statement.

[8] Loss, *Securities Regulation,* 2d ed., (1961), p. 290.
[9] A. A. Sommer, Jr., "Accountant's Counsel—Advice to My Client," *The Business Lawyer,* Jan. 1969, p. 594.

For obvious reasons, accountants' letters issued pursuant to these require-ments are usually called "comfort letters" (or, less often, "cold comfort letters"). The matters dealt with in a particular letter will ordinarily be confined to those specified in the underwriting agreement.

The accountants can normally furnish only "negative assurance" con-cerning items (c), (d), and (e) above. (Negative assurance consists of a statement to the effect that, as a result of specified procedures, nothing came to the accountants' attention that caused them to believe that specified mat-ters do not meet a specified standard, e.g., that unaudited financial state-ments were not prepared in conformity with generally accepted accounting principles applied on a consistent basis.)

A few investment bankers (including some of the most prominent in the business) do not make the receipt of comfort letters a condition of their formal underwriting agreements, but nevertheless ask for such letters. Ac-cordingly, in a given case if the underwriting agreement is silent with re-spect to comfort letters, the accountant should not conclude that such letters are not required.

Comfort letters are not required by the 1933 Act or by the SEC, and copies of the letters are not filed with the SEC. Nonetheless, as previously noted, it is a common provision in an underwriting agreement in connec-tion with an offering of securities registered with the SEC under the 1933 Act that a comfort letter will be furnished. Since the agreement itself is filed with the registration statement, the staff of the SEC are alerted to the fact that the agreement contemplates the issuance of a comfort letter. In such cases, the staff, on occasion, have asked to be furnished with a copy of the comfort letter—not as a part of the registration statement, to be sure, but as supplemental information for use only by the staff. This has hap-pened only seldom, but it seems clear that if it becomes the practice of the SEC to ask for these letters, accountants will give serious consideration to discontinuing them. The letters are clearly intended for the benefit of the underwriters. Most certainly there is no intention to expose the writers of such letters to the liabilities of the Securities Act or to enlarge the circle of persons for whose benefit the letters are written.

Statement on Auditing Procedure No. 48.—For several years the issuance of comfort letters by independent auditors was governed by SAP No. 35, issued in 1965 by the AICPA Committee on Auditing Procedure. This statement contained many suggestions regarding the form and content of such letters.

In recent years—and especially since the BarChris decision—there has been an enormous proliferation in underwriters' requests for matters to be included in comfort letters. The accountants involved felt that some of these requests could be complied with, but that there were others which were beyond their professional competence. As a result of extensive experience with SAP No. 35 and because of the uncertainty among accountants, clients, and underwriters as to the nature and proper scope of comfort letters, the AICPA Committee on Auditing Procedure reconsidered the entire subject, and, in October 1971, issued SAP No. 48, "Letters for Underwriters."

As compared with the statement which it superseded, the new statement made these changes:

a. Makes it clear that the underwriters are responsible for the sufficiency of the procedures employed by the independent auditors in furnishing negative assurance with respect to unaudited interim financial statements and other matters included in the comfort letters.

b. Eliminates the use of the term "material adverse changes" in dealing with changes in operations and financial condition subsequent to the statements included in the prospectus, and substitutes therefor "decreases" in specified financial statement items.

c. Discusses how to deal with statistical tables and other text material and what kind of items may be appropriately covered in the comfort letter.

The new statement made many other changes, but those listed above were the principal changes. The comments and discussion which follow were taken largely from that statement.

Statements on Auditing Procedure are generally effective at the time of their issuance. Inasmuch, however, as clients, underwriters, and accountants normally reach agreement about the procedures to be performed and the content of comfort letters well in advance of the letters being issued, SAP No. 48 was not effective with respect to comfort letters in connection with registration statements initially filed on or before March 31, 1972.

Underwriters have little or no liability with respect to information in a registration statement filed under the 1933 Act which is made on the authority of an "expert." Under the statute, an accountant whose certificate is included in a registration statement with his consent is an expert. When financial statements in a registration statement are certified by an independent public accountant, the statements are said to be "expertized." With respect to the portions of the registration document that are not expertized, the underwriter is obligated to make a reasonable investigation. The underwriter's request for a comfort letter springs from his need to make a reasonable investigation of financial and accounting data that are not certified by independent auditors.

Accountants also have an obligation to make a reasonable investigation of the audited financial statements that are included in a registration statement in reliance upon their report. As SAP No. 48 points out, the accountants' reasonable investigation must be based upon an audit made in accordance with generally accepted auditing standards; the investigation can not be accomplished by measures short of an audit. In contrast, what constitutes a reasonable investigation of unaudited financial and accounting data, sufficient to satisfy an underwriter's purposes, has never been clearly delineated. It seems clear, however, that the purposes of the investigations by the underwriter on the one hand and by the accountant on the other hand are quite different.

Accountants are normally willing to assist the underwriters in any way consistent with their professional capabilities, but the assistance which they can furnish in the form of comfort letters is limited in the following respects:

a. An independent accountant can properly comment in his professional capacity only on matters with respect to which his professional expertise is relevant. Accordingly, he is no more expert than the underwriter to verify the registrant's representations with respect to the number of square feet of floor space in a factory building.

b. Procedures that fall short of an audit made in accordance with generally accepted auditing standards (which is all that a comfort letter calls for) by their nature ordinarily do not furnish accountants with a basis for a positive opinion, but at the most negative assurance. Although SAP No. 48 furnishes illustrations of procedures which are often followed by accountants as a basis for their comments in comfort letters, *it is important to understand that the statement does not prescribe such procedures.*

c. The AICPA Committee on Auditing Procedure concluded that it is not practicable to establish standards comparable to generally accepted auditing standards by which the sufficiency of procedures to support the negative assurance contained in comfort letters can be measured. Therefore, negative assurances in specific situations cannot reasonably imply any definite or uniform degree of certainty concerning the matters to which they relate. Accordingly, the Committee said, there is necessarily a risk that matters against which negative assurance is sought may be present even though such assurance has been received.

When the underwriting agreement provides for the receipt from the independent accountants of a comfort letter which will include negative assurance on some matters, the accountants should suggest that there be a meeting of the underwriter, the client, and the accountants to discuss the procedures that will be employed in connection with the letter. In the course of such a meeting the accountants may describe the procedures commonly followed in connection with the issuance of comfort letters. Because of the accountants' familiarity with the client's business and its accounting principles and procedures, such a meeting can be helpful to the underwriter in reaching his decision as to the procedures which the accountants are to follow for the purpose of the comfort letter. However, because of the lack of standards by which the sufficiency of the procedures employed can be tested, it should be made clear that the accountants can not furnish any assurance as to the adequacy of the procedures for the underwriter's purpose.

Because the receipt of a satisfactory comfort letter from the independent auditors is an essential condition in most underwriting agreements, it is highly desirable that the auditors obtain a draft of the agreement as soon as the underwriter and the issuer have reached an understanding in principle as to what the agreement will provide. Although, as indicated in Chapter **11**, there are several reasons why the accountants should read the tentative underwriting agreement as soon as possible, it is especially important for them to read it promptly because of its bearing on the comfort letter they are expected to furnish. The accountants' primary concern is that the provisions in the agreement relating to comfort letters will not make demands on them that are impossible of performance, and that they will be able to furnish the letter on time and in acceptable form.

After they have read the tentative agreement, the accountants should prepare a draft of the letter they expect to furnish. To the extent possible, the draft should cover all the matters that will be dealt with in the final letter and should use the exact language they expect to use in the final letter, with the understanding, of course, that the comments in the final letter can not be determined until the procedures underlying it have been performed. The draft should be identified as a draft in order to avoid giving the impression that the procedures described in it have been carried out.

The draft of the comfort letter should avoid statements or implications that the accountants are carrying out such procedures as they consider necessary since this may lead to a misunderstanding about the responsibility for the sufficiency of the procedures for the underwriter's purposes.

Copies of the draft of the comfort letter should be furnished to the underwriter and to the client as soon as possible. This enables the underwriter and the client to know at an early point what they may expect of the accountants, and gives the underwriter and the client an opportunity to revise the tentative underwriting agreement if they wish to do so. In addition, it gives the underwriter the opportunity of discussing further with the accountants the procedures which they expect to follow and, if necessary, of adding to those procedures. If the additional procedures are relevant to the accountants' professional competence, they would ordinarily agree to perform them ; in that event, they should revise the draft of their comfort letter and furnish copies of it to the underwriter and to the client.

If the underwriter accepts the draft of the comfort letter and subsequently accepts the letter in its final form, the accountants may reasonably conclude that the underwriter considers the procedures described in the letter sufficient for his purposes. It is important, therefore, as SAP No. 48 points out, that the procedures employed by the accountants be clearly described in the comfort letter, in both draft and final form, so that there will be no misunderstanding of the basis upon which the accountants' statements have been made, and so that the underwriter can decide whether such procedures are sufficient for his purposes.

A legend should be placed on the draft of the letter for identification and to explain its purposes and limitations. A suggested form of such a legend (taken from SAP No. 48) follows:

> This draft is furnished solely for the purpose of indicating the form of letter which we would expect to be able to furnish [name of underwriter] in response to their request, the matters expected to be covered in the letter and the nature of the procedures which we would expect to carry out with respect to such matters. Based on our discussions with [name of underwriter], it is our understanding that the procedures outlined in this draft letter are those they wish to follow. Unless [name of underwriter] informs us that there are additional procedures they wish us to follow, we shall assume that they consider those procedures outlined sufficient for their purposes. The text of the letter itself will of course depend upon the results of the procedures, which we would not expect to complete until shortly before the letter is given and in no event before the cutoff date indicated therein.

In the absence of any discussions with the underwriter, the accountants should outline in the draft letter those procedures specified in the underwriting agreement which they are willing to perform. In that event, the second sentence in the foregoing legend should be revised as follows: "In the absence of any discussions with [name of underwriter], we have set out in this draft letter those procedures referred to in the draft underwriting agreement (of which we have been furnished a copy) which we are willing to follow."

DATE OF THE COMFORT LETTER.—The comfort letter is usually dated at or shortly before the "closing date" (which is the date on which the issuer or selling stockholder delivers the securities to the underwriters in exchange for the proceeds of the offering). The underwriting agreement ordinarily specifies the date to which the letter is to relate (e.g., a date five business days before the date of the letter)—often referred to as the "cutoff date." The auditors should make sure that the cutoff date will not place an unreasonable burden on them. The letter should state that the procedures carried out in connection with the letter did not cover the period from the cutoff date to the date of the letter.

Comfort letters may also be requested at or shortly before the effective date of the registration statement and, less frequently, at or shortly before the filing date of the registration statement. For each of such letters, it will be necessary to carry out the procedures and inquiries as of the cutoff date of the letter.

ADDRESSEE OF THE COMFORT LETTER.—Inasmuch as the comfort letter is issued as a result of the underwriter's request, many accountants address the letter only to them, and furnish a copy to their client. When this is done, the letter is addressed to the underwriter who has negotiated the underwriting agreement with the client—usually in his capacity "as Representative of the Several Underwriters." Ordinarily the accountants' discussions as to the scope and sufficiency of the letter will be conducted with the representative of the underwriting group rather than with the group itself.

Some accountants prefer to address the comfort letter to their client, or to both the client and the underwriter. SAP No. 48 suggests that if the accountants are requested to address the letter to any person other than the client or the underwriter, the accountants would do well to consult their counsel.

INTRODUCTORY PARAGRAPH OF COMFORT LETTER.—SAP No. 48 states that it is desirable to include an introductory paragraph in the comfort letter substantially as follows:

We have examined the [here identify the financial statements and schedules examined] included in the registration statement (SEC File No. 2- _____) on Form ___ filed by (name of company) under the Securities Act of 1933 (the "Act"); our reports with respect thereto are also included in such registration statement. Such registration statement, as amended as of (date), is referred to herein as the "registration statement."

This introductory paragraph is presumably intended to provide the audit base which is prerequisite for the issuance of any comfort letter.

ACCOUNTANTS' INDEPENDENCE.—The underwriting agreement will usually provide that the accountants must make a representation that they are independent within the meaning of the 1933 Act and the SEC's regulations. This matter need not be covered in the comfort letter, but is most often included in that letter.

The accountants' representation as to their independence may be along the following lines:

We are independent public accountants with respect to (name of company) within the meaning of the Act and the applicable published rules and regulations thereunder, and the answer to [here identify the item number of the applicable form that refers to the relationship with registrant of experts named in the registration, e.g., Item 24 of Form S-1] of the registration statement is correct insofar as it relates to us.

Comfort letters are sometimes requested from more than one accountant, as, for example, when a registration statement is filed in connection with the sale of securities issued in a merger. In these circumstances, each accountant must be sure he is independent within the meaning of the Act and the rules and regulations thereunder. The accountants for Company A which has been merged into Company B but was previously not affiliated need not have been independent with respect to Company B whose securities are being registered. To avoid any misunderstanding, the accountants for Company A should modify the language of the independence representation suggested above, somewhat as follows:

As of [here insert the date of the accountants' most recent report on the financial statements of their client] and during the period covered by the financial statements on which we reported, we were independent public accountants with respect to [insert here the name of their client] within the meaning of the Act and the applicable published rules and regulations thereunder, and the answer . . .

COMPLIANCE WITH THE SEC's REQUIREMENTS.—The underwriting agreement may provide that the accountants are to express an opinion concerning compliance as to form of the financial statements covered by their report with the pertinent published accounting requirements of the SEC. (The word "published" is used because the SEC staff sometimes has informal requirements which they apply administratively but which the SEC has not published. Accountants should not be expected to be familiar with, or express assurances as to compliance with, such informal requirements.)

The matter of compliance with the SEC's requirements need not be included necessarily in a comfort letter and therefore subject to the restrictions on the use of such a letter. Most often, however, the compliance representations are included in the comfort letter as a matter of convenience.

The representation as to compliance may be along the following lines:

In our opinion, [here include the phrase "except as disclosed in the registration statement," if applicable] the [here identify the financial statements and schedules covered by the auditors' report] examined by us and included or incorporated by reference in the registration statement comply as to form in all material respects with the applicable accounting requirements of the Act and of the published rules and regulations thereunder.

If there is a material departure from the pertinent published requirements, the departure should be disclosed in the letter. Normally, representatives of the SEC will have agreed to such departure; when this occurs, such agreement should be mentioned in the comfort letter. The following typical language may be added at the end of the compliance paragraph quoted above:

. . . thereunder; however, as agreed to by representatives of the SEC, separate parent company financial statements and schedules as required by Instruction 1 as to Financial Statements for Form S-1 have been omitted.

Since the published SEC requirements do not deal with the form of pro forma financial statements, there is no basis for accountants to comment on whether such pro forma information complies as to form with SEC requirements.

OTHER ACCOUNTANTS.—There may be situations in which more than one accountant is involved in the examination of the financial statements of an enterprise, and where more than one accountant's report appears in the registration statement; this subject is discussed in Chapter **24**. At the earliest practicable date, the client should advise any other accountants who may be involved in the registration engagement as to any letters that may be required from them, and should arrange to send them a draft of the underwriting agreement so that they can arrange to prepare the draft of their comfort letter (a copy of which should be given to the principal accountants) and to perform the procedures referred to in their letter.

In addition, the underwriter may desire to meet with the other accountants for the purpose of discussing with them the procedures he wishes them to follow in connection with their comfort letter. In the case of a worldwide enterprise employing several different accounting firms, a meeting of the underwriters with the other auditors may be impracticable.

The principal accountants (who report on the consolidated financial statements and consequently are asked to give a comfort letter with regard to information expressed on a consolidated basis) should read the letters of other accountants reporting on significant units of the enterprise. These letters should contain statements similar to those in the principal accountants' comfort letter, including representations as to their independence.

The principal accountants should state in their letter that (a) the procedures followed included reading the letters of other accountants, and (b) the procedures performed by the principal accountants (other than reading the other accountants' letters) relate solely to (i) companies audited by the principal accountants, and (ii) the consolidated financial statements.

If the other accountants' letters disclose decreases in financial statement items or any other matters that affect the negative assurance that is given, the principal accountants should mention these matters in their letter. Where appropriate, the principal accounts may comment that there were no decreases in the consolidated financial statement items despite the decreases mentioned by the other auditors.

RESTRICTIONS ON USE OF COMFORT LETTER.—In order to avoid misunderstanding as to the purpose and intended use of the comfort letter, it is desirable that the letter conclude with a paragraph restricting its use along the following lines:

This letter is solely for the information of, and assistance to, the underwriters in conducting and documenting their investigation of the affairs of the Company in connection with the offering of the securities covered by the registration statement, and is not to be used, circulated, quoted, or otherwise referred to within or without the underwriting group for any other purpose, including but not limited to the registration, purchase or sale of securities, nor is it to be filed with or referred to in whole or in part in the registration statement or any other document, except that reference may be made to it in the underwriting agreement or in any list of closing documents pertaining to the offering of the securities covered by the registration statement.

When the letter is furnished by the auditors for a subsidiary who are not the auditors for the parent company, the beginning of the above paragraph should be modified as follows:

This letter is solely for the information of, and assistance to, the underwriters and for the use of the accountants for [name of issuer] in furnishing their letter for the underwriters in conducting . . .

EFFECT OF QUALIFIED OPINION ON COMFORT LETTER.—As will be seen from the discussion in Chapter **25**, the SEC does not permit a registration statement under the 1933 Act to become effective when the accountants' report is qualified as to the scope of their examination or as to the accounting principles reflected in the financial statements, except in unusual circumstances as set forth in that chapter. Such unusual circumstances do arise occasionally, however, and although the SEC may permit the registration statement to become effective with a qualified opinion, the accountants may not be able to report in their comfort letter that the financial statements comply as to form in all material respects with the published rules and regulations of the SEC under the 1933 Act.

If the accountants' opinion is qualified, the qualification should be referred to in the opening paragraph of the comfort letter by saying, for example, ". . . our reports with respect thereto (which contain a qualification as set forth therein) are also included in such registration statement."

The accountants should also consider the effect of the subject matter of the qualification if they are asked to furnish negative assurance with respect to subsequent unaudited financial statements included in the registration statement.

REPETITION OF ACCOUNTANTS' OPINION IN COMFORT LETTER.—Underwriters sometimes ask that the accountants repeat in the comfort letter their opinion with respect to the audited financial statements included in the registration statement. SAP No. 48 states that because of the special significance of the date of an accountant's report, the accountants should not repeat their opinion in the comfort letter, since the latter is usually dated more recently than the former.

Unaudited Financial Statements and Subsequent Changes.—IN GENERAL.—Comments in comfort letters will often relate to one or more of the following items:

a. Unaudited financial statements, earnings summaries, and supporting schedules included in the registration statement
b. Changes in capital stock and long-term debt
c. Decreases in other specified financial statement items
d. Pro forma financial statements.

In commenting on the foregoing matters, SAP No. 48 points out that the following guides are important:

a. Any statements by the accountants regarding unaudited financial statements and schedules and subsequent changes and decreases in financial statement items should be limited to negative assurance.
b. The agreed upon procedures performed by the accountants should be set forth in the letter. This may be done along the lines of the example on page **12**·37.
c. The accountants' letter should identify the unaudited statements and schedules to which it relates, and should state that the accountants have not made an examination of such statements and schedules in accordance with generally accepted auditing standards and do not express an opinion concerning them. Paragraph 3 in the example on page **12**·37 illustrates how this may be done.
d. The accountants should not give negative assurance regarding unaudited financial statements, changes, or decreases unless they have made an examination of the issuer's financial statements for a period including or immediately prior to that to which the negative assurance relates or, less commonly, have made an examination for a later period.
e. Accountants should not give negative assurance regarding financial statements that have been examined by other accountants whose report appears in the registration statement.
f. The procedures followed will not necessarily disclose changes in capital stock or long-term debt, decreases in certain financial statement items, inconsistencies in the application of generally accepted accounting principles, instances of failure to comply with the SEC's requirements, or other matters concerning which the underwriter seeks negative assurance. This should be made clear in the letter, and one way of doing it is shown in paragraph 4 of the example on page **12**·37.
g. Accountants should not give negative assurance regarding pro forma adjustments applied to historical financial statements unless they

have audited the historical statements (or, in the case of business combinations, a significant constituent part of the combined statements) (i) for the period presented, or (ii) in the case of interim periods, for the latest fiscal period which includes or precedes the interim period.

h. The accountants' working papers should contain adequate evidence of the work that was done.

i. SAP No. 48 states that terms of indefinite meaning such as "review," "general review," "limited review," "check," or "test" should not be used in describing the work unless the procedures comprehended by the term are described in the comfort letter.

UNAUDITED FINANCIAL STATEMENTS.—Comfort letter comments concerning the unaudited financial statements and schedules *should always be made in the form of negative assurance.* Such comments usually relate to (a) conformity with generally accepted accounting principles, (b) consistency with the audited statements, and (c) compliance with the SEC's requirements. Paragraph 5a of the example on page **12·38** shows how this negative assurance may be phrased.

When the most recent figures in the earnings summary are for a period less than a year, the SEC usually requires that figures be shown for the corresponding period of the preceding year. The latter are ordinarily unaudited even though the period is part of a full year that has been audited. Consequently, the unaudited status of the figures of the earlier period should be made clear along the lines indicated in paragraph 3 of the example on page **12·37**.

CAPSULE INFORMATION.—The information shown in earnings summaries (or income statements) is often supplemented by unaudited condensed information concerning recent operations—commonly called "capsule information." This later information is often shown after the summary, either in narrative or in tabular form, for a recent period of the current year and for the same period of the previous year. The information ordinarily consists of selected income statement items—often limited to sales and total and per share amounts of extraordinary items and net income.

Since the term "fair presentation" (or variations thereof) as used by independent public accountants relates to the presentation in accordance with generally accepted accounting principles of financial statements as a whole, including the applicable notes, in giving negative assurance regarding selected income statement items, accountants should not employ the term "fair presentation," but should refer to whether the dollar amounts are stated on a basis consistent with that of the corresponding amounts in the audited statement.

In connection with capsule information, underwriters sometimes ask accountants to give negative assurance with respect to the related unaudited financial statements from which the capsule information is taken but which do not appear in the registration document, and to state that the capsule information agrees with amounts set forth in such statements. If such financial statements are prepared in conformity with generally accepted accounting principles (including the applicable notes), it is appropriate for the accountants to comply with the underwriter's request.

SUBSEQUENT CHANGES.—Comfort letter comments concerning subsequent changes should also be in the form of negative assurance. The comments should not employ the term "adverse changes" (or "material adverse changes") because despite the long use of that term under SAP No. 35 and prior thereto, the term does not have a clearly understood meaning in an accounting sense. In fact, it appears that the term may, on some occasions, have been misinterpreted by underwriters as encompassing judgments and conclusions not intended by the accountants.

There is disagreement, for example, as to whether the term as applied to results of operations relates only to absolute changes as between periods or whether it also includes trends in amounts or ratios. By way of illustration, assume that in the current interim period sales have increased as compared with sales in the corresponding period of the preceding year. The cost of sales percentage increased in the current period, however, as a consequence of which *net income this year is the same as last year*. Has there been an "adverse change" in the results of operations? Some say yes; some say no.

The term "adverse change" has sometimes been construed as contemplating comments by the accountants on matters concerning which their professional competence has little relevance, such as evaluating certain types of expenses that may decrease current income but are intended to increase future income. For example, net income of the current interim period is below that of the same period last year; the decrease is due principally to a substantial increase in research and development expenses, or a major advertising campaign—all of which have a depressing effect on current net income, but were incurred in the expectation of benefiting future net income. Has there been an "adverse change" in the results of operations on the basis of comparing the current interim period with the corresponding period a year earlier? Some say yes; some say no.

In the case of a company whose earnings summary shows a remarkable growth pattern, assume that the interim period this year shows net income that exceeds net income in the same period last year but there has been a deceleration of growth, has there been an "adverse change" this year as compared with last year? Here also there is disagreement as to what the term means.

In order that comments on subsequent changes will not be ambiguous and their determination will be within the accountants' professional competence, the comments should relate to the absence of any change in capital stock or long-term debt, or "decreases" in other identified financial statement items, during a period referred to as the "change period" as explained below. Usually these identified items would include the amounts of net current assets (working capital), net assets (stockholders' equity), net sales, and the total and per share amounts of income before extraordinary items, and net income. An appropriate way of making these comments when there has been no decrease is shown in paragraph 5b of the example on page **12·**39.

In the context of a comfort letter, a decrease occurs when the amount of a financial statement item at the cutoff date or for the change period (as if financial statements and their notes had been prepared at that date and for that period) is less than the amount of the same item at a specified earlier date or for a specified earlier period. With respect to the items mentioned in the preceding paragraph, the term "decrease" means:

  a. Any combination of changes in the amounts of current assets and current liabilities that results in a decrease in net current assets;
  b. Any combination of changes in the amounts of assets and liabilities that results in a decrease in net assets;
  c. Decreased net sales; and
  d. Any combination of changes in the amounts of sales and expenses and/or outstanding shares that results in a decrease in total and/or per share amounts of income before extraordinary items and of net income (including, in each instance, a greater loss or other negative amount).

The change period for which the accountants' comfort letter gives negative assurance ends on the cutoff date and ordinarily begins (a) as to balance sheet items, immediately after the date of the latest balance sheet included in the registration statement, and (b) as to income statement items, immediately after the latest period for which such items are presented in the registration statement. The comparison relates to the entire period and not to portions of it. A decrease during one part of a period may be offset by an equal or larger increase in another part of the period; however, because there was no decrease for the period as a whole, the comfort letter would not ordinarily report the decrease during one part of the period.

Underwriters sometimes ask that the change period begin immediately after the date of the latest *audited* balance sheet which is usually also the end of the latest audited income statement in the registration statement, even though it includes a more recent unaudited balance sheet and income statement. The use of the earlier date might defeat the underwriter's purpose since it is possible that an increase in one of the items occurring between the dates of the two balance sheets might more than offset a decrease occurring after the later balance sheet. A similar situation might arise in the comparison of income statement items, as a result of which a decrease occurring after the date of the latest financial statements included in the registration statement would not be reported in the comfort letter. If, however, the underwriter nonetheless requests the use of a change period or periods other than those described in the preceding paragraph, the accountants may comply with that request.

The underwriting agreement usually specifies the dates and periods with which data at the cutoff date and for the change period are to be compared. For balance sheet items, the comparison date is normally that of the latest balance sheet included in the registration document; for income statement items, the comparison period or periods might be one or more of the following:

a. The corresponding period of the preceding year;
b. A period of corresponding length immediately preceding the change period;
c. A proportionate part of the preceding fiscal year; or
d. Any other period of corresponding length chosen by the underwriter.

The date and period used in making the comparison should be stated in the comfort letter so that there is no misunderstanding as to what has been compared, and so that the underwriter can decide whether those dates and periods are suitable for his purposes.

In addition to making the comparisons indicated above using the financial statements made available to them, the accountants will usually be asked to read minutes and make inquiries of company officials relating to the entire change period. For the period between the date of such latest statements and the cutoff date, the accountants have to base their comments necessarily on the limited procedures performed with respect to the period (which in most cases will be limited to reading the minutes and making inquiries of company officials as referred to in the preceding sentence), and their comfort letter should make this clear.

The matters to be commented upon in the comfort letter should be agreed upon in the meetings with the underwriters and made clear in the letter. Since there is no way of anticipating other matters that might interest an underwriter, accountants should not make a general statement in their comfort letters that, as a result of carrying out the specified procedures, nothing else came to their attention which might be of interest to the underwriter.

Tables, Statistics, and Other Financial Information.—Underwriting agreements sometimes call for the accountants to comment in their comfort letter on tables, statistics, and other financial information included in the registration statement.

The Committee on Auditing Procedure took the position in SAP No. 48 that accountants should not comment in comfort letters on matters with respect to which their competence as independent public accountants has little relevance. The Statement provided:

Accordingly, except as indicated in the next sentence, they should comment only with respect to information (a) which is expressed in dollars (or percentages derived from such dollar amounts) and has been obtained from accounting records which are subject to the internal controls of the company's accounting system, or (b) which has been derived directly from such accounting records by analysis or computation. The accountants may also comment on quantitative information which has been obtained from an accounting record if the information is of a type that is subject to the same controls as the dollar amounts.

Accountants should not comment on matters involving primarily the exercise of business judgment of management. For example, changes between periods in gross profit ratios or net income may be caused by factors that are not necessarily within the accountants' expertise. Similarly, even though the accountants might appropriately comment on amounts shown as profit contributions for each line of business as defined by management, it would seldom be appropriate for them to comment on the reasonableness of management's determination of what constitutes a line of business.

Accountants should not comment on other types of matters merely because they happen to be present and are capable of reading, counting, measuring, or performing other functions which might be applicable. Examples of matters that, unless subjected to the internal controls of the company's formal accounting system (which is not ordinarily the case), should not be commented on by the accountants include the square feet of facilities, number of employees (except as related to a given payroll period) and backlog information.

The accountants should not comment on tables, statistics and other financial information relating to an unaudited period unless they have made an examination of the client's financial statements in conformity with generally accepted auditing standards for a period including or immediately prior to the unaudited period or, less commonly, have made an examination for a later period.

As with comments relating to financial statements, the procedures followed by the accountants with respect to other information should be clearly set out in the comfort letter (in both draft and final form) so that there will be no misunderstanding with respect to the basis of comments thereon, and no implication that the auditors are furnishing any assurance as to the sufficiency of such procedures for the underwriter's purposes.

In order to avoid any ambiguity, the accountants' letter should identify the specific information covered by the letter, by reference to captions, tables, page numbers, specific sentences or paragraphs. It should not refer, for example, to "all financial and statistical information" set forth (a) in the registration statement, (b) under specific captions, or (c) in response to specific item numbers in the registration statement.

Comments in comfort letters regarding tables, statistics, and other financial information in the registration statement should be in the form of a description of the procedures employed, the findings (ordinarily expressed in terms of agreement between the items compared), and in some cases statements as to the acceptability of methods of allocation used in deriving the figures commented upon. Whether comments upon the allocation of income or expense items between such categories as military and commercial sales, or lines of business, may appropriately be made will depend upon the extent to which such allocation is made in, or can be derived directly by analysis or computation from, the accounting records. In any event, if such comments are made, they should make it clear—if it is true—that the allocations are to a considerable extent arbitrary, that the method of allocation used is not the only acceptable one, and that other acceptable allocation methods might produce significantly different results.

The expression "presents fairly" (or a variation of it) should not be used in connection with comments on tables, statistics, and other financial information. When an independent accountant uses the expression "presents fairly," ordinarily it is in relation to financial statements; SAP No. 48 states that it should not be used in commenting on other types of information. Except as to the requirements for financial statements, the question of what constitutes appropriate information for the purpose of complying with the instructions of a specific item of the registration form is a matter of legal interpretation outside of the competence of accountants as such. Consequently, the accountants' letter should say that they make no representations as to any matter of legal interpretation.

Since the accountants will not be in a position to make any representations as to the adequacy of the disclosures or as to the procedures followed, the letter should so state. It should also point out that the procedures would not necessarily disclose material misstatements or omissions in the information to which the comments relate.

Example of a Typical Comfort Letter.—As previously indicated, the matters covered in a typical comfort letter are as follows:

a. Accountants' independence.

   b. Compliance as to form of the audited financial statements with the 1933 Act and the published rules and regulations thereunder.

   c. Negative assurance as to whether the unaudited financial statements included in the registration statement:

     i. Comply as to form with the Act and the published rules and regulations.

     ii. Are fairly presented in conformity with generally accepted accounting principles on a basis substantially consistent with that of the audited financial statements.

   d. Negative assurance as to whether during a specified period following the date of the latest financial statements in the registration statement, there has been any change in capital stock or long-term debt, or any decrease in other specified financial statement items.

The example of a typical comfort letter which follows covers all of the items described immediately above and is taken from SAP No. 48. Letters which cover some of the items may be developed by omitting portions of the letter which are not applicable. The example does not include coverage of statistical and tabular material; these are covered in the example beginning on page **12·40**.

The example which follows assumes the following circumstances:

   a. The prospectus (Part I of the registration statement) includes consolidated balance sheets at December 31, 1970 (audited), and March 31, 1971 (unaudited), consolidated statements of income, retained earnings, and changes in financial position for the three years ended December 31, 1970 (audited), and the three months ended March 31, 1971 (unaudited), and a consolidated summary of earnings for the five years ended December 31, 1970 (audited), and the three-month periods ended March 31, 1970 and March 31, 1971 (both unaudited).

   b. Part II of the registration statement includes consolidated financial schedules for the three years ended December 31, 1970 (audited), and the three months ended March 31, 1971 (unaudited).

   c. The effective date is June 23, 1971.

   d. The cutoff date is June 25, 1971.

   e. The letter is dated June 30, 1971.

Frequently the income statement is expanded to include all of the periods for which a summary of earnings is required, and a separate summary of earnings is omitted. In that case, the example which follows would be modified by expanding the references to the consolidated statements of income to cover the appropriate periods, and the references to the summary of earnings would be omitted.

For the purpose of the example, the income statement items of the current interim period are to be compared with those of the corresponding period of the preceding year.

Example of Typical Comfort Letter

June 30, 1971

[Addressee]
Dear Sirs:

We have examined the consolidated financial statements and schedules of The Blank Company, Inc. (the "Company") and subsidiaries as of December 31, 1970 and for the three years then ended and the related summary of earnings for the five years then ended included in the registration statement (SEC File No. 2-   ) on Form S-1 filed by the Company under the Securities Act of 1933 (the "Act"); our reports with respect thereto are also included in such registration statement. Such registration statement, as amended as of June 23, 1971, is herein referred to as the "registration statement." In connection with the registration statement:

1. We are independent public accountants with respect to the Company within the meaning of the Act and the applicable published rules and regulations thereunder, and the answer to Item 24 of the registration statement is correct insofar as it relates to us.

2. In our opinion, [here include the phrase "except as disclosed in the registration statement," if applicable], the financial statements and schedules and the summary of earnings examined by us and included or incorporated by reference in the registration statement comply as to form in all material respects with the applicable accounting requirements of the Act and of the published rules and regulations thereunder.

3. We have not examined any financial statements of the Company as of any date or for any period subsequent to December 31, 1970; and although we have made an examination for the year ended December 31, 1970, the purpose (and therefore the scope) of such examination was to enable us to express our opinion as to the financial statements as of December 31, 1970 and for the year then ended but not as to the financial statements for any interim period within such year. Therefore, we are unable to and do not express any opinion on the unaudited consolidated balance sheet as of March 31, 1971, interim consolidated statements of income, retained earnings and changes in financial position for the three months then ended, and interim consolidated summary of earnings for the three month periods ended March 31, 1971 and 1970, and related schedules included in the registration statement, or on the financial position or results of operations as of any date or for any period subsequent to December 31, 1970.

4. For purposes of this letter we have read the 1970 minutes of the stockholders, the Board of Directors, and [here include other appropriate committees, if any] of the Company and its subsidiaries as set forth in the minute books at June 25, 1971, officials of the Company having advised us that the minutes of all such meetings through that date were set forth therein, and have carried out other procedures to June 25, 1971 (our work did not extend to the period from June 26, 1971 to June 30, 1971, inclusive), as follows:

a. with respect to the three month periods ended March 31, 1970 and 1971:

(1) read the unaudited consolidated summary of earnings for these periods included in the registration statement;

(2) read the unaudited consolidated balance sheet as of March 31, 1971, and unaudited consolidated statements of income, retained earnings and changes in financial position for the three months then ended and the related unaudited schedules included in the registration statement; and

(3) made inquiries [if written representations were obtained from Company officials, they may be referred to here] of certain officials of the Company who have responsibility for financial and accounting matters as to (i) whether the unaudited financial statements, summary of earnings, and schedules referred to under a(1) and a(2) above comply as to form in all material respects with the applicable accounting requirements of the Act and the published rules and regulations thereunder, (ii) whether said financial statements are fairly presented, and the information in said summary is fairly summarized, in conformity with generally accepted accounting principles applied on a basis substantially consistent with that of the audited financial statements and summary of earnings included in the registration statement, and (iii) whether said unaudited schedules, when considered in relation to the basic unaudited financial statements, present fairly in all material respects the information shown therein;

b. with respect to the period from April 1, 1971 to May 31, 1971:

(1) read the unaudited consolidated financial statements of the Company and subsidiaries for April and May of both 1970 and 1971 furnished us by the Company, officials of the Company having advised us that no such financial statements as of any date or for any period subsequent to May 31, 1971 were available; and

(2) made inquiries of certain officials of the Company who have responsibility for financial and accounting matters as to whether the unaudited financial statements referred to under b(1) above are stated on a basis substantially consistent with that of the audited financial statements included in the registration statement.

The foregoing procedures do not constitute an examination made in accordance with generally accepted auditing standards. Also, they would not necessarily reveal matters of significance with respect to the comments in the following paragraph. Accordingly, we make no representations as to the sufficiency of the foregoing procedures for your purposes.

5. Nothing came to our attention as a result of the foregoing procedures, however, that caused us to believe that:

a. (i) the unaudited financial statements, summary of earnings, and schedules described in 4(a)(1) and (2) above, included in the registration statement, do not comply as to form in all material respects with the applicable accounting requirements of the Act and of the published rules and regulations thereunder, (ii) said financial statements are not fairly presented, or the information in said summary is not fairly summarized, in conformity with generally accepted accounting principles applied on a basis substantially consistent with that of the audited financial statements and summary of earnings, or (iii) said unaudited schedules, when considered in relation to the basic unaudited financial statements, do not present fairly in all material respects the information shown therein; or

b. (i) at May 31, 1971, there was any change in the capital stock or long-term debt of the Company and subsidiaries consolidated or any decrease in consolidated net current assets or net assets as compared with amounts shown in the March 31, 1971 balance sheet included in the registration statement or (ii) for the period from April 1, 1971 to May 31, 1971, there were any decreases, as compared with the corresponding period in the preceding year, in consolidated net sales or in the total or per share amounts of income before extraordinary items or of net income, except in all instances for changes which the registration statement discloses have occurred or may occur.

6. As mentioned under 4b, Company officials have advised us that no consolidated statements as of any date or for any period subsequent to May 31, 1971 are available; accordingly, the procedures carried out by us with respect to changes in financial statement items after May 31, 1971 have, of necessity, been even more limited than those with respect to the periods referred to in 4. We have made inquiries of certain officials of the Company who have responsibility for financial and accounting matters as to whether (i) there was any change at June 25, 1971 in the capital stock or long-term debt of the Company and subsidiaries consolidated or any decreases in consolidated net current assets or net assets as compared with amounts shown on the March 31, 1971 balance sheet included in the registration statement or (ii) for the period from April 1, 1971 to June 25, 1971, there were any decreases, as compared with the corresponding period in the preceding year, in consolidated net sales or in the total or per share amounts of income before extraordinary items or of net income. On the basis of these inquiries and our reading of the minutes as described in 4, nothing came to our attention that caused us to believe that there was any such change or decrease, except in all instances for changes which the registration statement discloses have occurred or may occur.

7. This letter is solely for the information of, and assistance to, the underwriters in conducting and documenting their investigation of the affairs of the Company in connection with the offering of the securities covered by the registration statement, and is not to be used, circulated, quoted or otherwise referred to within or without the underwriting group for any other purpose, including but not limited to the registration, purchase or sale of securities, nor is it to be filed with or referred to in whole or in part in the registration statement or any other document, except that reference may be made to it in the underwriting agreement or in any list of closing documents pertaining to the offering of the securities covered by the registration statement.

Example of Coverage of Statistical and Tabular Material in Comfort Letters.—As previously noted, following the decision in the BarChris case, there was an enormous increase in the requests from underwriters to have the independent auditors give some sort of a blessing to every number and every percentage appearing in a registration statement. The number or percentage might have no relation whatever to the accounting process, but the underwriters frequently asked that the auditors verify it in some way. For example, the prospectus might disclose the number of square feet in the various buildings owned by the registrant and its subsidiaries, or the number of employees classified as to plant locations and as between union and non-union, or the amount of unfilled orders, and so on. These are matters which ordinarily are not verified by the independent auditors in the course of their examination. Although accountants can measure and count, they are no more qualified than the underwriters themselves to give comfort on the number of square feet in a building. Consequently, SAP No. 48 laid down some ground rules with respect to those matters which could appropriately be covered by the accountant in his comfort letter, as previously discussed in this chapter.

When the accountant has determined that the statistical and tabular material on which he has been asked to comment has some relevance to his professional competence and has been obtained from accounting records which are subject to the internal controls of the companies' accounting system, or has been derived from such records by analysis or computation, he may cover such information in his comfort letter. Following is an example (taken from SAP No. 48) showing how the accountant may comment on such statistical and tabular material. The following paragraphs are intended to follow paragraph 6 in the preceding example:

7. For purposes of this letter, we have also read the following, set forth in the registration statement on the indicated pages.

Item	Page	Description
a	4	"Capitalization." The amounts under the captions "Amount Outstanding as of June 15, 1971" and "As Adjusted." The related notes, except as to the following in Note 2: "See 'Transactions with Interested Persons.' From the proceeds of this offering the Company intends to prepay $90,000 on these notes, pro rata. See 'Use of Proceeds.'"
b	13	"History and Business—Sales and Marketing." The table following the first paragraph.
c	22	"Remuneration." The table at the bottom of the page, except as to estimated annual benefits upon retirement.
d	33	"Revenue Sources." The amounts in the first paragraph and the table following that paragraph.

8. Our examination of the financial statements for the periods referred to in the introductory paragraph of this letter comprised audit tests and procedures deemed necessary for the purpose of expressing an opinion on such financial statements taken as a whole. For neither the periods referred to therein nor any other period did we perform audit tests for the purpose of expressing an opinion on individual balances of accounts or summaries of selected transactions such as those enumerated above and, accordingly, we express no opinion thereon.

9. However, for purposes of this letter we have performed the following additional procedures, which were applied as indicated with respect to the items enumerated above:

Item number in 7 above	Procedures and Findings

a   We compared the amounts and numbers of shares listed under the caption "Amount Outstanding as of June 15, 1971," with the balances in the appropriate accounts in the Company's general ledger at May 31, 1971 (the latest date for which postings had been made), and found them to be in agreement. We were informed by officials responsible for financial and accounting matters that there had been no changes in such amounts and numbers of shares between May 31, 1971, and June 15, 1971. We compared the amounts and numbers of shares listed under the caption "Amount Outstanding as of June 15, 1971," adjusted for the issuance of the debentures to be offered by means of the registration statement and for the proposed use of a portion of the proceeds thereof to prepay portions of certain notes, as described under "Use of Proceeds," with the amounts and numbers of shares shown under the caption "As Adjusted" and found such amounts and numbers of shares to be in agreement (however, we make no comments as to the reasonableness of the "Use of Proceeds" or whether such use will actually take place). We compared the description of the securities and the information (except as to certain information in Note 2 referred to in 7 above) included in the notes to the table with the corresponding descriptions and information in the Company's consolidated financial statements, including the notes thereto included in the registration statement, and found such descriptions and information to be in agreement.

b   We compared the amounts of military sales, commercial sales and total sales shown in the registration statement with the balances in the appropriate accounts in the Company's general ledger for the respective fiscal years and for the unaudited interim periods and found them to be in agreement (however, we make no comments as to the appropriateness of such classification or the manner in which such classification has been made). We computed the approximate percentages of such amounts of military sales and commercial sales to total sales for the respective fiscal years and for the unaudited interim periods. We compared the computed percentages with the corresponding percentages appearing in the registration statement and found them to be in agreement.

c   We compared the amounts of direct remuneration listed in the registration statement with the corresponding amounts shown by the individual employee earnings records for the year 1970 and found them to be in agreement.

d   We compared the amounts of sales and contributions to profit for each line of business for the years 1968, 1969 and 1970 and the three months ended March 31, 1971, appearing in the registration statement with the corresponding amounts shown by an analysis prepared by the Company and found such amounts to be in agreement (however, we make no comments as to the appropriateness of the determination by the Company as to what constitutes its lines of business). We compared the aggregate of the amounts of sales and contributions to profit, respectively, for the several lines of business for each of the periods mentioned in the preceding sentence with the corresponding amounts shown in the financial statements for such periods appearing in the registration statement and found such amounts to be in agreement. We computed the approximate percentages of the total amounts of sales and net income for each line of business for each of the periods mentioned in the preceding sentence. We compared the computed percentages with the corresponding percentages appearing in the registration statement and found them to be in agreement. We compared the sales and cost of sales shown in the analysis referred to above for each line of business with the balances in the appropriate accounts in the Company's general ledger for the respective fiscal years and for the unaudited interim periods and found them to be in agreement. Officials responsible for financial and accounting matters described to us the methods used in the analysis referred to above in allocating certain costs and expenses, including income tax expense, among the several lines of business; but we did not test the application of the procedures. Although nothing came to our attention as a result of the foregoing that caused us to believe that the method of allocation employed is not acceptable, it should be understood that the allocations are to a substantial extent necessarily arbitrary and that other acceptable methods of allocation might produce significantly different results.

10. It should be understood that we make no representations as to questions of legal interpretation or as to the sufficiency for your purposes of the procedures enumerated in the preceding paragraph; also, such procedures would not necessarily reveal any material misstatement of the amounts or percentages listed above. Further, we have addressed ourselves solely to the foregoing data as set forth in the registration statement and make no representations as to the adequacy of disclosure or as to whether any material facts have been omitted.

In some cases it might be considered desirable to combine in one paragraph the substance of paragraphs 7 and 9 in the foregoing example. This may be done by expanding the identification of items in paragraph 9 to provide the identification information contained in paragraph 7. In such cases, the introductory sentences in paragraphs 7 and 9 and the text of paragraph 8 might be combined as follows:

For purposes of this letter, we have also read the following information and have performed the additional procedures stated below with respect to such information. Our examination of the financial statements. . . ."

Other Examples of Comfort Letters in SAP No. 48.—The foregoing examples of comfort letters were taken from the AICPA Statement

(SAP No. 48) which also contains other examples of letters appropriate to certain designated situations, such as:

a. When the summary of earnings covers the twelve-month period to the date of the latest balance sheet furnished in lieu of earnings data for both the interim period between the end of the latest fiscal year and the date of the latest balance sheet and the corresponding interim period of the preceding fiscal year.

b. When comfort letters are to be furnished at more than one date.

c. When there is a departure from the applicable accounting requirements of the 1933 Act and the published rules and regulations thereunder, and the SEC staff have agreed to such departures.

d. When the information shown in the earnings summary (or income statement) is supplemented by later information (usually in capsule form) as to sales and earnings, and the accountants are asked to comment on such information.

e. When there has been a decrease in a financial statement item on which the accountants have been requested to comment.

f. When the accountants' opinion on the audited financial statements included in the registration statement contains a qualification regarding a matter that may also affect the unaudited financial statements included in the registration statement.

g. When more than one accountant is involved in the overall examination, and the principal accountants have obtained a copy of the comfort letter of the other accountants.

Comfort Letter Review of Unaudited Financial Statements.— From what has been written on the preceding pages based on the provisions of SAP No. 48, "Letters for Underwriters," it will be apparent that the most important part by far of a comfort letter is that portion which deals with the unaudited interim financial statements—those that are included in the registration statement as well as those that are not included. Concerning such unaudited financial statements, the independent auditors customarily say in their comfort letters (see the example of a typical letter on page **12·38**) that they have "made inquiries of certain officials of the Company who have responsibility for financial and accounting matters . . ."

In relation to the example of the letter on page **12·38**, it will be seen that the accountants' inquiries were on three levels:

1. The unaudited statements as of March 31, 1971 and for the three-month periods ended March 31, 1970 and 1971 which were included in the registration statement.

2. The unaudited statements for April and May of both 1970 and 1971 which were not included in the registration statement and were said to be the latest available.

3. The period from May 31, 1971 to June 25, 1971 (the cutoff date).

With regard to the interim financial statements included in the registration statement, the accountants stated that they read the statements and made inquiries concerning them as follows:

(i) whether the statements comply as to form in all material respects with the applicable accounting requirements of the Act and the published rules and regulations thereunder;

(ii) whether the financial statements are fairly presented and the information in the earnings summary is fairly summarized, in conformity with generally accepted accounting principles applied on a basis substantially consistent with that of the audited financial statements and earnings summary included in the registration statement; and

(iii) whether the unaudited schedules, when considered in relation to the basic unaudited financial statements, present fairly in all material respects the information shown therein.

With regard to the unaudited financial statements which the company had prepared for the months of April and May of 1970 and 1971 but which were not included in the registration statement, the procedures were more limited. The accountants stated that they read the statements and made inquiries as to whether the statements were stated on a basis substantially consistent with that of the audited financial statements included in the registration statement.

With regard to the period after May 31, 1971 to the cutoff date, the procedures were even more limited than those for the periods for which statements were available. For the post-statement period the accountants made inquiries as to:

(i) whether there was any change at the cutoff date in the capital stock or long-term debt or any decreases in net current assets or net assets as compared with the March 31, 1971 balance sheet included in the registration statement; or

(ii) for the period from April 1, 1971 to the cutoff date, whether there were any decreases, as compared with the corresponding period in the preceding year, in consolidated net sales or in the total or per share amounts of income before extraordinary items or of net income.

What were the "inquiries" which the accountants said they made with respect to the unaudited interim statements included in the registration statement, the unaudited interim statements not included in the registration statement, and the post-statement period? In other words, what is contemplated when the accountants say they made "inquiries"?

Let it be clear at the outset, that the term "inquiries" has no more clearly defined meaning than the term "adverse changes" which the AICPA Committee on Auditing Procedure decided to eliminate from comfort letters on the grounds that there was significant disagreement as to what it means.

SAP No. 48 does not define "inquiries" which forms the basis for most of the representations in a comfort letter. There is also no other authoritative pronouncement as to the meaning of "inquiries" in the context of a comfort letter. The meaning of the word is obviously important because it represents a distillation of all the procedures applied by the accountants with respect to the unaudited interim financial statements and to the post-statement period.

Although the author is unable to explain what is meant by the term "inquiries" in the recommended form of comfort letter, he is reasonably sure of what it does *not* mean. It does not mean asking a few perfunctory questions and making note of the answers as to the make-up of the statements and what happened in the post-statement period.

On the other hand, an "inquiry" for the purpose of negative assurance in a comfort letter is certainly far short of a conventional audit.

Somewhere in between the two extremes, there should be a point at which the underwriter (who is responsible for the procedures performed) can draw a line and say that an inquiry which includes certain specified procedures should suffice for the purpose of his reasonable investigation.

Set forth below are the programs used by the author's firm in connection with its inquiries into the unaudited interim financial statements of three companies that filed registration statements under the 1933 Act. The inquiries were made for the purpose of issuing comfort letters. The first program relates to a manufacturing company, the second to a telephone company, and the third to a company operating a chain of retail discount department stores. The programs are presented for illustration only to show the scope of the work done in specific cases, and not with the thought that they should be followed in any other case.

Although all of the programs were used in 1971, they were used before SAP No. 48 was issued. If, in the future, an underwriter reading these programs were to conclude that he wanted more done in specified areas, the programs would have to be altered accordingly (assuming, of course, that the additional procedures involved matters with respect to which the accountants' competence was relevant as provided in SAP No. 48).

A Manufacturing Company

A multiplant operation, with numerous divisions and subsidiaries, operating principally in the United States but to some extent in foreign countries. The company has an excellent accounting department, which is decentralized, and an effective internal audit department.

1. Select the major division and subsidiary accounting offices to be visited for review of their interim statements. Advise the company and the underwriters of the locations selected and the approximate percentage of consolidated sales accounted for at the locations which are not to be visited. (The underwriting agreement provided that

this percentage would be given in the comfort letter describing the auditors' review.)

2. Obtain copies of the interim financial statements for the divisions and subsidiaries selected for visit.

3. Forward the above copies of statements, together with instructions, to the persons responsible for the field reviews.

Work to be done at division and subsidiary accounting offices selected for visit:

1. Compare the details of amounts included in the interim financial statements with the related general ledger account balances.

2. Obtain explanations for any significant new accounts opened during the periods or accounts with no balance at the close of the periods.

3. (a) Compare the interim financial statements with those for the corresponding period of the preceding year and with the most recent audited financial statements for a full year. Note unusual variations or relationships in the interim statements and obtain explanations for the changes.

   (b) Inquire regarding any significant changes in accounting principles or policies during the interim periods and consider their effect upon the interim statements.

   (c) Inquire as to the effect, if any, on the interim statements, of seasonal factors and controllable costs such as advertising, research and development, etc.

4. Inquire of responsible employees regarding any significant adverse events or abnormal conditions in the interim periods. In this connection, questions to be considered should include the following:

   (a) Accounts receivable:

   1. Has the ratio of past due accounts increased significantly? If so, is the allowance for doubtful accounts adequate?

   2. Has there been any loss of important customers?

   3. Have there been any significant changes in sales prices or terms of sale?

   (b) Inventories:

   1. Are interim inventory amounts based upon book or physical inventories? If based upon book amounts, does past experience as to difference between book and physical inventories when taken, indicate that book inventories are reliable?

   2. Have there been any significant changes in cost methods or basis of inventory valuation?

   3. Have there been changes in major products or methods of manufacture? If so, do they create inventory obsolescence which requires adjustment?

        4. Have there been significant changes in the cost of raw materials or other costs?

        5. Are there any significant unfavorable purchase commitments?

  (c) Fixed assets:

        1. Have any plants or major departments become permanently inactive? If so, is provision necessary for loss on sale or abandonment?

        2. Have there been significant losses of fixed assets resulting from fire, flood, or other catastrophes?

        3. Have there been changes in depreciation rates or methods?

        4. Are there any profits or losses from disposal of fixed assets included in earned surplus?

        5. Have commitments for acquisition of fixed assets increased significantly since the most recent year end?

  (d) Prepaid expenses and accrued liabilities:

        1. Were the methods used in computing these amounts consistent with those followed at year end?

  (e) Accounts payable:

        1. Were the cut-off procedures for recording accounts payable consistent with those at the year end?

  (f) Labor matters:

        1. Have there been new union contracts or major amendments to existing contracts during the interim periods and, if so, what is the financial effect thereof?

        2. Have there been significant work stoppages resulting from labor disagreements during the interim periods which might require disclosure in the financial statements?

        3. Are there unresolved liabilities for retroactive wages or other benefits?

5. (a) Review client's working papers in support of any schedules required to be filed with the interim financial statements.

  (b) Compare amounts in the schedules with the related financial statements.

  (c) Check to see that requirements of SEC are complied with.

Work to be done at the parent company's principal accounting office:

1. (a) Obtain copies of the consolidating financial statements supporting the interim consolidated financial statements.

  (b) Compare the interim financial statements and schedules for the divisions and subsidiaries visited with the related amounts in the consolidating statements and schedules.

  (c) Review the consolidating eliminations to determine consistency of the basis of consolidation, intercompany eliminations, etc.

(d) Check mathematics of statements and cross-references.

2. (a) Compare the consolidated interim financial statements with those for the corresponding period of the preceding year and with the most recent audited financial statements for a full year. Note unusual variations or relationships in the interim statements and obtain explanations for the changes. (Information obtained at division and subsidiary offices which were visited should explain some of these variations.)

(b) Inquire about and note any evidence of material amounts in the interim figures that are applicable to prior periods.

(c) Inquire whether changes in bank loans or funded debt involve related changes in dividend restrictions.

3. Review the client's internal reports to management for the interim periods and note any comments regarding unusual conditions relating to sales, costs, expenses, operations, acquisition or disposal of major properties, legal suits, etc.

4. Review the reports rendered by internal auditors since the most recent annual examination.

5. Read the minutes of all meetings of stockholders, directors, and related committees subsequent to the year end and inquire whether important actions are properly reflected in the financial statements or notes.

6. (a) Review the computation of federal income tax provision for the interim periods to see that the provision is on a basis consistent with the prior year.

(b) Inquire regarding any Revenue Agent's examination or report since the year-end audit.

7. Obtain a letter from company's counsel regarding pending litigation, claims, etc., and consider the possible effect thereof upon the interim and certified financial statements.

8. (a) Discuss with the controller and other accounting personnel questions developed in the review of the interim financial statements.

(b) Questions regarding significant events or abnormal conditions during the interim periods, such as those previously suggested for investigation at division and subsidiary locations, should also be discussed with the controller.

9. Obtain a letter, signed by the controller and the treasurer, giving current information regarding the company's contingent liabilities and commitments as well as a description of any mate-

rial changes in the company's accounting principles and procedures since the previous year end.

10. By reference to Regulation S-X and the instructions as to financial statements of Form S-1, ascertain that SEC's requirements are complied with.

A Telephone Company

A company operating directly and through subsidiaries in several states and having connections with numerous other telephone companies. The company has excellent accounting and internal auditing departments. The accounting is decentralized on a company and area basis.

The following procedures relate to the records of the registrant as well as to all significant consolidated and unconsolidated subsidiaries :

1. Trace the details of amounts included in the interim financial statements (including notes and schedules) to the general ledger accounts or other appropriate accounting records and determine consistency with respect to report classifications for each period.

2. Check the mathematics of the statements and schedules and verify all cross-references included therein.

3. Review consolidating working papers to determine consistency with respect to the basis of consolidation, intercompany eliminaations, account classifications, etc.

4. Read the minutes of all meetings of stockholders, directors, and Executive Committee held subsequent to the year-end audit and prior to the effective date of the registration statement, and determine that important actions are properly reflected in the financial statements or notes.

5. Scan journal entries other than standard entries for the current interim period. Investigate transactions unusual in nature or amount, and determine whether transactions have been reflected in the proper period. Reference should also be made in this connection to the investigation of nonstandard journal entries in the audit working papers of the previous year.

6. Compare balance sheets at the current interim date and at the prior year end, and income statements for the interim period of the current and prior years. Such comparisons should include the related information in the notes and schedules. Note and obtain explanation for significant variations.

7. In conjunction with the investigation of questions developed in the review, specific inquiry should be made of accounting officers and other persons responsible for financial operations as to the following

matters and as to the effect thereof on earnings of prior, current, and future periods:

  (a) Pending or concluded hearings before regulatory bodies regarding changes in rates for services to customers or changes in the basis of settlement of revenues from business conducted jointly with non-affiliated companies.

  (b) Pending or approved applications for changes in depreciation rates prescribed by regulatory bodies.

  (c) Modifications in salary and wage agreements and the resulting estimated annual increases in costs.

  (d) Non-routine transactions, including prior-year adjustments, affecting miscellaneous income deductions or credits, retained earnings, and capital surplus.

  (e) Major additions or retirements of plant in service resulting from conversion or replacement of equipment formerly in use, such as conversion of central offices to electronic switching system operation.

  (f) Significant changes in method of apportionment of cost of facilities between intrastate and interstate services.

  (g) Significant factors affecting the computation of the federal income tax provision and the results of any Revenue Agent's examination or report since the year-end examination.

  (h) Adequacy of provision for uncollectibles in light of current collection experience.

  (i) Non-routine transactions affecting prepaid, deferred, and accrued items, such as redemption or refunding of bond issues, proration of annual expenses through clearing accounts, accruals for pension fund, and provisions for contested or contingent liabilities.

  (j) Significant changes in interest rate or amount of intercompany borrowings and the reasons therefor.

  (k) Significant internal audit findings.

  (l) Any other matters which could affect the comparability of the financial statements.

  8. Obtain a liability certificate in regular year-end audit form, and a letter from the company's counsel regarding pending litigation, claims, and other liabilities. Consider the effect of the information therein on the financial statements.

  9. By reference to Regulation S-X and other applicable rules and regulations of the SEC, ascertain that all required information has been disclosed and that all necessary schedules have been prepared.

  10. With respect to the interim statements of any significant consolidated or unconsolidated subsidiary reviewed by other accountants,

obtain copies of such statements, together with a copy of the "conformity and review" letter of the other accountants.

A Chain of Retail Department Stores

A publicly-owned company operating a chain of retail discount department stores is registering debt and equity securities with the Securities and Exchange Commission. The company has an adequate centralized accounting system, but no internal auditing department. The company operates at numerous store locations where sales are largely for cash, but with credit sales increasing in volume.

The following program was used in reviewing the unaudited financial statements of May 1, 1971 and for the three-month periods ended May 2, 1970 and May 1, 1971 (the "interim periods"), the summarized results of which were included in capsule form in the registration statement. The certified financial statements in the registration statement were as of January 30, 1971 and for full fiscal years then ended.

General

1. Obtain the comparative financial statements and trial balance grouping sheets for the interim periods. Agree the statements to the grouping sheets.
2. Verify the computation of income per share for the interim periods.
3. Compare the financial statements with the published statements for the interim periods.
4. Determine whether the principles of consolidation were the same for all periods.
5. Trace the details of the financial statements to the books and records of the company including supporting schedules and workpapers for both interim periods.
6. Inquire as to whether there are any deviations from generally accepted accounting principles not evident from a review of the financial statements.
7. Review major transactions during the interim periods with company officials and determine the propriety of the related accounting treatment.
8. Read the minutes of the Board of Directors, stockholders' and executive committee meetings through the effective date of the registration statement, and ascertain that all financial matters are properly reflected in the financial statements.
9. Confirm capital stock outstanding with the company's transfer agents as of the date of the Capitalization Table and within five days of the effective date of the registration statement. Reconcile capital stock purchases and sales since January 30, 1971 to the confirmed amounts and the books and records of the company.

10. Inquire concerning tax examinations since the year-end audit and determine the effect, if any, of such examinations on the company's tax provisions.

11. Obtain letters from the company's legal counsel regarding litigation, judgments or other information that might affect the financial statements through the effective date of registration.

12. Confer with company officials regarding new commitments for store openings (annual minimal rent for real estate), fixture purchases, and financing commitments. Verify the data obtained and prepare a summary to be presented in the registration statement.

13. Ascertain whether the company complies with the restrictions of its loan agreements at May 1, 1971, as well as through the effective date of the registration. Review the client's calculations supporting such compliance.

14. Obtain liability certificates signed by responsible officials of the company.

15. Determine that the client has not changed accounting principles or practices during the period or (if they have) the effect of such changes upon the financial statements.

16. Correlate the information in the financial statements and supporting schedules with representations in other parts of the registration statement.

Fixed Charge Ratios and Income Per Share

1. Review the client's calculation of the ratio of both historical and pro forma (for the most recent year) earnings to fixed charges.

2. For the income per share data, determine whether the Company has conformed with the requirements of APB Opinion No. 15 for calculating primary and fully diluted income per share.

Fluctuation Analyses

1. Prepare an analysis of Balance Sheet account fluctuations between January 30, 1971 and May 1, 1971. Obtain explanations for each account variance and relate such explanations to ongoing business trends, as well as the year-end fluctuation analyses.

2. Perform a comparative ratio analysis of the income statements by major account classification for the interim periods. Determine the causes of major fluctuations.

3. Compare the quarterly income statement ratios with those of the immediately preceding annual statements for both quarters. Determine the reasons for major differences.

Leased Department Income

1. Review the accounting for leased department sales, costs and expenses, and rental income for propriety and consistency.

2. Make over-all test of leased department income by applying average lease rate to leased department sales.

Expenses

1. Through the use of expense trial balances or management reports for the interim periods and the year ended January 30, 1971, compare the store expenses, account by account, on an individual store basis, and by comparison with other stores. For stores opened during each interim period, give consideration to the time of opening and obtain explanations for any unusual amounts.
2. For administrative, warehouse, and buying expense (home office overhead), compare the detail expenses for each of the two periods and the full year and obtain explanations for unusual fluctuations.
3. Determine whether the ratios of the major account classifications of selling, general, and administrative expense to net sales were reasonable in the light of all conditions.

Sales

1. Review cut-off procedures for interim periods for propriety and consistency with those of year-end.
2. Compare the total sales in each interim period in light of the number of stores operated in each period.
3. Reconcile sales for the interim periods with the general ledger, sales reports and the retail ledger.
4. For stores which were operated in both interim periods, compare the sales, on a store by store basis, for reasonableness.
5. For new stores, consider whether the sales in each store were reasonable in the light of sales in other stores and the impact of grand opening(s).
6. Obtain analyses of comparable store sales by month for the past two years. Arrange to receive monthly reports of comparative sales and gross profit up to the effective date of the registration. Determine ongoing sales to ascertain whether there are any adverse changes inherent in operational results. Ascertain reasons for increases and decreases in comparable sales.

Cash

Inquire whether all bank accounts were reconciled during each interim period and that adjustments were booked.

Accounts Receivable

1. Compare the composition of Accounts Receivable—due from landlords, vendors and employees with the year-end amounts. Inquire if there have been any loans to officers, directors and stockholders in the three months ended May 1, 1971.

2. Review reasons for fluctuations in customer receivables and ascertain that an aging of accounts has been prepared and that an adjustment for the allowance for bad debts has been made.

Inventories and Gross Profits

Inventories at interim dates were based on the departmental amounts reflected in the retail ledger.

1. Markdowns—Review markdowns taken during three months ended May 1, 1971, and relate such markdowns to sales in the period. Compare the amounts and the ratios with the comparable amounts and ratios during the preceding full year and first three months of the preceding year. Review the markdowns in May and June to determine whether required markdowns were being deferred beyond the close of the fiscal period and whether markdowns subsequent to May 1, 1971 were normal.

2. Allowance for shortages—Review the adequacy of the estimated per cent of sales used for allowance for shortages by comparison with the actual shortage per cent for the preceding year, and the comparable period of the preceding year, and by studying the trend. Review and discuss the shortage allowance with key personnel.

3. Compare the gross profit used in the financial statements with the gross profit per the retail ledger.

4. Ascertain the reasons for gross profit differences between year-end results and the first quarter of 1971 by reviewing the available data of all elements entering into gross profit (initial markon, retail losses, etc.), and relate it to internal statistical data.

5. Obtain explanations for large increases in inventory levels by department.

6. Determine that the markon applied to the interim accruals for merchandise purchases are consistent with actual markons for the subsequent month. Determine the profit effect, if any, of any differences.

Supplies and Prepaid Expenses

1. Compare the total amount of the store supplies at the interim dates with the year-end balances and make inquiries as to increases.

2. For all prepayments compare year-end and interim balances, and obtain explanations for unusual fluctuations.

Preopening Costs and Deferrals

1. Review the preopening costs deferred in each interim period and relate it to the number of new stores opened in each period and to the average amount of preopening costs deferred during the year ended January 30, 1971, to see that the amounts and types of expenses are in line with past experience.

2. Review amortization of preopening costs in each interim period for consistency and for reasonableness of amounts.

3. Review the client's method of determining other expense deferrals. Ascertain the consistency of those methods for the interim and year end periods for both years and verify the accuracy of the calculations.

Fixed Assets and Accumulated Depreciation

1. Review the reasonableness of the amounts of leasehold improvements and furniture and fixtures capitalized in the three months ended May 1, 1971, in relation to the number of stores opened in the period and to be opened in the subsequent month. Correlate this work with review of additions to equipment notes payable (general method of financing).
2. Review the retirements made in the period for propriety and reasonableness and ascertain whether related reserves were appropriately adjusted.
3. Review the computation of depreciation in each interim period, bearing in mind the depreciation policy, number of stores opened, dates they were opened, and consistency.
4. Inquire whether any assets had been pledged as collateral, beyond that at January 30, 1971.
5. Determine the extent of store refurbishment, and ascertain if abandonments have been properly accounted for.
6. Ascertain how stores and warehouses opened were financed and review reasonableness of costs incurred to comparable costs of prior years.

Other Assets

1. Review the increment in cash surrender value of life insurance.
2. Compare the amounts of organization expense deferred for new corporations with average (per corporation) deferred in the past year. Review amortization.
3. Inquire regarding nature of lease acquisition costs capitalized and amortization of such costs.
4. Review the analyses of all other assets for propriety and consistency of treatment, and compare interim balances with amounts at year-end. Obtain explanations for unusual amounts or changes.

Accounts Payable

1. Review cut-off procedures at May 1, 1971, to determine that the books had been kept open a sufficient length of time to pick up all known accounts payable.
2. Ascertain whether the company had tested open (unmatched) receiving reports to be sure that the liability for merchandise received was reflected in payables.

3. Make similar inquiries regarding liabilities for expenses, and correlate with review of expenses.

Notes Payable (Including Long-Term Debt)

1. Compare detailed note schedule at May 1, 1971, with the schedule of notes payable at year-end, and obtain explanation of changes in view of maturities and in view of capital expenditures required for new stores opened since January 30, 1971.
2. Review the schedule of short-term borrowings and correlate with review of prepaid interest.
3. Review provisions relating to new equipment notes—particularly with respect to assets pledged as collateral.
4. Inquire whether the company was complying with requirements of the proposed indenture relating to its long-term debt.
5. Review computation of interest accrual.
6. Review the description of notes and amounts of long-term debt included in the Capitalization Table in the registration statement. Review the reconciliation of the Capitalization Table to the General Ledger.
7. Continue to monitor the Company's debt and lease commitments through the effective date of the registration to verify that there has been no significant increase in debt outstanding since the date of the Capitalization Table.

Other Payables

Compare the balances in the vendors' leased departments' liability, payroll tax withholding, sales tax withholding, customers' deposits, liability for lay-aways, and similar accounts at May 1, 1971, with those at January 30, 1971, for reasonableness in light of the number of employees at both dates, sales volume, and time of year.

Accrued Liabilities

1. Ascertain adequacy of the amounts accrued for major expenses by:
   (a) Correlation with the review of the accounts payable cut off procedures.
   (b) Comparison with the types and amounts of adjusting entries made at the closings for year-end and interim periods.
   (c) Comparison of the balances in each of the accrued expense accounts at interim and year-end dates.
2. Obtain explanations for variances.

Capital

1. Determine that major transactions in the company's common and preferred stocks between January 30, 1971 and May 1, 1971, were properly accounted for.

2. Review the computation of retained earnings restricted under debt indenture.

Intercompany

1. Inquire regarding elimination of intercompany sales, purchases, and profit in inventory, and of service fees.
2. Review computation of intercompany service fees for each interim period and compare with method used for full year.
3. Review accounting for investments in subsidiaries.

Claims Based on Comfort Letters.—The question of accountants' legal liability to clients, underwriters, and the public is one of serious, continuing concern to the accounting profession in the United States. Chapters **27** and **28** contain a discussion of liabilities arising out of the Federal securities laws and regulations.

As previously noted in this chapter, the Securities Act does not provide for the issuance of comfort letters, and there is no requirement for them to be filed with the SEC.

When accountants issue a comfort letter, they know it is for the underwriter's benefit, and that the letter may influence the underwriter's decisions and actions. Since the letter is not based on an audit made in accordance with clearly defined professional standards (such as generally accepted auditing standards) but rather on a limited number of procedures, the accountants may well be concerned about the consequences which might flow from the letter. While it is true that the most important parts of the letter that have the potential for liability are stated in terms of negative assurance, there may be a risk if the work underlying the issuance of the letter was negligently performed.

There may also be a risk if it should turn out that the procedures performed in connection with the issuance of the letter were not the right ones —that if other procedures had been employed, a matter of great importance to the underwriter might have been brought to light. In this respect, however, the accountants will be the recipients of comfort in the sense that they know that the underwriter is responsible for the procedures which are performed by the accountants at his request. As part of his obligation to employ due diligence, which includes the obligation to make a reasonable investigation of financial statements that are not expertized, the underwriter has to decide what procedures he wants the accountants to perform in connection with unaudited financial statements, for example, for the purpose of their comfort letter.

The matter of accountants' liability based on comfort letters has not been thoroughly tested, and the author is aware of only one decided lawsuit and one SEC decision which involved such letters to a material extent.

THE BARCHRIS CASE.—For a discussion of the BarChris case, the reader is referred to Chapter **28**. The independent auditors in that case had issued a comfort letter the last paragraph of which restricted its use and said it was for the information of the underwriters and was not to be used in connection with the sale of securities.

It is not clear when the plaintiffs became aware of the existence of the comfort letter. In any event the judge ruled that they could not take advantage of any undertakings or representations in the letter. This may have been on the basis that they had not seen the letter since it had not been filed with the SEC and was not a public document. If they had seen it, they were not entitled to rely on it, since its use was clearly restricted to the underwriters.

As to any claims that the underwriters may have had against the accountants, the judge said he would decide this matter at a later date. The case was settled, however, and so this question was not judicially determined.

THE ULTRASONIC CORPORATION CASE.—In the stop-order proceedings involving Ultrasonic Corporation [37 SEC 497–506 (1957)], the principal issue was the amount reported as net income for the interim period of six months ended March 31, 1954. The prospectus showed a profit for that period of $49,715. The figures for this period had not been audited by independent public accountants, but the company made the customary representation that the figures included all adjustments necessary to a fair statement of the results of operations for the period.

In partial defense of its position, the company asserted that it had relied upon a comfort letter obtained by it from the accountants who had assisted in preparing the registration statement, approving the accounting followed by the company. This letter dealt with the unaudited interim figures, and its wording was arrived at by the accountants after discussions with the attorneys employed at the time in connection with the preparation of the registration statement. During their review of the company's books, the accountants had questioned various matters and had made several suggestions that were disregarded. In its final form, the letter noted that the accountants' review and investigation had been limited and that they did not have sufficient information on some of the matters; it was further qualified in various respects which were clearly in the nature of exceptions to the opinions expressed therein, and specifically stated that it was not to be used or referred to in the registration statement or offering literature. The SEC said it was clear that the letter could not relieve the company of its responsibility for the accuracy of the information in the registration statement, including the financial statements.

Letter to SEC Concerning Adjustments Reflected in Unaudited Interim Statements

In Chapter **10** reference was made to the fact that, with respect to unaudited figures in an earnings summary, the registrant must write to the SEC setting forth in detail the nature and amount of all adjustments (other than normal recurring adjustments) entering into the determination of the results shown. This must be done despite the fact that the earnings summary is required to contain a statement that all adjustments necessary to a fair statement have been made. If the summary of earnings states that there were no adjustments other than normal, recurring adjustments, the letter referred to below can be omitted.

The representation and letter requirements referred to in the preceding paragraph are not new. They have been informal administrative requirements of the SEC for several years and were formalized when Form S–1 was revised in 1955. When the SEC proposed to include these requirements in the revised form, it received objections from a number of different sources.

. . . Experience has shown that the requirement has caused many registrants to take a good hard second look at unaudited interim periods. It is common practice for the certifying accountants to assist the registrant in preparing the required letter to the Commission. And of course we assume that the accountants wish to know that the interim periods are prepared on a basis comparable to the certified statements, and, if not, that changes in the application of accounting principles are appropriate. He also wants to be sure that no event has occurred between the date of the certified statements and the effective date of the registration statement that should be disclosed or that should be reflected in the statements he has certified. This Commission places great reliance upon the independent public accountant. This applies to the principles reflected in the uncertified financial statements as well as to the audited statements required to be certified. In a recent case, for example, the accountants' certificate called attention to the fact that the unaudited interim period reflected an important change in accounting. Conferences resulted in a significant change in presentation. . . . A part of your "reasonable investigation" as certifying accountants prior to the effective date should be directed to uncovering such efforts. The management's statement on adjustments in the prospectus and its letter on this subject to the Commission are required by the Commission for the purpose of assuring that the interim unaudited statements do not suffer from errors of omission or commission.[10]

When there are no adjustments other than normal recurring adjustments reflected in the unaudited financial statements, the registrant's letter to the SEC may be in the following form :

[10] J. Sinclair Armstrong, former Chairman of the SEC, address before Houston Chapter of the Texas Society of CPAs, December, 1955.

Securities and Exchange Commission,
500 N. Capitol St.
Washington, D.C. 20549.

Dear Sirs:
    We are writing with reference to the summary of earnings appearing in our registration statement (Form S-1), (SEC File No. ——) filed with you on (date).
    The aforesaid summary of earnings contains unaudited financial data for the (periods) ended (date) and (date). There were no adjustments other than normal recurring adjustments entering into the determination of the results reported for such periods.

Very truly yours,
(Name of registrant and authorized officer)

When, however, the unaudited interim figures do include adjustments other than normal recurring adjustments, the registrant's letter to the SEC may be as follows:

Securities and Exchange Commission,
500 N. Capitol St.
Washington, D.C. 20549.

Dear Sirs:
    The undersigned, as (title of officer) of (name of company), states that no adjustments other than normal recurring adjustments were made in determination of the results of the unaudited interim periods of nine months ending September 30, 19——, and 19——, included in the summary of earnings of the registration statement filed by this company and appearing on page —— of the prospectus, except that an unfavorable adjustment to inventories of imported ores was made in accordance with practices normally followed at year end but not normally accounted for in interim statements.

Very truly yours,
(Name of registrant and authorized officer)

CHAPTER 13

REGISTRATION PROCEDURE UNDER THE 1933 ACT, CONCLUDED

Part 3. Full Disclosure: Some Suggestions

CONTENTS

True Statements May Be Misleading.—The public accountant's examination should enable him to form an opinion not only whether the financial statements, taken as a whole, present fairly what they purport to present, but also whether the statements are not misleading. A possibility to bear in mind is that a statement, though literally true, may at the same time be a half-truth and consequently misleading.

The SEC considered this very question in one of its earliest decisions [*Charles A. Howard,* 1 SEC 11 (1934)] in a stop-order proceeding under the 1933 Act. A registration statement had been filed covering a proposed issuance of certificates of deposit by a bond-holders' protective committee against certain first mortgage bonds. Item 13 of the registration form asked: "If known, state whether or not any other person or persons are soliciting the deposit of any securities of the original issuer, and, if known, state the name and address of such person or persons." To this item the registrant answered: "Unknown." At the hearing it was shown that the registrant knew that a competing protective committee had filed a registration statement seeking the right to solicit the deposit of the same first mortgage bonds. The SEC conceded that a literal and technical construction of Item 13 would support the view that no other person or persons at that time were soliciting the deposit of the securities in question, inasmuch as the solicitation by the competing committee could not lawfully begin until after their registration statement became effective.

The SEC said:

> Such construction, however, ignores the obvious purpose of the item to elicit information as to whether any other protective committees are in the field. The fact that registrants knew that solicitation by others was planned, and that in all probability 'another protective committee would be actively soliciting deposits before the registrants themselves made their call for deposits, would certainly not be the conclusion that would be drawn by the average mind from the registrant's answer to Item 13. But the half-truth embodied in the registrant's answer is the very type of untruth to which the language of the Securities Act relating to omissions of material fact has reference. In the language of Mr. Justice Avory, the registrant's statement is "false in a material particular in that it conveyed a false impression." *Rex v. Kylsant* (1932) 1 K.B. 442, 448.

Another example of an innocent half-truth occurred in a registration statement and was referred to in a decision of the SEC subsequent to stop-order proceedings. [*Columbia Baking Company,* 38 SEC 217 (1958)]. The SEC commented about a statement in the text of a prospectus. The statement was to the effect that, in a five-year period, the company's sales had increased from $16,486,000 to $24,620,000—an increase of $8,134,000, or over 49 per cent. There was no mention at this point of the prospectus that net income had declined in the same period from $432,000 to $323,000. The net income figures were shown in a table presented on the facing page of the prospectus. Nonetheless the SEC found the prospectus materially misleading in presenting in the text thereof the favorable factor of a substantial increase in sales without *at that point* also disclosing the decline in earnings over the same period.

Although the Commission's opinions referred to above were directed to items in the narrative portion of a registration statement, the principle that they enunciate is equally applicable to financial statements.

The SEC requires statements of past earnings to be included in registration statements. All who have a hand in drafting the document, however, should (for reasons which appear below) consider carefully (1) whether the circumstances that existed during the period of the income statement are substantially the same at the effective date or the time of the proposed offering, and (2) whether they are likely to continue. A number of examples from the author's experience and from published SEC decisions will serve to illustrate the point involved.

Case No. 1. For many years, Company S was in the business of manufacturing principally refrigerators and air conditioning equipment and, during the Korean War, had a substantial amount of defense business. Beginning with the year 1953, the company sustained very substantial operating losses in its civilian business, with its defense business continually decreasing at the same time, so that its combined operating results showed very substantial losses. The company's tax loss carry-forward credit (about $15,000,000) resulted from some of these losses. The company finally decided to sell such business, with a view to entering another business or businesses of more profitable and stable character.

There were three principal sales: (1) the sale of the Commercial Refrigeration Division in September, 1956; (2) the sale of the Air Conditioning Division and defense plant in September, 1957; and (3) the sale of the bulk of the facilities and assets of the Home Appliance Division in January, 1958. These sales provided cash of $12,850,000 plus consultation fees of $1,000,000 payable over a five-year period beginning October, 1957. In connection with each sale, the company agreed it would not, for a period of five years thereafter, again engage in the same type of business in competition with the purchaser. There were also other sales of properties of relatively insignificant amounts.

In December, 1958, the company purchased the business and assets of the B Corporation for about $17,000,000 in cash, and the assumption of all liabilities of B.

In September, 1960, Company S filed a registration statement with the SEC under the 1933 Act. Prior to the filing, representatives of S and its independent auditors discussed the content of the financial statements with the staff of the SEC. The staff agreed to the omission of financial statements with respect to S's businesses which had been sold since they were not deemed to have any pertinency or materiality from the viewpoint of S's then business and operations. The prospectus, however, disclosed all of the foregoing history and stated that the annual reports on Form 10–K filed by S with the SEC and the New York Stock Exchange could be inspected at the SEC and the Exchange, and that copies thereof could be obtained from the Commission.

The financial statements in the registration statement with the consent of the SEC were those for S's fiscal year ended October 31, 1959 (which included B's operations from date of acquisition in December, 1958) plus a subsequent interim period, together with a balance sheet at the end of such period. In addition, an income statement of B was included for the four years and nine months prior to its acquisition by S.

Case No. 2. A corporation, organized during World War II, had a phenomenal war production record, and, with a very small capital investment, realized substantial profits. After the war, the company was faced with serious problems in converting to peacetime production of a device used on internal combustion engines (in which it had no special expertise) and in obtaining scarce materials because of the loss of wartime priorities. The owners of the company sold their stock to an underwriting group and began the preparation of a registration statement in anticipation of a public offering of the stock. The income statement required to be included in the registration statement covered the war period. In the circumstances the auditors believed that the income statement could serve no useful purpose. The auditors recommended, therefore, that the income statement should be included in Part II of the registration statement and omitted from the prospectus. The advice of others prevailed, however, and the prospectus as initially filed included the income statement with appropriate precautionary disclosures. The SEC in due course issued a letter of comment recommending among other things that "in the circumstances of this particular registration, all statements setting forth operating results should be omitted from the prospectus and filed as an exhibit." The registration statement and prospectus were amended accordingly.

Case No. 3. In July, 1946, a corporation organized in April of that year filed a registration statement. In 1941 and 1942, a predecessor of the registrant manufactured prefabricated houses and had constructed and sold about 300 of such houses. In the latter part of 1942, owing to wartime conditions, the business was converted to the manufacture of ammunition crates under contracts with several ordnance plants. During 1943, 1944, and the first half of 1945, the company sold large quantities of these ammunition containers and realized substantial profits. In June, 1945, the contracts were terminated, and in August of that year the company ceased production and began work preparatory to re-entering the business of manufacturing prefabricated houses. In April, 1946, all the physical property used by the predecessor was transferred to the company together with certain cash, securities, and accounts in exchange for common stock of the company.

The instructions for financial statements called for an income statement of the predecessor company for the war period, when the predecessor was making ammunition crates, although the company planned to make prefabricated houses. It appeared to the certifying accountants that an income statement in these circumstances could serve no useful purpose and might, in fact, be misleading. In view of the SEC instructions permitting the omission of financial statements in certain circumstances, the accountants suggested that the question be discussed with the SEC with a view to securing approval of the omission from the prospectus of all statements showing operations during the war period, that is, the income and surplus statements, but not the balance sheet. Representatives of the registrant (not the accountants) took the matter up with SEC representatives on two occasions, and each time the staff of the Commission ruled that the income and surplus statements of the predecessor company—despite their short-comings—had to be included in the prospectus.

In the original filing the prospectus contained an income statement followed by a note reading as follows: "The operations of [Predecessor] Company for the period prior to August 31, 1945, consisted principally of the production of ammunition crates and boxes under Government contracts, and for the period subsequent to that date of designing and engineering prefabricated homes. [Successor] Corporation is preparing to produce and sell prefabricated homes, and the above statement of income of the prede-cessor cannot be considered as indicative of operations or net income of the business to be conducted by the corporation." In addition, the accountants inserted a middle paragraph in their report which practically repeated the foregoing note. In all other respects, the report of the certifying accountants was conventional.

In due course, the Commission's deficiency memorandum was received. Concerning the financial statements, the memorandum had only one com-ment: The Commission suggested that the predecessor's income statement and summary of earnings be deleted from the prospectus and put in Part II of the registration statement. Apparently on reconsideration the SEC staff had reached the same conclusion as the certifying accountants. The registration statement was appropriately amended, after which the only financial statement in the prospectus was the balance sheet of the successor corporation.

It will be noted that in Case 1 the SEC permitted the statements of businesses that had been sold to be omitted from the prospectus as well as from the registration statement. In Cases 2 and 3, however, the SEC agreed that operating statements could be omitted from the prospectus but had to be included in Part II of the registration statement. The distinction between the first and the other two cases appears to be that Case 1 involved a listed company concerning which information was available at the SEC and the exchange on which the company's securities were listed, and the prospectus so disclosed. Cases 2 and 3, however, related to companies con-cerning which there was no information available previously. In these cases, the staff of the SEC felt that, although the information as to operations need not be included in the prospectus, compliance with statutory standards demanded that the operating information be included somewhere in the registration document.

Case No. 4. In 1943 the SEC issued a decision in *Colorado Milling and Elevator Company.* [15 SEC 20 (1943)] Resulting from a stop-order pro-ceeding, the decision is probably the definitive SEC pronouncement on the matter of important changes in financial condition and capital structure of a registrant before and after the balance sheet date.

In February, 1943, Union Securities Corporation bought from the stockholders of Colorado 98 per cent of the stock of Colorado for $13,800,000. A new board of directors, nominated by Union, was elected immediately, and Colorado's certificate of incorporation was amended, reducing the par value of the company's stock and transferring $7,800,000 from capital stock to capital surplus.

On May 26, 1943, a cash dividend of $7,000,000 was declared, of which Union received $6,886,000. To pay the dividend, Colorado sold over $5,-000,000 of marketable securities which it owned at the time Union bought control of the company. The balance of the dividend came from a bank loan of $2,000,000. On the same date, the directors of Colorado authorized the creation of an issue of $6,500,000 principal amount of 5 per cent convertible debentures and declared a dividend payable in such debentures. Union's share of the debenture dividend was $6,400,000.

On June 12, 1943, Union sold $3,410,000 principal amount of the debentures to four underwriting firms at par plus interest. Union also sold some of its Colorado common stock but retained control. In July, Colorado authorized an issue of $3,000,000 principal amount of 4 per cent debentures for sale to insurance companies and a new issue of $3 convertible preferred stock for sale to the public. The proceeds from the sale of the preferred stock and new debentures, together with additional necessary funds in treasury, were to be used to redeem the outstanding 5 per cent debentures held by Union and the four firms.

A registration statement was filed with the SEC on August 6, 1943, covering the new $3 convertible preferred stock. The registration statement contained a consolidated income statement of Colorado for the nine years ended May 31, 1943, and a balance sheet at that date. The balance sheet reflected the 5 per cent debentures issuable in payment of the dividend declared May 26, 1943. The balance sheet also reflected capital surplus in the amount of $986,000, with a disclosure that there was no earned surplus at May 31, 1943. All the marketable securities having been disposed of, none was shown on the balance sheet. Under other income, the income statement showed interest of $194,000 in 1935, decreasing to $121,000 in 1943, on United States Government and municipal securities. Results of operations during the nine years ranged from income of $1,515,000 in 1937 to a loss of $858,000 in 1938. The surplus statements disclosed the large dividends in 1943 in cash and in 5 per cent debentures, the aggregate of which was charged first to earned surplus (exhausting that account) and the balance to capital surplus.

After reviewing the registration statement, the SEC's Division of Corporation Finance charged that the registration statement was materially deficient and stop-order proceedings were instituted. The Division alleged that the failure to state that the data included in the nine-year income statements represented the results of operations for a period during which Colorado's capital structure, financial condition, and arrangements differed considerably from that which existed on and after May 31, 1943, constituted a material deficiency. By reason of the sale of its investment portfolio, Colorado would no longer receive the income on these investments by way of dividends and interest, which, in the most recent year, aggregated $123,-000. In the past, Colorado's bank loans were made on the collateral of the marketable securities owned by it at interest rates which averaged less than 1 per cent per annum. The registrant's new line of credit provided for an interest rate on future loans of 1½ per cent. The SEC also observed that the liquidation of the investment portfolio, the payment of the $7,000,000 cash dividend, and the proposed issuance of $3,000,000 principal amount of 4 per cent debentures would probably alter the federal excess profits tax base and increase Colorado's tax liability.

The Commission's decision also pointed out other factors which would adversely affect the registrant's future income and which were not disclosed in connection with the nine-year income statement: (1) the interest charges on the $3,000,000 of new 4 per cent debentures; (2) the increase in executive compensation from $56,800 in the year ended May 31, 1943, to $105,600 for the year ended May 31, 1944; (3) an increase of $76,000 in the cost of insurance for the year ended May 31, 1944, because of a substantial extension in coverage. "The net effect of the foregoing will be to diminish the net income available for dividends."

The SEC said:

Profit and loss statements are required in the registration statement as an indication to prospective investors of the registrant's earning power. The nine years' profit and loss statement contained in this registration statement reflected the results of operations during a period when the registrant had maintained continuously a financial status substantially equivalent to that existing immediately prior to this financing. By reason of the changes effected since May 22, that financial status bears little resemblance to that which obtains presently. Where such changes will have a material effect on prospective earnings, the omission to disclose those changes and their effect with relation to the profit and loss statements is as misleading as if the registrant's past earnings had been misrepresented.

In the meantime the registration statement had been amended along the lines suggested by the SEC's comments, and the registration was allowed to become effective.

Case No. 5. A company distributing liquid propane gas at retail was reorganized to engage in the distribution of natural gas. Because of this change in the nature of the company's business, and the fact that its new operations would be substantially extended and subject to rate regulation, the Commission acquiesced in the suggestion of the company itself that its past earnings record would be of little value to the investor and permitted its omission from the registration statement.[1]

The reader is also referred to the discussion under "Transactions and Events Subsequent to the Statement Date" in Chapter **12**, and "Predecessor Business Operated as a Partnership or Sole Proprietorship" in Chapter **21**.

Misleading Inferences from Interim Statements.—Accountants know that the value of an income statement as an indication of earning power is in direct proportion to the length of the period covered by the statement —the longer the period, the better. The shorter the period, the more apt it is to be influenced by unusual, extraneous, or non-recurring factors and by errors in estimates and apportionments. Registrants are accordingly reluctant to present income statements for periods as short as, say, one month. On the other hand, they are often willing to present statements of, say, the first three months of a year and the first four months of the same year. They sometimes overlook the fact that by subtracting one statement from the other, the difference represents the result of the fourth month.

This kind of situation was the subject of comment by the SEC in one of its annual reports [18 SEC Ann. Rep. 14 (1952)] to Congress. The registration statement as originally filed by a company deriving its income principally from long-term contracts included in the summary of earnings and in the financial statements unaudited interim figures for the twelve-week period subsequent to the close of its last fiscal year. The summary, in addition to its figures for ten full fiscal years and the twelve-week interim period, also included figures for the sixteen-week period subsequent to the close of the fiscal year. Comparison of the two interim periods disclosed net income in the last four weeks of the sixteen-week period approximately equal to the net income in the first twelve weeks. In view of the possible interpretation that this comparison indicated a substantial improvement in earnings, which was unwarranted because of the nature of the business, it was agreed, in a discussion between members of the SEC staff and counsel for the company, to delete the twelve-week figures from the summary of earnings and to substitute the sixteen-week for the twelve-week figures in the financial statements.

Sometimes the bare interim figures may lead the reader to conclude that an adverse trend in a company's affairs has set in when this is not true. If the figures are capable of misleading the reader, the necessary explanation should be made.

An illustration of the kind of explanation that should be made occurred

[1] Source: Harry Heller, "Disclosure Requirements Under Federal Securities Regulation," *The Business Lawyer,* Jan. 1961, p. 311.

in the November, 1960, prospectus of Ginn and Company which contained a summary of earnings covering the calendar years 1955–59 and the eight months ended August 31, 1959 and 1960. In the narrative material following the summary and the notes thereto, the company disclosed that in the two months ended October 31, 1960, net sales (unadjusted for consigned inventories) amounted to $3,902,702 compared with similar sales for the same period in 1959 of $4,785,484. Net income figures for such periods were not available.

The company apparently believed that the decrease in sales in the two-month period of almost $900,000 (or 18 per cent) might mislead the reader, and explained the situation as follows:

In the opinion of the company, this decrease does not indicate a trend, but reflects a correction of internal conditions which existed in 1959. In December, 1958, the company's Eastern warehouse was discontinued and this service added to the Central warehouse in Indianapolis. This change adversely affected order preparation and shipping throughout 1959 for the whole company with the result that shipping was delayed for the peak season during June, July, August and September of that year, with a corresponding delay in recording of sales. In 1960 this situation was corrected.

Unadjusted net sales for the ten months ended October 31, 1960 are $26,236,008, a gain of $973,314 over the corresponding period in 1959.

The Kaiser-Frazer Case.—The classic example of misleading inferences from interim statements was the Kaiser-Frazer case. Because of the nature of the dispute, the case was followed with interest not only by accountants but also by investment bankers, lawyers, and the SEC. The background of the case follows.

Kaiser-Frazer Corporation, an automobile manufacturer, entered into a contract on February 3, 1948, to sell shares of its common stock to Otis and Company and two other underwriters. The obligation of the underwriters to accept and pay for the stock was subject to certain conditions. One of the principal conditions was this: The registration statement (including the prospectus) filed under the 1933 Act was to comply with the Act and the regulations of the SEC and neither the registration statement nor the prospectus was to contain any untrue statement of a material fact nor were they to omit to state any material fact required to be stated therein or necessary in order to make the statements therein not misleading.

The registration statement became effective on February 3, 1948, the day the contract was signed. The contract set February 9, 1948, as the closing date at which time K-F was to deliver the stock and the underwriters were to pay for it. On the day of the closing, however, Otis and one other underwriter refused to accept the stock, and shortly thereafter K-F brought suit against Otis.

In its answer to the complaint, Otis claimed it was relieved of the obligation to perform because the registration statement contained false and misleading statements. The trial judge found in favor of K-F and entered judgment for over $3,000,000. Otis appealed claiming several errors, but the Court of Appeals discussed only one of the alleged errors, namely, whether the District Court was correct in finding that K-F had not misrepresented but had adequately disclosed its profit for the month of December, 1947, in the statement of earnings in the prospectus. If the prospectus contained such a misrepresentation, Otis was not obligated to pay for the stock.

In order to follow the reasoning in the upper court, some additional background information must be presented. In the early part of 1948, when the issue in question was contemplated, K-F was as yet a newcomer in the automobile industry. Production of its cars did not get under way until late 1946. Volume production was not achieved until the spring of 1947. While the postwar period in the automobile industry was abnormal in the sense that a strong seller's market prevailed, nevertheless the problems of production and competition confronting one in K-F's position were in sufficient magnitude, said the Court, to make the venture highly speculative. In these circumstances, the Court said, it was evident that the prospective purchaser of the K-F stock would rely heavily on the corporation's sales and earnings during the last quarters of 1947 as the best, and perhaps the only, available indication of its ability to compete with the established automobile manufacturers. The prospectus included a summary of earnings which (with certain irrelevant deletions) is reproduced on the following page.

The earnings summary contains no figure showing the results for the month of December, 1947, as such. However, the Court said, "by subtracting the profit for the two months ending November 30, 1947 from the quarter ending December 31, 1947 profit, a figure of $4,009,383 is obtained which one would naturally assume to represent the profit of the Corporation for the single month of December, 1947." K-F argued that the average person reading the prospectus would not make this arithmetical computation and hence his judgment would not be affected by any consideration of what the December profit was represented to be. The Court thought otherwise: "Because of the comparatively brief earnings record of the Corporation and the speculative nature of the venture in which it was engaged, we think that the average prospective purchaser of K-F stock would have made a subtraction and would have concluded that the December earnings totaled nearly $4,000,000."

The corporation's earnings for December were actually in the neighborhood of $900,000. The difference in amount was due to the fact that, as mentioned in Note 4 of the summary, a physical inventory was taken in the latter part of December, 1947, at which time it was discovered that the

SUMMARY OF CONSOLIDATED SALES AND EARNINGS

The following summary reflects consolidated sales and earnings of the Corporation from its inception to December 31, 1947. . . . The information shown in the table for the eleven months ended November 30, 1947, and the breakdown into the three fiscal quarters and the two months period comprising such eleven months, have been taken from profit and loss statements prepared by the Corporation from its books and accounts, without audit, and should be read in conjunction with the unaudited eleven months financial statements and schedule included herein. The tentative information shown in the table for the quarter and for the year ended December 31, 1947, has been prepared by the Corporation from its books and records, without audit, on the basis of a preliminary 1947 closing made at January 23, 1948.

Period	Sales and Miscellaneous Income	Cost of Sales	Selling and Adminis- trative Expenses	Other Deductions or Credits* — Net	Net Profit or Loss*
From August 9 to December 31, 1945	$ 10,979	$ 224,607	$ 551,988	$ 7,104	$ 772,720*
Year ended December 31, 1946	11,657,972	28,092,530	2,940,877	90,754*	19,284,681*
Eleven months ended November 30, 1947	227,560,032	204,674,595	6,751,960	637,729	15,495,748
Quarter ended March 31, 1947	27,305,035	29,366,660	1,093,542	81,127	3,236,294*
Quarter ended June 30, 1947	53,142,946	50,255,274	1,640,776	198,641	1,048,255
Quarter ended September 30, 1947	78,527,735	67,890,777	2,150,261	209,388	8,277,309
Two months ended November 30, 1947	68,584,316	57,161,884	1,867,381	148,573	9,406,478
Quarter ended December 31, 1947 (4)	101,999,563	84,519,665	3,850,916	213,121	13,415,861
Year ended December 31, 1947 (4)	260,975,279	232,032,376	8,735,495	702,277	19,505,131

NOTES:
   (4) The tentative information for the quarter and year ended December 31, 1947, reflects various substantial year-end adjustments including provision for certain reserves and a material increase in inventories to conform to the results of the complete physical inventory taken by the Corporation as of December 31, 1947.

actual inventory was much larger than the book inventory. The book inventory was adjusted accordingly in the amount of $3,371,000, and this amount was included in the final quarter's earnings in the summary. The Court observed:

Actually, the increase in profit resulting from the larger inventory was allocable not only to the month of December or the last quarter of 1947, but to the entire year's operations and in part to prior years; for in effect the larger inventory meant that K-F had been charging too much to cost of sales for these periods. Indeed, the Corporation's "Consolidated statement of income and expense" for December, 1947, prepared for its own use, summarized the month's operation as follows:

"Net profit (or loss) for the month of December, 1947 .... $ 638,226[2]
Prior months' adjustments ...... 3,371,155"

K-F's own expert accounting witness did not deny that the inventory write-up should have been allocated to prior periods. He did, however, testify that a complete reallocation of its expenses that had been charged to December would yield a profit of $2,900,000, "which in turn would mean that the amount of the overstatement of December earnings was only a little over $1,000,000." The Court rejected this testimony because the method of reallocation was entirely opposed to the accounting system that had been utilized by K-F and upon which the summary was based.

The District Court had found that the summary of earnings was computed in accordance with accepted accounting procedures and that it was not misleading. The Court of Appeals, however, did not agree. The upper court said: "For, regardless of whether its accounting system was a sound one, K-F stated its earnings in such a way as to represent that it had made a profit of about $4,000,000 in December, 1947. This representation was $3,100,000 short of the truth."

The Court conceded that the profits for the year as a whole were substantially unaffected by the overstatement of the earnings for the month of December, 1947, but stated that the prospective purchaser was entitled to a full disclosure of all the facts that were known to the corporation at the time the prospectus was issued, "and the Corporation knew on February 3, 1948 that its profit for the month of December, 1947 was less than $1,000,000." The Court continued:

> The source of the profit as stated in the prospectus for December could have been readily disclosed by a footnote to the earnings table. The footnote (4) that appeared in the prospectus as issued was entirely insufficient for this purpose. No one reading it would have been put on notice that the actual profit for December was less than a fourth of what was indicated by the table.

The Court concluded that the contract was unenforceable and that K-F was not entitled to recover damages.

AFTERMATH OF THE KAISER-FRAZER CASE: THE HELLER COMMITTEE REPORT.—In 1951, the Committee on Interstate and Foreign Commerce of the House of Representatives appointed a subcommittee with authority to investigate the SEC and the exercise by the Commission of the duties and functions granted to it by law. The subcommittee was frequently referred to as the Heller Committee, after its chairman. Among other things, the Committee investigated the Kaiser-Frazer registration statement and the handling thereof by the SEC. A large part of the inquiry was directed to Note 4 of the earnings summary in the K-F prospectus (see page **13·11**) which disclosed that, "The tentative information for the quarter and year

---

[2] Some of the inventory write-up, approximately $260,000, was allocable to the month of December, which accounts for the difference between $638,226 shown in this statement as December profit and the $900,000 figure referred to earlier.

ended December 31, 1947, reflects various substantial year-end adjustments including . . . a material increase in inventories to conform to the results of the . . . physical inventory taken . . . as of December 31, 1947."

The Heller Committee issued a report[3] in 1952 on its findings and conclusions. The report indicated that the Committee had attempted to find out whether the SEC and its personnel who handled the K-F registration statement knew that the December profit of $4,000,000 included inventory and other adjustments of $3,100,000. The testimony on this question was sharply contradictory.

The Committee was critical of the manner in which the SEC had processed the K-F registration statement.[4] Subsequent to the preparation of the Committee's report, the then chairman of the SEC wrote to the Committee advising of the steps taken by the SEC to tighten up its administrative procedures in the processing of registration statements under the 1933 Act. The SEC chairman said:

. . . The Commission has supplemented its long-standing direction to the staff, to make appropriate inquiry, in connection with all summaries of financial information for interim periods, to determine the existence of unusual conditions which may affect the propriety of the presentation of the summary of earnings. This has been accomplished by further directing that the registrant be required to represent specifically in the registration statement, with respect to any unaudited interim period included therein, that all adjustments necessary to a proper presentation have been made and that the staff obtain from the registrant a letter describing in detail the nature and amounts of any adjustments other than normally occurring accruals entering into the determination of the results reported in the summary of earnings. . . . In this fashion, the Commission will be assured that its permanent files will contain the necessary information. More importantly, the receipt of a written communication concerning these matters will bring directly to the attention of the staff the necessity for considering the question of whether additional or other disclosures should be required.[5]

As a result of the K-F case, the SEC adopted two informal administrative requirements in respect of unaudited interim periods in earnings summaries. First, registrants are required to represent with respect to such periods that all adjustments necessary for a fair presentation of the results for the periods are included. Second, registrants are required to set forth in a letter to the SEC the adjustments other than normal recurring accruals entering into the results shown. (Although the SEC requirement refers to "accruals," obviously "adjustments" is a better term. In practice the latter is substituted for the former with no objection from the SEC's staff.) With the revision in 1955 of the requirements for earnings summaries in Form

---

[3] *Study of the Securities and Exchange Commission, Report of the Committee on Interstate and Foreign Commerce* (1952).

[4] *Ibid.*, p. 91.

[5] *Ibid.*, p. 95.

S–1, these requirements became formalized. For a suggested form of letter to the SEC setting forth unusual adjustments and the SEC's views regarding the importance of this requirement, see page **12**·59.

The Globe Aircraft Case.—A registration statement under the 1933 Act was filed by Globe Aircraft Corporation. As originally filed, the registration statement included a certified income statement for the last four months of 1945 which showed a loss of $540,000 as compared with net income of $53,000 for the full year. Of the $540,000 loss, there was a disclosure that $439,000 represented a write-down of inventories from cost to replacement values. At the request of the Commission an income statement for the month of January, 1946, was included in an amended prospectus. While disclosing a loss of $17,000 for the month, this *unaudited* statement made no reference to additional inventory write-downs necessitated by the continuation of excess costs for work-in-process inventory incurred throughout January and February, 1946. Despite the assertion that there was a probability that a tax refund would offset a substantial part of the indicated inventory losses, the Commission held that the failure to disclose the situation made the income statement for the month of January, 1946, materially false and misleading.

At the proceeding which resulted in the issuance of a stop-order, the underwriters contended that under accepted accounting principles it was not required that a write-down be made of the inventory at the end of January, 1946. They argued that actual profit and loss depends upon the price at which the planes manufactured from the work-in-process inventories are ultimately sold and not upon the replacement cost of the inventory. The SEC brushed this argument aside:

> The question here is not whether from an accounting standpoint there should have been an actual inventory write-down in January, but whether the existence of additional inventory losses of which the management was cognizant, should have been disclosed. A full and fair presentation of the company's financial status would have required that this condition be brought to the attention of investors. Similarly, it is immaterial whether or not an inventory write-down is viewed as an operational loss. The significant fact is not whether the loss has in fact been actually realized by sale, but that the loss has accrued and is inherent on the basis of the company's current operations. . . .
>   . . . The question here is not one of accounting procedure whereby a corporation makes certain accounting adjustments at specified times thereby giving formal recognition to the cumulative effect of prior operations. Our inquiry is directed to the problem whether, in connection with the public offering of securities, adequate disclosure of the company's financial condition is furnished if the company merely shows the carrying value per books, of its inventories without indicating the existence of losses inherent in its operations due to non-recoverable costs incurred in acquiring those inventories. We do not believe that under such circumstances the disclosure standards of the Securities Act

are met where investors are presented with financial statements which merely reflect the carrying value of such inventories without disclosing that such carrying value contains costs which, on the basis of present indications, would not be recovered. The failure to disclose the existence of such facts creates a misleading picture of the company's position and operations.

Moreover, the possibilities for misleading investors in this respect were greatly emphasized by the fact that the figures for the last four months of 1945 contained specific reference to inventory losses for that period; the obvious implication from the failure to make any reference to such losses for the month of January, 1946, was that there were no similar losses in the latter period. As we have indicated, this implication was wholly false [26 SEC 46 (1947)].

Interim Statements of Companies Subject to Seasonal Factors.— The reader is referred to the discussion beginning on page **10·**39 regarding the effect of seasonal factors on the business of a registrant in relation to the summary of earnings included in a registration statement. As there stated, when the summary includes data for an interim period, it will ordinarily be necessary to furnish data for the corresponding period of the preceding fiscal year. As far as the summary of earnings is concerned, if interim data are furnished, they are furnished for two comparable periods.

Frequently income statements are included in registration statements in addition to earnings summaries. Such income statements often include the most recent interim period, but there is no formal SEC requirement to furnish an income statement for the corresponding interim period of the preceding year. As stated in the discussion referred to above, statements for interim periods are apt to be misleading when they relate to businesses affected by seasonal factors, and therefore consideration needs to be given to what disclosure should be made of the seasonal influences. When an income statement is submitted for an interim period of less than one year, and when there is reason to believe that the income and expenses for the interim period may not be indicative of the rate of yearly earnings owing to seasonal factors or other reasons, it is important that a note to that effect be appended.

An aggravated instance was found in the case of a registrant that had shown a very rapid expansion during the last five years. The financial statements of this company as initially filed revealed that the net profit for the first five months of the current fiscal year amounted to approximately $1,500,000 and indicated that, owing to the seasonal nature of the business, earnings for the first five months of a fiscal year had historically been materially greater than for the balance of the year. The extent of the past seasonal variation could not be determined from the financial data furnished. Therefore a danger existed that the five-month earnings of $1,500,000 would be misinterpreted as indicating an annual rate grossly in excess of the amount that reasonably could be anticipated. In order to avoid this danger, the registrant was required to furnish the results of operations for the same period of the previous fiscal year for comparison with the first five months of the current fiscal year. When the comparison was furnished, it was obvious that the net profit for the first five months of the previous fiscal year was approximately equal to the net profit for the entire fiscal year. The registrant was thereupon requested also to add a statement in respect of the net profit reported for the first five months of the current fiscal year indicating that substantially all earnings for the entire fiscal year had historically been made during the first five months. [20 SEC Ann. Rep. 15 (1954)]

Because of the fact that summaries of earnings that contain interim financial data present such information for two corresponding periods, it should not be necessary in the ordinary case to furnish income statements for both periods. Except in an aggravated case, all that is necessary is to comply with the formal SEC requirements for financial statements and to disclose the seasonal aspects of the company's operations.

Restatement of Previously Reported Financial Statements.—The question of when should previously reported financial statements be restated has been one of continuing concern not only to the accounting profession but also to the SEC. A related question is: when *may* previously reported financial statements be restated?

In recent years, these questions have become more pressing—largely as the result of changes in accounting principles adopted by several publicly-owned corporations. In some of these cases, the changes were from one generally accepted accounting principle to another principle which, although generally accepted, was less preferable. Some companies also in making a change in their accounting principles restated retroactively their financial statements for a period of years, which sometimes had the effect of charging to past years deferred costs that the company's operations would otherwise have to absorb in the current and future years, and a retroactive adoption of new principles seemed like an expeditious way of getting these costs behind them.

It was apparent that the APB had to consider the problems involved in when should companies be permitted to change their accounting principles, and when should retroactive restatements of prior years' financial statements be required or permitted. When the Board issued its Opinion No. 20, "Accounting Changes," in July 1971, it was with the purpose of dealing with these matters. The Board's earlier Opinion No. 9 on "Reporting the Results of Operations" (December 1966) had touched on these matters only incidentally.

The Board stated in APB No. 20 that, in the preparation of financial statements, there is a presumption that a generally accepted accounting principle once adopted should not be changed in accounting for similar events and transactions. This presumption may be overcome only if the enterprise justifies the use of an alternative acceptable accounting principle on the basis that it is preferable. The burden of justifying accounting principle changes rests with the entity proposing the change. The issuance of an opinion by the APB that creates a new accounting principle, or that expresses a preference for an accounting principle, or that rejects a specific accounting principle is sufficient support for a change in principle. The issuance of an industry audit guide by a committee of the AICPA may also prescribe the manner of reporting a change in accounting principle; such a guide also constitutes sufficient support for a change.

Opinion No. 20 discusses how a change in accounting principle should be disclosed and the treatment to be accorded the change. The APB concluded that most changes in accounting should be recognized by including the cumulative effect, based on a retroactive computation, of changing to a new accounting principle in net income of the period of the change, but that a few specific changes in accounting principles should be reported by restating the financial statements of prior periods.

When the cumulative effect of a change is to be included in income, it should be positioned between extraordinary items and net income. Financial statements of periods prior to the one in which the change occurred, which are presented for comparative purposes, should be presented as previously reported. The effect of adopting the new principle on income before extraordinary items and on net income (and on the related per share amounts) of the period of the change should be stated. Disclosure must be made of the pro forma effect of the change on all periods presented in the statements. (Chapter **21** contains a discussion of the pro forma presentation in these circumstances.) Thus, income before extraordinary items and net income (exclusive of the cumulative adjustment) for the period of the change should be reported on the new basis.

It will sometimes not be possible to compute the effect on retained earnings at the beginning of the period in which a change in principle is made. The principal example of this type of change is a change in inventory method from FIFO to LIFO. In these situations, disclosure will be limited to showing the effect of the change on the results of operations of the period of change and to explaining the reason for omitting the cumulative effect and disclosure of pro forma amounts for prior years.

As previously stated, the adoption of certain specified changes in accounting principles requires retroactive application of the new method in restatements of prior periods, rather than absorbing the cumulative effect of the change in the income statement of the period in which the change is made. The accounting changes that require retroactive application are:

    a. A change from the LIFO method of inventory pricing to another method.

    b. A change in the method of accounting for long-term construction-type contracts.

    c. A change to or from the "full cost" method of accounting which is used by some companies in the extractive industries.

When any of the three aforementioned changes have been adopted, the Opinion discusses the disclosures that have to be made regarding the nature of and the justification for a change in accounting principle. In addition, the effect of the change on income before extraordinary items, net income, and the related per share amounts, has to be given for all periods presented.

In issuing Opinion No. 20, the Board recognized that a company owned by a few individuals might decide to change from one acceptable accounting principle to another acceptable principle in connection with a forthcoming public offering of its equity securities. In recognition of this situation, the Board decided that financial statements for all prior periods presented may be restated to reflect the new principle. The Board felt that potential investors might be better served by statements of income for a period of years reflecting the use of the newly adopted accounting principles because they will be the same as those expected to be used in future periods. Accordingly, a special exemption permitting retroactive restatement of financial statements for any changes in accounting principles was provided for companies first issuing their financial statements for any one of the following purposes:

    (a) obtaining additional equity capital from investors,

    (b) effecting a business combination, or

    (c) registering securities.

With respect to (c) above, although the Opinion does not so state, presumably the exemption would also be available in connection with an offering which is not registered with the SEC but is made pursuant to one of the exemptions contained in the 1933 Act—as, for example, when the amount of the public offering is under $500,000.

The special exemption provided in APB Opinion No. 20 and discussed above is available only once for changes made at the time a company's financial statements are first used for any of those purposes and is not available to companies whose securities currently are widely held. When using this exemption, companies should disclose the nature of the change in accounting principle and the justification for it, including an explanation of why the newly adopted accounting principle is preferable.

Previously reported financial statements should also be retroactively recast for prior period adjustments as indicated in APB Opinion No. 9, paragraph 18, and for the correction of errors.

Accounting changes that result in financial statements that are in effect the statements of a different reporting entity should also be reported by restating the financial statements of all prior periods presented. This type of change occurs when (a) consolidated or combined statements are presented in place of statements of individual companies, (b) a change in the make-up of the group of companies for which consolidated statements are furnished, and (c) a change in the companies included in combined statements. A different group of companies comprise the reporting entity after each change. A business combination accounted for by the pooling of interests method also results in a different reporting entity.

Shown below are some examples of the disclosures made when financial statements are restated under varying circumstances. Further examples illustrating the required disclosures may be found in Exhibit C to Opinion No. 9 and in the appendices to Opinion No. 20.

Example 1—Change in accounting entity as the result of poolings of interest

The most common circumstance which causes a restatement of financial statements of prior years is when there has been a pooling of interests. The prospectus of Litton Industries, Inc., dated December 15, 1970, disclosed the effect on sales and service revenues and on net income resulting from poolings of interest. The disclosures were made on the face of the income statement rather than in a note to the statement. The sales reconciliation was made as follows:

	Year Ended July 31,				
	1970	1969	1968	1967	1966
Sales and service revenues:		(thousands of dollars)			
Litton Industries, Inc. and subsidiary companies—as reported in the Company's reports to shareholders	$2,404,327	$2,176,598	$1,855,007	$1,561,510	$1,172,233
Businesses acquired in poolings of interests—sales for years prior to year of acquisition:					
1969			75,419	73,986	62,781
1968				217,291	203,674
1967					168,731
	2,404,327	2,176,598	1,930,426	1,852,787	1,607,419

Following the information as to ratio of earnings to fixed charges was the reconciliation of earnings with previously reported amounts as follows:

Reconciliation of net earnings with net earnings as reported in the Company's reports to shareholders:					
Litton Industries, Inc. and subsidiary companies—as reported	$ 68,751	$ 82,258	$ 58,456	$ 70,070	$ 55,614
Businesses acquired in poolings of interests—earnings for years prior to year of acquisition:					
1969			2,481	4,077	3,463
1968				13,129	16,052
1967					5,314
Net earnings, as above	$ 68,751	$ 82,258	$ 60,937	$ 87,276	$ 80,443

Example 2—Change in inventory method from LIFO to FIFO

The following extract from a note to the financial statements of Chrysler Corporation appeared in a May 11, 1971 prospectus of Chrysler Financial Corporation:

Inventories are stated at the lower of cost or market. For the period January 1, 1957 through December 31, 1969 the last-in, first-out (LIFO) method of inventory valuation had been used for approximately 60% of the consolidated inventory. The cost of the remaining 40% of inventories was determined using the first-in, first-out (FIFO) or average cost methods. Effective January 1, 1970 the FIFO method of inventory valuation has been adopted for inventories previously valued using the LIFO method. This results in a more uniform valuation method throughout the Corporation and its consolidated subsidiaries and makes the financial statements with respect to inventory valuation comparable with those of the other United States automobile manufacturers. As a result of adopting FIFO in 1970, the net loss reported is less than it would have been on a LIFO basis by approximately $20.0 million, or $0.40 a share. Inventory amounts at December 31, 1970 are stated higher by approximately $150.0 million than they would have been had the LIFO method been continued. The Corporation has retroactively adjusted financial statements of prior years for this change. Accordingly, the 1969 and 1968 financial statements have been restated resulting in an increase in Net Earnings of $10.2 million and $12.2 million, respectively, and Net Earnings Retained for Use in the Business at December 31, 1969, 1968 and 1967 have been increased by $53.5 million, $43.3 million and $31.1 million, respectively.

APB Opinion No. 20, which was issued subsequent to the date of this prospectus, would also require disclosure of the effects of the change on 1968 and 1969 earnings per share.

Example 3—Correction of an error

The following extract from a note to the financial statements of Alloys Unlimited Inc. and subsidiaries appeared in a March 11, 1971 prospectus of The Plessey Company Limited:

Subsequent to June 30, 1970, a subsidiary of Alloys included in the combined financial statements of Universal Titanium Corp. and Universal Titanium International, Inc. (not presented separately herein), discovered that accounts payable of $210,000 (attributable to cost of sales) had not been recorded as of August 31, 1969. The financial statements for the year ended August 31, 1969 have been restated to reflect the additional liabilities and net income for 1969 has been reduced $99,000 (net of the applicable federal income tax benefit of $111,000) from the amount previously reported.

The absence of disclosure of the effects of the error on earnings per share, as required by APB Opinion No. 20, was accounted for by another note to the financial statements which stated, in part, that all of Alloys' subsidiaries were wholly owned.

Restatements by Closely-Held Companies When Going Public.—
The previous pages of this chapter have discussed Opinion No. 20 issued
by the APB in July 1971. That discussion indicated that, in general, accounting principles should not be changed by a reporting entity unless it
could be demonstrated that the change was from one generally accepted
accounting principle to a better one. Furthermore, except as provided in
the Opinion, the effect of the change has to be included in the income statement of the year in which the change is made, and statements of prior years
may not be restated on account of the change but its effect must be shown
pro forma on the face of the statement.

One of the exceptions provided for in the Opinion was for closely-held
companies that file registration statements with the SEC—usually in connection with a plan for going public. It is no secret that the accounts of
many of these closely-held companies—especially privately-owned companies—are maintained on a basis that will show the smallest amount of
net income, and hence the minimum amount of income tax. This is not
to suggest that there is anything necessarily wrong in keeping records on
that basis. For example, a company can avail itself of the accelerated depreciation methods permitted by the Internal Revenue Code and thereby postpone a portion of the income tax that would otherwise be payable. The
company can deduct interest charges and other costs in its tax returns
which, alternatively, could be amortized over longer periods. For these and
other reasons, statements prepared on a tax basis may not fairly reflect a
company's earning potential. Some companies therefore adopt alternative
accounting concepts in their registration statements when they go public.
If the revised statements reflect an attempt to more clearly match costs and
revenues, or to follow acceptable alternative accounting methods, the Commission will accept them.

Here are a few of the areas in which closely-held companies followed
one method for tax purposes and another for their SEC statements:

1. Some companies follow accelerated depreciation for tax purposes
   and straight-line depreciation for financial accounting purposes.
2. Research and development costs which are written off currently for
   tax purposes may be capitalized and amortized for statement purposes.
3. Subscription income of publishers must be deferred over the life
   of the subscription. Related subscription expense may also be
   capitalized and amortized.
4. Some real estate developers who purchase acreage for the purpose
   of building a specified number of homes have felt it preferable to
   defer selling, general, and administrative expenses connected with
   the development, and amortize such costs as homes are sold.

5. Some finance corporations defer the first year of operating losses of newly opened offices and amortize such amounts over a period not in excess of three years.

6. Some companies with multiple retail locations (particularly bowling and discount operations) defer certain of their preopening costs to be recovered against future operations.

7. Newly organized companies may defer starting-up costs prior to commercial operations to be amortized over a period not in excess of five years.

8. Some companies under fixed price contracts have found that percentage of completion accounting presents a more realistic operating trend than completed contract accounting.

Disclosure of Declining Trend.—As might be expected, the staff of the SEC is keenly aware of changes in business conditions. Although the Commission requires financial statements filed with it to be as of a date within 90 days of filing in some cases and within six months of filing in others, the staff is alert to the fact that recent developments in the affairs of a company may give a picture quite different from that exhibited in the financial statements required to be filed.

A commissioner of the SEC pointed out the consequences which might result from the failure to disclose a declining trend in the issuer's operations in the period following the latest financial statements included in a registration statement:

. . . In a recent instance, a registration statement which became effective on September 5, 1967 contained an Income Statement showing that for the six-month period ending May 31, 1967, the issuer had earnings for the first time in its history. Within 10 days of the effective date of the registration statement, the underwriter and issuer decided to withdraw the offering, cancel all transactions, and bring to the Commission's attention facts that had not previously been disclosed—that the company had operated at a loss in June and July of 1967. By the time this action was taken, the entire offering had been sold out at the offering price of $22.50 per share and active trading was in progress at prices up to $49.00 per share. As a result of the cancellation, no securities were delivered and no transactions were consummated.

This case primarily illustrates the adverse consequence that can result from the failure to amend a registration statement in a timely fashion.[6]

The prospectus filed in January, 1954, as part of the registration statement of a company engaged in a highly competitive line of manufacture contained somewhat broad generalizations under "recent developments" indicating that the volume of sales and level of earnings had fallen off. After the staff of the SEC elicited from representatives of the company details con-

[6] Hugh F. Owens, "A Regulator's Look at Quick Profit Fever—Some Disquieting Reactions," address before Mississippi Valley Group, Investment Bankers Association of America, Hot Springs, Ark., Oct. 20, 1967.

cerning the extent and effect of this downward trend, the prospectus was amended to include the specific statement that "sales for the month of December, 1953, approximated 62 per cent of average monthly sales for the six months ended August 31, 1953, earnings for the quarter ended November 30, 1953, approximated 52 per cent of average quarterly earnings for the six months ended August 31, 1953, and sales backlog at January 31, 1954, approximated 62 per cent of such backlog at August 31, 1953." [20 SEC Ann. Rep. 14 (1954)].

A corporation prepared a registration statement and filed it with the SEC in March, 1968. The company was on a calendar year for fiscal reporting purposes, and the financial statements filed were as of December 31, 1967, and for the five fiscal years then ended. These statements complied with the requirements for financial statements in the applicable registration form. In due course the SEC issued its memorandum of comments which contained the following in relation to the summary of earnings:

If net sales and net income for the three months ended December 31, 1967 were materially below those for the same three months in the preceding year, it is suggested that such figures on a comparative basis for the two three-months periods be given.

The obvious purpose of this comment was to elicit information with respect to a material dip in sales or net income in the last quarter of 1967 as compared with the corresponding quarter of the preceding fiscal year. Accountants and registrants would be well advised to keep in mind the matter of recent adverse changes in the financial affairs of a company even though the formal requirements of the SEC do not specifically call for such current information.

THE HAYES MANUFACTURING CORPORATION CASE.—What would the situation be under the 1933 Act if a company reported profits in the registration statement but had losses in the succeeding interim period that were not reported? Would the omission to report a change in the company's affairs existing at the effective date constitute a material omission that would render the registration statement misleading? The Commission discussed this question in *Hayes Manufacturing Corporation* [23 SEC 586 (1946)] in connection with a registration statement under the 1933 Act.

Hayes Manufacturing Corporation proposed to issue shares of its common stock in exchange for all the common stock of American Engineering Company. The stockholders of the latter planned to sell the Hayes stock so acquired to the public through underwriters, and Hayes filed a registration statement on February 27, 1946, to cover the proposed offering. On March 29, 1946, prior to the effective date, the SEC directed that a public examination be held, and on April 24, 1946, instituted stop-order proceedings. Material amendments were filed in April, May, and July, 1946, which substantially corrected the deficiencies complained of by the

SEC. The Commission therefore determined not to issue the stop-order but commented upon certain deficiencies in the original filing.

The original filing included financial statements of Hayes and American which showed that the companies had earned net income as follows:

Hayes:
- Fiscal year ended September 30, 1943 . . . . $284,973
- Fiscal year ended September 30, 1944   735,522
- Fiscal year ended September 30, 1945   436,446

American:
- Parent company alone:
  - 11 months ended November 30, 1944   427,277
  - Year ended November 30, 1945   480,055
- Consolidated basis:
  - Year ended November 30, 1945   197,373

The SEC said, "However the registration statement did not indicate that, since the date of the latest profit and loss statements, the companies were operating at a loss."

In the latest amendment to the registration statement filed on July 12, 1946, Hayes showed a net loss from operations of $247,868 for eight months ended May 31, 1946, which was offset by a credit of $318,860 for estimated refund of prior years' taxes arising from carry-back of operating loss and unused excess profits credit, resulting in net income for the period of $70,992. For the six months ended May 31, 1946, American had net income of $140,876 on a parent company basis, and a net loss of $36,919 on a consolidated basis.

The SEC said that it seemed clear that the managements of both companies were aware of the drastic changes in the results of operations as of the date when the registration statement was filed, *and the statement should have disclosed the changes.*

THE ELASTIC STOP NUT CORPORATION CASE.—Elastic Stop Nut Corporation of America (ESNA) filed a registration statement under the 1933 Act covering an issue of debentures with warrants attached for the purchase of common stock [19 SEC 412 (1945)]. The registration statement became effective on January 14, 1944. On August 29, 1944, ESNA made application to list its common stock on the New York Stock Exchange. This application became effective on September 29, 1944.

On November 29, 1944, the president of the company, William T. Hedlund, took his own life. On that day the SEC suspended exchange trading in ESNA common stock, and on December 8, 1944, ordered an investigation under the 1933 and the 1934 Acts to determine the adequacy and accuracy of the information contained in the material filed by ESNA under the SEC laws.

ESNA manufactured elastic stop nuts, the principal consumer of which was the aircraft industry. Prior to World War II over 70 per cent of the company's products went into aircraft; by 1943 this had increased to over 95 per cent. The production facilities of the entire lock nut industry were greatly increased under the impetus of the war, but were sufficient to supply the demand by May, 1943. The net sales of ESNA increased from $621,000 in 1938, to $3,922,000 in 1940, and $42,072,000 in 1943. ESNA's unfilled orders likewise reached a peak in May, 1943, aggregating in excess of two billion nuts at May 31. In order to take care of these orders, ESNA increased its own production and by December, 1943, was manufacturing 300,000,000 nuts a month.

The average of monthly orders booked by ESNA in 1942 was nearly 200,000,000 nuts. This average remained about the same for 1943, but orders received in the summer of 1943 declined. ESNA officials, concerned about the decline, discussed the problem with representatives of the Army Air Force. In September, 1943, Hedlund wrote to them that, after review of orders on hand, previous estimates of required production were not warranted. He stated that incoming orders for the summer months of 1943 averaged only 150,000,000 nuts, and that, while he had planned a production of up to 375,000,000 nuts in December, he would review the situation every 30 days.

In October and November, 1943, the company attempted to obtain the approval of the Air Force for financial assistance with respect to the company's working capital, but the request was not approved. The government's position was that it could furnish financial assistance only for the purpose of increasing production facilities of the entire lock nut industry whose facilities were already more than adequate. The Air Force advised the company that the downward trend of orders would probably continue throughout the fourth quarter of 1943 and into the first quarter of 1944. While ESNA received net orders in excess of 400,000,000 nuts in September, 1943, the net orders received in the last quarter of 1943 were: October—98,000,000, November—37,000,000, and December—97,000,000.

In September, 1943, Hedlund estimated that, under the proposed renegotiation of war contracts for 1942 under the War Profits Control Act, the current asset ratio of ESNA would be reduced to less than 1.1 to 1. He felt therefore that there was some question as to whether the company should secure public financing, the proceeds of which would be used as working capital for a war operation, when a loss of less than 25 per cent in the inventory valuation would result in a negative working capital. On December 15, 1943, ESNA as a result of renegotiation made a gross settlement of $8,000,000 which after tax credits resulted in a net refund to the government of $1,953,000.

In January, 1944, the company revised its V-Loan agreement increasing the banks' commitments from $7,000,000 to $15,000,000. Under the new agreement the interest rate was 3¾ per cent with a provision, however, that if the company sold its debentures to the public, the interest rate was to be reduced to 3¼ per cent. An official of the agent for the lending banks stated that the problem of the company was to tide itself over its weakest period, which was to come in 1944, and therefore the company would want a bank credit that would not put it in default from settlement of renegotiation for 1943. He further stated that the company was warned of the problem that would arise if orders were canceled during 1944, and the company was then trying to attract new capital to the business.

When the company filed its registration statement under the 1933 Act, it was aware that its inventory position was abnormal. The comptroller of ESNA commented in October, 1943, that the inventory converted to a selling price basis indicated that it was equivalent to the company's entire backlog of orders. As at the end of the fiscal year ended November 30, 1943, the comptroller found that inventory plus commitments for material represented a sales volume of over $50,000,000.

In the registration statement, which became effective January 14, 1944, the company made no mention of the decline in incoming orders or of its abnormal inventory and commitment position. The SEC said that the implications in the registration statement were that the business was still expanding. The summary of earnings included in the prospectus showed sales increasing from $107,000 in 1934 to about $42,000,000 in 1943, the sales of each year representing a substantial increase over the preceding year (with one minor exception in 1938).

The narrative section of the prospectus made the following statement:

Since 1934 the growing demand of aircraft manufacturers for Elastic Stop Nuts has consumed most of the company's production. Between 1940 and November, 1942, the productive facilities and the production of the company have been greatly expanded to meet the increasing demand for Elastic Stop Nuts by the aircraft industry required for the production of military aircraft. Since substantially all of the company's greatly increased production has been consumed by the aircraft industry, the company has not had full opportunity to exploit the possibility of supplying its products for equipment made by other industries.

The SEC said that the implication in this statement in the January, 1944, prospectus that the demand for Elastic Stop Nuts was still increasing and the company's production was still increasing "is obviously misleading."

The balance sheet of the company at November 30, 1943, reflected a general purpose contingency reserve of $1,500,000 which the company said had been set aside "against future unknown contingencies" and constituted a "surplus reserve." The downward trend of incoming orders and of the backlog of orders and the abnormal inventory situation created contingencies, the SEC said, "which the company knew or should have known might result in future losses."

The text of the prospectus stated that "in view of lower costs effected through increased volume of production and through the development of more economical manufacturing methods, the company has made various price reductions to its customers." While price reductions were in fact made, the SEC said, "It is clear that costs had not been lowered but had substantially increased."

The 1934 Act application for registration (Form 10) of the common stock of the company on the New York Stock Exchange was prepared by the vice president and treasurer of the company in cooperation with the certifying accountants and attorneys representing the company. The financial statements included in the application were the balance sheet at November 30, 1943, and the income and surplus statements for the years 1941, 1942, and 1943 which had been previously filed in the 1933 Act registration statement and were incorporated in the 1934 Act application by reference to the earlier registration statement. In the Form 10 the certifying accountants consented to the use of their report attached to the financial statements previously filed.

In the interim between the effective date of the 1933 Act registration and the filing of the Form 10, the company's situation had deteriorated rapidly, and the company's operations had become a matter of serious concern to the management. In the monthly report of the comptroller for May, 1944, it was stated:

Net orders entered for the six months averaged 129,000,000 [nuts] per month and shipments and production control corrections averaged 266,000,000 [nuts] per month. The continuation of this trend means that by the end of September we will be depending upon current bookings to operate the plant.

For the period from June 1 to June 11, 1944, cancellations entered exceeded orders entered by 9,918,000 nuts.

One effect of this trend may be noted in the excess manufacturing costs other than subcontracting. For the six months ended May 31, 1944, manufacturing costs in excess of standard totaled $3,719,000 compared with $1,443,000 for the first six months of 1943, an increase of $2,276,000. As our production decreases these costs are likely to increase unless rigidly controlled, and the seriousness lies in the fact that at the current level of excess manufacturing costs the company would sustain a loss on a monthly sales volume of $2,500,000.

Inventory and outstanding commitments less reserves as of May 31, 1944, totaled $12,855,000.

Assuming we can recover, in the event of severe cutbacks, substantially all of our investment in costs applicable to orders scheduled for delivery up to September 30, 1944, and also assuming incoming orders at the rate of 100,000,000 nuts per month for delivery up to September 30, 1944, our inventory investment at May 31, 1944, to cover these requirements would be $3,009,000. To this might be added a normal inventory not covered by orders, and for this purpose the inventory as of November 30, 1941, is used, which totaled

$2,067,000. Thus we have a total of $5,076,000 compared to the $12,855,000 mentioned above, or an excess of $7,779,000. The raw material content of $5,076,000 is $2,212,000 compared to raw material inventory and commitments at May 31, 1944, of $4,004,000, or an excess of $1,792,000.

* * *

In view of the foregoing data it is our recommendation that a reserve for raw material liquidation of $1,500,000 be established at midyear to cushion, in part at least, the possible impact of substantial contract cancellations. We also recommend treating this amount as a valuation reserve and giving full tax effect, which means working capital would not be appreciably affected.

Up to the time the Form 10 became effective, no progress had been made with respect to control of the inventory situation. On August 28, 1944, the president reported to the management committee of the company that it would be necessary to dispose of between $3,000,000 and $4,000,000 of excess and obsolete inventory. An officer of one of the V-Loan banks, after discussion of this situation with an official of the company, commented that the working capital of $5,250,000 at the end of August, as reflected on the books, would be substantially reduced if there were a proper valuation reserve against inventory.

The monthly average of orders received, net of cancellations, for the months of June, July, August, and September was less than 20,000,000 nuts as contrasted with a monthly average for each of the years 1942 and 1943 of nearly 200,000,000 nuts. Unfilled orders on the books of the company had declined from about 1,500,000,000 nuts at the end of November, 1943, to about 300,000,000 nuts at the end of August, 1944. The value in dollars of unfilled orders decreased from about $25,000,000 at November 30, 1943, to about $8,000,000 at the end of August, 1944, and of this latter amount approximately $7,000,000 was regular business, the balance being for ordnance contracts.

From discussions with the larger aircraft companies and other informed agencies, ESNA knew that there was an enormous surplus of stop nuts in the hands of industry.

For the quarter ending August 31, 1944, net sales were $7,419,000, or an average of $2,473,000 per month. For the month of August the sales were $1,693,000, and there was a net operating loss of approximately $470,000. For the month of September there was a net operating loss of $116,000. On August 14, 1944, the comptroller reported that "if the present trend of shipments continued on an average price of $2, there would be a loss of $300,000 to $500,000 for the month of August." In November the president of the company stated that the losses of the company were due in part to mistake in relying upon the estimates of the Army Air Force, to overbuying by customers with resulting cancellations, to unsatisfactory production control, and to increase of costs to such a point that when volume was cut back, losses resulted.

No disclosure was made in Form 10 with respect to the operating losses in August and September, the excess and obsolete inventory conditions, the surplus stocks in the hands of the industry which would constitute a block to new business, the drastic decline in the volume of incoming orders, and the amount of unfilled orders on the books of the company.

While no criticism was made by the SEC concerning the work of the certifying accountants, a partner of the accounting firm apparently testified at the SEC investigation. He said it was his opinion that if a certifying accountant had any knowledge of a material adverse change in the business of a company, some mention should be made of it in Form 10. As of May 31, 1944, a special reserve of $1,500,000 was created by ESNA for inventory liquidation. The accountant agreed that it would have been preferable to have mentioned the creation of this reserve in the Form 10, but stated that it had not occurred to him. He said that he had had no knowledge of the operating losses of the company in August until October and that he had felt that the excess and obsolete inventory situation was not too serious.

At the completion of its investigation the SEC decided not to institute stop-order proceedings with respect to the debenture registration statement and lifted the suspension of exchange trading in the company's securities. Although the SEC's report makes no clear-cut statement to that effect, it appears to the author that the SEC believed that the company should have disclosed the adverse change in its results of operations, financial condition, incoming orders, backlog, and inventory.

Increases in Costs Subsequent to Statement Date.—In *Potrero Sugar Company* [5 SEC 982 (1939)] the SEC considered whether an income statement is misleading if it does not disclose subsequent increases in costs.

The balance sheet included in the registration statement was as of January 31, 1936. There was a strike of employees at the Mexican properties of the company from January 7, 1936, to February 21, 1936. In connection with the settlement of the strike the company agreed to pay higher wages and made various concessions which would increase future costs of operations. In its decision the Commission said that the purpose of the income statements is to reflect the results of operations during the periods they purport to cover, that there is no proof that the registrant's income statements did not accomplish that purpose, and that the statements accurately represented the results of operations for their particular periods.

The SEC concluded that the statements were not made misleading by failure to disclose the probable effect upon future operations of higher wages and various concessions to employees.

The SEC observed that:

> There is expert testimony by accountants in the record to the effect that factors arising subsequent to the date of the balance sheet and which do not affect the position of the company on the given date should not be included in financial statements. It is claimed that to include such factors would be to undertake to prognosticate the future, which is outside the province of an accountant. Inclusion of some of such material and failure to mention other facts would result in a misleading impression. Increased costs may be offset by rising prices or other factors.
>
> However, authoritative writers on accounting principles agree that extraordinary circumstances occurring between the stated date of the balance sheet and the date of certification of the balance sheet may make necessary disclosure of the effect of such circumstances. Thus, if assets of material amount which existed on the date of the balance sheet had been destroyed prior to the date of certification, it would be the duty of the certifying accountant to call attention to that fact. Whether disclosure is required in a given case depends upon the facts of that particular case. To our belief, the accountant should adopt a liberal attitude towards the problem and make appropriate disclosures even though in an individual case the clear necessity therefor might not appear.

Three years later the SEC considered a similar question in *Central Specialty Company* [10 SEC 1102 (1942)]. Subsequent to the period covered by the income statement the company had granted wage increases and paid vacations to employees and there was no disclosure of these cost increases in the income statement in the registration statement. There was also no disclosure of the possibility of further cost increases arising out of negotiations with the company's union employees who had demanded wage adjustments.

The SEC commented that the question of responsibility for disclosure in this area had not yet been subjected to hard and fast rules, and consequently it had to be determined in the light of all the circumstances of a particular case.

No question was raised that the registrant's income statement did not accurately reflect the results of operations of the period it purported to cover. While the vacations and wage increases which had been granted would increase annual labor costs by about 9 per cent, it appeared that this increase had been offset by higher selling prices for the company's products. Under the facts of this case, the SEC did not believe that the increased labor costs represent the type of "extraordinary circumstances" (apparently referring to its observation in the Potrero Sugar case) occurring after the date of the statements which need be disclosed in the statements. On the assumption that a proper registration statement and prospectus would state elsewhere complete information with respect to the registrant's labor relations, the SEC held that the income statement was not deficient by reason of its omission to disclose the increase in labor costs resulting from higher wages and vacations which had been granted or by reason of its failure to mention the possibility of further wage increases.

One may speculate as to what the decision in the Central Specialty case would have been: (1) if the cost increases had not been offset by increased selling prices, or (2) if the narrative section of the registration statement did not contain complete information as to the company's labor situation. If the SEC's decision does nothing else, it demonstrates that the financial statements are an integral part of the registration document.

The reader is referred to the discussion regarding earnings summaries in Chapter **10** where it is suggested that disclosures should be made which, in the Potrero Sugar and Central Specialty cases, the SEC ruled were not essential in relation to income statements.

Discontinued Operations.—When preparing an income statement or summary of earnings, consideration should be given to important changes during the period in the company's business or operations. If, for example, the company had sold or abandoned an important segment of its business, disclosure of that fact may have to be made along the lines of the recommendations in APB Opinion No. 9 (1966) on "Reporting the Results of Operations."

A prospectus of Fibreboard Corporation, dated October 15, 1968, included an income statement for the years 1963–1967 and for the six months ended June 30, 1967 and 1968. A note to the income statement disclosed that the company had sold certain of its facilities and abandoned others. Accordingly, the discontinued operations were shown on one line of the income statement as follows (amounts are omitted because they are not important for the purpose of the illustration):

> Revenues (excluding discontinued
> operations):(E)
> Net sales ....
> Selling commissions ....
> Interest earned ....
> Other, net ....
> Costs and expenses (excluding dis-
> continued operations):(E)
> Cost of goods sold ....
> Selling, general and administrative
> expenses ....
> Interest and debt expense ......
>
> Income before federal in-
> come taxes (excluding dis-
> continued operations) (E)

Income (Loss) from discontinued
operations before federal income
taxes (E)

Income before federal in-
come taxes and extraor-
dinary items ....

Federal income taxes:
Current ....
Deferred to future years ....

Income before extraor-
dinary items ....
Extraordinary items ....
Net income ....

Note E, referred to in the above statement, discussed the sales and abandonments and gave the details of the discontinued operations which were shown on one line of the above statement. The note follows:

(E) In December 1967, the Company sold three of its four gypsum plants together with quarries and inventories but retained its gypsum plant at Newark, California and an interest in the gypsum quarry at Apex, Nevada. Certain closed facilities were abandoned, including the felt mill and power plant at Emeryville, California and the buildings on property at Redwood City, California.

The Company sold substantially all of the assets of its Paint Division in July 1968 and the assets of its Roofing Division in September 1968.

The detail of sales, costs and expenses of these discontinued operations, excluded from the Consolidated Statement of Income for the periods reported, is as follows:

	Year Ended December 31					6 Months Ended June 30	
	1963	1964	1965	1966	1967	1967 (unaudited)	1968
	(In thousands of dollars)						
Net sales	$21,648	$18,905	$16,095	$14,701	$14,301	$6,266	$5,557
Cost of goods sold	(17,337)	(14,635)	(13,607)	(12,864)	(12,628)	(5,528)	(4,739)
Direct selling and administrative expenses	(2,170)	(2,418)	(2,392)	(2,752)	(2,497)	(1,111)	(804)
Operating income (loss)	$ 2,141	$ 1,852	$ 96	$ (915)	$ (824)	$ (373)	$ 14

For the above summary, only cost of goods sold and direct selling and administrative expenses have been deducted in arriving at operating income (loss); such indirect selling, general and administrative expenses that may have been either reduced or eliminated as a result of the discontinued operations are not material.

Concentration of Sales.—It is not unusual for a company to sell a disproportionately large part of its production to one or two customers. In preparing financial statements solely for the company's benefit, there is not much purpose in having the accountant tell the client that a large portion of his sales are to a single customer or to a small group of customers. There is a different situation, however, when the client's financial statements are in a registration statement for the purpose of making a public offering of the client's securities. Unless the reader of the registration statement or prospectus is informed otherwise, he may have no reason to suspect that there is a concentration of sales to a few customers. If there is such a concentration, this is information that it is important to disclose, since the loss of one or two customers might be a serious blow to the enterprise if the sales to them could not be replaced. All other things being equal, an investor would prefer to buy the securities of a company with a large list of customers, rather than the securities of a company whose output is taken largely by one or two customers.

The author does not believe that the matter of a concentration of sales is one to be disclosed solely or primarily in the financial statements. Item 9(c) of Form S-1, for example, provides as follows:

If a material part of the business of the registrant and its subsidiaries is dependent upon a single customer, or a very few customers, the loss of any one of which would have a materially adverse effect on the registrant, the name of the customer or customers and other material facts with respect to their relationship, if any, to the registrant and the importance of the business to the registrant shall be stated.

This disclosure should be made in the narrative section of the prospectus, and the financial statements may make cross-reference to the portion of the text dealing with this question.

Concentration of Raw Materials Sources.—In a rare situation the accountant may find that his client is completely dependent upon one source for an important raw material used in the client-company's manufacturing processes and that no alternative sources are available from which such raw materials can be obtained. While this is not a matter of primary importance in relation to the financial statements, the situation may be such that the accountant may wish to call the matter to the attention of his client or the client's counsel for appropriate disclosure in the prospectus.

CHAPTER 14

1934 ACT REGISTRATION AND REPORT FORMS

CONTENTS

Under the authority conferred by the Securities Exchange Act of 1934, the SEC has adopted a number of forms for registering securities of issuers for trading on securities exchanges; periodic reports of such issuers; reports of certain members of securities exchanges, brokers, and dealers; reports of trading by corporate insiders, and others. The registration and report forms are also applicable to a large number of publicly-owned unlisted companies whose securities are traded over-the-counter and which are required to register pursuant to Section 12(g) of the 1934 Act as amended in 1964.

This chapter lists the registration and report forms with which the public accountant should be familiar and briefly describes those most commonly used. The procedure for listing on the New York Stock Exchange and the American Stock Exchange is described in Chapter **29**.

As in the case of a filing under the 1933 Act, the decision as to which

SEC form to use should be made by the company or its counsel—not by the accountant.

Forms for Registration Under 1934 Act.—Listed below are the forms for registering securities under the 1934 Act.

Form 10. This form is used for registration of securities of issuers for which no other form is prescribed.

Form 12. For registration of securities by issuers which file reports with certain other federal agencies.

Form 14. This form is used to register certificates of deposit issued by a committee.

Form 16. This form is used to register securities evidencing a participation in a voting trust agreement or similar agreement for the holding of securities for voting purposes and of securities held subject to such agreements. An application on this form consists of two parts: Part I, for the registration of voting trust certificates; and Part II, for the registration of securities held subject to the voting trust agreement.

Forms 18, 19, and 20. These forms are for the registration of securities of certain foreign governments, foreign private issuers, and American certificates against foreign issues and for the underlying securities. The provisions of these forms are discussed in Chapter **31**.

Form 8–A. This form may be used for registration pursuant to Section 12(b) or (g) of the 1934 Act of any class of securities of any issuer that is required to file reports pursuant to Section 13 or 15(d) of that Act.

Form 8–B. This form may be used for registration pursuant to Section 12(b) or (g) of the 1934 Act of securities of an issuer which has no securities so registered but which has succeeded to an issuer which at the time of the succession had securities so registered, or to such an issuer and one or more other persons, subject to certain conditions. Among the stated conditions is this: the capital structure and balance sheet of the successor issuer immediately after the succession were substantially the same as those of the single predecessor or, if more than one predecessor, the combined capital structures and balance sheets of all the predecessors. The other conditions for use of Form 8–B relate to the solicitation of proxies with respect to the succession and the registration under the 1933 Act of the securities issued in connection with the succession.

FORM 10.—It will be apparent from the foregoing that the majority of listed corporations and those unlisted corporations subject to the 1934 Act are registered on Form 10. The form was extensively revised in 1970 as a result of the recommendations in "Disclosure to Investors: A Reappraisal of Federal Administrative Policies under the '33 and '34 Acts" (more commonly known as The Wheat Report).

A brief indication of the content of Form 10 is given by the following listing of the items of information required to be included in a registration statement on this form.

Item 1.   General information as to date and form of organization, a brief description of the business done and intended to be done by the affiliated group, and its development in the last five years. This item contains the disclosure requirements with respect to the principal lines of business in which the companies are engaged, which are discussed in Chapter **23**.

Item 2.   Summary of operations for each of the last five fiscal years (or for the life of the registrant and its predecessors, if less) and any additional years which may be necessary to keep the summary from being misleading. See the discussion in Chapter **10**.

Item 3.   Location and character of the principal plants, mines, and properties.

Item 4.   List of parents and subsidiaries.

Item 5.   Voting securities owned by principal holders and equity securities owned by management.

Item 6.   List of directors and executive officers.

Item 7.   Remuneration of each director of the registrant who received more than $40,000 from the affiliated group in the last fiscal year, each of the three highest paid executive officers who received more than that amount, and the remuneration of all directors and officers as a group.

Item 8.   Management options to purchase securities from the registrant or subsidiaries.

Item 9.   Interest of management and others in certain transactions.

Item 10. Material pending legal proceedings.

Item 11. Number of holders of equity securities of the registrant.

Item 12. For securities to be registered pursuant to Section 12(g) of the 1934 Act, a description of the nature of the trading market in such securities.

Item 13. Recent sales of securities by the registrant not registered under the 1933 Act.

Item 14. Information as to capital stock to be registered.

Item 15. Information as to debt securities to be registered.

Item 16. Information as to other securities to be registered.

Item 17. Indemnification arrangements for directors and officers.

Item 18. List of financial statements (see Chapter **15**) and exhibits.

One of the general instructions relating to the use of Form 10 contains provisions making it possible to limit some of the disclosures with respect

to foreign subsidiaries, but applies only to the narrative section of the form
—not to the financial statements. The instruction is as follows:

E. OMISSION OF INFORMATION REGARDING FOREIGN SUBSIDIARIES.

Information required by an item or other requirement of this form with
respect to any foreign subsidiary may be omitted to the extent that the required
disclosure would be detrimental to the registrant. However, financial statements, otherwise required, shall not be omitted pursuant to this instruction.
Where information is omitted pursuant to this instruction, a statement shall be
made that such information has been omitted and the names of the subsidiaries
involved shall be separately furnished to the Commission. The Commission may,
in its discretion, call for justification that the required disclosure would be
detrimental.

Attention is directed to Rule 12b–23 which provides for the incorporation by reference of information contained in certain documents in answer
or partial answer to any item of a registration statement (including financial statements). The rule is reproduced on page **14·21**.

FORM 12.—Form 12 is used for the registration under the 1934 Act of
securities issued by any of the issuers specified below:

  (a) Any issuer which files annual reports with the Federal Power
      Commission on FPC Form No. 1 or Form No. 2 and whose
      annual report to stockholders for its last three fiscal years con-
      tained financial statements (other than schedules) prepared and
      certified substantially in accordance with Regulation S–X.
  (b) Any issuer which files annual reports with the Interstate Com-
      merce Commission pursuant to Sections 20, 220, or 313 of the
      Interstate Commerce Act.
  (c) Any issuer which files annual reports with the Federal Commu-
      nications Commission pursuant to Section 219 of the Communica-
      tions Act of 1934.

The content of a registration statement on Form 12 is indicated by
the brief summary that follows:

  Item 1. Number of holders of equity securities.
  Item 2. If capital stock is to be registered, information with respect
      to such stock.
  Item 3. If debt securities are to be registered, information with respect
      to such securities.
  Item 4. Other securities to be registered.
  Item 5. Exhibits.

Included in the exhibits called for by Item 5, are copies of the annual
reports filed with other Federal agencies, annual reports sent to stock-

holders, and, in some cases, financial statements of certain majority-owned subsidiaries. These requirements are discussed in Chapter **15**.

SEC Registration Forms Are in Addition to Requirements of Exchanges.—When a corporation desires to list securities for trading on an exchange, two sets of requirements must be complied with: (1) those of the SEC (involving the preparation of Form 10 and similar forms), and (2) those of the exchange. The SEC registration form is not filed in lieu of the exchange's listing application; nor does the exchange's listing application serve as a substitute for the SEC requirements.

In an original application for listing, this duplicate set of requirements may involve a certain amount of duplication of effort, since some of the information called for by the SEC is also required by the exchange. The requirements for listing of the New York Stock Exchange are summarized, beginning on page **29·**6. The requirements for listing of the American Stock Exchange are summarized, beginning on page **29·**17. These are the two principal securities exchanges in the United States. Both exchanges have made provisions in their rules for listing to avoid unnecessary duplication of effort in preparing a listing application. This is true to some degree in the preparation of an application for original listing; it is true to an even greater degree in the preparation of an application subsequent to original listing.

Normally, securities are admitted to trading 30 days after the exchange certifies the registration form. In practice, the SEC's registration form and the exchange's listing application are prepared simultaneously and filed concurrently.

Annual Reports.—Every issuer having securities registered pursuant to Section 12 of the 1934 Act must file an annual report for each fiscal year after the last full fiscal year for which financial statements were filed in its registration statement. Companies that registered on Form 8–B (for successor issuers) must file an annual report for each fiscal year beginning on or after the date as of which the succession occurred. Annual reports have to be filed within the period specified in the appropriate form.

The prescribed forms for annual reports are as follows:

Form 10–K. This is the general report form to be used by companies for which no other report form is authorized or prescribed.

Form 11–K. For reports of employee stock purchase, savings, and similar plans.

Form 12–K. For issuers which file reports with certain other federal agencies.

Form 14–K. For certificates of deposit issued by a committee.

Form 16–K. For voting trust certificates and underlying securities.

Form 18–K. For foreign governments and political sub-divisions thereof.

Form 19–K. For American certificates against foreign issues and for underlying securities.

Form 20–K. For securities of certain foreign private issuers.

FORM 10–K.—Form 10–K is the principal form of annual report filed by commercial and industrial companies and is designed to bring up to date much of the information filed in the registration statement. The form was extensively revised in 1971.

Form 10–K consists of two parts: Part I includes Items 1 through 10, and Part II includes Items 11 through 15. (The financial statements are in Item 10(a)). Part I is to be furnished by all registrants that have to file Form 10–K. If, however, the answers to Items 4, 5, or 9 would be unchanged from that given in a previous report, a reference to the previous report which includes the required information will suffice. Part II may be omitted from the report by any registrant which, since the end of the fiscal year, has filed with the SEC a definitive proxy statement pursuant to Regulation 14A (discussed in Chapter **22**) or a definitive "information statement" pursuant to Regulation 14C (also discussed in Chapter **22**) which involved the election of directors, or which files such a proxy or information statement not later than 120 days after the end of the fiscal year.

The content of the 10–K annual report is indicated briefly by the following listing of the items of information required to be furnished.

PART I

Item 1.   Principal products and services rendered; changes in products, services, markets, or method of distribution since beginning of year. (This is the item which calls for information regarding principal lines of business discussed in Chapter **23**.)

Item 2.   Summary of operations for each of the last five fiscal years (or for the life of the registrant and its predecessors, if less) and any additional years which may be necessary to keep the summary from being misleading. (See the discussion in Chapter **10**.)

Item 3.   Location and general character of principal plants, mines, and properties.

Item 4.   List of parents and subsidiaries.

Item 5.   Material pending legal proceedings.

Item 6.   Increases and decreases during the year in outstanding securities of the registrant.

Item 7. Number of holders of equity securities of the registrant.
Item 8. Executive officers of the registrant.
Item 9. Indemnification arrangements for directors and officers.
Item 10. Financial statements (see Chapter **15**) and exhibits.

PART II

Item 11. Principal holders of voting securities of the registrant, and holdings of equity securities of the registrant by directors and officers.
Item 12. Information regarding directors of the registrant.
Item 13. Remuneration of directors and officers.
Item 14. Options granted to management to purchase securities from the registrant or its subsidiaries.
Item 15. Interest of management and others in certain transactions.

Reports on Form 10–K must be filed within 90 days (prior to the 1971 revision, it was 120 days) after the end of the fiscal year covered by the report. However, all of the supporting schedules to the financial statements called for by Regulation S–X may, at the registrant's option, be filed as an amendment to the report not later than 120 days after the end of the fiscal year covered by the report. (The amendment is filed under cover of Form 8.) See page **14·23** for the procedure to be followed in requesting an extension of time.

The instructions for Form 10–K contain a provision with respect to omission of information (other than financial information) regarding foreign subsidiaries. This provision is identical with that in Form 10 which appears on page **14·4**.

Except where information is required to be given for the fiscal year or as of a specified date, it has to be given as of the latest practicable date.

Three complete copies of the 10–K report, including financial statements, exhibits, and all other papers and documents filed as a part thereof, and five additional copies which need not include exhibits, must be filed with the SEC. At least one complete copy of the 10–K report, including financial statements, exhibits, and all other papers and documents filed as a part thereof, has to be filed with each exchange on which any class of securities of the registrant is registered. At least one complete copy filed with the SEC and one such copy filed with the exchange have to be manually signed. Copies not manually signed must bear typed or printed signatures.

FORM 11–K.—This form is to be used for annual reports with respect to employee stock purchase, savings, and similar plans, interests in which constitute securities that have been registered under the 1933 Act. Such a report is required to be filed even though the issuer of the securities offered to employees pursuant to the plan also files annual reports under the 1934 Act. Rule 15d–21 provides that in certain cases the information required by this form with respect to the plan may be furnished as a part of the annual report of such issuer. Reports on Form 11–K are due within 90 days after the end of the fiscal year of the plan.

The requirements for financial statements in Form 11–K are discussed in Chapter **15**.

FORM 12–K.—This form may be used by the issuers specified below for annual reports pursuant to Section 13 or 15(d) of the 1934 Act:

(1) Any issuer which files annual reports with the Federal Power Commission on that agency's Form No. 1 or Form No. 2 and whose annual report to stockholders for its last fiscal year contains financial statements (other than schedules) prepared and certified substantially in accordance with Regulation S–X;

(2) Any issuer which files annual reports with the Interstate Commerce Commission pursuant to Section 20, 220, or 313 of the Interstate Commerce Act; or

(3) Any issuer which files annual reports with the Federal Communications Commission pursuant to Section 219 of the Communications Act of 1934.

Reports on Form 12–K are due to be filed with the SEC within 120 days after the end of the fiscal year covered by such reports. If, however, the time for filing an annual report with the ICC or the FCC is extended beyond the end of the 120-day period in any year, the registrant may file its Form 12–K report within ten days after the extended date, provided the SEC is promptly advised of the extension.

Reports on Form 12–K must include as exhibits copies of the annual reports filed with other Federal regulatory commissions and annual reports sent to stockholders together with additional financial statements of unconsolidated subsidiaries. The requirements regarding such reports and statements are discussed in Chapter **15**.

Current Reports (Form 8–K).—A so-called "current report" (Form 8–K) must be filed only when certain significant events occur. The report must be filed by issuers having securities listed and registered on a national securities exchange and also by publicly-owned, unlisted companies that are registered pursuant to Section 12(g) of the 1934 Act. The report need not be filed, however, by foreign governments, foreign private issuers required to make reports on Form 6–K, issuers of American Depositary Receipts (ADRs) for securities of any foreign issuer, or investment companies required to report quarterly under Rule 13a–12.

In 1969, in connection with its announcement of the adoption of two new forms (10–Q and 7–Q), the Commission also announced that it had under consideration a proposal to rescind Form 8–K (Release Nos. 34–8683 and 34–8684). At the date of this writing, the Commission had not acted on the proposal.

A brief indication of the scope of the Form 8–K report follows.

Item 1. Changes in control of the registrant.

Item 2. Acquisition or disposition of a significant amount of assets otherwise than in the ordinary course of business.

Item 3. Material legal proceedings.

Item 4. Changes in registered securities.

Item 5. Changes in collateral for registered securities.

Item 6. Material defaults upon senior securities.

Item 7. Material increases in amounts of outstanding securities.

Item 8. Material decreases in amounts of outstanding securities.

Item 9. Granting or extension of options to purchase securities of the registrant or its subsidiaries.

Item 10. Material charges or credits of an unusual nature (such as write-downs, write-offs or abandonments of assets or obsolescence of inventory), material credits to income from disposition of assets, or material restatements of capital share accounts.

Item 11. Matters submitted to vote of security holders.

Item 12. Changes in registrant's certifying accountant. This is a new item of information which was added to Form 8–K in 1971. Because of its unusual nature and its significance to accountants, the item is quoted in full below :

If an independent accountant has been engaged as the principal accountant to audit the registrant's financial statements who was not the principal accountant for the registrant's most recently filed certified financial statements, state the date when such independent accountant was engaged. The registrant shall also furnish the Commission with a separate letter stating whether in the eighteen months preceding such engagement there were any disagreements with the former principal accountant on any matter of accounting principles or practices, financial statement disclosure, or auditing procedure, which disagreements if not resolved to the satisfaction of the former accountant would have caused him to make reference in connection with his opinion to the subject matter of the disagreement. The registrant shall also request the former principal accountant to furnish the registrant with a letter addressed to the Commission stating whether he agrees with the statements contained in the letter of the registrant and, if not, stating the respects in which he does not agree; and the registrant shall furnish such letter to the Commission together with its own.

Item 13. The registrant may, at its option, report under this item any events, with respect to which information is not otherwise called for by the form, that the registrant deems of material importance to security holders.

Item 14. Financial statements (see Chapter **15**) and exhibits.

Form 8–K must be filed within 10 days after the end of any month during which any of the events listed above occurs, unless substantially the same information as that required by Form 8–K has been previously reported by the registrant to the SEC.

Quarterly Reports on Form 10–Q.—Every issuer of a security that is registered pursuant to Section 12 of the 1934 Act which is required to file annual reports with the SEC on Forms 10–K, 12–K, or U5S, has to file a quarterly report on Form 10–Q.

Form 10–Q was adopted by the Commission in 1970. At the same time the Commission rescinded Form 9–K, a semi-annual reporting form. Both of these actions are a reflection of some of the recommendations made by the Wheat Report ("Disclosure to Investors—A Reappraisal of Administrative Policies Under the '33 and '34 Acts").

Form 10–Q is filed for each of the first three quarters of the fiscal year of the issuer, beginning with the first of such quarters that ends after securities of the issuer become registered.

The following issuers, however, are exempt from the requirement to file these quarterly reports:

(1) Investment companies required to file quarterly reports under SEC Rule 13a–12;

(2) Real estate companies that file quarterly reports on Form 7–Q;

(3) Foreign private issuers that file reports on Form 6–K;

(4) Life insurance companies and holding companies having only life insurance subsidiaries; or

(5) Companies in the promotional or development stage to which paragraph (b) or (c) of Rule 5A–01 of Article 5A of Regulation S–X is applicable.

In lieu of furnishing the information called for by Form 10–Q, certain public utilities may, at their option, file as exhibits to Form 10–Q copies of their reports to regulatory authorities for the preceding fiscal quarter or for each month of such quarter, as the case may be, together with copies of their quarterly reports, if any, for such periods sent to their stockholders. The utilities to which this provision applies are public utilities, common carriers, and pipe line carriers that submit reports to the Civil Aeronautics Board, the Federal Communications Commission, the Federal Power Commission, or the Interstate Commerce Commission.

The requirement to file quarterly reports on Form 10–Q is also applicable to every issuer that registered securities pursuant to the Securities Act of 1933 and is required to file annual reports pursuant to Section 15(d) of the 1934 Act on Form 10–K, 12–K, or U5S. The kinds of companies exempt from this requirement are the same as those in the five categories listed, and there are similar optional filing provisions for certain public utilities that report to other regulatory authorities.

The report on Form 10–Q is due to be filed within 45 days after the end of each of the first three fiscal quarters of each fiscal year. A report need not be filed for the fourth quarter.

The 10–Q report is largely financial in nature, and its content is discussed in Chapter **15**.

Quarterly Reports of Certain Real Estate Companies (Form 7–Q).

—Quarterly reports on Form 7–Q have to be filed by issuers of securities that are registered under Section 12 of the 1934 Act and a substantial portion of whose business is that of acquiring and holding for investment real estate or interests in real estate, or interests in other issuers a substantial portion of whose business is that of acquiring and holding for investment real estate or interests in real estate, and which as a matter of policy or practice make cash distributions from any source other than current or retained earnings. The report must also be filed by such real esate companies that register securities under the 1933 Act and are obligated to file reports pursuant to Section 15(d) of the 1934 Act.

Form 7–Q was adopted by the SEC in 1970. It replaced Form 7–K, a quarterly reporting form that had previously been used by certain real estate companies.

Form 7–Q has to be filed for each of the first three fiscal quarters of each fiscal year of the issuer, commencing with the first such quarter that ends after securities of the issuer become registered. No report need be filed for the fourth quarter of any fiscal year.

Form 7–Q need not be filed with respect to any investment company that has an obligation to report quarterly pursuant to Rule 13a–12, foreign private issuers required to file Form 6–K, or any partnership all of whose properties are under long-term net leases to other persons.

The 7–Q report is due to be filed within 45 days after the end of each quarter.

Interim Reports When Fiscal Year Is Changed.

—When an issuer of securities that are registered under Section 12 of the 1934 Act changes its fiscal closing date, an interim period is created as to which statements may or may not have to be filed in a separate report, depending on the circumstances. SEC Rule 13a–10 deals with interim reports by issuers so registered, and provides as follows:

Rule 13a-10. Interim Reports.

(a) Every issuer which changes its fiscal closing date after the last fiscal year for which financial statements were filed in its registration statement pursuant to Section 12 of the Act shall file a report covering the resulting interim period not more than 120 days after the close of the interim period or after the date of the determination to change the fiscal closing date, whichever is later. [*Author's note*: But see (d) below.]

(b) Every issuer having securities registered pursuant to an application on Form 8-B shall file an interim report for the period, if any, between the close of the fiscal year covered by the last annual report of its predecessor or predecessors and the beginning of the first fiscal year of the registrant subsequent to the succession. The report shall be filed within 120 days after the close of the period. It shall include information regarding the predecessor or predecessors from the close of the most recent fiscal year prior to the succession as if such predecessor or predecessors were the registrant. The financial statements filed with the report shall give effect to the operations of, and transactions by the predecessor or predecessors during the period as if they were the registrant. A statement that effect has been given to such operations and transactions shall be made in a note or otherwise. Separate financial statements for the predecessor or predecessors need not be filed.

(c) A report pursuant to this rule shall be filed on the form appropriate for annual reports of the issuer and shall clearly indicate the period covered. If the report covers an interim period of less than six months, the financial statements filed therewith need not be certified but, if they are not certified, the issuer shall file with its next annual report certified financial statements covering the interim period.

(d) Notwithstanding the foregoing, a separate report need not be filed for any period of less than three months if the annual report of the issuer or predecessor for the preceding fiscal year or the annual report of the issuer for the succeeding fiscal year covers the interim period as well as the fiscal year. In such case balance sheets need be furnished only as of the close of the entire period but all other financial statements, including balance sheet schedules, shall be filed separately for both periods.

A similar rule (designated Rule 15d–10) is applicable to companies that registered securities under the 1933 Act and are required to file reports with the SEC pursuant to Section 15(d) of the 1934 Act.

Reports of Companies Registered Under 1933 Act.—The Securities Exchange Act of 1934 was extensively amended in 1964 by the passage of the Securities Acts Amendments of 1964. Prior to the 1964 Amendments, many issuers with securities traded in the over-the-counter markets were subject to the reporting requirements of the 1934 Act pursuant to the provisions of Section 15(d) of that Act. That section contained a provision requiring that a registration statement filed under the 1933 Act contain an undertaking to comply with the reporting requirements of Section 13 of the 1934 Act if the value of the securities offered, plus the value of all other outstanding securities of the same class, was at least a specified amount and did not drop below another specified amount. The duty to comply also ceased if the issuer became subject to a corresponding reporting requirement, which would be the case, for example, if the issuer listed its securities for trading on a securities exchange.

Under the 1964 Amendments, the requirement of an undertaking to file reports was deleted with respect to registration statements filed after August 20, 1964. As amended, Section 15(d) of the 1934 Act now automatically requires issuers filing 1933 Act registration statements to file reports under the 1934 Act as would be required in respect of a company having securities registered under Section 12 of the 1934 Act. Although the obligation of issuers to file reports pursuant to Section 15(d) is suspended while they have a class of securities registered under the 1934 Act, they nevertheless are required to file reports by virtue of being registered under the 1934 Act. An issuer which is not registered under the 1934 Act but which filed a 1933 Act registration statement on or before August 20, 1964 generally is obligated to file reports pursuant to the terms of the undertaking contained in its 1933 Act registration statement. However, in addition to the provisions for suspension of the duty to file reports specified by the undertaking, the duty to file reports is also suspended for any fiscal year if, at the beginning of such year, the securities of each class to which the registration statement relates are held of record by less than 300 persons, unless a 1933 Act registration statement of the issuer becomes effective during that fiscal year. Thus, the obligation of an issuer presently filing reports under Section 15(d) may now be automatically suspended if it has not offered securities under a 1933 Act registration statement within its last fiscal year and if, at the beginning of its last fiscal year, it did not have any class of securities offered under a 1933 Act registration statement which was held by 300 or more persons.

Special Financial Report of Registrants Under 1933 Act.—The requirements for financial statements in the principal registration forms under the 1933 Act are discussed in Chapter **9**. From the discussion in that chapter it will be apparent that, in some circumstances, the financial statements of the most recent fiscal year included in the registration statement may not be certified by independent public accountants. This might be the case, for example, if a company filed a registration statement within 90 days after the close of its fiscal year. The statements of that latest fiscal year would be included in the registration statement, but they would not have to be certified. The SEC is concerned that those statements be certified since the registrant's obligation to file certified statements in its annual 10–K reports would apply to the following fiscal year.

Consequently, there is an SEC rule (designated Rule 15d–2) to deal with this situation. The text of the rule follows:

Rule 15d-2. Special Financial Report.

(a) If the registration statement under the Securities Act of 1933 did not contain certified financial statements for the registrant's last full fiscal year (or for the life of the registrant if less than a full fiscal year) preceding the fiscal year in which the registration statement became effective, the registrant shall, within 90 days after the effective date of the registration statement, file a special report furnishing certified financial statements for such last full fiscal year or other period, as the case may be, meeting the requirements of the form appropriate for annual reports of the registrant.

(b) The report shall be filed under cover of the facing sheet of the form appropriate for annual reports of the registrant, shall indicate on the facing sheet that it contains only financial statements for the fiscal year in question, and shall be signed in accordance with the requirements of the annual report form.

Applications and Reports of Certain Members of National Securities Exchanges, Brokers, and Dealers (Forms BD and X–17A–5).— Section 15 of the 1934 Act requires certain brokers and dealers to register with the Commission. Registration is accomplished by filing Form BD with the SEC. This form is used not only for original registrations of brokers and dealers but also to amend or supplement such applications. When Form BD is filed as an application of registration, it must contain a statement of financial condition; when the form is used as an amendment or as a supplement, it need not contain a statement of financial condition.

The statement of financial condition filed as part of Form BD must include in such detail as will disclose the nature and amount of assets and liabilities and the net worth of the broker or dealer as of a date within 30 days of the date on which the statement is filed. Securities of the broker or dealer or in which the broker or dealer has an interest must be listed in a separate schedule and valued at market. The schedule of securities shall be deemed confidential if bound separately from the balance of such statement, except that it shall be available for official use by any official or employee of the United States or any state, by national securities exchanges and national securities associations of which the person filing such statement is a member, and by any person to whom the Commission authorizes disclosure of such information as being in the public interest. The statement of financial condition is not required to be certified by an independent public accountant, but attached to it must be an oath or affirmation that the statement is true and correct to the best knowledge and belief of the person making such oath or affirmation (Rule 15b1–2).

Annual reports of financial condition must be filed with the SEC by every member of a national securities exchange who transacts a business in securities directly with the public, by every broker or dealer who transacts a business in securities through any such member, and by brokers and dealers registered pursuant to Section 15 of the 1934 Act (Rule 17a–5). Such persons must file reports of financial condition containing the information required by Form X–17A–5 as follows:

(i) a report shall be filed as of a date within each calendar year, except that (a) the first such report of a member, broker or dealer (other than one succeeding to and continuing the business of another member, broker or dealer) shall be as of a date not less than one nor more than five months after the date on which such member, broker or dealer becomes subject to Rule 17a–5 (in the case of a registered broker or dealer this shall be the date the registration becomes effective) and (b) a member, broker or dealer succeeding to and continuing the business of another member, broker or dealer need not file a report as of a date in the calendar year in which the succession occurs if the predecessor member, broker or dealer has filed a Form X–17A–5 report in compliance with the rule as of a date in such calendar year;

(ii) such reports shall be filed not more than 45 days after the date of the report of financial condition; and

(iii) reports for any two consecutive years shall not be as of dates within four months of each other.

See Chapter **15** for a discussion of the contents of Form X–17A–5 and the requirements as to audit and certification by independent public accountants.

Information Required of Exchange Members, Brokers, and Dealers Under Section 17 of 1934 Act and Rule 17a–10 (Form X–17A–10).— A report of his income and expenses and related financial and other information has to be filed annually on Form X–17A–10 by every member of a national securities exchange and every broker or dealer registered pursuant to Section 15 of the 1934 Act. The report covers the calendar year, and is due to be filed not later than 120 days after the close of the year. There are provisions in the SEC rules, however, for extension of time for filing the report to a specified time not later than 150 days after the end of the year for which the report is made.

The report on Form X–17A–10 does not have to be filed by a member of a national securities exchange or a registered national securities association which maintains records containing the information required by the form as to each of its members, and which transmits to the SEC a copy of the record as to each such member pursuant to a plan the procedures of which have been approved by the SEC. Under SEC Rule 17a–10, any such plan filed by an exchange or association may provide that, in transmitting copies of such records to the SEC, the names and addresses of members as to whom such information is transmitted may be omitted. Individual reports filed by, or on behalf of, brokers, dealers, or members of securities exchanges are to be considered non-public information, except in cases where the SEC determines that it is in the public interest to direct otherwise.

Form X–17A–10 consists of an Introduction and three Parts. All reporting firms must complete the Introduction.

The following persons are exempt from filing Parts I, II, and III (but not the Introduction) : a reporting member, broker, or dealer whose gross securities income during the year was less than $20,000 or who effected no securities transactions with or for any person other than a broker or dealer during the year, and underwriters of shares of open-end investment companies and variable annuities who did not themselves effect retail sales of such securities during the year.

All other reporting firms are required to complete and file the Introduction and *one* Part of the form as follows :

(a) Part I is to be completed by any reporting firm which :
   (1) is not a member of the New York Stock Exchange *and*
   (2) had gross securities income of at least $20,000 but less than $100,000 during the year, *or,*
   (3) had gross securities income of at least $20,000 and received 80% or more of his gross securities income from *one or more* of the following : retail mutual fund sales ; municipal bonds ; fractional interests in oil, gas, or other mineral rights ; variable annuities ; savings and loan placements ; real estate syndications.

(b) Part II is to be completed by any reporting firm which :
   (1) does not qualify to complete Part I *and*
   (2) had gross securities income of at least $100,000 but less than $1 million during the year, *and*
   (3) is not a member of the New York Stock Exchange.

(c) Part III is to be completed by any reporting firm which :
   (1) does not qualify to complete Part I or II *or*
   (2) is a member of the New York Stock Exchange.

(As used above "gross securities income" does not include fees received solely for investment advisory services.)

The form contains special instructions where the reporting firm was subject to the reporting requirements for less than a full year, where there has been a change in the form of its organization during the year (e.g., from a partnership to a corporation), or where there has been an acquisition by merger, consolidation, or otherwise.

Only majority-owned subsidiaries that are exchange members, brokers, or dealers may be consolidated in the Form X–17A–10 report.

All money amounts in the report are to be expressed in dollars; cents are to be omitted.

The report does not have to be certified by independent public accountants.

The Introduction of the report consists of 19 items of information. Following is a brief indication of the scope of these items:

Item 1. Name of exchange member or registrant.

Item 2. Name under which business is conducted, if different from Item 1.

Item 3. Address of principal place of business.

Item 4. Name of person to contact regarding the report.

Item 5. List of subsidiaries which are exchange members or registered broker-dealers.

Item 6. Type of organization.

Item 7. Names of exchange members, brokers, or dealers acquired during the year, and period for which included in report.

Item 8. Specify whether report is initial, regular or final.

Item 9. Number of years engaged in securities business.

Item 10. Number of branch offices engaged in securities business.

Item 11. Exchange memberships.

Item 12. NASD membership.

Item 13. For exchange members, designate whether commission broker, specialist, floor trader, etc.

Item 14. Percent of gross securities income from foreign sources.

Item 15. Primary and secondary sources of gross securities income.

Item 16. Major source of respondent's income if not from securities.

Item 17. Amount of gross securities income during year (exclusive of fees from investment advisory services).

Item 18. During the year, whether there were one or more securities transactions with or for any person who was not a broker or dealer.

Item 19. During the year, whether income from securities activities was derived solely from sales, as underwriter, of shares of open-end investment companies and variable annuities to brokers and/or dealers.

Parts I, II, and III of Form X–17A–10 are almost entirely financial in nature, and are discussed in Chapter **15**.

Reports of Directors, Officers, and Principal Stockholders.—Section 16(a) of the 1934 Act provides for the filing of reports in certain circumstances by officers and directors of listed companies and by persons owing more than 10% of any class of any equity security registered on a national securities exchange. Section 16(a) is also applicable to the officers and directors and 10% owners of securities of unlisted companies registered with the SEC pursuant to Section 12(g) of the 1934 Act. Accountants are rarely concerned with the preparation or filing of reports under this section, but they should be familiar in a general way with their content.

The reports on which the required information is furnished are designated Forms 3 and 4. They are multipurpose forms in the sense that they are also used to report similar information required to be filed in connection with the Holding Company Act and the Investment Company Act.

For several years Forms 3 and 4 did not reflect the changes flowing from the Securities Acts Amendments of 1964 which extended the SEC's jurisdiction to many publicly-owned unlisted companies. Accordingly, the forms were extensively revised in February 1972 to make it clear that they applied not only to securities of listed companies but also to securities of companies that are traded over-the-counter and are registered with the SEC pursuant to Section 12(g) of the 1934 Act.

The forms (and the related SEC rules) were also amended to provide for reporting the ownership, acquisition, and disposition of certain puts, calls, options, etc. In addition, in the case of securities bought or sold for cash, Form 4 as amended provides that the price per share or other unit shall be reported.

Form 3. Form 3 is designated "Initial Statement of Beneficial Ownership of Securities." The form must be filed by each of the following persons:

(a) Every person who, at the time any class of equity securities (other than exempt securities) becomes registered pursuant to Section 12 of the 1934 Act, (i) is directly or indirectly the beneficial owner of more than 10% of such class, or (ii) is a director or officer of the company which is the issuer of such securities; and every person who thereafter becomes such a beneficial owner, director or officer;

(b) Every person who, at the time a public utility holding company becomes registered under the Holding Company Act, is a director or officer of such company, and every person who thereafter becomes such a director or officer;

(c) Every person who, at the time a closed-end investment company becomes registered under the Investment Company Act, (i) is directly or indirectly the beneficial owner of more than 10% of any class of outstanding securities (other than short term paper) of which such company is the issuer, or (ii) is a director, officer, member of an advisory board, investment adviser, or affiliated person of an investment adviser, of such company; and every person who thereafter becomes such a beneficial owner, director, officer, member of an advisory board, investment adviser, or affiliated person.

Form 4. Form 4 is designated "Statement of Changes in Beneficial Ownership of Securities." It must be filed by each of the following persons:

(a) Every person who at any time during any calendar month was (i) directly or indirectly the beneficial owner of more than 10% of any class of equity securities (other than exempt securities) registered pursuant to Section 12 of the 1934 Act, or (ii) a director or officer of the company which is the issuer of such securities, *and* who during such month had any change in his beneficial ownership of any class of equity securities of such company;

(b) Every person who at any time during any calendar month was a director or officer of a public utility holding company registered under the Holding Company Act, *and* who during such month had any change in his beneficial ownership of any class of securities of such registered company or of any of its subsidiaries;

(c) Every person who at any time during any calendar month was (i) directly or indirectly the beneficial owner of more than 10% of any class of outstanding securities (other than short term paper) of a closed-end investment company registered under the Investment Company Act, or (ii) a director, officer, member of an advisory board, investment adviser or affiliated person of an investment adviser, of such company, *and* who during such month had any change in his beneficial ownership of any class of securities (other than short term paper) of such company.

SEC's Instructions Represent Minimum Requirements.—A rule of the SEC under the 1934 Act relates to the furnishing of information in addition to what is expressly required to be included in a statement or report that may be necessary to make the required statements, in the light of the circumstances under which they are made, not misleading. The rule, designated Rule 12b–20, is as follows:

Rule 12b–20. Additional Information.

In addition to the information expressly required to be included in a statement or report, there shall be added such further material information, if any, as may be necessary to make the required statements, in the light of the circumstances under which they are made, not misleading.

For an indication of the Commission's thinking on this subject, the reader is referred to the discussion under "True Statements May Be Misleading" in Chapter **13**.

Information Unknown or Not Available to Registrant.—Occasionally a registrant under the 1934 Act may find that some of the information that must be furnished in a registration statement or report is not known or is not available without incurring unreasonable effort or expense to obtain it, or for other reasons. Rule 12b–21 was promulgated by the SEC under the 1934 Act to deal with these circumstances. The text of the rule follows:

Rule 12b–21. Information Unknown or Not Available.

Information required need be given only insofar as it is known or reasonably available to the registrant. If any required information is unknown and not reasonably available to the registrant, either because the obtaining thereof would involve unreasonable effort or expense, or because it rests peculiarly within the knowledge of another person not affiliated with the registrant, the information may be omitted, subject to the following conditions:

(a) The registrant shall give such information on the subject as it possesses or can acquire without unreasonable effort or expense, together with the sources thereof.

(b) The registrant shall include a statement either showing that unreasonable effort or expense would be involved or indicating the absence of any affiliation with the person within whose knowledge the information rests and stating the result of a request made to such person for the information.

The rule is applicable not only to the narrative section of registration statements and reports, but also to the financial section. In the author's experience, it has not been necessary to invoke the rule on many occasions in relation to the financial statements. There are times, however, when the existence of this rule has saved substantial amounts of time that would otherwise be required to dig out relatively inconsequential information. In some cases, for example, companies do not maintain their accounts in a way that would furnish all the information relating to maintenance and repairs required by Schedule XVI, Supplementary Income Statement Information, in Regulation S–X. In those rare instances where this situation exists, the author has advised his clients to furnish the information that is available and, as required by the rule, disclose that the information is incomplete and the reason therefor. It is suggested, however, that the rule be availed of only when the obtaining of information would involve effort and expense out of proportion to its value.

The following illustrates how the SEC applied the rule in an actual case. A company was required to file a Form 10 registration statement. During the period covered by the required income statement, the company had pooled with a smaller company whose financial statements had been examined and certified by an independent public accountant. The accountant's manually signed certificate had to be filed along with the certificate of the principal accountant covering the pooled figures. The accountant for the smaller company (an individual practitioner), however, had died. The registrant obviously could not comply with the requirement for a certificate covering the operations of the pooled company unless it incurred the expense of another independent audit of that company. In view of the relative insignificance of the pooled company to the total enterprise, the SEC, relying on Rule 12b–21, waived the requirement for a certificate with respect to the pooled company.

Incorporation by Reference.—The Commission and its staff have long been aware that some of the information called for by a given item in a registration statement or report may duplicate information called for by another item in the same document. Also, a financial statement filed under one of the laws administered by the SEC may have to be filed under another of the SEC-administered statutes. With a view to avoiding unnecessary repetition and duplication of information, the SEC promulgated Rule 12b–23 under the 1934 Act. The text of the rule (as extensively amended in 1971) follows:

Rule 12b–23. Incorporation by Reference.

(a) Information contained in any part of a registration statement or report, other than exhibits, may be incorporated by reference in answer or partial answer to any item of the same statement or report. Information contained in an exhibit may be so incorporated to the extent permitted by Rule 12b–24.

(b) Any information, other than financial statements, contained in any of the following documents may be incorporated by reference in answer or partial answer to any item of a registration statement or report:

(1) A definitive proxy statement filed pursuant to Section 14(a) of the Act or a definitive information statement filed pursuant to Section 14(c) of the Act;

(2) A report to security holders; or

(3) A prospectus filed pursuant to Rule 424(b) or (c) under the Securities Act of 1933.

(c) Any financial statement contained in any document referred to in paragraph (b) or filed with the Commission pursuant to any Act administered by the Commission may be incorporated by reference in a registration statement or report if such financial statement substantially meets the requirements of the form on which the statement or report is filed. Financial statements or other financial data required to be given in comparative form for two or more fiscal years or periods shall not be incorporated by reference unless the material incorporated by reference includes the entire period for which the comparative data is required to be given.

(d) Copies of any information or financial statement incorporated by reference pursuant to paragraph (b) or (c), or copies of the pertinent pages of the document containing such information or statement, shall be submitted with the statement or report and shall be deemed to be filed with the Commission for all purposes of the Act.

(e) Matter incorporated by reference shall be clearly identified in the reference by page, paragraph, caption or otherwise. Where only certain pages of a document are incorporated by reference and filed with the statement or report, the document from which the material is taken shall be clearly identified in the reference. An express statement that the specified matter is incorporated by reference shall be made at the particular place in the statement or report where the information is required. Matter shall not be incorporated by reference in any case where such incorporation would render the statement or report incomplete, unclear or confusing.

To illustrate how the incorporation by reference rule operates in practice, assume that a company files a registration statement on Form S–1 under the 1933 Act. At a later date, the securities having been distributed, the company desires to list its securities for trading on an exchange, and proceeds with the preparation of a registration statement on Form 10 under the 1934 Act. Many of the financial statements in Form S–1 are also required to be included in the Form 10 registration. In such circumstances, the SEC permits the registrant to incorporate the financial statements required in the 1934 Act filing by reference to the financial statements contained in the 1933 Act filing but a copy of the statements so incorporated must be submitted with the Form 10 filing (see paragraph (d) of the rule).

Probably the most likely situation in which Rule 12b–23 (incorporation by reference) would be appropriate is in connection with the preparation of the annual report to the SEC—Form 10–K. Over the years, the financial statements in published annual reports to stockholders have come more and more into agreement with those in 10–K, so that, except for the so-called "compliance" notes required by Regulation S–X (referred to below) there is very little substantive difference in the financial statements in the two reports.

Despite this fact, most companies have been reluctant to comply with the SEC's financial requirements by the process of incorporating by reference the financial statements in their published annual reports to stockholders. Their reluctance was based on the fear that, by so doing, the published report might be deemed to be "filed" under the 1934 Act, and therefore the entire published report—President's letter, "highlights," statistical tables, charts, and so on—would be subject to the liabilities provided in the Act. Under the amended rule (quoted above), it is now possible to remove the financial statements from the published report and incorporate only those pages of the published report by reference. Nonetheless some lawyers advise against incorporating by reference even to this extent; consequently, before going down this road, the registrant should obtain competent legal advice.

If legal counsel has no objection to incorporating in Form 10–K the financial statements in the published annual report by reference to that document, it may be that the time actually saved is significantly less than at first expected for the following reasons:

1. The financial statements in the stockholders' report may not be completely in accord with Regulation S–X. This may require the presentation of supplemental data in the Form 10–K report (e.g., the separate disclosure of accounts payable and various items of accrued expenses) ;

2. In many cases the footnotes in the stockholders' report have to be

expanded in the Form 10–K report by the use of supplemental footnotes to cover the so-called "compliance" aspects of Regulation S–X
(e.g., five-year maturities of long-term debt, certain pension information, stock options, excess of investment over equity in underlying
net assets of unconsolidated subsidiaries, etc.) ;

3. The accountant's opinion will have to be expanded to cover the
   supplemental footnotes and data referred to in Items 1 and 2 preceding, as well as the supporting schedules ; and
4. The separate financial statements of the registrant (unconsolidated),
   unconsolidated subsidiaries, fifty per cent owned companies, etc.,
   may require separate preparation and presentation.

It is also possible to incorporate by reference the accountant's certificate
appearing in the Form S–1 filing. If such certificate is incorporated by
reference, the accountant (pursuant to Rule 12b–36) must give his consent.
The consent may be in the following form :

We consent to the incorporation by reference in this registration statement
of our report dated _____ appearing in the registration statement on
Form S–1 (SEC File No. _____) of (Name of Company) filed with the Securities and Exchange Commission pursuant to the Securities Act of 1933.

The consent should be dated and manually signed by the certifying accountant. While the foregoing consent is written for inclusion in a registration
statement, the form may be adapted for inclusion in any other document ;
for example, an annual report on Form 10–K. In the latter event, appropriate revision should be made in the consent—by substituting "annual
report" for "registration statement."

The issuer cannot incorporate an accountant's certificate without obtaining the written consent of the accountant under the circumstances described above. However, incorporation by reference to financial statements
filed under the same Act does not require consent.

Extension of Time for Furnishing Information.—The Commission
has a rule under the 1934 Act relating to requests for extension of time if
it is impracticable to furnish information within the time specified, but it is
not applicable to an initial registration statement under Secton 12(g) of
the Act. The rule specifies the procedures to be followed in requesting an
extension of time, and provides for an initial extension of not more than
30 days, and, in certain circumstances, an additional extension of not more
than 30 days. If the request for an extension is made because of the independent auditor's inability to furnish a required report by the due date, a
statement from the auditor must accompany the request from the registrant.
The rule is designated Rule 12b–25 and is as follows :

Rule 12b–25. Extension of Time for Filing Information.

Note: The disclosures required in reports filed with the Commission are essential to the preservation of free, fair and informed securities markets. It is of critical importance that such reports be filed with the Commission on or before their respective due dates under the Commission's rules. Only the most compelling and unexpected circumstances justify a delay in the filing of a report and the dissemination to the public of the factual information called for therein.

(a) If any required information, document or report, other than an initial registration statement under Section 12(g) of the Act, cannot, without unreasonable effort or expense, be furnished at the time it is required to be filed, the registrant shall, prior to such time, file with the Commission, as a separate document, an application (1) identifying the information, document or report in question, (2) stating in detail the specific reasons why the filing thereof at the time required cannot be made without unreasonable effort or expense, (3) requesting an extension of time for filing the information, document or report to a specified date not more than 30 days after the date it would otherwise have to be filed and (4) showing that such extension is consistent with the public interest and the protection of investors.

(b) If the requested extension is necessitated by the inability of any person other than the registrant to furnish any required opinion, information, report or certification (1) the application shall be accompanied by a statement signed by such person stating the specific reasons why such person is unable to furnish the required opinion, information, report or certification within the required time; and (2) the application shall state whether the registrant has published a preliminary release of sales and earnings and mailed an annual report to shareholders containing financial statements certified by independent accountants relating to the registrant's latest fiscal year.

(c) The application shall be deemed granted unless the Commission within 15 days after the receipt thereof shall enter an order denying the application or shall notify the registrant that the application does not meet the requirements of the rule.

(d) One additional extension of not more than 30 days may be applied for following the same procedure as for the initial application. An application for any further extension of time shall be deemed to have been denied unless the Commission shall enter an order granting such application within 15 days after its receipt.

(e) If the application, or the extension of time granted, relates only to a portion of the required information, document, or report, the registrant shall file the remaining portion, and the portion filed shall prominently indicate the nature of the omitted portion.

One of the criticisms of the Commission's requirements made by the Wheat Report ("Disclosure to Investors") was that annual reports to the SEC on Form 10–K were filed too late. In many cases the 10–K reports were filed as much as two months after the company had released its published annual report to security holders. One result of this criticism was that the filing date for 10–K was accelerated to 90 days instead of the previous period of 120 days after the close of the company's fiscal year.

One further result of the criticism in the Wheat Report and its emphasis on timeliness of filing, is that the SEC has become very hard-boiled about granting extensions of time for filing, and registrants should not take it for granted that extensions can be had just for the asking. Recent experience indicates that extensions are granted only in exceptional and meritorious circumstances, as contemplated in the headnote to Rule 12b–25 quoted above.

In case it becomes necessary to apply for an extension of time for filing a document with the SEC, it can be done in the form of a letter written by the registrant to the Commission, of which the following is an example:

Securities and Exchange Commission
500 N. Capitol St.
Washington, D. C. 20549.

Dear Sirs:
This company is registered under the Securities Exchange Act of 1934 and accordingly is required to file an annual report on Form 10–K for the year ended (date). The report is due to be filed on (date), but, for the reasons stated below, the registrant requests an extension of (number) days for filing the financial statements required by Items 2 and 10 of the report. The balance of the report will be filed on or before (date), the normal due date.

On (date) there was a fire in our Accounting Department, in the course of which several of our records relating to (subjects) were either destroyed or seriously damaged. With the help of a service bureau, we are reconstructing such records from alternate and source data, and expect to have this work accomplished so that our report to shareholders can be released on (date) and Items 2 and 10 of Form 10–K can be filed as an amendment to Form 10–K on (date).

In view of the circumstances, we believe that this request for an extension in the date for filing of part of our Form 10–K is consistent with the public interest and the protection of investors.

> Very truly yours,
> (Name of registrant)
> By (name of person signing and title)

Issuers Subject to Dual Federal Regulation.—There are a number of companies that have securities registered with the SEC under the 1934 Act that are also subject to the jurisdiction of other Federal agencies. A railroad company, for instance, may be subject to the Interstate Commerce Commission, and, having securities listed for trading on a securities exchange, is also subject to the 1934 Act and the SEC. The accounting requirements of the two Federal agencies may not be the same. Accordingly, the SEC promulgated a rule (designated Rule 13b–1) giving priority to the accounting requirements of the other Federal agency to the extent that their requirements are inconsistent. The text of the SEC rule follows:

Rule 13b–1. Carriers and Other Persons Subject to Federal Regulation.

(a) If a person's methods of accounting are prescribed under any law of the United States or any rules and regulations thereunder, the requirements imposed by such law or rules and regulations shall supersede the requirements prescribed by the rules and regulations of the Commission with respect to the same subject matter, insofar as the latter are inconsistent with the former.

(b) Carriers reporting under Section 20 of the Interstate Commerce Act, as amended, and carriers required by any other law of the United States to make reports of the same general character as those required under Section 20, may file duplicate copies of the reports filed pursuant to such Acts in lieu of any reports, information or documents required by the rules and regulations of the Commission in regard to the same subject matter.

Confidential Treatment of Information Under 1934 Act

The 1934 Act contains provisions authorizing the Commission to grant confidential treatment to information filed with it. The law states in Section 24(b) that:

Any person filing any such application, report, or document may make written objection to the public disclosure of information contained therein, stating the grounds for such objection, and the Commission is authorized to hear objections in any such case where it deems it advisable. The Commission may, in such cases, make available to the public the information contained in any such application, report, or document only when in its judgment a disclosure of such information is in the public interest; and copies of information so made available may be furnished to any person at such reasonable charge and under such reasonable limitations as the Commission may prescribe.

The 1934 law provides in Section 24(a) that trade secrets or processes are not to be revealed. The applicable provision of the 1934 law is as follows: "Nothing in this title shall be construed to require, or to authorize the Commission to require, the revealing of trade secrets or processes in any application, report, or document filed with the Commission under this title."

The SEC has adopted a rule of general application (designated Rule 6) pertaining to the non-disclosure of information the publication of which would be detrimental to the national security. The text of the rule follows:

Rule 6. Disclosure Detrimental to the National Security.

(a) Any requirement to the contrary notwithstanding, no registration statement, report, proxy statement or other document filed with the Commission or any securities exchange shall contain any document or information which, pursuant to Executive order, has been classified by an appropriate department or agency of the United States for protection in the interests of national defense or foreign policy.

(b) Where a document or information is omitted pursuant to paragraph (a) of this section, there shall be filed, in lieu of such document or information, a statement from an appropriate department or agency of the United States to the effect that such document or information has been classified or that the status thereof is awaiting determination. Where a document is omitted pursuant to paragraph (a) of this section, but information relating to the subject matter of such document is nevertheless included in material filed with the Commission pursuant to a determination of an appropriate department or agency of the United States that disclosure of such information would not be contrary to the interests of national defense or foreign policy, a statement from such department or agency to that effect shall be submitted for the information of the Commission. A registrant may rely upon any such statement in filing or omitting any document or information to which the statement relates.

(c) The Commission may protect any information in its possession which may require classification in the interests of national defense or foreign policy pending determination by an appropriate department or agency as to whether such information should be classified.

(d) It shall be the duty of the registrant to submit the documents or information referred to in paragraph (a) of this section to the appropriate department or agency of the United States prior to filing them with the Commission and to obtain and submit to the Commission, at the time of filing such documents or information, or in lieu thereof, as the case may be, the statements from such department or agency required by paragraph (b) of this section. All such statements shall be in writing.

Quite apart from matters affecting national security and foreign policy, there are many matters that the managements of publicly-owned corporations would like not to disclose. They consider, for example, that the public disclosure of their sales, cost of sales, and gross profit may injure the corporation in its relations with customers. In their view, such information is also exceedingly helpful to competitors. The SEC is mindful of these and other reasons for objecting to the public disclosure of some of the information which the SEC requires to be filed with it.

The SEC promulgated a rule many years ago setting forth the procedure to be followed by any company that objected to the public disclosure of information filed with the Commission under the 1934 Act. The text of the rule (designated Rule 24b–2) follows:

Rule 24b–2. Non-disclosure of Information Filed with the Commission and with an Exchange.

Any person filing any registration statement, report, material contract, or other document (hereinafter referred to as the material filed) under the Act may make written objection to the public disclosure of any information contained therein in accordance with the procedure set forth below:

(a) The person shall omit from the material filed the portion thereof which it desires to keep undisclosed (hereinafter called the confidential portion). In lieu thereof, it shall indicate at the appropriate place in the material filed that the confidential portion has been so omitted and filed separately with the Commission.

(b) The person shall file with the copies of the material filed with the Commission—

(1) As many copies of the confidential portion, each clearly marked "CONFIDENTIAL TREATMENT", as there are copies of the material

filed with the Commission and with any exchange. Each copy shall contain an appropriate identification of the item or other requirement involved and, notwithstanding that the confidential portion does not constitute the whole of the answer, the entire answer thereto; except that in case the confidential portion is part of a financial statement or schedule, only the particular financial statement or schedule need be included. All copies of the confidential portion shall be in the same form as the remainder of the material filed.

(2) An application making objection to the disclosure of the confidential portion. Such application shall be on a sheet or sheets separate from the confidential portion, and shall contain: (i) an identification of the portion of the material filed which has been omitted; (ii) a statement of the grounds of objection; (iii) either a consent that the Commission shall determine the question of public disclosure upon the basis of the application and without a hearing, or a request for a hearing on the question of public disclosure, if that is desired; and (iv) the name of each exchange, if any, with which the material is filed.

The copies of the confidential portion and the application filed in accordance with this paragraph (b) shall be enclosed in a separate envelope marked "CONFIDENTIAL TREATMENT" and addressed to The Secretary, Securities and Exchange Commission, Washington, D. C. 20549.

(c) Pending the determination by the Commission as to the objection filed in accordance with paragraph (b), the Confidential Portion will be kept undisclosed.

(d) If the Commission determines that the objection shall be sustained, a notation to that effect will be made at the appropriate place in the material filed.

(e) Prior to any determination overruling the objection, if a hearing shall have been requested in accordance with paragraph (b), at least ten days' notice of the time and place of such hearing will be given by registered or certified mail to the person or his agent for service. Failure of any person making an application pursuant to paragraph (b) to request a hearing, to appear at such hearing, or to offer evidence at the hearing in support of his application, shall be deemed a consent by such person to the submission of his objection for determination by the Commission. In any case in which a hearing has been held, the Commission need consider only such grounds of objection as shall have been supported by evidence adduced at the hearing and the failure at the hearing to adduce evidence in support of any ground of objection may be deemed by the Commission a waiver thereof.

(f) If after such hearing the Commission determines that the objection shall be sustained, a notation to that effect will be made at the appropriate place in the material filed.

(g) If such hearing either (1) shall not have been requested, or (2) if requested, shall have been held, and the Commission shall have determined that disclosure of the Confidential Portion is in the public interest, a finding and determination to that effect will be entered and notice of the finding and determination will be sent by registered or certified mail to the person or his agent for service.

(h) If such finding and determination are made with respect to the confidential portion of material filed by the issuer of a security registered on any exchange, the registration of securities on each exchange with respect to which the material filed relates may be withdrawn at any time within fifteen days of the dispatch of notice by registered or certified mail of such finding and determination. Such withdrawal shall be effected as follows:

(1) The issuer shall file with the Commission a written notification of withdrawal.

(2) Upon receipt of such notification, the Commission will send confirmed telegraphic notice thereof to each exchange on which the securities are registered.

(3) The registration shall continue in effect until, and shall terminate on, the close of business on the tenth day after the dispatch of such telegraphic notice to the exchange by the Commission.

(4) All material filed in connection with the registration shall be retained by the Commission and the exchange on which filed, and shall be plainly marked: "Registration withdrawn as of _____ (date of termination of registration)" except that all copies of the confidential portion will be returned to the issuer.

(i) The Confidential Portion shall be made available to the public at the time and according to the conditions specified in subparagraphs (1)–(3) of this paragraph:

(1) Upon the lapse of fifteen days after the dispatch of notice by registered or certified mail of the finding and determination of the Commission described in paragraph (g), if prior to the lapse of such fifteen days the person shall not have filed a written statement that he intends in good faith to seek judicial review of the finding and determination;

(2) Upon the lapse of sixty days after the dispatch of notice by registered or certified mail of the finding and determination of the Commission, if the statement described in subparagraph (1) of this paragraph shall have been filed and if a petition for review shall not have been filed within such sixty days; or

(3) If such petition for review shall have been filed within such sixty days, upon final disposition, adverse to the person, of the judicial proceedings.

(j) If the Confidential Portion is made available to the public, one copy thereof shall be attached to each copy of the material filed with the Commission and with each exchange.

There have been numerous instances in which companies, pursuant to SEC Rule 24b–2 quoted above, have filed requests with the Commission for the confidential treatment of information and documents filed under the 1934 Act. Many of these requests have centered on the financial statements—specifically the information with regard to sales, cost of sales, and gross profits, since many companies consider these to be the most sensitive items of information in their financial statements.

In its 1936 annual report, the SEC reported that requests for confidential treatment of information had been filed under the 1934 Act by 849 issuers. The requests of 225 issuers were granted; the requests of 400 issuers were denied. Twenty-five years later, in its 1961 report, the SEC reported that 12 requests for confidential treatment were received during the year and one had been pending at the beginning of the year. Of this number, four were granted, one denied, and eight were pending at the year end. In the Commission's 1969 fiscal year, the number of requests for confidential treatment had apparently decreased to the point where it was no longer the subject of comment in the annual report.

The author knows of cases where requests for confidential treatment were granted for a period and then denied. In one case, for example, the company was the only company in its industry having securities listed for trading on a national securities exchange. The company contended that its competitors did not reveal, either to the public or to their stockholders, information as to sales, cost of sales, and gross profit. The release by the Commission, the company maintained, of information concerning the company's sales, cost of sales, and gross profit would put the company at a disadvantage as compared with all of its competitors. The company's request for confidential treatment of such information was granted by the SEC for several years. Eventually, however, the Commission denied the company's request for confidential treatment of financial information. In view of the lack of success other companies had had in contesting the Commission's authority, this company decided not to challenge that authority.

On the other hand, the author knows of a real estate company that was granted a request for confidential treatment of a portion of the information in one of the supporting schedules that it was required to include in its annual report on Form 10–K, and the request has been renewed and granted each year. The request in this case related to the schedule furnished pursuant to Rule 12–42 of Regulation S–X. The company is required to list each of its properties, the mortgages thereon, and the cost of each property. The amount of the mortgage on a particular property is based principally on the lender's appraisal of the property—not on the cost to the owner. The registrant had no objection to showing the mortgage on each property, but maintained that disclosure of the cost of each individual property could hurt the company (and hence its security holders) in its relations with the lending institutions. The company disclosed the *aggregate* cost of all its properties both in the balance sheet and in the supporting schedule, but the SEC granted the company's application to omit the cost of *individual* properties.

The American Sumatra Tobacco Corporation Case.—In the American Sumatra Tobacco Corporation case [7 SEC 1033 (1940)] the SEC denied the company's request for confidential treatment of information as to sales and cost of goods sold. The Commission's decision said that the first question to be answered was whether such information is "necessary, or useful, to investors, present or prospective."

The Commission continued:

As a part of the information designed to assure investors the protection and benefits of adequate corporate publicity, Congress prescribed the filing of "profit and loss statements for not more than the three preceding fiscal years". And the Commission, by virtue of the authority granted to it in Sections 12 and 13 of the Act, has by rule required to be included in such statements the registrant's figures of sales and cost of goods sold. The importance of this disclosure can readily be demonstrated by the functions of a profit and loss statement.

The profit and loss statement is designed to disclose for the period selected the amount of net profit or loss, the sources of revenue, and the nature of expenses. It thereby provides a basis for analyzing the results of operation and the course of the business; and in addition, it may be utilized in forecasting the future revenues, expenses, and operating results of the enterprise. It is generally agreed among accountants and analysts that in order to perform these functions the statement of profit and loss should show, as a minimum requirement, the dollar volume of commodities or services, the cost of goods sold and operating expenses of the business, income from other sources, income deductions of nonoperating charges, and net profit for the period.

To particularize, one of the essential purposes of the profit and loss statement is to furnish the investor or prospective investor with adequate historical data definitive of past earning power, and of prime importance in forecasting future earning power. In order either to judge the past or to forecast intelligently, an investor must have not only a record of past earnings or losses, but also the significant details as to how the particular results were obtained. The starting point in forecasting earning power is, of course, sales and operating revenues. Moreover, since earning power results from the sale of commodities or services for an amount greater than the cost of producing or distributing such commodities or services, the next essentials are the cost of goods sold and operating expenses. Similarly, selling and administrative expenses are of prime significance. If there is made available the historical record of sales, cost of sales, and the resultant profit margin, the investor is provided an important guide in calculating future costs in relation to future sales.

If, however, sales and cost of sales in dollars are not included in the profit and loss statement, information essential for analysis is absent. In the first place, there is no possibility of gauging the effect of changes in selling prices, wage rates, material costs and similar items upon the undisclosed primary elements—sales and revenues, and cost of goods sold—upon which the profit figure is partially based. Likewise, the possibility of gauging the probable effect of such changes upon the resultant profit figure itself becomes less likely. The relationship of the trends of the primary elements from which the resultant profit figure is derived varies under different business and economic conditions. The effects of variations in this relationship cannot be measured by study of the trend of the gross profit on sales or of the net operating profit alone.

In the second place, the investor is also directly concerned with the relative size of an enterprise's profit margin, since it may be vital in appraising the significance to the particular enterprise of other known factors and trends. A business enterprise may manifest particular efficiency of production, purchasing or distribution; its location, cost of capital, personnel, patents, trademarks may all be highly favorable. If the factors contributing to the wide profit margin cannot be duplicated, strength may be indicated. But, to the extent that the contributing factors may not be lasting, weakness may be indicated. So a wide profit margin constitutes a warning signal; the investor must determine to what extent the margin is likely to continue. A narrow profit margin may likewise be indicative of strength or weakness. If the narrow profit margin represents the choice of the management to do a large volume of business at prices but little above the cost of production and if this method has resulted in a large scale, integrated, efficient business, the very narrowness of the margin may be an effective barrier to competition. On the other hand, a narrow profit margin may be indicative of a variety of causes, such as strong or even destructive competition, managerial inefficiency, increasing prices of raw materials relative to selling price. It follows, therefore, that, unless the *size* of the profit margin is known to the investor, a vital element of the information necessary for informed judgment and for this minimum protection is lacking. Moreover, in either case the extent of fluctuations in sales and cost of sales is itself an important factor in appraising the degree of fluctuations in the profit margin.

In the third place, knowledge of sales is vital also if the quality of various balance sheet items is to be tested. The comparison of sales to receivables, inventories, fixed assets, and net worth is ordinarily one of the first steps taken in attempting to appraise the results of operations, and to predict their future course.

Unless, in short, an adequate profit and loss statement including gross sales and cost of sales, is made available, a sound appraisal of the management is likely to be impossible. . . .

When the SEC denied the company's request for confidential treatment of its information as to sales and cost of goods sold, the company brought suit. The Court upheld the SEC and said that the SEC properly issued the order denying confidential treatment. The Court further stated that the delegation by Congress to the Commission of the power to determine what shall or shall not be given confidential treatment under Section 24(b) of the 1934 law is a constitutional delegation of power [*American Sumatra Tobacco Corporation v. SEC*, 110 F. (2d) 117 (1940)].

The Allegheny Ludlum Steel Corporation Case.—The American Sumatra Tobacco case (discussed above) was a landmark case in which the SEC set forth its views regarding the importance to investors of sales and cost of sales information. More recently—in 1969—the SEC set forth similar views in denying a request for confidential treatment of the financial statements of a 50% owned company.

The registrant in this case was the Allegheny Ludlum Steel Corporation (as it was then known). Allegheny was the owner of one-half of the stock of Titanium Metals Corporation of America (Timet), the other half being owned by National Lead Company (as it was then known). Allegheny had included the financial statements of Timet in the Allegheny 10–K report filed with the SEC for 1966 and 1967, but they were filed under separate cover as confidential material with a request, pursuant to SEC rules, that the Timet statements not be publicly disclosed. Allegheny requested a hearing on the question of public disclosure of Timet's financial statements. The SEC held private hearings for the purpose of determining whether the disclosure of the Timet material was in the public interest.

In a decision dated July 25, 1969, the SEC's hearing examiner denied Allegheny's request for confidential treatment. The information about the case which follows is taken from that decision.

Allegheny's principal contention was that disclosure of Timet's financial statements would adversely affect its competitive position in its industry, would be detrimental to Allegheny and its shareholders, and was not necessary for the protection of investors.

Timet was engaged principally in the manufacture and sale of titanium mill products made from titanium ingots. The ingots were produced from rutile, a titanium bearing ore. After processing the raw material in Timet's Nevada plant, the ingots were shipped to Timet's plant in Ohio and to certain of Allegheny's plants and fabricated into finished mill products of pure titanium and titanium alloys.

The titanium industry was young, having begun in 1951 when an interest developed in titanium sponge for aircraft and the use of titanium and its alloys in jet engines and aircraft frames. In the early years, the United States Government was the principal consumer, but more recently the output was released for commercial and non-government consumption and had increased although the growth had been uneven resulting in periods of oversupply and over-demand. As a result it was claimed that there was especially keen competition among the companies in the industry. Timet was the most completely integrated producer in the industry, had the broadest product line, and about one-half of the market for titanium mill products.

Allegheny contended that disclosure of Timet's financial statements would place Timet at a competitive disadvantage since Timet's principal competitors did not disclose similar financial information. If Timet's statements were disclosed, competitors would make certain calculations and "get a fair idea of Timet's average unit production costs." It was testified that a competitor could arrive at such unit costs by taking the information from the financial statements, combine it with information obtainable from Government reports and other sources, and since Timet accounted for one-half of the industry, could ascertain fairly accurate unit costs. The competitor could then adjust its prices to Timet's detriment. Timet's president testified at length as to how knowledgeable competitors could make use of various items in Timet's income statement and balance sheet to Timet's disadvantage.

Allegheny had disclosed Timet's expansion plans and was willing to disclose Timet's net earnings and the dividends paid to its two parents, and Timet's gross sales. Allegheny argued that all this represented sufficient information to permit an investment evaluation of Allegheny's stock. Although Timet's gross revenues and assets ranged between 15% and 20% of the combined revenues of Allegheny and its subsidiaries, Allegheny contended that the interest of its stockholders in Timet was relatively insignificant and, in any case, they were given enough information to evaluate properly their interest in Timet.

In opposition to Allegheny, the SEC's Division of Corporation Finance argued before the SEC's hearing examiner that the claimed competitive harm to Timet was neither real nor imminent, but a matter of speculation and conjecture, and did not outweigh the public interest which it sought to protect by requiring disclosure of Timet's statements. The Division said that the fears that competitors could combine information from various sources to Timet's disadvantage was based on assumptions and merely established that competitors might be able to make better guesses with the statements than without them. The Division characterized some of the testimony as purely a guess not supported by the record.

The hearing examiner referred to and quoted from the SEC's decision in *American Sumatra* and said that the problem in the Timet case, therefore, was whether such positive equities had been presented to entitle the applicant to an exception from the general rule of disclosure. In his view the primary objection to disclosure was that Timet was a single product company, and accordingly the information in its financial statements, combined with other information, would put Timet at a competitive disadvantage—particularly in the light of the fact that corresponding information about competitors was not available to Timet. "Testing the facts in the instant case against the principles of the *Sumatra* case," he said, "leads to the conclusion that the instant application should be denied."

According to the hearing examiner, the record failed to establish that Timet's competitors could with any certainty determine the unit cost for each mill product produced from the information in Timet's financial statements even on the assumption that it could be combined with information from other sources. This claim, he said, depended "on many assumptions and conjectures and is not persuasive." While Timet had one-half of the titanium market, it did not have that proportion in each of the four categories of mill products which it manufactured. For each of the Allegheny arguments, the examiner had a counter-argument. Some of the Allegheny arguments he rejected as being "without substance."

The principles laid down by the SEC in the *Sumatra* case, said the hearing examiner, were "equally applicable here." The application for confidential treatment was denied. The decision became effective after no appeal was made, and the SEC did not review the decision on its own initiative (*The Wall Street Journal,* August 26, 1969).

CHAPTER 15

FINANCIAL STATEMENTS REQUIRED BY PRINCIPAL 1934 ACT FORMS AND REPORTS

CONTENTS

Scope of This Chapter.—The information to be included in a registration statement under the 1934 Act is set forth in Sections 12(b) and

(g) of the law, but the Commission has broad powers as to what a registration statement for a given class of issuer shall contain. The law gives the SEC authority to require certified balance sheets for the three preceding fiscal years, certified income statements for the three preceding fiscal years, and any other financial statements it may deem necessary or appropriate for the protection of investors. Although the SEC is authorized by law to require these financial statements, anyone preparing a registration statement is more interested in the requirements of the form he is using—Form 10, for example. Chapter **14** contains a list of the registration forms under the 1934 Act, with instructions regarding their applicability.

The law also provides for the filing of current and annual reports with the SEC by every issuer of a security registered under Section 12 of the 1934 Act. If the issuer has securities listed for trading on a national securities exchange, copies of such reports must also be filed with the exchange. The Commission has broad authority to prescribe the requirements as to information to be included in such reports, and the items and details to be shown in financial statements. The Commission is authorized to prescribe the methods to be followed in the preparation of reports, in the appraisal or valuation of assets and liabilities, in the determination of depreciation and depletion, in the differentiation of recurring and non-recurring income, in the differentiation of investment and operating income, and in the preparation of separate and/or consolidated financial statements. The statute also authorizes the SEC to require certification of financial statements by independent public accountants. Whereas these are the statutory provisions, the issuer, because of the discretionary powers vested in the SEC, is more immediately concerned with the requirements of the form prescribed by the SEC applicable to his situation—for example, Form 10–K, the annual report form filed by most registered companies. Chapter **14** contains a list of annual and other report forms with instructions for their use.

This chapter contains the requirements for financial statements in the following forms, which are the ones most often filed under the 1934 Act and which concern the practicing public accountant:

Form 10	Form 8–K
Form 10–K	Form X–17A–5
Form 11–K	Form X–17A–10
Form 12–K	
Form 10–Q	
Form 7–Q	

Any reader who is interested in the requirements for financial statements in other registration or report forms under the 1934 Act may obtain them from the SEC or may see them described in the loose-leaf services.

The reader should bear in mind that the following SEC rules under the 1934 Act, discussed in Chapter **14**, may be applicable in whole or in part not only to the narrative section of a registration statement, report, or document, but also to the financial statements:

SEC Rule	Subject
12b–20	Additional information
12b–21	Information unknown or not available
12b–23	Incorporation by reference
12b–25	Extension of time for filing information
24b–2	Non-disclosure of information filed with the Commission and with an exchange

Financial Statements Required by Form 10

The principal form for registration of securities under the 1934 Act is Form 10. The SEC's instructions as to financial statements to be filed as part of Form 10 were extensively revised in 1970. As amended, they relate to the following:

Financial statements of the registrant

Consolidated financial statements

Financial statements of unconsolidated subsidiaries, 50 per cent owned companies, and other companies

Financial statements of affiliates whose securities are pledged as collateral

Special provisions in connection with reorganization of registrant

Special provisions in connection with succession by the registrant to other businesses

Special provisions in connection with acquisition of other businesses

Special provisions for financial statements of banks and insurance companies

Registrants not in the production stage

Historical financial information

Filing of other statements in certain cases

Financial Statements of the Registrant.—A certified individual (unconsolidated) balance sheet of the registrant is required to be filed as of the close of its latest fiscal year unless such fiscal year has ended within 90 days prior to the date of filing the Form 10 registration, in which case the balance sheet may be as of the close of the preceding fiscal year. (The reader may note that this requirement is less stringent than a filing under the 1933 Act inasmuch as the Form 10 balance sheet need not be as of a date within 90 days or six months of the filing date.) If the latest fiscal year of the registrant has ended within 90 days prior to the date of filing the Form 10 registration, and the required balance sheet is filed as of the end of the preceding fiscal year, there must be filed as an amendment to the registration, within 90 days after the date of the latest fiscal year, a certified balance sheet of the registrant as of the end of the latest fiscal year.

The registrant must file certified income and source and application of funds statements (unconsolidated) for each of the three fiscal years preceding the date of the balance sheet specified in the preceding paragraph, and, by amendment, for the year, if any, preceding the aforementioned balance sheet which is required to be filed as an amendment within 90 days after the date of the latest fiscal year. Certified statements of retained earnings and other additional capital must be filed for the same periods as the aforementioned statements. The retained earnings statement may be furnished either as a separate statement or as a continuation of the income statement.

Notwithstanding the two preceding paragraphs, the individual (unconsolidated) financial statements of the registrant may be omitted if (1) consolidated statements of the registrant and one or more of its subsidiaries are filed, *and* (2) the conditions specified in *either* of the following paragraphs are met:

(a) The registrant is primarily an operating company, and all subsidiaries included in the latest consolidated financial statements filed are wholly-owned subsidiaries, and are not indebted to any person other than the parent or the consolidated subsidiaries in an amount which is material in relation to the total consolidated assets at the date of the latest balance sheet filed, except indebtedness incurred in the ordinary course of business which is not overdue and which matures within one year from the date of its creation, whether evidenced by securities or not. Indebtedness of a subsidiary which is guaranteed by, or secured by leases of, its parent or the parent's consolidated subsidiaries is to be excluded for the purpose of this determination.

(b) The registrant's total assets, exclusive of investments in and advances to the consolidated subsidiaries, constitute 75% or more of the total assets shown by the consolidated balance sheet filed, and the registrant's total gross revenues for the latest period for which income statements would be filed, exclusive of interest and dividends received, or equity in income, from the consolidated subsidiaries, constitute 75% or more of the total gross revenue shown by the consolidated income statements filed.

For a discussion of what is meant by "primarily an operating company," see page **9·52**   See also the discussion beginning on page **9·48** regarding the possibility of omitting parent company financial statements in circumstances not complying strictly with the instructions.

Consolidated Financial Statements.—The Form 10 registration statement must include a certified consolidated balance sheet of the registrant and its subsidiaries as of the close of the latest fiscal year of the registrant, unless such fiscal year has ended within 90 days prior to the date of filing the registration statement, in which case this balance sheet may be as of the close of the preceding fiscal year. If the latest fiscal year of the registrant has ended within 90 days prior to the date of filing, and the required balance sheet is filed as of the end of the preceding fiscal year, there must be filed as an amendment to the registration statement, within 90 days after close of registrant's fiscal year, a certified consolidated balance sheet of the registrant and its subsidiaries as of the close of the latest fiscal year.

The registration statement must also contain certified consolidated statements of income, source and application of funds, retained earnings, and other additional capital of the registrant and its subsidiaries for each of the three fiscal years preceding the balance sheet mentioned in the first sentence of the preceding paragraph. If, pursuant to the instructions in the preceding paragraph, an amendment must be filed within the prescribed 90 days containing a more recent balance sheet, then the amendment must also contain certified consolidated statements of income, source and application of funds, retained earnings, and other additional capital for the latest fiscal year.

Financial Statements of Unconsolidated Subsidiaries, 50 Per Cent Owned Companies, and Other Companies.—For each majority-owned subsidiary of the registrant not consolidated, there must be filed the financial statements which would be required if the subsidiary were itself a registrant. Insofar as practicable these statements must be as of the same dates and for the same periods as those of the registrant. If the fiscal year of any unconsolidated subsidiary has ended within 90 days prior to the date of filing the registration statement, or ends after the date of filing, the financial statements of the subsidiary may be filed as an amendment to the registration statement within 90 days after the end of the subsidiary's fiscal year. See Rule 4–03 in Chapter **17** regarding group statements of unconsolidated subsidiaries.

If the registrant owns, directly or indirectly, approximately 50 per cent of the voting securities of any company and approximately 50 per cent is owned, directly or indirectly, by another single interest, or if the registrant takes up the equity in undistributed earnings of any other unconsolidated company, there must be filed for each such company the financial statements that would be required if it were a registrant. (In view of the position taken by the APB in its Opinion No. 18 (1971), prescribing equity accounting on an enlarged scale, the SEC's financial instructions will require the filing in many cases of financial statements of companies in which the investor owns as little as 20 per cent of the voting securities of the "investee.") The statements of each 50 per cent owned company must identify the "other single interest" which owns the remaining 50 per cent of the voting securities. See Rule 4–03 regarding the filing of group statements. See also the definition of "fifty per cent owned person" on page **16·7**.

Notwithstanding the instructions in the two preceding paragraphs, there may be omitted from the registration statement all financial statements of any one or more unconsolidated subsidiaries or 50 per cent owned companies or other companies: (1) if all such subsidiaries and 50 per cent owned companies and other companies for which statements are so omitted, considered in the aggregate as a single subsidiary, would not constitute a "significant subsidiary" (see definition on page 16· 8) ; or (2) if the investments in and advances to such company (companies) by its parent and the parent's other subsidiaries, and the parent's and the other subsidiaries' equity in the net income of the company (companies) does not exceed 10% of the total consolidated assets at the date of the latest balance sheet filed or the consolidated net income for the latest fiscal year for which income statements are filed, respectively. See page 9· 8 regarding a similar requirement in Form S–1.

Financial Statements of Affiliates Whose Securities Are Pledged as Collateral.—For each affiliate, securities of which constitute or are to constitute a substantial portion of the collateral securing any class of securities being registered, there must be filed the financial statements that would be required if the affiliate were a registrant. However, statements need not be filed pursuant to this instruction for any company whose statements are otherwise filed with the registration statement on an individual, consolidated, or combined basis. For the purpose of this instruction, securities of a company shall be deemed to constitute a substantial portion of the collateral if the aggregate principal amount, par value, or book value as shown by the books of the registrant, or market value, which ever is the greatest, of such securities equals 20 per cent or more of the principal amount of the class secured thereby.

Special Provisions in Connection with Reorganization of Registrant.—If during the period for which its income statements are required the registrant has emerged from a reorganization in which substantial changes occurred in its asset, liability, capital stock, surplus, or reserve accounts, a brief explanation of such changes shall be set forth in a note or supporting schedule to the balance sheets filed.

If the registrant is about to emerge from such a reorganization, there shall be filed, in addition to the balance sheets of the registrant otherwise required, a balance sheet giving effect to the plan of reorganization. These balance sheets shall be set forth in such form, preferably columnar, as will show in related manner the balance sheet of the registrant prior to the reorganization, the changes to be effected in the reorganization, and the balance sheet of the registrant after giving effect to the plan of reorganization. By a footnote or otherwise a brief explanation of the changes shall be given.

Special Provisions in Connection with Succession to Other Businesses.—If during the period for which its income statements are required, the registrant has by merger, consolidation, or otherwise succeeded to one or more businesses, the additions, eliminations, and other changes effected in the succession shall be appropriately set forth in a note or supporting schedule to the balance sheets filed. In addition, income statements for each constituent business, or combined statements if appropriate, must be filed for such period prior to the succession as may be necessary when added to the time, if any, for which income statements after the succession are filed to complete the three-year period.

If the registrant by merger, consolidation, or otherwise is *about* to succeed to one or more businesses, such financial statements as would be required in a registration of securities under the 1934 Act shall be filed for each of the constituent businesses. The statements may be combined if appropriate. In addition, there must be filed a balance sheet (pro forma) of the registrant giving effect to the plan of succession. These balance sheets are to be set forth in such form, preferably columnar, as will show in related manner (1) the balance sheets of the constituent businesses, (2) the changes to be effected in the succession, and (3) the balance sheet (pro forma) of the registrant after giving effect to the plan of succession. By a footnote or otherwise, a brief explanation of the changes shall be given. (See the discussion of pro forma statements in Chapter **21**.)

These instructions do not apply with respect to the registrant's succession to the business of any totally-held subsidiary or to any acquisition of a business by purchase if such businesses, considered in the aggregate as a single subsidiary, would not constitute a significant subsidiary.

Special Provisions in Connection with Acquisition of Other Businesses.—For any business directly or indirectly acquired by the registrant *after* the date of the balance sheet filed pursuant to the instructions relating to the registrant and the consolidation and for any business *to be* directly or indirectly acquired by the registrant, there must be filed the financial statements that would be required if such business were a registrant.

The acquisition of securities is deemed to be the acquisition of a business if such securities (combined with securities already held) give control of the business. In addition, the acquisition of securities which will extend the registrant's control of a business is deemed the acquisition of the business if any of the securities being registered by means of the Form 10 filing are to be offered in exchange for the securities to be acquired.

No financial statements need be filed, however, for any business acquired or to be acquired from a totally-held subsidiary. In addition, the statements of any one or more businesses may be omitted if such businesses, considered in the aggregate as a single subsidiary, would not constitute a significant subsidiary.

(See the discussion beginning on page **9·12** regarding SEC Release No. 4950 under the *1933* Act setting forth the Commission's requirements for certified statements of acquired businesses where a registration statement is to be filed under the *1933* Act. According to its terms, the requirements of the release do not apply to Form 10.)

Statements of Banks and Life Insurance Companies.—Notwithstanding the requirements of the foregoing instructions, financial statements filed for banks for periods ending on or before November 30, 1971 and for life insurance companies need not be certified. (On July 19, 1971 the SEC revised the previously existing exemption from certification of banks' financial statements (ASR No. 121). Instead of deleting entirely the exemption from certification, the Commission determined that the amendment in the instructions would not apply to financial statements of banks for periods ending on or before November 30, 1971 so that a reasonable period of time will be provided for affected registrants to plan and arrange for appropriate audit work and because of the difficulties that may be encountered by registrants if retroactive independent audits for periods ending prior to the amendment of the instructions were required.)

Registrants Not in the Production Stage.—Notwithstanding the foregoing instructions, if the registrant falls within the terms of paragraphs (b) or (c) of Rule 5A–01 of Regulation S–X (see page **19·2**), the following statements, all of which shall be certified, shall be filed for the registrant and each of its significant subsidiaries, if any:

(a) The statements specified in

Rule 5A–02(Statement of assets and unrecovered promotional, exploratory, and development costs),
Rule 5A–03 (Statement of liabilities),
Rule 5A–04 (Statement of capital shares),
Rule 5A–05 (Statement of other securities), and
Rule 5A–07 (Supporting schedules),

shall be filed as of the end of the registrant's latest fiscal year unless such fiscal year has ended within 90 days prior to the date of filing the registration statement, in which case such statements may be as of the close of the preceding fiscal year.

(b) If the latest fiscal year of the registrant has ended within 90 days prior to the date of filing the registration statement and the statements required by paragraph (a) are filed as of the end of the preceding fiscal year, statements as of the end of the latest fiscal year shall be filed as an amendment to the registration statement within 90 days after the close of registrant's fiscal year.

(c) The statement of cash receipts and disbursements specified in Rule 5A–06 shall be filed for each of the three fiscal years preceding the date of the statements required by paragraph (a) above, and for the fiscal year immediately preceding the date of any statements filed pursuant to paragraph (b).

Filing of Other Statements in Certain Cases.—The Commission may, upon the request of the registrant and where consistent with the protection of investors, permit the omission of one or more of the statements required by the instructions for Form 10 or the filing in substitution therefor of appropriate statements of comparable character. The Commission may also require the filing of other statements in addition to, or in substitution for, the statements required by the instructions for Form 10 in any case where such statements are necessary or appropriate for an adequate presentation of the financial condition of any company for which financial statements are required or for which such statements are otherwise necessary for the protection of investors.

Historical Financial Information.—The information required by the instructions referred to below must be submitted in respect of each company for which a balance sheet is being filed. The information is to cover the seven-year period preceding the three-year period for which the related income statements are filed. The information must be given as to all of the accounts specified below whether or not they are presently carried on the books of account. The information required by these instructions does not call for an audit, but only for a survey or review of the accounts named. For a form of report covering this type of information, see page **24·** 19.

The information should not be detailed beyond a point material to an investor, and may be omitted as to any company for which equivalent information for the period has been filed with the Commission pursuant to the 1933 or 1934 Acts.

The items of information called for are the same as those in a registration statement on Form S–1 under the 1933 Act, which are set forth beginning on page **9·** 16.

Supporting Schedules.—In addition to the financial statements indicated above, the Form 10 registration statement must contain certain supplemental schedules. These schedules, insofar as they relate to a commercial and industrial company, are set forth beginning on page **18·** 39, together with the related instructions and the requirements as to the form and content of such schedules. See also the SEC rule concerning the possibility of incorporating these schedules by reference to information already on file with the SEC.

Form and Content of Financial Statements.—Form 10 contains the requirements as to what financial statements are to be filed in that form; that is, the date as of which balance sheets are to be furnished and the periods to be covered by the income, source and application of funds, and surplus statements. The requirements as to the form and content of such financial statements are set forth in Regulation S–X. The requirements of Regulation S–X are included in Chapters **16** through **20**, except that the requirements as to certification by and independence of accountants are set forth in Chapters **24** through **26**.

Disclosure with Respect to Foreign Subsidiaries.—Form 10 contains a number of instructions. Instruction E deals with the disclosure requirements with respect to foreign subsidiaries in recognition of the fact that, in the case of some registrants, the disclosures concerning foreign subsidiaries may be detrimental to the company. The instruction follows:

E. Omission of information regarding foreign subsidiaries.

Information required by any item or other requirement of this form with respect to any foreign subsidiary may be omitted to the extent that the required disclosure would be detrimental to the registrant. *However, financial statements, otherwise required, shall not be omitted pursuant to this instruction.* Where information is omitted pursuant to this instruction, a statement shall be made that such information has been omitted and the names of the subsidiaries involved shall be separately furnished to the Commission. The Commission may, in its discretion, call for justification that the required disclosure would be detrimental. [Emphasis added.]

At first glance it might appear that the italicized portion of the instruction quoted above is contrary to the letter as well as the spirit of the remainder of the instruction. But this is not so as will be seen from an illustration. Assume, for instance, that the registrant has a majority-owned foreign subsidiary that is not consolidated but is significant. Assume also that, pursuant to the Form 10 instructions, it is permissible to omit all information about the subsidiary (including its name) on the ground that disclosure of the relationship would be detrimental to the registrant. The financial statements of the subsidiary would nonetheless have to be furnished, but the name of the subsidiary could be omitted from the title of the statements. In that event, the subsidiary's statements would be entitled somewhat as follows: "Unconsolidated Subsidiary of (Name of Registrant) Name of Subsidiary Omitted Pursuant to Instructions for Form 10."

Summary of Operations.—The summary of operations required to be included in Form 10 is discussed in Chapter **10**.

Principal Lines of Business.—The information regarding principal lines of business called for by Item 1 of Form 10 is discussed in Chapter **23**.

Financial Statements Required by Form 12

The requirements applicable to companies that register under the 1934 Act using Form 12 are commented upon in Chapter **14**. As indicated in that chapter, a Form 12 registration statement must be accompanied by numerous exhibits, including copies of annual reports filed with other Federal regulatory commissions, annual reports furnished to stockholders, and other financial statements of unconsolidated subsidiaries in certain circumstances. The following comments relate to the requirements for such annual reports and statements.

Companies Reporting to Federal Power Commission.—If the registrant filed annual reports with the FPC, the company's Form 12 registration statement must include as exhibits the following reports and statements:

(a) The registrant's annual report to the FPC for the last three fiscal years;

(b) The registrant's annual report to stockholders for its last three fiscal years (the manually signed copies of the Form 12 registration statement must contain manually signed certificates of the certifying accountants);

(c) The annual reports to the FPC on Form No. 1 or Form No. 2 filed by each majority-owned subsidiary of the registrant, which filed such a report, for each of its last three fiscal years; and

(d) For each other majority-owned subsidiary of the registrant whose financial statements were not included, on either an individual or a consolidated basis, in the registrant's annual report to stockholders, the financial statements called for by the form appropriate for registration of securities of such subsidiary.

Notwithstanding the foregoing, annual reports and financial statements of subsidiaries may be omitted to the extent that all subsidiaries for which they are so omitted, considered in the aggregate as a single subsidiary, would not constitute a significant subsidiary.

Companies Reporting to Interstate Commerce Commission or Federal Communications Commission.—If the registrant files annual reports with the ICC or FCC, the Form 12 registration statement must include:

(a) The registrant's annual reports to the ICC or the FCC on either a separate or system basis for each of the last three fiscal years;

(b) Its annual reports to stockholders, if any, covering the comparable period (if no such reports were published, the registrant should so state in the list of exhibits called for by Item 5 of Form 12) ;

(c) The annual reports to the ICC or the FCC (on either a separate or system basis) for each of the last three fiscal years of each majority-owned subsidiary of the registrant which filed such reports and which is not included in the system reports filed pursuant to (a) above; and

(d) For each majority-owned subsidiary of the registrant which does not file reports with the ICC or the FCC and whose financial statements are not included on either an individual or consolidated basis in the annual reports filed pursuant to (a), (b) or (c) above, the financial statements (which need not be certified) called for by the appropriate form for registration of securities of such subsidiary.

Notwithstanding the foregoing, annual reports and financial statements of subsidiaries may be omitted to the extent that all subsidiaries for which they are so omitted, considered in the aggregate as a single subsidiary, would not constitute a significant subsidiary.

Financial Statements Required by Form 10–K

The principal annual report form required to be filed by companies registered under the 1934 Act and by certain companies that registered under the 1933 Act is Form 10–K. (See the discussion of the form in Chapter **14**.) The SEC's instructions for financial statements to be filed as part of an annual report on Form 10–K (which were materially revised in 1970) relate to the following :

Financial statements of the registrant
Consolidated financial statements
Financial statements of unconsolidated subsidiaries, 50% owned companies, and other companies
Financial statements of affiliates whose securities are pledged as collateral
Financial statements of banks and life insurance companies
Registrants not in the production stage
Filing of other statements in certain cases

Financial Statements of the Registrant.—The annual report on Form 10–K must contain certified balance sheets of the registrant as of the close of the last two fiscal years, in comparative columnar form, and certified statements of income, source and application of funds, retained earnings, and other additional capital for each of such fiscal years.

Notwithstanding the preceding paragraph, the individual financial statements of the registrant may be omitted if (1) consolidated statements of the registrant and one or more of its subsidiaries are filed, *and* (2) the conditions specified in *either* of the following paragraphs are met:

(i) The registrant is primarily an operating company, and all subsidiaries included in the consolidated financial statements filed are wholly-owned subsidiaries and are not indebted to any person other than the parent or the consolidated subsidiaries in an amount which is material in relation to the total consolidated assets at the date of the latest balance sheet filed excepting indebtedness incurred in the ordinary course of business which is not overdue and which matures within one year from the date of its creation, whether evidenced by securities or not. Indebtedness of a subsidiary which is guaranteed by or secured by leases of its parents or the parent's consolidated subsidiaries is to be excluded for the purpose of this determination.

(ii) The registrant's total assets, exclusive of investments in and advances to the consolidated subsidiaries, constitute 75% or more of the total assets shown by the latest consolidated balance sheet filed, and the registrant's total gross revenues for the latest period for which income statements would be filed, exclusive of interest and dividends received, or equity in income, from the consolidated subsidiaries, constitute 75% or more of the total gross revenues shown by the consolidated income statements filed.

For a discussion of what is meant by "primarily an operating company," see page **9·52**.   See also the discussion beginning on page **9·48** regarding the possibility of omitting financial statements of the parent company in circumstances not complying strictly with the instructions.

Consolidated Financial Statements.—The annual report on Form 10–K must also contain certified consolidated balance sheets of the registrant and its subsidiaries as of the close of the last two fiscal years, in comparative columnar form, and certified consolidated statements of income, source and application of funds, retained earnings, and other additional capital for each of such fiscal years.

Financial Statements of Unconsolidated Subsidiaries, 50 Per Cent Owned Companies and Other Companies.—For each majority-owned subsidiary of the registrant not consolidated, there must be filed the financial statements which would be required if it were a registrant. If the fiscal year of any unconsolidated subsidiary ends within 90 days before the date of filing the annual report, or after the date of filing, the statements of the subsidiary required by the preceding sentence may be filed as an amendment to Form 10–K within 90 days after the end of the subsidiary's fiscal year.

If the registrant owns, directly or indirectly, approximately 50 per cent of the voting securities of any company, and approximately 50 per cent of the voting securities of such company is owned, directly or indirectly, by another single interest, or if the registrant takes up the equity in undistributed earnings of any other unconsolidated company, there has to be filed for each such company the financial statements that would be required if it were a registrant under the 1934 Act. (In view of the issuance by the APB of Opinion No. 18 (1971) prescribing equity accounting on an enlarged scale, it is to be expected that financial statements will be filed for many companies in which the investment represents as little as 20 per cent of the voting securities of the "investee.") The statements filed for each such company must identify the other single interest, or other interests in any company operated jointly.

Notwithstanding what has been said in the two preceding paragraphs, there may be omitted from the annual report all financial statements of any one or more unconsolidated subsidiaries, 50% owned companies, or other companies: (1) if all such subsidiaries, 50% owned companies, and other companies for which statements are so omitted, considered in the aggregate as a single subsidiary, would not constitute a "significant subsidiary" (as defined on page **16·** 8) ; or (2) if the investments in and advances to such company by its parent and the parent's other subsidiaries, and the parent's and the other subsidiaries' equity in the net income of the company, does not exceed 10% of the total consolidated assets at the date of the latest balance sheet filed or the consolidated net income for the latest fiscal year for which income statements are filed, respectively.

See Rule 4–03 in Chapter **17** regarding the filing of combined or group statements. See also page **9·** 8 for a discussion of the omission of statements of unconsolidated subsidiaries and 50% owned companies in Form S–1.

Financial Statements of Affiliates Whose Securities Are Pledged as Collateral.—For each affiliate of the registrant whose securities constitute a substantial portion of the collateral securing any class of registered securities, financial statements must be filed that would be required if the affiliate were a registrant. However, statements need not be filed pursuant to this instruction for any company whose statements are otherwise filed with the report on an individual, consolidated, or combined basis. For the purposes of this instruction, securities of a company are deemed to constitute a substantial portion of the collateral if the aggregate principal amount, par value, or book value as shown by the books of the registrant, or market value, whichever is the greatest, of such securities equals 20 per cent or more of the principal amount of the class secured thereby.

Statements of Banks and Life Insurance Companies.—Notwithstanding the requirements of the foregoing instructions, financial statements filed for banks for periods ending on or before November 30, 1971 and for life insurance companies need not be certified. (On July 19, 1971 the SEC revised the previously existing exemption from certification of banks' financial statements (ASR No. 121). Instead of deleting entirely the exemption from certification, the Commission determined that the amendment in the instructions would not apply to financial statements of banks for periods ending on or before November 30, 1971 so that a reasonable period of time will be provided for affected registrants to plan and arrange for appropriate audit work and because of the difficulties that may be encountered by registrants if retroactive independent audits for periods ending prior to the amendment of the instructions were required.)

Registrants Not in the Production Stage.—Notwithstanding the foregoing instructions, if the registrant falls within the terms of paragraph (b) or (c) of Rule 5A–01 of Regulation S–X (see page **19**·2), the following statements, all of which shall be certified except as provided below, shall be filed for the registrant and each of its significant subsidiaries, if any :

(a) The statements specified in
    Rule 5A–02 (Statement of assets and unrecovered promotional, exploratory, and development costs),
    Rule 5A–03 (Statement of liabilities),
    Rule 5A–04 (Statement of capital shares),
    Rule 5A–05 (Statement of other securities), and
    Rule 5A–07 (Supporting schedules)
    shall be filed in comparative columnar form, as of the end of the last two fiscal years ; and
(b) The statement of cash receipts and disbursements specified in Rule 5A–06 shall be filed, in comparative columnar form, for such fiscal years.

The financial statements prescribed above need not be certified if all of the following conditions are met by the registrant and each of its significant subsidiaries, if any :

(a) Gross receipts from all sources for the fiscal year are not in excess of $5,000.
(b) The registrant has not purchased or sold any of its own stock, granted options therefor, or levied assessments upon outstanding stock.
(c) Expenditures for all purposes for the fiscal year are not in excess of $5,000.
(d) No material change in the business has occurred during the fiscal

year, including any bankruptcy, reorganization, readjustment, or succession, or any material acquisition or disposition of plants, mines, mining equipment, mining rights, or leases.

(e) No exchange upon which the shares are listed, or governmental authority having jurisdiction, requires the furnishing to it, or the publication of, certified financial statements.

Notes to Financial Statements.—Notes to financial statements must be furnished for both of the two years for which such statements are required to be furnished. Preferably such notes should be integrated. (Release No. 34–9083, Feb. 18, 1971)

When, pursuant to Rule 12b–23 (see Chapter **14**), financial statements contained in a prospectus, proxy statement, or report to security holders are incorporated by reference in a report on Form 10–K (and copies of the statements are filed with the report as required by that rule) any so-called compliance or supplemental notes required by Regulation S–X which are not included in the prospectus, proxy statement, or report to security holders, as the case may be, must be filed with the report on Form 10–K within 90 days after the end of the fiscal year covered by the report on Form 10–K. The instructions to Form 10–K with respect to the filing of schedules within 120 days after the end of the fiscal year does not apply to such notes. (Release No. 34–9083, Feb. 18, 1971)

Filing of Other Statements in Certain Cases.—The Commission may, upon the informal written request of the registrant and where consistent with the protection of investors, permit the omission of any statements required by the instructions for Form 10–K or the filing in substitution therefor of appropriate statements of comparable character. The Commission may also by informal written notice require the filing of other statements in addition to, or in substitution for, the statements required by the instructions for Form 10–K in any case where such statements are necessary or appropriate for an adequate presentation of the financial condition of any company whose financial statements are required, or whose statements are otherwise necessary for the protection of investors.

Supporting Schedules.—In addition to the financial statements indicated above, an annual report on Form 10–K must include certain supplemental schedules. These schedules, insofar as they relate to a commercial and industrial company, are set forth in Rule 5–04 of Regulation S–X entitled "What Schedules Are to Be Filed," beginning on page **18·39** together with the related instructions and the requirements as to the form and content of such schedules.

Paragraph (a) (1) of Rule 5–04 provides that certain schedules shall be filed as of the date of the most recent balance sheet filed, and paragraph (a) (3) provides that certain other schedules shall be filed for each period for which an income statement is filed. As applied to Form 10–K, which requires financial statements for two fiscal years, this means that the schedules called for by paragraph (a) (1) need be furnished only as of the end of the latest fiscal year, but that those called for by paragraph (a) (3) are to be furnished for both fiscal years. (Release No. 34–9083, Feb. 18, 1971)

See also page **14·21** concerning the possibility of incorporating these schedules by reference to information already on file with the SEC. See also the comments on page **14·7** regarding the possibility of filing the schedules at a later date than the principal statements.

Form and Content of Financial Statements.—The instructions for financial statements in Form 10–K set forth above list the financial statements required to be filed and the dates and periods they are to cover. As to the form and content of such financial statements, however, Regulation S–X is applicable. The requirements of Regulation S–X are set forth in Chapter **16** through **20**, except the requirements as to certification by and independence of accountants, which are set forth in Chapters **24–25** and **26**. respectively.

Financial Statements of Acquired Businesses.—See the discussion beginning on page **9·12** regarding SEC Release No. 4950 under the 1933 Act setting forth the Commission's requirements for certified statements of acquired businesses where a registration statement is to be filed under the 1933 Act. The requirements of this release do not apply to Form 10–K.

Disclosure with Respect to Foreign Subsidiaries.—The reader is referred to the discussion on page **15·10**—regarding the possibility of omitting information with respect to foreign subsidiaries from Form 10. There is an identical provision in the instructions for the use of Form 10–K.

Summary of Operations.—The summary of operations called for by Item 2 of Form 10–K is discussed in Chapter **10**.

Principal Lines of Business.—The information regarding principal lines of business called for by Item 1 of Form 10–K is discussed in Chapter **23**.

Subsequent Transactions and Events in Form 10–K Filings.—In Chapter **12** it was indicated that in a filing under the 1933 Act the truthfulness of the statements made will be tested in the light of the situation as it existed on the *effective date* of the registration statement. What is the situation in respect of the filing of an annual report on Form 10–K under the 1934 Act?

Assume, for example, a company that has an obligation to file Form 10–K and has a fiscal year ending December 31. The company publishes an annual report which it sends to stockholders early in the following February. The financial statements in the published report are accompanied by a certificate of an independent public accountant which bears a date late in January. The company's Form 10–K report must cover the most recent year as well as the preceding year, and (except for the supporting schedules) is due to be filed before the end of March. Ordinarily, the auditor's report in the Form 10–K filing will bear the same date as the report in the published report to security holders. Is there any obligation on the part of the independent auditor to review the events and transactions between the date of his certificate in the published report and the date of filing the Form 10–K?

According to SAP No. 47 (1971) there is no such obligation. The statement deals with subsequent events and transactions, and considers specifically the question of the auditor's obligation in connection with the reissuance of an auditor's report, which is what Form 10–K involves. The statement observed that use of the original report date in a reissued report removes any implication that records, transactions or events after that date have been examined or reviewed. The statement continues: "In such cases, the independent auditor has no responsibility to make further investigation or inquiry as to events which may have occurred during the period between the original report date and the date of the release of additional reports." The statement points out, however, that there are special requirements if the reissued report is included in a registration statement filed under the 1933 Act; this matter is discussed in Chapter **12.**

If, however, the independent auditor has become aware of an event that occurred after the date of his original report that requires adjustment or disclosure in the financial statements, it may not be possible for him to reissue his report as stated in the preceding paragraph. In that case, adjustment of the financial statements or additional disclosure in the statements should be made as indicated in SAP No. 47, paragraph 8, and the auditor will have to give some thought to the dating of the report in view of the fact that it covers events which occurred after the date of the original report.

When a subsequent event has a material effect on operations of a year previously reported upon to stockholders, some companies have found it advisable to report that fact to their stockholders. In June, 1955, for example, Section 452 and 462 of the 1954 Internal Revenue Code were repealed retroactive to January 1, 1954. Companies which, in good faith, had made an accrual for estimated expenses, found in June, 1955, that, because of the retroactive repeal, the provisions for income taxes in their balance sheets were inadequate. A few companies reported that fact in letters to stockholders. Some companies sent revised financial statements to their stockholders and also amended their Form 10–K filings because of the repeal of the aforementioned sections of the Code.

Companies filing proxy statements (under the 1934 Act) or registration statements (under the 1933 Act) after the repeal of the Code sections in question were required either to amend their financial statements for 1954 or to state the effect of repeal where the amounts involved were material. The SEC, however, did not require these companies to amend their Form 10–K filings. The SEC apparently took the position that the 10–K filings were correct in the light of the situation as it existed at the time of filing.

Financial Statements Required by Form 11–K

Chapter **14** contains a description of the circumstances under which an annual report on Form 11–K is required to be filed with respect to employee stock purchase plans, savings, and similar plans. Where such plans exist, most companies furnish to their employees annual reports covering the operation of the plans. Four copies of such annual reports to employees have to be furnished to the Commission for its information not later than the date on which the report is furnished to the employees. These reports so furnished to the Commission are not deemed to be "filed" with the SEC or otherwise subject to the liabilities of Section 18 of the 1934 Act except to the extent that it is requested that such report be treated as a part of the annual report on Form 11–K or is incorporated in 11–K by reference. Financial statements in the report to employees may be incorporated by reference in 11–K if they substantially meet the requirements of the latter.

The following certified financial statements must be included in Form 11–K:

> Statement of financial condition as of the end of the fiscal year of the plan
>
> Statement of income and changes in plan equity of the plan for the fiscal year

Regulation S–X is applicable to the form and content of the financial statements named above. The regulation also governs the requirements for certification by independent public accountants, and specifies the schedules that have to be submitted in support of the principal financial statements.

Financial Statements Required by Form 12–K

There is a large number of companies which, in addition to being subject to the jurisdiction of the SEC, is also subject to regulation by other agencies of the United States Government, such as the Federal Power Commission, Interstate Commerce Commission, and Federal Communications Commission. In lieu of the Form 10–K annual report that would otherwise have to be filed by such companies, they may file annual reports with the SEC on Form 12–K as discussed in Chapter **14**. When a company decides to file Form 12–K, a copy of its report to the other Federal agency must be included as an exhibit in Form 12–K, together with a copy of the annual report to stockholders. In addition, it may have to furnish financial statements of majority-owned subsidiaries that were not included in the annual report to stockholders. A discussion of these requirements follows:

Companies Reporting to Federal Power Commission.—If the registrant files annual reports with the FPC, the company's report on Form 12–K must include:

(a) The registrant's annual report to FPC for its last fiscal year;

(b) The registrant's annual report to stockholders for its last fiscal year (the manually signed copies of the Form 12–K reports have to contain manually signed certificates of the certifying accountants);

(c) The annual reports to the FPC on Form No. 1 or Form No. 2 filed by each majority-owned subsidiary of the registrant, which filed such a report, for its last fiscal year; and

(d) For each other majority-owned subsidiary of the registrant whose financial statements were not included, on either an individual or a consolidated basis, in the registrant's annual report to stockholders, the financial statements called for by the form appropriate for an annual report by such subsidiary to the SEC.

Notwithstanding the foregoing, annual reports and financial statements of subsidiaries may be omitted from the 12–K report to the extent that all subsidiaries for which they are so omitted, considered in the aggregate as a single subsidiary, would not constitute a significant subsidiary.

Companies Reporting to Interstate Commerce Commission or Federal Communications Commission.—If the registrant files annual reports with the ICC or the FCC, its annual report on Form 12–K must include:

(a) The registrant's annual report to the appropriate Commission on either a separate or system basis for the last fiscal year;

(b) Its annual report to stockholders, if any, covering the comparable period (if no such report is published, the registrant has to so state in answer to Item 3 of Form 12–K);

(c) The annual report to the appropriate Commission on either a separate or system basis for the last fiscal year of each majority-owned subsidiary of the registrant which files such a report and which is not included in a system report filed pursuant to (a) above, and

(d) For each majority-owned subsidiary of the registrant which does not file reports with the FCC or the ICC and whose financial statements are not included on either an individual or consolidated basis in the annual reports filed pursuant to (a), (b), or (c) above, the financial statements (which need not be certified) called for by the form appropriate for an annual report by such subsidiary to the SEC.

Notwithstanding the foregoing, annual reports and financial statements of subsidiaries may be omitted to the extent that all subsidiaries for which they are so omitted, considered in the aggregate as a single subsidiary, would not constitute a significant subsidiary.

Financial Statements Required by Form 10–Q

As indicated in Chapter **14**, Form 10–Q is a relatively new form, having been adopted by the SEC in 1970. It is a quarterly reporting form, and, at the time of its adoption, the SEC rescinded Form 9–K, a semi-annual reporting form.

Form 10–Q calls for two kinds of financial information:

A. Summarized profit and loss information.
B. Summarized capitalization and stockholders' equity information.

In addition, in Part C it calls for information concerning sales of unregistered securities.

Only the information specified in the form has to be furnished, and it need not be certified. A notation to the effect that the data are not certified is permitted together with any other qualification considered necessary or appropriate. Losses or other negative amounts have to be clearly indicated in the caption, and the amounts should be shown in parentheses.

The required information is to be given as to the registrant or, if the registrant includes consolidated financial statements in its annual reports filed with the Commission, it shall be given for the registrant and its consolidated subsidiaries. If the information is given for the consolidated group, it need not be given separately for the registrant.

The required information must also be given separately as to each unconsolidated subsidiary, or 50% owned company, or other company, or group of such subsidiaries, 50% owned companies, or other companies, for which separate individual or group statements are required to be included in the registrant's annual reports filed with the Commission. It need not be furnished, however, for any such unconsolidated subsidiary or company which would not be required pursuant to Rule 13a–13 or 15d–13 to file quarterly financial information if it were a registrant.

If the registrant makes available to its stockholders or otherwise publishes, within the period prescribed for filing the 10–Q report, a financial statement containing the information required by Form 10–Q, the information called for may be incorporated by reference to such published statement provided copies thereof are filed as an exhibit to the 10–Q report.

The information required may be omitted with respect to foreign subsidiaries not consolidated or other foreign companies if it is impracticable to furnish it within the time specified for filing the report, provided it is indicated that such information has been omitted. The omitted information must be furnished by amendment when available. Apart from the foregoing, requests for extension of time for the filing of the report or the furnishing of any of the required information is made pursuant to Rule 12b–25.

The summarized financial information called for by Part A of the form has to be furnished in comparative columnar form, in the manner indicated, for (1) the interim period between the end of the last fiscal year and the end of the latest fiscal quarter, and (2) the corresponding period of the preceding fiscal year.

In the case of reports for the second and third fiscal quarters, the summarized financial information may also be furnished, *at the registrant's option,* for the most recent fiscal quarter and the corresponding period of the preceding fiscal year.

For registrants having material seasonal cycles, or material variations in operating results from other causes, comparable figures may be given for the 12 months to the end of the period for which the report is filed and for the corresponding 12 months in the preceding fiscal year in addition to the required information. For registrants engaged in the seasonal production and the seasonal sale of a single-crop agricultural commodity, the summarized financial information may include information for the 12 months ended with the current interim quarter, with comparative data for the corresponding period of the preceding fiscal year in place of the year-to-date information specified in the preceding paragraphs.

The financial information to be included in Form 10–Q must be prepared in conformity with the accounting principles or practices, or methods of applying accounting principles or practices (including consolidation practices), reflected in the financial statements included in the annual report filed with the Commission for the preceding fiscal year, except for a change reported as required by the SEC's instruction which is quoted below:

Describe any such change in accounting principles or practices followed by the registrant, or any change in the method of applying any such accounting principles or practices, which will materially affect the financial statements filed or to be filed for the current year with the Commission and which has not been previously reported hereunder. State the date of the change and the reasons therefor. A letter from the registrant's independent accountants, approving or otherwise commenting on the change, shall be filed as an exhibit.

Variations in the captions and content of the form may be made to conform to the nature of the business of the registrant and its subsidiaries. Additional captions may also be used where appropriate. In addition there has to be furnished any material information necessary to make the information called for not misleading, such as a statement that the results for interim periods are not necessarily indicative of results to be expected for the year, due to seasonal or other specified factors, or an explanation of any unusual increase or decrease in net sales or income.

The information furnished has to reflect all adjustments which are, in the opinion of management, necessary to a fair statement of the results for the interim periods; a statement to that effect must be included. Such adjustments have to include, for example, appropriate estimated provisions for bonus and profit sharing arrangements normally determined or settled at year end.

Any material retroactive prior period adjustment made during any period included in this report needs to be disclosed, together with the effect thereof upon net income—total and per share—of any prior period included in the report and upon the balance of retained earnings. If results of operations for any period reported in the report have been adjusted retroactively by such an item subsequent to the initial reporting of such period, similar disclosure of the effect of the change has to be made.

The registrant may furnish any additional information related to the periods being reported on which, in the opinion of management, is of significance to investors, such as a statement of source and application of funds, the dollar amount of backlog of firm orders, and an explanation of commitments and contingent liabilities.

If appropriate, the summary of income information must be prepared to show earnings applicable to common stock. Per share earnings and dividends declared for each period of the summary must be included and the basis of the computation stated together with the number of shares used in the computation. The registrant has to file as an exhibit a statement setting forth in reasonable detail the computation of per share earnings, unless the computation is otherwise clearly set forth in the 10–Q report.

Part A of the report on Form 10–Q contains the requirements for summarized income information as follows:

A. Summarized Financial Information

Company or group of companies for which report is filed:

Profit and Loss Information   For the.......Months Ended:

	(Current Year)	(Preceding Year)
1. Gross sales less discounts, returns and allowances	$..............	$..............
2. Operating revenues	$..............	$..............

Instruction. If income is derived from both gross sales and operating revenues, captions 1 and 2 may be combined, provided the lesser amount is not more than 10 percent of the sum of the two captions.

3. Total of captions 1 and 2	$..............	$..............

Instruction. If the total of gross sales and operating revenues includes excise taxes in an amount equal to 10 percent or more of such total, the amount of such excise taxes shall be stated separately.

4. Costs and expenses—		
(a) Cost of goods sold*	$..............	$..............
(b) Operating expenses*	$..............	$..............
(c) Selling, general and administrative expenses*	$..............	$..............
(d) Interest expense	$..............	$..............
(e) Other deductions, net*	$..............	$..............
Total costs and expenses	$..............	$..............
5. Income (or loss) before taxes on income and extraordinary items	$..............	$..............
6. Provision for taxes on income	$..............	$..............

Instruction. If the provision for taxes on income includes any material provisions for deferred income taxes resulting from allocations, they shall be disclosed and explained. The methods used (e.g., proportion of year expired, or estimated annual effective tax rate) in the allocation to the interim periods of the income tax effects of operating loss carrybacks, carry-forwards or other tax credits shall be described.

7. Minority interest	$..............	$..............

8. Income (loss) before extraordinary items $. . . . . $. . . . .

9. Extraordinary items, less applicable income tax . . . . $. . . . . $. . . . .

   Instruction. State separately under this caption any material amounts of an unusual or non-recurring nature which qualify as extraordinary items included in the determination of net income or loss during the period covered by the report. The amount of income tax applicable shall be disclosed.

10. Net income (or loss) . . . . $. . . . . $. . . . .

11. Earnings per share

12. Dividends per share

* Items so marked may be combined or omitted.

Where there have been acquisitions of other businesses (by pooling or otherwise) or dispositions of significant portions of the registrant's business, the following additional instructions are applicable:

If, during the current period covered by the 10–Q report, the registrant or any of its consolidated subsidiaries, entered into a business combination treated for accounting purposes as a pooling of interests, the results of operations reported in Form 10–Q—for both the current year and the preceding year—must reflect the combined results of the pooled businesses. Supplemental disclosure of the separate results of the combined entities for periods prior to the combination must be given, with appropriate explanations.

In case the registrant has disposed of any significant portion of its business or has acquired a significant amount of assets in a transaction treated for accounting purposes as a purchase, during any of the periods covered by the report, the effect thereof on revenues and net income—total and per share—for all periods has to be disclosed.

Part B of Form 10–Q provides for the furnishing of a summary of capitalization and stockholders' equity as at the end of the latest fiscal quarter insofar as practicable in the manner called for by the form. The requirements of Part B follow:

B. Capitalization and Stockholders' Equity

. . . .
(Date)

Debt	*Amount*
Short-term loans, notes, etc.	$. . . . .
Long-term debt, including parenthetically portion due within one year (list separately convertible and subordinated debt).	$. . . . .
Total debt	$. . . . .

Deferred credits .... $...........
Minority interest .... $...........
Stockholders' equity

	Shares issued or outstanding	Amount
Preferred stock		
(list separately convertible and non-convertible preferred stock)	....	$...........
Common stock	....	$...........
Capital in excess of par value		$...........
Retained earnings—		
Balance at beginning of current fiscal year		$...........
Prior period adjustments, if any (show credits (and charges) separately)		$...........
Net income (Caption 10, above)		$...........
Dividends		
(state cash and stock dividends on common stock separately, indicating amount per share —dividends on preferred stocks may be shown in one amount)		$(........)
Other credits (charges)		
(explain nature and amounts)		$...........
Balance at end of interim period		$...........
Treasury stock		
(identify class of security, number of shares and basis at which stated)	....	$(.........)
Total stockholders' equity		$...........

Instructions. 1. The form and content shall conform generally with that in the balance sheet and notes thereto appearing in the annual report filed with the Commission.

2. The number of shares of each class of securities reserved for conversion, warrants, options and other rights shall be separately disclosed.

Part C of Form 10-Q calls for information (including an EDP attachment) regarding securities of the registrant sold by the registrant during the period which were not registered under the 1933 Act in reliance upon an exemption from registration.

Eight copies of the Form 10-Q report are to be filed with the Commission and at least one copy with each exchange on which any class of securities of the registrant is listed.

Financial Statements Required by Form 7–Q

As indicated in Chapter **14**, Form 7–Q is a quarterly financial report adopted by the SEC in 1970 for reports of certain real estate companies. The new form replaced Form 7–K which was also a quarterly reporting form previously filed by real estate companies.

The report on Form 7–Q is entirely financial in nature and consists of four parts:

A. Profit and loss information prepared on an accrual basis.

B. Funds generated and funds disbursed.

C. Cumulative amounts of excess (deficiency) of funds generated over distributions after realized gains (losses) on investments (exclusive of minority interests).

D. Summary of capitalization and stockholders' equity.

Only the items of information specified in the form have to be furnished. The information in the report does not have to be certified by independent public accountants, and may carry a notation to that effect. Amounts may be stated in thousands of dollars (000 omitted) provided it is stated that this has been done. Losses or other negative amounts have to be clearly indicated in the caption and the amounts shown in parentheses.

The required information is to be given as to the registrant or, if the registrant includes consolidated financial statements in its annual reports filed with the SEC, it shall be given for the registrant and its consolidated subsidiaries. If the information is furnished for the consolidated group, it need not be given for the registrant separately.

The required information also has to be given separately as to each unconsolidated subsidiary, or 50% owned company, or other company, or group of such subsidiaries, and 50% owned companies, or other companies for which separate individual or group statements are required to be included in the registrant's annual reports filed with the Commission. It need not be furnished, however, for any such unconsolidated subsidiary or company which would not be required to file quarterly financial information if it were a registrant.

If the registrant makes available to its stockholders or otherwise publishes, within the period prescribed for filing Form 7–Q, a financial statement containing the information required by the form, the information called for may be incorporated by reference to such published statement provided copies of the published report are filed as an exhibit to the Form 7–Q report.

The information required may be omitted with respect to foreign subsidiaries not consolidated or foreign companies if it is impracticable to furnish it within the time specified for filing Form 7–Q. In that event, the report must indicate that the information has been omitted, and the omitted information must be filed by amendment when available.

The summarized financial information called for by Parts A and B of the form has to be furnished for (1) the interim period between the end of the last fiscal year and the end of the latest fiscal quarter, and (2) the corresponding period of the preceding fiscal year. In the case of reports for the second and third fiscal quarters, the information may also be furnished *at the registrant's option* for the most recent fiscal quarter and the corresponding quarter of the preceding year.

The information must be furnished in comparative columnar form in the manner indicated, but appropriate variations may be made to conform to the nature of the business.

The financial information to be included in the 7–Q report must be prepared in conformity with the accounting principles or practices, or methods of applying accounting principles or practices (including consolidation practices), reflected in the financial statements included in the annual report filed with the Commission for the preceding fiscal year, except for a change reported as required by the SEC's instruction which is quoted below:

> Describe any such change in accounting principles or practices followed by the registrant, or any change in the method of applying any such accounting principles or practices, which will materially affect the financial statements filed or to be filed for the current year with the Commission and which has not been previously reported hereunder. State the date of the change and the reasons therefor. A letter from the registrant's independent accountants, approving or otherwise commenting on the change, shall be filed as an exhibit.

Any material information that is needed to make the required information not misleading should also be furnished.

The financial information in Form 7–Q has to reflect all adjustments which are, in the opinion of management, necessary to a fair statement of the results for the interim periods. A statement to that effect must be included. Such adjustments might include, for example, appropriate estimated provisions for bonus and profit sharing arrangements normally determined or settled at year-end.

Any material retroactive prior period adjustment made during any period included in the report needs to be disclosed, together with the effect thereof upon net income—total and per share—of any prior period included in the report and upon the balance of retained earnings. If results of operations for any period reported in the report have been adjusted retroactively by such an item subsequent to the initial reporting of such period, similar disclosure of the effect of the change must be made.

The registrant may furnish any additional financial information related to the periods being reported upon which, in the opinion of management, is of significance to investors.

If appropriate, the summary must show earnings applicable to common stock. Per share earnings and dividends declared for each period of the summary shall be included and the basis of the computation stated together with the number of shares used in the computation. The registrant has to file as an exhibit a statement setting forth in reasonable detail the computation of per share earnings, unless the computation is otherwise clearly set forth.

Parts A, B, and C of the summarized financial information in Form 7–Q follow:

Summarized Financial Information

Company or group of companies for which report is filed:

For the.......Months Ended:

....
(Current Year)   (Preceding Year)

A. Profit and Loss Information Prepared on an Accrual Basis.

1. Revenues:
   Rental income
   Mortgage interest income
   Management fees
   Others $.............. $..............
        Total $.............. $..............

2. Deductions:
   Operating expenses
   Real estate taxes
   Depreciation
   Interest expense
   General and administrative expenses
   Others $.............. $..............
        Total $.............. $..............

3. Income before income taxes, extraordinary items and realized gain or loss on investments $.............. $..............

4. Provision for taxes on income $.............. $..............
   Instruction. If the provision for taxes on income includes any material provisions for deferred income taxes resulting from allocations, they shall be disclosed and explained. The methods used (e.g., proportion of year expired, or estimated annual effective tax rate) in the allocation to the interim periods of the income tax effects of operating loss carry-backs, carry-forwards or other tax credits shall be described.

5. Minority interests $.............. $..............

6. Income before extraordinary items and realized gain or loss on investments $.............. $..............

7. Extraordinary items $.............. $..............

8. Income (loss) before realized gain or loss on investments $.............. $..............

9. Realized gain or loss on investments $.............. $..............
   Instruction. State separately and describe each material item not included in caption 8. Profits or losses from sales of

properties or other assets shall be included herein.

10. Net income $............. $.............

11. Earnings per share

B. Funds Generated and Funds Disbursed.

Instruction. In captions 11 to 25 inclusive, where applicable, the minority interests shall be segregated from the consolidated results shown and stated in a separate column, if material. If not material, the amount of minority interests reported in caption 5 shall be added back or deducted, as appropriate, under caption 15 and distributions made to minority interests shall be deducted separately under caption 17.

12. Income (loss) as reported in caption 8 $............. $.............
    Instruction. Changes in funds resulting from transactions reported in caption 9 are not to be reported here but shall be reported under caption 19.

13. Cash distributions to shareholders $............. $.............
    Instruction. Include a tabulation of the amounts per share and the number of shares outstanding at each distribution date. A note to this item shall indicate the amounts representing accumulated income and the amounts representing a return of capital and shall be computed on the accounting basis rather than the income tax basis.

14. Excess (deficiency) $............. $.............

15. Add: A. Depreciation or amortization of property.
         B. Charges (credits) for deferred income taxes.
         C. Amortization of debt discount and expense.
         D. Other. (Describe) $............. $.............
    Instruction. A. The amount reflected hereunder for depreciation or amortization of property shall be the amount deducted in caption 2 and shall be stated separately by major classes such as depreciation on fixed property, depreciation of personal property and amortization of leases.
       B. Amortization of deferred charges other than debt discount and expense shall be provided for under caption 21.

16. Total $. . . . . $. . . . .

17. Deduct: A. Principal payments on mortgages and installment notes.
B. Replacements of personal and
other property and payments
into funds for such replace-
ments. $. . . . . $. . . . .

Instruction. Other payments and
amounts specifically called for under captions 21 and 23 shall be excluded here.

18. Excess (deficiency) of funds generated
over distributions before realized gain or
loss on investments $. . . . . $. . . . .

19. Realized gain (or loss) on investments—
funds generated $. . . . . $. . . . .

Instruction. State separately any material item. The computation of funds generated from property sales shall be reflected hereunder in tabular form indented
under this caption beginning with the
profits or losses reported under caption 9
with respect thereto, deducting therefrom
the amount of accumulated depreciation
applicable to the property sold and adding
back the recovery of principal payments
on mortgages previously deducted under
caption 17 with respect to the property
sold. Any other adjustments made in arriving at funds generated from property
sales shall also be separately stated.
Where a purchase money mortgage is received as part of the consideration in the
sale of property, the portion of the profit
as computed above represented by the
purchase money mortgage shall be recognized thereunder as funds generated only
as cash collections are received. If the
profit as computed above is less than the
purchase money mortgage, no amount
shall be reflected hereunder until cash collections reduce the purchase money mortgage to the amount of the profit. Thereafter, funds generated shall be reflected
hereunder as cash collections are received.
Any balance of cash proceeds from sales of
properties shall be given under caption 21.

20. Excess (deficiency) of funds generated
over distributions after realized gain (loss)
on investments $. . . . . $. . . . .

21. Other sources of funds $............. $.............

    Instruction. State separately any item of a material amount. Net proceeds of refinancing of mortgages shall be included here. The change in net current assets (other than cash) and other miscellaneous items shall be reflected here or under caption 23 as appropriate.

22. Total $............. $............:....

23. Other disposition of funds $............. $.............

    Instruction. State separately any item of a material amount. "Balloon" payments on mortgages not refinanced shall be reflected here.

24. Net increase (decrease) in cash during period $............. $.............

25. Cash balance at beginning of period covered by this report $............. $.............

26. Cash balance at close of period covered by this report $............. $.............

    C. Cumulative Amounts of Excess (Deficiency) of Funds Generated Over Distributions After Realized Gains (Losses) on Investments (Exclusive of Minority Interests).

27. Cumulative excess (deficiency) of funds generated over distributions after realized gain (loss) on investments at the beginning of the fiscal year $............. $.............

    Instructions. 1. The amount reflected hereunder shall be computed from the beginning of the first fiscal year ending on or after January 1, 1959, or the date of organization of the registrant, whichever is later.

    2. The cumulative amount hereunder and the amount reflected under caption 28 shall be computed in the same manner as is the amount shown in caption 20 above.

28. Net increase (decrease) in excess (deficiency) of funds generated over distribution after realized gain (loss) on investments from beginning of the fiscal year to end of period covered by this report $............. $.............

29. Cumulative excess (deficiency) of funds generated over distribution after realized gain (loss) on investments at end of fiscal period to date $............. $.............

30. Per share amounts declared at the date of this report for distribution in the forth-

coming period(s). List separately the declaration by payment period

REMARKS: ....
....
....
....

Following are the requirements if there has been an acquisition of a business during the period covered by Form 7–Q:

If a business has been acquired for cash or debt during the period, the net current assets acquired at date of acquisition shall be stated separately under caption 21. Cash and current obligations used for the purchase shall be shown separately under caption 23. The operations of a purchased business from date of acquisition shall be reflected in other captions of the form.

For a business acquired in an exchange of shares during the period, complete separate statements may be presented in an additional column on this form, or the operations of the acquired business may be included with those of the registrant in the proper captions for the entire period or from date of acquisition as appropriate. The beginning balance of cash (caption 25) shall reflect separately the amounts contributed by the acquired business. The operations of the acquired business shall be reflected in captions 28 and 29 only for the period included in the operations of the registrant during the period.

The requirements with regard to the summary of capitalization and stockholders' equity are as follows:

Furnish, insofar as practicable in the manner described below, a summary of capitalization and stockholders' equity as at the end of the latest fiscal quarter.

D. Capitalization and Stockholders' Equity

....
(Date)

Debt

	Amount
Short-term loans, notes, etc.	$........
Long-term debt, including parenthetically portion due within one year (list separately convertible and subordinated debt)	$........
Total debt	$........
	$........
	....
Deferred credits	$........
Minority interests	$........

Stockholders' equity—

	Shares Issued or Outstanding	Amount
Preferred stock (list separately convertible and nonconvertible preferred stock)	....	$........

Common stock	. . . .	$. . . . .
Capital in excess of par value		$. . . . .
Retained earnings—		
Balance at beginning of current fiscal year		$. . . . .
Prior period adjustments, if any (show credits (and		
charges) separately)		$. . . . .
Net income (Item 10, above)		$. . . . .
Dividends		
(State cash and stock dividends on common stock		
separately, indicating amount per share—dividends		
on preferred stocks may be shown in one amount)		$(. . . . . .)
Other credits (charges)		
(Explain nature and amounts)		$. . . . .
Balance at end of interim period		$. . . . .
Treasury stock		
(Identify class of security, number of shares and		
basis at which stated)	. . . .	$(. . . . . .)
Total stockholders' equity		$. . . . .

Instructions. 1. The form and content shall conform generally with that in the balance sheet and notes thereto appearing in the annual report filed with the Commission.

2. The number of shares of each class of securities reserved for conversion, warrants, options and other rights shall be separately disclosed.

Eight copies of the Form 7–Q report have to be filed with the Commission and at least one copy with each exchange on which any class of securities of the registrant is listed and registered. At least one copy of the report filed with the SEC and one copy filed with each such exchange must be manually signed. Copies not signed manually have to bear typed or printed signatures.

Financial Statements Required by Form 8–K

In Chapter **14** the requirements for filing current reports on Form 8–K are described briefly. In certain circumstances a report on this form must contain financial statements. As stated in Chapter **14**, the SEC announced in 1969 that it had under consideration a proposal to rescind Form 8–K. Before using the form, therefore, it is suggested that the reader inquire concerning the status of the form.

Financial Statements of Businesses Acquired.—The financial statements specified below must be filed for any business the acquisition of which by the registrant or any of its majority-owned subsidiaries is required to be described in answer to Item 2 of Form 8–K. Item 2 calls for information with respect to acquisitions or dispositions of assets otherwise than in the ordinary course of business. For this purpose an acquisition or disposition is deemed to involve a significant amount of assets (1) if the net book value of such assets or the amount paid or received therefor upon such acquisition or disposition exceeded 15 per cent of the total assets of the registrant and its consolidated subsidiaries, or (2) if it involved the acquisition or disposition of a business whose gross revenues for its last fiscal year exceeded 15 per cent of the aggregate gross revenues of the registrant and its consolidated subsidiaries for the registrant's last fiscal year.

A balance sheet of an acquired business must be filed as of a date reasonably close to the date of acquisition. This balance sheet need not be certified, but if it is not certified, there shall also be filed a certified balance sheet as of the close of the preceding fiscal year. Income and surplus statements of the business must be filed for each of the last three full fiscal years and for the period, if any, between the close of the latest of such fiscal years and the date of the latest balance sheet filed. The income and surplus statements must be certified up to the date of the certified balance sheet. If the business was in insolvency proceedings immediately prior to its acquisition, the balance sheets referred to above need not be certified. In such case, the income and surplus statements required must be certified to the close of the latest full fiscal year. Except as otherwise provided in the instructions, the principles applicable to a registrant and its subsidiaries with respect to the filing of individual, consolidated, and group statements in an original registration statement or annual report are applicable to the statements required to be filed.

Regulation S–X contains the requirements as to certification and form and content of balance sheets and of income and surplus statements that are required as set forth in the preceding paragraph. No supporting schedules need be filed. The instructions for Form 8–K also contain provisions relating to the filing of other statements or the omission of statements similar to those appearing in Form S–1 set forth on page **9·14** and are not repeated here.

Deficiency Letters and Amendments

As in the case of filings under the 1933 Act, the SEC also examines the financial statements included in filings under the 1934 Act. In the former case, however, because an effective date is involved, SEC examines promptly the material filed with it and communicates its findings to the registrant. (The foregoing references to the SEC's examination of material filed under the 1933 Act should be qualified in view of its cursory review procedures when the backlog of registration statements is heavy; this matter is discussed in Chapter **7**.) In the case of filings under the 1934 Act, however, no such urgency exists, except in the case of proxy statements and information statements when proxies are not solicited. As a result, the SEC's comments, if any, with respect to a filing (other than a proxy statement or information statement) under the 1934 Act may be received several months after the registration statement or report has been filed.

Frequently the SEC's comments with respect to material in an annual report on Form 10–K, for instance, may be relatively unimportant, involving perhaps the failure to comply with an immaterial technical requirement of Regulation S–X. In that case, the Commission's comments are usually in the form of "suggestions" for future reports and do not require the material previously filed to be amended. When, however, the Commission indicates that the information filed is deficient and must be amended, the registrant's management must decide whether or not they agree with the views of the Commission. If the Commission's comments were not "suggestions" of the order mentioned above, and if the management concludes that the Commission's comments are well founded, they will proceed with the preparation of amended financial statements. The amended material should be filed as soon as practicable after the Commission's comments are received. If the management wishes to contest the Commission's views, they should proceed promptly to take the matter up with the appropriate persons in the Commission.

If a registrant has received "suggestions" from the SEC staff for future reports, and these suggestions are ignored in the subsequent filing, the "suggestion" in the previous filing often becomes a "deficiency" in the current filing. For this reason, it is desirable to consider the SEC's suggestions carefully. If it is expected that the suggestion will not be followed in future reports, the author would recommend that this fact be communicated to the Commission together with the reasons therefor.

If the original financial statement had to be certified by an independent public accountant, then the amended financial statement must also be certified. Some accountants accomplish the latter certification by means of a letter or communication that, in effect, says that the accountant's certificate previously filed is applicable to the amended financial statement involved. In a typical case, assuming that a balance sheet and a supporting schedule are amended, the letter or authorization of the certifying accountant would be somewhat along the lines of the following:

We consent to the substitution of the following financial statement and schedule for the corresponding financial statement and schedule previously filed by you as part of your annual report (Form 10–K) for the fiscal year ended (date):

> Balance sheet (date)
> Schedule (number and title)

and to the use of our opinion dated _____ included in the said annual report after such substitution.

> (Signature of certifying accountant)

Assume that the financial statements as originally filed required the certifying accountant to take exception to an accounting principle reflected in the financial statements. Assume also that the SEC's comment required the financial statements to be amended so as to remove the need for the exception by the certifying accountant. If the registrant accedes to the view of the SEC, then the accountant's certificate as originally filed would no longer apply to the amended financial statements. In that case, in addition to filing amended financial statements, the registrant will have to include in the amendment a revised accountant's certificate. Frequently the accountant will also include a letter to the effect that the amended certificate is applicable to the financial statements originally filed as amended by the financial statements now being filed. A typical letter used in that situation would be somewhat as follows:

We consent to the substitution of the accompanying report dated _____ and the following financial statements and schedules for those previously filed by you as part of your annual report (Form 10–K) for the fiscal year ended (date):

(Here list financial statements and schedules which are being amended)

The accompanying report dated _____ is applicable to the financial statements and schedules included in the said annual report (Form 10–K) as amended by the financial statements and schedules listed above.

(Signature of certifying accountant)

All Amendments on Form 8.—All amendments to registration statements or reports filed pursuant to Sections 12, 13, or 15(d) of the 1934 Act are filed on Form 8. This form is, in effect, a covering page that identifies the items of information in a registration statement or report which it is desired to amend. Thus, for example, if it is desired to amend Item 1 of Form 10, the item as amended would be filed attached to Form 8. Similarly, if it is desired to amend a balance sheet submitted previously as part of Form 10–K, the amended balance sheet would be submitted under cover of Form 8.

Reports of Certain Exchange Members, Brokers, and Dealers (Form X–17A–5)

The report of financial condition on Form X–17A–5 is almost entirely financial in nature and must comply with Rule 17a–5. Paragraph (b) of the rule follows:

(b) *Nature and Form of Reports.* Each report of financial condition filed pursuant to paragraph (a) of this section shall be prepared and filed in accordance with the following requirements:
(1) The report of a member, broker or dealer shall be certified by a certified public accountant or a public accountant who shall be in fact independent; *Provided, however,* that such report need not be certified if, since the date of the

previous financial statement or report filed pursuant to [Rule 15b1–2] or this section, (i) said member has not transacted a business in securities directly with or for others than members of a national securities exchange; has not carried any margin account, credit balance or security for any person other than a general partner; and has not been required to file a certified financial statement with any national securities exchange; or (ii) his or its securities business has been limited to acting as broker (agent) for the issuer in soliciting subscriptions for securities of such issuer, said broker has promptly transmitted to such issuer all funds and promptly delivered to the subscriber all securities received in connection therewith, and said broker has not otherwise held funds or securities for or owed money or securities to customers; or (iii) his or its securities business has been limited to buying and selling evidences of indebtedness secured by mortgage, deed of trust, or other lien upon real estate or leasehold interests, and said broker or dealer has not carried any margin account, credit balance, or security for any securities customer. A member, broker or dealer who files a report which is not certified shall include in the oath or affirmation required by paragraph (b)(2) of this rule a statement of the facts and circumstances relied upon as a basis for exemption from the certification requirements.

(2) Attached to the report shall be an oath or affirmation that, to the best knowledge and belief of the person making such oath or affirmation, (i) the financial statement and supporting schedules are true and correct and (ii) neither the member, broker, or dealer, nor any partner, officer, or director, as the case may be, has any proprietary interest in any account classified solely as that of a customer. The oath or affirmation shall be made before a person duly authorized to administer such oaths or affirmations. If the member, broker, or dealer is a sole proprietorship, the oath or affirmation shall be made by the proprietor; if a partnership, by a general partner; or if a corporation, by a duly authorized officer.

(3) If the schedules furnished pursuant to the requirements of items (a), (b), and (c) of part II are bound separately from the balance of the report, they shall be deemed confidential, except that they shall be available for official use by any official or employee of the United States or any state, by national securities exchanges and national securities associations of which the person filing such report is a member, and by any other person to whom the Commission authorizes disclosure of such information as being in the public interest. Nothing contained in this paragraph shall be deemed to be in derogation of the rules of any national securities association or national securities exchange which give to customers of a member, broker, or dealer the right, upon request to such member, broker, or dealer, to obtain information relative to his financial condition. [*Author's note:* The reader is referred to the addendum at the end of this chapter.]

Use of Statements Filed with State Commissions and Securities Exchanges.—Any member, broker, or dealer required to file Form X–17A–5 may file in lieu of the report required by the SEC's rules a copy of any financial statement he is, or has been, required to file with any national securities exchange of which he is a member, or with any agency of any state as a condition of doing business in securities therein, provided that (a) the copy so included reflects his financial condition as of a date not more than 45 days prior to the filing thereof with the Commission; and

(b) the report, as filed with the Commission, meets the requirements of the SEC rules and Form X–17A–5 and contains the information called for by the form.

Content of Form X–17A–5. Form X–17A–5, the financial questionnaire, was extensively revised by the SEC in 1967. A principal purpose of the form is to furnish certified financial information to the SEC in order to enable that agency to check compliance with the applicable net capital rules and other aspects of investor protection. In its present form, the questionnaire consists of two parts. Part I consists of 16 so-called "questions"; Part II consists of information supplementary to the "questions."

PART I. The requirements of Part I follow:

Question 1. Bank Balances and Other Deposits.

State separately total of each kind of deposit (cash and/or market value of securities) with adequate description. This shall include cash on hand; cash in banks representing general funds subject to immediate withdrawal; cash in banks subject to withdrawal restrictions; funds segregated pursuant to regulations of any agency of the Federal government, any state, any national securities exchange or national securities association; contributions to clearing organizations incident to membership; deposits with clearing organizations in connection with commitments; guaranty and margin deposits; good faith deposits (see note 3 to Question 14); drafts with securities attached deposited for collection.

Question 2. Money Borrowed, and Accounts Carried for Respondent by Other Banking or Brokerage Houses, Secured by or Containing Customers' Collateral.

State separately totals of ledger net debit balances; ledger net credit balances; long security valuations; short security valuations; spot (cash) commodity valuations; net losses and net gains in future commodity contracts, and classify as follows:

A. Money borrowed:
  1. From banks, trust companies and other financial institutions
  2. From others

B. Accounts carried for respondent by other banking or brokerage houses, including omnibus accounts:
  1. Securities accounts:
    a. Accounts with net debit balances
    b. Accounts with net credit balances
  2. Commodities accounts:
    a. Regulated commodities futures accounts:
      i. Accounts liquidating to an equity
      ii. Accounts liquidating to a deficit
    b. Nonregulated commodities futures accounts:
      i. Accounts liquidating to an equity
      ii. Accounts liquidating to a deficit

    c. Spot (cash) commodity accounts:
      i. Accounts with net debit balances
      ii. Accounts with net credit balances

Notes:

1. To the extent that the collateral for the loan, or other amount payable, also includes additional collateral owned by others than customers, the valuation of such collateral shall be shown separately and designated as owned by respondent, general partners, officers, directors, or others, including securities covered by subordination agreements.

2. If collateralized entirely by "exempted securities," the amount of the borrowing, or amount payable to a banking or brokerage house, and the valuation of the collateral shall be stated separately.

Question 3. Money Borrowed, and Accounts Carried for Respondent by Other Banking or Brokerage Houses, Unsecured, or Secured Entirely by Collateral Owned by Respondent and Its Partners or Its Officers and Directors, or by Securities Covered by "Satisfactory Subordination Agreements."

State separately totals of ledger net debit balances; ledger net credit balances; long security valuations; short security valuations; spot (cash) commodity valuations; net losses and net gains in future commodity contracts, and classify as follows:

  A. Money borrowed:
    1. From banks, trust companies and other financial institutions
    2. From officers and directors
    3. From others

  B. Accounts carried for respondent by other banking or brokerage houses:
    1. Securities accounts:
      a. Accounts with net debit balances
      b. Accounts with net credit balances
    2. Commodities accounts:
      a. Regulated commodities futures accounts:
        i. Accounts liquidating to an equity
        ii. Accounts liquidating to a deficit
      b. Nonregulated commodities futures accounts:
        i. Accounts liquidating to an equity
        ii. Accounts liquidating to a deficit
      c. Spot (cash) commodity accounts:
        i. Accounts with net debit balances
        ii. Accounts with net credit balances

Note:

State separately borrowings under A or credit balances under B.1.b. and/or B.2.c.ii:

1. Unsecured
2. Not adequately collateralized under Rule 15c3–1(c)(6)
3. Collateralized in whole or in part by securities and/or commodities reportable under 8 or 9B. Designate valuation of such collateral, and state separately amounts adequately collateralized by "exempted securities."

Question 4. Other Open Items with Brokers and Dealers.

State separately totals of ledger debit balances; ledger credit balances; long security valuations; short security valuations, and classify as follows:

A. Securities borrowed (i.e., amount to be received from others upon return to them of securities borrowed by respondent)

B. Securities failed to deliver (i.e., amount to be received from brokers and dealers upon delivery of securities sold by respondent)

C. Securities loaned (i.e., amount to be paid to others upon return of securities loaned by respondent) :
   1. Customers' securities
   2. Securities reportable under 8 or 9B
   3. Securities reportable under 9A, 10, 11, and 12

D. Securities failed to receive (i.e., amount to be paid to brokers and dealers upon receipt of securities purchased by respondent) :
   1. For customers
   2. For accounts reportable under 8 or 9B
   3. For accounts reportable under 9A, 10, 11, and 12:
      a. Sold at date of report
      b. Unsold at date of report

Notes:
   1. Where it is impractical or unduly expensive to allocate all securities loaned and all securities failed to receive to each category in C and D, proper allocation shall be made to the extent feasible and all other such credit balances and short security valuations shall be reported under C.1. and/or D.1., respectively.
   2. State separately or in a footnote the totals of ledger debit balances; ledger credit balances; long security valuations; short security valuations, for transactions outstanding 30 calendar days or longer included in the answers to Question 4.B. (Securities Failed to Deliver) and Question 4.D. (Securities Failed to Receive). The amounts reported for Question 4.B. shall be classified in accordance with the period that the transactions have been outstanding: 30 to 39 calendar days; 40 to 49 calendar days; 50 to 59 calendar days; and 60 or more calendar days.

Question 5. Valuations of Securities and Spot (Cash) Commodities in Box, Transfer and Transit.

State separately the total valuation of:

A. Negotiable securities in box, transfer, and in transit between offices of respondent.

B. Spot (cash) commodities represented by warehouse receipts or bills of lading in box and in transit between offices of respondent.

Note: Question 5 requires entries in short valuation column only.

Question 6. Customers' Security Accounts.

State separately totals of ledger debit balances; ledger credit balance; long security valuations; short security valuations, and classify as follows:

A. Bona fide cash accounts (i.e., accounts having both unsettled money balances and positions in securities which are current items within the meaning of section 4(c) of Regulation T of the Board of Governors of the Federal Reserve System):
  1. Accounts with debit balances
  2. Accounts with credit balances

B. Secured accounts:
  1. Accounts with debit balances
  2. Accounts with credit balances

C. Partly secured accounts (accounts liquidating to a deficit):
  1. Accounts with debit balances
  2. Accounts with credit balances

D. Unsecured accounts

E. Accounts with credit balances having open contractual commitments

F. Accounts with free credit balances

G. Fully paid securities not segregated

Notes:
  1. Cash accounts which are not "bona fide cash accounts" shall be reported under B, C, or D as appropriate.
  2. Do not combine the accounts of customers except as permitted by General Instruction B.6.
  3. Each joint account carried by respondent in which respondent has an interest shall be so stated, separately, as a customer's account in the proper classification and the status of the respondent's interest therein shall be stated. Funds received by respondent as margin in these accounts shall be separately stated by account. If any funds have been provided by the respondent as margin, these shall be clearly indicated here and in the answer to Question 13.
  4. With respect to contractual commitments state as a footnote or in a separate schedule the total of:
    a. Deficits in the accounts of the respective customers reported in the answers to B and/or E after application of net losses in open contractual commitments in securities carried for each such customer.
    b. Net losses in open contractual commitments in securities carried for each customer whose account is reported in the answers to C or D.
  In computing net losses, gains at market and profits on such sales may be applied against losses only in the same security in each customer's account.
  5. See General Instruction B.11 for definition of the term "contractual commitments."

Question 7. Customers' Commodity Accounts.

State separately totals of ledger debit balances; ledger credit balances; spot (cash) commodity valuations; net losses and net gains in future commodity contracts, and classify as follows:

A. Accounts with open future contracts liquidating to an equity:
  1. Regulated commodities
  2. Nonregulated commodities

B. Accounts with open future contracts liquidating to a deficit:
   1. Regulated commodities
   2. Nonregulated commodities

C. Accounts with spot (cash) commodity positions:
   1. Hedged:
      a. Secured
      b. Partly secured
   2. Not hedged:
      a. Secured
      b. Partly secured

D. Unsecured debit balance

E. Accounts with free credit balances:
   1. Regulated
   2. Nonregulated

Note: See notes 2 and 3 to Question 6.

Question 8. Accounts of Officers and Directors.

State separately, in accordance with the applicable classifications and instructions of Questions 6 and 7, totals of ledger debit balances; ledger credit balances; long security and spot (cash) commodity valuations; short security and spot (cash) commodity valuations; net losses and net gains in future commodity contracts in the accounts of:

A. Officers
B. Directors

Note: If an individual is both an officer and a director, classify the accounts under 8A.

Question 9. General Partners' Individual Accounts.

State separately totals of ledger debit balances; ledger credit balances; long security and spot (cash) commodity valuations; short security and spot (cash) commodity valuations; net losses and net gains in future commodity contracts, and classify as follows:

A. Individual accounts of general partners who have signed specific agreements that cash, securities, commodities, and equities recorded in these accounts are to be included as partnership property.

B. All other accounts of general partners. (These accounts shall be classified in accordance with the applicable classifications and instructions of Questions 6 and 7.)

Notes:
1. Total valuations of "exempted securities" reported in answer to Question 9A, shall be stated separately.
2. The noncapital accounts of partners other than general partners shall be included either with customers' accounts in the appropriate classifications of Questions 6 and 7 or, where applicable, in Question 12.

Question 10. Trading and Investment Accounts of Respondent.

State separately totals of ledger debit balances; ledger credit balances; long security and spot (cash) commodity valuations; short security and spot (cash) commodity valuations; net losses and net gains in future commodity contracts, and classify as follows:

A. Securities accounts:
   1. Exempted securities
   2. Other securities

B. Commodities accounts:
   1. Future commodities contracts
   2. Spot (cash) commodities;
      a. Hedged
      b. Not hedged

C. Other

Notes:
   1. Ledger balances may be combined with respect to all security accounts and also with respect to all spot (cash) commodity accounts.
   2. Treasury stock of respondent shall not be included hereunder.
   3. In the case of a sole proprietor, see General Instruction B.9.

Question 11. Capital Accounts.

State separately totals of ledger debit balances; ledger credit balances; long security and spot (cash) commodity valuations, short security and spot (cash) commodity valuations, and classify as follows:

A. Sole proprietorship:
   1. Capital account
   2. Undistributed profit and loss accounts, including balances remaining in income and expense accounts. (This question may be answered by giving one net amount.)

B. Partnership:
   1. Capital accounts of general partners
   2. Capital accounts of special or limited partners
   3. Undistributed profit and loss accounts, including balances remaining in income and expense accounts. (This question may be answered by giving one net amount.)

C. Corporation or similar entity:
   1. Capital stock (detail by class of stock showing number of shares and par value.):
      a. Authorized (state parenthetically.)
      b. Issued
      c. Treasury stock
   2. Capital surplus
   3. Earned surplus or deficit, including balances remaining in income and expense accounts. (This question may be answered by giving one net amount.)

D. Capital reserves (State nature and amount of each reserve. Valuation reserves and liability reserves shall be reported in answer to Question 13).

Note: Total valuations of "exempted securities" shall be stated separately.

Question 12. Subordinated Accounts.

State separately for all accounts covered by "satisfactory subordination agreements," totals of ledger debit balances; ledger credit balances; long security and spot (cash) commodity valuations; short security and spot (cash) commodity valuations; net losses and net gains in future commodity contracts, and classify as follows:

A. Subordinated accounts:
   1. Accounts with debit balances
   2. Accounts with credit balances

B. Subordinated borrowings.

Notes:
   1. Total valuations of "exempted securities" shall be stated separately.
   2. Any subordinated account reported under this question must be subject to an agreement which complies with the requirements of Rule 15c3–1 (c) (7) or, if the respondent is a member of an exchange whose members are exempt from Rule 15c3–1 by subparagraph (b) (2) thereof, complies with the rules regarding subordination agreements of all the exchanges therein listed of which respondent is a member. Subordinated accounts with agreements that do not comply with the above requirements must be reported in the answers to Questions 2 through 9, as appropriate.

Question 13. Other Accounts, etc.

State details (ledger balances; valuations of securities and spot (cash) commodities; status of future commodity positions; and any other relevant information) of any accounts which have not been included in one of the answers to the above questions. These shall include: accounts for exchange memberships; furniture, fixtures, and other fixed assets; valuation reserves; funds provided or deposited by the respondent as margin in joint accounts; revenue stamps; dividends receivable, payable, and unclaimed; floor brokerage receivable and payable; commissions receivable and payable; advances to salesmen and other employees; commodity difference account; goodwill; organization expense; prepaid expenses and deferred charges; liability reserves; mortgage payable; other liabilities and deferred credits; market value of securities borrowed (other than for delivery against customers' sales) to the extent to which no equivalent value is paid or credited; long security count difference valuations; short security count difference valuations; and other accounts not specifically mentioned herein.

Notes:
   1. Any liability reported under this question secured by collateral in any form shall be identified by reference to the related collateral.
   2. State in a footnote (a) long security count difference valuations and short security count difference valuations classified in accordance with the date of the physical count and verification pursuant to Rule 17a–5 or 17a–13 in which they were discovered, and (b) the value of long security count differences sold and

short security count differences bought-in to resolve differences since the last report on Form X–17A–5 classified in accordance with the date that the related differences were discovered.

3. State in a footnote the number of securities in which there were long security count differences; the number in which there were short security count differences; and the total number of securities in which there were positions as of the audit date.

Question 14. Contractual Commitments That Are Not Recorded in a Ledger Account for Money.

State separately for each type of commitment total cost; total proceeds; valuation of net long and/or short position for the following:

A. Respondent (see notes 2 and 3)

B. General partners who have signed specific agreements that cash, securities, commodities and equities recorded in these accounts are to be included as partnership property.

C. Subordinated accounts.

D. Other general partners, officers and/or directors:
    1. Accounts not fully secured (including unsecured accounts)
    2. Commitments which are substantial in view of the capital of the respondent

E. Customers:
    1. Accounts not fully secured (including unsecured accounts)
    2. Commitments which are substantial in view of the capital of the respondent

Notes:
1. See General Instruction B.11 for definition of term "contractual commitments."
2. As to underwriting commitments, the amounts reported shall represent the respondent's interest in the entire account.
3. Related good faith deposits shall be clearly indicated; the total thereof shall be included in the amount reported in answer to Question 1.
4. The details required by Part (a) may be reported herein.

Question 15. Participations of the Respondent in Joint Trading and Investment Accounts Carried by Others that are not Recorded in a Ledger Account for Money.

State separately for each joint account (1) the account balance, exclusive of deposits; (2) the total market valuations of long securities, short securities, and commodities; and (3) the respondent's share of such account balance and each such market valuation. Any related deposits reported in answer to Question 13 shall be clearly indicated hereunder.

Question 16. Unrecorded Assets, Liabilities and Accountabilities.

Submit a separate schedule containing a description of any assets, liabilities and accountabilities of the respondent, actual or contingent, which are not included in a ledger account or reported in answer to Questions 14 and 15. Only such items which in the aggregate are material in relation to net capital need be reported. Accountabilities shall include cash and/or other property including securities held for customers by or on behalf of respondent, which are not included in a ledger account. Contingent liabilities may include lawsuits pending against the respondent, accommodation endorsements, rediscounted notes, and guarantees of accounts of others.

PART II. The requirements of Part II of Form X–17A–5 follow:

Submit the following information:

(a) Separate schedules giving adequate description including quantity, price, and valuation of each security and commodity position supporting each total valuation reported in answer to the following:

Questions 6 and 7—Joint accounts in which respondent has an interest.

Questions 6C., 7C.1.b., and 7C.2.b.—Customers' partly secured accounts.

Question 8—Partly secured accounts of officers and directors.

Question 9A.—Individual accounts of general partners who have signed specific agreements that cash, securities, commodities, and equities recorded in these accounts are to be included as partnership property.

Question 9B.—Partly secured accounts of partners reported in response hereto.

Question 10—Trading and investment accounts of respondent.

Question 11—Capital accounts.

Question 12—Subordinated accounts and borrowings.
The schedule shall show with respect to each borrowing or claim the name of the lender, the relationship to respondent, the amount of the borrowing or claim and the maturity date of the agreement.

Question 14—Contractual commitments that are not recorded in a ledger account for money reported in answer to Questions 14A., 14B., 14C., 14D.1., and 14E.1., Part I.
In addition to the details of securities and commodities positions, report the total cost and total proceeds for each security and commodity; the totals thereof shall agree with the amounts reported in answer to Question 14, Part I.
Where contractual commitments exist in puts or calls, or any combination thereof, the details shall include separately with respect to puts or calls in each separate security of the same class: quantity, description of security, expiration date or range of expiration dates, indicated contract cost or proceeds, market valuation and indicated unrealized profit or loss. This information shall be reported in separate columns, classified separately and grouped as puts or calls.
Where contractual commitments are related to positions in other securities reflected in the answers to questions in Part I such relationship shall be clearly described.
The above information may be reported in Part II(a) or in the answer to Question 14 Part I.

Question 15—Participations of the respondent in joint trading and investment accounts carried by others that are not recorded in a ledger account for money.

Notes:

1. "Exempted securities" and "securities not readily marketable" shall be stated separately.

2. If the respondent is not exempt from the provisions of Rule 15c3–1 but desires that, where allowed, greater than 70% of the market valuation of certain securities be included in the computation of net capital under that rule, such securities shall either be listed by groups in accordance with the classifications of Rule 15c3–1 (c) (2) (C) or the applicable percentages allowable under that rule shall be stated with respect to each security and a summary of valuations by such percentages shall be given.

(b) A schedule showing in detail ledger balances, valuations of long and short securities and spot (cash) commodities, and net losses and net gains in future commodity contracts and other open contractual commitments (other than those reported in the answers to Part I of this Form) in any accounts carried by other brokerage houses in which a sole proprietor or any general partner of the respondent has an interest. (Accounts containing only free securities or free credit balances need not be reported.)

(c) (i) A separate schedule showing the market value of all long and all short future commodity contracts in each account other than customers' commodity accounts reported in answer to all Questions in Part I of this Form (contracts representing spreads or straddles in the same commodity and those contracts offsetting or hedging any "spot" commodity positions, and accounts of general partners, officers or directors not subject to percentage deduction shall be so designated).

(ii) A separate schedule showing the market value of all customers' long and all customers' short future contracts in each commodity reported in answer to all Questions in Part I of this Form.

(d) If the answer to Question 11 includes amounts authorized or proposed to be distributed or withdrawn within the next 6 months, furnish the details.

(e) If respondent is a sole-proprietor state whether any liabilities which are not reflected in the answers to Part I of this form would materially affect net worth as reported; if such liabilities would materially affect net worth as reported, the statement required by Item 7 of the Audit Requirements shall be furnished as a schedule.

(f) If the respondent has met the conditions specified in subparagraph (a) (2) of Rule 15c3–1 throughout the year and desires that the lower net capital requirements apply, a specific statement to that effect shall be furnished as a schedule.

GENERAL INSTRUCTIONS FOR FORM X–17A–5.—The general instructions with respect to Form X–17A–5 follow:

A. Rules as to use of Form X–17A–5:

1. This form shall be used by every member, broker or dealer required to file reports under Rule 17a–5(a). It is not to be used as a blank form to be

filled in but only as a guide in the preparation of the report. No caption need be shown as to which the items and conditions are not present.

2. The name of the respondent and date of report shall be repeated on each sheet of the answers and schedules submitted.

3. If no answer is made to a question or subdivision thereof it shall constitute a representation that respondent has nothing to report.

B. Presentation of information (including definitions) :

1. The information presented shall be sufficient to permit the determination of the financial condition of the respondent.

2. The valuations of customers' securities in segregation or safekeeping need not be included in the answers.

3. Use separate pairs of columns for ledger debit and ledger credit balances; long security and spot (cash) commodity valuations and short security and spot (cash) commodity valuations; net losses in future commodity contracts and net gains in future commodity contracts. All columns must be totaled. The total of debit balances must equal the total of credit balances. The total of long security and spot (cash) commodity valuations must equal the total of short security and spot (cash) commodity valuations; the total losses and the total gains in future commodity contracts must be in agreement after consideration of "commodity difference accounts." The answers to Questions 14, 15 and 16 shall not be included in the totals.

4. Security and spot (cash) commodity valuations and losses and gains in future commodity contracts shall be based upon current market prices; fractions and accrued interest may be omitted except where such procedure in the case of short positions would have a material effect upon net capital.

5. "Securities not readily marketable" shall be so designated. The term "securities not readily marketable" shall include, but not be limited to, (a) securities, except "exempted securities," for which there is no market on a securities exchange or no independent publicly quoted market; (b) securities which cannot be publicly offered or sold unless registration has been effected under the Securities Act of 1933 (or the conditions of an exemption such as Regulation A under Section 3(b) of such Act have been complied with) ; and (c) securities which cannot be offered or sold because of other arrangements, restrictions, or conditions applicable to the securities or to the respondent.

6. All accounts (other than regulated commodity accounts) of any one customer may be combined and reported under any appropriate classification other than Question 6.A. Customers' accounts related by bona fide written guarantees may be combined.

7. For the purpose of this questionnaire, the term "customer" shall not include the respondent, general partners, officers, or directors. An account covered by a "satisfactory subordination agreement" shall be reported in answer to Question 12.

8. Foreign currency may be expressed in terms of United States dollars at the current rate of exchange and where carried in conjunction with the United States dollar balances for the same customer may be consolidated with such United States dollar balances and the gross or net position reported in its proper classification, provided the foreign currency is not subject to any restrictions as to conversion. If the foreign currency position so treated is substantial, some indication of its size shall be given.

9. If the respondent is a sole proprietor, all accounts carried by brokers, dealers, or others for the respondent which contain money balances and/or

securities allocated to or otherwise used in connection with his business shall be reported in the answers to Questions 1 through 16, as appropriate.

10. "Exempted securities" are those securities defined as such under the provisions of Section 3(a)(12) of the Securities Exchange Act of 1934 other than securities designated for exemption by action of the Securities and Exchange Commission.

11. The term "contractual commitments" shall include underwriting, when-issued, when-distributed and delayed delivery contracts, repurchase agreements, endorsements of all puts and all calls, commitments in foreign currencies, and spot (cash) commodity contracts, but shall not include future commodity contracts and uncleared regular way purchases and sales of securities. A series of contracts of purchase or sale of the same security conditioned, if at all, only upon issuance may be treated as an individual commitment.

12. For the purpose of this questionnaire securities sold as principal under an agreement to repurchase shall be stated separately and clearly indicated as such in the answers to Questions 3.A. and 10.

Audit Requirements of Form X–17A–5.—The audit requirements applicable to Form X–17A–5 are set forth beginning on page **5·54**.

Accountants' Certificate Applicable to Form X–17A–5.—The accountants' certificate applicable to Form X–17A–5 and the accountants' qualifications for the purpose of furnishing such a certificate are set forth in Chapter **25**.

Information Required of Exchange Members, Brokers, and Dealers Under Section 17 of the 1934 Act and Rule 17a–10 (Form X–17A–10).—Chapter **14** of this book contains a brief discussion of a report required to be filed annually with the SEC by exchange members, brokers, and dealers on Form X–17A–10. As stated in Chapter **14**, the form consists of an Introduction and three Parts. All reporting firms must complete and file the Introduction. No firm has to complete more than one Part, and, in some cases, some respondents need not complete any of the Parts—all as set forth in Chapter **14**. Since the contents of Parts I, II, and III are almost entirely financial in nature, their scope is described below.

Only majority-owned subsidiaries that are exchange members, brokers, or dealers may be consolidated in Form X–17A–10.

All money amounts are to be expressed in dollars; cents are to be omitted.

The information in the report is not required to be certified by independent public accountants.

Part I of the report consists of the following statements and schedule:

Statement AAA—Statement of Income and Expenses
Schedule AAA–1—Number Count of Personnel

Statement BBB—Statement of Capital Funds
Statement CCC—Statement of Financial Condition

Part II of the report consists of the following statements and schedules:

Statement AA—Statement of Income and Expenses
   Schedule AA–1—Number Count of Personnel
   Schedule AA–2—Transaction Count
Statement BB—Statement of Capital Funds
Statement CC—Statement of Financial Condition
   Schedule CC–1—Securities and Commodities Positions in Investment, Trading and Other Accounts

Part III of the report consists of the following statements and schedules:

Statement A—Statement of Income and Expenses
   Schedule A–1—Brokerage Commissions
   Schedule A–2—Gain or Loss from Principal Transactions in Securities in Trading Accounts
   Schedule A–3—Profit or Loss from Management of and Participation in Underwriting Syndicates and Selling Groups
   Schedule A–4—Income from Sale of Investment Company Securities
   Schedule A–5—Income from Other Sources
   Schedule A–6—Employee Compensation and Employment Costs
   Schedule A–7—Interest Expense
   Schedule A–8—Transaction Count
Statement B—Statement of Capital Funds
Statement C—Statement of Financial Condition
   Schedule C–1—Securities and Commodities Positions in Investment, Trading and Other Accounts

There is little similarity between the statements and schedules in Parts I, II, and III other than their titles. The statement of income and expense in Part I is much less detailed, has far fewer supplementary schedules, and has far fewer instructions than its counterpart in Part III. The same is true of the statements of capital funds and financial condition.

Addendum to the discussion of reports of exchange members, brokers, and dealers.—The SEC on June 30, 1972 adopted important amendments to Rule 17a–5. Persons affected by the amendments are required:

   1. To file with the SEC a complete set of financial statements (including income statements) in addition to those contained in Form X–17A–5. These statements are filed on a confidential basis and, depending on the circumstances, may have to be certified.
   2. To send unconsolidated balance sheets and other financial information

to their customers. These statements may have to be certified. If the most recent report on Form X–17A–5 contained an auditor's report commenting on inadequacies in the accounting system, internal control, and other specified procedures, the member, broker, or dealer shall notify the customer of the report and comments and where it may be inspected. In addition, persons affected by the new rule have to send their customers quarterly financial information which need not be certified.

For further information, readers are referred to SEC Release No. 34–9658, June 30, 1972.

CHAPTER 16

REGULATION S–X (ANNOTATED)

Part 1. The Rules of General Application

CONTENTS

Scope of Regulation S–X.—Regulation S–X is the principal accounting regulation of the SEC in its administration of the Securities Act of 1933, the Securities Exchange Act of 1934, the Public Utility Holding Company Act of 1935, and the Investment Company Act of 1940. Promulgated originally in 1940, the regulation has been amended numerous times since that date—most recently in 1972. *No public accountant should at-*

tempt an examination of financial statements intended for filing under any of these Acts without having an up-to-date copy of Regulation S–X at hand. The 1972 amendments of the regulation are effective with respect to financial statements for periods ending on or after December 31, 1972 in registration statements and reports filed with the Commission.

The regulation does not specify whether balance sheets, income statements, surplus or other financial statements are to be furnished for the registrant, for the registrant and its subsidiaries consolidated, for unconsolidated subsidiaries, etc.; these requirements appear in the instructions applicable to the particular registration or report form involved. Similarly, the regulation does not specify the dates of financial statements or the periods they are to cover; these also appear in the instructions accompanying the applicable registration statement or report forms. To illustrate, Form S–1 (applicable to the registration of certain securities under the 1933 Act) contains the instructions as to what statements are to be filed, the dates of the balance sheets, and the periods to be covered by the income statements; but Regulation S–X governs the form and content of these balance sheets and income statements. Similarly, Form 10–K (one of the annual report forms under the 1934 Act) contains the instructions as to what financial statements are to be filed, the form and content of which are governed by Regulation S–X.

This chapter and following chapters give numerous citations of SEC decisions and reports that antedate the adoption of Regulation S–X. These citations are furnished as historical background of the regulation and to explain some of its requirements. The reader may observe inconsistencies between the dicta in some of the citations—particularly the older ones—and the requirements of Regulation S–X. Where these inconsistencies appear, it may be assumed that the regulation is controlling.

It should also be remembered that Regulation S–X does not include all the SEC's views on accounting principles; see, for example, the discussion in Chapters **3** and **4**.

Information Unknown or not Reasonably Available.—The requirements of Regulation S–X should be considered in the light of a general rule of the SEC under the Securities Act of 1933, which deals with the omission of information—including financial information—that is unknown or not reasonably available.

Rule 409. Information Unknown or not Reasonably Available.

Information required need be given only insofar as it is known or reasonably available to the registrant. If any required information is unknown and not reasonably available to the registrant, either because the obtaining thereof would involve unreasonable effort or expense, or because it rests peculiarly within the knowledge of another person not affiliated with the registrant, the information may be omitted, subject to the following conditions:

(a) The registrant shall give such information on the subject as it possesses or can acquire without unreasonable effort or expense, together with the sources thereof.

(b) The registrant shall include a statement either showing that unreasonable effort or expense would be involved or indicating the absence of any affiliation with the person within whose knowledge the information rests and stating the result of a request made to such person for the information.

Rule 12b–21 under the 1934 Act is similar to Rule 409 above.

Conflict Between Regulation S–X and Uniform Systems of Accounts

The accounts of public utility companies and the statements prepared from such accounts are closely regulated by state and federal authorities, such as the public utility commissions of the various states, the Federal Power Commission, the Federal Communications Commission, and other authorities. Many of these commissions have promulgated Uniform Systems of Accounts that specify in great detail the manner in which the company's accounts shall be maintained and the manner in which statements compiled from such accounts shall be prepared. In certain respects, the requirements in the Uniform Systems of Accounts conflict with those of the SEC as provided in its Regulation S–X. For example, some public utility commissions provide that utility companies subject to their jurisdiction shall file statements in which the reserve for depreciation is shown on the liability side of the balance sheet. Some uniform systems also require that earned surplus be charged or credited with a wide variety of items of profit and loss given recognition in the accounts during the period. Both of the aforementioned provisions are at variance with the requirements of Regulation S–X. The question naturally arises as to how financial statements of a regulated public utility company should be prepared if they are to be filed with SEC pursuant to the Securities Act of 1933 or any other statute administered by the SEC.

Presentation of Reserve for Depreciation.—The SEC requires that the reserve be deducted from the related fixed asset account despite contrary provisions in the Uniform Systems of Accounts of state or federal authorities having jurisdiction over the company. Regulated companies customarily report to their stockholders on the basis of the provisions of the applicable Uniform Systems of Accounts. Consequently, the total assets shown in a published report to stockholders of a regulated company differ from the amount of total assets shown in the financial statements filed with the SEC, the difference being measured by the amount of the reserve for depreciation, which in one filing is shown among the liabilities, whereas in the other it is deducted from fixed assets.

Treatment of Credit for Deferred Taxes.—Another important area of conflict between the requirements of Regulation S–X and those of state regulatory commissions occurs in relation to the presentation in balance sheets of the credit for deferred taxes that arises from the deduction of certain costs for tax purposes at rates faster than they are charged off for financial reporting purposes. The principal source of such difference is depreciation, with respect to which accelerated write-off methods are permitted under the Internal Revenue Code although straight-line depreciation may be reflected in the books and financial statements. This subject is discussed on page 3·10 in conjunction with the SEC's statement of administrative policy regarding the showing of the credit for deferred taxes in balance sheets filed with the Commission. Under ASR No. 85, the credit may not be included with earned surplus, nor may it be shown in any manner as part of equity capital.

This is a matter of some concern especially to companies in the public utility field, many of whom are either permitted or ordered to show the deferred credit in balance sheets filed with state regulatory commissions in a manner that is not acceptable to the SEC. This is not an academic question, because the manner of presentation has a direct effect on the computation of capitalization ratios.

On January 16, 1961, in proceedings involving Kentucky Power Company, the SEC agreed that a designation of the deferred tax credit account as "Accumulated amount invested in the business equivalent to reduction in Federal income taxes resulting from accelerated amortization and liberalized depreciation, which is recorded as earned surplus restricted for future Federal income taxes in accounts maintained pursuant to state regulatory requirements" would be an acceptable caption for SEC filing purposes. The SEC also indicated that while it would not regard the credit, when considering capitalization ratios, as being either debt or equity, it would—so long as the credit was substantial in amount—approve capital structures in which common stock equity was not less than 30% of total capitalization, mortgage debt was not in excess of 60% of capitalization, and total debt did not exceed 65%.

Although the decision involving Kentucky Power Company was under the Public Utility Holding Company Act (Kentucky being a subsidiary of American Electric Power Company, a holding company), the SEC, acting under the 1933 Act, has since that time permitted a registration statement of Atlantic City Electric Company to become effective in which a similar caption was used.

Familiarity with Regulation S–X

An accountant undertaking an examination of financial statements filed under the 1933 and 1934 Acts should have knowledge of the requirements of the Acts and of the rules and regulations thereunder. The accountant who participates in a registration engagement is charged not only with a knowledge of the Commission's formal requirements, but also with its pronouncements on accounting matters. In 1938 the Commission issued a statement of its administrative policy with respect to financial statements; the statement, known as ASR No. 4, appears on page **2·**6. Because of its importance, accountants should know that release.

Under the 1933 Act, the SEC is empowered to declare the registration statement effective at a date earlier than the usual 20 days after the date of filing. To issuers and underwriters desiring to have a registration statement become effective at the earliest possible date, it is important that the registration statement as originally filed be free from errors of omission or noncompliance. This is further reason why public accountants should be thoroughly familiar with the requirements of Regulation S–X and with the applicable form and instruction book, all of which are published in the loose-leaf services or may be obtained from the SEC. Because it is a basic tool with which he must work constantly, the accountant must be thoroughly familiar with Regulation S–X. In most respects the requirements of this regulation are not much different from those of good practice generally; the regulation, however, contains certain provisions—particularly in the area of footnote disclosure—that are not presently required by good accounting practice, and for this reason alone the accountant should have a thorough working knowledge of the regulation. There are differences, however, between the requirements of generally accepted accounting practice and those of the SEC that, although minor in nature, cannot be ignored. For example, capital stock subscriptions may be carried as an asset, but in an SEC filing they must be deducted in the capital section from capital stock subscribed for but not issued; see the comment on page **18·**17.

Content of Regulation S–X

Regulation S–X consists of a number of "articles." Each article, in turn, consists of a number of "rules." The articles are as follows:

1. Application of Regulation S–X
2. Qualifications and reports of accountants
3. Rules of general application
4. Consolidated and combined financial statements
5. Commercial and industrial companies other than those classified below

   5A. Commercial, industrial, and mining companies in the promotional, exploratory, or development stage

    6. Management investment companies

   6A. Unit investment trusts

   6B. Face-amount certificate investment companies

   6C. Employee stock purchase, savings, and similar plans

    7. Insurance companies other than life and title insurance companies

   7A. Life insurance companies

    8. Committees issuing certificates of deposit

    9. Bank holding companies and banks

  10. Natural persons

  11. Content of statements of other stockholders' equity

 11A. Statement of source and application of funds

  12. Form and content of schedules

It will be noted that Articles 5 through 10 are applicable to specific kinds of businesses or forms of organization. These distinctions recognize that what may be significant for one kind of business or organization may not be for another.

Important Definitions

Rule 1–02 of Regulation S–X contains the definitions of some of the terms used in the regulation. Because of their importance, they appear below.

Accountant's report.—The term "accountant's report," when used in regard to financial statements, means a document in which an independent public or certified public accountant indicates the scope of the audit (or examination) which he has made and sets forth his opinion regarding the financial statements taken as a whole, or an assertion to the effect that an overall opinion cannot be expressed. When an overall opinion cannot be expressed, the reasons therefor shall be stated.

Affiliate.—An "affiliate" of, or a person "affiliated" with, a specific person, is a person that directly, or indirectly through one or more intermediaries, controls, or is controlled by, or is under common control with, the person specified.

Amount.—The term "amount," when used in regard to securities, means the principal amount if relating to evidences of indebtedness, the number of shares if relating to shares, and the number of units if relating to any other kind of security.

Audit (or examination).—The term "audit" (or "examination"), when used in regard to financial statements, means an examination of the statements by an accountant in accordance with generally accepted auditing standards for the purpose of expressing an opinion thereon.

Bank holding company.—The term "bank holding company" means a person which is engaged, either directly or indirectly, primarily in the business of owning securities of one or more banks for the purpose, and with the effect, of exercising control.

Certified.—The term "certified," when used in regard to financial statements, means examined and reported upon with an opinion expressed by an independent public or certified public accountant.

Control.—The term "control" (including the terms "controlling," "controlled by" and "under common control with") means the possession, direct or indirect, of the power to direct or cause the direction of the management and policies of a person, whether through the ownership of voting shares, *by contract, or otherwise.* [Emphasis supplied.]

Equity security.—The term "equity security" means any stock or similar security; or any security convertible, with or without consideration, into such a security, or carrying any warrant or right to subscribe to or purchase such a security; or any such warrant or right.

Fifty-percent-owned person.—The term "50-percent-owned person," in relation to a specified person, means a person approximately 50 percent of whose outstanding voting shares is owned by the specified person, either directly, or indirectly through one or more intermediaries. [The definition would appear not to include a 50% interest in an unincorporated joint venture.]

Fiscal year.—The term "fiscal year" means the annual accounting period or, if no closing date has been adopted, the calendar year ending on December 31.

Insurance holding company.—The term "insurance holding company" means a person which is engaged, either directly or indirectly, primarily in the business of owning securities of one or more insurance companies for the purpose, and with the effect, of exercising control.

Majority-owned subsidiary.—The term "majority-owned subsidiary" means a subsidiary more than 50 percent of whose outstanding voting shares is owned by its parent and/or the parent's other majority-owned subsidiaries.

Material.—The term "material," when used to qualify a requirement for the furnishing of information as to any subject, limits the information required to those matters about which an average prudent investor ought reasonably to be informed.

Parent.—A "parent" of a specified person is an affiliate controlling such person directly, or indirectly through one or more intermediaries.

Person.—The term "person" means an individual, a corporation, a partnership, an association, a joint-stock company, a business trust, or an unincorporated organization.

Principal holder of equity securities.—The term "principal holder of equity securities," used in respect of a registrant or other person named in a particular statement or report, means a holder of record or a known beneficial owner of more than 10 percent of any class of equity securities of the registrant or other person, respectively, as of the date of the related balance sheet filed.

Promoter.—The term "promoter" includes—

(a) Any person who, acting alone or in conjunction with one or more other persons, directly or indirectly takes initiative in founding and organizing the business or enterprise of an issuer;

(b) Any person who, in connection with the founding and organizing of the business or enterprise of an issuer, directly or indirectly receives in consideration of services or property, or both services and property, 10 percent or more of any class of securities of the issuer or 10 percent or more of the proceeds from the sale of any class of securities. However, a person who receives such securities or proceeds either solely as underwriting commissions or solely in consideration of property shall not be deemed a promoter within the meaning of this paragraph if such person does not otherwise take part in founding and organizing the enterprise.

Registrant.—The term "registrant" means the issuer of the securities for which an application, a registration statement, or a report is filed.

Share.—The term "share" means a share of stock in a corporation or unit of interest in an unincorporated person.

Significant subsidiary.—The term "significant subsidiary" means (1) a subsidiary or (2) a subsidiary and its subsidiaries, which meets either of the conditions described below based on (i) the most recent annual financial statements, including consolidated financial statements, of such subsidiary which would be required to be filed if such subsidiary were a registrant and (ii) the most recent annual consolidated financial statements of the registrant being filed:

(a) The parent's and the parent's other subsidiaries' proportionate share of the total assets (after intercompany eliminations) of the subsidiary, or their investments in and advances to the subsidiary exceed 10 percent of the total assets of the parent and consolidated subsidiaries.

(b) The parent's and the parent's other subsidiaries' proportionate share of the total sales and revenues (after intercompany eliminations) of the subsidiary exceed 10 percent of the total sales and revenues of the parent and consolidated subsidiaries.

Subsidiary.—A "subsidiary" of a specified person is an affiliate controlled by such person directly, or indirectly through one or more intermediaries.

Totally-held subsidiary.—The term "totally-held subsidiary" means a subsidiary (1) substantially all of whose outstanding equity securities are owned by its parent and/or the parent's other totally-held subsidiaries, and (2) which is not indebted to any person other than its parent and/or the parent's other totally-held subsidiaries, in an amount which is material in relation to the particular subsidiary, excepting indebtedness incurred in the ordinary course of business which is not overdue and which matures within one year from the date of its creation, whether evidenced by securities or not. Indebtedness of a subsidiary which is secured by its parent by guarantee, pledge, assignment or otherwise is to be excluded for purposes of (2) above.

The definition of the term "totally-held subsidiary" is important since, as will be seen from the instructions as to financial statements in the SEC forms, it may be a factor in determining whether unconsolidated statements of a registrant may be omitted from a registration statement or report. As indicated in the definition, whether or not a subsidiary is totally held depends in part on the relationship of its publicly held debt to the subsidiary itself. This literal interpretation could lead to some ridiculous results.

Assume, for instance, a consolidated group of companies which includes a truly insignificant subsidiary. All of the subsidiary's stock is held within the affiliated group, but it has some mortgage debt held by outsiders. The debt is "material in relation to the particular subsidiary" and hence, under a literal reading of the definition, the subsidiary is not totally held. The debt held by outsiders, however, is trifling in relation to the consolidated group, and, under a rule of reason, should not—of itself—cause the submission of a complete set of unconsolidated financial statements of a registrant.

The staff of the SEC interpret the definition with reasoned judgment, and not literally. The author, for example, put the following circumstances before the staff for a decision as to whether the subsidiary involved in the question was a "totally held subsidiary." The published consolidated financial statements of a listed company showed the following:

Total assets	$100,000,000
Current assets	40,000,000
Current liabilities	17,000,000
Parent company long-term debt	20,000,000
Capital and surplus	60,000,000
Net income	9,000,000

The company had a consolidated subsidiary, the minority interest in which was $500,000 at the balance sheet date. The report to shareholders did not contain parent company (unconsolidated) statements, since neither the company nor its certifying accountants thought such statements to be either necessary or desirable. In the circumstances of this case the staff of the SEC agreed that holdings of outsiders were of insufficient consequence in relation to the consolidated picture to require the submission of parent company financial statements, and, accordingly, such statements were omitted from the report filed with the Commission. In the author's opinion, it should make no difference for this purpose whether the holdings of outsiders are represented by debt securities, preferred stock, or common stock. The significant matter is the relationship of the interests of third parties to the interests of the consolidated group.

The author also discussed another problem with the accounting staff of the SEC where the resolution of the problem depended on the interpretation of the term "totally-held subsidiary." The subsidiary in question had an issue of long-term debt outstanding amounting to $20 million, held by the public. The subsidiary's common stock (all held by the parent company) and retained earnings aggregated $80 million. The subsidiary was included in the consolidated financial statements of one of the world's largest manufacturing enterprises. Was the subsidiary "totally-held"? The SEC held that: net assets in the amount of $80 million certainly constituted a significant amount of capital junior to the publicly-held debt; therefore the publicly-held debt of $20 million was not "an amount which is material in relation to the particular subsidiary"; and therefore the subsidiary in question was a totally-held subsidiary.

Voting shares.—The term "voting shares" means the sum of all rights, other than as affected by events of default, entitled to vote for election of directors and/or the sum of all interests in an unincorporated person.

Wholly-owned subsidiary.—The term "wholly-owned subsidiary" means a subsidiary substantially all of whose outstanding voting shares are owned by its parent and/or the parent's other wholly-owned subsidiaries.

Applicability of Regulation S–X

Regulation S–X was adopted originally in 1940 and has been amended several times—most recently in 1972. At the time of its adoption, the regulation was applicable to a majority of the Commission's registration and report forms under the 1933 and 1934 Acts. At a later date the regulation was amended to make it applicable to filings under the 1935 and 1940 Acts. Prior to its adoption, the rules and instructions governing financial statements were scattered among the various SEC registration and report forms. The regulation is (together with the Accounting Series Releases) presently applicable to the form and content of all financial statements and supporting schedules required to be filed as part of:

(1) Registration statements under the Securities Act of 1933, except as otherwise specifically provided in the forms which are to be used for registration under this Act;

(2) Registration statements under Section 12, annual or other reports under Sections 13 and 15(d) and proxy and information statements under Section 14 of the Securities Exchange Act of 1934, except as otherwise specifically provided in the forms which are to be used for registration and reporting under these sections of this Act;

(3) Registration statements and annual reports filed under the Public Utility Holding Company Act of 1935 by public utility holding companies registered under such Act; and

(4) Registration statements and annual reports under the Investment Company Act of 1940.

The term "financial statements" as used in the Regulation is deemed to include all notes to the statements and all related schedules.

Article 2. Certification

Article 2 of Regulation S–X contains the requirements applicable to accountants' certificates and qualifications of certifying accountants. Chapters **24** and **25** of this volume deal with certification by independent public accountants; Chapter **26** deals with independence of certifying accountants.

Article 3. Rules of General Application

Article 3 contains the rules of general application which are listed below to show their scope:

3–01 Form, order, and terminology; rounding of money amounts; negative amounts

3–02 Items not material

3–03 Omission of inapplicable captions; omission of unrequired or inapplicable statements and schedules and listing of such schedules

3–04 Omission of substantially identical notes

3–05 Omission of names of certain subsidiaries

3–06 Additional information

3–07 Changes in accounting principles and practices and retroactive adjustments of accounts

3–08 Summary of accounting principles and practices

3–09 Valuation and qualifying accounts

3–10 Basis of determining amounts—"book value"

3–11 Current assets

3–12 Current liabilities

3–13 Reacquired evidences of indebtedness

3–14 Reacquired shares

3–15 Discount on capital shares

3–16 General notes to financial statements

    (a) Principles of consolidation or combination

    (b) Principles of translation of items in foreign currencies

    (c) Assets subject to lien

    (d) Intercompany profits and losses

    (e) Defaults

    (f) Preferred shares

    (g) Pension and retirement plans

    (h) Restrictions which limit the availability of retained earnings for dividend purposes

    (i) Commitments and contingent liabilities

    (j) Bonus, profit sharing, or other similar plans

    (k) Significant changes in bonds, mortgages, and similar debt

    (l) Bases of revenue recognition

    (m) Depreciation, depletion, obsolescence, and amortization

    (n) Capital stock optioned, sold or offered for sale to officers, directors, and key employees

    (o) Components of income tax expense

    (p) Warrants or rights outstanding

Form, Order, and Terminology (Rule 3–01).—Financial statements may be filed in such form and order, and may use such generally accepted terminology, as will best indicate their significance and character in the light of the provisions applicable to such statements. This provision of Regulation S–X permits some latitude in the form of financial statements filed with SEC. For a long time SEC did not accept the "single step" form of income statement and insisted on fairly close observance of the form and captions prescribed in Rule 5–03 (see page **18·22**). In recent years, however, the SEC changed its policy and now accepts the single step form of statement so long as it furnishes the essential information specified in Rule 5–03.

Similarly, the SEC for a period did not accept "statements of financial position" or "statements of investment" in lieu of its requirements for balance sheets as set forth in Regulation S–X. (Statements of financial position or investment are those that begin with current assets, deduct current liabilities, add other assets, deduct other liabilities, to arrive at stockholders' investment.) Particularly where substantial amounts of long-term debt were involved, the staff of the SEC, for a time, insisted on balance sheets meeting the requirements of its regulation. In recent years, however, relying on Rule 3–01, the SEC has accepted statements of financial position and statements of investment in fulfillment of the requirements for balance sheets provided all the other information specified in its regulation is furnished.

All money amounts required to be shown in financial statements may be expressed in whole dollars, in thousands of dollars or in hundred thousands of dollars, as appropriate; provided that, when stated in other than whole dollars, an indication to that effect is inserted immediately beneath the caption of the statement or schedule, or at the top of the money columns, or at an appropriate point in narrative material. The individual amounts shown need not be adjusted to the nearest dollar, or thousand or hundred thousands if in a note it is stated that the failure of the items to add to the totals shown is due to the dropping of amounts less than $1.00, $1,000 or $100,000, as appropriate.

Negative amounts—that is, red figures—have to be shown in brackets or parentheses and so described in the related caption, columnar heading, or a note to the statement or schedule, as appropriate.

As will be seen in Rule 5–02 of Regulation S–X, commercial and industrial companies are ordinarily expected to show the amounts of total current assets and current liabilities in their balance sheets filed with the SEC. Company X, which was in the business of owning and operating bowling centers, had been reporting to its security holders and the SEC for many years on the usual basis showing total current assets and total current liabilities. In 1968, however, the company reconsidered the matter and, with the concurrence of its independent public accountants, decided that it was inappropriate to show current assets and current liabilities in view of the circumstances peculiar to companies in that industry. Accordingly, the current assets and current liability classification were omitted from its published balance sheets and from the 10–K balance sheets.

As expected, the company received a letter from the SEC requesting that the 10–K report be amended to show current asset and current liability totals as required by Regulation S–X. The company wrote to the SEC as follows:

> The company decided, with the concurrence of its independent public accountants, to revise the format of the September 30, 1968 balance sheet included in the Annual Report to Stockholders and in the Annual Report (Form 10–K) to the Commission because it considered that the revised format more clearly presents the company's financial position in the circumstances under which it operates. In prior years the company's balance sheets were prepared in the usual format presenting current assets and current liabilities, and in every year current liabilities on this basis were considerably in excess of current assets. We do not believe that this represented a realistic picture of the company's position, since the major portion of the liabilities due within one year comprise payments on equipment obligations which will be met from operating revenues in the ensuing year rather than from resources existing at the balance sheet date.
>
> Paragraph 7 of Chapter 3 of Accounting Research Bulletin No. 43, issued by the American Institute of Certified Public Accountants, states that "the term current liabilities is used principally to designate obligations whose liquidation is reasonably expected to require the use of existing resources properly classifiable as current assets." We do not believe that current maturities of equipment obligations fall within this definition, and we therefore elected to adopt the format used in our September 30, 1968 balance sheet as being more appropriate to our circumstances. We have, of course, indicated parenthetically the amount of long-term debt expected to be payable within one year, as well as the related deferred interest expense to be amortized currently. It is, therefore, possible for the reader to determine the company's current position if such a determination is considered to be useful or desirable.
>
> Rule 3.01(a) of Regulation S–X states that financial statements may be filed in such form and order, and may use such generally accepted terminology, as will best indicate their significance and character in the light of the provisions applicable thereto. It is our opinion, in which our independent public accountants concur, that the format of the September 30, 1968 balance sheet best complies with this rule.
>
> For the reasons outlined above, we believe that the financial statements in our September 30, 1968 Annual Report (Form 10–K) were appropriate as filed.

On reconsideration apparently the SEC's accounting staff decided to withdraw the deficiency letter, because the company had no further communication from the Commission on this subject.

Items Not Material (Rule 3–02).—If the amount that would otherwise be required to be shown with respect to any item is not material, it need not be separately set forth. Thus, for example, although the rules relating to the balance sheet call for a separate showing of investments in securities of affiliates, if, in a particular case, a company's investments in affiliates are trifling, they need not be shown as a separate item. The Commission has stated, however, that the significance of an item may be independent of the amount involved.

For example, amounts due to and from officers and directors, because of their special nature and origin, ought generally to be set forth separately even though the dollar amounts involved are relatively small. Likewise, disclosure of the various types of surplus, the important reserve accounts, and, under present conditions, the accrued liability for taxes is of importance. In the same way, in the corporate income statement of a company having large investments in subsidiaries or in the securities of unaffiliated companies, the disclosure of income from dividends and interest is necessary irrespective of the amount, since the absence or smallness of dividend and interest income is of as great importance as the exact amount thereof. (ASR No. 41).

The Commission has gone even further. In *Poulin Mining Co., Ltd.*, [8 SEC 116 (1940)], the balance sheet listed a liability to a creditor of the company. The SEC said the statement was deficient for not disclosing that the company's president and chief promoter controlled the creditor-corporation.

The SEC's position with respect to immaterial items is similar to that taken by the AICPA Committee on Accounting Procedure. In its first accounting research bulletin the Committee said: "The committee contemplates that its pronouncements will have application only to items large enough to be material and significant in the relative circumstances. It considers that items of little or no consequence may be dealt with as expediency may suggest."

Inapplicable Captions (Rule 3–03).—Some accountants approach financial statements for filing with SEC much as they do the preparation of a tax return. They turn to Rule 5–02, which indicates the captions in a balance sheet of an ordinary commercial or industrial company, and attempt to fill in amounts for each caption. As stated above, if the amount for a stated caption is not material, the item need not be separately shown. No caption need be shown in any financial statement as to which the items and conditions are not present.

Omission of Unrequired or Inapplicable Financial Statements (Rule 3–03).—Financial statements not required or inapplicable because the required matter is not present need not be filed. Financial statements omitted and the reasons for their omission shall be indicated in the list of financial statements required by the applicable form. In Form S–1 the list of financial statements appears in Item 31; in Form 10–K the corresponding list is in Item 10. In respect of a 10–K filing, see the suggested form of response on pages **24**·16-1⁄. With suitable modification, this suggested response may be used in filings on other forms.

Omission of Substantially Identical Notes (Rule 3–04).—If a note covering substantially the same subject matter is required with respect to two or more financial statements relating to the same or affiliated companies, for which separate sets of notes are presented, the required information may be shown in a note to only one of such statements, provided that a clear and specific reference thereto is made in each of the other statements with respect to which the note is required. In the interest of brevity, accountants should make every effort to avoid needless repetition. This applies not only to material within the financial statements, but also to information in the balance of the document of which the financial statements are only a part. One of the general instructions of Form S–1 provides:

Unless clearly indicated otherwise, information set forth in any part of the prospectus need not be duplicated elsewhere in the prospectus. Where it is deemed necessary or desirable to call attention to such information in more than one part of the prospectus, this may be accomplished by appropriate cross reference. *In lieu of restating information in the form of notes to the financial statements, references should be made to other parts of the prospectus where such information is set forth.* [Emphasis supplied.]

Omission of Names of Certain Subsidiaries (Rule 3–05).—Notwithstanding the requirements as to particular statements, subsidiaries the names of which are permitted to be omitted from the list of affiliates required by the applicable form, need not be named in any financial statement. Reasonable grouping of such subsidiaries may be made, with an explanatory group caption that shall state the number of subsidiaries included in the group.

In Form S–1 the list of subsidiaries appears in Item 27. In Form 10–K the corresponding list is in Item 4.

Additional Information (Rule 3–06).—The information required with respect to any statement must be furnished as a minimum requirement, to which shall be added such further material information as is necessary to make the required statements, in the light of the circumstances under which they are made, not misleading. This rule is applicable to all statements required to be filed, including copies of statements required to be filed in the first instance with other governmental agencies.

Changes in Accounting Principles and Practices and Retroactive Adjustments of Accounts (Rule 3–07).—Any change in an accounting principle or practice, or in the method of applying any accounting principle or practice, made during any period for which financial statements are being filed which materially affects comparability of such financial statements with those of prior periods, and the effect thereof upon the net income of the period in which such change is made, shall be disclosed in an appropriate manner. If practicable, the effect of the change upon the net income of the prior periods for which financial statements are being filed shall also be disclosed.

Any material retroactive adjustment made in income statements during any period for which financial statements are being filed, and the effect thereof upon net income of prior periods must be disclosed in a note to the appropriate financial statements. Such disclosures need not be made, however, (1) if they have been made in filings with the Commission in prior years, or (2) the financial statements which are being retroactively adjusted have not previously been filed with the Commission or otherwise made public.

Just prior to a public offering of securities a company changed its method of handling development costs so that the income figures for the latest period showed, because of the change in method, a sharp increase in earnings over prior periods. The SEC said that the failure to disclose fully, by footnote to the income statement, the change in the method of handling the account rendered the statement misleading. *Metropolitan Personal Loan Corp.,* 7 SEC 234 (1940).

Summary of Accounting Principles and Practices (Rule 3–08).— Information required in notes as to accounting principles and practices reflected in the financial statements may be presented in the form of a single statement, that is, in one note. In such case specific references shall be made in the appropriate financial statements to the applicable portion of such single statement.

In this connection it may be appropriate to consider the views expressed by the APB in its Opinion No. 22 (April 1972) on "Disclosure of Accounting Policies." The Board stated that a description of all significant accounting policies of a reporting entity should be included as an integral part of financial statements which purport to present fairly financial position, changes in financial position, and results of operations. The disclosure is particularly useful, in the Board's view, if given in a separate *Summary of Significant Accounting Policies* preceding the notes to the financial statements or as the initial note, and expressed a preference for that format under the same or a similar title.

Valuation and Qualifying Accounts (Rule 3–09).—Valuation and qualifying accounts must be shown separately in the financial statements as deductions from the specific assets to which they apply. (A similar requirement is set forth in APB Opinion No. 12, paragraph 3.)

For many years the regulatory commissions of many states required, in their Uniform Systems of Accounts, that depreciation reserves be shown on the liability side of balance sheets filed with the commissions. The Federal Power Commission, on the other hand, requires that the reserve be shown as a deduction on the asset side of the balance sheet, and most of the state commissions have changed their requirements in this respect to conform with those of the FPC. A few state commissions, however, still require the reserve to be included among the liabilities. A public utility company subject to the reporting requirements of one of the latter commissions (and not subject to FPC jurisdiction) would nonetheless have to conform with Rule 3–09 of Regulation S–X in filing with the SEC. In that event the company might want to explain the difference in presentation of its depreciation reserve in a note to the financial statements in its filing with the SEC. Following is a suggested form of such a note:

In order to conform to the regulations of the Securities and Exchange Commission, concerning the form of financial statements, the reserve for depreciation is shown in the accompanying balance sheet as a deduction from the recorded amount of utility plant. The Company considers that the practice of reflecting such reserve for depreciation on the liability side of the balance sheet under "Reserves" is proper and is in accord with the systems of accounts prescribed for utilities in the State of————.

Basis of Determining Amounts—Book Values (Rule 3–10).—If an instruction requires a statement as to "the basis of determining the amount," the basis must be stated specifically, that is, cost, market, lower of cost or market, and so on. The term "book value" will not be sufficiently explanatory unless, in a particular instruction, it is stated to be acceptable with respect to a particular item.

Current Assets (Rule 3–11).—Assets and other resources classed with cash and its equivalent as current assets shall be reasonably expected to be realized in cash or sold or consumed within one year. However, if the normal operating cycle of the company is longer than one year, generally recognized trade practices may be followed with respect to the inclusion of items such as instalment receivables or inventories long in process, provided an appropriate explanation of the circumstances is made and, if practicable, an estimate is given of the amount not realizable within one year. The captions specified under Rules 3–11 and 3–12 are not required for companies which do not normally distinguish current assets and liabilities from noncurrent.

A cigarette company filing with the SEC made this statement with respect to its inventory of leaf tobacco:

It is a generally recognized trade practice to classify the total amount of leaf tobacco inventory as a current asset although part of such inventory, because of the duration of the aging process, ordinarily would not be realized within one year. It is impracticable to estimate the amount of leaf inventories not realizable within one year.

A company that sells machinery to customers and receives their instalment notes made this disclosure concerning its receivables:

Following generally recognized trade practice, instalment notes receivable maturing more than one year from date of the balance sheet are included in current assets. It is not practicable, without unreasonable effort and expense, to estimate the amount of such notes not realizable within one year.

In similar circumstances, another company said:

In accordance with the general practice of the sales finance business, all retail notes receivable (paper) are shown as current assets regardless of maturity. At (date) retail notes included $ maturing after (one year from date of balance sheet), of which $ will mature after (two years from date of balance sheet).

See the discussion on page **16·12** with respect to a company in the bowling alley business that omitted the current asset and current liability classifications from its balance sheets. The SEC objected to this omission, but, on reconsideration, withdrew its objection.

Current Liabilities (Rule 3–12).—Obligations which are payable within one year or whose liquidation is reasonably expected to require the use of existing current assets (see Rule 3–11) or the creation of other current liabilities shall be classed as current liabilities. However, if the normal operating cycle of the company is longer than one year, generally recognized trade practices may be followed with respect to the exclusion of items such as customers' deposits and deferred income, provided an appropriate explanation of the circumstances is made.

See the discussion on page **16·12** with respect to a company in the bowling alley business that omitted the current asset and current liability classifications from its balance sheets. The SEC objected to this omission, but, on reconsideration, withdrew its objection.

The reader is also referred to the discussion beginning on page **3·10** regarding ASR No. 102 dealing with the balance sheet classification of deferred taxes where the related asset (such as instalment receivables) is classified as a current asset.

Reacquired Evidences of Indebtedness (Rule 3–13).—Reacquired evidences of indebtedness (such as bonds, debentures, and the like) shall be deducted from the appropriate liability caption. However, reacquired evidences of indebtedness held for pension and other special funds not related to the particular issues may be shown as assets of such funds, provided that there be stated parenthetically the amount of such evidences of indebtedness, the cost thereof, and the amount at which stated.

Reacquired Shares (Rule 3–14).—Reacquired (treasury) shares not· retired have to be shown separately as a deduction from capital shares, or from the total of capital shares and other stockholders' equity, at either par or stated value, or cost, as circumstances require.

These instructions imply that treasury stock may not be shown as an asset. This is generally—but not always—true. An exception to the general rule may occur when a corporation reacquires some of its outstanding stock for prompt distribution to officers or employees pursuant to a bonus or stock purchase plan. In the case of a registration statement filed by one of the largest American corporations its balance sheet included among the assets the following:

> Common stock in treasury:
> Held for bonus purposes (shares) $

A note to the financial statements described briefly the provisions of the corporation's bonus plan, and stated:

> Common stock held in treasury for bonus purposes at (date) includes (number) shares carried at $ representing undelivered instalments of bonus awards for (years) held for future delivery under the earning out provisions of the Bonus Plan.

Discount on Capital Shares (Rule 3–15).—Discount on capital shares, or any unamortized balance thereof, is to be shown separately as a deduction from capital shares or from other stockholders' equity, as circumstances require. Commissions and expenses on capital shares, however, may be carried as an asset. If such commissions and expenses are carried as an asset and are material in amount, they should be shown as a separate item in the balance sheet together with a disclosure of the method of amortization, if any.

General Notes to Financial Statements (Rule 3–16).—Rule 3–16 specifies the information that is required to be set forth on the face of the appropriate financial statement (if it is relevant in relation to the company for which the statement is filed) or in notes appropriately captioned and referred to in the statement. The information has to be provided for each statement that is required to be filed, except that the information required by the following items has to be provided as of the most recent audited balance sheet and any subsequent unaudited balance sheet being filed: (c) (assets subject to lien), (e) (defaults), (f) (preferred shares), (g)(3) (excess of vested pension benefits), (h) (dividend restrictions), (i) (commitments and contingent liabilities), (k) (changes in funded debt), and (p) (information as to warrants or rights). When specific statements are presented separately, the pertinent notes must be attached unless cross-referencing is appropriate. The rule is divided into sixteen subdivisions— (a) through (p)—which are considered separately below.

PRINCIPLES OF CONSOLIDATION OR COMBINATION (RULE 3–16(a)).— With regard to consolidated or combined financial statements refer to Article 4 for the requirements for supplemental information in notes to the financial statements. This subject is discussed in Chapter **17**.

PRINCIPLES OF TRANSLATION OF ITEMS IN FOREIGN CURRENCIES (RULE 3–16(b)).—When items in foreign currencies are included in the financial statements being presented, a brief description has to be furnished of the principles followed in translating the foreign currencies into United States currency and the amount and disposition of the unrealized gain or loss.

When separate financial statements are furnished by a foreign company that is itself the registrant, they shall be stated in its local currency; and, when deemed appropriate, translation into United States currency shall be shown on a supplemental basis. If financial statements are shown separately for a foreign company that is a subsidiary not consolidated, a 50 percent owned company, or a company acquired or to be acquired, the financial statements of the foreign company may be in United States currency only.

The following are examples showing compliance with Rule 3–16(b):

Example 1

Translation of foreign currencies. The consolidated financial statements include the following United States dollar amounts in respect of the four consolidated foreign subsidiaries; net current assets and deferred charges, $; net plant assets, $; long-term notes payable to bank, $; and net income, $

Foreign currency amounts have been translated into United States dollars on the following bases:

(a) Current assets and liabilities, and deferred charges—at $ to the £ sterling and at $ to the Canadian dollar.
(b) Fixed assets—generally at rates in effect at dates of acquisition.
(c) Income and expense items—at $ to the £ sterling and $ to the Canadian dollar, except for depreciation, which has been translated on the basis at which the fixed assets are carried. A foreign exchange difference of $ has been charged to income.

Example 2

Translation of foreign currency items. In the translation of foreign currency items, the general policy followed is that current assets and other assets (except real estate, plants, and equipment and accumulated depreciation and obsolecence), prepaid expenses and deferred charges, current liabilities, other liabilities, and reserves are translated at the official rates of exchange prevailing at the end of the period except where there is a wide spread between this rate and the free or curb rate of exchange. When the free or curb rate is significantly lower than the official rate of exchange and if the investment is substantial, the free or curb rate of exchange is used. In stating Canadian accounts in United States dollars at (date) and (date), Canadian funds have been translated at par. Real estate, plants, and equipment and accumulated depreciation and obsolescence are translated on the basis of the rate in effect at the time of acquisition. Cumulative unrealized profits arising from translation of foreign currency accounts into United States dollar equivalents are credited to reserves. In the event that changes in foreign exchange rates result in a reduction in the value, as measured in dollars, of the net working capital of any foreign subsidiary or branch, the reduction becomes a charge against consolidated net income to the extent that it exceeds available reserves. These translations have resulted in net credits or (charges) to income as follows: 19   (nine months)—$; 19 —$; 19 —$; 19 —$; 19 —$; 19 —$

ASSETS SUBJECT TO LIEN (RULE 3–16(c)).—The amounts of assets mortgaged, pledged, or otherwise subject to lien, and the approximate amounts thereof, shall be designated, and the obligations collateralized briefly identified.

A company failed to indicate in its balance sheet that certain of its investments stated therein were held in escrow and were pledged for the benefit of a special class of its existing security holders. The SEC said the balance sheet was misleading since the investments were represented as general assets of the company. *Bankers Union Life Co.,* 2 SEC 63 (1936).

Omission of facts concerning a subsidiary of the registrant's predecessor, which, in its early history, issued bonds constituting a first lien on mining equipment included among registrant's assets, some of which bonds were still outstanding, has been held to be a material omission. *Livingston Mining Co.,* 2 SEC 141 (1937).

Failure to disclose that 80 per cent of the assets of a business to be acquired were pledged to secure an indebtedness was held by the SEC to be a material omission. *Mutual Industrial Bankers, Inc.,* 1 SEC 271 (1936).

This is how one company disclosed the amount of its assets pledged against its notes payable:

> Note to financial statements:
> *Assets pledged as collateral.* U.S. Government securities costing $ ($ at market quotations) and $ of receivables due from customers are pledged as collateral against the Company's notes payable to banks in the amount of $

A company disclosed the pledge of a portion of its inventory thus:

> Note to financial statements:
> *Inventory pledged under bankers' acceptances.* In connection with

its liability under bankers' acceptances, the Company received coffee in trust [$ at (date)] under agreement to hold the coffee or proceeds thereof as the property of the bank which issued the acceptances.

INTERCOMPANY PROFITS AND LOSSES (RULE 3–16(d)).—When there have been profits or losses resulting from transactions with affiliated companies that have not been eliminated, there must be a disclosure of the amounts of such profits or losses and the effect thereof upon any balance sheet items. If the amounts are impracticable of accurate determination, without unreasonable effort or expense, an estimate or an explanation must be given.

Whether subsidiaries are included or not included in the consolidated statements, if intercompany profits and losses *are* eliminated, a notation is *not* required.

In one case filed with the SEC consolidated balance sheets were held to be deficient for failure to disclose that fixed capital included substantial intercompany profits arising from engineering fees paid to subsidiaries. *Associated Gas and Electric Co.*, 11 SEC 975 (1942).

American Telephone and Telegraph Company owns all of the stock of Western Electric Company, Incorporated. The principal business of Western is manufacturing communications equipment and apparatus and cable for the Bell System telephone companies, procuring and selling to such companies supplies not of its own manufacture, and installing central office equipment for such companies. The consolidated financial statements of AT&T consolidate the accounts of the company and those of the principal operating telephone companies in which AT&T owns securities representing more than 50% of the voting power, but not the accounts of Western.

In a prospectus of AT&T dated June 1971, the company stated that most of the telephone equipment, apparatus, and material used by the companies consolidated was manufactured or procured for them by Western, a subsidiary not consolidated. These items are entered in the accounts of the telephone companies at cost to them, and are included in the consolidated financial statements at such cost. This cost includes the return realized by Western on its investment devoted to this business. A note keyed to the telephone plant account in the balance sheet stated in part:

Practically all of the material purchased for the construction and maintenance of telephone plant, other than buildings, has been obtained from Western Electric. . . . It is impossible to identify the particular purchases from Western Electric over a long period of years which were charged to the plant accounts and now remain therein, but the Company considers that such purchases made by it represent about 65% of its plant investment and that such purchases made by the companies consolidated represent about 55% of the consolidated plant investment. Western Electric advises that its rate of profit (before interest charges) has varied by years and by classes of sales but that such profit attributable to all sales of material and services to affiliated telephone companies (including items chargeable to other than plant accounts) has been approximately 5% of such sales over the twenty-five year period ended December 31, 1970 and approximately 5¼% of such sales over the five year period then ended. Western Electric considers that its profit ratio on those items which have been charged to the plant accounts is somewhat higher than its profit ratio on total sales to such companies.

DEFAULTS (RULE 3–16(e)).—Disclosure must be made of the facts and amounts concerning any default in principal, interest, sinking fund, or redemption provisions with respect to any issue of securities or credit agreements, or any breach of covenant of a related indenture or agreement, which default or breach existed at the date of the most recent balance sheet being filed and which has not been subsequently cured.

Notation of such default or breach of covenant has to be made in the financial statements, and the entire amount of obligations to which the default or breach relates must be classified as a current liability if the default or breach accelerates the maturity of the obligations and makes it current under the terms of the related indenture or agreement. Classification as a current obligation is not required if the lender has waived the accelerated due date or otherwise agreed to a due date more than one year from the balance sheet date. If a default or breach exists but acceleration of the obligation has been waived for a stated period of time beyond the date of the most recent balance sheet being filed, the amount of the obligation and the period of the waiver must be stated.

Where property was set up as an asset, with disclosure that it secured a debt but without disclosure that default on the debt had taken place, the SEC ruled that it was misleading despite the fact that creditors, at the Commission's hearing, assert that they have no intention of foreclosing at present or at all if the company can float sufficient securities to repay the loan. *Mining and Development Corp.,* 1 SEC 786 (1936).

Material defaults in the interest payments occurring before the date of the accountant's certificate must be disclosed in the balance sheet or by way of a note thereto. *Oklahoma Hotel Building Co.,* 4 SEC 580 (1939).

Failure to make the required deposits under a sinking fund arrangement must be disclosed. *Oklahoma Hotel Building Co.,* 4 SEC 580 (1939).

PREFERRED SHARES (RULE 3–16(f)).—If callable, the date or dates and the amounts per share at which preferred shares are callable shall be stated. This provision differs slightly from the requirements of APB Opinion No. 10 (1966) which provides that disclosure shall be made of the aggregate or per share amounts at which preferred shares may be called or are subject to redemption through sinking fund operations or otherwise.

Following is an example showing compliance with the requirements of both the SEC rule and the APB Opinion:

The Corporation each year must redeem (number) shares of its preferred stock at not more than $ a share and, at its option, may redeem its preferred stock at $ a share until (date), when the redemption price will be $ a share.

If the preferred stock is convertible, the conversion terms have to be stated briefly.

Arrears in cumulative dividends per share and in total for each class of shares shall also be stated.

Aggregate preferences on involuntary liquidation, if other than the par or stated value, *shall be shown parenthetically in the equity section of the balance sheet.* When the excess involved is material, there shall be shown (1) the difference between the aggregate preference on involuntary liquidation and the aggregate par or stated value; (2) a statement that this difference, plus any arrears in dividends, exceeds the sum of the par or stated value of the junior capital shares and other stockholders' equity applicable to junior shares, if such is the case; and (3) a statement as to the existence of any restrictions upon retained earnings growing out of the fact that upon involuntary liquidation the preference of the preferred shares exceeds its par or stated value.

This is how this disclosure was made in two cases—one involving a restriction, the other, no restriction.

Example 1. Where the preference on involuntary
liquidation may result in a restriction on surplus.

Convertible preferred shares. The convertible preferred shares, par value $25 each, are entitled in involuntary liquidation to $50 per share ($1,386,000 for all such shares outstanding) plus accrued dividends in arrears as stated in Note 2, or an aggregate preference of $2,631,149. This aggregate preference is $1,938,-149 more than the par value of such shares, and the latter amount is $266,806 more than the total of the common stocks and retained earnings before giving consideration to the unrealized net appreciation ($1,356,425) of securities owned at June 30, 19——, based on market quotations.

Under the Certificate of Incorporation, no dividend may be declared on the common stock of the Company if, after the payment of such dividend and after deducting the sum of the par value of the first preferred stock, if any, then outstanding, and an amount equivalent to $50 per share of convertible preferred stock then outstanding, the net assets of the Company, based on market values as of the date of such declaration, are less than $10 per share of common stock.

Example 2. Where the preference on involuntary
liquidation does not result in a restriction on retained earnings.

Class A Stock. Upon involuntary liquidation, holders of Class A stock (par value $2.50 per share) shall be entitled to receive an amount equal to $15 per share, together with all unpaid cumulative dividends. The aggregate of the preference in excess of par value upon involuntary liquidation to which holders of Class A stock, excluding shares in treasury, are entitled is $5,752,550. In the opinion of the corporation's counsel, the existence of this excess imposes no restriction upon retained earnings.

PENSION AND RETIREMENT PLANS (RULE 3–16(g)).—A brief description of the essential provisions of any employee pension or retirement plan and of the accounting and funding policies related thereto has to be furnished.

The estimated cost of the plan for each period for which an income statement is presented has to be given.

If a plan has not been fully funded or otherwise provided for, the estimated amount that would be necessary to fund or otherwise provide for the past service cost of the plan needs to be disclosed as of the date most recently determined. (This disclosure represents an important difference between the requirements of the SEC and those of the APB as indicated in its Opinion No. 8 (1966) which dealt with the accounting for the cost of pension plans. The APB apparently believed that this information with respect to unfunded past service cost was not essential to a showing of financial position or results of operations, but the SEC has made it clear that the information has to be included in financial statements filed with it.)

The excess, if any, of the actuarially computed value of vested benefits over the total of the pension fund and any balance sheet pension accruals, less any pension prepayments or deferred charges, has to be given as of the most recent practicable date.

Also to be given is a statement of the nature and effect of significant matters affecting comparability of pension costs for any periods for which income statements are presented.

An important point to bear in mind is whether a company may account for its pension plan on a "pay as you go" basis, or whether there is an inescapable liability. For example, a registration statement was filed by a gas company that had guaranteed annuities for life to certain former employees who had retired and to others who were eligible to retire. Annual payments to those retired were charged to income only when made. However, the company did not carry any liability in its balance sheet for the estimated amount of the cost of future payments of annuities for past services in the financial statements originally filed in connection with its public offering of securities. Following discussions held between the Commission's staff, representatives of the issuer and the certifying accountants, an actuarial study was made to ascertain the estimated liability representing the cost of these annuities. This cost was found to approximate $1,500,000 and was consequently so recorded on the balance sheet as a liability, with a corresponding reduction of earned surplus. [15 SEC Ann. Rep. 20 (1949).]

In another instance reported by the SEC, involving liability under pension plans, a registrant had adopted a five-year plan to become effective on a date within an interim period for which financial statements were furnished. The statements included a charge to income for the interim period proportionate to the total estimated cost for the five-year period with an equivalent amount reflected in the balance sheet as a liability. The SEC's examination of the plan indicated that in the first year a much larger number of employees would be eligible under the plan than in the succeeding years because of the fact that all employees over the required age and term of service for eligibility could claim their pension rights immediately, although not all of them were expected to do so. When this feature was called to the attention of the registrant, the financial statements were amended to increase the liability shown in the balance sheet under the pension plan from the previous estimate of approximately $500,000 to $2,000,000, of which $400,000 was classified as current. The previously determined accrual was charged to income and the remaining $1,500,000 was set up as a deferred charge to be allocated against future operations. A comprehensive footnote described the pension plan and indicated that the liability included in the balance sheet was based upon the best indication at the date of filing of the intention of eligible employees to retire within the terms of the plan. [16 SEC Ann. Rep. 16 (1950).]

Ordinarily a company's pension or retirement plan is set forth in the prospectus. The "brief description" of the plan required by Regulation S–X can usually be complied with, in the case of 1933 Act registrations, by a cross-reference in the notes to the financial statements to the appropriate section of the prospectus, provided this section contains the information required by Rule 3–16(g). Such cross-reference cannot be made in most annual reports filed with the SEC, in which event the required note may be patterned on the following examples:

Example 1. A retail company

Employees' retirement plan.—Effective February 28, 19——, with subsequent revisions, the Company and its domestic subsidiaries adopted (subject to the right reserved therein to discontinue at any time) an employees' retirement plan to which the employees and the companies contribute. All contributions are committed in trust to an independent trustee to be held for the exclusive benefit of employees who qualify as members or retired members under the plan. In general, employees are to be retired at age 65. The present annual gross cost of the plan to the companies as revised effective March 1, 19——, is estimated at $294,-700 (subject to actual determination upon completion of the actuary's review of the plan each fiscal year), of which $55,700 represents cost of prior service benefits which is borne entirely by the companies. It is the companies' intention to pay the unpaid prior service benefit cost (estimated at $557,000 plus interest) over a period of 10 years.

Example 2. An industrial company

Retirement plan.—The company's retirement plan (noncontributory) covers all full-time and seasonal employees. The plan presently provides that after ten years of service, employees may retire at the age of 65, or under certain circumstances, at a reduced retirement allowance at the age of 55. Retirement allowances for service prior to January 1, 19———, are computed on the employee's rate of annual compensation at January 1, 19———, in an amount equal to ¾ths of 1 per cent of the first $3,000, plus 1½ per cent of the balance, multiplied by the number of years of service to January 1, 19———. Retirement allowances for service after January 1, 19———, are computed in an amount equal to 1 per cent of the first $3,600, plus 1½ per cent of the balance, of each year's annual compensation, including bonus, except that the amount of bonus for this purpose shall not exceed $25,000. The plan is subject to discontinuance at any time.

Prior service benefits as established under the plan as of April 1, 19———, were completely funded at March 31, 19———. As a result of amendments to the plan, approved by stockholders in July, 19———, additional unpaid prior service benefit costs of $ were created as of April 1, 19———. It is the present intention of management to fund such costs, together with interest, over a ten-year period, although it is not required to do so.

During the seven months ended October 31, 19———, the company's contributions to the plan were $ for current services and $ for prior services.

Example 3. An industrial company with two plans, one for salaried employees and one for hourly employees

Pension plans.—The Company has two noncontributory pension plans, one for salaried employees and one for hourly employees, established September 1, 19———, and April 1, 19———, respectively. Both are qualified under Section 165(a) of the Internal Revenue Code.

The September 1, 19———, plan provides for the payment of premiums to an insurance company, under a group annuity contract, for the purchase of retirement annuities for salaried employees, thirty years of age and over, who have completed at least one year of service with the Company; the interest of the employee is partially vested after five years of service and fully vested after ten years of service.

Under the April 1, 19———, plan, premium deposits are being made with an insurance company to provide for the payment of pensions to hourly employees when they reach sixty-five years of age, if they have completed at least fifteen years of continuous service. This plan, created pursuant to a Union agreement, is to continue in effect until April 1, 19———, and each year thereafter, unless forty-five days prior to any expiration date, written notice is given by either the Company or the Union of its desire to amend or modify the agreement. The Company expects to continue the plan beyond April 1, 19———, but it is required by the Union agreement to provide for pension payments only to the employees who become eligible during the original five-year term of the plan or any extension thereof. Premium deposits heretofore made to the insurance company are in excess of the maximum reserve needed for employees eligible to retire prior to April 1, 19———.

Premiums paid or accrued during the three years and two months ended February 28, 19———, are as follows:

	Total	Current Service		Past Service
		Salaried Employees	Hourly Employees	Hourly Employees
19____				
19____				
19____				
Two months ended				
February 28, 19____				

The amount required at February 28, 19——, to complete the funding of the past service cost of the hourly employees' plan is approximately $265,000, assuming that the plan continues beyond the five-year period ending April 1, 19——. Past service premium costs for the salaried employees' plan were paid in prior years ($ in 19—— and $ on September 1, 19——).

[Author's note: Three-year information is not required in annual reports.]

RESTRICTIONS WHICH LIMIT THE AVAILABILITY OF RETAINED EARN-INGS FOR DIVIDEND PURPOSES (RULE 3–16(h)).—If there are restrictions which limit the availability of retained earnings for dividend purposes, there must be furnished a description of the most restrictive of such restrictions, other than as reported pursuant to Rule 3–16(f). The description should include the source of the restriction, its pertinent provisions, and, where appropriate and determinable, the amount of retained earnings (i) so restricted or (ii) free of such restrictions.

In ASR No. 35 (1942) the Chief Accountant of the SEC discussed a number of situations that limit the availability of retained earnings (surplus) for dividend purposes and the requirements for disclosure of the restrictions in statements prepared for filing with the SEC. The Chief Accountant concluded as follows:

Minimum disclosure, in my opinion, would consist of a description of the restriction, indicating briefly its source, its pertinent provisions, and, where appropriate and determinable, the amount of the surplus so restricted. Such disclosure should be made either in a note to the balance sheet or in an appropriate place in the surplus section of the balance sheet. Also, any statement of surplus, such as is prescribed in Rule 11–02 of Regulation S–X, should contain similar information or should refer to the disclosure made in the balance sheet. Since the declaration and payment of dividends depends on many factors, other than the mere absence of restrictions of the type under discussion, disclosure pursuant to the above requirements should not be made in such a way as improperly to leave an inference that dividends will or may necessarily be declared from surplus in excess of the restrictions noted.

Examples follow showing how these restrictions have been disclosed in practice.

Example 1. Restrictions on common dividends in
indenture and preferred stock provisions

Common stock dividend restrictions.—The terms of issue of the Sinking
Fund Debentures include certain restrictions with respect to dividends (other
than stock dividends) on the common stock of the company, and to the purchase,
redemption or retirement of its capital shares. At October 31, 19——, approximately $　　　　of the retained earnings was free of such restrictions. Under
similar restrictions in the terms of issue of the cumulative preferred stock, the
amount of retained earnings free of such restrictions was in excess of the aforementioned $

Example 2. Disclosure of formula

Common stock dividend restrictions.—Under mortgage restrictions cash dividends on common stock after January 1, 19——, may be paid only from Net Income Available for Common Dividends for the Accounting Period as defined,
plus $　　　　. Retained earnings unrestricted as to payment of dividends on
common stock amounted to $　　　　at February 28, 19——.

Commitments and Contingent Liabilities (Rule 3–16(i)).—If
material in amount, the pertinent facts regarding firm commitments for
the acquisition of permanent or long-term investments and property, plant
and equipment and for the purchase, repurchase, construction, or rental of
assets under material leases have to be disclosed.

Where the annual rentals or obligations under noncancelable leases
which have not been recorded as assets and liabilities are more than one per
cent of total sales and revenues of the most recent fiscal year, there must be
shown (1) the minimum annual rentals for the current and each of the
five succeeding years; (2) the nature and effect of any provisions that
would cause the annual rentals to vary from the minimum rentals; and
(3) a description of the types of property leased, important obligations
assumed or guarantees made, and any other significant provisions of such
leases.

A brief statement has to be made as to contingent liabilities not reflected
in the balance sheet. In the case of guarantees of securities of other issuers, periodic reports filed with the Commission must include a reference
to Schedule XI (guarantees of securities of other issuers) and reports or
prospectuses which do not include that schedule must include a brief description of such guarantees; where only consolidated financial statements
are presented, such information shall relate solely to guarantees of securities
of companies not included in the consolidation.

A retail chain store organization described its lease commitments in
this way:

Leases on retail stores.—The Company and its subsidiaries have (number)
leases on retail store properties expiring in the period 19—— to 19——. The
rentals payable under such leases are generally a percentage of sales with pro-

vision for minimum rentals. The minimum rentals payable for the current and each of the next five years are as follows: $, $, $, $, $, and $ The leases are net leases providing for the payment of taxes, insurance, etc.; in the current year, such additional payments aggregated $

Following is the description of an oil company's lease commitments as stated in its registration statement:

Lease commitments.—The Company and its subsidiaries lease numerous properties for terms expiring more than three years after (year), many of which cover properties in foreign countries. The leases cover producing, sales, pipe line, and other properties and vary widely as to their conditions. Certain of the leases provide for rentals based on the volume of gasoline sold or handled at the particular location while others are on a flat rental basis or are based on gasoline volume with provision for a flat rental, etc. Minimum annual rentals under leases (other than oil and gas leases) expiring after 19—— average: 1964–1973, $; 1974–1983, $. The rentals actually paid in recent years in excess of minimum requirements are not significant in amount. Annual payments under marine charter parties expiring after 19—— average: 1964–1970, $; 1971–1983, $; 1984–1985, $

Commitments for the purchase of fixed assets have been described in this way:

Example 1. An industrial company

Machinery commitments.—The company had commitments at (date) of approximately $ for purchases of machinery and equipment.

Example 2. An electric utility company

Construction commitments.—The company has a construction program involving estimated expenditures of $ during (year) and has made substantial commitments (most of which can be canceled) for equipment.

Examples follow showing how contingent liabilities have been disclosed in financial statements filed with SEC:

Example 1. Guarantee of subsidiary's bank loans

Contingent liability.—The Company has guaranteed bank loans to (name of company), an unconsolidated foreign subsidiary, under a $ bank credit agreement. At December 31, 19——, such loans amounted to $

Example 2. Guarantee of subsidiary's funded debt

Contingent liability.—In connection with a mortgage loan on property of (subsidiary), the unpaid balance of which on December 31, 19——, amounted to $ bearing interest at   per cent, maturing December 1, 19——, but subject to principal amortization payments at rate of $ annually until maturity, and with prepayment privilege, this corporation guarantees the payment of principal and interest on the loan, as well as the performance of all the covenants and conditions of the mortgage including the payment of real estate taxes.

Example 3. Guarantee of debt of a municipality

Contingent liability.—The Company is contingently liable under an agreement to purchase, at face value, any bond and/or coupon attached thereto, of   per cent City of   Industrial Water Revenue Bonds, Series of 19 , maturing serially from (date) to (date) ($ outstanding at December 31, 19——) which, upon being duly presented, is not paid by the City of

Bonus, Profit Sharing, and Other Similar Plans (Rule 3–16(j)).—There must be furnished a description of the essential provisions of any bonus, profit sharing, and other similar plans in which only directors, officers, or key employees may participate. The disclosure also has to include the aggregate amounts provided under all plans by charges to expense in each of the fiscal periods for which income statements are required to be filed.

Following is a typical note conforming with the above requirements:

Bonus and profit sharing plan.—The Company and its subsidiaries have a bonus and profit sharing plan providing for the payment of bonuses to officers and employees (brief statement of those eligible to participate). The total of the fund which may be disbursed in respect of the operations of a given year is based on (brief statement of how the total is computed, such as, a percentage of pretax income after allowing % of stockholders' equity at the beginning of the year). The amounts provided in each of the last five years and charged to expense in those years follow: (years and amounts).

Significant Changes in Bonds, Mortgages, and Similar Debt (Rule 3–16(k)).—The notes to financial statements must include a disclosure of significant changes in the authorized or issued amounts of bonds, mortgages, and similar debt since the date of the latest balance sheet being filed for a particular company or group.

Bases of Revenue Recognition (Rule 3–16(l)).—If sales are made on a deferred basis (such as instalment sales), or if there are sales of equipment long in process of manufacture (such as ocean going tankers), or if sales or revenues are otherwise subject to alternative methods of revenue recognition, the basis of taking profits into income shall be stated.

A company sold land contracts and took the profits into income at the time of sale although the payments were to be received over a three-year period. Without passing on the propriety of the method employed, the SEC said it was misleading to employ the procedure without a full explanation of its character and effect. *American Tung Grove Developments, Inc.,* 8 SEC 51 (1940). See also "Accounting for Transactions Involving Real Estate" on page **4·1**.

A company which sold equipment under long-term conditional sales contracts described its accounting policy in its prospectus as follows:

Instalment Notes Receivable: These receivables, which include accrued interest of $, are secured by equipment sold under conditional sales contracts. In accordance with generally recognized trade practice, all notes, including those which mature for collection subsequent to one year amounting to $ at (date) have been included in current assets. It is the policy to include profits from such sales in income when the sales are made.

It should be borne in mind that the APB has stated that, in the absence of special circumstances, the instalment method of recognizing revenue is not acceptable. In Opinion No. 10 (1966) the APB recognized that there are exceptional cases where receivables are collectible over an extended period of time and, because of the terms of the transactions or other conditions, there is no reasonable basis for estimating the degree of collectibility. When such circumstances exist, and as long as they exist, the APB said that either the instalment method or the cost recovery method of accounting may be used.

A shipbuilding company described the basis on which it took profits into income as follows:

Profits on long-term contracts.—The Company records profits on its long-term shipbuilding contracts through estimates on the percentage-of-completion basis, and on its other long-term contracts as billings are made thereon. The profits so estimated and recorded are subject to the provision of such allowances as may be considered advisable, taking into account the stage of completion of each contract, possible increases in costs not included in the estimates, guarantee liabilities, unsettled contract adjustments and other factors. The performance of such contracts may extend over periods as long as several years, and revisions in the contract estimates and allowance requirements during performance and upon final contract settlements have the effect of including in subsequent accounting periods adjustments necessary to reflect the results indicated by the revised estimates and allowances. The amounts reserved as allowances reflect the reductions in Federal and state income taxes which would result if the matters covered by the allowances materialize, and aggregated $ at (date) and $ at (date).

A 1969 prospectus of Convalariums of America, Inc. furnished a good example of "dollarizing" the effect of alternative methods of recognizing income. The prospectus included an income statement for the five years ended March 31, 1968, and for the nine months ended December 31, 1967 and 1968. For the 1968 interim period, net income was reported as $204,000. A note to the statement indicated that the company in 1968 began constructing health care facilities, and had elected to recognize profits on construction contracts under the completed contract method, under which profits from contracts are reflected only in the periods in which the contracts are completed. Since none of the construction contracts had been completed by December 31, 1968, no construction income was included in the income statement, and all other operating expenses of the construction business were deferred. The note continued that the company could have employed the percentage of completion method and described that method briefly. If the company had employed that method, according to the note, net income for the most recent interim period would have been approximately $11,000 more than was shown by the statement.

The SEC's Chief Accountant said in a 1961 speech that it helps the staff examiners when they find a clear explanation of the method of accounting followed by finance companies (determination of income) and real estate development companies (basis for costing sales and properties in inventory).

An example of the explanation contemplated by the foregoing reference occurred in the prospectus of Continental Leasing Company, Inc., dated August 6, 1970. A note to the income statement explained the method followed by the company in accounting for finance leases and rentals as follows:

The Company uses the finance method of accounting for equipment leased under full-pay-out leases. Under this method of accounting, total unearned lease income from finance leases is represented by the difference between the total lease receivable under the lease contract and the cost of the related equipment (after deduction of estimated residual value). The Company records a portion of unearned lease income (1965—$5,500; 1966—$3,500; 1967—$11,500; 1968—$49,000; 1969—$420,000; five months ended May 31, 1969 and 1970— $100,200 and $209,900 (unaudited), respectively) as income upon commencement of each lease to offset lease acquisition and administrative expenses incurred during the period. The balance of unearned lease income is amortized over the term of the lease using the sum-of-the-month's-digits method. Under this method, the balance of unearned lease income is recorded on a declining basis over the life of the lease in proportion to the lease instalments outstanding. The cost of equipment under finance leases at December 31, 1969 and May 31, 1970 amounted to $7,092,400 and $9,094,700 (unaudited), respectively.

Rental equipment is rented on a short-term basis on which the customer pays a monthly rental charge and may terminate the rental arrangement at any time. Income on rental equipment is recorded in the month earned, based on the terms of the rental contracts. The related equipment is recorded in the balance sheet at cost and is depreciated on the straight-line method based on an 8-year life with a 4% residual value.

DEPRECIATION, DEPLETION, OBSOLESCENCE, AND AMORTIZATION (RULE 3–16(m)).—The notes to the financial statements must contain a statement of the policy followed with respect to:

(1) The provision for depreciation, depletion, amortization, and obsolescence of physical properties and capitalized leases, including the methods and, if practicable, the rates used in computing the annual amounts;

(2) The provision for depreciation and amortization of intangible as-

sets or the lack of such provision, including the methods and, if practicable, the rates used in computing the annual amounts;

(3) The accounting treatment for maintenance, repairs, renewals, and betterments; and

(4) The adjustment of accumulated depreciation, depletion, obsolescence, and amortization at the time the properties are retired or otherwise disposed of, including the disposition made of any gain or loss on sale of such properties.

For a discussion of the SEC's views regarding depreciation based on current cost or replacement value of assets, see the discussion beginning on page **3·**32.

Examples follow showing typical depreciation disclosures:

Example 1. An industrial company

Depreciation policy.—The company follows the policy of providing for depreciation on the straightline method by charges to costs or expenses at rates based on the estimated useful lives of the respective properties applied to the gross book amounts thereof.

The rates used for computing depreciation on the properties are as follows:

Class of Property	Rates per Annum
Land improvements	4%
Buildings—other than warehouses	2%
Warehouses	4%
Building equipment	5 and 6⅔%
Machinery and equipment	6⅔%
Office furniture and fixtures	6⅔%
Automobiles and trucks	25%

Maintenance, repairs, and minor renewals are charged to income as incurred except that expenditures which substantially increase the useful lives of the buildings, machinery, and equipment are capitalized.

As a general rule, when items are retired or otherwise disposed of, the reserves for depreciation are charged with the accumulated amount of depreciation applicable thereto and any gain or loss on such retirement or disposal is credited or charged to income.

Example 2. A telephone company using straight-line depreciation

Policies as to depreciation, etc.—It is the long-established policy of the Company to provide for depreciation of its depreciable telephone plant on the straight-line basis, which is the method prescribed by the Uniform System of Accounts and which is designed to distribute the amounts at which such plant is carried in the Telephone Plant in Service account, less salvage, as evenly as possible throughout its service life. Stated in percentages of average depreciable telephone plant, provisions for depreciation, which are charged to the expense and clearing accounts, amounted to 3.70 per cent (annual basis) for the 6 months ended June 30, 19   , 3.69 per cent for each of the years 19   , 19   , 19   , and 19   , and 4.02 per cent for 19   . When depreciable plant, other than minor items thereof which are replaced, is retired, the amount at which such plant has been carried in the Telephone Plant in Service account (estimated if not known) is charged against the reserve accumulated, whether or not the particular item retired has attained the average service life of its class, and the salvage value is credited to the reserve.

The cost of maintenance and repairs of Telephone Plant, including the cost of replacing minor items not effecting substantial betterments, is charged to operating expense, principally to Current Maintenance, except that maintenance and repairs of vehicles and other work equipment used both in maintenance and construction work and repairs of certain furniture and office equipment are charged initially to clearing accounts and distributed to Current Maintenance, Telephone Plant, and other accounts. When station apparatus is removed from customers' premises, the original cost of the installation and wiring is credited to Telephone Plant and charged to Current Maintenance. If wires left in place are subsequently reused in connection with another installation at the same location, the cost of an installation and wiring (based on the average cost of units in service) is charged to Telephone Plant and credited to Current Maintenance.

Example 3. An oil company using both the unit
of production and straight-line methods of depreciation, depletion, and amortization

Depreciation, depletion and amortization.—(a) The policy with respect to fixed assets, except undeveloped leases (domestic undeveloped leases are amortized over the periods of the leases but foreign undeveloped leases are not amortized) is, in general, to charge profit and loss or income over the estimated life of such assets by the application of either the unit method or the straight-line method. Rates under the unit method of depreciation and depletion are based upon quantities of recoverable oil estimated by the Company. The rates used under the straight-line method are based upon the expected life of the facilities, grouped in some instances but viewed as individual plant items in the majority of cases. These rates are revised for either the group or the item whenever a different life expectancy is recognized. In view of the variety of properties included in the fixed assets and the wide range of depreciation rates applicable thereto, it is not considered practical to set forth herein the rates or range of rates used in computing the provision for depreciation. In every case, the rates are designed to accumulate a reserve sufficient to provide for cost, less salvage, at the termination of the expected life of the item or group. Upon the retirement of any facility, the accumulated depreciation is charged against the reserve for depreciation, except that in the case of items depreciated at group rates, the cost, less salvage, is charged to the reserve. Differences between cost, less salvage, and the accumulated depreciation on items depreciated individually are charged or credited to profit and loss.

Provisions for depreciation, depletion, and amortization for interim periods are based on estimates which are revised during the year as circumstances require and adjusted at the year end on the basis of known asset balances and production and estimated underground reserves.

Maintenance and repairs are charged to expense, except that occasional substantial renewals, which prolong life of the facility beyond the date previously contemplated, are charged to the reserve for depreciation; betterments are capitalized as plant additions.

(b) Intangible development costs incurred prior to January 1, 19   , were charged to expense. Such costs incurred on and after that date, which are applicable to wells completed as producers, have been capitalized on the books and are being amortized on the basis of the quantities of recoverable oil as estimated by the Company and the production for the period. Costs incident to the drilling of development wells are initially capitalized but are charged to expense when the hole is determined to be dry. Costs of drilling exploratory wells are charged to expense as incurred but are capitalized and credited to expense when the well proves to be productive. Geological and geophysical expenses are charged to expense.

Some companies provide reserves out of income for certain major maintenance and repair items, such as relining a blast furnace. In that case the company may describe its accounting policy in terms such as the following:

Maintenance and repairs are charged to income as incurred except that the costs of relining blast furnaces and glass furnaces are charged to reserves provided out of income.

Prior to the issuance of APB Opinion No. 17 (1970), there was no requirement to amortize goodwill and similar intangible assets having an indeterminate life unless and until it became apparent that there had been a decline in the value of such assets. With the issuance of Opinion No. 17, however, there was a significant change in generally accepted accounting principles affecting such assets, although the Opinion, by its terms, is not to be applied retroactively. The Opinion provided that such intangible assets acquired after the effective date have to be amortized over the period estimated to be benefited, but that the amortization period should not exceed 40 years. Consequently, when a company has goodwill and similar intangible assets on its balance sheet, in the note required by Rule 3–16(m) of Regulation S–X, it will have to distinguish between goodwill and similar intangibles acquired before November 1, 1970 (which are subject to the pre-Opinion No. 17 rules) and intangibles acquired after October 31, 1970 (which are subject to the rules in Opinion No. 17).

CAPITAL STOCK OPTIONED, SOLD OR OFFERED FOR SALE TO OFFICERS, DIRECTORS, AND KEY EMPLOYEES (RULE 3–16(n)).—A note to the financial statements has to furnish information with respect to capital stock optioned, sold or offered for sale to officers, directors, and key employees. The information must include at least the following:

A brief description of the terms of each option arrangement, including (i) the title and amount of securities subject to option; (ii) the year or years during which the options were granted; and (iii) the year or years during which the optionees became, or will become, entitled to exercise the options.

A statement of (i) the number of shares under option at the balance sheet date, and the option price and the fair value thereof, per share and in total, at the dates the options were granted; (ii) the number of shares with respect to which options became exercisable during each period presented, and the option price and the fair value thereof, per share and in total, at the dates the options became exercisable; (iii) the number of shares with respect to which options were exercised during each period, and the option price and the fair value thereof, per share and in total, at the dates the options were exercised; and (iv) the number of unoptioned shares available at the beginning and at the close of the latest period presented for granting of options under an option plan.

A brief description of the terms of each other arrangement covering shares sold or offered for sale to only officers, directors and key employees, including the number of shares, and the offered price and the fair value thereof, per share and in total, at the dates of sale or offer to sell, as appropriate.

The required information has to be summarized and tabulated, as appropriate, with respect to all option plans as a group and other plans for shares sold or offered for sale as a group.

The basis of accounting for such arrangements and the amount of charges, if any, reflected in income with respect thereto has to be stated.

If the financial statements are filed as part of a prospectus or proxy statement which contains information regarding stock options in the narrative section, cross-reference may be made in the notes to financial statements to such information and thereby avoid needless repetition.

The following is a suggested form of a note to financial statements dealing with a stock option plan only, which complies with the requirements of Rule 3–16(n). The form covers a three-year period on the assumption that it would be included in a registration statement under the 1933 Act. If the note were included in an annual report on Form 10–K under the 1934 Act, the period covered would be reduced to one year.

At (balance sheet date), (number) shares of common stock of the Company were reserved for sale to officers and employees under a stock option plan approved by stockholders on (date). The plan provides that the option price shall be fixed by a committee of the Board of Directors, but shall not be less than —% of the market value of the stock at date of grant. Options are exercisable —— months after grant and may not be exercised after —— years. Options were granted for (number) shares in 19——, (number) shares in 19——, and (number) shares in 19——.

Information as of (balance sheet date) and for the years 19—— through 19—— with respect to options granted under the plan is as follows:

	Number	*Option Price*		*Market Value*	
	of Shares	*Per Share*	*Total*	*Per Share*	*Total*
Shares under option at (balance sheet date) ..	———	$_ to $_	$_____	$_ to $_(a)	$_____
Options which became exercisable during:					
19_	———	$_ to $_	$_____	$_ to $_(b)	$_____
19_	———	$_ to $_	$_____	$_ to $_(b)	$_____
19_	———	$_ to $_	$_____	$_ to $_(b)	$_____
Options exercised during:					
19_	———	$_ to $_	$_____	$_ to $_(c)	$_____
19_	———	$_ to $_	$_____	$_ to $_(c)	$_____
19_	———	$_ to $_	$_____	$_ to $_(c)	$_____

(a) At the dates options were granted.
(b) At the dates options became exercisable.
(c) At the dates options were exercised.

The number of shares and prices in the preceding tabulation have been adjusted to reflect subsequent stock dividends paid through (date).

At the beginning of (period), there were (number) unoptioned shares available for the granting of options under the plan; at the end of such period there were (number) unoptioned shares available.

The Company makes no charges to income in connection with the plan.

The disclosure provisions of Rule 3–16(n) relating to stock options go beyond those of generally accepted accounting principles as expressed in ARB 43, Chapter 13, Section B. On the other hand, for a company that has securities listed for trading on the New York Stock Exchange, there are additional requirements which, in some respects, differ from those in the SEC rule. The Exchange's current requirements for listing contain a provision with regard to the information to be disclosed in annual reports to security holders concerning the operation of stock option plans. The applicable portion of the listing agreement follows:

6. The Corporation will disclose in its annual report to shareholders, for the year covered by the report, (1) the number of shares of its stock issuable under outstanding options at the beginning of the year; separate totals of changes in the number of shares of its stock under option resulting from issuance, exercise, expiration or cancellation of options; and the number of shares issuable under outstanding options at the close of the year, (2) the number of unoptioned shares available at the beginning and at the close of the year for the granting of options under an option plan, and (3) any changes in the exercise price of outstanding options, through cancellation and reissuance or otherwise, except price changes resulting from the normal operation of anti-dilution provisions of the options.

It may be noted that the Exchange's requirement is for disclosure of the information in question—but not necessarily as a part of the financial statements. Some companies do, in fact, furnish the required information in the text portion of their annual reports; others, however, include it in their financial statements and combine it with the information otherwise required to be furnished in respect of stock options.

Some insurance companies have adopted compensation plans for their agents which, in addition to commission on policies sold, include stock options. The options generally give the holder the right to purchase shares of the insurance company or of the parent holding company at a price which is less than the market price at the date of grant of the option, say 75% to 80% of market. In a typical plan, options are granted to agents as policies are issued with the number of options per $1,000 of insurance in force declining as the total of insurance in force increases. The options are generally not exercisable for specified periods of time, often three years, and their exercise is frequently conditioned upon the related policy remaining in force. The insurance company is allowed a deduction as compensation for the difference between the option price and the fair market value of the stock at the exercise date.

Because of the significance of the additional compensation amounts involved, the SEC has required recognition of the value of the options at the date of grant in the financial statements or in supplementary statements which adjust the accounts on a regulatory basis to the basis of generally accepted accounting principles. Recognition of the value of the options should be made by a charge to income and a corresponding credit to capital surplus. Where the option must be held for a period of time before it becomes exercisable, it is appropriate to amortize the charge over that period. (Walter Mickelsen, "Recent Developments in the SEC Accounting Field," May 24, 1966.)

INCOME TAX EXPENSE (RULE 3–16(o)).—Disclosure has to be made, in the income statement or in a note thereto, of the components of income tax expense, including (1) taxes currently payable; (2) the net tax effects, as applicable, of (i) timing differences and (ii) operating losses; and (3) the net deferred investment tax credits. Amounts applicable to Federal income taxes and to other income taxes shall be stated separately for each component, unless the amounts applicable to other income taxes do not exceed 5 per cent of the total for the component and a statement to that effect is made.

WARRANTS OR RIGHTS OUTSTANDING (RULE 3–16(p)).—Information with respect to warrants or rights outstanding at the date of the related balance sheet has to be set forth as follows:
(1) Title of issue of securities called for by warrants or rights.
(2) Aggregate amount of securities called for by warrants or rights outstanding.
(3) Date from which warrants or rights are exercisable and expiration date.
(4) Price at which warrant or right is exercisable.

CHAPTER **17**

REGULATION S-X (ANNOTATED), CONTINUED

Part 2. The Rules Relating to Consolidated and Combined Statements

CONTENTS

Article 4. Rules Relating to Consolidated and Combined Statements

When a company files financial statements with the SEC for the first time, some of the questions that most frequently arise are these: What are the SEC's requirements as to consolidation of subsidiary financial statements with those of the parent company? If subsidiaries are not consolidated, to what extent must their financial statements be furnished? If statements of unconsolidated subsidiaries must be furnished, to what extent, if any, may they be combined?

The registration and report forms of the SEC contain the instructions as to what financial statements (consolidated and unconsolidated) are to be filed and the dates and periods of the statements (see Chapters **9** and **15**

17·1

for details). The SEC's rules as to consolidation and combination are contained in Article 4 of Regulation S–X.

Article 4 consists of the following rules:

4–01   Application of Article 4

4–02   Consolidated financial statements of the registrant and its subsidiaries; principles to be followed

4–03   Group financial statements of subsidiaries not consolidated and 50% or less owned companies

4–04   Statement as to principle of consolidation or combination followed

4–05   Reconciliation of investment of parent in subsidiaries not consolidated and 50% or less owned companies accounted for by the equity method and equity in their net assets

4–06   Intercompany items and transactions

4–07   Consolidation of financial statements of a registrant and its subsidiaries engaged in diverse financial activities

4–08   Special requirements as to public utility holding companies

4–09   Special requirements as to commercial, industrial, and mining companies in the promotional, exploratory, or development stage subject to Article 5A

Consolidated Statements of the Registrant and Its Subsidiaries (Rule 4–02).—The registrant is required to follow in the consolidated statements principles of inclusion or exclusion that will clearly exhibit the financial position and results of operations of the registrant and its subsidiaries; provided, however, that the registrant shall not consolidate:

(1) Any subsidiary which is not majority owned; or

(2) Any subsidiary whose financial statements are as of a date or for periods different from those of the registrant, unless all the following conditions are met: (i) such difference is not more than 93 days; (ii) the closing date of the subsidiary is expressly indicated; and (iii) the necessity for the use of different closing dates is briefly explained.

Notwithstanding the 93-day requirement specified in (2) above, in connection with the retroactive combination of the financial statements of entities following a "pooling of interests," the financial statements of the constituents may be combined even if their respective fiscal periods do not end within 93 days, except that the financial statements for the latest fiscal year shall be recast to dates which do not differ by more than 93 days, if practicable. Disclosure shall be made of the periods combined and of the sales or revenues, net income before extraordinary items, and net income of any interim periods excluded from or included more than once in results of operations as a result of such recasting.

The 93-day requirement specified above is not applicable to the recognition of earnings or losses of 50 per cent or less owned companies the investments in which are accounted for by the equity method of accounting.

Due consideration shall be given to the propriety of consolidating with domestic corporations foreign subsidiaries which are operated under political, economic, or currency restrictions. If consolidated, disclosure should be made as to the effect, insofar as this can reasonably be determined, of foreign exchange restrictions upon the consolidated financial position and operating results of the registrant and its subsidiaries.

It should be borne in mind that the ownership of a majority of the voting stock in a company does not automatically qualify the company for inclusion in consolidated statements. In a given case, *control* of the company may vest somewhere else. The company may be a wholly-owned subsidiary but it may be in bankruptcy proceedings and its affairs under court jurisdiction. In other cases involving solvent entities, control may vest in the holders of the minority interest by virtue of a contract or other arrangement which gives the minority interest the power to direct the management, policies, and activities of the company. In any of these situations, the ownership of a majority of the voting power does not carry with it the factor of control, and therefore the company is not a subsidiary.

Sometimes a company may have majority ownership of voting power, but a minority interest in the equity in net assets of a distant subsidiary, as in this situation: A owns 51% of the voting common stock of B; B owns 51% of the voting common stock of C. A therefore has a 26% interest in the net assets of C. Since B is a majority-owned subsidiary of A, and C is a majority-owned subsidiary of B, all three companies may be included in consolidated financial statements.

See page **24**·56 regarding the disclosure requirements and those applicable to the accountant's certificate when there has been a change in the principle of consolidation.

This is how one company (which is on a calendar year basis) complied with the requirement to explain the necessity for the use of a different fiscal year by its consolidated subsidiary:

The financial statements of the consolidated subsidiary in England are included at its regularly scheduled closing date, December 23, 19___. This practice is necessary for the prompt reporting of consolidated monthly results. The accounts of the remaining subsidiary companies and branches were closed at December 31, 19___.

Assume a parent company having a December 31 fiscal year. It has a subsidiary with a September 30 fiscal year and another subsidiary with a

January 31 fiscal year. Could all the companies in the affiliated group be consolidated on the basis of their respective fiscal years despite the fact that the closing dates of the subsidiaries are four months apart? In the author's opinion, Rule 4–02—setting forth the 93 day limitation—does not prohibit such full consolidation, assuming that all the other conditions in the rule are complied with.

The SEC permits reasonable deviation from its rule prohibiting consolidation of a subsidiary as of a date more than 93 days from that of the parent. In the prospectus of William J. Burns International Detective Agency, Inc. (1961), for example, subsidiaries were included in consolidated statements on the basis of their fiscal years ended June 30 and April 30 whereas the fiscal year of the parent company was December 31. It was stated in a note, however, that the subsidiaries "are not significant subsidiaries."

The SEC has generally taken the position that the investor can most readily appraise the financial condition of a company and of his investment in the company if all majority owned subsidiaries are consolidated. See, for example, the comment beginning on page **30**·10 regarding the SEC's suspension of trading in the common stock of Atlantic Research Corporation. The SEC alleged that the company's published financial statements for 1961 were misleading. The statements in the published report were those of the parent company alone and showed *net income* of $1,473,000. The company's annual report (Form 10–K) for that year filed with the SEC, on the other hand, included consolidated financial statements of the company and its subsidiaries, and these showed a *net loss* of more than $1,000,000. See also the discussion in this chapter under "Consolidation of Unacknowledged Subsidiaries," also involving Atlantic Research Corporation, regarding the SEC's criticism of the company for failure to consolidate a subsidiary, control of which was exercised otherwise than through record ownership of voting stock.

Where an operating function of a company is separated from the parent and is performed by a subsidiary, ordinarily the subsidiary should be included in the consolidated statements. An example is the real estate subsidiary which is normally heavy with fixed assets and long-term debt. A former Chief Accountant of the SEC said:

Omitting the real estate subsidiary and its debt from consolidation results in a "clean balance sheet" but does not disclose the impact of the debt on the consolidation. On the other hand, where the subsidiary is consolidated the reader is properly informed as to the debt for which the parent company's rental payments are usually collateral . . . [Author's note: See, however, page **17**·12.]

Some accountants . . . have contended that a finance subsidiary should not be consolidated, even where it is financing primarily sales of the parent, on the ground that the finance subsidiary's operations are of a banking nature and are too unlike the operations of the parent to make it advisable to consolidate. The typical finance company has a heavy debt/equity ratio, although the argument is made here that this should not be considered where the parent has no liability on the accounts. In my opinion, where the finance company is handling primarily the accounts of the parent and affiliates, it constitutes an integrated part of total operations and should be consolidated even though the parent is not subject to recourse on the accounts . . .

Some industrial companies acquire or establish subsidiaries for the production of their raw materials. Where this stage of vertical integration is not common in the industry, some companies are reluctant to consolidate such subsidiaries and argue that their statements would no longer be comparable with those of other firms in the industry. With the possible rare exception it would appear that consolidation is in order.[1]

The SEC's rule as to consolidation, stripped of its prohibitions, is substantially this: Principles of inclusion or exclusion must be followed that will clearly exhibit the financial position and results of operations of the affiliated group represented by the registrant and its majority owned subsidiaries. How does the rule work in practice?

Assume that Company A is contemplating filing a registration statement with the SEC. Company A is an operating company and has investments in Subsidiaries X, Y, and Z. The subsidiaries are engaged in lines of business similar to that of the parent, employ the same fiscal period, and all are significant, domestic corporations. X and Y are wholly owned subsidiaries but Z is owned 95 per cent by A, the other 5 per cent being owned by the general manager of Z.

In its financial statements, A customarily consolidates X and Y. As far as the investment in Z is concerned, A follows the recommendations in APB Opinion No. 18 (1971) with respect to accounting for unconsolidated domestic subsidiaries, that is, the investment is carried at cost plus or minus the equity in earnings or losses of Z since acquisition, and the income statement reflects the equity in Z's earnings or losses for the period.

In its filing with the SEC, A would like to continue its policy of consolidating wholly owned subsidiaries, but has no objection to furnishing statements of the unconsolidated 95% owned subsidiary. The management of A believes that this proposed presentation "clearly exhibits the financial condition and results of operations of the registrant and its subsidiaries."

Would the SEC agree?

The probabilities are that the SEC would not agree. In circumstances similar to those described above, it is probable that the SEC would require that Subsidiary Z be consolidated as well as X and Y. *The burden of justifying the exclusion of any majority owned subsidiary from consolidation must always be assumed by the registrant.* In this case it would not

[1] Andrew Barr, "Disclosure in Theory and Practice," *The New York CPA,* Sept. 1959, p. 640.

suffice to say that Z was excluded from consolidation because it was A's policy to consolidate only wholly owned subsidiaries. The fact that Z's statements are also filed as part of the registration will not relieve the company from the necessity of consolidating Z.

Prior to the issuance of Opinion No. 10 by the APB in 1966, and later Opinion No. 18 in 1971, many companies carried their investments in unconsolidated subsidiaries at cost and disclosed in footnotes the equity in the net assets of such subsidiaries. Dividends received from such subsidiaries were included in income with disclosure of the related equity in earnings or losses of the subsidiaries. The APB Opinions caused many companies that were on the cost basis to revise their accounting for the investments in unconsolidated subsidiaries (foreign as well as domestic). The Commission's consolidation policy was even more rigid in the period before Opinions 10 and 18 than it is today, for the reason that under the equity method recommended by the Opinions net assets and net income are not affected by whether or not the subsidiaries in question are consolidated.

See the comment of the SEC's Chief Accountant on page **3**·24 regarding companies that filed registration statements with the SEC and had never before prepared consolidated statements.

A company stated in its registration statement under the 1933 Act that a named subsidiary was not consolidated because it was insignificant. The SEC's letter of comment said that it was not requesting a change in the consolidated statements, but that "it is not our policy to consider the mere insignificance of a subsidiary as the basis for omission from consolidation." In the author's opinion, this is the type of comment that the SEC could well dispense with. The registrant had taken the position that it did not consolidate a subsidiary because it was insignificant. The SEC did not challenge the fact of insignificance, but chose instead to make a gratuitous policy observation having no relation to the registration statement and no interest to the company.

Following are examples from actual practice in which the SEC forced companies to consolidate subsidiaries in financial statements filed with the Commission. These cases give an insight into SEC's thinking on the question of consolidated statements.

Example 1

A company registered on Form 10 under the 1934 Act had been filing annual reports with the SEC on Form 10–K for several years. The company did not consolidate a subsidiary 95 per cent owned which was in a similar line of business. Separate statements were furnished for the subsidiary. There were numerous complicated transactions between parent and subsidiary, all of which had been disclosed in the Form 10–K's. The SEC had not challenged any of these filings under the 1934 Act. When, however, the parent company filed a registration statement under the 1933 Act in which the financial statements were prepared on the same basis as in Form 10–K, the SEC had only one comment on the financial statements: "Consolidate the subsidiary." It did not matter to SEC that the company was following in the registration statement the same practice it had followed for years in annual reports filed with the SEC. It also did not matter to the SEC that the task of consolidating the subsidiary would cause a delay of about one week in a debenture offering of $100,000,000. The statements were appropriately amended to consolidate the subsidiary which up to that time had never been consolidated.

Example 2

An American corporation had a wholly owned Canadian subsidary. Parent and subsidiary were engaged in the same line of business. The parent company was registered with the SEC under the 1934 Act and filed annual reports with the SEC on Form 10–K. In its financial statements the parent company had regularly followed the practice of consolidating the Canadian subsidiary. In 1950, however, the company decided that it would no longer include the Canadian subsidiary in the consolidation and based its decision on the restriction at that time on transfers of funds from Canada. For some time the SEC raised no objection to this change in principle of consolidation. In 1953, however, with the removal of restrictions on transfers of funds from Canada, the SEC wrote the company and "suggested" that the Canadian subsidiary be restored to the consolidation.

Example 3

A company registered with the SEC under the 1934 Act owned 67 per cent of the voting stock of a subsidiary. The companies operated independently of each other, but the parent made sales in substantial amounts to the subsidiary. Because of the large outside interest in the subsidiary, the parent company did not consolidate the statements of the subsidiary, but furnished separate financial statements of the subsidiary in the report to stockholders of the parent company. The parent's financial statements also disclosed information concerning its equity in the subsidiary's net assets and earnings. The same procedure was followed in the annual reports (Form 10–K) filed with the SEC, without objection from the SEC. After a few years the company received a letter from the Commission commenting on the reports filed with SEC. After noting what the company's practice had been, the SEC said:

> . . . it is contemplated by Rule 4–02 of Regulation S–X that consolidated financial statements of the registrant and its subsidiary should be furnished unless such consolidation would not clearly exhibit the financial condition and results of operations. In our opinion consolidated statements of the registrant and its subsidiary would clearly exhibit the financial condition and results of operations of such companies. Therefore, it appears in order to meet the requirements of Rule 4–02 of Regulation S–X, consolidated statements should be furnished in the annual report for the fiscal year ended (date).

The company was not disposed to take issue with the SEC, and subsequent reports were prepared on the basis suggested by the SEC.

Example 4

A retail merchandising company, registered with SEC under the 1934 Act, had a subsidiary which owned the real estate in which the parent conducted its operations. All the subsidiary's stock was owned by the parent, but mortgages on the property were held by outsiders. For many years, the parent had consolidated the subsidiary in reporting to stockholders and SEC. In 1954, however, the parent decided not to consolidate the subsidiary. Its decision was based on the fact that the inclusion in the consolidated balance sheet of the subsidiary's fixed assets and debt tended to obscure the real nature of the business, which was a merchandising business, not one of operating real estate, the principal owners of which were the outside holders of the mortgage debt. Separate statements of the subsidiary were furnished. Although not requiring the 1954 statements to be amended, SEC did "suggest" that the company in future filings consolidate the subsidiary.

Example 5

A large grocery chain-store corporation, as a part of the preliminary proxy material relating to a proposal to increase its authorized preferred stock, filed consolidated financial statements of the parent company and certain subsidiaries. However, the accounts of three major subsidiaries, one financing fixture and equipment purchases, the second purchasing merchandise for the registrant, and the third operating a chain in Canada, were not included in the consolidated financial statements. The effect was that neither a substantial amount of property and other assets used in the registrant's business nor senior securities of the unconsolidated subsidiaries were shown in the consolidated balance sheet. The SEC's staff took the position that in view of the importance of the three unconsolidated subsidiaries to the integrated operations of the registrant, the financial statements should be on a complete consolidated basis. The definitive proxy material was appropriately revised. [17 SEC Ann. Rep. 45 (1951)].

Improper Elimination of Investment Account in Consolidation. —In ASR No. 3 (1937) the SEC's Chief Accountant stated his view regarding a procedure followed in consolidating subsidiaries through the elimination of only a portion of the parent's investment account. In the case in question, a company had acquired investments in subsidiaries at a cost which was in excess of its proportionate interest in the equity in the net assets of the subsidiaries as shown on the books of the latter. In consolidation, there was eliminated only the par or stated value of the stock of the subsidiaries. The parent's equity in the acquisition surplus of the subsidiaries was included in consolidated surplus, and the uneliminated investment was shown as an asset in the consolidated balance sheet and designated "Excess of cost over par or stated value of the securities of subsidiaries eliminated in consolidation." This had the effect of overstating both the consolidated assets and surplus. The Chief Accountant said:

> The purpose of a consolidated balance sheet is to reflect the financial condition of a parent company and its subsidiaries as if they were a single organization. Thus, in such a balance sheet, the parent company's equities in net assets of subsidiaries are substituted for its investments therein. This substitution is effected by eliminating from the parent company's investment account an amount equal to the par or stated value of the subsidiaries' stocks owned by the parent and its proportionate share of their surpluses at acquisition. Any

part of the parent's investment account remaining (representing the excess cost thereof over the equities in the net assets represented thereby) may properly be retained among the consolidated assets.

CONSOLIDATION OF FOREIGN SUBSIDIARIES.—In 1949–50 there were widespread devaluations of currencies by foreign governments with the result that a large number of domestic corporations engaged in business in these countries were presented with problems as to how to state the accounts of their foreign subsidiaries and branches in terms of United States currency. A principal problem was whether to continue the previous practice of consolidating foreign and domestic operations. The Commission recognized that the decision on this point is one primarily to be reached by the company and its independent accountants, having due regard for all the facts, and having in mind the objective of most clearly exhibiting the financial condition and results of operations of the parent company and its subsidiaries. In answer to a number of inquiries, the SEC's staff indicated its general conclusion that the consolidation question might well be determined upon the basis of the degree of integration of the foreign operations with domestic operations. If such foreign operations are essentially an arm or extension of domestic operations, and are actively being conducted, the SEC's view is that there is a presumption in favor of the consolidation thereof, despite the probable impact upon the foreign operations of unfavorable political and economic factors. If, in an instance of this kind, remittances to the parent company are restricted, appropriate disclosure of the facts would be necessary and the consolidated income statement should reflect only earnings of foreign subsidiaries which are available to the parent in terms of United States dollars. If, on the other hand, the foreign operations constitute a complete and separate business unit in and of themselves, and serious economic problems are presented, nonconsolidation would generally appear to be indicated. [16 SEC Ann. Rep. 158 (1950)].

WHEN DOES SEC NOT INSIST ON CONSOLIDATION?—The SEC rules set forth above contain prohibitions as to consolidation of subsidiaries in certain circumstances: when a subsidiary, for example, is not majority-owned, or when it operates in a foreign country having severe restrictions on the remittance of funds to the parent. Assuming these prohibitions are not applicable, when does the SEC not insist on consolidation?

There are some formal SEC rules on this subject. See, for example, "Special Requirements as to Public Utility Holding Companies" on page **17·23**. Also "Special Requirements as to Commercial, Industrial, or Mining Companies in the Promotional, Exploratory, or Development Stage" on page **17·23**.

In addition, experience indicates:

1. SEC will probably not insist on consolidating a subsidiary which is in a business totally different from that of the parent and the parent's other subsidiaries. Even this statement may have to be hedged, however, in view of the increasing tendency among American businesses to diversify their operations.
2. SEC will probably not insist on consolidating a subsidiary where it is clear that the investment in the subsidiary is a temporary one which the parent intends to dispose of as soon as circumstances permit.
3. SEC will probably not insist on consolidating a finance subsidiary with a manufacturing company.
4. SEC will probably not insist on consolidating a trifling subsidiary, although, as previously noted, the Commission stated in its letter of comment that "it is not our policy to consider the mere insignificance of a subsidiary as the basis for omission from consolidation."

As an indication of circumstances in which the SEC does not insist on consolidating a subsidiary, it may be informative to describe an actual case in which a subsidiary was consolidated and then, with the SEC's consent, was deconsolidated.

The Hotel Company (not its real name) was a large, publicly-owned company that directly and through subsidiaries was engaged in the business of operating hotels, apartments, and restaurants. It also had an investment of $300,000 (a relatively minor amount) in a wholly-owned subsidiary. The subsidiary was the owner of a specialized plant built by the subsidiary and costing $12,000,000 that produced chemicals. The construction funds had come from Hotel Company's investment of $300,000 and $11,700,000 loaned to the subsidiary on its notes. The debt was a lien on the property, but Hotel Company was not liable for the subsidiary's debt.

The subsidiary's plant was leased for 20 years to a prominent United States corporation. The lease was a net lease, and the rental payments were a fixed sum annually calculated to pay the interest and retire the subsidiary's debt over the period of the lease.

The Hotel Company filed a registration statement with the SEC which became effective in May 1964. The subsidiary was included in the consolidated financial statements from the beginning of operations on July 1, 1963. Consequently, the subsidiary's income from rent of the chemical plant and related expenses were included in the 1963 results for about a half year. Both for financial reporting and tax purposes, the chemical plant was depreciated on an accelerated basis, and this had the effect of transforming a pretax profit on the Hotel Company's operations in the amount of $443,000 to a consolidated net loss of $11,000 for 1963.

For a full year, it was estimated that the depreciation deduction applicable to the chemical plant would be $1,600,000. The use of accelerated depreciation would have the effect of showing a loss from the subsidiary's ownership of the chemical plant for about nine years, after which it would turn around, and for the remaining eleven years there would be profits. The inclusion of the subsidiary's chemical plant in the consolidated tax return would enable the Hotel Company to defer the payment of income taxes for several years. For the 20-year period of the lease, there was every expectation that the Hotel Company would come out whole as far as its $300,000 investment in the subsidiary was concerned, and that it might even realize a substantial profit on the investment.

The Hotel Company's normal operations were shown separately from the lease of the chemical plant in the earnings summary. As noted above, however, the inclusion in the consolidation of the lease of the subsidiary's plant had the effect of transforming a profitable hotel-apartment-restaurant operation into a consolidated loss. It was conceivable that an informed, sophisticated reader or analyst would comprehend what was involved in the situation and the tax deferment that flowed from it, and would make a mental adjustment for the substantial depreciation charge applicable to the chemical plant lease. On the other hand, because of the tendency of financial publications to report only the consolidated net income or loss, in total and per share, the management of Hotel Company had reason to believe that the market price of the company's stock had suffered from the financial presentation that it had followed.

It was also possible that stockholders who had sold their Hotel Company stock may have been hurt if they sold based on a misunderstanding of the consolidated operating results of Hotel Company and its subsidiaries.

Furthermore, investment advisers are reluctant to recommend the securities of a company whose financial statements have to be explained for the benefit of unsophisticated readers.

For these and other reasons, the Hotel Company wished to deconsolidate the subsidiary's chemical plant operations from the consolidated financial statements. The investment in the subsidiary that owned the chemical plant would be carried at cost with disclosure in a footnote or otherwise of the financial condition and operating results of the subsidiary. The change in Hotel Company's principles of consolidation would also be disclosed together with the reason therefor, namely, that the subsidiary's operations were not an integral part of the principal operations of Hotel Company. It would be stated also that, despite the subsidiary's indicated loss from operations, neither the Hotel Company nor its independent auditors considered it necessary to provide a reserve for loss on the investment in the subsidiary. In the year of change, the financial statements of the preceding year would be restated to the new basis for comparative purposes. (This incident occurred before the issuance of APB Opinion No. 10 which required equity accounting for domestic subsidiaries.)

The Hotel Company's independent auditors approved the deconsolidation proposal and the related changes. The matter was discussed with the staff of the SEC which also agreed with all aspects of the proposal.

As a further indication of the SEC's policy in permitting certain subsidiaries to be excluded from consolidated statements, the following incident might be mentioned. The GHI Manufacturing Company (not its real name) was in the business of manufacturing a product which it sold to dealers who, in turn, sold it to the public. The company also had a finance subsidiary a major purpose of which was to furnish financial services to the parent company's dealers—principally the rediscounting of notes received from their retail customers. In a few cases, GHI operated dealer outlets, but as a matter of policy, it made every effort to transfer its ownership of such dealerships to unaffiliated responsible individuals as soon as practicable.

GHI published financial statements in which it consolidated all its manufacturing and distributing activities up to and including the wholesale level. It did not consolidate the finance subsidiary or the retail dealerships.

With a view to securing the best possible locations for present and future dealerships, the company organized a subsidiary to acquire real estate in choice locations. These would be used for the establishment or relocation of retail dealerships. It was planned to lease the real estate to the independent dealers that handled the company's products. The subsidiary would be financed principally through outside borrowings which would be guaranteed by GHI and it was expected that the subsidiary's eventual debt-to-equity ratio could be as high as 10-to-1.

GHI planned to exclude the new real estate subsidiary from consolidation but would pick up in income its equity in the subsidiary's profits (or losses). When and if the subsidiary became significant, appropriate information with regard to it would be furnished in the same manner as the information concerning the finance subsidiary. (The subsidiaries that operated retail dealerships had never been material.) The principal reason for placing the real estate operation in an unconsolidated subsidiary was to account for it in the same manner as GHI's other financial service activities on behalf of its customers and to segregate it from GHI's manufacturing and selling activities which had distinctly different operating and financial characteristics.

The GHI Manufacturing Company discussed its plans with the SEC which stated that it had no objection to the omission of the real estate subsidiary from the consolidated statements in view of the planned disclosures regarding its financial position and operating results.

In this connection it is worth noting that there are several prominent publicly-owned companies that also have substantial investments in real estate subsidiaries which own and operate properties not involved in the operations of the parent company or its other subsidiaries, and that such real estate subsidiaries are not included in the consolidated financial statements. One such company is Aluminum Company of America.

CONSOLIDATION OF A COMPANY NOT TECHNICALLY A SUBSIDIARY.— Rule 4–02 referred to above would seem to prohibit the consolidation of a company which is not a majority owned subsidiary. In general this is true and as it should be, but the SEC has permitted deviation from this rule where literal enforcement of the rule would violate common sense. For example, a parent company loaned each of three employees $1,000, receiving their non-interest-bearing notes. The employees invested the funds in the common stock of a new venture and gave options to the company to buy the stock in the venture for their cost, namely, $1,000 each, or a total of $3,000. By exercising the option the parent company could convert a receivable of $3,000 due from employees into an investment in a wholly owned subsidiary. The parent company was a multi-million dollar company and the loan to the employees was purely nominal—both in form and intent as well as in amount. The venture company had accumulated many millions of retained earnings all of which would be applicable to the parent company's investment the moment it exercised its unqualified option to buy the shares held nominally by its employees. In these circumstances, the SEC staff agreed that the venture company should be consolidated even though it was not technically a "majority-owned subsidiary."

The SEC also permitted a relaxing of its Rule 4–02 in connection with a registration statement filed in April, 1962, by Philips Gloeilampenfabrieken, a large electrical manufacturing company with headquarters in The Netherlands. The company has subsidiaries all over the free world, but has none in the United States. Prior to World War II Philips did own properties in the U.S.A. but transferred them to The American Trust which transferred them in 1956 to a newly established trust, known as The United States Philips Trust. A Connecticut bank, as trustee, administers the affairs of the Trust in conjunction with a consulting committee all of the members of which are required to be citizens of the U.S.A. Philips does not control, and does not have the power to control, the Trust. Some of the companies owned by the Trust, however, do business with companies in the Philips group.

The stockholders of Philips are, as such, beneficiaries of the Trust. Thus a Philips shareholder has an interest in two things: (1) a direct interest as a shareholder in Philips and its subsidiaries, and (2) a beneficial interest in the Trust. In order to ascertain his total interest, the statements of the Trust would have to be combined with those of Philips and its subsidiaries. This was the approach taken in the registration statement. In addition to the combined financial data, there was a full disclosure of the portion relating to the Trust. Apparently, the Commission did not object to the presentation because the financial statements in the registration statement as it became effective were in the form just described.

CONSOLIDATION OF 50% OWNED COMPANIES AND JOINT VENTURES.— Despite the language of Rule 4–02 of Regulation S–X, which would appear to restrict consolidation to majority-owned subsidiaries, the SEC, in a few instances, has permitted the consolidation of 50% owned companies. For example, the prospectus of El Paso Natural Gas Company, dated January 17, 1968, indicates that the consolidated financial statements include the accounts of all 50% or more owned subsidiaries.

Also, where two companies each own an undivided one-half interest in an unincorporated joint venture, the SEC has permitted the participants in the venture to reflect in their financial statements their one-half interest in the venture. This is an unusual method of consolidation because it includes one-half of the venture's cash, one-half of the venture's receivables, and so on, but as far as the consolidated net assets and net income of the co-venturers are concerned, it has the same effect as though all the cash, all the receivables, and so on, were included and provision made for the interest of the other co-owner.

The A Company and the S Company entered into precisely that kind of joint venture agreement with each company having a one-half interest, for the manufacture of a product of which it was expected that A would take about half the production and S would furnish most of the basic raw material. The operations of the joint venture were directed by a policy committee on which A and S each had an equal number of representatives. A chief executive officer had general supervision of the venture subject to the direction of the policy committee.

Positive action of the co-venturers had to be taken to commit the venture to major courses of action, such as expansion of facilities. The earnings of the venture were regularly distributed to the participants, unless the policy committee directed otherwise. In essence, each participant had an undivided one-half interest in the venture's assets; each participant was liable for the full amount of liabilities incurred by the venture but each had a claim against the other party to the extent of one-half thereof so that for practical purposes it could be said that each participant was liable for one-half of the venture's liabilities.

There were "put-sell" provisions in the agreement whereby one party could buy the other's one-half interest or sell its interest to the other party in the event of a dispute between the parties.

For tax purposes, each participant accounted for one-half of the venture's operations in its corporate federal income tax returns.

Pursuant to a lease and agreement between the A Company and the S Company (not the joint venture) and a mid-Western city, the city sold an issue of industrial development revenue bonds, maturing in annual amounts with a final maturity 25 years after issuance. The proceeds of the bonds were used to build the plant owned by the city. The lease was a net lease, and the basic rental was an amount equal to the interest and principal payments on the bonds. The companies' obligations were several rather than joint, so that each company was responsible for basic rental payments equal to one-half of the interest and principal of the bonds. The companies had the option to acquire title to the property at any time upon payment of an amount sufficient to redeem the bonds outstanding and accrued interest, plus $1.

The companies had secured a ruling from the U. S. Treasury Department to the effect that the lease transaction with the city was a financing arrangement and the companies would be treated for federal tax purposes as the owners of the facilities. Accordingly, they were entitled, among other things, to deductions for interest and depreciation and the investment credit related to the plant facilities. Under these circumstances, the companies considered it preferable that the obligation under the lease be carried as a liability in the companies' financial statements, that the interest on the bonds be considered as interest expense of the companies and classified as such in their financial statements, that the plant facilities be considered fixed assets of the companies, and that depreciation be so classified in the companies' financial statements.

The arrangements were discussed with the accounting staff of the SEC, and the companies stated their intention to reflect their liability under the lease as indebtedness, to carry their undivided interest in the plant facilities as fixed assets, to classify interest on the bonds and depreciation of the fixed assets as expenses of that nature, and to include one-half of the other assets, liabilities, income, and expenses of the joint venture with footnote disclosure that this had been done. The companies' independent auditors approved the treatment, and the SEC's staff, after considering the matter, wrote to the companies that the staff also agreed with the accounting.

The annual report of Rexall Drug and Chemical Company for 1964 indicated that the unusual method of consolidating an unincorporated joint venture (described above) was also followed by Rexall in the case of a corporation in which it held a 50% interest and another company owned the other 50% interest. A note in Rexall's 1964 report described how its ownership in a subsidiary was reduced to 50% and the accounting therefor as follows:

(3) CONSOLIDATED THERMOPLASTICS COMPANY. In 1963 and prior years Rex-all sold minority interests in the stock of a consolidated subsidiary, Consolidated Thermoplastics Company, to El Paso Natural Gas Products Company. An additional sale in 1964 reduced Rexall's ownership to 50%. No further sales are contemplated. In recognition of this new 50-50 ownership, only 50% of the assets, liabilities, income, costs and expenses of Thermoplastics are included in the accompanying 1964 statements. Comparative 1963 figures have been restated to the same 50% basis with no change in net earnings.

CONSOLIDATION OF UNACKNOWLEDGED SUBSIDIARIES.—In Chapter **30** is a discussion concerning Atlantic Research Corporation and the circumstances which caused the SEC to suspend trading in the company's securities on the American Stock Exchange. The SEC said that the company's annual report to shareholders for 1961 was materially misleading because of the failure to consolidate the operations of subsidiaries that had suffered substantial losses, or otherwise to disclose those losses. In the annual report to the Commission on Form 10–K the operations of the subsidiaries were consolidated, as a result of which the picture shown in the published report was vastly different from the picture shown in the report filed with the SEC.

Atlantic was also the subject of another SEC decision which had important accounting implications (Release Nos. 33–4657 and 33–4657A, dated December 6, 1963 and December 7, 1963). The principal point of the decision involves the existence of a parent-subsidiary relationship by means of control exercised otherwise than through record ownership of voting stock. When such effective control exists, consideration should be given to the inclusion of the controlled subsidiary in the consolidated statements.

The SEC decision in this instance was issued in connection with a registration statement filed by Atlantic under the 1933 Act. The registration did not become effective and consequently the securities were not sold. The SEC began stop-order proceedings and on December 6, 1963 issued an order suspending the effectiveness of the registration statement.

According to the SEC's findings, Atlantic failed to reveal its control and manipulation of several "satellite" or "straw" corporations and thereby concealed material aspects of its assets, obligations and operations. Under the circumstances of this case, the SEC said that it was immaterial that neither the registrant nor any of its officers or directors were the *record* owners of stock in the satellite companies. The SEC said that the facts demonstrated Atlantic's all-encompassing influence, interest and control in the affairs and management of all the satellite companies.

The nub of the SEC's reasoning is contained in the following excerpt from the decision. In this excerpt, "TCI" refers to Texas Capital Investments, Inc., one of the satellite companies; "Scurlock" is Dr. Arch C. Scurlock, the then president and a director of Atlantic; and "Bowers" is William O. Bowers III, president, treasurer and a director of TCI.

There can be no doubt as to registrant's possession, and its actual exercise, of the power to direct the management and policies of each of the satellite companies. With specific reference to TCI, we have noted that Bowers, a long-time close, personal friend of Scurlock and the record holder of the TCI stock, made no contribution of funds to TCI's capital; that TCI in effect had no funds other than those supplied to it or procured for it by registrant; that TCI's affairs were managed from registrant's offices by registrant's employees; that TCI had no employees of its own and its officers and directors, other than Bowers, were totally uninformed of its activities; that even Bowers on occasion was informed of transactions effected in TCI's name only after they had been executed by registrant's employees; that Bowers signed various documents pursuant to registrant's instructions, including checks signed in blank to be filled in as to important matters by registrant's employees; that the initiative for TCI's activities came solely from registrant and Scurlock; that various transactions directed by registrant were potentially or actually detrimental to TCI; and that TCI was heavily indebted to registrant. It is clear that TCI had no function or existence other than to be utilized by registrant to achieve registrant's objectives; its sole raison d'etre was to act as a nominee or repository which registrant could use to create or carry out transactions in which for one reason or another registrant did not wish to appear directly.

Disclosure of the facts regarding the controlled satellites, said the SEC, "would have pointed to the conclusions which the facts compel; namely, that (the) satellite companies were and are in fact extensions of the registrant which under the Act and rules and regulations promulgated thereunder should have been treated as subsidiaries *and that their financial statements should properly have been included as part of the consolidated financial statements of registrant.*" (Emphasis added.)

The SEC described a long series of transactions and operations of TCI which, in the words of the Commission, were "conceived, planned and consummated" by Atlantic "to carry out registrant's own objectives and serve registrant's own interests." The SEC said that treating TCI and the other satellites as independent corporations "was a sham and fictitious."

The decision itself makes no reference to Rule 4–02 of SEC Regulation S–X which prohibits consolidation of subsidiaries unless they are majority-owned. A majority-owned subsidiary was defined in the regulation as being a subsidiary more than 50% of whose outstanding securities representing the right, other than as affected by events of default, to vote for the election of directors, was owned by the subsidiary's parent and/or one or more of the parent's other majority-owned subsidiaries.

The SEC concluded that TCI was effectively controlled by, and was therefore a subsidiary of, Atlantic. The record ownership of the TCI stock by Bowers was brushed aside by the SEC. The decision does not discuss whether or not TCI was a majority-owned subsidiary of Atlantic but seems to suggest that TCI was wholly owned by Atlantic.

ACCOUNTING TREATMENT OF INVESTMENT IN 50 PER CENT OWNED COMPANIES.—Corporate expansion in recent years has increasingly taken the form of investments in jointly owned enterprises. These enterprises have often been set up in the form of a corporation in which each of the organizers owns a 50 per cent interest. Companies are motivated to enter into such an arrangement for a variety of reasons:

1. The risk associated with the new activity may be too great for one company to assume by itself.
2. The capital requirements of the new venture may be more than one company would wish to allocate from its own resources.
3. The new venture may develop a source of raw materials that are in common need by two companies.
4. When one party possesses the "know how" and the other party has the production facilities or other resources, the 50–50 arrangement may enable both parties to exploit their combined resources, tangible and intangible, more fully.

Under Rule 4–02 of Regulation S–X, a subsidiary may not be consolidated unless it is majority owned. As noted in this chapter, however, the SEC has permitted the consolidation of 50% owned companies, but this consolidation practice is not widespread.

Most companies in the past carried their investments in 50% owned companies at cost. There has been an increasing tendency, however, to depart from this practice and to employ the equity method. Under the equity method, the investor picks up in income its share of the current earnings or losses of the investee and adjusts the investment to the basis of cost plus (or minus) the share of income (or loss) and minus distributions. With the issuance of APB Opinion No. 18 in 1971, the equity method of accounting was formally approved by the arm of the AICPA authorized to promulgate accounting principles.

At what place in the investor's income statement should the equity in the earnings of the 50% owned company be shown? This matter was specifically dealt with in the 1972 revision of Regulation S–X. Under Rule 5–03, caption 17, the adjustment of the equity in 50% owned companies is to be shown just before income or loss before extraordinary items. The applicable instructions provide, however, that it may be shown in a different position and in a different manner if justified by the circumstances.

Group Financial Statements of Subsidiaries Not Consolidated and 50 Per Cent or Less Owned Companies (Rule 4–03).—There may be filed statements in which majority-owned subsidiaries not consolidated with the parent are consolidated or combined in one or more groups pursuant to principles of inclusion or exclusion which will clearly exhibit the financial position and results of operations of the group(s). There may also be filed financial statements in which 50% or less owned companies the investments in which are accounted for by the equity method are consolidated or combined in one or more groups pursuant to principles of inclusion or exclusion which will clearly exhibit the financial position and results of operations of the group(s).

This rule not only permits the registrant to combine statements of unconsolidated, majority owned subsidiaries; it also serves as a warning that, in certain circumstances, the SEC may insist on a reasonable grouping of the statements of such subsidiaries. Suppose, for example, that a company employing a calendar year as its fiscal year has a large number of subsidiaries with fiscal years ranging from April 30 to August 31. Under SEC rules the subsidiaries may not be consolidated. If they are significant, their statements must be filed. In the ordinary case there would be no objection to combining the subsidiaries' statements and furnishing a single statement. This is so even though the subsidiaries have different fiscal years. In that event the only requirement is that disclosure be made of the different fiscal years.

What has been said in the preceding paragraph about combining the financial statements of unconsolidated subsidiaries applies also to the financial statements of 50% or less owned companies the investments in which are accounted for by the equity method. If the statements of such companies have to be furnished because they are significant, the statements may be grouped or combined on a reasonable basis.

Statement as to Principles of Consolidation or Combination Followed (Rule 4–04).—A brief description has to be furnished of the principles followed in consolidating or combining the separate financial statements, including the principles followed in determining the inclusion or exclusion of (1) subsidiaries in consolidated or combined financial statements, and (2) companies in consolidated or combined financial statements. The description has to be furnished in the notes to the respective financial statements.

As to each consolidated financial statement and as to each combined financial statement, if there has been a change in the companies included or excluded in the corresponding statement for the preceding fiscal period filed with the Commission which has a material effect on the financial statements, the companies included and excluded have to be disclosed. If there have been any changes in the respective fiscal periods of the companies included made during the periods of the report which have a material effect on the financial statements, the changes and the manner of treatment have to be clearly indicated. The SEC does not require an affirmative statement where there have been no changes in the consolidated or combined group.

Corporations disclose their principles of consolidation in various ways. The following are typical:

Example 1. A telephone company

The consolidated financial statements shown on pages ——— and ——— consolidate the accounts of the Company and the accounts of the principal operating telephone companies in which the Company owns, directly or indirectly, securities representing more than 50 per cent of the voting power. The total investment of the companies consolidated in operating telephone subsidiaries which are not consolidated is less than $———. The subsidiaries whose accounts are so consolidated are listed below:
[Listing omitted here]

Example 2. An automobile manufacturer

The consolidated financial statements include all subsidiaries which are wholly owned, or practically so, and which are engaged in the manufacture or wholesale marketing of the Corporation's United States and Canadian products.

The SEC requirement as to disclosure of changes in the consolidated or combined group has its principal application in relation to annual reports filed with the SEC and stock exchanges—Form 10–K, for example. The note is intended to elicit information as to changes in the make-up of the consolidated or combined group. When a subsidiary is consolidated that was not previously consolidated, the following language would be an appropriate addition to the immediately preceding paragraph:

. . . except that ——— Company is included in consolidation for the first time. Prior to (date) this subsidiary was owned   per cent by the parent company; on that date the parent company acquired the remaining voting shares of the subsidiary.

When a subsidiary ceases to be consolidated, the note would read:

. . . except that Subsidiary Company is no longer included in the consolidated financial statements. Prior to (date) this subsidiary was a majority owned subsidiary. Since that date, however, due to the sale by Subsidiary Company to the public of additional shares of its common stock, the parent company owns less than a majority of the voting shares of Subsidiary Company.

When a subsidiary is liquidated or merged into the parent (registrant), and the operations are continued by the parent, there would seem to be no practical purpose served by making a notation as to a change which, in effect, is merely one of form and does not have a material effect on the financial statements.

Reconciliation of Parent's Investment in Subsidiaries not Consolidated and 50% or Less Owned Companies Accounted for by the Equity Method and Parent's Equity in Their Net Assets (Rule 4–

05).—The notes to financial statements have to include information with respect to the difference between the investments in certain companies and the equities in their net assets as follows:

Subsidiaries not consolidated and 50% or less owned companies accounted for by the equity method.—A statement shall be made in a note to the latest balance sheet of the amount and the accounting treatment of any difference between (1) the investment of the parent and its consolidated subsidiaries, as shown in the consolidated balance sheet, in the unconsolidated subsidiaries and 50% or less owned companies accounted for by the equity method and (2) their equity in the net assets of such unconsolidated subsidiaries, and 50% or less owned companies as shown in their financial statements.

Prior to the 1972 amendments of Regulation S–X, Rule 4–05 also called for a statement of the difference between the investments in *consolidated* subsidiaries and the equity in their net assets, together with the disposition of the difference in the consolidated statements. Most accountants considered this information to be relatively useless, and were glad to see the rule amended to eliminate this provision. As will be seen from the foregoing discussion, however, the rule still applies to unconsolidated subsidiaries and 50% or less owned companies accounted for by the equity method.

The contents of a note furnished pursuant to Rule 4–05 would depend on the circumstances. The following are the bare bones of such a note to which would be added the information needed to complete it:

The Company's investment in unconsolidated subsidiaries and 50% or less owned companies as shown in the accompanying balance sheet at (date) is $ more than the Company's equity in their net assets as shown in their financial statements at that date. In the accompanying balance sheet, the accounting treatment accorded such difference has been as follows:
(Details regarding accounting treatment to be furnished)

Intercompany Items and Transactions (Rule 4–06).—In general, there must be eliminated intercompany items and transactions between companies included in the (1) consolidated financial statements being filed, and as appropriate, (2) unrealized intercompany profits and losses on transactions between companies for which financial statements are being filed and companies the investment in which is presented in such statements by the equity method. If they are not eliminated, a statement of the reasons and the methods of treatment has to be made. In this connection, see also the discussion of Rule 3–16(d), also dealing with intercompany profits and losses.

If intercompany items and transactions are eliminated, there is no need to make a statement to that effect. A notation must be made only if intercompany items and transactions are *not* eliminated. See, for example, the discussion on page **16·22** relating to American Telephone and Telegraph

Company and its unconsolidated subsidiary, Western Electric Company, Incorporated.

When a statement has to be made regarding intercompany items and transactions, it is often included as part of the note dealing with the principles of consolidation. The following are typical notes furnished in compliance with Rule 4–06:

Example 1.

Certain intercompany profits, considered not to be material, have not been eliminated from inventories in the accompanying financial statements.

Example 2.

Construction and maintenance materials, supplies and equipment purchased by [regulated natural gas company] from its manufacturing subsidiaries are purchased at prices generally no less favorable than prices available to non-affiliated companies for comparable items, are recorded in the accounts of [the Company] at cost to such Company and are included in the consolidated financial statements at such cost. This cost includes the return on investment realized by the manufacturing subsidiaries and the Company believes that such cost is properly included in the consolidated accounts.

Example 3.

[A parent company in the oil business has a shipbuilding subsidiary which sells tankers to the parent.]

[Note to fixed assets:]

Included in fixed assets are plant and equipment purchased from [shipbuilding subsidiary] at cost to [parent company], less depreciation. It has been the consistent policy of the company to pay this subsidiary the same price for its work as is paid by outside companies for similar work. At (date) the cost of such assets (including profit of $ to [subsidiary] before consideration of income taxes) aggregated $ and accumulated depreciation thereon amounted to $.

[Note regarding intercompany transactions:]

. . . Intercompany profits arising from sales by [shipbuilding subsidiary] of equipment purchased and capitalized by [parent company] (see note above), before consideration of income taxes, amounted to approximately $ in (year). Depreciation charges by [parent company] applicable to such profits capitalized in fixed assets in current and prior years amounted to approximately $ in (year).

Consolidation of Financial Statements of a Registrant and Its Subsidiaries Engaged in Diverse Financial Activities (Rule 4–07).— In connection with the revision of Regulation S–X in 1972 a new rule was adopted permitting the consolidation of a registrant and its subsidiaries that are engaged in diverse financial activities. The new rule formalizes what had previously been informally permitted by the Commission. The rule follows:

(a) If the registrant and its subsidiaries are engaged in one or more types of financial activities, e.g., banking, insurance, finance, and savings and loan subsidiaries, consolidated financial statements may be filed unless deemed inappropriate; provided that, when more than one type of financial activity is involved, separate audited financial statements for each significant financial subsidiary or each significant group of financial subsidiaries shall be presented. Banks and other direct or indirect subsidiaries of bank holding companies engaged in bank related finance activities are considered to be one type of financial activity for the purpose of this rule.

(b) If the registrant and its subsidiaries are engaged in (1) manufacturing, merchandising or other nonfinancial activities as well as in (2) financial activities as described in (a) above, the subsidiaries related to whichever of group (1) or (2) is less significant shall not be consolidated with the operations of the major group; however, the group of lesser significance may be included in the consolidated financial statements if its activities are principally for the benefit of the operations of the major group. In interpreting the significance of the groups above, the registrant should consider factors in addition to those in the definition of significant subsidiary including the primary business activities of the registrant, trends, and other pertinent matters.

Special Requirements as to Public Utility Holding Companies (Rule 4–08).—In the consolidated balance sheet of a public utility holding company there must be shown the difference between the amount at which the parent's investment is carried and the underlying book equity of subsidiaries as at the respective dates of acquisition.

As an example, the consolidated balance sheet of General Public Utilities Corporation and its domestic subsidiaries included in its prospectus dated December 30, 1959, showed the following item among the consolidated assets at that date:

Excess of aggregate recorded amounts of investments in subsidiaries over related combined net assets of such subsidiaries $29,801,620

Special Requirements as to Commercial, Industrial, and Mining Companies in the Promotional, Exploratory, or Development Stage Subject to Article 5A (Rule 4–09).—The financial statements required by Article 5A must, insofar as practicable, be prepared so as to show the information for the registrant and each of its subsidiaries separately or on a consolidating basis in parallel columns. (Article 5A of Regulation S–X is applicable to commercial, industrial, and mining companies in the promotional, exploratory, or development stage. Registration statements of such companies under the 1933 Act are filed on Forms S–2 and S–3.)

Special Requirements for Investment Companies.—See Article 6 of Regulation S–X for the special consolidation requirements applicable to investment companies.

CHAPTER 18

REGULATION S–X (ANNOTATED), CONTINUED

Part 3. Form and Content of Prime Financial Statements for Commercial and Industrial Companies

CONTENTS

Article 5. Financial Statements of Commercial and Industrial Companies[1]

[Article 5 of Regulation S–X contains the requirements applicable to the form and content of balance sheets and income statements of commercial and industrial companies, except the following for which the articles indicated are applicable:

(1) Commercial, industrial and mining companies in the promotional, exploratory or development stage (see Article 5A).

[1] In the following pages of this chapter, the annotations enclosed in brackets—thus, [ ]—are not part of the Regulation S–X; they are the author's.

(2) Management investment companies (see Article 6).

(3) Unit investment trusts (see Article 6A).

(4) Face-amount certificate investment companies (see Article 6B).

(5) Employee stock purchase, savings and similar plans (see Article 6C).

(6) Insurance companies other than title insurance companies (see Articles 7 and 7A).

(7) Committees issuing certificates of deposit (see Article 8).

(8) Banks (see Article 9, Rule 9–05).

(9) Brokers and dealers when filing Forms X–17A–5 and X–17A–10 (see Rules 17a–5 and 17a–10 under the Securities Exchange Act of 1934).

Financial statements and schedules filed for bank holding companies have to be prepared in accordance with Article 5 except that Rules 9–01 to 9–04, inclusive, of Article 9 are applicable thereto.

[In Chapter **8** reference was made to the registration statements filed under the 1933 Act by brokers and dealers in securities relating to public offerings of their own securities. In connection with such registration statements, the SEC published in Release No. 33–5222 (January 3, 1972) the comments and suggestions of its staff concerning the special disclosure requirements (including those relating to financial statements) applicable to such registration statements. In view of the limited number of such registration statements, the contents of that release are not included in this book.]

Rule 5.02 Balance Sheets.—[Set forth below are the required items of information that must be shown in balance sheets together with the applicable instructions. It should be borne in mind that the form of balance sheets and the captions below are not hard and fast requirements (see Rule 3–01. It should also be remembered that if the amount to be shown for any item is not material, the item need not be shown separately (Rule 3–02). Also, inapplicable captions need not be shown (Rule 3–03).]

ASSETS AND OTHER DEBITS

Current Assets, when appropriate (see Rule 3-11 regarding items classed as current assets)

1. **Cash and cash items.**—State separately (a) cash on hand and demand deposits; (b) funds subject to repayment on call or immediately after the date of the balance sheet required to be filed; (c) time deposits; and (d) other funds, the amounts of which are known to be subject to withdrawal or usage restrictions, e.g., as compensating bal-

ances or special purpose funds. The general terms and nature of such repayment provisions and withdrawal or usage restrictions shall be described in a note referred to herein. Funds subject to withdrawal or usage restrictions shall not be included under this caption unless they are reasonably expected to become available for current operations within one year.

[The SEC has said that, prior to the McKesson & Robbins case (see Chapter **5**), accountants depended too much upon the verification of cash as the basis for the whole auditing program and hence as underlying proof of the authenticity of all transactions. Where physical contact with the operations of a business was limited to examination of supposed documentary evidence of transactions carried on completely offstage through agents unknown to the auditors, the reliability of these agents must be established by independent methods. ASR No. 19 (1940).]

2. **Marketable securities.**—Include only securities having a ready market and which represent the investment of cash available for current operations; securities which are intended to be used for nonworking capital purposes shall be excluded. Securities of affiliates shall not be included here. State, parenthetically or otherwise, the basis of determining the amount shown in the balance sheet and state the alternate of the aggregate cost or the aggregate amount on the basis of market quotations at the balance sheet date. When the original cost of securities purchased on a yield basis has been properly adjusted to reflect amortization of premium or accumulation of discount since acquisition, the basis of determining their amount may be described "at cost."

[Stock of an insolvent subsidiary may not be carried as a current asset at value at which it was received in payment for moneys advanced. Securities of subsidiaries may be carried as current assets only if they are bonds or other funded obligations or preferred stock that can be sold in open market in a short space of time without affecting the market. *American Gyro Co.,* 1 SEC 83 (1935).

A company reported large holdings of municipal bonds in part under current assets as "short-term securities (at cost plus accrued interest, which approximates market)" and in part as "other investments (at cost)." The principal basis for the inclusion of the bonds in current assets was an agreement with a brokerage firm which had sold the bonds to the company to repurchase them at the cost to the company, but the brokerage firm was financially unable to meet its repurchase obligations. Certain of the bonds were delinquent as to interest and in default as to principal which made them publicly saleable only at an amount below their cost to the company.

The SEC held the presentation in the company's balance sheet to be materially misleading. (Release No. 34–9536, March 20, 1972.)

A corporation included among "Investments, at cost" the following item: "Securities in escrow under option to the ———— Railway Co. at $13.25 per share (the aggregate option price being $5,065,475 against which aggregate payments of $3,440,700 have been made), $34,677,600." The SEC maintained the arrangement was not an "option" as described in the contracts and in the balance sheet, but a contract of sale, or a contract to sell, which involved a loss of $29,612,125. This loss should have been reflected in the accounts at the time the agreement was entered into. *Alleghany Corp.,* 6 SEC 960 (1940).]

3. **Accounts and notes receivable.**—(a) State separately amounts receivable from (1) customers (trade); (2) parents and subsidiaries; (3) other affiliates and other persons the investments in which are accounted for by the equity method; (4) underwriters, promoters, directors, officers, employees, and principal holders (other than affiliates) of equity securities of the person and its affiliates; and (5) others. Exclude from (4) amounts for purchases by such persons subject to usual trade terms, for ordinary travel and expense advances and for other such items arising in the ordinary course of business. With respects to (2) and (3), state separately in the registrant's balance sheet the amounts which in the related consolidated balance sheet are (i) eliminated and (ii) not eliminated.

(b) If receivables maturing after one year are included here under a longer current operating cycle (see Rule 3–11), state in a note to the financial statements the amount thereof and, if practicable, the amounts maturing in each year. Interest rates on major receivable items maturing after one year, or classes of receivables so maturing, shall be set forth, or an indication of the average interest rate, or the range of rates, on all receivables shall be given.

(c) Receivables from a parent, a subsidiary, an affiliate or other person designated under (a)(2) and (a)(3) above shall not be considered as current unless the net current asset position of such person justifies such treatment.

(d) If the aggregate amount of notes receivable exceeds 10 per cent of the aggregate amount of receivables, the above information shall be set forth separately for accounts receivable and notes receivable.

[Amounts due from officers and directors, because of their special nature and origin, ought generally to be set forth separately even though the dollar amounts involved are relatively small. ASR No. 41 (1942).

Where a company's business is the curing, dressing, and dyeing of fur skins, the inclusion of amounts advanced in a joint merchandising venture in which it participated among "notes receivable (trade)" or "loans receivable" is a concealment of a material item. *A. Hollander & Son, Inc.,* 8 SEC 586 (1941).

Inclusion as a current asset at face value in the balance sheet of a note given by an underwriter to cover up the improper diversion of proceeds from the sale of securities with the understanding that it would not have to be paid is false and misleading. *National Boston Montana Mines Corp.,* 2 SEC 228 (1937).

Rent and royalties not earned at the balance sheet date may not be included in the balance sheet except to the extent that collections have been made in advance of the due date. 17 SEC Ann. Rep. 18 (1951).]

4. **Allowances for doubtful accounts and notes receivable.**— Accounts and notes receivable known to be uncollectible shall be excluded from the assets as well as from the allowance accounts.

5. **Unearned income.**—Unearned discounts, finance charges and interest included in receivables shall be shown separately and deducted from the applicable receivable caption.

6. **Inventories.**—(a) State separately here, or in a note referred to herein, if practicable, the major classes of inventory such as (1) finished goods; (2) work in process (see Rule 3–11); (3) raw materials; and (4) supplies.

(b) The basis of determining the amounts shall be stated. If a basis such as "cost," "market," or "cost or market whichever is lower" is given, there shall also be given, to the extent practicable, a general indication of the method of determining the "cost"; e.g., "average cost," "first-in, first-out," "last-in, first-out," and the method of determining "market" if other than replacement or current cost. If the LIFO method is used, the excess of replacement or current cost over stated LIFO value shall, if material, be stated parenthetically or in a note to the financial statements.

[If the information required by the instructions is given in a note, it is often combined with the information required by Rule 5–03, caption 2A. The following are examples showing compliance with the instructions:

Example 1.

Inventories of raw materials, work in process, finished goods and supplies are stated at the lower of cost or market. Cost is determined substantially by the first-in, first-out method and market is based on replacement cost or realizable value.

The amounts of inventories, determined on the foregoing basis, entering into the computation of cost of goods sold, were as follows:

Beginning of Year 1	$———
End of Year 1	$———
End of Year 2	$———
End of Year 3	$———

Example 2.

Inventories have been stated at the lower of cost or market. Cost was determined by the last-in, first-out method as to inventories of approximately $ at (date). Cost of other inventories represented average or standard (approximate production) cost.

If all costs determined by the LIFO method at (date) had been determined by the first-in, first-out method, inventories would have been greater by approximately $. Working capital, after giving effect to applicable taxes on income, would have been greater by approximately $ at (date).

Example 3.

Ores, metals, and metal-bearing products have been valued at the lower of cost or market which has been reduced to state basic quantities of lead and zinc at fixed prices, based on 6.5 cents per pound for lead (New York) and 5 cents per pound for zinc (East St. Louis), under the base stock method of inventory valuation adopted at (base date). At (current date) basic quantities were 7,000 tons of lead and 18,000 tons of zinc, the same as at the end of the preceding year.

See the adverse comment of the SEC's Chief Accountant on page **3·23** regarding the omission of overhead, and sometimes even direct labor, from inventory.

See also the comment of the SEC's Chief Accountant on page **16·33** regarding the desirability of disclosure by real estate development companies of the basis of costing sales and the basis of their properties in inventory.

A company reported a loss of $17,000 for the month of January, 1946, based on book inventory, but failed to disclose that there were additional losses in the inventory accounts. It is not important whether the loss has in fact been actually realized by sale, but that the loss has accrued and is inherent on the basis of the company's current operations. "We do not believe that . . . the disclosure standards of the Securities Act are met where investors are presented with financial statements which merely reflect the carrying value of such inventories without disclosing that such carrying value contains costs which, on the basis of present indications, would not be recovered." *Globe Aircraft Corp.,* 26 SEC 45 (1947).]

7. **Other current assets.**—(a) State separately any amounts in excess of five per cent of total current assets. The remaining items may be shown in one amount.

8. **Prepaid expenses** (see Rule 5–02.19).

9. **Total current assets, when appropriate.**

[Some companies—such as real estate development companies and real estate operating companies—are not required to show a total of current assets, presumably on the basis that the information is not significant with respect to such companies.

The SEC held that a corporation's total current assets were overstated because of the inclusion therein of "Bond Expense." *Dixie Land and Timber Corp.,* ——SEC——(1966).]

INVESTMENTS

10. **Securities of affiliates and other persons.**—Include under this caption amounts representing investments in affiliates and investments in other persons which are accounted for by the equity method, and state the basis of determining these amounts. State separately in the registrant's balance sheet the amounts which in the related consolidated balance sheet are (a) eliminated and (b) not eliminated.

[See the discussion in Chapter **17** regarding the accounting for investments in 50% owned companies.

With regard to the investments of life insurance holding companies in their life insurance subsidiaries, the Chief Accountant of the SEC's Division of Corporation Finance has said: "It is our present thinking that life insurance subsidiaries should be carried at cost plus or minus changes in equity as adjusted to include those non-admitted assets which would be properly includible in a balance sheet and reflected in equity except for insurance regulatory requirements. If investments are carried at cost, disclosure is necessary in the holding company statements as to underlying equity in investments and equity in losses or profits by years." (Walter Mickelsen, "Recent Developments in the SEC Accounting Field," May 24, 1966.)

When the life insurance holding company carries its investments in life insurance companies at equity values, the statements are not generally deemed to be in accordance with generally accepted accounting principles since the insurance companies follow accounting prescribed by the regulatory authorities having jurisdiction. (*Ibid.*)

The corporate (unconsolidated) balance sheet of a corporation was held to be deficient for failure to recognize the existence of losses in the company's investments in subsidiaries, as indicated by the large excess of carrying value over equity in underlying assets, and by the limited earning power of the investments whether based upon earnings during the period under consideration or upon future earnings as projected by the company. *Associated Gas and Electric Co.,* 11 SEC 975 (1942) ; *Suburban Electric Securities Co.,* 11 SEC Ann. Rep. 87 (1945) ; also 18 SEC 216 (1945).

A company filed a registration statement which, in addition to a consolidated balance sheet, included an unconsolidated balance sheet of the registrant. In the latter statement, investments in subsidiaries were carried at cost, which was considerably more than the equity in the net assets of the subsidiaries. The SEC requested in its letter of comments that the investments in subsidiaries be carried at the amount of the underlying equity. (The author is unaware of any instance in which the SEC made this kind of suggestion when the equity in subsidiaries was *more* than the carrying value of the investments.) In discussing this matter with the SEC's staff, it appeared that their position was based principally on the views expressed in APB Opinion No. 10, paragraph 3 (which was later reaffirmed by the APB in Opinion No. 18, paragraph 14) which provides that, *in consolidated statements,* investments in unconsolidated subsidiaries should be carried at cost plus or minus the equity in their undistributed earnings.

See the comment on page **17·8** giving the SEC's views on elimination of investments in subsidiaries in a consolidated balance sheet.]

11. **Indebtedness of affiliates and other persons—not current.**—Include under this caption indebtedness of affiliates and indebtedness of other persons the investments in which are accounted for by the equity method. State separately in the registrant's balance sheet the indebtedness which in the related consolidated balance sheet is (a) eliminated and (b) not eliminated.

12. **Other security investments.**—State the basis of determining the amount shown in the balance sheet and state, parenthetically or otherwise, the alternate of the aggregate cost or the aggregate amount on the basis of market quotations at the balance sheet date.

13. **Other investments.**—State separately, by class of investments, any items in excess of five per cent of total assets.

PROPERTY

[See the discussion in Chapter **3** regarding the SEC's views as to the accounting for property acquired for stock, property under option, promotional services, appraisals, and the like.]

14. **Property, plant and equipment.**—(a) State separately here, or in a note referred to herein, if practicable, each major class, such as land, buildings, machinery and equipment, leaseholds, or functional grouping such as revenue producing equipment or industry categories, and the basis of determining the amounts; i.e., cost, cost plus manufacturing profit, etc.

(b) Tangible and intangible utility plant of a public utility company shall be segregated so as to show separately the original cost, plant acquisition adjustments, and plant adjustments, as required by the system of accounts prescribed by the applicable regulatory authorities. This rule shall not be applicable in respect of companies which are not otherwise required to make such a classification or have not completed the necessary original cost studies. If such classification is not otherwise required or if such original cost studies have not been completed, an appropriate explanation of the circumstances shall be set forth in a note which shall include a specific statement as to the status of the original cost studies and, to the extent practicable, the results indicated thereby.

[Registrant capitalized in the property account a loss incurred during a preliminary trial period. Even though it might be permissible to capitalize such losses in some cases, it is improper to place such capitalized losses in a property account. *Illinois Zinc Co.,* 6 SEC 861 (1940).]

15. Accumulated depreciation, depletion and amortization of property, plant and equipment.

[See the comment on page **16·** 17 regarding the practice of some public utility companies that are required or permitted to show their reserves for depreciation on the liability side of their balance sheets.]

INTANGIBLE ASSETS

16. Intangible assets.—State separately each major class, such as goodwill, franchises, patents or trade-marks, and the basis of determining their respective amounts.

[The SEC disapproves of writing down or writing off purchased goodwill by means of charges to *capital surplus.* ASR No. 50 (1945). See also APB Opinion Nos. 16 and 17.

Where the registrant in 1925 acquired the goodwill, processes, and formulae of a business for $460,000, and in 1931, in consideration of the payment of $75,000 to it, entered into an agreement permitting the former owner of such business to re-enter the business and, as part of such transaction, registrant agreed that its subsidiary would refrain from using the name of such person, SEC held that the $75,000 was in effect consideration for the reconveyance of at least some of the rights which were acquired in 1925 and should have been credited to the original $460,000. *A. Hollander & Son, Inc.,* 8 SEC 586 (1941).

The designation of patent *applications* as "patents" or "patent rights" is misleading. *Lewis American Airways, Inc.,* 1 SEC 330 (1936). *Petersen Engine Co., Inc.,* 2 SEC 893 (1937).

An arbitrary setting of "goodwill" value to an untried invention by those in control of a newly formed corporation, based on a mere guess with no sound basis, renders the balance sheet misleading. *American Gyro Co.,* 1 SEC 83 (1935).

A corporation operating a bus transportation system reflected in its balance sheet an intangible asset item "franchise and organization expense," which represented the capitalized cost of an abandoned street railway system which was supplanted by the bus system. The SEC said it was misleading to reflect the book value of the abandoned railway properties as an asset. 6 SEC Ann. Rep. 120 (1940).]

17. Accumulated depreciation and amortization of intangible assets.

OTHER ASSETS AND DEFERRED CHARGES

[See the discussion in Chapter **3** regarding the SEC's views as to accounting for property acquired for stock, promotional services, appraisals, and the like.

See also the comment of the SEC's Chief Accountant on page **3·24** regarding the inclusion in balance sheets of dubious deferred charges which are amortized over excessively long periods in the future.

When deferred Federal income taxes are included among the deferred charges, the nature of the transactions giving rise thereto should be stated.]

18. **Other assets.**—State separately (a) noncurrent receivables from persons specified in captions 3(a)(1) and (4); (b) each pension or other special fund; and (c) any other item not properly classed in one of the preceding asset captions which is in excess of five percent of total assets.

[Amounts due from officers and directors, because of their special nature and origin, ought generally to be set forth separately even though the dollar amounts involved are relatively small. ASR No. 41 (1942).

Financial statements that did not reflect advances to promoters were held to be deficient. *International Spa, Inc.,* 36 SEC 625 (1956).]

19. **Prepaid expenses and deferred charges.**—State separately any material items. Items properly classed as current may, however, be included under caption 8.

[A prospectus of Donaldson, Lufkin & Jenrette, Inc., dated Oct. 7, 1969, indicated that the company in May 1969 sold shares of common stock at a price of $1.00 per share to officers, directors, and employees pursuant to restrictive shareholder agreements with the company. The agreements provided that the restricted stock may not be sold, transferred, or otherwise disposed of for five years from the date of purchase. The balance sheet included an item of deferred compensation expense which was keyed to a note. The note said that the additional compensation, represented by the difference between the price paid per share and the then fair value of the shares, had been deferred and was being amortized over a five year period, the term of the restrictive feature of the shares issued.]

20. **Deferred research and development expenses, preoperating expenses and similar deferrals.**—State separately each major class and, in a note referred to herein, the policy for deferral and amortization. Where the amounts deferred or amortized are material, such amounts as shown by Rule 12–08 shall be stated in the note for each period reported on.

[When a balance sheet included in a registration statement filed under the 1933 Act reflects a material amount of "Research and Development Expense," the SEC's staff has generally requested that an analysis of the account be included in the notes to the financial statements. The analysis should include the following:

(a) Additions and amortization for a minimum of three years;

(b) Policy of amortization followed;

(c) A representation that such amounts relate to items being commercially produced or are deemed to be commercially feasible; and

(d) Upon determination that any amounts capitalized cannot be recovered by future sales, a representation as to immediate write-off to income.

The balance sheet of a company included in a registration statement included the following deferred charge:

Research and development, less related provision for deferred
federal income taxes of $——— (Note 3)

Note 3 disclosed that R & D was expensed for tax purposes as incurred, and that the company provided for the related deferred tax liability to the extent that income in a current year benefits from the tax deferment. With respect to this item, the SEC's letter of comment said "the reserve for deferred Federal income taxes should be shown under 'Liabilities and Capital' rather than as a deduction from deferred research and development."

Capitalized expenses incurred in connection with experimentation and attempted development of inventions that have been found to be worthless may not be included in the balance sheet. *American Gyro Co.,* 1 SEC 83 (1935).

Operating expenses of a coal terminal, incurred during the construction period, were charged to development, but all operating income during the construction period was included in income. The income statement and development cost item were held to be untrue. *American Terminals and Transit Co.,* 1 SEC 701 (1936).

Capitalization of net operating losses as an asset entitled "development" for period during which registrant was engaged solely in the production of ore for profit is a misrepresentation. *Virginia City Gold Mining Co.,* 2 SEC 855 (1937).

It is misleading to include in "models, experiment, development expense, etc." a charge creating a reserve for depreciation of real property not used in development or experimental work. *Lewis American Airways, Inc.,* 1 SEC 330 (1936).

Inclusion in "models, experiment, development expense, etc." of a material amount of stock selling expense is misleading. *Lewis American Airways, Inc.,* 1 SEC 330 (1936).

Where a company adopts a policy of amortizing deferred development expenses over a stated number of units to be produced, and represents that it has firm orders for that number, if, because of defects in the product, the number of orders is reduced substantially by cancellations, the amortization rate should be increased. *Drayer-Hanson, Inc.,* ASR No. 64 (1948).]

21. Deferred organization expense.—State, in a note referred to herein, the policy for deferral and amortization.

[An example of a note showing compliance with the above requirement follows: "Amounts incurred in connection with the organization of the Company have been deferred and are being amortized on a straight-line basis over a five year period ending in (year) by charges to income."

Where the amount of promoters' fees included in the asset "organization expense" is so indefensibly large as to be outside the range of reasonable difference of opinion as to the value of the services performed by the promoters, the conclusion must be that some of the stock issued to the promoter represented a donation to the promoter—not an asset of the corporation. *Brandy-Wine Brewing Co.,* 1 SEC 123 (1935).]

22. Deferred debt expense.—State, in a note referred to herein, the policy for deferral and amortization.

[Following is an example of a note showing compliance with this requirement: "Expenses incurred in connection with the issuance by the Company of long-term debt have been deferred and are being amortized on a straight-line basis by charges to income over the life of the respective bond issues."

See caption 30 regarding the showing of debt discount.

Unamortized balance of debt discount and expense, applicable to bonds retired prior to maturity with proceeds from the sale of capital stock, should be written off when the old bonds are retired. ASR No. 10 (1938). See also ARB No. 43, Chapter 15 (1953) as amended by APB Opinion No. 9 (1966).]

23. **Deferred commissions and expense on capital shares.**—
State in a note referred to herein, the policy for deferral and amortization. These items may be shown as deductions from other stockholders' equity.

[The following are examples showing compliance with the requirements:

Example 1.

No provision has been made for amortization of capital stock expense.

Example 2.

Preferred stock issue expense is written off to capital surplus on a pro rata basis as shares are acquired to meet sinking fund requirements. The amount so written off in (most recent fiscal year) was $.]

24. **Total assets and, when appropriate, other debits.**

LIABILITIES, RESERVES AND STOCKHOLDERS' EQUITY
Current Liabilities, when appropriate
(See Rule 3–12 regarding items classified as current liabilities)

25. **Accounts and notes payable.**—(a) State separately amounts payable to (1) banks, for borrowings; (2) trade creditors; (3) parents and subsidiaries; (4) other affiliates and other persons the investments in which are accounted for by the Equity Method; (5) underwriters, promoters, directors, officers, employees, and principal holders (other than affiliates) of equity securities of the person and its affiliates; and (6) others. Exclude from (5) amounts for purchases from such persons subject to usual trade terms, for ordinary travel expenses, and for other such items arising in the ordinary course of business. With respect to (3) and (4), state separately in the registrant's balance sheet the amounts which in the related consolidated balance sheet are (i) eliminated and (ii) not eliminated.

(b) If the aggregate amount of notes payable exceeds 10 percent of the aggregate amount of payables, the above information shall be set forth separately for accounts payable and notes payable.

[Amounts due to officers and directors, because of their special nature and origin, ought generally to be set forth separately even though the dollar amounts involved are relatively small. ASR No. 41 (1942).

A balance sheet listed a liability to a creditor of the registrant. The SEC said the statement was deficient for not disclosing that the president and chief promoter of the registrant controlled the creditor-corporation. *Poulin Mining Co., Ltd.,* 8 SEC 116 (1940). See also *Red Bank Oil Co.,* 21 SEC 695 (1946).]

26. **Accrued liabilities.**—State separately (a) payrolls; (b) taxes, indicating the current portion of deferred income taxes (see ASR No. 102); (c) interest; and (d) any other material items, indicating any liabilities to affiliates.

[See the SEC's comment in ASR No. 41 quoted in Chapter **30** regarding the importance of disclosing the liability for taxes.]

27. **Other current liabilities.**—State separately (a) dividends declared; (b) current portion of bonds, mortgages and similar debt; and (c) any other item in excess of five per cent of total current liabilities, indicating any liabilities to affiliates. The remaining items may be shown in one amount.

[A company held property on lease with option to purchase at any time during the lease term upon payment of option price, and reflected such amount in its balance sheet as a liability "due on purchase contract real estate." SEC said this was misleading, since there was nothing "due." *American Terminals and Transit Co.,* 1 SEC 701 (1936). *Canusa Gold Mines, Ltd.,* 2 SEC 549 (1937). *Franco Mining Corp.,* 1 SEC 289 (1936). *Poulin Mining Co., Ltd.,* 8 SEC 116 (1940).]

28. **Total current liabilities, when appropriate.**

[Some companies—such as real estate development companies and real estate operating companies—are not required to show a total for current liabilities, presumably on the basis that the information is not significant with respect to such companies.]

LONG-TERM DEBT

29. **Bonds, mortgages and similar debt.**—State separately here, or in a note referred to herein, each issue or type of obligation and such information as will indicate (see Rule 3–13) (a) the general character of each type of debt including the rate of interest; (b) the date of maturity, or if maturing serially, a brief indication of the serial maturities, such as "maturing serially from 1980 to 1990"; (c) if the payment of principal or interest is contingent, an appropriate indication of such contingency; (d) a brief indication of priority; (e) if convertible, the basis; and (f) the combined aggregate amount of maturities and sinking fund requirements for all issues, each year for the five years following the date of the balance sheet. For amounts owed to affiliates, state separately in the registrant's balance sheet the amounts which in the related consolidated balance sheet are (1) eliminated and (2) not eliminated.

[A company sold its bonds, repayable in cash and stock, to investors. The company deposited with trustees shares of stock to secure the company's liability to deliver the stock upon payment of the purchase price of the bonds. SEC ruled it was misleading to deduct the stated value of the deposited shares from the cash liability on the bonds. *Bankers Union Life Co., 2 SEC 63 (1937).*

Where a company has bonds outstanding that are repayable in cash and stock, a balance sheet that expresses only the obligation to pay cash is misleading for failure to indicate the obligation to deliver stock. *Bankers Union Life Co., 2 SEC 63 (1937).*

Unissued notes "in the treasury" of the company, shown as asset on balance sheet, were held to be misleading. *National Boston Montana Mines Corp., 2 SEC 228 (1937).*]

30. **Unamortized debt discount and premium.**—The amounts applicable to debt issues under captions 5–02.29, 31, 32 or 33 shall be deducted from or added to the face amounts of the issues under the particular caption either individually or in the aggregate, but if the aggregate method is used, the face amounts of the individual issues and the applicable unamortized discount or premium shall be shown parenthetically or otherwise.

[Caption 30 reflects one of the changes effected in the 1972 revision of Regulation S–X. Although the concept of deducting debt discount from the related debt issue is not a new one, it has had little support in authoritative accounting literature until recently. The APB stated in its Opinion No. 21 (1971) that discount and premium on debt should be reported in the balance sheet as a deduction from or addition to the face amount of the note—not as a deferred charge or credit.]

31. **Indebtedness to affiliates and other persons—not current.** —Include under this caption indebtedness to affiliates and indebtedness to other persons the investments in which are accounted for by the equity method. State separately in the registrant's balance sheet the indebtedness which in the related consolidated balance sheet is (a) eliminated and (b) not eliminated.

32. **Other long-term debt.**—Include under this caption all amounts of long-term debt not provided for under captions 29 and 31 above. State separately amounts payable to (a) persons specified in captions 25(a)(1), (2) and (5); and (b) others, specifying any material item. Indicate the extent that the debt is collateralized. Show here, or in a note referred to herein, the information required under caption 29.

[Amounts due to officers and directors, because of their special nature and origin, ought generally to be set forth separately even though the dollar amounts involved are relatively small. ASR No. 41 (1942).

See the comment on page **12·4** regarding the acceleration (subsequent to the date of the balance sheet) of payment of non-current liabilities due to officers of a registrant, and the consequent diminution of working capital.]

OTHER LIABILITIES AND DEFERRED CREDITS

33. **Other liabilities.**—State separately any item not properly classed in one of the preceding liability captions which is in excess of five percent of total liabilities.

34. **Commitments and contingent liabilities.**—(See Rule 3–16(i).

[A balance sheet was held to be deficient for failure to indicate the existence of contingent liabilities arising out of the sale of securities in violation of the Securities Act of 1933. *American Tung Grove Developments, Inc.,* 8 SEC 51 (1940). *Canusa Gold Mines, Ltd.,* 2 SEC 549 (1937). *Cristina Mines, Ltd.,* 18 SEC Ann. Rep. 12 (1952). *Petersen Engine Co., Inc.,* 2 SEC 893 (1937). *Resources Corporation International,* 7 SEC 689 (1940). *National Security Life Insurance Co.,* 41 SEC 628 (1963).

A balance sheet of a railroad in bankruptcy that fails to disclose a contingent liability of a large amount and unusual nature in accordance with requirements of the Interstate Commerce Commission is materially false and misleading. *Missouri Pacific Railroad Co.,* 6 SEC 268 (1939).

A company offered to permit previous purchasers of its securities to rescind their purchases and recover the purchase price. The omission of this contingent liability from the company's balance sheet was held to render the statement incomplete. *Bering Straits Tin Mines, Inc.,* 2 SEC 486 (1937).

Failure to disclose in a post-effective amendment that previous sales of stock under a registration statement and prospectus containing materially misleading statements created possible civil liabilities is an omission of a material fact. *United States Molybdenum Corp.,* 10 SEC 796 (1941).

The SEC was critical of a company that omitted all mention of contingent liabilities for the payment of illegal dividends and the failure to inform stockholders as to the source of dividend payments as required by Michigan law. *Consolidated Grain Corp.,* 6 SEC 597 (1940).

Omission to state that a minority of the stockholders of a subsidiary of the registrant's predecessor never accepted terms of reorganization, together with omission to indicate whether this minority stock which remains outstanding has any legal rights, have been held to be an omission of a material fact. *Livingston Mining Co.,* 2 SEC 141 (1937).]

35. **Deferred credits.**—State separately amounts for (a) deferred income taxes, (b) deferred tax credits, and (c) material items of deferred income. The current portion of deferred income taxes shall be included under caption 26 (see ASR No. 102).

RESERVES

36. **Reserves.**—State separately each major class and indicate clearly its purpose (see Rule 3–09).

[Financial statements were held to be misleading by reason of failure to provide for unrecoverable costs which might arise under the company's guaranty of its product, the management knowing of the defects in its product and the necessity for making expenditures to correct these defects. *Drayer-Hanson, Inc.,* ASR No. 64 (1948).

If the contingency or condition against which a reserve is provided is so indefinite and problematical that the reserve is in effect no more than earmarked earned surplus, it can best be shown as a sub-division thereof. ASR No. 42 (1943).

See the SEC's comment in ASR No. 41 quoted in Chapter **30** regarding the importance of showing reserve amounts.]

MINORITY INTERESTS

37. **Minority interests in consolidated subsidiaries.**—State separately in a note referred to herein amounts represented by preferred stock and the applicable dividend requirements if the preferred stock is material in relation to the consolidated stockholders' equity.

STOCKHOLDERS' EQUITY (see Rule 3–01(a))

38. **Capital shares.**—State for each class of shares the title of issue, the number of shares authorized, the number of shares issued or outstanding, as appropriate (see Rules 3–14 and 3–15), and the dollar amount thereof, and, if convertible, the basis of conversion (see also Rule 3–16(f)(3)). Show also the dollar amount, if any, of capital shares subscribed but unissued, and show the deduction of subscriptions receivable therefrom. Show here, or in a note or statement referred to herein, the changes in each class of capital shares for each period for which an income statement is required to be filed.

[Consistent with the provisions of Regulation S–X, the policy of the SEC's staff with respect to amounts receivable from the sale of capital stock may be summarized as follows:

1. All amounts receivable from the sale of capital stock should be deducted in the equity section of the balance sheet unless paid by cash prior to issuance of the auditors' report or filing the registration statement.

2. Issuance of notes evidencing the indebtedness does not constitute payment for this purpose. A legal conclusion that receipt of a note makes the stock "fully paid and nonassessable" does not constitute the receipt of funds for purposes of increasing the company's equity.

3. Financial responsibility of the subscriber, or obligor on the note or contract, is not relevant to the issue because the capital accounts of the company can not be increased until the funds are actually made available for use in the business.

In its decision in *Republic Co.,* 6 SEC 1062 (1940), the SEC said that where notes were accepted in part payment for sale of stock, the preferable accounting procedure is to set up the capital account for the full amount of the subscriptions and to show as a deduction therefrom the amounts remaining unpaid.

When a company sells its securities under instalment contracts that by their terms are not enforceable, treatment of the total amount receivable on such subscriptions as an asset without indicating that the amount may be reduced at the election of the subscriber is misleading. *Bankers Union Life Co.,* 2 SEC 63 (1937).

Financial statements that did not reflect obligations to issue stock were held to be deficient. *International Spa, Inc.,* 36 SEC 625 (1956).

It is misleading to state in financial statements that stock was issued for cash when, in fact, it was issued for property. *Platoro Gold Mines, Inc.,* 3 SEC 873 (1938).

In a transaction between a corporation and its management or parent whereby the corporation issued its stock in return for assets, it is misleading to set the stock up at its par value (indicating that the equivalent had been paid in to the company) when the assets had been acquired by the parent or management for a fraction of that amount. *Red Bank Oil Co.,* 21 SEC 695 (1946).

Where securities of a registrant have been bought for registrant's benefit in a security trading account carried on with registrant's funds, although not in registrant's name, the SEC ruled such securities must be shown on financial statements as re-acquired securities. *Kenneth N. Logan,* 10 SEC 982 (1942).

Some companies that have par value capital stock outstanding show the capital stock account in their balance sheets at the amount paid in for such stock when that amount exceeds the par value. (In California this is the required method of presentation.) In the case of one publicly-owned company, however, that filed a 10–K report with the SEC, the capital section of its balance sheet was shown thus:

Common stock, carried at	$
Authorized, (number) shares of $1 par value per share; issued (number) at (date) and (number) at (date)	
Capital in excess of carrying value of common stock	$
Retained earnings	$

The SEC reviewed the company's annual report, Form 10–K, and objected to the presentation of the capital section. In a letter to the company, the SEC said: ". . . it is our position that the carrying value of par value stock represents the dollar equivalent of the number of shares issued and outstanding multiplied by the par value per share. Any capital contributions in excess of such par value per share are required to be credited to capital surplus . . . Accordingly, it is requested that in future reports filed with this Commission, the equity section of the balance sheet be presented in conformity with the foregoing."

The company arranged a conference with the accounting staff of the SEC to discuss the suggested change. The company took the position that the presentation followed by it gave all the pertinent information, was not misleading, conformed with the requirements of generally accepted accounting principles, had substantial authoritative support, and did not violate any published rule of the Commission. The accounting staff withdrew the suggestion for future reports.]

39. **Other stockholders' equity.**—(a) Separate captions shall be shown for (1) paid-in additional capital, (2) other additional capital and (3) retained earnings (i) appropriated and (ii) unappropriated.

(b) If undistributed earnings of unconsolidated subsidiaries and 50% or less owned persons are included, state the amount in each category parenthetically or in a note referred to herein.

[This instruction is a considerable expansion of a corresponding instruction which existed before the 1972 revision of Regulation S–X. The old rule created problems; the new rule will create even greater problems. The problems arise out of the difficulty in tracing the source of earnings when dividends are declared. In conformity with the recommendations of APB Opinion No. 18, companies adjust their investments in subsidiaries, 50% owned companies, corporate joint ventures, and in certain other common stock holdings to reflect the equity in the earnings of such companies, and the adjustments are reflected initially in income and ultimately in retained earnings. When the parent company declares a dividend, what is the source of the dividend, that is, what portion is chargeable to earnings of subsidiaries, etc., and what portion is chargeable to other sources of retained earnings? This information is not required by the APB Opinion No. 18, and the SEC's instructions furnish no guidance in dealing with the matter.

Where the information required by caption 39 represents a real problem, the company might choose to adopt an arbitrary method of dealing with it—such as first-in, first-out—and disclose what was done. Alternatively, the registrant has available to it Rule 409 under the 1933 Act and Rule 12b–21 under the 1934 Act, each of which deals with information neither known nor available without unreasonable effort and expense and are set forth in this book on pages **16·2** and **14·20**, respectively.]

(c) For a period of at least 10 years subsequent to the effective date of a quasi-reorganization, any description of retained earnings shall indicate the point in time from which the new retained earning dates and for a period of at least three years shall indicate the total amount of the deficit eliminated.

(d) A summary of each account under this caption setting forth the information prescribed in Rule 11–02 shall be given for each period for which an income statement or summary of operations is being filed.

[See the SEC's comment in ASR No. 41, quoted in Chapter **30**, regarding the importance of disclosing the various types of surplus.

Write-downs or write-offs of purchased goodwill should be accomplished through timely charges preferably to income, but in no event would it be permissible to charge the loss to capital surplus. ASR No. 50 (1945). See also APB No. 17 (1970).

Write-downs of fixed assets in recognition of accumulated depreciation in values should not be charged to capital surplus. Capital surplus should under no circumstances be used to write off losses that, if currently recognized, would have been chargeable against income. ASR No. 1 (1937).

See the comment on page **17·8** giving the SEC's views disapproving of the inclusion of acquisition surplus of subsidiaries in consolidated surplus.

For a summary of the SEC's views relating to "quasi-reorganizations," see Chapter **4**.

See the discussion in Chapter **21** regarding small business corporations which elect to be taxed under Sub-Chapter S of the Internal Revenue Code. The SEC has taken the position in connection with several filings with it that the undistributed earnings of such corporations are capital surplus. This is presumably on the theory that the earnings of such corporations were, in effect, distributed to shareholders, and those not actually distributed represent a contribution to the capital of the corporation. An alternative method of accounting for Sub-Chapter S earnings that has been filed with and cleared by the SEC is to credit capital surplus with the tax benefit to the corporation resulting from the assumption of tax liability by the stockholders, which amount would also be deducted in the income statement to arrive at corporate net income.

Under certain circumstances, the "short swing" profits realized by corporate insiders are, pursuant to Section 16(b) of the 1934 Act, recoverable by the issuer. In several instances which have come to the author's attention, the SEC insisted that profits from this source received by a registrant be credited to capital surplus, and not included in income as an extraordinary gain or windfall.

In *Alleghany Corp.*, 6 SEC 960 (1940), the SEC criticized the practice under which a company charged off bond discount and expense to paid-in surplus at the time the bonds were sold. The discount and expense should have been allocated to income over the life of the bonds. In *Associated Gas and Electric Co.*, 11 SEC 1034 (1942), the SEC was even more critical. This company, prior to 1927, amortized debt discount and expense through charges to income. As at December 31, 1926, the then unamortized balance of debt discount and expense was charged to capital surplus, and in the years 1927, 1928, 1929, and 1930 annual amortization charges were made to earned surplus and were offset by credits to capital surplus. From 1931 through 1936 no amortization charges were made for debt discount and expense. In 1932 approximately $2,000,000 which had been amortized by charges to earned surplus prior to 1931 was restored to earned surplus and was offset by a charge to capital surplus.

Where stock has been sold at a premium and partly for notes receivable, and the notes are doubtful of collection, it is improper to credit paid-in surplus with the first monies paid in. Premiums should be credited to paid-in surplus only after full payment of par and stated value of securities sold. *Republic Co.,* 6 SEC 1062 (1940).

It is misleading to include in a balance sheet as "capital surplus" the valuation of development work done previously upon property under lease but representing no present-day value. *Great Dike Gold Mines, Inc.,* 1 SEC 621 (1936).

Excess of proceeds from the sale of treasury stock over the cost thereof should be treated as capital stock or capital surplus as the circumstances require. ASR No. 6 (1938).

In the case of property acquired for stock, it is improper to include in donated surplus the shares issued to the vendor and concurrently donated back to the issuer. *Bering Straits Tin Mines, Inc.,* 2 SEC 486 (1937). *Thomas Bond, Inc.,* 5 SEC 60 (1939). *Virginia City Gold Mining Co.,* 2 SEC 855 (1937).

Mortgages totaling $5,500 were received in payment of a $2,000 claim, the excess being carried to income and included in the balance sheet as earned surplus. There was evidence of an intention to contribute the excess to the recipient. The excess should have been credited to "donated surplus." *General Income Shares, Inc.,* 1 SEC 110 (1935). *National Educators Mutual Association, Inc.,* 2 SEC 212 (1935).

Financial statements that fail appropriately to disclose a question as to the propriety of dividend payments previously made, where such payments were questionable under charter provisions and involved distributions to common stock (principally held by officers and directors) of a portion of the original contribution of the preferred shares, were held by the SEC to be false. *Metropolitan Personal Loan Corp.,* 7 SEC 234 (1940).

On redemption of preferred stock, if the redemption price exceeds the amount paid in on such shares, the excess should ordinarily be charged to earned surplus. If less than an entire issue were redeemed, it would not be proper to charge against capital surplus contributed by the preferred stock an amount per share in excess of the pro rata portion of such capital surplus applicable to each share of preferred stock outstanding prior to the redemption in question. If capital surplus resulted from prior acquisition and retirement of preferred or common shares at less than amounts paid in, the redemption premium may be charged against such capital surplus. If preferred stock is replaced by a new issue bearing a lower dividend rate and there is no earned surplus available, the Commission has permitted the redemption premium to be offset against subsequent earnings in annual amounts not less than the savings effected by the lower dividend rate on the new stock. ASR No. 45 (1943).

While it may be entirely appropriate to use the increase or decrease in net asset value between two periods as a standard for the company's progress on a market value basis, it is misleading to label the increase in net asset value as "earnings" or "profits." The concept of "profits" does not include an appreciation in market value that is not realized. *Free Traders, Inc.,* 7 SEC 926 (1940).]

40. Total liabilities, reserves and stockholders' equity.

Rule 5–03. Income Statements.—[The items of information that must be set forth in the income statement, together with the related instructions, follow. See Rule 3–01 as to the flexibility of the requirements, Rule 3–02 regarding immaterial items, and Rule 3–03 as to inapplicable captions.

For a long time the SEC did not accept the "single step" form of income statement and insisted on fairly close observance of the form and captions provided in Rule 5–03. The SEC changed its policy in this respect and now accepts the single step form of statement so long as it furnishes all the information specified in Rule 5–03.]

Except as otherwise permitted by the Commission, the income statements filed for persons to whom this article is applicable shall comply with the provisions of this rule (see Rule 3–01(a) and ASR No. 41).

(a) All items of profit and loss given recognition in the accounts during each period covered by the income statements, except retroactive adjustments, shall be included in the income statement for each such period (see Rule 3–07).

(b) Only items entering into the determination of net income or loss may be included.

[The effect of this instruction is to exclude from the income statement provisions for general purpose contingency reserves, for example, that represent appropriations of surplus. The SEC rule is in harmony with ARB No. 43, Chapter 6, which provides:

7. The Committee is therefore of the opinion that reserves such as those created:
    (a) for general undetermined contingencies, or
    (b) for any indefinite possible future losses, such as, for example, losses on inventories not on hand or contracted for, or
    (c) for the purpose of reducing inventories other than to a basis which is in accordance with generally accepted accounting principles, or
    (d) without regard to any specific loss reasonably related to the operations of the current period, or
    (e) in amounts not determined on the basis of any reasonable estimates of costs or losses
   are of such a nature that charges or credits relating to such reserves should not enter into the determination of net income.
8. Accordingly, it is the opinion of the Committee that if a reserve of the type described in paragraph 7 is set up:
    (a) it should be created by a segregation or appropriation of earned surplus,
    (b) no costs or losses should be charged to it and no part of it should be transferred to income or in any way used to affect the determination of net income for any year,
    (c) it should be restored to earned surplus directly when such a reserve or any part thereof is no longer considered necessary, and
    (d) it should preferably be classified in the balance sheet as a part of shareholders' equity.

While it may be entirely appropriate to use the increase or decrease in net asset value between two periods as a standard for the company's progress on a market value basis, it is misleading to label the increase in net asset value as "earnings" or "profits." The concept of "profits" does not include an appreciation in market value that is not realized. *Free Traders, Inc., 7* SEC 926 (1940).]

(c) If income is derived from sales of tangible products (caption 1A below) and/or operating revenues of public utilities (caption 1B below) and/or other revenues (caption 1C below), each class which is not more than 10 percent of the sum of the items may be combined with another class. If these items are combined, the cost of tangible goods sold (caption 2A below), operating expenses of public utilities (caption 2B below), and costs and expenses applicable to other revenues (caption 2C below) may be combined in the same manner.

[The prospectus of National Cash Register Company, dated April 12, 1967, included an income statement for the years 1962–1966. The statement showed separate amounts for (1) net sales, and (2) service income and equipment rentals—in compliance with the instructions of Rule 5–03. The company was unable to make a similar break-down of related costs which were shown in one amount for each year and explained in a note as follows: "Under the Company's system of accounting and due to the nature of the Company's business, a break-down of cost of products and services sold applicable to net sales, service income and equipment rentals is not practicable."]

1A. **Net sales of tangible products (gross sales less discounts, returns and allowances).**—State separately, if practicable, (a) sales to unconsolidated affiliates, including 50-percent-owned persons, and (b) sales to others. If the total sales and revenues under captions 1A, 1B and 1C includes excise taxes in an amount equal to 10 percent or more of such total, the amount of such excise taxes shall be shown parenthetically or otherwise.

[In the case of retail organizations having leased departments, the sales of such leased departments should be shown separately in the income statement.]

2A. **Cost of tangible goods sold.**—(a) State the amount of cost of tangible goods sold as regularly computed under the system of accounting followed. State separately here or in a note referred to herein, if practicable, (a) purchases from unconsolidated affiliates, including 50-percent-owned persons, and (b) purchases from others. Indicate the amount of beginning and ending inventories and state the basis of determining such amounts.

(b) Merchandising organizations, both wholesale and retail, may include occupancy and buying costs under this caption. However, publicity costs shall be included under caption 4 below or shown separately.

[In practice the inventory information required by the instructions for caption 2A is frequently combined with the information required by Rule 5–02, caption 6 ("Inventories").

See the adverse comment of the SEC's Chief Accountant on page **3·23** regarding the omission of overhead, and sometimes even of direct labor, from inventory, and the comment on page **10·30** regarding the exclusion from gross profits of non-recurring gains.

See also the comment on page **16·33** regarding the desirability of disclosure by real estate development companies of the basis of costing sales.

If cost of tangible goods sold includes allocations of selling, general, and administrative expenses, see the comment below following caption 4.

Some manufacturing companies state their cost of goods sold at an amount that excludes depreciation, and show depreciation expense as a separate item (usually immediately after cost of goods sold) at an amount that includes, not only the portion applicable to cost of goods sold, but also to other profit and loss accounts. Some accountants maintain that "cost of goods sold" as so stated is not a correct figure, but this presentation has been permitted by the SEC.

The following note is an example of compliance with the inventory and purchase disclosure requirements of the instructions for caption 2A:

Inventories used in the computation of cost of goods sold are on the basis stated in Note —— to the financial statements. The amounts of such inventories were as follows:

Beginning Year 1	$
Ending Year 1	
Ending Year 2	
Ending Year 3	
Ending Interim Periods:	
Last Year	
This Year	

During the (period) purchases were made as follows:

	From unconsolidated affiliates, including 50% owned companies	From others
Year 1	$	$
Year 2		
Year 3		
Interim periods:		
Last year		
This year		

In the preceding note regarding inventories, the information need be given only for periods for which an income statement is *required* even though the instructions imply that it is to be furnished for each period for which an income statement is *filed*. For example, if a three-year income statement is *required,* but a five-year income statement is *given* (i.e., *filed*) in lieu of an earnings summary, the compliance information regarding inventories is needed only for three years.]

1B. **Operating revenues of public utilities.**—State separately, if practicable, revenues from (a) unconsolidated affiliates, including

50-percent-owned persons, and (b) others. A public utility company using a uniform system of accounts or a form for annual report prescribed by Federal or state authorities, or a similar system or report, shall follow the general segregation of operating revenues prescribed by such system or report.

2B. **Operating expenses of public utilities.**—State separately, if practicable, purchases from and services rendered by (a) unconsolidated affiliates, including 50-percent-owned persons, and (b) others. A public utility company using a uniform system of accounts or a form for annual report prescribed by Federal or state authorities, or a similar system or report, shall follow the general segregation of operating expenses prescribed by such system or report.

1C. **Other revenues (such as royalties, rents and the sales of services and intangible products, e.g., engineering and research and development).**—State separately, if practicable, revenues from and sales to (a) unconsolidated affiliates, including 50-percent-owned persons, and (b) others.

2C. **Costs and expenses applicable to other revenues (caption 1C).**—State the amount of costs and expenses applicable to other revenues as regularly computed under the system of accounting followed. State separately here or in a note referred to herein, if practicable, purchases from and services rendered by (a) unconsolidated affiliates, including 50-percent-owned persons, and (b) others.

3. **Other operating costs and expenses.**—State separately any material amounts not included in caption 2A, 2B or 2C above.

[Some real estate companies show depreciation expense in their published financial statements as the last, or next to the last, item in their income statements just before net income. This is intended to downgrade the importance of the expense because of its non-cash nature and to achieve, as a result, a mongrel sort of a cash flow statement which, of course, it is not. The SEC's staff object to this form of presentation and insist that depreciation be presented like any other ordinary expense of operation in statements filed with the Commission.

Operating expenses of a coal terminal, incurred during the construction period, were charged to development and not included in income, but all operating income during the construction period was included in income. The income statement and development cost item were held to be untrue. *American Terminals and Transit Co.,* 1 SEC 701 (1936).]

4. **Selling, general and administrative expenses.**—Any unusual material items shall be disclosed parenthetically or otherwise.

[Companies that are engaged in defense work under certain types of contracts with the United States government are entitled to recover all, or a portion of, their general and administrative expenses. Some of these companies therefore allocate such expenses to inventories and cost of sales. They are unable to state the amount of such expenses charged to income in any period since the inventories include allocations of such expenses. They are able to state the amount of such expenses incurred during a period, but this may differ materially from the amount ultimately absorbed in income through the cost accounts.

Companies in these circumstances should have no difficulty in complying with Rule 5–03 despite the specific requirement to state separately any unusual material items included in selling, general, and administrative expenses.

There have been several cases in which companies have combined cost of sales and selling and administrative expenses, showing one amount for the total. In a typical case, a note to the statement stated that "it is impracticable to segregate selling and administrative expenses from cost of sales, since allocations of such expenses have been made to inventories and cost of sales in accounting for government contract business." The company then stated the gross amounts of selling and administrative expenses incurred in each period covered by the statement.

In other instances the inability to separate general and administrative expenses from direct operating expenses may be due to the nature of the company's operations—not because of the accounting records—as in the case of service companies.

An income statement was held to be defective for failure to disclose that management fees had been paid in excess of the amount apparently permitted. *W. Wallace Alexander, Inc.,* 6 SEC 127 (1939).]

5. **Provision for doubtful accounts and notes.**

6. **Other general expenses.**—Include items not normally included in caption 4 above. State separately any material amount.

OTHER INCOME

7. **Dividends.**—State separately, if practicable, the amount of dividends from (a) securities of affiliates, (b) marketable securities, and (c) other securities. Exclude from this caption dividends from both subsidiaries and investments which are accounted for by the equity method.

[Dividends on a corporation's own stock held in its treasury or in sinking or other special funds should not be included in income. ASR No. 5 (1938).

Where stock normally is sold in part for notes that are doubtful of collection and the stock is held as security for payment of the notes, crediting dividends on such stock to income improperly inflates income. *Republic Co.,* 6 SEC 1062 (1940)].

8. **Interest on securities.**—State separately, if practicable, the amount of interest from (a) securities of affiliates, (b) marketable securities, and (c) other securities. Disclose, parenthetically or in a note referred to herein, interest from securities of companies the investments in which are accounted for by the equity method.

[The SEC has stated its opinion concerning interest collected on defaulted bonds applicable to a period prior to the date on which such bonds and defaulted interest were purchased. Collections on account of the principal of the bonds and the defaulted interest coupons should not be treated as income until such time as the full purchase price has been recovered. The opinion related specifically to the accounting treatment by an investment company, but the principle enunciated has broader application. ASR No. 36 (1942).

Where accrued interest was reflected in the market price of bonds at time purchased, and such interest was received shortly after date of purchase, the interest should have been applied as a reduction of the cost of the bonds, rather than as a credit to income. *National Securities and Research Corp.,* 12 SEC 173 (1942).]

9. **Profits on securities.**—Profits shall be stated net of losses. No profits on the person's own equity securities, or profits of its affiliates on their own equity securities, shall be included under this caption. State here or in a note referred to herein, the method followed in de-determining the cost of securities sold, e.g., "average cost," "first-in, first-out," or "identified certificate." Consideration should be given to reporting such transactions under caption 19, when appropriate.

[Excess of proceeds from the sale of treasury stock over the cost thereof should be treated as capital stock or capital surplus as the circumstances require—not as corporate profits or earned surplus. ASR No. 6 (1938).]

10. **Miscellaneous other income.**—State separately any material amounts, indicating clearly the nature of the transactions out of which the items arose. Miscellaneous other income may be stated net of miscellaneous income deductions, provided that any material amounts are set forth separately.

[The inclusion in "other income" of unusual and non-recurring income of material amounts, without further explanation, is misleading. *American Terminals and Transit Co.,* 1 SEC 701 (1936).

Where registrant, a small loan business, acquired overdue notes of a face value of $41,000 for $12,000 and reflected these notes on its books at a net amount of $30,000, crediting the excess of $18,000 to income and surplus in the amount of $7,000 and $11,000, respectively, the SEC held that the statements were misleading. *Metropolitan Personal Loan Co.,* 2 SEC 803 (1937).

Mortgages totaling $5,500 were received in payment of a $2,000 claim, the excess being carried to income. There was evidence of an intention to contribute the excess to the recipient. The excess should have been credited to donated surplus. *General Income Shares, Inc.,* 1 SEC 110 (1935). *National Educators Mutual Association, Inc.,* 1 SEC 212 (1935).

A registrant's income statement included as income the profits resulting from the sale of certain properties to insiders. The SEC held that under the circumstances the profits constituted a capital contribution rather than income. *Ambrosia Minerals, Inc.,* 26 SEC Ann. Rep. 75 (1960).]

INCOME DEDUCTIONS

11. **Interest and amortization of debt discount and expense.** —State separately (a) interest on bonds, mortgages and similar debt, (b) amortization of debt discount and expense (or premium), and (c) other interest.

12. **Losses on securities.**—Losses shall be stated net of profits. No losses on the person's own equity securities, or losses of its affiliates on their own equity securities, shall be included under this caption. State here or in a note referred to herein, the method followed in determining the cost of securities sold, e.g., "average cost," "first-in, first-out," or "identified certificate." Consideration should be given to reporting such transactions under caption 19, when appropriate.

13. **Miscellaneous income deductions.**—State separately any material amounts, indicating clearly the nature of the transactions out of which the items arose. Miscellaneous income deductions may be stated net of miscellaneous other income, provided that any material amounts are set forth separately.

[In payment of a debt of $13,000 owing to its management, a corporation turned over property having a book value of $145,000 as security for the debt, and charged off the loss to "sale of capital assets," lumped together with other losses. The statement was defective for not disclosing full details as to the nature of the transaction. *Reiter-Foster Oil Corp.,* 6 SEC 1028 (1940).]

14. **Income or loss before income tax expense and appropriate items below.**

15. **Income tax expense.**—Include under this caption only taxes based on income. [See Rule 3–16(o).]

[In the case of a company for which individual statements are filed but that pays its tax as a member of a consolidated group of companies, there should be disclosed by means of a note the estimated amount of taxes applicable to the company had it filed on an individual basis. ASR No. 52 (1945). (Although this is a published requirement of the SEC, the staff has not been enforcing it—presumably on the basis that the information called for by ASR 52 is not material as long as consolidated returns are permitted, and the company will continue as a member of the affiliated group.)

Where there are unusual relationships of taxes to pre-tax income, the reasons therefor should be stated in the notes to the financial statements.

In addition, if the tax provision is low or non-existent because of exemption from Puerto Rican taxes, the amount of such taxes that would have been applicable if the exemption were not available should be set forth in the notes to the financial statements.

In an interim financial statement covering a three-month period following a loss year, a company computed income taxes on the basis of deducting the full amount, rather than one-quarter of the amount, of operating loss carry-over. The SEC required the statement to be revised, on the presumption of continuing profitable operations which the company did not disclaim, to show the taxes for the three-month period computed on the basis of deducting only one-quarter of the operating loss carry-over. 17 SEC Ann. Rep. 17 (1951).]

16. **Minority interest in income of consolidated subsidiaries.**

17. **Equity in earnings of unconsolidated subsidiaries and 50 per cent or less owned persons.**—The amount reported under this caption shall be stated net of any applicable tax provisions. State, parenthetically or in a note referred to herein, the amount of dividends received from such persons. If justified by the circumstances, this item may be presented in a different position and in a different manner. [See Rule 3–01 (a).]

18. **Income or loss before extraordinary items.**

19. **Extraordinary items, less applicable tax.**—State separately any material items and disclose, parenthetically or otherwise, the tax applicable to each.

20. **Cumulative effects of changes in accounting principles.** —State separately any material items and disclose, parenthetically or otherwise, the tax applicable to each.

21. **Net income or loss.**—See Rule 5–02 (caption 39(d)).

22. **Earnings per share data.**—Refer to the pertinent requirements in the appropriate filing form.

[If discontinued operations during the period covered by the income statement have been material, the SEC frequently requires that such discontinued operations be shown separately from continuing operations in the statement.   The discontinued operations should be shown on one line on an after-tax basis following income from continuing operations, arriving at income (loss) before extraordinary items. Where this presentation is followed, there should be an accompanying note setting forth sales; cost of goods sold; selling, general and administrative expenses; interest expense; and income taxes, arriving at the one line item shown in the income statement. This is necessary in order to meet the requirements of the rule as to disclosure of these various items of income and expense.

Under certain circumstances, the "short swing" profits realized by corporate insiders are, pursuant to Section 16(b) of the 1934 Act, recoverable by the issuer. In several instances with which the author is familiar, the SEC insisted that profits from this source received by a registrant be credited to capital surplus and not included in income as an extraordinary gain or windfall.]

Rule 11–02. Statement of Other Stockholders' Equity.—An analysis of each class of other stockholders' equity has to be furnished for each period for which an income statement or summary of operations is filed. The other stockholders' equity accounts are set forth in the related balance sheet; in the case of commercial and industrial companies, they appear as caption 39 of Rule 5–02. The statement of other stockholders' equity for such companies must show (1) paid-in additional capital, (2) other additional capital, and (3) retained earnings (i) appropriated and (ii) unappropriated.

The statement of other stockholders equity is also prescribed by caption 26 of Rule 6–22, caption 19 of Rule 7–03, and caption 20 of Rule 7A–03.

The information to be furnished in respect of each class of other stockholders' equity follows:

1. **Balance at beginning of period.**—State separately the adjustments to the balance at the beginning of the first period of the report for items which were retroactively applied to periods prior to that period. (See Rule 5–03(a).)

2. **Net income or loss from income statement.**

3. **Other additions.**—State separately any material amounts, indicating clearly the nature of the transactions out of which the items arose.

4. **Dividends.**—For each class of shares state the amount per share and in the aggregate.

(a) Cash.

(b) Other.—Specify.

5. **Other deductions.**—State separately any material amounts, indicating clearly the nature of the transactions out of which the items arose.

6. **Balance at end of period.**—The balance at the end of the most recent period shall agree with the related balance sheet caption.

Dividends Charged to Capital Surplus.—The Commission has consistently held that the charging of dividends to capital surplus when earned surplus exists is a form of skullduggery for which there is rarely any justification. The Commission's position may be stated in this manner: Where a company purports to segregate earned and capital surplus, the financial statements are perverted when dividends are charged to capital surplus while there is an earned surplus credit balance, and the showing of an earned surplus credit balance after the payment of dividends gives a false picture of corporate strength when the earned surplus credit remains only because the dividends have been charged to capital surplus. *Associated Gas and Electric Corp.,* 6 SEC 605 (1940). Under the Public Utility Holding Company Act of 1935 the SEC has authority to regulate the payment of dividends of regulated companies [Sec. 12(c)]. Regulation 250.46(a) prohibits the declaration or payment of dividends by registered holding companies or their subsidiaries out of capital or unearned surplus except as may be permitted pursuant to an order of the Commission.

The Commission does not have the same authority over the accounting for dividends of companies not subject to the Holding Company Act, but some idea of the Commission's influence in this area may be gained from the following incident which was reported in *The Journal of Accountancy* (August, 1937, p. 87).

In 1935 a corporation charged ordinary dividends first to capital surplus, exhausting that account, and the balance to earned surplus. Apparently in explanation of their certification, the independent public accountants addressed the following letter to the SEC:

We have been advised by [name of company] of [city], regarding your request that we, as auditors for the company, furnish you with a letter explaining the propriety of a charge made to capital surplus in the year 1935 of $284,025.43, representing a portion of the cash dividends paid within that year.

We recognize that under ordinary circumstances accounting procedure requires that cash dividends be charged to earned surplus. It was the desire, however, of some of the officers and directors of the company to eliminate the capital surplus item from the accounts and, after some discussion, the legal phases of the question were referred to the company's attorneys. The attorneys stated that in their opinion it is proper, under Michigan law, to declare dividends out of capital surplus when the balance in the capital surplus account is not composed of items out of which, under Michigan law, dividends may not be paid. From the legal point of view, the balance in the capital surplus account of the company contained no items out of which dividends could not be paid.

Under the circumstances, the directors passed resolutions authorizing the payment of cash dividends out of capital surplus, which dividends were specifically paid out of such surplus. In view of the action of the directors in authorizing the payment of dividends out of capital surplus and the payment thereof out of capital surplus, it seems that the effect of the action taken must be reflected in the accounts in the manner prescribed.

The attorney for the company also wrote the SEC, and said, "the item in question has never been anything other than earned surplus, having been earned by [a predecessor company], prior to its merger by exchange of shares in 1929 with the [present company]." He continued:

By some vagaries of accounting, two surplus accounts were set up; one consisting of the surplus account earned prior to the merger and the other of surplus earned after the merger. This, naturally, led to numerous inquiries as to why we had two surplus accounts, and it was in an effort to consolidate the two accounts that it was proposed to charge dividends against the so-called "capital surplus" until it was depleted, and I know no reason, under the statutes of this state, why the procedure is not perfectly lawful, whether according to approved accounting or not, a matter about which I have no knowledge. . . . I believe that the same result could have been attained by a resolution of the board consolidating the two surplus accounts, but this was not done.

A few years later the company transferred to earned surplus the charge for the dividend which had previously been recorded in capital surplus.

The author believes that many United States accountants support the SEC's position on accounting for ordinary cash dividends, but that this support is based on common sense grounds rather than pure accounting theory. Lenhart and Defliese acknowledge that dividends have been charged to paid-in surplus or to a surplus other than earned surplus without violating state regulations. They maintain, however, that this reflects no great credit on the lawmakers, "since the incongruity of contributing to the capital of a corporation and then receiving part of it back in the guise of ordinary dividends should be sufficiently evident to encourage making the practice legally impossible." [2]

Blough, on the other hand, recognizes that the type of surplus that can be used as a basis for cash dividend declarations is a legal matter and if the directors specify that a dividend shall be paid out of a certain type of surplus—and if their action is legal—"the financial statements would contain a misrepresentation if they reflected the dividend as having been charged to any other account. . . ." [3]

[2] Lenhart and Defliese, *Montgomery's Auditing*, 8th ed. (1957), p. 407.
[3] Carman G. Blough, "Accounting and Auditing Problems," 108 *The Journal of Accountancy* 70 (Oct. 1959).

Stock Dividends.—The SEC is in agreement with the AICPA pronouncements on accounting for stock dividends. The Institute's Committee on Accounting Procedure stated that the issuer should charge its earned surplus account with the fair value of the shares issued as a stock dividend. (ARB No. 43 (1953), p. 51; see that bulletin for the distinction between a stock dividend and a stock split.)

In a case considered by the SEC a company that was going to issue a stock dividend indicated that the dividend would be charged to earned surplus at a per share amount representing the fair value of the shares to be issued. The company later amended the statement to indicate that the charge to earned surplus would be the par value of the shares (which was less than the fair value). SEC advised the company that applicable accounting principles required a charge against earned surplus in the amount of the fair value of the shares. However, in the company's annual report filed shortly thereafter the accounting treatment to which the SEC had objected was followed. Moreover, the report of the independent public accountants accompanying the company's financial statements contained an explicit exception to the company's failure to account for the dividend at fair value rather than the lower par value figure. The company was again requested to change its accounting treatment of the transaction, but declined to do so. After reconsidering its position and reviewing the case in detail, the SEC again advised the company that the annual report should be amended in accordance with its earlier recommendations and those of the independent accountants. Failing this, the staff indicated it would consider the report false and misleading and would accordingly recommend that appropriate formal action be taken by the Commission to determine whether the company had failed to comply with the provisions of the Securities Exchange Act and the rules and regulations thereunder. Following this interchange of views the statements were amended without resorting to formal action. (12 SEC Ann. Rep. 116 (1946).)

The SEC instituted stop-order proceedings against Monmouth Capital Corporation on the basis of allegations by the Commission's staff that the company had made a series of stock distributions without adequate undistributed earned surplus to capitalize such distributions as required by proper accounting principles, which rendered misleading the financial statements of the company included in a registration statement filed by it under the 1933 Act. In connection with an offer of settlement, the company consented to the Commission's findings that generally accepted accounting principles were not followed with respect to the various stock distributions since it did not have the requisite earned surplus. (SEC Ann. Rep. year ended June 30, 1970, p. 156.)

United States accountants are far from unanimous in their views regarding the position taken by the AICPA with respect to accounting for stock dividends.[4] Some are frankly puzzled by the rationale in the AICPA bulletin; others are in complete disagreement. Many foreign accountants— even those who admire most the United States advances in accounting and auditing—are strongly opposed to the bulletin, and are at a complete loss to understand the reasoning on which it is based. The Institute's bulletin, however, has the enthusiastic support of the New York Stock Exchange, as well as the SEC. The Commission insists that United States registrants comply with the AICPA pronouncement, but is slightly more flexible where foreign registrants are involved. For comment on this matter in relation to foreign corporations, see Chapter **31**.

When a stock dividend is declared payable at a specified future date, how should it be reflected in a balance sheet prior to the issuance of the additional shares? Such dividends are not shown among the liabilities. The amount to be capitalized may be shown as a separate classification in the capital section with an indication of the number of shares expected to be issued. Some accountants contend that it is permissible not to reflect any change in the balance sheet as a result of the declaration other than to disclose by footnote the nature of the declaration and the amount of surplus to be capitalized.[5]

In some cases it may not be possible to determine the amount of the charge to surplus until the record date of the dividend has passed. This would be the case, for example, when there is an issue of convertible bonds outstanding; if a holder of a bond exercises his right to convert before the record date for the stock dividend, he would be entitled to the dividend.

Assuming, however, that the amount of the dividend can be reasonably estimated—that is, the number of shares to be issued has been reasonably fixed—the staff of the SEC has indicated a preference for dealing with the amount of the dividend by a charge to surplus and not by a footnote to the financial statements. The staff believes that as far as it relates to the *time* when surplus is charged, there is no difference between a cash dividend and a stock dividend.

Proposed Rule 10b–12.—As an indication of the SEC's thinking with respect to stock dividends, mention might be made of an announcement by

---

[4] In an address before the annual meeting of the AICPA, entitled "Challenges to the Accounting Profession in the United States," Carman G. Blough, the then director of research of the AICPA, said: ". . . It is a generally accepted practice today that if a corporation having a public issue of securities declares a small stock dividend, it should charge to retained earnings, not only the par or stated value of the stock issued, but should transfer enough more to capital surplus so that the charge to retained earnings will be no less than the fair market value of the stock. The propriety of treating this as an accounting principle has been challenged on more than one occasion." [Reprinted in 108 *The Journal of Accountancy* 41 (Dec. 1959).]

[5] See, for example, Lenhart and Defliese, *Montgomery's Auditing,* 8th ed., p. 431 (1957).

the Commission on March 7, 1968 (Release No. 34–8268). The SEC said it had under consideration a proposal to adopt a rule under Section 10(b) of the 1934 Act. (This section makes it unlawful to use or employ, in connection with the purchase or sale of any security, any manipulative or deceptive device or contrivance in contravention of SEC rules.) The proposed rule (which would be designated Rule 10b–12) would preclude an issuer whose stock is publicly offered or traded from misrepresenting the results of its operations by distributing stock dividends unless the issuer has earned surplus sufficient to cover the fair value of the shares distributed. The rule would not affect stock splits involving the distribution of at least an additional share for each share outstanding.

The SEC pointed out that pro rata stock distributions to stockholders in amounts which are small in relation to the number of shares outstanding are a means of conveying the impression that a distribution is being made out of the earned surplus of the company without the drain on current assets that would result from the distribution of a cash dividend. The SEC said that instances had come to its attention in which such distributions were utilized by companies having little or no earned surplus, "thus creating a misleading impression concerning the results of operations of the company."

Paragraph (a)(1) of the proposed rule would provide that any pro rata stock distribution to stockholders shall be a manipulative or deceptive device if it be designated as a stock dividend, unless the issuer has earned surplus in an amount not less than the fair value of the shares so distributed and unless it transfers such amount from earned surplus to permanent capitalization. This paragraph also declares that, regardless of how designated, if the number of shares to be so distributed be less than 25% of the number of shares of the same class prior to the distribution, the transaction would constitute a manipulative or deceptive device if the distribution be made in the absence of earned surplus in an amount not less than the fair value of the shares so distributed and in the absence of the transfer by the issuer of such amount from earned surplus to the permanent capitalization of the issuer.

Paragraph (a)(2) deals with distribution of that type in a quantity of 25% or more but less than 100% of the number of shares outstanding prior to the distribution. In such a case, if the distribution is part of a plan for recurring pro rata distributions to stockholders without consideration, the issuer would be prohibited from making it in the absence of earned surplus in an amount not less than the fair value of the distributed shares and in the absence of the capitalization by the issuer of such amount out of earned surplus. This paragraph also provides that the issuer shall have the burden of proving that any given distribution of shares of that kind is not part of a program of recurring pro rata distributions.

Paragraph (b) provides that the term "fair value" covered by the provisions of the rule means an amount determined in accordance with good accounting practice, which closely approximates the current per share market price adjusted to reflect issuance of the additional shares. This standard applies only when the shares being issued are of a previously outstanding class for which a market exists. The proposed rule is also applicable to a distribution of shares of a class not previously outstanding or for which no market exists, but the rule does not prescribe a specific standard for valuation in these circumstances.

At the date of this writing, the proposed rule had not been adopted nor has the Commission made any public announcement with regard to it. The author believes that the proposal gave rise to many problems—including its applicability to foreign issuers whose securities are traded in the United States but which do not follow United States principles in accounting for stock dividends.

On June 1, 1972, however, the Commission issued Accounting Series Release No. 124 which dealt with pro rata stock distributions to stockholders. The Commission said that if the distribution is less than 25% of shares of the same class outstanding, the fair value of the shares issued must be transferred from retained earnings to other capital accounts. Failure to make this transfer in connection with a distribution, or making a distribution in the absence of retained or current earnings "is evidence of misleading practice." The release also pointed out that, in situations where companies did not have retained or current earnings, the declaration of a dividend not warranted by the business condition of a company "is characteristic of a manipulative scheme."

Distribution of Warrants to Shareholders.—Several publicly-owned companies in recent years have distributed to their shareholders long-term warrants which entitle the holders for a specified period—say, ten years—to purchase the issuer's stock at a fixed price. Usually the purchase price is a price above the market price at the time the warrants are issued. At the present time there is no requirement in generally accepted accounting principles that any accounting be made for the issuance of these warrants since the issuer neither receives consideration nor diminishes its assets as a result of the distributions. On the other hand, the New York Stock Exchange has been adamant with respect to companies having securities listed on the Exchange, and has insisted that the appropriate accounting is to capitalize the fair value of the warrants distributed by a transfer from retained earnings to other capital. This position is largely a policing action, and is wholly consistent with the Exchange's attitude on stock dividends.

The Exchange has indicated that unless some accounting were ordered for the distribution of warrants, a company could elect to make periodic distributions of warrants to shareholders in lieu of stock dividends.

In an informal poll, most of the members of the APB indicated that they could not support the Exchange's position on a logical basis, but as long as the requirement for accounting for stock dividends existed, they could not take a contrary position with respect to warrant distributions.

While the initiative in this instance was taken by the New York Stock Exchange, it is known that the SEC agrees with the Exchange's position, which is not surprising in view of the SEC's position with respect to accounting for stock dividends.

Rule 11A–02. Statement of Source and Application of Funds (Statement of Changes in Financial Position).—The statement of source and application of funds is prescribed in the instructions for financial statements of the applicable registration and report forms. In APB Opinion No. 19 (March 1971) it was recommended that the title of the funds statement be changed to "Statement of Changes in Financial Position," and it is to be expected that the statement prescribed by Rule 11A–02 will be so designated in most cases.

The requirements as to the form and content of the funds statement are set forth in Rule 11A–02 which follows, except that certain real estate companies that have to file quarterly reports on Form 7–Q must comply in all filings with the requirements as to form and content of a funds statement specified in that form.

Rule 11A–02 follows:

The statement of source and application of funds shall summarize the sources from which funds or working capital have been obtained and their disposition. (See Rule 3–01.)

Material changes in the components of net funds or working capital shall be shown in the statement or in a supporting tabulation.

As a minimum, the following shall be reported:

(a) Sources of funds:
    (1) Current operations (showing separately net income or loss and the addition and deduction of specific items which did not require the expenditure or receipt of funds; e.g., depreciation and amortization, deferred income taxes, undistributed earnings or losses of unconsolidated persons, etc.)
    (2) Sale of noncurrent assets (identifying separately such items as investments, fixed assets, intangibles, etc.)
    (3) Issuance of debt securities or other long-term debt
    (4) Issuance or sale of capital stock
(b) Disposition of funds:
    (1) Purchase of noncurrent assets (identifying separately such items as investments, fixed assets, intangibles, etc.)
    (2) Redemption or repayment of debt securities or other long-term debt
    (3) Redemption or purchase of capital stock
    (4) Dividends
(c) Increase (decrease) in net funds or working capital

Rule 5–04. What Schedules Are to Be Filed.—[Schedules must be furnished in support of the balance sheets and income statements required by Rules 5–02 and 5–03. The purpose of the schedules is to furnish the prospective investor or security analyst with information in addition to that contained in the prime statements. The schedules furnish two types of information: (1) they indicate the *makeup* of amounts in the prime statements, or (2) they give an indication of the *activity* of an account during the entire period for which income statements are required. In Instruction (a)(1) below is a list of those schedules that must be furnished as of the date of the most recent audited balance sheet and any subsequent unaudited balance sheet being filed. The schedules listed in Instruction (a) (1) need not be certified if the related balance sheet is not certified. All other schedules required to be filed must be furnished for each period covered by the income statements and shall be certified if the related income statement is certified.]

(a) Except as expressly provided otherwise in the applicable form—

    (1) The schedules specified below in this rule as Schedules I, IX, XI, XIII, XIV, XV, XVII, XVIII and XIX shall be filed as of the date of the most recent audited balance sheet and any subsequent unaudited balance sheet being filed for each person or group, provided that any such schedule (other than Schedules I, XIII, XVII, XVIII, and XIX) may be omitted if both of the following conditions exist:

    (i) The financial statements are being filed as part of an annual or other periodic report; and

    (ii) The information that would be shown in the respective columns of such schedule would reflect no changes in any issue of securities of the registrant or any significant subsidiary in excess of five per cent of the outstanding securities of such issue as shown in the most recently filed annual report containing the schedule.

    (2) Schedule XIII, Capital Shares, may also be omitted if the above two conditions exist and any information required by column G of the schedule is shown in the related balance sheet or in a note thereto.

    (3) *All other schedules* specified below in this rule as Schedules II, III, IV, V, VI, VII, VIII, X, XII and XVI shall be filed *for each period for which an income statement is required to be filed* for each person or group.

(b) When information is required in schedules for both the registrant and the registrant and its subsidiaries consolidated, it may be presented in the form of a single schedule, provided that items pertaining to the registrant are separately shown and that such single schedule affords a properly summarized presentation of the facts. If the information required by any schedule (including the notes thereto) may be shown in the related financial statement or in a note thereto without making such statement unclear or confusing, that procedure may be followed and the schedule omitted.

(c) Reference to the schedules shall be made in the appropriate captions of the financial statements. Where, pursuant to the applicable instructions, the supporting schedules do not accompany the financial statements, references to such schedules shall not be made.

(d) The schedules shall be examined by the independent accountant if the related financial statements are so examined.

[If a registrant voluntarily furnishes a ten-year income statement in a registration statement, in lieu of the required three-year income statement, the schedules need be furnished only for the required three-year period.

In the detailed instructions relating to schedules which follow, provision is made for the omission of the schedules in specified circumstances when the information is not material. For example, Schedule V ("Property, plant, and equipment") may be omitted depending on whether the amount shown by balance sheet caption 14 does not exceed 5% of total assets as shown by the related balance sheet at *both* the beginning and end of the period, and if neither total additions nor total deductions during the period exceeded 5% of total assets as shown by the related balance sheet at *either* the beginning *or* end of the period. Where the schedules are furnished as part of a registration statement and cover, say, three years, there may be a question in interpreting the SEC's instruction. In order to omit the schedule, must there be compliance with the specified conditions in *all three years?* The answer is no; each year stands on its own, and hence it would be possible, for example, to omit the property schedule for Years 1 and 3 and to furnish it for Year 2, except for Schedule II ("Amounts receivable from underwriters, promoters, directors, officers, employees, and principal holders (other than affiliates) of equity securities of the person and its affiliates"), with respect to which a different interpretation applies; see the comment on page 18·42 interpreting the requirements applicable to that schedule.

Assume that a company files a registration statement under the 1933 Act on Form S–1, and that, under the financial instructions, its financial statements may be as of a date within six months of filing in lieu of the 90-day requirement applicable to other companies—in other words, the company is of the requisite size, is registered under the 1934 Act and files reports under the Act, and has no funded debt in default. The company's fiscal year is a calendar year, and normally the year-end statements would not have to be updated if filed before June 30. The company, however, has released interim first quarter information following its year end together with information for the corresponding quarter of the preceding year, and therefore plans to furnish a balance sheet at March 31 of the current year, income and other stockholders' equity statements for the quarter then ended, and first quarter information for this year and last year in the summary of earnings. Does the company have to furnish supporting schedules for the first quarter of this year down to the date of the latest balance sheet submitted? The answer is no; the supporting schedules need be furnished only in support of the year-end balance sheet. The SEC takes the position that the year-end financial statements and schedules meet the Commission's requirements, and if the company furnishes statements as of a later date, this is gratuitous information and need not be accompanied by supporting schedules as of the later date.

On the other hand, this interpretation should be considered in the light of two factors:

1. See the SEC's administrative policy on page **9**·3 regarding the need for updating financial statements in certain circumstances.

2. If a comparison of the balance sheets at December 31 and March 31 indicates that significant information might be revealed by the supporting schedules, the SEC would reserve the right to request that supporting schedules be submitted down to the date of the latest balance sheet filed.

The reader is referred to the discussion beginning on page **10**·9 regarding the submission by certain utility companies of earnings summaries for a *twelve-month period* ending on an interim date in lieu of the summaries both for the interim period between the close of the last fiscal year and the date of the latest balance sheet and for the corresponding period of the preceding fiscal year. When the earnings summary is furnished in sufficient detail so that it meets the requirements of an income statement, such companies need not furnish the income statement that would otherwise be required for the most recent short interim period. If the income statement for the short interim period is omitted, supporting schedules for that period may also be omitted.]

SCHEDULE I. MARKETABLE SECURITIES—OTHER SECURITY INVESTMENTS.—The schedule prescribed by Rule 12–02 shall be filed—

(1) In support of caption 2 of a balance sheet, if the greater of the aggregate cost or the aggregate market of marketable securities based

on market quotations as of the balance sheet date constitutes 10 per cent or more of total assets.

(2) In support of caption 12 of a balance sheet, if the amount at which other security investments is shown in such balance sheet constitutes 10 per cent or more of total assets.

(3) In support of captions 2 and 12 of a balance sheet, if the amount at which other security investments is shown in such balance sheet plus the greater of the aggregate cost or the aggregate market of marketable securities based on market quotations as of the balance sheet date constitutes 15 per cent or more of total assets.

SCHEDULE II. AMOUNTS RECEIVABLE FROM UNDERWRITERS, PROMOTERS, DIRECTORS, OFFICERS, EMPLOYEES, AND PRINCIPAL HOLDERS (OTHER THAN AFFILIATES OF EQUITY SECURITIES OF THE PERSON AND ITS AFFILIATES.—The schedule prescribed by Rule 12–03 shall be filed with respect to each person among the underwriters, promoters, directors, officers, employees, and principal holders (other than affiliates) of equity securities of the person and its affiliates, from whom an aggregate indebtedness of more than $20,000 or one per cent of total assets, whichever is less, is owed, or at any time during the period for which related income statements are required to be filed, was owed. For the purposes of this schedule, exclude in the determination of the amount of indebtedness all amounts receivable from such persons for purchases subject to usual trade terms, for ordinary travel and expense advances and for other such items arising in the ordinary course of business.

[The requirements applicable to Schedule II are to be distinguished from those applicable to any other schedule insofar as the period to be reported upon is concerned. If the limit of $20,000 or 1 per cent of total assets, whichever is less, is met in *any* of the three years covered by the income statement in the usual registration statement, then the schedule must be furnished for *each of the three years* (plus the interim period, if applicable). This is different from Schedule V ("Property, plant and equipment"), for example, where it would be possible to furnish the schedule for one year and omit it for the others.]

SCHEDULE III. INVESTMENTS IN, EQUITY IN EARNINGS OF, AND DIVIDENDS RECEIVED FROM AFFILIATES AND OTHER PERSONS.—The schedule prescribed by Rule 12–04 shall be filed in support of caption 10 of each balance sheet. This schedule may be omitted if (1) neither the sum of captions 10 and 11 in the related balance sheet nor the amount of caption 31 in such balance sheet exceeds five per cent of total assets as shown by the related balance sheet at either the beginning or end of the period or (2) there have been no material changes in the information required to be filed from that last previously reported.

Schedule IV. Indebtedness of Affiliates and Other Persons— Not Current.—The schedule prescribed by Rule 12–05 shall be filed in support of caption 11 of each balance sheet; however, the required information may be presented separately on Schedule III or Schedule X. This schedule may be omitted if (1) neither the sum of captions 10 and 11 in the related balance sheet nor the amount of caption 31 in such balance sheet exceeds five percent of total assets as shown by the related balance sheet at either the beginning or end of the period, or (2) there have been no material changes in the information required to be filed from that last previously reported.

Schedule V. Property, Plant and Equipment.—The schedule prescribed by Rule 12–06 shall be filed in support of caption 14 of each balance sheet, provided that this schedule may be omitted if the total shown by caption 14 does not exceed five per cent of total assets as shown by the related balance sheet at both the beginning and end of the period and if neither the additions nor the deductions during the period exceeded five per cent of total assets as shown by the related balance sheet at either the beginning or end of the period.

Schedule VI. Accumulated Depreciation, Depletion and Amortization of Property, Plant and Equipment.—The schedule prescribed by Rule 12–07 shall be filed in support of caption 15 of each balance sheet. This schedule may be omitted if Schedule V is omitted.

Schedule VII. Intangible Assets, Deferred Research and Development Expenses, Preoperating Expenses and Similar Deferrals.—Part A of the schedule prescribed by Rule 12–08 shall be filed in support of caption 16 and Part B shall be filed in support of caption 20 of each balance sheet, provided that either part may be omitted if the total shown by the related balance sheet caption does not exceed five percent of total assets as shown in the related balance sheet at both the beginning and end of the period and if neither the additions nor the deductions during the period exceeded five percent of total assets as shown by the related balance sheet at the beginning or end of the period.

Schedule VIII. Accumulated Depreciation and Amortization of Intangible Assets.—The schedule prescribed by Rule 12–09 shall be filed in support of caption 17 of each balance sheet. This schedule may be omitted if Schedule VII is omitted.

SCHEDULE IX. BONDS, MORTGAGES AND SIMILAR DEBT.—The schedule prescribed by Rule 12–10 shall be filed in support of caption 29 of a balance sheet.

SCHEDULE X. INDEBTEDNESS TO AFFILIATES AND OTHER PERSONS— NOT CURRENT.—The schedule prescribed by Rule 12–11 shall be filed in support of caption 31 of each balance sheet; however, the required information may be presented separately on Schedule III or Schedule IV. This schedule may be omitted if (1) neither the sum of captions 10 and 11 in the related balance sheet nor the amount of caption 31 in such balance sheet exceeds five percent of total assets as shown by the related balance sheet at either the beginning or end of the period, or (2) there have been no material changes in the information required to be filed from that last previously reported.

SCHEDULE XI. GUARANTEES OF SECURITIES OF OTHER ISSUERS.—The schedule prescribed by Rule 12–12 shall be filed with respect to any guarantees of securities of other issuers by the person for which the statement is filed.

SCHEDULE XII. VALUATION AND QUALIFYING ACCOUNTS AND RE- SERVES.—The schedule prescribed by Rule 12–13 shall be filed in support of valuation and qualifying accounts and reserves included in each balance sheet but not included in Schedule VI or VIII. (See Rule 3–02.)

SCHEDULE XIII. CAPITAL SHARES.—The schedule prescribed by Rule 12–14 shall be filed in support of caption 38 of a balance sheet.

SCHEDULE XIV. WARRANTS OR RIGHTS.—The schedule prescribed by Rule 12–15 shall be filed with respect to warrants or rights granted by the person for which the statement is filed to subscribe for or purchase securities to be issued by such person.

SCHEDULE XV. OTHER SECURITIES.—If there are any classes of securities not included in Schedules IX, XI, XIII or XIV, set forth in this schedule information concerning such securities corresponding to that required for the securities included in such schedules. Information need not be set forth, however, as to notes, drafts, bills of exchange, or bankers' acceptances, having a maturity at the time of issuance of not exceeding one year.

SCHEDULE XVI. SUPPLEMENTARY INCOME STATEMENT INFORMATION. —The schedule prescribed by Rule 12–16 may be omitted for each income statement in which sales or operating revenues were not of significant amount. This schedule may also be omitted if the information required by column B and instructions 3 and 4 thereof is furnished in the income statement or in a note thereto.

SCHEDULE XVII. REAL ESTATE AND ACCUMULATED DEPRECIATION.— The schedule prescribed by Rule 12–42 shall be filed for real estate (and the related accumulated depreciation) held by persons a substantial portion of whose business is that of acquiring and holding for investment real estate or interests in real estate, or interests in other persons a substantial portion of whose business is that of acquiring and holding real estate or interests in real estate for investment. Real estate used in the business shall be excluded from the schedule.

SCHEDULE XVIII. MORTGAGE LOANS ON REAL ESTATE.—The schedule prescribed by Rule 12–43 shall be filed by persons specified under Schedule XVII for investments in mortgage loans on real estate.

SCHEDULE XIX. OTHER INVESTMENTS.—If there are any other investments, under caption 5–02.13 or elsewhere in a balance sheet, not required to be included in Schedule I or III, there shall be set forth in a separate schedule information concerning such investments corresponding to that prescribed by Schedule I. This schedule may be omitted if the total amount of such other investments does not exceed five per cent of total assets as shown by such balance sheet.

CHAPTER **19**

REGULATION S–X (ANNOTATED), CONTINUED

Part 4. Form and Content of Prime Financial Statements for Companies other than Commercial and Industrial Companies

C O N T E N T S

Article 5A. Commercial, Industrial, and Mining Companies in the Promotional, Exploratory, or Development Stage

Rule 5A–01. Application of Article 5A.—This article shall be applicable to the financial statements filed as a part of:

   (*a*) Registration statements on Form S–2 or Form S–3, except as otherwise specifically provided in such forms, under the Securities Act of 1933;

   (*b*) Applications for registration and annual reports pursuant to sections 12, 13, and 15 (*d*) respectively of the Securities Exchange Act of 1934 filed by commercial and industrial companies in the promotional or development stage which, if registering under the Securities Act of 1933, would be required to use Form S–2.

(c) Applications for registration and annual reports pursuant to sections 12, 13, and 15 (d) respectively of the Securities Exchange Act of 1934 filed by mining companies not in the production stage[1] but engaged primarily in the exploration for or the development of mineral deposits other than oil, gas or coal, if all of the following conditions are met:

(1) The registrant has not been in production during the period of the report or the two years immediately prior thereto; except that being in production for an aggregate period of no more than eight months over the three-year period shall not affect the use of the form.

(2) Receipts from the sale of mineral products or from the operation of mineral producing properties by the registrant and its subsidiaries combined have not exceeded $500,000 in any of the most recent six fiscal years and have not aggregated more than $1,500,000 in the most recent six fiscal years.

Rule 5A–02. Statement of Assets and Unrecovered Promotional, Exploratory, and Development Costs.—The statement of assets and unrecovered promotional, exploratory, and development costs filed for persons to whom this article is applicable shall comply with the following provisions:

[Despite what is said in Rule 5A–02, the staff of the SEC prefers to have a balance sheet (together with a statement of cash receipts and disbursements) in every case where it is feasible to reduce the promotional stage accounts to balance sheet format.]

CURRENT ASSETS

1. **Cash and cash items.**

2. **Marketable securities.**—Include only securities having a ready market. Securities of affiliates shall not be included here. State here the basis of determining the amount at which carried. The aggregate cost and aggregate amount on the basis of current market quotations shall be stated parenthetically or otherwise.

3. **Accounts and notes receivable.**

4. **Reserve for doubtful accounts and notes receivable.**

5. **Inventories.**—State separately each major class of inventory and the basis of determining the amounts shown. Any classification that is reasonably informative may be used.

[1] For the purpose of financial statements prepared pursuant to the instructions contained in this article a mine will be considered to have passed from a development to a production stage when the major portion of the mineral production is obtained from workings other than those opened for the purpose of exploration or development or when the principal activity of the mine becomes the production of developed ore rather than the development of additional ores for mining.

6. **Amounts due from underwriters, promoters, directors, officers, employees. and principal holders of equity securities other than affiliates.**—State separately the total amount, if significant, due from each class of persons named in the caption to this paragraph. Exclude from the amounts set forth hereunder trade accounts subject to the usual trade terms.

7. **Other current assets.**—(*a*) State separately (1) total of current amounts due from parents and subsidiaries; and (2) any other amounts in excess of five percent of total current assets, indicating when any such amount is due from affiliates other than parents and subsidiaries; (b) indebtedness of a parent or subsidiary, or an affiliate designated under (*a*) (2) shall not be considered current unless the net current asset position of such person justifies such treatment.

8. **Total current assets.**

OTHER ASSETS AND UNRECOVERED PROMOTIONAL, EXPLORATORY, AND DEVELOPMENT COSTS

9. **Securities of affiliates.**

10. **Indebtedness of affiliates—Not current.**

11. **Other security investments.**—In a note herein referred to state the basis of determining the amount. If available, state parenthetically or otherwise the aggregate amount on the basis of market quotations.

12. **Amounts due (not current) from underwriters, promoters, directors, officers, employees, and principal holders of equity securities other than affiliates.**—The instruction to caption 6 shall apply here.

13. **Property, plant, and equipment.**[2]—(*a*) Identify separately intangible property and property held under lease, option, and lease and option agreements. Identify items acquired from persons having a material relationship to the registrant. Extend only the total number of units of each class of securities, the amount of cash, and/or an indication of anything else, given by the registrant therefor. Except as stated in footnote 2, dollar amounts shall be extended only for cash transactions.

(*b*) In a note state as to property held under lease, option, or lease and option agreements or purchase contracts (1) the nature and amount of future payments to be made, (2) whether the property on default will revert to the seller, and (3) whether any assets constructed on or attached to the property will become the property of the seller on default.

---

[2] **Special instructions regarding this caption for mining companies using Article 5A.**—Include hereunder only depreciable mine plant and equipment. See caption 13A for the disposition of mine property subject to depletion. In those situations where depletable mine property and depreciable mine plant and equipment and other assets were acquired in one transaction in exchange for capital stock of the registrant or for cash, capital stock, or other securities of the registrant and any other consideration, the assets acquired such as accounts receivable, supplies, buildings, mining and mill equipment, which have a fixed or objectively determinable value should be valued on those bases. The dollar amounts assigned to these properties shall be extended.

13A. **Mine property.**—Set forth hereunder property usually extinguished by depletion such as mines, mining claims, water rights, land for waste dumps, and similar property. The instructions set forth under caption 13, including footnote 2 if applicable, shall also apply to this caption.

14. **Unrecovered promotional, exploratory, and development cost.** —Set forth under this caption unrecovered costs incurred in promotion, exploration and development.

State separately (*a*) development expenses, (*b*) plant and equipment maintenance expenses, (*c*) rehabilitation expenses, (*d*) general administrative expenses incurred in a period when there was little or no actual mining and (*e*) other expenses. Do not include securities selling costs under this caption but include them under caption 17 or 18. General administrative expenses incurred in connection with subcaptions (*a*), (*b*), and (*c*) should be included therein. Any other general administrative expenses not chargeable to those subcaptions nor written off as costs or other operating charges (including taxes, protection and conservation of property when inactive) shall be included under subcaption (*d*). Extend only the total number of units of each class of securities, the amount of cash and/or an indication of anything else, given by the registrant. Dollar amounts shall be extended only for cash transactions, including, when appropriate, depreciation, depletion, and amortization of assets extended at dollar amounts under captions 13 and 13A. The instructions set forth under caption 13, footnote 2 to caption 13 and caption 13A, if appropriate, should be applied also to any unrecovered promotion, exploratory, and development costs incurred by predecessors of the registrant.

15. **Reserves for depreciation, depletion, and amortization of property, plant, and equipment and unrecovered promotional, exploratory, and development costs (or reserves in lieu thereof).**—Set forth hereunder only the amount of the reserve for depreciation, depletion, and amortization of property, plant, and equipment and unrecovered costs incurred in promotion, exploration, and development applicable to the dollar amounts extended under captions 13, 13A, and 14 above.

16. **Prepaid expenses and other deferred items.**—State separately any significant items not shown elsewhere. Prepayments of services to be received within one year may, however, be included under caption 7.

17. **Debt discount and expense.**—State in a note referred to in the statement of assets and unrecovered promotional, exploratory, and development costs the method used in amortizing such debt discount and expense.

18. **Commissions and expense on capital shares.**—Explain in a note referred to in the statement of assets and unrecovered promotional, exploratory, and development costs what provisions have been made for writing off these items.

19. **Other assets.**—State separately any other item in excess of five percent of the amount of all assets other than fixed and intangible ones.

Rule 5A–03. Statement of Liabilities.—The statement of liabilities filed for the persons to whom this article is applicable shall comply with the following provisions:

CURRENT LIABILITIES

1. **Notes payable.**—State separately amounts payable (*a*) to banks; (*b*) for merchandise, materials, supplies, and expenses incurred in the ordinary course of business; and (*c*) to others.

2. **Accounts payable.**—State separately amounts payable (*a*) for merchandise, materials, supplies, and expenses incurred in the ordinary course of business; and (*b*) to others.

3. **Accrued liabilities.**—State separately (*a*) accrued payrolls; (*b*) tax liability; (*c*) interest; (*d*) rents and royalties; and (*e*) any other significant items. If the total under this caption is not significant it may be stated as one amount.

4. **Amounts due to underwriters, promoters, directors, officers, employees, and principal holders of equity securities other than affiliates.**—State separately the total amount, if significant, due to each class of persons named in the caption to this paragraph. Exclude from the amounts set forth hereunder trade accounts subject to the usual trade terms.

5. **Other current liabilities.**—State separately (*a*) dividends declared; (*b*) notes and mortgages instalments, mortgages due within one year, and payments on other long-term debt due within one year; (*c*) total of current amounts due to parents and subsidiaries; and (*d*) any other item in excess of five percent of total current liabilities indicating any such liability due to affiliates other than parents and subsidiaries. Remaining items may be shown in one amount.

6. **Total current liabilities.**

DEFERRED INCOME

7. **Deferred income.**

LONG-TERM DEBT AND OTHER LIABILITIES

8. **Bonds, notes, and other liabilities represented by securities.**— Show for each class (*a*) title of the class; (*b*) the amount authorized; (*c*) the amount issued; and (*d*) the amount reacquired and held in the treasury (show such amount as a deduction). As to issued securities, show separately in a note the amount issued for (1) cash, (2) property, and (3) services. The facts and amounts with respect to any defaults in principal, interest, sinking fund, or redemption provisions shall be stated.

9. **Indebtedness to affiliates—Not current.**

10. **Amounts due (not current) to underwriters, promoters, direc-**

tors, officers, employees, and principal holders of equity securities other than affiliates.—The instruction to caption 4 above shall apply here.

11. **Other liabilities—Not current.**—State separately any significant items. State whether accrued, and the interest rate if any.

12. **Total liabilities.**

Rule 5A–04. Statement of Capital Shares.—The statement of capital shares filed for the persons to whom this article is applicable shall comply with the following provisions:

1. State for each class of capital shares the title and number of shares (*a*) authorized, (*b*) issued, (*c*) reacquired and held in the treasury, (*d*) outstanding, and (*e*) reserved for option, warrant, conversion, and other rights to acquire such shares.

2. As to each class of issued shares state the number of shares issued for (*a*) cash, (*b*) services, and (*c*) property.

3. If there are any shares subscribed for but unissued, state the number of shares of each class subscribed for, the subscription price, the total amount receivable thereon, and the approximate due dates. If payable otherwise than in cash, explain. If any unpaid amounts on such shares are past due, state the number of shares and amounts involved.

4. If any shares are assessable, state the aggregate and per-share amounts of assessments levied. If any such assessments have not been paid, state the number of shares and amounts involved, indicating separately any amounts past due.

5. If any shares have been issued subject to a liability for further calls, state the number of shares so issued and the aggregate and per-share amounts of such liability. State also the aggregate amount of any past due calls.

6. If any shares have been forfeited for non-payment of assessments or calls thereon, state the number of shares involved and the present status of such shares.

7. State the total amount of underwriting discounts and commissions incurred on sale of capital shares.

8. As to any arrears in cumulative dividends, the amount per share and in total shall be stated.

9. If preferred shares are callable, the date or dates and the amount per share and in total at which such shares are callable shall be stated. Preferences on involuntary liquidation, if other than par or stated value, shall be shown. A statement shall be made as to the existence, or absence, of any restrictions upon surplus growing out of the fact that upon involuntary liquidation the preference of the preferred shares exceeds its par or stated value.

Rule 5A–05. Statement of Other Securities.—If the persons to whom this article is applicable have any securities with respect to which information is not called for in the statement of liabilities or in the statement of capital shares, furnish as to such securities information corresponding to that required in those statements.

Rule 5A–06. Statement of Cash Receipts and Disbursements.[3]— The statement of cash receipts and disbursements filed for persons to whom this article is applicable shall comply with the following provisions:

RECEIPTS

Sale of securities .... $..........
        (Itemize receipts by classes of securities.)
Assessments .... $..........
Loans by banks .... $..........
Loans by others .... $..........
Sale of products .... $..........
Donations .... $..........
Royalties .... $..........
Rents, tolls, and similar receipts .... $..........
Other receipts .... $..........

     (Specify and show separately any items of significant
     amount. Details may be given in a separate schedule if
     referred to under this caption.)

        Total receipts .... $..........

DISBURSEMENTS

Loans repaid .... $..........
Commissions and other selling expenses in connection with
    the sale of securities .... $..........
Legal and accounting fees .... $..........
Fees of engineers, appraisers, and other similar experts ... $..........
Payments on options, leases, lease and option agreements,
    and purchase contracts .... $..........

     (Show separately each payment of significant amount
     and identify the property for which paid.)

Royalties .... $..........
Contract work (specify) .... $..........
Purchase of equipment .... $..........
Salaries of directors and officers .... $..........
Other salaries and wages .... $..........
Merchandise, materials, and supplies .... $..........

---

[3] If the registrant maintains its books on the accrual basis, items of income and expense reported in the statement of cash receipts and disbursements may be presented on such basis, provided entries are introduced in the statement to reconcile the figures in total to the cash receipts and cash disbursements respectively.

Taxes	$...........
Dividends	$...........
Other disbursements	$...........

> (Specify and show separately any items of significant amount. Details may be given in a separate schedule if referred to under this caption.)

Total disbursements	$...........

Net increase (or decrease) in cash during period	$...........
Cash and cash items balance at beginning of period	$...........
Cash and cash items balance at close of period	$...........

Rule 5A–07. What Schedules Are to Be Filed.—The following schedules are required to be filed as a part of an application for registration on Form 10 and as part of an annual report on Form 10–K by companies to whom this article is applicable.

(*a*) The schedules specified below in this rule as schedules I, II, and III shall be filed as of the date of the statement of assets and unrecovered promotional, exploratory, and development costs and statement of liabilities filed for each person.

Such schedules shall be certified.

(*b*) The information required in schedules for the registrant and for its subsidiaries may be presented in the form of a single schedule, provided that items pertaining to the registrant and those pertaining to each subsidiary are separately shown and that such single schedule affords a properly summarized presentation of the facts.

(*c*) References to the schedules shall be made against the appropriate captions of the statement of assets and unrecovered promotional, exploratory, and development costs.

(*d*) If the information required by any schedule (including the footnotes thereto) may be shown in the related statement of assets and unrecovered promotional, exploratory, and development costs, without making such statement unclear or confusing, that procedure may be followed and the schedule omitted.

(*e*) If schedules, other than those specifically called for by paragraph (*a*) of this rule, are required to make clear and not confusing certain material items appearing in the financial statements, the registrant may use the appropriate schedule set forth in article 12 to present the additional information required by rule 3–06.

SCHEDULE I. PROPERTY, PLANT, AND EQUIPMENT.—The schedule prescribed by rule 12–06 shall be filed in support of caption 13 and caption 13A of each statement of assets and unrecovered promotional, exploratory, and development costs.

SCHEDULE II. UNRECOVERED PROMOTIONAL, EXPLORATORY, AND DEVELOPMENT COSTS.—The schedule prescribed by rule 12–06A shall be filed in support of caption 14 of each statement of assets and unrecovered promotional, exploratory, and development costs.

SCHEDULE III. RESERVES FOR DEPRECIATION, DEPLETION, AND AMORTIZATION OF PROPERTY, PLANT, AND EQUIPMENT AND UNRECOVERED PROMOTIONAL, EXPLORATORY, AND DEVELOPMENT COSTS (OR RESERVES IN LIEU THEREOF).—The schedule prescribed by rule 12–07 shall be filed in support of caption 15 of each statement of assets and unrecovered promotional, exploratory, and development costs.

Article 6. Management Investment Companies

Rule 6–01. Application of Article 6.—This article shall be applicable to financial statements filed for management investment companies other than those which are issuers of periodic payment plan certificates.

Rule 6–02. Special Rules Applicable to Management Investment Companies.—The financial statements filed for persons to which this article is applicable shall be prepared in accordance with the following special rules in addition to the general rules in articles 1, 2, 3, and 4. Where the requirements of a special rule differ from those prescribed in a general rule, the requirements of the special rule shall be met.

1. **Content of financial statements.**—The financial statements shall be prepared in accordance with the requirements of Regulation S–X notwithstanding any provision of the articles of incorporation, trust indenture or other governing legal instruments specifying certain accounting procedures inconsistent with those herein required.

2. **Certification.**—Where, under the applicable form, financial statements are required to be certified, the certifying accountant shall have been selected and ratified in accordance with section 32 of the Investment Company Act of 1940 and the applicable rules thereunder.

3. **Consolidated and combined statements.**—(*a*) Consolidated and combined statements filed for management investment companies shall be prepared in accordance with article 4 except that (1) statements of the registrant may be consolidated only with the statements of subsidiaries which are investment companies; (2) a consolidated statement of the registrant and any of its investment company subsidiaries shall not be filed unless accompanied by a consolidating statement which sets forth the individual statements of each significant subsidiary included in the consolidated statement, *provided, however,* that a consolidating statement need not be filed if all included subsidiaries are totally held; and (3) consolidated or combined

statements filed for subsidiaries not consolidated with the registrant shall not include any investment companies unless accompanied by consolidating or combining statements which set forth the individual statements of each included investment company which is a significant subsidiary.

(*b*) If consolidated statements are filed, the amounts included under each caption in which financial data pertaining to affiliates is required to be furnished shall be subdivided to show separately the amounts (1) eliminated in consolidation and (2) not eliminated in consolidation.

4. **Affiliates.**—The term "affiliate" means an "affiliated person" as defined in section 2 (*a*) (3) of the Investment Company Act of 1940. The term "control" has the meaning given in section 2 (*a*) (9) of that Act.

5. **Value.**—As used in this article 6, the word "value" shall have the meaning given in section 2 (*a*) (39) (B) of the Investment Company Act of 1940.

6. **Valuation of assets.**—(*a*) The balance sheets of open-end companies shall reflect all assets at value, showing cost parenthetically.

(*b*) The balance sheets of closed-end companies shall either (1) reflect all assets at cost, showing value parenthetically, or (2) reflect all assets at value, showing cost parenthetically. If assets are reflected at cost, however, due consideration shall be given to evidence of probable loss and, where such evidence indicates an apparently permanent decline in underlying value and earning power, recognition thereof shall be made by means of an appropriate write-down or the establishment of an appropriate reserve.

(*c*) The balance sheet shall clearly disclose whether assets are carried at cost or value.

[ASR Nos. 113 and 118 contain comprehensive statements of the SEC's views regarding the valuation of investments in securities (including restricted securities) and in other assets of investment companies, and the auditor's examination of such investments. These matters are discussed in Chapter **4**.]

7. **Cost in case of reorganizations, exchanges of investments, syndicate operations, etc.**—Where information as to the cost of investments is required to be furnished, the term "cost" shall have the indicated special meaning in the following instances:

(*a*) **Reorganizations and quasi-reorganizations.**—Where investments have been adjusted in the course of a reorganization or quasi-reorganization of the registrant, "cost" shall mean such adjusted amount. The date of and a brief statement as to such adjustment shall be given in a note referred to in the balance sheet.

(*b*) **Exchanges of investments.**—(1) Where investments have been acquired in exchange for other investments as a result of a reorganization, consolidation or merger of a portfolio company, "cost" of the investments acquired shall be the cost of the investments released. Due consideration shall, however, be given to evidence of probable loss and, where such evidence indicates an apparently permanent decline in underlying value and earning power, "cost" of the investments acquired shall be the value, on the effective date of the transaction, of the investments released or of the investments received, as appropriate. (2) In other cases in which investments have been acquired in exchange for assets other than cash, "cost" of the investments acquired shall be the value, on the effective date of the exchange, of the assets released or of the assets received, as appropriate.

(c) **Syndicate operations.**—In the case of securities acquired through joint syndicate operations, "cost" shall be net of syndicate discounts and commissions applicable thereto.

8. **Issuance and repurchase of securities by a management investment company.**—In a footnote or statement referred to in the balance sheet or other appropriate statement, show for each class of the company's securities (1) the number of shares or principal amount of bonds sold during the period of report, the amount received therefor, and, in the case of shares sold by closed-end companies, the difference, if any, between the amount received and the net asset value or preference in involuntary liquidation (whichever is appropriate) of securities of the same class prior to such sale; and (2) the number of shares or principal amount of bonds repurchased during the period of report and the total or average cost thereof. Closed-end companies shall furnish the following additional information as to securities repurchased during the period of report:

(a) as to bonds and preferred shares, the aggregate difference between cost and the face amount or preference in involuntary liquidation and, if applicable net assets taken at value as of the date of repurchase were less than such face amount or preference, the aggregate difference between cost and such applicable net asset value;

(b) as to common shares, the weighted average discount per share, expressed as a percentage, between cost or repurchase and the net asset value applicable to such shares at the date of repurchases.

The information required by 2 (a) and (b) may be based on reasonable estimates if it is impracticable to determine the exact amounts involved.

9. **Federal income taxes.**—Appropriate provision shall be made, on the basis of the applicable tax laws, for Federal income taxes that it is reasonably believed are, or will become, payable in respect of (a) current net income, (b) realized gain on investments and (c) unrealized appreciation on investments. The company's status as a "regulated investment company" as defined in Subtitle A, Chapter 1, Subchapter M of the Internal Revenue Code as amended shall be stated in a note referred to in the appropriate statements. Such note shall also indicate briefly the principal present assumptions on which the company has relied in making or not making

provisions for such taxes. However, a company which retains realized capital gains and designates such gains as a distribution to shareholders in accordance with Section 852(b)(3)(D) of the Code shall, on the last day of its taxable year (and not earlier), make provision for taxes on such undistributed capital gains during such year.

10. **Balance sheets; statements of assets and liabilities.**—As used herein the term "balance sheets" shall include statements of assets and liabilities unless the context clearly indicates the contrary.

11. **Inapplicable captions.**—Attention is directed to the provisions of rule 3–02 which permit the omission of separate captions in financial statements as to which the items and conditions are not present, or the amounts involved not significant. However, amounts involving directors, officers, and affiliates shall nevertheless be separately set forth except as otherwise specifically permitted under a particular caption.

Rule 6–03. Balance Sheets; Statements of Assets and Liabilities.

—Balance sheets and statements of assets and liabilities filed under this rule shall comply with the following provisions:

ASSETS

1. **Cash and cash items.**—State separately (*a*) cash on hand, demand deposits, and time deposits; (*b*) call loans; and (*c*) funds subject to withdrawal restrictions. Funds subject to withdrawal restrictions and deposits in closed banks shall not be included under this caption unless they will become available within 1 year.

2. **Dividends and interest receivable.**—(*a*) Dividends shall not be included before the ex-dividend date, nor unless payment is reasonably assured by past experience, guaranty, or otherwise. No dividend shall be included on stocks issued or assumed by the company and held by or for it, whether held in its treasury, in sinking or other special funds, or pledged as collateral.

(*b*) Interest due or accrued on bonds, notes, deposits, open accounts, and other interest-bearing obligations owned, shall not be included unless payment is reasonably assured by past experience, guaranty, or otherwise. No interest shall be included on securities issued or assumed by the company and held by or for it, whether held in its treasury, in sinking or other special funds, or pledged as collateral.

3. **Notes receivable.**

4. **Accounts receivable.**

5. **Reserves for doubtful receivables.**—Notes and accounts receivable known to be uncollectible shall be excluded from the asset as well as from the reserve account.

6. **Sundry assets of a current nature.**—State separately (*a*) total of current amounts due from directors and officers; (*b*) participation in syndicates; and (*c*) any other significant amount.

7. **Investments in securities of unaffiliated issuers.**—See rule 6–02–6.

(*a*) **United States Government bonds and other obligations.**—Include only direct obligations of the United States Government.

(*b*) **Securities of other investment companies.**—Such securities may be included under (*c*) if they amount in the aggregate to less than 5 per cent of total assets.

(*c*) **Other securities.**

(*d*) Such further classification may be used as is appropriate under the circumstances.

(*e*) **Reserves for unrealized depreciation in value of securities.**—If assets are reflected at cost, any reserve for unrealized depreciation shall be shown here as a deduction from the items to which applicable.

[ASR Nos. 113 and 118 contain comprehensive statements of the SEC's views regarding the valuation of investments in securities (including restricted securities) and in other assets of investment companies, and the auditor's examination of such investments. These matters are discussed in Chapter **4**.]

8. **Investments—Other than securities.**—State separately each major class. See rule 6–02–6.

9. **Investments in affiliates.**—State separately investments in (*a*) controlled companies and (*b*) other affiliates. See rule 6–02–6.

10. **Prepaid expenses and other deferred items.**—(*a*) State separately each of the following items if significant: (1) debt discount and expense, (2) organization expense, (3) commissions and expense on capital shares, and (4) other prepaid and deferred items showing separately any significant items. Explain in a note to this caption the provisions which have been made to write off or amortize such items.

(*b*) Recurrent costs of issuing shares, such as registration fees and expenses, shall be charged off in the statement of income and expense for the period in which such costs are incurred.

[The Excise Tax Technical Changes Act of 1958 increased materially the tax upon original issue of stock. The effect on open-end investment companies is apt to be substantial. The National Association of Investment Companies (NAIC) suggested that, in view of the change in the law, the charging of original issue taxes to paid-in surplus be accepted as a permissible procedure by investment companies. The Chief Accountant of the SEC wrote to the NAIC on May 8, 1959, and said that in view of the general acceptability of the principle involved, no objection would be raised to charging the tax to paid-in surplus as an alternative to charging such amount to income as has been the generally accepted interpretation of Rule 6–03–10(b), although original issue taxes are not mentioned in the rule. If a change in reporting is made, the amount of the tax should be shown as a deduction on either the statement of capital surplus required by Rule 6–07–1 or on the statement of changes in net assets under Rule 6–08 in sub-caption (b)(5) ("Securities issued and repurchased").]

11. **Other assets.**—State separately (*a*) total of amounts due from directors and officers, not included under caption 6 above; (*b*) each special fund of a significant amount; (*c*) real estate and improvements not included under caption 8 above; (*d*) furniture and fixtures; and (*e*) any other significant amounts.

LIABILITIES

12. **Notes payable.**—State separately amounts payable within 1 year (*a*) to banks, and (*b*) to others. See caption 16 (*a*).

13. **Accounts payable.**—State separately (*a*) the total of amounts payable for purchase of securities, and (*b*) other accounts payable.

14. **Accrued liabilities.**—State separately (*a*) accrued salaries, (*b*) tax liability, (*c*) interest, and (*d*) any other significant items. If the total under this caption is not significant, it may be stated as one amount.

15. **Sundry liabilities of a current nature.**—State separately (*a*) dividends declared; (*b*) bonds, notes, mortgage installments, and mortgages due within 1 year; (*c*) total of current amounts due to affiliates, excluding any amounts owing to non-controlled affiliates which arose in the ordinary course of business and are subject to usual trade terms; (*d*) total of current amounts (other than as required under caption 14) due directors and officers; and (*e*) any other items of significant amount. Remaining items may be shown in one amount.

16. **Long-term debt.**

(*a*) **Funded debt.**—If any amount included herein will fall due within 1 year, indicate such amount and explain in a footnote the reason for not including such amount as a current liability under rule 6–03–15. See also caption 19 (*c*) (2).

(*b*) **Indebtedness to affiliates—not current.**—State separately amounts due to (1) controlled companies and (2) other affiliates.

(*c*) **Other long-term debt.**—Indicate whether secured. State separately (1) total of amounts due directors and officers; and (2) other long-term debt, specifying any significant item. State separately by years, in the balance sheet or in a note therein referred to, the total amounts of the respective maturities for the 5 years following the date of the balance sheet.

17. **Other liabilities.**—State separately any significant amounts.

18. **Reserves, not shown elsewhere.**—State separately the total of each major class and describe each such major class by using an appropriate caption or by a footnote referred to in the caption.

19. **Net assets applicable to outstanding capital shares.**—(*a*) This caption may be used only by companies which reflect assets at value, showing cost parenthetically.

(*b*) **Companies having only one class of outstanding capital securities.**—Such companies may conclude the statement with this caption and give the number of outstanding shares and the net asset value per share. In such case the statement shall be entitled "Statement of Assets and Liabilities" and the information required by captions 20 to 24 below shall be set forth in the form of a separate schedule immediately following this statement and referred to under this caption.

(*c*) **Companies having more than one class of outstanding capital securities.**—(1) Such companies may conclude the statement at this point and in such case shall furnish in tabular form immediately following this caption the following information as to each class of capital securities: (*i*) title of issue; (*ii*) in the case of funded debt treated as a capital security the total face amount outstanding and the asset coverage per unit; (*iii*) in the case of preferred shares, the par or stated value, the number of shares outstanding, the total preference thereof in involuntary liquidation, and the asset coverage per share and (*iv*) in the case of common shares, the par or stated value, the number of shares outstanding and the net asset value per share and in the aggregate. In such case the statement shall be entitled "Statement of Assets, Liabilities and Capital Securities" and the information required by captions 20 to 24 below shall be set forth in the form of a separate schedule immediately following this statement and referred to under this caption.

(2) If funded debt is outstanding and is to be treated as a capital security, caption 16 (*a*) may be omitted if appropriate adjustment of related captions is made.

CAPITAL SHARES AND SURPLUS

20. **Capital shares.**—State for each class of shares the title of issue, the number of shares authorized, the number of shares outstanding and the capital share liability thereof. See also rule 6–09.

21. **Surplus.**—(*a*) Show the division of this item into (1) capital surplus; (2) balance of undistributed net income; and (3) accumulated net realized gain or loss on investments. The information required by rule 6–02–8 shall be given in a footnote to this statement, or in a footnote to the statement permitted by rule 6–08.

(*b*) Except as permitted by rule 6–08, an analysis of each surplus account setting forth the information prescribed in rule 6–07 shall be given, for each period for which a statement of income and expense is filed, in the form of a separate statement of surplus, and shall be referred to under this caption.

22. **Total capital and surplus.**—Companies which reflect assets at cost, showing value parenthetically, shall furnish the following information in a separate statement immediately following this statement and referred to herein:

(*a*) The amount of unrealized appreciation or depreciation of the assets, taken at value, as compared to the amount at which such assets are reflected in the balance sheet, together with the increase or decrease thereof during the period of report.

(*b*) An appropriate provision for taxes in respect of appreciation if required by rule 6–02–9.

(*c*) If total assets at value are less than cost, the adjustment that would have to be made to reflect such depreciation in the surplus accounts.

(*d*) The net asset coverage per unit of each class of bonds and per share of each class of preferred shares.

(*e*) The net asset value per share of the outstanding common shares, computed on the basis of assigning to prior securities their preference in involuntary liquidation.

23. **Unrealized appreciation or depreciation of assets.**—Companies which reflect assets at value showing cost parenthetically shall include this item as an addition to or deduction from caption 22. See rule 6–06. Appropriate provision shall be made for applicable income taxes if required by rule 6–02–9.

24. **Net assets applicable to outstanding capital shares.**—The amount of this caption should agree with the amount shown under caption 19.

Rule 6–04. Statement of Income and Expense.—(*a*) Statements required by this rule and by rules 6–05 and 6–06 shall be shown on the same or on consecutive pages. If not shown on the same page, however, the items required to be set forth by caption 5 of rule 6–05 and caption 2 of rule 6–06 shall be appended immediately following the information required by caption 7 of this rule.

(*b*) Statements filed under this rule shall comply with the following provisions:

1. **Income.**—(*a*) State separately income from (1) cash dividends, (2) interest, and (3) other income. If income from investments in or indebtedness of affiliates is included hereunder, such income shall be segregated under an appropriate caption subdivided to show separately income from (*i*) controlled companies and (*ii*) other affiliates.

(*b*) Due consideration shall be given to the propriety of treating, as income, dividends on stock acquired or disposed of during the period of report.

(*c*) Due consideration shall be given to the propriety of treating extraordinary dividends as income. For the purpose of this rule the term "extraordinary dividends" shall mean (1) dividends which are known to have been declared out of sources other than current earnings or earned surplus and (2) dividends which are declared otherwise than out of earnings of the current or preceding year and are abnormal in size in relationship to the value of the securities upon which declared.

(*d*) Dividends in arrears on preferred stock may not be treated as income in an amount which exceeds an amount arrived at by applying the stated dividend rate to the period during which the stock has been held, *provided,* that, in computing the period held, periods of more than one-half of a quarter year may be treated as full quarter years, if periods of less than one-half of a quarter year are not counted. Any such dividends which are treated as income but which are applicable to periods prior to the current fiscal year shall be included under caption 1 (*a*) (3) above.

(*e*) Dividends by controlled companies may be treated as income only to the extent that they are out of earnings subsequent to (1) the date of acquisition or (2) the effective date of a reorganization or quasi-reorganization of the receiving company if such date is subsequent to the date of acquisition.

(*f*) Due consideration shall be given to the propriety of treating, as income, interest received on bonds which were in default when acquired. Any such interest which may be treated as income shall not be treated as ordinary interest income in an amount in excess of the amount arrived at by applying the stated interest rate to the period of report, and any excess thereof shall be included under caption 1 (*a*) (3) above. The policy followed in accounting for such interest shall be stated in a footnote.

(*g*) Common stock received as a dividend on common stock of the same issuer shall not be treated as income, and no amount shall be debited to investments or credited to income or surplus at the time such dividend is received.

(*h*) State as to any noncash dividends, other than stock dividends referred to in paragraph (*g*), and as to preferred stock received as a stock dividend, the basis on which taken up as income. If any such dividends received from controlled companies have been credited to income in an amount different from that charged to income or earned surplus by the disbursing company, state the amount of such difference and explain.

(*i*) State separately each category of other income representing more than 5 per cent of the total shown under caption 1 of rule 6–04 (*b*).

(*j*) Proceeds from the sale of new capital shares which represent payment on account of accrued undivided income shall not be included in the statement of income and expense. See rule 6–07–2.

(*k*) Dividends and interest applicable to an issuer's own securities held in its treasury or in sinking or other special funds shall not be treated as income.

2. **Expenses.**—State separately each category of expense representing more than five per cent of the total expenses. There shall also be shown in an appropriate manner (*a*) the total of management and other service fees to unaffiliated persons; (*b*) the total of management and other service fees to affiliated persons, indicating in a note or otherwise (1) the name of each such person accounting for 10 per cent or more of the total under this sub-caption, (2) the nature of the affiliation between the investment company and each such person, and (3) the amount applicable to each such person; and (c) other expenses within the person's own organization in connection with research, selection and supervision of investments. The total of management and service fees shall be included herein regardless of the basis used for, or the method of, computation thereof. State in a note referred to under this item the basis and methods of computing management or service fees and if none was incurred for the period of report, the reason therefor. If any of the expenses were paid otherwise than in cash, state the details in a note referred to under this caption.

3. **Taxes—Other than taxes on income.**

4. **Interest and debt discount and expense.**—State separately (*a*) interest on funded debt, (*b*) amortization of debt discount and expense or premium, and (c) other interest.

5. **Balance before provision for taxes on income.**

6. **Provision for taxes on income.**—State separately (*a*) Federal taxes on income, and (*b*) other taxes on income. If the amount to be shown under this caption is less than 5 per cent of caption 7, it may be combined with caption 3 and in such case caption 5 may be omitted. See rule 6–02–9.

7. **Net income.**—The amount included under this caption shall be carried to the related subdivision of surplus or to the statement of changes in net assets, as appropriate. See rules 6–07–2 and 6–08 (*b*) (2).

Rule 6–05. Statement of Realized Gain or Loss on Investments.
—Statements filed under this rule shall comply with the following provisions:

1. **Realized gain or loss on sales of investments.**—(*a*) State separately the aggregate cost, the aggregate proceeds, and the net gain or loss from sales of each of the following classes of investments: (1) investments in securities of affiliates, (2) investments in other securities, showing United States Government bonds and other direct obligations separately, and (3) other investments.

(*b*) Transactions in shares of the person for which the statement is filed shall not be included here.

(*c*) State in a footnote the aggregate cost of securities acquired during the period, showing separately United States Government bonds and other direct obligations.

(*d*) State the basis followed in determining the cost of securities sold. If a basis other than average cost is used, state, if practicable, the gain or loss computed on the basis of average cost.

2. **Realized gain or loss on other transactions.**—(*a*) Include under this caption exchanges of investments. Show the aggregate cost of the investments released and, as the proceeds of the exchanges, the aggregate amount at which the investments acquired were recorded in the accounts. See rule 6–02–7.

(*b*) Include also under this caption any write-downs required by rule 6–02–6 (*b*). Show the aggregate cost and the aggregate adjusted cost of the investments involved.

3. **Realized gain or loss on investments, before provision for income taxes.**

4. **Provision for income taxes.**

5. **Net realized gain or loss on investments.**—The amount included under this caption shall be carried to the related section of surplus or to the statement of changes in net assets, as appropriate. See rules 6–07–3 and 6–08 (*b*) (3).

Rule 6–06. Statement of Unrealized Appreciation or Depreciation of Investments.—This statement may be omitted by companies reflecting assets at cost, showing value parenthetically, provided the information called for by the second sentence of rule 6–04 (*a*) is given. Statements filed under this rule shall comply with the following provisions:

1. **Unrealized appreciation or depreciation of investments.**—State the amount of unrealized appreciation or depreciation of investments as shown in caption 23 of the balance sheet (*a*) at the beginning of the period of report, and (*b*) at the end of the period of report.

2. **Increase or decrease of unrealized appreciation or depreciation.**

Rule 6–07. Surplus Statements.—Surplus statements filed under this rule shall comply with the following provisions:

1. **Capital surplus.**—(*a*) The analysis of capital surplus shall show separately for each period (1) balance at beginning of period, (2) additions during period due to (*i*) sale of capital shares, and (*ii*) other additions described in reasonable detail, (3) deductions during period due to (*i*) repurchase of capital shares, (*ii*) distributions to shareholders from capital sur-

plus, and (*iii*) other deductions, described in reasonable detail, and (4) balance at end of period. State in a footnote or otherwise the aggregate amount per share of dividends paid during the period of the report.

(*b*) There shall be shown, parenthetically or otherwise, the total dividend distributions to shareholders made from capital surplus since the date of organization or the date of the most recent reorganization, whichever is later; provided that companies organized prior to January 1, 1925, need show only such dividends paid since that date if that fact is indicated.

2. **Balance of undistributed net income.**—The analysis of the balance of undistributed net income shall show separately for each period of report (*a*) balance at beginning of period, (*b*) net income as shown under rule 6–04–7, (*c*) other additions described in reasonable detail, (*d*) distributions to shareholders, (*e*) other deductions described in reasonable detail, and (*f*) balance at end of period. State in a footnote or otherwise the aggregate amount per share of dividends paid during the period of the report.

Open-end companies which follow the policy of recording separately a part of the sale and repurchase price of capital shares as an adjustment on account of undivided income shall include, as a separate item hereunder, the difference between the amount received from the sale of new capital shares which represent payment on account of accrued undivided income and the amount paid on the repurchase of capital shares which represent payment on account of accrued undivided income.

3. **Accumulated net realized gain or loss on investments.**—The analysis of accumulated realized gain or loss on investments shall show separately for each period of report (*a*) gain or loss on investments prior to the period, (*b*) distributions to shareholders made therefrom prior to the period, (*c*) balance at the beginning of the period, (*d*) gain or loss on investments as shown under rule 6–05–5, (*e*) distributions to shareholders, and (*f*) balance at end of period. Captions (*a*) and (*b*) of this paragraph may be omitted by companies organized or most recently reorganized, prior to January 1, 1925, provided there is given in a footnote (*i*) total distributions made to shareholders out of realized gain on investments during the period from January 1, 1925, to the beginning of the period of report, and (*ii*) total realized gain or loss on investments for the same period. State in a footnote or otherwise the aggregate amount per share of dividends paid during the period of the report.

4. **Opening balances.**—Companies may accept balances of surplus accounts at January 1, 1925, as per the accounts.

5. See also rules 6–03–19 and 6–03–21.

Rule 6–08. Statement of Changes in Net Assets.—(*a*) Companies which in statements filed pursuant to rule 6–03 reflect assets at value, showing cost parenthetically, may file statements of changes in net assets in lieu of the surplus statements required by rule 6–07, *provided,* there is shown under caption 21 (*a*) of rule 6–03 the amount of dividends previously paid from (1) capital surplus, and (2) realized gain on investments. See rules 6–07–1 (*b*) and 6–07–3.

(*b*) Statements of changes in net assets filed under this rule shall comply with the following provisions:

(1) **Net assets at beginning of period.**—The amount shown shall agree with caption 19 of the related statement filed pursuant to rule 6–03 as of the beginning of the period of report. Show parenthetically or otherwise the balance of undistributed net income included in net assets at the beginning of the period.

(2) **Income.**—State separately (*a*) net income as shown by caption 7 of rule 6–04; (*b*) net accrued undivided earnings included in price of capital shares issued and repurchased; (*c*) distributions paid; and (*d*) balance of income undistributed, or decrease in prior balance of undistributed net income, as appropriate.

(3) **Realized gain or loss on investments.**—State separately (*a*) net realized gain or loss on investments as shown by caption 5 of rule 6–05; (*b*) distributions paid; and (*c*) balance of realized gain on investments for the period, or decrease in prior accumulated realized gain on investments, as appropriate.

(4) **Increase or decrease of unrealized appreciation or depreciation of assets.**—The amount shown should agree with caption 2 of rule 6–06.

(5) **Securities issued and repurchased.**—State separately for each issue (1) amount issued, and receipts therefrom on account of principal; (2) amount repurchased, and payments therefor on account of principal; and (3) net increase or decrease in amount outstanding and the difference between receipts and payments in respect thereof.

(6) **Distributions of capital.**

(7) **Other items.**—If during the period there have been any charges or credits to surplus accounts not specifically provided for in captions (2) to (6), include such items under an appropriate caption and explain clearly their nature.

(8) **Net assets at close of period.**—The amount shown shall agree with caption 19 of rule 6–03. Show parenthetically or otherwise the balance of undistributed net income included in net assets at the end of the period.

State in a footnote or otherwise to captions (2), (3), and (6) the aggregate amount per share of dividends paid during the period of the report.

Captions (*b*) (3) to (6), inclusive, may be shown subordinate to a general caption "Capital." If appropriate, the term "Principal" may be used in place of "Capital."

Rule 6–09. Statement of Sources of Net Assets.—Companies having only one class of outstanding capital securities, and reflecting all assets at value, may combine captions 20 and 21 (*a*) (1) of rule 6–03, *provided* (1) the analyses prescribed by rule 6–03–21 (*b*) are furnished and (2) other information comparable to that prescribed by captions 20 to 24 of rule 6–03 is set forth in substantially the following form :

(1) **Capital.**—If appropriate, the term *Principal* may be used in place of this caption.

(*a*) **Excess of amounts received from sale of capital shares over amounts paid out in redeeming or reacquiring shares.**—State here or in a footnote the number of shares authorized, the number of shares outstanding, and the capital shares liability thereof. The information required by rule 6–02–8 shall be given in a footnote or by reference to the statement of changes in net assets.

(*b*) **Aggregate distributions from net proceeds from sale of capital shares.**—See also rule 6–07–1 (*b*).

(*c*) **Balance of capital paid in on shares.**

(*d*) **Accumulated net realized gain or loss on investments.**

(*e*) **Accumulated distributions of realized gain on investments.**— The amount shown under this caption (*e*) shall be added to or deducted from caption (*d*) as appropriate to give a single total which need not be separately designated. See rule 6–07–3 with respect to companies organized or most recently reorganized prior to January 1, 1925.

(*f*) **Unrealized appreciation or depreciation of assets.**—See rule 6–02–9.

(*g*) **Total of captions (*a*) to (*f*), inclusive.**

(2) **Balance of undistributed net income.**

(3) **Net assets applicable to outstanding shares.**

Rule 6–10. What Schedules Are To Be Filed.—(*a*) Except as otherwise expressly provided in the applicable form :

(1) The schedules specified below in this rule as schedules I, VII, VIII, and IX shall be filed as of the date of the most recent balance sheet filed for each person and for each group for which separate statements are filed. Such schedules shall be certified if the related balance sheet is certified.

(2) All other schedules specified below in this rule shall be filed for each period for which a statement of income and expense is filed. Such schedules shall be certified if the related statement of income and expense is certified.

(*b*) The information required in schedules for the registrant, for the consolidated subsidiaries and for the registrant and its subsidiaries consolidated may be presented in the form of a single schedule, *provided,* that items pertaining to the registrant and to each consolidated subsidiary or group for which separate statements are required are separately shown and that such single schedule affords a properly summarized presentation of the facts.

(*c*) If the information required by any schedule (including the footnotes thereto) may be shown in the statements required by rules 6–03 to 6–09 without making such statements unclear or confusing, that procedure may be followed and the schedule omitted.

(*d*) Reference to the schedules shall be made against the appropriate captions of the balance sheet and the statement of income and expense.

A. Investment Schedules

Schedule I. Investments in Securities of Unaffiliated Issuers. —The schedule prescribed by rule 12–19 shall be filed in support of caption 7 of each balance sheet.

Schedule II. Investments—Other than Securities.—The schedule prescribed by rule 12–21 shall be filed in support of caption 8 of each balance sheet. This schedule may be omitted if the investments, other than securities, at both the beginning and end of the period amount to less than 1 per cent of total assets or $50,000 whichever is less.

Schedule III. Investments in Affiliates.—The schedule prescribed by rule 12–22 shall be filed in support of caption 9 of each balance sheet.

B. Miscellaneous Schedules

Schedule IV. Amounts Due from Directors and Officers.—The schedule prescribed by rule 12–03 shall be filed with respect to each person among the directors and officers from whom any amount was owed at any time during the period for which related statements of income and expense are filed.

Schedule V. Indebtedness to Affiliates.—The schedule prescribed by rule 12–11 shall be filed in support of caption 16 (*b*). This schedule and schedule III may be combined if desired.

Schedule VI. Reserves.—The schedule prescribed by rule 12–13 shall be filed in support of all reserves included in the balance sheet.

C. Capital Securities

Schedule VII. Funded Debt.—The schedule prescribed by rule 12–10 shall be filed in support of caption 16 (*a*) of each balance sheet.

Schedule VIII. Capital Shares.—(*a*) Open-end companies, all of whose outstanding securities are redeemable at the option of the holder thereof, need not file this schedule.

(*b*) Closed-end companies shall file the schedule prescribed by rule 12–14 in support of caption 20 of each balance sheet.

SCHEDULE IX. OTHER SECURITIES.—Schedules shall be filed in respect of any classes of securities issued by the person for whom the statement is filed, but not included in schedules VII and VIII. As to guarantees of securities of other issuers, furnish the information required by rule 12–12. As to warrants or rights granted by the person for whom the statement is filed, to subscribe for or purchase securities to be issued by such person, furnish the information called for by rule 12–15. As to any other securities, furnish information comparable to that called for by rules 12–10, 12–12, 12–14 or 12–15, as appropriate. Information need not be set forth, however, as to notes, drafts, bills of exchange or bankers' acceptances having a maturity at the time of issuance of less than 1 year.

Article 6A. Unit Investment Trusts

Rule 6–10A. Application of Article 6A.—This article shall be applicable to financial statements filed for unit investment trusts, including those which are issuers of periodic payment plan certificates, and financial statements filed for unincorporated management investment companies which are issuers of periodic payment plan certificates.

Rule 6–11. Statements of Condition.—Statements of condition filed for persons to whom this article is applicable shall comply with the following provisions:

TRUST PROPERTY

1. **Investment in securities.**—The aggregate cost and the aggregate value of investments included under this caption and caption 2 below shall be shown in the statement of condition parenthetically or otherwise. The method used in determining the "cost" shall be stated. For the purpose of this rule 6–11, "value" has the meaning defined in Section 2 (*a*) (39) (B) of the Investment Company Act of 1940. State in the statement of condition for each caption the basis of determining the amount at which investments are carried.

(*a*) **Securities of investment companies.**—State separately (1) trust shares in trusts created or serviced by the depositor or sponsor of this trust; (2) trust shares in other trusts; and (3) securities of other investment companies.

(*b*) **Securities of other companies.**—State separately (1) marketable securities and (2) other securities.

[ASR Nos. 113 and 118 contain comprehensive statements of the SEC's views regarding the valuation of investments in securities (including restricted securities) and in other assets of investment companies, and the auditor's examination of such investments. These matters are discussed in Chapter **4**.]

2. **Investments other than securities.**—State separately each major class. See instructions to caption 1.

3. **Dividends and interest receivable.**

4. **Cash.**

5. **Other property.**—State separately each significant item. State the basis of determining the amounts.

LIABILITIES, TRUST SHARES, AND DISTRIBUTABLE FUNDS

6. **Liabilities.**—State separately amounts payable to (a) trustee and custodian; and (b) depositor, sponsor, and their associates. State separately any other significant items.

7. **Reserves not shown elsewhere.**—State separately each significant item. If the caption used for each reserve stated separately is not clearly indicative of the purpose for which the reserve was created, explain the purpose in a note referred to under this caption.

8. **Trust shares.**—State for each class of trust shares (a) the title of issue, the number of trust shares outstanding and the total cost to the investors of such trust shares; (b) the adjustment for market depreciation or appreciation; (c) other deductions from the total cost to the investors for fees, loads, and other charges; and (d) the net amount applicable to the investors. Explain in a note referred to under this caption the deductions for fees, loads, and other charges from the total cost to the investors.

9. **Balance of income and distributable funds applicable to trust shares.**—The amount shown here shall agree with that shown in caption 19 of the related statement of income and distributable funds.

Rule 6–12. Statements of Income and Distributable Funds.—The statements of income and distributable funds filed for persons to whom this article is applicable shall comply with the following provisions:

INCOME

1. **Distributions and dividends.**—State separately (a) distributions received on shares of investment trusts, and (b) dividends on other securities. Exclude any distribution or portion thereof received on shares of investment trusts which is known to represent the return of any amount invested in the shares upon which such distribution was paid. Also indicate the basis upon which dividends and distributions are taken into income (e.g., "cash" or "accrual"; and if accrual whether as of declaration or record date); and, as to any distributions and dividends other than cash, the basis on which they have been taken up as income.

2. **Interest.**—State separately interest from (*a*) securities and (*b*) other sources.

3. **Other income.**—State separately by class of income each significant amount.

4. **Total income.**

EXPENSES

5. **Taxes.**

6. **Fees of the trustee and custodian.**

7. **Fees of the depositor and sponsor.**

8. **Legal fees and expenses.**—State separately each significant amount.

9. **Auditing fees and expenses.**—State separately each significant amount.

10. **Other expenses.**—State separately by class of expense each significant amount.

11. **Total expenses.**

12. **Balance of income before gain or loss realized from security transactions.**—See caption 13 below.

13. **Gain or loss realized from security transactions.**—State separately the net of gains and losses arising from transactions in (*a*) trust shares of trusts created or serviced by the depositor or sponsor of this trust; (*b*) trust shares in other trusts; and (*c*) other investments in securities. State here or in a note herein referred to the principle followed in determining the cost of securities sold, *e.g.,* "average cost" or "first-in, first-out." This caption, and caption 12 above, may be omitted by unit investment trusts provided the information herein required is contained in Schedule III of rule 6–13, and provided there be given in a footnote in the financial statements (*a*) the aggregate amount received from sale of securities; (*b*) the aggregate cost of the securities sold; (*c*) the realized gain or loss thereon; and (*d*) the principle followed in determining the cost of securities sold, *e.g.,* "average cost" or "first-in, first -out."

14. **Net income for the period.**—If captions 12 and 13 are omitted by unit investment trusts, this caption shall be changed to **Net income for the period excluding gain or loss realized from security transactions.**

15. **Balance of income and distributable funds applicable to trust shares at the beginning of the period.**

16. **Additions to distributable funds.**—State separately (*a*) that portion from the sale of trust shares which represents payments for participation in the balance of income and distributable funds; and (*b*) any other significant amounts.

17. **Deductions other than distributions.**—State separately (*a*) amounts withheld (1) for reserves and (2) for investments, and (*b*) any other significant amounts.

18. **Distribution to shareholders.**—For each class of trust shares state the amount per share and in the aggregate. State, as to any distributions other than cash, the nature of the distributions and the basis of determining the amount charged to income and distributable funds. Indicate here or in a note herein referred to the aggregate distributions made upon the surrender and cancellation of trust shares which represent income and distributable funds applicable thereto at the date of surrender and cancellation.

19. **Balance of income and distributable funds applicable to trust shares at close of the period.**

Rule 6–13. What Schedules Are to Be Filed.—(*a*) Schedule IV, specified below, shall be filed as of the date of the most recent statement of condition filed. The other schedules specified shall be filed for each period for which a statement of income and distributable funds is filed. All schedules shall be certified.

(*b*) Reference to the schedules shall be made against the appropriate captions of the statement of condition and the statement of income and distributable funds.

SCHEDULE I. INVESTMENT IN SECURITIES.—The schedule prescribed by rule 12–33 shall be filed in support of caption 1 of each statement of condition and of captions 1 and 2 of each statement of income and distributable funds.

SCHEDULE II. TRUST SHARES.—The schedule prescribed by rule 12–34 shall be filed in support of caption 8 of each statement of condition.

SCHEDULE III. GAIN OR LOSS FROM TRANSACTIONS IN TRUST PROPERTY.—A schedule shall be submitted showing for each investment set forth in Schedule I in which there were any sales or redemptions during the period: (*a*) the aggregate amount received from sale; (*b*) the aggregate cost of the investment sold; and (*c*) the realized gain or loss thereon.

SCHEDULE IV. ALLOCATION OF TRUST ASSETS TO SERIES OF TRUST SHARES.—If the trust assets are specifically allocated to different series of trust shares, and if such allocation is not shown in the statement of condition in columnar form or by the submission of separate statements for each series of trust shares, a schedule shall be submitted showing the amount of trust assets, indicated by each statement of condition filed, which is applicable to each series of trust shares.

SCHEDULE V. ALLOCATION OF TRUST INCOME AND DISTRIBUTABLE FUNDS TO SERIES OF TRUST SHARES.—If the trust income and distributable funds are specifically allocated to different series of trust shares and if such allocation is not shown in the statement of income and distributable funds in columnar form or by the submission of separate statements for each series of trust shares, a schedule shall be submitted showing the amount of income and distributable funds, indicated by each statement of income and distributable funds filed, which is applicable to each series of trust shares.

Article 6B. Face-Amount Certificate Investment Companies

Rule 6–20. Application of Article 6B.—This article shall be applicable to financial statements filed by investment companies which are issuers of face-amount certificates.

Rule 6–21. Special Rules Applicable to Face-Amount Certificate Investment Companies.—The financial statements filed by persons to which this rule is applicable shall be prepared in accordance with the following special rules in addition to the general rules in articles 1, 2, 3, and 4. Where the requirements of a special rule differ from those prescribed in a general rule, the requirements of the special rule shall be met.

1. **Content of financial statements.**—The financial statements shall be prepared in accordance with the requirements of Regulation S–X notwithstanding any provision of the articles of incorporation, trust indenture or other governing legal instruments specifying certain accounting procedures inconsistent with those herein required.

2. **Certification.**—Where, under the applicable form, financial statements are required to be certified, the certifying accountant shall have been selected and ratified in accordance with section 32 of the Investment Company Act of 1940 and the applicable rules thereunder.

3. **Consolidated and combined statements.**—(a) Consolidated and combined statements filed for face-amount certificate investment companies shall be prepared in accordance with article 4 except that statements of the registrant which is a face-amount certificate investment company and engages in no business of a material amount other than issuing or servicing of face-amount certificates, may be consolidated only with the statements of subsidiaries which are also face-amount certificate investment companies; *provided, however,* that (i) the subsidiaries are totally held, except as to outstanding face-amount certificates, by the parent, (ii) each face-amount certificate investment company maintains certificate reserves and qualified assets as provided by section 28 of the Investment Company Act of 1940, and (iii) separate financial statements for each company are filed.

(b) Any face-amount certificate investment company may, however, file a consolidating statement which may include totally-held subsidiary companies, except face-amount certificate investment companies, the inclusion of which in consolidation is prohibited by the provisions set forth in paragraph (*a*). Such consolidating statement shall set forth the individual statement of the parent company and each other company or groups of similar other companies.

4. **Affiliates.**—The term "affiliate" means an "affiliated person" as defined in section 2 (a) (3) of the Investment Company Act of 1940. The term "control" has the meaning given in section 2 (a) (9) of that Act.

5. **Qualified assets.**—(*a*) *For companies issuing face-amount certificates subsequent to December 31, 1940 under the provisions of sections 28 of the Investment Company Act of 1940,* the term "qualified assets" means qualified investments as that term is defined in section 28 (b) of the Act. A statement to that effect shall be made in the balance sheet.

(*b*) *For other companies,* the term "qualified assets" means cash and investments which such companies do maintain or are required, by applicable governing legal instruments, to maintain in respect of outstanding face-amount certificates. State in a note to the balance sheet the nature of the investments and other assets so maintained or required to be maintained by such legal instruments. If the nature of the qualified assets and amount thereof are not subject to the provisions of section 28 of the Investment Company Act of 1940, a statement to that effect shall be made.

(*c*) Loans to security holders may be included as a qualified asset in an amount not in excess of certificate reserves carried on the books of account in respect of each individual certificate upon which the loans were made.

6. **Valuation of qualified assets.**—(*a*) The balance sheet shall reflect all qualified assets at cost or amortized cost whichever is appropriate. Such basis shall be explained in a note which should also state the policy followed in writing off or amortizing any premium included in the cost of interest-bearing obligations. State, also, in an appropriate manner the amount of each kind of investments acquired from controlled companies and other affiliates, if material, during the period covered by the profit and loss or income statement, and the method used in determining the cost of any such investments.

(*b*) Market value of securities shall be stated parenthetically.

(*c*) Due consideration shall be given to evidence of probable loss and, where evidence indicates an apparently permanent decline in underlying value and earning power, recognition thereof shall be made by means of an appropriate write-down or the establishment of an appropriate reserve.

7. **Certificate reserves.**—(*a*) *For companies issuing face-amount certificates subsequent to December 31, 1940 under the provisions of section 28 of the Investment Company Act of 1940,* balance sheets shall reflect reserves for outstanding certificates computed in accordance with the provisions of section 28 (a) of the Act.

(b) *For other companies,* balance sheets shall reflect reserves for outstanding certificates determined as follows:

(i) For certificates of the installment type, such amount which, together with the lesser of future payments by certificate holders or such portion thereof as is credited to the account of certificate holders as and when accumulated at a rate not to exceed 3½ per centum per annum (or such other rate as may be appropriate under the circumstances of a particular case) compounded annually, shall provide the minimum maturity or face amount of the certificate when due.

(ii) For certificates of the fully paid type, such amount which, as and when accumulated at a rate not to exceed 3½ per centum per annum (or such other rate as may be appropriate under the circumstances of a particular case) compounded annually, shall provide the amount or amounts payable when due.

(iii) Such amount or accrual therefor, as shall have been credited to the account of any certificate holder in the form of any credit, or any dividend, or any interest in addition to the minimum maturity or face amount specified in the certificate, plus any accumulations on any amount so credited or accrued at rates required under the terms of the certificate.

(iv) An amount equal to all advance payments made by certificate holders, plus any accumulations thereon at rates required under the terms of the certificate.

(v) Amounts for other appropriate contingency reserves, for death and disability benefits or for reinstatement rights on any certificate providing for such benefits or rights.

8. **Inapplicable captions.**—Attention is directed to the provisions of rules 3–02 and 3–03 (a) which permit the omission of separate captions in financial statements as to which the items and conditions are not present, or the amounts involved are not material. However, amounts involving directors, officers and affiliates shall nevertheless be separately set forth except as otherwise specifically permitted under a particular caption.

Rule 6–22. Balance Sheets.—Balance sheets filed under this rule shall comply with the following provisions:

ASSETS AND OTHER DEBITS

QUALIFIED ASSETS
(See rule 6–21–5 (a) and (b))

1. **Cash and cash items.**—State separately (a) cash on hand, demand deposits, and time deposits; (b) call loans; and (c) funds subject to withdrawal restrictions.

2. **Dividends and interest receivable.**—(*a*) Dividends shall not be included before the ex-dividend date, nor unless payment is reasonably assured by past experience, guaranty, or otherwise. No dividend shall be included on stocks issued or assumed by the company and held by or for it, whether held in its treasury, in sinking or other special funds, or pledged as collateral.

(*b*) Interest due or accrued on bonds, notes, deposits, loans, open accounts, and other interest-bearing obligations owned, shall not be included unless payment is reasonably assured by past experience, guaranty, or otherwise. No interest shall be included on securities issued or assumed by the company and held by or for it, whether held in its treasury, in sinking or other special funds, or pledged as collateral.

3. **Notes receivable.**

4. **Accounts receivable.**

5. **Reserves for doubtful receivables.**—Notes and accounts receivable known to be uncollectible shall be excluded from the assets as well as from any reserve account.

6. **Investments in unaffiliated issuers.**—See rule 6–21–6.

(*a*) **Securities.**—State separately investments in (i) United States Government bonds and other obligations (including only direct obligations of the United States Government); (ii) other bonds; and (iii) other securities.

(*b*) **First mortgage loans on real estate.**—State separately (i) mortgages insured by an agency acting as an instrumentality of the United States Government; (ii) mortgages guaranteed by an agency acting as an instrumentality of the United States Government; and (iii) other first mortgages. There shall also be shown in an appropriate manner (1) the aggregate amount of self-amortizing mortgages, and (2) the amount of mortgages in respect of which interest or principal payments are past due for more than three months.

(*c*) **Other mortgage loans on real estate.**—Such classification shall be used as is appropriate under the circumstances.

(*d*) **Reserves for investments in unaffiliated issuers.**

(*e*) There shall be shown in an appropriate manner the average gross rates of return realized by the company, for each period for which profit and loss or income statements are filed, on each class of investment shown in this caption.

7. **Real estate owned.**—State separately (*a*) real estate acquired through foreclosure of mortgages; and (*b*) other real estate investments.

8. **Reserve for real estate owned.**

9. **Loans to certificate holders secured by certificate reserves.**—See rule 6–21–5 (*c*).

10. **Other qualified assets.**—State separately (*a*) investments in and advances to controlled companies and (*b*) other affiliates; (*c*) each special fund of a material amount; (*d*) unamortized premium on mortgages; and (*e*) any other material amounts.

11. **Total qualified assets.**—State in a note the amount of qualified assets on deposit classified as to general classes of assets and as to general types of depositaries, such as banks and states, together with a statement as to the purpose of the deposits.

Other Assets

12. **Investments in unaffiliated issuers, not included in total of caption 11.**—State separately each class of investment.

13. **Investments in and advances to affiliates.**—State separately investments in (*a*) controlled companies and (*b*) other affiliates. The basis of determining the amount shall be explained in an appropriate manner.

14. **Prepaid expenses and other deferred items.**—State separately any material items. State in a note to this caption the provisions which have been made to write off or amortize such items.

15. **Other assets.**—State separately (*a*) amounts due from directors and officers, and (*b*) any other item in excess of 5 per cent of the amount of all assets other than qualified assets.

LIABILITIES, CAPITAL SHARES, AND SURPLUS

Certificate Reserves and Current Liabilities

16. **Certificate reserves.**—State separately reserves for (*a*) certificates of the installment type; (*b*) certificates of the fully paid type; (*c*) advance payments; (*d*) additional amounts accrued for or credited to the account of certificate holders in the form of any credit, dividend, or interest in addition to the minimum maturity amount specified in the certificate; and (*e*) other certificate reserves. State in an appropriate manner the basis used in determining the reserves, including the rates of interest of accumulation.

17. **Current liabilities, exclusive of certificate reserve liabilities.**

(*a*) **Notes payable.**—State separately amounts payable within one year (i) to banks and (ii) to others.

(*b*) **Accounts payable.**—State separately (i) amounts payable for purchase of securities and (ii) other accounts payable.

(*c*) **Accrued liabilities.**—State separately (i) accrued salaries; (ii) tax liability; (iii) interest; and (iv) any other material item. If the total under this subcaption is not material, it may be stated as one amount.

(*d*) **Sundry liabilities of a current nature.**—State separately (i) dividends declared; (ii) serial bonds, notes and mortgages installments and mortgages due within one year; (iii) total of current amounts due to affiliates; (iv) total of current amounts due directors and officers; and (v) other items of material amount.

18. **Total certificate reserves and current liabilities.**

OTHER LIABILITIES

19. **Funded debt.**—If any amount included herein will fall due within one year, indicate such amount and explain in a note the reason for not including such amount as a current liability.

20. **Indebtedness to affiliates—Not current.**—State separately amounts due to (*a*) controlled companies, and (*b*) other affiliates.

21. **Other long-term debt.**—Indicate whether secured. State separately (*a*) total of amounts due directors and officers; and (*b*) other long-term debt, specifying any material item. State separately by years, in the balance sheet or in a note therein referred to, total amounts of respective maturities for the 5 years following the date of the balance sheet.

22. **Other liabilities.**—State separately any amount in excess of 10 per cent of the total of liabilities other than certificate reserves, funded debt, capital shares and surplus.

DEFERRED INCOME

23. **Deferred income.**—State separately each material item and the basis of taking amounts reported under this caption into income.

RESERVES NOT SHOWN ELSEWHERE

24. **Reserves not shown elsewhere.**—State separately each major class and indicate clearly its purpose.

CAPITAL SHARES AND SURPLUS

25. **Capital shares.**—State for each class of shares (*a*) the title of issue; (*b*) the number of shares authorized; and (*c*) the number of shares outstanding and the capital share liability thereof. Show also the dollar amount, if any, of capital shares subscribed but unissued, and of subscriptions receivable thereon.

26. **Surplus.**—(*a*) Show the division of this item into (i) paid-in surplus; (ii) other capital surplus; (iii) earned surplus.

(*b*) If undistributed earnings of subsidiaries are included, state the amount thereof parenthetically, or otherwise. Due consideration shall be given to the propriety of including any undistributed earnings on which restrictions are imposed.

(*c*) An analysis of each surplus account setting forth the information prescribed by rule 11–02 shall be given for each period for which a profit and loss or income statement is filed, as a continuation of the related profit and loss or income statement or in the form of a separate statement of surplus, and shall be referred to in the balance sheet.

Rule 6–23. Profit and Loss or Income Statements.—Statements filed under this rule shall comply with the following provisions:

INVESTMENT INCOME AND EXPENSES
(Including Servicing and Loading Income and Expenses)

1. **Income.**—(*a*) State separately (i) interest on mortgages; (ii) interest on securities; (iii) cash dividends; (iv) rentals; and (v) other investment income. If income from investments in or indebtedness of affiliates is included hereunder, such income shall be segregated under an appropriate caption subdivided to show separately income from controlled companies and from other affiliates.

(*b*) Due consideration shall be given to the propriety of treating as income, dividends on stock acquired or disposed of during the period of report.

(*c*) Due consideration shall be given to the propriety of treating extraordinary dividends as income. For the purpose of this rule the term "extraordinary dividends" shall mean (i) dividends which are known to have been declared out of sources other than current earnings or earned surplus and (ii) dividends which are declared otherwise than out of earnings of the current or preceding year and are abnormal in size in relationship to the value of the securities upon which declared.

(*d*) Dividends in arrears on preferred stock may not be treated as income in an amount which exceeds an amount arrived at by applying the stated dividend rate to the period during which the stock has been held, *provided,* that, in computing the period held, periods of more than one-half of a quarter-year may be treated as full quarter-years, if periods of less than one-half of a quarter-year are not counted. Any such dividends which are treated as income but which are applicable to periods prior to the current fiscal year shall be included under caption 1 (a) (v).

(*e*) Dividends by controlled companies may be treated as income only to the extent that they are out of earnings subsequent to (i) the date of acquisition or (ii) the effective date of a reorganization or quasi-reorganization of the receiving company, if such date is subsequent to the date of acquisition.

(*f*) Due consideration shall be given to the propriety of treating, as income, interest received on investments which were in default when acquired. Any such interest which may be treated as income shall not be treated as ordinary interest income in an amount in excess of the amount arrived at by applying the stated interest rate to the period of report, and any excess thereof shall be included under caption 1 (a) (v) above. The policy followed in accounting for such interest shall be stated in a note.

(*g*) Common stock received as a dividend on common stock of the same issuer shall not be treated as income, and no amount shall be debited to investments or credited to income or surplus at the time such dividend is received.

(*h*) State as to any non-cash dividends, other than stock dividends referred to in paragraph (*g*), and as to preferred stock received as a stock dividend, the basis on which taken up as income. If any such dividends received from controlled companies have been credited to income in an amount dffierent from that charged to income or earned surplus by the disbursing company, state the amount of such difference and explain.

(*i*) State separately each category of other investment income representing more than 5 percent of the total of such income shown under caption 1 (a) (v).

(*j*) Dividends and interest applicable to an issuer's own securities held in its treasury or its sinking or other special funds shall not be treated as income.

2. **Service fees on certificate installment payments.**—State in a note the basis on which taken up as income.

3. **Loading credits on certificate installments.**—State separately (*a*) the portion of initial loading credits applicable to the current year, and (*b*) other loading credits. State in a note the basis on which taken up as income.

4. **Other income.**—State separately each material item.

5. **Total investment income.**

6. **Investment expenses.**—State separately each category of expense representing more than 5 percent of the total expense. There shall also be shown in an appropriate manner (*a*) the amount of management, service and other fees to unaffiliated persons; (*b*) the amount of management, service and other fees to affiliated persons, indicating in a note or otherwise (i) the name of each such person accounting for 10 percent or more of the total under this subcaption, (ii) the nature of the affiliation between the company and each such person, (iii) the amount applicable to each such person, and (iv) the basis and methods of computing management or service fees; and (*c*) other expenses within the person's own organization in connection with research, selection, and supervision of investments. State in a note referred to under this item the basis and methods of computing management, service and other fees and if none was incurred for the period of report, the reason therefor. If any of the expenses were paid otherwise than in cash, state the details in a note referred to under this caption.

7. **Taxes.**—The amount included under this caption shall represent taxes (other than taxes on income) applicable to investment income.

8. **Interest and debt discount and expense.**—State separately (a)

interest on funded debt; (*b*) amortization of debt discount and expense or premium; and (*c*) other interest.

9. **Total investment expenses.**

10. **Investment income less investment expenses.**

11. **Provision for certificate reserves.**—State separately provision for additional credits, or any dividends, or any interests, in addition to the minimum maturity or face amount specified in the certificates. State also in an appropriate manner reserve recoveries from surrenders or other causes.

12. **Net investment income less provision for certificate reserves.**

OTHER INCOME AND EXPENSES

13. **Income from other operations.**—State separately, with explanation, any material amounts, designating clearly the nature of the transactions out of which the items arose. Income from operations with affiliated companies shall be stated separately. Realized gain or loss on sale of mortgage loans on real estate shall be included under this caption, *provided,* such sales are part of the ordinary and recurring operations of the business.

14. **Expenses applicable to income from other operations.**—State separately, with an explanation, any material amounts. Information comparable to that required under caption 6 of this rule shall be given for items shown under this caption.

15. **Net income from other operations.**

16. **Net investment income and net income from other operations before realized gain or loss on investments.**

GAIN OR LOSS ON INVESTMENTS

17. **Realized gain or loss on sales of investments.**—(*a*) State in an appropriate manner the aggregate cost, aggregate proceeds, and net gain or loss from sales of each of the following classes of investments; (i) investments in securities of affiliates; (ii) investments in other securities, showing United States Government bonds and other direct government obligations separately; and (iii) other investments, exclusive of gain or loss on sale of mortgage loans on real estate. See text under caption 13 above.

(*b*) Transactions in shares of the person for which the statement is filed shall not be included here.

(*c*) State in a note the aggregate cost of securities acquired during the period, showing separately (i) United States Government bonds and other direct government obligations; (ii) other securities; and (iii) mortgages on real estate.

(*d*) State the basis followed in determining the cost of investments sold. If a basis other than average cost is used, state, if practicable, the gain or loss computed on the basis of average cost.

18. **Realized gain or loss on other transactions.**—(*a*) Include under this caption exchanges of investments. Show the aggregate cost of the investments released, stating, as to interest-bearing obligations, principal and interest separately and, as to the proceeds of the exchanges, the aggregate amount at which the investments acquired were recorded in the accounts.

(*b*) Include also under this caption any write-downs required by rule 6–21–6. Show the aggregate cost and the aggregate adjusted cost of the investments involved.

19. **Net income before provision for income taxes.**

20. **Provision for taxes on income.**—State separately (*a*) Federal income taxes, and (*b*) other income taxes.

21. **Net income or loss.**—The amount included under this caption shall be carried to the related subdivision of surplus.

Rule 6–24. What Schedules Are to Be Filed.—Except as otherwise expressly provided in the applicable forms:

(1) The schedules specified below in this rule as schedules I, V, XI, XII, and XIII shall be filed as of the date of the most recent balance sheet filed for each person and for each group for which separate statements are filed. Such schedules shall be certified if the related balance sheet is certified.

(2) All other schedules specified below in this rule shall be filed for each period for which a profit and loss or income statement is filed, except as indicated below for schedules III and IV. Such schedules shall be certified if the related profit and loss or income statement is certified.

(*b*) The information required in schedules for the registrant, for the consolidated subsidiaries and for the registrant and its subsidiaries consolidated may be presented in the form of a single schedule, *provided,* that items pertaining to the registrant and to each consolidated subsidiary or group for which separate statements are required are separately shown and that such single schedule affords a properly summarized presentation of the facts.

(*c*) If the information required by any schedules (including the notes thereto) may be shown in the statements required by rule 6–22 and 6–23 without making such statements unclear or confusing, that procedure may be followed and the schedule omitted.

(*d*) Reference to the schedules shall be made against the appropriate captions of the balance sheet and the profit and loss or income statement.

A. INVESTMENT SCHEDULES

SCHEDULE I. INVESTMENT IN SECURITIES OF UNAFFILIATED ISSUERS.—The schedule prescribed by rule 12–35 shall be filed in support of captions

6 (*a*) and 12 of each balance sheet. Separate schedules shall be furnished in support of each caption, if applicable.

SCHEDULE II. INVESTMENTS IN AND ADVANCES TO AFFILIATES AND INCOME THEREON.—The schedule prescribed by rule 12–36 shall be filed in support of captions 10 and 13 of each balance sheet and caption 1 (a) of each profit and loss or income statement. Separate schedules shall be furnished in support of each caption, if applicable.

SCHEDULE III. MORTGAGE LOANS ON REAL ESTATE AND INTEREST EARNED ON MORTGAGES.—The schedule prescribed by rule 12–37 shall be filed in support of captions 6 (b) and (c) and 12 of each balance sheet and caption 1 (a) (i) of each profit and loss or income statement, except that only the information required by column G and note 8 of the schedule need be furnished in support of profit and loss or income statements for years for which related balance sheets are not required.

SCHEDULE IV. REAL ESTATE OWNED AND RENTAL INCOME.—The schedule prescribed by rule 12–38 shall be filed in support of captions 7 and 12 of each balance sheet and caption 1 (a) (iv) of each profit and loss or income statement for rental income included therein, except that only the information required by columns H, I, and J, and item "Rent from properties sold during the period" and note 4 of the schedule need be furnished in support of profit and loss or income statements for years for which related balance sheets are not required.

B. MISCELLANEOUS SCHEDULES

SCHEDULE V. QUALIFIED ASSETS ON DEPOSIT.—The schedule prescribed by rule 12–41 shall be filed in support of note required by caption 11 of rule 6–22 as to total amount of qualified assets on deposit.

SCHEDULE VI. AMOUNTS DUE FROM DIRECTORS AND OFFICERS.—The schedule prescribed by rule 12–03 shall be filed with respect to each person among the directors and officers from whom any amount was owed at any time during the period for which related profit and loss or income statements are filed. The schedule shall include also amounts due from employees. These amounts may be shown in an aggregate amount setting forth separately the amount due (1) from office employees and (2) sales employees, stating the total number of employees in each class. State if an exemption has been granted by the Commission with respect to amounts included in this schedule.

SCHEDULE VII. INDEBTEDNESS TO AFFILIATES—NOT CURRENT.—The schedule prescribed by rule 12–11 shall be filed in support of caption 20 of each balance sheet. This schedule and schedule II may be combined if desired.

SCHEDULE VIII. SUPPLEMENTARY PROFIT AND LOSS INFORMATION.—The schedule prescribed by rule 12–39 shall be filed in support of each profit and loss or income statement.

C. RESERVE SCHEDULES

SCHEDULE IX. CERTIFICATE RESERVES.—The schedule prescribed by rule 12–40 shall be filed in support of caption 16 of each balance sheet.

SCHEDULE X. RESERVES—OTHER.—The schedule prescribed by rule 12–13 shall be filed in support of all other reserves included in the balance sheet.

D. CAPITAL SECURITIES

SCHEDULE XI. FUNDED DEBT.—The schedule prescribed by rule 12–10 shall be filed in support of caption 19 of each balance sheet.

SCHEDULE XII. CAPITAL SHARES.—The schedule prescribed by rule 12–14 shall be filed in support of caption 25 of each balance sheet.

SCHEDULE XIII. OTHER SECURITIES.—Schedules shall be filed in respect of any classes of securities issued by the person for whom the statement is filed, but not included in schedules XI and XII. As to guarantees of securities of other issuers, furnish the information required by rule 12–12. As to warrants or rights granted by the person for whom the statement is filed, to subscribe for or purchase securities to be issued by such person, furnish the information called for by rule 12–15. As to any other securities, furnish information comparable to that called for by rules 12–10, 12–12, 12–14 or 12–15, as appropriate. Information need not be set forth, however, as to notes, drafts, bills of exchange or bankers' acceptances having a maturity at the time of issuance of less than one year.

Article 6C. Employee Stock Purchase, Savings and Similar Plans

Rule 6–30. Application of Article 6C.—This article shall be applicable to financial statements filed for employee stock purchase, savings and similar plans.

Rule 6–31. Special Rules Applicable to Employee Stock Purchase, Savings and Similar Plans.—The financial statements filed for persons to which this article is applicable shall be prepared in accordance with the following special rules in addition to the general rules in Articles 1, 2, 3, and 4. Where the requirements of a special rule differ from those prescribed in a general rule, the requirements of the special rule shall be met.

1. **Investment programs.**—If the participating employees have an option as to the manner in which their deposits and contributions may be invested, a description of each investment program shall be given in a footnote or otherwise. The number of employees under each investment program shall be stated.

2. **Net asset value per unit.**—Where appropriate, the number of units and the net asset value per unit shall be given by footnote or otherwise.

3. **Federal income taxes.**—(a) Appropriate provision shall be made, on the basis of the applicable tax laws, for Federal income taxes that it is reasonably believed are, or will become, payable in respect of (1) current net income, (2) realized net gain on investments, and (3) unrealized appreciation on investments. If the plan is not subject to Federal income taxes, a note shall so state indicating briefly the principal present assumptions on which the plan has relied in not making provision for such taxes.

(b) State the Federal income tax status of the employee with respect to the plan.

4. **Valuation of assets.**—The statement of financial condition shall reflect all assets either (1) at value, showing cost parenthetically, or (2) at cost, showing value parenthetically.

Rule 6–32. Statements of Financial Condition.—Statements of financial condition filed under this rule shall comply with the following provisions:

PLAN ASSETS

1. **Investments in securities of participating employers.**—State separately each class of securities of the participating employer or employers.

2. **Investments in securities of unaffiliated issuers.**

(a) **United States Government bonds and other obligations.**—Include only direct obligations of the United States Government.

(b) **Other securities.**—State separately (1) marketable securities and (2) other securities.

3. **Investments—Other than securities.**—State separately each major class.

4. **Dividends and interest receivable.**

5. **Cash.**

6. **Other assets.**—State separately (a) total of amounts due from participating employers or any of their directors, officers and principal holders

of equity securities; (*b*) total of amounts due from trustees or managers of the plan; and (*c*) any other significant amounts

LIABILITIES AND PLAN EQUITY

7. **Liabilities.**—State separately (*a*) total of amounts payable to participating employers; (*b*) total of amounts payable to participating employees; and (*c*) any other significant amounts.

8. **Reserves and other credits.**—State separately each significant item and describe each such item by using an appropriate caption or by a footnote referred to in the caption.

9. **Plan equity at close of period.**

Rule 6–33. Statements of Income and Changes in Plan Equity.—Statements of income and changes in plan equity filed under this rule shall comply with the following provisions:

1. **Net investment income**

(*a*) **Income.**—State separately income from (1) cash dividends; (2) interest; and (3) other sources. Income from investments in or indebtedness of participating employers shall be segregated under the appropriate subcaption.

(*b*) **Expenses.**—State separately any significant amounts.

(*c*) **Net investment income.**

2. **Realized gain or loss on investments.**—(*a*) State separately the net of gains or losses arising from transactions in (1) investments in securities of the participating employer or employers; (2) other investments in securities; and (3) other investments.

(*b*) State in a footnote or otherwise for each category of investment in paragraph (*a*) above the aggregate cost, the aggregate proceeds and the net gain or loss. State the principle followed in determining the cost of securities sold, e.g., "average cost" or "first-in, first-out."

3. **Unrealized appreciation or depreciation of investments.**—(*a*) State the amount of increase or decrease in unrealized appreciation or depreciation of investments during the period.

(*b*) State in a footnote or otherwise the amount of unrealized appreciation or depreciation of investments at the beginning of the period of report, at the end of the period of report, and the increase or decrease during the period.

4. **Contributions and deposits.**—(*a*) State separately (1) total of amounts deposited by participating employees, and (2) total of amounts contributed by the participating employer or employers.

(*b*) If employees of more than one employer participate in the plan, state in tabular form in a footnote or otherwise the amount contributed by each employer and the deposits of the employees of each such employer.

5. Withdrawals, lapses and forfeitures.—State separately (a) balances of employees' accounts withdrawn, lapsed or forfeited during the period; (b) amounts disbursed in settlement of such accounts; and (c) disposition of balances remaining after settlement specified in (b).

6. Plan equity at beginning of period.

7. Plan equity at end of period.

Rule 6–34. What Schedules Are to Be Filed.—(a) Schedules I and II, specified below, shall be filed as of the date of each statement of financial condition filed. Schedule III shall be filed for each period for which a statement of income and changes in plan equity is filed. All schedules shall be certified if the related statements are certified.

(b) Reference to the schedules shall be made against the appropriate captions of the statements of financial condition and income and changes in plan equity.

SCHEDULE I. INVESTMENTS.—A schedule substantially in the form prescribed·by Rule 12–19 shall be filed in support of captions 1, 2 and 3 of each statement of financial condition unless substantially all of the information is given in the statement of financial condition by footnote or otherwise.

SCHEDULE II. ALLOCATION OF PLAN ASSETS AND LIABILITIES TO INVESTMENT PROGRAM.—If the plan provides for separate investment programs with separate funds, and if the allocation of assets and liabilities to the several funds is not shown in the statement of financial condition in columnar form or by the submission of separate statements for each fund, a schedule shall be submitted showing the allocation of each caption of each statement of financial condition filed to the applicable fund.

SCHEDULE III. ALLOCATION OF PLAN INCOME AND CHANGES IN PLAN EQUITY TO INVESTMENT PROGRAMS.—If the plan provides for separate investment programs with separate funds, and if the allocation of income and changes in plan equity to the several funds is not shown in the statement of income and changes in plan equity in columnar form or by the submission of separate statements for each fund, a schedule shall be submitted showing the allocation of each caption of each statement of income and changes in plan equity filed to the applicable fund.

Article 7. Insurance Companies Other Than Life and Title Insurance Companies

Rule 7–01. Application of Article 7.—This article shall be applicable to financial statements filed for insurance companies other than life and title insurance companies. (Title insurance companies shall comply with the requirements of Article 5.)

Rule 7–02. General Requirement.—Except as otherwise provided in this article, persons subject to this article shall follow the rules and instructions governing the definition and computation of items in annual statements to their State regulatory authority. If the registrant deviates from such rules and instructions of its State regulatory authority, except in accordance with the provisions of this article, the reason for and effect of such deviation shall be stated.

Rule 7–03. Balance Sheets.—Balance sheets filed for insurance companies other than life and title insurance companies shall comply with the following provisions:

ADMITTED ASSETS

1. **Bonds.**
2. **Investments in stocks other than stocks of affiliates.**—State separately: (*a*) preferred stocks and (*b*) common stocks.
3. **Investments in stocks of affiliates.**

   (*a*) **In insurance companies.**—Include only stocks of insurance companies under this subcaption.

   (*b*) **In other affiliates.**—Include under this subcaption stocks of other affiliates. If any such "other affiliate" controls insurance companies, the stock of such "other affiliate" shall be included under this subcaption, and the fact of such control shall be stated in a note to the balance sheet.

4. **Mortgage loans on real estate.**—State separately (*a*) first liens and (*b*) other than first liens.
5. **Real estate.**—State parenthetically the amount of encumbrances deducted.
6. **Cash and cash items.**—State separately (*a*) cash on hand, demand deposits, and time deposits and (*b*) call loans.
7. **Agents' balances and/or gross premiums in course of collection.**—State parenthetically the amount of ceded reinsurance balances payable deducted, if material.
8. **Due from other insurance companies.**—Include reinsurances recoverable on losses paid, etc.; do not include premium balances.
9. **Interest, dividends and real estate income due and accrued.**
10. **Other assets.**—State separately any significant items.

LIABILITIES, CAPITAL SHARES AND SURPLUS

11. **Losses and claims.**
12. **Loss adjustment expenses.**

13. **Unearned premiums.**

14. **Dividends declared and unpaid.**—State separately amounts payable to (*a*) policyholders and (*b*) stockholders.

15. **Borrowed money.**—State here or in a note as to each loan (*a*) from whom borrowed, (*b*) date of loan, (*c*) repayment terms and other conditions governing each loan, (*d*) due date, (*e*) extensions granted, (*f*) original amount, and (*g*) interest rate.

16. **Other liabilities.**—State separately any significant items.

17. **Commitments and contingent liabilities.**—See rule 3–16(i) and 7–05–4.

18. **Capital shares.**—State for each class of shares the title of issue, the number of shares authorized, the number of shares outstanding and the capital share liability thereof, and, if convertible, the basis of conversion. Show also the dollar amount, if any, of capital shares subscribed but unissued, and of subscriptions receivable thereon.

19. **Surplus.**—(*a*) Separate captions shall be shown for (1) paid-in surplus, (2) surplus arising from revaluation of assets, (3) other capital surplus, and (4) earned surplus (i) appropriated and (ii) unappropriated. There shall be included under earned surplus, appropriated, all reserves and segregations of surplus, mandatory or voluntary, which are general contingency reserves whose purposes are not specific, or reserves for indefinite possible future losses, such as, for example, for future decline in value of investments or for contingencies.

(*b*) If undistributed earnings of subsidiaries are included, state the amount thereof parenthetically or otherwise. However, in a consolidated statement the preceding sentence shall have reference only to the undistributed earnings of subsidiaries not consolidated in such statement.

(*c*) An analysis of each surplus account setting forth the information prescribed in Rule 11–02 shall be given for each period for which a profit and loss statement is filed, as a continuation of the related profit and loss statement or in the form of a separate statement of surplus, and shall be referred to here. In this statement caption 3, *Other additions to surplus,* shall be subdivided to show (1) unrealized gain on bonds and stocks from change in market values, (2) unrealized gain on other investments from change in market values, and (3) all others, designating clearly the nature thereof. Likewise, caption 5, *Other deductions,* shall be subdivided to show (A) unrealized loss on bonds and stocks from change in market values, (B) unrealized loss on other investments from change in market values, and (C) all others, designating clearly the nature thereof.

(*d*) If separate balances are not shown in the accounts for the divisions of surplus in (*a*) above other than for earned surplus appropriated, i. e., if the company has not, up to the opening of the period of report, differentiated in its accounting for surplus as indicated, then the unsegregated surplus may be stated in one amount, and, in lieu of such segregation, there shall be given as a note an analysis of surplus since organization. Such analysis shall show (1) total net income after income taxes, (2) aggregate dividends paid (A) in cash, and (B) in capital stock, (3) total paid-in surplus, (4) unrealized gain or loss from change in market values, (5) aggregate transfers to reserves, (6) change in non-admitted assets, and (7) other additions or deductions of material amount, indicating clearly the nature of the item.

Rule 7–04. Profit and Loss or Income Statements.—Profit and loss or income statements filed for insurance companies other than life and title insurance companies shall comply with the following provisions:

UNDERWRITING PROFIT OR LOSS

1. **Net premiums written.**—State premiums written including reinsurance assumed less reinsurance ceded.
2. **Increase or decrease in unearned premium reserve.**
3. **Premiums earned.**
4. **Losses incurred.**
5. **Loss expense incurred.**
6. **Balance.**
7. **Commissions and brokerage.**—State commissions and brokerage less amount received on return premiums and reinsurance.
8. **Salaries and other compensation.**—State the total amount paid to directors, officers, employees and agents not paid by commission other than amounts allocable to loss and investment expense.
9. **Taxes, licenses and fees.**—State the total amount excluding income taxes.
10. **All other underwriting expenses.**—Include hereunder all other underwriting expenses not included above. State separately any material amount. Do not include investment expense under this caption.
11. **Other underwriting profit or loss.**—Include the income or loss from unusual or nonrecurring contingent profits or reinsurance agreements, pools and other miscellaneous contracts, licenses and agreements, etc. Give in a note a brief explanation of any items included in this account.
12. **Profit or loss from underwriting.**

INVESTMENT INCOME OR LOSS

13. **Interest on bonds.**
14. **Dividends.**—State separately dividends from (*a*) unaffiliated companies and (*b*) affiliated companies.
15. **Interest on mortgage loans.**

16. **Real estate income.**

17. **Other investment income.**—State separately any material amount.

18. **Total investment income.**

19. **Investment expense.**—Include interest on encumbrances, real estate expense, supervisory service, other fees, salaries, administrative expenses, etc. State separately any material amounts.

20. **Net investment income.**—Realized gains or losses on investments, shall be reported in caption 26 below. Unrealized gains or losses resulting from change in market values shall be reported in the appropriate surplus account.

21. **Total income and profit or loss from underwriting and investment.**

22. **Dividends to policyholders.**

23. **Net income or loss before provision for income taxes.**

24. **Provision for income taxes.**—State separately (*a*) Federal normal income tax and surtax, and (*b*) other income taxes. Amounts allocable to realized gains or losses on investments shall be reported in caption 26 below.

25. **Net income or loss.**

26. **Realized gains or losses on investments.**—State parenthetically or otherwise the amount of income taxes deducted

27. **Net income or loss and realized gains or losses on investments.**

Rule 7–05. Special Notes to Financial Statements.—1. Assets shall be set forth in the balance sheet at admitted asset values. Book values of assets included under captions 1, 2, 3(a), 3(b), 4 and 5 shall be shown parenthetically or in a note.

The total amount of non-admitted assets shall be stated in a note, and if such amount exceeds one percent of the total admitted assets then a separate statement shall be presented showing the details of such assets. State in a note or otherwise the amount of assets charged to income or surplus immediately upon acquisition during the period, if significant.

There shall also be added as a note to the financial statements the following:

"The term 'admitted assets' means the assets stated at values at which they are permitted to be reported to the respective domiciliary State regulatory authority for balance sheet purposes in the annual report in accordance with the rules and regulations of such regulatory authority.

"The term 'non-admitted assets' means assets other than assets which are so permitted to be reported."

2. State in tabular form in a note or otherwise, together with appropriate explanation, a reconciliation of material differences between (*a*) capital share equity as reported on the balance sheet and capital share equity as determined in accordance with generally accepted accounting principles and practices, and (*b*) net income or loss as reported on the profit and loss or income statement and net income or loss as determined in accordance with generally accepted principles and practices.

3. State in a note the amount of surplus not available for payment of dividends to stockholders. See rule 3–16(h).

4. Explain in a note the basis of determining the unearned premiums and the estimated liability for losses and claims and state the amounts deducted in respect of reinsurance carried with other companies.

5. If the company wrote mortgage guaranty surety bonds during the period of report, state the amount of liability in force therefor as of the date of the balance sheet.

Rule 7–06. What Schedules Are to Be Filed.—(*a*) Except as expressly provided otherwise in the applicable form:

(1) The schedules specified below in this rule as schedules I, II, III, IV, V, VI, VIII, and IX shall be filed as of the date of the most recent balance sheet filed for each person or group. Such schedules shall be certified if the related balance sheet is certified.

(2) All other schedules specified below in this rule shall be filed for each period for which a profit and loss statement is filed. Such schedules shall be certified if the related profit and loss statement is certified.

(*b*) Reference to the schedules shall be made against the appropriate captions of the balance sheet and the profit and loss statement.

(*c*) If the information required by any schedule (including the footnotes thereto) may be shown in the related balance sheet or profit and loss statement without making such statement unclear or confusing, that procedure may be followed and the schedule omitted.

SCHEDULE I. BONDS.—The schedule prescribed by rule 12–23 shall be filed in support of caption 1 of each balance sheet.

SCHEDULE II. STOCKS—OTHER THAN STOCKS OF AFFILIATES.—The schedule prescribed by rule 12–24 shall be filed in support of caption 2 of each balance sheet.

SCHEDULE III. MORTGAGE LOANS ON REAL ESTATE.—The schedule prescribed by rule 12–25 shall be filed in support of caption 4 of each balance sheet.

SCHEDULE IV. REAL ESTATE.—The schedule prescribed by rule 12–26 shall be filed in support of caption 5 of each balance sheet.

SCHEDULE V. SUMMARY OF INVESTMENTS IN SECURITIES—OTHER THAN SECURITIES OF AFFILIATES.—The summary schedule prescribed by rule 12–27 shall be filed in conjunction with schedules I and II.

SCHEDULE VI. INVESTMENTS IN STOCKS OF AFFILIATES.—The schedule prescribed by rule 12–28 shall be filed in support of caption 3 of each balance sheet.

SCHEDULE VII. PREMIUMS, LOSSES AND UNDERWRITING EXPENSE.— The schedule prescribed by rule 12–29 shall be filed in support of caption 13 of each balance sheet and captions 1, 3, 4, 5, 7, 8, 9, and 10 of each profit and loss statement.

SCHEDULE VIII. CAPITAL SHARES.—The schedule prescribed by rule 12–14 shall be filed in support of caption 18 of each balance sheet.

SCHEDULE IX. OTHER SECURITIES.—If there are any classes of securities not included in schedule VII, set forth in this schedule information concerning such securities corresponding to that required for the securities in such schedule. If the securities required to be reported on the schedules prescribed by rules 12–10, 12–12 or 12–15 are present, those schedules should be used. Information need not be set forth, however, as to notes, drafts, bills of exchange or bankers' acceptances having a maturity at the time of issuance of not exceeding one year.

SCHEDULE X. INCOME FROM DIVIDENDS—EQUITY IN NET PROFIT AND LOSS OF AFFILIATES.—The schedule prescribed by rule 12–17 shall be filed in support of caption 14(b) of each profit and loss statement.

SCHEDULE XI. SUMMARY OF REALIZED GAINS OR LOSSES ON SALE OR MATURITY OF INVESTMENTS.—The schedule prescribed by rule 12–30 shall be filed in support of caption 26 of each profit and loss statement.

Article 7A. Life Insurance Companies

Rule 7A–01. Application of Article 7A.—This article shall be applicable to financial statements filed for life insurance companies.

Rule 7A–02. General Requirement.—Except as otherwise provided in this article, persons subject to this article shall follow the rules and instructions governing the definition and computation of items in annual statements to their State regulatory authority. If the registrant deviates from such rules and instructions of its State regulatory authority, except in accordance with the provisions of this article, the reason for and effect of such deviation shall be stated.

Rule 7A–03. Balance Sheets.—Balance sheets filed for life insurance companies shall comply with the following provisions:

ADMITTED ASSETS

1. **Bonds.**
2. **Investments in stocks other than stocks of affiliates.**—State separately (*a*) preferred stocks and (*b*) common stocks.
3. **Investments in stocks of affiliates.**

(*a*) **In insurance companies.**—Include under this subcaption only stocks of insurance companies.

(*b*) **In other affiliates.**—Include under this subcaption stocks of other affiliates. If any such "other affiliate" controls insurance companies the stock of such "other affiliate" shall be included under this subcaption, and the fact of such control shall be stated in a note to the balance sheet.

4. **Mortgage loans on real estate.**—State separately (*a*) first liens and (*b*) other than first liens.
5. **Real estate.**—State separately if material (*a*) property occupied by the company; (*b*) property acquired by foreclosure; and (*c*) investment property. The amount of encumbrances deducted shall be stated parenthetically.
6. **Policy loans.**
7. **Cash and bank deposits.**
8. **Premiums and other considerations deferred and uncollected.**
9. **Investment income due and accrued.**
10. **Other assets.**—State separately any significant items.

LIABILITIES, CAPITAL SHARES AND SURPLUS

11. **Aggregate reserves for all policies.**—State separately reserves for (*a*) life insurance; (*b*) accident and health insurance; (*c*) supplementary contracts without life contingencies; and (*d*) policyholders' dividend accumulations.
12. **Policy and contract claims.**
13. **Other policyholders' funds.**—Include premiums paid in advance, premium deposit funds, and dividends to policyholders declared and unpaid

and estimated amounts provided for payment in the following year. State separately any material amounts.

14. **Dividends to stockholders declared and unpaid.**

15. **Borrowed money.**—State here or in a note as to each loan (*a*) from whom borrowed; (*b*) date of loan; (*c*) repayment terms and other conditions governing each loan; (*d*) due date; (*e*) extensions granted; (*f*) original amount; and (*g*) interest rate.

16. **Other liabilities.**—State separately any significant items.

17. **Commitments and contingent liabilities.**—See Rules 3–16(i) and 7A–05–3.

18. **Mandatory securities valuation reserve.**—See Rule 7A–05–2(d).

19. **Capital shares.**—State for each class of shares the title of issue, the number of shares authorized, the number of shares outstanding and the capital share liability thereof, and, if convertible, the basis of conversion. Show also the dollar amount, if any, of capital shares subscribed but unissued and of subscriptions receivable thereon.

20. **Surplus.**—(*a*) Separate captions shall be shown for (1) paid-in surplus, (2) surplus arising from revaluation of assets, (3) other capital surplus, and (4) earned surplus (i) appropriated and (ii) unappropriated. There shall be included under earned surplus, appropriated, all special surplus funds. That portion of the surplus allocable to participating policies should be included in caption 21 below.

(*b*) If undistributed earnings of subsidiaries are included, state the amount thereof parenthetically or otherwise.

(*c*) An analysis of each surplus account setting forth the information prescribed in Rule 11–02 shall be given for each period for which a profit and loss statement is filed, as a continuation of the related profit and loss statement or in the form of a separate statement of surplus, and shall be referred to here. In this statement caption 3, **Other additions,** shall be subdivided to show (1) unrealized gain on bonds and stocks from change in admitted asset values; (2) unrealized gain on other investments from change in admitted asset values; (3) realized gain on investments; and (4) all others, designating clearly the nature thereof. Likewise, caption 5, **Other deductions,** shall be subdivided to show (A) unrealized loss on bonds and stocks from change in admitted asset values; (B) unrealized loss on other investments from change in admitted asset values; (C) realized loss on investments; and (D) all others, designating clearly the nature thereof.

(*d*) If separate balances are not shown in the accounts for the divisions of surplus in (*a*) above other than for earned surplus appropriated, i.e., if the company has not, up to the opening of the period of report, differentiated in its accounting for surplus as indicated, then the unsegregated surplus may be stated in one amount, and, in lieu of such segregation, there shall be given as a note an analysis of surplus since organization. Such analysis shall show (1) total net income after income taxes; (2) aggregate dividends paid (A) in cash and (B) in capital stock; (3) total paid-in surplus; (4) realized gain or loss on investments; (5) unrealized gain or loss from change in admitted asset values; (6) increase in reserves on account of change in valuation basis; (7) non-admitted assets; and (8) other additions or deductions of material amount, indicating clearly the nature of the item.

21. **Surplus allocable to participating policies.**—State the amount of surplus required to be allocated to participating policies and not available for dividends to stockholders.

Rule 7A–04. Profit and Loss or Income Statements (Summary of Operations).—Profit and loss or income statements (summary of operations) filed for life insurance companies shall comply with the following provisions:

1. **Premiums and other considerations.**—State separately the amount arising from (*a*) life insurance; (b) accident and health insurance; and (*c*) considerations for supplementary contracts.

2. **Investment income.**

  (*a*) **Investment income.**

    (1) **Interest on bonds.**

    (2) **Dividends.**—State separately dividends from (i) unaffiliated companies and (ii) affiliated companies.

    (3) **Interest on mortgage loans.**

    (4) **Real estate income.**

    (5) **Interest on policy loans.**

    (6) **Other investment income.**—State separately any material amounts.

    (7) **Total investment income.**

  (*b*) **Investment expense.**—Include investment expense, investment taxes, and depreciation on real estate. State separately any material amounts.

  (*c*) **Net investment income.**

3. **Other income.**—State separately any significant items.

4. **Total.**

5. **Death and other benefits.**

6. **Increase in aggregate reserves for all policies.**

7. **Total.**

8. **Balance.**

9. **Commissions.**

10. **General insurance expenses.**—Amounts allocable to investment expense shall be excluded from this caption and captions 11 and 12 below.

11. **Insurance taxes, licenses and fees.**—Income taxes shall not be included under this caption.

12. **Other insurance expense.**

13. **Increase in loading on and cost of collection on deferred and uncollected premiums.**

14. **Total income and profit and loss from insurance and investment.**

15. **Dividends to policyholders.**

16. **Net income or loss before provision for income taxes.**

17. **Provision for income taxes.**—State separately (*a*) Federal normal income tax and surtax and (*b*) other income taxes. Amounts allocable to realized gain or loss on investments shall be excluded from this caption and reported as deductions or additions to the related captions on the analysis of surplus.

18. **Net income or loss (net gain from operations).**—State here or in a note the amount of net income allocated to participating policies.

Rule 7A–05. Special Notes to Financial Statements.

1. Assets shall be set forth in the balance sheet at admitted asset values. Book values of assets included under captions 1, 2, 3(a), 3(b), 4, 5, and 6 shall be shown parenthetically or in a note.

The total amount of non-admitted assets shall be stated in a note, and if such amount exceeds one per cent of the total admitted assets then a separate statement shall be presented showing the details of such assets. State in a note or otherwise the amount of assets charged to income or surplus immediately upon acquisition during the period if significant.

There shall also be added as a note to the financial statements the following:

"The term 'admitted assets' means the assets stated at values at which they are permitted to be reported to the respective domiciliary State regulatory authority for balance sheet purposes in the annual report in accordance with the rules and regulations of such regulatory authority.

"The term 'non-admitted assets' means assets other than assets which are so permitted to be reported."

2. State in notes or otherwise:

(*a*) The general policy of the company in determining dividends and profits allocable to participating policies.

(*b*) The amount of surplus not available for payment of dividends to stockholders. See Rule 3–16(h).

(*c*) The addition to the "policyholders surplus account" (under the sections of the Internal Revenue Code applicable to life insurance companies on which payment of income taxes has been deferred) for each period for which a profit and loss statement is filed and the total thereof accumulated as of the date of the most recent balance sheet filed. The income taxes, at current rates, which would become payable on these amounts upon distribution thereof to shareholders shall also be stated.

(*d*) The amount of income tax which would accrue if the unrealized gain from change in admitted asset value of investments were realized by sale or maturity.

3. State in a note the names of mortality tables and rates of interest most generally used in calculating reserves and whether the net level premium or a modified reserve valuation method is used. Explain the policy with regard to reinsurance and the amount of such reinsurance.

Rule 7A–06. What Schedules Are to Be Filed.—(*a*) Except as expressly provided otherwise in the applicable form:

(1) The schedules specified below in this rule as Schedules I, II, III, IV, V, VI, VIII, and IX shall be filed as of the date of the most recent balance sheet filed for each person or group. Such schedules shall be certified if the related balance sheet is certified.

(2) All other schedules specified below in this rule shall be filed for each period for which a profit and loss statement is filed. Such schedules shall be certified if the related profit and loss statement is certified.

(*b*) Reference to the schedules shall be made against the appropriate captions of the balance sheet and the profit and loss statement.

(*c*) If the information required by any schedule (including the footnotes thereto) may be shown in the related balance sheet or profit and loss statement without making such statement unclear or confusing, that procedure may be followed and the schedule omitted.

SCHEDULE I. BONDS.—The schedule prescribed by Rule 12–23 shall be filed in support of caption 1 of each balance sheet.

SCHEDULE II. STOCKS—OTHER THAN STOCKS OF AFFILIATES.—The schedule prescribed by Rule 12–24 shall be filed in support of caption 2 of each balance sheet.

SCHEDULE III. MORTGAGE LOANS ON REAL ESTATE.—The schedule prescribed by Rule 12–25 shall be filed in support of caption 4 of each balance sheet.

SCHEDULE IV. REAL ESTATE.—The schedule prescribed by Rule 12–26 shall be filed in support of caption 5 of each balance sheet.

SCHEDULE V. SUMMARY OF INVESTMENTS IN SECURITIES—OTHER THAN SECURITIES OF AFFILIATES.—The summary schedule prescribed by Rule 12–27 shall be filed in conjunction with Schedules I and II.

SCHEDULE VI. INVESTMENTS IN STOCKS OF AFFILIATES.—The schedule prescribed by Rule 12–28 shall be filed in support of caption 3 of each balance sheet.

SCHEDULE VII.—POLICY RESERVES, BENEFITS, AND INSURANCE IN FORCE.—The schedule prescribed by Rule 12–31 shall be filed in support of caption 11 of each balance sheet and captions 5 and 6 of each profit and loss statement. The schedule prescribed by Rule 12–29 shall be used insofar as it may more appropriately present those reserves of accident and health business which are based on unearned premiums and the related benefits paid.

SCHEDULE VIII. CAPITAL SHARES.—The schedule prescribed by Rule 12–14 shall be filed in support of caption 19 of each balance sheet.

SCHEDULE IX. OTHER SECURITIES.—If there are any classes of securities not included in Schedule VIII, set forth in this schedule information concerning such securities corresponding to that required for the securities in such schedule. If the securities required to be reported on the schedules prescribed by Rules 12–10, 12–12 or 12–15 are present, those schedules should be used. Information need not be set forth, however, as to notes, drafts, bills of exchange or bankers' acceptances having a maturity at the time of issuance of not exceeding one year.

SCHEDULE X. INCOME FROM DIVIDENDS—EQUITY IN NET PROFIT AND LOSS OF AFFILIATES.—The schedule prescribed by Rule 12–17 shall be filed in support of caption 2(a)(2)(ii) of each profit and loss statement.

SCHEDULE XI. SUMMARY OF REALIZED GAINS OR LOSSES ON SALE OR MATURITY OF INVESTMENTS.—The schedule prescribed by Rule 12–30 shall be filed in support of the related amount shown on each analysis of surplus required under caption 20(c) of each balance sheet.

Article 8. Committees Issuing Certificates of Deposit

Rule 8–01. Application of Article 8.—This article shall be applicable to financial statements filed for committees issuing certificates of deposit.

Rule 8–02. Statements of Assets and Liabilities.—Statements of assets and liabilities shall be in the following form:

STATEMENT OF ASSETS AND LIABILITIES

As of ....

ASSETS

Cash ....
Receivables (specify) ....
Advances to committee members or secretary ....
Investments in securities (specify)[4] ....
Miscellaneous other assets (specify)[5] ....

Subtotal ....
Expenses of committee chargeable against deposited securities[6] ....

Total ....

LIABILITIES

Notes payable:
    To banks (detail security) ....
    To others (specify and detail security) ....
Accounts payable ....
Other liabilities[7] ....

Total ....

[4] Each issue of securities shall be shown either here or in a schedule herein referred to. State the basis of determining the amount at which carried and, if available, the aggregate amount at current market quotations.

[5] Each class of "Miscellaneous Other Assets," if significant, shall be specified either here or in a schedule herein referred to. State the basis for determining the amount at which carried.

[6] State in a note to this item any limits fixed by the deposit agreement or otherwise upon the compensation and expenses of the Committee, and also the nature and extent of any lien of the Committee on the deposited securities for such compensation and expenses.

[7] (a) Each class of "Other Liabilities" shall be specified either here or in a schedule herein referred to.

(b) In a note describe briefly the nature of any commitment for compensation or other expenditures not included in "Other Liabilities," and state the amount or any basis agreed upon for determining the amount thereof. Describe briefly the general nature of any services rendered to the Committee, the cost of which is not included in "Other Liabilities" and as to which no commitment for compensation has been made. Separate descriptions of the services of the Committee, the secretary thereof, counsel, accountants, appraisers, depositary, and persons performing similar functions shall be given.

Rule 8–03. Statements of Cash Receipts and Disbursements.—Statements of cash receipts and disbursements shall be in the following form:

STATEMENT OF CASH RECEIPTS AND DISBURSMENTS [8]

RECEIPTS

Proceeds from loans and advances[9]—
    Against deposited securities ....
    Other ....
Assessments—
    On withdrawn securities ....
    Others (specify) ....
        Total ....

Other receipts—
Dividends ....
Interest ....
All other (specify) ....
    Total ....

Total receipts ....

DISBURSEMENTS

For committee expenses—
Compensation and fees to:
    Committee members ....
    Secretary ....
    Attorneys ....
    Solicitors for deposits ....
    Depositary ....
    Others[10] ....
        Total ....
Interest ....
Other committee expenses[9]— ....
        Total committee expenses ....

Other disbursements—
Purchase of securities called for deposit ....
Purchase of other securities ....
All other (specify) ....
    Total other disbursements ....

    Total disbursements ....

SUMMARY

Cash balance at beginning of period ....
Add total receipts ....
    Total ....

Deduct total disbursements ....
    Cash balance at close of period[11] ....

[8] If statements are required for different periods the statements shall be presented in columnar form, if practicable.

[9] Include under this caption only advances to be reimbursed by the Committee. Under each of the two sub-captions state separately amounts received from (a) banks, (b) original underwriters of issues called for deposit, (c) individuals, (d) committee members and (e) others (specify).

[10] Such expenses shall be specified in reasonable detail either here or in a schedule herein referred to, indicating amounts for clerical, statistical, and other expenses paid to (a) original underwriters of issues called for deposit and any affiliates of such underwriters and (b) affiliates of committee members.

[11] The cash balance at the close of the most recent period shall agree with the cash shown in the statement of assets and liabilities as of the same date.

Article 9. Bank Holding Companies and Banks

Rule 9–01. Application of Article 9.

    (a) **Bank holding companies.**—Financial statements filed for bank holding companies shall be prepared in accordance with Article 5 and Rule 9–02, 9–03 and 9–04 of this article.

    (b) **Banks.**—Financial statements filed for banks shall be prepared in accordance with Rule 9–05 of this article.

(c) **Consolidated and combined financial statements.**—Article 4 is applicable to the preparation of consolidated and combined financial statements. If consolidated financial statements are prepared for a bank holding company and its bank and other subsidiaries, consideration shall be given to utilization of the bank format for financial statements and schedules as prescribed in Rule 9–05.

Rule 9–02. Balance Sheets of Bank Holding Companies.

(a) Notwithstanding the provisions of Rule 5–02, current assets and current liabilities need not be separately classified as such.

(b) Any amount representing balances on deposit with or indebtedness to or from affiliated banks under the following captions prescribed by Rule 5–02 shall be set forth separately under the respective captions:

(1) Caption 1—**Cash and cash items.**

(2) Subdivisions (2) and (3) of caption 3—**Accounts and notes receivable.**

(3) Caption 10—**Securities of affiliates.**

(4) Caption 11—**Indebtedness of affiliates—not current.**

(5) Subdivisions (3) and 4) of caption 25—**Accounts and notes payable.**

(6) Subdivision (c) of caption 27—**Other current liabilities.**

(7) Caption 31—**Indebtedness to affiliates—not current.**

(c) Amounts required to be reported under caption 5–02.39(b) shall be stated separately for bank subsidiaries, and 50-per cent and less-than-50-per-cent-owned banks.

Rule 9–03. Income Statements of Bank Holding Companies.—The following captions shall be in complete substitution for Rule 5–03.

1. **Income.**—(a) State separately the total of income from (1) equity in earnings of unconsolidated subsidiaries, 50-per-cent-owned persons and other persons (showing dividends and interest received parenthetically), (2) dividends, (3) interest, (4) management and service fees, and (5) other income (specifying any significant items), exclusive of profits and losses under caption 6, **Profits on securities,** and caption 7, **Losses on securities.**

(b) State separately amounts included under item (1) which are material in relation to caption 5 below.

(c) Exclude from dividends included under item (2) amounts from investments in affiliates and others which are accounted for by the equity method and state separately, if significant, the amounts from (1) securities of other affiliates, (2) marketable securities, and (3) other securities.

In regard to any dividends other than cash, state the basis on which they have been taken up in the accounts and the justification, if any, for such action. If any such dividends received from affiliates have been credited in the accounts in an amount different from that charged to retained earnings by the disbursing company, state the amount of such difference and explain.

(d) State separately, if significant, the amounts of interest included under item (3) from (1) securities of affiliates other than unconsolidated subsidiaries, 50-per-cent-owned persons and other persons, the investments in which are accounted for by the equity method; (2) marketable securities; and (3) other securities.

2. **Expenses for salaries.**—State separately the total of salaries (a) to directors and officers and (b) to others. If paid in other than cash, state the details in a note referred to in the income statement.

3. **Taxes.**—Other than income tax expense.

4. **Other expenses.**—State separately the amount of interest and debt discount and expense and any significant amounts of other classes of expense.

5. **Income or loss before provision for taxes on income and appriate items below.**

6. **Profits on securities.**—Profits shall be stated net of losses. No profits on the person's own securities, or profits of its affiliates on their own securities, shall be included under this caption. State here or in a note herein referred to the method followed in determining the cost of securities sold, e.g., "average cost," "first-in, first-out," or "identified certificate." Consideration should be given to reporting such transactions under caption 11, when appropriate.

7. **Losses on securities.**—Losses shall be stated net of profits. No losses on the person's own securities, or losses of its affiliates on their own securities, shall be included under this caption. State here or in a note herein referred to the method followed in determining the cost of securities sold, e.g., "average cost," "first-in, first-out," or "identified certificate." Consideration should be given to reporting such transactions under caption 11, when appropriate.

8. **Income tax expense.**—State separately (a) Federal taxes on income currently payable; (b) related net tax effects, as appropriate, of (1) timing differences, (2) deferred investment tax credits, and (3) operating losses; and (c) other taxes based solely on in-

come, including foreign, state and local taxes and the related net tax effects, as appropriate, of timing differences and operating losses. Taxes on earnings of affiliates shall be included in timing differences.

9. **Minority interest in income of consolidated subsidiaries.**
10. **Income or loss before extraordinary items.**
11. **Extraordinary items, less applicable tax.**—State separately and describe any material items and disclose parenthetically or otherwise the tax applicable to each.
12. **Net income or loss.**—See Rule 5–02 [caption 39(d)].
13. **Earnings per share data.**—Refer to the pertinent requirements in the appropriate filing form.

Rule 9–04. What Schedules Are To Be Filed For Bank Holding Companies.—The following special provisions shall be applicable to the schedules specified in Rule 5–04:

SCHEDULE I.—The schedule prescribed by Rule 12–02 shall be filed in support of captions 2 and 12 of the latest balance sheet required to be filed.

SCHEDULE III.—The schedule prescribed by Rule 12–04 shall be presented in two parts as follows: Part 1 for banks and part 2 for other than banks.

Rule 9–05. Financial Statements and Schedules of Banks.

(a) Statements of banks need not be certified for periods ending on or before November 30, 1971.
(b) Financial statements and schedules of banks shall be furnished in substantially the same form as prescribed in Forms F–9, F–9A, F–9B, F–9C and F–9D of Regulation F of the Board of Governors of the Federal Reserve System issued pursuant to Section 12(i) of the Securities Exchange Act of 1934, except as otherwise provided in this rule
(c) The financial statements and schedules required to be filed shall be supplemented as follows:
   (1) The aggregate amount on the basis of market quotations at the balance sheet date shall be shown parenthetically for each category of investment securities reported under caption 2 of each balance sheet required to be filed.
   (2) The aggregate amount on the basis of market quotations at the balance sheet date shall be stated for each type and maturity grouping of securities listed on Schedules I and II prescribed under Form F–9D.

(3) SCHEDULE VIII.—AMOUNTS RECEIVABLE FROM DIRECTORS, OFFICERS AND PRINCIPAL HOLDERS OF EQUITY SECURITIES OTHER THAN AFFILIATES OF THE PERSON AND ITS AFFILIATES.—A schedule in the format prescribed by Rule 12–03 of Regulation S–X shall be filed showing the aggregate amounts in excess of $20,000 or one percent of total assets, whichever is less, that are receivable or were receivable at any time during the period for which income statements are required to be filed from each director, officer and principal holder of equity securities other than affiliates of the person and its affiliates. For the purpose of this schedule, exclude in the determination of indebtedness all amounts receivable from such persons for ordinary travel expense advances and for other such items arising in the ordinary course of business.

Article 10. Natural Persons

Rule 10–01. Financial Statements of Natural Persons.—A natural person may file the following financial statements in place of any balance sheets and profit and loss statements otherwise required in the applicable form or instructions thereto.

(*a*) A statement of his assets and liabilities as of a date within 93 days and statements of his income (1) for the calendar year ended prior to such statement of assets and liabilities, and (2) for the two preceding calendar years if the applicable form requires profit and loss statements for three fiscal years. These statements shall be set forth in reasonable detail and need not be certified.

(*b*) Balance sheets and profit and loss or income statements of—

(1) Every business of which he is sole proprietor;
(2) Every partnership in which he has a controlling interest;
(3) Every business trust, unincorporated association, or similar business organization in which he has a controlling interest; and
(4) Every corporation in which he owns directly or indirectly securities representing more than fifty percent of the voting power.

(*c*) Financial statements need not be filed, however, with respect to any corporation or other business organization designated in (3) or (4) of paragraph (*b*) above if both of the following conditions exist:

(1) His total investment in such corporation or business organization does not exceed five percent of his total assets; and,
(2) His total income from such corporation or business organization does not exceed five percent of his gross income:

Provided, That his aggregate investment in all such corporations and business organizations whose statements are omitted pursuant to this paragraph (*c*) shall not exceed fifteen percent of his total assets, and that his aggregate income from all such corporations and business organizations shall not exceed fifteen percent of his gross income.

(*d*) Financial statements required by paragraph (*b*) above shall be for the dates and periods prescribed for the financial statements of an unconsolidated subsidiary in the applicable form. Such statements shall also conform, so far as practicable, to all other requirements as to financial statements, including requirements as to certification, as set forth in such form.

Article 11. Content of Statements of Other Stockholders' Equity

Rule 11–01. Application of Article 11.—This article prescribes the content of the statements of other stockholders' equity specified in Rules 5–02 (caption 39), 6–22 (caption 26), 7–03 (caption 19), and 7A–03 (caption 20).

Rule 11–02. Statements of Other Stockholders' Equity.—A summary shall be given for each class of other stockholders' equity set forth in the related balance sheet. The information to be furnished in the statement is set forth on page **18**·31.

Article 11A. Statement of Source and Application of Funds

[As a result of the recommendations made by the APB in its Opinion No. 19 (March 1971), it is to be expected that, in most cases, the statement called for by Article 11A will be designated "Statement of Changes in Financial Position."]

Rule 11A–01. Application of Article 11A. This article shall be applicable to statements of source and application of funds (or statement of changes in financial position) filed pursuant to requirements in registration and reporting forms under the Securities Act of 1933 and the Securities Exchange Act of 1934, except that companies which are required to file quarterly reports on Form 7–Q shall comply, in all filings, with the requirements as to type, form and content of a funds statement specified in that form.

Rule 11A–02. Statement of Source and Application of Funds. The statement of source and application of funds (or statement of changes in financial position) shall summarize the sources from which funds or working capital have been obtained and their disposition. (See Rule 3–01.) The information that must be included in the statement is set forth on page **18**·38.

CHAPTER 20

REGULATION S–X (ANNOTATED), CONCLUDED

Part 5. Form and Content of Supporting Schedules

CONTENTS

Article 12. Form and Content of Supporting Schedules

[**The Numbering System for Schedules.**—Regulation S–X contains a number of "rules" that set forth the form and content of certain schedules when and if the schedules are required to be furnished in support of balance sheets and income statements. For example, if a capital shares schedule must be furnished, its form and content will be governed by Rule 12–14 (see page **20**·19). In the case of the ordinary commercial and industrial company, the list of supporting schedules that must be furnished is set forth in Rule 5–04, and in that rule the capital shares schedule is designated as Schedule XIII.

On the other hand, a capital shares schedule is also required to be submitted in support of the balance sheet of an insurance company (other than a life or title insurance company). In that case the list of schedules that must be furnished appears in Rule 7–06 and the capital shares schedule is designated as Schedule VIII.

Similarly, the content of the schedule of amounts due from underwriters, promoters, directors, officers, employees, and principal holders (other than affiliates) of equity securities of the company and its affiliates is governed by Rule 12–03. When this schedule is furnished for ordinary commercial and industrial companies, it is Schedule II; for a management investment company, it is Schedule IV; and for a face-amount certificate investment company, it is Schedule VI. In other words, the number of a schedule in a given case is derived from the article in Regulation S–X that governs that filing.

The requirements for supporting schedules applicable to different types of companies are set forth in the articles of Regulation S–X applicable to such companies as follows:

	Rule	*Page*
Commercial and industrial companies	5–04	**18**·39
Commercial, industrial, and mining companies in the promotional, exploratory, or development stage	5A–07	**19**·9
Management investment companies	6–10	**19**·23
Unit investment trusts	6–13	**19**·28
Face-amount certificate investment companies	6–24	**19**·38
Employee stock purchase, savings and similar plans	6–34	**19**·43
Insurance companies other than life and title insurance companies	7–06	**19**·48
Life insurance companies	7A–06	**19**·54
Bank holding companies and banks	9–04	**19**·60

Rule 12–02. Marketable Securities—Other Security Investments.

Column A	Column B	Column C	Column D[3]
Name of issuer and title of each issue[1]	Number of shares or units—principal amount of bonds and notes	Amount at which shown in the balance sheet[2]	Value based on market quotations at balance sheet date

1. (a) Each issue shall be stated separately, except that reasonable groupings, without enumeration, may be made of (1) securities issued or guaranteed by municipalities, states, the United States Government or agencies thereof and (2) securities issued by others for which the amounts shown in column C in the aggregate are not more than two percent of total assets.

(b) In the case of bank holding companies group separately (1) securities of banks and (2) other securities, and in column C show totals for each group.

2. State the basis of determining the amounts in column C. Column C shall be totaled to correspond to the respective balance sheet captions.

3. This column may be omitted if all amounts that would be shown are the same as those shown in column C.

Rule 12–03. Amounts Receivable from Underwriters, Promoters, Directors, Officers, Employees, and Principal Holders (Other Than Affiliates) of Equity Securities of the Person and Its Affiliates.

Column A	Column B	Column C	Column D		Column E	
			Deductions		Balance at close of period	
Name of debtor[1]	Balance at beginning of period	Additions	(1) Amounts collected[2]	(2) Amounts written off	(1) Current	(2) Not current

1. Include in this schedule both accounts receivable and notes receivable and provide in a note hereto pertinent information, such as the due date, interest rate, terms of repayment and collateral, if any, for the amounts receivable from each person named in column A as of the date of the most recent balance sheet being filed.
2. If collection was other than in cash, explain.

[In connection with the preparation of the information for inclusion in the schedule of Amounts Due From Underwriters, Promoters, Directors, Officers, etc., the first question that occurs is: officers and directors of what? Is the schedule intended to elicit information with respect to officers and directors of *the registrant?* Or is it intended to cover officers and directors of all companies *in the affiliated group?*]

The author is unaware of any official interpretation on this point, and, in his practice, has construed the reference to officers and directors as applying to officers and directors *of the registrant.* This conclusion is based in part on the responses to the items in the SEC registration and report forms dealing with remuneration of officers and directors. In these items it is clear that the *persons* for whom the information is to be reported are the officers and directors *of the registrant,* but that the *amount* to be reported is the aggregate compensation they receive from all companies in the affiliated group.

Consequently, when the schedule is furnished in support of consolidated statements, the author believes that the information should be furnished in respect of officers and directors of the parent company, but that the amounts in the schedule should reflect borrowings, repayments, etc., for all companies in the consolidation.

The information called for by Schedule II is often distasteful to the individuals involved, but it is particularly so in the case of a privately-owned company that is going public. The owners of privately-owned companies sometimes use their companies like a private bank—borrowing money from the company when they need it and paying it back when convenient. In one case of a privately-owned company that filed a registration statement under the 1933 Act, the schedule disclosed the required information for the individuals involved *in the aggregate—not by individuals* as clearly required by the instructions—and this was accepted by the SEC. The pertinent part of the schedule in the form in which it became effective was as follows:

Col. A	Col. B	Col. C	Col. D		Col. E
	Balance Receivable at Beginning of Period	Additions	Deductions		Balance Receivable at Close of Period
			(1) Amounts Written Off	(2) Collections	

Prior to (date) when it was a closely-held company, (name of company) made tax and other noninterest-bearing advances to a limited number of corporate officials. Such advances to each of such officials having at any time outstanding advances of more than $20,000 may be summarized in the aggregate as follows:

Year 19	None	$		$	None
Year 19	None	$		$	None
Year 19	None	$		$	None
Quarterly period ended (date)	None	$		$	None

Another example (also taken from actual practice) will illustrate the SEC's interpretation of its requirements. John P. Smith was the sole owner of Smith's Tool Works, Inc. (none of the names is real), a highly successful business that "went public" a few years before the incident described below. Mr. Smith sold only a portion of his STW shares and retained control of the company after the sale. He remained president and a director and actively in charge of the business which continued to prosper and grow.

Mr. Smith is an internationally known art collector, and parts of his collection of paintings are often on loan to museums all over the world. He frequently made trips to foreign countries to visit museums and dealers for the purpose of adding to his collection. In May 1970 Mr. Smith was vacationing in France, and in the course of buying some paintings, he overdrew his personal bank account by about $100,000.

When his checks were presented for payment, his bank informed the company about the overdraft, and the company, without Mr. Smith's knowledge, gave the bank its check for $100,000, and charged it to Mr. Smith's personal account as an advance. One week later, Mr. Smith, having returned from abroad, gave his personal check to the company in repayment of the amount that it had advanced to the bank on his behalf.

It was apparent that Mr. Smith was indebted to STW for one week in the amount of $100,000 but that at the end of the company's fiscal year (June 30) there was no balance owing to the company.

In connection with the preparation of the company's proxy statement for its annual meeting, this incident came to the attention of the company's lawyer. He considered the matter in relation to the requirement to disclose material transactions between the company and insiders, and concluded that the advance of $100,000 to Mr. Smith for one week did not have to be disclosed, and the definitive proxy statement made no mention of the matter.

The independent auditors learned of the short-term advance to Mr. Smith in the course of their audit for the year ended June 30, 1970. Since the company had to file an annual report on Form 10–K for that year with the SEC, the auditors considered whether Schedule II (Amounts receivable from underwriters, etc.) applied in view of the peculiar circumstances. The schedule is obviously designed to disclose loans to an insider even though there is no amount owing by such person at the year-end. A technical reading of the instructions to the schedule might support the view that the one week advance had to be reported, which, of course, might raise a question as to the completeness of the proxy statement. The independent auditors and counsel were both of the opinion that the spirit—if not the letter—of the instructions for Schedule II would not call for the inclusion of what was at best an accidental loan—particularly in view of the fact that the president of STW was a very wealthy man who would never dream of borrowing $100,000 from the publicly-owned company that he headed. It was decided to discuss the matter with the accounting staff of the SEC.

The independent auditor and the company's lawyer met with representatives of the accounting staff of the SEC and discussed the matter freely. On the day of the meeting, a large metropolitan newspaper carried a news article to the effect that Mr. Smith had made a cash gift of $1,000,000 to the Ivy League school from which he had graduated. This supported the view of all involved in the discussion that the $100,000 advance was an unfortunate accident, and had occurred partly because the company had been privately-owned for many years, and the company's employees had not learned all the fine points of operating as a publicly-owned company.

The SEC representatives inquired as to what procedures or controls the company had set up to prevent this kind of situation from recurring. Assured on this point, the SEC representatives said they had no objection to the omission of the information concerning the $100,000 advance from Schedule II in the company's 10–K.]

Rule 12–04. Investments in, Equity in Earnings of, and Dividends Received from Affiliates and Other Persons.

Column A	Column B		Column C		Column D		Column E		Column F
	Balance at beginning of period		Additions		Deductions		Balance at end of period		Dividends received during the period from investments not accounted for by the equity method[5]
Name of issuer and description of investment[1]	(1) Number of shares or units,[2] Principal amount of bonds and notes	(2) Amount in dollars	(1) Equity taken up in earnings (losses) of affiliates and other persons for the period[3]	(2) Other[4]	(1) Distribution of earnings by persons in which earnings (losses) were taken up[5]	(2) Other[6]	(1) Number of shares or units,[2] Principal amount of bonds and notes	(2) Amount in dollars[7]	

1. (a) Group separately securities of (1) subsidiaries consolidated; (2) subsidiaries not consolidated; (3) other affiliates; and (4) other persons, the investment in which is accounted for by the equity method, showing shares and bonds separately in each case. Investments in individual affiliates which, when considered with related advances, exceed two percent of total assets shall be stated separately. Dividends from (1) marketable securities and (2) other security investments shall also be included and may be shown in separate aggregate amounts.

(b) Those foreign investments, the enumeration of which would be detrimental to the registrant, may be grouped.

2. Disclose, in the column or in a note hereto, the percentage of ownership interest represented by the shares or units, if material.

3. The total of column C(1) shall be reconciled with the amount of the related income statement caption.

4. Briefly describe each item in column C(2); if the cost thereof represents other than a cash expenditure, explain. If acquired from an affiliate (and not an original issue of that affiliate) at other than cost to the affiliate, show such cost, provided the acquisition by the affiliate was within two years prior to the acquisition by the person for which the statement is filed.

5. As to any dividends other than cash, state the basis on which they have been taken up in the accounts, and the justification for such action. If any such dividends received from affiliates have been credited in the accounts in an amount differing from that charged to retained earnings by the disbursing company, state the amount of such difference and explain.

6. Briefly describe each item in column D(2) and state: (a) cost of items sold and how determined; (b) amount received (if other than cash, explain); and (c) disposition of resulting profit or loss.

7. The total (or a sub-total) of column E(2) shall be reconciled with the amount reported under caption 10 of the related balance sheet.

Rule 12–05. Indebtedness of Affiliates and Other Persons—Not Current.

Column A	Column B	Column C
Name of person[1]	Balance at beginning of period	Balance at end of period[2]

1. The persons named shall be grouped as in the related schedule required for investments in affiliates and other persons. The information called for shall be shown separately for any persons whose investments were shown separately in such related schedule.

2. For each person named in column A, explain in a note hereto the nature and purpose of any increase during the period that is in excess of 10 percent of the related balance at either the beginning or end of the period.

Rule 12–06. Property, Plant and Equipment.[1]

Column A	Column B	Column C	Column D	Column E	Column F
Classification[2]	Balance at beginning of period[3]	Additions at cost[4]	Retirements[5]	Other changes— add (deduct)— describe[6]	Balance at end of period

1. Comment briefly on any significant and unusual additions, abandonments, or retirements, or any significant and unusual changes in the general character and location, of principal plants and other important units, which may have occurred within the period.

2. (a) Show by major classifications, such as land, buildings, machinery and equipment, leaseholds, or functional groupings. If such classification is not present or practicable, this may be stated in one amount. The additions included in column C shall, however, be segregated in accordance with an appropriate classification. If property, plant and equipment abandoned is carried at other than a nominal amount indicate, if practicable, the amount thereof and state the reasons for such treatment. Items of minor importance may be included under a miscellaneous caption.

   (b) *Public utility companies.*—A public utility company shall, to the extent practicable, classify utility plant by the type of service rendered (such as electric, gas, transportation and water) and shall state separately under each of such service classifications the major subclassifications of utility plant accounts.

   (c) *Mining companies using Article 5A.*—Such mining companies shall include herein only depreciable mine property, plant and equipment at dollar amounts required by the instructions set forth under caption 13, property, plant and equipment, of Article 5A. A mining company falling into this category shall also, to the extent practicable, observe the other instructions set forth under this rule.

3. If neither the total additions nor total deductions during any of the periods covered by the schedules amount to more than 10 percent of the ending balance of that period and a statement to that effect is made, the information required by columns B, C, D and E may be omitted for that period, provided that the totals of columns C and D are given in a note hereto and provided further that any information required by instructions 4, 5 and 6 shall be given and may be in summary form.

4. For each change in accounts in column C that represents anything other than an addition from acquisition, and for each change in that column that is in excess of two percent of total assets at either the beginning or end of the period, state clearly the nature of the change and the other accounts affected. If cost of property additions represents other than cash expenditures, explain. If acquired from an affiliate at other than cost to the affiliate, show such cost, provided the aquisition by the affiliate was within two years prior to the acquisition by the person for which the statement is filed.

5. If changes in column D are stated at other than cost, explain if practicable.

6. State clearly the nature of the changes and the other accounts affected. If provision for depreciation, depletion and amortization of property, plant and equipment is credited in the books directly to the asset accounts, the amounts shall be stated in column E with explanations, including the accounts to which charged.

[If a new group of assets is included in the schedule for the first time as a result of acquisition, merger, pooling of interests, change in principle of consolidation, or similar event, it is desirable to state such amounts separately by subdividing either column B or column C into two columns with appropriate headings; footnote disclosure is also acceptable.]

Rule 12–06A. Unrecovered Cost Incurred in the Promotional, Exploratory, and Development Stage.[1]

[For commercial, industrial, and mining companies specified in paragraphs (b) and (c) of rule 5A–01 when filing registration statements on Form 10 and annual reports on Form 10–K, pursuant to the provisions of the Securities Exchange Act of 1934]

Column A	Column B	Column C	Column D	Column E
Classification[2]	Balance at beginning of period[3]	Additions at cost[4]	Deductions[5]	Balance at close of period[6]

1. Include in this schedule only unrecovered cost incurred in promotional, exploratory, and development work paid for in cash, or to be paid for in cash, and, when appropriate, depreciation, depletion, and amortization of assets extended at dollar amounts under captions 13 and 13A of Rule 5A–02.

2. Show by major classifications under (1) development expenses, (2) plant and equipment maintenance expenses, (3) rehabilitation expenses, (4) general administrative expenses incurred in a period when there was little or no actual mining, and (5) other expenses. If unrecovered cost incurred in exploration and development work abandoned is carried at other than a nominal amount indicate, if practicable, the amount thereof and state the reason for such treatment. Items of minor importance may be included under a miscellaneous caption.

3. The balance at the beginning of the period of report may be as per the accounts. If neither the total additions nor the total deductions during the period amount to more than 10 percent of the closing balance and a statement to that effect is made, the information required by columns B, C, and D may be omitted provided that the totals of columns C and D are given in a footnote and provided further that any information required by notes 4, 5, and 6 shall be given and may be in summary form.

4. If the changes in unrecovered cost incurred in promotional, exploratory, and development work in column C represent anything other than additions from acquisitions, state clearly the nature of the changes and the other accounts affected. If acquired from an affiliate at other than cost to the affiliate, show such cost, provided the acquisition by the affiliate was within two years prior to the acquisition by the person for which the statement is filed.

5. (a) Include in this column unrecovered cost incurred in development and exploratory work abandoned and written off. If such abandonments are stated at other than cash cost, explain if practicable.

(b) Include in this column proceeds from ore sales and other income if so credited on the books; state separately and describe.

(c) If provisions for amortization of unrecovered cost incurred in promotional, exploratory, and development work are credited in the books directly to such deferred expense accounts, the amounts shall be stated in column D with explanations, including the accounts to which charged.

6. The balance at the close of the period for each major classification set forth in this schedule shall be subdivided and presented in three additional columns, if practicable, to show the amount of unrecovered cost incurred in promotional, exploratory, and development work accumulated and added during (a) the five years prior to the date of the related statement of assets and unrecovered promotional, exploratory, and development costs, (b) the period of the sixth to fifteenth year inclusive prior to the date of the related statement of assets and unrecovered promotional, exploratory, and development costs, and (c) the period from the inception of the registrant and its predecessors to the fifteenth year prior to the date of the related statement of assets and unrecovered promotional, exploratory, and development costs. If it is impracticable to subdivide the total of each major classification set forth in column E, the grand total of such column shall nevertheless be subdivided in the manner indicated in the immediately preceding sentence in which case the information may be furnished in a footnote to this schedule.

Rule 12–07. Accumulated Depreciation, Depletion and Amortization of Property, Plant and Equipment.[1]

Column A	Column B	Column C	Column D	Column E	Column F
Description[2]	Balance at beginning of period	Additions charged to costs and expenses	Retirements	Other changes—add (deduct)—describe	Balance at end of period

1. (a) Insofar as amounts for depreciation, depletion and amortization are credited to the property accounts, such amounts shall be shown in the schedule of property, plant and equipment, as there required.

(b) *Mining companies using Article 5A.*—Such mining companies shall include herein only the amount of the accumulated depreciation, depletion and amortization of mine property, plant and equipment, and unrecovered promotional, exploratory and development costs applicable to the amounts set forth in the schedule filed pursuant to Rule 12–06 and Rule 12–06A. A mining company falling into this category shall also, to the extent practicable, observe the other instructions set forth under this rule.

2. If practicable, accumulated depreciation shall be shown to correspond with the classifications of property set forth in the related schedule of property, plant and equipment, separating especially depreciation, depletion, amortization and provision for retirement.

Rule 12–08. Intangible Assets, Deferred Research and Development Expenses, Preoperating Expenses and Similar Deferrals[1,2]

Column A	Column B	Column C	Column D		Column E	Column F
			Deductions[6]			
Description[3]	Balance at beginning of period[4]	Additions at cost— describe[5]	(1) Charged to costs and expenses	(2) Charged to other accounts— describe	Other changes— add (deduct)— describe	Balance at close of period

1. The information required shall be presented in two parts:
   Part A—Intangible assets.
   Part B—Deferred research and development expenses, preoperating expenses and similar deferrals.

2. If in the accounts it is not practicable to separate intangible assets from property, plant and equipment, the information here required may be included in the schedule for property, plant and equipment. In such event state in the balance sheet any known amount of intangibles so included with an indication that a further unknown amount of intangibles is also so included.

3. Show by major classifications in each part, such as franchises, goodwill, deferred research and development expenses, etc. If such classification is not present or practicable, each part may be stated in one amount. The additions included in column C shall, however, be segregated in accordance with an appropriate classification. Items of minor importance may be included under a miscellaneous caption in each part.

4. If neither the total additions nor total deductions of a part during any of the periods covered by the schedules amount to more than 10 percent of the closing balance of the part for that period and a statement to that effect is made, the information required by columns B, C, D and E may be omitted for that part for that period by any company other than a public utility company. Any information required by instruction 5 or 6 shall, however, be given and may be in summary form.

5. For each change in intangible asset accounts in column C that represents anything other than an addition from acquisition, and for each change in that column in either Part A or B that is in excess of two percent of total assets at either the beginning or end of the period, state clearly the nature of the change and the other accounts affected. If cost of additions represents other than cash expenditures, explain. If acquired from an affiliate at other than cost to the affiliate, show such cost, provided the acquisition by the affiliate was within two years prior to the acquisition by the person for which the statement is filed.

6. If provision for depreciation and amortization of intangible assets is credited in the books directly to the intangible asset account, the amounts shall be stated in column D with explanations, including the accounts to which charged. If the changes in column D represent anything other than regular amortization in either Part A or B, state clearly the nature of the changes.

7. If an account for accumulated depreciation or amortization is maintained for any item of deferred research and development expenses, preoperating expenses and similar deferrals, Rule 12–09 shall apply to such accounts and that schedule shall be divided into parts A and B as shown above.

Rule 12–09. Accumulated Depreciation and Amortization of Intangible Assets.[1]

Column A	Column B	Column C Additions		Column D	Column E
		(1) Charged to costs and expenses	(2) Charged to other accounts— describe		
Description[2]	Balance at beginning of period			Deductions— describe	Balance at end of period

1. Insofar as amounts for depreciation and amortization are credited to the intangible asset accounts, such amounts shall be shown in the schedule of intangible assets, as there required.

2. If practicable, accumulated depreciation and amortization shall be shown to correspond with the classifications set forth in the related schedule of intangible assets.

3. See Instruction 7 of Rule 12–08.

Rule 12–10. Bonds, Mortgages and Similar Debt.

Column A	Column B	Column C	Column D		Column E	Column F	Column G	Column H	
			Amount included in column C, which is					Amount held by affiliates for which statements are filed herewith[4]	
Name of issuer and title of each issue[1]	Amount authorized by indenture	Amount issued and not retired or cancelled	(1) Held by or for account of issuer thereof	(2) Not held by or for account of issuer thereof	Amount included in sum extended under caption "bonds, mortgages and similar debt" in related balance sheet[2]	Amount in sinking and other special funds of issuer thereof[3]	Amount pledged by issuer thereof[3]	(1) Persons included in consolidated statements[5]	(2) Others

1. Include in this column each issue authorized, whether issued or not and whether eliminated in consolidation or not. For each issue listed give the information called for by columns B to H, inclusive.

2. This column is to be totaled to correspond to the related balance sheet caption. If amounts shown in this column differ from face amounts shown in column C or D, explain.

3. Indicate by means of an appropriate symbol any amounts not included in subcolumn D(1).

4. Affiliates for which statements are filed herewith shall include affiliates for which separate financial statements are filed and those included in consolidated or combined statements, other than the issuer of the particular security.

5. Include in this subcolumn only amounts held by persons included in the consolidated statement in support of which this schedule is being filed. If not eliminated in the consolidation, explain in a note.

Rule 12–11. Indebtedness to Affiliates and Other Persons—Not Current.

Column A	Column B	Column C
Name of person[1]	Balance at beginning of period	Balance at end of period[2]

1. The persons named shall be grouped as in the related schedule required for investments in affiliates and other persons. The information called for shall be shown separately for any persons whose investments were shown separately in such related schedule.

2. For each person named in column A explain in a note hereto the nature and purpose of any increase during the period that is in excess of 10 percent of the related balance at either the beginning or end of the period.

Rule 12–12. Guarantees of Securities of Other Issuers.[1]

Column A	Column B	Column C	Column D	Column E	Column F	Column G
Name of issuer of securities guaranteed by person for which statement is filed	Title of issue of each class of securities guaranteed	Total amount guaranteed and outstanding[2]	Amount owned by person or persons for which statement is filed	Amount in treasury of issuer of securities guaranteed	Nature of guarantee[3]	Nature of any default by issuer of securities guaranteed in principal, interest, sinking fund or redemption provisions, or payment of dividends[4]

1. Indicate in a note to the most recent schedule being filed for a particular person or group any significant changes since the date of the related balance sheet. If this schedule is filed in support of consolidated statements or combined statements, there shall be set forth guarantees by any person included in the consolidation or combination, except that such guarantees of securities which are included in the consolidated or combined balance sheet need not be set forth.

2. Indicate any amounts included in column C which are included also in column D or E.

3. There need be made only a brief statement of the nature of the guarantee, such as "Guarantee of principal and interest," "Guarantee of interest" or "Guarantee of dividends." If the guarantee is of interest or dividends, state the annual aggregate amount of interest or dividends so guaranteed.

4. Only a brief statement as to any such defaults need be made.

Rule 12–13. Valuation and Qualifying Accounts and Reserves.

Column A	Column B	Column C		Column D	Column E
		Additions			
Description[1]	Balance at beginning of period	(1) Charged to costs and expenses	(2) Charged to other accounts— describe	Deductions— describe	Balance at end of period

1. List, by major classes, all valuation and qualifying accounts and reserves not included in specific schedules. Identify each such class of valuation and qualifying accounts and reserves by descriptive title. Group (a) those valuation and qualifying accounts which are deducted in the balance sheet from the assets to which they apply and (b) those reserves which support the balance sheet caption, Reserve. Valuation and qualifying accounts and reserves as to which the additions, deductions, and balances were not individually significant may be grouped in one total and in such case the information called for under columns C and D neet not be given.

Rule 12–14. Capital Shares.[1]

Column A	Column B	Column C	Column D		Column E		Column F		Column G	
			Number of shares included in column C which are		Shares issued or outstanding as shown on or included in related balance sheet under caption "capital shares"		Number of shares held by affiliates for which statements are filled herewith[4]		Number of shares reserved for options, warrants, conversions and other rights	
Name of issuer and title of issue[2]	Number of shares authorized by charter	Number of shares issued and not retired or cancelled	(1) Held by or for account of issuer thereof	(2) Not held by or for account of issuer thereof	(1) Number	(2) Amount at which shown[3]	(1) Persons included in consolidated statements[5]	(2) Others	(1) Directors, officers and employees	(2) Others

1. Indicate in a note to the most recent schedule being filed for a particular person or group any significant changes since the date of the related balance sheet.

2. Include in this column each issue authorized, whether issued or not and whether eliminated in consolidation or not, provided that when this schedule is filed in support of a consolidated statement the information required by columns A to G, inclusive, need not be given as to any consolidated subsidiary if substantially all of the outstanding shares of each issue of capital shares (other than directors' qualifying shares) of such subsidiary are held by one or more of the persons included in such consolidated statement; if the answer to columns G(1) and (2) would be none; and if a note indicating such omission is given. For each issue or group listed give the information called for by columns B to G, inclusive.

3. This column is to be totaled to correspond to the related balance sheet caption. In the case of consolidated subsidiaries only the minority interest need be set forth.

4. Affiliates for which statements are filed herewith shall include affiliates for which separate financial statements are filed and those included in consolidated or combined statements, other than the issuer of the particular security.

5. Include in this subcolumn only amounts held by persons included in the consolidated statement in support of which this schedule is being filed. If not eliminated in the consolidation, explain in a note.

[A comparison of the instructions applicable to Rule 12–14 ("Capital Shares") with those applicable to Rule 12–04 ("Investments in Affiliates, etc.") will reveal important differences insofar as they relate to disclosing the names of foreign affiliates. The instructions for Rule 12–04 contain a provision to the effect that those foreign investments, the enumeration of which would be detrimental to the registrant, may be grouped. This provision is consistent with the requirements of the registration forms generally which permit the omission of names of foreign subsidiaries in certain cases. For example, General Instruction E of Form S–1 provides that information required by any item or other requirement of the form with respect to any foreign subsidiary may be omitted to the extent that the required disclosure would be detrimental to the registrant, provided a statement is made that such information has been omitted. There is no instruction in Rule 12–14 corresponding to the one in Rule 12–04.

The author discussed the conflicting requirements with the staff of the SEC in relation to a company that had foreign subsidiaries and was planning to file a registration statement with the SEC. The company was required to furnish both parent company and consolidated statements. In support of the parent company balance sheet, the schedule of investments in affiliates would be submitted, and the company would omit the names of certain foreign subsidiaries in reliance upon the specific instructions of that schedule. There were minority interests in these foreign subsidiaries, and the company wanted to omit the names of these subsidiaries and the minority interests therein from the consolidated capital shares schedule, but the instructions for the schedule did not specify that such an omission might be made.

The SEC staff stated that it would be inconsistent to require disclosure in the capital shares schedule of information which, by specific instructions, could be omitted elsewhere in the registration statement. In the staff's view it is permissible to group subsidiaries in the capital shares schedule in the same manner as in the investment schedule or in any other way that would accomplish the desired objective. Thus, it would be acceptable in the investment schedule to say "Five foreign subsidiaries" and give the dollar amount, and the same or similar presentation may be followed in the capital shares schedule.]

Rule 12–15. Warrants or Rights.[1]

Column A	Column B	Column C	Column D	Column E	Column F	Column G
Title of issue of securities called for by warrants or rights	Amount of securities called for by each warrant or right	Number of warrants or rights outstanding[2]	Aggregate amount of securities called for by warrants or rights outstanding	Date from which warrants or rights are exercisable	Expiration date of warrants or rights	Price at which warrant or right exercisable

1. Indicate in a note to the most recent schedule being filed for a particular person or group any significant changes since the date of the related balance sheet.

2. State separately amounts held by persons for which separate financial statements are filed or which are included in consolidated or combined statements, other than the issuer of the particular security.

Rule 12–16. Supplementary Income Statement Information.[1]

Column A	Column B[2]
Item	Charged to costs and expenses
1. Maintenance and repairs..............................	....
2. Depreciation, depletion and amortization of property, plant and equipment..................................	....
3. Depreciation and amortization of intangible assets......	....
4. Taxes, other than income taxes[3].....................	....
5. Rents[4]...	....
6. Royalties...	....
7. Advertising costs[5]................................	....
8. Research and development costs.....................	....

1. State, for each of the items noted in column A which exceeds one percent of total sales and revenues as reported in the related income statement, the amount called for in column B.

2. Totals may be stated in column B without further designation of the accounts to which charged.

3. State separately each category of tax which exceeds one percent of the total sales and revenues.

4. Include rents applicable to leased personal property.

5. This item shall include all costs related to advertising the company's name, products or services in newspapers, periodicals or other advertising media.

[Items 7 and 8 of the foregoing schedule were added in the 1972 revision of Regulation S–X.

In the case of a "net lease" of real property, a question may arise as to the amount to be reported as rent. In such a lease, a common provision is for the tenant to pay all costs of maintenance, repairs, real estate taxes, and certain other expenses, in addition to the basic rent provided in the agreement. If the amount reported in the schedule as rent does not include such other costs, the author would recommend that that fact be indicated together with a statement that the amounts for maintenance and taxes are included in those captions of the schedule.]

Rule 12–17. Income from Dividends—Equity in Net Profit and Loss of Affiliates.

For the (period)

Col. A	Col. B			Col. C
	Amount of dividends (Note 2)			
Name of issuer and title of issue (Note 1)	(1) Cash	(2) Other (Note 3)	(3) Total of related captions of profit and loss or income statement	Amount of equity in net profit and loss for the period (Notes 2 and 4)

Note 1. The shares of affiliates shall be listed as in the related schedules required for investments in securities of affiliates. Dividends from (1) marketable securities and (2) other security investments shall also be included, and may be shown in separate aggregate amounts: *Provided, however,* That securities held in issuers as to which securities representing exactly fifty percent of the voting power are held directly or indirectly by the person for which the statement is filed and those representing the other fifty per cent are held by another single interest, shall be separately stated and are, within the group, to be listed separately as to each major investment, the balance to be stated in a single aggregate.

Note 2. The information called for in columns B and C may be shown in total for any two or more totally held subsidiaries included in a consolidated statement.

Note 3. State as to any dividends other than cash, the basis on which they have been taken up as income, and the justification, if any, for such action. If any such dividends received from affiliates have been credited to income in an amount differing from that charged to income or earned surplus by the disbursing company, state the amount of such difference and explain.

Note 4. (*a*) The information required by column C need be furnished only (1) as to affiliates and (2) as to issuers securities of which representing exactly fifty percent of the voting power are held directly or indirectly by the person for which the statement is filed and those representing the other fifty per cent are held by another single interest. If the answer required in column B is in the negative as to any particular person, the information called for in column C shall nevertheless be furnished.

(*b*) The equity in the net profit and loss of each person required to be listed separately shall be computed on an individual basis. In addition, there may be submitted the information required as computed on the basis of statements of each such person and its subsidiaries consolidated.

Rule 12–19. Investments in Securities of Unaffiliated Issuers.

(For Management Investment Companies Only)

COL. A	COL. B	COL. C	COL. D
Name of issuer and title of issue [1]	Balance held at close of period. Number of shares—principal amount of bonds and notes [2]	Cost of each item [3][4]	Value of each item at close of period [3][5]

[1] (a) The required information is to be given as to all securities held as of the close of the period of report. Each issue shall be listed separately: *Provided, however,* That an amount not exceeding five percent of the total of column D may be listed in one amount as "Miscellaneous securities," provided the securities so listed have been held for not more than one year prior to the date of the related balance sheet, and have not previously been reported by name to the shareholders of the person for which the statement is filed or to any exchange, or set forth in any registration statement, application, or annual report or otherwise made available to the public.

(b) Indicate by an appropriate symbol those securities which are non-income-producing securities. Evidences of indebtedness and preferred shares may be deemed to be income-producing if, on the respective last interest payment date or date for the declaration of dividends prior to the date of the related balance sheet, there was only a partial payment of interest or a declaration of only a partial amount of the dividends payable; in such case, however, each such issue shall be indicated by an appropriate symbol referring to a note to the effect that, on the last interest or dividend date, only partial interest was paid or partial dividends declared. If, on such respective last interest or dividend date, no interest was paid or no dividends declared, the issue shall not be deemed to be income-producing. Common shares shall not be deemed to be income-producing unless, during the last year preceding the date of the related balance sheet, there was at least one dividend paid upon such common shares. List separately (1) bonds; (2) preferred shares; (3) common shares. Within each of these subdivisions classify according to type of business, insofar as practicable; e.g., investment companies, railroads, utilities, banks, insurance companies, or industrials. Give totals for each group, subdivision, and class.

[2] Indicate any securities subject to option at the end of the most recent period and state in a note the amount subject to option, the option prices, and the dates within which such options may be exercised.

[3] Columns C and D shall be totaled. The totals of columns C and D should agree with the correlative amounts required to be shown by the related balance sheet captions. As to what is "cost" where there has been a reorganization or quasi-reorganization, see rule 6–02–7 (a). State in a footnote to column C the aggregate cost for Federal income tax purposes.

[4] *Closed-end companies reflecting investments at cost, showing value parenthetically.*—If any investments have been written down or reserved against by such companies pursuant to rule 6–02–6 (b), indicate each such item by means of an appropriate symbol and explain in a footnote.

[5] Where value is determined on any other basis than closing prices reported on any national securities exchange, explain such other bases in a footnote.

Rule 12–21. Investments—Other Than Securities.

(For Management Investment Companies Only)

COL. A	COL. B	COL. C	COL. D	COL. E	COL. F	COL. G
Description [1]	Balance held at beginning of period —quantity [2]	Gross purchases and additions during period —quantity [2]	Gross sales and reductions during period —quantity [2]	Balance held at close of period —quantity [2][3]	Cost of items included in column E [4][5]	Value of each item at close of period [4][6]

[1] The required information is to be given as to all investments which were held at any time within the period. List each major class of investments by descriptive title.

[2] If practicable, indicate the quantity or measure in appropriate units.

[3] Indicate any investments subject to option at the end of the most recent period and state in a note the amount subject to option, the option prices, and the dates within which such options may be exercised.

[4] Columns F and G shall be totaled and should agree with the amounts required to be shown by the related balance sheet caption. As to what is "cost" where there has been a reorganization or quasi-reorganization, see rule 6–02–7 (a). State in a footnote the aggregate cost for Federal income tax purposes.

[5] *Closed-end companies reflecting investments at cost showing value parenthetically.*—If any investments have been written down or reserved against by such companies pursuant to rule 6–02–6 (b), indicate each such item by means of an appropriate symbol and explain in a footnote.

[6] State the basis of determining the amount shown in column G.

Rule 12–22. Investments in Affiliates.

(For Management Investment Companies Only)

COL. A	COL. B	COL. C	COL. D	COL. E		COL. F
				Amount of dividends or interest [4][6]		
				(1)	(2)	
Name of issuer and title of issue or amount of indebtedness [1]	Balance held at close of period. Number of shares—principal amount of bonds, notes and other indebtedness [2]	Cost of each item [3][4]	Value of each item at close of period [4][5]	Credited to income	Other	Amount of equity in net profit and loss for the period [7]

[1] (a) The required information is to be given as to all investments in affiliates as of the close of the period. List each issue and group separately (1) investments in majority-owned subsidiaries, segregating subsidiaries consolidated; (2) other controlled companies; and (3) other affiliates. Give totals for each group. If operations of any controlled companies are different in character from those of the registrant, group such affiliates within divisions (1) and (2) by type of activities.

(b) *Changes during the period.*—If during the period there has been any increase or decrease in the amount of investment in any affiliate, state in a footnote (or if there have been changes as to numerous affiliates, in a supplementary schedule) (1) name of each issuer and title of issue; (2) balance at beginning of period; (3) gross purchases and additions; (4) gross sales and reductions; (5) balance at close of period as shown in column B. Include in such footnote or schedule comparable information as to affiliates in which there was an investment at any time during the period even though there was no investment in such affiliate as of the close of such period.

2 Indicate any securities subject to option at the end of the most recent period and state in a note the amount subject to option, the option prices, and the dates within which such options may be exercised.

3 If the cost in column C represents other than cash expenditure, explain.

4 (a) Columns C, D, and E shall be totaled. The totals of columns C and D should agree with correlative amounts required to be shown by the related balance sheet captions. As to what is "cost" where there has been a quasi-reorganization, see rule 6–02–7 (a).

State in a footnote the aggregate cost for Federal income tax purposes.

(b) Closed-end companies reflecting investments at cost showing value parenthetically.—If any investments have been written down or reserved against by such companies pursuant to rule 6–02–6 (b), indicate each such item by means of an appropriate symbol and explain in a footnote.

5 State the basis of determining the amounts shown in column D.

6 Show in column E (1) as to each issue held at close of period, the dividends or interest included in caption 1 of the statement of income and expense. In addition, show as the final item in column E (1) the aggregate dividends and interest included in the statement of income and expense in respect of investments in affiliates not held at the close of the period. The total of this column should agree with the amounts shown under such caption. Include in column E (2) all other dividends and interest. Explain briefly in an appropriate footnote the treatment accorded each item. Identify by an appropriate symbol all noncash dividends and explain the circumstances in a footnote. See rules 6–03–2 and 6–04–1.

7 The information required by column F need be furnished only as to controlled companies. The equity in the net profit and loss of each person required to be listed separately shall be computed on an individual basis. In addition, there may be submitted the information required as computed on the basis of the statements of each such person and its subsidiaries consolidated.

Rule 12–23. Bonds.[1]

(For Insurance Companies)

COL. A	COL. B	COL. C	COL. D	COL. E	COL. F	COL. G
Name of issuer and title of issue [2]	Principal amount of bonds and notes	Actual cost (excluding accrued interest)	Book value [3]	Market value [4]	Amortized or investment value [5]	Admitted asset value [6]

[1] (a) In lieu of this schedule there may be filed schedule D, part 1, of the annual statement filed with the respective domiciliary State regulatory authority. In such case the method of determining market value shown in column 7 of that schedule shall be stated in a note.

(b) All money columns shall be totaled.

[2] (a) Bonds shall be grouped in accordance with the classification required under rule 12–27 and listed alphabetically in each group.

(b) Indicate by appropriate symbol those bonds which are non-income producing or in default as to principal or interest.

[3] State the basis of determining the amount.

[4] State the method of determining market value.

[5] Indicate by a symbol whether amortized or estimated value. State the basis of determining estimated value.

[6] If admitted asset value is different from the amount shown in either column C, D, E, or F, state the basis of determining such value.

Rule 12–24. Stocks—Other than Stocks of Affiliates.[1]

(For Insurance Companies)

COL. A	COL. B	COL. C	COL. D	COL. E	COL. F
Name of issuer and title of issue [2]	Number of shares	Actual cost	Book value [3]	Market or estimated value [4]	Admitted asset value [5]

[1] (a) In lieu of this schedule there may be filed schedule D, part 2, of the annual statement filed with the respective domiciliary State regulatory authority: *Provided,* (1) That from the totals of the proper columns there be deducted the amounts represented by the investment in stocks of affiliates called for in the schedule prescribed by rule 12–28; and (2) the method of determining market value shown in column 6 of schedule E, part 2, be stated.

(b) All money columns shall be totaled.

[2] (a) Stocks shall be grouped in accordance with the classification required under rule 12–27 and listed alphabetically in each group.

(b) Indicate by appropriate symbol those stocks which are non-income producing.

[3] State the basis of determining the amount.

[4] Indicate by a symbol whether market or estimated value. State the basis of determining such value.

[5] If admitted asset value is different from the amount shown in either column C, D, or E, state the basis of determining such value.

Rule 12–25. Mortgage Loans on Real Estate.[1]

(For Insurance Companies)

COL. A Summarize by State and classification indicated below[2]	COL. B Amount of principal indebtedness	COL. C Book value of mortgages	COL. D Admitted asset value[3]	COL. E Appraised value of land and buildings
NAME OF STATE				
Farm mortgages—insured .... (total)	....	....	....	....
Farm mortgages—other .... (total)	....	....	....	....
City mortgages—insured .... (total)	....	....	....	....
City mortgages—other .... (total)	....	....	....	....
Total	....	....	....	....
Total, all states	....	....	....	....

[1] All money columns shall be totaled.

[2] (a) Mortgage loans shall be grouped by States and in accordance with the classifications indicated in column A above.
  (b) Mortgage loans other than first liens shall be listed separately in a like manner.
  (c) State in a note the amount of mortgage loans in each state and classification (1) upon which interest is overdue more than three months; and (2) which are in the process of foreclosure.

[3] If admitted asset value is different from the amount shown in either column B or C, state the basis of determining such value.

Rule 12–26. Real Estate Owned.[1]

(For Insurance Companies)

COL. A Summarize by State and classification of property as indicated below	COL. B Amount of encumbrances	COL. C Actual cost	COL. D Book value less encumbrances	COL. E Market or fair value less encumbrances [2]	COL. F Admitted asset value [3]
NAME OF STATE					
Farms ....(total)	....	....	....	....	
Residential ....(total)	....	....	....	....	
Apartments and business ---(total)	....	....	....	....	
Unimproved ....(total)	....	....	....	....	....
Total	....	....	....	....	....
Total, all states	....	....	....	....	....

[1] All money columns shall be totaled.

[2] State the basis of determining such value.

[3] If admitted asset value is different from the amount shown in either column C, D, or E, state the basis of determining such value.

Rule 12–27. Summary of Investments in Securities—
Other than Securities of Affiliates.[1]

(For Insurance Companies)

COL. A	COL. B	COL. C	COL. D	COL. E	COL. F
Type of Security	Actual cost	Book value	Market value	Amortized or investment value of bonds and notes	Admitted asset value
1. BONDS AND NOTES					
(a) Government	....	....	....	....	....
(b) States, Territories and possessions ..	....	....		....	....
(c) Political subdivisions of States, Territories and possessions	....	....	....	....	....
(d) Government agencies and authorities	....	....		....	....
(e) Railroads	....	....	....	....	....
(f) Public utilities ...	....	....	....	....	....
(g) Industrial and miscellaneous	....	....	....	....	....
Total bonds and notes	....	....	....	....	....
2. STOCKS					
Preferred stocks:					
(h) Railroad	....	....	....	XXXXXXXXXX	
(i) Public utilities ...	....	....	....	XXXXXXXXXX	
(j) Banks, trust and insurance companies	....	....	....	XXXXXXXXXX	....
(k) Industrial and miscellaneous	....	....	....	XXXXXXXXXX	....
Total preferred stocks	....	....	....	XXXXXXXXXX	....
Common stocks:					
(l) Railroad	....	....	....	XXXXXXXXXX	....
(m) Public utilities ...	....	....	....	XXXXXXXXXX	....
(n) Banks, trust and insurance companies	....	....	....	XXXXXXXXXX	....
(o) Industrial and miscellaneous	....	....	....	XXXXXXXXXX	....
Total common stocks	....	....	....	XXXXXXXXXX	....
Total stocks ...	....	....	....	XXXXXXXXXX	....
Total investments in securities other than securities of affiliates	....	....	....	XXXXXXXXXX	....

[1] All money columns shall be totaled.

Rule 12–28. Investments in Stocks of Affiliates.[1]

(For Insurance Companies)

COL. A	COL. B	COL. C	COL. D	COL. E	COL. F
Name of issuer and title of issue [2]	Number of shares	Actual cost	Book value [3]	Market or estimated value [4]	Admitted asset value [5]

[1] All money columns shall be totaled.

[2] Group separately (a) stocks of insurance companies and (b) stocks of other affiliates. Within group (b) classify according to type of business. Give totals for each group and class.

[3] State the basis of determining the amount.

[4] Indicate by a symbol whether market or estimated value. State the basis of determining such value.

[5] If admitted asset value is different from the amount shown in either column C, D, or E, state the basis of determining such value.

Rule 12–29. Premiums, Losses, and Underwriting Expense.[1]

(For Insurance Companies Other Than Life and Title Insurance Companies)

	Part 1—Premiums				Part 2—Losses and Underwriting Expenses[2]			
COL. A	COL. B	COL. C	COL. D	COL. E	COL. F	COL. G	COL. H	COL. I
Line of insurance	Unearned premiums beginning of period	Net premiums written	Unearned premiums end of period	Premiums earned during period	Losses incurred during period	Loss expense incurred during period	Commissions and brokerage incurred during period	Other underwriting expense incurred during period[3]

[1] All money columns shall be totaled.

[2] Fire insurance companies may furnish information under columns G, H, and I by totals only, if the information required by such columns is not available by lines of insurance.

[3] Include in this column all amounts set forth in the related profit and loss statement under captions 8, 9, and 10.

Rule 12–30. Summary of Realized Gains or Losses on Sale or Maturity of Investments.[1]

(For Insurance Companies)

COL. A	COL. B	COL. C	COL. D
Type of security	Aggregate cost	Aggregate proceeds	Gain or loss
Bonds			
Stocks—other than stocks of affiliates			
Stocks—affiliates			
Mortgage loans			
Real estate			
Other			
Total			
Income taxes allocable to realized gains	xxxxxx	xxxxxx	
Net realized gains or losses	xxxxxx	xxxxxx	

[1] All money columns shall be totaled.

Rule 12–31. Policy Reserves, Benefits, and Insurance in Force.[1]

(For Life Insurance Companies)

Policy Reserves:
1. Additions .... $........
    (a) Tabular net premiums and other considerations .. ..
    (b) Tabular interest ....
    (c) Other [2] ....
2. Deductions $........
    (a) Tabular cost .... $........ ....
    (b) Reserves released ....
    (c) Annuity, supplementary contract and other payments ....
    (d) Other [2] .... $........
3. Increase in policy reserves ....
4. Policy reserves at beginning of period ....
5. Policy reserves at end of period .... $........
Death and other benefits .... $........ ....
Insurance in force .... $........ ....

[1] This schedule shall be prepared from and be in substantially the same form as the analysis of increase in reserves during the year (gain and loss exhibit) of the annual statement filed with the respective domiciliary State regulatory authority. If the company writes more than one line of business, e.g., industrial, ordinary, group life insurance, the schedule shall show in columnar form the changes in the policy reserves and the amounts of benefits and insurance in force allocable to each line of business. In lieu of this schedule there may be filed the aforementioned analysis of increase in reserves during the year (gain and loss exhibit) of the annual statement filed with the respective domiciliary State regulatory authority together with the information required regarding death and other benefits and insurance in force.
[2] State separately any significant items.

Rule 12–32. Investments in Securities of Affiliates—Banks.[1]

(For Bank Holding Companies Only)

COL. A	COL. B		COL. C						COL. D	COL. E	COL. F	COL. G
	Shares owned by the person for which statement is filed		Total capital, surplus, and undivided profits of affiliated banks [3]									
	(1)	(2)	(1)	(2)	(3)	(4)	(5)	(6)				
Name of issuer and title of issue [2]	Number	Percent of total outstanding	Preferred shares, capital notes, or debentures	Common shares	Surplus and undivided profits	Total common shares, surplus, and undivided profits	Adjustments, if any, necessary to arrive at net tangible asset value [4]	Net tangible asset value	Amount of net tangible asset value applicable to shares owned by others	Amount of net tangible asset value applicable to shares owned by person for which statement is filed	Amount at which carried in balance sheet of person for which statement is filed [5]	Net additions to profits of each affiliate for period [5][6]

[1] Subcolumns C (1), (2), (3), (4), (5) and (6) and columns D, E, F, and G shall be totaled.

[2] Each issue shall be separately listed. Group according to combined statements, if any; otherwise group by States. Within each group segregate national banks from State banks. Designate by an appropriate method those banks which are (a) not members of the Federal Reserve System, and (b) not insured with the Federal Deposit Insurance Corporation. If preferred shares, state par value and if the redemption or retirable value is other than par value, state such other value.

[3] The information called for in subcolumns C (1), (2), (3), and (4) and column G shall be as shown by the "Reports of Condition" and the "Reports of Earnings and Dividends" submitted by the affiliate to a Federal authority, or if it does not report to a Federal authority, to its respective State authority.

[4] Describe briefly the nature of the adjustments. Deduct here any excess of redemption or retirable value over par value of preferred shares or principal amount of capital notes and debentures.

[5] If the amount shown in column F differs from the amount shown in column E, state the basis of determining the amount in column F.

[6] The information required by column G shall be shown separately for each period for which a profit and loss statement is filed.

Rule 12–33. Investments in Securities.[1]

(For all Unit Investment Trusts, and for those Unincorporated Management Investment Companies which are Issuers of Periodic Payment Plan Certificates)

| | Part 1 | | | | | | | Part 2 | | |
COL. A	COL. B	COL. C	COL. D	COL. E	COL. F	COL. G	COL. H	COL. I	COL. J	COL. K
Name of issuer and title of issue [2]	Balance held at beginning of period. Number of shares—principal amount of bonds and notes	Gross purchases and additions as to each issue during period. Number of shares—principal amount of bonds and notes [3]	Gross sales and reductions as to each issue during period. Number of shares—principal amount of bonds and notes	Balance held at close of period. Number of shares—principal amount of bonds and notes	Cost of items included in column E [4][5]	Amount at which each issue was carried at close of period [5]	Market value of each issue at close of period [5][6]	Distribution received on trust shares	Dividends on other shares [7]	Interest

[1] The required information is to be given as to each issue of securities held at any time during the period.

[2] Group separately (a) shares of investment companies; and (b) other securities. As to securities set forth in group (a) list separately (1) trust shares in trusts created or serviced by the depositor or sponsor of this trust; (2) trust shares in other trusts; and (3) securities of other investment companies. As to securities set forth in group (b) list (1) evidences of indebtedness; (2) preferred shares; (3) common shares; and (4) other securities. Within each of these subdivisions classify according to type of business, insofar as possible, e.g., railroads, utilities, banks, insurance companies, industrials. Give totals of each group, subdivision, and class.

[3] Describe briefly the nature of any additions otherwise than through cash purchases.

[4] State the basis upon which cost has been determined. State in a footnote to this column the aggregate cost for purposes of the Federal income tax.

[5] Columns F, G, and H shall be totaled. The total of column G at the close of the most recent period shall agree with the related caption in the statement of condition. If the amount shown in column G differs from the amount shown in either column F or H, state the basis of determining the amount in column G. If the amounts to be shown in column G are identical with the amounts to be shown in columns F or H, a statement to that effect will suffice.

[6] If market value is determined on any basis other than closing prices reported on any national securities exchange, explain such other basis in a note.

[7] Identify all dividends other than cash taken up in income, and state the basis on which so taken up.

Rule 12–34. Trust Shares.

(For all Unit Investment Trusts, and for those Unincorporated Management Investment Companies which are Issuers of Periodic Payment Plan Certificates)

1. Amount at which .... trust shares are carried at beginning of period.[1] [2] .... $........

2. Additions during period resulting from:
    (a) Creation of .... trust share [1] .... $........
    (b) Allocation of trust income for reinvestment ....
    (c) Other additions [3] ....

3. Total additions ....

4. Deductions during period resulting from:
    (a) Surrender and cancellation of .... trust shares [1] ... .
    (b) Other distributions (or transfers to distributable funds) of amounts credited to trust shares ....
    (c) Other deductions [4] ....

5. Total deductions ....

6. Amount at which ...... trust shares were carried at end of period [1] [5] .... $........

[1] Insert the applicable number of trust shares.

[2] State the basis of determining the amount.

[3] State separately all significant items. If market appreciation of underlying trust property is included, the amount thereof shall be shown separately. Income required to be set forth in the statement of income and distributable funds shall not be set forth here.

[4] State separately all significant items. If market depreciation of underlying trust property is included, the amount thereof shall be shown separately. Expenses required to be set forth in the statement of income and distributable funds shall not be set forth here.

[5] The balance at the close of the most recent period shall agree with caption 8 of the related statement of condition.

Rule 12–35. Investments in Securities of Unaffiliated Issuers.

(For Face-Amount Certificate Investment Companies)

COL. A	COL. B	COL. C	COL. D
Name of issuer and title of issue [1]	Balance held at close of period. Number of shares—principal amount of bonds and notes [2]	Cost of each item [3] [4]	Value of each item at close of period [3] [5]

[1] (a) The required information is to be given as to all securities held as of the close of the period of report. Each issue shall be listed separately.

(b) Indicate by an appropriate symbol those securities which are non-income-producing securities. Evidences of indebtedness and preferred shares may be deemed to be income-producing if, on the respective last interest payment date or dates for the declaration of dividends prior to the date of the related balance sheet, there was only a partial payment of interest or a declaration of only a partial amount of the dividends payable; in such case, however, each such issue shall be indicated by an appropriate symbol referring to a note to the effect that, on the last interest or dividend date, only partial interest was paid or partial dividends declared. If, on such respective last interest or dividend date, no interest was paid or no dividends declared, the issue shall not be deemed to be income-producing. Common shares shall not be deemed to be income-producing unless, during the last year preceding the date of the related balance sheet, there was at least one dividend paid upon such common shares. List separately (1) bonds; (2) preferred shares; (3) common shares. Within each of these subdivisions classify according to type of business, insofar as practicable: e.g., investment companies, railroads, utilities, banks, insurance companies, or industrials. Give totals for each group, subdivision, and class.

[2] Indicate any securities subject to option at the end of the most recent period and state in a note the amount subject to option, the option prices, and the dates within which such options may be exercised.

[3] Columns C and D shall be totaled. The totals of columns C and D should agree with the correlative amounts required to be shown by the related balance sheet captions. State in a footnote to column C the aggregate cost for Federal income tax purposes.

[4] If any investments have been written down or reserved against by such companies pursuant to rule 6–21–6, indicate each such item by means of an appropriate symbol and explain in a footnote.

[5] Where value is determined on any other basis than closing prices reported on any national securities exchange, explain such other bases in a footnote.

Rule 12–36. Investments in and Advances to Affiliates and Income Thereon.

(For Face-Amount Certificate Investment Companies)

COL. A	COL. B	COL. C	COL. D	COL. E		COL. F
				Amount of dividends or interest [4][6]		
				(1) Credited to income	(2) Other	
Name of issuer and title of issue or amount of indebtedness [1]	Balance held at close of period. Number of shares, principal amount of bonds, notes and other indebtedness [2]	Cost of each item [3][4]	Amount at which carried at close of period [4][5]			Amount of equity in net profit and loss for the period [7]

[1] (a) The required information is to be given as to all investments in affiliates as of the close of the period. See captions 10, 13, and 20 of rule 6–22. List each issue and group separately (1) investments in majority-owned subsidiaries, segregating subsidiaries consolidated; (2) other controlled companies; and (3) other affiliates. Give totals for each group. If operations of any controlled companies are different in character from those of the registrant, group such affiliates within divisions (1) and (2) by type of activities.

(b) *Changes during the period.*—If during the period there has been any increase or decrease in the amount of investment in any affiliate, state in a footnote (or if there have been changes as to numerous affiliates, in a supplementary schedule) (1) name of each issuer and title of issue; (2) balance at beginning of period; (3) gross purchases and additions; (4) gross sales and reductions; (5) balance at close of period as shown in column C. Include in such footnote or schedule comparable information as to affiliates in which there was an investment at any time during the period even though there was no investment in such affiliate as of the close of such period.

[2] Indicate any securities subject to option at the end of the most recent period and state in a footnote the amount subject to option, the option prices, and the dates within which such options may be exercised.

[3] If the cost in column C represents other than cash expenditure, explain.

[4] (a) Columns C, D, and E shall be totaled. The totals of columns C and D should agree with correlative amounts required to be shown by the related balance sheet captions. State in a footnote the aggregate cost for Federal income tax purposes.

(b) If any investments have been written down or reserved against by such companies pursuant to rule 6–21–6, indicate each such item by means of an appropriate symbol and explain in a footnote.

5 State the basis of determining the amounts shown in column D.

6 Show in column E (1) as to each issue held at close of period, the dividends or interest included in caption 1 of the profit and loss or income statement. In addition, show as the final item in column E (1) the *aggregate* dividends and interest included in the profit and loss or income statement in respect of investments in affiliates not held at the close of the period. The total of this column should agree with the amounts shown under such caption. Include in column E (2) all other dividends and interest. Explain briefly in an appropriate footnote the treatment accorded each item. Identify by an appropriate symbol all non-cash dividends and explain the circumstances in a footnote. See rules 6–22–2 and 6–23–1.

7 The information required by column F need be furnished only as to controlled companies. The equity in the net profit and loss of each person required to be listed separately shall be computed on an individual basis. In addition, there may be submitted the information required as computed on the basis of the statements of each such person and its subsidiaries consolidated.

Rule 12–37. Mortgage Loans on Real Estate and Interest Earned on Mortgages.[1]

(For Face-Amount Certificate Investment Companies)

COL. A	COL. B[2]	COL. C	COL. D		COL. E	COL. F	COL. G
			Amount of principal unpaid at close of period			Part 2—Interest Earned on Mortgages	
List by classification indicated below [2][3][7]	Prior liens	Carrying amount of mortgages [8][9][10][11]	(1) Total	(2) Subject to delinquent interest [4]	Amount of mortgages being foreclosed	Interest due and accrued at end of period [6]	Interest income earned applicable to period [5][6]
Liens on:							
Farms .... (total)	....	....	....	....	....	....	....
Residential .... (total)	....	....	....	....	....	....	....
Apartments and business .... (total)	....	....	....	....	....	....	....
Uninproved ...... (total)	....	....	....	....	....	....	....
Total [12]	....	....	....	....	....	....	....

Part 1—Mortgage Loans on Real Estate at Close of Period

[1] All money columns shall be totaled.

[2] If mortgages represent other than first liens, list separately in a schedule in a like manner, indicating briefly the nature of the lien. Information need not be furnished as to such liens which are fully insured or wholly guaranteed by an agency of the United States Government.

[3] In a separate schedule classify by States in which the mortgaged property is located the total amounts in support of columns B, C, D, and E.

[4] (a) Interest in arrears for less than 3 months may be disregarded in computing the total amount of principal subject to delinquent interest.

(b) Of the total principal amount, state the amount acquired from controlled and other affiliates.

5 In order to reconcile the total of column G with the amount shown in the profit and loss or income statement, interest income earned applicable to period from mortgages sold or canceled during period should be added to the total of this column.

6 If the information required by columns F and G is not reasonably available because the obtaining thereof would involve unreasonable effort or expense, such information may be omitted if the registrant shall include a statement showing that unreasonable effort or expense would be involved. In such an event, state in column G for each of the above classes of mortgage loans the average gross rate of interest on mortgage loans held at the end of the fiscal period.

7 Each mortgage loan included in column C in an amount in excess of $500,000 shall be listed separately. Loans from $100,000 to $500,000 shall be grouped by $50,000 groups, indicating the number of loans in each group.

8 In a footnote to this schedule, furnish a reconciliation, in the following form, of the carrying amount of mortgage loans at the beginning of the period with the total amount shown in column C:

```
Balance at beginning of period ................... $........
Additions during period:
    New mortgage loans .......... $........
    Other (describe) .......... ........
                                          $........

Deductions during period:
    Collections of principal ............ $........
    Foreclosures .......... ........
    Cost of mortgages sold .......... ........
    Amortization of premium .......... ........
    Other (describe) .......... ........
                                          $........

Balance at close of period ................... $........
```

If additions represent other than cash expenditures, explain. If any of the changes during the period result from transactions, directly or indirectly with affiliates, explain the bases of such transactions, and the amounts involved. State the aggregate amount of mortgages (a) renewed and (b) extended. If the carrying amount of the new mortgages is in excess of the unpaid amount (not including interest) of prior mortgages, explain.

9 If any item of mortgage loans on real estate investments has been written down or reserved against pursuant to rule 6–21–6, describe the item and explain the basis for the write-down or reserve.

10 State in a footnote to column C the aggregate cost for Federal income tax purposes.

11 If the total amount shown in column C includes intercompany profits, state the bases of the transactions resulting in such profits and, if practicable, state the amounts thereof.

12 Summarize the aggregate amounts for each column applicable to captions 6(b), 6(c), and 12 of rule 6–22.

Rule 12–38. Real Estate Owned and Rental Income.[1]

(For Face-Amount Certificate Investment Companies)

| | Part 1—Real Estate Owned at End of Period | | | | | | Part 2—Rental Income | | |
COL. A	COL. B	COL. C	COL. D	COL. E	COL. F	COL. G	COL. H	COL. I	COL. J
List classification of property as indicated below [2] [3]	Amount of encumbrances	Initial cost to company	Cost of improvements, etc.	Amount at which carried at close of period [4] [5] [6] [7]	Reserve for depreciation	Rents due and accrued at end of period	Total rental income applicable to period	Expended for interest, taxes, repairs, and expenses	Net income applicable to period
Farms	......	......	......	......	......	......	......	......	......
Residential	......	......	......	......	......	......	......	......	......
Apartments and business .	......	......	......	......	......	......	......	......	......
Unimproved	......	......	......	......	......	......	......	......	......
Total [8]	xxxxxxxx	xxxxxxxx	xxxxxxxx	xxxxxxxx	xxxxxxxx	xxxxxxxx	......	......	......
Rent from properties sold during period	......	......	......	......	......	xxxxxxxx	......	......	......
Total	xxxxxxxx	xxxxxxxx	xxxxxxxx	xxxxxxxx	xxxxxxxx	xxxxxxxx	......	......	......

[1] All money columns shall be totaled.
[2] Each item of property included in column E in an amount in excess of $100,000 shall be listed separately.

3 In a separate schedule classify by states in which the real estate owned is located the total amounts in support of columns E and F.

4 In a footnote to this schedule, furnish a reconciliation, in the following form, of the total amount at which real estate was carried at the beginning of the period with the total amount shown in column E:

Balance at beginning of period .... $.........

Additions during period:

Acquisitions through foreclosure .... $.........

Other acquisitions ....

Improvements, etc. ....

Other (describe) ....

$.........

Deductions during period:

Cost of real estate sold .... $.........

Other (describe) ....

$.........

Balance at close of period .... $.........

If additions, except acquisitions through foreclosure, represent other than cash expenditures, explain. If any of the changes during the period result from transactions, directly or indirectly, with affiliates, explain and state the amount of any intercompany gain or loss.

5 If any item of real estate investments has been written down or reserved against pursuant to rule 6–21–6, describe the item and explain the basis for the write-down or reserve.

6 State in a footnote to column E the aggregate cost for Federal income tax purposes.

7 The amount of all intercompany profits included in the total of column E shall be stated if material.

8 Summarize the aggregate amounts for each column applicable to captions 7 and 12 of rule 6–22.

Rule 12–39. Supplementary Profit and Loss Information.

(For Face-Amount Certificate Investment Companies)

COL. A	COL. B	COL. C		COL. D
Item [1]	Charged to Investment Expense	Charged to Other Accounts		Total
		(1) Account	(2) Amount	
1. Legal expenses (including those in connection with any matter, measure or proceeding before legislative bodies, officers or government departments)		....	....	....
2. Advertising and publicity	....	....	....	....
3. Sales promotion [2]	....	....	....	....
4. Payments directly and indirectly to trade associations and service organizations, and contributions to other organizations	....	....	....	....

[1] Amounts resulting from transactions with affiliates shall be stated separately.

[2] State separately each category of expense representing more than 5 percent of the total expense shown under this item.

Rule 12–40. Certificate Reserves.

(For Face-Amount Certificate Investment Companies)

COL. A	COL. B Balance at Beginning of Period			COL. C Additions			COL. D Deductions			COL. E Balance at Close of Period		
Description [1]	(1) Number of accounts with security holders	(2) Amount of maturity value	(3) Amount of reserves [2]	(1) Charged to profit and loss or income	(2) Reserve payments by certificate holders	(3) Charged to other accounts— Describe	(1) Maturities	(2) Cash surrenders prior to maturity	(3) Other— Describe	(1) Number of accounts with security holders	(2) Amount of maturity value	(3) Amount of reserves [2]

[1] (a) Each series of certificates shall be stated separately. The description shall include the yield to maturity on an annual payment basis.

(b) For certificates of the installment type, information required by columns B, D (2) and (3) and E shall be given by age groupings, according to the number of months paid by security holders, grouped to show those upon which 1–12 monthly payments have been made, 13–24 payments, etc.

[2] (a) If the total of the reserves shown in these columns differs from the total of the reserves per the accounts, there should be stated (i) the aggregate difference and (ii) the difference on a $1,000 face-amount certificate basis.

(b) There shall be shown by footnote or by supplemental schedule (i) the amounts periodically credited to each class of security holders' accounts from installment payments and (ii) such other amounts periodically credited to accumulate the maturity amount of the certificate. Such information shall be stated on a $1,000 face-amount certificate basis for the term of the certificate.

Rule 12–41. Qualified Assets on Deposit.[1]

(For Face-Amount Certificate Investment Companies)

COL. A	COL. B	COL. C	COL. D	COL. E	COL. F
Name of Depositary[2]	Cash	Investments in Securities	First Mortgages and Other First Liens on Real Estate	Other	Total[3]

[1] All money columns shall be totaled.
[2] Classify names of individual depositaries under group headings, such as banks and states.
[3] Total of column F shall agree with note required by caption 11 of rule 6–22 as to total amount of qualified Assets on Deposit.

Rule 12–42. Real Estate and Accumulated Depreciation[1]

(For Certain Real Estate Companies)

Column A	Column B	Column C		Column D		Column E			Column F	Column G	Column H	Column I
Description[2]	Encumbrances	Initial cost to company		Cost capitalized subsequent to acquisition		Gross amount at which carried at close of period[3,4,5,6,7]			Accumulated depreciation	Date of construction	Date Acquired	Life on which depreciation in latest income statements is computed
		Land	Buildings and improvements	Improvements	Carrying costs	Land	Buildings and improvements	Total				

1. All money columns shall be totaled.
2. The description for each property should include type of property (e.g., unimproved land, shopping center, garden apartments, etc.) and the geographical location.
3. The required information is to be given as to each individual investment included in column E except that an amount not exceeding five percent of the total of column E may be listed in one amount as "miscellaneous investments."
4. In a note to this schedule, furnish a reconciliation, in the following form, of the total amount at which real estate was carried at the beginning of each period for which income statements are required, with the total amount shown in column E:

Balance at beginning of period.......... $..........
Additions during period:
  Acquisitions through foreclosure.......... $..........
  Other acquisitions.......... ....
  Improvements, etc.......... ....
  Other (describe).......... .... $..........

Deductions during period:
  Cost of real estate sold.......... $..........
  Other (describe).......... ....
Balance at close of period.......... $..........

If additions, except acquisitions through foreclosure, represent other than cash expenditures, explain. If any of the changes during the period result from transactions, directly or indirectly with affiliates, explain the basis of such transactions and state the amounts involved.
  A similar reconciliation shall be furnished for the accumulated depreciation.
5. If any item of real estate investments has been written down or reserved against, describe the item and explain the basis for the write-down or reserve.
6. State in a note to column E the aggregate cost for Federal income tax purposes.
7. The amount of all intercompany profits included in the total of column E shall be stated if material.

Rule 12–43. Mortgage Loans on Real Estate[1]

(For Certain Real Estate Companies)

Column A	Column B	Column C	Column D	Column E	Column F	Column G	Column H
Description[2][3][4]	Interest rate	Final maturity date	Periodic Payment Terms[5]	Prior liens	Face amount of mortgages[10]	Carrying amount of mortgages[3][6][7][8][9]	Principal amount of loans subject to delinquent principal or interest[10]

1. All money columns shall be totaled.

2. The required information is to be given for each individual mortgage loan which exceeds three percent of the total of column G.

3. If the portfolio includes large numbers of mortgages most of which are less than three percent of column G, the mortgages not required to be reported separately should be grouped by classifications that will indicate the dispersion of the portfolio, i.e., for a portfolio of mortgages on single family residential housing. The description should also include number of loans by original loan amounts (e.g., over $100,000, $50,000–$99,999, $20,000–$49,000, under $20,000) and type loan (e.g., VA, FHA, Conventional). Interest rates and maturity dates may be stated in terms of ranges. Data required by columns D, E and F may be omitted for mortgages not required to be reported individually.

4. Loans should be grouped by categories, e.g., first mortgage, second mortgage, construction loans, etc., and for each loan the type of property, e.g., shopping center, high rise apartments, etc., and its geographic location should be stated.

5. State whether principal and interest is payable at level amount over life to maturity or at varying amounts over life to maturity. State amount of balloon payment at maturity, if any. Also state prepayment penalty terms, if any.

6. In a note to this schedule, furnish a reconciliation, in the following form, of the carrying amount of mortgage loans at the beginning of each period for which income statements are required, with the total amount shown in column G:

Balance at beginning of period.................................... $............
Additions during period:
  New mortgage loans...................................... $............
  Other (describe).. $............

Deductions during period:

Collections of principal.............................. $............

Foreclosure.. ....

Cost of mortgages sold.............................. ....

Amortization of premium............................ ....

Other (describe)................................... ....

Balance at close of period............................. $............

If additions represent other than cash expenditures, explain. If any of the changes during the period result from transactions, directly or indirectly with affiliates, explain the bases of such transactions, and the amounts involved. State the aggregate mortgages (a) renewed and (b) extended. If the carrying amount of new mortgages is in excess of the unpaid amount of the extended mortgages, explain.

7. If any item of mortgage loans on real estate investments has been written down or reserved against, describe the item and explain the basis for the write-down or reserve.

8. State in a note to column G the aggregate cost for Federal income tax purposes.

9. The amount of all intercompany profits in the total of column G shall be stated, if material.

10. (a) Interest in arrears for less than three months may be disregarded in computing the total amount of principal subject to delinquent interest

(b) Of the total principal amount, state the amount acquired from controlled and other affiliates.

CHAPTER 21

PRO FORMA FINANCIAL STATEMENTS; BUSINESS COMBINATIONS

CONTENTS

Pro Forma Statements Widely Used and Abused.—Although pro forma financial statements are not of importance solely in relation to documents prepared for filing with the SEC, they are often used in registration statements and proxy statements prepared for SEC filing.

Pro forma statements are of many kinds. For example, there are pro forma balance sheets which give effect to the receipt of funds from the proposed sale of new securities and the application of the proceeds toward payment of liabilities or purchase of new assets. There are pro forma balance sheets which set forth the financial position of two or more business enterprises whose merger is proposed. There are pro forma income statements of merged companies which previously operated as separate enterprises; the combined statement of their operations for the period prior to merger is intended to portray the operating results which might have been achieved had the companies been merged at the beginning of, or prior to, the period covered by the statement. When a company is no longer affiliated with other companies, pro forma statements may attempt to present the operating results that would have obtained had the company not enjoyed the benefits of consolidated tax returns. The number and variety of pro forma statements is almost endless. However, recognition of prior period charges and credits, adjustments of federal income taxes, and other similar adjustments in the years to which they apply does not change the essentially historical character of financial statements, and statements so adjusted should not be labeled "pro forma."

Pro forma statements often help the reader to comprehend an otherwise confusing situation; sometimes they are essential to a proper understanding of financial statements. Often pro forma statements are more illuminating than the so-called "actual" (or historical) statements on which they are based, and the public accountant must be alert to see that the prospective investor is furnished not only with all the financial information he needs but also that the information is presented in the most convenient and useful form. This latter consideration frequently dictates the use of pro forma statements, and in recent years prospectuses and proxy statements have placed increasing emphasis on these statements.

In its findings and opinion in the case of Faradyne Electronics Corporation [40 SEC 1053 (1962)], the SEC was highly critical of the company for having failed to present a pro forma earnings statement in its registration statement. The registration statement had been filed in connection with a proposed public offering of $2,000,000 of convertible subordinated debentures. Of the proceeds, $1,200,000 was to be used to discharge an interest-free obligation of the company. The replacement of the interest-free debt by interest-bearing obligations would result in an increase in expenses of $78,000 per year plus amortization of the expenses of the proposed offering. This amount was substantial in relation to the reported earnings of the company but was not disclosed in the prospectus. The Commission said: "Also making the summary of earnings materially misleading [was] the failure to present a pro forma earnings statement to reflect debenture interest chargeable to the replacement of the $1,200,000 interest-free obligation . . . with an interest-bearing obligation . . . ."

When pro forma statements are not furnished voluntarily and the SEC thinks they are essential, the registrant will be requested to submit them. The proxy rules of the SEC contain instructions for the submission of pro forma financial statements where mergers and acquisitions are involved;

see the discussion in Chapter **22**. Filings with the SEC under the 1933 Act must also contain pro forma financial statements when a registrant is about to succeed to one or more businesses through merger, consolidation, or otherwise; see, for example, the discussion of the requirements of Form S–1 in Chapter **9**.

Particularly in acquisitions and mergers, pro forma statements may be essential to an understanding of the proposed action. A steel company, for example, proposed to acquire the business and assets of another company in a related business by issuing additional capital shares in an aggregate amount which the acquiring company considered represented fair value for the acquisition. These securities were to be distributed to the stockholders of the company being acquired according to a fixed pro rata basis, thereby effecting the dissolution of the company. The purchase price of the assets being acquired, paid by the issuance of capital stock, was substantially in excess of the book value of the assets. This excess was allocated to fixed assets since the amount was approximately equivalent to the difference between the independent currently appraised values and book values. In the preliminary proxy material proposed to be submitted to the stockholders of the respective companies, statements of earnings and of assets, liabilities, and capital of the respective companies were furnished in conventional form. However, the proposed data did not readily demonstrate the impact of the acquisition upon the acquiring company resulting from (1) the new capital structure and (2) the new valuation placed upon the fixed assets to be acquired. Specifically the stockholders would be unable to determine readily (A) the coverages of liquidating values and of dividend requirements of the increased preferred shares, and (B) the earnings per share of the increased common stock as affected by the increased amount of the preferred stock. Accordingly, the respective companies were requested by the SEC staff to furnish, in the proxy statements, a pro forma consolidating balance sheet giving effect to the recapitalization and acquisition, together with a pro forma income statement for the year 1950 of both companies combined, calculating the income and excess profits taxes under the Revenue Act of 1950 for the entire year, and calculating depreciation charges upon the basis of the increase in valuation of the fixed assets. Also upon such request the pro forma net income, applicable to common stock in the aggregate and in per share amounts after provision for preferred stock dividends, was stated and accompanied by an explanation that this information was not necessarily indicative of the results of future operations or the availability of net income for dividend purposes. [17 SEC Ann. Rep. 45 (1951).]

There has been some abuse of pro forma financial statements, principally in the direction of stating past financial statements in the light of present or assumed future conditions. To attribute to a past period certain conditions which exist currently, or which will exist in the future and, at the same time, to ignore other changed conditions may be misleading. Such adjustments of earnings should ordinarily be avoided, but if used, the statements should clearly disclose the adjustments that have been made.

This was the subject of extended discussion at a meeting several years ago attended by representatives of investment banking, legal, and accounting firms. It was the consensus of those present that it is not desirable to restate in an earnings summary extending back over several years interest and other fixed charges on the basis of securities to be outstanding in the future. When it is considered necessary to make such a computation in order to indicate the balance of earnings applicable to equity securities, the computation should be limited to the current and immediately preceding periods, as indicated later in this chapter.

AICPA Pronouncements.—In 1923, long before the enactment of the SEC laws, the membership of the AICPA adopted the recommendations of a special committee on the subject of pro forma statements.[1] Such statements, the committee said, should be issued only under proper safeguards and rules for the guidance of professional public accountants to insure as far as possible sound standards and uniformity of practice. The committee recommended the following rules concerning pro forma financial statements, and the Institute membership adopted the rules:

I. The accountant may certify a statement of a company giving effect as at the date thereof to transactions entered into subsequently only under the following conditions, viz:

    (a) If the subsequent transactions are the subject of a definite (preferably written) contract or agreement between the company and bankers (or parties) who the accountant is satisfied are responsible and able to carry out their engagement;

    (b) If the interval between the date of the statement and the date of the subsequent transactions is reasonably short—not to exceed, say, four months;

    (c) If the accountant, after due inquiry, or, preferably, after actual investigation, has no reason to suppose that other transactions or developments have in the interval materially affected adversely the position of the company; and

    (d) If the character of the transaction to which effect is given is clearly disclosed, i.e., either at the heading of the statement or somewhere in the statement there shall be stated clearly the purpose for which the statement is issued.

II. The accountant should not *certify* a statement giving effect to transactions contemplated but not actually entered into at the date of the certificate, with the sole exception that he may give effect to the proposed application of the proceeds of new financing where the application is clearly disclosed on the

---

[1] *1923 Institute Year-Book,* pp. 90, 96, 167–70.

face of the statement or in the certificate and the accountant is satisfied that the funds can and will be applied in the manner indicated. It is not necessary that the precise liabilities shown in the balance sheet before adjustment should actually be paid out of the new money. It is sufficient, for instance, where the balance sheet before the financing shows bank loans, if the proceeds are to be applied to bank loans which are either identical with or have replaced the bank loans actually outstanding at the date of the balance sheet. Ordinarily, however, the accountant should not apply the proceeds of financing to the payment of current trade accounts payable, at least not against a normal volume of such current accounts payable, because there must always be such accounts outstanding, and the application of new moneys against the outstandings of the date of the balance sheet results in showing a position which in fact could never be attained. The accountant may usually best satisfy himself that the funds will be applied as indicated by getting an assurance from the issuing house on the point.

III. In any description of a statement or in any certificate relating thereto, it is desirable that the past tense should be used. It should also be made clear that the transactions embodied have been definitely covered by contract.

IV. When the accountant feels that he cannot certify to such a hypothetical statement, probably because of the length of the period which has elapsed since the accounts have been audited, he may be prepared to write a letter, not in certificate form, stating that at the request of the addressee a statement has been examined or prepared in which effect is given, in his opinion correctly, to proposed transactions (which must be clearly specified). Such letters should be given only in very special cases and with the greatest care.

One of the rules in the Code of Professional Ethics relates to the use of names of members of the AICPA in conjunction with forecasts. It is Rule 2–04 of the Code and provides as follows:

A member or associate shall not permit his name to be used in conjunction with any forecasts of the results of future transactions in a manner which may lead to the belief that the member or associate vouches for the accuracy of the forecast.

In amplifying this rule, the Ethics Committee of the AICPA stated in its Opinion No. 10 that it was well aware that pro forma statements of financial position and results of operation are important tools of management. The committee was of the opinion that Rule 2–04 does not prohibit a member from preparing, or from assisting a client in the preparation of, such statements. However, when a member associates his name with such statements, or permits his name to be associated therewith, there shall be the presumption that such data may be used by parties other than the client. In such cases, full disclosure must be made of the source of the information used, or the major assumptions made, in the preparation of the statements, the character of the work performed by the member, and the degree of responsibility he is taking. Such disclosure should be made on each statement, or in the member's letter or report attached to the statements. The letter or report of the member must also clearly indicate that the member does not vouch for the accuracy of the forecast. (This does not refer to the accuracy of the mathematical computations but rather to whether or not the prediction itself will come true.)[2] It was the opinion of the Committee that full and adequate disclosure would put any reader of such statements on notice and restrict the statements to their intended use.

SEC Formal Rules.—The SEC rule under the 1933 Act relating to pro forma statements is as follows:

Rule 170. Prohibition of Use of Certain Financial Statements.

Financial statements which purport to give effect to the receipt and application of any part of the proceeds from the sale of securities for cash shall not be used unless such securities are to be offered through underwriters and the underwriting arrangements are such that the underwriters are or will be committed to take and pay for all of the securities, if any are taken, prior to or within a reasonable time after the commencement of the public offering, or if the securities are not so taken to refund to all subscribers the full amount of all subscription payments made for the securities. The caption of any such financial statement shall clearly set forth the assumptions upon which such statement is based. The caption shall be in type at least as large as that used generally in the body of the statement.

Rule 170 represents a substantial revision and relaxation of an earlier SEC rule on the same subject. The old rule prohibited the use of pro forma financial statements giving effect to the receipt and application of proceeds from the sale of securities unless the sale was underwritten and the underwriters were to be irrevocably bound, on or before the date of the public offering, to take the issue. Presumably the SEC believes that with the safeguards built into the present rule, investors are not likely to be hurt by reading a pro forma balance sheet which complies with the new rule. If the financial condition portrayed in the pro forma balance sheet is not ultimately realized because of the failure of the underwriter to take and pay for all the securities, those investors who bought the securities will have their money returned.

If an accountant is called upon to assist in the preparation of a pro forma balance sheet of the type under consideration, he should ascertain the nature of the underwriting commitment, whether it complies with SEC Rule 170, and whether the statement complies with AICPA pronouncements previously referred to in this chapter. An underwriting commitment on a "best efforts" basis would not comply with Rule 170.

The SEC has a similar rule under the 1934 Act relating to pro forma financial statements. The rule follows:

[2] Carey and Doherty, *Ethical Standards of the Accounting Profession,* AICPA, 1966.

Rule 15c1–9

The term "manipulative, deceptive, or other fraudulent device or contrivance," as used in Section 15(c)(1) of the Act, is hereby defined to include the use of financial statements purporting to give effect to the receipt and application of any part of the proceeds from the sale or exchange of securities, unless the assumptions upon which each such financial statement is based are clearly set forth as part of the caption to each such statement in type at least as large as that used generally in the body of the statement.

It will be seen that the rule under the 1933 Act relates to the receipt and application of the proceeds from the sale of securities *for cash*, whereas the rule under the 1934 Act applies to the receipt and application of the proceeds from the sale *or exchange* of securities.

Pro Forma Statements Used in Connection with Exchange Offers. —Neither Rule 170 under the 1933 Act nor Rule 15c1–9 under the 1934 Act prohibits the use of pro forma financial statements in the case of an exchange offer, that is, one in which Company A offers its securities to the security holders of Company B in exchange for the holdings of the latter in Company B. Occasionally the exchange offer is made in connection with an unfriendly take-over which is opposed by the management of the target company, and consequently there is no assurance that the exchange offer will be successfully consummated.

A typical example of such an exchange offer occurred in 1968 when Loew's Theatres, Inc. (as it was then known) offered to exchange its convertible debentures for shares of common stock of Commercial Credit Company, the offering being made directly to the common stockholders of Commercial. In the prospectus filed with the SEC and used in connection with the exchange offer, Loew's stated that it owned 1,000,700 shares of common stock of Commercial which at December 31, 1967 had 10,538,000 common shares outstanding. Loew's said that it had requested information from Commercial for use in connection with the prospectus, but that Commercial had refused to comply. The reaction of Commercial's Board of Directors to Loew's exchange offer, according to the prospectus, was unfavorable. Through the exchange offer, Loew's said that it wished to increase its holdings in Commercial by purchasing as many shares as might be tendered and, although it was not a condition of the offer, Loew's intention was to achieve at least majority ownership of Commercial.

The prospectus used in the exchange offer included conventional, historical financial statements of Loew's and Commercial. In addition it included a pro forma statement of income which combined the operations of the two companies for one year and gave effect to the assumptions that Loew's, after the exchange offer, would own (1) 52.7% (which represented 51% of the outstanding voting stock) and (2) 100%, of the outstanding common stock of Commercial. There were several pro forma adjustments reflected in the statement, the principal one being for the interest on the convertible debentures proposed to be issued, and the related tax effect. A pro forma balance sheet giving effect to the exchange offer was also included in the prospectus on the basis of the same assumptions as used in the pro forma income statement, namely, 52.7% and 100% ownership, respectively, of Commercial's common stock.

(Loew's exchange offer was defeated when Control Data Corporation made a competing exchange offer that was successful.)

SEC Formal Decisions.—There have been relatively few published decisions by the SEC involving pro forma financial statements. Probably the most glaring case reported by the SEC was *Leedy, Wheeler & Company* [16 SEC 299 (1944)]. This company was a broker-dealer registered with the SEC under the 1934 Act. The Commission had instituted proceedings against the company under that Act to determine whether its registration as a broker-dealer should be revoked because the firm had sold certain bonds of a gas company by means of false and misleading statements. The bonds of the gas company were believed to be exempt from the registration requirements of the 1933 Act and were therefore not registered under that Act.

Under the 1934 Act it is unlawful to use or employ any manipulative or deceptive device in the sale of securities. In Rule 15c1–9 the term "manipulative, deceptive, or other fraudulent device or contrivance" includes the use of financial statements purporting to give effect to the receipt and application of any part of the proceeds from the sale of securities, unless the assumptions upon which the statement is based are set forth as part of the caption of the statement. (The text of Rule 15c1–9 is given on a preceding page.)

In the *Leedy* case the offering circular relating to the gas company bonds included a pro forma balance sheet that had been prepared on the assumption that an informal oral agreement would be carried out. The balance sheet disclosed that it gave effect "to present financing" with no further indication of the nature of the financing. The balance sheet also gave effect to the discharge of indebtedness to officers and others by issuance of preferred stock but gave no indication that such adjustment had been made. Furthermore, the agreement to issue the preferred stock was of doubtful enforceability.

Other adjustments were reflected in the pro forma balance sheet, also without disclosure. In the preparation of the pro forma balance sheet a deficit in earned surplus had been eliminated. The deficit was charged partly to capital stock and partly to reserve for depreciation. The reader of the balance sheet had no way of knowing that a deficit had been eliminated. The pro forma balance sheet showed that the gas company was in a liquid position whereas the actual balance sheet (which was not included in the offering circular) told a different story. A prospective investor could not ascertain the gas company's condition from the information given in the offering circular or in the pro forma balance sheet.

In finding the documents misleading and deceptive, the Commission said:

A pro forma balance sheet does not portray the actual financial condition of an enterprise. It is a statement based on a balance sheet taken from the books of account, but adjusted to incorporate various hypothetical transactions which have not in fact occurred at the date of the balance sheet, but whose occurrence is contemplated. Since such a balance sheet does not purport to portray the actual financial condition of a company at the balance sheet date, it is plainly necessary that it indicate the assumptions which underlie its preparation, so that one examining the statements will be fully apprised as to which items in it are based on fact and which on assumption. Without such disclosure a pro forma statement is meaningless and deceptive.

In *Marquette Mines, Inc.* [8 SEC 172 (1940)] a registration statement was filed, under the 1933 Act, which included a pro forma balance sheet giving effect to the receipt and application of cash proceeds from the proposed offering and sale of stock. Inasmuch as no underwriter was committed to take any of the issue, the use of this balance sheet was plainly misleading and a violation of the Commission's Rule 170 (quoted previously). Even before the Commission adopted Rule 170, it had consistently held that the use of pro forma balance sheets in similar circumstances (that is, where there was no firm commitment by a responsible underwriter to take the securities) was misleading. (See, for example, *Haddam Distillers Corp.*, 1 SEC 52 (1934); *Continental Distillers & Importers Corp.*, 1 SEC 78 (1935); and *Bering Straits Tin Mines, Inc.*, 2 SEC 497 (1937).)

Predecessor Business Operated as Partnership or Sole Proprietorship.—Occasionally the owners of a business desire to sell all or a portion of their interests in that business. If the business is conducted as a partnership or as a sole proprietorship, the owners may form a corporation to take over the assets and operations of the business. They may then cause the corporation to file a registration statement covering the portion of the securities of the new corporation which they desire to dispose of by means of a public offering. This is the typical situation of a privately owned business, the owners of which decide to "go public." If the successor corporation has been recently incorporated, the only financial operating information of the business would be that for the period during which it was conducted as a partnership or as a sole proprietorship. Financial statements of a partnership or a sole proprietorship necessarily do not contain some of the expense items which would apply in the case of a corporation. For example, the statements of a partnership or proprietorship ordinarily do not contain charges for salaries to the owners which, in the case of a corporation, would probably be reflected as officers' salaries. Similarly, since federal income taxes on the income of partnerships and sole proprietorships are assessed against the owners as individuals, the financial statements of partnerships or proprietorships may not contain a charge for federal income taxes and certainly would not contain a charge for federal income taxes which would be appropriate in the case of a corporation.

Although financial statements of a partnership or sole proprietorship reflect the actual operating results of the predecessor business entity, they have limited value to the prospective investor contemplating the purchase of shares of the successor corporation. Where this situation exists, the SEC ordinarily requires that the actual statements be appropriately modified to reflect the operations of the predecessor adjusted to the new form of organization—that is, with appropriate deductions for officers' salaries, federal income taxes, and state franchise taxes.

In one case filed with the SEC, the registrant had succeeded to the business of a partnership. Financial statements of the partnership included in the registration statement reflected net income of $251,000, $452,000, $236,000, and $406,000, for the four most recent fiscal periods of the predecessor partnership. By amendment the income statements were supplemented to show as deductions certain items of expense which would have been incurred had the business been operated as a corporation throughout the period. As a consequence, the net income as previously reported was reduced to $61,000, $114,000, $56,000, and $128,000, respectively. No question was raised as to the accuracy of the financial statements of the predecessor partnership, but it must be agreed that the more meaningful statements to the prospective investor were the pro forma statements, that is, those which were adjusted to reflect the operations as they would have appeared had the business enterprise been conducted as a corporation instead of as a partnership.

A company filed a registration statement with SEC in connection with the proposed sale of equity securities, the principal purpose of which was to acquire certain assets of a partnership and certain real estate from the partners. The amount to be paid for the partnership assets exceeded the amount at which they were carried on the partnership books, the excess being related to depreciable property. The prospectus included a summary of earnings of the partnership for the 10½ years ended June 30, 1947. The Commission pointed out that the summary of partnership income did not properly show the earning power of the assets to be acquired, as recognition was not given to the additional depreciation charge resulting from the excess payment for property or to income taxes which would have been incurred had the partnership been operated as a corporation. As amended, the summary of earnings showed for each period the effect of additional depreciation and of income taxes computed on a pro forma basis of rates applicable to corporations. [15 SEC Ann. Rep. 21 (1949).]

With respect to the summary of earnings referred to in the preceding case, the author believes that the current preferred practice would sanction the adjustment of the summary for all periods only for income taxes since this is apparently the sole adjustment necessary to place the operating results of all years of the partnership on the corporate basis of the acquirer. The pro forma adjustment for additional depreciation resulting from the acquisition should be applied only in the last full fiscal year and in any subsequent interim period presented.

In another registration statement filed with SEC, a corporation presented the financial statements of a predecessor partnership. The financial statements were the actual financial statements of the partnership and, while they included partners' salaries, they did not include any provision for federal income taxes. The income statement of the partnership was followed by a footnote reading as follows:

The costs and expenses of the partnership include partners' salaries of $ for the respective periods from (date) to (date). The Board of Directors of the corporation has authorized officers' salaries at the annual rate of $ starting (date). Since federal income taxes on partnership income are assessed against the individual partners, no provision for such taxes appears in the above statement of income.

Were the differences between the amount of officers' salaries and directors' fees established by the corporation and partners' salaries paid, and were an estimated amount of federal and state taxes that would have been applicable had the business been conducted by a corporation, applied to the above partnership net income, the following would result:

Net income, as above ....
    Deduct:
        Excess of officers' salaries (at annual rate established by
           the corporation effective (date) over partners' salaries
           charged to costs and expenses) ....
        Directors' fees—estimated ....
        Federal capital stock tax, state franchise tax, and social
           security taxes applicable to officers' salaries ......
        Provision for federal income taxes ....
    Adjusted net income ....

Many believe that the adjusted (pro forma) net income is more significant than the actual (historical) net income. (The SEC, in fact, in many cases has suggested that per share amounts be furnished only in respect of the pro forma earnings since these are the more meaningful figures from the point of view of the investor.) For that reason they believe that the information in the footnote above should be made a part of the summary itself. Since the difference in presentation is one of form—not substance—

there can be no valid objection to presenting the information in a form which will be most useful to the reader. Examples conforming to this point of view follow.

The following is an acceptable form for presenting the historical operations of a business previously operated as a partnership (now operated as a corporation), and the pro forma results of the business on the basis of operating as a corporation:

Historical:
Net sales ....
Cost of sales ....
    Gross profit on sales ....
Selling, general, and administrative expenses ....
Other income ....
Other deductions ....
        Income before taxes on income ....
Pro forma adjustments:
Pro forma adjustments to reflect partnership operations
        above on a corporate basis:
Estimated salaries to Messrs. A and B as officers (with
    reference to note explaining basis of this assumption) ......
Estimated federal and state taxes on income ....
Total pro forma adjustments ....
Pro forma net income ....
Pro forma net income per share ....

Similar adjustments would also be made in the case of a business previously operated as a sole proprietorship.

The business of the sole proprietor (or partnership, as the case may be) may have been conducted from premises owned by him. It is possible either that no rent was paid by the business or that the rent was inadequate as compared with the rent which will be paid by the business after incorporation. In either case, the pro forma adjustments should also include, if material, an adjustment for building rentals. In an actual case, involving predecessor corporations and proprietorships, the pro forma adjustments were summarized and explained as follows:

Combined (historical) earnings:
Net sales ....
Cost of sales ....
    Gross profit on sales ....
Selling, general, and administrative expenses ....
    Income from operations ....
Other income or (expense): ....
    Interest expense ....
    Other ....
    Income before income taxes ....
Provision for income taxes: ....
    Federal ....

Other ....
    Net Income ....
Pro forma adjustments—to adjust proprietorship operations
    included above to a corporate basis (see note below) :
Building rental ....
Adjustment of salaries of officers ....
Estimated taxes on income ....
Pro forma net income ....
Per common share (based on shares outstanding after con-
    summation of transactions referred to in Note — to the
    financial statements) on basis of pro forma net income above ....

NOTE: The operations of a predecessor proprietorship included in the (years) above have been adjusted to reflect (1) payment of rent to the proprietor at the current rate of rental plus certain maintenance expenses net of other rentals received, (2) payment of salary to the proprietor (who during the period of proprietorship operation did not receive a salary as such) at his current rate, and (3) the provision of income taxes at the rate currently applicable to corporations.

Objection has sometimes been made that the pro forma net income and adjustments discussed above leave something to be desired. It is true that the pro forma net income is a meaningful figure, but often all the figures which precede the pro forma adjustments, while actual, are not the most useful figures from the viewpoint of the prospective investor. In that event, it might be desirable to furnish an earnings summary entirely on a pro forma basis (including pro forma net income), showing the pro forma adjustments given effect to, and the amount of historical net income. A prospectus of Vahlsing, Inc. (1961) included a pro forma earnings summary presented on this basis, as follows:

Net sales ....
Cost of goods sold ....
    Gross profit ....
Brokerage charges ....
Other selling, general and administrative expense ....
Other income, net ....
    Income before federal income taxes ....
Provision for federal income taxes ....
    Net income (pro forma) ....
Deduct, Adjustments to restore pro forma net income to an
    historical basis (Note C) ....
    Net income of Vahlsing, Inc. (historical) ....
    Net income (pro forma) per share ....

Note C contained a detailed explanation of each of the adjustments given effect to, and the amounts thereof, year by year, and the total of all such adjustments, which total agreed with the adjustment line in the summary that restored pro forma net income to historical net income.

In presenting a pro forma balance sheet when a partnership acquisition is accounted for as a pooling of interests, the SEC has required that the balance of the partners' capital accounts be added to contributed capital in the combination. Therefore, any partnership earnings that may be included in the partners' capital accounts may not be added to the pooled retained earnings account.

Sub-Chapter S Corporations.—Some corporations can elect not to be subject to Federal income tax. When the election is made under Sub-Chapter S of the Internal Revenue Code, the shareholders include in their own income for tax purposes the current taxable income of the corporation, both the part which is distributed and the part which is not. The tax option is available only to corporations meeting the requirements, including these: (1) The corporation must be a domestic corporation not eligible to file a consolidated return with any other corporation. (2) The corporation may not have more than one class of stock. (3) The corporation must not have more than ten shareholders. (4) All of the shareholders must consent to the election.

In the case of a tax-option corporation meeting the requirements of the Code, it is not necessary to provide for Federal income taxes other than certain capital gains taxes under Section 1378, since the remainder of the tax burden is assumed by the company's shareholders. When a company of this kind goes public, however, it will lose its tax option in the future by the mere fact of becoming a publicly owned company. Therefore, in addition to showing the historical earnings of the corporation, it will ordinarily be necessary to make pro forma provision for the taxes that would have been required if the corporation had not had the benefit of the tax option which it will lose in the future. One way of accomplishing this adjustment in an earnings summary follows:

> *Historical earnings:*
>   Sales . . . .
>   Cost of sales . . . .
>   Gross profit on sales . . . .
>   Selling, general and administrative expenses . . . .
>   Other income and (expense) . . . .
>   Income before income taxes . . . .
> *Pro forma adjustment:*
>   Deduct—Pro forma adjustment to reflect the provision for
>   income taxes that would have been required had the corporation not elected to be exempted under Sub-Chapter
>   S of the Internal Revenue Code . . . .
>   Pro forma net income . . . .
>   Pro forma net income per share . . . .

Following is the summary of earnings (with irrelevant information and certain dollar amounts omitted) that appeared in a registration statement filed with the SEC, in which the registrant had elected to be taxed under Sub-Chapter S of the Internal Revenue Code for part of the period under report:

	Year Ended November 30,					Three Months Ended February 28, 1966	13 weeks Ended March 4, 1967
	1962	1963	1964	1965	1966	(Unaudited)	
Net sales							
Cost of sales							
Gross profit							
Selling, general, and administrative expenses							
Operating income ..							
Other expense—interest..							
Income (loss) before federal income taxes(a)..........							
Pro forma provision for (refund of) federal income taxes (Note c) ..							
Pro forma net income (loss)	$ 71,293	$ 45,521	$ (13,778)	$ 11,826	$ 69,091	$ 1,068	$ 23,245
Income (loss) per share before federal income taxes (a) (b)					(a)		(a)
Pro forma net income (loss) per share (b) ...	$ .100	$ .064	$ (.019)	$ .017	$ .091	$ .002	$ .023

(a) Income (loss) before federal income taxes is historical net income (loss) except for the period ended March 4, 1967 and the year ended November 30, 1966 in which case historical net income is $23,245 ($.   per share) and $81,091 ($.   per share) respectively. See Note c.

(b) Based on the number of shares outstanding at the end of each period after giving effect to the reclassification described in Note — to the financial statements.

(c) During the four years ended November 30, 1965 and the six months ended May 31, 1966, the Company elected to be taxed as a small business corporation under SubChapter S of the Internal Revenue Code. Under Sub-Chapter S, the corporate income is taxable to the shareholders individually and the distributions made to shareholders have not been in the form of usual corporate dividends. Subsequent to May 31, 1966, the Company will be subject to taxation at usual corporate rates and, accordingly, such taxes have been provided for. However, where applicable, a pro forma provision for federal income taxes on a regular corporate basis has been reflected in the summary of earnings.

One of the SEC's unwritten requirements is to the effect that no part of the retained earnings of a Sub-Chapter S corporation may be added to pooled retained earnings in a business combination to which the pooling of interests concept is applicable. This position apparently rests on the assumption that the earnings, in effect, have been distributed, the income taxes paid by the shareholders, and the remainder has been reinvested in the company.

Predecessor Business Previously Operated as a Division.—Occasionally a public offering is made of securities of a company organized for the purpose of acquiring and operating a going business. If the business had been a separate corporation, the problem of presenting informative financial statements would be relatively simple, although consideration might have to be given, among other things, to the cost of the business to the new owners as compared with the net assets of the business as shown by its books.

When the business has been operated as a division of a larger enterprise, the problem of presenting financial statements of the division—that is, the portion of a larger enterprise which is acquired by the new owners —is compounded. As a division, there may not have been arm's-length apportionments and allocations of costs and expenses. In some cases, in fact, there is no allocation at all of federal income taxes. These are matters which will have to be considered in furnishing financial statements of the division to the prospective investor as an indication of how the division might have operated if it had stood on its own feet as a separate corporation.

A good case study of this kind of situation occurred in the registration statement filed by Special Metals, Inc. (prospectus dated June 28, 1961). Special Metals, Inc., was incorporated on March 22, 1961, to investigate the business and properties of the Metals Division of Kelsey-Hayes Company with a view to purchasing the assets of the division. Special Metals acquired the assets of the Metals Division as of June 1, 1961. Prior to such acquisition, Special Metals was a nominal corporation with a small amount of cash, offset by capital stock of the same amount.

A summary of earnings was furnished which was historical (actual) but reflected one significant pro forma adjustment:

The Metals Division had not previously recorded federal income taxes since the net income of such division was included with the overall net income of Kelsey-Hayes for purposes of computing federal income taxes. State taxes based on income were allocated between the Metals Division and other divisions of Kelsey-Hayes located in New York State. The state taxes were eliminated, and, in lieu thereof, there was substituted a pro forma provision for federal and state taxes based on income computed to be the amounts that would have been applicable if the Division had been a separate company.

A note to the summary disclosed the amounts, year by year, allocated by Kelsey-Hayes and affiliates representing the Metals Division's portion of certain expenses. The note further stated that, in the opinion of the Division's management, such allocated expenses "approximate the expenses which would have been incurred by the Metals Division had such Division been operated as a separate company during such periods."

The accountants' report repeated the information in the notes to the summary relating to taxes and allocations of expenses and said, "while we believe that the pro forma provision for Federal and state taxes based on income and the allocation of expenses have been made on a reasonable basis, such charges may or may not be representative of the expenses that would have been incurred had the Metals Division operated as a separate and independent company." The opinion paragraph was "with the foregoing ex-

planations concerning provisions for taxes and allocation of expenses . . ."
(The phrase "with the foregoing explanations, etc." may create uncertainty
in the mind of the reader as to the accountants' opinion and, therefore, the
phrase should not be used to qualify an opinion; see Statement on Auditing
Procedure No. 33.)

In addition to the summary of earnings discussed above, the prospectus
contained a further pro forma summary in which adjustment was made for
(1) depreciation and amortization based on estimated valuation of the
properties acquired by the new company, (2) estimated increased compensation, and (3) interest on the proposed long-term financing incurred in
connection with the acquisition of the business.

Acquisition or Disposition of Part of a Business.—Somewhat similar considerations apply in the case of an acquisition or disposition of part
of a business. As in the case of a business previously operated as a division,
here also an effort should be made to show the results that might have been
achieved by the business which is to be acquired or sold if it had been an
independent company. In order to produce a meaningful statement, pro
forma adjustments often need to be made to the historical figures of the
part of the business in question. This kind of situation is well illustrated
in the proxy statement of General Refractories Company, dated March 22,
1966, used to solicit shareholder approval of the proposed acquisition of the
Mining and Mineral Products Division of Great Lakes Carbon Corporation and certain affiliated companies in consideration of the issuance of
shares of capital stock of General Refractories.

The proxy statement contained conventional financial statements of
General Refractories and pro forma financial statements of the businesses
to be acquired, namely, the Mining and Mineral Products Division of Great
Lakes and certain affiliated companies. Notes to the pro forma statements
set forth the adjustments reflected in the statements. The income statement
adjustments were described as follows:

Pro forma adjustments applicable to Mining and Mineral
   Products Division of Great Lakes Carbon Corporation:
     Corporate selling, administrative and research expenses attributable to Division ....
     Elimination of nonrecurring gains on sales of land ..
       Less related federal income taxes* ....
     Other miscellaneous adjustments ....
        Net decrease in income before taxes on income
     Provision (credit) for federal income taxes* ....
        Net decrease in net income ....

* The Mining and Mineral Products Division follows the consistent practice of providing for federal income taxes
solely in respect of gains on dispositions of property. All other provisions for federal income taxes are reflected
on the books of Corporate Headquarters.

In addition, the proxy statement included a pro forma income statement
which combined the historical income statement of General Refractories and
the pro forma income statement of the business proposed to be acquired

(on a pooling of interests basis) as if the acquisition had been consummated at the beginning of a five year period. (While this type of business combination can not be accorded pooling treatment under the conditions set forth in APB Opinion No. 16, it does illustrate the pro forma adjustments applicable to the income statement of part of a division of a business.)

In another case, the registrant, The Dexter Corporation, filed a registration statement under the 1933 Act in 1970 covering a proposed offering of common stock. The prospectus disclosed that part of the proceeds would be used to repay short-term bank loans in the amount of $8,400,000, and that the company had used $7,000,000 of such loans to provide most of the purchase price for the business of the Adhesives Department of Shell Chemical Company, a division of Shell Oil Company. In addition to financial statements of Dexter, the registration statement included financial information regarding the business acquired from Shell as of October 1, 1969. This information consisted of a statement of income before allocation of division and head office expenses and income taxes for the period of nine months ended September 30, 1969 and a statement of assets acquired at October 1, 1969.

An introductory headnote to the income statement stated that it did not include all costs incident to the operations of the Adhesives Department, as described in Note 1 to the statement. Note 1 indicated that the Adhesives Department for the most part was operated as a separate department of Shell Chemical Company, which was a division of Shell Oil Company. The note continued:

However, the headquarters office of the division as well as the corporate headquarters (head office) of Shell Oil Company provide the Adhesives Department with certain executive, administrative, financial, marketing, legal and general management services as well as certain other services performed on a centralized basis such as insurance and tax matters. Such services performed by the corporate headquarters are also performed for other divisions and departments of Shell Oil Company. These corporate and divisional services either substitute functions which the Adhesives Department does not perform or supplement functions performed by the Adhesives Department and which are necessary for its operations. It is not practical to identify the actual costs of these services allocable to the Adhesives Department and such costs are not included in the above statement. The above statement also does not include allocations of Shell Oil Company's interest on long term debt or federal and other income taxes.

The statement of assets acquired from Shell listed the assets (1) at their book values, and (2) at their cost to Dexter. The excess of Dexter's cost over book values was allocated to (1) property, plant and equipment, (2) patents, license agreement, formulae and other amortizable intangibles, and (3) excess of cost over book value of assets acquired.

The registration statement included a pro forma income statement which combined the operations of Dexter and the Adhesives Department of Shell for the nine months ended September 30, 1969. This statement gave pro forma effect to the increased cost to Dexter of the acquired Shell assets and was reflected by an increase in depreciation expense, and an increase in the write-off of amortizable intangible assets. There was also an adjustment of income taxes computed by applying Dexter's effective tax rates to the Adhesives Department's adjusted pre-tax income.

Elimination of Loss of Discontinued Business.—Chapter **13** made reference to disclosing in the summary of earnings the results of operations of a discontinued department or division of the business, and discussed the manner of disclosing such discontinued operations. Some might contend that, since the company is no longer engaged in the discontinued business, a pro forma earnings summary should be prepared which would eliminate the profits or losses incident to the discontinued business. The manner of presenting the loss of a discontinued business shown in Chapter **13** is consistent with APB Opinion No. 9 (1966). Profits of a discontinued business, although not occurring as often as losses, should be reported in the same manner as losses.

Company Previously Included in Group Filing Consolidated Tax Return, Now Not Included.—A significant change in conditions under which a corporation operates may indicate the desirability of furnishing pro forma financial statements in addition to the actual financial statements of the corporation, but the point which it is desired to emphasize can be shown by actual statements as in the following illustration. A public utility operating company was a subsidiary of a holding company which also had a number of other operating company subsidiaries. The operating company joined with its parent and the other affiliates in consolidated federal income tax returns. The filing of consolidated returns resulted in important tax savings to the operating company. Ultimately, the parent company sold all its holdings in the operating subsidiary and the subsidiary thereafter became ineligible to join in further consolidated tax returns with its former parent and affiliates. After the former parent company had sold its holdings in the subsidiary, the latter filed a registration statement with the SEC under the 1933 Act covering an additional issue of common stock. Inasmuch as the company would no longer be eligible to join in consolidated tax returns, the company (with the approval of its certifying accountants) furnished a summary of earnings on an actual basis but with adequate disclosure in respect of the changed tax situation. The summary of earnings was presented in the following form (dollar amounts being omitted here as not material to the illustration) :

Operating revenues:
  Electric ....
  Gas:
    Manufactured ....
    Natural ....
  Steam ....
      Total operating revenues ....
Operating revenue deductions:
  Operating expenses (other than shown below) ....
  Electricity and gas purchased for resale ....
  Maintenance ....
  Provision for depreciation of property, plant, and equipment ...
  Provision for taxes:
    Federal income (on separate return basis) before
      reductions shown separately below ....
    Other taxes ....
      Total operating revenue deductions ....
Operating income ....
Other income (net) ....
Gross income ....
Income deductions:
  Interest on long-term debt ....
  Interest on notes payable ....
  Other interest charges ....
  Amortization of premium, discount, and expense on debt, net ...
  Interest charged to construction ....
  Miscellaneous income deductions ....
      Total income deductions ....
Income, before reductions in taxes shown below ....
Reductions in federal taxes on income, resulting from
  joining in consolidated returns with former parent
  company and others ....
Net income ....

NOTE: As a result of the sale of the Company's common stock by its former parent, the Company became ineligible after (date) to join in further consolidated tax returns with such parent and its affiliates. See Note — to the Financial Statements.

It will be noted that the net income shown in the statement was actual —not pro forma—although the reduction in taxes resulting from joining in consolidated tax returns was clearly set out as a separate item.

Preceding the summary of earnings in the case mentioned above was a narrative discussion concerning earnings and dividends per share based on the assumption that federal income taxes had been provided for on a separate return basis.

Acquisition of Real Property by Real Estate Company.—The reader is referred to the discussion in Chapter **8** regarding the use of Form S–11 by certain real estate investment trusts and other issuers whose business is primarily that of acquiring and holding real estate for investment. Occasionally a company using Form S–11 will indicate that the proceeds, or part of the proceeds, of the proposed offering will be used to acquire a specific parcel of real estate. Unless the proposed acquisition is clearly insignificant, the registration statement will have to include an operating statement of the property.

The operating statement will cover a minimum of five years and be essentially historical in character, but it will exclude items not comparable to the proposed future operation of the property, such as mortgage interest, depreciation, leasehold rental, corporate expense, and income taxes. The basis for excluding these expenses is that such expenses, when the property is in the hands of the new owner, will, in all likelihood, be significantly changed from what they were under the prior ownership. Depreciation, for example, will change as a result of a change in the cost of the property to the new owner as compared with the prior owner.

An example of this situation occurred in a registration statement filed by Prudential Real Estate Trust on Form S–11 in 1966. The prospectus indicated that part of the proceeds would be used to consummate the purchase of a shopping center known as the Seven Grand Shopping Center. The prospectus included a "statement of operating income" of the shopping center, and was limited to the following items of information:

Gross income:
    Rents . . . .
    Rent overages . . . .
    Other . . . .
        Total gross income . . . .
Operating costs and expenses:
    Interest . . . .
    Real estate taxes . . . .
    Insurance . . . .
    Repairs and maintenance, building . . . .
        Total operating costs and expenses . . . .
Operating income exclusive of depreciation and amortization, advertising, parking lot maintenance, management fee, legal and auditing fees, administration expenses and federal income taxes . . . .

The basis on which the statement was prepared was stated in a footnote to the effect that it excluded expenses incurred by the present owner of the property which may not be comparable to the operation of the property by the new owner.

The reader will note that the statement includes interest expense. This was explained in a footnote which stated that "Interest at $5\frac{1}{2}\%$ on the existing mortgage is deducted in arriving at operating income because the new owner will take title subject to the present mortgage on the property."

Another footnote explained the exclusion of parking lot maintenance as follows:

Parking lot maintenance expenses 'are generally chargeable to tenants on a pro rata basis. The parking lot is maintained by an affiliate of the present owner. Maintenance costs billed by the affiliated company and related tenant reimbursements for such costs are excluded from this statement. Tenant reimbursements for maintenance costs aggregated approximately $7,500 for each of the years shown above.

In addition to the historical statement, the SEC's instructions call for a pro forma statement of operations of the property in certain circumstances. The applicable instructions (taken from Form S–11) follow:

(2) If the property is to be operated by the registrant, there shall be furnished a statement showing the estimated taxable operating results of the registrant based on the most recent twelve month period including such adjustments as can be factually supported. If the property is to be acquired subject to a net lease the estimated taxable operating results shall be based on the rent to be paid for the first year of the lease. In either case the estimated amount of cash to be made available by operations shall be shown. There shall be stated in an introductory paragraph the principal assumptions which have been made in preparing the statements of estimated taxable operating results and cash to be made available by operations.

Pro Forma Statements in Connection with Accounting Changes. —In July 1971 the APB issued its Opinion No. 20 on "Accounting Changes." The Board said that in preparing financial statements there is a presumption that an accounting principle once adopted should not be changed in accounting for similar events and transactions. This presumption may be overcome only if the use of another principle can be justified on the basis that it is preferable. The nature of, and justification for, a change in accounting principle and its effect on income should be disclosed in the financial statements of the period in which the change is made. This subject is more fully discussed in Chapter **13**.

Most changes in accounting principles, said the APB, should be recognized by including the cumulative effect, based on a retroactive computation, of changing to a new principle in net income of the period of the change. An exception was provided for a few specific accounting changes and for certain events, however, all of which should be reported by restating the financial statements of prior periods; these are also discussed in Chapter **13**.

For all changes in accounting principle not coming within the scope of the exceptions:

  a. Financial statements for prior periods included for comparative purposes should be presented as previously reported.
  b. The cumulative effect of the change on the amount of retained earn-

ings at the beginning of the period in which the change is made should be included in net income of the period of the change.

   c. The effect of adopting the new principle on income before extraordinary items and on net income (and on the related per share amounts) of the period of the change should be disclosed.

   d. Income before extraordinary items and net income, computed on a pro forma basis, should be shown on the face of the income statements for all periods presented as if the newly adopted accounting principle had been applied during all periods affected. The pro forma amounts include both (a) the direct effects of a change, and (b) nondiscretionary adjustments such as profit sharing expense and certain royalties, and related taxes, that would have been recognized if the newly adopted principle had been followed in prior periods.

The pro forma effects of retroactive application referred to above should be shown on the face of the income statement for income before extraordinary items and net income. The per share amounts on this basis (both primary and fully diluted) should also be shown on the face of the statement. If space does not permit, such per share amounts may be disclosed in a separate schedule or in the notes to the statements with appropriate cross reference; when this is done, the actual per share amounts should be repeated for comparative purposes.

In rare situations the pro forma effects of retroactive application cannot be computed or reasonably estimated for individual prior periods, although the cumulative effect on retained earnings at the beginning of the period of change can be determined. The cumulative effect should then be reported in the income statement as previously noted, and the reason for not showing the pro forma amounts by periods should be explained because the disclosure of these amounts is otherwise required and is expected by users of financial statements.

Computing the effect on retained earnings at the beginning of the period in which a change in accounting is made may sometimes be impossible. In those rare situations, disclosure will be limited to showing the effect of the change on the results of operations of the period of change (including per share data) and to explaining the reason for omitting accounting for the cumulative effect and disclosure of pro forma amounts for prior years. The principal example of this type of accounting change is a change in inventory pricing method from FIFO to LIFO.

Appendix A of Opinion No. 20 contains an example illustrating the disclosures required when there has been a change in accounting principle (including the pro forma disclosures) the cumulative effect of which is included in income.

Business Combinations

One of the most significant pronouncements on accounting matters by the AICPA was Opinion No. 16 issued in 1970 by the APB. This opinion was issued to promote uniformity in practice in determining whether a business combination should be accounted for as a purchase or as a pooling of interests and to prescribe the appropriate disclosures applicable in the circumstances. The preparation of pro forma statements, supplementing the usual historical statements of the constituents of a business combination, is usually necessary to obtain an understanding of the impact of the combination.

Business combinations may be consummated in a variety of ways. For example, a new corporation may be formed to take over the assets and operations of two or more existing businesses, or one or more corporations may merge into another under the applicable state laws. It is important to ascertain whether the combination represents a purchase or a pooling of interests, since the accounting treatment appropriate to a purchase is often vastly different from that appropriate to a pooling.

When a combination is deemed to be a purchase, the assets purchased should be recorded on the books of the acquiring company at cost, that is, cost to the purchasing company. When a combination is deemed to be a pooling of interests, there is no necessity for a new basis of accountability. In a pooling the carrying amounts of the assets of the constituent companies, if stated in conformity with generally accepted accounting principles, should be carried forward by the continuing company, and retained earnings and deficits of the constituent companies should also be carried forward. When a combination results in carrying forward the retained earnings and deficits of the constituent companies, statements of operations issued by the continuing business for the period in which the combination occurs and for any preceding period should ordinarily show the results of operations of the combined interests.

Where the market value of the stock to be issued in a business combination is substantially in excess of the book amount of the net assets of the business to be acquired, it will manifestly be to the advantage of the acquiring company to structure the transaction to qualify as a pooling of interests, since in that event there will be no necessity to account for the excess of such market value over the net assets acquired, the excess will not have to be allocated to tangible and intangible assets, and there will be no need to amortize or depreciate the portion assigned to those assets. In many cases involving business combinations, if the excess cost were to be assignable to such assets, the impact on future earnings would be so great that the transaction, if accountable as a purchase, could not be consummated; it would have to be changed in whatever respects necessary so that it would meet the criteria of a pooling of interests.

Pooling Criteria and Practice under ARB 48.—APB Opinion No. 16 superseded Accounting Research Bulletin No. 48 issued in 1957 by the AICPA's then Committee on Accounting Procedure. ARB No. 48 contained various criteria for determining when a combination could be treated as a pooling of interests. These criteria included continuity of management, relative size of the constituents, and continuity of interests.

Over the years, these criteria became severely eroded in practice. The Chief Accountant of the SEC's Division of Corporation Finance commented on this erosion in 1966. On the matter of *continuity of management,* he said:

The continuity of management standard formerly used in many cases was evidenced by representation on the boards of directors of the combined enterprises. With increasing disparities in the relative sizes of the pooling partners, representation on the Board of Directors is no longer practicable and we have agreed that if the direct operating management of the minor business remains in such capacity, the continuity of management standard for a pooling is satisfied.[3]

On the matter of *relative size,* he said:

The 90%-to-95% test set forth in Bulletin 48 has been eroded to the situation where a contribution as little as ½% by the minor party to a pooling is deemed acceptable.

On the matter of *continuity of interests,* he said:

The continuity of ownership by the former stockholders of Company B in a Company A—Company B merger is a key factor which we have deemed crucial in all poolings. The disposition by the former control group in B of more than 25% of the A shares received by the former B control group has been considered fatal to a pooling of interests by the SEC, absent very unusual circumstances. In a great many more instances, old Group B shareholders have scaled down their disposition plans for the A shares received by them. Among the unusual circumstances where a greater than 25% disposition has occurred in poolings are advanced ages of inactive B control group members with attendant potential estate problems, and ownerships of shares through long established trusts with independent trustees having supervision over trust investment decisions. In other instances a major interest may have been bought out shortly prior to the proposed pooling.

In actual practice, the SEC's holding requirements were less stringent than indicated in the foregoing quotation. The SEC had acquiesced in

[3] Walter Mickelsen, "Recent Developments in the SEC Accounting Field," prepared for AICPA course on "Filing with the SEC," May 24, 1966.

many cases in pooling treatment with respect to an acquisition if a sell-off of the shares received by the controlling group of the acquired entity did not exceed 25% of the total shares of the group in the first year following the combination and an additional 25% in the second year.

Further indications of the deterioration in the application of the pooling criteria under ARB No. 48 may be seen in illustrations from actual practice relating to continuity of ownership, that is, continuity of stock ownership. It was recognized that there could be some immaterial deviations from a rule of 100% continuing ownership without prohibiting the use of·the complete pooling concept. Thus, in a merger transaction in which it was hoped to acquire all of the outstanding stock of the target company, the continuation of a 5% or 6% minority interest was not deemed to destroy the pooling. This permitted deviation from the 100% rule was increased when the SEC did not object to the use of complete pooling accounting in cases involving the severance of a part of stock ownership through cash purchases aggregating 12½% of the total consideration.

An extreme illustration of the erosion of the criteria for pooling accounting may be found in a prospectus issued by N Company (not its real name) late in 1969 in connection with a proposed offering of stock and debentures. The prospectus included a consolidated statement of earnings for "predecessor and pooled companies" for the calendar years 1964 through 1968, for the eight-month periods ended August 31, 1968 and 1969, and also for the calendar year 1968 as adjusted on a pro forma basis primarily with respect to two purchases, one during the year 1968 and one at year-end.

The notes to the consolidated financial statements of N Company and the comments in the prospectus reveal that the results of operations of two companies *purchased for cash* near the end of 1967 were included in the historical consolidated statement of earnings beginning in 1964 (the earliest year in the statement) and until April 1, 1969, when they were sold. However, no justification can be found in AICPA or SEC pronouncements or in accounting practice for including the earnings of purchased companies in a historical earnings statement of the acquiring company for any period prior to the date of purchase. The fact that the earnings of these two acquired companies were shown in the historical consolidated statement of earnings as a one-line item before the determination of net earnings was not a mitigating factor. If there was a rationale justifying the inclusion in historical earnings of the pre-acquisition earnings of companies *purchased for cash,* it is not apparent to the author.

With all the abuses in the application of ARB No. 48, the pressure mounted, and it was apparent that something had to be done. At one point the then chairman of the SEC indicated to a Congressional committee that the SEC might have to step in if the APB did not act expeditiously. Ultimately the APB did act. It adopted two opinions—No. 16 dealing with business combinations, and No. 17 dealing with intangible assets. The SEC worked closely with the APB in developing the opinions. The SEC's suggestions for inclusion in the opinions were somewhat comparable to those finally adopted, except that a suggested requirement for a size test for the utilization of pooling accounting was dropped, and a suggested maximum period for amortization of purchased goodwill was increased to 40 years. In the words of Commissioner Hugh F. Owens, "These were compromises that were necessary to make the opinions acceptable to a majority of accountants and businessmen affected by them, and the Commission supports them." [4]

Pooling Conditions Under APB Opinion No. 16.—APB Opinion No. 16 provides that business combinations which meet *all* of the specified conditions *must* be accounted for by the use of the pooling of interests method; all other business combinations must be accounted for as purchases. The use of the pooling method is mandatory—not optional—where the indicated conditions exist.

The fact that *all* of the conditions requisite to a pooling must be present is a significant change from the position previously taken by the AICPA in ARB No. 48. That pronouncement had provided that the absence of one or more of the pooling criteria would not destroy the pooling, and that the determination as to whether a particular combination was a purchase or a pooling had to be made in the light of all the circumstances. The change effected in APB Opinion No. 16 is obviously an important one and, without doubt, is a direct result of the erosion in practice of the pooling criteria in ARB No. 48.

(In the author's opinion, the fact that the new Opinion insists on compliance with *all* of the stated conditions in order to qualify for pooling treatment may prove to be a weakness in the Opinion. There will be cases where pooling treatment of an acquisition is not desired—as, for example, where a bargain purchase is involved and pooling accounting would be disadvantageous. In that event, the transaction will in all likelihood be structured in such a way that it does not meet all of the pooling conditions and consequently purchase accounting will have to be followed.)

Also, under ARB No. 48 pooling accounting was considered to be optional; accordingly, purchase accounting was sometimes employed even though the transaction qualified for pooling treatment. In a few cases the SEC did not permit this optional treatment if the use of the purchase method gave rise to a "bargain purchase" under which the excess of the book value of net assets acquired over the cost to the acquiring company

---

[4] Hugh F. Owens, speech before Accounting and Auditing Symposium of Texas CPAs, May 25, 1971.

would be amortized as an addition to income (often with no income tax effects) in future years. There have been cases in which the SEC has argued, sometimes successfully and sometimes unsuccessfully, that a transaction qualified for pooling treatment even though the acquiring company felt very strongly that one or more of the pooling criteria had not been met.

In one case, for example, the X Company acquired another company in a transaction which met all the criteria for a pooling under the old rules except one—the consideration issued in the acquisition consisted of *nonvoting* preferred stock. On a purchase basis, it represented a bargain purchase and there would have been a substantial excess of net assets acquired over cost to be taken into future income. The Commission rejected the theory that the use of nonvoting preferred stock eliminated the possibility of employing the pooling method, and insisted that pooling be employed.

In highly condensed form, the conditions requiring pooling of interests accounting under APB Opinion No. 16 are stated below:

1. Each of the combining companies must be autonomous and must not have been a subsidiary or division of another corporation within two years before the plan of combination is initiated (Par. 46a).

This condition is not applicable when a combination is effected with a former subsidiary divested by governmental order or with a company created to hold assets so divested. Under ARB No. 48 poolings with subsidiaries and divisions or other parts of a business were permitted.

2. Each of the combining companies must be independent of the other combining companies (Par. 46b).

An intercorporate investment of 10% or less will not defeat this condition; when the plan of combination is initiated and when it is consummated, there can be no intercorporate investment of more than 10%. Practice under ARB No. 48 permitted complete pooling treatment where there was an exchange of stock following prior acquisitions for cash or non-pooling securities even though such acquisition might have been in excess of 10% of the total outstanding stock of the acquired company. Where this type of acquisition substantially exceeded 10%, practice previously permitted the use of the so-called "part purchase, part pooling" method discussed in this chapter. In the case of transactions of this kind, that is, where the intercorporate holdings exceed 10%, both the complete pooling treatment and the "part purchase, part pooling" treatment are prohibited by APB Opinion No. 16.

3. The combination must be effected in a single transaction or be completed in accordance with a specified plan within one year after the plan is initiated (Par. 47a).

If, for any reason, the terms of the plan are revised, it constitutes a new plan for purposes of testing compliance with this condition. Thus, if a company is acquired 100% as the result of a series of partial exchanges on differing terms, it could not be treated as a pooling. If, on the other hand, the delay in completing the combination is beyond the control of the companies involved (for example, delays caused by governmental proceedings or litigation), it would not defeat the pooling.

4. A corporation offers and issues only common stock with rights identical to those of the majority of its outstanding voting common stock in exchange for substantially all of the voting common stock interest of another company at the date the plan of combination is consummated (Par. 47b).

This provision of the Opinion eliminates the possibility of issuing voting preferred stock and non-voting convertible preferred stock in connection with an acquisition if pooling of interests accounting is desired. Acquisitions using such securities were frequently given pooling treatment under ARB No. 48. "Substantially all of the voting common stock" means 90% or more for this condition.

5. None of the combining companies, in contemplation of effecting the combination, can change the equity interest of the voting common stock by means of abnormal distributions to stockholders or additional issuances, exchanges and retirement of securities within the preceding two year period, or between the dates the combination is initiated and consummated (Par. 47c).

Distributions to shareholders which are no greater than normal are not changes for this condition.

6. Each of the combining companies can reacquire shares of voting common stock only for purposes other than business combinations, and no company can reacquire more than a normal number of shares between the dates the plan is initiated and consummated (Par. 47d).

Under ARB No. 48 corporations frequently reacquired their own shares in the open market for cash, used such shares to acquire other companies, and accounted for such acquisitions as poolings of interest with the specific concurrence of the SEC's accounting staff. The APB now views the acquisition of treasury stock and their use in such circumstances as what they really are, namely, the purchase of a business for cash.

7. The ratio of the interest of an individual common stockholder to those of other common stockholders in a combining company remains the same as a result of the exchange of stock to effect the combination (Par. 47e).

This condition means that each individual common stockholder who ex-changes his stock receives a voting common stock interest exactly in pro-portion to his relative voting common stock interest before the combination is effected. Thus no common stockholder is denied or surrenders his po-tential share of a voting common stock interest in a combined corporation. Because of this provision, for pooling accounting to be available, all com-mon stockholders of the combining company have to be treated exactly alike, and there can be no offers of special rights or packages of securities to certain stockholders that are different from what is offered to other stock-holders.

> 8. The voting rights of common shares issued in connection with a pooling must be exercisable by the stockholders, and the stockholders must not be deprived of or restricted in exercising those rights (Par. 47f).

This condition is not met, for example, if shares of common stock issued in connection with the business combination are transferred to a voting trust, or if the voting rights of shares issued in the combination may not be exercised for a period.

> 9. The combination is resolved at the date the plan is consummated, and no provisions of the plan relating to the issuance of securities (such as contingently issuable shares) or other consideration are pend-ing (Par. 47g).

This condition prevents the use of pooling accounting if shares are con-tingently issuable in the future depending on the attainment of certain earnings levels, or if the market prices of shares issued in the combination meet certain predefined amounts. However, if the transaction provides for placing in escrow a part of the shares issuable in the transaction for release upon resolution of a contingency (litigation or income taxes, for example), pooling treatment will not be denied.

> 10. There must be an absence of certain future planned transactions which would have the effect of negating the entire pooling concept, namely, the uniting of ownership interests and the sharing of the risks and rewards of ownership. The future transactions include: (a) re-acquisition of common stock issued in the combination; (b) financial arrangements for the benefit of former stockholders of a combining company (such as a guaranty of loans secured by stock issued in the combination); or (c) a plan or intention to dispose of a significant part of the assets of the combining companies within two years after the combination other than disposals in the ordinary course of business or to eliminate duplicate facilities or excess capacity (Par. 48).

The last-named provision is intended to prevent the creation of "instant earnings" following a pooling which could have occurred under ARB No. 48 as a result of the sale, shortly after the effective date of a combination, of assets of the acquired company having substantial unrealized appreciation. Even though there is no plan or intention to dispose of a significant portion of the assets, circumstances may arise where a disposal must be made within the two-year period after the pooling combination. If the profit or loss from the disposition has a material effect on the combined net income, separate disclosure of the profit or loss, less applicable tax effect, as an extraordinary item, must be made in the year the disposition occurs. (Par. 60).

APB Opinion No. 16 is not applicable to a group of companies under common control which are being put together for the purpose of a public offering. Thus, companies owned by the same financial interests may be merged and accounted for on a pooling basis even though the conditions set forth in the Opinion are not met (Par. 5). This matter is discussed at greater length on page **21**·50.

Date of Recording Combination.—A business combination accounted for under the pooling method is to be recorded only as of the date the combination is effected (APB Opinion No. 16, Par. 61). This procedure bars the practice followed by a few companies of presenting year-end financial statements adjusted for poolings consummated after the year-end. A combining company should, however, disclose as supplemental information, in notes to financial statements or otherwise, the substance of a combination consummated before financial statements are issued and the effects of the combination on reported financial position and results of operations. Comparative financial statements presented in reports of the resulting combined corporation *after* a combination is consummated should combine earlier financial statements of the separate companies (Par. 61).

An acquisition accounted for as a purchase is to be recorded ordinarily when the assets are received and other assets are given or securities issued (Par. 93).

No Restrictions on Disposition of Shares Issued in a Pooling.—APB Opinion No. 16 does not contain any requirements as to continuity of ownership after a pooling as a condition for pooling accounting. In view of the erosion of that criterion under ARB No. 48, this should not cause surprise. Restrictions on the sale of stock received in a pooling have proved impracticable and arbitrary in the past and had the effect of treating some stockholders differently from others.

The SEC had an unpublished administrative rule under the old pooling rules that restricted controlling stockholders of an acquired company from disposing of stock received in a pooling. The rule was to the effect that such stockholders could sell only 25% of the shares in the first year after a pooling, another 25% in the second year, and without limit thereafter, but exceptions were permitted in certain instances involving very old or very ill controlling persons. Since the SEC concurred in the adoption of APB Opinion No. 16, it is reasonable to assume that the Commission has scrapped—for the present, at least—its previous rules restricting sales by controlling persons.

Accounting for the Pooling.—In general, APB Opinion No. 16 does not provide new rules relating to the preparation of pooled financial statements. The recorded assets and liabilities of the separate companies generally become the recorded assets and liabilities of the combined corporation (Par. 51).

The separate companies may have recorded assets and liabilities under differing methods of accounting, and the amounts may be adjusted to the same basis of accounting if the change would otherwise have been appropriate for the separate company. A change in accounting method to conform the individual methods should be applied retroactively, and financial statements presented for prior periods should be restated (Par. 52).

Effective Date of APB Opinion No. 16.—Opinion No. 16 is effective for business combinations initiated after October 31, 1970. Combinations initiated before November 1, 1970 and consummated on or after that date under the terms prevailing on October 31, 1970 may be accounted for in accordance with the Opinion or the applicable previous pronouncements of the APB and its predecessor committee (Par. 97). Transitional rules are provided for a business combination where a corporation has a minority interest in or exactly 50% of the common stock of a company at October 31, 1970 and thereafter initiates a plan of combination (Par. 99).

Letters to New York Stock Exchange in Connection with Poolings.—Since the adoption of APB Opinion No. 16 on "Business Combinations," the New York Stock Exchange has requested each company applying to list additional shares to be issued in a pooling transaction to furnish the Exchange with a letter from the company setting forth the requirements for pooling of interests accounting together with an indication that the contemplated transaction meets each of those requirements. The Exchange also requests a letter from the issuer's independent public accountants approving the applicability of pooling accounting in relation to the proposed transaction.

The Exchange issues an information sheet outlining the material to be included in the company's letter showing compliance with the pooling conditions. The information sheet follows closely the wording of Opinion No.

16 which has been discussed in the preceding pages. The content of the Exchange's information sheet is reproduced below:

REQUIRED INFORMATION TO BE INCLUDED IN LETTERS OF COMPLIANCE WITH POOLING OF INTERESTS CRITERIA

Each Letter of Compliance with Pooling of Interests Criteria submitted to the New York Stock Exchange by companies wishing to have additional shares of stock listed for the purpose of a business combination to be accounted for as a pooling of interests, must contain the following information (references are to paragraphs of APB Opinion No. 16):

General

A brief statement identifying the companies involved, the date of inception of the plan, the proposed date of consummation of the plan, the number of shares to be issued, and the per cent of ownership to be obtained in the transaction.

Combining Companies (Par. 46)

  (a) A statement that each company is autonomous and is not currently and was not for the two years preceding the initiation of the plan of combination a division or subsidiary of another corporation. The allowed exceptions to the rule are itemized as follows, and should be disclosed:

    1. A new company formed within the preceding two years.

    2. A wholly owned subsidiary distributing voting common stock of its parent and the parent meets the pooling criteria (a Letter of Compliance with Pooling of Interests criteria from the parent must be attached).

    3. A company formed from a division or subsidiary of another corporation (within the past two years prior to the initiation of the plan) in compliance with an order from a governmental authority or judicial body.

  (b) A statement to the effect that the combining companies are independent of each other, i.e. no more than a 10% ownership of one combining company by another combining company at the dates the plan was initiated and when consummated.

Combining of Interests (Par. 47)

  (a) A statement to the effect that the combination will be effected in a single transaction or by a specific plan within 1 year after the plan is initiated.

  (b) A statement to the effect that:

    1. The common stock to be offered and issued carries the same identical rights as the majority of the then outstanding common stock of the issuing corporation and,

    2. At least 90% of the outstanding common stock of the combining corporation will be obtained in the transaction. (If there are intercorporate investments, a schedule showing the computation of compliance with the 90% requirement must be included.)

  (c) A statement to the effect that:

    1. None of the combining companies has changed the equity interest of the voting common stock in contemplation of effecting the combination within two years prior to the initiation of the plan or between the date of initiation and the date of the letter of compliance, and

2. None of the combining companies will effect such a transaction in the period from the date of the letter to the date of consummation. (Normal recurring dividend policy is not considered to violate this rule.)

'(d) A statement to the effect that treasury stock purchased by any of the combining companies between the dates of initiation and consummation is for business purposes other than the business combination and such purchases are in normal and/or nominal amounts in accordance with a systematic pattern of reacquisitions. Include schedules of treasury shares reacquired during the two-year period prior to initiation of the plan and during the period from initiation to the date of the letter, indicating the purpose of such reacquisitions.

(e) A statement to the effect that the ratio of interest of one stockholder to the other stockholders of a combining company will remain the same as a result of the exchange of stock to effect the combination.

(f) A statement that the voting rights, to which the ownership interests in the resulting combined corporation are entitled, are fully exercisable by by the stockholders and the stockholders are neither deprived nor restricted in exercising those rights.

(g) A statement to the effect that the combination will be resolved at the date of consummation and the only contingencies (if any) relate to the settlement of an event prior to the initiation of the plan and not to the anticipation of a future event.

Absence of Planned Transactions (Par. 48)

A statement to the effect that the combining companies, after the consummation of the combination, and acting as the combined company, do not intend and have not agreed to effect the following transactions:

(a) Retire or reacquire, directly or indirectly, all or part of the common stock issued to effect the combination.

(b) Enter into financial arrangements for the benefit of the former stockholders of a combining company.

(c) Dispose of a significant part of the assets of the combining companies within two years after the combination other than disposals in the ordinary course of business of the formerly separate companies and to eliminate duplicate facilities or excess capacity.

The letter, written by the issuing (listing) corporation, must contain the assent of the combining corporation and be accompanied by an opinion of the issuing corporation's independent accountants stating the acceptability of the "pooling of interest" accounting treatment for the proposed combination. This does not preclude, however, the issuing of separate letters by each combining corporation accompanied by an opinion from their respective independent accountants, providing that, in summary, the same conclusion can be reached.

EXAMPLE OF COMPANY'S LETTER TO NYSE SHOWING COMPLIANCE WITH POOLING CRITERIA.—Following is an example of a letter written by a company having securities listed for trading on the New York Stock Exchange in connection with an application to list additional shares of its common to be issued in connection with the acquisition of a company which is to be accounted for as a pooling of interests:

ABC Corporation
(Name of issuing corporation)

(Date)

New York Stock Exchange
11 Wall Street
New York, New York 10005

LETTER OF COMPLIANCE
WITH POOLING OF INTERESTS CRITERIA

ABC Corporation (ABC) has entered into an Agreement dated   (date) with XYZ Corporation (XYZ) pursuant to which ABC will issue, on or about (date), (number) shares of its Common Stock in exchange for __% of the outstanding shares of common stock of XYZ.

The transaction with XYZ will be treated for accounting purposes as a "pooling of interests" in conformity with the requirements of APB Opinion No. 16. The criteria for the "pooling of interests" method of accounting and their relevance to this exchange are outlined below.

Attributes of the Combining Companies

ABC was incorporated in (year) and has never been a subsidiary or division of another corporation. At the dates of initiation of the plan of combination, ABC had no investment in XYZ and has not acquired any investment in XYZ to date.

XYZ was incorporated in (year), resulting from an anti-trust action against NOP Corporation where, in compliance with a court order, NOP was required to divest itself of its XYZ division. XYZ owns shares (__%) of the outstanding common stock of ABC which was acquired prior to the initiation of the plan of combination.

The requirement that 90% of the outstanding voting common stock of the investor combining company be acquired by the issuing company is met as follows:

90% of outstanding common stock (400,000 shares) of the investor combining corporation (XYZ)	360,000
Number of shares of the investor combining corporation to be exchanged.	380,000
Less: The number of shares of voting common stock of the issuing corporation held by the investor combining company (10,000 shares) equated to its own shares by the exchange ratio (1:2).	(20,000)
To be compared with 90% of outstanding common stock (above).	360,000

Manner of Combining Interests

The combination is to be effected in a single transaction on or about (date) as stated in the plan of combination.

The common stock to be issued in the combination is authorized but unissued common stock of ABC Corporation with rights identical to those of the currently outstanding shares as described in the Articles of Incorporation.

Neither ABC nor XYZ has had any transactions changing the total equity interest of the common stock from (date) [(date) for XYZ] to present nor are any equity transactions of this type planned prior to consummation.

ABC acquired, on (date) (number) shares of its common stock in the market for purposes of funding its new stock option plan. This transaction was for a business purpose other than the combination, was of nominal amount, and consequently does not violate paragraph 47d of APB Opinion 16.

XYZ has purchased no treasury shares to date.

The exchange ratio of one share of ABC for two shares of XYZ is applicable to all common stockholders of XYZ and, consequently, the stockholders' relative position within XYZ will remain the same.

The voting rights granted by the provisions of the common stock in the resulting combined corporation will be exercisable by the stockholders.

XYZ is currently in litigation involving the insurance recovery from a building destroyed by fire. The plan provides for an adjustment of the number of shares issued by the issuing corporation if the final settlement of the insurance litigation is different from that currently estimated by XYZ.

Absence of Planned Transactions

The following transactions are not provided for in the Agreement and the combining companies, after the consummation of the combination, and acting as the combined company, do not intend and have not agreed to effect any of the following transactions:

    a. Retire or reacquire, directly or indirectly, all or part of the common stock issued to effect the combination.
    b. Enter into financial arrangements for the benefit of the former stockholders of a combining company.
    c. Dispose of a significant part of the assets of the combining companies within two years after the combination other than disposals in the ordinary course of business of the formerly separate companies, and to eliminate duplicate facilities or excess capacity.

The foregoing is based on facts and conditions known to the combining companies at the date of this letter. Neither company has agreed or intends to agree to any event which would change the criteria between the date of this letter and the date of consummation of the plan. If, however, any events occur during the period from the date of this letter to the consummation of the plan which could bear on the pooling of interests treatment, we will notify you.

                                    ABC Corporation
                                    President

ASSENTED TO:

_____
XYZ Corporation
President

EXAMPLE OF ACCOUNTANT'S LETTER TO NYSE CONCURRING IN POOL-
ING.—As noted in the preceding pages, the New York Stock Exchange
requires not only a letter from the listed corporation showing compliance
with the pooling criteria in APB Opinion No. 16, but also a letter from
the issuing corporation's independent accountants stating the acceptability
of pooling accounting in relation to the proposed transaction. Following is
an example of such an accountant's letter:

New York Stock Exchange
11 Wall Street
New York, New York 10005

We have reviewed the Agreement and Plan of Reorganization between
ABC Corporation and XYZ Corporation along with information and representations submitted to us by the companies, and the accompanying Letter of
Compliance with Pooling of Interests Criteria. This Agreement is to be consummated through the issuance of (number) shares of ABC Corporation Common Stock on or about (date).

In our opinion, based upon the information presented to us as of (date),
this combination conforms in substance with the principles, guides, rules and
criteria of APB Opinion No. 16, and we concur in the treatment of this combination as a pooling of interests.

(Signature of independent accountant)

Before the independent accountant issues such a letter, he should obtain and read copies of the merger or other agreements and the company's
letter to the Exchange. In many cases the accountant will be asked to assist
in drafting the company's letter to the Exchange. In that event, the accountant should make certain that the company's legal counsel reviews and
passes on all matters of legal interpretation.

**Letters to American Stock Exchange in Connection with Pool-
ings.**—The preceding pages of this chapter contain a discussion of the
letters that are required to be furnished to the New York Stock Exchange
in connection with applications to list securities to be issued in a business
combination that is to be accounted for as a pooling of interests. As indicated, letters are required to be furnished (1) by the acquiring company
showing compliance with the pooling conditions set forth in APB Opinion
No. 16, and (2) by the company's independent accountants in support of
the company's position.

The requirements of the American Stock Exchange in this respect are
the same as those of the New York Stock Exchange, although, at the date
of this writing, these requirements have not been formalized.

Pro Forma Statements Under Pooling Method.—In recent years
there has developed reasonable uniformity in practice with respect to the

pro forma financial statements and disclosures required when the pooling method of accounting is to be used. Generally, where a proposed combination is to be accounted for under the pooling method, practice in the preparation of prospectuses or proxy statements has called for the presentation of a pro forma balance sheet at a current date giving effect to the combination as if it had occurred at that date. In addition, pro forma statements of earnings have been presented, usually for the preceding five fiscal years and for any interim periods deemed appropriate, giving effect to the combination as if it had occurred at the beginning of the earliest period included in the statements.

APB Opinion No. 16 requires certain disclosures in the notes to financial statements in the period in which a combination occurs, and calls for similar information on a pro forma basis in data to be given shareholders in connection with a proposed business combination. These disclosures include the following:

1. Details of results of operations of the previously separate companies prior to an actual combination. Details should at least include revenue, extraordinary items, net income, other changes in stockholders' equity and amount and manner of accounting for intercompany transactions (Par. 64d).
2. Description of the nature of adjustments of net assets of the combining companies to adopt the same accounting practices and of the effects of changes on net income previously reported by the separate companies (Par. 64e). See the discussion of this matter on page **21·32**.
3. Details of increases or decreases in retained earnings from changing the fiscal year of a combining company (Par. 64f).

In addition, for the year in which the pooling combination is effected, the notes to the financial statements should contain a reconciliation of the revenue and earnings previously reported by the acquiring company with the pooled amounts currently shown in the financial statements (Par. 64g).

With regard to a pooling that is consummated before financial statements are issued but which was incomplete at the balance sheet date or was initiated after that date, APB Opinion No. 16 provides for certain disclosures in the notes to financial statements with respect to the details of the effect of the pooling. The details should include revenue, net income, earnings per share, and the effects of anticipated changes in accounting methods as if the combination had been consummated at the date of the financial statements (Par. 65). A pro forma balance sheet should be furnished as of the same date to comply with SEC practice.

Accounting Policy Changes in Pooled Pro Forma Statements.— As previously stated, when a business combination qualifies for pooling treatment, a change in accounting method to conform the individual methods of all constituent companies on a uniform basis should be applied retroactively, and financial statements presented for prior periods should be restated (APB Opinion No. 16, par. 52).

In a recent merger with which the author is familiar, the proxy soliciting material filed with the SEC included a pro forma statement of income combining Company A and Company B with adjustments to conform the accounting followed by Company B to the accounting followed by Company A. The SEC took the position initially that the *historical* earnings per share of Company B also had to be restated for the effect of the accounting policy changes that were reflected in the pro forma statements. Before the proxy statement was issued, however, the SEC changed its position and did not require the historical statements of Company B to be adjusted to conform the accounting. The SEC's staff accepted the arguments that the accounting principles which had been consistently followed by Company B (as well as by Company A) were generally accepted, and it would be difficult to justify changing these principles retroactively merely because of a proposed merger that might not be consummated. Furthermore, it was shown that the income of Company B was not affected by more than 5% in any one year presented in the proxy statement (although there was a material adjustment to retained earnings at the beginning of the period). The SEC required the notes to the pro forma statements to contain a disclosure of the reasons for not conforming the historical accounting.

Pro Forma Statements Under Purchase Method.—APB Opinion No. 16 sets forth the disclosures that have to be made when a business combination, to be accounted for as a purchase, has been effected. The notes to financial statements should include supplemental information on a pro forma basis of the following:

a. Results of operations for the current period as though the companies had combined at the beginning of the period, unless the acquisition was at or near the beginning of the period.

b. Results of operations for the immediately preceding period as though the companies had combined at the beginning of that period if comparative financial statements are presented.

As a minimum, the supplemental pro forma information should show revenue, income before extraordinary items, net income, and earnings per share. Interest and preferred stock dividends, income taxes, depreciation, and amortization of assets (including goodwill) should be adjusted to their accounting basis recognized in recording the combination. Pro forma presentation of results of operations of periods prior to the combination transaction should be limited to the immediately preceding period (Par. 96).

It has been the administrative practice of the SEC to require an acquiring company to disclose the contribution to sales and earnings of the acquired company for the year in which a purchase occurs *and in the succeeding year*. It would seem reasonable to expect that the retroactive disclosures required by APB Opinion No. 16 would be considered by the SEC as a substitute for the disclosures for future periods now required under its administrative practice. However, similar disclosures in subsequent years may be required by the SEC if the acquisition represents a separate line of business. (See Chapter **23** for a discussion of lines of business reporting.)

As noted above, the pro forma presentation of results of operations of periods prior to the purchase transaction is limited by the Opinion to the immediately preceding period. This limitation is intended to apply to the presentation of pro forma *combined* results of operations. It does not apply to the presentation of pro forma statements of sole proprietorships, partnerships, Sub-Chapter S corporations, and segments of a business entity to be included in a combination. Where such pro forma statements are to be prepared for a series of years for inclusion in a prospectus or proxy statement filed with the SEC relative to a contemplated purchase combination with a corporation, it is necessary to reflect pro forma adjustments in all years presented for such items as owners' or partners' salaries, income taxes, and, where applicable, home office administrative expense. This procedure is necessary so that each year reflects the results of operations of a business organization on a basis comparable with that of the acquiring corporation. Upon combining these pro forma statements with those of the acquiring corporation, the additional pro forma adjustments giving effect to the new accounting basis recognized in recording the combination should be limited to the current and immediately preceding periods. Further discussion of pro forma statements of sole proprietorships, partnerships, Sub-Chapter S corporations, and segments of a business entity appears elsewhere in this chapter.

The Opinion is silent as to the pro forma financial statements or disclosures to be furnished when (a) a purchase combination is proposed for consideration by shareholders, (b) a purchase combination is effected after the year-end but before the financial statements for the year are issued, and (c) historical financial statements are presented for interim periods. In each of these instances, it would be expected that existing practices would be continued. This would mean that a condensed pro forma balance sheet, together with any explanatory disclosures deemed appropriate, would be presented giving effect to the combination as if it had occurred at the date of the latest balance sheet forming a part of the historical statements which are issued. Where the combination is effected after the year-end, the disclosures would be in the notes to the financial statements.

Example of Purchase Combination.—As an example of a business combination that was accounted for as a purchase, the acquisition by the SUY Oil Producing and Refining Company of the BRN Oil Corporation may be cited. (The names are not real, and the author has taken minor liberties with the facts to bring them into conformity with current requirements of the APB and the SEC.) SUY and BRN were both in all branches of the oil business. Both were producers and refiners and operated retail marketing facilities. SUY had a relatively greater refining and marketing capacity than BRN, whereas the latter had relatively greater producing capability.

SUY acquired approximately one-half of the capital stock of BRN for $45,000,000 in cash. Of the total purchase price, SUY obtained $33,000,000 on a long-term note and pledged the shares of BRN as collateral for the loan. The directors of both companies agreed to merge the companies and submitted the merger proposal to their respective stockholders for approval. The merger agreement provided for the continued existence of SUY and for the conversion of the capital stock of BRN held by outside interests into preferred stock of SUY. Preliminary proxy statements were filed with the SEC.

SUY also filed a registration statement with the SEC under the 1933 Act covering an additional issue of common stock. The proceeds from the sale of the common stock were to be used principally to redeem a portion of the new SUY preferred stock into which BRN's capital stock would be converted pursuant to the terms of the merger. The merger and the financing were mutually interdependent; that is, the merger would not be consummated unless the financing was consummated and vice versa.

Because of the large initial acquisition of BRN's stock for cash, and because the remaining capital stock interests in BRN would, upon the merger becoming effective, be converted into preferred stock of SUY some of which would be redeemed for cash on completion of the common stock financing, it was apparent that the combination of the businesses of SUY and BRN represented, for accounting purposes, a purchase of BRN by SUY. In the circumstances, a new basis of accounting would arise for BRN's assets in the hands of SUY. The consideration paid for BRN's net assets was deemed to be (1) the cash paid on the initial acquisition of about one-half of BRN's stock, plus (2) the value of SUY's preferred stock to be issued in the merger. The total consideration paid and payable by SUY was estimated to be $70,000,000 more than the amount at which BRN's net assets were carried on its books.

Based on a survey of BRN's properties and operations, it was determined that the excess cost of $70,000,000 was applicable entirely to BRN's oil producing properties and related fixed assets, and that the book amounts of the remainder of BRN's assets and liabilities represented fair values. Accordingly, BRN's assets would continue to be carried by SUY at the amounts at which they appeared on BRN's books except that the excess cost ($70,000,000) to SUY of BRN's net assets would be added to the net book amount of BRN's producing properties and fixed assets to be amortized by charges to future periods on the basis of the estimated recoverable units in each property.

The proxy statements and the prospectus contained virtually identical financial statements. Financial statements in conventional form, on a historical basis, were furnished for SUY, and, on a similar basis, for BRN. In addition, pro forma financial statements were furnished to show the effect of the acquisition of BRN by SUY. Inasmuch as interim financial statements were neither required nor furnished, the pro forma balance sheet was based on the balance sheets of the respective companies at the end of their most recent fiscal years included in the proxy statements and prospectus. The pro forma balance sheet contained separate columns for (1) SUY, (2) BRN, (3) adjustments in connection with the merger and financing, and (4) pro forma combining SUY and BRN and giving effect to the merger and financing.

The pro forma income statement was based on the historical (actual) income statements of SUY and BRN, but covered only the most recent fiscal year. It was also prepared on a columnar basis and the adjustments given effect to in the adjustment column were described in detail in a note to the statement as follows:

(1) Depletion and depreciation of the cost to SUY of BRN's producing properties have been recomputed at —— cents per barrel of production. Included in such cost are (a) approximately $70,000,000 representing the excess of cost to SUY of BRN's producing properties over the unamortized cost thereof to BRN, and (b) an allowance of $—— for future development costs required to realize reserves classified as "proven undeveloped" at (date) by (consulting engineers).

(2) Abandoned leases, geophysical research expense, amortization of drilling expenses and dry holes, as reflected in BRN's statements, have been adjusted to SUY's accounting basis.

(3) Annual interest charges on long-term debt have been recomputed to reflect the interest which would have accrued if the full principal amount of (the new debt) had been outstanding during the (year).

(4) Amortization of financing expense has been increased to reflect the cost of issuing the (new debt).

(5) The annual cost of service annuities, including payments for past service annuities covering SUY's employees and for the modification of BRN's pension plan to cover death benefits has been added to "costs and operating expenses." See the information under "Pension Plan" in this (proxy statement/prospectus) as to the status of SUY's and BRN's pension plans.

(6) BRN's selling, general, and administrative expenses and provisions for state income taxes have been reclassified to accord with SUY's classifications; nonrecurring profit of $——— realized by BRN in (year) has been eliminated.

(7) Provisions for income taxes have been increased or decreased, as appropriate, to reflect the above adjustments.

The pro forma income statement also stated that the accounting of each company reflected in the historical statements of each company had been on a consistent basis, but that the accounting practices of the companies had not been identical in that lease rentals, which ultimately are reflected in abandonment or depletion costs, had been capitalized by SUY but had been charged to expense by BRN, and this difference had not been adjusted in the pro forma income statement.

In the foregoing example, the principal adjustments were for depletion and depreciation (arising out of the allocation of the excess cost to fixed assets), interest charges, and income taxes. Frequently it is not possible in the early stages of an acquisition to allocate the excess cost because the studies requisite to such an allocation have not been made or have not been completed. Where this is the case, the SEC has required merely a disclosure of that fact in terms that will put the reader of the pro forma statement on notice. An example of this situation occurred in the prospectus of General Host Corporation (1969) used in connection with its offer to issue its debentures and warrants for common stock in exchange for the outstanding common stock of Armour and Company.

The General Host prospectus included pro forma statements prepared on the basis that the acquisition would be accounted for as a purchase. The pro forma statements were prepared on four sets of assumptions: that Armour would be 51% owned, 60% owned, 80% owned, and 100% owned. It was estimated that the purchase price would exceed the net assets of Armour by $73,248,000 on the 51% basis, $86,249,000 on the 60% basis, $115,152,000 on the 80% basis, and $143,994,000 on the 100% basis. A note to the pro forma combined income statement disclosed these amounts and said, in bold face type, that the statement did not include any amounts for amortization of the estimated excess of the purchase price over the net assets of Armour, because the company (General Host) did not have sufficient information at that time to make any allocation of such excess. The note continued:

> When such allocation can be made, it is intended that the excess will be allocated among Armour's assets based on their present values. To the extent such allocation is made to depreciable or amortizable assets, increased depreciation and amortization could have a material effect on future earnings of General Host Corporation.

Combination of Purchase and Pooling.—Sometimes a business combination may have been effected under circumstances in which it appeared that the combination resulted, in part, from a purchase and, in part, from a pooling. Assume, for example, that Corporation A acquires for cash a majority of the stock of Company S, which thereupon becomes a subsidiary of A and is included in the consolidated financial statements of A and its subsidiaries. Thereafter it is decided to merge S into A by having the shares of S held by the minority interest convert into shares of A. If all the other attributes of a pooling are present, the combination could have been treated for accounting purposes as part-purchase and part-pooling under practice considered consistent with the provisions of ARB No. 48. Except in certain transitional cases, *this accounting treatment is prohibited under APB Opinion No. 16* which requires complete purchase accounting for this kind of transaction.

Because this form of business combination has occurred many times in the past, it deserves some comment. In one such case, Triangle Conduit & Cable Co., Inc. acquired the business of Plastic Wire & Cable Corporation in 1965.

An agreement was entered into between Triangle and Plastic under which Plastic agreed to sell, subject to the approval of its stockholders, substantially all of its assets to a subsidiary of Triangle. In consideration of the sale, Triangle agreed to issue shares of its capital stock plus cash to Plastic which would distribute the stock and cash to its stockholders and dissolve.

Both Triangle and Plastic sought the approval of their shareholders of the proposed transaction and solicited proxies for use at the meetings at which the agreement of sale would be considered. Both companies prepared proxy statements in that connection pursuant to SEC requirements, and the financial statements in both proxy statements were identical. In addition to conventional, historical financial statements of each constituent, the proxy statements contained pro forma financial statements, in which it was indicated that the cash portion of the transaction would be accounted for as a purchase and the stock portion as a pooling—in other words, a part-purchase and part-pooling transaction.

The pro forma balance sheet was prepared in columnar form and showed (1) Triangle at June 30, 1965, (2) Plastic at July 3, 1965, (3) pro forma adjustments, and (4) pro forma combined. It was estimated that the cash portion of the purchase represented 59.2% of the total, and that the remainder of Plastic (40.8%) would be acquired for Triangle stock. The pro forma adjustments reflected in the balance sheet were as follows:

1. The borrowing of $10,000,000 by Triangle on senior notes and convertible subordinated notes; placement expenses incurred were $87,500 which would be amortized over the life of the debt.

2. Cash of $10,081,000 used for the purchase of 59.2% of the net assets of Plastic. The excess ($5,566,000) of the cash purchase price over the underlying book value of 59.2% of the net assets of Plastic was allocated to goodwill.

3. The issuance of 408,000 shares of Triangle (stated value $1 per share) for 40.8% of the net assets of Plastic represented by 1,389,000 of the par value of Plastic's common stock, and the transfer of the difference of $980,000 to capital surplus.

There were other adjustments reflected in the pro forma balance sheet, but they are not relevant to the present discussion. Of the amount assigned to goodwill, it was stated that a portion would be allocated to fixed assets on the basis of an appraisal which, it was estimated, would be completed by November 30, 1965; no reasonable estimate could be made at that time of the amount to be so allocated. Triangle said that it did not intend to amortize the excess of the cash paid for 59.2% of the net assets of Plastic over the book value of such assets except as to that portion which would be allocated to tangible assets as above indicated. (While a failure to amortize goodwill was acceptable procedure at that time, under current practice this would not be acceptable. As a result of the issuance of APB Opinion No. 17, goodwill would have to be amortized over a period not exceeding 40 years.)

The pro forma combined income statement covered the years 1960–1964 and the first half of 1965. As far as the first four years were concerned, the statement combined the income statements of Triangle and Plastic arriving at combined net income before eliminating pre-acquisition earnings applicable to the purchased portion (59.2%) of Plastic. From this amount there was deducted 59.2% of Plastic's earnings, to arrive at the pro forma pooled earnings for the first four years covered by the statement.

Insofar as the pro forma income statement related to 1964 and the first half of 1965, the assumption was made that Plastic was acquired by Triangle on January 1, 1964 partly as a purchase and partly as a pooling. On this basis the combined earnings of the companies were adjusted for the interest expense on the loans incurred in order to buy Plastic. In addition, adjustment was made for the related income tax effect. A note to the pro forma income statement also discussed the impact on future income statements of the excess cost applicable to the portion of Plastic's net assets acquired for cash; the note follows:

> (b) Of the cash consideration being paid by Triangle it is contemplated that a portion will be allocated to property, plant and equipment. When this amount is allocated to specific assets additional charges to depreciation will result. It is not practical to. compute the amounts of such additional depreciation on an annual basis because allocation to specific assets has not progressed to the point where a reasonable estimate can be made. However, because the tax basis of assets will be greater than the book basis arising from this allocation, the effect of such additional depreciation will not be material.

SEC Decisions Distinguishing Between Purchase and Pooling. —A foreign company filed with its registration statement under the 1933 Act a prospectus in which it was stated that the registrant was formed for the purpose of amalgamating a number of existing companies engaged in the oil business. The registrant urged before the Commission that the transaction was a purchase of assets (as distinguished from a pooling of interests) and that therefore the assets of the amalgamation should be stated on the basis of an amount, agreed upon by the several constituents, representing the value of the registrant's shares issued in the transaction. On this basis the consolidated balance sheet would have reported total assets of approximately $14,500,000 and capital surplus in excess of $10,000,000.

The Commission, giving consideration to the nature and effect of the transactions resulting in the formation of the registrant and its absorption of the businesses of its predecessor and subsidiary companies, concluded that the transaction in substance involved a pooling of interests, and that accounting procedures applicable to such a transaction should be followed in setting up the balance sheet of the new company. As a result the consolidated balance sheet of the registrant reported total assets of approximately $8,400,000 and capital surplus of approximately $4,100,000. The Commission did not elaborate on the nature and effect of the transactions which led to the conclusion that the combination was a pooling. [18 SEC Ann. Rep. 14 (1952)]

A company having total assets of $95,000,000 submitted preliminary proxy-soliciting material containing a pro forma balance sheet giving effect to the acquisition of the net assets of a company with total assets of approximately $15,000,000. The registrant issued 115,000 shares of its common stock, $25 par value, for substantially all of the net assets of the company to be acquired. This represented the issuance of approximately 20 per cent additional stock. The sum of $2,296,000, representing the excess of the common stock equity of the company to be acquired over the aggregate par value of registrant's common stock issued therefor, was reflected in the registrant's earned surplus account. The SEC's staff took the position that the business combination represented a purchase and that the accumulated earnings of the company to be acquired in excess of the credit to registrant's common stock account, $2,875,000, should be credited to capital surplus instead of to registrant's earned surplus since the transaction appeared to be, and was represented as, a purchase of net assets. Consequently the pro forma balance sheet was amended to reduce earned surplus by $2,296,000 and to credit capital surplus with the same amount. [18 SEC Ann. Rep. 60 (1952)]

The SEC also considered the accounting implications in a merger resulting in the acquisition of the assets of Company A by the issuance of preferred stock of Company B in exchange for all of the common stock of Company A, which was to be dissolved and its plant operated as a division of Company B. The net assets to be obtained after assumption of liabilities amounted to $1,667,000 less than the aggregate par value of the preferred stock to be issued, and Company B, the registrant, indicated it would charge off this difference of $1,667,000 to earned surplus. SEC advised the registrant that the proposed accounting treatment appeared to be inappropriate since it appeared that the merger plan was developed primarily for the purpose of acquiring additional plant. The registrant stated that the other company was acquired in order to obtain urgently needed building space and that the past earnings of the acquired company did not justify capitalization of any part of the consideration as having been paid for goodwill or for any other intangible. Accordingly, the registrant filed an amendment in which it was stated that the difference would be added to the cost of buildings. [19 SEC Ann. Rep. 20 (1953)]

Significant Acquisiton During Latest Fiscal Year.—Company A acquired for cash 82 per cent of the common stock (constituting the only class of stock) of Company B. The acquisition of control was made in the latter part of A's fiscal year. Company A assumed the management of Company B and operated it as a subsidiary until its merger into Company A just before the end of A's fiscal year. In the merger the shares of B held by the minority stockholders were converted into shares of common stock of A.

For the fiscal year prior to acquisition of control of B, that company had sales which were approximately one-half those of A. B's total assets and net assets were also material in relation to those of A. By any measure of significance the acquisition of control of Company B was a major event in the corporate history of Company A. The acquisition of the initial controlling block of B was financed by cash in A's treasury.

Company A filed a registration statement with the SEC under the 1933 Act for the purpose of refunding its outstanding long-term debt and preferred stock. The offering prospectus contained a consolidated summary of earnings of Company A including the earnings of B from the date of acquisition of control. Also in the prospectus was a summary of earnings of Company B for the period prior to acquisition of control by Company A. Both of the aforementioned summaries were "actual." Also included in the prospectus was a pro forma summary of earnings which combined the two summaries aforementioned. Presumably this pro forma summary was furnished with the thought that the earning power of the enterprise as then constituted was more fairly presented by a pro forma summary which combined the earnings of Company A and Company B.

The requirements of APB Opinion No. 16 applicable to the financial statements of an acquiring company for the period in which a purchase combination occurs (including the furnishing of pro forma information) are set forth on page **21**·39.

Pro Forma Statements Giving Effect to Purchase Transaction Completed Subsequent to Statement Date.—Subsequent to the date of a balance sheet and before its issuance, a transaction may be consummated (or an event may occur) which is so material that the transaction (or the event) should be disclosed as supplementary information in pro forma financial statements or in notes to the financial statements. Assume, for example, that a company having a fiscal year ending September 30 acquires on the following November 1 the assets of another company. The acquisition increases the company's assets from $15,000,000 to $26,000,000. The acquisition also increases the company's liabilities since it is financed largely by borrowing. Currently, general practice would require that a consummated transaction of such significance be disclosed in some way in a balance sheet prepared as of September 30. Some accountants also believe that, in addition to presenting the actual balance sheet at September 30, there should also be presented a pro forma balance sheet at that date giving effect to the November 1 acquisition and the related financing. Frequently these balance sheets are presented in columnar form, the first column showing the actual balance sheet at September 30 and the second column a pro forma balance sheet at that date. The headnote of the statement would indicate that the pro forma balance sheet gives effect to the acquisition of certain assets on November 1 and the method by which the acquisition was financed. The headnote would also make reference to a note to the financial statements which would describe the acquisition and related financing in some detail. Alternatively, the pro forma information could be furnished in condensed form in a note to the September 30 financial statements.

In an actual case filed with the SEC, the detailed note to the financial statements read as follows:

Under the provisions of a contract dated September 23, 19_____, the company purchased on November 1, 19_____, the assets of (name of company) including plants in (cities), inventories, and certain other assets; assumed certain liabilities of that company and paid the balance of the purchase price from funds borrowed from a bank. These transactions are reflected in the accompanying pro forma balance sheet which gives effect as of September 30, 19_____, to (a) the loan of $ from (name of bank), (b) the purchase of the assets of (name of company) for $, and (c) the settlement of the purchase price by (1) the assumption of $ liabilities and (2) the payment of $ in cash, all of which transactions were consummated as of November 1, 19_____.

Inasmuch as this was a completed transaction, the certifying accountant had no difficulty in expressing an opinion on the pro forma balance sheet which gave retroactive effect to a subsequent transaction. The certificate related to both the actual and pro forma balance sheets as follows:

We have examined the balance sheet of (name of company) as of September 30, 19_____, and the related statements of income, earned surplus and changes in financial position for the years ended September 30, 19_____ and 19_____. Our examination was made in accordance with generally accepted auditing standards and accordingly included such tests of the accounting records and such other auditing procedures as we considered necessary in the circumstances. We have also examined the accompanying pro forma balance sheet which is based upon the aforementioned balance sheet and gives effect to the transactions set forth in Note 1.

In our opinion, (a) the accompanying balance sheet and statements of income, earned surplus and changes in financial position present fairly the financial position of (name of company) at September 30, 19_____, and the results of their operations and changes in financial position for the years ended September 30, 19_____ and 19_____, in conformity with generally accepted accounting principles applied on a consistent basis, and (b) the accompanying pro forma balance sheet presents fairly the financial position of the company as it would have appeared at September 30, 19_____, had the transactions set forth in Note 1 been consummated at that date.

That portion of APB Opinion No. 16 relating to the accounting for business combinations on the basis of a purchase requires, as supplemental information, additional disclosures concerning earnings of the purchased entity. This requirement is discussed on page **21·39**.

The reader is also referred to the discussion under "Events Subsequent to the Statement Date" beginning on page **12·1** particularly as it refers to SAP No. 47 (1971). As that statement pointed out, certain subsequent events may be so significant that disclosure can best be made by supplementing the historical financial statements with pro forma financial data giving effect to the event as if it had occurred on the balance sheet date.

Two or More Businesses Under Common Control Combined Into One Corporation.—Two corporations which were under common ownership and control were combined into a single corporation. A new corporation was formed which issued its common stock for the assets and business of the two predecessor corporations, and assumed their liabilities. In addition to being affiliated in the sense that the predecessors were under common control, the businesses of the predecessors were similar in some respects and complementary in others. The successor corporation filed a registration statement with the SEC under the 1933 Act covering a new issue of preferred stock. At the date of the public offering, the business previously conducted by the two predecessor companies was being conducted by the successor corporation.

In its Opinion No. 16, the APB said that the term "business combination" as used in the Opinion did not include a transfer of net assets or exchange of shares between companies under common control such as between two subsidiaries of the same parent (par. 5 of the Opinion). Nonetheless, in the case cited above the financial statements presented in the registration statement were on a pooled basis which simply combined the amounts in the statements of the predecessors with appropriate eliminations for intercompany transactions.

Furthermore, the financial statements were not designated "pro forma" since the position was taken that they were historical statements in that they merely combined the historical figures of two companies which were combined and operated as one.

This situation is frequently encountered when the owner of a group of companies decides to go public. In that connection, he combines the various businesses into a single enterprise, and the financial statements he furnishes are those of the combined companies on a pooled basis with a disclosure of the method of their preparation.

Pro Forma Earnings Per Share.—The computation of earnings per share is commented upon in Chapter **10** in connection with the discussion of the summary of earnings.

In the preparation of financial statements relating to proposed business combinations, pro forma earnings per share data must be shown in the statement of income for all years which give effect to the business combination. In addition, the registrant should be prepared, if requested, to furnish to the staff of the SEC, as supplemental information, the computations of the per share data.

Apart from business combinations, pro forma earnings per share must also be shown as supplementary data (preferably in a note to the financial statements) when certain transactions occur during the latest period or shortly after the close of the period but before completion of the financial reports. These transactions include conversions of securities, either with dilutive or incremental effect, and cash sales of common stock or common stock equivalents where a portion or all of the proceeds is to be used to retire preferred stock or debt. In each case there must be disclosed the effect on primary earnings per share as if the conversion or the retirement had taken place at the beginning of the period or at the date of the issuance of the convertible security or retired security if the issuance occurred within the period.

PROXIES AND PROXY STATEMENTS

CONTENTS

What Is a Proxy?—A proxy is a device whereby a security holder authorizes another person or group of persons to act for him at a meeting of security holders—in effect a power of attorney. With the tremendous increase in ownership of American corporations, it is doubtful whether a large corporation could assemble a quorum at stockholders' meetings unless the stockholders authorized other persons to vote their shares at the meeting.

If the only business to be transacted at a meeting related to the election of directors, a typical form of proxy would read somewhat as follows:

PROXY

Annual meeting of stockholders of (name of company)

The undersigned, revoking all prior proxies, hereby appoints (names of persons), or any one of them, proxies with full power of substitution to vote all of the shares the undersigned is entitled to vote at the annual meeting of stockholders to be held at (location of meeting) on (date) at (time), and all adjournments thereof, and to vote upon the following matters:

(1) The election of directors;
(2) Upon such other business as may properly come before the meeting or any adjournment or adjournments thereof; all as more fully set forth

in the Notice of Meeting and Proxy Statement, receipt of which is hereby acknowledged.

This proxy is solicited on behalf of the management.

Dated _____

_____
(Signature(s))

In the case of solicitations subject to the SEC's proxy rules, the request for the proxy is accompanied by a proxy statement, which is discussed in this chapter.

In a more complicated situation, involving not only the election of directors but also certain proposals made by management, the proxy might read as follows:

(Name of company)
PROXY—ANNUAL MEETING—(Date)

The undersigned hereby appoints (names of persons), and each of them, proxies, with power of substitution, to vote for the undersigned at the Annual Meeting of Shareholders of (name of company), to be held at (city), on (date), or any adjournments thereof, with all the powers the undersigned would possess if personally present:

(1) For the election of a Board of (number) Directors to serve until the next Annual Meeting, and until their successors are elected and shall qualify; or check here ☐ if authority is to be withheld;

(2) FOR ☐ or AGAINST ☐ approval of a Reorganization Agreement providing for the acquisition of substantially all of the assets of (company) by (company), as described in the accompanying Proxy Statement.

(3) FOR ☐ or AGAINST ☐ a proposed increase in (company's) authorized Common Stock from (number) to (number) shares, as described in the accompanying Proxy Statement.

(4) FOR ☐ or AGAINST ☐ a proposed Qualified Stock Option Plan for the benefit of selected (company) employees (including Officers and Directors), as described in the accompanying Proxy Statement.

(5) Upon all matters which may properly come before the meeting.

This proxy is solicited by the management and will be voted for the Election of Directors and FOR Proposals 2, 3 and 4 unless otherwise specified. The undersigned acknowledges receipt of the accompanying Notice of the Meeting and Proxy Statement.

Dated .... ,

....
(*Signature of Stockholder*)

Proxy Solicitation Required by New York and American Stock Exchanges.—The SEC does not require corporations or their managements to solicit proxies. For many years, however, the New York Stock Exchange, in the interest of public policy and improved stockholder relations, urged that all listed companies make it a regular practice to solicit proxies for all meetings of stockholders. The Exchange believes that this practice, now followed by the great majority of listed companies, should be normal procedure for publicly owned companies. Accordingly, a new agreement, which provides for solicitation of proxies as a matter of agreement with the Exchange, was added, effective June 1, 1955, to the Exchange's standard listing agreements. Its purpose and intent is to afford stockholders a convenient method of voting, after full disclosure of relevant information, on matters which may be presented at stockholders' meetings. The Exchange states that exceptions to the new policy will be made only under unusual and special circumstances.

The listing agreement requiring proxy solicitation is Agreement No. 5 of Section III of the current form of listing agreements and reads as follows: "5. The Corporation will solicit proxies for all meetings of Stockholders."

Acting on the recommendation of the Special Committee for Study of the American Stock Exchange, the listing agreements of the American Stock Exchange have been revised to include a provision relating to the solicitation of proxies. Agreement No. 6 of the current form of listing agreements is as follows: "The Corporation will solicit proxies (pursuant to proxy statements conforming to the proxy rules of the Securities and Exchange Commission) for *all* meetings of stockholders at which holders of securities listed on the Exchange have the right to vote."

Although *preliminary* proxy material must be filed with the SEC, such material, under SEC rules, does not have to be filed with the exchanges. The *definitive* proxy material must be filed both with the SEC and the exchanges. The exchanges, however, are glad to review and comment on preliminary or draft copies of the proxy material if action is to be taken at the stockholders' meeting relating to matters which may affect the rights of the company's listed securities, or if it will result in the creation of new securities which the company may desire to list on the exchanges. Review by the exchanges may be helpful to the company in avoiding actions or situations which conflict with the requirements or policies of the exchanges.

Statutory Basis for Proxy Regulation.—The Securities Exchange Act of 1934 contains provisions relating to solicitation of proxies. Section 14(a) provides as follows:

It shall be unlawful for any person, by the use of the mails or by any means or instrumentality of interstate commerce or of any facility of a national securities exchange or otherwise, in contravention of such rules and regulations as the Commission may prescribe as necessary or appropriate in the public interest or for the protection of investors, to solicit or to permit the use of his name to solicit any proxy or consent or authorization in respect of any security (other than an exempted security) registered pursuant to section 12 of this title.

A similar statutory provision exists in Section 20(a) of the Investment Company Act of 1940, which provides as follows:

It shall be unlawful for any person, by use of the mails or any means or instrumentality of interstate commerce or otherwise, to solicit or to permit the use of his name to solicit any proxy or consent or authorization in respect of any security of which a registered investment company is the issuer in contravention of such rules and regulations as the Commission may prescribe as necessary or appropriate in the public interest or for the protection of investors.

Pursuant to the authority contained in the laws which it administers, the SEC promulgated Regulation 14A (formerly designated Regulation 14), relating to solicitation of proxies.

See also the discussion in this chapter relating to Regulation 14C pursuant to which companies may have to send an "information statement" to security holders if proxies are *not* solicited.

Proxy Requirements and Foreign Issuers.—For a discussion of proxies in relation to foreign issuers, see the discussion in Chapter **31**.

Regulation 14A.—Regulation 14A is the SEC's comprehensive regulation relating to the solicitation of proxies with respect to the securities of companies registered under Section 12 of the 1934 Act. The regulation is also applicable in respect of any security of which a registered investment company is the issuer. The regulation does not apply to the securities of unregistered issuers or to certain other exceptions noted in the rules.

Regulation 14A consists of a number of rules, a brief indication of the scope of which is indicated by the following listing:

Rule No.	Subject
14a–1	Definitions
14a–2	Solicitations to which the rules apply
14a–3	Information to be furnished to security holders
14a–4	Requirements as to the form of proxy
14a–5	Presentation of information in proxy statement
14a–6	Material required to be filed
14a–7	Mailing communications for security holders
14a–8	Proposals of security holders
14a–9	False or misleading statements
14a–10	Prohibition of certain solicitations
14a–11	Special provisions applicable to election contests
14a–12	Solicitation prior to furnishing required proxy statement

INFORMATION TO BE FURNISHED SECURITY HOLDERS; RULE 14a–3.— The proxy regulation provides in Rule 14a–3 that proxies subject to the regulation may not be solicited unless each person solicited is concurrently furnished or has previously been furnished with a written proxy statement containing the information specified in Schedule 14A, which is part of the regulation. The scope and content of Schedule 14A are described in this chapter.

There is an important distinction between proxies and proxy statements on the one hand and all other registration and report forms on the other hand which corporations are required to file under the 1934 Act. The registration statements and reports are filed with the SEC and, if the company's securities are listed on an exchange, with the exchange, whereas the proxies and proxy statements *must be furnished to security holders*. Not only are the proxy statements an exceedingly effective disclosure instrument but, what may be equally important, the proxy materials are furnished to the shareholder *at the time* when he has to make a decision.

If the solicitation is made on behalf of the management of the issuer and relates to an annual meeting of security holders at which directors are to be elected, each proxy statement furnished pursuant to the rules must be accompanied or preceded by an annual report to such security holders which complies with specified requirements among which the most important are described below.

The annual report has to contain, in comparative columnar form, such financial statements for the last two fiscal years, prepared on a consistent basis, as will in the opinion of the management adequately reflect the financial position of the issuer at the end of each such year and the results of its operations for each year. (This SEC requirement reflects and makes mandatory what had previously been an AICPA recommendation. ARB No. 43 in 1953 recommended the use of comparative financial statements in annual and other reports.) At the request of the issuer, the SEC may permit the omission of financial statements for the earlier of the two years upon a showing of good cause therefor. Investment companies subject to the Investment Company Act of 1940 need include financial statements only for the last fiscal year.

Consolidated financial statements of the issuer and its subsidiaries must be included if they are necessary to reflect adequately the financial position and results of operations of the issuer and its subsidiaries. In that case, however, the individual (unconsolidated) statements of the issuer may be omitted even though they are required to be included in reports to the Commission (in Form 10-K, for instance).

Any differences, reflected in the financial statements included in the report to security holders, from the principles of consolidation or other accounting principles or practices, or methods of applying accounting principles or practices, applicable to the financial statements of the issuer filed (or proposed to be filed) with the SEC, which have a material effect on the financial position or results of operations of the issuer, have to be noted and the effect thereof reconciled or explained in such report.

The meaning and significance of this requirement can be clarified by an example, which follows.

Example 1. Omission of cost of goods sold.

A company furnishes its security holders with an annual report that includes an income statement. The statement differs from the one furnished to the SEC in that the latter, in conformity with the requirements of Regulation S–X, will show cost of goods sold. The report to security holders shows the details of cost and expenses as follows:

	This Year	Last Year
Cost of goods sold and expenses, exclusive of items listed below	$762,802,287	$720,126,302
Taxes, except Federal income taxes	21,467,617	18,703,953
Rent expense—net	14,649,510	14,510,567
Depreciation	12,702,677	11,479,256
Maintenance and repairs	6,769,564	6,923,472
	$818,391,655	$771,743,550

A note to the financial statements in the published report indicates that the foregoing amounts of costs and expenses will be reported differently in the financial statements filed with the SEC. The note reads as follows:

Costs and expenses are reported to the Securities and Exchange Commission in accordance with its requirements as follows:

	This Year	Last Year
Cost of goods sold, including occupancy and buying costs	$650,702,300	$613,146,836
Selling, publicity, general, and administrative expenses	162,115,073	153,675,841
Provision for doubtful accounts	5,574,282	4,920,873
	$818,391,655	$771,743,550

The statements in the annual report to security holders may omit such details or employ such condensation as may be deemed suitable by the management of the issuer, provided, that such statements, considered as a whole in the light of other information contained in the report may not by such procedure omit any material information necessary to a fair presentation or to make the financial statements not misleading under the circumstances.

The SEC has emphasized on many occasions the importance of disclosing sales and cost of goods sold in income statements, and has taken the position that such information is essential for financial analysts and security holders. When this information is omitted from an income statement, in the eyes of the SEC the statement does not fairly present results of operations. Consequently, when there is a solicitation of proxies in circumstances where the SEC's Rule 14a–3 is applicable, the published report to security holders must disclose sales and cost of goods sold. As noted in the above-noted example, however, the presentation of cost of goods sold in the published report need not conform precisely with the presentation in the SEC report, but, when it differs, it must be explained in the published report along the lines of the explanation in the example.

Depending on their materiality, financial statements of unconsolidated subsidiaries and 50% owned companies may have to be included in the SEC annual report, even though they are not included in the published report to security holders. In the published report, the significant information with respect to such companies—that is, the equity in their net assets and in their undistributed earnings for the year(s)—is often given in notes to the financial statements. Despite this difference in presentation, it has not been the policy of the SEC to insist on conforming the published report in this respect with the presentation in the document filed with the Commission, nor is it necessary to disclose in the published report the difference in presentation.

As a result of the issuance of APB Opinion No. 18 (effective for fiscal periods beginning after December 31, 1971), there should be a lessening of the differences between annual reports to the SEC and those to security holders, as well as in the content of the notes referred to above. Opinion No. 18 requires that the equity method of accounting be used with respect to (1) unconsolidated subsidiaries (both domestic and foreign), (2) corporate joint ventures, and (3) corporate investments in voting stock where such investment permits significant influence over operating and financial policies even if 50% or less of the voting stock is held. (A holding of 20% or more is presumed to create such influence.) Under the equity method, the holder of the investment recognizes its share of earnings or losses in the period for which they are reported by the entity in which the investment is owned. Thus, at least as to earnings, the effect will be the same as in a consolidation. In addition, the Opinion may well result in a reduction in the subsidiaries not included in consolidation.

One of the most obvious differences between financial statements in published reports to security holders and those in reports filed with the SEC is in the volume of so-called "compliance" notes in the latter which are not ordinarily included in published reports. These are the notes to financial statements called for by Regulation S–X, some of which have become necessary disclosure items in published reports, but others have not been considered that essential. An example of the latter is the description of some of the details relating to a company's stock option plan which, pursuant to Regulation S-X, must be included in financial statements filed with the SEC, whereas the accounting profession does not agree that this information is needed by the average reader of financial statements. Despite the omission of this information from the published report, it does not require comment in that report.

The financial statements in the annual report to security holders have to be certified by independent public accountants for at least the last fiscal year unless (1) the corresponding statements included in the issuer's annual report filed (or to be filed) with the SEC for the same fiscal year are not required to be certified, or (2) the SEC finds in a particular case that certification would be impracticable or would involve undue effort or expense.

Subject to the requirements for financial statements which have been summarized above, the annual report to security holders may be in any form deemed suitable by the management.

If the issuer has not previously submitted to its security holders an annual report pursuant to the rules and regulations under Section 14 (relating to solicitation of proxies) of the 1934 Act, the report must also contain such information as to the business done by the issuer and its subsidiaries during the fiscal year as will, in the opinion of the management, indicate the general nature and scope of the business of the affiliated group.

The foregoing requirements with respect to the furnishing of an annual report and its content do not apply to solicitations made on behalf of the management before the financial statements are available (1) if solicitation is being made at the time in opposition to the management, and (2) if the management's proxy statement includes an undertaking in bold-face type to furnish such annual report to all persons being solicited, at least twenty days before the date of the meeting. (The requirements with respect to a participant in a contested election are discussed briefly under "Election Contests.")

Seven copies of each annual report sent to security holders pursuant to Rule 14a–3 have to be mailed to the Commission, solely for its information, not later than the date on which such report is sent to security holders or the date on which preliminary copies of solicitation material are filed with the Commission, whichever date is later. The annual report is not deemed to be "soliciting material" or to be "filed" with the Commission or subject to this regulation otherwise than as provided in Rule 14a–3 or to the liabilities of Section 18 of the Act, except to the extent that the issuer specifically requests that it be treated as a part of the proxy soliciting material or incorporates it in the proxy statement by reference.

A note to Rule 14a–3 requests the managements of issuers to assist the SEC's staff by indicating in a letter transmitting to the SEC copies of their annual reports, or in a separate letter, whether the financial statements in the report reflect a change from the preceding year in any accounting principles or practices or in the method of applying any such principles or practices.

Following is the relevant portion of a letter that one company wrote to the SEC with respect to accounting changes in the current year:

. . . Pursuant to Rule 14a–3, we also enclose seven copies of the Company's (year) annual report to stockholders, which was also mailed yesterday. The annual report is not deemed to be a part of the proxy soliciting material.

Certain accounting changes have been made in the financial statements from the preceding year, as are presented in Notes _____ and _____ to the consolidated financial statements in the annual report. These changes refer to the adoption of the percentage of completion method of accounting for long-term contracts and the adoption of a policy of expensing all research and development costs as incurred . . .

MATERIAL REQUIRED TO BE FILED; RULE 14a–6.—Five *preliminary* copies of the proxy statement and form of proxy and any other soliciting material to be concurrently furnished to security holders must be filed with the Commission at least 10 days prior to the date definitive copies of such material are first sent to security holders, or such shorter period prior to that date as the Commission may authorize. Five preliminary copies of any additional soliciting material, relating to the same meeting or subject matter, furnished to security holders subsequent to the proxy statement must be filed with the Commission at least two days prior to the date copies of such material are first sent to security holders, or such shorter period prior to such date as the Commission may authorize.

Eight *definitive* copies of the proxy statement, form of proxy, and all other soliciting material, in the form in which such material is furnished to security holders, must be filed with the Commission not later than the date such material is first sent to security holders. Three copies of such material shall at the same time be filed with each national securities exchange upon which any security of the issuer is listed and registered.

The definitive material filed with the Commission should be accompanied by a letter indicating any material changes which have been made therein, other than those made in response to the staff's comments, and, whenever possible, should also be accompanied by a marked copy of the definitive material indicating the changes made therein.

FALSE OR MISLEADING STATEMENTS; RULE 14a–9.—The regulation provides (in Rule 14a–9) that no solicitation subject to the regulation shall be made by means of any proxy statement, form of proxy, notice of meeting, or other communication containing any statement which, at the time and in the light of the circumstances under which it is made, is false or misleading with respect to any material fact, or which omits to state any material fact necessary in order to make the statements therein not false or misleading or necessary to correct any statement in any earlier communication with respect to the solicitation of a proxy for the same meeting or subject matter which has become false or misleading.

The rule also states that the filing of proxy material with the Commission, or the examination of such material by the Commission, is not to be deemed a finding by the Commission that such material is accurate or complete or not false or misleading or that the Commission has passed upon the merits of the statements contained therein or any matter to be acted upon by security holders. Representations to the contrary are prohibited.

Schedule 14A.—Rule 14a–3 (noted above) provides that no solicitation subject to the proxy regulation shall be made unless each person solicited is concurrently furnished, or has previously been furnished, with a written proxy statement containing the information specified in Schedule 14A. The schedule is a part of the total scheme of proxy regulation and sets forth the requirements as to the content of proxy statements subject to the regulation. The schedule contains 22 "items" of information and related instructions which are applicable in specified situations depending on the particular matters to be acted upon at the meeting of security holders.

The scope of Schedule 14A is indicated by the following listing of items of information to be furnished when applicable:

Item No.	*Subject*
1	Revocability of proxy
2	Dissenters' rights of appraisal
3	Persons making the solicitation
4	Interest of certain persons in matters to be acted upon
5	Voting securities and principal holders thereof
6	Nominees and directors
7	Remuneration and other transactions with management and others
8	Selection of auditors
9	Bonus, profit sharing and other remuneration plans
10	Pension and retirement plans
11	Options, warrants, or rights
12	Authorization or issuance of securities otherwise than for exchange
13	Modification or exchange of securities
14	Mergers, consolidations, acquisitions, and similar matters
15	Financial statements
16	Acquisition or disposition of property
17	Restatement of accounts
18	Action with respect to reports
19	Matters not required to be submitted
20	Amendment of charter, by-laws, or other documents
21	Other proposed action
22	Vote required for approval

The principal items of interest to accountants are Items 8, 12, 13, 14, 15, and 17. These items and their requirements are discussed in the following pages.

ITEM 8, SELECTION OF AUDITORS.—There is no law or SEC rule requiring corporations to submit to stockholders the question of electing independent auditors or ratifying the selection of auditors by a committee, except in the case of regulated investment companies. Section 32(a) of the Investment Company Act of 1940 contains provisions relating to the selection or ratification of independent public accountants. That section of the 1940 law provides as follows:

. . . It shall be unlawful for any registered management company or registered face-amount certificate company to file with the Commission any financial statement signed or certified by an independent public accountant, unless—

1. Such accountant shall have been selected at a meeting held within thirty days before or after the beginning of the fiscal year or before the annual meeting of stockholders in that year by a majority of those members of the Board of Directors who are not investment advisers of, or affiliated persons of an investment adviser of, or officers or employees of, such registered company;
2. Such selection shall have been submitted for ratification or rejection at the next succeeding annual meeting of stockholders if such meeting be held, except that any vacancy occurring between annual meetings, due to the death or resignation of the accountant, may be filled by the Board of Directors;
3. The employment of such accountant shall have been conditioned upon the right of the company by vote of a majority of the outstanding voting securities at any meeting called for the purpose to terminate such employment forthwith without any penalty; and
4. Such certificate or report of such accountant shall be addressed both to the Board of Directors of such registered company and to the security holders thereof.

The 1940 Act also contains provisions where the selection of accountants has been rejected or their employment terminated.

Despite the fact that it may not be required by law or regulation, many corporations submit to vote of their stockholders the matter of election of auditors or ratification of their appointment. In this situation, Item 8 of the proxy regulation is applicable. If action is to be taken with respect to the selection or approval of auditors, or if it is proposed that particular auditors shall be recommended by any committee to select auditors for whom votes are to be cast at the meeting of stockholders, the auditors must be named, and there must be a brief description of any direct financial interest or any material indirect financial interest in the issuer or any of its parents or subsidiaries, or any connection during the past three years with the issuer or any of its parents or subsidiaries in the capacity of promoter, underwriter, voting trustee, director, officer, or employee.

The instructions of Item 8 are intended to elicit information bearing on the question of the independence of the accountants to be selected or approved by stockholders at the meeting, either directly or through a committee to select the auditors. The SEC, as a major matter of policy, has been particularly insistent that accountants who certify statements for filing with it be, in fact, independent. (See the discussion of this subject in Chapter **26**.) In the proxy statement the management (or any other person making the solicitation) will usually make an inquiry to determine whether the auditors have a direct financial interest or a material indirect financial interest in the companies, and whether the auditors had any connection with the companies in the capacities named. If the response on all these points is negative, a statement to that effect is not required in the proxy statement. A disclosure must be made only if there *is* a financial interest or if there *was* a connection in the capacities named. Whether or not a disclosure must be made of such an interest or connection, the persons making the solicitation will frequently ask the accountant to furnish a letter setting forth the interest or connection, if any. A typical form of letter for this purpose follows:

We understand that the Audit Committee of the Board of Directors of your company has designated our firm to act as independent auditors of the company for the year 19___, subject to ratification by the stockholders at their meeting to be held on (date). In that connection, we advise you as follows:

1. Neither the firm nor any of its partners has any direct financial interest or any material indirect financial interest in the company or any of its parents or subsidiaries; and
2. Neither the firm nor any of its partners has had any connection during the years 19___, 19___, and 19___ with the company or any of its parents or subsidiaries in the capacity of promoter, underwriter, voting trustee, director, officer, or employee.

Item 12, Authorization or Issuance of Securities Otherwise than for Exchange.—If action is to be taken at the meeting with respect to the authorization or issuance of any securities otherwise than for exchange for outstanding securities of the issuer, there must be furnished the following information:

(a) State the title and amount of securities to be authorized or issued.

(b) Furnish a description of the securities such as would be required to be furnished in an application on the appropriate form for their registration on a national securities exchange. If the terms of the securities cannot be stated or estimated with respect to any or all of the securities to be authorized, because no offering thereof is contemplated in the proximate future, and if no further authorization by security holders for the issuance thereof is to be obtained, it should be stated that the terms of the securities to be authorized, including dividend or interest rates, conversion prices, voting rights, redemption prices, maturity dates, and similar matters will be determined by the board of directors. If the securities are additional shares of common stock of a class outstanding, the description may be omitted except for a statement of the pre-emptive rights, if any. Where the statutory provisions with respect to pre-emptive rights are so indefinite or complex that they cannot be stated in summarized form, it will suffice to make a statement in the form of an opinion of counsel as to the existence and extent of such rights.

(c) Describe briefly the transaction in which the securities are to be issued, including a statement as to (1) the nature and approximate amount of consideration received or to be received by the issuer, and (2) the approximate amount devoted to each purpose so far as determinable, for which the net proceeds have been or are to be used. If it is impracticable to describe the transaction in which the securities are to be issued, state the reason, indicate the purpose of the authorization of the securities, and state whether further authorization for the issuance of the securities by a vote of security holders will be solicited prior to such issuance.

(d) If the securities are to be issued otherwise than in a general public offering for cash, state the reasons for the proposed authorization or issuance and the general effect thereof upon the rights of existing security holders.

See Item 15 for the financial statements required if action is to be taken with respect to any matter specified in Item 12.

ITEM 13, MODIFICATION OR EXCHANGE OF SECURITIES.—If action is to be taken with respect to the modification of any class of securities of the issuer, or the issuance or authorization for issuance of securities of the issuer in exchange for outstanding securities of the issuer, the following information must be furnished:

(a) If outstanding securities are to be modified, state the title and amount thereof. If securities are to be issued in exchange for outstanding securities, state the title and amount of securities to be so issued, the title and amount of outstanding securities to be exchanged therefor, and the basis of exchange.

(b) Describe any material differences between the outstanding securities and the modified or new securities in respect of any of the matters concerning which information would be required in the description of the securities in an application on the appropriate form for their registration on a national securities exchange.

(c) State the reasons for the proposed modification or exchange and the general effect thereof upon the rights of the existing security holders.

(d) Furnish a brief statement as to arrears in dividends or as to defaults in principal or interest in respect to the outstanding securities which are to be modified or exchanged, and such other information as may be appropriate in the particular case to disclose adequately the nature and effect of the proposed action.

(e) Outline briefly any other material features of the proposed modification or exchange. If the plan of proposed action is set forth in a written document, file copies thereof with the Commission in accordance with Rule 14a–6.

See Item 15 for the financial statements required if action is to be taken with respect to any matter specified in Item 13.

ITEM 14, MERGERS, CONSOLIDATIONS, ACQUISITIONS, SALE OF ASSETS, LIQUIDATIONS, AND SIMILAR MATTERS.—The following information must be furnished if action is to be taken with respect to any plan for (1) the merger or consolidation of the issuer into or with any other person or of any other person into or with the issuer, (2) the acquisition by the issuer or any of its security holders of securities of another issuer, (3) the acquisition by the issuer of any other going business or of the assets thereof, (4) the sale or other transfer of all or any substantial part of the assets of the issuer, or (5) the liquidation or dissolution of the issuer :

(a) Outline briefly the material features of the plan. State the reasons therefor and the general effect thereof upon the rights of existing security holders. If the plan is set forth in a written document, file three copies thereof with the Commission at the time preliminary copies of the proxy statement and form of proxy are filed pursuant to Rule 14a–6(a).

(b) Furnish the following information as to the issuer and each person which is to be merged into the issuer or into or with which the issuer is to be merged or consolidated or the business or assets of which are to be acquired or which is the issuer of securities to be acquired by the issuer in exchange for all or a substantial part of its assets or to be acquired by security holders of the issuer. What is required is information essential to an investor's appraisal of the action proposed to be taken.

(1) Describe briefly the business of such person. Information is to be given regarding pertinent matters such as the nature of the products or services, methods of production, markets, methods of distribution and the sources and supply of raw materials.

(2) State the location and describe the general character of the plants and other important physical properties of such person. The description is to be given from an economic and business standpoint, as distinguished from a legal standpoint.

(3) Furnish a brief statement as to dividends in arrears or defaults in principal or interest in respect of any securities of the issuer or of such person, and as to the effect of the plan thereon, and such other information as may be appropriate in the particular case to disclose adequately the nature and effect of the proposed action.

(4) Furnish a tabulation in columnar form showing the existing and the pro forma capitalization.

(5) Furnish in columnar form for each of the last five fiscal years a historical summary of earnings and show per-share amounts of net earnings, dividends declared for each year, and book value per share at the end of the latest period.

(6) Furnish in columnar form for each of the last five fiscal years a combined pro forma summary of earnings, as appropriate in the circumstances, indicating the aggregate and per-share earnings for each such year and the pro forma book value per share at the end of the latest period. If the transaction establishes a new basis of accounting for assets of any of the persons included therein, the pro forma summary of earnings shall be furnished only for the most recent fiscal year and interim period and shall reflect appropriate pro forma adjustments resulting from such new basis of accounting.

(7) To the extent material for the exercise of prudent judgment in regard to the matter to be acted upon, furnish the historical and pro forma

earnings data specified in (5) and (6) above for interim periods of the current and prior fiscal years, if available.

Instructions. 1. The earnings per share and dividends per share amounts required by paragraphs (b) (5) and (6) shall be presented in tabular form where appropriate and equated to a common basis in exchange transactions. [For a discussion of "equated to a common basis," see the comments in Chapter **10**.]

2. Include comparable data for any additional fiscal years necessary to keep the summary from being misleading. Subject to appropriate variation to conform to the nature of the business or the purpose of the offering, the following items shall be included: net sales or operating revenues; cost of goods sold or operating expenses (or gross profit); interest charges; income taxes; net income; special items, and net income and special items. The summary shall reflect the retroactive adjustment of any material items affecting the comparability of the results.

[*Author's note:* The reference to "special items" in the aforementioned instructions of the SEC is an indication of the fact that the proxy regulation is out-of-date and needs to be revised. The instruction for the showing of "special items" was a technique developed by the SEC during the period when generally accepted accounting principles permitted certain gains and losses to be entered directly in retained earnings. With the issuance of APB Opinion No. 9 (1966) on "Reporting the Results of Operations", which requires such gains and losses to be shown in the income statement as "extraordinary items", the SEC abandoned its requirement for the showing of "special items", but has not revised its published rules to conform them with its current administrative practice.]

3. In connection with any unaudited summary for an interim period or periods between the end of the last fiscal year and the balance sheet date, and any comparable unaudited prior period, a statement shall be made that all adjustments necessary to a fair statement of the results for such interim period or periods have been included. In addition, there shall be furnished in such cases, as supplemental information but not as a part of the proxy statement, a letter describing in detail the nature and amount of any adjustments, other than normal recurring accruals, entering into the determination of the results shown.

4. Paragraph (b) shall not apply if the plan described in answer to paragraph (a) involves only the issuer and one or more of its totally-held subsidiaries.

(c) As to each class of securities of the issuer, or of any person specified in paragraph (b), which is admitted to dealing on a national securities exchange or with respect to which a market otherwise exists, and which will be materially affected by the plan, state the high and low sale prices (or, in the absence of trading in a particular period, the range of the bid and asked prices) for each quarterly period within two years. This information may be omitted if the plan involves merely the liquidation or dissolution of the issuer.

See Item 15 for additional financial statements required if action is to be taken with respect to any matter specified in Item 14.

ITEM 15, FINANCIAL STATEMENTS.—Item 15 of Schedule 14A gives the requirements for financial statements. If action is to be taken with respect to any matter specified in Items 12, 13, or 14 of Schedule 14A, certified financial statements of the issuer and its subsidiaries must be furnished such as would currently be required in an original registration statement for registration of securities of the issuer under the 1934 Act—Form 10, for example. Such statements may be omitted with respect to a plan described in answer to Item 14(a) if the plan involves only the issuer and one or more of its totally-held subsidiaries. All schedules other than the schedules of supplementary income statement information may be omitted. All required statements must be prepared and certified in accordance with Regulation S–X. One copy of the definitive proxy statement filed with the Commission shall include a manually signed copy of the accountant's certificate.

If action is to be taken with respect to any matter specified in Item 14(b), there must be furnished for each person specified therein (other than the issuer), such financial statements as would currently be required in an original registration statement for registration of securities of such person pursuant to Section 12 of the 1934 Act—Form 10, for example. *Such statements shall be certified if practicable.* All schedules other than the schedules of supplementary income statement information may be omitted. Furthermore, there may be omitted: (1) statements for any totally-held subsidiary of the issuer which is included in the consolidated statement of the issuer and its subsidiaries, and (2) statements for a person which is to succeed to the issuer, or to the issuer and one or more of its totally-held subsidiaries, provided the capital structure and balance sheet of the successor immediately after the succession will be substantially the same as those of the issuer or the combined capital structures and balance sheets of the issuer and its totally-held subsidiaries, as the case may be. The statements shall be prepared in accordance with Regulation S–X and, *if certified,* shall be certified in accordance with that regulation. One copy of the definitive proxy statement filed with the Commission shall include a manually signed copy of the accountant's certificate.

As noted above, if action is to be taken with respect to a proposal coming within the scope of Item 14(b), the financial statements of the other party to the proposed merger or acquisition have to be furnished, and such statements have to be certified if practicable. If certified, the requirements of Regulation S–X applicable to certification by independent public accountants are applicable. It is clear from the instructions, however, that if it is not practicable to furnish a certificate covering such financial statements, this will not be fatal to the proposed transaction or action by the security holders; the statements may be submitted on an uncertified basis. Also, if it is practicable to furnish a qualified certificate, such a certificate—depending on the extent of the qualification—may be acceptable for inclusion in the proxy statement. This seems like a reasonable approach because the security holders may want to approve the proposed transaction despite the absence of a conventional, unqualified auditors' certificate. While such a qualified certificate might not be acceptable for purposes of registration under the 1933 Act, there have been many cases in which they have been accepted by the SEC for inclusion in proxy statements.

In all other respects, however, the staff of the SEC views a proxy statement in a merger situation in much the same light as a filing under the 1933 Act. Accordingly, the staff looks beyond the instructions in the proxy rules, and, as an administrative matter, expects the proxy statement to meet the same high standards as a prospectus.

The Commission may, upon the request of the issuer, permit the omission of any of the statements referred to above where such statements are not necessary for the exercise of prudent judgment in regard to any matter to be acted upon, or may permit the filing in substitution therefor of appropriate statements of comparable character. The Commission may also require the filing of other statements in addition to, or in substitution for, the statements required by Item 15 in any case where such statements are necessary or appropriate for an adequate presentation of the financial condition of any person whose financial statements are required, or whose statements are otherwise material for the exercise of prudent judgment in regard to any matter to be acted upon. In the usual case, financial statements are deemed material to the exercise of prudent judgment where the matter to be acted upon is the authorization or issuance of a material amount of senior securities, but are not deemed material where the matter to be acted upon is the authorization or issuance of common stock, otherwise than in an exchange, merger, consolidation, acquisition, or similar transaction.

The Commission has called for financial statements in circumstances in which it appeared from the instructions that statements were not required. Take the case, for instance, of Company A which is seeking shareholder approval of an increase in the authorized issue of common stock, such approval being required either by state law or the company's charter. A will ask its shareholders to approve the increase in the authorized issue. Accordingly, the information called for by Item 12 of Schedule 14A will be furnished in A's proxy statement, together with A's financial statements called for by Item 15.

Assume also that the increase in the authorized issue of common stock is principally for the purpose of acquiring Company B, but that the approval of A's shareholders of the *acquisition* is not required and is not sought. Since the shareholders of A are not being asked to approve the acquisition of B, it would appear that B's financial statements need not be included in A's proxy statement. This is not so, however. The staff of the Commission has stated that, in such cases, the shareholders of A are, in effect, being asked to approve not only the increase in authorized stock, but also the proposed acquisition, even though their approval of the acquisition is neither sought nor required. Accordingly, the proxy statement must include all the financial statements that would be required if shareholders were being asked to approve the acquisition.

The proxy statement may incorporate by reference any financial statement contained in an annual report sent to security holders pursuant to the proxy rules with respect to the same meeting as that to which the proxy statement relates, provided such financial statements substantially meet the requirements of this item. See Chapter **30** for the Commission's views as to what constitutes substantial compliance with the requirements.

See also the discussion on page **9**.3 regarding the need for updating the financial data in registration statements filed with the SEC under the 1933 Act.

ITEM 17, RESTATEMENT OF ACCOUNTS.—If action is to be taken at the meeting with respect to the restatement of any asset, capital, or surplus account of the issuer, the following information must be furnished:

(a) State the nature of the restatement and the date as of which it is to be effective.

(b) Outline briefly the reasons for the restatement and for the selection of the particular effective date.

(c) State the name and amount of each account (including any reserve accounts) affected by the restatement and the effect of the restatement thereon. Tabular presentation of the amounts shall be made when appropriate, particularly in the case of recapitalizations.

(d) To the extent practicable, state whether and the extent, if any, to which, the restatement will, as of the date thereof, alter the amount available for distribution to the holders of equity securities.

FLEXIBILITY OF REQUIREMENTS FOR FINANCIAL STATEMENTS.—As previously noted. Items 14 and 15 of Schedule 14A contain the requirements for financial statements to be included in a proxy statement. It is worth emphasizing that the requirements are somewhat flexible. The instructions provide that the Commission, upon the request of the issuer, may permit the omission of any of the statements specified in the proxy rules where such statements are not necessary for the exercise of prudent judgment in regard to any matter to be acted upon, or may permit the filing in substitution therefor of appropriate statements of comparable character. The Commission may also require additional or substitute statements where necessary or appropriate.

The instructions recite certain instances in which financial statements are deemed material for the exercise of prudent judgment, and other instances in which such statements are not deemed material. In a particular case, the persons making the solicitation, their accountants, attorneys, and advisers, may believe that financial statements are not necessary in the circumstances of that case, and have good reasons for so believing. In that event, the reasons for omitting the financial statements should be made known to the staff of the SEC. If the SEC does not agree, it will so inform the persons making the solicitation. It is desirable to obtain the Commission's views in this respect *in advance* of filing the preliminary proxy material rather than learning at the eleventh hour that the Commission believes financial statements to be material. It is suggested that the Commission's views be obtained in advance of filing by communicating with the Chief Accountant of the Commission's Division of Corporation Finance.

The following example illustrates a case in which SEC waived the requirement for a pro forma combined summary of earnings (or income statement). Pfeiffer Brewing Company proposed to acquire the E & B Brewing Co., Inc., by merger, and prepared a proxy statement in connection with soliciting the approval of Pfeiffer's stockholders to the merger. For accounting purposes, the proxy statement indicated that the merger was in effect a purchase, and in the pro forma balance sheet E & B's fixed assets were reduced $387,000 and intangible assets of $154,000 were eliminated. The proxy statement also indicated that it was the intention to consolidate in Pfeiffer's Detroit brewery the production of the brands produced by E & B and to continue the separate distribution of such brands. Accordingly, the E & B brewery in Detroit would cease operations as soon as practicable after the merger and would be retained as an idle brewery or disposed of as management determined, which determination had not yet been made. Following the summaries of earnings of the individual parties to the merger, the company (Pfeiffer) made cross-reference to the section of the proxy statement disclosing its plans for the E & B brewery and said the consolidation was not expected to result in significant changes in operating costs. The company added, however, that in the light of the changes in operations and the accounting treatment being afforded the merger, "it is considered that a pro forma combined statement of income and expense of Pfeiffer and E & B would not be representative and accordingly none is presented herein." The SEC did not object to the omission of the combined income statement.

The following is another example illustrating the omission of a portion of the historical financial statements that would ordinarily be required in a proxy statement. The B Company prepared a proxy statement in connection with a meeting called to vote upon its proposed acquisition of the G Company. The assets of the latter consisted entirely of cash, U.S. government securities, other investments, and accrued interest and dividends. The G

Company had been a heavy industrial enterprise but had sold all of its property, plant, equipment, and inventories four years previously. Financial information on the G Company was therefore furnished only for the most recent one and one-half years, the Commission having been furnished with a statement of the reason for omitting earlier information, as follows:

> Information is furnished only for the year ended December 31, 19———, and six months ended June 30, 19———, since the Company was engaged in the manufacture of steel forgings and other related products until December 30, 19———, when it sold and transferred to (name of buyer) all of its property, plant, and equipment and inventories. The period between December 30, 19———, and October 1, 19———, was a transitional period during which the Company's principal assets were cash and U.S. government securities.

In one case reported by the SEC, a registrant engaged in real estate operations submitted preliminary draft copies of proxy solicitation material without complete financial statements, seeking among other matters authorization of stockholders to amend the company's certificate of incorporation so as to reduce the par value of capital stock by a split-up from $10 per share to $1 per share; to reduce correspondingly the capital of the company from $4,255,000 to $425,000; to execute 18 separate mortgages, together covering all of the company's real properties and aggregating $5,000,000 in principal amount to mature in 10 years, with interest at the rate of 4 per cent per annum; to distribute forthwith to stockholders the $5,000,000 of mortgage proceeds and other funds of the company aggregating $5,250,000. The company stated that financial statements had not been included for the reason that they were not deemed material for the exercise of prudent judgment in regard to the matters to be acted upon at the meeting. The company had included a summary of the balance sheet at the close of its last fiscal year and a table showing for ten years the "net income after operating expenses, adjusted to exclude interest on indebtedness, depreciation, and income taxes." The SEC's first letter of comment indicated the need to furnish to stockholders in this connection certified financial statements for three fiscal years, unaudited statements of a more recent date, and a pro forma balance sheet as of such recent date showing the effect of the proposed transactions covered by the proxy statement. The company was also requested to furnish to stockholders a complete summary of earnings for the last ten fiscal years. The most recent balance sheet indicated a stockholders' equity of $6,236,000; the pro forma balance sheet, as of the same date, after giving effect to mortgaging of properties, reduction of capital, and distribution to stockholders, indicated a stockholders' equity of $835,000. The table of "adjusted income" originally submitted averaged $729,000 per year (with a minimum of $688,000 and maximum of $787,000) compared with interest and amortization of the proposed mortgages of $350,000. The revised summary of earnings for ten years and six months afforded adequate material for analysis of the effect of the change in capital structure of the company. [17 SEC Ann. Rep. 46 (1951).]

WAITING PERIOD FOR PROXY STATEMENTS.—As has already been stated, preliminary copies of the proxy statement, form of proxy, and other soliciting material must be filed with the SEC at least ten days before definitive copies of such material are sent to security holders, or such shorter period as the Commission may authorize. During this ten-day period, the staff of the Commission examines the proxy statement, form of proxy, and soliciting material. As a result of the examination by the staff, the SEC frequently sends an informal letter of comment setting forth its criticisms and suggestions. Sometimes, because of the work load, the SEC is unable to complete its examination within the ten-day period, and the Commission's comments may therefore be delayed beyond that period. In the opinion of this author, it is not advisable to proceed with the printing of the proxy material until the Commission's comments have been received. Especially when the time schedule is very tight (as is frequently the case) the Commission's letter of comments is apt to upset the schedule. It is well to remember, however, that the Commission's comments represent the combined views of a number of experienced persons—accountants, lawyers, and analysts. Their opinions are often constructive and helpful. For that reason alone, if for no other reason, the author recommends that the printing of the proxy material be delayed until the Commission's comments have been received.

FORM OF FINANCIAL STATEMENTS AND CERTIFICATES IN PROXY STATEMENTS.—In the preceding pages there have been set forth the requirements for financial statements contained in Schedule 14A of the SEC's proxy regulation. If action is to be taken at the meeting of stockholders with respect to any matter specified in Items 12, 13, or 14 of the schedule, certified financial statements of the issuer and its subsidiaries must be furnished such as would currently be required in an original registration of securities of the issuer under the 1934 Act. Most companies filing registration statements under the 1934 Act do so on Form 10. A complete listing of forms for registration of securities under the 1934 Act appears in Chapter **14**.

If a company is required to include financial statements in a proxy statement, reference must be made to the appropriate registration form for the financial requirements applicable to the proxy statement. If, for example, the company would be required to file its registration statement on Form 10, then the financial statements in its proxy statement would be those in Form 10. The requirements for financial statements in Form 10 are set forth in Chapter **15** of this volume. That chapter also describes the requirements for certification of financial statements. The form of certificate of independent public accountants is governed by Regulation S–X. See Chapters **24** through **26** as to the requirements for certification by and qualifications of independent public accountants.

Relationship of Proxy Statement to Registration Statement Under 1933 Act.—Proxy statements are frequently prepared concurrently with the preparation of a registration statement under the Securities Act of 1933. As an illustration, a corporation may wish to issue a class of senior securities, such as bonds or preferred stock. For that purpose the corporation may have to seek the approval of its common stockholders and, in that connection, would prepare a proxy statement. If the senior securities (bonds or preferred stock) are to be sold to the public, and an exemption from registration under the 1933 Act is not available, the corporation would proceed with the preparation of the registration statement at or about the same time as it prepares the proxy statement. Insofar as the same financial statements appear in both documents, it is desirable that the statements be the same as far as their form and content is concerned.

Certifying Accountants' Review of Preliminary Proxy Material. —There have been instances when the SEC has not been certain that an accountant has agreed to the use of his opinion on audited financial statements which have been included in *preliminary* proxy material filed with the Commission. This is due to the fact that the 1934 Act, which governs proxy solicitations, does not require the filing of an accountant's consent to the use of his opinion in the proxy statement, and the accountant's opinion included in the *preliminary* filing does not have to be manually signed. This situation has caused some concern not only to accountants but also to the SEC because there have been cases where accountants have not been aware that preliminary proxy filings have been made that included their opinions.

In order to resolve this problem, the Commission issued Release No. 8881 under the 1934 Act on May 13, 1970. The text of the release follows:

CERTIFYING ACCOUNTANTS' REVIEW OF FINANCIAL STATEMENTS IN PRELIMINARY PROXY MATERIAL

Preliminary proxy material containing certified financial statements, or incorporating such statements by reference, frequently is filed with the Securities and Exchange Commission before the material has been presented to the certifying accountants for their consideration. We understand that certifying accountants review the textual disclosure in proxy soliciting material before permitting the use of their opinion with respect to the financial statements and that they frequently are able to offer comments helpful to those charged with preparation of such material.

In order to facilitate the staff's review of preliminary proxy material, especially during the present period of heavy demands on the staff, it is requested that such material be considered by the certifying accountants and any resulting revisions be made, wherever practicable, before the material is filed with the Commission. It is also requested that such preliminary material be accompanied by a letter advising the staff whether such material has been considered by the accountants and whether the accountants are prepared to permit the use of their opinion with regard to the financial statements. This procedure may substantially assist the staff in its consideration of preliminary proxy material.

This procedure is not a substitute for furnishing the accountants' certificate in the definitive proxy material filed with the Commission under Rule 14a–6(c). Under Rule 2–02(a) of the Commission's Regulation S–X, relating to the form and content of financial statements, the manual signature is necessary. At least one of the eight definitive copies filed under Rule 14a–6(c) must contain a manually signed opinion of the certifying accountant. Identification of the manually signed copy on the outside cover thereof will facilitate the Commission's filing processes.

The foregoing release effectively disposes of one problem—that is, whether the accountant is aware of the fact that his opinion is included in the preliminary filing of proxy material. But the release also raises a number of questions and potential problems.

First of all, the title of the release refers to "review of financial statements," whereas the body of the release deals with a review of "textual disclosure." In addition, the second paragraph of the release requests that the preliminary proxy material be "considered" by the certifying accountants and "any resulting revisions be made . . . before the material is filed . . ." The conflicts of subject matter (financial statements vs. textual disclosure) and terminology (review vs. consider), and the emphasis placed on "resulting revisions" have created uncertainty as to the intent of the release and confusion as to the accountants' responsibility, if any, for textual disclosures. Since the issuance of the release, some persons have stated that, in complying with the release, the accountants may be giving negative assurance as to the adequacy of the textual disclosures. Some feel that it may be tantamount to a positive assurance. Others have interpreted the release as placing a responsibility on the accountant actually to revise the textual material.

Although there is some basis in the release for the foregoing views, it should be clear that *accountants can not give such assurances, nor can they be relied upon as "experts" in the area of textual disclosures.* Such disclosures are made in response to legal requirements and involve substantial legal interpretation. Accordingly, the completeness and adequacy of textual disclosures are outside the area of the accountants' professional competence, and this should not come as a surprise to the Commission and its staff.

The accountant reads the textual portion of proxy material—or any other SEC filing—in which his opinion appears for the reasons indicated in Chapter 11. Primarily the accountant is interested in knowing whether there are any disclosures in the text that conflict with those in the financial statements. If such conflicts exist, they must be resolved. Also, as a result of reading the text material, an accountant may have an opinion as to its adequacy or completeness, and he may be able to make helpful comments or suggestions in this respect because of his familiarity with the issuer's financial affairs and because of his objective viewpoint which is independent of those who prepared the material. Such views and comments, however, helpful though they may be, can not be relied upon as the opinion of an expert in this area.

The author does not believe that the release was intended to impose on accountants the obligation of revising text material. Revision is not far different from preparation, and the preparation of the text portion of a proxy statement is most certainly not the responsibility of the accountant.

The second paragraph of Release No. 8881 requires that the preliminary proxy material filed with the Commission "be accompanied by a letter advising the staff whether such material has been considered by the accountants and whether the accountants are prepared to permit the use of their opinion with regard to the financial statements." The release does not state who is to furnish the letter—the accountants or the issuer. The author understands that the Commission intended that the *issuer* and not the accountants should write the required letter to the SEC. Since the issuer's counsel would probably advise the issuer not to furnish such a representation letter to the SEC unless the issuer receives a similar letter from the accountants, the accountants may be expected to write such a letter to their client (the issuer).

A letter of the kind contemplated must be carefully prepared to avoid any misunderstanding as to what it represents. It should avoid any direct or implied approval of the adequacy or completeness of the textual disclosures for the reasons discussed above. Even the most carefully prepared letter may be subject to misunderstanding, and those who receive the letter may be inclined to read into it more than is intended due, in part, to the ambiguous wording of the SEC's release. For this reason, the following alternative procedure was proposed to the staff of the SEC which they agreed informally to accept:

The staff will accept a manually signed opinion of the accountant in the preliminary proxy material in lieu of the letter contemplated by the second paragraph of the release.

The author recommends the foregoing alternative in satisfying the requirements of Release No. 8881. This procedure is simpler, less time-consuming, and should avoid the misunderstandings that could result from the letter contemplated by the release. (In addition to providing a manually signed opinion for inclusion in the *preliminary* proxy material, it will also be necessary for the accountant to sign manually his opinion in at least one copy of the *definitive* (final) proxy statement.)

Despite the Commission's acceptance of the alternative procedure described above, some issuers, on advice of their counsel, will request a letter from the certifying accountants as indicated in the release. The accountant should be able to convince the issuer and/or its counsel that the letter is not necessary. If they insist on it, however, a letter along the lines of the following may be furnished by the accountants to the issuer:

(Name of company)

We have read a copy of your preliminary proxy statement dated (date) relating to the meeting of stockholders on (date), and we are prepared to permit the use therein of our opinion dated (date) with respect to the following financial statements:

(Itemize statements, dates, and periods, covered by the accountants' opinion.)

It should be understood that our reading of the aforementioned proxy material was not for the purpose of expressing an opinion on the completeness or adequacy of the textual disclosures therein and this letter should not be relied on for that purpose.

We are aware that a copy of this letter may be furnished to the Securities and Exchange Commission pursuant to the provisions of Release No. 8881 under the Securities Exchange Act of 1934.

(Signature of accountants)

With respect to the foregoing letter, in a merger (or other acquisition) proxy statement, the first sentence of the letter should be limited to the company with whose affairs the accountants are familiar. Also, if the accountants are not the continuing accountants and accordingly have not participated in the preparation of any pro forma statements included in the proxy statement, they should so state in their letter.

It will be noted that the suggested form of letter uses the word "read" rather than the SEC's words "review" and "consider." The SEC's language should not be used because it may give rise to misunderstanding as to what the accountants have actually done and its purpose.

While the "keeping current" requirements of the 1933 Act do not apply to proxy materials filed under the 1934 Act, the accountants should read the text of the preliminary and definitive proxy materials carefully for information which may affect financial statements covered by the accountants' opinion.

Proposals of Security Holders.—One of the most interesting developments in recent years in connection with proxies and proxy solicitations has been the increasing number of proposals sponsored by persons not connected with the management of the issuer. Often the proposal is sponsored by a stockholder owning only one share of common stock of the issuer which he acquired very recently for the sole purpose of presenting a proposal for action by shareholders of the company. In some cases, the same shareholder has purchased a single share in many other companies—also for the sole purpose of presenting the same or similar proposals at their shareholder meetings. But whether he owns one share or a thousand shares, he has the same right to present a proposal for action by the shareholders and to insist upon the inclusion of his proposal in the management's proxy and proxy statement.

The right of the security holder to insist on inclusion of his proposal in management's proxy is contained in Rule 14a–8 of the SEC's proxy regulation. The rule provides that if any security holder entitled to vote at a meeting of security holders of the issuer shall submit to the management of the issuer a proposal which is accompanied by notice of his intention to present the proposal for action at the meeting, the management shall set forth the proposal in its proxy statement. The proposal has to be identified in the management's proxy and means provided by which shareholders can vote on it.

If the management opposes the proposal, it shall, at the request of the stockholder, include in its proxy statement a statement of the stockholder (in not more than 100 words) in support of the proposal. The reasons for management's opposition may also be set forth in the proxy statement.

The rule also sets forth the conditions under which management may omit a shareholder's proposal and any statement in support thereof from its proxy statement. A shareholder's proposal may be omitted, for instance, if, under applicable state law, it is not a proper subject for shareholder action. Also, a proposal may be omitted if it is submitted primarily for the purpose of enforcing a personal claim or redressing a personal grievance against the issuer or its management.

If the proposal was submitted at previous meetings and failed to receive specified percentages of the votes cast, it may be omitted. Also, if management has included proposals of the security holder at recent meetings and the security holder has failed to present the proposal for action at the meeting, there are restrictions on his right to include his proposals in management's proxy statement. The sincerity of some shareholders who include proposals in management's proxy statements may be questioned when they do not appear at the meeting either in person or by proxy to present their proposals, which are therefore not submitted to a vote.

In several instances corporations have excluded shareholder proposals from proxy statements with the SEC's concurrence, but the matter has been taken to court and the shareholder has won, with the result that there has been increasing reluctance on the part of issuers to oppose shareholders' proposals and thereby become embroiled in a legal fracas. This undoubtedly accounts for the explosive increase in recent years in the number and variety of shareholder proposals that are currently included in management's proxy statements.

Election Contests.—Not surprisingly, the SEC's proxy rules also deal with situations in which a person or group of persons opposes a solicitation subject to the rules with respect to the election of directors at a meeting of security holders. The provisions applicable to election contests are set forth in Rule 14a–11. Persons who solicit proxies in opposition to the management of an issuer are required to file with the SEC a statement in duplicate setting forth the information specified by Schedule 14B.

In addition to identifying the issuer, Schedule 14B calls for information concerning the solicitor—his name, business and residence addresses, and his principal occupation or employment currently and in the last ten years. He is required to state whether he has been a participant in any other proxy contest involving *any* issuer in the last ten years, and, if so, information with respect thereto. If he has been convicted of a crime in the last ten years, disclosure must be made of certain facts including dates, name and location of court, penalties, and so on.

The solicitor must state his ownership of securities of the issuer (record and beneficial) and transactions in the last two years, and funds borrowed to finance such acquisitions, together with the amount of such indebtedness as of the latest practicable date. If he was a party to any contract or arrangement with any person with respect to any securities of the issuer within the past year, the details must be stated. His interest in transactions, or proposed transactions, to which the issuer or its subsidiaries was or is to be a party, must be furnished, including his relationship to the issuer, and the nature and amount of his interest. If he has an arrangement or understanding with respect to future employment by the issuer or its affiliates, the facts must be disclosed. If he has an arrangement or understanding with respect to any future transactions to which the issuer or its affiliates will or may be a party, the details must be furnished. If he has contributed or proposes to contribute an aggregate of more than $500 in connection with the solicitation, his aggregate contribution must be stated.

Regulation 14C.—With the passage of the Securities Acts Amendments of 1964, the SEC's proxy rules were extended to a large number of publicly-owned, unlisted companies that had never made public disclosure of some of the information that must be set forth in a proxy statement subject to SEC rules. The managements of these companies are usually under no compulsion to solicit proxies. They may, in fact, find it to their advantage not to solicit if thereby they can avoid making the disclosures required by the proxy regulation. With this situation in mind, the 1964 Amendments added a section (Section 14(c)) to the 1934 Act which authorizes the Commission to adopt rules to require issuers that do not solicit proxies in connection with an annual or other meeting of shareholders to send to shareholders information substantially equivalent to what would be required in a proxy statement if a solicitation were made. The SEC adopted Regulation 14C which requires the distribution to security holders of an "information statement" with respect to annual and other meetings where proxies are not solicited on behalf of the management. The regulation is applicable to issuers of securities listed for trading on an exchange as well as to companies whose securities are traded over-the-counter but which are registered pursuant to Section 12(g) of the 1934 Act.

Security Holders Information Statement.—The security holders information statement is required to contain substantially the same information as that which would be required in a proxy statement if proxies were solicited. In the case of an annual meeting, the issuer is also required to transmit to security holders an annual report including financial statements certified by independent accountants, similar to the annual report required to be transmitted by issuers that solicit proxies.

Five preliminary copies of the information statement are required to be filed with the SEC at least ten days before the statement is sent to security holders, or such shorter period as the Commission may authorize. Eight copies of the information statement in definitive form must also be filed with the Commission. One unusual feature of the regulation is that the first page of the information statement must contain the following statement in bold-face type:

WE ARE NOT ASKING YOU FOR A PROXY AND YOU ARE REQUESTED NOT TO SEND US A PROXY.

CHAPTER **23**

LINE OF BUSINESS REPORTING

CONTENTS

Segmented Reporting Recommended by Wheat Report.—In 1969 the SEC adopted a new requirement that caused publicly-owned companies engaged in more than one line of business to disclose the sales and revenues and pre-tax earnings attributable to each of the principal components of their businesses. The new requirement (sometimes called "line of business reporting" or "segmented reporting") was adopted only after a great deal of soul searching by the members of the Commission and its staff, in the course of which the SEC publicly made a complete reversal of its position.

The Commission's action gave effect to one of the many recommendations of *The Wheat Report* which said "For many of today's corporate enterprises, the key to an understanding of the business and an appraisal of its future prospects is a breakdown of revenues and, to the extent feasible, of profits by separate lines of business." [1]

Reporting Practice Prior to 1970.—Before the new requirements were adopted in 1969, it had been a rule of long standing that companies registering under the Securities Acts had to disclose the relative importance of each product or service, or class of similar products or services, that contributed 15% or more of the total gross volume of business. This

[1] *Disclosure to Investors: A Reappraisal of Federal Administrative Policies under the '33 and '34 Acts (The Wheat Report)*, Commerce Clearing House, Inc., 1969, p. 338.

disclosure was required in the narrative or text portion of a registration statement—not in the financial statements. (This requirement still exists but, for companies whose volume is more than $50 million, the percentage has been lowered to 10%.) In addition, if income was derived from the sale of products as well as revenues for services, Regulation S–X called for a separate reporting in the formal income statement of such sales and revenues if either item was more than 10% of the combined total. The regulation also calls for a separate showing of cost of goods sold and operating expenses where sales and revenues are shown separately, but there was no requirement for a breakdown of net income by product lines or services.

In recent years, companies have in a very few instances voluntarily disclosed the relative contributions of particular parts of their business to the overall net profit. Martin Marietta, for instance, in 1965 showed sales and earnings separately for its space and missile division, its cement and lime division, its chemical division, and its rock products division. Also in 1965, Kaiser Industries summarized its earnings showing operating results (before interest expense) in four broad categories of operations. In subsequent years a few more companies reported their operations on the basis of their principal products or lines of business.

It has long been customary for the great majority of publicly-owned corporations in the United States to include in their annual reports consolidated financial statements of the reporting corporations and their majority-owned subsidiaries. (There have been some noteworthy exceptions to this general observation, but they are not relevant or significant to the present discussion.) In recent years there has been an increasing tendency to furnish voluntarily a breakdown of consolidated sales classified by lines of business, divisions, industry groups, or product lines, but this breakdown —except in rare instances—does not extend to net income. In a very few instances, companies also include in their reports information supplementing the formal financial statements to show the profit contributions of subsidiaries classified by principal industry groups.

One writer[2] surveyed the 1968 published annual reports of 506 United States corporations engaged primarily in manufacturing activities, and his findings may be summarized as follows:

Nearly half (47 per cent) of the companies showed contributions to sales by division, major markets, geographical areas (domestic), product lines, or operating groups.

Some breakdown of contributions to income was shown by nearly 9 per cent of these companies. In most cases, this was pre-tax income.

Nearly one-quarter reported sales outside the U.S. separately.

[2] George Hobgood, "Voluntary Disclosure in 1968 Annual Reports," *Financial Executive,* August 1969, pp. 64–69.

Thirty of the companies (6 per cent) showed sales made to a single customer. In most instances, these were sales to the U.S. government.

Eighteen companies (4 per cent) revealed assets employed by a product line or operating group.

Those companies which segmented sales appeared to break them down into much smaller components than in the past. Of these 233 companies, 41 per cent showed contributions by two or more components whose contributions were 15 per cent or less of total sales; 28 per cent showed two or more components contributing 10 per cent or less.

The resistance to reporting net income by product lines or lines of business has been widespread and understandable. Ignoring for the moment the problems and costs inherent in reporting on that basis, managements of publicly-owned companies have strongly opposed the disclosure of information that would put them at a disadvantage with respect to their competitors or their customers—both of which would be quick to obtain any useful information that is available or furnished to security holders as a class.

Well-managed companies have for a long time prepared, for internal use, reports on their separate lines of business, or divisions, or product lines, and even on individual products. Most companies, however, would never dream of publishing such information—and thereby subjecting themselves to the liabilities of the SEC statutes—for the simple reason that it is just not accurate enough for publication. One lawyer commented on the legal exposure as follows:

> One of the concerns of those pondering the problems of conglomerate reporting is litigation. In view of the rising tide of suits under Rule 10b-5 and other security enactments, it is little wonder that this aspect looms large. The concern is that the additional information may be misleading or deceptive unless it is so heavily enshrouded in qualifications, definitions and caveats that it becomes meaningless and detracts from the comprehensibility of the conventional portions of the report. Whether this is a real concern will depend largely on the methods of disclosure sought to be applied and the extent to which they are qualified.[3]

The limitations and imperfections inherent in segmented reports prepared for internal use are well understood by management. Although such reports are useful—and sometimes essential—for operating purposes, they are often not suitable for public release. In order to release these reports to the public, the basis of their preparation would have to be very carefully reconsidered, the methods of allocation studiously refined, more records kept, and more reports prepared—all of which can be very costly. Furthermore, since there are no authoritative guidelines for reporting the operating

[3] A. A. Sommer, Jr., "Conglomerate Disclosure: Friend or Foe?," *The Business Lawyer*, January 1967.

results of separate parts of a business, it would be impossible to make meaningful comparisons between the segmented reports of different companies—even of companies in the same industry.

There is no denying, however, that there has been continuing pressure for a long time for reporting the operating results of diversified or conglomerate companies on the basis of their principal lines of business. The pressure has come very largely from security analysts and persons connected with the stock brokerage business, who claimed that, without this information, they could not properly analyze a business enterprise that was engaged in several different lines of business. Consolidated figures, they say, by their very nature sometimes conceal a sorry situation by combining the good and the bad and showing only aggregate amounts.

Hearings of the Senate Subcommittee on Antitrust and Monopoly.—In April 1965 Senator Russell Long (Louisiana) introduced bills to amend the Clayton Antitrust Act. The bills were referred to the Senate Subcommittee on Antitrust and Monopoly, Committee on the Judiciary, which held hearings on them. It was these hearings which ultimately caused the SEC to prescribe a form of segmented reporting by publicly-owned, diversified companies.

Senator Long's proposed bills would have imposed extensive disclosure requirements on companies that were engaged in dual distribution, that is, companies which through vertical integration sell to affiliated companies and also to independent firms, who, in turn, sell in competition with the affiliated firms. Under the proposed bills, each affiliated firm would have been required to report annually its sales, cost of goods sold (broken down by source), operating overhead, and net profit or loss.

During the course of the hearings, there was considerable testimony concerning the effects of conglomerate acquisitions on the American economy. Among other witnesses, a university professor stressed the absence of factual information from which appropriate conclusions might be drawn concerning the effects of such acquisitions. He also said:

The relative profitability of different divisions and product lines should be brought out in order to appraise the competitive tactics utilizing diversification. We are operating in almost complete ignorance in this area when we do not know even the sales of many of the major firms in different lines, let alone the profitability or losses incurred in these lines. . . . I would speak also on behalf of the average investor who does not know what he is buying into when he purchases one of these large diversified firms. He has only the overall statement to go by. He judges then not the industry but the behavior of the firm itself, and he stakes his money on the management with a minimum of information. . . . On a more limited scale, I do think that an amendment to the Securities and Exchange Act [sic] could require that corporations disclose on a fuller basis than they do now their sales and operating income from different activities in which they may be engaged. . . .[4]

Although the proposed bills would have covered only vertically integrated companies, the then Chairman of the Federal Trade Commission, Paul R. Dixon, advocated extending the reporting requirements to cover the diversified company. He said that ". . . better and more detailed financial information would serve a great prophylactic purpose in forestalling or eroding monopoly power, by encouraging new entrants to move in and compete, and at the same time giving the antitrust agencies insight into the problem areas. He also said that corporations :·

. . . should be required to publish divisional statements which would reflect their profits or losses in major industries or categories of their operations. Ideally the public interest would be well served if information were available as to operations of the larger corporations in terms of each of the major product or geographic markets they serve. . . . I think it would be sufficient if the public had information as to the broad types of accounting information that are normally published in profit and loss statements and balance sheets, if organized and delineated by product and geographic markets.[5]

Senator Philip A. Hart (Michigan), Chairman of the Subcommittee, requested the SEC's views on reporting by diversified or conglomerate enterprises. He thought that the SEC might already have the authority to require division-by-division reports.

The SEC's Initial Response to Product Line Reporting.—In June 1965, Manuel F. Cohen, the then Chairman of the SEC, submitted a report in response to Senator Hart's request. Mr. Cohen stated that the SEC did indeed have the authority to require more detailed disclosure but had refrained from requesting it for a number of reasons:

There was a question as to whether the value of this information would be worth the cost of obtaining it;
There was a question of the reliability and meaningfulness of the information because of variations in cost determination methods and the procedures in allocating certain expenses among product lines;
The dangers, especially to small companies required to report on a product line, in disclosing strategic information to competitors;
The difficulty in making rules as to reporting in order to elicit meaningful information from all companies, that is, should the information be furnished by company, division, product line, or industry group;
The problems of uncertain and probably increased potential liability of accountants and issuers; and

[4] Joel Dirlam, Hearings, Subcommittee on Antitrust and Monopoly, Committee on the Judiciary, United States Senate, 89th Congress, First Session, 1965, p. 769.
[5] Paul R. Dixon, Hearings, Subcommittee on Antitrust and Monopoly, Committee of the Judiciary, United States Senate, Part 2, p. 209.

The fact that there had been a tendency among corporations to furnish more product line data voluntarily in published reports.[6]

In reply to the SEC's views, the Subcommittee received the comments of two investment analysts, both of whom felt very strongly that a divisional breakdown would be a desirable step in the area of corporate disclosure. The Subcommittee also heard from a professor who was highly critical of all of the SEC's arguments. Other persons also testified in favor of the proposal, including the president of a prominent U.S. corporation who said that product line reports were desirable and that there were no insurmountable problems in preparing them.

Some Additional Arguments in Opposition to Line of Business Reporting.—In its letter to the Senate Subcommittee, the SEC set forth the principal arguments that are ordinarily raised in opposition to proposals for segmented reporting. There are other arguments, however, that could be mentioned.

Segmented reporting might have the tendency to emphasize short-term results. Consider, for instance, the company that is thinking of entering a new line of business or of developing a new product where the immediate prospects are poor, but where the long-term prospects are promising. Management is understandably hesitant about embarking on such a project if the poor or subnormal results have to be separately disclosed.

Writing about the legal implications of segmented reporting, a law professor with considerable experience in the securities field has commented that such reporting might disclose management's errors of judgment. Thus, he said, an acquisition may turn out badly, and this would be revealed, whereas in consolidated figures the results of the acquired company would be concealed. Or, product line reporting may show a large loss in a developmental program and encourage a lawsuit for waste. To the extent that product line reporting poses a serious new threat to management from shareholders' derivative suits, thereby deterring management's venturesomeness, he observed that there might be a social loss. He added nonetheless that "while there is no way of knowing if there would be an increase in litigation, there does not seem to be any real danger of increased liability." [7]

Sometimes a company enters a new line of business deliberately with the knowledge that it will be a loser. This may be because of a policy decision: the new business may be needed, for instance, to offer a line as broad as one offered by a competitor. The stockholder may conclude, however, after a year or two that the company went into a new line of business,

---

[6] Hearings, Subcommittee on Antitrust and Monopoly, Committee on the Judiciary, U.S. Senate, 89th Congress, 1965, pp. 1070–71.

[7] Donald E. Schwartz, "Legal Implications of Product Line Reporting." *The Business Lawyer*, Jan. 1968, p. 540.

has been doing poorly in it, and apparently has no plans for getting out of it.

Even assuming that all the preparation problems for product line or line of business reports have been solved, they fall short of telling the whole story. A most important ingredient, namely, return on investment, would be missing. Can the reader of a segmented income statement be expected to know why Line A which contributed 50% of the sales makes only 5% of the net profit? How can he know that the investment in Line A is relatively very small and that the inventory of that line turns over weekly or, perhaps, daily?

Even the advocates of line of business reports concede that there are enormous problems in preparing income statements on that basis for publication. There are infinitely greater problems in allocating assets and liabilities to lines of business or products. Nonetheless, a breakdown of the income statement is only part of the story; such a statement is incomplete unless it is accompanied by information showing the return on investment of the various lines of business. A university professor of accounting made the same point when he observed that the demand for divisional reporting does not end with the reporting of sales and earnings. "Investment or capital employed in each division must also be shown if stockholders are to be informed about the rate of return on investment from each division." [8]

Arguments for Line of Business Reports.—Investment analysts have an insatiable appetite for information, and it is to be expected that they would be in favor of an income statement prepared in a way that shows the relative contributions to overall income of a company's principal lines of business. They point out that the different operations of a diversified company enjoy different price/earnings ratios. The chemical division, for instance, would be valued at a relatively high P/E ratio as compared with another division that operates, say, a chain of supermarkets. In order to evaluate the total enterprise, say the analysts, they must evaluate each of the operations that make up the total.

If one of the lines of business contributes 5% of the sales but 30% of the profit, the analysts say this is an important fact that they need to know. It might indicate not only that the rest of the business is doing poorly, but also that the profitable portion may be vulnerable and exposed to increased pressure from present and potential competitors, and to pressure for price reductions from customers. Indeed, one argument that was raised in favor of segmented reporting in the Senate hearings was that the disclosure of a highly profitable product line would invite more competition in that line with resulting benefit to the public.

[8] David Solomons, "Accounting Problems and Some Solutions," in *Public Reporting by Conglomerates,* ed. by Rappaport, Firmin, and Zeff, Prentice-Hall, Inc., 1968, p. 103.

From the discussion of Regulation S–X in Chapter **18**, it will be remembered that the SEC requires a separate showing in income statements of sales of *products* and revenues from *services* where either of these items is more than 10% of the aggregate amount. As far back as 1939, some writers contended that investors are not so much interested in whether income comes from the sale of goods or from the sale of services, as they are in knowing from *what goods* and *what services* the income is derived.[9] In the case of General Motors, for instance, the investor is more interested in knowing the income from the sale of cars, from the sale of appliances, and from the corporation's other major activities, than to know that a certain amount was derived from the sale of "goods" and the remainder from services, such as the operation of a railroad. In large corporations, with many diversified types of operations, it is not especially important or significant to the investor to know the amounts of sales of product and revenues from services, and the costs of goods and services sold. It is the breakdown within these amounts that is necessary for intelligent evaluation.

Robert T. Sprouse observed that in analyzing the investment potential of a conglomerate enterprise, it was reasonable to expect that the impact of the diverse elements in the enterprise would change with time. "That is precisely why the investor needs information about the magnitude and change in the diverse elements that comprise the conglomerate." Sprouse maintained that the investor must predict which elements will provide stability, which will provide growth, which will involve great risk, or which will affect other investment qualities that he (the investor) considers important. In most cases, Sprouse continued, measurements of past magnitudes and changes would be helpful as bases for making such predictions.[10]

The answer frequently made in reply to the foregoing argument is that the stockholder is investing in the total enterprise, not in particular parts of it, and therefore it should not concern him very much how the individual parts are doing as long as the overall performance is good. On the other hand, it is undoubtedly true, as a former chairman of the SEC observed, that segmented reporting "serves as an important control on corporate managers by requiring them to justify the results of their stewardship." He added:

There may be diversified companies which are maintaining low-profit or money-losing operations for reasons which would not be persuasive to stockholders or financial analysts, and requiring separate disclosure might well result in the improvement or elimination of the substandard operation, to the ultimate benefit of the stockholders . . .[11]

[9] Kaplan and Reaugh, "Accounting, Reports to Stockholders and the SEC," 48 *Yale Law Journal* 935 (1939).

[10] Robert T. Sprouse, "Chop Suey, Chain Stores, and Conglomerate Reporting," *The Journal of Accountancy,* April 1968, pp. 35–42.

[11] Manuel F. Cohen, address before AICPA, Oct. 5, 1966.

Advocates of segmented reports say that such reports might go a long way toward exposing a weak management to shareholders who might, as a result, give closer attention to proposed new acquisitions, especially in unrelated fields, and thereby remove the incentive to expand simply for the sake of expansion.

If a company acquires an unrelated business that turns out poorly, segmented reporting might highlight the error, whereas under present reporting practice, management's acquisition mistakes are buried in consolidated figures. (This argument cuts both ways, since, under present practice, the results of successful acquisitions are also not separately disclosed.)

Support for product line reporting also comes to a certain extent from industry. Take the case, for example, of a company that is engaged in only one line of business—a so-called "unitary" company. Its reports, prepared on a conventional basis, necessarily disclose the results of its operations in that line of business. Suppose the unitary company competes with a diversified company that is also in that line of business. Does not the absence of line of business reporting result in a competitive disadvantage to the unitary company?

Assume also that a small company in one line of business buys its raw materials from a huge, diversified company. Without segmented reporting, the small company has no way of knowing how profitable its business is to the big company, whereas the big company knows exactly how much profit the small company earns. In their price negotiations, the small company is obviously at a disadvantage as compared with its big supplier.

Support for segmented reporting also came from a prominent CPA who said that the reporting of meaningful data about major separable segments of an entire enterprise deserves careful consideration by all corporate management. He acknowledged that disclosures that would lose or reduce a competitive advantage would not be in the stockholder's overall best interest and should be avoided. However, he said, this point needs to be realistically evaluated in terms of what competitors already know. There are other cases, he said, in which operations are so interrelated that the segmenting would require the making of such major arbitrary assumptions that the meaningfulness of the results would be dubious. In still other cases, he added, "reluctance to make disclosures stems solely from the management's embarrassment that downward trends are hidden in the whole; in these cases, the health of the entire corporation-stockholder-society relationship calls for the disclosure." [12]

Proponents of segmented reporting also point to requirements of the London Stock Exchange adopted in 1965 and applicable to companies making an application for original listing of securities on the Exchange. In

[12] Herman W. Bevis, *Corporate Financial Reporting in a Competitive Economy,* 1965, pp. 155–56.

the case of such a company, or group of companies, the requirement is to give, wherever possible, a statement showing the sales turnover figures or gross trading income during the preceding three financial years which should contain a reasonable breakdown between the more important trading activities. In addition, in the case of applications for listing additional issues of securities on the Exchange, if the company, or group, carried on widely different operations, the requirement is to include in the annual audited accounts, or Chairman's statement, a statement showing the contributions to "trading results" of such respective differing operations. Also, if the company, or group, trades outside the United Kingdom, a statement showing geographical analysis of its trading operations must be included in the annual report either as part of the audited accounts or in the Chairman's statement. The required information can be indicated either by figures or percentages.

In keeping with the normal practice of the Exchange, flexibility has been maintained. The requirements may be altered or waived in the case of hardship or where it is shown that the disclosures would not be meaningful or would be damaging.

The London Stock Exchange requirements were echoed in provisions of the United Kingdom Companies Act of 1967. Clause 17 of the Act provides in part as follows:

If, in the course of a financial year, a company . . . has carried on business of two or more classes . . . that, in the opinion of the directors, differ substantially from each other, there shall be contained in the director's report relating to that year a statement of

a. the proportions in which the turnover [i.e. sales] for that year . . . is divided amongst those classes (describing them) ; and
b. as regards business of each class, the extent or approximate extent (expressed, in either case, in monetary terms) to which, in the opinion of the directors, the carrying on of business of that class contributed to, or restricted, the profit or loss of the company for that year before taxation.

A lawyer who is well-informed on the subject of product line reporting has raised the question: Is not the *absence* of this kind of information likely in some circumstances to give rise to litigation? He illustrates the point involved with a hypothetical case.[13] A corporation has two divisions whose sales volumes are approximately equal and employ the same amount of assets. One division is very profitable, the other a loser. The corporation sells the profitable division and continues to operate the loser. While the sale is pending or after it is consummated but before the corporation makes a disclosure of corporate—now single division—results,

---

[13] A. A. Sommer, Jr., "Conglomerate Disclosure: Friend or Foe?," *The Business Lawyer*, January 1967.

an investor, unaware of the sharply differing profitability, purchases securities from an insider or simply in the open market. The writer raised the question: Is there liability on the part of the corporation or the insider for failure to disclose the very material fact that the remaining enterprise is and has been a loser?

In October 1966, the then Chairman of the SEC, Manuel F. Cohen, asked the same question in another context. Assume, he said, a company engaged in two distinct lines of business, each of which accounted for about half of its volume and that this fact is disclosed in the prospectus or report that the company files with the SEC under its then existing disclosure rules. However, all, or substantially all, of the company's net income is derived from one of these two lines. "I am not sure," he said, "that financial statements which do no more than report sales, cost of sales, expenses and net income for the two divisions combined, 'fairly present' the results of operations of the company." [14] When the figures published in the income statement combine the results of operations in different lines of business in which gross profit margins and net income differ sharply, "they may be inadequate to convey meaningful information about the manner in which the company derives its income and may be more misleading than any of the alternative ways in which the divisional breakdown might be presented."

These are astonishing statements, to say the least. The SEC has accepted without comment or criticism literally thousands of financial statements which purported to "fairly present" the results of operations of the companies involved and which were prepared precisely in the manner that Mr. Cohen questioned. In presenting this argument, he may have realized that he was undercutting the significance of consolidated financial statements, and he added that he did not wish to detract in any way from the importance that the SEC attached to the publication of consolidated statements for a corporation and its subsidiaries. He acknowledged that the development of consolidated statements as the appropriate method for presenting the financial picture of an affiliated group was an important victory for the investing public. (In a 1968 speech, Mr. Cohen said that the development of consolidated financial statements, "in the context of the rapid changes in the last several years, has been a bit too successful.") [15] But the problem of conglomerates was a newer one—the other side of the coin. "An increasing number of companies . . . are spreading themselves over a variety of entirely different kinds of operations, and it is no longer enough for the investing public to know the overall results in consolidated form." If investors are to make meaningful decisions, Mr. Cohen asserted, they had to know the respective contributions of the various categories to the consolidated figures.

[14] Manuel F. Cohen, address before annual meeting of AICPA, Oct. 5, 1966.
[15] Manuel F. Cohen, address before Financial Executives Institute, Oct. 26, 1968.

SEC Reverses Its Position.—By May 1966 it became apparent that the SEC had had a change of heart. Speaking before the Financial Analysts Federation, Manuel F. Cohen, chairman of the SEC at the time, said that with the examples of voluntary reporting already in evidence and the English precedents, the next objective beyond the breakdown of sales for the conglomerate company should be the "defined" operating profit and loss statement on a divisional basis. He recognized that disclosure of divisional profits for the conglomerate company introduced the risk that indirect expenses could be allocated in a way designed more to produce a desired result than to effect a fair financial presentation. But this, he said, was the kind of risk always incident to progress, and that professionalism in accounting should keep this problem within bounds.

The SEC's emphasis in the beginning was on the necessity of obtaining more financial information of the kind that was needed to evaluate the experience and prospects of *conglomerate companies*. But once the SEC was launched in this direction, it became apparent that there could not be one set of disclosure rules for conglomerate companies and another set of rules for diversified companies. Consequently, what started out as a campaign with conglomerates as the target, changed into a broad-based program to obtain sales and profit information about the principal components of any corporation or affiliated group engaged in more than one line of business.

Resort to the Securities Acts.—Whatever may have been Senator Long's purpose in proposing to amend the antitrust laws, it appeared that new legislation might not be needed to accomplish that purpose, since the SEC had the authority under the Securities Acts to require companies subject to the statutes to make the kind of disclosures that Senator Long and Chairman Dixon had in mind in connection with the proposed amendments. The SEC had only to promulgate rules requiring companies subject to its jurisdiction to report the information. For the SEC to promulgate such a rule, presumably there would have to be a showing that it was in the interest of investors. This presented no problem, since, at the Senate Subcommittee hearings, several investment-oriented individuals testified that product line information was in the interest of investors—that without such information, they were handicapped in weighing the investment merits of a company's securities.

Research Underlying Segmented Reporting.—As has been stated earlier in this chapter, the matter of segmented reporting has been the subject of a great deal of study not only by the SEC and its staff but also by other organizations. A major effort in this respect was made by the Financial Executives Institute which, through the Financial Executives Research

Foundation, sponsored a study on the subject of segmented reporting. The study was headed by Professor Robert K. Mautz, and the report which followed is often referred to as the Mautz Report.[16]

The APB issued a statement on the subject entitled "Disclosure of Supplemental Financial Information by Diversified Companies" in September 1967. This statement (not one in the series of APB formal opinions) encouraged the voluntary disclosure of the operating results of the industry segments of a business.

Other organizations also conducted research on the subject of segmented reporting[17] but it was the Mautz study which was the most impressive and, as it developed, the most influential. The study recommended that companies engaged in more than one industry disclose for each component the sales (or revenues) and contribution to income. It took the position that "unitary" companies, that is, companies almost entirely engaged in a single industry, should not have to fractionalize themselves for reporting purposes. Other recommendations of the study were: (1) management, because of its familiarity with the business, is in the best position to determine the number and scope of components of a diversified company for reporting purposes; (2) if the methods of pricing intracompany transfers or of allocating costs affect significantly the reported contributions to income, the methods used should be disclosed; and (3) if the recommended disclosures would be detrimental to the interests of shareholders, a statement to that effect should be made in lieu of the disclosures.

The Line of Business Reporting Requirements.—In 1969 the SEC announced amendments to three of its registration forms: Forms S–1 and S–7 under the 1933 Act, and Form 10 under the 1934 Act. The amendments related to Item 9 of Form S–1, Item 5 of Form S–7, and Item 3 of Form 10, all of which require a brief description of the business done and intended to be done by the registrant and its subsidiaries. The effect of the amendments was to include a requirement for comprehensive line of business information to be disclosed by registrants who, with their subsidiaries, are engaged in more than one line of business.

[16] R. K. Mautz, *Financial Reporting by Diversified Companies,* Financial Executives Research Foundation, 1968.

[17] See, for example, the research study entitled *External Reporting for Segments of a Business,* by Morton Backer and Walter B. McFarland, published by National Association of Accountants, 1968. Readers interested in excellent presentations of developments in this new area of reporting are referred to *Public Reporting by Conglomerates,* containing the papers presented at a symposium organized by Tulane Graduate School of Business Administration in 1967, edited by Alfred Rappaport, Peter H. Firmin, and Stephen A. Zeff. These papers and other matters are commented upon by Robert T. Sprouse, "Diversified Views about Diversified Companies", *Journal of Accounting Research,* Spring, 1969, pp. 137–159.

In 1970 the Commission revised its annual report form (Form 10–K) to include a requirement for annual reporting of line of business information identical with the requirements in the three registration statements referred to above.

Briefly stated, the new provisions are intended to elicit information with respect to those lines of business that contributed, during either of the last two fiscal years, a certain proportion of (1) the total of sales and revenues, or (2) income before income taxes and extraordinary items and without deduction of loss resulting from operations of any line of business. For companies with total sales and revenues of more than $50 million, the proportion is 10%; for smaller companies, 15%. Similar disclosure is also required with respect to any line of business which resulted in a loss of 10% or more (15% or more for smaller companies) of income before income taxes, extraordinary items, and loss operations. The period to be covered by the information is each of a maximum of the last five fiscal years subsequent to December 31, 1966. (This paragraph is an attempt to simplify the requirements, the text of which is set forth below.)

Many companies will have serious problems in stating the contribution to income by lines of business because of the difficulty in allocating certain items of income and expense—for example, investment income, royalty income, interest expense, research and development costs, and so on. Some companies may presently allocate such items to existing lines of business on many different bases; some may find it almost impossible to do this on any but an arbitrary basis. The SEC is aware of this situation, and its instructions give the registrant some latitude by permitting it to report the contributions to results of operations "most closely approaching" income before income taxes, extraordinary items, and loss operations.

In its releases (No. 33–4988 and No. 34–8650, July 14, 1969) announcing the amendments to the registration forms, the SEC said that it had received various suggestions to be more specific as to the meaning of "line of business." The SEC indicated, however, that in view of the numerous ways in which companies are organized to do business, the variety of products and services, the history of predecessor and acquired companies, and the diversity of operating characteristics, such as markets, raw materials, manufacturing processes, and competitive conditions, "it is not deemed feasible or desirable to be more specific in defining a line of business." The Commission stated that management, because of its familiarity with company structure, is in the most informed position to separate the company into components on a reasonable basis for reporting purposes. Accordingly, discretion is left to the management to devise a reporting pattern appropriate to the particular company's operations and responsive to its organizational concepts.

Although some might think the SEC was reasonable in permitting management to define the lines of business in which it operates, this decision was not universally applauded. One writer said, ". . . although it may generally be true that managements are in the most informed position for making judgments about 'realistic components,' even the most scrupulous and conscientious managers are likely to lack objectivity." [18]

The instructions provide, however, that in grouping products or services as lines of business, appropriate consideration shall be given to all relevant factors, including rates of profitability of operations, degrees of risk, and opportunity for growth. Furthermore, the basis for grouping such products or services and any material changes between periods in such groupings shall be briefly described.

Because of the disclosure requirements with respect to lines of business that result in losses, it is possible that information may have to be furnished for more than ten lines of business. In that situation the registrant may, at its option, furnish the required information for only the ten lines of business deemed most important to an understanding of the business. If this option is availed of, a statement to that effect has to be made in the registration statement or annual report.

The text of the line of business requirements follows:

(b) (1) *Information as to lines of business.* If the registrant and its subsidiaries are engaged in more than one line of business, state, for each of the registrant's last five fiscal years, or for each fiscal year ending after December 31, 1966, or for each fiscal year the registrant has been engaged in business, whichever period is less, the approximate amount or percentage of (i) total sales and revenues, and (ii) income (or loss) before income taxes and extraordinary items, attributable to each line of business which during either of the last two fiscal years accounted for—

(A) 10 percent or more of the total of sales and revenues,
(B) 10 percent or more of income before income taxes and extraordinary items computed without deduction of loss resulting from operations of any line of business, or
(C) a loss which equalled or exceeded 10 percent of the amount of income specified in (B) above;

provided, that if total sales and revenues did not exceed $50,000,000 during either of the last two fiscal years, the percentages specified in (A), (B) and (C) above shall be 15 percent, instead of 10 percent.

If it is impracticable to state the contribution to income (or loss) before income taxes and extraordinary items for any line of business, state the contribution thereof to the results of operations most closely approaching such income, together with a brief explanation of the reasons why it is not practicable to state the contribution to such income or loss.

Instructions. 1. If the number of lines of business for which information is required exceeds ten, the registrant may, at its option, furnish the required

[18] Robert T. Sprouse, "Chop Suey, Chain Stores, and Conglomerate Reporting," *The Journal of Accountancy,* April 1968, p. 39.

information only for the ten lines of business deemed most important to an understanding of the business. In such event, a statement to that effect shall be set forth.

2. In grouping products or services as lines of business, appropriate consideration shall be given to all relevant factors, including rates of profitability of operations, degrees of risk and opportunity for growth. The basis for grouping such products or services and any material changes between periods in such groupings shall be briefly described.

3. Where material amounts of products or services are transferred from one line of business to another, the receiving and transferring lines may be considered a single line of business for the purpose of reporting the operating results thereof.

4. If the method of pricing intra-company transfers of products or services or the method of allocation of common or corporate costs materially affects the reported contribution to income of a line of business, such methods and any material changes between periods in such methods and the effect thereof shall be described briefly.

5. Information regarding sales or revenues or income (or loss) from different classes of products or services in operations regulated by Federal, State or municipal authorities may be limited to those classes of products or services required by any uniform system of accounts prescribed by such authorities.

It will be noted that, in the case of a diversified company having total sales of $90 million and pre-tax income of $9 million, it would have to disclose the operating results of a line of business in which the sales were $10 million or the pre-tax income was $1 million. The information would not have to be reported for this segment of the business if the sales of the entire enterprise were more than $100 million or the pre-tax income were more than $10 million.

It will also be noted from the text of the SEC's instructions, that the information as to lines of business does not have to be certified by independent public accountants. Many companies, however, have called and probably will continue to call on their auditors for advice and assistance in connection with preparing the information on a basis responsive to the SEC's requirements. In addition, underwriting agreements in connection with public offerings of securities are often conditioned on the underwriters receiving some kind of assurance ("comfort") from the independent accountants with respect to such information included in the registration statement. A member of the APB who is also a CPA and a university professor and was a participant in the Tulane symposium said that he looked forward to the time when there will be full, or relatively full, divisional reporting by all diversified enterprises and that the reports would be covered by the independent CPA's opinion.[19]

[19] Sidney Davidson, "Implications of Conglomerate Reporting for the Independent CPA—Comments", in *Public Reporting by Conglomerates,* ed. by Rappaport, Firmin, and Zeff, Prentice-Hall, Inc., 1968, p. 87.

In the early stages of the SEC's proposal to adopt a form of product line or line of business reporting requirement, the SEC had under consideration a requirement to report the amount of assets employed in each segment of the business for which operating results are furnished. In the final version of the line of business requirements, the SEC dropped the proposal relating to assets employed.

Breakdown of Total Volume of Sales and Revenues.—The revisions in the registration and report forms previously referred to in this chapter continued the existing disclosure requirements with respect to the breakdown of total volume of sales and revenues by principal classes of similar products or services, except that the percentage test was reduced from 15% to 10% in the case of companies having total sales and revenues of more than $50 million during either of their last two fiscal years. "This continued requirement is appropriate," the Commission said, "in view of the relative freedom given management in determining 'line of business'." For a company using classes of similar products or services as its basis for determining lines of business, repetition of the disclosure will not be necessary. To the extent that such classification is not coincident with the company's line of business determination or where the company is not engaged in more than one line of business, disclosure is limited to the proportion of sales and revenues and does not require a showing of the contribution to earnings.

Omission or Substitution of Information.—The instructions for all of the registration and report forms discussed in this chapter (Forms S–1, S–7, 10, and 10–K) contain provisions for the omission of line of business information called for by the SEC's instructions or the substitution of comparable information, if the registrant so requests and the SEC determines that the request is consistent with investor protection.

The Commission, on its own initiative, may call for the furnishing of other information in addition to, or in substitution for, what is called for by the instructions of the applicable form where such information is necessary or appropriate for an adequate description of the business done or intended to be done.

The Measure of Product Line Significance.—As indicated in the preceding discussion, the SEC has determined that a line of business is a material part of an enterprise when the line has 10% or more of the total sales or revenues, 10% or more of the pre-tax income (before extraordinary items and before deducting the loss from operations of any line of business), or a loss which equalled or exceeded 10% of the immediately preceding amount of income. For companies whose volume of sales or revenues are below $50 million, the corresponding percentage figure is 15%.

In general terms, therefore, the measure of materiality for a line of business is 10% in the case of the largest companies. Many interested persons and organizations have felt that the 10% breaking point is too low. As reported in *The Journal of Accountancy,* the APB noted that many of its members thought the 10% rule was too low.[20] The study sponsored by the Financial Executives Institute recommended that conglomerates report sales and profit contributions for any segment of their businesses generating 15% or more of gross sales.

Under ex-President Lyndon B. Johnson, a Cabinet Committee on Price Stability studied the merger movement, the growth of conglomerates, and the effect on competition and prices. Among other things, the Cabinet Committee recommended more detailed product-line reporting than that adopted by the SEC. Also, the Committee believed that the SEC's cut-off point of 10% was too high because some conglomerate enterprises sell literally thousands of products falling into numerous "product classes" few of which would constitute as much as 10% of total sales. Based on a survey by the Bureau of the Census, the Committee maintained that if the 10% rule were followed, the 50 largest United States manufacturing companies would be required to disclose product line earnings for only 14% of the Census Bureau categories in which they operated.

Instead of the 10% rule, the Cabinet Committee recommended disclosure of earnings by industry category for any product line that accounted for 5% of sales or any product line having sales over a specified minimum, say $25 million. On the basis of a 5% rule, the 50 largest manufacturers would disclose product line earnings in 42% of the Census Bureau categories in which they operate.

As previously noted, the SEC may have listened to the APB, the FEI, the Cabinet Committee, and others, but, in the end, made up its own mind as to where to draw the line on materiality.

Examples of Compliance with Line of Business Requirements.— The following pages of this chapter set forth examples, taken from recent prospectuses, showing various ways in which companies registering with the SEC have attempted to comply with the Commission's line of business reporting requirements. In some of the examples, it will be noted, no information was furnished with regard to the issuer's principal lines of business, presumably on the basis that the company involved was engaged in a single industry, that is, a "unitary" company.

[20] Paul A. Pacter, "News Feature," March 1969, p. 26.

Example 1. Disclosure of sales and pre-tax income.

Whittaker Corporation is a highly diversified company which grew rapidly in the period 1964 through 1970 primarily through acquisitions. In connection with the registration of its common stock, it issued a prospectus dated May 13, 1971 which disclosed that the company was not currently pursuing an active acquisition program, and, in fact, was in the process of identifying and disposing of a number of unprofitable operations or operations that were only marginally profitable.

The text of the prospectus indicated that the company and its subsidiaries are engaged primarily in the fields of materials, housing, recreation, transportation, and scientific and technical products and services. In materials, the company is engaged in the processing and distribution of metals, textiles, plastics, and other chemicals. In housing, it is a developer of low-income dwellings under government sponsored and subsidy programs, and manufactures building supplies. In recreation, it produces pleasure boats, physical conditioning equipment, and patio furniture. In transportation, it makes railroad freight cars, mining cars, and equipment, hydraulic truck equipment, cargo containers, and automotive trim and accessories. In the scientific and technical field, it renders research and development services. The company's activities also include pipeline construction, lithographic printing, and equipment leasing.

The text of the prospectus contained a table showing the sales (excluding discontinued operations) and income from continuing operations (before federal income taxes and extraordinary items) during each of the last four fiscal years in each of the major areas in which the company and its subsidiaries operated. With dollar amounts omitted, the table follows:

	Fiscal years ended October 31							
	1967		1968		1969		1970	
Line of business	Sales	Pre-tax income	Sales	Pre-tax income	Sales	Pre-tax income	Sales	Pre-tax income
Metal forming and conversion								
Metal finishing and distribution								
Chemicals and textiles								
Housing								
Recreation								
Transportation								
Scientific, technical & other								
Total								

Example 2. Disclosure of net sales and approximate contribution to net income.

The Singer Company issued a prospectus dated April 15, 1971 in connection with an underwritten offering of its common stock. In the text portion of the prospectus, under the caption "Business—General," the company disclosed the net sales and the approximate contribution to *net income* of its principal lines of business for the four years ended December 31, 1970. With amounts omitted, the form of the tabular disclosure was as follows:

	Net Sales			
	1970	1969	1968	1967
Consumer products	$	$	$	$
Industrial products				
Information systems				
Aerospace and marine systems				
Education and training products				
Total	$	$	$	$

	Approximate contribution to net income			
	1970	1969	1968	1967
Consumer products	$	$	$	$
Industrial products				
Information systems				
Aerospace and marine systems				
Education and training products				
Total	$	$	$	$

In a headnote to the tabular material, the company explained that, in the determination of approximate contribution to net income, allocations of corporate administrative expense and corporate interest expense were made to the principal lines of business based on their relative sales and assets, respectively. It also stated that income taxes were generally identifiable and allocated to the actual tax expense of or credit to each line of business.

Indicative of the broad range of products included in "consumer products" was the fact that it included sales of household sewing machines and related goods and services, furniture and wood products, KLH stereo systems, television sets, radios, phonograph records, refrigerators, washing machines, kitchen ranges, portable power tools, knitting machines, European mail order division, and the operations of the recently acquired Besco Organization (development, construction, and sale of homes, garden apartments, and shopping centers in Northern California).

Example 3. Disclosure of net revenues and income.

Kenton Corporation issued a prospectus dated May 4, 1971 which indicated that it was incorporated in 1968 as the successor to The Family Bargain Centers, Inc. The mass market retail business formerly conducted by Kenton's predecessor is being performed by a subsidiary, FBC Stores, Inc. The company also operates a wholesale business through a subsidiary, Republic-Cellini Corp. In recent years the company acquired a number of businesses, now operated as subsidiaries, which merchandise on a retail and wholesale basis products appealing to the affluent customer, including Cartier jewelry, Ben Kahn furs, Georges Kaplan furs, Mark Cross leather goods, Valentino Couture fashions, and Kenneth Jay Lane fashion jewelry.

In the narrative portion of the prospectus, Kenton stated that it was engaged principally in the business of wholesale and retail distribution. Retail products include jewelry, leather goods, furs and clothes, as well as a broad range of department store merchandise, including housewares, soft goods, and hardware. Wholesale products include imported sportswear, fashion jewelry, furs, and designer clothes.

The company furnished a table showing the approximate percentages of total net revenues and income (before income taxes, and unallocated administrative, general and net corporate interest expenses) attributable to the retail line of business and the wholesale line of business (which together encompass substantially all of the company's operations). With the percentage amounts omitted, the table was as follows:

	Net revenues					Income				
	1966	1967	1968	1969	1970	1966	1967	1968	1969	1970
Retail operations	%	%	%	%	%	%	%	%	%	%
Wholesale operations	%	%	%	%	%	%	%	%	%	%
Other	%	%	%	%	%	%	%	%	%	%
	100%	100%	100%	100%	100%	100%	100%	100%	100%	100%

[Footnotes to the table are omitted here.]

Following the above table, the company stated that it wholesaled and retailed two classes of products: those which are designed to sell in the mass market, and those designed to sell to the affluent consumer. In the last five years, sales of products for the mass market represented 93%, 94%, 89%, 82%, and 81% of total sales, respectively. The company also disclosed that profit margins on sales to the affluent consumer market have been historically higher than those on sales for the mass market, although in 1970 the opposite was true.

Example 4. Multidivision enterprise considered unitary.

Broadway-Hale Stores, Inc. issued a prospectus dated May 25, 1971 in connection with an offering of its debentures due in 1996. The text of the prospectus stated that the business of the company is carried on by six autonomous divisions. The general department store operations are conducted by the Broadway division in Southern California, Arizona, and Las Vegas; by the Emporium Capwell division in the San Francisco Bay area; and by the Weinstock's division in central California and Reno. Specialty department stores are operated in Texas and Florida by Neiman-Marcus. Other divisions are Sunset House (mail order business) and Walden Book Company (retail book stores). According to the prospectus, for each of the past five years more than 90% of the company's net sales and earnings before extraordinary items have been derived from the department store business. Accordingly, the company must have considered that it was in a "unitary" business, and it furnished no further break-down of its principal lines of business.

Example 5. Disclosure of sales and earnings before taxes.

Grolier Incorporated is in the business of publishing and distributing encyclopedias and reference works by door-to-door sales representatives and the sale of publications and other merchandise by mail. The company also distributes juvenile books and large type reading materials. Other activities include the sale of bookcases and water skis, the sale and servicing of vending machines, and the development and operation of mobile home parks.

According to the company's prospectus dated May 26, 1971, only two of its principal lines of business accounted for more than 10% of sales and pre-tax income in the years 1967–1970. The prospectus included the following tabulation of sales and pre-tax earnings for that period:

	Sales				Earnings before taxes			
	1967	1968	1969	1970	1967	1968	1969	1970
Encyclopedias and reference works:								
United States and Canada	%	%	%	%	%	%	%	%
International	%	%	%	%	%	%	%	%
	%	%	%	%	%	%	%	%
Mail order publications and merchandise:								
United States and Canada	%	%	%	%	%	%	%	%
International	%	%	%	%	%	%	%	%
	%	%	%	%	%	%	%	%
Other	%	%	%	%	%	%	%	%
Total	100%	100%	100%	100%	100%	100%	100%	100%

The above table was followed by an explanation as follows: "Earnings before taxes are computed after a charge by the parent company to its subsidiaries of a management fee based on net sales. Because of this method of allocation, this charge may not necessarily reflect the actual cost of services and expenses incurred by the parent company with respect to domestic as compared with international operations."

Example 6. Manufacturing enterprise considered unitary.

The prospectus of Garlock Inc., dated May 25, 1971, stated that the business was started in 1887 to manufacture packing and sealing materials and devices to control or prevent leakage of liquid and gaseous fluids in machinery and equipment. Since that time the company has broadened its product line through acquisitions, internal product development, and, to a lesser extent, licensing arrangements.

The company manufactures and sells annually over 100,000 kinds and sizes of individual and assembled engineered components for industry. During each of the last five years, the company derived more than 95% of its revenues and income before taxes from the sale of products which are related by way of function, manufacturing technology or customer to the company's packing and sealing devices and materials.

Because many of the products manufactured by the company are replaced during the life of the unit of which they are a part, a substantial portion of Garlock's business is derived from the sale of items which are used in maintenance applications, and is estimated to account for about one-half of the company's business.

The prospectus discloses some of the items produced by the company which include industrial rubber products, pipe couplings, gaskets, expansion joints, mechanical seals, leather packings, oil seals, metal packings, engine valves, power transmission components, speed reducers, gears, mufflers, and wire springs. There is no disclosure, however, of the sales and earnings of principal lines of business, from which it would appear that the company regarded itself as a "unitary" company, and the SEC's staff agreed.

Example 7. Disclosure of revenues and sales and net income.

A prospectus of General Telephone and Electronics Corporation, dated August 5, 1970, analyzed the consolidated operations by principal lines of business for the six months ended June 30, 1969 and 1970. The information appeared in the text of the prospectus as follows:

	Revenues and Sales		Net Income	
	Six Months Ended June 30, (Unaudited)		Six Months Ended June 30, (Unaudited)	
	1970	1969	1970	1969
Telephone Operations				
Manufacturing Operations				
Domestic				
Telecommunications ....:.....				
Sylvania				
International				
Intercompany eliminations				
Total				
Combined				
Parent Company interest expense, preferred stock dividend requirements, etc.				
Consolidated				

Example 8. Disclosure of net sales and operating income.

The Dow Chemical Company, in a prospectus dated April 22, 1970, stated that it had three principal lines of business: the manufacture and sale of chemicals and metals; plastic materials and products; and bioproducts/consumer products. The company set forth in the narrative portion of the prospectus the net sales and operating income of products and services for each of the years 1967, 1968, and 1969 for each of these lines of business, as follows:

	Products and services					
	Net Sales			Operating Income		
Lines of Business	1967	1968	1969	1967	1968	1969
Chemicals and metals	$	$	$	$	$	$
Plastic materials and products						
Bioproducts/consumer						
	$	$	$	$	$	$

The amounts in the table were not covered by the report of the independent public accountants, but the totals in the table agreed with the consolidated amounts shown in the income statement which was covered by the accountants' report. From the income statement, it was apparent that "operating income" was arrived at as follows:

Products and services:
Net sales
Operating costs and expenses:
Cost of sales
Depreciation

Selling and administrative
Total operating costs and expenses
Products and services operating income

The "operating income" so arrived at was before investment and financial costs and income (including equity in earnings of Swiss banking subsidiary), other income and expenses (including interest), taxes on income, and minority interests' share in income.

Example 9.   Disclosure of contributions of product categories to sales volume.

The Black and Decker Manufacturing Company is one of the leading manufacturers of portable power tools and accessories. In a prospectus dated May 13, 1971, the company stated that it was engaged in the manufacture of portable electric tools and accessories, portable air tools and accessories, and stationary woodworking and metalworking equipment.

Portable electric tools include electric drills, shears, nibblers, screwdrivers, impact wrenches, hammers, grinders, sanders, polishers, saws, routers, vacuum cleaners, valve refacers, valve seat grinders, lawn mowers, lawn trimmers, and hedge trimmers.

Portable air tools include pneumatic drills, screwdrivers, nut setters, impact wrenches, die grinders, grinders, sanders, hammers, rammers, and power chisels.

Stationary woodworking and metalworking equipment include bench grinders, radial arm saws, and panel saws.

The company disclosed the relative contributions of the various product categories (including product service related thereto) to the consolidated sales volume for the last five years as follows:

	1966	1967	1968	1969	1970
Portable electric tools and accessories	90%	91%	91%	91%	93%
Portable air tools and accessories	3%	3%	4%	4%	3%
Stationary woodworking and metalworking tools, equipment and accessories	7%	6%	5%	5%	4%

The prospectus did not contain information regarding the contributions to pre-tax income of the various product categories, or of the portable electric tool business which, as noted above, contributed in each year 90% or more of the consolidated sales.

Example 10. Disclosure of sales and other revenues
and some income statement details.

General Cigar Co., Inc. issued a prospectus dated May 17, 1971 in connection with an offering of its common stock. The company is engaged primarily in the tobacco business through the manufacture and sale of cigars, the growing of wrapper tobacco for use on its own cigars and for others, and as a distributor of cigars, cigarettes, health and beauty aids, candy, and other items. As a part of its tobacco business, the company licenses the manufacture of, or sells to others, HTL tobacco binder and Ultra Tobacco wrapper. It also licenses brand names, and certain of the machinery it has developed. Incidental to growing wrapper tobacco, the company operates a commercial tree and shrub nursery. Through its subsidiary, Ex-Lax, Inc., the company is engaged in the proprietary drug business.

The company furnished a table in the text portion of the prospectus setting forth the operations of the two principal lines of business for the two most recent fiscal years, as follows (with dollar amounts omitted):

| | Year ended | | | |
| | Jan. 3, 1970 | | Jan. 2, 1971 | |
	Tobacco business	Propri- etary drug business	Tobacco business	Propri- etary drug business
Total sales and other revenue	$	$	$	$
Income before interest expense, minority interest, taxes, and extraordinary items				
Less:				
Interest expense chargeable against operations of tobacco business				
Subtotal				
Interest on indebtedness incurred to purchase proprietary drug business				
Minority interest (before taxes)				
Income before taxes and extraordinary items	$	$	$	$

Example 11. Disclosure of line of business data within the income statement.

The prospectus of CIC Industries, Inc., dated June 16, 1970, contained an income statement for the years 1965–1969 and the four months ended April 30, 1969 and 1970. The line of business information appeared on the face of the income statement as follows:

Net Sales:
    Petroleum ....
    Manufacturing ....
    Chemical ....
    Other ....
Costs and Expenses:
    Cost of sales (exclusive of depreciation, depletion and amortization and taxes shown below) (Note) ....
    Selling, general and administrative expenses ....
    Nonproductive exploratory costs and delay rentals ......
    Depreciation, depletion and amortization (Note) ......
    Taxes, other than income—
        Real estate and personal property taxes ....
        Payroll taxes ....
        Other taxes ....
Operating Income ....
Other Income and Expense:
    Equity in net income of Jayhawk Pipeline Corporation
    Other, net ....
Division Income (Note 4):
    Petroleum ....
    Manufacturing ....
    Chemical ....
    Other ....
Financial Costs (Note 4):
    Interest on debt ....
    Interest charged to construction ....
    Amortization of debt expense ....

Other, net ....

Income, before income taxes and extraordinary charge ......

Income Taxes (Notes 4 and   )...........................

Income, before extraordinary charge ....

Extraordinary Charge, net of Federal income taxes (Note   ) .

Net Income ....

Note 4 to the income statement explained the basis on which the Division Income was stated, as follows:

(4) Division Income:

Division income is reported before financial costs and income taxes. Capital flows among the respective divisions in such a manner that divisional capitalization, financial costs and income taxes are not necessarily representative of, or comparable with, those of companies in similar industries. Reference is made to Note 1 of the Notes to Financial Statements which describes a capital contribution made by Colorado Interstate Corporation on February 10, 1970, part of which was contributed in turn by CIC Industries, Inc. to certain of its subsidiaries, thereby substantially changing their capital structures and related financial costs.

CHAPTER 24

ACCOUNTANT'S CERTIFICATES AND LETTERS

Part 1

CONTENTS

Importance of Accountant's Certificates.—Long before the SEC was thought of, there was general recognition of the importance of the accountant's certificate. Although offering circulars of the pre-1929 era bear little resemblance to today's statutory prospectuses, they have one thing in common: the financial statements in both are accompanied by accountant's certificates. Published reports of most publicly owned corporations contained accountant's certificates even before the 1934 Act required listed companies to file annual reports containing certified financial statements. It cannot be denied, however, that since the enactment of SEC legislation, there has been even greater recognition of the importance of accountant's certificates.

In one of its earliest decisions the SEC indicated the importance which it attached to the accountant's certificate. In this case, the registrant's financial statements were not in issue, but there was a question as to the independence of the certifying accountants. Since no questions had been raised concerning the financial statements, counsel for the registrant attempted to minimize the importance of the certificate, saying that certification by and of itself is not a material fact, that it is a "tag" attached to financial statements, and that its only significance is to induce reliance upon, and to guarantee the propriety of, the statements. The SEC did not agree with this concept of certification. The Commission said:

A certification is a material fact. It signifies that the contents of the financial statements to which it is appended have been checked and verified within the limits stated in the certificate. To make such certification truly protective of the interests of security holders and investors, the requirement under the Securities Act of 1933, as amended, is that it be made by an "independent public or certified accountant." The insistence of the Act on a certification by an "independent" accountant signifies the real function which certification should perform. That function is the submission to an independent and impartial mind of the accounting practices and policies of registrants. The history of finance well illustrates the importance and need for submission to such impartial persons of the accounting practices and policies of the management to the end that present and prospective security holders will be protected against unsound accounting practices and procedure and will be afforded, as nearly as accounting conventions will permit, the truth about the financial condition of the enterprise which issues the securities. Accordingly, the certification gives a minimum of protection against untruths and half-truths which otherwise would more easily creep into financial statements. Hence, a statement which serves such a high function cannot be dismissed under the Act as a mere "tag" attached to financial statements. It is a material fact, for it gives meaning and reliability to financial data and makes less likely misleading or untrue financial statements. [*Cornucopia Gold Mines,* 1 SEC 364 (1936).]

Not only is the certificate a material fact, but it has also been held that it is materially misleading for an accountant to represent himself as a CPA when, in fact, he is not. In *National Electric Signal Company* [8 SEC 160 (1940)] the accountant who certified the financial statements signed as a certified public accountant. The secretary of the State Board of Public Accountancy of Texas testified that the accountant was not a CPA in Texas, nor did the record indicate that the accountant was a CPA in any other state. (Apparently the accountant was a resident of, or had his office in, Texas.) The SEC held that the accountant was not a CPA within the meaning of its rules and that his signature as such in the registration statement was an untrue and materially misleading statement of fact. (It should be noted, however, that public accountants practicing before the SEC need not be certified.)

Statutory Basis for Accountant's Certificate

This book is concerned primarily with the operations of the SEC under the Securities Act of 1933 and the Securities Exchange Act of 1934, and only incidentally with the Commission's functions under the Public Utility Holding Company Act of 1935 and the Investment Company Act of 1940. All these laws employ the registration statement device and provide for the filing of periodic reports. The documents filed contain financial information, and the Commission is authorized to require that the financial statements be certified by independent public accountants.

The 1933 Act provides that a registration statement shall contain the information specified in Schedule A of the Act. Schedule A specifies, among other things, the financial statements which the SEC is authorized to require and the certification requirements. The SEC has broad authority to add to the list of items in Schedule A and to omit some of them. The SEC has issued a number of forms for registration of securities under the Act, the financial requirements in some of which are set forth in Chapter **9**, together with the requirements for certification by independent public accountants.

The 1934 Act provides for the registration of securities listed for trading on national securities exchanges and for the registration of securities of certain publicly-owned unlisted companies. The law authorizes the Commission to specify the information to be included in the registration statement, including financial statements "certified, if required by the rules and regulations of the Commission, by independent public accountants." Similarly, the Commission is authorized to prescribe the information to be contained in annual reports of issuers so registered. One of the registration forms is Form 10, the financial requirements of which are set forth in Chapter **15**, together with the certification requirements. One of the annual report forms is Form 10-K, the financial requirements of which are also set forth in Chapter **15**, together with the instructions as to certification.

The 1935 Act provides for registration of holding companies. Section 5(b) of the Act lists the items to be contained in such a registration statement, including financial statements "certified, if required by the rules and regulations of the Commission, by an independent public accountant." Section 14 requires registered holding companies to file with the Commission such periodic reports as the Commission may require, and authorizes the Commission to prescribe that the financial statements in such reports be certified by an independent public accountant. Registration statements of holding companies are filed on Form U5B, and their annual reports are filed on Form U5S. In both of these forms the principal financial statements must be certified by independent public accountants.

The 1940 Act provides for the registration of investment companies with the Commission and the filing of periodic reports with the Commission by such registered investment companies. A number of registration and annual report forms have been promulgated by SEC under the 1940 Act. All such forms require the financial data contained therein to be certified by independent public accountants.

Regulation S–X

Several chapters of this book deal with Regulation S–X of the SEC. This is the principal accounting regulation of the SEC in its administration of the Securities Act of 1933, the Securities Exchange Act of 1934, the Public Utility Holding Company Act of 1935, and the Investment Company Act of 1940.

Article 2 of the regulation gives the Commission's formal requirements as to certification of financial statements by independent public accountants. Rule 2–01 of the regulation recites the Commission's formal requirements as to the qualifications of accountants; the rule appears on page **26**·18. Rule 2–02 contains the Commission's formal requirements as to accountants' certificates (reports) and is quoted below:

Rule 2–02. Accountants' Reports.

(a) *Technical requirements.*—The accountant's report (1) shall be dated; (2) shall be signed manually; (3) shall indicate the city and state where issued; and (4) shall identify without detailed enumeration the financial statements covered by the report.

(b) *Representations as to the audit.*—The accountant's report (1) shall state whether the audit was made in accordance with generally accepted auditing standards; and (2) shall designate any auditing procedures deemed necessary by the accountant under the circumstances of the particular case, which have been omitted, and the reasons for their omission.

   Nothing in this rule shall be construed to imply authority for the omission of any procedure which independent accountants would ordinarily employ in the course of an audit made for the purpose of expressing the opinions required by paragraph (c) of this rule.

(c) *Opinion to be expressed.*—The accountant's report shall state clearly: (1) the opinion of the accountant in respect of the financial statements covered by the report and the accounting principles and practices reflected therein; and (2) the opinion of the accountant as to the consistency of the application of the accounting principles, or as to any changes in such principles which have a material effect on the financial statements as required to be set forth in Rule 3–07(a).

(d) *Exceptions.*—Any matters to which the accountant takes exception shall be clearly identified, the exception thereto specifically and clearly stated, and, to the extent practicable, the effect of each such exception on the related financial statements given. (See ASR No. 4.)

Is It a Certificate, Opinion, or Report?

Most accountants prefer that their reports be referred to as "reports" or "opinions." They would like to avoid using the term "certificate," since "certificate" implies a degree of exactness which is certainly not present in financial statements.

Some lawyers, however, point out that the 1933 Act and the 1934 Act call for a "certificate" of independent public accountants. These lawyers therefore request that the auditor's report or opinion be labeled a "certificate" so as to conform to the language of the statute. No difficulty is involved, as far as the SEC is concerned, whether the auditor's report is captioned a "report," an "opinion," or a "certificate." The SEC accepts all three designations.

Disclosure of Departures from Opinions of APB

In October 1964 the Council of the AICPA adopted recommendations that members of the Institute should see to it that departures from opinions of the APB (as well as bulletins issued by the former Committee on Accounting Procedure and still in effect) are disclosed, either in notes to financial statements or in audit reports.

If an accounting principle reflected in financial statements differs materially in its effect from one accepted in an APB Opinion, AICPA members must decide whether the principle has substantial authoritative support and is applicable in the circumstances.

If the accountant concludes that it *does not* have such support, he must qualify his opinion, disclaim an opinion, or give an adverse opinion as appropriate.

If the accountant concludes that the principle *does* have such support, he may give an unqualified opinion and disclose the fact of the departure from the APB opinion either in his report or in notes to the statements and, when practicable, give also the effect of the departure on the financial statements. A special bulletin to AICPA members in October 1964 gave an illustration of language to accomplish the disclosure contemplated as follows:

The company's treatment of (describe) is at variance with Opinion No. — of the Accounting Principles Board (or Accounting Research Bulletin No. — of the Committee on Accounting Procedure) of the American Institute of Certified Public Accountants. This Opinion (Bulletin) states that (describe the principle in question). If the Accounting Principles Board Opinion (Accounting Research Bulletin) had been followed, income for the year would have been increased (decreased) by $, and the amount of retained earnings at (date) increased (decreased) by $. In our opinion, the company's treatment has substantial authoritative support and is an acceptable practice.

If the disclosure is made in a footnote, the last sentence might be changed to read: "In the opinion of the independent auditors, (name), the company's treatment has substantial authoritative support and is an acceptable practice."

Use of Accountant's Name in Connection with Earnings Summaries

In ASR No. 62 the SEC's Chief Accountant set forth his opinion as to the circumstances under which independent public accountants may express an opinion, and the form of such opinion, with respect to earnings summaries included in registration statements filed under the 1933 Act. The release stated that the use of an accountant's name in connection with an earnings summary is designed to give added authority to the material presented. Like all other financial statements the earnings summary is primarily a representation of management, and the proper function of the independent accountant with respect to the summary is necessarily limited to an expression of his expert and professional opinion.

It has long been recognized that an independent public accountant cannot properly undertake to express an opinion as to financial statements except on the basis of an adequate examination conducted with professional skill and acumen. The code of professional ethics of the AICPA makes it an act discreditable to the profession if the auditor in expressing his opinion on financial statements fails to acquire sufficient information to warrant expression of an opinion. [Article 2–02(d).] In other words, an independent accountant is not in a position to express an opinion on financial statements except on the basis of an examination made in accordance with generally accepted auditing standards and including all procedures which he deems necessary in view of the circumstances of the particular case.

The SEC's Chief Accountant summarized his views as follows:

In view of the foregoing, it is my opinion that it is generally improper and misleading for an accountant to permit his name to be used in connection with any period covered by a summary earnings table or to undertake to express his professional opinion as to the fairness of the representations made for such period in a summary earnings table unless he has made an examination for such period in accordance with generally accepted auditing standards applicable in the circumstances. When the independent accountant has been the auditor for the company throughout the entire period covered by the summary, and his several examinations conformed to generally accepted auditing standards, he would ordinarily need to make only such additional review as would be necessary to satisfy himself as to whether any recasting of the statements originally prepared would be necessary to reflect transactions and adjustments recorded in later years but clearly applicable to prior operations. If the instant work represents the first engagement of the accountant by the registrant and he is to express his expert opinion with respect to the earlier periods contained in the summary, it would, in my opinion, be necessary for him to apply to the operations and transactions of each of the earlier periods with respect to which he is to express an opinion substantially the same auditing procedures as those employed with respect to the first two years of the three-year certified profit and loss or income statement included in the registration statement.

In cases where the accountant has performed sufficient work to make it appropriate for him to permit the use of his name in connection with a summary earnings table, there remains to be considered the form in which he should indicate his opinion. Under the rules promulgated by this Commission, the customary method used by accountants in expressing their expert opinion takes the form of a certificate conforming to the requirements of Rule 2–02 of Regulation S–X. Such certificates make appropriate representations as to the work done, state the opinion of the accountants as to the fairness of the statements presented, and describe clearly any exceptions which the accountants may wish to make. Since, as pointed out earlier, summary earnings tables are a species of income statement, it would appear that the accountant's certificate thereon should assume a comparable form, and should be included with the summary or made a part of his report as to the three-year certified statement. . . .

Forms of Certificates

The AICPA has recommended to its members the use of a standard so-called "short" form of report. The recommended form of report appears in SAP No. 33 (1963) and is widely used in the United States. As modified to cover comparative financial statements for two years, the statements of changes in capital shares and other stockholders' equity called for by Regulation S–X, and the statement of changes in financial position (sometimes called the statement of source and application of funds), the standard short-form certificate would read as follows:

We have examined the balance sheets of (name of company) as of (date) and (date), and the related statements of income, capital shares, other stockholders' equity, and changes in financial position for the years then ended. Our examination was made in accordance with generally accepted auditing standards, and accordingly included such tests of the accounting records and such other auditing procedures as we considered necessary in the circumstances.

In our opinion, the aforementioned financial statements present fairly the financial position of (name of company) at (date) and (date), and the results of its operations and changes in its financial position for the years then ended, in conformity with generally accepted accounting principles applied on a consistent basis.

(Signature of accountants)

(City, state, and date)

In the foregoing form of certificate and in some of the suggested forms that follow, the scope paragraph and the opinion paragraph include references to statements of changes in capital shares and other stockholders' equity. This is on the assumption that such statements have to be furnished pursuant to the instructions of Regulation S–X, Rule 5–02, captions 38 and 39. In practice the language of the scope and opinion paragraphs will be modified according to the financial statements covered by the certificate.

As stated in the AICPA statement previously referred to, because of the weight which the independent auditor's opinion carries with the investing and lending public and the responsibilities he assumes in expressing it, reasonable uniformity in the manner of stating the opinion is important both to the auditor and to those who rely on his findings.

Some accountants employ a variation of the AICPA short-form report. Apparently, they reason that there is more interest in the accountant's opinion than in the scope of his examination. Consequently, they reverse the usual order of the standard short-form report, and their certificates read thus:

> In our opinion, the accompanying financial statements (pages   through) present fairly the financial position of (name of company) at (date) and (date) and the results of its operations and the changes in its financial position for the years then ended, in conformity with generally accepted accounting principles applied on a consistent basis. Our examinations of these statements were made in accordance with generally accepted auditing standards and accordingly included such tests of the accounting records and such other auditing procedures as we considered necessary in the circumstances.

This form of report also complies with SEC requirements.

Form S–1.—In Chapter **9** consideration was given to the requirements for financial statements in a registration statement on Form S–1. As stated there, the registration statement consists of two parts: Part I, consisting of the prospectus, and Part II, consisting of information not contained in the prospectus. Certain of the financial statements contained in the prospectus must be certified by independent public accountants; most of the supporting schedules in Part II must also be certified. It is permissible to have one certificate cover both the financial statements in the prospectus and the supporting schedules in Part II. In many cases, however, underwriters object to this procedure. They contend that the accountant's certificate in the prospectus should not refer to something that is not in the prospectus. Since the supporting schedules are not included in the prospectus, underwriters urge that the accountant furnish two certificates: one applying to the financial statements in the prospectus, and another covering the supporting schedules in Part II. The latter certificate should be filed in Part II with the supporting schedules.

Rule 5–04(c) of Regulation S–X states that reference to the supporting schedules shall be made in the appropriate captions of the financial statements. Where, pursuant to the applicable instructions, the supporting schedules do not accompany the financial statements, references to such schedules shall not be made. The suggested forms of certificate given below assume that there will be no references in the main financial statements to the supporting schedules.

In the ordinary case the accountant's certificate appearing in the prospectus may take the following form:

We have examined the balance sheet of (name of company) as of (date) and the related statements of income, capital shares, other stockholders' equity, and changes in financial position for the (period). Our examination was made in accordance with generally accepted auditing standards, and accordingly included such tests of the accounting records and such other auditing procedures as we considered necessary in the circumstances.

In our opinion, the aforementioned financial statements present fairly the financial position of (name of company) at (date) and the results of its operations and the changes in its financial position for the (period), in conformity with generally accepted accounting principles applied on a consistent basis.

If the financial statements are preceded by a list or index of financial statements, the certificate may refer to that list or index in the scope and in the opinion paragraphs instead of identifying the statements as in the foregoing example. In that case, the certificate may read as follows:

We have examined the financial statements of (name of company) as listed in the accompanying Index of Financial Statements. Our examination was made, etc.

In our opinion the financial statements listed in the accompanying Index of Financial Statements present fairly, etc.

If the financial statements listed in the index of financial statements include unaudited as well as audited statements it is desirable to limit the reference to the index along the lines of the following:

We have examined the financial statements of (name of company) as of (date) and for the (period), as listed in the accompanying Index of Financial Statements. Our examination was made, etc.

In our opinion, the financial statements as of (date) and for the (period) listed in the accompanying Index of Financial Statements present fairly, etc.

The certificate relating to the supporting schedules filed in Part II would be along the lines of the following:

We have examined the balance sheet of (name of company) as of (date) and the related statements of income, capital shares, other stockholders' equity, and changes in financial position for the (period), and the supporting schedules. Our examination was made in accordance with generally accepted auditing standards and accordingly included such tests of the accounting records and such other auditing procedures as we considered necessary in the circumstances.

In our opinion, the supporting schedules (pages —— to ——, inclusive) present fairly the information required to be set forth therein, in conformity with generally accepted accounting principles applied on a consistent basis.

The SEC also accepts a variation of the opinion paragraph above reading as follows: "In our opinion, the supporting schedules (pages _____ to _____, inclusive) present fairly the required information." When, in the case of Form S–1, the supporting schedules (whether furnished or incorporated by reference to other SEC filings) are listed in Item 31(a) of the registration statement, the opinion paragraph above may be changed to read as follows: "In our opinion, the supporting schedules listed in Item 31(a) of the registration statement present fairly, etc."

Some accountants furnish a report covering the supporting schedules included in Part II of the registration statement, which differs somewhat from the form suggested above. A typical form of report would be as follows:

In connection with our examination of the financial statements of (name of company) as of (date), and for the (period) then ended, which are included in the Prospectus, we have also examined the supporting schedules listed above. In our opinion, these schedules present fairly the financial data required to be set forth therein, and were prepared in conformity with generally accepted accounting principles applied on a consistent basis during the (period) ended (date).

Many accounting, law, and underwriting firms contend that the earnings summary is usually the most important financial statement in the entire registration statement. It may, in fact, be of more interest to the investor than the other formal financial statements. Because of the importance attaching to such summaries, it is felt that they should be presented in sufficient detail so that the independent public accountant can properly express the opinion that they fairly present results of operations. In most cases this would not add materially to the earnings summaries now being furnished for prospectus purposes, but minor revisions (such as, for example, disclosure of dividends and other charges or credits to retained earnings) would be required to enable the accountant properly to render an opinion that they fairly present results of operations. In the opinion of many accountants (including the author) changes in retained earnings are essential to a showing of results of operations. In further support of this position it might be pointed out that APB Opinion No. 9 (1966) states "The statement of income and the statement of retained earnings (separately or combined) are designed to reflect, in a broad sense, the 'results of operations'."

Practice by the profession generally has not yet reached the point where the accountant can insist that his client furnish tabulations of earnings conforming to the views expressed above. In the opinion of this writer, however, this matter is important enough so that in all cases where an accountant's name is used in connection with an earnings summary, he should urge his client to furnish a tabulation which does fairly present results of operations and not merely limited income data. Most clients and underwriters appreciate the significance of the earnings summary and will accede to the suggestion.

The summary of earnings may or may not have to be certified, depending on the requirements of the form which is used to register the securities. If, however, an accountant's name is associated with the summary, then his opinion must be given. [ASR No. 62 (1947).] It is the practice of many accountants to give an opinion with respect to their examination of the summary of earnings, limited, of course, to the particular years for which they have made examinations of sufficient scope to justify certification. The opinion may be furnished either as a part of the certificate on the formal financial statements for the three-year period appearing in the prospectus or in a separate report. If the summary conforms to the recommendations made in the two preceding paragraphs, the accountant's certificate may take the following form:

We have made an examination of the consolidated balance sheet of (name of company) and its subsidiaries as of (date), and the related statement of income and retained earnings for the (period), which latter statement is included in this prospectus under "Summary of Earnings" and the statements of capital shares, other stockholders' equity and changes in financial position for the (period). Our examination was made in accordance with generally accepted auditing standards and accordingly included such tests of the accounting records and such other auditing procedures as we considered necessary in the circumstances.

In our opinion, the financial statements (pages _____ to _____, inclusive, of this prospectus) and the statement of income and retained earnings (page _____) present fairly the consolidated financial position of (name of company) and its subsidiaries at (date), and the consolidated results of their operations and the changes in their financial position for the (period), in conformity with generally accepted accounting principles applied on a consistent basis.

In the opinion of the author, information as to dividends and other changes in retained earnings is essential to a showing of results of operations. If the summary of earnings does not contain such information, or if it contains only selected data which do not present fairly the results of operations, the accountant's certificate may take the following form:

Certificate in the usual form relating to the years 19___, 19___, and 19___, followed by—

We had previously made yearly examinations similar in scope to that indicated in the first paragraph above, of the financial statements which were reported by the company for the years 19___ through 19___. We have examined the summary of earnings which appears under (caption) in this prospectus, and, in our opinion, it presents fairly the net income and the other data shown therein for the years 19___ to 19___, inclusive, in conformity with generally accepted accounting principles applied on a consistent basis.

Some accountants who agree with the views expressed above write their opinion paragraphs a little differently but with the same effect. Their reports say that the summary "presents fairly the information contained therein" or employ slight variations of such language.

Form S–2.—The requirements for certification of the financial statements included in a registration statement on Form S–2 are contained in Regulation S–X. The following is a suggested form of certificate which meets the SEC requirements. It should be revised in a manner appropriate to the nature of the financial statements to which it relates.

We have examined the accompanying statements of assets and unrecovered promotional and development costs, of liabilities, and of capital shares and contributed capital of (name of company) at (date) and the related statement of cash receipts and disbursements for the period from (date) through (date). Our examination was made in accordance with generally accepted auditing standards, and accordingly included such tests of the accounting records and such other auditing procedures as we considered necessary in the circumstances.

In the accompanying financial statements, assets acquired for capital shares and capital shares issued for services and property have been stated in numbers of capital shares rather than in dollars. This is in accord with the applicable regulations of the Securities and Exchange Commission, and, in our opinion, represents an acceptable method of presenting the accounts of the Company at this time.

In our opinion, the statements mentioned above present fairly the assets and unrecovered costs, the liabilities and the capital shares and contributed capital of (name of company) at (date), and the cash transactions of the Company for the period from (date) through (date).

The reader will note that the form of certificate suggested above is unusual in three respects:

1. The middle paragraph which deals with the omission of dollar amounts for assets and services acquired for capital stock
2. The omission from the last paragraph of the usual references to "financial position" or "results of operation"
3. The omission from the last paragraph of any references to "generally accepted accounting principles" or consistency.

This form of certificate has evolved over a period of many years, and is acceptable to the SEC as well as to certifying accountants. The reasons for the unusual features of the certificate will be apparent when consideration is given to the type of business enterprise for which Form S–2 was designed (see page **8·**4) and to the requirements of Article 5A of Regulation S–X (see page **19·**3) applicable to registrations filed on that form. The principal difference between the asset side of a conventional balance sheet and a statement of assets and unrecovered costs in Form S–2 is that the latter statement does not contain dollar amounts for certain property acquired for capital stock. If dollar costs of property are omitted from the asset amounts, the statement does not present "financial position." (In this connection, see caption 13 of Rule 5A–02 on page **19**·4 and the instructions applicable thereto, regarding the presentation of assets acquired for stock.) As far as the statement of cash receipts and disbursements is concerned, it does no more than summarize the cash transactions and is not expected to portray "results of operations."

Forms S–7 and S–9.—The conditions under which Forms S–7 and S–9 may be used for registration of securities under the 1933 Act are described in Chapter **8**. From the discussion in that chapter it will be apparent that S–9 is used to register high-grade, nonconvertible, debt securities of substantial companies with respect to which much information is publicly available. S–7 is also intended for use by seasoned issuers but is not limited to debt securities.

The requirements for financial statements in Forms S–7 and S–9 are set forth in Chapter **9**. While these requirements are the same in many respects, they also differ in some respects. In both of these forms, all the financial statements (including some schedules as indicated in Chapter **9**) must be included in the prospectus; hence there is no provision for including financial data in Part II of the registration statement. Consequently, only one accountant's certificate needs to be furnished. Following is a typical certificate for use in these circumstances:

We have examined the balance sheet of (name of company) as of (date) and the related statements of earnings (or income), capital shares, other stockholders' equity, and changes in financial position for the (period). Our examination was made, etc.

In our opinion, the financial statements (pages X and Y to Z, inclusive) present fairly the financial position of (name of company) at (date) and the results of its operations and the changes in its financial position for the (period), in conformity with generally accepted accounting principles applied on a consistent basis.

In the foregoing example, X refers to the page number of the summary of earnings, and Y to Z are the page numbers of the balance sheet and other prime financial statements.

Form S–8.—The instructions for financial statements to be included in Form S–8 are discussed beginning on page **9**·36 As there indicated, it is possible in many cases to incorporate the financial statements in the issuer's annual report to shareholders as a basic element of the Form S–8 prospectus. When this procedure is followed, the only financial statement in the prospectus is the summary of earnings.

When the financial statements in the annual report are incorporated in the prospectus, it is accomplished by means of a declaration in the prospectus reading somewhat as follows:

The Company's annual report to its stockholders for (period), a copy of which accompanies this prospectus, contains on pages _____ through _____ a consolidated balance sheet as at (date) and consolidated statements of income, capital shares, other stockholders' equity, and changes in financial position for the (period), and the report of (name of accountants), independent public accountants. Such financial statements and report are hereby made a part of this prospectus.

Where this procedure is followed, the accountant must furnish a certificate covering the summary of earnings for inclusion in the prospectus. This certificate may be along the lines of the following:

We have made annual examinations of the consolidated financial statements of (name of company) and its subsidiaries for the (period) and have examined the Summary of Consolidated Earnings for those years which appears under that caption in this prospectus. Our examinations were made in accordance with generally accepted auditing standards and accordingly included such tests of the accounting records and such other auditing procedures as we considered necessary in the circumstances.

In our opinion, the Summary of Consolidated Earnings in this prospectus presents fairly the consolidated net income and other data shown therein of (name of company) and its subsidiaries for (period) in conformity with generally accepted accounting principles applied on a consistent basis.

If the Form S–8 prospectus does not incorporate the financial statements in the annual report to shareholders, but in lieu thereof furnishes the statements required by Item 17 of the form, then the accountants' certificate will follow the lines of a certificate for inclusion in a Form S–1 prospectus (see page **24·8**).

Form 10.—Chapter **15** contains the requirements for financial statements to be included in a registration statement on Form 10. Unlike a registration statement, for example, on Form S–1, the financial data in Form 10 are not divided into a prospectus and Part II. In Form 10 all the financial statements and supporting schedules are submitted as part of one document. The accountant therefore need furnish only one certificate covering all the financial data covered by his report and included in Form 10.

Many accountants believe that, except in highly unusual circumstances, the supporting schedules are not essential to a showing of either financial position or results of operations. A typical form of accountant's report reflecting this view, for inclusion in Form 10, would be as follows:

We have examined the balance sheet of (name of company) as of (date), the related statements of income, capital shares, other stockholders' equity, and changes in financial position for the (period), and the supporting schedules. Our examination was made in accordance with generally accepted auditing standards, and accordingly included such tests of the accounting records and such other auditing procedures as we considered necessary in the circumstances.

In our opinion, the accompanying financial statements (pages — to —, inclusive) present fairly the financial position of (name of company) at (date) and the results of its operations and the changes in its financial position for the (period), and the accompanying supporting schedules (pages ___ to ___, inclusive) present fairly the information required to be included therein, all in conformity with generally accepted accounting principles applied on a consistent basis.

Some accountants who do not share the views expressed above furnish reports containing an opinion paragraph which differs from the one quoted immediately above and reads as follows:

In our opinion, the financial statements and schedules referred to above present fairly the financial position of (name of company) at (date) and the results of its operations and the changes in its financial position for the (period), in conformity with generally accepted accounting principles applied on a consistent basis.

Although both forms are acceptable to the SEC, the author's preference is for the first alternative inasmuch as the author believes that the supporting schedules ordinarily are not essential to a showing of financial position or results of operations.

As a variation of the form of certificate shown immediately above, some accountants, in the opinion paragraph of their reports, remove the schedules from the matter of conformity with generally accepted accounting principles. The opinion paragraphs of their certificates read as follows:

In our opinion, the financial statements referred to above present fairly the financial position of (name of company) at (date) and the results of its operations and the changes in its financial position for the (period), in conformity with generally accepted accounting principles applied on a consistent basis; and the schedules present fairly the required information.

This form of certificate is also acceptable to the SEC.

Form 10–K.—The requirements for financial statements to be included in an annual report on Form 10–K are set forth in Chapter **15**. Since the financial data to be covered by the report of the certifying accountant are submitted as part of a single document, the accountant need furnish only one report.

Form 10–K is unique among the SEC's forms in that, although an "annual" report, it calls for balance sheets as of the close of the last *two* fiscal years and statements of income, capital shares, other stockholders' equity, and changes in financial position for such fiscal years.

Item 10 of Form 10–K calls for a listing of all financial statements and exhibits filed as part of the annual report. There must also be furnished a listing of the financial statements and schedules omitted, together with the reasons for such omission. Inasmuch as the financial statements and schedules are, as a matter of convenience, often prepared or typed by the certifying accountants, these accountants have suggested to their clients or their attorneys who prepare the "narrative" section of the Form 10–K report, that Item 10, insofar as it relates to the financial statements, be answered by making a cross-reference to the financial section of the report, thus: "See page F–1." Page F–1 would be a listing of the financial statements and schedules which are filed as part of Form 10–K. The listing of statements and schedules that are furnished is followed immediately by a listing of statements and schedules that are omitted and the reasons for their omission. In a typical case the index page (F–1) of the financial section may be in the following form:

INDEX OF FINANCIAL STATEMENTS AND SCHEDULES

Financial statements: PAGES
    Consolidated balance sheets ....
    Consolidated statement of income ....
    Consolidated statement of capital shares ....
    Consolidated statement of other stockholders' equity ....
    Consolidated statement of changes in financial position ....
    Notes to financial statements ....
Consolidated schedules:
    V. Property, plant, and equipment ....
    VI. Reserves for depreciation and amortization of property,
        plant, and equipment ....
    IX. Bonds, mortgages, and similar debt ....
    XII. Reserves ....
    XIII. Capital shares ....
    XVI. Supplementary income statement information ....

LIST OF STATEMENTS AND SCHEDULES OMITTED

Financial statements of the Company (separately) are omitted for the reason that (reason to be furnished, based on instructions for financial statements in Form 10–K).

Financial statements of an unconsolidated subsidiary are omitted because (reason to be furnished, based on instructions for financial statements in Form 10–K).

Supporting schedules other than those listed above are omitted for the reason that they are not required or are not applicable.

The accountant's certificate in Form 10–K may be the conventional short-form report recommended by the AICPA appropriately modified to cover two years. It should be clear that the certificate applies to the supporting schedules as well as the principal financial statements. A typical report covering parent company and consolidated statements would read as follows:

We have examined the balance sheets of (name of company) and the consolidated balance sheets of that company and subsidiaries as of (date) and (date), and the related statements of income, capital shares, other stockholders' equity, and changes in financial position for the years then ended, and the supporting schedules. Our examination was made in accordance with generally accepted auditing standards, and accordingly included such tests of the accounting records and such other auditing procedures as we considered necessary in the circumstances.

In our opinion, the accompanying financial statements (pages   to   , inclusive) present fairly the financial position of (name of company) and the consolidated financial position of that company and subsidiaries at (date) and (date) and the results of their operations and the changes in their financial position for the years then ended, and the accompanying supporting schedules (pages   to   , inclusive) present fairly the information required to be included therein, all in conformity with generally accepted accounting principles applied on a consistent basis.

If, in the interests of brevity, it is desired to incorporate the index of financial statements and schedules as part of the accountant's report, the report would read as follows:

We have examined the financial statements and schedules listed in the accompanying index on page F–1. Our examination was made, etc.

In our opinion, the financial statements listed on page F–1 present fairly the financial position of (name of company) and the consolidated financial position of that company and subsidiaries at (date) and (date), and the results of their operations and the changes in their financial position for the years then ended, and the supporting schedules listed on page F–1 present fairly the information required to be included therein, all in conformity with generally accepted accounting principles applied on a consistent basis.

The foregoing reports for Form 10–K reflect the views indicated on page **24**·14 (which the author shares) to the effect that the supporting schedules ordinarily are not essential to a showing of financial position or results of operations. If the certifying accountant does not concur in this view, he may furnish a report along the lines of the following, which is also acceptable to the SEC:

Scope paragraph similar to the foregoing examples, followed by:

In our opinion, the accompanying statements and schedules (pages F– to F–   , inclusive) present fairly the financial position of (name of company) and the consolidated financial position of that company and subsidiaries at (date) and (date), and the results of their operations and the changes in their financial position for the years then ended, in conformity with generally accepted accounting principles applied on a consistent basis.

Certificate Covering Summary of Earnings in Summary Prospectus

On page **11**·26 of this volume is a discussion of the summary prospectus, which is a highly condensed form of the official or statutory prospectus, and may be used only in circumstances set forth in the SEC rules. If the summary prospectus is used, the only financial statements which it may contain are those listed on page **11·27**. It will be noted that the requirements vary somewhat, depending on which registration form is used. If the registration form used is Form S–1, the only financial statement that may be included in the summary prospectus is the earnings summary.

In a summary prospectus used in connection with Form S–1, the earnings summary is customarily preceded by a headnote which states that the earnings summary has been examined by independent public accountants, whose report appears in the "complete" prospectus, or words to that effect. In these circumstances, the accountant must make it clear in his certificate that it covers the earnings summary in the statutory prospectus as well as in the summary prospectus. Following is an example of a certificate written with this object in mind for inclusion in the complete prospectus:

> We have examined the balance sheet of (name of company) as of (date), and the related statements of income (which appears in this prospectus and in the summary prospectus), capital shares, other stockholders' equity, and changes in financial position for the (period). Our examination was made, etc.
>
> In our opinion, the above-mentioned financial statements present fairly the financial position of (name of company) at (date) and the results of its operations and changes in its financial position for the (period), in conformity, etc.

Certificate Covering Amended Financial Statements

The information in documents filed with the SEC frequently has to be amended, either as the result of a suggestion from the Commission, or because the registrant desires to amend something previously filed. The amendment may relate to financial statements as well as information contained in the so-called "narrative" section. Sometimes also it is necessary to amend the accountant's certificate.

1933 Act Filings.—In a 1933 Act filing, if financial data covered by the accountant's certificate are amended, it must be made clear whether the amended data are also covered by the accountant's certificate. This can be accomplished simply by having the accountant re-sign his consent and filing it as part of the amendment. The new consent must bear a current date.

If the certificate itself is to be amended—by way of updating it or otherwise—a similar procedure is followed: the certificate in the prospectus or in Part II is appropriately revised, manually signed together with a new consent (the latter bearing a current date), and filed as part of the amendment.

1934 Act Filings.—When financial statements covered by an accountant's certificate in a 1934 Act filing are amended, it must be made clear whether the amended financial statements are also certified. Assume, for example, that the balance sheet of a registrant in Form 10–K is to be amended. The amendment would be filed under cover of Form 8, which is the form used for amending any filing under the 1934 Act. Form 8 need contain only the balance sheet which is being amended and none of the other financial statements previously filed. In this situation the accountant who certified the financial statements in the original filing signs a "consent to substitution" which may read somewhat as follows:

We consent to the substitution of the following financial statement for the corresponding financial statement previously filed by you as part of your annual report (Form 10–K) for the fiscal year ended (date) :

Balance Sheet, (date)

and to the use of our opinion, dated (date), included in the said annual report after such substitution.

A slightly more complicated situation is involved when the accountant's certificate as well as the financial statement(s) are amended. Assume for example, that a registrant files its annual report on Form 10–K and that the form includes a certificate in which the accountant takes exception to an accounting principle reflected in the income and retained earnings statements. At a later date the company decides to amend the financial statements in its original filing so as to eliminate the basis for the accountant's exception. The amendment on Form 8 would contain amended income and retained earnings statements and an amended accountant's certificate which would be the conventional short-form report. In order to make it clear that the amended certificate applies to all the financial data in the original filing as amended by the financial data in the current filing on Form 8, the accountant furnishes a "consent to substitution" reading as follows:

We consent to the substitution of the accompanying opinion, dated _____ _____, and the following financial statements for those previously filed by you as part of your annual report (Form 10–K) for the fiscal year ended (date) :

Consolidated statement of income for the (period) ;
Consolidated statement of retained earnings for the (period).

The accompany report, dated (date), is applicable to the financial statements and schedules included in the said annual report (Form 10–K) as amended by the accompanying financial statements.

Report Covering Historical Financial Information

A registration statement on Form S–1 under the 1933 Act calls for information concerning certain asset revaluations and unusual adjustments of surplus during the seven-year period preceding the required three-year income statement included in the prospectus. This information is not required in the prospectus, but is submitted in Part II and, in the case of a company for whom equivalent information has been filed with SEC previously pursuant to the 1933 or 1934 Acts, may be omitted entirely. Similar information as to asset revaluations and surplus adjustments is required in a registration statement on Form 10, but may be omitted if corresponding information has previously been filed by the registrant pursuant to another filing with the Commission. The information which must be reported under "Historical Financial Information" is set forth beginning on page **9·16** of this volume.

The information dealing with historical financial information does not have to be certified, but, when practicable, the registrant or underwriters usually desire to have the response reviewed and signed by independent accountants, not on the basis of an audit but on the basis of a survey of the accounts named. Below is a suggested form of opinion covering such review:

> We have made a review, but not an audit, of the accounts maintained by (name of company) for the period from (date) through (date) corresponding to those named in Instructions as to Financial Statements on Form S–1 of the Securities and Exchange Commission covering matters to be reported under "Historical Financial Information" and, in our opinion, the information required to be reported under such heading is fairly presented above.

If the company's accounts were audited by the accountant during the period covered by the above report, the phrase "but not an audit" in the above report should be deleted.

When the above report is furnished in connection with a filing on Form 10, the reference to the instructions of Form S–1 would be deleted and there would be substituted ". . . those named in Instructions as to Financial Statements on Form 10 . . ."

Accountant's Opinion as to Changes in Accounting Principles

Rule 2–02 of Regulation S–X contains the requirements for the accountant's certificate and is set forth on page **24·4**. Paragraph (c) of the rule states the requirements for the opinions to be expressed in the certificate. Among other things, the accountant is required to state his opinion as to the accounting principles and practices reflected in the financial statements covered by his certificate and as to the consistency of the application of the accounting principles, or as to any changes in such principles which have a material effect on the financial statements.

Where there has been a change in accounting principle, the accountant, pursuant to the specific requirements of Rule 2–02(c), states his opinion regarding the change, frequently in language somewhat as follows:

> In our opinion, the accompanying financial statements present fairly the financial position of (name of company) at (date) and the results of its operations and the changes in its financial position for the (period) in conformity with generally accepted accounting principles applied on a consistent basis, except as to the change in (accounting principle or practice) referred to in Note ___ to the financial statements, in which change we concur.

It has seemed to many accountants that the provision in Rule 2–02(c)(2) is unnecessary and redundant. Where there has been change in accounting principle which the accountant could not approve, it would seem that his disapproval would also apply to the fairness of the presentation of the financial statements. It is difficult to imagine a case in which the accountant would disapprove of a change in principle and yet approve the fairness of the presentation of the statements. It seems to follow, then, that if the accountant is in a position to give affirmative approval to the financial statements as being in accordance with generally accepted principles of accounting, it is unnecessary and superfluous for him to state specifically his opinion of the change in principle.

Accountants have grumbled for some time about the provision in Rule 2–02(c)(2), but it remains an SEC requirement which must be complied with.

Elimination of Opinion as to Differences Between Books and Statements

Prior to the 1972 revision of Regulation S–X, the SEC's rules relating to accountants' reports required the auditor to state in his report the nature of any differences between the accounting principles and practices reflected in the financial statements and those reflected in the accounts, and the auditor's opinion as to such differences.

In the view of many persons (including the author), this requirement (which was contained in Rule 2–02) had no merit, since the reader of a financial statement is interested only in what the statements show; he is not interested to know how the statements may differ from the books of account. In addition, the SEC's previous requirement gave rise to many questions as to what constituted the "books of account." Some companies (especially real estate companies) maintain their books of account on a tax basis but also have available the information which makes it possible to prepare financial statements that conform with generally accepted accounting principles. The question arose whether the "books of account" was limited to the basic tax records, or whether the term included the supplemental information.

The 1972 revision in Rule 2–02 of Regulation S–X fortunately eliminated the requirement for the independent auditor to comment on the book/statement differences.

Certificate Where Part of Examination Is Made by Another Auditor

It is not unusual for a public accountant to report on financial statements, part of the examination of which has been made by other public accountants. The accounts of an out-of-town branch, division, or subsidiary may be examined by auditors located in or near the branch, division, or subsidiary. Sometimes the out-of-town auditor is engaged by the principal accountant, who reviews the work of the other accountant and pays his fee. In other cases the client engages the out-of-town accountant, whose report is made available to the principal accountant as a basis for reporting upon the over-all or consolidated financial statements. The variations in these arrangements are almost endless.

Also, in the case of business combinations that are treated for accounting purposes as poolings of interest (discussed in Chapter **21**), the independent auditors may be different for each of the constituent companies whose figures are combined in the pooled figures.

SAP No. 45.—With the view of establishing guidelines for reporting on financial statements when the principal auditor utilizes the work and reports of other independent auditors, the AICPA Committee on Auditing Procedure issued an important pronouncement in July 1971 entitled "Using the Work and Reports of Other Auditors" (SAP No. 45). The discussion that follows is taken largely from that statement.

When material portions of an examination have been performed by other auditors, the principal auditor must decide whether his own participation in the total examination is sufficient to enable him to serve as the principal auditor and to report as such on the financial statements. Although SAP No. 45 contains no quantitative tests to determine when that participation is "sufficient," it does indicate what the principal auditor should take into consideration in this regard. Among other things, he should consider the relative materiality of the portion of the statements he has examined and its importance to the total enterprise as compared with the portion examined by other auditors, and the extent of his knowledge of the overall financial statements.

If the auditor concludes that he can serve as the principal auditor, he must then decide whether or not to refer in his report to the fact that part of the total examination was made by another auditor (or other auditors). If the principal auditor concludes that he can assume responsibility for the work done by the other auditor insofar as that work relates to the principal auditor's expression of an opinion on the financial statements taken as a whole, he should not refer in his report to the other auditor's examination since that might cause a reader to misinterpret the degree of responsibility assumed. If he concludes that he can not assume that responsibility, his report should refer to the other auditor's examination and should indicate the division of responsibility between himself and the other auditor. A typical report in which the principal auditor refers to the participation in the overall examination by other auditors appears on page **24·25**.

DECISION NOT TO REFER TO OTHER AUDITORS.—The principal auditor may be able to report on the financial statements without making reference to the other auditor's examination if he takes steps to assure himself regarding the other auditor's examination, independence, and professional reputation. The principal auditor ordinarily need not refer to the other auditor's report when:

a. The other auditor is an associated or correspondent firm whose work is acceptable to the principal auditor based on his knowledge of the professional standards and competence of that firm; or
b. The other auditor was retained by the principal auditor, and the work was performed under his guidance and control; or
c. Whether or not the principal auditor selected the other auditor, he (the principal auditor) satisfies himself as to the other auditor's examination and is satisfied as to the reasonableness of the accounts for inclusion in the financial statements on which he is reporting; or
d. The portion of the financial statements examined by the other auditor is not material in relation to the statements covered by the principal auditor's opinion.

DECISION TO REFER TO OTHER AUDITORS.—The principal auditor may decide, on the other hand, to refer in his report to the other auditor's examination. This may be due to a number of factors, such as the impracticability of reviewing the other auditor's work, or to do whatever else would be necessary to satisfy him with regard to the other auditor's examination. Also, if the part of the enterprise examined by the other auditor is material in relation to the total enterprise, the principal auditor may decide, regardless of any other consideration, to refer to the other auditor's work.

When the principal auditor refers to the other examination, he should indicate in both the scope and opinion paragraphs of his report the division of responsibility as between that portion of the statements covered by him and that covered by the other auditor, including the magnitude of the latter portion. This may be done by stating the dollar amounts or percentages of one or more of the following: total assets, total revenues, or other criteria, whichever reveals most clearly the portion of the statements examined by the other auditor.

The other auditor may be referred to by name in the principal auditor's report, but only (according to SAP No. 45) if the other auditor has expressly permitted this to be done, and provided further that his report is furnished along with the principal auditor's report.

PROCEDURES APPLICABLE TO BOTH METHODS OF REPORTING.—Whether or not the principal auditor refers to the work of the other auditor, he should inquire regarding the latter's professional reputation and standing. Such inquiries may be addressed to professional organizations, other practitioners, credit grantors, and other appropriate sources. (This would not be necessary if the principal auditor already knows the reputation and standing of the other auditor, and (according to SAP No. 45) if the latter practices primarily in the United States.)

The principal auditor should also obtain a representation from the other auditor that he is independent as required by the rules of the AICPA and, if appropriate, the requirements of the SEC.

In addition, the principal auditor should ascertain through communication with the other auditor:

    a. That he (the other auditor) is aware that the financial statements which he is to examine will be included in statements on which the principal auditor will report, and that the other auditor's report will be relied upon (and, where applicable, referred to) by the principal auditor.

    b. That the other auditor is familiar with accounting principles generally accepted in the United States and with the generally accepted auditing standards promulgated by the AICPA, and will conduct his examination and will report accordingly.

    c. That the other auditor knows the requirements for statements to be filed with regulatory agencies (such as the SEC), if appropriate.

    d. That a review will be made of matters affecting the consolidation, such as the elimination of intercompany transactions and accounts, and uniformity of accounting practices among the companies in the total enterprise.

(Inquiries as to b and c would not be necessary if the principal auditor knows the professional reputation and standing of the other auditor, and, according to SAP No. 45, if the latter practices primarily in the United States.)

If the principal auditor's inquiries and procedures cause him to conclude that he can not assume responsibility for the other auditor's work, and that he (the principal auditor) can not report in the manner contemplated by the example of a report which follows, he should qualify his opinion or disclaim an opinion on the statements. He should state his reasons for qualifying his opinion or disclaiming an opinion, together with the magnitude of the portion of the statements to which his qualification applies.

ADDITIONAL PROCEDURES UNDER DECISION NOT TO REFER TO OTHER AUDITORS.—When the principal auditor concludes that he will not refer to the other auditor's examination, in addition to satisfying himself as to the matters described under "Procedures Applicable to Both Methods of Reporting," he should also consider whether to do any of the following:

a. Visit the other auditor and discuss the audit procedures followed and the results thereof.

b. Review the audit programs of the other auditor. In some cases, it may be appropriate to instruct the other auditor as to the scope of the work he is to perform.

c. Review the working papers of the other auditor, including his evaluation of internal control and his conclusions as to significant aspects of the audit engagement.

The principal auditor may decide in some circumstances to participate in discussions regarding the accounts with management personnel of the subsidiary, division, or other component examined by the other auditor and/or to make supplemental tests of such accounts. The extent of additional procedures, if any, to be applied is determined by the principal auditor because he is reporting without referring to the other auditor's examination. If additional procedures are undertaken, that fact is not a reflection on the work of the other auditor.

FORM OF REPORT REFERRING TO OTHER AUDITOR.—Following is an example of a report of the principal auditor which refers to the other auditor's examination:

We have examined the consolidated balance sheet of X Company and subsidiaries as of (date) and the related consolidated statements of income, capital shares, other stockholders' equity, and changes in financial position for the (period). Our examination was made in accordance with generally accepted auditing standards and accordingly included such tests of the accounting records and such other auditing procedures as we considered necessary in the circumstances. We did not examine the financial statements of B Company, a consolidated subsidiary, which statements reflect total assets and revenues constituting __% and __%, respectively, of the related consolidated totals. These statements were examined by other auditors whose report thereon has been furnished to us, and our opinion expressed herein, insofar as it relates to the amounts included for B Company, is based solely upon the report of the other auditors.

In our opinion, based upon our examination and the report of other auditors, the accompanying consolidated balance sheet and consolidated statements of income, capital shares, other stockholders' equity, and changes in financial position present fairly . . .

If a report such as the foregoing is included in a document filed with the SEC, it would have to be accompanied by the report of the other auditors since the principal auditor does not assume responsibility for that portion of the work performed by them. For the form of such a report, see the discussion under "Certificate Covering Financial Statements Not Presented Separately" on page **24·33**.

QUALIFICATIONS IN OTHER AUDITOR'S REPORT.—If the other auditor's report is qualified, the principal auditor has to decide whether the qualification is of such nature and significance in relation to the statements on which he is reporting that he has to qualify his report. If the qualification is not material in relation to such statements and the other auditor's report is not presented, the principal auditor need not refer in his report to the qualification; if the other auditor's report is presented (as is often the case in SEC filings), the principal auditor may wish to refer in his report to the qualification and its disposition.

RESTATED FINANCIAL STATEMENTS FOLLOWING A POOLING OF INTERESTS.—After a transaction that, for accounting purposes, has been treated as a pooling of interests (see the discussion thereof in Chapter **21**), an auditor may be asked to report on restated financial statements of prior years when, in all likelihood, other accountants examined some of the entities included in the pooled statements. As mentioned in the preceding discussion, the auditor must first decide whether he has examined a sufficient portion of the pooled statements so that he can serve as the principal auditor. Also, in such cases, it is often not possible for the auditor to satisfy himself with respect to the restated financial statements; an important pooled entity, for example, may be included in the combined figures on the basis of unaudited figures. In these circumstances, it may be appropriate for the auditor to report solely with respect to the manner of compiling the statements. Under the strictures of SAP No. 45, no opinion of any kind should be expressed unless the auditor has examined at least one of the entities included in the restatement for at least the latest period presented.

The following is an illustration of appropriate reporting on compilation which can be presented in an additional paragraph of the auditor's report following the standard scope and opinion paragraphs covering the financial statements of the current year:

We previously examined and reported upon the consolidated statements of income, capital shares, other stockholders' equity and changes in financial position of XYZ Company for the year ended December 31, 19_____ prior to its restatement for 19_____ poolings of interests. The contribution of XYZ Company to revenues and net income represented _____% and _____% of the respective restated totals. Separate financial statements of the pooled companies included in the 19_____ restated consolidated statement of income were examined and reported upon separately by other auditors. We also have reviewed, as to compilation only, the accompanying consolidated statements of income, capital shares, other stockholders' equity and changes in financial position for the year ended December 31, 19_____ after restatement for 19_____ poolings of interests;

in our opinion, such consolidated statements have been properly compiled on the basis described in Note X of notes to consolidated financial statements.

In reporting on the compilation as described above, the auditor does not assume responsibility for the work of other auditors or the responsibility for an opinion on the restated financial statements taken as a whole. His review is directed toward procedures which will enable him to express an opinion as to proper compilation only. These procedures include checking the compilation for mathematical accuracy and for conformity of the compilation methods with generally accepted accounting principles. The auditor should review and make inquiries, for example, regarding such matters as the following:

   a. Elimination of intercompany transactions and accounts.
   b. Combining adjustments and reclassifications.
   c. Adjustments to treat like items in a comparable manner, if appropriate.
   d. The manner and extent of presentation of disclosure matters in the restated financial statements and notes thereto.

Code of Professional Ethics.—It should not be overlooked that there are also provisions in the AICPA Code of Professional Ethics specifying what the principal auditor must do when he utilizes the work of another auditor. These provisions appear in Rule 2.01 of the Code.

The rule provides that, in obtaining sufficient information to warrant the expression of an opinion, a member or associate of the AICPA "may utilize, in part, to the extent appropriate in the circumstances, the reports or other evidence of auditing work performed by another certified public accountant, or firm of public accountants, at least one of whom is a certified public accountant, who is authorized to practice in a state or territory of the United States or the District of Columbia, and whose independence and professional reputation he has ascertained to his satisfaction."

Where the secondary auditor practices in a foreign country, the rule is more extensive, and is calculated to ascertain that the audit and the financial statements conform to United States standards. Insofar as it pertains to foreign auditors, the rule provides that a member or associate of the AICPA "may also utilize, in part, to the extent appropriate in the circumstances, the work of public accountants in other countries, but the member or associate so doing must satisfy himself that the person or firm is qualified and independent, that such work is performed in accordance with generally accepted auditing standards, as prevailing in the United States, and that financial statements are prepared in accordance with generally accepted accounting principles, as prevailing in the United States, or are accompanied by the information necessary to bring the statements into accord with such principles."

The Red Bank Oil Case.—The SEC has said little in its published decisions about an accountant reporting on financial statements where part of the examination is made by another accountant. The Commission, however, issued a decision in *Red Bank Oil Company* which involved a number of accounting questions including reliance upon other auditors. [21 SEC 695 (1946)].

The principal accountant in this case was an accountant in Dallas, Texas. This accountant did not audit the Houston unit of a consolidated subsidiary, which unit was audited by a firm of accountants located in that city. The principal accountant incorporated in his work papers the audit report for that unit prepared by the Houston auditors. The Houston unit accounted for 70 per cent of consolidated sales and 45 per cent of consolidated assets. The Dallas auditors did not disclose in their certificate the fact that they relied on other accountants. The SEC said that it doubted the propriety of the principal accountant undertaking to express his opinion with respect to financial statements when, as to so large a percentage of the revenues and assets, his opinion is founded "merely on the reports of other accountants not subject to his supervision, control or direction."

According to the SEC, the principal accountant was not familiar with the Houston unit's accounts and he was satisfied merely to incorporate them bodily in his working papers and over-all statements without further study. It appeared that he did not make any effort to determine whether the federal government sales were subject to renegotiation but accepted the Houston auditor's footnote to the effect that no provision had been made for renegotiation. The Dallas auditors did not know what inventory procedures were followed by the Houston auditors—did not, in fact, even know the basis used in determining costs. The SEC observed:

> We think it wholly clear that where an accountant undertakes to express his opinion in part in reliance on reports of other accountants, it is essential that he have far more knowledge of the underlying facts and of the accounting principles followed than was exhibited here. Lacking such knowledge, it is impossible for him to express an informed judgment as to whether the figures reported to him by other accountants have been properly included in the consolidated statements. . . . We also believe that the principal accountant is not in a position to express an informed opinion as to the financial statements where he excluded from his review so large a part of the revenues and assets.

Regulation S–X.—In 1950 (about four years after the Red Bank Oil case) the SEC revised its basic accounting regulation, Regulation S–X, and inserted a provision (Rule 2–05) dealing with certification of financial statements by more than one accountant. Minor revisions in the rule were made in 1972; as revised the rule is as follows:

Rule 2–05. Examination of Financial Statements by More Than One Accountant.

If, with respect to the examination of the financial statements of any person, the principal accountant relies on an audit made by another accountant of certain of the accounts of such person or its subsidiaries, the report of such other accountant shall be filed (and the provisions of Rules 2–01 and 2–02 shall be applicable thereto); however, the report of such other accountant need not be filed (1) if no reference is made directly or indirectly to such other accountant's audit in the principal accountant's report, or (2) if, having referred to such other accountant's audit, the principal accountant states in his report that he assumes responsibility for such other accountant's audit in the same manner as if it had been made by him.

Rule 2–05 (quoted above) is the most recent formal expression by the SEC on an examination made by more than one accountant. To the extent that it conflicts with the decision in the Red Bank Oil case, Rule 2–05 is controlling.

The AICPA Committee on Auditing Procedure, following its custom, consulted with the accounting staff of the SEC (among others) before issuing SAP No. 45. The staff indicated their concurrence in the Statement which, it should be apparent, goes considerably beyond the requirements of Rule 2–05. Accordingly, it may be expected that the SEC's staff will take exception to any reports which contravene the recommendations in the Statement.

The Atlantic Acceptance Corporation Case.—SAP No. 45 superseded that portion of an earlier AICPA pronouncement (SAP No. 33) which also dealt with the procedures to be followed by an independent auditor when part of the overall examination is made by other independent auditors. While it had been recognized for some time that that portion of the earlier statement was in need of updating and revision, the matter became urgent following the collapse of Atlantic Acceptance Corporation Limited, a Canadian finance company, which was placed in receivership in June 1965 with enormous losses to stockholders and subordinated lenders.

Writing in 1965 about the Atlantic collapse, F. J. McDiarmid said that it was too early at that time to assess the extent of the loss to creditors and investors, but that it stood to become "the biggest single financial debacle to take place in Canada for many years." [1]

Pursuant to The Business Inquiries Act, a royal commission was constituted to investigate the cause and effect of the Atlantic Acceptance group failure. Justice S. H. S. Hughes of the Ontario Supreme Court was appointed the commissioner, and his report was issued in September 1969. Most of the information which follows concerning the case was taken from

---

[1] F. J. McDiarmid, "After the Fall," *Barron's,* August 16, 1965, p. 9.

that report[2] except where the context indicates otherwise. The accounting and auditing practices of the Atlantic companies and their auditors were very much involved in the report. When the facts regarding the case became known, it had as much an effect on accounting in Canada and elsewhere as the McKesson and Robbins case had in the United States. As the report said:

> After Atlantic Acceptance had defaulted, and after the full implications of what had happened became known to the public mainly as a result of this Commission's proceedings, these rules [relating to reliance on other auditors] were changed, as will be seen, and it may be said that the Atlantic failure was as much of a watershed in the history of accounting in Canada, and perhaps abroad, as was that of McKesson & Robbins Inc. in the United States, on which the Securities and Exchange Commission reported in 1939.

Atlantic Acceptance began in a small way in Hamilton, Ontario, in 1953. It grew rapidly, however, and at the time of its collapse had total assets of $155,000,000, of which $149,000,000 consisted of notes and accounts receivable. At the same date, the company had liabilities of $137,000,000, of which $134,000,000 was owed to creditors who had purchased its notes. Stockholders' equity was $18,000,000. The notes were divided into three categories: senior, subordinated, and junior subordinated.

On June 14, 1965 a check for $5,010,000 drawn by Atlantic on a Canadian bank was not honored when presented for payment. The check was in payment of an Atlantic note payable that was due that day. As a result of the default, all of Atlantic's notes in all categories became due and payable, and the company collapsed.

Atlantic Acceptance was owned 52% by Great Northern Capital Corporation; the remaining 48% was publicly-owned. Great Northern's independent auditors were a large firm with international affiliations. The independent auditors for Atlantic were two Canadian firms—Firm A which examined Atlantic and some of the subsidiaries, and Firm B which examined the remaining subsidiaries. In June 1964 the auditors for Great Northern were also appointed auditors for Atlantic and some of the subsidiaries—replacing Firm A—but Firm B was continued as auditors for the other subsidiaries.

When Atlantic's report for 1964 was issued, it included only the audit report of the large international firm (the "primary auditors"). As Justice Hughes' report stated, the primary auditors, in accordance with Canadian practice, did not examine the audit working papers of Firm B (the "secondary auditors") relating to the audit of certain subsidiaries. The primary auditors made no reference in their report on the consolidated financial state-

---

[2] The Hon. S. H. S. Hughes, *Report of the Royal Commission Appointed to Inquire into the Failure of Atlantic Acceptance Corporation Limited* (Toronto: Queen's Printer, 1969), 4 volumes.

ments to the proportion of the total assets or income covered by the companies they had not examined, but said that with respect to certain subsidiaries (which were not identified), they had relied on the opinion of other chartered accountants (whom they did not name). In this respect, the primary auditors followed the practice, with minor variations, observed by the auditors they had replaced. Justice Hughes said "the evidence before the Commission is generally to the effect that this was acceptable at the time." His report continued:

. . . In view of the practice which prevailed and was acceptable at the time, it would seem that [the primary audit firm] were entitled, as auditors of the consolidated accounts of the parent company, to rely upon the opinion of auditors about which nothing discreditable was known, and they were not bound to make the enquiries which prudence, certainly, and even common sense would evidently require; but in failing to do so they ignored the advice of their own internal procedural manual . . .

The Hughes report was highly critical of the accounting practices of the Atlantic companies in two respects:

(1) The inadequacy of the allowance for bad debts against "the many large and imprudent loans made on the sole authority of C. P. Morgan, president of Atlantic . . . "; and

(2) The inflation of the companies' reported income growing out of the accounting treatment of the pre-computed interest charge added to the principal sum of the purchased receivables which were secured by conditional sales contracts.

Atlantic took into income immediately an excessive portion of this pre-computed interest charge to offset the cost of acquisition of the receivables, which had the effect of inflating current income at the expense of later periods. (As the report pointed out, Morgan, being a chartered accountant, was "familiar with the devices which might be resorted to to give a false appearance of profitableness to a company's operations, and resort to them he did.")

As for the allowance for bad debts, according to the judge, even without the benefit of hindsight, it was far too low. The deficiency, however, occurred principally on the books of the subsidiaries examined by Firm B— the allowance on Atlantic's books being adequate.

The report discussed at length the method of recognizing interest income and the inadequacy of the allowance for bad debts. For the purpose of the present discussion, however, the focus will be on the portion of the Hughes report relating to the use by one audit firm of the work done by another audit firm.

Justice Hughes pointed out that two things were essential to the success of Morgan's scheme: the auditors of the "Adelaide Street subsidiaries" (the secondary auditors) had to be Morgan's confederates, and the primary auditors had to be kept at a safe distance from the secondary auditors and from such subsidiaries. In fact, Morgan, a chartered accountant, reacted sharply to a suggestion by the primary auditors that their report should mention the names of the subsidiaries of which they were not the auditors, refusing to consider such a proposal because it was not Canadian practice, a contention with which the primary auditors had to agree.

If the primary firm had audited the subsidiaries which were examined by the secondary firm, they would have discovered that the secondary firm were also the auditors of a large number of the subsidiary companies' debtors—in particular Aurora Leasing Corporation which was the largest, "and would have been bound to enquire into the state of that company's accounts receivable, and the adequacy of its allowance for doubtful accounts which was virtually non-existent."

Justice Hughes commented critically in his report on the change in the Canadian practice where more than one auditor participates in an examination:

. . . Since the collapse of Atlantic the views of the accounting profession, as propounded by the Canadian Institute of Chartered Accountants, in company with those of other governing bodies in the English-speaking world, have altered to reflect the opinion that the primary auditor should take more responsibility for the auditing procedures applied by the auditors of subsidiary companies . . . The final determination of what can be described as a polite controversy, cautiously undertaken and replete with hair-splitting refinements, has yet to be declared, even after the lapse of four years, and it is perhaps time that public regulatory authorities concerned themselves with this vital aspect of the preparation of published financial statements.

The judge stated that he was in sympathy with the view that the auditor of the parent company should not necessarily be the auditor of the subsidiary. Nevertheless, he said, if there is any lesson to be learned from the Atlantic disaster, "it is that the auditor of a parent company, in expressing an unqualified opinion on consolidated financial statements, must take full responsibility for the opinions of auditors of subsidiary companies, and that he should be liable within the framework of the law of agency, for the consequences of their shortcomings."

The judge commented on why it was necessary for the primary auditors to satisfy themselves concerning the reputation and reliability of the secondary auditors. Had the primary auditors done so in the Atlantic case, he said, they would have found that the secondary firm had been reconstituted because a senior partner of its predecessor firm (whose name appeared first in the firm's name) had left the firm as the result of an investigation of a tax fraud for which he was convicted on November 29, 1965, resulting in his expulsion from the Institute of Chartered Accountants. Further inquiry would have shown that the same senior partner and a brother of a partner in the successor firm had been reprimanded by the president of the Institute at a meeting of its Council on February 16, 1962, having acknowledged the correctness of charges involving breach of the Institute's rules. A senior partner of Atlantic's primary auditors was a member of the disciplinary committee and attended the meeting at which the reprimand was issued.

A professor of accounting wrote an article on the Atlantic case, and among other things, commented on the failure of the primary auditors to obtain assurance that the subsidiary's auditors were independent. In the Atlantic case, he said, no such inquiry was made by the primary auditors. "Had such inquiries been made," he said, "it would have shown that individual partners of a subsidiary auditing firm were so immersed in the activities of the Atlantic Group or of companies associated with or dealing with the group, that they completely lost their independence, and were associated with [Morgan] in many transactions which were 'mostly dishonest and undertaken at the expense of Atlantic Acceptance . . . ' " [3]

A Canadian chartered accountant who had devoted over a year and a half to the investigation of Atlantic Acceptance—particularly the subsidiaries—wrote that the auditors of the subsidiaries "broke every rule of independence that one could imagine." [4] These auditors' sins, he said, were serious, "and I do not believe that all the professional and legal independence rules we have since invoked would have changed things in Atlantic in any way." He also observed that two of the senior partners of the secondary auditing firm have been expelled from the Canadian Institute of Chartered Accountants and have served prison terms.

Certificate Covering Financial Statements Not Presented Separately.—As previously noted, when the principal accountant discloses in his certificate that part of the over-all examination was made by other auditors (as in the case of a foreign subsidiary, for example) and the principal accountant does not accept responsibility for that portion of the total examination, the certificate of the other auditor must be furnished in the SEC filing. If the other auditor's certificate relates to the statements of an *unconsolidated* subsidiary, ordinarily the certificate will accompany the financial statements of that subsidiary as part of the total filing if the subsidiary is significant.

If the other auditor's certificate, however, relates to the statements of a *consolidated* subsidiary, special attention must be given to his certificate. Since the subsidiary is consolidated, the statements of that subsidiary are

---

[3] A. Beedle, "The Atlantic Acceptance Corporation—A Sorry Affair," *The Accountant*, December 10, 1970, pp. 801–805.

[4] William A. Farlinger, CA, "Atlantic Acceptance—Calamity or Catalyst?", *Canadian Chartered Accountant*, May 1971, pp. 339–345.

not required to be furnished separately and, almost without exception, the statements of the subsidiary are not filed with the SEC. The certificate has to be filed nonetheless, and since it does not accompany the statements to which it relates, the opinion paragraph should be written along the lines of the following:

In our opinion, the aforementioned financial statements (which are not presented separately in this prospectus [or other document]) present fairly, etc.

Unless this or a similar procedure is followed, the SEC's letter of comments is apt to say, "Since the financial statements of certain subsidiaries are not presented separately in the prospectus, the accountants' reports thereon should so indicate."

Certificate Covering Portion of Period Under Report

Occasionally a company which is no longer a client of the accountant files a registration statement the financial statements in which include the period when the accountant served the client, and the company asks the accountant to certify the statements for periods previously audited by him. For example, a company files a registration statement which contains an earnings summary (income statement) covering the Years 1, 2, 3, 4, and 5. The accountant had examined and reported upon Years 1, 2, and 3; a successor firm examined and reported upon Years 4 and 5. The company asks the first accountant for a certificate covering the years examined by him and a consent to the inclusion of his certificate in the registration statement. Because of the passage of time since he was in touch with the company and its affairs, the accountant should take steps to assure himself that his certificate may properly be issued. He would be concerned with what happened in Years 4 and 5 and subsequent interim periods, if any, for whatever light it might throw on Years 1, 2, and 3. He would want to know that the accounting principles followed in Years 1, 2, and 3 were also followed in Years 4 and 5; if not, the reason for the change and the effect thereof. If a prior period adjustment in Year 5 is retroactively applied to Years 1, 2, or 3, the accountant should inquire into the nature of the transaction and the basis and method of its application. He should also review the entire registration statement and prospectus. In the opinion of the author, the first accountant should also obtain a letter from the successor firm along the lines of the following:[5]

[5] The desirability of obtaining a letter along the lines indicated is suggested by SAP No. 47 (1971), paragraph 24. See the discussion on page **12·15** of this book.

Predecessor Firm
  City and state.

Dear Sirs:

This letter is furnished in connection with the opinion you have been requested to furnish with respect to the statements of income and retained earnings (and/or other statements) of (name of company) for the Years 1, 2, and 3, which statements are to be included by the company in its proposed registration statement to register under the Securities Act of 1933 an issue of (description of securities).

We have examined the balance sheet of (name of company) as at December 31, Year 5 and the statements of income and retained earnings (and/or other statements) for the Years 4 and 5, all as included in the aforementioned registration statement. Our examinations of such financial statements did not disclose any events or transactions subsequent to Year 3 which, in our opinion, would have a material effect upon the financial statements of (name of company) for the Years 1, 2, and 3 or (except as stated in the notes to the financial statements included in the proof dated [date] of the registration statement which has been furnished to you) would require mention in notes to the financial statements for the Years 1, 2, and 3.

(Signed) Successor Firm

In the circumstances described above, the certificate of the accountant who examined the Years 1, 2, and 3 may be in the form of the following:

We have made an examination of the financial statements of (name of company) for the Years 1, 2, and 3, and have examined the statements of income (or summary of earnings) and retained earnings (and/or other statements) for such years appearing in this prospectus. Our examination was made in accordance with generally accepted auditing standards, and accordingly included such tests of the accounting records and such other auditing procedures as we considered necessary in the circumstances.

In our opinion, the accompanying statements of income (or summary of earnings) and retained earnings (and/or other statements) present fairly the results of operations (and changes in financial position) of (name of company) for the Years 1, 2, and 3, in conformity with generally accepted accounting principles applied on a consistent basis.

If a certificate is required covering the supporting schedules insofar as they relate to Year 3, it can be patterned along the lines suggested elsewhere in this chapter.

When the accountant no longer serves the company whose statement he is asked to certify, he may, out of an abundance of caution, indicate in his certificate that he has made no examination since his examination covering the year 19___. Although no objection can be made to such declaration, it is unnecessary, in the opinion of this author, inasmuch as no one is entitled to assume that the accountant examined any periods other than those specified in his certificate.

One accounting firm follows the practice, when it is the successor firm, of practically combining a comfort letter with its letter to the predecessor firm. A sample of its letter addressed to the predecessor firm follows:

Predecessor Firm
  City and state.

Dear Sirs:
  This letter is furnished in connection with the report you are to give with respect to the financial statements of (name of company) for the (period). We understand that these statements are to be included by the company in its proposed registration statement to be filed under the Securities Act of 1933.
  We have examined the financial statements of (name of company) as of (date) and for the (period). We have not made an examination of financial statements or audited the records of transactions of the company subsequent to (date); accordingly, we express no opinion on financial statements or transactions of the company subsequent to that date.
  We have made a review for the period from (date) to (date) which does not constitute an examination in accordance with generally accepted auditing standards. Accordingly, we have:

  (a) read the interim unaudited financial statements as of (date) and for the (period);
  (b) read the minutes of the meetings of the stockholders, Board of Directors, and Executive Committee held during the period from (date) to (date) included in the minute books at (date), officials of the company having advised us that the minutes of all meetings through that date were set forth therein; and
  (c) had discussions with officials of the company responsible for financial and accounting matters as to transactions and events subsequent to (date of certified balance sheet). Our review for the period subsequent to (date of unaudited interim statements) has necessarily been confined largely to consultation with responsible officers and employees.

  Based upon our examination of (name of company) for the (period), and our aforementioned limited review, nothing has come to our attention which caused us to believe that there were any significant adjustments which were applicable to the period prior to (the beginning of the period covered by the successor auditor).
  Should anything come to our attention prior to the effective date of the registration statement which, in our judgment, would have a material effect on the financial statements covered by your report, we shall notify you promptly.
  It is understood that this letter is for your information and is not to be quoted, or referred to, in whole or in part, in the registration statement or prospectus or otherwise in connection with the registration under the Securities Act of 1933 or the sale of the securities.

Very truly yours
(Signed) Successor Firm

  The form of letter from the successor accountant (referred to above) obviously can be issued only if he has completed one or more audits of the company's financial statements. It is the fact of his having made an audit which gives him a basis for issuing such a letter, and which furnishes a basis for reliance by the predecessor accountant that there have been no material transactions or events which affect the statements previously certified by him. If the successor accountant has not made an audit, what kind of assurance can he give to his predecessor? In the author's opinion, if the successor accountant has completed an audit, he is in a position to give assurance to his predecessor. If he has not completed an audit, he would ordinarily not be in a position to furnish a letter which serves as an adequate basis for reliance by the predecessor accountant.

The predecessor auditor may have a difficult problem in certifying the figures of the years he previously examined if those figures have been revised in ways that do not lend themselves readily to verification by him. In an actual case, an accountant was asked to furnish his certificate (for inclusion in a prospectus) covering two years he had previously examined and reported upon. Another firm of accountants examined and reported upon the operations of the three succeeding years.

Subsequent to the predecessor accountant's contact with the company, it had acquired another company in a pooling of interests transaction; accordingly the financial statements of all prior years were retroactively restated to reflect the pooling. The company had discontinued retroactively the LIFO method of pricing inventories and had readopted the FIFO method. The accountant could not certify the adjusted figures of the years he had examined because of the effect of the pooling and the retroactive change in accounting for inventories. In addition, the company had retroactively adopted the equity method of accounting for investments in unconsolidated subsidiaries. Consequently, he furnished a certificate as follows:

> We have examined, etc. (as in a conventional certificate).
> As indicated in Notes — and — to the Summary of Earnings, subsequent to (date) [which was the date of the most recent balance sheet he had examined] retroactive adjustments were made to the two fiscal years ended (date) for the pooling of (name of company), discontinuance of the LIFO method of pricing merchandise inventories and readoption of a FIFO method of pricing such inventories, and the reflection in income of the Corporation's equity in the undistributed net earnings of its unconsolidated subsidiaries. We are not in a position to express, and we do not express, an opinion as to the propriety of these changes or as to their effect on the fairness of presentation of the results of operations for the two years ended (date).
> In our opinion, the financial statements as originally examined (which are not presented separately herein) presented fairly, under the then existing circumstances and conditions, the results of operations of (name of company) for the two years ended (date), in conformity with generally accepted accounting principles applied on a consistent basis.

It is clear from the foregoing certificate that it covered the amounts originally certified by the accountants, and therefore did not cover the changes effected in arriving at the revised amounts shown in the prospectus. These changes were covered by the certificate of the successor accountants whose certificate contained a final paragraph as follows:

We have also reviewed the information for the five years ended (date) included in the tabulation under "Summary of Earnings." The information for the three years ended (date) has been prepared from financial statements previously examined by us, as described above. The information for the two years ended (date), before the retroactive adjustments indicated in Notes — and — to the Summary of Earnings is based on, and has been prepared from, statements of income previously examined by (name of accountants) whose report appears in this prospectus. In our opinion, relying upon the accountants who examined the statements of income for the two years ended (date), the tabulation under "Summary of Earnings" presents fairly the information set forth therein, in conformity with generally accepted accounting principles applied on a consistent basis.

In another case, the successor accountants covered the same situation as the one above in a different way. The successors had examined only the year 1970. Their certificate concluded with the following paragraph:

During 1969 and 1970 XYZ & Company, Inc. (XYZ) acquired a number of companies in transactions accounted for as poolings of interests. The statements of consolidated operations, paid-in surplus and earnings retained in the business and the summary of consolidated earnings for the four years ended December 31, 1969 of XYZ and consolidated subsidiaries, represent combinations of the separate financial statements of XYZ and the companies referred to above for various fiscal years as set forth in Note 1 to Consolidated Financial Statements. These separate financial statements were examined by other public accountants to the extent set forth in Note 1, and subsequently restated by XYZ to reflect certain adjustments as set forth in Note 1. We did not examine the financial statements referred to in this paragraph for any of the periods prior to 1970, and accordingly we express no opinion thereon. However, in our opinion, the adjustments set forth in Note 1 have been reasonably applied to the years to which they relate and the amounts included in the statements referred to in this paragraph have been properly compiled from the amounts in the underlying statements, as covered to the extent set forth in Note 1 by the opinions of other public accountants and as subsequently restated by XYZ to reflect the adjustments set forth in Note 1.

Certificate Covering Income Statement Which Excludes Certain Items.—The reader is referred to the discussion in Chapter **21** regarding the acquisition by a registrant (Dexter) of a department that was part of a division of a company (Shell Oil). The registration statement included a historical statement of the operations of the department computed before the deduction of a significant number and amount of expenses. The statement was accompanied by an accountants' certificate as follows:

We have examined the statement of financial condition of Shell Oil Company and consolidated subsidiary companies at December 31, 1968 and the related statement of income and retained earnings for the year (none of these statements are presented herein) and have previously rendered our opinion thereon. We have also examined the statement of income before allocation of division and head office expenses and income taxes of the Adhesives Department of Shell Chemical Company, a division of Shell Oil Company, for the nine months ended September 30, 1969. Our examination of this statement was made in accordance with generally accepted auditing standards and accordingly included such tests of the accounting records and such other auditing procedures as we considered necessary in the circumstances.

In our opinion, the above-noted statement of income before allocation of division and head office expenses and income taxes (as described in Note 1 to the financial statement) presents fairly the data shown therein for the nine months ended September 30, 1969 in conformity with generally accepted accounting principles applied on a consistent basis.

The discussion in Chapter **21** also relates to a "statement of operating income" prepared for a parcel of real property proposed to be acquired by an issuer registering on Form S–11 under the 1933 Act. As explained in that chapter, this statement is a modified form of historical statement which excludes certain expenses (such as interest and depreciation) which are expected to be materially different when the property is in the hands of the new owner as compared with the amounts in the hands of the prior owner. Following is a typical form of accountants' certificate applicable to this kind of statement:

We have examined the statement of operating income of (name of company or property) for the (period). Our examination was made in accordance with generally accepted auditing standards, and accordingly included such tests of the accounting records and such other auditing procedures as we considered necessary in the circumstances.

Operating income has been stated before interest, depreciation and amortization, advertising, management fee, legal and auditing fees, administrative expenses and federal income taxes, in order to exclude expenses incurred by the present owner of the property which may not be comparable to the operation of the property by (new owner).

In our opinion, the aforementioned statement of operating income presents fairly the operating income, as defined above, of (name of company or property) for the (period), in conformity with generally accepted accounting principles applied on a consistent basis.

Date of Certificate

The usual practice of accountants is to date their certificates upon completion of the examination, that is, when they have completed all important audit procedures necessary to enable them to form an opinion. When the statements and the accountants' report are included in an annual report to security holders, there is ordinarily not much time lag between the date of the accountants' certificate and the issuance of the report to security holders. When these statements are included in the company's annual report to the

SEC (e.g., Form 10–K), it is customary and proper for the auditor to use the same date on his report included in the SEC filing as he used in reporting on the financial statements previously released. Statement on Auditing Procedure No. 47 provides that the auditor has no responsibility to make a further investigation or inquiry as to events which may have occurred between the time of issuance of his report on the financial statements initially released and the issuance of his report on the financial statements in the annual report to the SEC.

These same statements, however, may be used at a much later date in a registration statement to be filed under the 1933 Act. Question is sometimes raised concerning the date of the accountants' report which, because of the passage of time, may be quite old.

Most accountants prefer not to change the date of their reports although they recognize the objections on the part of the company and underwriters to using a report bearing an old date. These accountants sometimes meet these objections and retain the old date by dating their reports as follows: "August 15, 19___ as of January 21, 19___."

Information contained in notes to financial statements is sometimes brought up to the most recent practicable date, which may be subsequent to the date on which the auditor formed his opinion regarding the financial statements taken as a whole. The auditor may none the less wish to retain the original date of his certificate but may be troubled by the fact that the information in the notes speaks as of a more recent date. If this causes the auditor some concern, he can overcome it in several ways:

> He can date his certificate "January 29, 19___, except as to Note ___, with respect to which the date of this report is March 10, 19___."
> The certificate can be dated "February 14, 19___ (August 4, 19___ as to certain information referred to in Note ___)."
> The certificate can be dated "January 29, 19___ (Information in Note ___ being as of the later dates therein indicated)."

The reader is referred to the discussion on page **15·17** dealing with the situation that might arise after the release of an auditor's report for use in a published annual report to security holders but before the filing of the company's annual report to the SEC (Form 10–K) if the auditor learns of a subsequent event that requires adjustment of the financial statements or disclosure therein. If the statements are adjusted for purposes of the 10–K filing, the auditor's report may then bear a current date, in which case the independent auditor has the same responsibility with respect to all subsequent events up to the revised date as he had up to the date of his original report. Alternatively, the report may continue to bear the original date supplemented by a current date limited specifically to the event requiring the adjustment, thus eliminating responsibility for other subsequent events. [SAP No. 47(1971)].

The significance which SEC attaches to the date of an accountant's certificate may be gathered from the following case [18 SEC Ann. Rep. 33 (1952)]. A company filed an annual report with the SEC. The notes to the financial statements disclosed that in the month subsequent to the date of the balance sheet, the company had made settlement in a substantial amount in respect of claims against the company arising from certain investments which had been sold several years previously. The accountants' certificate covering the financial statements was signed approximately seven weeks after the settlement date. On the basis that the accountants had knowledge of the final status of the claims prior to signing their opinion, the SEC requested and obtained the filing of revised financial statements reflecting the settlement.

In *Oklahoma Hotel Building Co.* [4 SEC 580 (1939)] the SEC held that material defaults in interest payments occurring before the date of the accountant's certificate must be disclosed in the balance sheet or in a footnote thereto.

Reliance Upon Actuary or Other Expert

When a public accountant examines the financial statements of a company, ordinarily it is expected that he will furnish a report covering the financial statements as a whole. Occasionally, however, there may be something in the statements which the accountant is not competent to pass upon. For example, the adequacy of the policy reserves provided by insurance companies is usually not within the competence of the average public accountant, unless he has had extensive actuarial training and experience. In these circumstances, the accountant generally relies upon the opinion of another expert—such as an independent actuary—with respect to a portion of the statements.

In the following certificate (taken from a prospectus filed with the SEC), the certifying accountant relied upon the certificate of actuaries with respect to the policy reserves of an insurance company:

We have examined the (list of financial statements) of (name of company) at (date) and for the (period). Our examination . . . in the circumstances. The amounts at which the actuarial items are stated at (dates) were certified by the Company's consulting actuaries, whose reports have been furnished to us.

In our opinion, relying upon the aforementioned certification of actuarially determined amounts, the aforementioned financial statements, etc. . . . .

The reference in the scope paragraph to the report of actuaries may take a variety of forms, such as, "We received the report of consulting actuaries on their examination of policy reserves and other actuarial items."

The reference to actuaries in the scope paragraph, viewed as a recitation of an auditing procedure, can not be said to be an essential reference. However, actuarially derived amounts of policy reserves and similar items are usually very significant in the financial statements of insurance companies. Because of this and since the reference may, possibly, remove some uncertainty in the mind of the reader as to what steps the auditor (presumably untrained in actuarial science) employed to obtain the necessary independent audit satisfaction concerning policy reserves and similar actuarially derived items, many accountants consider an appropriate reference to actuaries to be desirable in the scope paragraph of accountant's certificates.

A question might be raised as to the necessity of referring, in the *opinion* paragraph, to the report of actuaries, since the report is only one of the many things on which the auditor bases his opinion. In several cases, however, where the auditor has omitted such a reference in the opinion paragraph of his report, the SEC has said in its letter of comments, "Unless the certifying accountants desire to assume responsibility for the actuarial computations, the opinion paragraph of their report should be expanded to indicate their reliance on the actuaries."

When actuaries are referred to in the accountant's report, the SEC requires that the actuaries be independent and that their report or certificate be included in the document filed with the Commission. If the document is a registration statement under the 1933 Act, the actuaries must also consent to the inclusion of their report or certificate in the registration statement.

Certificates in First Examinations

A recurring problem in the practice of public accounting is the audit of opening inventories in the first examination of a company preparatory to certification of the company's income statement. Sometimes the accountant may have been making limited examinations of his client's financial statements—limited usually with respect to observation of inventories and confirmation of receivables. As far as inventories are concerned, the auditing problem is the same whether it arises in connection with a first examination or after a series of limited examinations which did not include any verification of inventories. If the limited examinations included some verification of inventories, the problem is likely to be less acute than if no work at all had been done.

It is probably fair to say that almost every practicing public accountant has had some experience with this kind of problem, that is, where he is making his first examination of a particular company. The examination may have nothing whatever to do with a plan or proposal to "go public," but certainly it is in that connection that accountants are most often called upon to make an examination leading to an unqualified certificate.

In public offerings of securities involving less than $500,000, there is ordinarily no need to prepare and file a full-scale registration statement. These offerings are subject to the SEC's exemptive regulations previously referred to in this book. Under these regulations, depending on the size of the issue, offering circulars may have to be prepared, but the financial statements therein need not be certified except as indicated in the discussion in Chapter **9** relating to Form 1–A. If the offering cannot be made under the exemptive regulations, a registration statement will have to be prepared on one of the forms prescribed therefor. These are also described earlier in this book, together with the requirements for financial statements and certification by independent public accountants.

As far as the balance sheet is concerned, the auditor ought not to have much of a problem in his first examination leading up to an unqualified report. With proper planning, he should be able to arrange to observe the taking of the physical inventory at, or near, the balance sheet date, and he should therefore have no insurmountable difficulty in certifying the closing inventory.

Where the accountant may run into difficulties is in the audit of inventories at dates prior to the balance sheet. Assume, for example, that the summary of earnings is to cover five years which, for simplicity, will be referred to as Year 1, Year 2, and so on. Years 3, 4, and 5 have to be certified. (This discussion is on the basis of the earnings summary, but the same considerations would apply to an income statement if one is furnished in addition to an earnings summary.) Assume also that the company and the underwriters are willing that Years 1 and 2 be submitted without audit by independent public accountants. Insofar as inventories are concerned, the auditor's principal problem will be in relation to the amounts at the beginning of Year 3, at the end of Year 3, and at the end of Year 4. These are the so-called "earlier inventories." To be sure, he is also concerned with the inventory at the end of Year 5, but it is assumed that he has been able to observe the taking of that inventory and will have no extraordinary auditing problem with respect to it.

The audit problem relating to the earlier inventories will vary depending on a number of factors:

1. Whether or not the company took physical inventories at the earlier dates, and retained the original inventory and tally sheets, summaries, and instructions relating to the physical counts;
2. Whether company personnel who participated in or supervised such earlier counts are available to discuss the procedures followed in taking such inventories;
3. Whether or not other independent public accountants participated in such inventory taking, whether they are available to discuss the

procedures they followed in observing the counts and the tests made by them to verify the counts made by company personnel, and whether their working papers relating to their audit procedures are available for inspection;

4. Whether or not the company maintains adequate accounting records of inventories, including cost records and perpetual inventory records, and whether such records are integrated with the general accounting records;

5. Whether or not the company has an internal audit group which attempts to establish the accuracy and reliability of the accounting records in general and the inventory records in particular;

6. Whether or not satisfactory statistical and operating data exist in addition to the general accounting records, which serve as a check on the accounting information.

Generally accepted auditing standards require the auditor to observe the taking of inventories and to confirm receivables where either of these assets is material in relation to the financial position or results of operations of a business entity. By vote of the membership of the AICPA in 1939, these procedures were adopted as "generally accepted auditing procedures." In 1966 the AICPA Executive Committee approved the issuance of statements on auditing procedure which may modify or revise pronouncements on matters of auditing, previously approved by AICPA members, as consistent with the authority granted to the Committee on Auditing Procedure by the AICPA Council.

In September 1970 the Committee on Auditing Procedure issued its SAP No. 43 on "Confirmation of Receivables and Observation of Inventories." The Committee's statement reaffirmed the importance of the procedures with respect to inventories and receivables and emphasized that the independent auditor who issues an opinion when he has not employed them must bear in mind that he has the burden of justifying the opinion.

SAP No. 43 was issued for the purpose of providing additional guidelines for the independent auditor in confirming receivables and observing inventories and to modify existing reporting requirements. Paragraphs 9–13, inclusive, of the statement deal with inventory procedures:

Paragraph 9 describes the procedures to be followed when inventory quantities are determined solely by means of a physical count.

Paragraph 10 modifies the observation requirements when the client has well-kept perpetual inventory records.

Paragraph 11 states the procedures applicable to companies that have developed inventory controls or methods of determining inventories, including statistical sampling, which are highly effective in determining inventory quantities and which are sufficiently reliable to

make unnecessary an annual physical count of each item of inventory.
Paragraph 12 indicates what needs to be done when the auditor has not
satisfied himself as to inventories through the procedures described
in Paragraphs 9–11.

Paragraph 13 deals with examinations where the auditor has not observed or made physical counts of prior inventories. This paragraph
states that the auditor may, nevertheless, be able to become satisfied
as to such prior inventories through appropriate procedures, such as
tests of prior transactions, reviews of the records of prior counts, and
the application of gross profit tests, provided that he has been able to
become satisfied as to the current inventory.

The SEC recognizes that some auditing procedures commonly applicable
in the examination of financial statements for the latest year for which a
certified income statement is filed, such as the independent confirmation of
accounts receivable or the observation of inventory-taking, are either impracticable or impossible to perform with respect to the financial statements
of the earlier years and, hence, would not be considered applicable in the
circumstances. (ASR No. 62.)

In SAP No. 43 the AICPA Committee on Auditing Procedure stated
that if the auditor has been unable to apply the customary auditing procedures of confirming receivables or observing inventories because it was
impracticable or impossible to do so but nevertheless has satisfied himself by means of other auditing procedures, it is unlikely that disclosure
of that fact in the auditor's report has any significance to the reader.
("Impracticable" in auditing means "not capable of being done with the
available means or with reason or prudence.") The Committee concluded
that if the auditor has been unable to confirm receivables or observe the
taking of physical inventories solely because it was impracticable or impossible to do so, but has satisfied himself as to receivables or inventories
by means of other auditing procedures, no comment need be made in his
report, although he may wish to disclose the circumstances of the engagement and describe the other procedures. The omission of the receivable
and inventory procedures at the beginning of the year is also not required to
be disclosed in situations where the auditor has satisfied himself by means
of other auditing procedures, although the auditor may wish to disclose the
circumstances of the engagement and describe the other procedures he employed.

It is the opinion paragraph of the accountant's certificate that has given
rise to the greatest amount of confusion and difference of opinion. In an
initial examination, some accountants have certified "with the foregoing
explanation regarding earlier inventories," or "with the foregoing explanation as to the limitation on examination of earlier inventories," or they

used other language with similar effect. If the auditor has been able affirmatively to satisfy himself as to such earlier inventories, then to certify "with an explanation" is superfluous at best, and contradictory at worst. Nonetheless, the SEC, prior to March 1962 accepted literally hundreds of such certificates with "explanations" in the opinion paragraph as long as they were written as "explanations" and not as "exceptions." The SEC has consistently held that the accountant must be satisfied with the results of his inquiries and his opinion must be unqualified, or the certificate is not acceptable to the Commission. If the accountant certified "with the foregoing explanation," the SEC—*prior to March, 1962*—accepted the certificate with the understanding that it was an "explanation" and not an "exception."

It had become increasingly apparent that, in some cases, the certifying accountants intended the "explanation" to be read as an "exception": that the accountants, as a matter of fact, had *not* satisfied themselves completely with respect to the earlier inventories (and hence the income statement or earnings summary), and that their certificates were intended to be read as qualified certificates. *Certificates qualified in this respect are not acceptable for SEC purposes.* The SEC staff has made it abundantly clear that the accountant had to be satisfied with regard to the earlier inventories or he should not certify. The staff has also said that certificates relating to first examinations were acceptable provided that the disclosures in the certificates were presented as explanatory matter—not by way of an exception intended to qualify the accountant's opinion of the statements.

Accounting Series Release No. 90.—To remove any misunderstanding or ambiguity on this point, the SEC, on March 1, 1962, issued an opinion of its Chief Accountant dealing with this matter. The opinion was in the form of ASR No. 90. The most important statement in the release is the statement that the SEC would no longer accept certificates written along the lines of hundreds of similar certificates which had been filed with, and accepted without question by, the Commission. The release says in part that if an accountant reports that his examination was made in accordance with generally accepted auditing standards, and accordingly included such tests of the accounting records and such other auditing procedures as he considered necessary in the circumstances, a stated exception in the report as to failure to observe beginning inventories *is contradictory and should be omitted.*

A middle paragraph explaining that the certificate covers a first audit is informative and, the SEC says, in some cases is essential to describe the alternative procedures applied. *A negative type of conclusion to this paragraph,* that is, "nothing has come to my attention, etc.," *is not acceptable.* Lost and inadequate records may give rise to questions as to the reliability of the results shown in the financial statements and may make it impracticable to apply alternative audit procedures. The alternative procedures employed must be adequate to support an unqualified opinion as to the fairness of presentation of the income statements year by year.

If, as a result of the examination and the conclusions reached, the accountant is not in a position to express an affirmative, unqualified opinion as to the fairness of the presentation of earnings year by year, the registration statement is defective because the certificate does not meet the requirements of Regulation S–X. *If the accountant is not satisfied with the results of his examination, he should not issue an affirmative opinion.* If he is satisfied, any reference from the opinion paragraph to an explanatory paragraph devoted solely to the scope of the audit is inconsistent and unnecessary. Accordingly, phrases such as "with the foregoing explanation as to inventories" raise questions as to whether the certifying accountant intended to limit his opinion as to the fairness of the presentation of the results shown *and should be omitted.*

A "subject to" or "except for" opinion paragraph in which these phrases refer to the scope of the audit, indicating that the accountant has not been able to satisfy himself on some significant element in the financial statements, according to ASR No. 90, is not acceptable in certificates filed with the Commission in connection with public offerings. The "subject to" qualification is appropriate when the reference is to disclosures explaining the status of matters which cannot be resolved at the statement date. (There are also other situations in which the SEC accepts the "subject to" qualification in certificates filed with it; see the discussion of "subject to" certificates in Chapter 25.)

When the SEC issues a release on an accounting or auditing question having general application, a draft of the proposed release is usually submitted to professional groups and interested persons for comments and criticisms. This was not done, however, in the case of ASR No. 90. As a consequence, the issuance of the release took most accountants by surprise. Furthermore, the release was effective on issuance and was therefore applicable to registrations which had been filed literally months previously but had not yet become effective. The release created consternation and chagrin among public accountants because of its widespread application and because it said, in effect, that the Commission would no longer accept certificates which agreed, word for word, with literally hundreds of similar certificates which had been accepted, without question, by the Commission.

When the SEC takes such drastic action, it is generally safe to assume that something triggered it. It is known that the SEC had been dissatisfied for a long time with the certificates of accountants relating to first examinations. Many public accountants as well as persons within the Commission believed that many of the accountants' reports issued in such circumstances were actually "comfort letters" in the guise of certificates, and that the situation was one demanding attention and correction. The issuance of ASR No. 90 was prompted by what happened in the Londontown Manufacturing Company case. The case is discussed in Chapter **5**.

Inventory Problems of Companies Filing Under the 1934 Act.— In Chapter **1** a brief reference was made to the fact that certain unlisted companies are required to register with the SEC when their assets exceed $1,000,000 and they have a class of equity securities (other than an exempted security) held of record by 500 or more persons. This provision is contained in Section 12(g) of the 1934 Act.

In most cases, the issuer of the securities is required to file a registration statement on Form 10, which, as noted in Chapter **15**, calls for certified financial statements covering three years. What would the situation be if a company, having an obligation to register, is unable to furnish an unqualified certificate of an independent accountant because the accountant had not observed the taking of physical inventories? In ASR No. 90 (discussed in the preceding pages), the SEC said, in effect, that it would no longer accept certificates in which the accountant certified "with an explanation."

There seems to be no doubt that the Commission's basic position, as stated in ASR No. 90, is applicable to accountants' certificates included in Form 10 by over-the-counter companies required to register with the SEC. It may therefore also be a matter of some concern to an accountant whose examinations in prior years were not sufficiently comprehensive to enable him now to satisfy himself as to earlier inventories and, hence, to certify the income statement for all or part of the required three years. In its release the Commission said that it will not accept qualified certificates. On the other hand, there is nothing to compel the accountant to furnish an unqualified certificate in circumstances where it is inappropriate for him to do so.

As a minimum, it would seem that the accountant should be in a position to certify the inventory at the balance sheet date without qualification. With all the publicity that the 1964 amendments to the 1934 Act received, the issuer and its independent accountant should have arranged for the observation of physical inventories at or near the balance sheet date so that as far as the balance sheet is concerned the certificate is unqualified.

The earlier inventories, however, are another matter. The SEC has not announced a blanket waiver of the requirements as stated in its Release No. 90, and it is doubtful that any such waiver will be issued. It seems likely that the Commission will decide separately and on its merits each case involving a qualified certificate of the income statement in Form 10 arising from the fact that the accountant had not observed earlier physical inventories.

If this is a matter that causes the accountant some concern, he should give some thought to the matter at the earliest opportunity, to see what, if anything, can be done by way of reasonably satisfying himself with respect to those inventories. If the available alternative procedures do not furnish an adequate basis for a clean certificate, the accountant should take appropriate exception in his certificate. But at the same time he should be prepared to defend, if necessary, his inability to furnish a clean certificate. If his position is sound, it seems that the Commission will have no choice but to accept the exception in his report, knowing that this is something which, with the passage of time, will take care of itself. In the following year the accountant should be in a position to certify the income statement of that year without an exception running to inventories.

Certificate When Receivables Not Confirmed

By vote of the membership of the AICPA in 1939 confirmation of receivables became a required audit procedure; this step was taken by the accountancy profession following the McKesson and Robbins scandal, and the SEC's investigation of and report on that case.

In some circumstances it is not possible for the auditor to obtain confirmation of accounts receivable, and the auditor is compelled to satisfy himself with respect to such assets by alternative auditing procedures. Where this often happens is in the case of receivables due from the United States government. In many cases, such receivables are difficult—often impossible —to confirm, although the amounts involved may be very significant in relation to the enterprise being audited.

Until recently it had been mandatory for the auditor to disclose in his report that he was unable to confirm receivables even though he had substantiated them by the application of other auditing procedures and issued an unqualified opinion. The AICPA Committee on Auditing Procedure reconsidered the desirability of this reporting requirement which singled out this customary auditing procedure (together with the omission of physical inventory observation) for special reporting treatment to the exclusion of other customary procedures (SAP No. 43, 1970).

The Committee concluded that if the independent auditor has been unable to confirm receivables solely because it was impracticable or impossible to do so, but has satisfied himself as to such receivables by other means, no comment need be made in his report, although he may wish to disclose the circumstances of his audit engagement and describe the alternative auditing procedures which he employed in lieu of confirmation, but such disclosure is optional.

Before issuing its Statement, the Committee consulted with the staff of the SEC. In view of the option given the auditor of disclosing the omission of receivable confirmations, the staff stated that it would not take exception to the recommendations in the Statement. The staff wished to reserve the right to inquire in specific cases into the alternative procedures utilized by the auditor to substantiate receivables in the absence of confirmation.

Prior to the issuance of SAP No. 43, the SEC, in several cases, insisted that the auditors recite in some detail in their certificates why confirmation of receivables was not possible or practicable. In one case, for example, an auditor had reported in a company's published report to shareholders that it was not feasible to confirm accounts receivable by correspondence with customers, but that he satisfied himself as to such accounts by means of other auditing procedures. A similar report was included in the company's annual report on Form 10–K and filed with the SEC and the exchange on which the company's securities were listed. In due course the company received a deficiency letter from the SEC requesting that the accountant's certificate be expanded to indicate why it was not feasible to confirm customers' accounts receivable. Complying with this request the accountants furnished a new certificate, the pertinent portion of which, relating to scope, was as follows:

> . . . Our examination was made in accordance with generally accepted auditing standards and accordingly included such tests of the accounting records of the companies and such other auditing procedures as we considered necessary in the circumstances. Accounts receivable are composed principally of accounts of freight forwarding subsidiaries which use, as their detailed accounts receivable records, copies of issued way bills filed numerically by destination office. The use of such way bills, together with the fact that amounts receivable are recorded when the shipment is delivered to a common carrier, makes it impracticable to confirm accounts receivable balances by correspondence with customers. We have satisfied ourselves as to such accounts by means of other auditing procedures.

The foregoing certificate was acceptable to SEC.

As a consequence of the revised provision in SAP No. 43, the auditor in the case referred to above would not have to disclose the omission of receivable confirmations in his certificate and, in general, a certificate on this basis is acceptable to the SEC. If the staff, however, has reason to suspect that alternative procedures were employed in the absence of confirmation, they may require disclosure not only of the omission of confirmation but also a description of the circumstances which made confirmation impracticable.

Deficiencies Commonly Cited in Connection with Accountants' Certificates

The SEC in 1938 published an analysis of deficiencies commonly cited by the Commission in connection with financial statements filed under the

1933 and 1934 Acts (ASR No. 7). Among other things, the release contained a list of common deficiencies relating to accountants' certificates. The list follows:

1. Accountant's opinion in respect of (1) the financial statements of, and (2) the accounting principles followed by, the registrant not clearly stated.
2. Use of equivocal phrases such as "subject to the foregoing," "subject to the above comments," "subject to comments and explanations in exhibits," "subject to the accompanying comments," etc. [In some circumstances, however, the use of the words "subject to" is not objectionable; see the discussion in Chapter **25**.]
3. A reasonably comprehensive statement as to the scope of the audit made, not included in the certificate.
4. Adequate audit not made by certifying accountant. [In this connection attention is directed to the requirements of Regulation S–X, Rule 2–02.]
5. Failure to certify *all* financial statements required to be submitted; e.g., failure to certify income statement as well as balance sheet, and failure to certify statements of registrant as well as statements of registrant and subsidiaries consolidated.
6. Financial statements and supporting schedules covered by the certificate not clearly identified.
7. Certifying that the accounting principles followed by the registrant are in accordance with the system of accounts prescribed by a state regulatory body, or in a particular industry, but without indicating whether the practice of the registrant is in accordance with generally accepted accounting principles.
8. Effect upon the financial statements of substantial changes in accounting policies of the registrant not commented upon and explained by the certifying accountants.
9. Effect upon the financial statements of the registrant's failure to follow generally accepted accounting principles not commented upon and explained by the certifying accountants.
10. Disclaimer of responsibility on the part of the certifying accountants with respect to matters clearly within their province.
11. Reservations on the part of the certifying accountants with respect to matters not within their province which might indicate that apparently the accountants were not satisfied that such matters as legal titles, outstanding liabilities, etc., were properly reflected in the financial statements.
12. Certificate undated, or not manually signed.

Certificate Where Registrant's Records Are Inadequate or Are Not Maintained

When the independent public accountant has completed an examination of financial statements, usually there are proposed adjustments resulting from his audit. In many cases the adjustments may be so minor in character and amount that the auditor may voluntarily waive them as being not significant. In rare cases, however, the adjustments may be so significant that they amount, in effect, to a virtual reconstruction of the accounts. What, if any, disclosure should be made of the gross inadequacy of the registrant's accounting or the lack of accounting?

The SEC made public an opinion of its Chief Accountant dealing with an examination by an independent public accountant in the course of which the accountant was forced to make far-reaching adjustments of the accounts. [ASR No. 13 (1940)]. The concluding paragraph of the opinion is pertinent to this question:

In my opinion, when a registrant during the period under review has not maintained records adequate for the purpose of preparing comprehensive and dependable financial statements, that fact should be disclosed. If, because of the absence or gross inadequacy of accounting records maintained by a registrant, it is necessary to have essential books of account prepared retroactively and for the accountant to enlarge the scope of the audit to the extent indicated in order to be able to express his opinion, these facts also should be disclosed, and I believe it is misleading, notwithstanding partial disclosure by footnotes as in the instant case, to furnish a certificate which implies that the accountant was satisfied to express an opinion based on a test-check audit. Moreover, it is misleading, in my opinion, to state or imply that accepted principles of accounting have been consistently followed by a registrant during the period under review, if in fact during such period books of account were not maintained by a registrant or were grossly inadequate, or if it has been necessary for the accountant to make pervasive and extraordinary adjustments of the character under consideration.

A footnote to the above-quoted paragraph also made this comment: "Although not in question here, the status of accountants as independent experts may be jeopardized when employees of the certifying accountants prepare the registrant's ledgers and books of original entry or when the accountants' work becomes a substitute for management's accounting of its stewardship rather than a check upon that accounting."

It is not often that the accountant will be confronted with a situation requiring a disclosure in his certificate along the lines contemplated by the opinion quoted above. In one case, however, the accountant was faced with similar circumstances and his opinion was to be included in a registration statement. The accountant prepared a conventional short-form report except that he inserted a middle paragraph in his certificate which read as follows:

The accounting records of the Corporation were not maintained in conformity with generally accepted accounting principles. The principal items which required adjustment were as follows: (1) purchases of fixed assets were not capitalized in the accounts as acquired, but have now been capitalized retroactively and provisions have been made for related depreciation, (2) adjustment has been made for the re-allocation as required of income between fiscal periods and deferment of income at the end of the period, and (3) provision has been made for possible uncollectibility of charges made against certain affiliated companies for materials and advances.

Inasmuch as the financial statements had been properly adjusted, the opinion section of the report in question was unqualified.

One might well ask why any disclosure must be made of the fact that the record-keeping has been poor, inadequate, or lacking, if the financial statements included in the registration statement are such that the accountant can give an unqualified opinion. This question is difficult to resolve on its merits, since the accountant ordinarily reports not on the manner of keeping the records but on the financial statements included in the registration statement. As long as ASR No. 13 remains in effect and is not withdrawn by the SEC, it appears that the accountant should make the disclosure in his certificate contemplated by the release.

This view would seem to be reinforced by the Commission's decision in *National Electric Signal Company* [8 SEC 160 (1940)]. (See page **5**·39.)

In *Tucker Corporation* [26 SEC 249 (1947)] the SEC said that the auditor's certificate as originally filed [6] with the registration statement failed to reflect adequate information as to the condition of the corporation's books and records for the period under review. With respect to the condition of the accounting records, the *amended* accountant's certificate stated:

When we commenced our examination in April, 1947, a satisfactory system of internal control was in operation; however, we found that during the period

[6] The accountant's *original* certificate was as follows:
We have examined the balance sheet of Tucker Corporation as of April 21, 1947, and related statements of expenses and charges, surplus (deficit), and surplus arising from sales of franchises to distributors and dealers, for the period from inception of the company on July 8, 1946, to April 21, 1947, and the supporting schedules, included in the Registration Statement (Form S-1) about to be filed by Tucker Corporation under the Securities Act of 1933, have reviewed the system of internal control and the accounting procedures of the company and, without making a detailed audit of the transactions, have examined or tested accounting records of the company and other supporting evidence, by methods and to the extent we deemed appropriate. Our examination was made in accordance with generally accepted auditing standards applicable in the circumstances and included all procedures which we considered necessary.
In our opinion, the accompanying statements, specified above, present fairly the position of Tucker Corporation at April 21, 1947, and expenses and charges and surplus arising from sales of franchises to distributors and dealers for the period from July 8, 1946, to April 21, 1947, in conformity with generally accepted accounting principles applied consistently during the period; and the supporting schedules, in our opinion, present fairly the information required to be stated therein.

from the inception of the company on July 8, 1946 to March 31, 1947, no record known as the general ledger was maintained and that the accounting records during that period consisted solely of records of cash receipts and disbursements, the entries in which were posted to the general ledger on or about March 31, 1947; furthermore, at about this time provision was made to place the accounts on an accrual basis. Adopting the accrual basis, certain payments, a number major in amount, including payments to or on behalf of Mr. ———— and ——————— Machine and Tool Co. aggregating $160,692, although made in 1947 were entered in the general ledger as of December 31, 1946, for the reason that they were applicable to the period prior to that date.

In *Automatic Telephone Dialer, Inc.,* [10 SEC 707 (1941)] the testimony indicated that the company's accounting records were grossly inadequate. There appears to have been no journal kept, and the general ledger, after having been set up retroactively in 1935, had not been kept up since that date. Expenses admittedly were not properly classified. The books were kept with a minimum of detail and in what might be described as a homemade manner rather than in accordance with the usual bookkeeping and accounting practice. These facts, said the SEC, compelled the conclusion that the certificate did not conform to the requirements of Rule 651 of the general rules and regulations under the Securities Act. (Rule 651 is no longer in effect, having been replaced by Rule 2–02 of Regulation S–X. Rule 651 provided in part that the accountants' certificate "shall be reasonably comprehensive as to the scope of the audit made, and shall state clearly the opinion of the accountant or accountants in respect of the financial statements of, and the accounting principles *and procedures* followed by, the person or persons whose statements are furnished. . . .")

In *Livingston Mining Company* [2 SEC 148 (1937)] the registrant had no records of any kind except a stock certificate book, the minutes of directors' and stockholders' meetings (which were inadequate), and some stock sheets. The accountant had made changes quite freely in the minutes to reflect what in his best judgment had really taken place, occasionally ignoring what was recited in the minutes; and occasionally in making the changes he paid deference to what he wanted to happen in the future. "And yet," the SEC said, "nowhere in the registration statement or prospectus is there any intimation, either by the way the facts are stated or otherwise, that the facts contained therein are based largely upon conjecture, guess and inadequate records. . . . It is misleading merely to state the few facts about properties that are known, without making it clear that many facts are unknown, that the records are incomplete, and that part of what has been stated is mere guess; and we so find. The investor is entitled to know not only the facts which are established; it is frequently more vital for him to be cautioned that there are areas of information about which there is considerable doubt."

In *Platoro Gold Mines, Inc.,* [3 SEC 878 (1938)] it appeared from the testimony of the certifying accountant that the registrant was without books except for a stock certificate book (which the accountant did not see) and a minute book rewritten by officers of the registrant, because the original minute book had been lost. The accountants relied in part upon cancelled checks, agreements, and invoices, but largely upon representations of a promoter of the company, some substantiated by evidence and others not. In their certificate the accountants stated that they had relied upon sworn statements to them by the promoter. The SEC stated that this was not a fair disclosure of the fact that very little of the financial data had been verified from corporate records and that much of it was reconstructed on a basis which was largely arbitrary. Pointing out that the Commission had previously held (in *Livingston Mining Co.,* 2 SEC 1941) that an accountant certifying financial data in a registration statement is under a duty to disclose the existence of areas of information about which there is considerable doubt, the Commission concluded that the accountant's certification in this case was deficient in not doing so.

In *Petersen Engine Co., Inc.* [2 SEC 905 (1937)] the registration statement included a balance sheet of the predecessor companies certified by one public accountant, and a balance sheet of the registrant certified by another accountant. The latter balance sheet included an item for "Development and Experimental Engines, $40,918." A note to the balance sheet explained that this amount was a capitalization by the management of an equal amount of the total sum of $46,288 expended by the predecessor companies in the development of the Petersen engines. The remainder of the development cost was assigned to items appearing under "Fixed Assets." A break-down of the predecessor companies' development cost was contained in a note to the balance sheet. The accountant had made no attempt to verify these figures, and his certificate so stated. The Commission said the accountant should have made an attempt to verify the accuracy of the development expenses of the predecessor companies. "If, as the record indicates, the crudely kept records of the predecessor companies rendered these items impossible of verification except in the memories of the officers of the predecessor companies, the accountant's certificate should have so indicated."

In *American Trailer Rentals Company* [41 SEC 544 (1963)], the independent accountants stated in their report that they were unable to express an over-all opinion with respect to the summary of operations owing to the inadequacy of the company's accounting records. In a stop order decision, the SEC stated that because of the accountants' inability to give an over-all opinion, the summary failed to meet the Commission's requirements.

Negative Statements in Certificates

The SEC rule relating to accountant's certificates provides in part: "Nothing in this rule shall be construed to imply authority for the omission of any procedure which independent accountants would ordinarily employ in the course of an audit made for the purpose of expressing the opinions required by . . . this rule." The accountant's responsibility is to make a reasonable investigation. He cannot expect to lessen his responsibility by stating in his certificate that he has omitted procedures which he would have to admit were essential to a reasonable substantiation of any item in question and which he could reasonably have undertaken. A negative statement—to the effect that he has not followed this procedure or that procedure—should not be written into his certificate except in special cases and then only with adequate explanations. Any item which, for some reason, is not susceptible of reasonable investigation or concerning which he may have doubt, being unable to form his opinion about it even after making a comprehensive investigation, does call for an appropriate explanation, qualification, or reservation in his certificate.

It is not necessary for the accountant to disclaim in his certificate responsibility for titles to assets, or status of franchises, and like matters of law. The practice of disclaiming responsibility for such legal matters, followed by some accountants for a time out of extreme caution, has now been generally discontinued. In ASR No. 7 (see page **24·50**) the SEC lists among common deficiencies relating to certificates the reservation on the part of the certifying accountants with respect to matters not within their province.

Inconsistency Due to Change in Principles of Consolidation

The SEC published an opinion [ASR No. 32 (1942)] of its Chief Accountant in response to an inquiry as to whether, under Commission rules, it is necessary for an independent public accountant to indicate in his certificate that generally accepted accounting principles have not been applied on a basis consistent with that of the preceding year where a subsidiary consolidated in the preceding year is not to be consolidated in the year under review. The inquiry assumed that the registrant's policy in the past had been to consolidate all wholly owned subsidiaries and that the current exclusion of the subsidiary from consolidation was due to changed conditions and was made with a view to presenting more fairly the financial condition and results of operations of the registrant and its subsidiaries. The Chief Accountant said that the operation of the Commission's rules could be best indicated by an illustration.

Let us assume that a given registrant in its 1940 statements consolidated all of its wholly-owned subsidiaries. In the 1941 statements one significant wholly-owned foreign subsidiary was excluded by reason of the registrant's inability to obtain statements therefor. Under such circumstances Rule 4–04(b) [of Regulation S–X] would require that the name of the excluded subsidiary be given. The statement of the principles of consolidation required by Rule 4–04(a) [of Regulation S–X] would have to be appropriately modified to indicate that the wholly-owned subsidiary was not consolidated. Rule 3–07 [of Regulation S–X] would require, if the change substantially affected comparison with prior years, an appropriate explanation. Rule 2–02(c)(ii) [of Regulation S–X] would require a statement in the certificate of the accountant's opinion as to the change in the principles of consolidation employed.

Thus, it would not be proper, in my opinion, for the accountant to represent that the statements presented fairly the financial condition of the company and its consolidated subsidiaries and the results of their operations for the fiscal year, in conformity with generally accepted accounting principles and practices applied on a basis consistent with that of the preceding year. Instead, it would, in my opinion, be necessary to indicate that the principles of consolidation had been changed. If the new basis met with the approval of the accountant, as it presumably would, a positive statement to that effect should be made. If it did not, it would seem necessary to take an exception which would run to the fairness of the presentation.

The above conclusion may be contrasted with a case similar in all respects except that the subsidiary is dropped from consolidation because of sale of the investment therein. In cases such as this, no change in the principles of consolidation results, since all subsidiaries wholly-owned at the date of the statement are included in the consolidation. Disclosure that the former subsidiary is not included would, however, be required by Rule 4–04(b) and, under certain circumstances, Rule 3–06 [of Regulation S–X] might require that additional information, such as the reason for the change, be included either in the financial statements or in the accountant's certificate.

Accountant's Failure to Disclose Inconsistencies

In *Metropolitan Personal Loan Corporation* [7 SEC 245 (1940)] the company had changed its method of accounting for development costs just prior to a public offering of securities. Because of the change in method, earnings for the latest period showed a sharp increase over prior periods. Because full disclosure was not made of the effect of the change upon income, the SEC held the statements to be materially defective. The accountant's certificate, moreover, represented that the statements "fairly present, in accordance with accepted principles of accounting consistently maintained," the results of operations. The SEC also held that the accountant's certificate was materially misleading.

Certificates Involving Statement Comparability but not Principle Inconsistencies.—The generally accepted auditing standards as approved and adopted by the membership of the AICPA include (1) general standards, (2) standards of field work, and (3) standards of reporting. With respect to the reporting standards, the accountant's report is required to state whether the accounting principles followed in the preparation of financial statements have been consistently observed in the current period in relation to the preceding period; this is often referred to as the consistency standard.

The objective of the consistency standard is: (1) to give assurance that the comparability of financial statements as between periods has not been materially affected by changes in the accounting principles employed or in the method of their application; or (2) if comparability has been materially affected by such changes, to require a statement of the nature of the changes and their effects on the financial statements. (SAP No. 33, p. 42).

Comparability of financial statements may be affected by a change in the accounting principles employed—as when a company changes from the straight-line to the declining-balance method of depreciation. This requires disclosure in the notes to the financial statements and an exception as to consistency in the opinion paragraph of the standard short-form accountant's certificate.

Comparability of financial statements may also be affected by changed conditions which result in accounting changes but which do not involve changes in the accounting principles employed. A characteristic of this type of change is that it is caused by altered conditions. It involves no choice by management since the accounting principles have not changed; therefore, although comparability may be affected, the matter of consistency is not involved. An example of this kind of change occurs when the estimated remaining useful lives of fixed assets have been lengthened or shortened as a result of operating experience or obsolescence. When a change of this kind has a material effect on the financial statements, disclosure must be made in the financial statements, but it would not ordinarily have to be commented upon in the report of the independent auditor since it would not affect his opinion as to consistency. *The SEC, however, has a different view of this matter.*

Regulation S–X requires the independent auditor to disclose in his report and express his opinion as to the *consistency of application* of accounting principles or as to any changes in such principles which have a material effect on the financial statements. With respect to accounting changes which result from changed conditions (for example, changes in remaining useful lives of fixed assets), the SEC's requirements may be met by the use of a middle paragraph in the standard short-form certificate, in which the auditor describes the change and expresses his view thereon, in which event *the change should not be referred to in the opinion paragraph* of his certificate since the consistency standard is not involved. Following is an example of the middle paragraph of an accountant's certificate where the accounting changes which affect comparability result from extending the useful lives of fixed assets:

During the year ended (date), (name of company) extended the useful life of certain properties, as explained in Note — to the financial statements. These changes, in which we concur, do not represent a change in the consistent application of accounting principles, but do affect comparability of the financial statements with those of the prior year.

As stated above, in these circumstances the opinion paragraph makes no reference to the change since the accounting principle involved has not been changed.

CHAPTER **25**

ACCOUNTANT'S CERTIFICATES AND LETTERS

Part 2

CONTENTS

Qualifications and Exceptions

Occasionally, the public accountant may find that a company filing a registration statement or report with the SEC is required or desires to make certain representations or explanations in the financial statements which the accountant may be unable to verify and certify of his own knowledge. It may happen also that the accountant does not agree with the representations or with the accounting principles reflected in the financial statements. In all such instances, he should take care to write an appropriate qualification in his certificate.

In other cases the accountants' examination may disclose facts which cast doubt upon the truth of material representations in the financial statements. Where that situation exists, the SEC has said, the accountants are "under a duty to express such doubts in their report unless upon the basis of an investigation of available data such doubts are reasonably dispelled." [*Resources Corporation International,* 7 SEC 691 (1940)].

In *Republic Company* [6 SEC 1080 (1940)] the SEC said the company's accounting procedure was highly improper and criticized the accountant for not disclosing the accounting deficiencies in his certificate. The accountant sought to justify his certificate on two grounds: (1) the company's accounting procedure was proper, and (2) he felt obliged, under the circumstances, to follow the direction of management. As to the second defense, the SEC's decision quoted approvingly from the pamphlet entitled "Examination of Financial Statements" issued in 1936 by the AICPA:

> It is an important part of the accountant's duty, in making his examination of financial statements, to satisfy himself that accounting practices are being followed which have substantial recognition by the accounting profession. This does not necessarily mean that all companies will observe similar or equally conservative practices. Accounts must necessarily be largely expressions of judgment, and the primary responsibility for forming these judgments and preparing the financial statements in which they are reflected must rest on the management. . . . *But unless the difference is of minor importance the accountant must assume the duty of expressing his dissent through a qualification in his report or otherwise, if the conclusions reached by the management are, in his opinion, manifestly unsound,* though he is not entitled to substitute his judgment for that of the management when the management's judgment has reasonable support and is made in good faith. [Emphasis supplied.] (Pp. 4–5)

In *Poulin Mining Company, Limited* [8 SEC 116 (1940)], there were numerous deficiencies in the balance sheet. As was to be expected, the SEC ruled that the accountant's certificate, to the effect that the balance sheet set forth the financial position of the company, was misleading.

In *W. Wallace Alexander, Inc.* [6 SEC 144 (1939)], the registrant had been paid management fees in excess of the amount apparently permitted by a fund managed by the registrant. The SEC said that there should have been appropriate disclosure to that effect in the income statement of the fund. "Moreover," said the SEC, "we believe that it was incumbent upon the accountants to verify the management fees and under the circumstances of this case to include in their certificate, a disclosure of the precise method of computing the management fees." The SEC held that the failure of the accountants to include a full disclosure in their certificate of the method of computing the management fees rendered the accountants' certificate deficient in a material respect.

The SEC issued a decision in a proceeding to strike from listing and registration the securities of Associated Gas and Electric Company [11 SEC 975 (1942)]. The SEC held that the financial statements that had been filed by the company were materially deficient in several respects. Where the effects of the improper accounting practices followed by the company permeated the accounts to such an extent that the certifying accountants considered it impracticable to show the effect of such practices, the SEC held that the audits made by the accountants were not sufficiently comprehensive to justify their certifying the financial statements. The record in this case indicated also that the accountants did not "prefer" certain accounting practices followed by the company. The SEC held that the accountants' certificate was defective in not clearly stating the accountants' opinion of the practices reflected in the financial statements.

Effect of Accounting Series Release No. 4.—The reader is referred to Chapter **2** for a discussion concerning ASR No. 4 (1938) and its background. This is the release that sets forth the Commission's administrative policy with respect to financial statements. In brief, the release provides that, if a company files financial statements with the SEC and the statements reflect an accounting principle which has been formally disapproved by the SEC, the statements will be presumed to be misleading even though there is full disclosure of the accounting principle in question.

To observe the application of this policy in practice is both interesting and informative. Several instances are known where financial statements were filed by corporations accompanied by accountants' certificates in which the accountants took exception to the accounting principles followed in the preparation of the financial statements. In such cases the SEC usually requests that the financial statements be amended to conform with generally accepted accounting principles. When this has been accomplished, the accountant gives an unqualified certificate covering the amended statements.

There have been a few exceptions to the general rule that the statements have to be revised if the accountant certifies them with qualification; see the discussion on page **25·5** relating to accounting for pension costs, on page **25·16** relating to omission of charge for depreciation, and on page **31·14** relating to foreign companies. See also the discussion in this chapter of "subject to" certificates and qualifications caused by regulatory authorities.

A few examples will serve to illustrate how the Commission's policy works in practice.

Example 1

The O. M. Scott & Sons Company, a company engaged in the lawn seed and fertilizer business, filed its annual report (Form 10–K) with the SEC for its fiscal year ended September 30, 1968. In that year the company provided a "revenue reserve" in the amount of $443,000 by charge to income. In the income statement the charge was described as a "provision for revenue allocable to future periods." Net income for that year was $3,676,000, equal to $2.36 per share, which compared with $2,507,000, or $1.61 per share, in the preceding fiscal year. The reserve appeared in the balance sheet as a separate liability classification between current and long-term liabilities.

In a note to the financial statements, the "revenue reserve" was explained as follows:

Provision for revenue allocable to future periods: The special revenue reserve provides adjustment of earnings due to dealer inventory carryover being at a level which might reduce Company sales in fiscal 1969. The effect of this statistically determined adjustment is to reduce earnings for the current year $0.14 per share of Common Stock.

The company's independent accountants took exception to this reserve; the opinion paragraph of their certificate follows:

In our opinion, except for the revenue reserve which is at variance with generally accepted accounting principles, and the effect of which was to reduce net income as explained in note (d), the [financial statements] present fairly . . . in conformity with generally accepted accounting principles applied on a basis consistent, except for the aforementioned change, with that of the preceding year.

In the text portion of the published report to shareholders, the reserve was further explained, and it was stated that neither the auditors nor the Internal Revenue Service "accept this particular method of accounting at this time." Nevertheless the management believed that it was in keeping with the economic realities of the company's unique business and that it was "sound, valid and proper" for the business of the company.

Apparently the SEC refused to accept the Form 10–K financial statements on the basis described above. Indicative of this is the fact that the financial statements were later amended to eliminate the reserve, as a result of which the auditors were able to furnish an unqualified certificate.

In the published annual report for the following year (ended September 30, 1969) the company furnished financial statements on a comparative basis for the fiscal years ended September 30, 1969 and 1968. The statements for fiscal year 1968 were restated, and the restatement explained in a note as follows:

Note 1—Restatement: In 1968, the Company provided a special revenue reserve in the amount of $443,000 (equal to 14¢ per share of Common Stock after applicable federal income tax) to provide for year-end adjustment of earnings due to dealer inventory carryover. This was deemed to be "at variance with generally accepted accounting principles" and, in order to eliminate an exception in the accountant's opinion in conformity with the interpretations of the Securities and Exchange Commission, the special revenue reserve has been restored to earnings in 1968 by a restatement of the 1968 figures.

Example 2

While the effect of ASR No. 4 is usually to back up the certifying accountant, this is not always the case, as will be seen from the following discussion relating to accounting for the current service costs of pensions in financial statements filed with the SEC.

The K Company filed its annual report on Form 10–K for 1958 with the SEC. The note relating to pension costs and arrangements stated in part:

On the basis of the [pension] plans as presently constituted and the present rates of compensation and levels of employment, the annual cost of these plans to [the companies] is estimated to be $6,535,000. This estimate includes normal costs and amortization of past service costs on a basis actuarially determined to fulfill the requirements of the various plans.

The amount necessary at December 31, 1958 to fund the past service costs of the various plans to the extent that they are not already funded is estimated to be $38,700,000.

Employer contributions to the various plans were temporarily suspended as of February 1, 1958 and no provision has been made in the accounts for the balance of the year. Contributions were resumed as of January 1, 1959 on a modified basis. Had this modified basis been adopted in 1958 for employer contributions, the net income reported for the year would have been reduced by $1,850,000.

The K Company reported consolidated net income for 1958 of $60,000,000 as compared with $80,000,000 in 1957.

The accountants' report covering the 1958 financial statements was qualified insofar as it related to pension costs. The accountants stated that "except as to the omission of pension plan provisions referred to in Note —— to the consolidated balance sheet," the financial statements presented fairly the companies' financial position and results of operations in conformity with generally accepted accounting principles applied on a basis consistent with that of the preceding year.

The SEC did not require the K Company to revise the 1958 financial statements in its Form 10–K despite the fact that the accountants had taken exception to the accounting for pension costs. The reason for not insisting on a revision may be apparent from consideration of another case where, in similar circumstances, other accountants furnished a "clean" certificate.

This case involved a prospectus filed in 1961 by the U Company. The summary of earnings disclosed, among other things, the following information:

| | (*In millions of dollars*) | | | | |
	1956	*1957*	*1958*	*1959*	*1960*
Products and services sold	$4,228	$4,413	$3,472	$3,643	$3,698
Pension costs	125	140	33	104	87
Net income	348	419	301	254	304

A note following the summary of earnings dealt with pension costs and, particularly, the decline in such costs in 1958 and 1960 as compared with the preceding year. The note stated:

In each of the years 1956–1960, inclusive, [the U Company] has funded the annual current service costs of pensions except for 1958 when the Board of Directors determined that $61 million of payments made in prior years towards the funding of past service cost would be used to cover a portion of the current service costs for that year. If provision had been made for current service costs in 1958 on the same basis as in the other years, the additional pension cost charged against income would have amounted to $61 million before the effect of income taxes and $29 million after such taxes.

During 1960, in the light of review of [the U Company's] actual experience, certain actuarial service and mortality tables and the interest rate were refined, and costs were more directly related to the level of operations. If these refinements had not been made, total pension costs in 1960 would have been increased to approximately $122 million because of increased pension benefits made effective following negotiations with labor unions during the year.

In each of the years 1956 and 1957 [the U Company] paid $38 million against past service cost of noncontributory pensions and these amounts were charged to income. No payments toward funding of past service cost were made for 1958, 1959 or 1960. Past service cost applies against the actuarial cost of noncontributory pensions for service rendered prior to March 1, 1950, the effective date of the present plan. The cost which had not been funded at that date was then estimated at $496 million of which approximately $207 million remained unfunded as of December 31, 1960.

There is no unfunded past service cost in connection with contributory pensions, since no service prior to the date of employee participation is involved in determining benefits.

The assets of the combined pension trusts . . . are solely for the payment of benefits under [the U Company] pension plan, and were adequate at December 31 of each year 1956 through 1960, respectively, to meet currently accruing pension costs incurred since the adoption of the present contributory and of the present noncontributory parts of the pension plan in 1940 and 1950, respectively, as well as to pay full pensions to all those then entitled to receive them.

The independent public accountants in their certificate stated that the U Company financial statements, "together with the explanation pertaining to pension costs" appearing under the caption "Pension Costs" in the prospectus, presented fairly the results of operations in conformity with generally accepted accounting principles applied on a consistent basis during the period. In short, this was a certificate with an explanation, but the opinion was unqualified.

In similar circumstances, therefore, the SEC was confronted with two different accountants' opinions: qualified in respect of the K Company, unqualified in the case of the U Company. Both certificates were accepted by the SEC.

The K Company's accountants apparently were of the opinion that recognition should be given in the income statement of the current service costs of pensions regardless of the funding arrangements. These costs represent actual, incurred costs which are a charge to the period whether or not payment therefor is made into the pension fund. In the absence of a provision for such costs, the accountants qualified their opinion of the statements.

In the case of the U Company, the accountants apparently held a different view and concluded that the circumstances merely called for a complete disclosure of the facts relating to pensions. The disclosure being adequate, they furnished an unqualified certificate covering the statements.

The rationale followed by the SEC in the face of these apparently conflicting certificates appears to be this:

> Accounting principles in the area of accounting for current service costs of pensions had not *at that time* been crystallized. It was not until November, 1966, in fact, that an authoritative statement on the subject was issued by the APB, in the form of Opinion No. 8, Accounting for the Cost of Pension Plans.
>
> The certificates referred to above were furnished by well-known, competent practitioners who obviously had given the matter a great deal of thought but had arrived at contradictory conclusions.
>
> The Commission's staff was not convinced prior to 1966 that only one method of accounting for pension plans was acceptable, and, if so, what that method should be. (At the present time, however, the SEC is in complete accord with the aforementioned APB Opinion No. 8.)

The K and U cases referred to above admittedly were unusual circumstances, and represent one of the few instances, to the author's knowledge, in which the SEC has accepted a qualified certificate without insisting on a revision of the financial statements.

Example 3

A more recent example illustrating the Commission's willingness to accept qualified certificates in some situations involves the investment credit fiasco, which is discussed in Chapter **3**. For background information regarding the comments below, the reader is referred to that discussion.

In brief, the APB, after long debate on the question, issued an opinion indicating that the investment credit should be amortized through income over the life of the property giving rise to the credit. Not long after that, the SEC issued its ASR No. 96 in which it said that it would accept either of two methods: (1) the method approved by the APB, or (2) flow-through on a 48–52 basis, which gave recognition to the then existing requirements of the Internal Revenue Code. In the case of certain regulated companies (such as public utilities), the SEC said it would accept full flow-through.

The SEC realized that it was placing the accountants in a difficult position in that the APB had approved only one method whereas the SEC had approved two methods (three in some cases). If a company decided to follow 48–52 flow-through, the accountant was obligated to take exception to the accounting followed despite the fact of its approval by the SEC.

In the last paragraph of ASR No. 96, the SEC indicated it was aware of the accountants' obligation to the APB:

It is recognized that an accountant who certifies to financial statements reflecting a method of reporting contrary to the majority opinion of the Accounting Principles Board is assuming the burden of justifying departure from the recommended procedure and must take into consideration whether he is departing from an accepted procedure and consequently whether he must qualify his certificate . . .

In order to reconcile the conflicting positions of the SEC and the APB, the SEC said in its release that it would accept qualified certificates with respect to the investment credit: ". . . if an accountant deems it necessary to qualify his opinion under various circumstances the Commission will accept certificates containing appropriately worded qualifications . . . when an alternative accounting treatment acceptable to the Commission is followed by the registrant."

When the APB revised its opinion on accounting for the investment credit to bring it into line with the SEC's views, the question of a qualified accountants' certificate became academic.

Example 4

Another example involves the Commission's acceptance of a qualified certificate where the exception in the accountants' certificate is material in relation to the company being reported upon, but is not material in relation to the over-all financial picture. In 1969 PMI acquired 55% of CBM for $130,000,000 in cash (none of the names is real). Shortly after the acquisition of control PMI registered $100,000,000 of debt securities to be sold through underwriters. The offering prospectus included financial statements of CBM, together with the certificate of independent auditors. The CBM income statement showed sales increasing from $123 million in 1964 to $184 million in 1968. In the same period net income increased from $4.5 million to $9.0 million. The accountants' certificate was qualified in respect of the 1968 operations as follows:

(Conventional scope paragraph followed by—)
Opinion No. 11 of the Accounting Principles Board of the AICPA, which became effective in 1968, provides for comprehensive tax allocation by recognition of the income tax effect in the current period for each income and expense item, regardless of when the income tax is actually payable. The company's accounting practices are consistent with this opinion excepting that,

consistent with prior years and then existing accepted accounting principles, the company, in 1968, provided for possible tax adjustments approximating $510,000, and thus reduced net income in 1968 and retained earnings at December 31, 1968 by a like amount. To this extent, the company's practice in 1968 is at variance with Opinion No. 11.

In our opinion, with the exception stated in the preceding paragraph, the financial statements present fairly, etc.

In other words, the accountants reported that, in their opinion, the reported net income of $9.0 million for 1968 was understated by $510,000. It should be pointed out, however, that PMI was a much larger company, and an extremely prosperous one. The sales of PMI had increased from $641 million in 1964 to $1,019 million in 1968; in the same period its net earnings had increased from $22 million to $49 million. In the over-all picture, therefore, the understatement of CBM's income in 1968 was not significant.

Denial of Over-all Opinion.—If the accountant was not in attendance when physical inventories were taken and there are no alternative methods by means of which he can satisfy himself as to the amounts of such inventories, the accountant drafts his report along the lines contemplated by the AICPA's SAP ·No. 33 (1963), No. 43 (1970), and No. 46 (1971). In these circumstances, if inventories are sufficiently material, the accountant might conclude that he should deny an over-all opinion, and in lieu thereof, give a piecemeal opinion limited to the parts of the financial statements which are not affected by inventories. The probabilities are that the SEC would not accept statements filed on this basis as complying with their requirements for "certified" statements. When the accountant's report denies an over-all opinion, the SEC says that the report does not constitute a "certificate" and the statements are not "certified." The SEC's attitude in this kind of situation may be gathered from the following case, which is taken from actual experience:

A company that was on a fiscal year ending March 31 decided in October, 1954, to file a registration statement with the SEC under the 1933 Act. The company notified the accountant that a registration statement was being prepared and that it would include a balance sheet as of September 30 and income and surplus statements and related schedules for the three years and six months then ended. The company had taken a physical inventory at September 30, but the accountant was not present at the time the inventory was taken nor could he satisfy himself as to the amount of such inventory by any other means. The accountant had been in attendance when physical inventories were taken at preceding year ends and consequently was in a position to give an unqualified certificate covering the three-year income and surplus statements. Because he could not give an unqualified certificate as to the balance sheet at September 30, 1954, the accountant suggested that it would be desirable also to include a balance sheet at March 31, 1954, although it did not appear to be required by SEC instructions. Accordingly, the financial statements in the initial filing with SEC consisted of two balance sheets—one at March 31, 1954, and another at September 30, 1954—and income and surplus statements for the three years and six months then ended.

The accountant's report included in the initial filing with the SEC was in two parts: In the first part the accountant gave a conventional, unqualified opinion as to the financial statements at March 31, 1954, and for the three years then ended; in the second part the accountant gave a qualified opinion as to the financial statements at September 30, 1954, and for the six months then ended. His report relating to September 30, 1954, and the six months then ended was as follows:

We have also examined the balance sheet of XYZ Company as of September 30, 1954, and the related statements of income and surplus, and summary of earnings for the six months then ended. Except as explained in the following paragraph, our examination was made in accordance with generally accepted auditing standards, and accordingly included such tests of the accounting records of the company and such other auditing procedures as we considered necessary in the circumstances.

Physical inventories at September 30, 1954 were taken by the Company. We were not present when the inventories were taken, nor did we make any tests of physical quantities. We made tests of inventory prices and of arithmetical accuracy of the inventories and nothing has come to our attention to indicate that they are unreasonable.

In view of the limitation in the scope of our examination and the materiality of inventories in relation to the company's financial position and in the determination of cost of sales and dependent taxes on income for the interim period ended September 30, 1954, we are not in a position to express an opinion as to the over-all financial position of the company at that date or the over-all results of its operations for the period then ended. However, in all other material respects, such interim statements and summary of earnings, in our opinion, present fairly the assets, liabilities and capital of the company at September 30, 1954, and the income and expenses for the six months then ended, in conformity with generally accepted accounting principles applied on a basis consistent with that of the preceding year.

The SEC had the following to say with respect to the financial statements included in the initial filing and the accountant's report with respect thereto:

It is noted that the accountants' certificate relating to the balance sheet of XYZ Company as of September 30, 1954 and the related statements of income, earned surplus, and summary of earnings for the six months then ended is qualified with respect to inventories. Also, it is stated that "In view of the limitation in the scope of our examination and the materiality of inventories in relation to the company's financial position and in the determination of cost of sales and dependent taxes on income for the interim period ended September 30, 1954, we are not in a position to express an opinion as to the over-all financial position of the company at that date or the over-all results of its operations for the period then ended." In view of the qualification it appears that such financial statements do not meet the requirements as to certification.

Under the circumstances, it appears that the above financial statements and the interim period ended September 30, 1954 included in the summary of earnings, *should be submitted on an uncertified basis.* In this connection, it should be noted that said statements and related schedules should clearly indicate as part of the heading thereof that they are not audited.

The SEC's position appears to be this: The company and its independent auditors are in a position to arrange the examination so that there is no necessity for a qualification relating to the balance sheet and running over into the income statement which is so material as to deny the expression of an over-all opinion covering such financial statements. With proper planning and coordination on the part of the company and its certifying accountants, such highly qualified certificates can, and should be, avoided.

On the other hand, the SEC has accepted accountants' reports which contained a denial of over-all opinion with respect to a major financial statement, as indicated by the following example which is also based on an actual case:

A company that had been in the development stage for several years filed a registration statement (Form S–2) with the SEC, which became effective in May 1968. The financial statements followed the customary Form S–2 format, that is, in lieu of balance sheets and income statements, there were submitted (1) a statement of assets and deferred product development costs, (2) a statement of liabilities, (3) a statement of capital shares, and (4) a statement of cash receipts and disbursements. As to the first-named statement, in accordance with SEC instructions, assets acquired for capital stock were not shown at a dollar amount; instead, there was disclosed the number of shares issued therefor. On this basis, the statement showed $2,566,666 as the total of assets and deferred product development costs. Of this total, $2,447,376 represented deferred product development costs. Note 1 to the financial statements dealt with this matter as follows:

1. [Name of company] was organized on March 13, 1952 and since that date has been engaged principally in the development of an air pollution control system which utilizes electronic precipitating devices . . . For financial reporting purposes, the Company has deferred all costs incurred since its inception. The amounts deferred represent the aggregate cost of research, development, engineering, fabricating and testing of the control system, the general and administrative expenses and financing costs incurred in anticipation of the sale of capital shares of the Company.

Such costs were incurred as follows:

	Research, Development, Engineering, Fabricating and Testing of the Hydro-Precipitrol System*	General and Administrative	
Prior to December 31, 1963			$1,211,887
Year Ended December 31:			
1964	$247,957	$ 95,987	343,944
1965	252,119	131,210	383,329
1966	75,099	71,818	146,917
1967	111,647	184,477	296,124
Two months ended February 29, 1968	25,453	39,722	65,175
			$2,447,376

* Net of proceeds ($47,000) realized on sale of three prototype units.

At February 29, 1968 the Company had 17 prototype units . . . in various stages of completion, and the related manufacturing costs were included in deferred product development costs. The Company has sold three prototype units, the proceeds from which have been deducted from deferred product development costs. The Company intends to continue the practice of deducting from deferred product development costs the proceeds realized on the sale of prototype units. When successful market exploitation of the product is achieved, the unrecovered balance of deferred product development costs will be amortized ratably over future sales. The 17 prototype units are pledged as collateral for notes payable, other.

The report of independent accountants was along the lines of the Form S–2 example appearing in Chapter **24**, but the opinion paragraph was decidedly different. The opinion was as follows:

Since deferred product development costs represent a substantial portion of the total assets of the Company and because recovery of these expenditures is dependent upon the extent of profitable future sales, we are not in a position to express an over-all opinion on the financial position of [name of company] at February 29, 1968. However, in our opinion, the amount of deferred product development costs shown in the accompanying statement of assets and deferred product development costs ($2,447,376) presents fairly the cash expenditures of the Company in connection with the development of its products from March 13, 1952 (the date of inception) to February 29, 1968, and the other assets and liabilities and statement of capital shares at February 29, 1968 and the cash transactions of the Company for the period from January 1, 1965 through February 29, 1968 are fairly presented.

Since the foregoing report appeared in the final offering prospectus, it is apparent that it was acceptable to the SEC despite the denial of an over-all opinion with respect to the statement of assets and deferred product development costs.

In *Resources Corporation International* [7 SEC 689 (1940)] the accountants issued a report that was qualified in major respects. Investments in Mexican timber properties constituted practically the sole asset of the company. The auditors said that, as auditors, it was not possible for them to make any determination of the value of such assets, and consequently they were in no position to express an opinion with respect to the balance sheet "that embraces the matter of value assigned therein to those assets and to the stated capital or the accounting principles followed in connection therewith." The remaining items in the balance sheet were, in the accountants' opinion, fairly stated in accordance with accepted principles of accounting. The SEC said that the exceptions in the accountants' certificate "exclude from the purview of the certificate all but approximately $35,000 of assets out of total stated assets of more than $9,000,000." Such a report, said the SEC, is clearly insufficient to satisfy the requirement that the registrant file a *certified* balance sheet and the accountants' report is not a "certificate."

Qualified Certificates When Physical Inventories Have Been Omitted.—In one case with which the author is familiar a corporation omitted to take physical inventories for three years at the request of the government, because of the urgent need by the government for the war material that the company was producing. The perpetual inventory records did not furnish a satisfactory substitute for physical inventories. In place of an accounting based on physical inventories, a formula based upon a uniform percentage of sales was consistently applied by the company in each of the three years in determining the portion of the cost of manufacture to be charged against sales and the portion to be carried forward to the succeeding year as deferred costs in lieu of inventory. The company followed the same "formula" method of accounting in the succeeding six-month period, at the end of which a physical inventory was taken. The difference ($1,095,000) between the amount of this inventory and the "deferred costs" calculated as of that date by "formula" was charged off in the statement of income for the six-month period and shown as a separate item.

With respect to the procedure followed by the company, the pertinent portion of the accountant's certificate filed with the SEC (and not objected to by the SEC) was as follows:

As explained in Note A to the financial statements, owing to the urgent demands for its products for war uses, XYZ Corporation did not take inventories of stock on hand (on various dates). The company has not maintained quantitative records in lieu of inventories or kept continuous account of the unit costs of the various products and components manufactured. Our examination was made in accordance with generally accepted auditing standards applicable in the circumstances and included a review of the estimated average costs used by the management in pricing the inventory of work in process and finished goods on hand (date) and all other procedures which we considered necessary.

We can form no opinion whether the statements of income and of surplus of XYZ Corporation, which are based upon the "formula" method of accounting described in Note A, fairly present the net income earned year by year or for the half year ended (date). However, in our opinion, the accompanying balance sheet presents fairly the position of XYZ Corporation as of (date), the statements of income and surplus *viewed in the aggregate* reflect fairly the results of operations of the companies named *for the whole period* of three years and six months ended (date), and said balance sheet, and the statements of income and surplus, except for the afore-mentioned use of the "formula" method of accounting, are in conformity with generally accepted accounting principles applied on a consistent basis.

The SEC has reported another case involving the omission of physical inventories where the accountant attempted to certify with qualification [15 SEC Ann. Rep. 23 (1949)]. An unnamed electrical products manufacturing corporation filed a registration statement under the 1933 Act. Some time prior to the date of filing the company had reported to its stockholders a net loss of $724,000 for the six-month period ended October 31, 1948. However, the certified financial data included in the proposed form of prospectus indicated a net loss of $3,108,000 for that period. The greater loss disclosed in the prospectus was due to additional inventory writedowns and reserves of $1,765,000, a provision of $396,000 for possible loss on an investment in an affiliated company, and other audit adjustments of $223,000.

The principal deficiency in respect of the financial statements related to inventories, which at October 31, 1948, after deducting a reserve of $2,200,-000, represented over 42 per cent of total assets and 64 per cent of total current assets.

The prospectus and the report of a management consultant retained by the corporation disclosed that the corporation was carrying excess inventories and had discontinued certain product lines and reflected obsolescence and faults in products. Further, the prospectus stated there was general inefficiency in purchasing, production, shipping, and warehousing.

The amounts stated in the balance sheet for inventories were based upon book records. The accountants in their certificates stated: " . . . such continuous records of quantities as are maintained by the Corporation with respect to certain portions of the inventories are not integrated in monetary amounts with the general accounting records. . . ." They also stated: "Assuming use and realization of the inventories in the regular course of business, we have no reason to believe that the inventory amounts at October 31, 1948, have not been fairly stated." Inventories had been written down by $1,268,700 during the year ended April 30, 1948, and by $1,700,967 during the six months ended October 31, 1948.

The Commission's letter of comment set forth that, in view of the statements in the prospectus and elsewhere in respect of the inventories, it did not appear that reliable and dependable financial statements could be prepared in the absence of a physical inventory as of the balance sheet date and questioned whether the accountants had followed generally accepted auditing procedures under the circumstances. This failure to take a physical inventory raised the serious question of whether the amount of inventories, and of the write-downs made therein, had been properly determined.

Qualified Certificates When Inventories Are Omitted Due to War Conditions.—During World War II the SEC liberalized its policy with respect to its requirements regarding verification of physical inventories by independent public accountants. The policy was adopted to avoid any possible interruption in the production or delivery of war materials, and is not applicable in times of peace. Readers interested in this expression of SEC policy are referred to ASR No. 30 (1942).

Qualified Certificates as to Adequacy of Depreciation.—Several years ago the accountants' certificate which accompanied the financial statements of public utility companies contained the following qualification, or one similar to it:

. . . subject to the adequacy of the provision and the reserve for depreciation, as to which we are not in a position to express an opinion, the accompanying financial statements present fairly . . .

In the distant past, said the SEC, this might have been a proper reservation for an accountant to make in his certificate covering the accounts of a public utility company. Depreciation accounting, however, has generally displaced the retirement reserve or other methods of providing for the exhaustion of the service life of utility property. Accountants have had much opportunity to familiarize themselves with the property accounts and depreciation problems of utilities. Under these circumstances, the Commission said, there would appear to be little, if any, justification for accountants to avoid the assumption of full responsibility for the adequacy of depreciation provisions or reserves of these companies except, perhaps, in very unusual situations. The Commission's policy as to the accountant's responsibility for depreciation is approximately this: if, in the opinion of the accountant, the depreciation reserve is inadequate, he should so state in his certificate; the amount of the inadequacy, if known, should be stated; in any event the reader of the certificate should be left with no doubts as to whether the depreciation reserve as shown on the balance sheet and the provisions for depreciation included in the income statement are, within reason, adequate. [13 SEC Ann. Rep. 130 (1947)].

The Form 10–K annual report of Detroit International Bridge Company for 1970 showed that land and the bridge structure were carried as follows:

Land and main bridge structure—less than cost	$2,600,000
Bridge property and equipment—at cost	1,789,763
Less accumulated depreciation	431,941
	$1,357,822

Note A to the financial statements explained the basis at which properties were carried, the write-down of the property in 1939, and the omission of depreciation on the written-down amount, as follows:

Note A—Property and Equipment, Depreciation, and Taxes

At July 1, 1939, land, bridge structure, and equipment were written down (by approximately $14,000,000) to $2,600,000 under a Plan of Reorganization confirmed by the United States District Court, and the By-Laws were amended to provide that no depreciation of the main bridge structure be charged in determining earnings available for dividends. Accordingly, no depreciation has been charged to earnings since 1939 on any portion of the written down amount of $2,600,000 which, except for the By-Laws and Plan of Reorganization, would normally be subject to depreciation on that portion in excess of land value.

Net earnings and earnings retained for use in the business since 1939 would be reduced by an estimated $33,800 each year if depreciation on the main bridge structure, omitted pursuant to the By-Laws and Plan of Reorganization, had been taken in the financial statements.

Depreciation for United States and Canadian income tax purposes, based on original cost, has exceeded the amount deducted in the statement of net earnings. The resulting tax benefit amounts to approximately $100,000 annually and has been included in the statement of net earnings.

In a middle paragraph of their certificate, the independent auditors directed attention to the company's depreciation practice as follows:

As explained in Note A to the financial statements, the Company carries its land and main bridge structure at less than cost and, pursuant to its By-Laws and a Plan of Reorganization ordered by the United States District Court in 1939, has omitted depreciation on the written down carrying amount of the main bridge structure.

The auditors' opinion of the company's financial statements was qualified as follows:

In our opinion, except for the absence of that part of depreciation required by generally accepted accounting principles but omitted pursuant to the By-Laws and Plan of Reorganization, the consolidated financial statements referred to above present fairly the financial position, etc.

The company's financial statements, similarly qualified, have been accepted for many years by the SEC.

Deviations from Generally Accepted Accounting Principles Caused by Regulatory Commissions.—The accounts of many companies operating in fields involving the public interest are regulated by federal and/ or state commissions. The regulatory commissions often prescribe in great detail the manner in which companies subject to their jurisdiction shall keep their accounts. The commissions frequently stipulate that the published statements of such companies shall not contravene the provisions of the uniform systems of accounts prescribed for such companies. Included among such regulated companies are railroads, airlines, and other common carriers, electric and gas utilities, telephone companies, and insurance companies.

Some of the accounting requirements of regulatory commissions are at variance with generally accepted accounting principles. It is not the author's purpose to discuss the merits or demerits of the various uniform systems of accounts, but rather to illustrate the accounting problems faced by regulated companies which file registration statements under the 1933 Act, and the problems of the accountant in certifying financial statements of such companies. The illustrative examples which follow have been taken from actual SEC filings.

1. An Insurance Company

A prospectus of The Old Line Life Insurance Company of America (1965) stated that the financial statements therein were prepared on the basis of the requirements of the Insurance Department of the State of Wisconsin and the National Association of Insurance Commissioners. The statements disclosed that the accounting practices followed by the company differ in certain respects from those generally accepted accounting principles commonly followed by non-regulated enterprises. The differences which may be material included the following: (a) investment securities are carried in accordance with valuations established by the National Association of Insurance Commissioners, i.e., bonds are carried at cost, adjusted where appropriate for amortization of premium or discount, and stocks generally are carried at market values or values established by a prescribed formula; (b) acquisition costs such as commissions, costs of medical examinations and investigations, are charged to current operations as incurred; and (c) certain assets designated as "non-admitted assets" (principally agents' balances and office furniture and equipment) are charged off against income or unassigned surplus.

The independent accountants reported in a middle paragraph of their certificate as follows:

These financial statements have been prepared in conformity with accounting practices prescribed by the Insurance Department of the State of Wisconsin and by the National Association of Insurance Commissioners. The accounting practices are designed primarily to demonstrate ability to meet claims of policyholders and, as described in Note 1, differ in certain respects from those generally accepted accounting principles commonly followed by non-regulated enterprises in the presentation of financial position and results of operations.

The accountants' opinion of the statements was to the effect that they were in conformity with accounting practices prescribed by the Insurance Department of the State of Wisconsin and by the National Association of Insurance Commissioners—with no further references to generally accepted accounting principles.

In the middle paragraph of their certificates, some accountants, after calling attention to the differences between the practices followed by the company and those of generally accepted accounting principles, add that "the overall effect of such differences is believed to be material although their amount has not been determined by the Company."

There are many variations in the opinion paragraphs of accountants' certificates caused by the circumstances referred to in the foregoing example. Some accountants phrase their opinions in this way: ". . . in conformity with generally accepted accounting principles except as affected by the accounting practices required for life insurance companies as explained in Note A . . ." or "(as mentioned in the next preceding paragraph)."

In a 1966 speech, the Chief Accountant of the SEC's Division of Corporation Finance said that some accounting firms had concluded that, under certain conditions, with or without certain adjustments, life insurance statements may be deemed to be in accordance with generally accepted accounting principles and that an opinion may be expressed that they fairly present the financial position and results of operation and changes in surplus ". . . in accordance with generally accepted accounting principles . . ." [1]

2. AN ELECTRIC UTILITY COMPANY

A prospectus of Southern California Edison Company (1960) stated, in a note to the financial statements, the company's depreciation policy. For income tax purposes certain properties (emergency facilities) were being amortized over 60 months. The income taxes deferred to future years were provided for by charges to income and credits to a balance sheet account "Accumulated Deferred Taxes on Income," all pursuant to orders of the Public Utilities Commission of the State of California.

The company claimed "liberalized" (accelerated) depreciation under Section 167 of the Internal Revenue Code in its federal income tax returns for the years 1954 through 1959, and the related provisions for deferred taxes had been accounted for in a manner similar to that followed for deferred taxes arising from accelerated amortization. On April 12, 1960, the California commission issued an order (the accompanying opinion indi-

---

[1] Walter Mickelsen, "Recent Developments in the SEC Accounting Field," May 24, 1966.

cated that it did not deal with accelerated amortization) stating that "for the purpose of rate-fixing, the Commission will not allow a public utility to charge to its operating expense for income taxes any amount in excess of the amount of income taxes lawfully assessed by the taxing authority and paid by said public utility."

Effective January 1, 1960, as a result of the commission's decision, the company discontinued providing for deferred income taxes arising from liberalized depreciation although continuing to claim it for tax purposes. The note to the statements disclosed the effect of the change in accounting treatment.

In their report, the certifying accountants referred to the discussion of deferred taxes in the notes and said:

> . . . The policy of currently claiming higher tax depreciation than is recorded on the books results in lower tax depreciation deductions in later years since the Company cannot deduct more than the cost of any property for income tax purposes. Hence, in our opinion, the taxes so deferred constitute current costs unless they can be recovered in the future. Such future recovery cannot be determined at this time.
>
> Subject to the effect of the matter described in the preceding paragraph, in our opinion, etc. . . .

It is worth noting that, in the circumstances discussed above, many accountants would have concluded that "flow through" accounting is appropriate and, except for pointing out an inconsistency due to a change in method as a result of commission order, would have furnished an unqualified certificate. In fact, in a more recent (March, 1970) prospectus of Southern California Edison Company it was disclosed that the Company's practice with respect to liberalized depreciation was essentially the same as it was in 1960. In 1970 the Company stated that it deducted additional depreciation in its income tax returns as the result of using liberalized depreciation methods and lives but made no provision to normalize the income tax effect of the additional depreciation for tax purposes. The accountants' certificate appearing in this 1970 prospectus was conventional in all respects.

In 1958 the Missouri Power & Light Company also discontinued the practice of recording deferred income taxes resulting from claiming accelerated depreciation, for federal income tax purposes, on its property. A 1959 prospectus of the Company stated that "This change was made to conform the Company's accounting principles with the rate making policy of the Public Service Commission of Missouri, which prohibits the allowance of provisions for deferred income taxes resulting from accelerated depreciation as an operating expense." The effect on income of the change was also disclosed.

The accountants in this case said the statements were in conformity with generally accepted accounting principles. They continued: "These principles have been applied on a consistent basis throughout the period except for the change, effective January 1, 1958, in the recording of the tax reduction resulting from accelerated depreciation, to an acceptable alternative method which is described in Note 3 [summarized above] to the financial statements."

"Subject To" Certificates.—Page **24·51** lists deficiencies commonly cited by the SEC in connection with accountants' certificates. Included in the list of deficiencies is the use of equivocal phrases in the opinion paragraph of the certificate, such as "subject to the foregoing," "subject to the above comments," and the like, where the meaning or purpose of the words "subject to" was not clear. In some cases, the words were probably intended to emphasize something which had preceded it. In other cases, the accountant probably intended to take exception to an accounting principle or practice, but the reader was left to figure out for himself what the accountant had in mind. It is for this reason that Rule 2–02(d), dealing with exceptions, provides that the accountants' exception shall be clearly stated.

In the case of a company in precarious financial condition, the independent auditor's opinion with respect to its financial statements may be subject to the company's ability to remain in business, either by attaining profitable operations or by obtaining additional capital. A certificate along these lines raises a question as to the appropriateness of using the going concern concept which is a basic assumption underlying the preparation of financial statements in most circumstances. This matter is discussed later in this chapter under the heading "Subject to the Appropriateness of the Going Concern Concept."

Because of the SEC's insistence that exceptions shall be clearly and understandably stated, some accountants have concluded that the phrase "subject to" may not be used in certificates filed with the SEC. This is not true. The words "subject to" may be used, for example, where the reference is to a matter, transaction, or event the accounting significance of which can not be resolved at the date of the statement. In ASR No. 90, the SEC said that the "subject to" qualification is appropriate when the reference is to disclosures explaining the status of matters which cannot be resolved at the statement date.

Some accountants contend that the "subject to" qualification in such circumstances is redundant and unnecessary. In most cases where it is used, there is a clear reference to information in the statements, indicating that the matter cannot be resolved. A lawsuit, for example, is awaiting judicial determination, and counsel is unable or unwilling to forecast the result. An important tax case is awaiting decision in the Tax Court. A company's claim for reasonable profits on government contracts is before the Renegotiation Board. A company's basic patents are being challenged by competitors. A company's application for rate increases is being heard by a regulatory commission having jurisdiction over rates. Where these or similar circumstances exist, in all likelihood they are set forth in the financial statements or in notes to the statements. Since the statements with their notes do set forth the company's financial position and results of operations, what good purpose is served by the "subject to" language in the accountants' certificate calling attention to what is in the statements? These accountants contend that qualifications and exceptions should be restricted to those matters with respect to which there is a disagreement between the accountant and his client. In the circumstances which we have been discussing there is no dispute; the accountant presumably is completely in agreement with the representations in the statements.

Other accountants, however, contend that in these circumstances the company's financial position and/or results of operations are indeterminate and they are therefore not in a position to form an opinion in respect of the matter in question. For that reason, and for reasons of emphasis, they believe the "subject to" qualification is appropriate. In any event, the practice of qualifying a report in this manner and in these circumstances has widespread acceptance. In fact, the author knows of cases where the accountant furnished an unqualified certificate in an SEC filing, and the SEC staff requested him to revise his certificate because of the indefinite status of certain important matters. This was accomplished by the use of the "subject to" phrase which referred to that portion of the notes which contained the necessary information.

This difference in viewpoint among accountants regarding the necessity of the "subject to" phraseology in certificates might cause uninformed readers to wonder what motivates accountants. For example, in 1970 the NPD Company (not its real name) filed a registration statement with the SEC under the 1933 Act. The financial statements of the most recent year (1969) were certified by Accounting Firm A; the financial statements of the two preceding years were certified by Accounting Firm B. The company was in the development stage, had experienced an unbroken string of operating losses, and had on its balance sheet an amount of unamortized license and product development costs which was very substantial in relation to the company's net assets and overall financial position. As might be expected, Firm A certified the financial statements "subject to the realizability of unamortized license and product development costs which is dependent upon future successful development of commercial products." Firm B, however, furnished a conventional, unqualified certificate, although the financial picture was substantially the same as the one which caused Firm A to qualify its report. Despite what is said in the following paragraph, it is worth noting, also, that the SEC in this case did not request

Firm B to qualify its report along the lines of the report furnished by Firm A.

Especially where a company's balance sheet shows deferred research and development which is substantial in relation to the company's net assets, the staff of the SEC is likely to suggest to the certifying accountant that his opinion of the statements should be "subject to" the company's ability to realize in the future on the products or projects to which the deferred costs relate. The justification for this suggestion is that the SEC wants the reader to understand, not only from the financial statements, but also from the accountants' certificate, the magnitude of the deferred costs which are at risk. Where this suggestion has been made, the accountant ordinarily complies. He reasons that the effect of the "subject to" phrase is merely to emphasize what is already in the statements.

In one case with which the author is familiar, the accountants furnished a conventional, unqualified report for inclusion in a registration statement under the 1933 Act despite the fact that the balance sheet of the company in question contained a substantial amount of deferred development costs. In due course, the SEC's letter of comments was received which contained this comment among others:

. . . Prior to amendment, please have the certifying accountants advise the staff as to why a "subject to" qualification in their report with respect to the recovery of deferred development costs is not appropriate since these items represent approximately 25% of total assets.

The accountants wrote to the Commission saying that the omission of the "subject to" phraseology was not an oversight, and that the matter had been carefully considered. In their view, "Where there is reasonable and sufficient indication based on present evidence that development costs incurred have produced, or can be reasonably expected to produce, the anticipated results, these costs would appear to have future value and are, as in the case of this company, properly deferrable"; accordingly the "subject to" phrase was not necessary. Nonetheless, the accountants said, such a qualification might assist the reader by emphasizing the uncertainty inherent in the nature of the deferred development costs, and consequently they would not object to a revision of their opinion with respect to such costs. They revised their certificate accordingly.

Following are examples taken from actual cases in which the "subject to" phrase was used in accountants' certificates filed with the SEC.

Example 1. Pending Rate Matters

A natural gas transmission company stated in its prospectus that the company and its subsidiary had filed with the Federal Power Commission general rate increases for gas sold and transported. The Commission authorized the companies to place the increased rates into effect, subject to refund of any amounts collected thereunder which were not finally approved. The company disclosed the amounts of conditionally refundable revenues included in operating revenues for each year of the earnings summary, together with the effect on net income. The FPC had authorized the company's gas suppliers to put rate increases into effect subject to the refund of any amounts collected thereunder which were not finally approved. The increased amounts paid by the company to its suppliers constituted a portion of its increased costs upon which its increased rates were based. The company disclosed the amounts paid by the company, year by year, which were subject to refund by the suppliers.

The opinion paragraph of the accountant's certificate began:

Subject to the effect of the final determination of the pending rate matters, referred to in Note _____ to the financial statements, on the balance sheets at (date), and the related statements of income and retained earnings for the (period), in our opinion, the accompanying balance sheets and related statements of income and retained earnings, present fairly etc.

Example 2. RENEGOTIATION AND RELATED TAX MATTERS

A company disclosed the status of its renegotiation and of related tax matters in its prospectus as follows:

Under the Renegotiation Act of 1951, the Company has received clearance from The Renegotiation Board for 19___ and prior years. The Renegotiation Board has made unilateral determinations that the Company's profits were excessive in the amounts of $3,162,759 ($3,500,000 before adjustment for state income taxes) for 19___ and $5,868,319 ($6,250,000 before adjustment for state income taxes) for 19___ which, after federal tax credits, would result in net refunds of $1,526,192 and $2,816,793, respectively. The amount of $3,162,759 for 19___ having been paid (under protest) the Company has a claim for federal income tax refundable in the amount of $1,636,567. The Company, believing that no excessive profits were realized, has appealed to the Tax Court for a redetermination of the Board's findings for the year 19___ and intends similarly to appeal for the year 19___. The Renegotiation Act provides that on appeal, if the Tax Court shall find excessive profits were realized, it has the power to determine that the amount of such excessive profits is less than, equal to or greater than that determined by the Board.

The income statements for 19___ and 19___ have been restated to reflect the Board's determinations in the accounts, and the federal taxes for 19___ and 19___ have been reduced by $1,000,000 and $3,688,093, respectively, to reflect the refundable federal taxes applicable to such renegotiation refunds.

Sales and profits for 19___ and subsequent years are also subject to renegotiation. The Company has no basis for anticipating the final actions of The Renegotiation Board and intends to take such actions as may be required to sustain its position that no excessive profits have been realized for any year. Accordingly, no provisions have been made in the accounts for 19___ or subsequent years.

The pertinent portion of the accountants' certificate was as follows:

In our opinion, subject to such adjustments (which neither we nor the Company are able to evaluate) as may be required as a result of renegotiation as described in Note _____, the accompanying balance sheet and statements of income (set forth in the Prospectus under the heading "Consolidated Statement of Income"), capital surplus and earned surplus present fairly etc.

Example 3. INCOME TAXES

A company disclosed in its prospectus that it had provided for income taxes at capital gains rates on a portion of its profits attributable to the sale of lots acquired from a subsidiary, and stated what the effect might be if ultimately the profit were held to be taxable as ordinary income. The note discussing the situation was as follows:

On a portion of the consolidated profit attributable to the sale of lots from land acquired from a subsidiary, Florida West Coast Land Company, by certain of the Company's predecessors and the Company (see "Transactions with Florida West Coast Land Company"), the provision for federal income tax has been computed at capital gains rates and, based on opinion of [name of law firm], tax counsel of the Company, capital gains treatment has been given to the profits includible in the tax returns of Florida West Coast Land Company. The Internal Revenue Service has not yet examined income tax returns in which this treatment has been significant. If the Service should contend that such profit is taxable as ordinary income and its contention should be upheld, provisions for federal income taxes would be deficient in an aggregate amount of approximately $3,700,000, exclusive of interest. Of this amount, 20% or $740,000, would be applicable to the minority interest. The remaining 80%, chargeable to net income, amounts to $560,000 and $255,000 for the seven months ended July 31, 19___ and 19___; $420,000, $757,000, $1,026,000 and $197,000 for the years ended December 31, 19___, 19___, 19___ and 19___, respectively (equivalent to 9¢, 4¢, 6¢, 12¢, 17¢ and 4¢, respectively, per share computed as in Note (b) below). Since, however, profits on the sales by the subsidiary are subject to current tax only as realized in the form of cash payments received, only a portion of the additional tax would be immediately payable. It is not possible at this time to predict the eventual outcome of this matter.

The accountants certified "subject to the determination of the income tax status of certain transactions to which reference is made in Note ___ to the consolidated statement of earnings."

Example 4. CLAIM IN DISPUTE

A company disclosed in a note to the financial statements the status of a claim included among the receivables in its balance sheet. The company had entered into a fixed-price contract for $146,000, under which it undertook to perform certain qualifying tests in connection with the design and development of an ejection seat component for supersonic aircraft. Having completed all tests and submitted all data and reports which it (the company) felt were called for under the contract, the company billed the contractor for the full amount of the contract price. The contractor disapproved the qualification reports and refused to pay the contract price, pending additional work which the company contended was not intended under the terms of the original contract. The company believed that it was entitled to the entire contract price of $146,000. However, pending settlement of the dispute, the financial statements reflected a receivable of $100,000 after allowing for the maximum costs of settlement which the company believed might be incurred.

The accountants certified "subject to the outcome of the dispute, referred to in Note ——, which we are not able to evaluate."

Example 5. MATERIAL AMOUNTS OF DEFERRED DEVELOPMENT COSTS

A company stated in a note to the financial statements in its prospectus that it had incurred certain product development costs in connection with rocket propellant and engine production, and other production, which, "based upon present forecasts will be applicable to future production costs." The note described the company's amortization policy, the amounts deferred, and its expectations as follows:

The company follows the policy of amortizing these costs, except with respect to propellants, at varying rates dependent on sales forecasts of the related items, but not to exceed two years from the completion of the related development projects. Propellant development is being amortized at 1½% of total company sales, which will result in approximate two year amortization based on present forecasts.

At (date) unamortized product costs included (amount) propellants and (amount) of other products, of which (amount) was in process. The estimated cost of completion of projects in process is (amount), and (amount) has been budgeted for new projects for the six months ended (date).

Amortization of product development costs charged to cost of sales during the (period) amounted to $————.

While it is believed that sales forecasts of products developed and in process of development are reliable based on current conditions, the recovery of such development costs is dependent upon the successful market exploitation of the products to which such costs relate.

The accountants' report was "subject to the successful market exploitation of products to which the deferred development costs referred to in Note —— relate."

In somewhat similar circumstances, another accountants' report stated that the ultimate value of deferred product development costs "is primarily dependent upon future events and consequently is not determinable at this time." The opinion was "subject to such adjustment, if any, as might be required as the result of future developments with respect to the deferred charges mentioned in the preceding paragraph."

Example 6. INVESTMENT IN A FIFTY-PER-CENT-OWNED COMPANY

A company furnished a note to its balance sheet describing the status of its investment in a fifty-per-cent-owned company as follows:

The Corporation's investment of $3,300,000 in Royal Precision Corporation, which is 50% owned by the Corporation, exceeded its equity in the net assets (which included $1,158,000 of certain deferred costs), as shown by unaudited financial statements as of December 31, 19___, by $1,568,000. Royal Precision has not reached a level of operations which would indicate the ultimate benefits to be derived from funds expended to date. The Corporation made further advances of $750,000 to Royal Precision Corporation in February 19___.

The accountants' opinion of the statements was "reserved to the extent that we are unable to evaluate the fairness of the amount at which an investment in a partly-owned company is carried in the attached balance sheets (see Note ___), etc."

"Subject to the Appropriateness of the Going Concern Concept."

—A basic assumption underlying the preparation of financial statements in most circumstances is that the company is a going concern and will not have to liquidate. Unless the statements indicate otherwise, the reader is entitled to assume that the statements are those of a going concern, and that the amounts at which the assets are carried do not represent liquidation values, but rather amounts that will have to be allocated to future years.

When a company is in a precarious financial condition, there may be a question as to its ability to remain in business. Consequently, unless the company can achieve profitable operations or raise additional capital (which the auditor is in no position to predict), the auditor may have serious doubts as to the appropriateness of applying the going concern assumption to that company's situation.

In these circumstances, an accountant in 1968 furnished the following certificate for inclusion in his client's registration statement under the 1933 Act:

(Conventional scope paragraph, followed by—)
The accompanying financial statements have been prepared on a going concern basis. The Company has sustained losses from operations in recent years and such losses have continued to date. As explained in Note 1 to the financial statements, realization of the major portion of the assets reflected in the balance sheet is dependent on continuation of the business which, in turn, is dependent on securing additional working capital and on future profitable operations. These matters are contingent on future events, which cannot be determined at this time.

In our opinion, subject to the effect of the outcome of the uncertainties described in the preceding paragraph, the statements mentioned above present fairly, etc.

The SEC did not challenge the certificate.

A company filed a registration statement under the 1933 Act which became effective in 1965 in connection with an exchange offer to the preferred and common stockholders of HTI Company (not its real name).

The prospectus contained financial statements of HTI and a report of independent accountants in which they disclaimed an opinion on the financial statements for the year 1964 but said they conformed with generally accepted accounting principles. They also reported on the operating statements of the four preceding years. The certificate did not employ the "subject to" phraseology but was otherwise qualified with respect to the appropriateness of the going concern concept. The opinion follows:

(Conventional scope paragraph, followed by—)
Continuation of the Company's operations appears to be dependent upon obtaining additional financing or early suitable agreements of merger or sale. Continuing substantial losses and the accumulated deficit, in conjunction with other aspects of the financial position of the Company as shown in the financial statements and related notes, raise a question as to whether or not principles of accounting applicable to a going concern should continue to be followed with respect to the carrying values of assets.

Operations at the Company's plant in (city) were discontinued in (period) and the plant and equipment are being offered for sale. Although it is impossible to determine at this time the amount of the loss which may be sustained on the sale or other disposition of such plant, equipment, inventories and other assets, a provision for losses presently determinable has been reflected in the accompanying financial statements, as described in Note ___ to the financial statements.

As indicated in Note ___, the Company did not meet certain requirements at (date) under the terms of the Agreement relating to the % Notes Payable and the Indenture relating to the % Convertible Subordinated Debentures. Accordingly, these debts may be declared due and payable.

In view of the uncertainties which exist with respect to the Company's ability to continue as a going concern and because of the possible material effect on the financial statements of the matters described above, we do not express an opinion on the Company's financial statements for the year 1964. However, we believe that on a going concern basis, except for the possible effect of matters referred to above, the 1964 financial statements are in conformity with generally accepted accounting principles applied on a basis consistent with that of the preceding year.

(Operations of four preceding years were certified on conventional basis.)

In a 1967 prospectus, the independent auditor's opinion was "subject to the successful development of a commercial market for the products referred to in Note B of the notes to balance sheet, *and to obtaining adequate financing.*" (Emphasis added.)

In a 1967 10–K filing, the report of the independent auditors contained the following middle paragraph:

The financial statements have been prepared by management on the basis of a going concern. Amounts on the balance sheet do not purport to represent liquidation values, present economic values or replacement values. The ability of the corporation to continue as a going concern is dependent upon the bank not demanding payment of the ___% note described in Note ___ and upon future profitable operations. A loss before extraordinary items was incurred in 1967.

The auditors' opinion was "subject to the ability of the Corporation to continue as a going concern."

A registration statement under the 1933 Act was filed in 1969 in which there was a balance sheet showing negative working capital and a negative stockholders' equity. The company had had an unbroken series of losses since its inception. The auditors' report, like many before it, included a middle paragraph indicating doubt as to the company continuing as a going concern and an opinion "subject to obtaining adequate financing and attaining a profitable level of operations."

"Subject to" certificates of the type discussed above had become a matter of increasing concern to the Commission and its staff. As an administrative matter, and without notice to the public, the accountancy profession, or the securities industry, the staff had started to move up on such certificates claiming that they did not meet the SEC's certification requirements notwithstanding that the Commission's files contained innumerable certificates of this kind.

In discussing the matter with the Commission's staff in connection with a specific case, the suggestion was made that the opinion be revised to make it "subject to obtaining adequate financing such as would be obtained from the net proceeds of the public offering." This the auditors refused to do and said that the reader of such a report would be entitled to believe that such additional financing would be adequate to allow the company to stay in business for a reasonable period of time, and they did not know what a reasonable amount of time would be in such cases.

After consideration of the matter by the full Commission, the auditors revised their certificate. The middle paragraph of their certificate was changed to read as follows:

> The accompanying financial statements have been prepared in conformity with generally accepted accounting principles which contemplate continuation of the Company as a going concern; however, the Company has sustained substantial operating losses during the past five years and continuation as a going concern is dependent upon future profitable operations and obtaining additional financing. We are not in a position to express an opinion as to the Company's ability to attain profitable operations and the effect such operations may have on financing requirements. Except for the effect of such future operations, the financing contemplated by the offering set forth in this Prospectus should enable the Company to meet the liabilities and proposed expenditures for the research and development projects and the marketing program in the amounts set forth under "Use of Proceeds" elsewhere herein.

The opinion was "subject to the Company's ability to continue as a going concern."

Not long after this incident, the SEC, in February 1970, issued ASR No. 115 entitled "Certification of Financial Statements." The release dealt with precisely the kind of situation discussed in the preceding pages, namely, the nature of the independent accountant's opinion when there is a doubt of the registrant's ability to continue as a going concern unless it attains profitable operations or raises additional capital. The release stated in part:

   . . . [W]here, as here, the financial statements are prepared on a "going concern" basis, while at the same time the accountant's opinion is so qualified as to indicate serious doubt as to whether or not the preparation of financial statements on that basis is warranted, then a significant question arises as to whether the financial statements are certified as required by Schedule A of the Securities Act of 1933 and the rules and regulations thereunder.

   . . . If the business will not continue and the proceeds of the present offering will simply be used to pay existing creditors, then the offering may be deceptive to the public. The Commission does not expect accountants to express opinions that are unwarranted in the circumstances . . .

The Commission has concluded that a registration statement under the 1933 Act will be considered defective because the certificate does not meet the requirements of Rule 2–02 of Regulation S–X when the accountant qualifies his opinion because of doubt as to whether the company will continue as a going concern . . .

The Commission also said in the release that it did not intend to preclude companies with pressing financial problems from raising funds by public offerings of securities, but that it was clear that an accountant's report did not meet the certification requirements of the 1933 Act unless the registrant "can arrange its financial affairs so that the immediate threat to continuation as a going business is removed." The independent accountant, said the SEC, must be satisfied that it is appropriate to use conventional principles and practices for stating the accounts on a going concern basis before a registration statement under the 1933 Act can be declared effective.

ASR No. 115 applies only to registration statements filed under the 1933 Act; it does not apply (for the time being, at least) to filings under the 1934 Act. Thus, if a company's situation is such that the independent auditor has to furnish a "subject to" opinion of the kind contemplated by the foregoing discussion, *the company can not register under the 1933 Act for an offering of its securities to the public, but the certificate is acceptable for filing under the 1934 Act so that the public can continue to trade in the securities.*

It is possible that the situation insofar as it relates to the 1934 Act may also change if the following incident is an indication of things to come. On April 2, 1971, the SEC announced the filing of a complaint in the U. S. District Court in Seattle seeking court orders directing Crown Drug Company to comply with the reporting requirements of the 1934 Act. (Litigation Release No. 4963.) Pending public dissemination of material facts regarding losses by Crown from its operations, the SEC ordered over-the-counter trading in Crown stock suspended for ten days.

The Commission's complaint alleged that Crown had failed to file the reports required by Section 13 of the 1934 Act. The Commission's release contained the following comment:

> The accounting firm of [name omitted here] in its financial reports attached to that report indicates that—in the absence of additional financing from sources which are not now known—Crown may be unable to survive as a going concern. As a result, [accounting firm] has declined to express an opinion on the financial statements. Therefore, the statements were not certified as required by Form 10–K of the annual report.

"Subject To" Certificates for Investment Companies.—Chapter **4** of this book contains a discussion of the SEC's views regarding the accounting for investment securities owned by investment companies registered under the Investment Company Act of 1940, as set forth in ASR No. 113 and ASR No. 118. These releases contain the SEC's opinions regarding the date as of which transactions involving the purchase and sale of securities should be recognized for the purpose of preparing financial statements of the company and for the purpose of computing net asset value of the company's shares. The releases also set out guidelines for valuing the portfolio of the investments (including restricted securities) owned by the company, and the procedures to be followed by the company's independent accountants in substantiating the existence of the portfolio and in valuing the securities. The question of valuation is especially important when market quotations are not available for the securities and their "fair value" has to be determined in good faith by the board of directors of the investment company.

As stated in Chapter **4**, in the case of securities carried at "fair value" the accountant does not function as an appraiser and is not expected to substitute his judgment for that of the company's directors; rather, he should review all information considered by the board or by analysts reporting to it, read relevant minutes of directors' meetings, and ascertain the procedures followed by the directors. If the accountant is unable to express an unqualified opinion because of the uncertainty inherent in the valuations of the securities based on the directors' subjective judgment, he should nevertheless make appropriate mention in his certificate whether in the circumstances the procedures appear to be reasonable and the underlying documentation appropriate.

ASR No. 118 states that the Commission considered the circumstances in which a "subject to" opinion would be appropriately issued by the investment company's independent accountant. The release states that the "subject to" form of qualified opinion may be used when an investment company's portfolio includes a *significant amount* represented by securities for which market quotations are not readily available *and* when the auditor is satisfied that the procedures followed and the information obtained are adequate to enable the board of directors to value the securities but is unable to form an opinion as to the fairness of the specific values determined in good faith by the board of directors.

In the interest of uniformity of language, an opinion in the following form, preceded by the standard scope paragraph, should be used:

As discussed more fully in Note 1 to the financial statements, securities amounting to $ . . . . (. . % of net assets) have been valued at fair value as determined by the Board of Directors. We have reviewed the procedures applied by the directors in valuing such securities and have inspected under-lying documentation; while in the circumstances the procedures appear to be reasonable and the documentation appropriate, determination of fair values involves subjective judgment which is not susceptible to substantiation by auditing procedures.

In our opinion, subject to the effect on the financial statements of the valua-tion of securities determined by the Board of Directors as described in the pre-ceding paragraph, the (financial statements) present fairly . . .

Qualified Certificates in Merger or Acquisition Proxy Statements.

—The reader is referred to the discussion in Chapter **22** regarding the financial statements required to be included in a proxy statement involving a merger or acquisition—particularly Item 15 of Schedule 14A which sets forth the instructions for financial statements. As stated in that connection, the financial statements of the company to be acquired or merged have to be certified *if practicable*. The SEC recognizes that the statements of such companies may not be able to be certified in conventional form, or may be able to be certified only with qualification. Accordingly, in these circum-stances, the SEC accepts for proxy statement purposes certificates which, in all likelihood, it would not accept for purposes of 1933 Act registration.

In August 1970 Honeywell, Inc. sent its stockholders a proxy state-ment in connection with a special meeting of stockholders to vote upon a proposal to combine under Honeywell's control the computer operations of General Electric Company and Honeywell. In addition to financial statements of Honeywell, the proxy statement contained financial statements of "General Electric Computer Components." With respect to the latter, Note 1 to the financial statements described the businesses and the portions of businesses included in the statements, and significant recent acquisitions, as follows:

1. BASIS OF STATEMENT PRESENTATION

A. The accompanying financial statements present the consolidated financial position and results of operations of the following:

(a) The portion of the domestic computer-equipment business which is pri-marily concerned with the manufacture, sale, maintenance, service and rental of business data processing computer equipment. Not included are those General Electric domestic operations providing time-sharing and other information services, industrial process control applications including process computers, data communication equipment and certain other computer activities specified in the Agreement. Assets, liabilities, revenues and expenses applicable to businesses and operations which are not being transferred and to discontinued operations of the transferred business have been excluded. Expenses applicable to headquarters organizations which are not being transferred have also been excluded.

(b) The portion of Canadian General Electric Company Ltd. engaged in the business data computer-equipment business.

(c) The portion of the Australian General Electric Pty., Limited engaged in the business data computer-equipment and service business.

(d) The portion of the South African General Electric Company (Pty.) Limited engaged in the computer-service business.

(e) General Electric Information Systems Italia S. p. A.

(f) G. E. I. S. Ltd. (U. K.)

(g) Compagnie Bull General Electric, S. A./Societe Industrielle Bull General Electric, S. A., and subsidiaries, sometimes referred to as "the Bull Companies."

Insofar as practicable, adjustments have been made so as to present the consolidated statement of earnings on a uniform accounting basis for all periods presented. All significant transactions among the businesses being transferred have been eliminated from the consolidated statements. Because only portions of certain corporate entities are being transferred, the financial statements are partially estimated.

B. During the five years and three months ended March 31, 1970, the following acquisitions affecting the financial statements were made by General Electric Company:

(a) A 75% interest was acquired on July 28, 1965 in General Electric Information Systems Italia S. p. A. (formerly Olivetti-General Electric S. p. A.), a company formed by Ing. C. Olivetti & C., S. p. A. During the year 1965, this acquisition contributed revenue of $10,908,000 and a net loss of $4,158,000. On April 18, 1968, the remaining 25% interest was acquired.

(b) A 25% interest in G. E. I. S. Ltd. was acquired on October 10, 1966 (formerly De La Rue Bull Machines Limited) from The De La Rue Company Limited, which resulted in a total interest in the Company (direct and indirect) of approximately 51% which has since been increased to 58%. During the year 1966, this acquisition contributed revenue of $997,000, and a net loss of $461,000.

In addition, ownership in Compagnie Bull General Electric, S.A. was increased from 51% to 66% and in Societe Industrielle Bull General Electric, S. A. from 49% to 66% in 1967 through purchases of additional shares from such companies.

Acquisitions have been accounted for as purchases and operations, with appropriate recognition of minority interests, have been included in the consolidated financial statements as of the respective effective dates.

The independent auditors of General Electric Computer Components reported on the financial statements as of December 31, 1969 and for the five years then ended. The auditors reported without qualification on the statements as of December 31, 1969 and for the year 1969. Because of inadequacies in the accounting, cost, and control systems of "the Bull Companies," the auditors were unable to express an opinion on the statements as a whole for the years 1965 through 1968. For that four-year period, the auditors reported as follows:

We have also examined the consolidated statement of earnings of General Electric Computer Components for the four years ended December 31, 1968. Selected components were examined each year in connection with our regular annual examinations of the consolidated financial statements of General Electric Company and its affiliates, and, in addition, selected auditing procedures have been applied to the accounts of the principal U. S. and certain foreign components for years not otherwise examined.

General Electric Company has, during the period since assuming control of the Bull Companies (see Note A of Notes to Consolidated Statement of Earnings) in 1964, developed improved accounting, cost and control systems to replace the inadequate ones originally in existence. Although we satisfied ourselves as to sales, service and rental income for all years, we were unable to satisfy ourselves as to the fairness of the year-to-year operating results prior to 1969, because of the earlier inadequacies in the accounting, cost and control systems of the Bull Companies. While we were satisfied that variations between years in the operating results of the Bull Companies were not material with respect to the consolidated results of operations of General Electric Company and its affiliates, we were unable to make a similar determination in relationship to the operating results of General Electric Computer Components, and accordingly, we are unable to express an opinion on the consolidated statement of earnings as a whole for the years 1965 through 1968. In our opinion, however, the consolidated statement of earnings for the four years ended December 31, 1968, insofar as it applies to components other than the Bull Companies, is stated fairly in conformity with generally accepted accounting principles applied on a consistent basis.

Note A to the income statement of General Electric Computer Components contained further information regarding the amounts of the net losses of the Bull Companies for the years 1965 through 1968 concerning which the auditors were unable to express an opinion. The note follows:

The net losses of the Bull Companies attributable to General Electric concerning which [the auditing firm] is unable to express an opinion are as follows: 1965—$15,363,000; 1966—$19,247,000; 1967—$23,438,000; and 1968—$3,659,-000. The foregoing amounts are before eliminations between the Bull Companies and other General Electric Computer Components. The comparable net earnings of the Bull Companies included in the consolidated statement of earnings for the year 1969, upon which statement [the auditing firm] has expressed an unqualified opinion, were $7,739,000. Sales, service and rental income of the Bull Companies, included in the consolidated statement of earnings, was [amounts omitted here]. The [auditing firm's] report included elsewhere in this Proxy Statement contains their unqualified opinion with respect to the total sales, service and rental income of the General Electric Computer Components.

Certificate Covering Examination of Investment Company Securities

The custody of securities of regulated investment companies is subject to SEC rules. If the securities are held by a member of a national securities exchange, the arrangement must be pursuant to a written contract meeting the requirements of Rule 270.17f–1 under the Investment Company Act. The securities of a regulated investment company may be maintained in its custody only in accordance with the provisions of Rule 270.17f–2. Certain provisions of these rules appear on page **5·52** and set forth the requirements as they pertain to examination of the securities by independent public accountants and the content of the accountants' certificate.

The following is a form of certificate meeting the requirements of Rule 270.17f–1 :

In compliance with Rule 270.17f–1 promulgated under the Investment Company Act of 1940, we made an unannounced visit to your office in order to account for securities owned by the corporation at the close of business on (date). In connection with our examination we counted securities held by (name of broker) as custodian as at (date) and also counted the treasury stock held at your office as at that date. Confirmation was received from the broker with respect to securities in transit, etc. Our examination also included inspection of brokers' bills and other appropriate evidence in support of all security transactions recorded on the corporation's records since (date), the date of our last examination.

All securities owned by the corporation as shown by the records at (date) were accounted for by us in the manner outlined in the preceding paragraph.

The foregoing certificate should be transmitted by the independent accountant directly to the SEC.

Following is a form of certificate meeting the requirements of Rule 270.17f–2 :

In compliance with Rule 270.17f–2 promulgated under the Investment Company Act of 1940, we made an unannounced visit to your office on (date) in order to account for securities owned by the corporation at the close of business (date). In connection with our examination we received confirmation as of (date) from (name of bank), custodian, as to securities held by them for your account. Our examination also included inspection of brokers' bills and other appropriate evidence in support of all security transactions recorded on the Corporation's records since (date), the date of our last examination.

All securities owned by the Corporation, as shown by the records at (date) were accounted for by us in the manner outlined in the preceding paragraph.

The foregoing certificate should be sent directly to the SEC by the independent accountant.

Accountant's Opinion Covering Evaluation of Internal Control and Information Items in Form N–1R.—In Chapter 1 reference was

made to the fact that management investment companies registered under the Investment Company Act had to file annual reports on Form N–1R with the SEC. This is a comprehensive report containing 39 "items" of information in Part I and 32 "items" in Part II, including financial statements. The report was designed to assist the SEC with its inspection program by providing information as to the investment company's compliance with the provisions of the Investment Company Act and the SEC's rules thereunder. The report was also intended to achieve a substantial degree of self-inspection by laying before persons responsible for the management and operations of an investment company information which would assist them in determining more readily whether the company was in fact complying with the law and the rules thereunder.

In addition to an accountant's certificate covering the financial statements in Part I of Form N–1R, the investment company must also include in Part II of the report an opinion of its independent public accountant covering certain of the items of information other than financial statements as stated below. (The discussion that follows reflects the July 1971 amendments made by the SEC in the requirements of Form N–1R and announced in ASR No. 120.) The accountant's opinion submitted in Part II must be dated and signed manually and has to be on stationery of the accountant which shows the city and state of issuance, and must be addressed to the investment company (the registrant under the Investment Company Act).

The examination underlying the accountant's opinion for the purpose of inclusion in Form N–1R has to be made in accordance with generally accepted auditing standards, and accordingly must include a review of the accounting system and the system of internal accounting control. The examination must include all procedures necessary under the circumstances to substantiate assets, liabilities, income and expense, realized gain or loss on investments, unrealized appreciation or depreciation of investments, and total and per share net assets as of the date of the financial statements prescribed by Item 1.39 as well as financial information in other specified items included in the Form N–1R report, and to permit the expression of an opinion by the accountant as to the financial condition of the registrant at that date.

Based on his review of the accounting system and the system of internal accounting control, the independent accountant is required to comment in his opinion upon any inadequacies found to exist in the accounting system and the internal accounting control which in his opinion are material in the circumstances. In addition, the accountant must indicate any corrective action taken or proposed. These comments have to be included in the body of the accountant's opinion.

The accountant's opinion has to cover the following subject matter and be in substantially the form indicated below. When the opinion on the financial statements in Part I is qualified in some manner, the qualification has to be repeated as to any item in Part I or Part II which is subject to the same qualification. The form of report which follows reflects the discussions between representatives of the SEC and the AICPA's committees on auditing procedure, investment companies, and stock brokerage accounting (reported in *The Journal of Accountancy,* June 1972, page 72) :

We have examined the financial statements of (name of company) for the (period) and have issued our opinion thereon dated (date). As a part of our examination, we reviewed and tested the company's system of internal accounting control to the extent we considered necessary to evaluate the system as required by generally accepted auditing standards. Under these standards the purpose of such evaluation is to establish a basis for reliance thereon in determining the nature, timing, and extent of other auditing procedures that are necessary for expressing an opinion on the financial statements.

The objective of internal accounting control is to provide reasonable, but not absolute, assurance as to the safeguarding of assets against loss from unauthorized use or disposition and the reliability of financial records for preparing financial statements and maintaining accountability for assets. The concept of reasonable assurance recognizes that the cost of a system of internal accounting control should not exceed the benefits derived and also recognizes that the evaluation of these factors necessarily requires estimates and judgments by management.

There are inherent limitations that should be recognized in considering the potential effectiveness of any system of internal accounting control. In the performance of most control procedures, errors can result from misunderstanding of instructions, mistakes of judgment, carelessness, or other personal factors. Control procedures whose effectiveness depends upon segregation of duties can be circumvented by collusion. Similarly, control procedures can be circumvented intentionally by management with respect either to the execution and recording of transactions or with respect to the estimates and judgments required in the preparation of financial statements. Further, projection of any evaluation of internal accounting control to future periods is subject to the risk that the procedures may become inadequate because of changes in conditions, and that the degree of compliance with the procedures may deteriorate.

Our study and evaluation of the company's system of internal accounting control for the (period) was made for the purpose set forth in the first paragraph above and would not necessarily disclose all weaknesses in the system. However, such study and evaluation disclosed certain ("no" if no weaknesses are disclosed) conditions that we believe to be material weaknesses. Such weaknesses, with an indication of any corrective action taken or proposed were as follows :

(Describe exceptions and corrective action)

We have also examined the answers to the items enumerated below which are included in the report of (state the exact name of the registrant) filed with the Securities and Exchange Commission on Form N–1R for the fiscal year ended _____ (state the same fiscal year as appears on the facing sheet of the report) ; in connection therewith, we have applied such supplemental tests and other auditing procedures as we considered necessary in the circumstances.

In our opinion, the answers set forth in the following items present fairly the information they purport to show:

Items 1.03; 1.05; 1.06; 1.07(a), (b)(2), (b)(3) (clause (i)), (c); 1.17; 1.18(a)(1), (3), (4); 1.22; 1.25; 1.26(a); 1.27(a)(2), (b)(1); 1.29(a); 1.36(a); 1.37 (clauses (1), (3), (4)); 2.02; 2.13; 2.15(a), (b)(1); 2.17(a), (b)(1); 2.18; 2.23(a), (b), (c)(1); 2.24(a); 2.28(a), (b)(1); and 2.30.

The answers set forth in the following items are in accordance with the minutes of (name of registrant) examined by us:

Items 1.19; 1.38; 2.06; 2.11(b).

The procedures which we applied were not of sufficient scope to enable us to express an opinion, and we do not express an opinion, as to the answers to the following items:

Items 1.13; 2.05; 2.24(b), (c); 2.25(a)(1), (b)(1), (c); and 2.32.

However, in connection with our examination, nothing came to our attention which causes us to believe that the accompanying answers to such items do not fairly set forth the information they purport to show.

We consent to the use of this opinion in connection with the filing of the report of (name of registrant) with the Securities and Exchange Commission on Form N–1R.

(City, state and date)   (Signature of independent public accountant)

In the portion of the report dealing with internal control, it will be noted that the clause ". . . was not designed for the purpose of expressing an opinion on internal accounting control . . ." (which appears in the last paragraph of the report in paragraph 24 of SAP No. 49, "Reports on Internal Control," November 1971) has been omitted. This modification is required for SEC reporting purposes.

If the accountant takes exception to any of the answers or information covered by his opinion, the exceptions have to be specifically and clearly stated, together with the reasons therefor.

Following is a brief indication of the nature of the items that must be covered by the foregoing accountant's opinion:

Item No.   *Subject Matter*

Items with respect to which the accountant must report that the answers present fairly the information they purport to show:

Item No.	Subject Matter
1.03	Underwriting commitments
1.05	Condensed financial information
1.06	Asset coverage of senior securities
1.07(a)	Issuance, reacquisition, and redemption of securities
(b)(2)	Shares registered under '33 Act sold during year and unsold
(b)(3)(i)	Shares sold in excess of shares registered under '33 Act
(c)	Issuance of securities for services or property
1.17	Fidelity bond
1.18(a)(1)	Name and address of investment adviser
(3)	Brief description of the investment advisory contract
(4)	Remuneration paid to investment adviser

1.22	Services supplied or paid for by investment adviser
1.25	Rate of portfolio turnover
1.26(a)	Securities purchased on margin; joint trading; short sales
1.27(a)(2)	Information as to restricted securities owned during year
(b)(1)	Restricted securities sold during the year
1.29(a)	Monthly sales of shares; dividends and other distributions
1.36(a)	Compensation paid to principal underwriters
1.37(1)	Name and address of underwriters receiving "other" payments
(3)	Amount paid
(4)	Basis of payment and consideration received
2.02	Purchase and sale transactions within six month period
2.13	Distributions requiring notification to stockholders
2.15(a)	Calculations of net asset value pursuant to Rule 2a–4
(b)(1)	Departures from procedures specified in Rule 2a–4
2.17(a)	Brokerage paid on portfolio transactions
(b)(1)	Ten largest participating brokers in commissions paid
2.18	Portfolio transactions with brokers acting as principal
2.23(a)	Procedures followed on sale or redemption of shares
(b)	Compliance with Rule 22c–1 in pricing shares
(c)(1)	Departures from procedures specified in Rule 22c–1
2.24(a)	Time lapse between sale of shares and receipt of proceeds
2.28(a)	Ten largest dealers in registrant's shares; amount sold
(b)(1)	Gross commissions to such dealers for portfolio trades
2.30	Unsettled portfolio transactions at end of quarter

Items with respect to which the accountant must report that the answers are in accordance with the minutes of the registrant examined by him:

1.19	Entry into, or renewal of, investment advisory contract
1.38	Entry into, or renewal of, principal underwriting contract
2.06	Board vacancies; percent of Board elected by security holders
2.11(b)	Board action regarding fidelity bond coverage

Items with respect to which the accountant furnishes negative assurance:

1.13	Remuneration of certain affiliated persons
2.05	Purchase of interest in investment company, investment adviser, broker, dealer, underwriter, or insurance company
2.24(b)	Unsettled sales of registrant's shares at month end
(c)	Loss on cancellations due to changes in net asset values
2.25(a)(1)	Suspension of redemptions; shares involved
(b)(1)	Delayed payment on repurchased shares
(c)	Unsettled share repurchases at month end
2.32	Transmission of transaction confirmations or share balance statements

With respect to that portion of the accountant's opinion in which he gives negative assurance concerning certain items of Form N–1R, a question may be raised as to whether it is appropriate to give such assurance in view of the restrictions contained in SAP No. 33, Chapter 10, paragraphs

19–21. These paragraphs severely limit the situations in which an accountant may give negative assurance. However, the language of paragraph 21 is sufficiently broad, in the opinion of the author, to permit the furnishing of negative assurance to the SEC in the circumstances noted. That paragraph is as follows:

21. In situations involving special reports covering data which do not purport to present financial position or results of operations, negative assurances may be given provided the auditing procedures followed are appropriate and reasonable in the circumstances and the scope of the examination is described in the report.

In announcing the revised requirements relating to the accountant's opinion in Part II of Form N–1R, the SEC said the amendments were caused by the need to obtain information about potential back-office problems from a source of sufficient independence, expertise, and judgment to provide an indication of the seriousness of such problems.

In addition to Form N–1R, the investment company must supplement the report with "EDP attachments." These are blank forms that have to be filled in by the registrant investment company; separate forms have been provided for open-end and closed-end companies. The EDP attachments duplicate much of the information in Form N–1R and facilitate the processing of company and industry information by electronic data processing equipment. Information required by an item of Form N–1R may be incorporated by specific reference in the answer to that item to the same information appearing in the same item of the EDP attachments for the same fiscal year. The opinion of the independent public accountant required by Form N–1R with respect to certain items of the annual report shall not be deemed to cover the answers to the comparable items of the EDP attachments except such answers as are incorporated by reference in answer to items of Form N–1R which require an opinion. However, the answer to any item of the EDP attachments shall not be inconsistent with the answer to the comparable item of Form N–1R relating to the same subject matter.

Certificate for Form X–17A–5

Under the 1934 Act, reports of financial condition must be filed by certain members of securities exchanges, brokers, and dealers in securities. The reports are filed on Form X–17A–5, the content of which is set forth beginning on page **15·39**.

The report is almost entirely financial in nature. The financial statements are required to be certified by independent public accountants, and, in that connection, the SEC has prescribed audit requirements for this special purpose. The statement of the audit requirements begins on page **5·54**.

Qualifications of Accountants.—The requirements as to qualifications of accountants for purposes of certifying financial statements in Form X–17A–5 are set forth in Rule 17a–5(f) as follows:

> The Commission will not recognize any person as a certified public accountant who is not duly registered and in good standing as such under the laws of his place of residence or principal office. The Commission will not recognize any person as a public accountant who is not in good standing and entitled to practice as such under the laws of the place of his residence or principal office.

It may be noted that the above is not the same as the corresponding provisions in Regulation S–X, but it should be remembered that that regulation is not applicable to Form X–17A–5.

Certificate Requirements.—The requirements applicable to the accountant's certificate in Form X–17A–5 are contained partly in Rule 17a–5 and partly in the audit requirements contained in the form itself. Based on the instructions in both sources, the requirements applicable to the accountant's certificate are discussed below.

The accountant's certificate must be dated, signed manually, and must identify without detailed enumeration the items of the report covered by the certificate.

The accountant's certificate must contain a reasonably comprehensive statement as to scope of the audit made, including a statement as to whether the accountant reviewed the procedures followed for safeguarding the securities of customers, and including, if with respect to significant items in the report covered by the certificate any auditing procedures generally recognized as normal have been omitted, a specific designation of such procedures and of the reasons for their omission. The certificate shall also state whether the audit was made in accordance with generally accepted auditing standards applicable in the circumstances and shall state whether the audit made omitted any procedure deemed necessary by the accountant under the circumstances of the particular case. Nothing in the SEC rules may be construed to imply authority for the omission of any procedure which independent accountants would ordinarily employ in the course of an audit made for the purpose of expressing the opinions required by the following paragraph.

The accountant's certificate must state clearly the accountant's opinion with respect to the financial statements covered by the certificate and the accounting principles and practices reflected therein. Any matters to which the accountant takes exception must be clearly identified, the exception must be specifically and clearly stated, and as far as practicable the effect of each such exception on the related item of the report must be given.

The audit requirements relating to Form X–17A–5 are discussed in Chapter **5**. In addition to stating the procedures to be followed in making an audit for the purpose of certifying the financial statements in the form, the audit requirements include the following:

. . . Based upon such audit, the accountant shall comment upon any material inadequacies found to exist in the accounting system, the internal accounting control and procedures for safeguarding securities, and shall indicate any corrective action taken or proposed. These comments may be submitted in a supplementary certificate and filed pursuant to Rule 17a–5(b)(3).

The reference to Rule 17a–5(b)(3) means that the comments on inadequacies may be included with certain of the schedules in Part II of the Form X–17A–5 report, separately bound from the rest of the report.

Form of Certificate.—The following is a suggested form of auditors' certificate meeting the requirements of Form X–17A–5:

(Name of firm)
(Address)
We have examined the answers to financial questionnaire of (name of firm) as of (date). Our examination was made in accordance with generally accepted auditing standards, and accordingly included a review of the accounting system, the internal accounting control and procedures for safeguarding securities and such tests thereof for the period since the prior examination date, (date), and of the accounting records and such other auditing procedures as we considered necessary in the circumstances. Our examination complied with the audit requirements prescribed by (jurisdictional agency).

In our opinion, the accompanying answers to financial questionnaire present fairly the financial position of (name of firm) at (date), in the form prescribed by the (jurisdictional agency), in conformity with generally accepted accounting principles applied on a basis consistent with that of the preceding year. The supplementary information included in Part II* has been subjected to the same auditing procedures and, in our opinion, is stated fairly in all material respects when considered in conjunction with the basic financial statement taken as a whole.

(Signature of independent auditors)
(City and date)

* Certain stock exchanges require additional supplementary information to be submitted, including information which is not readily subject to examination in accordance with generally accepted auditing standards. Such information should be noted as "unaudited" and the last sentence of the opinion paragraph should begin "Except where otherwise indicated."

Form of Supplemental Report on Inadequacies.—As indicated in the foregoing discussion, the audit requirements for Form X–17A–5 include a provision pursuant to which the accountant has to comment on inadequacies in the accounting system, internal accounting control, and procedures for safeguarding securities. In addition, the auditor must comment on corrective action taken or proposed to be taken.

The following is an example of such a supplemental report.

(Name of firm)
   (Address)

We have examined the answers to financial questionnaire of (name of firm) as of (date) and have issued our opinion thereon dated (date). This supplementary report, which contains comments not considered necessary for a fair presentation either of financial position, or of the schedules and other data and information included in the answers, is being furnished as required by the audit requirements of Securities and Exchange Commission Form X–17A–5*.

As a part of our examination, we reviewed and tested the firm's system of internal accounting control (including the accounting system, procedures for safeguarding securities, and the practices and procedures employed quarterly in counting or accounting for securities and resolving securities differences as required by Rule 17a–13) to the extent we considered necessary to evaluate the system as required by generally accepted auditing standards. Under these standards the purpose of such evaluation is to establish a basis for reliance thereon in determining the nature, timing, and extent of other auditing procedures that are necessary for expressing an opinion on the financial statements.

The objective of internal accounting control is to provide reasonable, but not absolute, assurance as to the safeguarding of assets against loss from unauthorized use or disposition and the reliability of financial records for preparing financial statements and maintaining accountability for assets. The concept of reasonable assurance recognizes that the cost of a system of internal accounting control should not exceed the benefits derived and also recognizes that the evaluation of these factors necessarily requires estimates and judgments by management.

There are inherent limitations that should be recognized in considering the potential effectiveness of any system of internal accounting control. In the performance of most control procedures, errors can result from misunderstanding of instructions, mistakes of judgment, carelessness, or other personal factors. Control procedures whose effectiveness depends upon segregation of duties can be circumvented by collusion. Similarly, control procedures can be circumvented intentionally by management with respect either to the execution and recording of transactions or with respect to the estimates and judgments required in the preparation of financial statements. Further, projection of any evaluation of internal accounting control to future periods is subject to the risk that the procedures may become inadequate because of changes in conditions, and that the degree of compliance with the procedures may deteriorate.

Our study and evaluation of the firm's system of internal accounting control (including the accounting system, procedures for safeguarding securities, and the practices and procedures employed quarterly in counting or accounting for securities and resolving securities differences as required by Rule 17a–13) as of (date) was made for the purpose set forth in the first paragraph above and would not necessarily disclose all weaknesses in the system. However, such study and evaluation disclosed certain ("no" if no weaknesses are disclosed) conditions that we believe to be material weaknesses. Such weaknesses, with an indication of any corrective action taken or proposed were as follows:

                                  (Weaknesses and corrective actions
                                      to be inserted here)

(City, state
  and date)
                                (Signature of independent
                                            auditors)

    * Or other jurisdictional agency.

The foregoing form of report reflects the results of discussions between representatives of the SEC and the AICPA's committees on auditing procedure, investment companies, and stock brokerage accounting and auditing (*The Journal of Accountancy,* June 1972, page 72). As compared with the recommendations in SAP No. 49, "Reports on Internal Control," (November 1971), it may be noted that the clause ". . . was not designed for the purpose of expressing an opinion on internal accounting control . . ." in the last paragraph of the report in paragraph 24 has been omitted. This modification will be required for SEC reporting purposes.

Accountant's Certificate Covering Funds and Securities of Clients Held by Investment Advisers.—Chapter **5** of this book includes a discussion of the SEC's requirements applicable to investment advisers who have in their custody funds or securities belonging to their clients. Included in such requirements is a provision for verification of such funds and securities by an independent public accountant. The Commission's views with respect to the nature of the examination to be made by the independent accountant are set forth in ASR No. 103 (1966) and are included in Chapter **5**.

The aforementioned release also included the SEC's views regarding the content of the accountant's certificate covering the examination under consideration. The Commission said:

The accountant's certificate should comply with the usual technical requirements as to dating, salutation, and manual signature and should include in general terms an appropriate description of the scope of the physical examination of the securities and examination of the related books and records. In addition, the certificate should set forth:

(a) the date of the physical count and confirmation of balances of clients' accounts;

(b) a clear designation of the place and manner in which funds and securities are maintained;

(c) whether the examination was made without prior notice to the adviser; and

(d) the results of the examination including an expression of opinion as to whether, with respect to the rules under the Investment Advisers Act of 1940, the investment adviser was in compliance with paragraphs (a)(1) and (a)(2) of Rule 206(4)–2 as at the examination date and had been complying with Rule 204–2(b) during the period since the prior examination date; and whether, in connection with the examination, anything came to the accountant's attention which caused him to believe that the investment adviser had not been complying with paragraphs (a)(3) and (a)(4) of Rule 206(4)–2 during the period since the prior examination date. Any material inadequacies found to exist in the books, records, and safekeeping facilities referred to in this paragraph (d) should be identified and any corrective action taken or proposed should be indicated.

It will be apparent that paragraph (d) of ASR No. 103 (quoted above) can not be understood without reference to the text of Rule 206(4)–2 which follows:

(a) It shall constitute a fraudulent, deceptive or manipulative act, practice or course of business within the meaning of Section 206(4) of the Act, for any investment adviser who has custody or possession of any funds or securities in which any client has any beneficial interest, to do any act or take any action, directly or indirectly, with respect to any such funds or securities, unless:

(1) all such securities of each such client are segregated, marked to identify the particular client who has the beneficial interest therein, and held in safekeeping in some place reasonably free from risk of destruction or other loss; and

(2) (A) all such funds of such clients are deposited in one or more bank accounts which contain only clients' funds, (B) such account or accounts are maintained in the name of the investment adviser as agent or trustee for such clients, and (C) the investment adviser maintains a separate record for each such account which shows the name and address of the bank where such account is maintained, the dates and amounts of deposits in and withdrawals from such account, and the exact amount of each client's beneficial interest in such account; and

(3) such investment adviser, immediately after accepting custody or possession of such funds or securities from any client, notifies such client in writing of the place and manner in which such funds and securities will be maintained, and thereafter, if and when there is any change in the place or manner in which such funds or securities are being maintained, gives each such client written notice thereof; and

(4) such investment adviser sends to each client, not less frequently than once every 3 months, an itemized statement showing the funds and securities in the custody or possession of the investment adviser at the end of such period, and all debits, credits and transactions in such client's account during such period; and

(5) all such funds and securities of clients are verified by actual examination at least once during each calendar year by an independent public accountant at a time which shall be chosen by such accountant without prior notice to the investment adviser. A certificate of such accountant stating that he has made an examination of such funds and securities, and describing the nature and extent of such examination, shall be filed with the Commission promptly after each such examination.

(b) This rule shall not apply to an investment adviser also registered as a broker-dealer under Section 15 of the Securities Exchange Act of 1934 if (1) such broker-dealer is subject to and in compliance with Rule 15c3–1 under the Securities Exchange Act of 1934, or (2) such broker-dealer is a member of an exchange whose members are exempt from Rule 15c3–1 under the provisions of paragraph (b)(2) thereof, and such broker-dealer is in compliance with all rules and settled practices of such exchange imposing requirements with respect to financial responsibility and the segregation of funds or securities carried for the account of customers.

Paragraph (d) of ASR No. 103 also makes reference to Rule 204–2(b); this is the rule which sets forth the books and records that are required to be maintained by an investment adviser under the Act.

Rule 206(4)–2 requires that the accountant's certificate be filed with the SEC promptly after the completion of the examination. The SEC suggested in ASR No. 103 that the certificate be filed in duplicate at the regional office of the Commission for the region in which the investment adviser has his principal place of business.

Certificate with Respect to Pro Forma Statements.—There is no objection to issuing a certificate covering a pro forma balance sheet included in a prospectus provided:

1. The underlying financial statements have been examined by the certifying accountant;
2. There is compliance with AICPA pronouncements referred to in Chapter **21**; and
3. There is compliance with SEC Rules 170 and 15c1–9, if applicable.

A suggested form of accountant's certificate covering a pro forma balance sheet follows:

We have examined the accompanying pro forma balance sheet of (name of corporation) as of (date). This balance sheet is based upon the accompanying balance sheet of (name of corporation) as of (date) (which appears hereinafter with our certificate) and the pro forma adjustments identified in the headnote.

In our opinion, the accompanying pro forma balance sheet of (name of corporation) presents fairly, in accordance with generally accepted accounting principles, the position of the company as it would have appeared at (date) had the transactions set forth in the related pro forma adjusting entries been consummated at that date.

At the time the pro forma balance sheet is prepared, the underwriting agreement is usually tentative—it does not become final, in fact, until shortly before the effective date of the registration statement when agreement is reached as to the price of the securities. Usually, however, there is agreement in principle as to the nature of the underwriting commitment, and the accountant may proceed on oral assurance from the company or its counsel that the underwriting arrangements will comply with SEC Rule 170. He can satisfy himself on this point by reading the final agreement before the effective date.

When the public accountant has not examined the underlying financial statements, he is in no position to certify the pro forma statements derived therefrom. He may, however, include in the letter covering his review for private information (see page **12·37**) a paragraph similar to the following:

We have also read the pro forma balance sheet as at (date) which is also included in the above-mentioned registration statement. In our opinion, the adjustments set forth in the pro forma adjusting entries have been properly applied in the pro forma balance sheet.

The certification of pro forma income statements or earnings summaries presents a more difficult problem for the public accountant. There are situations in which he may with justification object to having his name identified publicly with certain types of such statements or summaries. He should not refuse to certify pro forma income statements or earnings summaries that merely add the historical results of two or more businesses which have been combined into a single enterprise. This rule is not altered by the fact that intercompany transactions, if any, are eliminated in the pro forma statement. Other pro forma statements, however, should be considered on their merits, and the auditor should bear in mind that these statements are sometimes abused.

In Chapter **21** there is discussion concerning a company that filed a registration statement with the SEC, and during part of the period covered by the earnings summary the company had elected to be taxed as a small business corporation under Sub-Chapter S of the Internal Revenue Code. Accordingly, for that portion of the period provision was made on a pro forma basis for the income taxes that would have been payable on a regular corporate basis. The accountants' certificate in that case was as follows:

We have examined the balance sheet of (name of company) as of (date), the related statements of retained earnings and capital surplus and summary of earnings for the (period) then ended. Our examination was made in accordance with generally accepted auditing standards, and accordingly included such tests of the accounting records and such other auditing procedures as we considered necessary in the circumstances.

In our opinion, the statements mentioned above present fairly the financial position of (name of company) at (date), and the results of its operations for the (period) then ended, in conformity with generally accepted accounting principles applied on a consistent basis.

We have also read the pro forma adjustments to the historical net income (loss) for the (period) and, in our opinion, these adjustments have been properly prepared and applied.

Additional discussion with respect to certificates in pro forma situations appears in Chapter **21**. The discussion includes the form of opinion in connection with a pro forma balance sheet that gives effect to a purchase combination completed after the date of the statement.

Certificate Covering a Pooling (on a Pro Forma Basis) Not Consummated at Filing Date.—At the time of filing its registration statement, a company may have entered into an agreement to combine with another company in a transaction which, for accounting purposes, will be treated as a pooling of interests. At the filing date, the transaction has not been consummated, but it is expected that it will be consummated before the effective date of the registration statement, and there is no reason to doubt that it will be consummated on schedule.

With proper caveats, the most useful financial statements to be included in the registration statement would be those giving effect to the pooling on a pro forma basis. This procedure ordinarily causes no concern to the SEC, the registrant, or the underwriters. The accountant, however, does have a problem in certifying "pooled" figures when the transaction has not been consummated.

The following procedure has been used many times by accountants in the circumstances described above. In the initial filing, the accountants furnish a certificate reading as follows:

Report of Independent Public Accountants

As indicated in Note ＿ to the accompanying financial statements of (name of company), the statements give effect retroactively on a pro forma basis to the acquisition of (name of company) on a "pooling of interests" basis, which transaction is expected to be consummated on (date). When that transaction has been consummated, we would expect to be in a position to issue the following report:

"To the Board of Directors of (name of company)

"We have examined the financial statements of (name of company) as of (date) and for the (period) then ended, all as listed in the accompanying index of financial statements. Our examination was made in accordance with generally accepted auditing standards, and accordingly included such tests of the accounting records and such other auditing procedures as we considered necessary in the circumstances. The aforementioned financial statements give retroactive effect to the acquisition of (name of company) on a "pooling of interests" basis. We did not examine the financial statements of (name of company) which statements were examined by other public accountants whose reports thereon have been furnished to us and are included in this prospectus. Our opinion expressed herein, insofar as it relates to the amounts included for (name of company) is based solely upon such reports.

"In our opinion, the aforementioned financial statements present fairly the consolidated financial position of (name of company) and subsidiaries at (date) and the related results of their operations and changes in financial position for the (period) then ended, in conformity with generally accepted accounting principles applied on a consistent basis."

(Signature of auditors)

(City, State, and date)

Before the effective date of the registration statement, and after the transaction has been consummated, an amendment to the registration statement is filed which includes a new certificate of the principal accountant. The revised certificate is the same as in the original filing except that the first paragraph in the original certificate is removed in the amendment, and the quotation marks in the original filing are also removed.

Letter Acknowledging SEC's Cursory Review.— The reader is referred to the discussion in Chapter **7** in which it was indicated that the

SEC had adopted certain abbreviated review procedures in some instances in order to cope with the unprecedented number of registration statements filed under the Securities Act. In certain cases the registrant is requested by the SEC to furnish a letter from the auditors, as supplemental information, to the effect that they (the auditors) are aware that the staff has made only a cursory and not a customary review of the registration statement, which may not be relied upon in any degree to indicate that the registration statement is true, complete, or accurate, and are also aware of their statutory responsibilities under the Securities Act.

Following is a suggested form of a letter to the SEC which follows the language of the release and which may be used for this purpose when appropriate:

Securities and Exchange Commission
500 North Capitol St.
Washington, D. C. 20549.

Dear Sirs:

Re: (Name of Registrant)

We have received a copy of your letter dated _____ relating to registration statement (SEC File No. 2– _____) filed with the Commission by (name of registrant). Accordingly, we are aware that "the staff has made only a cursory and not a customary review of the registration statement, which may not be relied upon in any degree to indicate that the registration statement is true, complete, or accurate."

In connection with our reports on financial statements filed pursuant to Securities Act of 1933, we are aware of our statutory responsibilities under the Act.

Very truly yours,

(Signature of auditors)

Some accountants, in their letters to the SEC, have changed the last sentence in the foregoing example to read as follows:

. . . In connection with the expression of opinion on financial statements included in registration statements filed under the Securities Act of 1933, this firm is *of course* aware of its statutory responsibilities under the Act. (Emphasis added)

Questions have been raised as to whether the representation letters referred to above increase the independent auditor's responsibility. According to Richard A. Nest:

The legal counsel of the [AICPA] believes the answer to this question is clearly no. The independent auditor's responsibilities with regard to registration statements are spelled out in Section 11 of the 1933 Act. The only documents filed with the Commission which affect the scope of his liability are: (1) his opinion on the financial statements, (2) his written consent, (3) references to him as an expert in Part I of the registration statement and (4) the response to Item 24 of Form S–1 regarding his independence. (*The Journal of Accountancy,* February 1969, p. 63.)

Accountant's Letter to NYSE Concurring in Pooling Treatment.
—Chapter **29** of this book contains a discussion of the requirements of the New York Stock Exchange applicable to companies listed on the Exchange. When application is made to list additional shares to be issued in connection with a business combination that will be accounted for as a pooling of interests, the Exchange asks the issuing company for a letter setting forth in detail the manner in which the combination complies with the criteria for a pooling. In addition, the Exchange requires a letter from the issuing company's independent public accountants concurring in the proposed accounting treatment. The discussion in Chapter **21** includes a suggested form of letter from the accountants to the Exchange for use in that connection.

Accountants' Letter Covering Review of Preliminary Proxy Material.—The reader is referred to the discussion in Chapter **22** regarding the accountants' "review" of preliminary proxy material growing out of SEC Release No. 34–8881 (1970). As indicated in that connection, the apparent purpose of the release was the Commission's wish to know whether the certifying accountants had "reviewed" the preliminary proxy material, and whether the accountants were prepared to permit the use in the proxy statement of their opinion with regard to the financial statements. For an example of the letter that the accountants may issue in these circumstances, see Chapter **22**.

Comfort Letters.—The subject of comfort letters (or letters to underwriters) is discussed in Chapter **12** together with suggested forms of such letters.

Certificates of Foreign Auditors.—For a discussion of certificates of foreign auditors, see Chapter **31**.

CHAPTER **26**

INDEPENDENCE OF ACCOUNTANTS

CONTENTS

What Is Meant by Accountant's Independence?

The professional public accountant must possess certain basic and fundamental attributes. Above everything else, his integrity must be unquestioned. If he holds himself out as a public accountant, it may be assumed that, as a result of training and experience, he is familiar with accounting principles and auditing standards and procedures. Accordingly, his technical competence may be taken for granted. Among other things, he should have good judgment and be able to distinguish between what is material and what is immaterial. Of equal importance, however, is the fact that his opinions must be based on an objective and disinterested viewpoint. In brief, he should be independent.

Independence is an abstract concept, difficult to define, "a reflection of honesty and integrity." [1] It is a state of mind and not susceptible of precise determination or definition. Public accountants know that their reputation for independence and integrity is their principal stock in trade and the justification for their existence as a profession. They are impelled by enlightened self-interest, and admonished by rules of ethics and professional conduct to maintain their independence at all costs, since it is as obvious as can be that independence is the very foundation of the public accounting profession.

Speaking of the concept of independence, a former chairman of the SEC [2] observed that it is not tangible, nor even in most instances clearly demonstrable, that it represents a state of mind. "The independent accountant must combine the impartiality of a judge with the high sense of responsibility of a fiduciary. . . . Though hired and fired by management, he must divorce his mental processes from any bias in their direction when making accounting judgments. Such a standard of professional conduct must be maintained if the auditor's certificate is to be more than a snare and a delusion and the public obligation of the accountant satisfied."

The concept of independence on the part of the certifying accountants was not created by the SEC or by the draftsmen of the federal securities laws. According to another SEC Commissioner, however, the Securities Act of 1933 was the first Federal law to recognize the independent status of the public accountant—a relatively new profession at that time. [3]

It is clear that the SEC and its predecessor, the Federal Trade Commission, deserve much of the credit for focussing attention on the subject of independence, and for promulgating rules prohibiting accountants from having financial interests in their clients and from having certain relationships with them, such as being an officer or director.

The Profession's Early Attempts to Deal with Independence

In his immensely readable book, "The Rise of the Accounting Profession," John L. Carey described how the profession was slow to act on the subject of independence. After the 1929 stock market crash, public accountants began to engage in some self-examination. At the 1931 annual meeting of the American Institute of Accountants (predecessor of the AICPA), Frederick H. Hurdman, immediate past president, delivered an address on the relations of client and accountant. In conjunction with his address, he introduced a resolution to the effect that the maintenance of a dual relationship, that is, as director or officer of a corporation while acting

[1] Lenhart and Defliese, *Montgomery's Auditing* (8th Ed., 1957), p. 24.
[2] Donald C. Cook, "The Concept of Independence in Accounting," address before AICPA, October 3, 1950.
[3] James J. Needham, address before Illinois Society of CPAs, April 1, 1971.

as auditor of that corporation, "is against the best interests of the public and the profession and tends to destroy that independence of action considered essential in the relationship between client and auditor."

Mr. Carey quoted excerpts from the remarks made in the discussion of the resolution:

We have too many rules already.

* * *

I agree with the spirit of that resolution but I think it is far too broad and sweeping. I think if it has any force at all it is dangerous because it would prevent, or tend to prevent, a perfectly proper relationship that might come under it ethically.

* * *

If there was some other way this rule could be enforced, or if it could be done in really worthwhile cases, then I am for it. But, do not let us have any more rules that would hamper the small man . . .

After some parliamentary maneuvering, a motion was made and carried that the resolution be referred to the committee on professional ethics, with instructions to report back to the 1932 annual meeting.

In 1932 the ethics committee brought in a resolution disapproving joint service as auditor and director of a corporation. The resolution was defeated, according to Mr. Carey, after a debate which clearly indicated a lack of enthusiasm for too many restraints on the members' freedom of action.

In Mr. Carey's words:

The profession had missed a chance to take a forward step voluntarily. A year later the Securities Acts became law, and the Federal Trade Commission, under date of July 6, 1933, issued regulations including the rule on independence cited earlier, covering not only joint service as auditor and officer or director, but also financial interest of an auditor in a client corporation.

In 1933, as the result of a trial involving Institute members who had invested in a client's securities, the ethics committee was requested to draft a rule covering such circumstances. The committee presented a resolution which would prohibit Institute members from certifying the financial statements of an enterprise financed in whole or in part by the public distribution of securities if the member had a substantial financial interest in the enterprise or was committed to acquire such an interest. "By this time, however," wrote Mr. Carey, "the action might have seemed to outside observers only an echo of the SEC's requirements on independence."

Early Influence of the Stock Exchanges

Beginning in April, 1932, all corporations applying for the listing of their securities upon the New York Stock Exchange were asked to enter into an agreement to the effect that future annual financial statements would be audited by independent public accountants. Beginning in July,

1933, listing applications filed with the Exchange also had to contain the certificate of an independent public accountant. The current form of listing agreement between the American Stock Exchange and corporations listed on that exchange contains similar provisions. The New York Stock Exchange and certain other national securities exchanges require members doing any business with persons other than members and member firms to have annual audits made by independent public accountants. Many bond indentures and preferred stock and note agreements require that financial statements be furnished at specified intervals accompanied by a report of independent public accountants. The "blue-sky" laws of some states provide that the financial statements contained in applications filed pursuant to such laws shall be certified by independent public accountants.

Influence of Professional Organizations

Rules of Conduct and Professional Ethics.—The by-laws of the AICPA contain provisions under which a member of the Institute may be expelled or suspended for infringement of the Code of Professional Ethics. The rules of the Code emphasize, among other things, the importance of independence on the part of Institute members. Rule 2.02 requires Institute members in their capacity as independent auditors to be governed by generally accepted accounting principles and to do their work in conformity with generally accepted auditing standards. Because of the great importance that attaches to Rule 2.02, it is appropriate to quote it in full:

In expressing an opinion on representations in financial statements which he has examined, a member or associate may be held guilty of an act discreditable to the profession if

(a) he fails to disclose a material fact known to him which is not disclosed in the financial statements but disclosure of which is necessary to make the financial statements not misleading; or

(b) he fails to report any material misstatement known to him to appear in the financial statement; or

(c) he is materially negligent in the conduct of his examination or in making his report thereon; or

(d) he fails to acquire sufficient information to warrant expression of an opinion, or his exceptions are sufficiently material to negative the expression of an opinion; or

(e) he fails to direct attention to any material departure from generally accepted accounting principles or to disclose any material omission of generally accepted auditing procedure applicable in the circumstances.

Rule 1.04 of the Institute's Code of Professional Ethics prohibits the rendering or offering of service for a fee that is contingent upon the findings or results of such services, with certain exceptions relating to tax practice.

Rule 1.01 of the Code relates to certification of financial statements of an enterprise in which the accountant may have a financial interest, and it was extensively revised in 1962. As previously in effect, the rule prohibited a member of the Institute from expressing an opinion on financial statements of an enterprise financed in whole or in part by public distribution of securities if he owned or was committed to acquire a financial interest in the business that was substantial either in relation to its capital or to his own personal fortune. He was also prohibited from certifying such financial statements if a member of his immediate family owned or was committed to acquire a substantial interest in the enterprise. An Institute member was also prohibited from expressing an opinion on financial statements used as a basis of credit if he owned or was committed to acquire a financial interest in the enterprise that was substantial either in relation to its capital or to his own personal fortune, or if a member of his immediate family owned or was committed to acquire such an interest, unless in his report he disclosed such interest. Effective as of January 1, 1964, the membership of the Institute adopted a new rule that closely parallels the SEC rule. As now in effect, the AICPA rule is as follows:

Neither a member or associate, nor a firm of which he is a partner, shall express an opinion on financial statements of any enterprise unless he and his firm are in fact independent with respect to such enterprise.

Independence is not susceptible of precise definition, but is an expression of the professional integrity of the individual. A member or associate, before expressing his opinion on financial statements, has the responsibility of assessing his relationships with an enterprise to determine whether, in the circumstances, he might expect his opinion to be considered independent, objective and unbiased by one who had knowledge of all the facts.

A member or associate will be considered not independent, for example, with respect to any enterprise if he, or one of his partners, (a) during the period of his professional engagement or at the time of expressing his opinion, had, or was committed to acquire, any direct financial interest or material indirect financial interest in the enterprise, or (b) during the period of his professional engagement, at the time of expressing his opinion or during the period covered by the financial statements, was connected with the enterprise as a promoter, underwriter, voting trustee, director, officer or key employee. In cases where a member or associate ceases to be the independent accountant for an enterprise and is subsequently called upon to re-express a previously expressed opinion on financial statements, the phrase "at the time of expressing his opinion" refers only to the time at which the member or associate first expressed his opinion on the financial statements in question. The word "director" is not intended to apply to a connection in such a capacity with a charitable, religious, civic or other similar type of nonprofit organization when the duties performed in such a capacity are such as to make it clear that the member or associate can express an independent opinion on the financial statements. The example cited in this paragraph, of circumstances under which a member or associate will be considered not independent, is not intended to be all-inclusive.

What is the meaning of "indirect financial interest" as used in the AICPA and SEC rules? It includes a variety of situations, the most common one being this: an accountant owns shares of a mutual fund which is not his client; the fund owns securities of Corporation X which is his client. This represents an indirect financial interest on the part of the accountant in Corporation X.

In addition, Rule 3.04 prohibits the payment of any portion of an accountant's fee to non-accountants or the acceptance of any portion of the fees or profits received by non-accountants from work turned over to them by accountants as an incident of their services to a client, and Rule 4.04 discusses occupations incompatible with public accounting.

The Rules of Professional Conduct of the New York State Society of CPAs provide that:

A member shall not express his opinion on financial statements of an enterprise if he, a partner in his firm, or a member of his immediate family owns or is committed to acquire a financial interest in the enterprise, or if he or a partner in his firm is an employee or director of the enterprise, unless he discloses such interest, employment or directorship in his report. (Rule No. 13)

In New York State the public practice of accountancy is regulated by law. Under the statute, the State Board of Regents has the power to revoke or suspend the certificate of a certified public accountant or to censure or reprimand the holder of such certificate when the holder has been found guilty of unprofessional conduct. In accordance with the requirements of the statute, the Board of Regents has delegated to the State Education Department the administration of the various professions which are licensed or certified as provided by the Education Law—including public accounting. With the approval of the Regents, the Commissioner of Education has promulgated a number of regulations governing the accountancy profession and the conduct of practitioners. The regulations relate, among other things, to unprofessional conduct. Under the regulations, a CPA or a public accountant is guilty of unprofessional conduct if he:

Expresses an opinion or knowingly permits his firm to express an opinion on financial statements of an enterprise, if he, a partner in his firm, or a member of his immediate family, or a member of his partner's immediate family, owns or is committed to acquire a substantial financial interest in the enterprise, or if he, or a partner in his firm, is or during the period covered by the examination has been a director, officer, or employee of the enterprise, unless such interest or relationship is disclosed in the report; [Sec. 94(f) of the Commissioner's Regulations].

These provisions are similar to those of the New York State Society of CPAs, but, as will be seen, there are also differences.

In 1947 the Executive Committee of the AICPA issued a tentative statement on independence of the CPA. Intended as a guide to Institute members, the public, and others, the Committee's statement described briefly the background and growth of public accountancy and the part played by the profession in contemporary economic life. The Committee said, in part:

A most important function which the certified public accountant performs in our economic life today is the part he plays in the maintenance of mutual confidence which is necessary in business relationships and transactions. The relationship may be that between management and stockholders, especially in publicly-held corporations. The transactions may be those between borrowers and lenders, or between purchasers and sellers of a business enterprise or of shares in it. It has become of great value to those who rely on financial statements of business enterprises that they be reviewed by persons skilled in accounting whose judgment is uncolored by any interest in the enterprise, and upon whom the obligation has been imposed to disclose all material facts. With the growth of business enterprises, the public accountant makes a vital contribution in meeting the need for independent, impartial, and expert opinions on the financial position and the results of operations. This is his unique contribution, a service which no one else offers or is qualified to perform. [84 *The Journal of Accountancy* 51 (1947)].

The Committee pointed out that the professional CPA societies at the national and state levels established rules designed to insure the independence of their members in the field of professional conduct. These rules require the auditor to direct attention in his certificate to any material misstatement, either of omission or commission, and to any material departure from generally accepted accounting or auditing principles applicable in the circumstances. He must refrain from expressing any opinion whenever his exceptions are so far-reaching as to negate the opinion. These formal rules, which set certain objective standards which the independent accountant is bound to observe, presuppose that he has acquired a thorough knowledge of accounting and auditing principles.

The independent accountant will not be expected to depend solely upon the principles that have been formally expressed, although he must be prepared to justify any departure from them. "A real test of the accountant's independence," said the Committee, "is in the application of general principles." Written rules and principles are not to be followed blindly. In complex situations the CPA is often confronted with a difficult problem in discerning the proper application of a recognized principle or in making a choice of conflicting principles. Frequently, too, the extent of disclosure the accountant should insist upon in special situations tests his independence of decision. To reach a sound and impartial judgment in these matters, the accountant must consider carefully the actual facts in the case.

The Committee concluded:

Rules of conduct can only deal with objective standards and cannot assure independence. Independence is an attitude of mind, much deeper than the surface display of visible standards. These standards may change or become more exacting, but the quality itself remains unchanged. Independence, both historically and philosophically, is the foundation of the public accounting profession, and upon its maintenance depends the profession's strength and its stature.

In a somewhat similar vein, a member of the SEC has said that the real test of the accountant's independence often comes when he must make a decision with respect to an accounting treatment of a matter not covered by an opinion of the APB.[4] Too many times, the Commissioner said, the accountant rationalizes or justifies his decision by pointing to the fact that the problem has not been specifically dealt with in accounting literature. "This is the most specious form of reasoning." He continued:

> I believe that too many times when confronted with close questions some accountants ignore one of the fundamentals of accounting—namely that substance shall triumph over form. This means that despite complicated legal instruments and whatever other documentation presented by a client, the accountant is charged, in the first instance, with the responsibility of seeing to it that the business impact of the transaction in question is reported rather than a literal reflection of a legal document.
>
> Furthermore, structuring a "business deal" in an attempt to exploit unsettled accounting principles is unfair to everyone and at times can come perilously close to commercial fraud. Management, as well as accountants, has a responsibility to see to it that the real significance of financial transactions is set forth properly in financial statements.
>
> Truly independent accountants are well aware of their responsibilities in this area . . .

Generally Accepted Auditing Standards.—In the conventional, short form certificate, public accountants represent that their examinations were made in accordance with "generally accepted auditing standards." Auditing standards differ from auditing procedures in that the latter relate to acts to be performed, whereas the former deal with measures of the quality of the performance of those acts and the objectives to be attained by the use of the procedures. [Statements on Auditing Procedure, No. 33 (1963).]

The generally accepted auditing standards as approved and adopted by the membership of the AICPA include so-called "general standards," standards of field work, and standards of reporting. The general standards are personal in nature and are concerned with the qualifications of the auditor and the quality of his work as distinct from those standards which relate to the performance of his field work and to his reporting. These personal, or general, standards apply also to the areas of field work and reporting.

The general standards are as follows:

---

[4] James J. Needham, address before joint meeting of Tennessee Society of CPAs and three other groups, Oct. 20, 1970.

1. The examination is to be performed by a person or persons having adequate technical training and proficiency as an auditor.
2. In all matters relating to the assignment an independence in mental attitude is to be maintained by the auditor or auditors.
3. Due professional care is to be exercised in the performance of the examination and the preparation of the report.

With respect to the second of the aforementioned general standards, the AICPA Committee on Auditing Procedure stated in its Statement No. 33:

. . . [The auditor] must be without bias with respect to the client under audit, since otherwise he would lack that impartiality necessary for the dependability of his findings, however excellent his technical proficiency may be. However, independence does not imply the attitude of a prosecutor, but rather a judicial impartiality that recognizes an obligation for fairness not only to management and owners (shareholders) of a business, but also to creditors and those who may otherwise rely (in part, at least) upon the auditor's report, as in the case of prospective owners or creditors.

It is of utmost importance to the profession that the general public maintain confidence in the independence of independent auditors. Public confidence would be impaired by evidence that independence was actually lacking and it might also be impaired by the existence of circumstances which reasonable people might believe likely to influence independence. To *be* independent, the auditor must be intellectually honest; to be *recognized* as independent, he must be free from any obligation to or interest in the client, its management or its owners. For example, an independent auditor auditing a company of which he was also a director might be intellectually honest, but it is unlikely that the public would accept him as independent since he would be in effect auditing decisions which he had a part in making. Likewise, an auditor with a substantial financial interest in a company might be unbiased in expressing his opinion on the financial statements of the company, but the public would be reluctant to believe that he was unbiased. Independent auditors should not only be independent in fact; they should avoid situations that may lead outsiders to doubt their independence.

Narrowing of the Distinction Between SEC's and Profession's Views

While the accounting profession and industry have been aware of the importance of independence on the part of public accountants, the SEC deserves most of the credit for accelerating the development of the independence concept. In its regulations and decisions—both formal and informal—the SEC has been insistent that accountants who certify statements for filing with it be independent. The distinction between the SEC's view and the profession's view of independence has been stated in this way:

The SEC emphasizes the specific relationships between an accountant and his client which give rise to a presumption of lack of independence—the SEC will not recognize an accountant as independent if any of the proscribed relationships exist.

The Institute emphasizes the fact of independence—the state of mind which the word denotes. It recognizes that an accountant may be independent in spite of close relationships with his client—or that he may lack independence in spite of the most correct appearances. The Institute, therefore, has not chosen to prohibit a great variety of relationships which might conceivably tend to introduce a subconscious bias into the accountant's judgment, but rather relies mainly on [Rule 2.02 of the Code of Professional Ethics] to determine whether independence has actually been impaired or not. If accepted accounting and auditing standards are observed, and all material facts are fully disclosed, it may be presumed that independence exists.[5]

With the revision in Rule 1.01 of the Code of Professional Ethics effective January 1, 1964, the distinction between the views of the SEC and the accountancy profession on the question of independence was narrowed considerably; see Rule 2–01 of Regulation S–X on page **26·18**. As a practical matter it may be said that, as of January 1, 1964, the distinction was eliminated.

A former chairman of the SEC[6] has said that the Commission has attempted to adapt the concept of independence to the needs of investors. When a registration statement or annual report is filed with the Commission, it is designed for use by the public. In lieu of government examination of each financial statement, the certificate of an independent accountant is required. "I believe that the duties inherent in furnishing such a certificate impress upon the auditor a fiduciary obligation toward the public as well as toward the client if full confidence in the publicly held securities is to be maintained." He continued:

. . . Just as a trustee of an estate in reorganization under the Bankruptcy Act may not ally himself with any creditor or stockholder interest in the estate, trade in securities of the estate, or purchase trust property, the accountant may not have any financial interest in a client's enterprise, even if it can be shown that the personal financial stake of the trustee or the accountant will have no effect upon his judgment. As a matter of fact, persons sensitive to their obligations may lean over backwards and act in opposition to their personal interests.

Nevertheless, I believe it is a salutary principle which arbitrarily denies to fiduciaries or people in a quasi-fiduciary position such as accountants the right to risk their independence. Not all people are strong enough to resist temptation, particularly when it may easily be hidden behind a convincing rationalization. Even if there is no conscious attempt to favor a personal interest, unconscious pressures may cause a shift in the normal judgment exercised by the accountant. For both these reasons, and because the public will have greater confidence in certifications when they know there is no conflict between personal desires and professional opinions, the accountant must carefully scrutinize his relationships with his client.

[5] John L. Carey, "Practical Applications of Professional Ethics," in *CPA Handbook* (1952), Chap. V, p. 17.

[6] Donald C. Cook, "The Concept of Independence in Accounting," address before the AICPA, October 3, 1950.

Management Advisory Services and Independence

The basic service offered by the public accountancy profession is the examination and certification of financial statements and the preparation or review of tax returns. For many years, however, businessmen have looked to their public accountants for a wide variety of other services to assist them in the conduct of their business. This is to be expected since accounting is the language of business, and the public accountant, in the course of his work, acquires a considerable knowledge not only of his client's business but also about business in general.

Management is accustomed to regarding public accountants as experts in such matters as organizational planning, methods and procedures for accounting and record keeping, and the characteristics of various types of clerical labor-saving devices. Because of the intensely competitive conditions existing in business today and the tremendous strides which have been made in data processing methods, management is turning more and more to its certified public accountants for services not bearing directly on the examination of their financial statements.

There is nothing wrong in helping a client prepare a budget system, or in improving his cost accounting methods, or in suggesting improvements in clerical procedures which enable a job to be done faster, better or cheaper. But in furnishing these services, the accountant should not lose sight of his proper function. It is the accountant's rightful job to bring to his client's attention all ideas, facts and recommendations pertaining to the problem under consideration, in an advisory capacity without active participation in management's decision. This requires a fine sense of professional responsibility. As an independent professional man, the public accountant should not hesitate to make his recommendations and to discuss the pros and cons of various alternatives. But, having given his advice, he must be content to let management make the final decision. Otherwise he may find himself in the position of auditing his own work—namely, his own decisions.

A similar point of view was expressed by the AICPA's Committee on Professional Ethics which considered the propriety of furnishing tax and management advisory services to clients on whose financial statements the CPA expresses an independent opinion. So long as the CPA's services consist of advice and technical assistance, the Committee said it discerned no likelihood of a conflict of interest arising from such services. If, however, the CPA should make management decisions on matters affecting the company's financial position or results of operations, "it would appear that his objectivity as independent auditor of the company's financial statements might well be impaired." (Opinion No. 12.)

Management advisory services have become a significant part of the practice of many public accounting firms. At the same time the range of activities within this phase of practice has expanded materially beyond the traditional areas related to financial planning and controls. Accompanying this growth in scope and volume, there has arisen some controversy as to whether the independent public accountant can perform management advisory services and still maintain his independence in his auditing capacity.

The development of the issue may be seen from some of the comments of the SEC and its representatives.

In 1958 the SEC commented on the independence of the accountant who is so closely identified with his client that he makes decisions that should be made by management. The Commission said:

Another reason for finding a lack of independence . . . is the fact that some accountants intending to certify financial statements included in such filings have been interested in serving the client's management, or in some cases large stockholders, in several capacities and in doing so have not taken care to maintain a clear distinction between giving advice to management and serving as personal representatives of management or owners and making business decisions for them.[7]

A former Chief Accountant of the SEC said that the public accountant who furnishes management services should keep two questions in mind:

1. Am I remaining an adviser to management and not entering the decision-making area?
2. Am I sure that the audit of the financial statements will not involve checking my own work?[8]

Unless the accountant can answer "Yes" to both questions, according to the Chief Accountant, the accountant's independence as to furnishing an objective report on management is in question. He recognized that systems work, cost analysis, budgetary controls and other aspects of business management have long been the province of the public accountant. It could be possible, he said, for an accountant to become so deeply involved in performing managerial services for a client that he would lose his objective approach to his audit engagement. In such a case, he should concentrate on one activity or the other and not attempt to do both.

In 1966 the then chairman of the SEC ranged broader in his comments on the subject of management advisory services by independent accountants:

However, a word of caution is in order with respect to what one of your prominent members describes as "consulting services which cannot be related logically either to the financial process or to broadly defined information and

---

[7] Securities and Exchange Commission, *23rd Annual Report for fiscal year ended June 30, 1957* (U. S. Government Printing Office, 1958), p. 184.

[8] Andrew Barr, "Accounting—Changing Patterns; The Impact of Regulatory Agencies," address at the Art Institute of Chicago, Nov. 11, 1959.

control systems, [such as] market surveys, factory layout, psychological testing, or public opinion polls." And, I am disposed to add, executive recruitment for a fee. An accountant who directs or assists in programs of this kind raises serious questions concerning his independence when it comes time to render to creditors, to investors and to the public his opinion on the results of the programs. Public accountants should carefully reconsider their participation in these activities lest their continuation and extension undermine the main function of the independent accountant—auditing and the rendering of opinions on financial statements. On the other hand, the notion seems to persist in some quarters that an auditor's opinion amounts to nothing more than attesting to the arithmetic in the books. Those who share this view fail to recognize that the basis of the auditor's opinion is found in adequate records, properly maintained and supported by internal checks and controls which include administrative practices as well as the recording process.[9]

Executive recruitment is undoubtedly of minor importance even to the most aggressive public accountant. But the manner in which this branch of service has evolved might be considered typical of how other areas of management advisory services have developed over the years. At some time or other during his professional career, almost every public accountant has been asked by a client to assist him in screening a prospective employee, or to assist him in obtaining a competent employee, such as a controller, assistant controller, and the like. Sometimes also a person seeking employment or a position better than the one he has, will ask an accountant whether he knows of a possible opening. In recent years the number of these inquiries received by accountants has increased considerably, and, in the case of the larger accounting firms, has caused some of them to set up specialized recruitment or placement services within their organizations.

In the beginning, these recruitment services were usually furnished on a no-fee basis as an accommodation to clients seeking executives or other employees, and to individuals looking for positions or for better positions than the ones they had. This kind of service obviously competed with that offered by executive recruitment agencies (so-called "head hunters") who, of course, charge for their services. Some of the accountants who furnished this type of service began to charge for the service.

What is the reason for the SEC's concern? It apparently is based on the premise that an accountant may hesitate to criticize the work of an officer or an employee if the accountant was instrumental in placing that officer or employee with the client and received a fee in that connection. In the opinion of the author, this fear is more theoretical than real. If there were any basis for the SEC's apparent position, it should not be influenced by whether or not the accountant received a fee for his recruitment services. If an accountant fails to criticize the work done by a person he has helped to recruit, it will not be because he did or did not receive a fee for that

[9] Manuel F. Cohen, address before AICPA annual meeting, Oct. 5, 1966.

service. But the former SEC chairman in his comments referred to above did not question the propriety of recruitment services furnished free of charge by independent accountants.

Executive recruitment is but a fragment of the management advisory service issue which has since been debated at length. The challenge to independence has been raised largely by academicians, with practitioners hastening to the defense. Typical of the professorial view are the contentions of Dr. Arthur A. Schulte, Jr. He sees potential conflicts when public accountants engage in management consulting activities, and thinks they become business consultants, not independent attestors, with the resulting possible impairment of their audit independence. Various areas of concern are expressed by him. Although decision making is the responsibility of management, "management may, however, surrender its authority and responsibility to the consultant to make the final choice of action." In a small business, the consultant may be an alternative to an internal staff and become "in effect, the controller for his client." Even if he makes no decisions, the consultant participates in the decision-making process and "develops a close relationship with management" and therefore "he may lose his objectivity." The need to gain acceptance for his recommendations places the public accountant in an advocacy role and represents "a psychological burden on the CPA to be impartial and disinterested toward the results of his recommendations he subsequently audits." And finally, "If the reputation of the CPA as a consultant depends on results, then he has a direct financial stake in the outcome of his consulting activities and he may no longer maintain the 'lack of any self-interest' which audit independence demands." [10]

Those who question the independence of accountants who perform management advisory services often cite the statement of a former chairman of the AICPA's Committee on Professional Ethics: "There are actually two kinds of independence which a CPA must have—independence in *fact* and independence in *appearance*." [11] They then contend that even if management advisory services and auditing are compatible, the auditor who renders both services *appears* to third parties as something less than independent.

There is no shortage of articles by public accountants rebutting the views of those who doubt the compatibility of management advisory services and the auditor's attest function. One of the outstanding CPA consultants, Dr. Felix Kaufman (who also has impressive academic credentials), commented on the controversy involving the independence issue. He observed that some people have applied a rigorous logic to the issue and have concluded that to

[10] Arthur A. Schulte, Jr., "CPA's Independence Affected by Management Services?", *The New York CPA*, Jan. 1967.

[11] Thomas G. Higgins, "Professional Ethics: A Time for Reappraisal," *The Journal of Accountancy*, March 1962, p. 31.

really achieve audit independence an environment must be established in which the auditor never has advocacy sentiments about his client. In this framework, he said, the knowledge that the client was going bankrupt would obtain a "so what" attitude, and audit independence becomes an abstraction rather than a positive and viable personal attribute. "And it envisages the auditor as a virtual automaton bereft of capacity for perception, discrimination or moral judgment." He continued:

The accountant's self-imposed professional discipline is strict. Probably no contemporary group is asked to exercise greater objectivity in what is, in fact, an essentially tough, pragmatic, and even cynical economic environment. The accountant considers this objectivity equally applicable to all areas of his services, whether they relate to the credibility of financial reporting or to the improvement of industry controls and productivity.[12]

Recognizing the existence of the controversy and its significance, the AICPA appointed an ad hoc Committee on Independence in 1966. Its report was approved in 1969 by the AICPA's Executive Committee and indicates the scope of its efforts. It studied what had been written on the subject, interviewed authors whose articles were based on surveys and sought the views of representatives of groups who use accountant's reports. The Committee's report appeared in *The Journal of Accountancy* (December 1969). Excerpts from its Summary of Observations and Recommendations give the profession's current viewpoint:

1. There has been no allegation, and the committee has found no substantive evidence, that the rendition of management advisory services has impaired the independence of CPAs *in fact*. Nonetheless, the committee believes that so long as a significant minority of users of financial statements has a concern that the rendition of management advisory services (all or some), or the manner in which they are rendered, raises questions as to an auditor's independence, the profession needs to be sensitive to their concerns and address itself to them.

2. Subsequent to the formation of this committee (and subsequent to interviews with the user groups) the management services committee of the AICPA has issued three statements titled "Tentative Description of the Nature of Management Advisory Services by Independent Accounting Firms," "Competence in Management Advisory Services," and "Role in Management Advisory Services." The committee believes these statements will be helpful in guiding the profession in the rendition of management advisory services and in better interpreting to interested parties outside the profession the nature of such services as rendered by independent accounting firms and the role which they play. These statements stress the caveats implicit in our code of ethics to the effect that a CPA is prohibited from serving a client as independent auditor should he make management decisions or take positions that might impair his objectivity with respect to that client. . . .

3. The rendition of management advisory services by CPAs is not a static matter. Accordingly we recommend that both the committee on professional

[12] Felix Kaufman, "Professional Consulting by CPAs," *The Accounting Review*, Oct. 1967, p. 719.

ethics and the management services committee of the AICPA keep the practice of management advisory services under continual surveillance. This surveillance should give particular attention to compliance with our present rules of ethics as to maintenance of our independence in the attest function and the possible need to provide additional safeguards if further developments appear to warrant them. . . .

4. For the present, CPAs should recognize that peripheral management advisory services—i.e., those not "related logically either to the financial process or to broadly defined information and control systems" are raising questions with some users of financial statements. The problem here appears to be not so much that peripheral services really impinge on independence (for in actuality they pose a lesser threat than conventional "accepted" services) as that they seem to some to dilute the image of the CPA as an auditor. With this in mind, CPAs should consider seriously whether or not they should elect to render such services; if they do, we would encourage them to voluntarily limit the extent of such services.

5. Determination of the CPA's role in the performance of management advisory services is crucial to the maintenance of his objectivity as an independent auditor. CPAs involved in rendering such services should give particular attention to the guidance provided in Statement on Management Advisory Services No. 3 on the subject of role. This committee particularly endorses that statement's admonition to the CPA to ". . . always be alert to the way his role may be viewed by others and not permit himself to be placed in a posture . . . that could cause serious question regarding his objectivity and independence." In this regard, this committee believes that the greater the economic consequence of a decision of management in the matter to which the management advisory service relates, the greater the care that should be exercised by the CPA as to the way his role may be viewed by others.

6. . . . Where a CPA is requested to render a management advisory service, he has an obligation of deciding whether he believes the given service, or more particularly the role he is asked to play, might pose a serious question as to his independence; if he so decides, then he should decline either to render such service or the audit service. If the CPA believes that providing such service causes no problems of independence in fact, yet might cause a serious question to be raised, due to an appearance of lack of independence, he should (particularly in the case of "publicly held" companies) consider the advisability of conferring with the audit committee (or if there be no such committee, then with the full board of directors) to make certain that the audit committee, as representatives of the board of directors and hence of the stockholders, concurs as to the propriety of the rendition of the given service. . . .

Conclusion

As a result of its studies and particularly its exposure to representatives of user groups, the committee is of the opinion that the profession is fortunate in having achieved a remarkable reputation for integrity and independence. This is a valuable asset but it has not been granted the profession in perpetuity. The profession must continue to justify its reputation and, accordingly, has the obligation in all areas of its service, including the management advisory services area, to observe its self-imposed ethical restraint. Furthermore, it must be sensitive to public opinion, and respond to criticism in a constructive, rather than a defensive manner. This suggests careful consideration by each member of the nature of the services he chooses to offer, his appropriate role in performing such services, and the manner in which he describes them—all in the light of possible public reaction.

The author has only one purpose in introducing the subject of management advisory services in this volume. Regardless of the type of service he furnishes his client, the accountant should make sure that he does nothing to prejudice his status as an *independent* public accountant.

Statutory Basis for Requirement as to Independence

The 1933 Act authorizes the Commission to designate the financial information that must be included in a registration statement and whether it shall be "certified by an independent public or certified accountant." (Sec. 7 and Schedule A.) The 1934 Act authorizes the Commission to prescribe the financial data to be included in applications for registration "certified if required by the rules and regulations of the Commission by independent public accountants." (Sec. 12(b)(1).) The 1934 Act also authorizes the Commission to prescribe the information to be included in annual reports of issuers having securities listed for exchange trading and in such reports of certain publicly-owned, unlisted companies "certified if required by the rules and regulations of the Commission by independent public accountants." (Sec. 13(c)(2).) The 1940 Act gives the Commission authority to prescribe the content of annual reports of registered investment companies, including financial statements certified, if required by the rules and regulations of the Commission, by independent public accountants. (Sec. 30(e).)

Under its statutory authority the SEC has promulgated a number of registration and report forms. Most of the forms require the submission of certified financial statements. "Certified" is defined under the 1933 Act as meaning "certified by an independent public or independent certified public accountant or accountants." (Rule 405.) Under the 1934 Act the term "certified," when used in regard to financial statements, has the same meaning. (Rule 12b–2.)

It is clear that, as far as practice before the SEC is concerned, a public accountant has the same standing as a certified public accountant. Whether or not the accountant is certified, this much is certain: he must be independent.

Regulation S-X

Regulation S–X is the principal accounting regulation of the SEC. It sets forth the requirements as to the form and content of financial statements and supplemental schedules required to be filed with the SEC.

Rule 2–01.—This part of the regulation contains the Commission's formal requirements as to qualifications of accountants and their independence. The rule as revised in 1972 is quoted below:

Rule 2–01. Qualifications of Accountants.

(a) The Commission will not recognize any person as a certified public accountant who is not duly registered and in good standing as such under the laws of the place of his residence or principal office. The Commission will not recognize any person as a public accountant who is not in good standing and entitled to practice as such under the laws of the place of his residence or principal office.

(b) The Commission will not recognize any certified public accountant or public accountant as independent who is not in fact independent. For example, an accountant will be considered not independent with respect to any person or any of its parents, its subsidiaries, or other affiliates (1) in which, during the period of his professional engagement to examine the financial statements being reported on or at the date of his report, he or his firm or a member thereof had, or was committed to acquire, any direct financial interest or any material indirect financial interest; or (2) with which, during the period of his professional engagement to examine the financial statements being reported on, at the date of his report or during the period covered by the financial statements, he or his firm or a member thereof was connected as a promoter, underwriter, voting trustee, director, officer, or employee, except that a firm will not be deemed not independent in regard to a particular person if a former officer or employee of such person is employed by the firm and such individual has completely dissociated himself from the person and its affiliates and does not participate in auditing financial statements of the person or its affiliates covering any period of his employment by the person. For the purposes of Rule 2–01 the term "member" means all partners in the firm and all professional employees participating in the audit or located in an office of the firm participating in a significant portion of the audit.

(c) In determining whether an accountant may in fact be not independent with respect to a particular person, the Commission will give appropriate consideration to all relevant circumstances, including evidence bearing on all relationships between the accountant and that person or any affiliate thereof, and will not confine itself to the relationships existing in connection with the filing of reports with the Commission.

The inclusion of professional employees in the definition of "member" in Rule 2–01(b) is effective commencing January 1, 1973.

The reader's attention is directed to paragraph (b) of Rule 2–01 quoted above, which provides in part that an accountant "will be considered not independent" if he or his firm or a member thereof had, or was committed to acquire, a financial interest in the affiliated group, or had certain relationships with the group. Where the "accountant" is a firm, the SEC construes the restriction to apply to *each partner whether or not he has any connection with the audit.* Accordingly, when the partner in charge of an audit is disqualified because he is not independent in relation to the client, the requirement with respect to independence can not be satisfied by changing the partner in charge of the audit engagement.

As an aid in administering paragraph (a) of Rule 2–01, the office of the Chief Accountant attempts to keep a current file of accountants authorized to practice in the several states. Some states publish such lists for all licensed or registered accountants, both certified and not certified. State societies of CPAs cooperate by furnishing the SEC with copies of directories as they are published. If the certifying accountant who is unknown to the SEC cannot be identified in this way, the Commission asks for evidence of his qualification to practice. In a few cases state boards have challenged the accountant's right to certify. When the accountants were found not to be properly qualified, the registrants were requested to furnish financial statements certified by qualified accountants.

The Commission has not attempted to set up objective standards for measuring the qualifications of accountants other than requiring that they be in good standing and entitled to practice as independent accountants in their place of residence or principal office. It is expected, however, that they will have adequate technical training and proficiency and will conduct their examinations pursuant to generally accepted auditing standards.

Several years ago, the SEC issued cards to public accountants attesting the right of the holder of the card to practice before the SEC. Because the privilege was abused by some, all the cards were withdrawn. A public accountant now does not have to hold a card or otherwise be "admitted" to practice before the SEC in order to certify statements for filing with the Commission. The public accountant need not be a CPA, but he must be independent, in good standing, and entitled to practice as a public accountant under the laws of the place of his residence or principal office.

In adopting an earlier version of paragraph (c) of Rule 2–01 (since superseded) the SEC advanced as one of its reasons that the rule appeared to be required in view of cases in which substantial amounts due from officers and directors were shown separately in balance sheets filed with the SEC but, in the balance sheet contained in the annual report to stockholders, were included without disclosure under the caption "Accounts and notes receivable, less reserves." Since both balance sheets were certified by the same public accountants, the difference in presentation, said the SEC, had a definite bearing on the independence of the certifying accountants.

Perhaps the most critical test of the actuality of an accountant's independence is the strength of his insistence upon full disclosure of transactions between the company and members of its management as individuals; accession to the wishes of the management in such cases must inevitably raise a serious question as to whether the accountant is in fact independent. Moreover, in considering whether an accountant is in fact independent, such accession to the wishes of the management is no less significant when it occurs with respect to the financial statements included in an annual report to security holders or otherwise made public than when it occurs with respect to statements required to be filed with the Commission. [ASR No. 37 (1942).]

Financial Interest Held During Period Covered by Report.—Assume that an accountant owns shares of common stock of the X Corporation. In September 1971 he is engaged to examine and report upon the financial statements of X Corporation for the calendar year 1971 with the understanding that his certificate will be included in X Corporation's report to shareholders for 1971 and in the company's Form 10–K report to the SEC. Immediately upon being engaged as the company's independent auditor, he disposes of his holdings in X Corporation. He has no other interest in, or relationship with, X Corporation or its affiliates which would preclude him from acting as its independent auditor.

It will be apparent that the accountant had a financial interest in his client during part of the period that will be covered by his report, and so the question may arise: Does this disqualify him for the year 1971? The answer is "No, it does not disqualify him."

Prior to the 1972 revision of Regulation S–X, Rule 2–01(b) was to the effect that an accountant would be considered not independent with respect to a company or its affiliates in which he has, *or had during the period of report,* a direct financial interest or a material indirect financial interest. The words in italics created a minor problem in interpreting the rule. Inasmuch as the accountant had a financial interest in the company "during the period of report," it might appear that he would be disqualified, but the SEC has made it clear that the rule was not to be so interpreted. The SEC's position was that the accountant's independence before being employed as the company's auditor was not a factor of importance, and if he disposes of his holdings when he is engaged as auditor, his independence will not be questioned on that score.

It was for the purpose of clarifying Rule 2–01(b) that it was revised in 1972. Under the new rule an accountant will be considered not independent with respect to a company or its affiliates in which, during the period of his professional engagement or at the date of his report, he had, or was committed to acquire, a direct financial interest or a material indirect financial interest. In this connection, see the excerpt from ASR No. 79 on page **26·29**.

"Substantial Interest" in Form S–1.—Item 24 of a registration statement on Form S–1 calls for a statement concerning substantial interests held by experts:

If any expert named in the registration statement as having prepared or certified any part thereof was employed for such purpose on a contingent basis or, at the time of such preparation or certification or at any time thereafter, had a substantial interest in the registrant or any of its parents or subsidiaries or was connected with the registrant or any of its subsidiaries as a promoter, underwriter, voting trustee, director, officer, or employee, furnish a brief statement of the nature of such contingent basis, interest, or connection.

The instructions for this item provide that, in the case of an accountant, any direct financial interest or any material indirect financial interest *held during the period covered by the financial statements* prepared or certified shall be deemed a "substantial interest" for the purpose of this item. The reader is referred to Rule 2–01(b) of Regulation S–X (quoted earlier in this chapter) for the Commission's requirements as to qualifications of accountants, particularly as they relate to financial interests—direct or indirect—in clients and affiliates. The language of Rule 2–01(b) is significantly different from the language of Item 24.

The reader is also referred to the discussion in the preceding pages under "Financial Interest Held During Period Covered by Report," from which it will be seen that if the auditor disposed of his interest in the company immediately upon being engaged as its independent auditor, his independence will not be challenged on that score alone notwithstanding that he had a financial interest in the company during part of the period covered by his report. In the author's opinion, the holding of an interest in these circumstances and the disposition thereof do not have to be reported in Item 24 of Form S–1 since, prior to his being engaged as the company's auditor, his financial interest in the company was not a matter of consequence.

Independence of Accountants Who Examine a Non-Material Segment of an International Business.—When a company is engaged in international operations, it generally requires the services of independent auditors in all those countries in which its subsidiaries or divisions own properties or otherwise conduct business. A United States parent corporation may be engaged in business abroad in an area where its independent auditors do not practice. Frequently, the foreign subsidiary (or division) may not be important to the total enterprise, and another accounting firm (referred to hereafter as the "other accounting firm") acceptable to the parent company's independent accountants may be engaged to examine the financial statements of the foreign subsidiary (or division). In many cases, the other accounting firm which has been retained to do the examination will do so through one of its foreign affiliated firms.

When the financial statements of the foreign subsidiary or division which represent a non-material segment of an international business are examined by another accounting firm or its affiliated firm, is Rule 2–01 of Regulation S–X construed so as to preclude all the partners of such other accounting firm or its affiliated firm from owning any securities of the United States parent or the foreign subsidiary in order for the other accounting firm to be considered independent as to the parent company or the subsidiary?

The SEC answered this question in ASR No. 112, issued in 1968. The Commission said:

> We believe that the purposes of Rule 2–01 would be adequately served by a less restrictive construction. Insofar as ownership of securities by partners is concerned, the other accounting firm would be held to be not independent only if securities of the parent company or the subsidiary are owned by any of the partners of the other accounting firm or its affiliated firm who are located in the office which makes the examination of the division or subsidiary or who are otherwise engaged in such examination.

The SEC's release stated that it related only to the ownership of securities and did not extend to any other relationship prohibited by Rule 2–01.

Employment of Accountant's Employees by Client.—A matter of recurring concern to practicing public accountants is the pirating of their professional staffs by clients. Especially in recent years, with the competition for skilled accountants, clients have made increasing inroads on the staffs of their independent auditors by making offers of employment to accountants who happen to be working on the examination of the financial statements of the client company. Public accountants have long accepted this as a fact of life and realize that when a competent staff man is exposed to a client, they may lose that man to the client. Ordinarily this is not a matter of overriding concern, but it does become very important if the client and the staff man enter into or conduct their negotiations *while the audit is in progress.*

It seems self-evident that an accountant's audit judgments and decisions with respect to a company's financial statements may be influenced to some extent if he is concurrently engaged in discussions leading to possible employment by that company. And yet, it does sometimes happen in a way that can embarrass all concerned, and, in an extreme case, could torpedo all the work done to date on the audit engagement.

If the client is thinking of approaching a staff auditor, the client should, simply as a matter of courtesy, first contact a partner or other principal of the accounting firm and tell him what he has in mind. More often than not the partner will not stand in the way of the staff man but will ask the client not to make his approach until the audit has been completed and the firm has issued its report on the financial statements.

In one case with which the author is familiar, a prospectus indicated (in the section discussing the officers' backgrounds) that Mr. R, a principal officer, was prior to a specified date on the staff of the accounting firm. The date named was within the period covered by the earnings summary in the prospectus. In its letter of comments, the SEC inquired whether Mr. R was involved in the audit examination of the company's financial statements and, if so, the extent of that involvement. Fortunately the company was able to say that although Mr. R was the audit manager on the audit, the company and he did not enter into negotiations leading to his employment by the company until after the audit had been completed.

In another unreported case with which the author is familiar, a staff accountant had been negotiating while the audit was in progress with an officer of the client company, with a view to his employment by the company as controller. The negotiations were conducted without the knowledge of the accounting firm involved. There was no intent to withhold this information from the partner of the accounting firm, but the staff accountant and his prospective employer did not realize the implications of their negotiations. (It might also be mentioned that the company officer was himself a CPA, although not in public practice!) In due course, the staff man notified the accounting firm of his decision to accept a position with the client and said he would be leaving in two weeks. The audit engagement was a sizeable one and was about ten days short of completion. To make matters worse, the company was subject to SEC jurisdiction and, in fact, had planned to file a registration statement with the SEC under the 1933 Act using the financial statements of the latest year which were then being audited.

The partner of the accounting firm in charge of the engagement promptly removed the staff man from the audit of the company and replaced him with another manager. In addition, the partner asked another partner who had not participated in examinations of that company's financial statements to review not only the work of the staff man in question but all the work on the engagement. Also, the partner in charge discussed the situation fully and frankly with the SEC's Chief Accountant. In view of the steps taken by the accounting firm, the Chief Accountant said the SEC would raise no question as to the accounting firm's independence in relation to the company being discussed.

SEC Rulings in Specific Cases

The SEC has made a number of formal and informal rulings bearing on the question of an accountant's independence. The following pages of this chapter contain the facts and rulings in the principal cases decided by the SEC. An important point to bear in mind is that the cases often were not decided on the basis of a single circumstance, but rather on the basis of a number of circumstances. Thus, the Commission may have concluded in a given case that an accountant was not independent because of the cumulative effect of Fact A, Fact B, Fact C, and so on. It does not necessarily follow that the accountant would have been similarly disqualified if the only question bearing on his lack of independence had been Fact A, *or*

Fact B, *or* Fact C. The existence of any one of these facts standing alone may not necessarily lead to the same result as when all the facts exist. In reading the SEC decisions, it is well to bear this point in mind.

As an example, consider the *Southeastern Industrial Loan Company* case. [10 SEC 617 (1941)] The record showed that the registrant was part of a holding company system with which the accountant was actively associated. The accountant performed various acts for the system, such as arranging for renewal notes, extending maturity and payments, arranging for refinancing, insurance and printing of stationery, passbooks and stock certificates, and distributing funds to various subsidiaries in payment for loans. The accountant borrowed money from some of the system companies. His office rent was paid by one of the system companies. He was auditor for one company in the system and vice president and director of the entire system. He admitted that at no time did he confirm amounts due from borrowers; such confirmation would be a "terribly big job," outside the scope of an auditor's work. He acted as accommodation payee on certain notes. He participated in the affairs of certain large borrowers as a representative of the system. The Commission concluded:

> From this mass of facts, only one conclusion is possible: . . . the certified public accountant was not independent as to the registrant or as to any other person or company connected directly or indirectly with the Southeastern system. The registrant was but a segment of the system with which [the accountant] was actively associated. His close identity with the financial destinies and his personal concern with the managerial policies of the system and its distressed customers were in conflict with the duties of an independent accountant.

In this case there were a number of factors all of which were pertinent to consideration of the accountant's independence. If, however, the only criticism of the accountant had been that he arranged for the printing of his client's stationery requirements, it is doubtful that the accountant's independence would have been an issue in the consideration of the case.

A number of SEC interpretations and rulings relating to accountant's independence[13] follow.

Lack of Independence as Basis for Disciplinary Proceedings.— The matter of disciplinary proceedings instituted against accountants under the SEC's Rules of Practice is discussed in Chapter **27**. A number of these proceedings were based on the fact that, in the SEC's opinion, the accountants' examinations did not conform with generally accepted auditing standards. The question of what constitutes an adequate examination tends to merge with the question of independence. If the accountant lacks independence, it is a simple matter for him to cut corners in his examination.

---

[13] The source of most, but not all, of this information is the following: ASR No. 47 (1944); appendix to address by Donald C. Cook, then Vice Chairman of the SEC (1950); ASR No. 81 (1958); ASR No. 126 (1972).

In several of the disciplinary proceedings, the independence of the certifying accountants was a principal issue. The first of these proceedings grew out of the Commission's findings in *A. Hollander & Son, Inc.* [8 SEC 612 (1941)]. It appeared that the accountants had given an audit report to management that was materially different from that furnished to the public in the SEC filing. A false account showing a balance due the registrant from the accountant was carried on the books to help conceal market operations in the registrant's stock. It also appeared that the accountant knew of the false account and requested and received indemnification against liability from the principal stockholder of the registrant. The accountant permitted the account to be continued for a year following his protests. The accountants, according to the SEC, were guilty of concealing a joint venture in which the company lost approximately $150,000. Two members of the accounting firm and their wives owned substantial amounts of the registrant's stock, the amounts varying from one-half of 1 per cent to 9 per cent of their combined net worth during a four-year period when the stock was held. The management of the registrant and the accountants made substantial loans to each other.

The Commission also found that management and the accountants were fellow members of various civic, fraternal, and social organizations, were associated in numerous charity drives, and joined together in signing a bond to secure a mortgage on a clubhouse. Various personal services were performed by the accounting firm for management in their individual capacities, preparing their personal income tax returns, and auditing the books and preparing financial statements of real estate and security holdings of management. These factors, however, the SEC said, did not necessarily indicate a lack of independence.

The other factors did have a bearing on the question of the accountant's independence. The Commission held that neither the firm nor the individual partners involved were independent with respect to the financial statements filed by A. Hollander & Son, Inc. The accounting firm and a partner of the firm were subsequently suspended for three months from the privilege of appearing or practicing before the SEC. [Release No. 34–3073 (1941)].

In the second disciplinary proceeding involving accountant's independence, the record showed that over a period of 21 months the corporation's funds were used to carry on a trading account, in the name of the accountant, in its own securities. The SEC found that the accountant, with the knowledge of only two or three members of the registrant's staff, had allowed his name to be used in a trading account in the securities of the registrant and either approved or acquiesced in procedures which effectively concealed the existence of such account. The concealment was effected by means of a complicated series of transactions which, said SEC, illustrate how closely identified the accountant was with the management. In addition, the record showed that the accountant had bought shares of his client on seven different occasions and had never sold any stock. When he terminated his services as accountant, he owned 554 shares of its stock, purchased at a total cost of $10,754. This latter amount was, on the basis of his own figures, equivalent to about 8 per cent of the net worth of himself and his immediate family. The SEC ruled that the accountant was not independent and suspended for sixty days his right to practice before the Commission. [ASR No. 28 (1942) ; also 10 SEC 982 (1942)].

In the third disciplinary proceeding it was found that the resident partner in charge of one of the offices of the accounting firm conducted an audit and certified a statement valuing a leasehold at $100,000, which had been acquired for $15,000 and had been assessed at $5,250. A note to the balance sheet stated that the value of the leasehold was purely arbitrary and had been acquired at a cost which "exceeded $2,000." The balance sheet certified by the firm included various items which had not been verified. The resident partner of the accounting firm actively participated in the promotion of the registrant. Although the audit certificate stated that the accountants had reviewed the accounting system and procedures of the company, made an audit of the transactions, examined or tested accounting records, and made an examination in accordance with generally accepted auditing standards, it appeared that, in fact, the company had no books of account and no accounting system and had no accounting records other than a few vouchers and rough notes in the accountants' own files. The Commission found that the certification had not been prepared by an independent accountant and disciplined both the firm and the resident partner who actually made the audit. [ASR No. 68 (1949)].

In the fourth disciplinary proceeding the SEC said that the certifying accountant, Mr. S, was a partner of Mr. B in the accounting firm of B & S. Mr. B was the principal promoter, president, treasurer, director, and owner of the majority of the voting stock of the Motel Corporation of Italy, whose address was the same as that of the accounting firm. Mr. B caused the Motel company to file a registration statement under the 1933 Act, covering a proposed public issue of securities aggregating $1,000,000. The registration statement included the company's balance sheet, which was certified by Mr. S as a CPA. The registration statement was later withdrawn after the company had been advised that it failed to meet the requirements of the Act.

The SEC cited other cases in which it had held that the lack of independence of a partner in a public accounting firm affects the partnership and every other partner. Mr. B was admittedly not independent for purposes of SEC certification, and this made Mr. S equally lacking in the requisite independent capacity.

Knowing that he was not independent, Mr. B discussed the selection of Mr. S with his attorney, who helped prepare the registration statement and who was also secretary and a director of the registrant and signed the registration statement. The attorney had advised Mr. B that Mr. S was independent within the intent of the registration requirements. "In our opinion," the SEC said, "any common sense interpretation of independence would have led to the conclusion that the partner of the promoter and controlling stockholder of an enterprise is not independent with respect to the enterprise. . . ." The SEC concluded that Messrs. B and S had engaged in improper professional conduct, and suspended them temporarily from practice before the Commission. [ASR No. 82 (1959) ; see also ASR No. 87 (1961) reinstating one of the accountants].

Several other releases of the SEC in the Accounting Series also involved the independence of auditors in disciplinary proceedings. See, for example, the discussion of Release Nos. 91, 92, 97, and 108 in Chapter **27**.

It should be remembered, however, that the matter of independence tends to merge with the auditor's obligation to do a proper job. If an auditor has omitted a generally recognized procedure, has failed to ask perfectly obvious questions, has not insisted on disclosing important facts relating to the financial position or operating results of the enterprise being audited, it seems perfectly clear that such an auditor lacks independence even though he does not have a financial interest in the enterprise, is not an officer, director, or employee, and has no other relationship with the company which would preclude him from acting as its independent auditor.

This is not to suggest that every incompetent auditor is also lacking in independence. On the other hand, some of the SEC's reports on inadequate examinations do not charge the auditor with a lack of independence in precisely those words. But a reading of some of these cases leads to the conclusion that, in some of them, the auditor not only failed to do a proper job, but he was also completely lacking in independence.

Conscious Falsification of the Facts.—The most convincing demonstration of lack of independence occurs when the accountant deliberately falsifies the facts. In that situation there is no need for considering whether the accountant has an interest in or connection with a company which might conceivably color his opinion of the company's financial statements. In *American Terminals and Transit Company* [1 SEC 707 (1936)] it was shown that the accountant had knowingly falsified the amount of the registrant's cash and accounts receivable so as to show an amount for cash in the balance sheet when actually there was an overdraft. The Commission said:

. . . Not every error in a financial statement can be construed as reflecting a lack of independence on the part of the accountant who set it up. In some cases, an accountant is justified in accepting as facts certain types of information furnished him by others, and a false item on a financial statement may thus be due not to the fault of the accountant but of the person who furnished him with the information. Again, even should an accountant adopt a technique frowned on by all existing professional authority, this might indicate no more than incompetence. *But where the accountant has consciously falsified the facts, as here, an inference of actual absence of independence would seem to be justified. He who, as a result of connivance with, or loyalty or subservience to his client, purposely or recklessly misrepresents the facts, cannot be said to qualify as an "independent" expert.* Protection of investors in these situations requires not only that these fiduciaries be free of the entangling alliances which relational and contractual connections with registrants frequently engender, but also that they approach their task with complete objectivity—critical of the practices and procedures of registrants, and unwilling to aid and abet in making statements which the facts do not warrant. (Emphasis added.)

Financial Interest in Client.—Rule 2–01(b) of Regulation S–X provides that SEC will not consider an accountant independent with respect to any person, or any affiliate thereof, in whom he has any direct financial interest, or any material indirect financial interest. The holding of a financial interest in the company whose statements he certifies—no matter how small the interest—in general disqualifies the accountant. See also the discussion on page **26·20** regarding "substantial interest" in relation to Form S–1.

There are implications in the phrase "any financial interest" which are not intended. Inasmuch as the independent public accountant renders service for a fee, it might be argued that he has a "financial interest" in his client. A long series of informal rulings make it clear, however, that a financial interest involves something other than the ordinary and usual professional relationship of an accountant and his client.

When the fees for an audit or other professional service remain unpaid over an extended period of time and become material in relation to the current audit fee, it may raise questions concerning the accountant's independence because he appears to have a financial interest in his client. The SEC said that while no precise rules can be set forth, normally the fees for the prior year's audit should be paid prior to the commencement of the current engagement. When such unpaid fees become material, the accountant can not be considered independent because he may appear to have a direct interest in the results of operations of the company for the period to be audited. [ASR No. 126 (1972).]

An accountant may acquire a financial interest in a company that is no longer his client. Suppose, for example, that Accountant A examined the financial statements of a company for Years 1, 2, and 3, and that during these years he complied with all requirements as to independence. Another accountant examined Years 4 and 5. In Year 5, when the company was no longer his client, Accountant A bought some of the company's stock. In Year 6 the company files a registration statement and asks Accountant A to report upon the results of operations during Years 1, 2, and 3. Does the fact that Accountant A now has an interest in the company disqualify him from reporting on Years 1, 2, and 3?

The SEC has expressed itself clearly on this point:

> Situations arise in which it is not necessary to make a finding of lack of independence even though an accountant may have held a financial interest during the period of report but at a time when his independence was not a factor. For example, an accountant may be called upon to furnish a certificate in a registration statement for a former client in whom he now has a financial interest but with whom he maintained an independent relationship during the period covered by the audit and up to the date he issued his original certificate. Another example is where an accountant held stock in a company for which he had never had an engagement but sold it upon accepting an engagement. In these and other situations where it is clear from the facts that the independent status of the accountant is not prejudiced by a particular relationship, we will upon request advise the accountant that no action will be taken because of this relationship. [ASR No. 79 (1958)].

A partner of an accounting firm who held shares of a registrant's stock was elected a director of the registrant. Eight days later he was notified of his firm's appointment as accountants for the current year. He never attended any meetings of the board of directors and did not participate in the selection of his firm. Upon being notified of the appointment of his firm as accountants, he immediately resigned his directorship and sold his stock. The SEC said it would take "no action" to challenge his firm's independence.

In a case with which the author is familiar, A & B, a firm of certified public accountants, examined and reported upon the financial statements of XYZ Corporation for the Years 1, 2, and 3. There was no question about the independence of the accounting firm or its partners. In Year 4, B (a partner in the accounting firm) became a director of XYZ Corporation and an officer of one of its principal subsidiaries and acquired a substantial financial interest in XYZ. Another firm of accountants examined and reported upon the consolidated financial statements of XYZ Corporation and subsidiaries for the Year 4. In Year 5, XYZ Corporation filed a registration statement under the 1933 Act. Question was raised whether A & B could certify for the Years 1, 2, and 3 in view of the altered status of B. SEC ruled that A & B could certify those years as independent accountants and demanded only that their certificate be dated not later than their original certificate covering the Year 3.

An accountant took an option for shares of his client's common stock in settlement of his fee. The option subsequently appreciated in value. The question of independence arose in connection with a proposed merger and application for listing on an exchange. The SEC ruled that the accountant was not independent with respect to his client.

After a registration statement had become effective, the partners and staff members of an accounting firm (who had certified the financial statements in the registration statement) acquired shares of stock of the registrant. They were denied the privilege of certifying subsequent financial statements to be included in a post-effective amendment to the registration statement.

After the issuance of an offering circular, some partners of an accounting firm which had certified the financial statements acquired shares of the company. In connection with a subsequent application for listing, the SEC advised the registrant that the accountants had lost their independent status with respect to the registrant.

Accounting Firm A was considering a merger with Accounting Firm B, one of whose partners owned stock in a client of Firm A. The partner proposed to put the stock in an irrevocable trust for the benefit of his children and controlled by two unassociated trustees. The SEC held that the independence of the merged firms would be adversely affected if the shares were not sold. Putting the shares in an irrevocable trust would not be sufficient.

A partner in an accounting firm which certified financial statements of a registrant owned 11,000 shares of the registrant. In an apparent effort to avoid conflict, an amended financial statement was filed, which was prepared by an employee of the accountant and certified jointly by the employee of the accounting firm and the accounting firm. The employee received from the registrant a cash payment for his services and had no other interest in the registrant. The Commission held:

> The purpose and intent of [the rule requiring accountants to be independent] would be defeated and evaded if [the accountant] is to be disqualified by its provisions but his partner or employee is not. It must be concluded that the amended balance sheets are not certified by independent accountants . . . [*Rickard Ramore Gold Mines, Ltd.,* 2 SEC 377 (1937)].

An accountant had for some time endeavored to persuade a department store that was his client to add a new department to its business. The registrant finally agreed to set up the department provided the accountant would finance the cost thereof. The accountant advanced the necessary funds and the department proved successful. The new department contributed less than 5 per cent of the total revenues of the registrant. The SEC held that the accountant could not be considered independent for the purpose of certifying the financial statements of the registrant.

An accounting firm had rendered services to a registrant for which the registrant had not been able to pay. To guarantee payment of the account, the registrant had pledged shares of its own stock. In addition, it had given the accountants an option to purchase the pledged securities at the market price existing at the date the option was given. The Commission ruled that the accounting firm could no longer be considered independent for the purpose of certifying the financial statements of the registrant.

Recent operations of a company that was a client of an accounting firm have not been profitable. In order to improve its current working capital ratio, the company invited its unsecured creditors to extend their settlement dates and subordinate 'the amounts owing to them in exchange for which they would receive the first proceeds from a proposed offering of its securities. The accounting firm's fee was one of the debts to be subordinated. The SEC ruled that if the accounting firm subordinated the amount due to it, its independence would be adversely affected.

In the year of a proposed financing by a registrant, an accountant acquired about 1 per cent of the outstanding shares of capital stock of the registrant for an amount which represented less than 5 per cent of his net worth. After the proposed financing, the shares held by the accountant would have a market value of 10 per cent of his net worth. The accountant had audited the accounts of the registrant for several years prior to the acquisition of the stock. The SEC ruled the accountant could not be considered independent for the purpose of certifying financial statements of the registrant for the year in which the stock was acquired *or for the two immediately preceding years.* It was also held that the sale of the stock after the close of the latest fiscal year for which statements are required to be filed would not remedy the situation.

The preceding case constrasts with one reported by the SEC in ASR No. 81 (1958). An accounting firm and the individual practitioner who preceded it had audited the financial statements of a proposed registrant since 1949. At various times between 1954 and 1957, a partner and an employee on the audit each acquired small amounts of issues of debenture bonds and subordinated notes. The securities held by these persons were redeemed by the company in August, 1957, prior to certification of financial statements to be used in a proposed registration statement. The SEC took "no action" in this case, meaning that there was no finding of a lack of independence on the part of the accountants.

Company A proposed filing a registration statement for a securities issue, part of the proceeds of which was to be used to acquire the assets of Company B. The financial statements of Company B were required to be included in A's registration statement together with a certificate of B's auditors. The certificate of the accountants for Company B could not be accepted for inclusion in the registration statement because a partner of the firm owned stock of his client, Company B.

An accountant who certified the financial statements of a registrant was appointed treasurer of the registrant. The accountant therefore could not be considered independent for the purpose of certifying the financial statements of the registrant filed with the Commission. The SEC ruled further that the accountant could not be considered independent for the purpose of certifying the financial statements of another company registered with the

Commission, the outstanding shares of which were held in trust by officers of the registrant for the shareholders of the registrant.

A member of a firm of certifying accountants was a director of a registrant, owned stock in the registrant, and was one of the trustees under a testamentary trust which controlled a substantial portion of the stock of the registrant. Inquiry was made as to whether the accounting firm could certify the financial statements of the proposed registrant if the member resigned as director of the corporation, or failing this, whether one of the duly qualified members of the firm could certify if the designation of the accounting firm as accountants for the corporation was canceled. The SEC concluded that the accounting firm of which the director was a member and each of the members thereof could not be considered independent for the purpose of certifying the financial statements of the registrant even though the member of the firm resigned his directorship and the accounting firm was not designated accountants for the corporation.

A partner in an accounting firm loaned $600,000 to a former officer of a company which held a significant interest in the registrant. This loan was secured by substantial blocks of stock of the registrant and of an affiliate of the registrant together with options to purchase the shares pledged. The accounting firm of which this partner was a member withdrew from the audit of the registrant. Subsequently, question arose as to whether the accounting firm could certify to financial statements to be filed with the Commission by a subsidiary of the registrant. The SEC ruled that the accounting firm which was not independent with respect to a parent corporation could not be considered independent with respect to its subsidiary.

A partner in an accounting firm owned an undivided one-third interest in a block of a corporation's stock amounting to approximately 70 per cent of the stock outstanding. The accountant was also an officer-director of the corporation. The accountant's firm did not audit the accounts of the corporation. The block of stock was sold to a registrant, a client of the accountant's firm. The accountant resigned as officer-director of the corporation and the corporation was merged with the registrant. The SEC held that the accountant could not be considered independent for the purpose of certifying the financial statements of the registrant.

After the close of the fiscal year October 31, 1946, corporation A distributed most of the shares of its subsidiary to its shareholders and retained 50,000 shares to use in lieu of cash to discharge some of its obligations. On November 29, 1946, 5,642 shares were given the accounting firm which audited A's statements as part payment for fees due it. On December 8, 1947, these shares were sold. Inquiry was made as to whether the accountant could certify financial statements of A for the fiscal year ending October 31,

1947. The Commission's decision was favorable to the accountants.

The SEC does not recognize a difference between a corporation and a registered investment company which would permit the ownership of shares in the latter by the accountant certifying its financial statements. On the other hand, if accountant A owned a few shares of a diversified mutual fund which was not a client and which included in its portfolio shares of Corportation X for which A was the certifying accountant, this would not necessarily disqualify A from serving as the accountant for X.

A partner in an accounting firm is a member of an investment club. The club owns stock in a company which is a client of the accounting firm. Neither the number nor the value of the shares purchased is material to the club or the company. The SEC said that the accounting firm's independence would be adversely affected as a result of the partner's interest in the investment club. In this regard, an investment club does not stand on the same footing as a mutual fund because the former is comprised of relatively few members each of whom plays an active part in the selection of investments.

The following interpretations of the independence rule were given to an accounting firm which submitted two hypothetical situations:

(a) Company A proposed to file a registration statement and merge with or acquire Company X, which had been entirely independent of Company A. Financial statements of each company certified by different accounting firms were to be included in the registration statement.

In this situation, if partners of the firm of accountants for X had an interest in A, that accounting firm could be considered independent for the purpose of certifying the statements of X for inclusion in A's registration statement. This conclusion assumes that A's shares are widely held and the partners' interest is similar to any public investor's. A different conclusion would be indicated if the partners of the firm were in a position to influence the action of A.

If X were to continue as a subsidiary of A, the accounting firm would not be considered independent for subsequent audits unless the partners of the firm promptly disposed of their financial interest in A.

(b) In a situation similar to that described above, the accounting firm which had certified the statements of A generally would have no knowledge of the investments of its partners in non-client corporations such as X. In some large national accounting firms the determination of such holdings can be a time-consuming and burdensome task. Under these circumstances Item 24 of the requirements of a registration statement under the 1933 Act (dealing with relationships between registrant and experts whose opinions are included in the registration statement) may be answered in the negative with a disclaimer of knowledge as to whether or not the certifying accountants of A had any interest in X.

Registrants A and B each own 50 per cent of the outstanding stock of Company C, but are otherwise not related. The accounting firm which audits A would not be disqualified because of ownership of a small number of shares of stock of B. However, the accounting firm which audits C would not be considered independent if any of its partners had an interest in either A or B.

Partners in an accounting firm owned stock in a company in which a substantial minority interest was owned by a client. Both companies were large and their securities were listed on a national securities exchange. The SEC said no question would be raised regarding the accounting firm's independence with respect to its client.

Financial Interest Held by Accountant's Wife.—In general the SEC's decisions involving accountants' independence make no distinction between the financial interests held by accountants and financial interests held by their wives. A few of such rulings are presented below.

Using their own funds, the wives of partners in an accounting firm purchased stock in a client of the firm immediately prior to registration by the client with the SEC. The SEC held that this disqualified the accounting firm from certifying for SEC filing purposes.

The wives of partners in an accounting firm purchased about one-half of 1 per cent of the outstanding capital stock of a registrant at regular market prices and the funds so invested represented less than 5 per cent of the combined wealth of the partners and wives involved. These shares were held at the time of registration with the Commission. The SEC held that the accounting firm of which these partners were members could not be considered independent for the purpose of certifying financial statements of the registrant filed with the Commission. The Commission ruled also that the purchase and sale of a material amount of the registrant's stock by the wives of the partners of the certifying accounting firm during a period immediately prior to registration would adversely affect, if not destroy, the accounting firm's independence. "Speculation of this kind in a registrant's stock is incompatible with the maintenance of an objective and impartial viewpoint which is essential to an independent status."

The wife of an accountant held shares of stock in a proposed registrant. The stock had originally been received by the accountant in settlement of his audit fee. The SEC ruled that the accountant's certificate was not acceptable.

An accounting firm was held to be not independent because the wife of a partner owned stock in the registrant which had been acquired out of community earnings, and another accounting firm was engaged to audit the years in question. The wife disposed of the stock, and the firm was told that no objection would be raised to their certifying in subsequent years.

The wife of an accountant had a 47½ per cent interest in one of the three principal underwriters of a proposed issue by the registrant. The SEC took the position that the accountant could not be considered independent for the purpose of certifying financial statements of the registrant.

An accountant's wife held a trust certificate issued by an investment trust on which had been paid an amount equal to 3 per cent of the combined personal fortunes of the accountant and his wife. The withdrawal value of the trust certificate was less than $1,000 and was about 1½ per cent of their personal fortunes. The accountant certified the financial statements of the investment trust as well as the financial statements of the corporation that sponsored the trust. The sponsor had no equity in the assets of the trust, but derived virtually all of its income from its activities as sponsor. The SEC ruled that the accountant could not be considered independent with respect to the investment trust. The Commission also declared that the facts given tended to indicate that the accountant was not independent with respect to the sponsoring corporation.

Financial Interest Held by Accountant's Employee.—The SEC held that a registration statement was false and misleading in representing that the financial statements were certified by independent accountants where the employee of the accounting firm who was in charge of the audit of the registrant's books had purchased stock of the registrant for himself or members of his family. [*Sports Arenas (Delaware) Inc.,* 39 SEC 463 (1959)]

Financial Interest Acquired as Result of Client's Bankruptcy or Reorganization.—The SEC has made several unpublished rulings involving the acquisition by an independent accountant of a financial interest in his client as the result of the client's bankruptcy or reorganization. Two of these rulings have come to the author's attention.

The cases were alike in that, in each case, the accountant's client was in bankruptcy proceedings and the accountant was a creditor as the result of services furnished prior to the bankruptcy. In each case, pursuant to a plan of arrangement or reorganization under Chapter XI of the Bankruptcy Act, the indebtedness was to be settled by the issuance of equity securities of the debtor corporation—convertible preferred stock in one case, common stock in the other. Before accepting the securities, the accountants inquired of the SEC in order to learn whether the acceptance of the securities would have an adverse effect on the accountant's independence.

In each case, the accountant was informed that his independence would not be adversely affected by the acceptance of the securities in settlement of his claim provided that the accountant disposed of the securities as promptly as feasible either by sale or gift to a third party.

Connection with Company in Managerial or Other Capacities.— Rule 2–01 of Regulation S–X provides that an accountant will not be considered independent with respect to any person, or any affiliate thereof, with whom he is, or was, during the period of report, connected as a promoter, underwriter, voting trustee, director, officer, or employee. See, however, the discussion on page **26·29** concerning an accountant who was independent but then became a director of his client.

If a partner in an accounting firm serves on the board of directors of a company but does not participate in any way in his firm's audit of the company, would the firm be disqualified for purposes of an SEC filing? The SEC has taken the position that the accounting firm in these circumstances could not be considered independent for the purpose of certifying the registrant's financial statements.

In a slight variation of the foregoing situation, a partner in the accounting firm was serving as a member of a registrant's board of directors. Another partner in the same accounting firm conducted the audit of the registrant and certified the financial statements *in his own name,* not in the firm name. The SEC held that the certifying accountant could not be considered independent.

In another case a partner in an accounting firm had served on the board of directors of a registrant but had resigned from that position prior to the close of the most recent fiscal year. This accountant had not participated in any way in the accounting firm's audits of the registrant. The Commission ruled that the accounting firm could not be considered independent for any period during which a partner of the firm was a director of the registrant.

From the time of organization of a proposed registrant in November, 1952, until July, 1954, an accountant served the company as assistant treasurer, comptroller, and director with the responsibility of keeping the accounts of the company, and also acted as co-signer of checks. He also owned shares of the company's stock. In July 1954 arrangements were made for an issue of securities. The accountant severed his affiliation with the company as officer and director and made a gift of his shares of stock to his daughter. Nonetheless, the SEC held that his certificate was not acceptable.

The board of directors of a registrant had established an operating committee in which had been vested all powers necessary and appropriate to the supervision of the management of the business. It was intended that the principal duty of the committee would be the *making of recommendations to the board of directors.* The committee consisted of two members of the board of directors and a member of the accounting firm that regularly certified the financial statements of the registrant. The SEC held that neither the individual accountant nor his firm could be considered independent.

Company A owned a small percentage of the stock of a sales company that sold some of the products of Company A. The accountant who certified the financial statements of Company A was the treasurer and one of the stockholders of the sales company. The SEC ruled that if the shares held by Company A and the nature of the sales relationship were such as to give Company A a significant element of indirect control over the sales company, the accountant could not be considered independent for the purpose of certifying Company A's financial statements.

An accountant was co-executor of an estate which held approximately 15% of the stock of a registrant. He had audited the registrant's accounts for several years prior to the latest fiscal year. Another accountant had been engaged to certify the financial statements of the latest year for inclusion in a registration statement. The estate was being terminated and the registrant proposed engaging the accountant as auditor for subsequent years. The SEC said it would not challenge the accountant's independence.

A partner of an accounting firm acted as one of three executors of the will of a principal officer of a registrant and as one of three trustees of a trust established under the will. The principal asset of the trust was a substantial proportion of the voting stock of the registrant. The SEC held that the accounting firm was not independent in relation to the registrant.

Financial statements for the first two years of the three-year period required to be included in a registration statement had been certified by an individual practitioner who gave up his practice to become an executive of the registrant. The SEC held that his certificate was not acceptable.

An accountant certifying the financial statements of a broker-dealer was a co-signer on the broker's indemnity bond. The SEC ruled that this disqualified the accountant.

Company A acquired Company B in January, 1955. Financial statements of A for years ended June 30, 1954, and prior, and financial statements of B for the year ended July 31, 1952, had been certified by accounting firm X. Financial statements of both companies for subsequent years were certified by accounting firm Y. After completion of the last audits of the respective companies by X, a partner of that firm became a director of each company. The statements certified by X were accepted for inclusion in a registration statement of A because the accountants were independent at the time of their certification and more recent audits were made by Y.

One of two partners of an accounting firm formed in February, 1955, and dissolved in February, 1956, became secretary-treasurer of a company in July, 1955. He retained no interest in the partnership. The accounting practice was continued by the other partner, who was engaged to make a first audit of the company in June, 1956. The SEC said "no action" would be taken to challenge the accountant's independence in relation to the company.

In the following case the accountant's disqualification arose from the connection of an employee with a registrant. A senior staff member of an accounting firm was appointed controller of a registrant as successor to a controller who had entered the United States armed forces. This employee, who had formerly been in charge of the audit of the registrant, remained on the staff of the accounting firm but relinquished all responsibility for the audit of the registrant and did no work for the accounting firm in connection therewith. The SEC held that the accounting firm could not be considered independent for the purpose of certifying the financial statements of this registrant. The SEC also ruled in this case that the accounting firm could not be considered independent for the purpose of certifying the financial statements of the registrant if the senior staff member were to leave the employ of the accounting firm and be paid by the registrant, subject to the understanding among the several parties that upon the termination of the war emergency he would return to the staff of the accounting firm.

A staff member of an accounting firm who had prepared financial statements for a mining company in the development stage and had participated in the audit was offered a position as an officer of the company prior to the filing of a registration statement. The SEC ruled that acceptance of the position by the staff member would not of itself destroy the independence of the accounting firm in connection with the proposed registration statement.

A partner in an accounting firm had previously been an accountant on the staff of another accounting firm which certified the financial statements of a registrant. While with that firm, the accountant was in charge of the audit of the registrant for 1940 and 1941. On November 1, 1942, the accountant became treasurer of the registrant. He held this position until November 15, 1943. On or about that date, the accountant left the employ of the registrant and organized his own firm which audited the registrant's accounts for 1944. Inquiry was made as to whether in statements to be filed with the Commission the accounting firm of which the former treasurer of the registrant was a partner could certify to the financial statements of the registrant for 1945 and 1944 and refer to the audit made in 1943 by the independent firm, which it was willing to accept. The SEC decided that the accounting firm could not be considered independent with respect to the registrant for the purpose of certifying financial statements to be filed with the Commission.

A partner of an accounting firm was a director and member of the executive committee of a company for six years. In the year following his resignation, the firm was engaged to certify the company's financial statements, but the audit did not cover any of the time during which the accountant served as a director. The SEC said no question would be raised regarding the firm's independence.

From 1940 to September, 1946, a partner in an accounting firm was a director of a business corporation and during part of that time served as a member of its executive committee. Inquiry was made of the SEC as to whether the accounting firm was qualified to certify the financial statements of the corporation for the year 1947. The Commission's decision was favorable to the accountant but conditional. The Commission ruled that since the audit did not cover any of the time during which the accountant served as a director, no question would be raised with respect to the certification. However, since the independence of the accountant was a matter of fact, this opinion might be altered if it should develop that the 1947 audit was improperly influenced by the accountant's background of directorship or if any significant accounting policies formulated prior to 1946 persisted beyond that year.

An accountant certified financial statements used in a registration statement for the period ended December 31, 1947. His certificate was dated March 17, 1948. Because of the resignation of the general manager of the company on May 7, 1948, and the general knowledge possessed by the accountant of the company's activities, he was engaged by the directors to reorganize the office and reallocate the duties of the executive personnel. The SEC was asked whether the accountant was qualified to certify the financial statements used in the registration statement for the purpose of a post-effective amendment dated June 30, 1948. Here also the ruling was favorable to the accountant. The Commission said that the accountant could be considered independent with respect to the financial statements for the period ending December 31, 1947.

In addition to auditing the accounts of a hotel, an accounting firm provided the hotel with the services of a resident auditor and with a food controller who had no control over policies, personnel, or records and was responsible only for gathering statistical data. Both remained in the employ of the accounting firm. The SEC held that the accounting firm could not be considered independent with respect to the hotel for the purposes of certifying financial statements to be filed with the Commission.

In another case involving a hotel, however, the hotel had requested an accounting firm to assign to the hotel one of their senior accountants, experienced in hotel auditing, to make a continuous audit of transactions from day to day. The individual assigned to this work was not to administer the accounting office or to sign checks of the company, and he was not required to make any entries in the books of account. The hotel had on its staff another person with the title of chief accountant whose duty it was to administer the accounting office and to maintain the books of account. Inquiry was made as to whether the accounting firm would be qualified to certify the financial statements filed by the hotel company with the Commission. The SEC ruled that under all the circumstances the accounting firm could be considered independent.

An accounting firm is paid a retainer for consultation services and for making studies and investigations for a hotel company. In this case also the SEC ruled that the accounting firm may be considered independent.

From September, 1943, until January 31, 1946, a partner in an accounting firm was at all times available for conferences with the registrant on accounting matters. The corporation's accounting procedures were subject to the supervision of the partner acting in the capacity of quasi-controller during part of 1944, part of 1946, and all of 1945. The Commission concluded that the accounting firm of which the accountant was a partner could not be considered independent for the fiscal years ended March 31, 1944, 1945, or 1946.

An accountant was elected director of a company in which his client held a 30 per cent common stock interest. He submitted his resignation immediately after he was notified of his election. Inquiry was made of the SEC as to whether the accountant could withdraw his resignation and, if not, whether his election disqualified him for any period of time. The Commission held that if the client and the company to which the accountant was elected a director were "affiliated" within the meaning of that term as defined in the General Rules and Regulations under the Securities Act of 1933, service as a director of either company would disqualify the accountant from certifying financial statements to be filed with the Commission. With respect to the interval of time during which the accountant served as a director, no question was raised, since it was indicated that the accountant resigned as soon as he was notified of his election and did not participate in a directors' meeting or act in that capacity.

Original Work on Accounting Records.—The SEC has stressed the importance of separating the functions of record-keeping and independent auditing. In the Commission's view, an accountant may not hold himself out as independent in respect of financial statements prepared from accounting records which he has kept. In *Interstate Hosiery Mills*, for example, an employee of the certifying accountants had taken upon himself the function of bookkeeping as well as auditing. Condemning this procedure, the SEC said that an audit should be a check by an outsider of original work done by the client's employees. "If an accountant is permitted to do original work, the whole purpose of the audit is lost." [4 SEC 717 (1939)].

In another case the accounting firm that certified the financial statements of a particular registrant had in the past followed the practice of drawing up the monthly journal records of the company from underlying documents that had been prepared by the registrant's staff. These journal records were posted to the appropriate ledgers by the certifying accountants. At the end of the year the audit engagement was undertaken by personnel of the certifying accountant who were not connected with the original recording of the accounting data. The Commission ruled that the accounting firm could not be considered independent for the purpose of certifying the financial statements of this registrant.

A variation of the above involved a small loan company that kept its accounting records on a cash basis. The primary records of the company consisted of daily cash reports that were prepared by the cashier and signed by the manager. The accountant who certified the financial statements of this company took no part in the preparation of these basic records. However, he did audit these cash reports each month and then proceeded to enter the totals in a summary record which he in turn posted to the general ledger. The certifying accountant also made adjusting journal entries each month with respect to insurance, taxes, depreciation, and similar items. The company was small and did not require the services of a full-time bookkeeper. The certifying accountant devoted about one day a month to the clerical or bookkeeping tasks described above. The Commission held that the accountant could not be considered independent for the purpose of certifying the financial statements of this registrant.

Keeping books even on a temporary basis may raise a question as to the accountant's independence. In one case, members of a firm of certifying accountants set up a registrant's books and maintained them for about six months until the registrant engaged a bookkeeper. The SEC ruled that the accounting firm could not be considered independent with respect to the registrant for the purpose of certifying its financial statements for the year in which the accountants kept the books.

Even where the accountant's work on the records is exceedingly limited, it may disqualify him for purposes of an SEC filing. An accountant certified the financial statements of a registrant which were filed with the Commission. Prior to certification, the accountant posted to the general ledger entries covering a month's transactions and made all the closing entries. The SEC ruled that the accountant could not be considered independent for the purpose of certifying financial statements filed by the registrant.

On the other hand, in ASR No. 81 (1958) the SEC described three cases in which accountants did bookkeeping work but there was no question raised about their independence:

A. In addition to certifying the financial statements of a registrant, the accountant reviewed certain transactions of prior years, prepared fixed asset subsidiary ledgers, prepared the annual report to the state of incorporation, made recommendations for adjustments, and when consulted gave his professional opinion on the accounting treatment of particular transactions.

B. Due to the unexpected resignation of registrant's comptroller at the end of the year, the accountant was called upon to provide assistance in closing the books for the year. The work performed did not involve making decisions on a managerial level.

C. Following the death of the registrant's bookkeeper, an accounting firm posted the general ledger from the books of original entry and prepared periodic financial statements for the last eight months of the fiscal year. Registrant's bookkeeping staff had full charge of accounting journals and subsidiary ledgers and recorded all transactions. Financial statements certified by the accounting firm were accepted by the SEC, but the accountants were advised to discontinue the bookkeeping services immediately.

As B and C above indicate, the SEC has made exceptions in emergency situations to its general rule outlawing bookkeeping services by independent accountants. A former Chief Accountant of the SEC said, however, that the Commission's experience shows that continuous bookkeeping service may cause the accountant to become too closely identified, even in his own thinking, with the management.[14]

The bookkeeper-cashier of a registrant entered the armed forces, and a junior accountant on the staff of the accounting firm which audited the accounts of the registrant was loaned to the registrant one day a month to perform certain bookkeeping tasks. The following represented the maximum work done in any one month by the junior accountant. He footed the books of original entry, posted to the general ledger, took off trial balances, reconciled bank statements, occasionally made entries in the blotters from company records of purchases and sales, made journal entries for regular monthly accruals, prepared journal entries correcting errors and omissions made by company employees, and prepared and entered closing journal entries at the end of the year at the direction of the registrant. He also prepared balance sheets and profit and loss statements from book figures. The SEC ruled that the accounting firm of which this junior accountant was a member could not be considered independent with respect to the registrant.

In a proceeding under the 1933 Act, the SEC questioned the status of the accountant, who was represented to be independent. The record showed, however, that, among other things, the accountant had helped maintain the company's books, had advanced a small sum of money to the company, and was therefore not independent. [*Cristina Copper Mines, Inc.,* 33 SEC 397 (1952)].

In a proceeding to revoke a broker-dealer registration, the principal complaint against the firm was in respect to a prospectus relating to an issue of securities underwritten by the firm. The Commission said:

The prospectus filed as a part of the registration . . . falsely stated that the financial statements included in the registration statement had been exam-

[14] Andrew Barr, "Accounting and Auditing Problems with Particular Reference to New Registrants with the SEC," *The New York CPA,* January, 1961, p. 30.

ined by an independent public accountant. Respondents admit, and we find, that the accountant who certified the financial statements was not in fact independent, but had served as [the issuer's] principal bookkeeper in posting the monthly journals reflecting receipts and disbursements from subsidiary records and posting the journal records to ledger accounts, with the result that his certification of the financial statements amounted merely to authentication of his own accounting procedures. [Release No. 34–6684 (1961)].

Despite the discussion above with regard to the SEC's views on the independence of accountants who do original work on accounting records, it is necessary, in the interest of completeness, to say that the SEC's bark may be worse than its bite. The fact is that the SEC has accepted the certificates of several public accountants in documents filed with it knowing that the accountants had been involved to a slight degree with the record keeping of the companies whose statements they certified.

The author is aware of several public accountants (most of them individual practitioners) who learned too late of the SEC's rules relating to record keeping by public accountants and its effect on independence. In most cases, the accountants had been posting the general ledger, or had been keeping a private ledger, or had performed some other innocuous part of the recording function, which nonetheless did literally constitute original work on accounting records. Suddenly they were faced with the fact that their clients were going public, or had to register under the 1934 Act because of having grown to the required size in terms of total assets and number of shareholders. The accountants wondered whether the SEC would reject their certificates on the ground that their involvement in the clients' record keeping made them not independent in the eyes of the Commission.

In each of the cases of this kind with which the author is familiar, the accountant who was faced with the possibility that the SEC would reject his certificate, discontinued immediately the bookkeeping activity which gave rise to the problem, and then discussed the matter with a member of the Commission's staff. In each case, the SEC representative informed the accountant that the SEC would not object to the inclusion of his certificate in the document filed with the SEC by his client.

The author wishes it to be understood that he is not being critical of the SEC's staff for accepting accountants' certificates in circumstances that appear to contravene its own rules. The author believes that the acceptance of certificates in these circumstances is a reasonable and practical solution to a problem made more difficult by the fact that the SEC's rules in this area are not widely known. Apart from the SEC position, the author is not aware of any authoritative statement that links record-keeping to a lack of audit independence.

Carman G. Blough, the SEC's first Chief Accountant and former Director of Research of the AICPA, considered the question of "Should CPAs Audit Books They Have Kept?" in his book *Practical Applications of Accounting Standards.* He said that both the committee on professional ethics and the committee on auditing procedure had studied the question extensively over a considerable period. In their reports to the AICPA Council, both committees had been in agreement that if a CPA is in fact independent and if he has performed all the auditing procedures necessary to supplement the information obtained through keeping the books, he should be entitled to express any opinion he may have formed. As to the question of whether or not the auditor should disclose in his report the fact that he kept the books, the committee on professional ethics concluded that it was a question that should be left to the judgment of the CPA in the light of the facts in each case. It was the committee's belief that disclosure was not necessary as a general rule. Mr. Blough continued:

Thus, there exists strong authoritative support for the view that the CPA is not necessarily lacking in independence simply because he has kept the books, that he is entitled to express an opinion on the financial statements if he has made a satisfactory audit, and that disclosure of the fact that he has kept the books is not necessary as a general rule.[15]

Substantially similar views have been held by others qualified to speak with authority, such as John L. Carey and William O. Doherty in their *Ethical Standards of the Accounting Profession,* and the AICPA Committee on Auditing Procedure as set forth in its Statement on Auditing Procedure No. 28.

Accountant's Use of Client's Employees in Connection with Examination.—In a stop order decision involving Precision Microwave Corporation [41 SEC 971 (1964)], the SEC commented, among other things, on the fact that the certifying accountant, Mr. K, was not independent. This conclusion was based on the fact that K, at the suggestion of the company's president and principal stockholder, had engaged Mr. S (for a fee) to assist K in making the audit. S was the office manager and accountant of one of the company's subsidiaries, and as such he maintained or supervised the maintenance of the very books and records that K was required to review in connection with his audit. The employment of S by K, said the SEC, created a relationship which was inconsistent with the complete objectivity required of an independent accountant, since S was not independent in relation to the subsidiary (his principal and continuing employer) or in relation to the parent company, the registrant—a defect which K's supervision could not remedy.

Accountant's Fee Based on Sales.—One of the earliest published decisions of the SEC involved an accountant's independence where an unusual relationship existed between the accountant and the registrant [*Cornucopia*

[15] Pp. 67–69. (AICPA, 1957).

Gold Mines, 1 SEC 364 (1936)]. In their certificate the accountants said (for some reason which is not clear to the author) that their relationship with the registrant was "the usual relationship of independent accountants to their client." The accountants had entered into a contract with the registrant by the terms of which they were to receive a fixed annual fee plus 1 per cent of the gross proceeds of sales for one year. Under the contract the accountants were to install an accounting system, make audits, and furnish office space for the use of the registrant, and an employee of the accountants was made controller of the registrant. In that capacity he signed the registration statement as principal financial and accounting officer of the registrant. As controller of the registrant he exercised the usual functions of a controller with authority over employees regarding accounting matters. The accountants' employee owned 1,760 shares of the registrant which he had purchased before the filing of the registration statement. The SEC, in its decision, said that a person in this position would be apt to approach accounting problems of the registrant as one of its officers and stockholders, not as an "independent" accountant. The Commission continued:

It would be unreasonable to suppose that he could cast aside these relationships and view the accounting problems with the objectivity of an "independent" accountant, criticizing and correcting accounting practices and methods of the corporation's own staff, for in making an audit he would in fact be partly reviewing his own work. Hence in this case he cannot rid himself of the disabilities inherent in his office of controller and in his status of stockholder of the registrant, when, as employee of [the certifying accountants], he prepares or participates in the preparation of the accounting and audit. The existence of these disabilities thus prevents him from being an "independent" accountant. By the same token [the certifying accountants] fail to acquire the necessary independence since it is through him that [the certifying accountants] are making the accounting and the audit on the basis of which the certificate is drawn. . . . Furthermore, we conclude that the contract between the registrant and [the certifying accountants] by its very nature clothed [the accountants] with a disability which prevented them, during the duration of the contract, from being an "independent" accountant as respects the registrant. . . . [The accountants] . . . had a continuing pecuniary interest in the registrant for the terms of the contract. . . . A claim to 1 per cent of the . . . sales of a mining company is a substantial and material continuing pecuniary interest. The holder of such a claim has too close an identity with the financial destinies and too intimate personal concern with the managerial policies of the enterprise to bring to bear in his accounting and auditing work the objectivity which is the essence of an "independent" accountant.

Contingent Fees.—It will be noted that although Rule 2–01 of Regulation S–X disqualifies an accountant for a variety of reasons, the rule does not refer specifically to contingent fee arrangements. In this author's opinion, it is not necessary for the rule to refer to such fee arrangements.

In the first place, the rule is probably broad enough to include contingent fees. If an accountant's remuneration is contingent upon the happening of some transaction or event, it might be argued that he has a financial interest.

Second, Rule 2–01(c) provides that in determining whether an accountant is independent, the SEC will give consideration to all relevant circumstances including evidence bearing on all relationships between the accountant and the registrant. The existence of a contingent fee arrangement is certainly a "relevant circumstance," especially since it is prohibited by Rule 1.04 of the Code of Professional Ethics of the AICPA.

Third, there have been a few SEC decisions involving accountants' independence where there were contingent fee arrangements. In *Great Dike Gold Mines, Inc.* [1 SEC 625 (1936)] the Commission was critical of the work of the certifying accountant for several reasons and pointed out that he had been employed on a contingent fee basis to prepare all the financial statements except that of expenses, receipts, and disbursements. In *Cornucopia Gold Mines* [1 SEC 364 (1936)] the Commission ruled the accountants were not independent and mentioned several factors bearing on their lack of independence, including the fact that the accountants were to receive a fixed annual fee plus 1 per cent of the gross proceeds of sales for one year. (This case is discussed on pages **26**·44–45.)

Subordination of Judgment to Client's Desires; Reliance on Unverified Information.—In *Metropolitan Personal Loan Company* [2 SEC 813 (1937)] the SEC charged that the certifying accountants were not independent because they completely subordinated their judgment as accountants to the desires of their client in setting up the financial statements. A partner in the accounting firm testified that he was not sure of an accountant's function in this respect and that he generally did what his clients requested. Although he knew and admitted that to credit a certain item to income was improper, he allowed such credit to be made "because the registrant's officers so ordered." He accepted the statements of the registrant's president as to the worth of accounts and securities with little or no investigation. He further testified that he exercised "no independent judgment" with respect to the adequacy of the reserves. Although audit reports for 1933, 1934, and 1935 advised that the reserves of $4,916, $5,881, and $5,639, respectively, were inadequate, a partner of the accounting firm testified that he thought a reserve of $1,835 in 1936 was adequate "because the registrant's officers told him so." Quoting from an earlier decision [*American Terminals and Transit Co.*, 1 SEC 701 (1936)] (see page **26**·27) the SEC held the accountants were not independent.

In *Associated Gas & Electric Company* [11 SEC 1047 (1942)] the order for hearing raised no question as to the independence of the certifying accountants, and this matter was therefore not at issue. The Commission pointed out, however, that a partner of the accounting firm testified time and again that the principle of accounting which he preferred was not followed by the company or its subsidiaries. In its decision, the Commission stated that "an accountant who consistently submerges his preferences or convictions as to accounting principles to the wishes of his client is not in fact independent."

The National Boston Montana Mines Corporation case [2 SEC 249 (1937)] involved an accountant who had certified financial statements on the basis of unverified data. The only books or records available to the accountant in preparing a balance sheet consisted of uncertified consolidated balance sheets of the registrant's predecessor and subsidiaries, the registrant's minute book, and a cash book of the predecessor. The accountant had never audited the books of the registrant's predecessor, and he had no access to the predecessor's books to verify the items going into the consolidated balance sheet. In preparing a balance sheet, the accountant relied in great part upon unverified information furnished by the chairman of the board and by other officers and employees of the registrant. He rarely verified items of expenses, even when they amounted to a sizeable part of the total receipts. The accountant himself set up certain books of account for the registrant but, with the possible exception of a cash book, the books were not posted until the time of the audit, when an attempt was made to record what had already happened, in some cases from memory. The Commission held:

> We find that these circumstances cast further grave doubt on [the accountant's] independence . . . , and in any case establish his reckless disregard of careful accounting procedure.

In *Red Bank Oil Company* [21 SEC 695 (1946)] the accounting firm that certified the registrant's financial statements in one year engaged the treasurer and bookkeeper of the registrant to do the detailed auditing work, including the preparation of working papers and draft of financial statements. In four other years the detailed auditing work was done and working papers and draft financial statements were prepared by an accountant employed by the accounting firm who did not make "that critical and objective examination which is the obligation of an independent accountant." The accountant failed to investigate transactions between the registrant and its parent and affiliates so that there was no disclosure of substantial amounts of receivables and payables which were due from or to the parent and affiliates. In four years no adequate review of the auditing work was made by the head of the certifying firm. A close relationship existed between the certifying firm and the registrant. The SEC held:

The audits for the years under consideration were inadequate and not performed in a manner consistent with generally accepted auditing standards. The issues of independence and scope of audit tend to merge since it is highly doubtful whether an accountant lacking in independence can ever exercise the objectivity, vigilance, and inquisitiveness essential to his task and required by generally accepted auditing standards. . . . Since we have found that [the accountants] were not independent and that the scope of their audit was inadequate, we further find that the financial statements have not been certified by independent public accountants.

Family Relationships.—There are an infinite variety of family relationships which can raise a question as to the independence of the certifying accountant. It is also true that while some relationships do not create a problem for the accountant, others may, as in the case, for example, of the accountant whose wife was the only child of the owner of the client company. In this situation the SEC has ruled that the accountant was not independent in relation to the company.

An individual serving as assistant treasurer and chief accountant of a registrant was the son of a partner in the accounting firm that certified the financial statements of the registrant. The son was living with his father at the time. The son served the registrant under the direction and supervision of the treasurer of the company. The SEC ruled that the accounting firm could not be considered independent for the purpose of certifying the financial statements of the registrant.

An accountant who certified the financial statements of a registrant was the father of the secretary-treasurer of the registrant. The secretary-treasurer was employed by the registrant on a half-time basis. Prior to holding such position, the secretary-treasurer was employed by the registrant as its full-time principal accounting officer. The Commission held that the accountant could not be considered independent for the purpose of certifying the financial statements of the registrant.

In a proceeding to withdraw securities from listing and registration under the 1934 Act, the SEC alleged that the company had not complied with the requirement that its financial statements be certified by an independent accountant. The Commission found that the certifying accountant was not independent with respect to the company because he was the husband of the company's secretary and treasurer. [*In the Matter of American Metal Mining Co.,* Release No. 34–3537 (1944)].

A partner of an accounting firm was the brother of the holder of fifty per cent of the stock of a proposed registrant. The accountant was also counsel for the company, and his wife held $35,000 of its preferred stock. The audit of the registrant's financial statements was to be made by a branch office of the accounting firm in which the partner had only a financial interest. The SEC ruled that the accounting firm was not independent in relation to this client.

A publicly-owned corporation headquartered in Detroit and conducting all its operations in the Detroit area was audited by the Detroit office of an international firm of accountants. The president of the corporation was the brother of one of the partners of the accounting firm located in Pittsburgh. The brother in Pittsburgh was not involved in any way in the audit conducted by the Detroit office. Nonetheless, the SEC held that the accounting firm of which he was a member could not be considered independent for the purpose of certifying the corporation's financial statements for filing with the SEC.

The wife of an accountant who had certified the financial statements of a proposed registrant was the sister of a widow of the founder of the company. On the death of the founder, the widow had inherited 60 per cent of the company's stock, and her son 10 per cent. The SEC ruled that this disqualified the accountant.

An accountant certified the financial statements of a brokerage firm in which his father and uncle were officers and owners of substantially all the outstanding stock. The accountant was held to be not independent.

An accounting firm which had certified the financial statements of a broker-dealer for several years took the son-in-law of an officer of the registrant into their partnership. The SEC ruled that the accountants were no longer independent in relation to the broker-dealer.

A partner of the accounting firm which had certified the financial statements of a broker-dealer loaned securities to a partner of the registrant (the broker-dealer). The latter was the accountant's brother-in-law. The securities were put in the firm's capital account and were used as part of the collateral securing a bank loan. The SEC said the accountant was not independent.

In another case which has come to the author's attention, there was also a brother-in-law relationship, but, after discussion with the SEC's staff, the accountant was advised that the SEC would raise no question as to the accountant's independence. The facts in the case were as follows:

Mr. JYH was a tax partner in an office of a large accounting firm. One of the clients of that office of the firm was a construction company. Mr. HB, a vice president of the construction company, was the owner of 15% of its common stock. Mr. JYH and Mr. HB were brothers-in-law. Mr. HB's work as vice president meant that he was field man in charge of construction. Mr. JYH had given tax advice to the construction company and the firm had prepared tax returns for the company but not for the individual officers.

In the foregoing case, it is possible that the SEC might have had a different view of the accounting firm's independence if Mr. HB had been involved in the accounting or finance areas of the construction company's business.

Outside Business Relationships.—A partner in an accounting firm which audited a registrant's accounts was appointed agent in control of certain buildings by the trustee for the children of the controlling stockholder of the registrant. In such capacity, the accountant negotiated a lease with the registrant which occupied office space in one of the buildings. The partner in the accounting firm also acted as trustee of a trust of which the wife and children of the controlling stockholder of the registrant were the beneficiaries. The SEC ruled that the accounting firm of which this accountant was a partner could not be considered independent with respect to the registrant.

A partner in an accounting firm which certified the financial statements of a registered broker-dealer maintained a cash account with the broker. The accountant effected transactions through the broker and left the securities in his possession. It was held that the maintenance of an open account with a broker, represented by cash or securities, or both, by a partner of a certifying accounting firm, casts doubt upon the independence of the accountant and the firm of which he is a partner with respect to the broker.

A partner in an accounting firm responsible for the audit of the financial statements of an oil company and the son of the president of the company jointly acquired a 25 per cent stock interest in an oil equipment company. In connection therewith they obtained a bank loan of $200,000, signing a joint note and pledging the stock of the oil equipment business as collateral. The president of the oil company indorsed the $200,000 note and pledged as additional collateral 2,500 shares of the oil company's stock. Inquiry was made as to whether the partner in the accounting firm, who had resigned from the firm, was qualified to practice before the Commission. The SEC took the position that these actions on the part of the accountant prevent his recognition by the Commission as an independent accountant with respect to any financial statements which the oil company filed or may file covering the period of time when he was a member of the accounting firm which certified those statements.

An accounting firm which had certified the financial statements of a proposed registrant acquired a parcel of real estate for the purpose of selling or leasing it to the company. The total purchase price was $85,000, of which $26,000 was paid in cash and the balance by a note secured by a mortgage. In addition to providing his portion of the cash payment, the accountant loaned the others $21,000 on interest-bearing notes to cover their share of the down payment. It was also provided that the accountant would receive 25 per cent of any profit arising from sale of the property to an outsider. The SEC ruled that the accountant was not independent with respect to the proposed registrant.

A certifying accountant, together with certain officers of the registrant, organized a corporation which purchased property from the registrant for

$100,000, giving the registrant $25,000 cash and a purchase money mortgage for $75,000. The SEC held that the accountant was disqualified with respect to this registrant.

The partners of an accounting firm were considering investing in a finance company which operated a wholly owned insurance agency to arrange insurance on the property financed. It was contemplated that a substantial part of such insurance would be placed with an insurance company client of the accounting firm. The accountants were advised that, if the insurance were so placed, they would not be considered independent with respect to their client.

Connection with Lending Bank.—An accounting firm certified the financial statements of a bank. A partner in the accounting firm acted as representative of the directors' examining committee of the bank. In this capacity he reviewed the loans made by the bank and made reports to the committee with respect to loans requiring special attention. A registrant, which was indebted to the bank for a substantial amount and whose loan had been reviewed by the accountant, intended to issue preferred stock amounting to about 75 per cent of the loan. The preferred stock was to be junior to the bank loan and the proceeds from the sale of the stock were to be used for working capital purposes. The accounting firm of which this partner was a member had been asked to certify the financial statements to be included in the registration statement. The SEC ruled that the accounting firm of which this partner was a member could not be considered independent for the purpose of certifying the financial statements of the proposed registrant.

Indemnity Agreement Between Accountant and Client.—Question was raised with SEC as to whether an accountant who certifies financial statements filed with SEC may be considered to be independent if he has entered into an indemnity agreement with the registrant. In the particular illustration cited, the board of directors of the registrant formally approved the filing of a registration statement with the Commission and agreed to indemnify and save harmless each and every accountant who certified any part of such statement, "from any and all losses, claims, damages, or liabilities arising out of such act or acts to which they or any of them may become subject under the Securities Act of 1933, as amended, or at 'common law, other than for their wilful misstatements or omissions.'" The SEC made known its position with regard to such indemnity agreements in a published opinion of its Chief Accountant.

The Chief Accountant stated that, in his view, the purpose of requiring the certifying accountant to be independent is clear: Independence tends to assure the objective and impartial consideration which is needed for the fair solution of the complex and often controversial matters that arise in the course of an audit. On the other hand, he said, bias due to the presence of an entangling affiliation or interest, inconsistent with proper professional relations of accountant and client, may cause loss of objectivity and impartiality and tends to cast doubt upon the reliability and fairness of the accountant's opinion and of the financial statements themselves. The Chief Accountant said that the existence of the indemnity agreement referred to above removed or greatly weakened one of the major stimuli to objective and unbiased consideration of the problems encountered in a particular engagement.

Such condition must frequently induce a departure from the standards of objectivity and impartiality which the concept of independence implies. In such difficult matters, for example, as the determination of the scope of audit necessary, existence of such an agreement may easily lead to the use of less extensive or thorough procedures than would otherwise be followed. In other cases it may result in a failure to appraise with professional acumen the information disclosed by the examination. Consequently, on the basis of the facts set forth in your inquiry, it is my opinion that the accountant cannot be recognized as independent for the purpose of certifying the financial statements of the corporation. [ASR No. 22 (1941)].

Custody of Portfolio Securities.—An accounting firm certified the financial statements of a registered investment company. The stocks and bonds of the registrant were kept in a safety deposit box in a bank and the members of the accounting firm had exclusive custody of the key to the safety deposit box. The SEC ruled that the accounting firm acting as custodian of the registrant's portfolio securities could not be considered independent for the purpose of certifying the financial statements of the registrant.

Accountant Who Is Also Attorney for Client.—In the *American Finance Company, Inc.* case [40 SEC 1043 (1962)] the Commission had before it the important question of whether or not an accountant who is also an attorney for a registrant is independent within the meaning of the Securities Act and the SEC rules. The company's registration statement contained a summary of earnings and earned surplus. Insofar as the summary related to the three years ended June 30, 1960, and the six months ended December 31, 1959, it was certified by an accounting firm which we shall call A & B. Mr. B, a partner of the firm, acted as legal counsel for the Company from 1955 through 1956 and received fees during that period for his services as an attorney as well as an accountant. Although the Commission's release is silent on the point, the author understands that Mr. B did not render legal services in connection with the registration statement.

The Commission said:

Though owing a public responsibility, an attorney in acting as the client's advisor, defender, advocate and confidant enters into a personal relationship in which his principal concern is with the interests and rights of his client. The requirement of the Act of certification by an independent accountant, on the other hand, is intended to secure for the benefit of public investors the detached objectivity of a disinterested person. The certifying accountant must be one who is in no way connected with the business or its management and who does not have any relationship that might affect the independence which at times may require him to voice public criticisms of his client's accounting practices.

The Commission concluded that Mr. B's relationship as attorney for the registrant during the same period covered by his firm's certification disqualified him and the firm of which he was a partner from certifying the registrant's financial statements as independent accountants.

In ASR No. 81 (1958), the SEC reported a case involving two of the partners of an accounting firm certifying the financial statements of a registrant. The two partners were also partners of a law firm engaged by the registrant to pass upon the legality of the securities which were being registered. The SEC held that the accountants were not independent with respect to the registrant.

Also in ASR No. 81, the SEC discussed a case where a CPA who was also a lawyer practiced both professions as a partner in separate accounting and law firms. Both firms were approached by an investment company to accept engagements in their respective fields. The accountants were advised that they would be held not independent if the law firm of which one of their partners was a member served as counsel to the company.

Incompatible Occupation.—An accountant certified financial statements of securities dealers filed on Form X–17A–5 with the Commission. The accountant was considering an offer to serve as salesman for one of the securities dealers and inquired as to whether this would affect his independence with respect to dealers other than his prospective employer as to whom he acknowledged his lack of independence. The SEC ruled that accepting employment as a security salesman would place the accountant in the position of engaging in a line of endeavor incompatible with that of an independent public accountant and would affect his status with respect to certifying financial statements filed with the Commission. In this connection, the SEC cited Rule 4 of the Rules of Professional Conduct (now Rule 4.04 of the Code of Professional Ethics) of the AICPA. This rule provided that Institute members shall not engage in any business or profession conjointly with that of a public accountant "which is incompatible or inconsistent therewith."

The Keller Brothers Securities Co., Inc. case is discussed in Chapter **5**. Keller was a broker-dealer and the distributor of Mutual Securities Fund of Boston, a registered investment company. Through an affiliate,

Keller provided investment advice to Mutual until the middle of 1961. Keller's president was a member of Mutual's board of trustees.

Keller's financial statements were filed with the SEC on Form X–17A–5 and were certified by Mr. X, a certified public accountant. Mr. X was also the certifying accountant for Mutual. He was one of three stockholders of Trinity Investment Company, a finance company located in his offices. He was also an officer and co-manager of Trinity, which, during part of 1961, made loans to customers and employees of Keller collateralized by securities. The loans were arranged through one of Keller's salesmen, who was paid a commission of one-fifth of the interest charged the borrower.

The financial report of June 30, 1960 certified by Mr. X was the last report filed by Keller with the SEC because Keller was placed in receivership in May, 1961. At the time of the Trinity loan transactions, however, Mr. X was performing the same accounting services for Keller and Mutual that he had previously performed. His selection as Mutual's independent auditor was made on a year-to-year basis, and was ratified annually by vote of its shareholders. He certified Mutual's financial statements for periods when the loans were outstanding.

By virtue of the Trinity loans, Mr. X, as a principal stockholder of Trinity, assumed a relationship with Keller which, in the SEC's view, was inconsistent with his position as an independent accountant. He acquired a personal financial stake in the repayment of the Trinity loans by the borrowing Keller salesmen and customers. He thus had an interest in Keller's continued operation and solvency, on which the repayment of the loans by those persons might have been dependent. He also had an interest in the securities collateral, which was being delivered from and to Keller in connection with the loans.

The SEC ruled that Mr. X's activities on behalf of Trinity were incompatible with his role as independent accountant, and his relationship with Keller was not in accord with professional ethics. (ASR No. 97, May 21, 1963.)

Client as Tenant or Subtenant.—The partners of an accounting firm and their wives had created a trust. It was proposed that the trust would purchase a building occupied by a client of the firm under a 21-year lease. The building was owned by an unrelated person and the transaction would have involved a substantial sum of money. The accountants were advised that their independent status would be lost if the transaction were consummated.

A company which was liquidating and held only two blocks of securities had leased for a period not to exceed 18 months one room in a suite of offices held by an accounting firm. The company paid the same rental per square foot as the accounting firm for the remainder of the office space.

Inquiry was made of the SEC concerning the propriety of this arrangement, since the accounting firm certified the financial statements of the company. The SEC said that arrangements of this type cast doubt upon the independence of the accountant, but in view of the special circumstances of this case the accounting firm would be permitted to certify the company's financial statements.

Independence of Foreign Auditors.—For a discussion of the independence of foreign auditors, see Chapter **31**.

CHAPTER 27

LIABILITY OF ACCOUNTANTS

Part 1: Federal Securities Laws Affecting Accountants; SEC Injunction Suits; SEC Rules of Practice

CONTENTS

Since the author of this book is not a lawyer, it is not his purpose to present an exhaustive discussion of the legal responsibilities of public accountants. That subject has been ably dealt with by competent writers in that field. This chapter will present briefly those aspects of the 1933 and 1934 Acts which expose the accountant to liability, and the disciplinary proceedings involving accountants under the Commission's Rules of Practice. If one has a problem involving these statutes or proceedings, he should consult a lawyer.

Accountant's Liabilities Under the 1933 Act

Section 11(a) of the Securities Act of 1933 contains the provisions relating to civil liabilities on account of untrue statements or material omissions in registration statements. The section provides for liability of persons who signed the registration statement, directors of the issuer, underwriters, and "experts" (including accountants). Insofar as it relates to accountants, Section 11(a) provides, in part, as follows:

In case any part of the registration statement, when such part became effective, contained an untrue statement of a material fact or omitted to state a material fact required to be stated therein or necessary to make the statements therein not misleading, any person acquiring such security . . . may . . . sue . . . every accountant . . . who has with his consent been named as having . . . certified any part of the registration statement . . . with respect to the statement in such registration statement . . . which purports to have been . . . certified by him.

Under this section, it will be seen that the accountant may be liable to any *purchaser* of the security offered by means of the registration statement. This liability does not extend to a *seller* of the security covered by the registration statement. Furthermore, liability to the purchaser may be created without his having to prove that he relied on an untrue statement in the registration statement, or that he relied not knowing of a material omission. (See page **31·22** for a discussion of the liability of foreign auditors.)

The 1933 Act also contains a provision designed to ease the burden of liability when a corporation (or other issuer) has made generally available to its security holders an earnings statement covering a period of one year beginning after the effective date of the registration statement. Section 11(a) continues as follows:

If such person acquired the security after the issuer has made generally available to its security holders an earning statement covering a period of at least twelve months beginning after the effective date of the registration statement, then the right of recovery under this subsection shall be conditioned on proof that such person acquired the securities relying on such untrue statement in the registration statement or relying upon the registration statement and not knowing of such omission, but such reliance may be established without proof of the reading of the registration statement by such person.

The effect of this provision of Section 11(a) appears to be this: If the investor acquired the security after the issuer had made generally available to its security holders an earnings statement covering a period of at least one year beginning after the effective date of the registration statement, in order to recover damages he must prove that he acquired the security in reliance upon an untrue statement in the registration statement, or in reliance upon the registration statement and not knowing of a material omission. This paragraph has no effect on persons who acquired the security during the period when such reliance need not be proved, that is, prior to the publication of the earnings statement referred to above.

The financial pages of newspapers occasionally carry advertisements of which the following is typical:

(Name of company) has made generally available to its security holders an earnings statement for the period (date) to (date) pursuant to Section 11(a) of the Securities Act of 1933, as amended. Such earnings statement covers 52 weeks beginning after the effective date of the Corporation's Registration Statement for (quantity and type of security) which Registration Statement was filed on (date), with the Securities and Exchange Commission pursuant to the Securities Act of 1933, as amended, and became effective on (date).

The advertisement may contain the earnings statement referred to above, or it may say where the statement may be obtained. Some companies send copies of the statement to the SEC, stock exchanges, underwriters, and financial publishing houses (such as Standard and Poor's, Moody's, and Fitch) in the belief that this constitutes making the statement "generally available."

The Section 11(a) earnings statement need not be certified by independent public accountants. Some corporations, however, ask their independent accountants to review the manner of its preparation and its content. The statement need not follow any prescribed form. Some corporations endeavor to prepare the statement in the same form as the statement in the prospectus.

Section 11(e) of the 1933 Act provides, among other things, that the suit authorized under Section 11(a) may be to recover damages representing the difference between the amount paid for the security (not exceeding its public offering price) and (1) its value as of the time the suit was brought, or (2) the price at which the security shall have been disposed of in the market before suit, or (3) the price at which the security shall have been disposed of after suit but before judgment, if such damages shall be less than the damages representing the difference between the amount paid (not exceeding the public offering price) and the value of the security as of the time the suit was brought.

Defenses of Experts.—The 1933 Act provides that no person, other than the issuer, shall be liable who shall sustain the burden of proof that:

. . . as regards any part of the registration statement purporting to be made upon his authority as an expert . . . he had, after reasonable investigation, reasonable ground to believe and did believe, at the time such part of the registration statement became effective, that the statements therein were true and that there was no omission to state a material fact required to be stated therein or necessary to make the statements therein not misleading . . . (Section 11(b)(3)(B) of the 1933 Act.)

It will be seen from the statutory language of the defense section quoted above that the accountant must make a reasonable investigation, must actually believe, and must have reasonable grounds for his belief, that the statements made upon his authority as an expert are true, and that there are no omissions of material facts required to be stated or necessary to make the statements not misleading.

Standard of Reasonableness.—In determining, for the purpose of Section 11(b)(3) of the 1933 Act, what constitutes reasonable investigation and reasonable ground for belief, the law provides: " . . . the standard of reasonableness shall be that required of a prudent man in the management of his own property." (Section 11(c) of the 1933 Act.) As it was originally enacted, the law provided that the standard of reasonableness required was that of a "person occupying a fiduciary relationship." The standard presently prescribed by the Act was adopted in a subsequent amendment. The standard, according to one authority, was changed "largely for psychological reasons, so it seems." [1] He said that this was substantially the standard adopted in the *Restatement of Trusts* and applied under the English Companies Act.

A former chairman of the SEC said that reasonability will differ widely according to the person involved.[2]

Under some circumstances such a standard would require personal knowledge of the facts assumed to be true. Delegation to others of the duty to verify the facts would under other circumstances suffice to meet the requirements. A director, for example, would have little excuse for not having personal knowledge of what his stock holdings in the issuer and its subsidiaries were, but he should obviously be entitled to rely upon the statements of his fellow directors, as checked by the stock books, as to what their stock holdings were. Furthermore, the director who is also Chairman of the Board or Chairman of some special committee will stand in a different relationship as to the knowledge which is the special concern of his committee. Or take the situation of the underwriters. The type of investigation which can reasonably be demanded of the sponsoring or principal underwriters is one thing; that which the Act requires of the small participating underwriter in order that he shall satisfy its requirements is another thing; while an even less standard of investigation would be demanded of the dealer selling on commission, who, because of his relationship to the issuer, is considered as an underwriter by the Act.

Privity Not Essential Under 1933 Act.—If the registration statement under the 1933 Act contains an untrue statement or material omission, any person acquiring the security may sue the certifying accountant regardless of the fact that such person is not the client of the accountant. There need be no legal relationship between the investor and the accountant; in other words, there need be no showing of "privity."

THE ULTRAMARES CASE.—Until the passage of the 1933 Act, privity was an essential requirement of any suit brought against an accountant by third parties and based on negligence. The classic American case which illustrates this requirement is *Ultramares Corporation v. Touche.* [255 N. Y. 170 (1931)]. The defendants, a firm of certified public accountants, had furnished 32 copies of a certified balance sheet to their client knowing

---

[1] Loss, *Securities Regulation,* 2d ed. (1961), p. 1726.
[2] James M. Landis, Address before New York State Society of CPAs, October 30, 1933.

that it would be shown to creditors. The plaintiff was a creditor to whom the balance sheet had been shown, who claimed that he had relied on it in making substantial advances to the client. The balance sheet showed net assets of $1,070,000 when, as a matter of fact, the client was insolvent and its liabilities exceeded its assets by $200,000. The assets had been overstated by the inclusion of over $950,000 of fictitious receivables; liabilities had been understated by about $300,000 through failure to record accounts payable covering merchandise which had been purchased, received, and included in assets in the balance sheet. The audit had failed to detect these fraudulent entries, and the plaintiff-creditor brought suit against the accountants.

A jury found for the plaintiff on both the claims of fraud and negligence, but the trial judge dismissed the complaint and set aside the verdict. The case was eventually appealed to New York's highest court which affirmed the dismissal of the action on the basis of negligence, but ordered a new trial on the claim of fraud. Chief Judge Cardozo (his appointment at the time) wrote the opinion of the unanimous court and said in part:

> The assault upon the citadel of privity is proceeding in these days apace. . . . From the foregoing analysis the conclusion is, we think, inevitable that nothing in our previous decisions commits us to a holding of liability for negligence in the circumstances of the case at hand, and that such liability, if recognized, will be an extension of the principle of those decisions to different conditions, even if more or less analogous. The question then is whether such an extension shall be made.
>
> The extension, if made, will so expand the field of liability for negligent speech as to make it nearly, if not quite, coterminous with that of liability for fraud. Again and again, in decisions of this Court, the bounds of this latter liability have been set up, with futility the fate of every endeavor to dislodge them. . . . Even an opinion, especially an opinion by an expert, may be found to be fraudulent if the grounds supporting it are so flimsy as to lead to the conclusion that there was no genuine belief back of it. Further than that this Court has never gone. . . . This has not meant, to be sure, that negligence may not be evidence from which a trier of the facts may draw an inference of fraud, but merely that if that inference is rejected, or, in the light of all the circumstances, is found to be unreasonable, negligence alone is not a substitute for fraud. Many also are the cases that have distinguished between the wilful or reckless representation essential to the maintenance at law of an action for deceit, and the misrepresentation, negligent or innocent, that will lay a sufficient basis for rescission in equity. If this action is well conceived, all these principles and distinctions, so nicely wrought and formulated, have been a waste of time and effort. . . . A word of caution or suggestion would have set the erring suitor right. Many pages of opinion were written by judges the most eminent, yet the word was never spoken. We may not speak it now. A change so revolutionary, if expedient, must be wrought by legislation.

The change which the New York Court of Appeals thought so "revolutionary" as to be "wrought by legislation" has been made. The liability imposed by Section 11 is for the benefit of all innocent buyers of the security.

There is no requirement for privity. As was said of the 1933 Act shortly after its enactment:

> To say the least the Act goes as far in protection of purchasers of securities as plaintiff in *Ultramares Corp. v. Touche* unsuccessfully urged the New York Court of Appeals to go in the protection of a creditor. . . . The duty placed on experts such as accountants has not been measured by the expert's relation to his employer but by his service to investors.[3]

A member of the Illinois bar made this observation of the Ultramares decision which is indicative of the changing legal atmosphere involving public accountants:

> . . . [Judge] Cardozo did not hold for the accountant in *Ultramares* for lack of a logical basis for liability. That was quite clear. He thought the exposure to which accountants would be subject would be unreasonable, *but that kind of judicial restraint seems to be becoming increasingly less fashionable.*[4] (Emphasis supplied.)

THE RUSCH FACTORS CASE.—Indicative of the fact that the "judicial restraint" exhibited by Judge Cardozo is becoming "less fashionable" is the 1968 decision in *Rusch Factors, Inc. v. Levin* 284 F. Supp. 85 (D.R.I. 1968).

Rusch Factors was a banker and factor which was considering a loan to a Rhode Island business corporation. To measure the financial stability of the borrower, Rusch asked for certified financial statements of the borrower. The defendant, a Rhode Island CPA, prepared and certified financial statements of the borrower which showed that it was solvent by a substantial amount when, in fact, it was insolvent.

The borrower submitted the statements to the plaintiff which, in reliance on the statements, made a loan to the borrower. Later, the borrower went into receivership, and the plaintiff sued the accountant for its loss. The defendant accountant moved to dismiss claiming that the absence of privity of contract between him and the plaintiff was a complete defense. The Court denied this motion.

In deciding the motion, the Court discussed *Ultramares* and its implications. The Court said that privity of contract is clearly no defense in a fraud action, and that the question to be considered is whether the accountant's liability to his client for negligence should be extended to persons who the accountant knew would rely on the statements certified by him. The Court said there was no need to decide whether the Ultramares decision

[3] Douglas and Bates, "The Federal Securities Act of 1933," 43 *Yale Law Journal* 171 (1933).
[4] Ray Garrett, Jr., Panelist, American Bar Association National Institute, *The Business Lawyer,* Jan. 1969, p. 658.

should be overruled, because the case at bar was distinguishable from that case.

In *Ultramares,* "the plaintiff was a member of an undefined, unlimited class of remote lenders and potential equity holders not actually foreseen but only foreseeable." In the case at bar, according to the complaint, the defendent knew that potential financiers of the borrower would rely upon his certification.

The Court observed that no appellate court, English or American, has held an accountant liable in negligence to reliant parties not in privity. "The reluctance of the courts to hold the accounting profession to an obligation of care which extends to all reasonably foreseeable reliant parties is predicated upon the social utility rationale first articulated by Judge Cardozo in the Ultramares case." In that case, in holding the defendant accountants free from liability for their negligence, Judge Cardozo said:

If liability for negligence exists, a thoughtless slip or blunder, the failure to detect a theft or forgery beneath the cover of deceptive entries, may expose accountants to a liability in an indeterminate amount for an indeterminate time to an indeterminate class. The hazards of a business conducted on these terms are so extreme as to enkindle doubt whether a flaw may not exist in the implication of a duty that exposes one to these consequences.

The Court in *Rusch Factors* said that the wisdom of the decision in the *Ultramares* case has been doubted, and that "this Court shares the doubt." "Why," he asked, "should an innocent reliant party be forced to carry the weighty burden of an accountant's professional malpractice?"

Isn't the risk of loss more easily distributed and fairly spread by imposing it on the accounting profession, which can pass the cost of insuring against the risk on to its customers, who can in turn pass the cost on to the entire consuming public. . . . For these reasons *it appears to this Court that the decision in Ultramares constitutes an unwarranted inroad upon the principle that 'the risk reasonably to be perceived defines the duty to be obeyed.'* (Emphasis supplied.)

In *Rusch Factors,* the Court found that "an accountant should be liable in negligence for careless financial misrepresentations relied upon by actually foreseen and limited classes of persons."

Criminal Penalties Under the 1933 Act.—Section 24 of the 1933 Act contains the penalties for willful violation of the Act or the rules and regulations thereunder, or for a willful misstatement or omission in a registration statement filed under the Act. The section is as follows:

Sec. 24. Any person who willfully violates any of the provisions of this title, or the rules and regulations promulgated by the Commission under authority thereof, or any person who willfully, in a registration statement filed under this title, makes any untrue statement of a material fact or omits to state any material fact required to be stated therein or necessary to make the statements therein not misleading, shall upon conviction be fined not more than $5,000 or imprisoned not more than five years, or both.

Accountant's Liabilities Under the 1934 Act

Under Section 18 of the Securities Exchange Act of 1934:

Any person who shall make or cause to be made any statement in any application, report, or document filed pursuant to this title or any rule or regulation thereunder or any undertaking contained in a registration statement as provided in subsection (d) of section 15 of this title, which statement was at the time and in the light of the circumstances under which it was made false or misleading with respect to any material fact, shall be liable to any person (not knowing that such statement was false or misleading) who, in reliance upon such statement, shall have purchased or sold a security at a price which was affected by such statement, for damages caused by such reliance, unless the person sued shall prove that he acted in good faith and had no knowledge that such statement was false or misleading. . . .

It will be apparent from a reading of Section 18 that it establishes liability to both *purchasers* and *sellers* of securities arising out of the filing of a statement or other document under the 1934 Act which is false or misleading.

In a suit brought under this section, a plaintiff would have to prove reliance upon the financial statements and the damages caused thereby, but he would not have to prove fraud or negligence on the part of the accountant. The accountant, on the other hand would have the statutory defense that "he acted in good faith and had no knowledge that such statement was false or misleading." Levy wrote:

This quoted language is consistent with freedom from fraud rather than freedom from negligence. It would seem, therefore, that the rule of the *Ultramares* case has been here enacted and that there would not be liability to third parties for mere negligence where the good faith of the accountant is established.[5]

Section 10b and Rule 10b–5 under the 1934 Act.—Much of the litigation involving accountants has been based on Section 10b of the 1934 Act and Rule 10b–5 promulgated thereunder. That section and rule are as follows:

Section 10b of the 1934 Act

Sec. 10. It shall be unlawful for any person, directly or indirectly, by the use of any means or instrumentality of interstate commerce or of the mails, or of any facility of any national securities exchange—

(b) To use or employ, in connection with the purchase or sale of any security registered on a national securities exchange or any security not so regis-

---

[5] Levy, *Accountants' Legal Responsibility,* p. 50 (1954).

tered, any manipulative or deceptive device or contrivance in contravention of such rules and regulations as the Commission may prescribe as necessary or appropriate in the public interest or for the protection of investors.

Rule 10b-5 under the 1934 Act

It shall be unlawful for any person, directly or indirectly, by the use of any means or instrumentality of interstate commerce, or of the mails, or of any facility of any national securities exchange,

(a) to employ any device, scheme, or artifice to defraud,

(b) to make any untrue statement of a material fact or to omit to state a material fact necessary in order to make the statements made, in the light of the circumstances under which they were made, not misleading, or

(c) to engage in any act, practice, or course of business which operates or would operate as a fraud or deceit upon any person, in connection with the purchase or sale of any security.

The reader is referred to the discussion of the Olen Company case in Chapter **5** and the SEC's severe criticism of the audits made by the company's public accountants. H. L. Green Company, Inc. acquired the Olen Company by merger after the latter went public in 1958. The merger was accomplished in late 1958 by an exchange of stock. Proxy statements prepared in connection with the merger included the financial statements of Olen and the certificate of its public accountants. Green discovered the falsity of the Olen financial statements after the merger and sued the accountants for damages under Section 10(b) of the 1934 Act. Green alleged that the accountants knowingly prepared false financial statements and made other misrepresentations with the intent to induce Green to enter into the merger.

The accountants moved to dismiss the complaint on the ground that it did not state a claim under the 1934 Act and therefore, the court lacked jurisdiction. The accountants contended that (1) the transaction was a merger and not a "purchase or sale" of securities within the meaning of the 1934 Act, and (2) the preparation of a false and misleading financial statement by an accountant does not make him a participant in a sale induced by the use of such a statement.

The court said that "merger" is not a term of fixed and definite content, and that a transaction so described may or may not involve a purchase and sale within the meaning of Section 10(b) of the Act. The court ruled that the transaction appeared to be a purchase and sale.

The complaint also alleged that the accountants acted "knowingly . . . pursuant to a conspiracy to defraud." The court further ruled that the defendants' status as accountants and the fact that their activities were confined to the preparation of false and misleading financial statements and misrepresentations did not immunize them from civil suit for their alleged participation, and that the extent and culpability of that participation had to be determined at a trial. Accordingly, the court denied the accountants' motion. [*H. L. Green Company, Inc. v. Lewie F. Childree, et al.,* 185 F. Supp. 95 (S.D.N.Y. 1960).]

Practical Effect of Distinction Between Accountant's Liability Under 1933 and 1934 Acts.—As pointed out earlier in this chapter the 1933 and the 1934 Acts differ materially in respect of reliance and burden of proof. It should be observed that under the 1933 Act liability in respect of a misleading statement is imposed only in favor of a purchaser of a security. Under the 1934 Act, liability is imposed in respect of a misleading statement which results in a person buying or selling a security at a price affected by such statement. Since an income statement may be misleading whether it overstates or understates net income, it is possible that under the 1934 law an accountant may be vulnerable if he allows conservatism to influence his judgment to such an extent as to result in a material understatement of income. It appears likely that an accountant may not be liable to third parties by an understatement of earnings in a 1933 Act filing, whereas a similar understatement in a 1934 Act filing may subject him to damages. The decision on this matter, however, will be made by the courts—not by authors of books on accounting subjects.

There is no liability under the 1933 Act for any act done or omitted in good faith in conformity with any rule or regulation of the Commission notwithstanding that such rule or regulation may thereafter be amended or rescinded or determined to be invalid (Section 19(a) of the Act).

In Chapter **12**, it was stated that a registration statement under the 1933 Act speaks as of its effective date. The 1934 Act contains no similar provision. In order to furnish a basis for suit under the 1934 Act, the statement must be false or misleading "at the time and in the light of the circumstances under which it was made." See the discussion in Chapter **12** relating to the accountant's responsibility for events and transactions subsequent to the statement date.

Limitations of Actions to Recover.—Under the 1933 Act suit must be brought within one year of the discovery of the untrue statement or omission, or after such discovery should have been made by the exercise of reasonable diligence, and in any event within three years after the security was bona fide offered to the public. Section 13 of the 1933 Act provides as follows:

No action shall be maintained to enforce any liability created under Section 11 or Section 12(2) unless brought within one year after the discovery of the untrue statement or the omission, or after such discovery should have been made by the exercise of reasonable diligence, or, if the action is to enforce a liability created under Section 12(1), unless brought within one year after the violation upon which it is based. In no event shall any such action be brought to enforce a liability created under Section 11 or Section 12(1) more than three years after the security was bona fide offered to the public, or under Section 12(2) more than three years after the sale.

The reader's attention is directed to the phrase "after such discovery should have been made by the exercise of reasonable diligence." A former SEC Commissioner said that the greatest difficulty in the application of the limitations provided in Section 13 unquestionably will arise in determining when an untrue statement or omission could have been discovered "by the exercise of reasonable diligence." [6]

Under the 1934 Act suit must be brought within one year after the discovery of the facts constituting the cause of action and within three years after such cause of action accrued. Section 18(c) of the 1934 Act provides as follows:

No action shall be maintained to enforce any liability created under this section unless brought within one year after the discovery of the facts constituting the cause of action and within three years after such cause of action accrued.

Criminal Penalties Under the 1934 Act.—Section 32 of the 1934 Act sets forth the penalties for willful violation of the Act or the rules and regulations thereunder, and for willful false or misleading statements in documents filed pursuant to the Act. In addition the law provides penalties for failure to file information, documents, or reports required to be filed. Section 32 of the Act is as follows:

Sec. 32. (a) Any person who willfully violates any provision of this title, or any rule or regulation thereunder the violation of which is made unlawful or the observance of which is required under the terms of this title, or any person who willfully and knowingly makes, or causes to be made, any statement in any application, report, or document required to be filed under this title or any rule or regulation thereunder or any undertaking contained in a registration statement as provided in subsection (d) of section 15 of this title, which statement was false or misleading with respect to any material fact, shall upon conviction be fined not more than $10,000, or imprisoned not more than two years, or both, except that when such person is an exchange, a fine not exceeding $500,000 may be imposed; but no person shall be subject to imprisonment under this section for the violation of any rule or regulation if he proves that he had no knowledge of such rule or regulation.

(b) Any issuer which fails to file information, documents, or reports required to be filed under subsection (d) of section 15 of this title or any rule or regulation thereunder shall forfeit to the United States the sum of $100 for each and every day such failure to file shall continue. Such forfeiture, which shall be in lieu of any criminal penalty for such failure to file which might be deemed to arise under subsection (a) of this section, shall be payable into the Treasury

---

[6] Edward T. McCormick, *Understanding the Securities Act and the SEC* (New York: American Book Co., 1948), p. 184.

of the United States and shall be recoverable in a civil suit in the name of the United States.

(c) The provisions of this section shall not apply in the case of any violation of any rule or regulation prescribed pursuant to paragraph (3) of subsection (c) of section 15 of this title, except a violation which consists of making, or causing to be made, any statement in any report or document required to be filed under any such rule or regulation, which statement was at the time and in the light of the circumstances under which it was made false or misleading with respect to any material fact.

In the Continental Vending Machine case (discussed in Chapter **28**), the accountants were convicted of violating this section of the law, in addition to violating the Mail Fraud Statute.

SEC Injunction Suits as a Stimulus for Private Actions.—In connection with its administration of the Federal securities laws, the SEC occasionally brings an action in which it alleges that a company, or an individual, or both, have violated the Federal securities laws or the Commission's rules and regulations thereunder. Based on these allegations, the SEC seeks to enjoin the company or the individual, or both, from further violations of the statutes, rules, and regulations. Frequently the company or individual involved will consent to the entry of the injunction but without admitting the truth of the SEC's allegations simply as a means of disposing of the matter. Following such a consent decree, however, may be a whole series of private actions—many of them class actions—brought by security holders or others claiming that they have been damaged or have suffered losses as a result of the very things complained of in the SEC's action. A typical example of this situation occurred in 1971 in a matter involving Occidental Petroleum Corporation.

The Occidental Petroleum Corporation Case.—The SEC announced on March 4, 1971 that it had filed a complaint in a U. S. District Court seeking to enjoin Occidental Petroleum Corporation and Armand Hammer, its chairman and chief executive officer, from "further violations of the antifraud provisions of the federal securities laws." (SEC Litigation Release No. 4922, March 4, 1971.)

In its complaint, the SEC alleged that Occidental issued false and misleading earnings reports for each of the last three quarters of 1969, the first two quarters of 1970, and for the years 1969 and 1970. The SEC charged that the company structured certain financing transactions to take on the appearance of land sales and "improperly" recorded profits from these transactions. The complaint alleged that, in connection with these earnings figures, the company reported the "purported" profits from these financing transactions as current income for the first and second quarters of 1970, and improperly included other items as current income for the second and fourth quarters of 1969 and the first and second quarters of 1970.

The SEC also alleged that the company failed to disclose that for the third quarter of 1969, $14,042,000 of the $49,134,000 in net income which the company reported resulted from "extensive adjustments" and changes in accounting in one of its consolidated subsidiaries, and that a major portion of the adjustments and changes related to prior years and prior quarters of 1969.

Although the complaint alleged that the company issued false and misleading earnings reports for 1969 and 1970, the SEC did not seek to enjoin the independent public accountants who had certified those reports which had been filed with the SEC and the New York Stock Exchange.

The SEC's complaint also contained allegations not related to the company's financial statements.

Occidental's common stock was the most actively traded issue on the New York Stock Exchange in 1968 and 1969, and the second most active issue in 1970.

The company and its chairman consented to the entry of an injunction but did "not concede that [they had] violated any regulation of the SEC or any rule of law whatsoever or any proper accounting practices." (*The New York Times,* March 5, 1971.) In consenting to the injunction, the company and its chairman sought to avoid costly and protracted proceedings. "We also seek to save the time of our executives in vindicating our position by formal legal proceedings."

The company and its chairman also said they had consulted the company's independent auditors, "and the earnings reports wouldn't be changed." (*The Wall Street Journal,* March 5, 1971). The SEC's suit did not ask the court to require Occidental to revise its financial statements for the periods in question, as it does in some cases involving financial reports.

Within two weeks after the filing of the consent decree, eight lawsuits had been instituted against Occidental Petroleum Corporation in various U. S. District Courts alleging violation of the federal securities laws and the SEC's rules and regulations. In at least one of the suits, the company's independent public accountants were also named co-defendants although they had not been involved in the consent decree. The first of such suits, brought as a class action, is based on the same allegations as the SEC action, and followed by only *four* days the SEC's action (*Frank v. Occidental Petroleum Corporation,* complaint filed March 8, 1971, District of Columbia.)

Inasmuch as the issues involved in the complaints were before the courts at the date of this writing, they will not be discussed here. The only purpose of including the cases in this volume is to illustrate how an action by the SEC serves to stimulate civil suits by private parties. In fact, as one publication put it, "As a result of the SEC's action, a host of private suits against Occidental may be filed." (*Securities Regulation and Law Report,* March 10, 1971.)

SEC Injunction Suits Against Accountants.—In recent years the SEC has stepped up its legal barrage against corporations, firms, and individuals which it believed were violating the Federal securities laws. As previously noted, one of the principal weapons in the SEC's armory has been the injunction suit in which the SEC files a complaint alleging that the defendants have violated the securities laws or regulations and asks the court to enjoin the defendants from further violations.

In some of these suits the SEC has charged not only the companies involved with filing false and misleading financial statements, but also the public accountants who certified the financial statements.

One commentator on this situation as it affects public accountants has stated that the SEC, in its recent actions, seems to be adopting the view that the accountant has some sort of undefined stewardship or fiduciary obligation to stockholders and creditors. Since this view has not yet been expressed by statute or by amendment to Regulation S–X, he said it was difficult to see where the Commission is headed. He continued:

It may well be that the Commission hopes to encourage civil damage actions by bringing these situations to light in criminal prosecutions, "stop order" proceedings or by obtaining injunctions directed at public accountants. From these actions, in which the Commission may participate, as it has done in other areas, there may be developed the obligations the Commission has in mind.

It would appear that the Commission would like to impose a federal standard of liability on the [accountancy] profession and thus eliminate whatever limitations on the public accountants' liability which may exist under state law.[7]

Two of the injunction suits initiated by the SEC which involved CPA firms are described in the following pages: those relating to Liberty Equities Corporation and Utilities Leasing Corporation. These were not the only SEC injunction suits which involved certifying accountants, but these are discussed because, in each case, the accounting firm—without admitting the facts alleged in the SEC's complaint—consented to the entry of a final judgment enjoining them from future violations of the Federal securities laws and the SEC's rules and regulations. The amendment by the Commission of its Rules of Practice (discussed below), may affect an accountant's willingness in the future to consent to the entry of such injunctions.

The SEC amended its Rules of Practice in 1971 in important respects, particularly Rule 2(e). The amendments increased significantly the risk

---

[7] Thomas W. Hill, Jr., "The Public Accountants' Legal Liability to Clients and Others," *The New York CPA,* Jan. 1968, p. 26.

that an expert, including an attorney, accountant, engineer, or other professional would be denied the privilege of appearing or practicing before the SEC if, after July 1, 1971, he was enjoined from violating the Federal securities laws or regulations. The same result could occur if the accountant or other expert were found in an action brought by the SEC, or in an SEC administrative proceeding, to have violated the Federal securities laws, unless the violation was found not to have been willful. For the purpose of determining whether to suspend or disqualify the accountant or other expert, the SEC has said that no distinction will be made between injunctions and findings that are contested by the accountant and those which have been consented to by the accountant without admitting the facts alleged by the SEC in its complaint.

Consequently, it is to be expected that accountants who are charged by the SEC with misconduct will be much less likely in the future, than they have been in the past, to consent to the entry of an injunction without admitting the facts, and thereby dispose of the matter.

In the discussion of the Liberty Equities and Utilities Leasing cases which follows, the reader should bear in mind that *the accountants did not contest the SEC's action.* Therefore, while the discussion includes the facts alleged by the SEC, *it does not include the accountants' version of those facts* although the accountants in both cases withdrew their reports. As anyone who has had any experience with lawsuits knows, there is often a world of difference between the plaintiff's allegations and the whole truth.

THE LIBERTY EQUITIES CORPORATION CASE.—On August 6, 1970 the SEC filed a complaint in a U. S. District Court seeking to enjoin the defendants, Liberty Equities Corporation and others (including a firm of CPAs), from further violations of the registration, reporting, proxy and anti-fraud provisions of the Federal securities laws. The SEC alleged in its complaint that Liberty's financial statements for the fiscal periods ended March 31, 1967 and March 31, 1968 (which were audited by the defendant CPAs) were false and misleading and violated the anti-fraud provisions of the 1934 Act.

The SEC also alleged in its complaint that:

1. The balance sheets at March 31, 1967 and March 31, 1968 improperly reflected as a current asset 14-month, non-negotiable, *non-interest bearing* certificates of deposit (C/Ds) in the amount of $325,000 in 1967 and $300,000 in 1968, which had been purchased from National Savings and Trust Co. (NS&T), one of the defendants, on March 30, 1967 and March 28, 1968, respectively, from the proceeds of a 14-month 6% loan of $325,000 and $300,000 obtained from NS&T on the same day. There was no disclosure that the C/Ds

were pledged with NS&T as collateral for the loans, that the transactions would cost Liberty approximately $19,500 in 1967 and $18,000 in 1968 in interest payments, and that there was no legitimate business purpose that could be served by the transaction. The net effect of the reporting of these transactions was to "dress up" Liberty's financial statements by inflating current assets in order to show a favorable working capital ratio.

2. The income statement for fiscal 1968 improperly reflected as ordinary income the purported profit of $763,663 resulting from a transaction whereby Liberty sold for $808,663 certain options on real estate which it had purchased for $45,000 shortly before this transaction. The sale was to Real Estate Investors of Iowa, Inc., a subsidiary of Professional Investors of Iowa, Inc. Without this purported profit, Liberty would have reported a net operating loss for fiscal 1968. In addition, no disclosure was made with respect to the transactions to show that:

   (a) The sale transaction was unusual and nonrecurring; (b) it took place on the last day of Liberty's fiscal year; (c) Edward A. White, one of the defendants, who was vice-president and a director of Liberty as well as president of Professional Investors of Iowa, Inc., represented both parties to the transaction; (d) the transaction was consummated with a non-existent entity; (e) the transfer of the options was the first active step by Liberty and other defendants to form a joint venture of which Liberty was a 50% participant; and (f) the purpose of the transaction was to eliminate Liberty's net operating loss and to "dress up" its financial statements.

3. Current assets in the March 31, 1968 balance sheet improperly reflected as a note receivable the $708,663 [*Author's note:* So reported in the SEC's release; the amount probably should have been $808,663] promissory note of Real Estate Investors of Iowa, Inc., since it was unlikely that there would be any proceeds for that receivable because of the lack of financial responsibility of the purchaser and the intent of the parties.

4. Current assets in the balance sheets also reflected a *non-interest bearing* note receivable in the amount of $236,436, but there was no disclosure that the note receivable had been pledged with defendant NS&T as collateral for a short term *interest bearing* loan of the same amount obtained from NS&T.

The SEC's complaint contained other allegations which, however, did not appear to involve Liberty's financial statements or its independent CPAs. (SEC Litigation Release No. 4709, August 6, 1970.)

On November 16, 1970 the SEC announced that Liberty and several other defendants had consented to the entry of a final judgment of permanent injunction enjoining them from future violations of the Federal securities laws. In so consenting, however, the company and the defendants did not admit the allegations in the SEC's complaint. The Commission's announcement, however, made no mention of the CPA firm that had been named as a defendant in the complaint or of two other individual defendants. (SEC Litigation Release No. 4810 and 4811, November 16, 1970.)

On May 6, 1971 the SEC announced that a final judgment of permanent injunction had been entered by a Federal judge against the CPA firm in the Commission's injunctive action against Liberty Equities Corporation, et al. The accountants consented to the injunction enjoining the firm from future violations of the 1934 Act and the rules thereunder "in connection with Liberty Equities Corporation." (SEC Litigation Release No. 4999, May 6, 1971.)

Commenting on the SEC's announcement, the CPA firm's general counsel said:

We consented to entry of the judgment without admitting liability in order to dispose of the SEC action. I should point out charges identical to those in the SEC complaint have since been made in a class action for damages which the firm has denied in detail and which it is defending vigorously. (*Wall Street Journal,* May 7, 1971.)

On May 7, 1971 the SEC announced that the CPA firm had withdrawn its reports with respect to Liberty Equities Corporation's (now known as Smithfield Foods) financial statements "as of and/or [sic] the eight months ended March 31, 1967 and the twelve months ended March 31, 1968." The accountants took this action, according to the SEC, "in view of the allegations with respect to certain transactions reflected in said financial statements which have been made by the Commission in its injunctive action against Liberty Equities Corporation et al. . . . and in response to the request of the Commission's staff." (*SEC News Digest,* May 7, 1971.)

THE UTILITIES LEASING CORPORATION CASE.—The SEC filed a complaint with a U. S. District Court on February 26, 1971 seeking to enjoin Utilities Leasing Corporation, The Queen, Ltd., and eleven others from further violations of the registration, anti-fraud and reporting provisions of the Federal securities laws. The defendants included present or former officers and directors of Utilities Leasing and The Queen, Ltd., a CPA firm who were Utilities Leasing's auditors, and others.

In its complaint the Commission alleged that certain of the defendants filed or caused to be filed false and misleading registration statements and periodic reports with the Commission in 1969 and 1970. Pursuant to a registration statement covering a public offering of securities by Utilities Leasing, $8,000,000 was raised from the public. The SEC charged that Utilities

Leasing used the proceeds of this offering for purposes contrary to those described in its registration statement, and that part of those proceeds was placed in inactive, non-interest bearing accounts at various banks as compensating balances for personal loans to officers of Utilities Leasing.

As far as the independent CPAs were concerned, the SEC alleged that the company's financial statements included in Form 10–K for the fiscal year ended September 30, 1969 were false and misleading. The SEC said, among other things, that the financial statements failed to disclose certain liabilities that the company had incurred for the sole benefit of J. Gerald McElroy, the president of Utilities Leasing, and that the company had paid a corporation controlled by McElroy money for services which had not been rendered. (SEC Litigation Release No. 4916, February 20, 1971.)

According to the SEC's complaint, there were other allegations concerning the financial statements. Among other things, the annual report was said to have contained misleading statements concerning an unpaid loan to a company controlled by Utilities' former president, the use of corporate funds in connection with loans to corporate officers or their friends, payments made to a company controlled by the former president for services not rendered, and the cancellation of a receivable due from this company as an offset against services not rendered.

On March 24, 1971 the SEC announced that a Federal judge had signed a permanent injunction against the public accounting firm enjoining them from violating the 1934 Act and various rules thereunder in connection with annual reports on Form 10–K of Utilities Leasing. The accountants, without admitting the SEC's allegations and having withdrawn their report included in the Form 10–K of Utilities Leasing for fiscal 1969, consented to the issuance of the permanent injunction. (SEC Litigation Release No. 4952, March 24, 1971.)

SEC Decisions Involving Accountants

There have been a number of SEC decisions and reports involving public accountants. They have discussed in detail the inadequacies in examinations made by public accountants in specific instances, differences in viewpoint concerning the accounting principles reflected in financial statements filed with the Commission, cases in which the SEC found that the certifying accountants were not independent according to the Commission's standards, and so on. The more important of such decisions and reports are discussed or referred to in this book under the subject headings to which they relate.

The SEC Rules of Practice

Like many other government commissions, the SEC has rules governing persons who appear and practice before the Commission, informal procedures, and the conduct of SEC employees and former staff members. Rule 2 of the Rules of Practice relates to appearance and practice before the Commission. For the purpose of the rule, "practicing before the Commission" includes the preparation of any statement, opinion, or other paper by an accountant, filed with the Commission in any registration statement, application, report, or other document with the consent of such accountant.

Rule 2(e) provides that the Commission may deny, temporarily or permanently, the privilege of appearing or practicing before it to any person who is found by the Commission (1) not to possess the requisite qualifications to represent others, or (2) to be lacking in character or integrity or to have engaged in unethical or improper professional conduct, or (3) to have willfully violated, or willfully aided and abetted the violation of, any provision of the Federal securities laws, or the rules and regulations thereunder.

Under the rule, the privilege of appearing or practicing before the Commission is suspended in the case of any accountant whose license to practice as such is revoked by any State, Territory, District, Commonwealth, or Possession, or who has been convicted of a felony or of a misdemeanor involving moral turpitude.

The SEC made important amendments in Rule 2(e) in 1971 (Release No. 33–5147, May 10, 1971). The amendments provide for the suspension from appearing or practicing before the SEC of any attorney, accountant, engineer, or other professional or expert who, on or after July 1, 1971, "by name," has been permanently enjoined by reason of his misconduct, in an action brought by the SEC, from violating or aiding the violation of the Federal securities laws or the rules thereunder. The amendments also provide for the suspension of any accountant or other professional who has been found in an action brought by the SEC, or by the SEC in an administrative proceeding, to have violated or to have aided the violation of any such provision or rule, unless the violation was found not to have been willful.

Under the amendment, a temporary suspension will become permanent after 30 days unless a petition to lift the suspension is filed within that time. If a petition is filed, the SEC may lift the suspension or, after a hearing, may censure the petitioner or may suspend him (temporarily or permanently) from appearing or practicing before the SEC.

In a hearing, the burden will be upon the petitioner to show cause why he should not be censured or disqualified. Also, he will not be permitted to litigate factual questions that he litigated or, but for his consent, might have litigated in the earlier judicial or administrative proceeding. Moreover, a person will be presumed to have been enjoined by reason of the misconduct alleged in the complaint if he consented to an injunction without admitting the facts.

Under the amended Rule 2(e), a permanent injunction against securities laws violations, or a finding of such violations, will provide a basis for the SEC to start proceedings to censure or disqualify a person from SEC practice. For this purpose, no distinction will be made between injunctions and findings which have been contested and those which have been consented to without admitting the facts alleged in the complaint. In announcing the amendment to the rule, the SEC said that "Consequently, it will be incumbent upon any person who may be affected by the amended rule who does not wish to waive a hearing on the question of misconduct to avail himself of the opportunity for hearing provided in the action or proceeding in which a securities law injunction has been sought or in which securities laws violations have for other purposes been alleged; the Commission will afford a hearing only to consider mitigating or other factors why neither censure nor . . . disqualification should be imposed."

The Commission's release stated that the amended rule applies only to professionals or experts who are "by name" enjoined or the subject of a finding and not to partnerships (or corporations) of which they might be members, although a firm may itself be enjoined "by name" and thus come within the terms of the rule. Partners of a disqualified individual may not permit such person to participate to any extent in matters coming before the Commission, to participate in profits from their SEC business, or to hold himself out as entitled to practice before the SEC. Partners and associates of a disqualified firm may not practice before the SEC so long as they remain members of or associated with the firm.

Because of the importance of Rule 2(e), its text is reproduced below:

Rule 2(e) of the Rules of Practice

(e) *Suspension and Disbarment.* (1) The Commission may deny, temporarily or permanently, the privilege of appearing or practicing before it in any way to any person who is found by the Commission after notice of and opportunity for hearing in the matter (i) not to possess the requisite qualifications to represent others, or (ii) to be lacking in character or integrity or to have engaged in unethical or improper professional conduct, or (iii) to have willfully violated, or willfully aided and abetted the violation of any provision of the federal securities laws . . . , or the rules and regulations thereunder.

(2) Any attorney who has been suspended or disbarred . . . , or any person whose license to practice as an accountant, engineer or other expert has been revoked or suspended in any State, Territory, District, Commonwealth, or Possession, or any person who has been convicted of a felony, or of a misdemeanor involving moral turpitude, shall be forthwith suspended from appearing or practicing before the Commission. A disbarment, suspension, revocation or conviction within the meaning of this rule shall be deemed to have occurred when the disbarring, suspending, revoking or convicting agency or tribunal enters its judgment or order, regardless of whether appeal is pending or could be taken, and includes a judgment or order on a plea of *nolo contendere.*

(3) (i) The Commission, with due regard to the public interest and without preliminary hearing, may by order temporarily suspend from appearing or practicing before it any attorney, accountant, engineer or other professional or expert who, on or after July 1, 1971, has been by name

(A) permanently enjoined by any court of competent jurisdiction by reason of his misconduct in an action brought by the Commission from violation or aiding and abetting the violation of any provision of the federal securities laws . . . or of the rules and regulations thereunder; or

(B) found by any court of competent jurisdiction in an action brought by the Commission to which he is a party or found by this Commission in any administrative proceeding to which he is a party to have violated or aided and abetted the violation of any provision of the federal securities laws . . . or of the rules and regulations thereunder (unless the violation was found not to have been willful).

An order of temporary suspension shall become effective when served by certified or registered mail directed to the last known business or residence address of the person involved. No order of temporary suspension shall be entered by the Commission pursuant to this paragraph (i) more than three months after the final judgment or order entered in a judicial or administrative proceeding described in subparagraph (A) or (B) has become effective upon completion of review or appeal procedures or because further review or appeal procedures are no longer available.

(ii) Any person temporarily suspended from appearing and practicing before the Commission in accordance with paragraph (i) may, within thirty days after service upon him of the order of temporary suspension, petition the Commission to lift the temporary suspension. If no petition has been received by the Commission within thirty days after service of the order by mail the suspension shall become permanent.

(iii) Within thirty days after the filing of a petition in accordance with paragraph (ii), the Commission shall either lift the temporary suspension or set the matter down for hearing at a time and place to be designated by the Commission or both, and after opportunity for hearing, may censure the petitioner or may disqualify the petitioner from appearing or practicing before the Commission for a period of time or permanently. In every case in which the temporary suspension has not been lifted, every hearing held and other action taken pursuant to this paragraph (3) shall be expedited in every way consistent with the Commission's other responsibilities.

(iv) In any hearing held on a petition filed in accordance with paragraph (ii), the staff of the Commission shall show either that the petitioner has been enjoined as described in paragraph (i) (A) or that the petitioner has been found to have committed or aided and abetted violations as described in paragraph (i) (B) and that showing, without more, may be the basis for censure or disqualification; that showing having been made, the burden shall be upon the petitioner to show cause why he should not be censured or temporarily or permanently disqualified from appearing and practicing before the Commission. In any such hearing the petitioner shall not be heard to contest any findings made against him or facts admitted by him in the judicial or administrative proceeding upon which the proceeding under this paragraph (3) is predicated, as provided in subparagraph (i) hereof. A person who has consented to the entry of a permanent injunction as described in subparagraph (i) (A) of this paragraph (3) without admitting the facts set forth in the complaint shall be presumed for all purposes under this paragraph (3) to have been enjoined by reason of the misconduct alleged in the complaint.

(4)(i) An application for reinstatement of a person permanently suspended or disqualified under paragraphs (1) or (3) of this Rule may be made at any time, and the applicant may, in the Commission's discretion, be afforded a hearing; however, the suspension or disqualification shall continue unless and until the applicant has been reinstated by the Commission for good cause shown.

(ii) Any person suspended under paragraph (2) of this Rule shall be reinstated by the Commission, upon appropriate application, if all the grounds for application of the provisions of that paragraph are subsequently removed by a reversal of the conviction or termination of the suspension, disbarment or revocation. An application for reinstatement on any other grounds by any person suspended under paragraph (2) of this rule may be filed at any time and the applicant shall be accorded an opportunity for a hearing in the matter; however, such suspension shall continue unless and until the applicant has been reinstated by order of the Commission for good cause shown.

(5) Any person appearing or practicing before the Commission who has been the subject of an order, judgment, decree or finding as set forth above shall promptly file with the Secretary of the Commission a copy thereof (together with any related opinion or statement of the agency or tribunal involved). Failure to file any such paper shall not impair the operation of any other provision of this rule.

(6) Any proceeding brought under any of the above sections shall not preclude a proceeding under any other section.

(7) All hearings held under this Rule 2(e) shall be non-public unless the Commission on its own motion or the request of a party otherwise directs.

The above text of Rule 2(e) reflects the revisions made by the Commission in 1970 and 1971. In announcing the 1970 revisions, the Commission said that the need therefor was apparent from a recent case in which an attorney, who had been convicted of violating SEC statutes, was able to file numerous documents with the Commission during the approximately eleven months between the conviction and his disqualification by the Commission. The Commission also observed that the revisions should "prevent similar situations in which the Commission and the investing public places its trust in, or reliance upon, attorneys, accountants and other experts who have proved their untrustworthiness." (Release No. 33–5088, Sept. 24, 1970.)

From a reading of the rule it will be apparent that a person's privilege of appearing or practicing before the SEC will be "forthwith suspended" as the result of his conviction of a felony or of a misdemeanor involving moral turpitude, even though the conviction has nothing whatsoever to do with the statutes administered by the SEC. Furthermore, if the SEC learns that an accountant has committed a reprehensible act in the course of a professional engagement—even though it has no relationship whatsoever to the SEC or its functions—the Commission may institute proceedings to prevent that individual from appearing or practicing before the Commission. Not only is this a possibility, but, as will be seen from the decisions in Rule 2(e) proceedings summarized below, it has in fact occurred. In other words, the Commission's right to disqualify a person from practicing before the Commission is not limited to findings in connection with material filed with the Commission. The rule appears to be broad enough to cover the lack of integrity or professional misconduct wherever or however it occurs.

Proceedings under Rule 2(e) are private unless the Commission on its own motion or the request of a party to the proceedings directs otherwise. Consequently, the first public indication of proceedings under the rule is usually when the Commission makes known its findings. There have been a number of Rule 2(e) proceedings, but the number which have been made public is small indeed, considering the number of accountants who certify financial data in documents filed with the SEC. The number is also small considering the volume of registrations and reports filed with SEC, and the fact that the Commission had its origin in 1933.

The SEC has said that, while the Commission has cooperated with the accounting profession to secure a common objective of high professional standards, "yet it has, as it must, reserved to itself the right to invoke sanctions against accountants who wilfully or carelessly violate its rules." [8 SEC Ann. Rep. 45 (1942)].

If, as a result of its hearings under Rule 2(e), the SEC finds that the work of a public accountant does not measure up to professional standards, the SEC sends a report of its findings to the national and state societies of certified public accountants and state agencies for disciplinary action. The same procedure is followed where the Commission publicly criticizes the work of a public accountant as evidenced in a registration or report filed with the Commission.

From a reading of the cases involving accountants summarized on the following pages, it will be noted that there has been a growing tendency in recent years to terminate proceedings under Rule 2(e) when the accountant tenders his resignation from SEC practice and agrees that he will not thereafter appear or practice before the Commission. This does not prevent him from practicing his profession in the future (unless the state or territory in which he resides or practices takes further disciplinary action against him), but it certainly restricts him severely. If, in the future, any of his clients would have to file financial statements with the SEC—for whatever reason —the accountant's report covering such statements could not be filed with the SEC.

Disciplinary Proceedings Against Accountants Under Rule 2(e).
—It is not publicly known how many proceedings have been instituted by the

SEC against public accountants under Rule 2(e) of its Rules of Practice, inasmuch as there is no public record or disclosure of the fact that such proceedings have begun.

At the date of this writing, the SEC has made public the proceedings in 20 cases involving 22 public accountants. The SEC revealed the names of the accountants in all but two cases, but the names will not be disclosed in this book.

1. The first of the proceedings against accountants grew out of the A. Hollander and Son, Inc. case [8 SEC 586 (1941)]. In Release No. 3073 under the 1934 Act, the SEC in 1941 announced (without separate opinion) the results of the disciplinary proceedings under its Rule 2(e). The principal issue in the Hollander case, as far as the accountants were concerned, was the accountants' independence. The case is discussed on page **26**·25 of this book. The accounting firm and a partner of the firm were suspended for a period of three months.

2. In the second proceeding, the independence of the certifying accountant was also the principal issue. The facts appear in ASR No. 28 (1942) (also 10 SEC 982), and are briefly set forth on page **26**·25 of this volume. The accountant was suspended for sixty days.

3. An accountant was permanently disqualified from practice before the Commission following a false certification of the financial statements in a registration statement under the 1933 Act. The SEC found that the accountant had made no audit of the registrant's financial statements but had accepted without question the statements prepared by the registrant's own bookkeeper with whom the accountant had a practice of splitting fees. The accountant was wholly unfamiliar with SEC rules and showed lack of familiarity with rules of the state board of accountancy and the rules of professional conduct (now the Code of Professional Ethics) of the AICPA. The facts in the case are discussed in ASR No. 48 (1944) (also at 15 SEC 400).

4. A proceeding against an unnamed accountant was discontinued, following a stipulation that the accountant would never again practice before the Commission as an accountant. The facts in this case appear in ASR No. 51 (1945).

5. An accounting firm and a partner of the firm were suspended for a period of one year from the privilege of appearing and practicing before the SEC. The firm had certified the financial statements of a broker-dealer on Form X–17A–5, and their audit fell far short of the SEC's requirements. The case is discussed at length in ASR No. 59 (1947).

6. Proceedings against an accounting firm, the former manager of the firm's Los Angeles office, and a staff accountant were dismissed. The case arose out of the Drayer-Hanson, Incorporated matter [27 SEC 838 (1948); also ASR No. 64], which is discussed on page **5**·33 of this book. The

proceedings were the subject of ASR No. 67 (1949). Promptly after the discovery of the inventory shortage involved in the case, the accountants offered to contribute to the company approximately the amount of the shortage.

7. An accounting firm was suspended for a period of thirty days and a partner of the firm was suspended for one year from appearing or practicing before the SEC. The Commission held that the partner was virtually a promoter in relation to his client and, as such, was not independent. Further, the SEC ruled that the accountants had not made a proper audit of the amounts due the president and principal promoter of the issuer. The facts in the proceeding are set forth in ASR No. 68 (1949), and are referred to on page **26**·26 of this book.

8. An accounting firm and one of its partners were suspended for a period of ten days. This proceeding grew out of the Thomascolor, Incorporated, case [27 SEC 151 (1947)]. The principal issue in that case was the showing of intangible assets acquired for par value stock in the balance sheet of a corporation, the accounting for shares to be donated to the corporation, and the accounting for shares issued for promotional services. The proceedings were discussed at length in ASR No. 73 (1952). (It is noteworthy that the decision in the Rule 2(e) proceedings followed by *five years* the decision in the Thomascolor case.)

9. Proceedings against an unnamed accountant were dismissed. The accountant had certified the financial statements of a broker-dealer, and had failed to discover a shortage in the accounts of a branch office. The accountant qualified the opinion expressed in his certificate by indicating that his examination of the branch office was "limited to a verification of reported assets and liabilities." The SEC was of the opinion that while more thorough auditing procedures might have resulted in the discovery of the fictitious transactions, the record in this case did not disclose a lack of the requisite qualifications to represent others or a lack of integrity or improper professional conduct within the meaning of Rule 2(e). The proceeding is the subject of ASR No. 77 (1954).

10. As a result of proceedings in the Seaboard Commercial Corporation case, the SEC instituted Rule 2(e) proceedings against the certifying accountants. The Commission suspended the accounting firm and two of its partners from practice before the Commission for a period of fifteen days. The Commission's decision relating to the accountants was announced in ASR No. 78 (1957), a summary of which appears in this volume beginning on page **5**·18. The proceedings in this case were instituted in 1952, and the Commission announced its decision in 1957—*five years later.*

11. In ASR No. 82 (1959), the SEC reported its findings and opinion in Rule 2(e) proceedings following the withdrawal of the registration statement of Motel Corporation of Italy. The certifying accountant in this case

was a partner in a public accounting firm. The other partner of the firm was the principal promoter, president, treasurer, director, and owner of the majority of the voting stock of the registrant. The latter realized that he was not independent for SEC purposes, and the former therefore certified the company's balance sheet in his own name. The case is discussed on page **26·**26. The SEC ordered that the firm of B & S, and Mr. B, be denied the privilege of practicing before the Commission unless and until they shall have obtained the prior approval of the Commission, and Mr. S was denied the privilege of practicing for a period of thirty days. (In ASR No. 87 (1961) the SEC reported that Mr. B, "formerly a partner in [B & S], a firm of certified public accountants, now dissolved," had filed a petition for reinstatement of his privilege of practicing before the Commission. The Commission concluded that in the circumstances of the case it would not be inconsistent with the public interest to terminate its prior order, and granted the request for reinstatement.)

12. In connection with proceedings to determine whether to withdraw the listing of the common stock of Cornucopia Gold Mines on the American Stock Exchange, the Commission issued its findings and opinion. [40 SEC 177 (1960)]. The Commission determined that the listing should be withdrawn, and issued an opinion which, among other things, was highly critical of the company's financial reporting practices, and the examinations of the company's financial statements by three accountants. Subsequently the Commission instituted proceedings against the accountants under Rule 2(e) to determine whether the privilege of practicing before the SEC should be suspended or withdrawn. The Commission announced its decisions in three separate releases which are discussed below.

A. The decision involving Accountant A was reported in ASR No. 88 (1961). The SEC said that the accountant's conduct throughout his connection with the company and its parent was unethical, improper, and unprofessional. Without even seeing the books and records of Eastern (the parent), he certified financial statements of that company. He furnished Earl Belle (the principal architect of the false statements and later a fugitive from justice) with blank signed stationery which was later used to circulate false financial statements. Even assuming that the accountant did not appreciate fully what he was doing, he did nothing to make appropriate disclosures of the improprieties once he discovered them. On the contrary, he continued to perform services, including the preparation of certified financial statements which were stipulated to be incorrect and misleading. The SEC decided that Accountant A should be denied the privilege of practicing before the SEC in the future.

B. The decision involving Accountant B was announced in ASR No. 91 (1962). The accountant had certified financial statements of Cornucopia and Eastern and had represented that his examination was made in accordance with generally accepted auditing standards and accordingly included such tests of the accounting records and such other auditing procedures as he considered necessary in the circumstances. He admitted that he had made no audit of, nor had he ever seen, the books and records of either company. The Cornucopia statements certified by him were copied from statements prepared and certified by Accountant A. The Eastern statements certified by him (Accountant B) were copied from unsigned draft statements given to him by Belle. The SEC also determined that the accountant was not independent within the meaning of the SEC's rules. The Commission ordered that the accountant be denied the privilege of practicing before the Commission.

C. The decision involving Accountant C was announced in ASR No. 92 (1962). This accountant had prepared a balance sheet on the basis of information he had received over the telephone from an officer of Eastern. The accountant furnished a covering letter in which he stated that he had reviewed the books and records and had prepared therefrom a balance sheet as of December 31, 1956. In fact, the accountant had not seen any books or records of Eastern; his sole source of information for the balance sheet was his telephone conversation with Eastern's officer. The balance sheet was materially false and misleading, and was used to obtain a bank loan. The Commission concluded that Accountant C should be disqualified from practicing before the Commission "unless and until he shall obtain our prior approval, provided that no application for such approval will be entertained for a period of one year after the date of our order in this proceeding."

One of the most significant aspects of the SEC's decisions involving the three accountants in the Cornucopia case related to Accountant C. *To the author's knowledge, this was the first instance in which the SEC disciplined an accountant for misconduct in connection with something which was never filed with the Commission.* Granted that the balance sheet prepared by Accountant C was improper and misleading. Granted also that his covering letter was false in stating that he had reviewed books and records of the company. The statement and the letter were shown only to a bank as a basis for a loan and to a credit rating agency. The fact remains, however, that no public investor ever saw the balance sheet or the letter and hence was not misled by them. The staff of the SEC were never misled by them. The staff of the SEC did not know of the balance sheet or accountant's letter until they learned about them in their investigation of the Cornucopia matter. As a matter of fact, the statement was not a balance sheet of Cornucopia; it was a balance sheet of Eastern, the parent of Cornucopia, and Eastern was not a publicly owned company.

On March 31, 1965, Accountant C filed a request for reinstatement of his privilege of appearing and practicing before the SEC. He stated that since his suspension by the Commission he had conducted himself both personally and professionally in a way which has not been subject to criticism by any professional or regulatory body. The Commission granted the request for reinstatement. (ASR No. 101, Apr. 26, 1965.)

13. A Rule 2(e) proceeding was initiated against an accountant because the SEC's Office of the General Counsel charged him with conduct that should disqualify him from appearing or practicing before the Commission. The accountant denied the charges, the nature of which was not disclosed. He was in poor health, and it appeared that his condition would be worsened by a continuation of the proceedings. He agreed that he would not practice before the Commission in any way at any time in the future, and the proceedings were terminated. (ASR No. 94, Nov. 5, 1962.)

14. The Keller Brothers Securities Co., Inc. case is discussed in Chapter 5 because the SEC found material deficiencies in the audits made by the certifying accountant. The SEC also said that the accountant had certain business relationships which were incompatible with his status as an independent public accountant; these relationships are disclosed in Chapter **26**. The SEC said that the accountant co-operated completely and candidly with the SEC's staff in its investigation of his case, and no question was raised as to his personal integrity. Nevertheless he was denied the privilege of appearing or practicing before the Commission for a period of 60 days. (ASR No. 97, May 21, 1963).

15. The Miami Window Corporation case is discussed in Chapter **5** of this book. The company's registration statement under the 1933 Act was the subject of stop-order proceedings.

In August 1963 the SEC began proceedings under its Rule 2(e) to determine whether the certifying accountants in that case should be denied the right to appear or practice before the Commission. The charges arose from the certification of the financial statements in the registration statement in which the accountants represented that the financial statements fairly presented the company's financial position and results of operations, and that their audit had been made in accordance with generally accepted auditing standards.

The accountants filed a motion to discontinue the proceedings on the ground, among others, that the Commission lacked a quorum of Commissioners qualified to act in this matter. The SEC did not concede that any of the grounds urged for dismissal were valid. However, the SEC took into consideration the representations of the accountants: (1) that from the time of the institution of the public stop-order proceeding, and to some extent before that time during which a private investigation by staff of the Commission was being conducted, the accountants suffered the loss of a substantial portion of their practice before the Commission; (2) that the publication of the Commission's stop-order opinion on June 21, 1962 had a further adverse effect on their practice; and (3) that improved auditing procedures had been put into effect by the accounting firm.

In view of these circumstances and the fact that the inventory discrepancies had been called to the Commission's attention by the accountants and company officials, and also because of the possibility of extensive and time-consuming litigation on procedural matters not relating to the merits of the case and the resulting delay in the already protracted proceedings, the Commission terminated the Rule 2(e) proceedings without a hearing. (ASR No. 99, Feb. 28, 1964.)

16. On the basis of information furnished to the Commission in a non-public investigative proceeding, the SEC said that it had reason to believe that there may have been a lack of adherence to auditing standards by a CPA in connection with the preparation and submission of certain material to the Commission.

The CPA, without admitting any such lack of adherence, had tendered to the SEC his resignation in which he agreed that he would not appear or practice before the Commission in the future. The Commission decided to accept the accountant's resignation from SEC practice and to discontinue the Rule 2(e) proceedings. (ASR No. 104, June 2, 1966.)

17. One of the most widely publicized cases of false financial statements ever filed with the SEC occurred in the case of the registration statement of Olen Company, Inc. The case is discussed in Chapter 5.

After the start of Rule 2(e) proceedings against the certifying accountants in that case, the senior partner of the firm died. The remaining junior partner, a CPA, without admitting any of the allegations against him, tendered his withdrawal from practice and agreed not to appear or practice before the SEC in the future, with the understanding that the proceedings would be dismissed as to him and that the SEC could issue a statement with respect to the action taken. The Commission accepted the accountant's withdrawal from SEC practice and dismissed the proceedings. (ASR No. 105, July 29, 1966.)

18. On the basis of information furnished to the Commission, the SEC said that a CPA may have failed to comply with generally accepted auditing standards and its minimum audit requirements in connection with a filing on Form X–17A–5. It appeared that the audits may have been deficient in one or more of the following matters: (1) failure to obtain written confirmation of bank balances and to obtain the bank statements and cancelled checks from the depositaries and to reconcile the bank balances at the audit date; (2) the same procedures were omitted at an appropriate date subsequent to the audit date; (3) failure to obtain written confirmation of customers' accounts, open contractual commitments, etc., as at the audit date; (4) failure to review and, on a test basis, obtain written confirmation of customers' accounts closed during the period under review; (5) failure to

examine and confirm in writing subordination agreements covering indebtedness shown as subordinated in the financial statements; (6) failure to secure a written statement signed by the proprietor, a responsible partner, or an officer, as appropriate, as to the assets, liabilities, and accountabilities, contingent or otherwise, not recorded in the books; (7) the CPA appears not to have been independent in respect to the broker-dealer in that he owed money to the broker-dealer or one of its officers; and (8) the CPA appeared to have altered his audit working papers in at least two instances after the SEC's investigation began.

The CPA, without admitting or denying any of the charges, offered to resign from SEC practice. The SEC accepted the resignation and decided that no proceedings under its Rule 2(e) were necessary. (ASR No. 108, Feb. 9, 1967.)

19. In another case similar to the foregoing involving the financial statements of a broker-dealer filed with the SEC, the Commission said that it had information indicating that there may have been a failure to comply with generally accepted auditing standards and the Commission's minimum audit requirements, but the SEC did not specify the shortcomings. In this case also, the SEC accepted the accountant's resignation from practice before the Commission and concluded that an action under its Rule 2(e) was not necessary. (ASR No. 109, Sept. 25, 1967.)

20. ASR No. 110 (Jan. 18, 1968) also is concerned with sub-standard audits of two broker-dealers by a CPA. On the basis of a non-public investigation, the SEC's staff charged that the CPA willfully aided and abetted violations of the 1934 Act and its rules relating to Form X–17A–5. The staff alleged that the CPA certified without qualification a materially false and misleading statement of financial condition filed with the SEC by a broker-dealer (Sec. Exch. Act Release No. 7343, June 15, 1964). When the CPA, according to the staff, was not independent, he certified the financial statements of another broker-dealer. In connection with all of the foregoing, the staff charged that the CPA failed to comply with generally accepted auditing standards and did not observe the audit requirements applicable to Form X–17A–5.

It appeared that Broker No. 1 did not maintain a general ledger, and therefore the CPA did not compare the "ledger accounts" with a trial balance obtained from the general ledger and did not compare the aggregates of subsidiary ledgers with their respective control accounts. The CPA, it was said, did not balance securities positions at the audit date, and did not balance and confirm customers' money balances and securities positions. The staff asserted that the statement of financial condition of the broker omitted liabilities for loans payable aggregating $525,500, including about $34,000 payable to banks, and that the statement thereby showed a capital position of about $38,000. It was also charged that the CPA failed to check the proceeds of such loans into bank accounts and to verify expenditures therefrom, and that the CPA was not, in fact, independent.

Without admitting or denying the staff's charges, the CPA agreed that he would not practice before the SEC in the future. The SEC accepted his resignation and decided that Rule 2(e) proceedings were not necessary.

Effect of Suspension.—In several of the proceedings against accountants the SEC announced that it had "suspended" the accountants from appearing or practicing before the Commission. This means that, during the period of the suspension:

1. The accountants' certificate may not be included in any registration statement, application, or report filed with the Commission;
2. The accountants' certificate may not be included in any amendment to any of the afore-mentioned documents;
3. No registration statement which includes their certificate can become effective; and
4. The accountants may not discuss any problem with the Commission or its staff.

The author understands that after the "black out" is lifted, nothing filed with the Commission may include an accountants' certificate dated during the suspension period. It will be readily seen that a suspension for even a short period—say, ten days—is a very serious thing indeed, since it punishes not only the accountant involved *but also his clients.*

CHAPTER 28

LIABILITY OF ACCOUNTANTS

Part 2: Court Decisions Involving Accountants Under Federal Securities Laws; the Leading Cases

CONTENTS

Court Decisions Involving Accountants Based on Federal Securities Laws

The most authoritative work on the subject of securities law is *Securities Regulation* by Louis Loss, a law professor and former official of the SEC. In 1961 Loss wrote that the number of suits brought by investors under the 1933 Act was very small both in comparison with the mass of litigation under the state acts and in absolute terms.[1] He reported that the total number of cases of which any trace could be found in interlocutory or final court decisions, reported and unreported, was 77—less than three actions per year. He acknowledged that the statistics were faulty, and their completeness could not be assured.

Up to that time (1961) the only recorded case involving a claim against accountants based on the Federal securities statutes dealt with a lease commitment entered into between the balance sheet date and the effective date

[1] P. 1685.

of a registration statement under the 1933 Act.[2] The case is an unsatisfactory one as will be seen from the discussion of it in Chapter **12**.

Loss said it was difficult to account for the amazingly small amount of litigation in the aggregate—and this in a country in which several of the larger states (New York State, for example) have felt it necessary to erect legislative safeguards against "strike suits." He said:

> The bar and the accounting profession can presumably take a share of the credit, so far as Section 11 [of the 1933 Act] is concerned, because of the care with which most registration statements are prepared. But probably the greatest single deterrent to Section 11 actions has been the Commission's careful examination of registration statements. Both lawyers and clients have apparently been awake for some time to the realization that a scrupulous processing of the registration statement is the best sort of insurance they have against Section 11 actions. . . . Nothing else can account for the fact that some 18,000 registration statements have resulted in 2 adjudicated recoveries under Section 11, none since 1939.[3]

When, and if, Loss revises his 1961 publication, the section on litigation —particularly as it relates to public accountants—will require extensive revision and updating. The amount of litigation involving accountants has never been as high as it has been in recent years. The volume of litigation, the decisions by judges and juries, the amounts of settlements, the difficulties in obtaining adequate professional insurance coverage—all are currently matters of great concern to the public accounting profession.

As one writer put it, "Perhaps at no time since Luca Pacioli first published a description of double entry bookkeeping in 1494 has the ancient . . . profession of accounting been under as much scrutiny and as much pressure as it is presently." [4] All the dangers which accountants saw lurking in the statutory and common law extensions of their responsibilities, he said, have now begun to blossom. He continued:

> Despite protestations of accountants that they are not 'guarantors' or 'insurers' of the financial statements prepared by their clients with respect to which they render opinions, despite their insistence that their function is not to, and their methods are not designed to, encounter or uncover fraud and despite their most diligent efforts to limit the scope of their responsibility, they are increasingly the prey of purportedly damaged investors . . .[5]

An editorial in the accountancy profession's principal publication inquired as to the reasons for the sudden spurt in claims against auditors, and said that what seems to be happening is that banks and other financial institutions were increasingly hoping that accounting firms "can be made a

---

[2] *Shonts v. Hirliman,* 28 F. Supp. 478 (S. D. Cal. 1939).

[3] Pp. 1690–91.

[4] A. A. Sommer, Jr., "Accountant's Counsel—Advice to My Client," *The Business Lawyer,* Jan. 1969, p. 593.

[5] *Ibid.,* p. 593.

source of salvage when loans go bad or credit losses occur." [6] The editorial also pointed out that legal fees contingent on the success of litigation encourage naming as a defendant anyone (including accountants) related in any way to a case involving financial loss.

As an indication of the enormous increase in litigation involving public accountants, it is interesting to contrast the current climate with that existing at the time the McKesson & Robbins fraud was brought to light. The McKesson case is discussed in some detail in this book primarily because of the SEC's painstaking investigation of the fraud and the auditing practices of public accountants at the time—particularly with respect to the verification of receivables and inventories. As previously noted, the McKesson case and the SEC's report on its investigation had a profound effect on the practice of public accounting in the United States and, with the passage of time, on practice in foreign countries. And yet, despite the magnitude of the deception in the McKesson case, it is noteworthy that not a single lawsuit was brought against the accountants who certified McKesson's financial statements. According to the author's information, McKesson's independent auditors refunded the fees they had received from the company, and there was no litigation whatever involving them.

Contrast the relatively litigation-free atmosphere in the McKesson era with that existing today! As will be noted in the discussion of the BarChris case, there were over 60 plaintiffs who were joined in a "class action" at the time the case came to trial. In the Yale Express case (also discussed in this book), there were 17 actions instituted against some of the company's former officers and directors, its independent auditors, and the underwriters of its debenture offering.

It seems clear that the legal device known as a "class action" has contributed to the growth of a new specialization in the practice of law, as a result of which lawyers are willing to invest large amounts of their time and effort on behalf of a minor, allegedly injured security holder. They make that investment in the hope that, if their efforts are successful, there will be a sizeable award or settlement on behalf of *all* the security holders of that class. The lawyers' fees in cases of this kind have been known to be very substantial indeed since they are based on the amount of the recovery or settlement for the entire class—not merely on the recovery by the nominal plaintiff. Accordingly, lawyers specializing in this branch of the law are quick to welcome a plaintiff when there is a prospect of a class action, even when the possibility of success is somewhat remote. If it is possible to include the company's independent auditors in the list of defendants, the prospect of a suit becomes all the more attractive since it is common knowledge that public accountants, as a rule, carry substantial amounts of insur-

[6] *The Journal of Accountancy,* Sept. 1965.

ance. Even if the lawyers are not designated as lead counsel, in the event of a successful result, their share of the recovery is likely to be substantial.

(Federal Rule of Civil Procedure 23, which governs the bringing of class actions in federal court, was recently liberalized to facilitate the bringing of such actions.)

One result of the enormous increase in lawsuits against accountants is a re-awakening of interest in the possibility of conducting a professional accounting practice in corporate form. The possibility of practicing as a corporation is a subject that has interested other professional groups as well as accountants, but until recently the principal advantage which it was hoped would accrue from the change was in the area of taxation.

Especially in SEC practice, where the accountant's legal exposure may be as much as the entire amount of the public offering of securities, accountants are more interested than ever before in the possibilities of incorporating their practices. Other possibilities being considered are changes in the securities laws limiting the liability of experts at some percentage of the offering price, or at some figure related to the audit fees involved. At any rate, the subject of practicing in corporate form is being discussed in professional literature as it has never been discussed before.[7]

A professor of law, writing about the Yale Express case (see page **28·32** of this book), has observed that the court, in deciding many of the issues before it, would have to choose between the enormously diverse economic interests of the investor on the one hand, and, on the other hand, the public accountant. The writer said that a healthy economic climate requires not only the vigilant protection of the investing public from misleading information, but also maintenance of the solvency of the honest, conscientious accountant whose certification is greatly relied upon by the entire business community. "The time seems ripe, therefore, to strike for a meaningful compromise which achieves both ends."[8] The professor suggested integrating into one composite statute all the rules concerning the accountants' duties and liabilities arising out of the certification of financial statements filed with the SEC. In drafting such a statute, he said, the following might be considered:

1. The widely divergent substantive and procedural variations of the accountants' liability under the Federal securities statutes should be narrowed and in most cases eliminated.

2. The reporting methods should be tightened by a panel established under

[7] See, for example, Stewart Schackne, "Incorporating Accounting Practices: Good Idea? Bad Idea?", *The Journal of Accountancy,* Dec. 1968, pp. 33–39; also, Eli Mason, "Should CPAs Be Permitted to Practice in Corporate Form?", *The New York CPA,* Dec. 1969, pp. 938–943.

[8] Constantine N. Katsoris, "Accountants' Liability: Where Will It End?", *Trial Magazine,* June–July 1969, p. 51.

the statute and consisting of personnel from the SEC, the accounting profession, and the financial and business communities.

3. Create a pre-clearance board from which the accountant could seek guidance if a unique situation arises not then covered by the statute or the rules thereunder.

4. The accountant's duties should be more specifically outlined in such statute, instead of advising him in an *ex post facto* manner on such problems as: (a) after-acquired information, (b) interim financial statements, (c) effect of non-auditing services on accountants' independence, and (d) the desirability of specifying in-depth auditing procedures.

5. Grant the accountant immunity which, insofar as financial statements filed with SEC are concerned, absolves him from liability in any form to the extent he follows the reporting requirements and procedures outlined in the statute, or promulgated thereunder. (Cf. Section 19 of the 1933 Act).

Such a statute, in the professor's view, would achieve the dual purpose of aiding the investor before he is hurt, and tightening the sphere of the auditor's liability.

The Leading Decided Cases Involving Accountants

At the time this is written, there have been instituted and are pending more than 100 lawsuits against major United States accounting firms in which there are allegations of Federal securities laws violations. (In some of the cases, there are multiple separate actions in which the plaintiffs are different, but the allegations are similar, which will undoubtedly be consolidated into a single proceeding. In one such case, there are more than 50 separate actions. In all such instances, while there may be many separate actions, they are considered here as one case.) How many lawsuits involving the Federal securities laws have been initiated against smaller accounting firms is not known, but there are many.

The complaints in many of the cases have been widely publicized, and the developments in them will be watched with interest by lawyers as well as by accountants. The author has read many of the complaints, and although they do not disclose any particular pattern as far as the accountant-defendants are concerned, all of them, as might be expected, charge the accountants with negligent performance of their professional obligations. Allegations, however, are a long way from proof. Although the allegations in several of the more important cases have been reported in the press, they will not be discussed in this book. The author prefers to suspend judgment concerning the merits of a case until there is a decision with an accompanying written opinion.

The following pages of this chapter contain discussions of several leading cases involving public accountants under the Federal securities laws which have been decided or settled and in which there was a written opinion by a judge. Where a suit was instituted against accountants and it was decided or settled without a written opinion, the case is not discussed. Where an accountant was indicted criminally and there was no written decision, the case is also not discussed.

This chapter therefore contains discussions of the following cases:

(1) The BarChris case (the leading case dealing with civil liabilities under the 1933 Act) ;
(2) The Continental Vending Machine case (involving accountants' criminal liabilities under the 1934 Act) ; and
(3) The Yale Express case (in which the SEC took a position with respect to accountants' obligations when they learn that financial statements previously certified by them were materially incorrect).

The BarChris Case.—The most comprehensive decision in a lawsuit involving civil liability under the Securities Act of 1933 was in the BarChris case (cited *Escott, et al. v. BarChris Construction Corp., et al.* 283 F. Supp. 643 (S.D.N.Y. 1968)). It is a landmark case since it dealt extensively, for the first time, with the liabilities under the 1933 Act of officers and directors of an issuer, underwriters, accountants, and counsel for the issuer and the underwriters. As a consequence it has been widely discussed in journals, seminars, and in publications concerned with law, accounting, and investment banking. The discussion which follows, however, will be limited to the role played by the independent public accountants and their liabilities in connection with an offering of BarChris's securities which had been registered with the SEC under the 1933 Act.

BarChris Construction Corporation was in the business of constructing "bowling centers"—more commonly known as bowling alleys. BarChris was a minor factor in an industry that was completely overshadowed by two giants. In 1960 it constructed about 3% of all the lanes built in the United States. Its sales had increased dramatically from $819,000 in 1956 to $9,165,000 in 1960. To a minor extent, it also operated bowling alleys.

BarChris's method of doing business was to enter into a contract with a customer, receive a down payment, and proceed with the construction of the bowling center. On completion of the center, the customer would deliver its notes to BarChris for the balance due. BarChris would discount the notes with a factoring company. In some cases BarChris would sell the center to a factoring company. The factor, in turn, would lease the center either to the customer or to a BarChris subsidiary with the lease obligations being guaranteed by BarChris.

BarChris filed a registration statement under the 1933 Act which became effective on May 16, 1961, covering an issue of convertible debentures. The securities were sold through an underwriting group in May 1961. The proceeds were approximately $3,250,000.

By the offering date the company was having trouble collecting amounts due from its customers. Some of the customers were in arrears in payments due to factoring companies with whom the customers' notes had been discounted. As time went on, those difficulties increased. BarChris continued to build alleys in 1961 and 1962, but it became increasingly apparent that the industry was overbuilt. Operators of alleys began to fail. In several instances BarChris had to operate alleys it had built pursuant to contract for sale to others. When the tide turned is disputed, but it was painfully apparent in 1962 that the bowling boom was over.

In October 1962 BarChris came to the end of the road. On October 29, 1962 it filed under the Bankruptcy Act. Four days previously (October 25, 1962) a civil suit was instituted under Section 11 of the 1933 Act against the company, its officers and directors, the underwriters, and the independent public accountants. When the action was begun, there were nine plaintiffs. Others were subsequently permitted to intervene, and, at the time of the trial, there were over 60 plaintiffs who were joined in a "class action."

More than five years later (on March 29, 1968, to be exact), the judge who presided at the trial rendered his decision in which he ruled that all defendants were responsible to some extent, but reserved decision on the extent of liability attaching to each, which involved consideration of cross-claims filed among the defendants. (The case has since been settled out of court, and so there will not be a further judicial determination of the issues.)

The judge's decision is a long, complicated document (127 printed pages), that will be carefully read, re-read, and analyzed for years to come by accountants, lawyers, investment bankers, and others interested in the question of liability as it relates to the 1933 Act.

Summarized below are some of the principal findings involving the accountants and their responsibilities under the 1933 Act. It will be noted that some of them are favorable not only to the accountants involved in the BarChris case, but also to the accountancy profession in general.

The prospectus included a consolidated balance sheet as of December 31, 1960 and statements of earnings and retained earnings for the five years then ended. These statements were audited by the independent accountants whose report was dated February 23, 1961. The prospectus also contained "capsule" information for the first quarter of 1961 with respect to net sales, gross profit, and net earnings, together with the figures for the corresponding quarter of the preceding year—all of such capsule information being submitted on an unaudited basis.

PLAINTIFFS COULD NOT RELY ON COMFORT LETTER.—At the closing with the underwriters on May 24, 1961, the auditors delivered a comfort letter to the underwriters. The letter ended with this paragraph:

It is understood that this letter is for the information of the underwriters and is not to be quoted or referred to, in whole or in part, in the Registration Statement or Prospectus or in any literature used in connection with the sale of securities.

Although it is common knowledge that comfort letters are often furnished by accountants in connection with underwritten offerings, the judge said that the BarChris plaintiffs could not take advantage of any undertakings or representations in this letter. Presumably this was on the basis that the plaintiffs had not seen the letter and had not relied on it since it was not a public document and had not been filed with the SEC. As to claims, however, that the underwriters may have had against the accountants who signed the letter, the judge said that he would decide this matter at a later date. (Because of the settlement, the question of the accountants' liability, if any, to the underwriters, based on the comfort letter, was not judicially determined.)

ERRORS IN THE 1960 FINANCIAL STATEMENTS.—The plaintiffs made extravagant claims of errors and omissions in the 1960 audited financial statements. The judge's task was to sort out the claims, decide which were correct and which were not correct, and—as to those which were correct—to determine whether they were material.

The judge determined that the 1960 sales and earnings were overstated. Sales for that year were reported as $9,165,000, an overstatement of $654,000, or 8%.

"Net operating income" (consisting of income before adding other income and before deducting other deductions and Federal income taxes) for 1960 was stated to be $1,742,000 in the prospectus; according to the judge, the correct figure was $1,496,000, an overstatement of $246,000, or 16%. Net earnings per share were reported in the prospectus at 75 cents a share; the judge said the correct figure was 65 cents a share—an overstatement of 10 cents a share, or 15%. (In 1959 the net earnings were 33 cents a share.)

More detailed information regarding the errors in the 1960 financial statements appears in the following pages.

ERRORS IN THE 1961 CAPSULE DATA.—The prospectus included unaudited capsule data for the first quarter of 1961 relating to net sales, gross profit, and net earnings. The judge found this information to be materially incorrect due principally to the inclusion in sales of alleys which had originally been constructed for outsiders but were eventually acquired and operated by subsidiaries of BarChris.

Bridge Lanes, for example, was built for a company known as Biel Land and Development Co. At December 31, 1960 (the date of the balance sheet) this job was in process. On March 24, 1961 BarChris acquired the stock of Biel and subsequently operated the alley through a subsidiary. BarChris did not sell the alley at any time thereafter, and hence it was erroneous to include in sales $269,810 for Bridge Lanes.

Yonkers Lanes was in the same category. The amount included in 1961 sales for this alley was $250,000. On May 4, 1961 BarChris organized a subsidiary which eventually operated the alley. It was not clear from the testimony at the trial whether BarChris originally intended to operate the alley or whether, at the outset, it had a customer for it. However, the minutes of an Executive Committee meeting on March 18, 1961 showed that as of that date there was no contract with an outside customer, and it should not have been included in sales.

The information for the first quarter of 1961 as originally reported in the prospectus and as corrected by the judge follows:

	As reported in prospectus	As corrected by judge
Net sales	$2,138,455	$1,608,645
Gross profit	483,121	252,366
Net earnings	125,699	Not computed

Net earnings would have been reduced along with the correction in gross profit. The judge said the evidence did not permit calculation of the exact amount of the reduction, but it obviously would have been material.

WERE THE FALSITIES MATERIAL?—The next question to be decided was: were these falsities material facts? In deciding this question, the judge quoted from a 1934 SEC decision (In the *Matter of Charles A. Howard,* 1 SEC 6). A "material fact" was defined in that decision as ". . . a fact which if it had been correctly stated or disclosed would have deterred or tended to deter the average prudent investor from purchasing the securities in question." The judge then considered what the "average prudent investor" would be concerned with in the BarChris situation:

The average prudent investor is not concerned with minor inaccuracies or with errors as to matters which are of no interest to him. The facts which tend to deter him from purchasing a security are facts which have an important bearing upon the nature or condition of the issuing corporation or its business.

Judged by this test, there is no doubt that many of the misstatements and omissions in this prospectus were material. This is true of all of them which relate to the state of affairs in 1961, i.e., the overstatement of sales and gross profit for the first quarter, the understatement of contingent liabilities as of April 30, the overstatement of orders on hand and the failure to disclose the true facts with respect to officers' loans, customers' delinquencies, application of proceeds and the prospective operation of several alleys.

The misstatements and omissions pertaining to BarChris's status as of December 31, 1960, however, present a much closer question. The 1960 earnings figures, the 1960 balance sheet and the contingent liabilities as of December 31, 1960 were not nearly as erroneous as plaintiffs have claimed. But they were wrong to some extent, as we have seen. Would it have deterred the average prudent investor from purchasing these debentures if he had been informed that the 1960 sales were $8,511,420 rather than $9,165,320, that the net operating income was $1,496,196 rather than $1,724,801 and that the earnings per share in 1960 were approximately 65¢ rather than 75¢? According to the unchallenged figures, sales in 1959 were $3,320,121, net operating income was $441,103, and earnings per share were 33¢. Would it have made a difference to an average prudent investor if he had known that in 1960 sales were only 256 per cent of 1959 sales, not 276 per cent; that net operating income was up by only $1,055,093, not by $1,301,698, and that earnings per share, while still approximately twice those of 1959, were not something more than twice?

These debentures were rated 'B' by the investment rating services. They were thus characterized as speculative, as any prudent investor must have realized. It would seem that anyone interested in buying these convertible debentures would have been attracted primarily by the conversion feature, by the growth potential of the stock. The growth which the company enjoyed in 1960 over prior years was striking, even on the correct figures. It is hard to see how a prospective purchaser of this type of investment would have been deterred from buying if he had been advised of these comparatively minor errors in reporting 1960 sales and earnings.

Since no one knows what moves or does not move the mythical 'average prudent investor,' it comes down to a question of judgment, to be exercised by the trier of the fact as best he can in the light of all the circumstances. It is my best judgment that the average prudent investor would not have cared about these errors in the 1960 sales and earnings figures, regrettable though they may be. I therefore find that they were not material within the meaning of Section 11 [of the 1933 Act].

There was an understatement of contingent liabilities. These were reported as totalling $4,719,835—or $375,000 less than the correct figure. The Court characterized the reported amount as "huge" for a company with assets of $6,101,000 but added that knowledge of the correct amount of contingent liabilities would not have deterred a prospective purchaser of the debentures.

On the other hand, the judge found that certain errors in the 1960 (certified) balance sheet were material. Current assets, he said, were overstated by approximately $600,000; liabilities were understated by approximately $325,000, of which $65,000 should have been treated as current.

Cash was shown as $285,482. This amount included $145,000 which had been borrowed temporarily from a finance company by an unconsolidated subsidiary of BarChris and was to be returned by January 16, 1961 "so that realistically, cash value was only $140,482." (This matter is commented upon further below.)

Current assets also should have been reduced $50,000 for a reserve of the Federal Lanes receivable (further comment on this matter appears below).

An asset item in the balance sheet captioned "Financial institutions on notes discounted, $264,689" should have been treated, at least in part, as a noncurrent asset (commented upon further below).

Trade accounts receivable were overstated by $150,000 by including an alley (Howard Lanes Annex) which was not sold to an outside party. The property was owned by a BarChris subsidiary and leased to outsiders. It should not have been included in current assets or sales for 1960. (It should have been included in fixed assets.)

Summing up the balance sheet errors, the judge pointed out that the balance sheet showed total current assets of $4,524,000, and total current liabilities of $2,413,867—"a ratio of approximately 1.9 to 1." He commented:

. . . This was bad enough, but on the true facts, the ratio was worse. As corrected, current assets, as near as one can tell, were approximately $3,924,000, and current liabilities approximately $2,478,000, a ratio of approximately 1.6 to 1.

Would it have made a difference to a prospective purchaser of the BarChris debentures if he had been advised of these facts? The judge said that there must be some point at which errors in a company's balance sheet become material even to a growth-oriented investor, and he concluded that these errors in the balance sheet were material within the meaning of Section 11 of the 1933 Act.

(It seems to the author of this book that this finding with respect to the current ratio is naive, to put it mildly. If a prospective purchaser of the debentures would not have been dissuaded by the errors in the income statement, it is difficult, if not impossible, to believe that he would have decided against a purchase because of the balance sheet errors and the effect they had on the current ratio. The author believes that most equity investment decisions of the average prudent investor are made mainly on the basis of income information with little reference to balance sheets or working capital ratios. This observation may not apply to the average security analyst, but the BarChris judge was concerned with what motivates the average prudent investor—not the average security analyst.)

(The following statement, taken from a study by the Canadian Institute of Chartered Accountants, supports the views expressed by the author of this book:

An accounting error (or a total of accounting errors) is material if the distortion affects or should affect the decisions of an intelligent reader of the financial statements. Since the prime concern of most readers is the earning power of the enterprise, the most obvious type of error affecting the reader is *one which distorts reported net profit* . . .[9] (Emphasis added)

(The author is convinced that his view of the Court's ruling on the current ratio is shared by others. A lawyer, with much expertise in the securities field, expressed himself on this point in no uncertain terms when he said:

It is submitted that the Court's conclusion that the auditors were liable because of the error in the current ratio, even if it is concluded the auditors were negligent in the particulars the Court says they were, is incorrect. The Court first remarked that the ratio disclosed on the balance sheet at December 31, 1960, 1.9, was "bad enough." Was it so bad? Two-to-one is regarded as something of a standard. In the construction industry the median in 1959 was 1.81. Thus there is some question whether the ratio in the balance sheet or even as adjusted was as lamentable as the Court said.

Secondly, would this difference, 1.9 reduced to 1.6, have really affected an investor? The Court asked, "Would it have made any difference if a prospective purchaser of these debentures had been advised of these facts? There must be some point at which errors in disclosing a company's balance sheet position become material, even to a growth-oriented investor. . . ." Thus the Court, which had rejected a 14 percent discrepancy in earnings as "immaterial," concluded a 15 percent discrepancy in the current ratio was material! [10]

WHAT PORTION OF THE PROSPECTUS WAS "EXPERTIZED"?—Since there is a defense for certain persons when a statement is made "on the authority of an expert," several defendants in the BarChris case claimed that the lawyers for the company and for the underwriters were "experts" and that they (the defendants) should not be liable for portions of the prospectus prepared by the lawyers. The judge rejected this view and said that the lawyers were not experts within the meaning of the statute; the only expert in this sense was the firm of independent accountants.

The judge further asserted that the accountants' report related only to the consolidated balance sheet as of December 31, 1960 and the related statement of earnings and retained earnings for the five years then ended. This was all that the auditors purported to certify, and it was perfectly clear that they did not purport to certify the 1961 figures some of which were expressly stated in the prospectus as unaudited.

The plaintiffs claimed that the auditors were responsible for a portion of the text of the prospectus pertaining to "Methods of Operation" because

[9] *Materiality in Auditing,* Study Group on Audit Techniques, October 1965, p. 3. Quoted in Leopold A. Bernstein, "Materiality—The Need for Guidelines." *The New York CPA,* July 1969, p. 502.

[10] A. A. Sommer, Jr., "Accountant's Counsel—Advice to My Client," *The Business Lawyer,* January, 1969, pp. 599–600.

a reference to it was made in Note 9 to the balance sheet. In this connection, the judge made an important finding because it involves an area that concerns all accountants when, as a matter of convenience and in the interest of brevity, they make a cross-reference in a financial statement or note to a portion of the narrative section of the prospectus. The judge said:

. . . The cross reference in footnote 9 to the 'Methods of Operation' passage in the prospectus was inserted merely for the convenience of the reader. It is not a fair construction to say that it thereby imported into the balance sheet everything in that portion of the text, much of which had nothing to do with the figures in the balance sheet.

THE ACCOUNTANTS' DEFENSE OF DUE DILIGENCE.—The defense available to an expert under Section 11 of the 1933 Act is set forth earlier in Chapter **27**. Briefly stated, the expert's defense requires a showing of reasonable investigation and belief, with reasonable grounds to believe. The auditors for BarChris pleaded this defense.

The judge stated that since the statute required the court to determine the accountants' belief, and the grounds thereof, "at the time such part of the registration statement became effective," the matter had to be viewed as of May 16, 1961, the effective date of the registration statement. Also, since the only certified figures that were challenged were those for 1960, the question was whether, on the effective date, the auditors, after reasonable investigation, had reasonable ground to believe and did believe that the 1960 figures were true and that no material fact had been omitted from the registration statement which should have been included in order to make the 1960 figures not misleading. In deciding that issue, the judge said he had to consider not only what the auditors did in their 1960 examination, but also what they did in their subsequent so-called "S–1 review." (The "S–1 review" was a term used by the BarChris auditors and corresponds to the procedures contemplated in a "Keeping Current" review as discussed in Chapter **12** of this book.)

The audit engagement was in general charge of a partner of the auditing firm and more immediately in charge of a manager. Most of the actual work on the engagement was performed by a senior accountant who had junior assistants. The judge was concerned not with everything the senior did in the course of the audit, but rather with what he did or did not do with respect to those items that were found to be incorrectly reported in the 1960 figures and which were material.

The judge said that the 1960 sales figures were inflated by the inclusion therein of $653,900 for five alleys that had not been sold. Of this amount, $330,000 represented Capitol Lanes, which was also known as Heavenly Lanes. (It appeared that alleys often had more than one name.) BarChris originally had a contract to construct Heavenly Lanes for an outside customer who did not consummate the agreement. On July 29, 1960 BarChris entered into a contract with its wholly-owned subsidiary, BarChris Leasing Corporation, described in the contract as the purchaser, to build this alley. BarChris completed the contract before December 31, 1960 but "never sold it to any outside interest." "Purely as a financing mechanism, it sold the alley" to a factor who leased it back to Capitol Lanes, Inc., a newly organized BarChris subsidiary.

(The last two sentences in the preceding paragraph may appear to be contradictory; what the Court said, in effect, was that a sale to a factor with a leaseback is not a sale to an outside interest, and therefore should be accounted for as a financing or a loan, not a sale. Bearing in mind that the transaction in question occurred in 1960, the Court's ruling is particularly interesting. At that time generally accepted accounting principles permitted gains on sale-leaseback transactions to be included in income; the applicable provisions of ARB No. 43 merely called for disclosure of the principal details of important sale-leaseback transactions. In 1964, four years after the BarChris sale-leaseback, the APB revised the ground rules for accounting in sale-leaseback transactions, and provided, in Opinion No. 5, that material gains or losses on such transactions should be amortized over the life of the lease as an adjustment of the rental cost.)

Capitol Lanes, Inc. operated the alley beginning in December 1960. BarChris's minutes showed that it contemplated operating the alley as early as November 22, 1960. The judge was critical of the senior accountant's failure to discover that Capitol Lanes had not been sold. The error, said the judge, stemmed from the fact that the senior accountant never realized that Heavenly Lanes and Capitol were two different names for the same alley. He was shown the contract file, examined the contracts in the file, and made a list of them. The file must have included a contract with an outside purchaser for Heavenly Lanes because he included Heavenly on his list. Apparently there was no contract in the file for a lane named Capitol because that name did not appear on the senior's list.

BarChris's treasurer also made a list of jobs. Heavenly was on his list; Capitol was not. The senior accountant compared the two lists and satisfied himself that he had the proper jobs to be taken into account. He assumed that Heavenly was to be treated like any other completed job, and included it in all his computations. He was aware that there were references here and there in BarChris's records to Capitol Lanes. He also knew that Capitol Lanes, Inc. was paying rentals to the factoring company. The auditors also had other indications that the subsidiary was operating an alley.

The senior accountant testified that he understood that the alley had not been built and that he believed the rental payments were on vacant land. The judge was not satisfied with this testimony because the records should have alerted him to the fact that an alley existed. "In any case," said the judge, "he never identified this mysterious Capitol with the Heavenly Lanes which he had included in his sales and profit figures."

The burden of proof that they had made a reasonable examination, said the judge, was on the auditors, and he found that they had "not sustained that burden."

The senior accountant also failed to discover that the Howard Lanes Annex (included in 1960 sales in the amount of $150,000) was not sold, but here the evidence was much scantier. He saw a contract for this alley in the contract file. No one told him that it was to be leased rather than sold. There was no evidence to indicate that any record existed which would have put him on notice. The judge concluded that the auditor's investigation was reasonable as to this item.

CASH.—Cash was shown in the December 31, 1960 balance sheet at $285,482. This amount actually was on hand on that day but, according to the judge, "certain rather peculiar circumstances relating to this cash balance should have been disclosed."

BarChris had a wholly owned finance subsidiary, BarChris Financial Corporation, whose accounts were not consolidated with those of the parent company and the other subsidiaries. In the consolidated balance sheet it was shown as "Investments in (at Equity) and Advances to Non-Consolidated Subsidiary."

The finance subsidiary discounted customers' notes with a factoring company. The factor held certain reserves in the amount of $147,466.80 as security with respect to customers' notes discounted. On December 22, 1960, at the request of BarChris's executive vice-president, the factor released the $147,466.80 of reserves to the finance subsidiary temporarily, on the latter's agreement to redeposit it with the factor not later than January 16, 1961, so that the factor could continue to hold it as security. The finance subsidiary then paid $145,000 of this sum to its parent, BarChris, which put it into one of BarChris's bank accounts.

The plaintiffs claimed that this transaction was arranged by the executive vice president in order to increase BarChris's cash temporarily, so that its financial condition would look better on December 31, 1960. The judge said, "No other explanation was offered by defendants and I can see none."

The $145,000 was an asset of the finance subsidiary subject only to the factor's lien. "It would seem," the judge asserted, "that under the circumstances it would have been more accurate to include this amount, not in cash, but in 'investment in non-consolidated subsidiary'." The latter item was not a current asset, and to have put it there would have reduced cash and current assets by $145,000. "In any event, to treat it as cash on hand without some explanation of the temporary character of the deposit was misleading." The judge said also that the incident is important for the light that it shed upon BarChris's business practices, which "has a bearing upon the credibility of some of BarChris's officers and the weight to be given to their testimony in other respects."

The senior accountant properly obtained a confirmation from the bank as to BarChris's cash balance on December 31, 1960. He did not know that part of this balance had been temporarily increased by the deposit of reserves returned to BarChris by the factoring company conditionally and for a limited time. The judge did not believe that the senior accountant should have known this. "Although [the auditors'] work papers recorded the fact that these reserves were returned, there was nothing to indicate that the payment was conditional. [The executive vice-president, who had arranged the temporary return of reserves,] obviously did not reveal this fact [to the auditors, and] it would not be reasonable to require [that they] examine all of BarChris's correspondence files when [they] had no reason to suspect any irregularity."

RECEIVABLE FROM FEDERAL LANES.—The balance sheet at December 31, 1960 included in current assets a receivable due from Federal Lanes in the amount of $125,000 representing a down payment under its contract for the purchase of an alley. It had been overdue since July 31, 1960, but no reserve had been provided against it for possible uncollectibility. BarChris received 36,400 shares of Federal stock. The executive vice-president of BarChris thought that $100,000 of the $125,000 had been paid by the delivery of the stock, but the agreement between the parties on this subject was not clear. BarChris's accounting department did not treat the receipt of this stock as part payment. Instead, they treated it as security for an account receivable still unpaid in the amount of $125,000. It was because of the existence of this security, which on December 31, 1960 had some value, plus the existence of additional security in the form of a mortgage, that it was decided to treat this $125,000 as fully collectible.

Federal had also delivered notes to BarChris in payment of the balance of the purchase price over and above the down payment. These notes were discounted with a factor. On December 31, 1960 they were in arrears to the extent of $24,366—which was substantially more than the arrearages of any other customer on notes discounted with the factor. The judge said that this was a clear indication, if any were needed, that all was not right with Federal.

Even on December 31, 1960, the judge asserted, Federal's prospects were so bad that some reserve should have been set up against the $125,000. In view of the security in the form of the stock and the mortgage, a reserve of the entire $125,000 was not necessary. The judge determined that a reserve of at least $50,000 should have been created, with a corresponding decrease in current assets.

FACTOR'S RESERVES.—Among the current assets in the balance sheet at December 31, 1960 was "Financial Institutions on Notes Discounted," $264,689. This represented the amount of reserves withheld by factors on customers' notes discounted with them by BarChris and its consolidated subsidiaries. As the notes were paid by the customers to the factors, the reserves were released proportionately by the factors to BarChris.

There was no attack upon the accuracy of the figure or the propriety of carrying it as an asset. The claim was that it was not a current asset because (1) part of the reserve, in the normal course of events, would not have been released within one year; and (2) some of it might not be released at all, for some of the customers' notes held by the factors were already in arrears. The judge concluded that this item, in part at least, should not have been classified as a current asset. As to the auditors' performance with respect to this item, he said it was hard to understand how the senior accountant could have treated it entirely as a current asset "when it was obvious that most of the reserves would not be released within one year."

USE OF THE PERCENTAGE OF COMPLETION METHOD.—The Court ruled that it was proper to employ the percentage of completion method, and that it was properly applied in this case, despite the plaintiffs' contentions to the contrary. The evidence showed that generally accepted accounting principles sanctioned the inclusion in sales for one year of part of the consideration ultimately to be received for work in progress which spreads over more than one year. "Otherwise," the judge indicated, "the figures would be distorted by reflecting the entire consideration in the sales for the year in which the work was finally completed." The same principle had been employed by BarChris in 1959, with the auditors' knowledge and approval, and the judge said "it was proper to employ it also for 1960." He also found that, except for two specific instances, the principle had been correctly applied in determining the amount to be included in 1960 sales for uncompleted contracts. The two exceptions, however, were not of such a nature as to have rendered the financial statements incorrect or misleading.

THE "S–1 REVIEW."—The purpose of the "S–1 Review" (as previously indicated, this corresponds to the "Keeping Current Review" referred to in Chapter **12**) was to ascertain, in the judge's words, "whether any material change has occurred in the company's financial position which should be disclosed in order to prevent the balance sheet figures from being misleading." He said:

. . . The scope of such a review, under generally accepted auditing standards, is limited. It does not amount to a complete audit.

The audit firm had prepared a written program for such a review, and the judge found that the program conformed to generally accepted auditing standards. Among other things, it required the following:

1. Review minutes of stockholders, directors and committees . . .
2. Review latest interim financial statements and compare with corresponding statements of preceding year. Inquire regarding significant variations and changes.

* * *

4. Review the more important financial records and inquire regarding material transactions not in the ordinary course of business and any other significant items.

* * *

6. Inquire as to changes in material contracts . . .

* * *

10. Inquire as to any significant bad debts or accounts in dispute for which provision has not been made.

* * *

14. Inquire as to . . . newly discovered liabilities, direct or contingent . . .

The auditing firm's senior accountant made the S–1 review in May 1961 and devoted 20½ hours to it. He did not discover any of the errors or omissions pertaining to the state of affairs in 1961, "all of which were material," according to the judge.

(Although the Court's opinion mentions that a partner and a manager of the auditing firm were in charge of the BarChris audit, it reserves its criticisms almost entirely for the senior accountant. Nothing is said about the part played in the examination by the partner and manager, or the function they performed in supervising and reviewing the work of their subordinates. Also, the opinion is completely silent with respect to the review made by one of the firm's SEC specialists. The testimony at the trial, however, demonstrated that there was a substantial amount of time devoted to the engagement by the partner, manager, and SEC specialist.)

What the senior accountant did, the judge said, "was to look at a consolidating trial balance as of March 31, 1961 which had been prepared by BarChris, compare it with the audited December 31, 1960 figures, discuss with [BarChris's controller] certain unfavorable developments which the comparison disclosed, and read certain minutes." He did not examine any "important financial records" other than the trial balance (see step 4 of the auditing firm's review program). He did not read minutes of the Executive

Committee (see step 1 of the review program). (The author understands, however, that BarChris had supplied the senior accountant with a representation letter which said, among other things, that *the auditors had been furnished all minutes* covering a period that would have included the Executive Committee meeting.) The senior accountant did not know that there was an Executive Committee, hence he did not discover that an officer had notes of Executive Committee minutes that had not been written up. He did not read the minutes of any subsidiary.

The judge said that the senior accountant asked questions, got answers which he considered satisfactory, and did nothing to verify them. He noticed that there had been an increase in notes payable by BarChris and was told by an officer of BarChris that the company was "a bit slow" in paying its bills. He recorded in his notes that the company was in a "tight cash position."

The judge asserted that the senior accountant had no conception of how tight the cash position was. He did not discover that BarChris was holding up checks in substantial amounts because there was no money in the bank to cover them. He did not know of a bank loan or loans from officers. He had not read the prospectus, and so he was not aware that there had been a problem about loans from officers.

(The decision made no mention of whether any other representatives of the audit firm had read the prospectus. This is a significant matter inasmuch as reading the prospectus has been a required procedure both in SAP No. 33 (1963) and in its predecessor, SAP No. 25 (1954). The author understands that at least three highly placed individuals of the audit firm read the BarChris prospectus: the partner of the firm in charge of the examination, the manager, and one of the firm's specialists in SEC engagements. The Court, however, omitted to mention this material fact. Although as stated above, reading the prospectus is a required procedure, the author has not interpreted the requirement as applying to every person involved in the audit. It seems to the author that there is much more to be gained by having experienced partners, managers, and specialists read the prospectus than to have a senior accountant read it. On the other hand, if the Court was suggesting that this task should be performed by all persons involved in the engagement, then the profession has cause for concern, because it just is not done.)

During the 1960 audit, the senior accountant had obtained information from factors about delinquent notes. He made no similar inquiry in his S–1 review. Since he did not know about Executive Committee meetings, he did not know that the delinquency situation had worsened.

The judge observed that there had been a material change for the worse in BarChris's financial position. "That change was sufficiently serious so that the failure to disclose it made the 1960 figures misleading." With respect to this matter, Sommer made this significant observation:

> . . . Inferentially, of course, by its determination with regard to the responsibility of accountants subsequent to the opinion date or the balance sheet date the Court placed some responsibility upon the accountants with regard to post-balance sheet date events. Nonetheless the Court made clear that the responsibility with respect to post-balance sheet events existed only to the extent that such events rendered the financial statements as to which they rendered an opinion misleading.[11]

The Court said the senior accountant's S–1 review "was useless" as far as results were concerned. The Court's opinion continued with this extremely important holding:

> Accountants should not be held to a standard higher that that recognized in their profession. I do not do so here. [The senior accountant's] review did not come up to that standard. He did not take some of the steps which [the auditing firm's] written program prescribed. He did not spend an adequate amount of time on a task of this magnitude. Most important of all, he was too easily satisfied with glib answers to his inquiries.
>
> This is not to say that he should have made a complete audit. But there were enough danger signals in the materials which he did examine to require some further investigation on his part. Generally accepted accounting [sic] standards required such further investigation under these circumstances. It is not always sufficient merely to ask questions.

The judge concluded that the auditing firm had not established its due diligence defense, and that it was therefore liable under Section 11 of the 1933 Act.

EFFECTS OF THE BARCHRIS DECISION.—The discussion in this book of the BarChris case has been confined almost exclusively to the Court's findings with respect to accounting principles and auditing procedures. In so doing, the discussion has omitted some of the Court's most severe findings, which relate to the issuer's officers and directors and to the underwriters. The author does not propose to go into these findings because they are not an appropriate subject for this volume, and, in any case, they have already been covered by persons much more competent to do so than the author.

The Court's findings in these other areas, however, have had an important effect on the role of the independent public accountant insofar as it relates to filings with the SEC under the 1933 Act.

First, because of the demands of underwriters, there are many more interim audits than previously. In the BarChris case, it will be remembered, the Court's principal fire relating to financial statements was aimed at the

---

[11] A. A. Sommer, Jr., "Accountant's Counsel—Advice to My Client," *The Business Lawyer,* Jan. 1969, p. 595.

unaudited figures for the first quarter of 1961. Some of the leading under-writing firms, in fact, have adopted a policy that they will not proceed with an underwriting if the unaudited interim statements cover a period of more than six months.

Second, underwriting agreements are providing more and more as a condition of the agreements that they shall be furnished with *two* comfort letters—one to be furnished at or about the effective date, or the preceding day, when they sign the agreement, and one to be furnished as customary at the closing.

Third, underwriters are asking more and more that the accountants, in their comfort letters, cover almost every number and percentage which appears in the prospectus, whether or not such numbers and percentages are produced under the controls of the issuer's accounting system. This is a subject that is discussed at length in Chapter **12**, dealing with comfort letters.

The Continental Vending Machine Corporation Case[12].—Continental Vending Machine Corp. was a publicly-owned company, and its securities were listed for trading on the American Stock Exchange. Its principal business was the manufacture of vending machines and the maintenance of vending machine routes.

FACTUAL BACKGROUND OF THE CASE.—The president of Continental, Harold Roth, was also its largest stockholder, owning about 22% of the outstanding stock. An associate (who had served as chairman of the board for several years) owned 9%, and another associate (also a board member for a while) owned over 14%, making a total of about 45% owned by these three men. They were also officers, directors, and principal stockholders of a finance company, called Valley Commercial Corporation. The other principal stockholders of Valley were Arthur Field (counsel for Continental and, for some time, one of its directors) and Roth's father. Continental itself owned no stock of Valley, but was an "affiliate" because the companies were under common control.

Valley's main business had been the discounting of notes receivable arising from the sale by Continental of vending machines or vending machine routes; Valley generally discounted or rediscounted the notes with one of two banks, at each of which it had a $1 million line of credit. Most of the notes handled by Valley involved transactions of Continental, its subsidiaries, or other companies affiliated with Roth. Valley also made unsecured loans to other individuals and companies not affiliated with Continental. Valley's books and records were kept by Roth's secretary in her office at Continental's main plant.

[12] The case is cited *U. S. v. Simon, et al.* 425 F. 2d. 796 (2d Cir. 1969).

Continental's auditors were not the same firm as that which audited Valley. One of the partners in Valley's auditing firm was a director of Continental from 1956 to 1960; another partner was a director from 1960 to 1963.

In 1957, according to testimony, Roth started borrowing money from Valley, and instructed his secretary that, if Valley did not have enough cash to lend him what he needed, she should get the money for Valley from Continental. Thus was created the "Valley receivable," an open account on Continental's books bearing 12% interest which reflected frequent round-amount advances to Valley and frequent repayments. Roth told Continental's auditors that the purpose of these advances was to invest Continental's funds on a very short-term basis at 12% interest. (Continental's board knew that, from time to time, as money was available, it was advanced to Valley, and that the loans bore interest at 12%.) Continental's books also showed a "Valley payable" account, representing Continental's notes payable (interest bearing) to Valley. The balance in this account generally amounted to about $1,000,000.

At the end of each of Continental's fiscal years from September 30, 1960 to 1962, the balances in the Valley receivable and payable accounts were as follows:

September 30	Receivable from Valley	Payable to Valley
1960	$ 397,996	$ 949,852
1961	848,006	780,472
1962	3,543,335	1,029,475

On each of the Continental balance sheets, there was disclosure of the amounts of the receivable and the payable and the fact that Valley was an affiliate. At December 31, 1962, three months after the fiscal year end, the receivable balance had risen to about $3,900,000, while the payable remained at about $1,000,000.

In February 1963, the field work on the September 30, 1962 audit was almost complete. The company's trial balance showed a *profit* before taxes for fiscal 1962 of about $100,000; the auditors, however, had a substantial number of proposed audit adjustments. At a two-day conference attended by three directors of Continental (its president, executive vice-president, and treasurer) and its chief accountant, and, for the auditors, the two partners, manager and supervisor on the engagement, the proposed adjustments were discussed. The financial statements, as ultimately agreed upon, showed a *loss* for the year of $867,000 ($1,246,000 before tax credit) and, in addition, various write-offs of over $3,000,000 charged to retained earnings. (In the preceding fiscal year Continental had net income of $1,250,000.) The shareholders' equity at the end of fiscal 1962 was reduced to about one-half of the amount at the beginning of the year and retained earnings were eliminated completely.

Meanwhile, with regard to the Valley receivable, the auditors had confirmed in writing the balance due, reconciled the reported small differences reported by Valley, checked the interest accrual, and tested the checks payable to Valley for endorsements and supporting vouchers. They also confirmed the Valley payable. Similar procedures were performed in prior years.

In addition, for the first time, the auditors in December 1962 asked Roth for permission to see Valley's financial statements in order to assess the collectibility of the receivable, which at September 30, 1962, amounted to about 11% of Continental's total assets. Roth stated that Valley was then in the process of being audited and that he would provide the statements when they were completed. Two months later, after further requests from the auditors to see Valley's financial statements, Roth informed them that the audit was still not complete, that he owed money to Valley, and that Valley was not in a position to repay Continental, but that he would post sufficient collateral to secure the receivable.

About 80% of the collateral consisted of equity in Continental stock and debentures, owned by Roth, members of his family, and an associate, all assigned to Field as trustee for Valley. Field gave the auditors his legal opinion, in writing, setting forth the collateral arrangements and concluding ". . . it is our opinion that the securities assigned secure the loan due from Valley to Continental."

The auditors confirmed by telephone on February 15, 1963 the existence of the securities pledged and the equity therein which, on that day, had a value of about $2.9 million. On the following day they completed their field work.

Note 2 to the financial statements, written by the auditors and which was the central point in subsequent legal actions, read as follows:

The amount receivable from Valley Commercial Corp. (an affiliated company of which Mr. Harold Roth is an officer, director and stockholder) bears interest at 12% a year. Such amount, less the balance of the notes payable to that company, is secured by the assignment to the Company of Valley's equity in certain marketable securities. As of February 15, 1963 [the date of the auditors' opinion], the amount of such equity at current market quotations exceeded the net amount receivable.

In the balance sheet itself, there was no "netting" of receivables from and payables to Valley, despite the confusing wording at the end of the footnote which was inadvertent and conceded to be erroneous. On the contrary, they were shown "broad," that is, the receivable from Valley was included among the assets, and the payable to Valley was included among the liabilities.

The certified statements were released and almost immediately thereafter, frenzied trading in Continental's securities took place. Within three trading days, the quoted prices of Continental's securities had fallen so low that the collateral for all practical purposes was wiped out. Shortly thereafter, the Continental plant was padlocked because a check payable to the Internal Revenue Service had bounced. The auditors, who were preparing the annual report Form 10–K for submission to the SEC and the stock exchange by February 28, 1963, notified Continental and then the SEC that, because of the decline in value of the collateral, they would not certify the financial statements in the 10–K, thereby effectively withdrawing their report. Eventually bankruptcy ensued, and a trustee was appointed.

Two years later the trustee instituted a civil suit against the auditing firm, charging negligence, and two years after that, criminal indictments were handed down, naming Roth and the two partners and manager of the auditing firm, charging them with mail fraud and conspiracy. The mail fraud charge related to the mailing of false financial statements, and the other charge to a "conspiracy" to file a false Form 10–K, *even though it was never filed.* The civil suit was subsequently settled out of court.

Roth (who was also under indictment on other charges relating to his conduct as chief executive officer of Continental) pleaded guilty and testified as a witness for the government against the auditors. The first trial, which lasted two months, ended in a hung jury (deadlocked 11-to-1 for acquittal); the second trial, which lasted one month, resulted in guilty verdicts. The verdicts were appealed and upheld. The three auditors were fined an aggregate of $17,000, but there was no prison sentence. Roth, however, received a jail sentence on his guilty plea.

Discussion of the Decision and the Issues.—Because the verdicts against the accountants were made by a jury, the basis for their decision is not known. The trial judge, however, had a different view of the defendants than the jury. In ruling on a defense motion, the judge said, "Although the Court, had it been the trier of the facts, *would probably have found sufficient doubt to warrant acquittal . . .*" (Emphasis added.) With respect to this observation by the trial judge, the Court of Appeals said: "That some other jury might have taken a more lenient view, as the trial judge said he would have done, is a misfortune for the defendants but not one within our power to remedy."

It was indeed unfortunate for the auditors that the issues, which were extremely complicated and technical, were decided by a jury of laymen. (For example, the jury was obviously enmeshed in technical detail when at a critical point of its deliberations and in announced deadlock at 9:15 p.m., it asked three questions regarding the collateralization. The questions involved such delving into complex documents and the intricacies of marshalling collateral, that the trial judge and counsel for the government and the defendants were engaged for the next two hours that evening and for an hour the next morning in colloquy as to what the record showed and what the supplemental instructions to the jury should be. In the end, the judge refused to answer one of the questions because he could not understand its meaning.) The defendants had in fact pressed in both trials for a nonjury trial, but the government—without giving any reasons for its position—refused to waive its right to a jury trial.

The principal accounting issue in the trial was whether the 1962 financial statements of Continental were false and misleading because:

(1) They did not disclose Roth's borrowings from the affiliated company (Valley);

(2) They would mislead readers into believing that the Valley receivable was adequately secured by including the footnote quoted above, which should have disclosed:

(a) That the notes payable to Valley could not be offset against the amount receivable from Valley;

(b) That 80% of the collateral used to secure the Valley receivable consisted of Continental stock and debentures; and

(c) That between the balance sheet date and the date of certification, the Valley receivable had increased from $3,500,000 to $3,900,000.

The question as to whether Roth's borrowings from Valley should have been disclosed leads to the general accounting and auditing question as to whether, in reporting loans to an affiliate, accountants should also inquire into and require disclosure of the use made of the money by the affiliate. While agreeing that ordinarily such inquiry and disclosure would not be required, the Court of Appeals, in upholding the jury verdict, held otherwise in this case. The Court said:

. . . We join defendants' counsel in assuming that the mere fact that a company has made advances to an affiliate does not ordinarily impose a duty on an accountant to investigate what the affiliate has done with them or even to disclose that the affiliate has made a loan to a common officer if this has come to his attention. But it simply cannot be true that an accountant is under no duty to disclose what he knows when he has reason to believe that, to a material extent, a corporation is being operated not to carry out its business in the interest of all the stockholders but for the private benefit of its president. For a court to say that all this is immaterial as a matter of law if only such loans are thought to be collectible would be to say that independent accountants have no responsibility to reveal known dishonesty by a high corporate officer. If certification does not at least imply that the corporation has not been looted by insiders so far as the accountants know, or, if it has been, that the diversion has been made good beyond peradventure (or adequately reserved against) and effective steps taken to prevent a recurrence, it would mean nothing, and the reliance placed on it by the public would be a snare and a delusion. Generally accepted accounting principles instruct an accountant what to do in the usual case where he has no reason to doubt that the affairs of the corporation are being honestly conducted. Once he has reason to believe that this basic assumption is false, an entirely different situation confronts him. . . .

In that event, said the Court, the auditor must extend his procedures to determine whether or not his suspicions are justified. The Court continued:

If as a result of such an extension or, as here, without it, he finds his suspicions to be confirmed, full disclosure must be the rule, unless he has made sure the wrong has been righted and procedures to avoid a repetition have been established. At least this must be true when the dishonesty he has discovered is not some minor peccadillo but a diversion so large as to imperil if not destroy the very solvency of the enterprise.

The references in the Court's opinion above to "dishonesty" and "looting" are amazing and contrast sharply with the trial judge's charge to the jury that *there was no evidence of criminality or dishonesty on the part of Roth.*

With regard to the failure to describe the collateral, the Court of Appeals said, ". . . As men experienced in financial matters, they must have known that the one kind of property ideally unsuitable to collateralize a receivable whose collectibility was essential to avoiding an excess of current liabilities over current assets and a two-thirds reduction in capital already reduced would be securities of the very corporation whose solvency was at issue . . ."

There were a number of other accounting issues in the original indictment which were dropped or stricken during the course of the two trials. On the other hand, one accounting issue not mentioned in the indictment was introduced by the government and assumed some importance. This issue was that the auditors had a responsibility in the years 1958 to 1961 to find out what Valley was doing with the money advanced to it by Continental, either by insisting upon auditing Valley or at least by "looking" at Valley's books. If they had done so, the government claimed, they would have discovered Roth's *modus operandi,* and could have reported it to the Board of Directors or stockholders, thereby stopping his borrowing before the amount became critical. It was argued that the fear of discovery of their "negligence" in prior years motivated the auditors to conceal in the 1962 statements not only the fact that Roth owed money to Valley but also any other items, such as the nature of the collateral, which might lead to that fact being uncovered.

All of the accounting issues were discussed at length during the trial by witnesses for both government and the defendants. Expert witnesses called by the auditor-defendants, as the Court of Appeals noted in its opinion, were "an impressive array of leaders of the profession" and included a former president of the AICPA, a former Chief Accountant of the SEC, a former Chief Accountant of the SEC's Division of Corporation Finance, and highly qualified spokesmen for the country's leading accounting firms. They testified:

> that Continental's financial statements, taken as a whole, fairly presented its financial condition and results of operations in a manner consistent with generally accepted accounting principles;
>
> that there were no departures from generally accepted auditing standards or generally accepted accounting principles;
>
> that it was not required, nor would it have been appropriate, to disclose in Continental's financial statements the fact that Valley had loaned money to Roth;
>
> that it was not necessary to disclose the nature of the collateral or the increase in the Valley receivable after the balance sheet date; and
>
> that in the prior years there was no obligation to audit Valley or "look" at Valley's books.

There were only two accounting witnesses for the government. One was an SEC staff accountant, who testified on the direct case; the other was the SEC's Chief Accountant, who testified on rebuttal. As to these witnesses, the Court of Appeals said that "they hardly compared with defendants' witnesses in aggregate auditing experience or professional eminence." The government witnesses endorsed the government's contentions regarding what Note 2 should have disclosed and stated that the defendants should have either audited Valley or "looked" at Valley's books to investigate the propriety of Continental's advances to Valley. They did not give their opinion of the statements as a whole whereas (as noted above) the defense witnesses did.

Writing in *Notre Dame Lawyer* (Spring, 1971) about the Continental Vending case, Fred Kuhar contrasted the quality and quantity of expert testimony offered by the government and the defense. Kuhar wrote that the government made only a token effort to establish by expert testimony any departure from professional standards. He continued:

> [Name omitted here], an SEC staff accountant, the Government's sole expert witness on its direct case—a witness who "had never certified a financial statement or worked as a certified public accountant on an audit which had certification as its purpose"—testified that "practice" required the defendants to have *audited Valley's books*. He was quite sure of himself, indicating, "I don't believe anyone will follow me here and say to the contrary." He said this after nine distinguished experts *had* said to the contrary in his presence at the first trial. As was pointed out in the appellant's brief:
>
> > He could cite nothing in published standards or principles, accounting literature or precedent in support of his views, and all he ventured as any source of

authority for his views was the enigmatic statement that "in my conversations with partners of leading firms . . . I have formed in my own mind what I believe they think would be what they would have to do under similar circumstances." [Emphasis in the original; footnotes omitted here.]

Because there was such a sharp difference between the testimony of the defendants' expert witnesses and the SEC witnesses, the trial judge remarked during sentencing: "The fraud charged here involved a highly technical and complex area, about which there is room for considerable difference of opinion as to what balance sheet disclosure would have been appropriate." He also said: "If the SEC believes that disclosures of the type indicated by its officials here should have been made, it has the power to issue regulations. In the light of the jury's verdict, the American Institute of Certified Public Accountants would probably do well to revise the auditing standards and accounting principles sponsored by them."

In ruling on a defense motion, the trial judge said that the jury was entitled to weigh the extensive expert testimony adduced with respect to generally accepted auditing standards and accounting principles or practice. He noted that the defendants and the AICPA (appearing as *amicus curiae*) urged that the proof established that these standards and principles did not require the disclosures complained of and that it was error for the Court to refuse to charge that adherence to such standards and principles was a complete defense. The judge maintained that the jury was entitled, in determining whether or not a defendant knowingly concealed a material fact, to consider and weigh proof as to generally accepted auditing standards and accounting principles in effect at the time of their action, along with all of the other proof in the case, *but that proof of such standards and principles is not conclusive on the issue of fraud.* This permitted the jury to convict even though it found that the defendants' performance conformed in every respect with the standards of their profession.

(This action by the trial judge is in startling contrast with the view expressed by the judge in the *BarChris* case discussed beginning on page **28·6**. In *BarChris*—a civil case—the judge said, "Accountants should not be held to a standard higher than that recognized in their profession.")

In upholding the jury's verdict in the Continental Vending case, the Court of Appeals said:

We do not think the jury was also required to accept the accountants' evaluation whether a given fact was material to overall fair presentation, at least not when the accountants' testimony was not based on specific rules or prohibitions to which they could point, but only on the need for the auditor to make an honest judgment and their conclusion that nothing in the financial statements themselves negated the conclusion that an honest judgment had been made. Such evidence may be highly persuasive, but it is not conclusive, and so the trial judge correctly charged.

From the foregoing it might appear that the Court of Appeals might have taken a different approach if there had been a specific rule of the accounting profession that it was not necessary to disclose the matters involved in the case. In fact one highly qualified lawyer, who was very close to the case, has written that the case points out once more the very real advantage, at least from the viewpoint of legal responsibility, in having professional standards spelled out:

Had there been specific rules or prohibitions governing the matters about which there was dispute among the expert witnesses in this case, to which the defendants could refer, it is quite probable the result would have been different. There would very possibly have been different instructions; very likely a different verdict; and altogether likely, if neither of those had occurred, a different decision by the Court of Appeals.[13]

Counsel for the defendants, in a petition to the United States Supreme Court, for a writ of certiorari, pointed out that, so far as they knew, never before had any jury been permitted to determine the guilt or innocence of a professional man in the conduct of a professional engagement on any basis other than adherence or non-adherence to the standards of his profession, and continued:

The doctor, lawyer, engineer or accountant, accustomed and obliged to practice in accordance with the teachings of his profession, could not salutarily serve with the prospect that he must answer criminally—even if not civilly—to a lay judgment on lay standards conceived after the event.

In his charge to the jury, the trial judge acknowledged that the auditors had not profited, in any way, from the alleged fraud and conspiracy. The Court of Appeals also observed in its opinion:

None of the defendants made or could make a penny from Continental's putting out false financial statements. Neither was there evidence of motive in the sense of fear that telling the truth would lose a valuable account. Continental was not the kind of client whose size would give it leverage to bully a great accounting firm, nor was it important to the defendants personally in the sense of their having brought in the business.

The AICPA filed three briefs as *amicus curiae* with the various courts. The first was filed with the District Court where the trial was held; in that brief the Institute asked that the verdict be set aside, stating that its interest lay in the possible impact of the verdict beyond the Continental case itself upon other cases and upon the profession as a whole.

In its brief filed with the Court of Appeals, the Institute raised the question, among others, as to whether "the professional conduct of a pro-

[13] David B. Isbell, "The Continental Vending Case: Lessons for the Profession," *The Journal of Accountancy*, August 1970, p. 36.

fessional person may properly be measured against any standards other than those of the profession." It argued that professional standards should be the criteria, both in criminal and civil actions, because the professional accountant undertakes in the performance of his duties to conduct himself in accordance with such standards. Further, if criminal sanctions are involved, the Institute argued, there should be definite proof that the defendant's conduct had varied from a requirement established by an authoritative pronouncement of a body having competence to promulgate and enforce such standards, or from a requirement universally recognized within the profession, or from a requirement acknowledged by the defendant himself. When the charge is bad faith rather than the breaking of a specific requirement, the brief continued, then independent evidence of bad faith should be required or the action should be shown to be one that competent members of the profession could not have honestly taken. The Institute stated unequivocally that the convictions comported with none of these rules.

The Court of Appeals (as noted above) took a position almost diametrically opposite to that advanced by the Institute, stating that the decision as to what was material to fair presentation was properly up to the jury of laymen to decide, *unless* the accountant could point to a specific rule or prohibition supporting his actions.

In its brief filed with the United States Supreme Court, the Institute raised two questions, one of which related directly to the Appeals Court decision. The *amicus curiae* brief stated as follows:

> The Court of Appeals' approval of the leave given to the jury to disregard accepted professional standards and substitute its own notion of what standards should be not only is novel and unfair, but serves no substantial public interest. Professional standards should of course be open to challenge and change, but criminal prosecution and punishment are not appropriate methods for amending accepted professional standards or devising new ones. Not only are professional organizations ordinarily available as instruments of change—and in the case of accountancy the Institute has certainly performed this role—but governmental agencies, such as the Securities and Exchange Commission in the case of accounting, can where necessary compel needed reforms in professional standards. Such bodies are significantly better equipped to weigh all relevant considerations than a jury or judge hedged by the narrow confines of a criminal prosecution. Moreover, they can accomplish reforms in standards by means that are far more fair and even handed than retroactive imposition of criminal liability upon isolated individuals.

The Supreme Court on March 31, 1970 denied certiorari, and so the jury's verdict remains.

THE SIGNIFICANCE OF THE CASE.—The Continental Vending Machine case marks the first time that a United States court has suggested that professional men may be judged by a jury of laymen according to lay standards.

It is the first time also that a United States court has decided that professional men may be judged guilty of misconduct in a professional engagement even though their performance of that engagement was in conformity with the standards of their profession. In a very well-written and researched article on accountants' liability, Reiling and Taussig made this comment on the case: "Diligent research has uncovered no other criminal prosecution where the motive of personal gain was so lacking and the argument for conformity with generally accepted accounting principles so strong".[14]

It should be noted, however, that the Court of Appeals said that while "generally accepted accounting principles instruct an accountant what to do in the usual case where he has no reason to doubt that the affairs of the corporation are being honestly conducted," an accountant is confronted with "an entirely different situation" when "he has reason to believe that this basic assumption is false."

In so stating, the Court of Appeals was not making its own appraisal of the evidence since it was precluded from doing so. Once a jury has returned a verdict, after a fair trial that is reasonably free of legal error, a reviewing court may not substitute its judgment for that of the jury in assessing the credibility of witnesses or the weight to be given the evidence in the trial. An appellate court, in reviewing a jury verdict, is required to assume that the jury believed the evidence favorable to the prosecution and disbelieved the testimony given on behalf of the defendants. Thus the trial judge, in reviewing the evidence after trial, and the Court of Appeals, in reviewing the jury verdict, were both required to assume that the jury believed the testimony of the prosecution's witnesses that all of the facts had been disclosed to the auditors. Similarly, the reviewing court was required to assume that the jury disbelieved the contrary testimony of the defendants and gave little weight to the expert testimony given on behalf of the defendants by "an impressive array of leaders of the profession." If, in fact, the auditors knew that "the affairs of the corporation are being dishonestly conducted" and that such dishonesty was on so grand a scale "as to imperil if not destroy the very solvency of the enterprise," it is obvious now, under the Court of Appeals decision, that "full disclosure must be the rule."

The main conclusion to be drawn from the case is this: unless there is a specific, written rule embodied in the profession's rulebook that requires the auditor to do what he did, or prohibits him from doing what he did not do, he may be subject to second-guessing, from hindsight, by a jury of laymen as to whether what was done, or what was not done, was right. And this may be true despite anything to the contrary that may be stated orally by "an impressive array of leaders of the profession."

[14] Henry B. Reiling and Russell A. Taussig, "Recent Liability Cases—Implications for Accountants," *The Journal of Accountancy,* Sept. 1970, note 25, p. 52.

Admittedly, it required a strange set of circumstances to permit the jury and the courts to reach a decision against the auditors in the Continental Vending case, but the accountancy profession may well be concerned that in the next case (which will probably also have a strange set of circumstances) a lay jury may be permitted to override a written, specific rule of the profession as to disclosure or non-disclosure. The grounds for such overriding may be that the jury believes the profession's written rule to be unfair, unclear, wrong, or whatever a jury may think. It is possible that the conclusion will be rationalized on the theory that the accountancy profession can not create law, and that, as a matter of public policy, its professional rules and pronouncements should always be subject to review by a jury of laymen according to lay standards.

When, and if, that should come about, another Court of Appeals may conclude, as it did in the Continental Vending case, that it is a "misfortune for the defendants but not one within our power to remedy."

(This is by way of a footnote to the Continental Vending case. When a CPA of New York State has been convicted of a crime, the State's Board of Regents holds a hearing for the purpose of considering whether the accountant's CPA certificate should be revoked or suspended. In the case of the three defendants in the Continental Vending case (all of whom held New York State CPA certificates), the Board of Regents held such hearings and considered the matter for several months.

(In due course, the Board of Regents rendered its decision. They said they had studied the evidence very carefully and in great detail, and had very carefully considered the testimony at the criminal trial which was given by all of the expert witnesses, both for the prosecution and for the defendants in that proceeding. The Board made this observation:

> While as stated earlier in this report, we cannot and do not collaterally attack the judgment of conviction of crime, nevertheless, although we are in agreement that the respondent was negligent . . . in the preparation and issuance of the financial report of Continental, we do not feel that the respondent actually committed a crime.

(The Board of Regents concluded that the CPA certificates of the three individuals should not be suspended or revoked, but that they should receive a "Censure and Reprimand.")

The Yale Express Case.[15]—Yale Express System, Inc. and its subsidiaries were common carriers by motor vehicle and freight forwarders. Yale acquired about 97% of Republic Carloading & Distributing Co., the nation's third largest freight forwarder, in May 1963.

In August 1963 Yale sold an issue of convertible debentures and Class A

[15] The case is cited *Fischer, et al. v. Kletz, et al.* 266 F. Supp. 181 (S. D., N. Y. 1967).

stock to the public through underwriters for an aggregate offering price of $12,000,000. The securities were not registered with the SEC. The registration provisions of the 1933 Act were not applicable since the Interstate Commerce Commission (ICC) had approved the issuance of the securities.

Yale's Class A stock had been listed for trading on the American Stock Exchange; the listing was transferred to the New York Stock Exchange in December 1963. The debentures were listed on the latter exchange in February 1964.

The company's annual report to shareholders for the year 1963 was issued some time around April 9, 1964. The financial statements in that report were accompanied by a report of independent public accountants dated March 31, 1964. Subsequently, some time around June 29, 1964, Yale filed a Form 10–K report with the SEC and the stock exchange. This report contained essentially the same financial statements as the shareholders' report, and showed that the company had had consolidated net income of $1,140,000 in 1963.

It was subsequently ascertained that the 1963 financial statements were materially incorrect, and this fact was disclosed in the report to shareholders for the following year, namely, 1964. (The author has been informed that earlier disclosure was made to the SEC and to the New York Stock Exchange in February 1965.) The 1964 report also included revised amounts for the year 1963, and these showed that Yale had incurred a loss of $1,254,000 in 1963, and, in addition, had had losses aggregating $1,417,000 (or $629,000 after applicable taxes) which were treated as special charges not entering into the determination of the net loss.

A note to the financial statements discussed the revision of the 1963 figures and the nature and amount of the adjustments reflected in the revised amounts. The adjustments consisted, for the most part, of write-offs of uncollectible receivables, costs and expenses paid in 1964 but relating to 1963, additional provision for losses and claims, and related tax effects.

For the year 1964, the company reported a consolidated loss of $2,851,000.

The accountants' certificate in the 1964 report covered the restated amounts for 1963 as well as the figures for 1964. In that certificate, the accountants said that they originally reported on the 1963 financial statements under date of March 31, 1964. "As set forth in note 1 to the financial statements," they said, "it has since been ascertained that these financial statements were incorrect, principally due to the omission in the Company's statements of certain liabilities, information as to which was withheld or otherwise not made available to us by accounting personnel of the Company, and the inclusion, as assets, of receivables which were not subsequently collected. . . . "

In May 1965 Yale was placed in reorganization proceedings under Chapter X of the Bankruptcy Act. In the summer and fall of 1965 some 17 actions (later combined into one consolidated action) were instituted against some of the company's former officers and directors, its former auditors, and the underwriters of the debenture offering. The plaintiffs were said to be owners of Yale's capital stock or debentures.

The complaints were based upon various sections of the 1934 and 1933 Acts, the Interstate Commerce Act, SEC Rule 10b–5, and on principles of common law. Among other things, the complaints alleged that three sets of financial statements filed with the SEC, the ICC, and the stock exchanges, and distributed to the public, were false and misleading, and that the defendants were negligent in preparing and disseminating them. These statements were (1) the unaudited statements included in the August 1963 prospectus referred to above; (2) the audited statements for the year 1963; and (3) unaudited interim statements issued during 1964.

The case was settled in 1970 without a trial of the issues. Those issues, however, are important to practicing public accountants for a number of reasons. As will be seen from the discussion below, one of the issues related to the important question of information that comes to the auditor's attention after he has certified a company's financial statements. If the information indicates that the statements previously certified by him were materially inaccurate, what obligation, if any, does the auditor have to bring this information to the attention of persons who may be relying on the inaccurate statements? Stated differently, does the auditor's duty end when the financial statements have been certified, or does it continue after certification? (As stated in Chapter **5** of this book, the AICPA Committee on Auditing Procedure issued its Statement No. 41 in October 1969 dealing with these questions which constituted an important aspect of the Yale Express case.)

In the course of ruling on pre-trial motions, a Federal judge considered these questions among others. He also considered the auditor's responsibility for interim financial statements not compiled or certified by him but in the release of which he may have been involved. Much of the discussion that follows is taken from the judge's written opinion dated April 5, 1967. In ruling on defendants' motions, the judge was required "to view the facts in the light most favorable to the plaintiffs and to deny the motion if there was any viable legal theory for sustaining the plaintiffs." [16] Since the facts might have been disproved at a trial, the reader should bear in mind that, had there been a trial, the judge's views might have been different.

In connection with a pre-trial motion, the SEC, as *amicus curiae,* filed a memorandum with the court in opposition to a position taken by the audi-

---

[16] H. B. Reiling and R. A. Taussig, "Recent Liability Cases—Implications for Accountants," *The Journal of Accountancy,* Sept. 1970, pp. 50–51.

tor-defendants. The Commission's brief dealt with the auditor's duty to disclose his subsequently acquired knowledge that statements previously certified by him were false. The Commission's views are discussed in Chapter **5** of this book.

THE "SPECIAL STUDIES."—At an unspecified date "early in 1964," the auditors were engaged to conduct so-called "special studies" of Yale's past and current income and expenses. In the course of this non-audit engagement, the auditors discovered that the figures in the 1963 report (which had been certified by them) were substantially incorrect. There was a factual dispute as to when the auditors discovered the falsity of the 1963 figures: the auditors maintained that it was after the filing of the Form 10–K on June 29, 1964; the plaintiffs contended that the discovery was made before that date.

There was also a factual dispute as to when disclosure was made of the falsity of the 1963 figures. According to the judge (who was simply repeating the plaintiffs' allegations), "Not until May 5, 1965, however, when the results of the special studies were released," did the auditors disclose the falsity of the 1963 figures to the stock exchange, the SEC, or the public. (The auditors' report was dated May 4, 1965; it covered the figures for 1964 and the corrected figures for 1963.)

During the course of the special studies, Yale informed the auditors of its intention to issue interim reports of the company's 1964 operations. In at least two instances, according to the plaintiffs' allegations (disputed by the defendants), the auditors told the company that figures derived from the special studies could not be used as a basis for these interim reports. The auditors, it was alleged, recommended that the figures developed by Yale through its internal accounting procedures be used in the reports. The company thereupon issued several interim statements containing figures which were not compiled, audited, or certified by the auditors. Later developments revealed that the figures in these interim statements were, according to the judge, false and misleading

In ruling on a motion by the auditor-defendants to dismiss portions of the complaint, the judge discussed the auditors' obligation to disclose after-acquired information in connection with (1) annual reports containing financial statements certified by them, and (2) interim financial statements not compiled or audited by them.

ANNUAL REPORT LIABILITY.—The plaintiffs attacked the auditors' alleged silence and inaction after its employees discovered, during the special studies, that Yale's 1963 financial statements, certified by them, were incorrect. Inasmuch as the auditors knew that their certificate would be relied upon by the investing public, the plaintiffs contended, the auditors had a duty to alert the public that the statements were false. The auditors, on the other hand, contended that there was no common law or statutory basis for imposing such a duty on them, and that any duty they may have had to the investing public terminated once they certified the relevant financial statements.

The judge observed that the complaint attacked the auditors because they wore two hats in their business relations with Yale. As statutory independent public accountants, they certified the financial statements in the 1963 annual report and Form 10–K. Following the certification, they switched their role to that of an accountant (or consultant) employed to undertake special studies necessitated by business demands rather than by statutory or regulatory requirements. "In this sense," the judge said, "during the special studies [the auditing firm] was a 'dependent public accountant' whose primary obligations, under normal circumstances, were to its client and not to the public."

The judge referred to a number of cases in which plaintiffs had relied on representations that defendants later learned had become false and in which it had been held that the defendants were under a duty to notify the plaintiffs of the falsity of the earlier representations. He continued:

Generally speaking, I can see no reason why this duty to disclose should not be imposed upon an accounting firm which makes a representation it knows will be relied upon by investors. To be sure, certification of a financial statement does not create a formal business relationship between the accountant who certifies and the individual who relies upon the certificate for investment purposes. The act of certification, however, is similar in its effect to a representation made in a business transaction: both supply information which is naturally and justifiably relied upon by individuals for decisional purposes. Viewed in this context of the impact of nondisclosure on the injured party, it is difficult to conceive that a distinction between accountants and parties to a business transaction is warranted. The elements of "good faith and common honesty" which govern the businessman presumably should also apply to the statutory "independent public accountant."

Solely for the purpose of the motion, the judge ruled against the auditors. He said, "The common law has long required that a person who has made a representation must correct that representation if it becomes false and if he knows people are relying on it." He was aware of the many difficulties that a final determination of liability on the part of public accountants for nondisclosure would create for professional firms and others similarly situated. For example: How long does the duty to disclose after-acquired information last? To whom and how should disclosure be made? Does liability exist if the after-acquired knowledge is obtained from a source other than the original supplier of information? Is there a duty to disclose if an associate or employee of the accounting firm discovers the information but fails to report it to the firm members?

The judge said that, on the other side of the coin, is the fact that investors in publicly-held companies have a strong interest in being afforded some degree of protection by and from those professional and business persons whose representations are relied upon for decisional purposes. He continued:

> . . . In my view, resolution of the issues posed by the complaint allegations here in question must be made with these important but conflicting interests in mind. Proper reconciliation of these interests or policy considerations, however, can only be made after full development of the facts of this case during the discovery process and at trial.

As stated above, the case was settled without a trial and therefore the "proper reconciliation" of the conflicting interests contemplated by the judge could not be made.

The judge's opinion was silent with respect to the dilemma which faced the accountants growing out of the restraints imposed by professional organizations which have as their objective the preservation of the confidential relationship between accountants and their clients. The AICPA's Code of Professional Ethics, for instance, provides in Rule 1.03 that "A member [of the Institute] shall not violate the confidential relationship between himself and his client." The New York State Society of CPAs has an even more stringent disclosure prohibition; the State Society's Rule 1.03 of the Rules of Professional Conduct provides as follows:

> 1.03. A member shall not violate the confidential relationship between himself and his client. Therefore, a member shall not disclose, except as required by law, information acquired in the course of a professional engagement to anyone other than his client without the consent of the client or without the consent of both the client and third party when the accounts of such third party are examined at the request of a client.

[*Author's note:* At the date of this writing, both the AICPA rule and the NYSSCPA rule are under consideration for possible revision.]

The plaintiffs had based their suit in part on Section 10(b) of the 1934 Act and SEC Rule 10b–5. (The section and rule are quoted in Chapter **27**.) The judge observed that the defendants in cases involving Section 10(b) and Rule 10b–5 have tended to fall into four general categories. The first three are (1) corporate insiders, (2) brokers and dealers in securities, and (3) corporations whose securities are purchased or sold by plaintiffs. Common to each of these categories is the possibility that economic gain or advantage will result from the fraudulent practices complained of. The fourth category consists of those who "aid and abet" or conspire with a party who falls into one of the first three categories. Since the auditors did not appear to fit any of these categories, the central issue was whether a Section 10(b) action could be maintained against persons such as the auditors who, it appeared, did not gain from their failure to disclose the discovery of the falsity of the financial statements.

After discussing the precedents, the judge said that the auditors' motion to dismiss claims that were based on Section 10(b) and Rule 10b–5 raised novel and difficult issues. Because of the importance of the questions involved and the need for further factual and legal development of them, he denied this portion of the motion without prejudice to renew it at the trial which, as stated above, was not held because the case was settled.

INTERIM STATEMENT LIABILITY.—During the period in which the special studies were in progress, Yale compiled interim 1964 financial statements based on its internal accounting procedures. The complaint alleged that the earnings reported in these statements were overstated. The plaintiffs charged that the auditors knew the figures were false but did not disclose that knowledge to anyone, and that the auditors "recommended" that the false reports be issued. Accordingly, said the plaintiffs, the auditors should be held liable for "aiding and abetting" Yale's scheme to defraud.

The auditors moved to dismiss this portion of the claim saying that the complaint failed to spell out an actionable conspiracy, and that, in any event, it owed no duty to the investing public in respect of the special studies.

The judge observed that there was no allegation that the auditors compiled, audited, or certified any of the interim statements, nor was there indication that any of the statements contained material which an investor could justifiably attribute or relate to the auditors.

If the auditors' failure to disclose constituted a breach of its duty, it seems clear that the judge would have ruled for the plaintiffs. He said:

But, as indicated, no such duty can be found in the context of those facts pleaded here. Absent such a duty, there is no basis for transforming silence into actionable aiding and abetting.

The judge then considered whether, as alleged by the plaintiffs, the auditors aided and abetted Yale's alleged violation of Section 10(b) by recommending or sanctioning the release of statements containing figures compiled by Yale's own Accounting Department rather than those developed by the auditors during the course of the special studies. The plaintiffs' claim in this connection was said to be found in answers given to plaintiffs' interrogatories by certain individual defendants who were former officers and directors of Yale. These claims by the plaintiffs were hotly disputed by the auditors. For that reason and because the case was settled, the basis for the plaintiffs' allegations, although referred to in the judge's opinion, are omitted here.

Quoting from the Restatement of Torts, Sec. 876 (1939), the judge said:

For harm resulting to a third person from the tortious conduct of another, a person is liable if he

* * * * *

(b) Knows that the other's conduct constitutes a breach of duty and gives substantial assistance or encouragement to the other so to conduct himself . . .

If it was true that the auditors knew that Yale was breaching its duty to investors by issuing false financial statements, the question was whether the auditors gave "substantial assistance or encouragement" to Yale. The judge said that, even on the plaintiffs' allegations, it was difficult to characterize the auditors' action as "assistance or encouragement"; furthermore, doubt remained as to whether the term "substantial" could be added to them. He said, however, that it was inappropriate to make a determination of the "aiding and abetting" issue at that time because "Discovery is presently in a relatively inadvanced stage." While the plaintiffs could then show only minimal interaction between the auditors and the company in relation to the interim statements, "they must be given an opportunity to further explore this facet" of the relationship. Accordingly, he denied the auditors' motion to dismiss this portion of the complaint.

LISTING PROCEDURE

CONTENTS

Most of the larger American corporations have one or more classes of securities listed for trading on national securities exchanges. On the other hand, a number of large, publicly-owned corporations (notably banks, investment companies, and insurance companies) do not have any securities so listed; their securities are traded in the "over-the-counter" market.

A noteworthy development in recent years has been the increased interest of United States investors in the securities of Canadian and other foreign issuers. A glance at the portfolios of investment companies will indicate the extent of that interest on the part of substantial holders. In recognition of the increased ownership of their securities by United States investors, many foreign corporations have listed their securities for trading on United States securities exchanges. The securities of many other foreign corporations are actively traded in the over-the-counter markets in the United States.

Businessmen frequently seek their accountants' advice on a wide variety of matters, and it is not unusual for a businessman to ask his accountant, "What are the advantages or disadvantages of having securities listed on an exchange?" Some of the advantages and disadvantages of an exchange listing are discussed in the following pages.

Advantages to the Corporation

In order to become listed, a corporation must file a registration statement (usually on Form 10) to comply with requirements of the Securities Exchange Act of 1934, and in addition it must prepare an application for listing to comply with the requirements of the particular exchange on which listing is desired. From the viewpoint of future financing, it is a distinct advantage to a corporation to have had its registration statement or reports processed by the SEC. With the SEC filing, the company and its affairs become known to the SEC staff. The group at the SEC which processes the registration statement will, in the future, usually process everything filed by that registrant, regardless of the SEC statute involved. This means that if, at some future date, the company should have need for additional capital and decides to register under the 1933 Act for a public offering, the processing by the SEC will be expedited. Furthermore, much of the information in the company's registration statement and reports under the 1934 Act will be required in the registration statement under the 1933 Act. Also, many of the numerous exhibits filed with Form 10 are also required in connection with an S–1 filing but need not be duplicated if they have previously been filed with SEC. In other words, once a company is listed, much of the work involved in preparing a registration statement under the 1933 Act is reduced or eliminated.

The "blue-sky" laws of some states provide an exemption for securities listed on specified exchanges or securities senior to securities so listed. This also expedites the process of raising capital for listed companies.

There is a great deal of publicity value attaching to an exchange listing. Many newspapers and statistical services each day print complete quotations of securities listed on some exchanges and abbreviated listings of securities on other exchanges. Moreover, the financial writers and news services pay much more attention to listed securities than to unlisted securities. This publicity factor also has a bearing on future financing by the corporation. A well-known corporation is likely to find more acceptance among investors than one that is less well known. (This advantage may be more apparent than real. One writer[1] points out that officers of some leading companies traded over-the-counter insist their securities have become better known and more widely traded over the years than some listed shares. "American-Marietta [now Martin Marietta, a listed company], for in-

---

[1] Worth Seymour, "To List, or Not to List," *Investment Dealers' Digest,* November 20, 1961, p. 30.

stance, can claim about 50,000 shareholders while some of the long-time listed companies have barely maintained the minimum number of investors required."

Experience indicates that, in general, when a corporation has its securities listed on an exchange, it usually acquires more stockholders. Every stockholder is a potential customer.

Some investors (certain investment trusts, for example) will invest only in listed securities or, as a matter of policy, will give preference to such securities. They want to be assured of an exchange market for quick resale if necessary. That is why a prospectus relating to a new offering sometimes states on its cover whether application will be made for exchange listing.

Advantages to the Stockholder

The principal advantage of an exchange listing to the stockholder is the fact that transactions are in the open. The investor knows instantly the price at which his transaction was consummated and the price of preceding and following transactions. This price is also known at the same instant in the offices of thousands of brokers, financial institutions, investment companies, dealers, and investors by means of the quotation tickers.

Listed securities are more acceptable as collateral for loans than are unlisted securities. For certain types of loans, in fact, unlisted securities are not acceptable. One reason for this preference for listed securities is that the ticker tape furnishes a constant check to the lender on the value of the collateral. Quotations of listed securities are printed in many daily newspapers.

Since there is always a specialist on the floor of the exchange charged with the responsibility of maintaining a fair, orderly and continuous market in a particular security, the mere fact of listing provides a better market for the security.

Since an exchange listing provides a ready market, it facilitates the distribution of large holdings for estate liquidation, tax, or other reasons.

Exchange rules are designed to protect the public. Exchange members are under careful supervision by the exchanges and the SEC.

The investor in a listed company is furnished with financial and other information which he would not receive, as a matter of right, in respect of an unlisted security. (This would not be true, however, with respect to an unlisted company which, as a result of the Securities Acts Amendments of 1964, had to register with the SEC under the 1934 Act.)

Disadvantages To the Corporation and Its Executives

Prior to the enactment of the Securities Acts Amendments of 1964, a publicly-owned unlisted company enjoyed some distinct advantages as compared with a listed company. Before the 1964 Amendments, the unlisted company was not subject to the SEC's reporting requirements or to the Commission's regulations regarding the solicitation of proxies. Most important of all, the unlisted company was not subject to the provisions in Section 16 of the 1934 Act dealing with the recapture by a corporation of short-swing profits realized by its officers, directors, and principal holders of equity securities. Because it was felt that one set of rules should not apply to listed companies and another set of rules to companies whose securities were traded over-the-counter, the 1964 Amendments required unlisted companies to register under the 1934 Act when they had a certain number of holders of equity securities and had a stated amount of assets.

Once the publicly-owned but unlisted company had to register under the 1934 Act, many of the advantages accruing to it because of its unlisted status disappeared.

There are still many companies whose securities are traded over-the-counter which are not registered under the 1934 Act because they do not meet the requirements as to size in terms of assets and number of shareholders. Such companies, despite their size, may be considering the pros and cons of listing their securities for exchange trading. Registered but unlisted companies may also be considering the merits of listing.

For both groups of companies, the only significant disadvantage of listing is the cost, because listing is not cheap. There is an initial fee for listing, and some exchanges make an annual charge for a specified number of years for the privilege of having the company's securities traded on the exchange.

For companies not subject to the registration provisions of the 1934 Act, listing on an exchange would bring with it all the disadvantages of registration under that Act, because in order to be listed, companies must also be registered.

A listed and registered company must furnish much more information to the SEC, the exchange, and its stockholders than would be required if the company's securities were not listed and registered. Not only is this true with respect to annual and interim reports; it is especially true with respect to proxy-soliciting material. Corporate insiders (that is, officers and directors and holders of ten per cent of the company's equity securities) must report their holdings of, and transactions in, the company's stock if it is listed and registered.

A principal objection to listing and registration is the provision in the 1934 Act relating to "short-swing" profits. The law provides that profits arising from a purchase of a registered security and a sale within six months, or a sale and a purchase within six months, realized by an officer, director, or persons owning ten per cent or more of the equity securities of a registered corporation, shall inure to and be recoverable by the corporation. Many a corporation executive has congratulated himself on his sagacity in realizing short-term profits only to discover that he had to turn them over to the corporation.

The corporate insider may be liable not only for his short-swing profits, but also for interest thereon. In a 1962 decision, a judgment had been obtained against an officer-director of a corporation for recovery of short-swing profits plus interest. He moved for modification of the judgment to eliminate the interest. He argued, among other things, that the judgment obtained against him was equivalent to a penalty on which interest is not granted. The court denied the motion to eliminate the interest and said that an award for profits made by an insider in a short-swing transaction is not the imposition of a penalty but is compensation to a corporation for the breach of a statutory duty.[2]

Procedure for Listing

Before securities can be traded on a securities exchange, the company must comply with two sets of requirements: those of the particular securities exchange involved and those of the SEC. The exchange requires the submission of an application in conformity with the rules of the exchange. The SEC requires the preparation of a registration statement under the 1934 Act for filing both with the exchange and with the SEC. (The registration forms are listed in Chapter **14**.) Usually the listing application and the registration statement are prepared and filed concurrently. In due course the exchange approves the listing application submitted to it and certifies to the SEC that it has received its copy of the registration statement and has approved the company's securities for listing and registration. Ordinarily registration becomes effective automatically 30 days after receipt by the SEC of the exchange's certification but may become effective within a shorter period by order of the SEC following a request by the company or the exchange to that effect.

Each exchange has its own requirements for listing. The most stringent requirements are those of the New York Stock Exchange. This chapter sets forth briefly the listing requirements of that exchange and those of the American Stock Exchange, the two principal American exchanges.

The Listing Application

There are two kinds of listing applications: (1) the application for original listing, and (2) the application subsequent to original listing.

The application for original listing places before the exchange the essential information as to the suitability of the securities for exchange trading and provides the investing public such information as may be required to

[2] *Perfect Photo, Inc. v. Grabb,* U.S. District Court, Eastern District of Pa., June 20, 1962.

judge the merits of the security. The application subsequent to original listing gives information as to the purpose for which additional securities are to be issued, the consideration to be received therefor, and brings up to date significant data given in the company's previous applications. If the subsequent application relates to shares to be issued as stock dividends or in a split-up, the information to be furnished is usually limited to a few details bearing on the transaction of issuance.

The New York Stock Exchange

Eligibility for Listing.—The qualifications for listing on the New York Stock Exchange are somewhat flexible. The company must be a going concern, or the successor to a going concern, and must have substantial assets or demonstrated earning power, or both. The company should have a demonstrated earning power, under competitive conditions, of at least $2,500,000 *before* federal income taxes in the latest fiscal year, and $2,000,000 *before* federal income taxes in each of the two preceding years. Net tangible assets should be at least $16,000,000, but the Exchange places greater emphasis on the aggregate market value of the publicly-held common stock, where $16,000,000 or more at the time of listing will be looked for. While the amount of assets and earnings and the aggregate market value of the company's junior securities are considerations, the Exchange places greater emphasis on such questions as degree of national interest in the company, its standing in its particular field, the character of the market for its products, its relative stability and position in its industry, and whether or not it is engaged in an expanding industry with prospects of maintaining its position.

The securities to be listed must have a sufficiently wide distribution to offer reasonable assurance that an adequate auction market in the securities will exist. In the case of common stock issues, the Exchange will expect the total number of publicly held shares to be a minimum of 1,000,000. The shares must be held by at least 2,000 stockholders each owning 100 or more shares.

The Exchange will refuse to list non-voting common stock or any non-voting stock, however designated, which by its terms is, in effect, a common stock. The Exchange will also refuse to list the common voting stock of a company which also has outstanding in public hands a non-voting stock, however designated, which by its terms is in effect a common stock.

The Exchange will also refuse to list voting trust certificates (except in cases of reorganization proceedings under court direction) and common stock where the voting rights of shareholders in stock to be issued for assets or sold for cash would be restricted by the use of a voting trust, irrevocable proxy, or any similar arrangement to which the company or any of its officers or directors is a party, either directly or indirectly.

The Exchange may also refuse to list preferred stock not having certain minimum voting rights. To be acceptable for listing, a preferred stock should provide for:

1. The right of the preferred stock, voting as a class, to elect at least two directors upon default of the equivalent of six quarterly dividends;

2. The affirmative approval of at least two-thirds of the outstanding preferred stock as a prerequisite to any charter or by-law amendment altering materially any existing provision of such preferred stock.

In the application of its listing policy relating to preferred stock, the Exchange may make exceptions in highly unusual cases, as, for example, where the laws of the state of incorporation preclude, or make virtually impossible, the conferring of exclusive voting rights upon any particular class of stock.

In the case of a company contemplating filing of an application for listing on the Exchange, and particularly where there is any doubt as to its eligibility for listing, it is recommended that data first be presented informally for confidential study by the Exchange prior to the preparation of a complete formal application.

Submission of Application.—Four draft copies of the application should be submitted to the Department of Stock List of the Exchange at least two weeks in advance of the date on which it is desired to have the application acted upon, to allow time for preliminary examination and revision if necessary. A longer period is desirable, particularly in the case of original listings. The application should be in substantially its final revised form (and the file of required supporting documents complete) at least one week in advance of the date it is to be acted upon.

Printing of Application.—After listing has been authorized the Exchange distributes copies of the final listing application to all member firms of the Exchange and to others, including the general public, who may request a copy. A subscription service is available to those desiring to receive copies of all applications through the mail.

The applicant company pays all costs of printing the application.

Confidential Preliminary Review of Eligibility.—Upon request, the Exchange is willing to conduct an informal and confidential review of the applicant company's eligibility for listing. This procedure normally precedes a formal application for listing and is designed to avoid embarrassment to either the company or the Exchange in having an application filed which the Exchange may not be willing to approve for whatever reason.

Even though all original listings ultimately require approval by the Exchange's Board, the preliminary review will assure the company that the application will be reported on favorably by the staff. The Board generally follows the staff's recommendations on new listings. The preliminary review should be completed prior to any announcement in the press, annual report, prospectus, etc., of a company's intention to file a listing application.

Following is a general outline of the information needed by the Exchange for the purpose of the confidential preliminary review:

1. The charter and by-laws.
2. Specimens of bonds or stock certificates.
3. Annual reports to stockholders for last five years.
4. Latest prospectus covering an offering under the 1933 Act and latest Form 10–K filed with the SEC.
5. Proxy statement for most recent annual meeting.
6. Stock distribution schedule.
7. Supplementary data to assist the Exchange in determining the character of the share distribution and the number of publicly-held shares:
   (a) Names of 10 largest holders of record, and beneficial owners (if known) of holdings of record by nominees.
   (b) List of holdings of 1,000 shares or more in the names of Exchange member organizations.
   (c) Number of transfers and shares transferred during each of last two years.
   (d) Summary, by principal groups, of stock owned or controlled by:
       (i) Officers or directors and their immediate families.
       (ii) Other concentrated holdings of 10% or more.
       (iii) Shares held under investment letters (1933 Act) and not reported elsewhere under Item 7.
   (e) Estimate of number of non-officer employees owning stock and the total shares held.
   (f) Company shares held in profit-sharing, savings, pension, or other similar funds or trusts established for benefit of officers, employees, etc.
8. It is recognized that in a closely-held company, situations involving the personal interests of officers, directors, or principal share-owners are sometimes regarded as advantageous or convenient. Usually, the character and appropriateness of these relationships is reconsidered when a company goes public. Accordingly, the Exchange would look for information on any such relationships; for example, the leasing of property to or from the company, interests or options

in subsidiaries, interests (other than ordinary investments in widely-held, publicly-owned companies) in businesses that are competitors, suppliers, or customers of the company.

Action on Application by Exchange.—The Exchange will act on the application as soon as practicable after the necessary revisions have been made and the file of supporting documents completed. If the company already has securities listed, action on the application by the Board of Governors of the Exchange may not be required; in all other cases the application is submitted to the Board for final authorization of listing.

Applications for Original Listing.—The Exchange issues to all interested persons booklets of various kinds to help in the preparation of the listing application. In addition, the Exchange makes available copies of listing applications filed by other companies in the same or similar industry. The wide range of circumstances found among various industries, and among individual companies, makes it impossible to set forth all details which may finally be required in a listing application.

The following captions indicate the general scope of the information to be included in the application:

1. Name of company and formal title or designation of securities
2. Formal titles of the securities for which listing application is made and the amounts thereof; number of stockholders of record of common stock at latest available date
3. Opinion of counsel
4. Status under federal or state acts and authorities
5. History and business:
   Where and when organized
   Form of organization; duration of charter
   Principal products or services; annual output last five years
   Principal markets for products and raw material
   Operations conducted
   Merchandising methods
   Recent growth and development of the industry and of the company and the place it occupies in its field
   Importance of patents, formulae, or secret processes
6. Physical properties of the company and subsidiaries and whether owned or leased
7. Subsidiary and controlled companies
8. Names and addresses of directors and officers and their principal business affiliations
9. Capitalization

10. Funded debt
11. Stock provisions
12. Employees and labor relations:
    Number of employees
    Material work stoppages in last three years
    Provisions of pension, retirement, bonus, profit-participation, stock purchase, insurance, hospitalization, or other employees' benefit plans
13. Stockholder relations:
    Publicity given to interim statements and dividend declarations and omissions
14. Dividend record during last five years
15. Options, warrants, conversion rights, etc.
16. Litigation
17. Business, financial, and accounting policies (see below)
18. Financial statements (see page **29·**12)

Because of his familiarity with the company, it is advisable for the accountant to read the entire application—not merely the financial statements covered by his certificate.

PROSPECTUS INCORPORATED IN LISTING APPLICATION.—At the option of the company, the data required in the listing application may be furnished by reference to any prospectus relating to the company which was filed pursuant to the Securities Act of 1933 and issued not more than thirty days prior to the filing of the initial draft of the listing application. When this procedure is followed, the information required in addition to that included in the prospectus varies depending upon the contents of the prospectus itself. The additional information required is set forth in the detailed directions for the preparation of the application. This information is usually printed in the form of cover pages attached to the prospectus, and accordingly such applications are often referred to as "wraparound."

The instructions of the Exchange do not provide for the incorporation of a proxy statement in an original application for listing. In some circumstances, however, it is known that the Exchange does permit the use of a recent proxy statement for this purpose where the proxy statement serves as a satisfactory basis therefor. This would be true, for example, in the case of a proxy statement prepared in connection with a proposed merger which conforms with the requirements of the SEC's proxy regulation.

BUSINESS, FINANCIAL, AND ACCOUNTING POLICIES.—The textual material presented under this heading should be prepared or reviewed by the applicant's independent public accountant.

Independent Auditors.—There must be stated the name of independent public accountants, how long they have audited the company's accounts, when and by whom appointed, whether or not they report directly to the Board of Directors, whether they make a continuous or periodic audit, extent of their authority to examine all records and supporting evidence, whether or not they are authorized or invited to attend stockholders' meetings, whether they do attend such meetings and (if they do attend) whether or not they are authorized to answer questions raised by stockholders.

Chief Accounting Officer.—The name and title of the company's chief accounting officer must be stated, together with information as to when and by whom appointed, to whom he reports and the extent of his authority, and whether or not he attends the meetings of the Board of Directors.

Leases.—If the company conducts a substantial portion of its business in leased premises, as in the case of retail chain store organizations, the company must state its policy with regard to such leases, that is, whether, in general, the leases are long-term, whether rentals are at a flat rate or percentage of sales, etc. The total of rentals paid during the last year must be stated, together with the average term of leases.

Depreciation.—There must be furnished a description in reasonable detail of the company's policy as to depreciation. The description must state the method of depreciation followed, that is, "straight-line," etc., and the theory underlying such method. The rates employed as to major classes of property must be stated in tabular form.

Depletion.—If assets subject to depletion are material, the company must describe the basis on which depletion is charged and the theory underlying such basis.

Amortization (Other than Depreciation).—The company must state the policy followed with respect to those items which, in ordinary accounting practice, may be capitalized and amortized.

Commitments.—The company is required to state whether or not it is the company's policy to make future commodity commitments to an extent which may materially affect its financial position. The company must also indicate whether or not, in the normal course of the business, it is necessary to expand working capital through short-term loans (or otherwise) to a material extent.

Valuation of Inventories.—The practice followed in adjusting inventories to the lower-of-cost-or-market must be stated, that is, whether the adjustment is based on specific items, groups or classes, or the entire inventory. The term "market" must be explained, that is, whether it represents:

(a) Replacement market, and whether, in that event, allowance is made for any decline in price of basic commodities in finished goods and work in process; or

(b) Selling market, and whether, in that event, allowance is made for selling expense and normal margin of profit.

The company must state its practice if (a) and (b) are followed in respect of different parts of the inventory. The treatment of any intercompany profit on goods included in inventory must be described.

Method of Computing Cost of Goods Sold.—The general method of computing cost of goods sold must be stated, that is, whether computed on basis of "average cost," "standard cost," "last-in, first-out," "first-in, first-out," etc., and, if practicable, the year in which such method was adopted.

Marketable Securities.—If marketable securities are material in proportion to the total assets, the company must state the method of computing profit or loss on sale of securities.

Consolidation.—A statement must be made as to the principles followed with respect to consolidation, for accounting purposes, in the inclusion or exclusion of companies. There must also be stated whether all companies included in the consolidation employ the same principles of accounting; if not, the nature of any substantial divergence.

Other Policies.—In cases where (because of the nature of the industry or circumstances peculiar to the company) business, financial, or accounting policies other than those outlined above are considered to be of material effect in determination of the company's income or its financial position, or in interpretation of its financial statements, the company must describe such other policies.

FINANCIAL STATEMENTS.—The following financial statements must be included in the listing application:

1. A summarized statement of earnings, on a consolidated basis for the last ten fiscal years, showing sales, earnings before charges for depreciation, interest, and federal income taxes, the amount of each of these charges, and net earnings. This summary need not be certified by independent accountants.

2. Consolidated income and surplus statements for the last two fiscal years, with consolidated balance sheets as of the end of each of those years, together with the related certificate of the company's independent auditors. If practicable, these statements shall be in comparative form.

3. Any consolidated statement of earnings for any regular interim

period of the current fiscal year which may be available. If a consolidated balance sheet as of a date later than the close of the last fiscal year is available, it shall be included also. Such interim statements shall be certified, but certification may be made by the company's principal accounting officer; for a form of certificate, see page **29·**14.

4. A pro forma or "giving effect" consolidated balance sheet may also be required where there has been, or is contemplated, any major financing, recapitalization, acquisition, or reorganization.

Unconsolidated Subsidiaries.—If there are any subsidiary or controlled companies not included in the consolidated financial statements, the consolidated income statement shall include a footnote reflecting the parent company's proportion of the undistributed profits or of the losses of such companies. There shall also be a footnote to the consolidated balance sheet showing the amount by which the parent company's equity in the unconsolidated subsidiary or controlled companies has increased or decreased, since the date of acquisition, as a result of profits, losses, and distributions.

Separate financial statements of any such unconsolidated subsidiary or controlled company may be required in the application if the investment in such company represents a substantial part of the assets of the parent company, or if the parent company's proportion of the profits or losses of such company is substantial in relation to the consolidated net income.

Parent Company Statements.—There may also be required statements of the parent company as a separate corporate entity if such statements appear essential or desirable. In general, parent company statements are not required in cases where the subsidiaries are wholly owned and do not have any substantial amount of funded debt outstanding.

Form of Financial Statements.—The Exchange does not attempt to prescribe the form or detail of the financial statements included in listing applications. It is expected, however, that such statements will be reasonably informative and that the accounting policies of the company will conform to accepted practice.

The Exchange asks the applicant company to submit its financial statements, initially, in the form in which they have been published theretofore in the annual reports to stockholders. Those statements are examined by the Department of Stock List. Such changes as may seem desirable are discussed with the company's representatives.

When preparing financial statements for inclusion in a listing application, it should be borne in mind that, among the listing agreements filed by the company in support of the application, there is one requiring all financial statements contained in the company's future annual reports to stockholders to be in the same form as the statements contained in the listing application. In practice this agreement is construed as meaning that financial statements in future annual reports will contain substantially the same amount of detailed information as the statements included in the listing application. However, the agreement is not considered applicable to financial statements included in a prospectus incorporated in a listing application. In such a case, the Exchange usually assents to a modification of the agreement so as to make it relate to a form of financial statements agreed upon with the Exchange independently of the listing application in which such prospectus is incorporated.

ORIGINAL LISTING OF BONDS.—If the listing application relates to bonds, debentures, notes, or other securities evidencing indebtedness, the additional information outlined below shall be included in the application following "Funded Debt."

Title of issue; title of instrument under which created; name of trustee; dates of authorizations for issue by directors, stockholders and public authorities; amounts authorized, issued, retired, outstanding; date of issue and maturity; interest rate; places and dates for payment of principal and interest; currency in which payable; tax exemptions; whether coupon or registered form and whether exchangeable.

Indenture provisions—security; additional issues; sinking fund; redemption; default; release of pledged property; convertibility; modification of indenture; treatment of deposited funds; important covenants.

CERTIFICATE OF PRINCIPAL ACCOUNTING OFFICER.—Certain of the interim financial statements in the listing application must be certified, but the certificate may be made by the company's principal accounting officer. Following is a suggested form of certificate which complies with the requirements:

The accompanying financial statements of ABC Corporation as of (date) and for the (period) then ended were prepared under my control and direction.

In my opinion, such financial statements present fairly the position of ABC Corporation at (date) and the results of its operations for the (period) then ended, in conformity with generally accepted accounting principles applied on a basis consistent with that of the preceding fiscal year.

(Name and title)

Listing Agreements.—As a condition for listing, the applicant signifies concurrence in a number of agreements called "Listing Agreements." The agreements which have accounting significance and which are of most interest to accountants are the following:

1. The Corporation will publish at least once a year and submit to its stockholders at least fifteen days in advance of the annual meeting of such stockholders and not later than three months after the close of the last preceding fiscal year of the Corporation a Balance Sheet as of the end of such fiscal year, and a surplus and income statement for such fiscal year of the Corporation as a separate corporate entity and of each corporation in which it holds directly or indirectly a majority of the equity stock; or in lieu thereof, eliminating all intercompany transactions, a consolidated balance sheet of the Corporation and its subsidiaries as of the end of its last previous fiscal year, and a consolidated surplus statement and a consolidated income statement of the Corporation and its subsidiaries for such fiscal year. If any such consolidated statement shall exclude corporations a majority of whose equity stock is owned directly or indirectly by the Corporation: (a) the caption of, or a note to, such statement will show the degree of consolidation; (b) the consolidated income account will reflect, either in a footnote or otherwise, the parent company's proportion of the sum of, or difference between, current earnings or losses and the dividends of such unconsolidated subsidiaries for the period of the report; and (c) the consolidated balance sheet will reflect, either in a footnote or otherwise, the extent to which the equity of the parent company in such subsidiaries has been increased or diminished since the date of acquisition as a result of profits, losses and distributions.

Appropriate reserves, in accordance with good accounting practice, will be made against profits arising out of all transactions with unconsolidated subsidiaries in either parent company statements or consolidated statements.

Such statements will reflect the existence of any default in interest, cumulative dividend requirements, sinking fund or redemption fund requirements of the Corporation and of any controlled corporation, whether consolidated or unconsolidated.

2. All financial statements contained in annual reports of the Corporation to its stockholders will be audited by independent public accountants qualified under the laws of some state or country, and will be accompanied by a copy of the certificate made by them with respect to their audit of such statements showing the scope of such audit and the qualifications, if any, with respect thereto.

The Corporation will promptly notify the Exchange if it changes its independent public accountants regularly auditing the books and accounts of the Corporation.

3. All financial statements contained in annual reports of the Corporation to its stockholders shall be in the same form as the corresponding statements contained in the listing application in connection with which this Listing Agreement is made, and shall disclose any substantial items of unusual or non-recurrent nature.

4. The Corporation will publish quarterly statements of earnings on the basis of the same degree of consolidation as in the annual report. Such statements will disclose any substantial items of unusual or non-recurrent nature and will show either net income before and after federal income taxes or net income and the amount of federal income taxes.

5. The Corporation will not make, nor will it permit any subsidiary directly or indirectly controlled by it to make, any substantial charges against capital surplus, without notifying the Exchange. If so requested by the Exchange, the Corporation will submit such charges to stockholders for approval or ratification.

6. The Corporation will not make any substantial change, nor will it permit any subsidiary directly or indirectly controlled by it to make any substantial

change, in accounting methods, in policies as to depreciation and depletion or in bases of valuation of inventories or other assets, without notifying the Exchange and disclosing the effect of any such change in its next succeeding interim and annual report to its stockholders.

Listing Fees.—The listing fees of the New York Stock Exchange (in effect at the time of this writing) payable at the time of initial listing of stock, and the continuing annual fees, are summarized in the following schedule:

Fees for Stock—Per Share Issued

Fee Bracket	*Initial Fee	Continuing Annual Fee
First 2 million shares	1¢	1/10¢
3rd & 4th million shares	1/2¢	1/20¢
5th million to 300 million shares	1/4¢	1/20¢
In excess of 300 million shares	1/8¢	1/20¢

* For original listings of common stock there is a further one-time charge of $15,000.

Minimum fees: Initial —$1,000 per application for listing additional shares
Annual—$5,000 per common stock issue and
$1,000 for each issue or series other than common

The fees for listing of bonds and similar securities on the New York Stock Exchange are summarized in the following schedule:

Fees for Bonds and Similar Securities
per Million Principal Amount

Regular bonds, debentures, etc. $120
Short term—Maturity 5 years or less .... $ 60
Relisting previously listed bonds on assumption by another obligor involving no change in original terms .... $ 30

There is no continuing fee for the listing of bonds and similar securities.

Audit Requirements Affecting Listed Companies.—The current form of listing agreements of the New York Stock Exchange requires that all annual financial statements, as submitted to stockholders, be audited by independent accountants qualified under the laws of some state or country, and be accompanied by a copy of the certificate made by such independent accountants in respect of their audit of such statements, showing the scope of such audit and the qualifications, if any, with respect thereto. This agreement does not apply to interim financial statements.

Exceptions to this requirement have been made in the past in the case of railroads, banks, and insurance companies, but the Exchange now requires banks and insurance companies to be audited. As far as railroads are concerned, there are now very few whose annual financial statements are not audited.

The American Stock Exchange

Unlisted Trading on American Stock Exchange.—There are two kinds of securities traded on the American Stock Exchange: (1) those that are fully listed, and (2) those that are admitted to unlisted trading privileges. The second type are securities of companies which did not apply for listing and were admitted to unlisted trading privileges by the Exchange prior to the enactment of the Securities Exchange Act of 1934. Possibly because of constitutional questions involved, these companies retained their unlisted trading privileges when the 1934 Act was passed through a special provision in Section 12(f) of that Act. Further admission of securities to unlisted trading has been virtually terminated.

Since the adoption of the Securities Acts Amendments Act of 1964, most companies admitted to unlisted trading privileges on the Exchange have had to register with the SEC under Section 12(g) of the 1934 Act, and are subject to the same financial reporting, proxy statement, and insider trading requirements as apply to fully listed companies.

The number of companies with unlisted trading privileges on the American Stock Exchange has been substantially reduced as a result of recapitalizations, mergers, and—in a few cases—companies transferring to a fully listed status or moving to the "Big Board." As of December 31, 1970 only 61 companies' stocks continued to have unlisted trading privileges on the Exchange.

The American Stock Exchange issues on request several different kinds of booklets and other information describing its listing requirements, procedures, and fees, all of which are available on request at the Exchange. In addition, as a guide to the preparation of a listing application, the Exchange furnishes copies of applications filed by other issuers, including, if available, some in industries similar to that of the prospective applicant.

Eligibility for Listing.—Prior to 1962, the standards for listing on the American Stock Exchange were highly informal. There was no rigid policy as to size of applicant corporations from the viewpoint of either assets or earning power. Neither was there a formal Exchange rule or policy as to the minimum number of shares of stock which must be publicly distributed or the minimum number of public stockholders among whom such shares must be distributed in order to qualify for listing.

In 1962 the Board of Governors of the American Stock Exchange adopted formal listing standards and policies in line with the recommendations of the Special Committee for Study of the American Stock Exchange. The criteria for listing on the Exchange have been raised over the years, although they are considerably below those of the New York Stock Exchange. At the date of this writing, the requirements as to size and earnings for listing on the American Stock Exchange are as follows:

Size (Net Assets): Net tangible assets of at least $3,000,000.

Earnings: Net income of at least $300,000 *after all charges,* including Federal income taxes, in the fiscal year immediately preceding the filing of the listing application, and, except under special circumstances, net income *before income taxes* and extraordinary charges and credits, of at least $500,000.

There are additional criteria applicable to various classes of securities and issuers, the most significant of which are summarized below.

Companies applying for the listing of common shares are expected to comply with requirements as to distribution, price, and aggregate market value of publicly-held shares as follows:

Distribution of Common Stock Issues: Minimum public distribution of 300,000 shares (exclusive of the holdings of officers, directors, controlling shareholders and other concentrated or family holdings) among not less than 900 holders, including not less than 600 holders of lots of 100 shares or more.

Companies whose securities are concentrated in a limited geographical area, or whose securities are largely held in blocks by institutional investors, are normally not considered eligible for listing unless the public distribution appreciably exceeds 300,000 shares.

Price Per Share: A minimum of $5 per share for a reasonable period of time prior to the filing of the listing application. In the case of recent public offerings, a higher price will generally be expected.

Aggregate Market Value for Publicly Held Shares: $2,000,000 minimum.

The listing of preferred stock issues on the American Stock Exchange is considered on a case by case basis, in the light of the suitability of the issue for a continuous auction market, the public interest in having the same market place for two or more securities of the same company, and other factors. In general, the Exchange will not list the preferred stock of a company unless its common stock is also listed and unless:

Size and Earnings: The company appears to be in a financial position sufficient to service satisfactorily the dividend requirements of the preferred stock, and the company meets the size and earnings criteria for companies generally referred to above.

Aggregate Market Value: $2,000,000 minimum. Preferred stocks selling below $10 per share will not ordinarily be considered eligible for listing.

Convertible Issues: In the case of convertible issues, the Exchange may require a substantially larger distribution than in the case of non-convertible issues.

The listing of bonds and debentures is also considered on a case by case basis. As a general rule, the Exchange will not consider listing such securities of a company unless:

Size and Earnings: The company appears to be in a financial position sufficient to service satisfactorily the debt issue to be listed and the company meets the size and earnings criteria set forth above.

Distribution: The issue has a minimum distribution as follows:

Principal Amount Outstanding: $1,500,000.

Aggregate Market Value: $1,500,000.

Approximate Number of Holders: 300, subject to review on a case-by-case basis.

Convertible Issues: As in the case of preferred stock issues, the Exchange may require that convertible debt issues have a substantially larger distribution (aggregate market value of $2,000,000 or more) than the amount specified above for non-convertible issues.

The Exchange has special listing requirements applicable to long-term warrants and to securities of real estate investment trusts.

The approval of an application for the listing of securities on the American Stock Exchange is a matter solely within the discretion of the Exchange's Board of Governors. The guidelines listed above are considered in evaluating potential applicants for listing, but there are other relevant factors which the Board considers in determining whether a company qualifies for listing, such as the nature of its business, the market for its products, its future prospects, the reputation of its management, and so on. The fact that an applicant may meet the numerical guidelines referred to above does not necessarily mean that the Board will approve the application. Also, in special situations an application may be approved even though the company does not meet all of the statistical guidelines.

As stated above, one of the factors considered by the Board is the market for the applicant company's products. Thus, a company may not be eligible for listing if it (a) produces a single product or line of products or engages in a single service, and (b) sells such product or products to, or performs such service for, only one customer or a limited number of customers.

The Exchange generally will not list companies organized for the exploration and development of natural resources until they have reached the production stage and meet the other criteria specified above.

Listing of Non-Voting Stock.—The Exchange will not approve the listing of a non-voting common stock unless the listing application also includes the voting class of stock, which must also be eligible for listing. In addition, the applicant must agree to (a) solicit proxies from the voting class for all shareholder meetings, (b) furnish the holders of the non-voting class with copies of all proxy materials sent to the voting shareholders, and (c) give the holders of both classes the right to vote on certain important matters, such as stock option plans and significant acquisitions.

"Back-Door" Listing.—The Exchange will not approve an application to list additional shares of a listed company in any combination of a listed company with an unlisted company which, in the option of the Exchange, would result in the acquisition of the listed company by the unlisted company, except where:

(a) the company resulting from the combination meets the original listing standards of the Exchange in all respects; or

(b) the unlisted company meets the original listing standards of the Exchange in all respects except for share distribution and number of shareholders, and the company resulting from the combination would appear to have a substantially improved financial condition and earnings outlook as compared to the listed company; or

(c) the company resulting from the combination meets at least one-half of the prescribed standards for original listing, and would appear to have a substantially improved financial condition and earnings outlook as compared to the listed company.

The type of combination to which this policy relates is a so-called "back-door" listing generally resulting from a plan of acquisition, merger or consolidation the net effect of which is that a listed company is acquired by an unlisted company, regardless of which company is the survivor in the combination. In applying this policy consideration will be given to all relevant factors, including the proportionate amount of the securities of the resulting company to be issued to each of the combining companies, changes in ownership or management of the listed company, whether the unlisted company is larger than the listed company, the nature of the businesses being combined, and so forth. The Exchange recommends that any proposed plan of the above nature, including particularly any plan under which stockholders of the listed company would own less than 50% of the shares or voting power of the resulting company, be submitted to the Exchange for an informal opinion before its promulgation.

Shares Issued in Split-ups or as Stock Dividends.—The Exchange does not view favorably a split-up of a stock selling in a low price range or split-up or substantial stock dividend which may result in an abnormally low price range for the shares after the split or stock dividend. Any company considering a split-up (or a stock dividend of more than 5 per cent) which would result in an adjusted price of less than $7.50 per share for its stock should consult the Exchange before taking formal action.

Preliminary Opinion Prior to Preparation of Application.—An informal and confidential opinion as to the eligibility of a particular issue for listing may be obtained in advance of the preparation and filing of a complete listing application, by sending to the Division of Securities of the Exchange (a) a copy of the latest prospectus and proxy statement of the company (if available); (b) copies of printed annual reports distributed to stockholders for the past three years (if available) or financial statements for such years, and earnings statements for interim periods since end of latest fiscal year (if available); (c) a certificate showing the extent of the public distribution of the stock, to be furnished on a printed form (Listing Form K) supplied by the Exchange upon request; (d) number of transfers and number of shares transferred each year during the last two years and price range for last three years (applicable to companies dealt in over the counter only); (e) information with respect to personal interests, if any, of officers, directors or principal stockholders in any business arrangements involving the company such as the leasing of property to or from the company, interests in minority held subsidiaries, interests in businesses that are competitors, suppliers or customers of the company, loans to or from the company, etc.; and (f) information concerning material pending litigation if not included in prospectus or proxy statement.

Prospectus or Proxy Statement Incorporated in Listing Application.—The listing requirements of the American Stock Exchange permit the filing of a prospectus relating to the securities applied for if the prospectus is in process of issuance or has been issued in accordance with the requirements of the 1933 Act within a reasonably short period prior to the date on which the listing application is filed. In such cases, at the applicant's option, any of the data required in the listing application may be incorporated by reference to the prospectus. When this is done, the prospectus is attached to and made a part of the application. Any required information not contained in the prospectus must be contained in the application.

Where this procedure is followed, the application consists of little more than a wrapper around a prospectus. This is a "short-form" listing application and its content is limited to those few items of information required by the Exchange which are not ordinarily included in a prospectus.

The short form application is also permitted in cases where a proxy statement prepared in accordance with the SEC's proxy rules is available, describing the transaction pursuant to which the securities applied for are to be issued, provided that the proxy statement includes sufficient information with respect to the history, business and properties of the applicant corporation. The ordinary proxy statement prepared for an annual meeting would not be satisfactory for this purpose, but one prepared in connection with a special meeting in connection with a proposed merger might well serve as the basis for a short-form listing application.

Printing of Application.—Applications to list on the American Stock Exchange are printed in the final form in which they were signed by the applicant. Printing costs are paid by the applicant.

Action on Application by Exchange.—Preliminary drafts of the application including financial statements and supporting papers and documents are filed initially with the Division of Securities of the Exchange for examination. The Division furnishes the applicant with a list of deficiencies, if any, or changes which have to be made and additional data which must be furnished. After such corrected and additional data are furnished, the application is set up in the form of a printer's proof for presentation to the Board of Governors. Each application must be approved by the Board of Governors before the security may be listed.

Applications for Original Listing.—An application for original listing of stock must recite, in substantially the order given below, the following:

1. The title page, showing
    (a) Name of company, place and date of incorporation, and CUSIP number
    (b) Class of stock applied for and par value
    (c) Date of application.
2. Capitalization, number of stockholders of record as of a recent specified date, and the names of the principal stockholders who own of record or beneficially 10% or more of the applicants' shares.
3. Long-term or funded debt.
4. History and business. A brief history of the business or enterprise, including predecessors if organized as the result of mergers, etc. Nature of the business, including products and services, markets

for products and raw materials, method of marketing and distributing products, annual output for the last five years and for the current year to the·most recent practicable date (in units, if practicable, otherwise in dollars), backlog as of a recent date, if applicable, divided as between defense items and commercial items, and whether orders are firm. Competitive conditions in the industry. Patent information and licensing and royalty arrangement, if material.

5. Summary of earnings. A summary of earnings (on a consolidated basis, if the applicant has subsidiaries, to the degree required by Accounting Research Bulletin No. 51, as amended by APB Opinion No. 10) for the last five fiscal years, showing sales, earnings before charges of depreciation, interest, and Federal income taxes, the amount of each of those charges, net income before extraordinary items, extraordinary items, and net income. If supplementary financial statements for any interim period in the current fiscal year are submitted (as specified under "Supplementary Financial Statements"), the summary should also include a summary of the interim statement of earnings for the current fiscal year with comparative statement for the same interim period of the preceding fiscal year. Where there has been a very substantial increase or decline in sales and/or net income in a given year (or years) explain in a footnote to the summary the principal reasons for such change.

6. Properties. Brief description of the general character of the principal plants or properties, including location, land area, number of buildings, floor area, condition of equipment, transportation facilities, and capacity. Whether properties are owned or leased. If leased, rentals paid in last fiscal year and average term of lease.

7. Employees and labor relations. Number regularly employed. If seasonal, maximum and minimum employed. Dates and duration of material work stoppages due to labor disagreements in last three years, and terms of settlement of such disagreements.

8. Stock provisions. Rights, preferences, privileges, and priorities of the class of stock applied for and of each class on a parity therewith or senior thereto. Restrictions on dividends, voting rights, and pre-emptive rights.

9. Registration with SEC. Whether securities applied for have been registered under 1933 Act; if not, reason for not registering and applicable section of Act granting exemption. Whether application being currently applied for under 1934 Act.

10. Opinion of counsel.

11. Subsidiary and affiliated companies.

12. Sales of securities in last three years and use of proceeds.
13. Options, purchase warrants, and similar agreements.
14. Dividend record.
15. Bonus, profit-participation, pension, and retirement plans.
16. Litigation.
17. List of directors and officers.
18. Interest of management and others in certain transactions. Brief description of the nature and approximate amount of any material interest, direct or indirect, of management (officers, directors, principal stockholders and their associates) in any material transactions to which the applicant or any of its subsidiaries was or is to be a party. (Note: The information required in answer to this item is similar to that required to be submitted in support of a Form S–1 registration statement under the 1933 Act, or a Form 10 registration statement under the 1934 Act.)
19. General information. Address of principal executive offices, state and date of incorporation, date of fiscal year, date and place of annual stockholders' meeting, quorum requirements, names and addresses of transfer agents and registrars.
20. Business, financial and accounting policies (this section can be prepared or reviewed by the independent public accountant):
    (a) Consolidation. Principle followed in including or excluding companies from consolidation, whether all consolidated companies employ same accounting principles; if not, nature of substantial divergence.
    (b) Depreciation. Policy as to depreciation, method employed and basis therefor, and rates for major classes.
    (c) Depletion. Policy as to depletion, basis on which depletion is charged and theory underlying basis.
    (d) Amortization (other than depreciation). Policy followed with respect to patents or other items which in ordinary practice are capitalized and amortized.
    (e) In cases where, because of the nature of the industry or circumstances peculiar to the applicant, business, financial or accounting policies other than those outlined above are considered material in determining the applicant company's income or financial position, or in interpreting its financial statements, describe such policies.
21. Financial statements:
    (a) Applicants which use the short form of listing application incorporating a prospectus or proxy statement by reference must submit (separately) three copies of the prospectus or proxy statement in which the accountants have manually

signed their certificate relating to the financial statements contained therein. If the statements contained in the prospectus have been prepared as of and to a date more than 90 days prior to the date of the listing application, supplemental statements (referred to below) should also be submitted.

(b) If the applicant does not use the short-form listing application, the following financial statements must be submitted in triplicate. Such statements will be included as part of the listing application when the same is printed for distribution.

(c) Independently certified financial statements:

(1) Balance sheet, in reasonable detail, as of the close of the latest fiscal year ended prior to the date of the listing application.

(2) Comparative statements of income, in reasonable detail, for each of the three fiscal years preceding the date of the listing application (i.e., to the date of the above balance sheet), if the applicant has been in business that long, or for such lesser period as the applicant has been in business.

(3) Comparative analysis of surplus, in reasonable detail, for the same period covered by the income statement submitted pursuant to (2) above. Paid-in surplus, capital surplus, surplus arising from revaluations, and other increases must be clearly separated from earned surplus.

Where significant, schedules of details of items contained in the foregoing statements may be required.

The above financial statements must be certified by a "properly qualified practicing public accountant or certified public accountant" who shall, if requested, submit to the American Stock Exchange a statement setting forth his qualifications. The accountant's certificate should be manually signed and should conform to the standard prescribed by the AICPA.

Because of his familiarity with the company, it is desirable that the accountant read the entire application—not merely the financial statements he certifies.

SUPPLEMENTARY FINANCIAL STATEMENTS.—If the independently certified financial statements submitted pursuant to the above requirements have been prepared as of and to a date which is more than 90 days prior to the date of the listing application, such statements shall be supplemented by corresponding statements, similar in form and content, as of and to a date not more than 90 days prior to the date of the listing application with comparative income statements for the same interim period of the preceding year. The supplementary financial statements will, in ordinary cases, be accepted either (a) independently certified, or (b) certified by the chief accounting officer of the applicant corporation. (See page **29**·14 for a suggested form of officer's certificate.)

The financial statements should be prepared on a consolidated basis if the applicant has subsidiaries to the degree required by Accounting Research Bulletin No. 51 as amended by APB Opinion No. 10. If there are any subsidiary or controlled companies not included in the consolidated financial statements, the consolidated income statement should carry a footnote reflecting the parent company's proportion of the undistributed profit or of the losses of such companies for the period of the report. There should also be a footnote to the consolidated balance sheet showing the amount by which the parent company's equity in the unconsolidated subsidiary or controlled companies has increased or decreased since the date of acquisition as the result of profits, losses, and distributions. The Exchange may require that separate financial statements of any such unconsolidated subsidiary or controlled company be furnished for inclusion in the listing application if the investment in such company represents a substantial part of the assets of the applicant corporation.

All financial statements are submitted to the Consulting Accountants appointed by the American Stock Exchange for approval as to form, content, and agreement with the requirements. Any inquiries as to accounting procedures will be answered by them only through the medium of the Exchange.

ORIGINAL LISTING OF BONDS.—In the case of an application for original listing of bonds, Item 8 of the items of information on page **29**·23 would be appropriately modified. Instead of detailing the provisions relating to stocks, the following would be furnished: (1) full title of issue, (2) title of instrument under which created, (3) name of trustee, (4) dates of authorizations for issue, including directors, stockholders, and public authorities, (5) amount authorized, amount issued to date, amount retired, amount outstanding, (6) date of issue and maturity, (7) interest rate, (8) places and date for payment of principal and interest and standard of money in which payable, (9) tax exemptions, (10) whether issuable in coupon or registered form, (11) denominations issuable, (12) whether exchangeable as between registered and coupon form, and interchangeable as to denominations, together with places and times at which exchanges may be made, and (13) where registerable and transferable and if convertible, the places and times at which conversions may be made.

The provisions of the indenture relating to the issue would also be furnished as follows: (1) security (including a description of the lien, assets pledged, and underlying and prior liens), (2) whether additional debt may be issued, (3) sinking fund, (4) redemption provisions, (5) events of default and remedies of bondholders, (6) release of pledged property, (7) convertibility, (8) provisions for modification of indenture, (9) treatment of deposited funds, (10) summary of important covenants, and (11) names and addresses of trustee, fiscal and paying agents, and agents for registry, exchange, interchange and conversion of bonds.

The financial statements required to be submitted would be the same as those required in the case of an application for original listing of stock.

SPECIAL REQUIREMENTS.—In addition to the requirements set forth above, there are special requirements applicable to public utility corporations, mining corporations, and oil corporations. The requirements for financial statements, however, do not differ materially as between the different types of applicants.

Listing Agreements.—The listing agreements of the American Stock Exchange were revised on April 5, 1962, to make them more like those of the New York Stock Exchange than they were previously. The New York Stock Exchange agreements which are of greatest interest to accountants are presented on page **29·**14 of this book. Except for the first sentence relating to timing and publication of an annual report, the agreements of the American Stock Exchange are virtually the same—word for word—as those of the New York Stock Exchange on page **29·**14. The first sentence of the American Stock Exchange agreement follows:

The Corporation will publish at least once in each year and submit to its stockholders, and file with the Exchange, at least ten days in advance of the annual meeting of such stockholders and not later than four months after the close of the last preceding fiscal year of the Corporation a Balance Sheet as of the end of such fiscal year, and a Surplus and Income Statement for such fiscal year of the Corporation as a separate corporate entity, etc.

Listing Fees.—Following are the listing fees of the American Stock Exchange in effect at the date of this writing.

Original Listing Applications

(a) *Stock Issues*—The original listing fees for stock issues (including both issued shares and unissued shares to be added to the list on notice of issuance) are:

> 1¢   per share for the first 500,000 shares;
> ¾¢ per share for the second 500,000 shares;
> ½¢ per share for the third 500,000 shares;
> ¼¢ per share for the fourth 500,000 shares; and
> ⅛¢ per share for the balance of shares applied for.

There is no maximum fee.

(b) *Bond Issues*—The original listing fees for bond issues are:

$100 per million dollars ($1,000,000) face value, or fraction thereof.

The maximum fee applicable to bonds included in each application is $2,500, regardless of the number of bond issues (or the principal amount thereof) applied for. The minimum fee is $500.

(c) *Warrant Issues*—The original (as well as the continuing and supplemental) listing fees for long-term warrant issues are the same as those for stock issues, and are based upon the aggregate number of shares that the warrants evidence the right to purchase.

Continuing Annual Fee

(a) *Stock Issues*—

$\frac{1}{10}$¢ per share for the first 2,000,000 shares issued and outstanding (including shares held in the treasury), and
$\frac{1}{20}$¢ per share for the excess.

The minimum fee is $500 (for 500,000 shares or less) and the maximum fee is $3,500 (for 5,000,000 shares or over).

This fee is based on the total number of shares of all classes of stock dealt in on the Exchange on June 30 of each year, payable in July of each year.

The continuing annual fee is also required to be paid by companies with stock issues admitted to unlisted trading privileges on the Exchange, based on the number of outstanding shares of the issue admitted to unlisted trading privileges (including shares held in the treasury).

(b) *Bond Issues*—There is no continuing annual fee for Bonds.

(c) *Warrant Issues*—The schedule applicable to stock issues also applies to listed warrants, based on the aggregate number of shares to which the warrants evidence the right to subscribe.

Supplemental Listing Applications

(a) *Previously Listed Classes*—Listing of additional shares (of previously listed classes) subsequent to original listing—1¢ per share for shares in excess of amount previously listed to a maximum of $3,500 for all such additional shares per application. (If amount applied for in any one application exceeds 350,000 shares, the maximum of $3,500 is applicable.) The minimum fee on each application is $250. (If amount applied for is less than 25,000 shares, the fee is $250.)

(b) *Different Class*—Listing of securities (stocks or bonds) of an issue, class or series not previously listed—The schedule for original listing (see above) is applicable.

(c) *Substitution Listing*—In cases where, after original listing, a change is effected by charter amendment or otherwise under which shares listed upon the Exchange are reclassified, or changed into or exchanged for another security, either with or without a change in par value, the fee for the listing of such number of "new" substituted shares as is not in excess of the amount previously listed is ¼¢ per share to a maximum of $500. The full basic listing fee is charged, i.e., 1¢ per share, for all shares included in the application in excess of the amount previously listed. The maximum fee for the aggregate of all such "new" substituted shares and excess shares is $3,500.

In the case of an application for the relisting of previously listed bonds on their assumption by another obligor, the listing fee will be $500.

(d) *Reincorporation, Merger or Consolidation*—If a listed Company reincorporates, or merges with or consolidates into one or more corporations, the substitution listing fee (paragraph (c) above) is applicable.

Audit Requirements Affecting Listed Companies.—The current form of listing agreement of the American Stock Exchange contains a provision requiring the company to furnish annual reports (including financial statements) to stockholders. Furthermore, such financial statements must be audited by independent public accountants whose certificate shall accompany such statements in the annual report.

The listing agreement also requires the company to publish quarterly statements (unaudited) of sales and earnings on the basis of the same degree of consolidation as in the annual report. Such statements must disclose any substantial items of unusual or non-recurring nature and net income before and after Federal income taxes. The quarterly statements need not be detailed income statements, but merely summary statements of sales and net income, and may cover each quarter individually and/or the elapsed quarters of the current fiscal year on a cumulative basis. No statement is required for the fourth quarter. Each interim statement should show comparative figures for the same period of the previous year. These statements are to be published within 45 days after the end of each fiscal quarter. They need not be sent to stockholders, but should be distributed in the form of a press release to one or more newspapers of general circulation in New York regularly publishing financial news, or to one or more of the news-wire services, and to the news-ticker service operated by Dow Jones & Company, Inc. and Reuters Economic Services.

REPORTS TO STOCKHOLDERS

CONTENTS

Some Control by SEC of Stockholder Reports.—The typical annual report to stockholders includes narrative material (often in the form of a letter from the chairman or president), a "highlights" section, condensed summaries for a period of years of important financial and operating statistics, and formal financial statements. In most cases, the financial statements consist of two-year comparative balance sheets and statements of income, retained earnings, other changes in equity accounts, and sources and application of funds. Under APB Opinion No. 19, the funds statement, heretofore a merely recommended statement, became a mandatory statement for fiscal years beginning after September 30, 1971 with a considerable expansion in content and entitled "Statement of changes in financial position."

The SEC has considerable control over the published reports sent to shareholders by *regulated investment companies* and *registered public utility holding companies*. The SEC also has some control over the financial statements in reports to stockholders of listed and unlisted companies registered under Section 12 of the 1934 Act. The control is exercised principally through the Commission's proxy regulation (Regulation 14A) which is discussed in Chapter **22**, and partly through the registration procedure applicable to registration statements on Form S-8 under the 1933 Act. These matters are discussed in the following pages of this chapter. As will also be seen from this discussion, the Commission, in a few cases, has caused some corporations to revise and recirculate their annual reports to stockholders and, in exceptional cases, has suspended trading in the corporation's securities until the revised report had received adequate circulation and publicity.

One result of the Commission's review of proxy statements and Form S–8 registration statements has been to narrow the differences between the financial statements in published annual reports to security holders and those in documents filed with the SEC. This is especially true in the case of proxy statements, because if there are significant differences between the statements in the published reports and those filed with the SEC, disclosure of that fact must be made in the published report. This is the kind of a disclosure that the managements of many corporations would prefer not to make, and consequently the SEC's disclosure requirement operates as an incentive to eliminate significant differences.

Investment Company Act.—The Investment Company Act of 1940 [Section 30(d)] and the Commission's rules thereunder (Rules 270.30d–1 and 270.30d–2) require registered investment companies to send reports, at least semianually, to stockholders of management investment companies and shareholders of unit investment trusts. These reports may not be misleading in any material respect. The reports must be mailed within 45 days after the date as of which the report is made, with provision for a longer period as permitted by the Commission if the investment company is a so-called "non-diversified" company having one or more majority owned subsidiaries that are not investment companies. The report made as of the close of the investment company's fiscal year must cover the whole fiscal year and shall be accompanied by a certificate of an independent accountant; reports made as of any other date must cover a period beginning either (1) with the beginning of the fiscal year, or (2) with the close of the period covered by the last report.

The report of the investment company must contain a balance sheet and statement of income and surplus. The balance sheet must be accompanied by a list showing the amounts and values of securities owned on the balance sheet date. The income statement must be itemized at least with respect to each category of income and each expense representing more than 5 per cent of total income or expense. The statement of surplus must be similarly itemized. These reports to stockholders are not subject to Regulation S–X, but the stockholder reports may not be misleading in any material respect in the light of the reports filed with the SEC. The effect of these requirements, for all practical purposes, is that the financial statements in the stockholders' reports must be substantially the same as those included in reports filed with the Commission. Accordingly, although Regulation S–X does not apply to stockholders' reports, in preparing financial statements for inclusion in such reports, it is desirable to consult Article 6 of Regulation S–X which deals with the form and content of financial statements of management investment companies.

The investment company's report must contain a statement of the aggregate remuneration paid by the company during the period covered by the report (a) to all directors and to all members of any advisory board for regular compensation, (b) to each director and to each member of an advisory board for special compensation, (c) to all officers, and (d) to each person of whom any officer or director of the company is an affiliated person. A statement must also be made as to the aggregate dollar amounts of purchases and sales of investment securities, other than government securities, made during the period covered by the report.

Copies of every communication containing financial statements and transmitted by any registered investment company to its security holders must be filed with the SEC. [Sec. 30(b)(2) of the Act].

Public Utility Holding Company Act.—Under the Public Utility Holding Company Act of 1935, the SEC does not have jurisdiction or control over the reports sent to stockholders of such companies. One of the Commission's rules, however, relates to inconsistent financial statements and is as follows:

Except as otherwise authorized or required by the Commission by rule, regulation, order, statement of administrative policy, or otherwise, no registered holding company or subsidiary company thereof shall distribute to its security holders, or publish, financial statements which are inconsistent with the book accounts of such company or financial statements filed with this Commission by, or on behalf of, such company. This rule shall not be deemed to prevent the distribution or publication of reasonable condensations or of unaudited financial statements or of financial statements (on a cash or other basis) pursuant to the requirements of an indenture or mortgage given to secure bonds or similar instruments, or of appropriate financial statements of a receiver or trustee appointed by a court of the United States. (Rule 250.28; formerly Rule U–28)

Disclosure Regarding Annual Reports in Registration Statements.—When a prospective investor is considering whether or not to purchase a security offered to him by means of a prospectus, is it important to him to know what the issuer's practice is, or will be, with respect to the publication and distribution of annual reports to security holders? The SEC thinks this is a matter of some consequence.

The SEC published a release entitled "Guides for Preparation and Filing of Registration Statements" (Release No. 33–4936, December 9, 1968). The release set forth certain of the SEC's administrative policies as they relate to registration statements filed under the 1933 Act, and was intended to be helpful to prospective registrants under the Act and to their lawyers and accountants. As a corollary, the wide publicity given the release was expected to be helpful to the Commission's staff by relieving them of the necessity of commenting repeatedly on matters which were discussed in the release.

One of the items included in the Guides was as follows:

Annual Reports to Security Holders

The prospectus should disclose whether or not annual reports of the registrant will be furnished to security holders and whether or not such reports will contain certified financial statements. The nature and frequency of other reports to be issued by the registrant also should be disclosed. However, this disclosure is not required in the case of registrants required to send annual reports containing certified financial statements to security holders pursuant to the statutes or regulations administered by the Commission or pursuant to a listing agreement with a national securities exchange.

In an effort to comply with the foregoing requirement, some companies have stated in their prospectuses that annual reports will be issued to security holders, and that such reports will contain *audited* financial statements. This is not acceptable to the SEC; the registrant must state whether the report will contain *certified* financial statements. This raises a question as to whether the SEC would object if, in a future published annual report to stockholders, the accountant's report is qualified. According to the author's information, this matter has not been tested.

Influence of SEC and Stock Exchanges on Reports to Security Holders.—In the years since the SEC laws were passed there has been a marked and widespread improvement in the reporting practices of American corporations. How much of this improvement can be attributed to the SEC or to the stock exchanges, it is difficult to say, but it is clear that both the SEC and the exchanges share some of the credit for the improvement. It is also true that corporation managements and public accountants had a major role in bringing corporate reports up to their present standard.

The SEC, as previously noted, has a certain amount of authority to regulate the annual reports furnished by most publicly-owned corporations to their security holders. The SEC's jurisdiction, however, is complete as to financial statements filed with it pursuant to the various statutes which it administers. Any pronouncement by the Commission carries with it the weight of an authoritative body.

As a result of SEC requirements, many corporations, which had never done so before, were compelled to make public the amount of their sales and cost of sales. Some managements objected to the disclosure of this information in reports to security holders despite the fact that their competitors and other interested persons could get the information for a nominal sum simply by writing to the SEC and asking for copies of the statements that contained the information. Some managements realized that persons who were not entitled to the information were getting it from the SEC; those who were entitled to it were not getting it as a matter of course. Consequently these managements decided to include in reports to their security holders sales, cost of sales, and other information that had previously been included only in filings with SEC.

The SEC requirements also affected the listing requirements of securities exchanges. The New York Stock Exchange, for example, since the 1934 Act was passed, tightened up its rules relating to financial statements in listing applications. As a condition to listing, the Exchange now insists on disclosure of information that previously it did not consider essential and frequently bases its insistence on the fact that the applicant makes public the information requested in a filing with the SEC. Over the years therefore the requirements of the Exchange have come more and more to parallel those of the SEC. Since the listing agreements (see page **29·**14) provide, in effect, that the applicant will furnish in the future financial statements similar to those in the listing application, with the passage of time the SEC requirements are reflected increasingly in the published reports of listed corporations to their stockholders.

While there had been progress in the reporting practices of listed corporations, this was not true in the same degree of unlisted corporations. Although some unlisted corporations had also improved their reports to security holders, the progress had been notably slower than in the case of listed companies, due largely to the fact that, prior to 1965, the managements of unlisted companies were usually not answerable to the SEC or to the stock exchanges. The lag in the reporting practices of unlisted corporations was a major reason for the enactment of the Securities Acts Amendments of 1964 which extended the SEC's jurisdiction to cover many publicly-owned unlisted corporations.

Copies of Annual Stockholder Reports Furnished to SEC.—In Chapter **22** reference was made to proxies solicited in connection with an annual meeting of security holders at which the business to be transacted includes the election of directors. If the proxy solicitation is made on behalf of the management, the proxy statement furnished pursuant to Rule 14a–3 of the proxy rules must be accompanied or preceded by an annual report to security holders containing such financial statements for the last fiscal year as will, in the opinion of the management, adequately reflect the financial position and results of operations of the issuer. Seven copies of each annual report sent to security holders pursuant to the proxy regulation must be mailed to the Commission, solely for its information, not later than the date on which the report is sent to security holders, or the date on which preliminary copies of solicitation material are filed with the Commission, whichever date is later.

SEC requirements with respect to such reports deal with the period to be covered by the financial statements in the annual report, the consolidation of subsidiaries, certification by independent public accountants, and disclosure of significant differences between the financial statements in the annual report and those in the corresponding report (Form 10–K, for example) filed with the SEC. These matters are commented upon in Chapter **22** in connection with the discussion of the SEC's requirements relating to proxies and proxy statements. The reader is referred to that chapter for a discussion of the effect on a published annual report to security holders when the SEC's proxy rules are applicable.

In the case of companies registered under Section 12 of the 1934 Act which choose not to solicit proxies, Regulation 14C is applicable and an "information statement" must be furnished to shareholders. The information statement must be accompanied or preceded by an annual report to security holders similar to what would be required if proxies were being solicited for the election of directors. Seven copies of the annual report must be mailed to the Commission—similar to the requirements in the preceding paragraph.

Companies not registered under Section 12 of the 1934 Act but which are required to file reports (Form 10–K, for example) pursuant to Section 15(d) of the 1934 Act, must also send to the Commission (solely for its information) copies of annual reports sent to security holders.

Annual reports sent to the Commission pursuant to the requirements summarized above are not deemed to be "filed" with the SEC or otherwise subject to the liabilities of Section 18 of the 1934 Act (which relates to the liability for misleading statements), except to the extent that the issuer specifically requests that it be treated as a part of the proxy soliciting material or incorporates it in the proxy statement or Form 10–K by reference.

There may be a number of reasons which cause a corporation, in its proxy statement, to incorporate by reference in such statement something which appears in the published report. If the financial statements appearing in the published annual report are incorporated in the proxy statement, the accountant must manually sign his certificate in the copy of the published report thus filed with the Commission. This provision for manual signature is not merely for the purpose of furnishing the SEC with a signed copy of the accountant's certificate; it is also intended for the benefit of the certifying accountant as it puts him on notice that a report bearing his name is being filed with the SEC. There have been numerous instances in which annual reports were made a part of the proxy-soliciting material and no notice to that effect was given to the certifying accountant. In these instances the first knowledge the accountants had that their certificates were being so used was when the SEC asked that the accountants manually sign the certificates appearing in the published report filed with the Commission. See also the discussion of SEC Release No. 34–8881 in Chapter **22** regarding the accountant's review of preliminary proxy material and the letter from the accountant saying that he has read such material.

To assist the SEC's staff, issuers have been requested to indicate in a letter transmitting to the SEC copies of their annual reports to shareholders, or in a separate letter, at or about the time the annual report is furnished to the SEC, whether the financial statements in the report reflect a change from the preceding year in any accounting principles or practices, or in the method of applying any such principles or practices.

Filing of Published Annual Report in Lieu of SEC Report.—If comparison were made of the principal financial statements appearing in the published annual reports to stockholders of a representative group of companies with the financial statements appearing in the annual SEC reports of such companies on Form 10–K, it would probably be noted that, in most cases, there is not much difference between the two sets of financial data. Most of the differences are due to the fact that the financial statements in the SEC report contain more details and are supplemented by the so-called "compliance" notes dealing, for example, with the difference between the investment in consolidated subsidiaries and the equity in their net assets and the disposition of the difference in consolidation. In some cases, the differences are more significant, as, for example, when the published report contains no figure for cost of goods sold (or gross profit on sales) which information is included in the SEC report.

With a view to reducing the year-end work load of corporations registered with the SEC, the question has been raised as to whether it is possible to furnish the published report as partial compliance with the requirements for financial statements in the SEC report. In that connection, ASR No. 41 is pertinent. That release provides, in part, as follows:

A recent amendment of Form 10–K provides that in partial response to the requirements for filing financial statements a registrant may if it wishes file a copy of its regular annual report to stockholders and incorporate by reference the financial statements contained in such report. This procedure may be followed, however, only if the financial statements included in the report to stockholders substantially conform to the requirements of Regulation S–X. Of course, any financial statements or schedules required by the instructions that are not included in the stockholders' report must also be furnished.

A review of numerous stockholders' reports covering the year 1941 indicates that in many cases the financial statements included are identical with those filed subsequently as part of the annual report on Form 10–K except that a number of relatively minor items shown separately in the report on Form 10–K are grouped, or combined with closely similar items in the report to stockholders. Inquiries have been received as to whether, where condensation of this type exists, the statements may nevertheless be considered to conform substantially to the requirements of Regulation S–X.

The provisions of Article 5 of Regulation S–X contain a general statement of the details to be shown in balance sheets and income statements filed by commercial and industrial companies. Such requirements are, however, supplemented by and subject to the general rules contained in Article 3. Rule 3–06 thereof provides, on the one hand, that, in applying the requirements to the circumstances of an individual case, there shall be given, in addition to the required information, such further information as is necessary to make the required statements, in the light of the circumstances under which they are made, not misleading. On the other hand, Rule 3–02 provides that, if the amount to be shown under any particular caption is not significant, the caption need not be separately set forth. The effect of these two general requirements is to require the disclosure of significant information not specifically called for, but to permit the omission of information, even though covered by a specific requirement, if the item involved is not significant. It should be pointed out, however, that in some cases the significance of an item may be independent of the amount involved. For example, amounts due to and from officers and directors, because of their special nature and origin, ought generally to be set forth separately even though the dollar amounts involved are relatively small. Likewise, disclosure of the various types of surplus, the important reserve accounts, and, under present conditions, the accrued liability for taxes is of importance. In the same way, in the corporate income statement of a company having large investments in subsidiaries or in securities of unaffiliated companies, the disclosure of income from dividends and interest is necessary irrespective of the amount, since the absence or smallness of dividend and interest income is of as great importance as the exact amount thereof. In the income statement generally, it is important that the major elements such as sales and cost of sales, substantial items of other income and income deductions, and the provision for income and excess profits taxes be separately disclosed, unless to do so would violate the provisions of the Code of Wartime Practices. Finally, care should be taken that the necessary descriptive and explanatory footnotes applicable to the particular statements are set forth.

On the other hand, the combination under a miscellaneous caption of minor items among the current assets or liabilities resulting from the ordinary course of business, or their combination with closely similar items that are large in amount, is, in my opinion, permissible and, where minor items are numerous, would tend to improve the legibility of the statements. Similar combinations appear to be permissible within the other major categories of items customarily appearing in the financial statements, such as deferred charges, prepaid expenses, and fixed assets. Generally, however, condensation in the balance sheet would not appear appropriate with respect to an item amounting to more than 10 per cent of its immediate category, such as deferred charges, or more than 5 per cent of total assets. Where, however, the immediate category is less than 5 per cent of total assets, it would generally appear permissible to combine all components of the category under a suitable caption.

If such condensation as may exist in the financial statements included in the regular annual report to stockholders has been made along the lines indicated, such financial statements would in my opinion substantially conform to the requirements of Regulation S–X and could therefore, under the recent amendment to Form 10–K, be incorporated by reference in annual reports on that form. Of course, care should be taken that the captions used are not such as to be misleading.

Form N–30A–1, the annual report for investment companies subject to the Investment Company Act of 1940, has been amended in the same manner as Form 10–K. While the discussion above relates to the financial statements of commercial, industrial and utility companies using Form 10–K, comparable principles are applicable to investment companies using this form.

In the opinion of the author, few companies have taken advantage of the provision whereby their published reports may be furnished in partial compliance with the requirements for financial statements to be included in their SEC reports. (One writer reported that out of 150 corporations, only 17 exercised this option.)[1] There are several reasons why corporations have been slow to avail themselves of the permissive procedure stated in the release quoted above. In the first place, corporations are reluctant to "file" their annual reports to stockholders with SEC and thereby possibly make the entire report subject to the liabilities provided in the 1934 Act. In the second place, the possible saving involves principally the time of retyping or reprinting the statements in question. Since this does not require extensive time or effort, the saving is usually negligible.

If the stockholder report is filed with the SEC in satisfaction of the requirements for financial statements of Form 10–K, the accountant must manually sign his certificate appearing in such report.

Published Annual Reports in Employee Stock Offerings.—Under the 1933 Act, Form S–8 is the registration statement form used for certain types of unincorporated employees' stock purchase and savings plans. This form may also be used in connection with the sale by a corporation of its securities to employees under employee stock offerings.

Item 25 of Form S–8 relates to financial statements, and requires the company to include in the registration statement the certified financial statements of the issuer that are required to be included in the annual report which the issuer has filed or is required to file for its last fiscal year pursuant to the 1934 Act. (Form 10–K is an example of this type of annual report.) The instructions provide, however, that if the annual report of the issuer to its security holders for its last fiscal year includes certified financial statements substantially meeting the above requirements, such statements may be incorporated by reference in the prospectus. (For an interpretation of what constitutes "substantially" in this context, see the quotation from ASR No. 41 previously referred to.) The instructions also provide that if the annual report includes certified consolidated financial statements of the issuer and its subsidiaries, the latter must be furnished in lieu of the unconsolidated statements of the issuer.

---

[1] Surendra S. Singhvi, "Disclosure to Whom? Annual Financial Reports to Stockholders and to the Securities and Exchange Commission," *The Journal of Business,* July 1968, p. 350.

There have been innumerable cases where corporations filed registration statements on Form S–8 in connection with stock offerings to employees. These companies furnished copies of the published annual reports to stockholders in satisfaction of the requirement for financial statements in Item 25. Despite the fact that these reports lacked the "compliance" notes required by Regulation S–X, the SEC ruled informally that, for this purpose, the published reports substantially met the requirements of Form S–8. In several instances, however, where the published annual report did not disclose cost of goods sold as required by Regulation S–X, the SEC's comment was as follows: "In the future, cost of goods sold should be shown separately in the statement of income included in annual reports to stockholders."

Misleading Report as Basis for Suspension in Trading: The Atlantic Research Case.—On October 10, 1962, the SEC suspended trading in the common stock of Atlantic Research Corporation on the American Stock Exchange, and based its action on allegedly misleading financial statements. The financial statements that the SEC said were misleading were not those that the company had filed with the SEC, but rather those that the company had furnished to its stockholders for the year 1961.

The company's annual report on Form 10–K for 1961 filed with the SEC included consolidated financial statements of the company and its subsidiaries. These statements showed a consolidated net *loss* of $1,066,015. The annual report to shareholders for the same year, however, did not include consolidated statements; the report contained statements of the parent company alone, and these statements reported net *income* of $1,473,192.

The published report to shareholders showed a provision of $70,196 for "corporate income taxes." This seemed low in relation to the after-tax net income of $1,473,192, and a note to the financial statements explained the situation as follows:

The provision for corporate income taxes is based on the consolidated income of Atlantic Research Corporation and subsidiaries. Due to losses and write-offs reported by two of the subsidiaries, no substantial provision has been made for federal taxes on income . . .

The company's investments in subsidiaries were carried in its balance sheet at cost, and there was no disclosure in the financial statements of the underlying equity in net assets, earnings, or losses of the subsidiaries. Also, financial statements of the subsidiaries were not included in the stockholders' report. See also the discussion on page **17·16**.

In its release announcing the suspension, the SEC said:

The suspension order was based upon information developed in an investigation by the Commission's staff which raises serious question as to the accuracy and adequacy of available, public information concerning the financial condition of Atlantic Research. While this information presents no question as to the company's solvency, the suspension of trading was deemed necessary and appropriate in the public interest in view of the fact that an informed evaluation of the Atlantic Research stock could not be made upon the basis of published information. The Commission noted in this connection that while the report of Atlantic Research to its shareholders showed a net income of $1,473,192 for the year 1961, which figure also is carried in securities manuals, financial statements on file with the Commission reflect a loss in 1961 of $1,066,015 on a consolidated basis for Atlantic Research and its subsidiaries. (*SEC News Digest,* Oct. 10, 1962.)

On November 14, 1962, the SEC lifted the suspension order and trading was reinstated on November 16, 1962. The case is significant in that it is the first time, to the author's knowledge, in which a suspension order has been based, not on what is in the Commission's official files, but on information otherwise available to the public.

SEC Order to Revise Misleading Published Report.—Although most published reports to security holders are not legally or technically "filed " with the SEC, the Commission has taken action against a few companies that published reports which, in the Commission's view, were materially misleading. In these cases the SEC has caused the companies involved to revise and recirculate the reports in question. The number of instances in which the SEC has taken such action has not been publicized, but is believed to be small. A few of these cases have surfaced and will be discussed below as indications of the kind of situations that cause the SEC to demand revision and recirculation.

THE MARTIN MARIETTA CASE:—Martin Marietta Corporation owned 90% of Bunker-Ramo Corporation during the first six months of 1964 and became a 61% shareowner on July 1, 1964. Bunker-Ramo's loss for 1964 was $13,172,000, of which Martin Marietta's share was $9,608,000. These facts were fully disclosed in Martin Marietta's published report for 1964, but Bunker-Ramo was not consolidated with Martin Marietta nor was provision made in Martin Marietta's financial statements for its share of Bunker-Ramo's loss. Bunker-Ramo was consolidated for tax purposes, however, and the resulting reduction in tax liability ($2,800,000) was applied as a reduction in the carrying value of the investment in Bunker-Ramo. The financial statements of Bunker-Ramo were included in Martin Marietta's report to its security holders for 1964. On the basis indicated (that is, without taking into account its pro rata share of the Bunker-Ramo loss), Martin Marietta reported net earnings of $37,159,000 for 1964. The accountants' certificate relating to Martin Marietta's financial statements and included in the published report was unqualified.

The SEC took exception to the accounting followed by Martin Marietta in the published financial statements, and required the company to revise it. Under date of June 30, 1965, Martin Marietta sent its shareholders a "Special Report to Shareowners on Restatement of Earnings as Required by the Securities and Exchange Commission." The report stated that the SEC had required Martin Marietta to restate its balance sheet and statement of earnings to reflect a pro rata share of the operating losses of Bunker-Ramo for the year 1964 and the first quarter of 1965. The effect of the revised accounting treatment required by the SEC was to reduce the stated net earnings of the Corporation for 1964 from $37,159,000 to $30,-351,000, or from $1.67 per common share to $1.35 per common share. The investment in Bunker-Ramo was correspondingly reduced from $35,200,000 to $28,391,000. The report also stated that to the extent that Bunker-Ramo continued to operate at a loss and Martin Marietta continued to own more than 50% of its common stock, the stated earnings of the Corporation would be reduced by its pro rata amount of such losses.

The Corporation defended the accounting treatment in the original report for 1964. The Corporation said:

The management of the Corporation and its independent accountants believe that the financial statements previously presented were in accordance with sound accounting principles and properly reflect the results of the Corporation's operations. Further, they were of the opinion that full disclosure of all pertinent information relative to the investment in Bunker-Ramo was made in Martin Marietta's 1964 Annual Report and in other stockholder publications, and that all requirements of the New York Stock Exchange and the Securities and Exchange Commission were fulfilled insofar as they pertain to the accounting principles of consolidation.

The revised financial statements were not accompanied by an independent public accountants' certificate.

THE MAJOR REALTY CASE:—More recently the SEC caused Major Realty Corporation to revise its published annual reports to security holders for the fiscal years ended May 31, 1968 and 1969 because, according to the SEC, the company had improperly accounted for a real estate transaction in such reports. The facts in this case are discussed in Chapter **4**. Briefly stated, the SEC determined that the company's fiscal 1968 report improperly included $3.2 million as income from a transaction in which the buyer had so little economic interest in the property that it could not properly be deemed a sale for accounting purposes, and the error was carried over into the 1969 report. The transaction was subsequently rescinded.

The SEC ordered the company to send to its shareholders revised annual reports for fiscal 1968 and 1969 prior to its next annual meeting together with a copy of the Commission's findings and opinion in the case. The SEC said that its action was based on an offer of settlement under which the company consented to the Commission's findings and agreed to file amendments to the annual reports.

Inclusion in Annual Report of Misleading Information Not Covered by Accountants' Certificate.—A matter of recurring concern to the SEC is the inclusion of misleading information in the "highlights" or text portion of published annual reports to security holders. Usually this information is in the form of tables, charts, or figures, none of which is covered by the certificate of an independent public accountant. Sometimes this information may differ significantly from the information contained in the certified financial statements in the back of the report. A former SEC Commissioner, Francis M. Wheat, referred to this as a problem area which should concern not only the SEC but also the accounting profession.[2]

Mr. Wheat referred to a case involving a specific (but unnamed) company to illustrate the problem. The company in question published an annual report to shareholders for the year 1967. Inside the cover page appeared a "Highlights" section comparing results of operations for the years 1966 and 1967, with emphasis given to large percentage increases in both sales and earnings. Thus, sales were shown in the "Highlights" to have increased by 250 per cent and net income by 171 per cent. No reference was made to an extraordinary item which had increased 1967 earnings over 20 per cent.

There followed 14 pages of text, pictures, bar charts and so forth all emphasizing the astonishing growth of the company. It was only when one reached the audited income statement that the real story was revealed. There, in accordance with the strictures of APB Opinion No. 10, sales and earnings for 1966 were shown restated to include the accounts of a large company which had been acquired in 1967 in a pooling of interests transaction. On a "pooled back" basis, the reader learned that although sales had increased by about 3 per cent or so, net income had actually decreased in 1967. As mentioned above, the income for 1967 had also been given a material boost in the order of 20 per cent by an extraordinary item—gain on the sale of a stock investment. Excluding the extraordinary item, 1967 earnings per share were 30 per cent below those of 1966.

"In a nutshell," said Mr. Wheat, "the company had operated on the theory of the television commercial: 'It's what's up front that counts'."

The company happened to have a registration statement under the 1933 Act on file with the Commission, and the annual report was published while the registration statement was being processed.

[2] Francis M. Wheat, "Toward a More Rational Disclosure Policy," *The Journal of Accountancy*, Sept. 1968, pp. 56–59.

The Commission advised the company, in effect, to show cause why its request for acceleration of the pending registration statement should not be denied. Ultimately, the SEC granted acceleration after the company had sent to all its shareholders a special letter advising them to disregard the material in the "Highlights" section of the annual report and to rely solely on the data set forth in the audited income statement, a copy of which was attached to the letter. The company informed the SEC that the presentation which it had used in the "Highlights" section would not occur again.

The incident prompted the Commission to issue a release (No. 33–4910, June 18, 1968) which said in part:

"In the opinion of the Commission, it is misleading to make comparisons such as were made in this instance or to invite or draw conclusions as to improvement in a company's operations by comparing pooled figures for a particular year with unpooled figures for the prior year. Comparisons in such case should be made with financial data for the prior period restated on a combined (pooled) basis."

Mr. Wheat said that the case he had discussed was not an isolated example, and that the Commission had seen "numerous instances . . . of inconsistencies between the financial data in annual reports which are covered by the auditor's opinion and the figures accented in the text." Almost invariably, he said, these inconsistencies operate to dilute or even stultify the advance in accounting presentation made possible by a "landmark Opinion of the Accounting Principles Board, Opinion 9, which we at the Commission welcomed as a notable product of a great profession's efforts to improve its own standards" and also that portion of APB Opinion No. 10 requiring restatement of prior years' results following a pooling. (According to *Accounting Trends and Techniques,* out of 600 companies tested in 1968, 16 did not restate their uncertified historical summaries; in 1967 the corresponding number was 25.)

Mr. Wheat certainly makes a valid point, and the situation is one that accountants have been aware of for many years. Some accountants have made it a practice to read the text of the published annual report at or about the time they check the proof of the certified financial statements included in the report, but practice among accountants in this respect is far from uniform. In addition there is no professional requirement for them to read the president's letter, the highlights, or any other text material in the report.

When accountants do read the text of the report, the primary objective is to ascertain that it does not conflict with the certified financial statements and that it does not contain obvious errors. This kind of reading does not contemplate any investigation or examination by the accountant over and above what was required in order for him to certify the formal financial statements. From the standpoint of the company, the reading affords an additional safeguard against the possibility of unintentional error which may be embarrassing and in some instances may result in delay and additional expense if reprinting of the annual report would be necessary. From the accountant's viewpoint, the reading affords an opportunity to suggest the revision of information in the text which conflicts with representations in the financial statements or the need for clarification of ambiguities.

If a question is raised as to the accountant's responsibility in connection with reading the text of the annual report, the accountant should make it clear that he assumes no responsibility for any representations not covered by his certificate. As a corollary to the limitation on his responsibility, the accountant is certainly not in a position to insist on any changes in the text of the report which may occur to him as a result of reading it.

Commissioner James J. Needham noted that there had been some public discussion about the desirability of having independent public accountants certify more of the contents of a company's published reports. He said that one prominent financial executive had predicted that within five years certain non-monetary amounts in annual reports would be so certified. Initially the certification would be limited to data on employment, man hours, floor space, capital expenditures, basic raw materials used, and units of specific product produced or delivered, with the expectation that the auditor's attest function would be extended after five years. Commissioner Needham observed:

The fact that recommendations have been made that outsiders attest to data appearing in a company's report is indicative of certain opinions and attitudes towards management. To put it another way, the uncomfortable feeling some managements experience in dealing with the public is due to a "credibility gap"—real or imagined.[3]

Views similar to Commissioner Needham's have also been expressed by others.[4]

Until recently, the funds statement did not have to be certified; now it must be covered by the accountant's report. The profit contributions of the various lines of business of a diversified company are not now required to be certified, but several companies are now furnishing the information to their security holders on a certified basis, and the probabilities are that this development will spread.

[3] James J. Needham, speech before 51st Annual International Conference of National Association of Accountants, June 22, 1970.

[4] See, for example, "Measuring Management Efficiency" (editorial), *The Journal of Accountancy* (March 1961), p. 38; R. K. Mautz and Hussein A. Sharaf, *The Philosophy of Auditing* (American Accounting Association, 1961), p. 200; Robert W. Clarke, "Extension of the CPA's Attest Function in Corporate Annual Reports," *The Accounting Review*, Oct. 1968, pp. 769–776; Frank J. Imke, "The Future of the Attest Function," *The Journal of Accountancy*, Apr. 1967, pp. 51–58.

Finally, it is worth noting that the Wheat Report[5] considered the possibility of making it a requirement by rule that *all* financial disclosures in annual reports to shareholders, wherever located in the report, be reviewed by the auditors for consistency with the certified financial statements and covered by the opinion of the independent auditors. The opinion would be required to state that the auditor reviewed such disclosures and that they are fairly based on the certified statements. At the date of this writing, the Commission has not moved to implement this proposal.

[5] *Disclosure to Investors—A Reappraisal of Federal Administrative Policies under the '33 and '34 Acts (The Wheat Report)*, Commerce Clearing House, Inc. (1969), p. 371.

SEC PROBLEMS OF FOREIGN ISSUERS

CONTENTS

Lack of Uniformity in Accounting and Auditing Throughout the World.—Just as the laws and customs of nations all over the world differ in many respects from those in the United States, so also are there differences in accounting principles, auditing standards and procedures, and reporting practices all over the world. Financial statements prepared by a foreign corporation more than likely differ in many respects from financial statements prepared by a United States corporation. Not only are the statements different in their form and content, but there also may be significant differences in the accounting principles underlying their preparation.

These are some of the areas in accounting with respect to which conflicting—and sometimes contradictory—views are held throughout the world:

Certain methods of accounting for inventories are accepted in some countries and rejected in others. The LIFO method, which is permitted in the United States, is not accepted in some other nations. Conversely, arbitrary write-downs of inventory which are acceptable in some countries would not be permitted in the United States.

There are significant and widespread differences in accounting for fixed assets and in methods of computing depreciation. Write-ups to reflect replacement values (or current values)—with or without the benefit of government-computed "coefficients"—are followed by many foreign companies with the approval of their public accountants. In the United States, general price-level information may be presented as a supplement to the basic historical dollar financial statements in reports to stockholders, but the price-level financial statements would not be covered by the auditor's report. In many foreign countries depreciation is computed on fully depreciated assets which are still in use; in other countries it is not a generally accepted practice.

There are important differences in viewpoint throughout the world in the creation and use of reserves. This applies to disclosed reserves as well as secret reserves. Even with respect to disclosed reserves, there is no agreement as to whether allocations to, or withdrawals from, reserves should enter into the determination of net income.

Some of the views held in the United States regarding accounting for business combinations are either not accepted or not followed in many foreign nations.

Profits and losses arising from transactions in a company's own stock and in securities of other companies are accorded varying treatment in different nations.

Bonuses to management and employees are charged to income in some countries and to surplus in others.

The accounting for stock dividends generally accepted in the United States is virtually unheard of abroad.

There are also important differences in the nature and scope of the examinations of financial statements made by independent public accountants all over the world. The extended procedures with respect to the examination of receivables and inventories which have been generally accepted in the United States since 1939 have begun to spread to other countries of the world, but in most countries the procedures are not followed. Confirmation of receivables became a recommended practice in Canada in April, 1958,[1] and observation of physical inventories a recommended practice in May, 1959.[2] The Institute of Chartered Accountants in England and Wales issued a statement in July 1968 regarding the audi-

[1] Bulletin No. 15, The Canadian Institute of Chartered Accountants, April, 1958.
[2] Bulletin No. 16, The Canadian Institute of Chartered Accountants, May, 1959.

tor's observation of the client's stock-taking procedures. The statement said in part that ". . . wherever it is practicable and stock-in-trade and work in progress is a material factor in the business, the auditors should satisfy themselves as to the effectiveness of the application of the client's stock-taking procedures by observation on a test basis of these procedures whilst the stock-taking is in progress." [3] Other nations have been much slower in adopting these procedures, and in many countries they have not been adopted at all.

There are also other procedures which are taken for granted in the United States which would not normally be employed by foreign auditors unless special arrangements were made therefor. This should not be construed as reflecting on all examinations by foreign auditors; on the contrary, although the scope of their examinations and the procedures employed are different from those in the United States, in many cases their examinations are more than adequate.

There are significant variations in auditors' reports all over the world. Even where the objectives of the audit are similar, the reports in one country may bear no similarity to those in another country. The quality and objectives of British examinations are not markedly different from those made by United States auditors, and yet the reports of British auditors are distinctively different from those of United States CPAs. The differences have their roots in professional and statutory requirements as well as in custom and tradition.

It is regrettable, to say the least, that these differences should exist. Accounting is said to be the language of business, but an international language has not yet been developed either for communication purposes or for accounting.

The lack of uniformity in accounting principles and auditing procedures as between nations has been a cause of some concern to thoughtful accountants everywhere. This concern is not confined, by any means, to accounting practitioners alone; it is shared by others who have occasion to read and understand financial statements. One of the world's leading industrialists deplored the lack of uniformity in accounting and auditing and said that there was a real need for certainty as to the meaning of information embodied in financial statements. The development of the world economy, he said, places on those who are responsible for the preparation of financial statements the obligation of attaining the greatest possible uniformity in their form and content. He said:

. . . Only when this is achieved will the national boundaries in the field of reporting disappear and will it be possible for everyone to draw his conclusions from reports of any enterprise located in any country with understanding and

[3] Statement on Auditing No. 9, The Institute of Chartered Accountants in England and Wales, July, 1968.

confidence. Only then will readers place the same reliance on the auditor's certificate included therein. . . .[4]

One reason for the differences in point of view is that in some foreign countries—notably in Europe—accounting decisions are based to some extent on economic considerations. That is to say that economists and economic thought have had an influence in shaping accounting practices. The theory of depreciation based on replacement value (or current value) is a case in point. The economist is less concerned with the *original cost* of the assets consumed in the manufacturing process than he is with the *current value* of the assets consumed. It is the same kind of thinking which dictates that operations should be charged with depreciation on fixed assets used in the manufacturing process even though such assets may have been fully depreciated in the accounts.

It is obvious that there is a real need to develop uniformity in accounting and auditing on a world-wide basis. This is a long-range goal. For the immediate future the short-range goal should be the development of international understanding. Some steps in this direction have already been taken. In 1966, the three Institutes of Chartered Accountants in Great Britain and Ireland, the Canadian Institute of Chartered Accountants and the American Institute of Certified Public Accountants formed an International Study Group whose purpose is to publish comparative studies of accounting and auditing practice in the participating countries. The first four studies produced by this group include such subjects as accounting and auditing approaches to inventories and accounting for corporate income taxes in the three nations. More recently, these same Institutes agreed to cooperate with one another in developing common positions on accounting problems. To this end the accounting committees of each Institute will seek opportunities to issue pronouncements which would agree in substance to the extent practicable. However admirable these steps are, a great deal more must be done to achieve the long range goal of international harmonization of accounting principles and auditing standards and procedures.

All other considerations aside, the foreign auditor must be aware of United States requirements since they apply to his examinations of subsidiaries of American companies, and they also apply to those of his clients who contemplate registering with the SEC. Conversely, the United States CPA must be familiar with accounting and auditing in various foreign countries so that he can intelligently relate the statements of foreign subsidiaries to those of the United States parent company. The American CPA must also be familiar with accounting principles abroad when he is asked to assist

---

[4] P. F. S. Otten, former Chairman of the Supervisory Board of N. V. Philips Gloeilampenfabrieken, in an address before the Eighth International Congress of Accountants, New York, N.Y., September 24, 1962.

his client in connection with a proposed acquisition of a subsidiary in a foreign country or when he is asked to examine the financial statements of a United States subsidiary of a foreign parent company.

Progress in United States Has Not Been Duplicated Abroad.— The progress in accountancy in the United States has not been matched in foreign countries. Although much remains to be done, accountancy has made great strides in the United States. Largely as the result of activities of committees of the AICPA, the accounting profession can point with justifiable pride to progress in the formulation and adoption of accounting principles, in the examination of financial statements by public accountants, and in their reporting standards. The SEC, beyond doubt, deserves a measure of credit for some of this progress and particularly for having sharpened the concept of independence on the part of the certifying accountants.

Although there is ample room for further progress, certainly the profession in the United States cannot be accused of complacency. The AICPA sponsorship of an accelerated program of research in accounting principles in association with representatives of industry and the teaching profession is an indication of accountancy's recognition of the urgent need for moving forward—not movement for its own sake, but movement with progress. The accounting research program in the United States has no equal in any foreign country.

Some may say that developments in the United States affecting accounting are not necessarily synonymous with progress. They will refer to the issuance of a research bulletin by a committee of the AICPA dealing with stock options [ARB No. 37 (1948)] only to have the bulletin revised in important respects four years later [ARB No. 37 (Revised) (1953)]. They will also refer to the issuance of an opinion of the APB dealing, in part, with convertible debt and debt issued with warrants [APB Opinion No. 10, par. 8 and 9, (1966)] only to have that part of the opinion suspended one year later [APB Opinion No. 12, par. 11–15 (1967)] and revised in important respects a little more than two years later [APB Opinion No. 14 (1969)]. They will point to a bulletin on accounting for stock dividends [ARB No. 43, Chapter 7B (1953)] the reasoning in which defies understanding at home as well as abroad, but which has the enthusiastic support of the SEC and the stock exchanges.

But at least there has been a willingness to examine critically what has been done in the past to see whether or not a change is desirable or necessary. The road to progress has not been smooth. When errors are made, they have to be acknowledged, and a fresh start has to be made.

The relative lack of progress in some foreign countries may be due in part to the fact that these countries do not have the equivalent of an SEC to direct attention to weaknesses in accounting and auditing practices and suggest that something ought to be done about them. When the SEC has made such suggestions to the accounting profession in the United States, in the background there has been the understanding that if the profession did not do something in an area where something needed to be done, the SEC would do it if necessary. (See, for example, the discussion of the adoption of extensions of auditing procedures following the McKesson & Robbins disclosures, beginning on page **5·7**.)

There most assuredly has been progress in foreign countries, but it does not match the pace in the United States. In some foreign countries, almost anything may be done in financial statements so long as it is disclosed. In other countries, it is not even necessary to make the disclosure so long as the accounting is "conservative." One result is that not even a sophisticated reader can understand the financial statements of some foreign corporations, or compare them with those of a similar United States corporation.

SEC Statutes Do Not Distinguish Between Domestic and Foreign Private Issuers or Accountants.—The Securities Act of 1933 provides exemptions for the securities of domestic governmental units, but there is no similar exemption for the securities of foreign governments. Consequently securities of foreign governments which are publicly offered in the United States must be registered with the SEC. The registration requirements applicable to the securities of foreign governments are contained in Schedule B of the 1933 Act.

The 1933 Act makes no distinction, however, between domestic private issuers of securities and foreign private issuers. As a consequence, an offering of securities by a foreign private issuer is subject to the same requirements as would be applicable in the case of an offering by a domestic private issuer. In connection with public offerings by foreign enterprises in the United States, a major problem facing the issuer is the reconciliation of the information available to it with the requirements of the law and the SEC.

The 1933 Act provides for the filing of financial statements in such form and in such detail as the Commission may prescribe, and also provides for the certification of financial statements by independent public accountants. The Commission has considerable latitude in expanding or modifying the information requirements of the Act in order to be able to cope with the problems presented by particular classes of issuers or securities.

Reference has previously been made (see page **9·14**) to Instruction 13 of Form S–1 which provides for the filing of financial statements other than those specified in the instructions, or the filing of additional statements, when appropriate. Pursuant to this instruction, registrants—foreign as well as domestic—have been permitted to substitute, modify, or omit the financial statement disclosures specified in Form S–1 when necessary or appropriate.

The 1934 Act (which relates, among other things, to securities traded in the over-the-counter market and on exchanges) has substantially the same financial and certification provisions as the 1933 Act. The SEC's requirements for registration of foreign securities under the 1934 Act and listing on an exchange for trading are considerably more lenient, however, than its requirements under the 1933 Act, except in the case of foreign issuers domiciled in a North American country or Cuba. The requirements for registration of foreign issuers under the 1934 Act are discussed beginning on page **31**·39.

The 1933 and 1934 Acts make no distinction between domestic accountants and foreign accountants. A former chairman of the SEC observed:

> . . . There is nothing in the Congressional debates or Committee reports on the Acts to indicate that the acceptability of certificates of foreign accountants was ever considered. The statutes merely use the term "independent public or certified public accountant." [5]

The SEC's Dilemma.—While trying to do everything in its power to make it possible for United States investors to invest if they wish in foreign enterprises, the SEC has been pulled in many directions simultaneously. If replacement value depreciation is not permitted to be followed by a United States corporation, why should it be permitted for a foreign corporation that wishes to sell its securities to American citizens? If a United States auditor must observe the taking of physical inventories as an essential element of his examination, should not the SEC insist that foreign auditors follow the same procedures? If American public accountants are barred from having a financial interest in enterprises on which they report, should not the same standard of independence apply to foreign auditors? If American corporations registering with the SEC must disclose the remuneration of their highest-paid executives, should not the same disclosures be made by foreign registrants?

The fact of life is that many of the standards and customs in the United States simply do not exist in many foreign countries. If the SEC were to cling to a single standard for all registrants—United States and foreign —it would, in all probability, result in denying to United States residents the opportunity of investing in some foreign issuers. Take the case, for instance, of the foreign corporation some of whose shares are owned by

---

[5] J. Sinclair Armstrong, "Highlights in Current Financial Reporting," address before Illinois Society of CPAs, June 6, 1957.

United States residents. The corporation plans to make a rights offering to its shareholders. If the company decides to make the offering to its United States shareholders as well as all other shareholders, it would have to register with the SEC the shares to be offered in the United States. On the other hand, the company might decide that it does not wish to go to the trouble and expense of registering with the SEC or to incur the liabilities associated with the Securities Act. The company could ignore the American shareholders and let them make their own arrangements for exercising or selling their rights abroad.

The fact of the matter is that many foreign corporations do follow replacement value depreciation. Observation of physical inventories by auditors is still largely an American, Canadian and British practice which is not followed in many foreign countries. Foreign auditors are not only permitted to invest in securities of their clients, but in some cases they are expected to be shareholders. In many foreign countries it is simply out of the question to disclose the remuneration of top-echelon executives individually, and to make such disclosure might have serious repercussions.

The SEC, as a consequence, has had to walk a tight rope—pulled in one direction by those who maintain that there ought to be only one standard applicable to *all* registrants and in another direction by those who think that some accommodation should be made for the mores, standards, and procedures in foreign countries. The SEC has taken a middle course and has made concessions to foreign registrants which would not even be considered for United States registrants.

In the case of some foreign issuers, for example, the SEC has waived some of its disclosure requirements with respect to remuneration of officers and directors. Item 17 of Form S–1 calls for the names and amounts paid to each director and to each of the three highest-paid offiecrs of the registrant whose aggregate direct remuneration exceeded $30,000. In lieu of the disclosure normally required, the SEC has accepted a statement of the *aggregate* remuneration of all officers and directors as a group.

The SEC has accepted the certificates of foreign auditors who did not comply with the SEC's requirements as to independence. Some of these foreign auditors had had financial interests in their clients during the period covered by their reports, but disposed of the interests before their clients filed their registration statements with the Commission. If the auditors had been United States firms, there is no doubt that the SEC would have rejected their certificates.

In the case of issues by foreign governments, the SEC has waived certification by independent auditors of the financial statements of agencies of such governments if such statements are customarily examined and certified by the regular auditing staff of the government. The SEC has a rule in Regulation S–X to this effect reading as follows:

Rule 2–03. Examination of Financial Statements by
Foreign Government Auditors.

Notwithstanding any requirements as to examination by independent accountants, the financial statements of any foreign governmental agency may be examined by the regular and customary auditing staff of the respective government, if public financial statements of such governmental agency are customarily examined by such auditing staff.

An example of the certificate contemplated by the foregoing rule was in a Form 18 registration statement filed in 1968 by the Mortgage Bank and Financial Administration Agency of the Kingdom of Denmark. The accounts of the bank are audited by two auditors appointed by the Minister of Finance for terms of three years. The annual report of the auditors is submitted to the Folketing (the Danish legislature), the Minister of Finance, the Board of Directors of the bank, and the appropriate governmental audit department. The Form 18 filing included the following:

For the three fiscal years ended March 31, 1965, the auditors of the accounts of the Bank were Messrs. R_____ and J_____, and for the two fiscal years ended March 31, 1967, such auditors were Messrs. R_____ and V_____. Mr. J_____ is deceased. Messrs. R_____ and V_____, who are officials in the Ministry of Finance of the Kingdom, have furnished the following statements for inclusion herein.

I have reviewed the accompanying Balance Sheet as of March 31, 1967, and the accompanying Statements of Profit and Loss and Distribution of Surplus for the five fiscal years ended March 31, 1967, of The Mortgage Bank and Financial Administration Agency of the Kingdom of Denmark. In my capacity as one of the Auditors of the Bank, duly appointed by the Minister of Finance of the Kingdom of Denmark, and in accordance with my function as such, I have examined the accounts of the Bank at such date and for such periods. In my opinion, the above-mentioned Balance Sheet presents fairly the financial condition of the Bank as of March 31, 1967, and the above-mentioned Statements of Profit and Loss and Distribution of Surplus present fairly and on a consistent basis the results of its operations for the five fiscal years ended March 31, 1967.

O. R_____
Auditor

Copenhagen, Denmark
November 13, 1967.

(The report of Mr. V_____, the other auditor, is omitted here because, except for the fact that it covered a different period, it was the same as the report of Mr. R_____ above.)

The Abortive Attempt to Relax the Auditing Requirements for Certain Rights Offerings.—In December, 1956, the SEC gave notice of a proposal to amend Form S–1, which is the form of registration statement most often used to register securities under the 1933 Act (Release No. 33–3735). The proposal related to rights offerings by certain foreign private issuers and would have had the effect of waiving the requirements for certification by independent accountants and the requirements of Regulation S–X in connection with pro rata offerings by foreign issuers to their stockholders of securities of the same class as those listed and registered on a national securities exchange. The relaxed requirements would have applied where the proposed offering price was not more than 60 per cent of the market value and the amount offered to United States shareholders did not exceed 5 per cent of the total offering. The issuer would also have been required to be in business more than 25 years and to have had total assets of at least $100,000,000.

The proposal to waive the certification requirements and the requirements of Regulation S–X would have been subject to the fulfillment of certain conditions including the following:

(1) The financial statements are reviewed, reported upon and prepared in accordance with the standards, procedures and legal requirements prevailing in the country where the issuer is located and conform as nearly as practicable to the form and content prescribed by Regulation S–X, and disclosure is made of the basis upon which the accounts are stated and of the principal respects in which such prevailing standards and procedures do not conform to these instructions and the requirements of Regulation S–X.

The SEC made the proposal to relax its requirements in certain highly circumscribed cases because it wanted to know whether there was an overriding public interest in relaxing the requirements. The public response to the proposal demonstrated, to the contrary, that there was a strong opposition to setting up a different standard for foreign reporting. In April, 1957, the SEC withdrew the proposal. (Release No. 33–3782).

A former chairman of the SEC has been outspoken in his opposition to relaxing the registration requirements for the benefit and convenience of foreign issuers. In his view there should not be a double standard—one for domestic issuers and another for foreign issuers:

. . . Investors who place their savings at the disposal of industry in new issues of corporate securities are entitled to rely on the accounting rules developed by the Commission over nearly a quarter of a century and the principles and practices developed by the American accounting profession. Any failure to require financial statements of foreign corporations registering new issues of securities for sale to the American investing public to be certified by independent auditors in accordance with the standards applicable to American corporations would establish a double standard for reporting by domestic and foreign issuers. Such statements could also be misleading because the public, other than financial experts, might have the impression that American standards had been adhered to simply because the financial statements had been filed with the Commission in a registration statement under the Securities Act.

. . . As a matter of principle, I believe that any relaxation of the standards which the Commission has built up over the years under the Federal securities laws merely to accommodate the raising of capital by foreign corporations from public investors in this country would be most unwise.

. . . It is my belief that in our own national interest and the interest of American investors, and the interest of the American accounting profession to which the success of the capital markets owes so much, that the Commission should require, in statements filed with it, such companies to adhere to our auditing, certification and financial reporting standards.[6]

Another former chairman of the SEC took a decidedly different view of the "minor concessions" which the Commission has made to foreign corporations:

European laws and practices with respect to accounting standards, . . . and other matters are naturally very different from ours. These conditions, I may say, have caused us some concern from time to time when international corporations have sought to enter our capital markets either for new money or for exchange listing. It does not increase international good will for us to attempt to say that foreign corporations must do everything exactly our way, even though we are satisfied that our way is the best way. Some accommodation to foreign ways and foreign standards seems necessary in our increasingly inter-dependent world, but essential standards of investor protection must still be insisted upon. I trust that no one will feel that occasional minor concessions to foreign ways of doing things and to the problems these corporations encounter at home constitute unfair discrimination against domestic corporations.[7]

While public reaction to the SEC's proposal in 1956 apparently reinforced the SEC's determination to apply the same standards to domestic and foreign issuers, the Commission has occasionally made some concessions to foreign corporations. In the opinion of the author, the concessions of which he has knowledge have been relatively minor in character and have not resulted in the withholding of significant information from United States investors or a significant reduction in the protection afforded them by the 1933 Act.

Differences in Accounting Principles and Auditing Standards— U. S. and Abroad.—The previous edition of this book was published in 1963 and dwelt at some length on the differences in accounting principles generally accepted in the United States as compared with those generally accepted in foreign countries. Also, the previous edition discussed the differences in auditing standards generally accepted in the United States as compared with those generally accepted in foreign countries. In addition, the previous edition contained two appendices summarizing the principal differences in accounting principles and auditing standards as between the United States and several principal countries of the free world.

In November 1964 the AICPA published a volume entitled "Professional

---

[6] J. Sinclair Armstrong, "Highlights in Current Financial Reporting," address before Illinois Society of CPAs, June 6, 1957. When Mr. Armstrong spoke, he was no longer a member of the Commission, and he was speaking as a private individual.

[7] Edward N. Gadsby, "The Listed and Unlisted Securities Markets," 105 *The Journal of Accountancy,* 34–35 (April, 1958).

Accounting in 25 Countries." It represented the work of the AICPA Committee on International Relations, and included a comprehensive and authoritative discussion of the differences in accounting and auditing in 25 of the principal commercial countries of the world, including the United States as a basis of comparison. Because the AICPA volume duplicated much of the information dealing with accounting and auditing differences in foreign countries previously included in this book, this discussion and the aforementioned appendices have been omitted from this edition.

In consulting the summaries of accounting principles and auditing standards which appear in "Professional Accounting in 25 Countries," certain things have to be kept in mind:

(1) Like all generalizations, the summary may be an oversimplification and subject to numerous exceptions in specific instances. While the general level of accounting and auditing in a particular nation may be at an early stage of development, it might well be that the accounting of a particular company in that nation and the scope and quality of the examination of that company's financial statements could be very well developed indeed. One reason for this might be that the accounting and auditing policies of an international enterprise are often determined by the corporate headquarters of the enterprise. Thus for example, the accounting principles followed by a manufacturing entity in Italy and the scope and quality of the audit of that entity may be specified by the parent company in Canada. The accounting by and auditing of the Italian subsidiary therefore may bear no resemblance to Italian accounting and auditing in general.

(2) International firms of accountants have had, and are having, an important effect in raising the accounting and auditing standards all over the world. A business in Ghana, therefore, without international business connections but served by an international accounting firm may be served just as well as a similar business located, say, in the United States.

(3) Accounting principles and auditing standards and practices are not static; they are in a constant state of development in foreign countries as well as in the United States. For example, since the issuance of "Professional Accounting in 25 Countries," the Institute of Chartered Accountants in England and Wales has adopted observation of physical inventories as a required auditing procedure, wherever practicable, and has formed an Accounting Standards Steering Committee which, during the 1970's, expects to review existing accounting principles and reduce the number of alternatives available, issue new recommendations where variations exist at present, and recommend disclosure of the accounting bases adopted when significant items depend substantially on value judgments.

(4) Although there are differences in accounting principles and in auditing standards and procedures among the nations, this does not necessarily mean that the principles, practices and procedures used in the United States are superior—or inferior—to those in other countries. They are simply different. A Dutch accountant who believes strongly in replacement value accounting would probably not concede that accounting principles generally accepted in The Netherlands were inferior to those in the United States merely because the Dutch subscribe to the current cost theory. In view of our willingness to accept LIFO inventory methods, he might argue with some justification that Americans recognize the *principle* of replacement value accounting but are unwilling for the present to carry it to its logical conclusion.

On the following pages are some comments with respect to certain accounting principles followed by foreign companies which differ from those generally accepted in the United States. The comments are based on registration statements filed by these companies with the SEC under the 1933 Act. The author's purpose in discussing these cases is to illustrate how specific deviations from United States practice have been dealt with in actual cases.

DEPRECIATION ON A BASIS OTHER THAN COST; REPLACEMENT VALUE. —Perhaps the world's leading advocate of the theory of depreciation based on replacement value (or current value) of assets is a large international manufacturing organization with headquarters in The Netherlands—N. V. Philips Gloeilampenfabrieken, a company known in the United States as Philips Lamp. For many years the company has followed the replacement value theory in its accounts and published financial statements, and applies the theory, not only to fixed assets, but also to inventories.[8] The company believes in and employs replacement value accounting *despite the fact that its use is not permitted for tax purposes in The Netherlands.*

Philips filed a registration statement with the SEC which became effective in May, 1962. The registration statement is discussed at greater length beginning on page **31·32**; the discussion here will be limited to the company's use of replacement value accounting. The company disclosed in the registration statement the fact that its accounting for fixed assets and inventories was based on a replacement value concept. It also disclosed that it followed other accounting practices which likewise were not generally accepted in the United States. The company's summary of earnings was presented on the basis of the accounting principles customarily

[8] For a comprehensive discussion of the application of the replacement value theory in the Philips company, see Professor A. Goudeket, "An Application of Replacement Value Theory," *The Journal of Accountancy,* July 1960, pp. 37–47.

employed by the company, arriving at net income on that basis. A one-line adjustment which followed had the effect of converting the reported amount of net income to approximately net income on the basis of accounting principles generally accepted in the United States, that is, computing depreciation on a cost basis and inventories also on a cost basis.

The auditors reported that the unadjusted figures were "in conformity with generally accepted accounting principles in The Netherlands." They also stated that there were certain differences between the accounting principles followed by Philips and those generally accepted in the United States, and that those which had a material effect on net income were set forth in the notes following the summary of earnings. They concluded their report saying, "The application of accounting principles generally accepted in the United States of America would, in our opinion, have required the adjustments in net income which have been estimated and are reflected in the aforementioned summary of earnings."

The presentation by Philips is in interesting contrast with that of AKU, another Dutch company which had filed a registration statement in 1953. This company also followed replacement value depreciation; the financial statements in its prospectus are discussed beginning on page 31·26.

In certain foreign countries, businesses have been permitted to revalue their fixed assets for both book and tax purposes on the basis of indices ("coefficients") established by the governments in those countries. Where this situation exists, the SEC has accepted financial statements which disclosed the facts and has not required a restatement on the basis of cost depreciation.

An early example of an SEC filing illustrating this procedure occurred in connection with a registration statement filed in 1956 by SIMCA, a French corporation. The company stated that, under French tax laws, companies may recognize the loss in purchasing power of the French franc by revaluing their fixed assets based on estimates of current useful value with certain limitations. SIMCA revalued its properties on three separate occasions—1945, 1949, and 1951—on the basis of coefficients of revaluation authorized by the French government. Thereafter the company charged against earnings depreciation on the higher amounts, as permitted by French tax law. The certifying accountant in this filing reported that the statements fairly presented the company's financial position and results of operations, but said nothing about their conformity with generally accepted accounting principles.

The depreciation principle involved in SIMCA was also applicable in a filing by Montecatini, an Italian company (Montecatini Societa Generale per l'Industria Mineraria e Chimica Anonima), which filed a registration statement with the SEC in 1960. The company stated in the notes to financial statements that under Italian monetary and Belgian tax laws, companies had been permitted to recognize to some extent the loss in purchasing power of the respective country's currency through permission to restate assets and related reserves at amounts in excess of cost on the basis of coefficients established under the law. The last revalorization enactment in Italy was in 1952 and related only to assets acquired in 1946 or earlier. As to the Belgian affiliates, the last revalorization of assets was made in 1949. Depreciation charged to income was based on the higher amounts. In this case, however, the certifying accountants stated that the financial statements had, "in all material respects, been prepared in accordance with generally accepted accounting principles applied on a consistent basis."

The principle established in SIMCA and followed with some modification in Montecatini has also been followed by several Japanese corporations. A registration statement filed in 1967 by Komatsu Manufacturing Co., Ltd. is typical, and the following information is taken from its prospectus dated December 12, 1967. The consolidated assets at December 31, 1966 were $321,000,000, of which $53,000,000 was represented by fixed assets less depreciation (all amounts are translated from Japanese yen). A note to the financial statements indicated that fixed assets were stated at cost, except as stated in the following paragraph:

In Japan companies have been permitted by law to give accounting recognition to some extent to the loss in the purchasing power of the yen by upward revaluation of certain of their properties, and computing depreciation for tax purposes on the higher amounts. The Company and its consolidated subsidiaries increased their property and plant accounts ¥1,173 ($3,258 thousand) in the years 1950 to 1954 with corresponding credits to revaluation surplus and have computed depreciation charged to operations and deducted for tax purposes on the basis of the adjusted amounts.

Depreciation was a significant factor in the company's results of operations.

In this case, the certifying accountants reported that the statements were "in conformity with generally accepted accounting principles applied on a consistent basis."

In short, the SEC will accept price level depreciation in some form in the case of foreign issuers where the practice is sanctioned and controlled by the foreign government and results in a new depreciation base for tax purposes. This would be the case, for example, in filings by French, Italian, Belgian, Japanese, and Israeli companies, all of whom have been permitted to revalue their fixed assets on the basis of laws in effect in their respective countries.

ACCOUNTING FOR RESERVES.—One of the major differences in accounting principles generally accepted in the United States and those in foreign countries is in the area of accounting for reserves. In several foreign countries reserves are created, and utilized, in a manner which is not generally accepted in the USA. Prior to 1965, German companies often followed the practice of creating substantial hidden reserves through higher than reasonable depreciation charges, understatement of saleable inventory, accrual of excess provisions for expenses and similar means. In 1965, a corporation law was enacted, which, in part, attempted to regulate the abuse of reserves by forbidding AGs (public corporations) from setting up new reserves. It is doubtful whether the practice of setting up reserves has disappeared entirely in Germany and it is still possible, for example, to understate substantially work-in-process and finished goods inventories, and to estimate the useful lives of fixed assets rather conservatively, although concealment may be more difficult.

In some foreign countries reserves are sometimes created, not to provide for a specific purpose, but rather for a general purpose—to provide for a contingency which may arise, or for future losses on inventories not on hand, and so on. In many cases there is no desire to conceal the true nature of the reserves, and accordingly they are disclosed. When reserves of this nature are charged to retained earnings, there is no particular problem in terms of practice in the USA; it is when they are charged to income that a problem is apt to arise. When the reserves are provided out of income, the reader is often not competent to judge whether they are provided for specific known losses, or whether the real purpose is to reduce reported profits in fat years and to increase profits in lean years.

Sometimes the reserves are provided merely because the provisions therefor are deductible for tax purposes and the law provides that, in order to be entitled to the deduction, the reserve must be recorded in the books. For example, provisions for certain reserves in Japan which are placed on the books merely because they are tax deductible and are not otherwise required.

Where these circumstances exist, the foreign registrant may have a problem in conforming its principles to, or reconciling with, the requirements in the United States and those of the SEC.

The accepted practice in the United States regarding general purpose contingency reserves was stated in a bulletin of the AICPA as follows:

7. The committee is therefore of the opinion that reserves such as those created:
    (a) for general undetermined contingencies, or
    (b) for any indefinite possible future losses, such as, for example, losses on inventories not on hand or contracted for, or
    (c) for the purpose of reducing inventories other than to a basis which is in accordance with generally accepted accounting principles, or
    (d) without regard to any specific loss reasonably related to the operations of the current period, or

(e) in amounts not determined on the basis of any reasonable estimates of costs or losses

are of such a nature that charges or credits relating to such reserves should not enter into the determination of net income.

8. Accordingly, it is the opinion of the committee that if a reserve of the type described in paragraph 7 is set up:

(a) it should be created by a segregation or appropriation of earned surplus,

(b) no costs or losses should be charged to it and no part of it should be transferred to income or in any way used to affect the determination of net income for any year,

(c) it should be restored to earned surplus directly when such a reserve or any part thereof is no longer considered necessary, and

(d) it should preferably be classified in the balance sheet as a part of shareholders' equity. [ARB No. 43, Chap. 6 (1953)].

The AICPA position is reinforced by a one-sentence provision in the SEC's Regulation S–X:

Only items entering into the determination of net income or loss may be included [in the income statement]. [Rule 5–03(b)].

To sum up: Foreign registrants and their accountants should consider carefully their accounting for reserves in the light of United States requirements. To adjust the operating results to reflect accounting on a USA-basis may be a difficult—in some instances, an impossible—task.

STOCK DIVIDENDS.—For a discussion of the SEC's views regarding the accounting for stock dividends, see page **18·34**. As there stated, the SEC supports completely the AICPA pronouncement on the subject of accounting for stock dividends. Inasmuch as United States registrants and their accountants are presumed to be familiar with the AICPA bulletin, the SEC has insisted on compliance with the bulletin where such companies were involved. Where foreign registrants were involved, however, the SEC has not insisted on retroactive application of the bulletin in all cases, although it may have so insisted in some. It would appear that each of these cases involving a foreign registrant is dealt with individually by the SEC.

In the case of a filing in 1959 by Supercrete Ltd., a Canadian company, its prospectus disclosed that stock dividends had been reflected in its accounts at the par value of the shares issued in accordance with Canadian accounting practice. In the prospectus financial statements, however, the stock dividends were reflected at the market value of the shares of the company at date of declaration "in accordance with United States accounting practice." The author is unable to say whether the change was made voluntarily by the company or as the result of insistence by the Commission.

Royal Dutch Petroleum Company filed a registration statement with the

SEC in 1958 in which it appears that the company accounted only for the "nominal" (par) value of share distributions. In 1961, however, in connection with a 10 per cent share distribution, the company accounted for the fair value of the shares distributed. It seems reasonable to assume that the change in accounting may have been caused by the insistence of the SEC or the New York Stock Exchange, on which exchange the company's shares had been listed for trading.

The author acted as a consultant to a foreign corporation that filed a registration statement with the SEC under the 1933 Act in 1962. The company had made numerous distributions of common stock to its shareholders but, in keeping with the accounting principles generally accepted in the foreign country, had accounted only for the par value of such shares, and had not accounted for the excess of the market value over par value, which excess was considerable. The Commission advised the registrant that it would raise no objection to the accounting for stock dividends as recorded in the past but said that it was of the opinion that in the future recognition should be given to practices followed in the United States with respect to recording recurring stock dividends at fair value.

From a review of what practice has been over an extended period of years, it seems reasonable to conclude that, in general, the SEC will not require a foreign registrant to account for recurring stock dividends *retroactively* on the basis of practices followed in the United States but will expect the company to account for *future* dividends on such basis.

The reader's attention is especially directed to the discussion in Chapter **18** regarding the SEC's proposal (made in 1968 but not yet acted upon) to adopt Rule 10b–12 which, if adopted, would seriously affect issuers that violate United States rules on accounting for stock dividends.

Departures from Generally Accepted Auditing Standards by Foreign Auditors.—United States accountants are expected to be familiar with generally accepted auditing standards and to plan their work accordingly when they are engaged in examinations leading up to a filing with the SEC. The SEC generally insists that the auditing standards followed by foreign auditors be the same as those required of United States auditors. Foreign auditors, however, cannot be expected to plan their examinations to meet SEC requirements unless they are specifically instructed to that effect. Frequently the foreign auditors are not instructed that their reports are to be filed with the SEC, and they may not employ certain procedures which are necessary to comply with United States standards. In the past the SEC has demonstrated a willingness to adapt its requirements where consistent with the protection of investors. In such cases, the reports of foreign auditors would disclose deviations from United States practice as illustrated in the following examples taken from actual registration statements:

Example 1. Receivables from subscribers (customers) not confirmed.

We have examined the financial statements of (name of foreign company) as listed in the accompanying "Index of Financial Statements." Our examination was made in accordance with generally accepted auditing standards, and included such tests of the accounting records and such other auditing procedures as we considered necessary in the circumstances.

Accounts receivable from subscribers at (date), were not confirmed by direct correspondence with the subscribers, since such procedure is neither mandatory nor customary in present day practice of independent public accountants in (country). In the absence of such confirmation, we satisfied ourselves concerning such accounts receivable by means of alternative auditing procedures which we consider adequate.

In our opinion, the aforementioned statements present fairly the financial position of (name of foreign company), at (date), and the results of its operations for the (period) then ended in conformity with generally accepted accounting principles, etc.

Example 2. Physical inventories not observed.

We have examined the balance sheet of (name of foreign company), at (date) and the related statements of income and surplus for the (period) then ended. Our examination was made in accordance with generally accepted auditing standards, and accordingly included such tests of the accounting records and such other auditing procedures as we considered necessary in the circumstances.

We did not make any independent physical verification of the inventory, which procedure is not mandatory in present day practice of independent accountants in (country).

In our opinion, the above-described statements present fairly the financial position of (name of foreign company), at (date) and the results of its operations for the (period) then ended, in conformity with generally accepted accounting principles, etc.

There is no assurance, however, that this state of affairs will continue, and the reader should not assume that the SEC will permit deviations of the types illustrated in all cases. When a foreign auditor has not complied with United States standards, the situation should be discussed with the SEC in advance of filing to see whether or not the lack of compliance with such standards will render the auditor's report unacceptable.

To avoid any possible complication arising out of lack of compliance with United States auditing standards, foreign companies planning to register securities for sale in the United States should promptly inform their auditors of their plans. This may enable the foreign auditors to make provision for including in their examinations the extended procedures for observation of inventories and confirmation of receivables. Often this is all that is required to conform the foreign auditor's examination to United States standards.

Different Concept of Independence of Foreign Auditors.—The matter of accountants' independence is considered in Chapter **26** where the SEC's formal and informal rules dealing with independence are discussed in some detail. In the following pages, this subject is considered from the viewpoint of foreign auditors whose certificates are filed with the SEC.

The concept of independence is quite different in foreign countries from what it is in the United States. There can be no doubt that the development of the independence concept was hastened in the USA largely as a result of the statutes administered by the SEC and the rules and regulations of the Commission thereunder. These, in turn, sparked the professional organizations (notably the AICPA) to tighten their requirements. All these influences have been lacking abroad. As a consequence it is not uncommon for a foreign auditor to discover—much to his amazement—that he is not independent in relation to his client *according to SEC standards*.

The SEC statutes make no distinction between United States accountants and foreign accountants; the rules and regulations of the SEC also make no distinction between independence of domestic and foreign auditors. (However, as discussed in Chapter **26**, the SEC in ASR No. 112 permits a slightly less restrictive interpretation of independence in the case of accountants examining a nonmaterial segment of an international business.) The Commission expects all accountants—foreign as well as domestic—to comply with its rules on independence. In the interpretation of its rules, however, it has been slightly more lenient where foreign auditors were concerned. The SEC has recognized that USA standards of independence simply do not exist abroad. Accordingly, the SEC has accepted certificates from foreign auditors which would have been rejected if the auditors were United States accountants.

In one case with which the author is familiar a registration statement under the 1933 Act was filed by a Danish company in connection with a proposed offering of its debentures in the United States. The statement was interesting because the SEC had to consider the independence of the foreign accountants who certified the company's financial statements included in the document.

The financial statements were certified jointly by two certified public accountants of Denmark, this being a common arrangement in that country. Each of the CPAs was a member of a firm, but they certified as individual CPAs—this also being a common arrangement in Denmark where the appointment as auditor frequently is a personal one; that is, it runs to the individual and not to the firm of which he is a member. The certificate of the joint auditors was entitled "Report of Certified Public Accountants"—

not "Report of *Independent* Certified Public Accountants." In no part of the prospectus—including the headnote to the summary of earnings or under the caption "Experts"—were the accountants referred to as being "independent."

One of the Danish CPAs, Mr. E, was chairman of the board of directors of a publicly held corporation which performed independent auditing. Mr. E owned D.Kr. 6,500 par value (about $940) of the registrant's capital stock which he sold prior to the filing of the registration statement. One of Mr. E's fellow directors of the auditing firm also owned D.Kr. 8,000 par value (about $1,160) of the registrant's capital stock which he also sold before the registration statement was filed. The market value was not materially different from the par value. The registrant's capital stock outstanding was D.Kr. 200,000,000. All these facts were set forth in Item 24 of the registration statement (dealing with the relationship of experts named in the registration statement) or in the related prospectus. Item 24 also stated that in Denmark there is no law, regulation, or custom which prohibits a CPA from owning capital stock in a company which he audits. With these disclosures the SEC accepted the certificate but apparently stipulated that there be no representation to the effect that the accountants were independent.

In similar circumstance it is clear that the SEC would not accept the certificate of a United States CPA. It is true that this creates a double standard of independence, but the distinction has its roots in common sense and a practical solution to a difficult problem.

United States public accountants know, or should know, the requirements of the SEC and professional organizations relating to independence. It is not reasonable to expect foreign auditors to practice according to United States standards. When a foreign auditor's client makes its first registered offering in the United States, should the Commission insist on a re-audit of the company's financial statements by an accountant who meets completely the SEC's requirements with regard to independence? This involves not merely a question of cost, but also of time, and the latter may be as important as the former. Most certainly the degree of deviation and the nature of the deviation from the SEC's standards are matters which should be considered. In the opinion of the author, the SEC is to be commended for making a reasonable compromise in the case discussed above as between its stated requirements relating to independence and the practices and customs in foreign countries.

In another case with which the author is familiar, a United States company filed a registration statement under the 1933 Act. The company had a subsidiary in England which was audited by a firm of English accountants. During the period covered by the financial statements of the subsidiary, two of the partners of the firm of English auditors were substantial stockholders in the subsidiary. These partners sold the shares which they owned in the subsidiary before the registration statement was filed. The SEC accepted the certificate of the English accountants, but there was no representation that the English accountants were independent. In fact, Item 24 of the registration statement discussed the relationship with the registrant of experts named in the registration statement and made the following disclosure:

> During the period referred to in the report of [English auditors] on the financial statements of [English subsidiary] one partner owned   shares of stock and another partner owned   shares of stock of [English subsidiary]. The Company is advised that neither [English auditors] nor any partner in that firm now has any direct or indirect interest in [English subsidiary]. The Company understands that the ownership by English accountants of securities of their clients is neither unusual nor improper.

The reader should not assume, however, that all of the Commission's rulings bearing on independence of foreign auditors have been favorable to the accountants. In ASR No. 81 (1958), for instance, the SEC reported a case involving chartered accountants for a proposed registrant, a foreign corporation. The accountants owned a stock interest in the company. The SEC held that the accountants in that case were not independent with respect to their client for purposes of filing with the Commission.

American accountants may occasionally encounter situations in which the auditor of a foreign subsidiary is a stockholder in the foreign subsidiary or has some other relationship with the foreign subsidiary which may raise a question as to the foreign auditor's independence and hence the acceptability of his certificate for SEC filing. When this possibility exists, it is frequently desirable to discuss with the SEC in advance of filing the question of whether or not the existence of the conditions bearing on the independence of the foreign auditor will render his certificate unacceptable.

Liability of Foreign Auditors Under SEC Laws.—The liability of accountants under the Securities Act of 1933 and the Securities Exchange Act of 1934 is discussed in Chapters **27** and **28**. The views expressed in those chapters may not be applicable in the case of a foreign public accountant.

The prospectus of a foreign issuer must contain a statement regarding the enforceability of civil liabilities under the 1933 Act against the issuer and others connected with the issue. The SEC requires that:

> . . . the forepart of the prospectus should clearly state how the enforcement by investors of civil liabilities under the Act may be affected by the fact that the registrant is located in a foreign country, that certain of its officers and directors are residents of a foreign country, that certain underwriters or experts named in the registration statement are residents of a foreign country, and that all or a substantial portion of the assets of the registrant and of said persons are located outside the United States. Such disclosures should indicate: whether investors will be able to effect service of process within the

United States upon such persons; whether investors will be able to enforce against such persons judgments obtained in United States courts predicated upon the civil liability provisions of the Act; whether the appropriate foreign courts would enforce judgments of United States courts obtained in actions against such persons predicated upon the civil liability provisions of the Act, and whether the appropriate foreign courts would enforce, in original actions, liabilities against such persons predicated solely upon the Act. If any portions of such disclosures are stated to be based upon an opinion of counsel, such counsel should be named in the prospectus and an appropriate manually-signed consent to the use of such name and opinion should be included in the registration statement. ("Guides for Preparation and Filing of Registration Statements.")

The disclosure contemplated by the foregoing SEC requirement appears early in the prospectus and is prominently displayed. The following is typical of notices of this kind:

All of the directors, all of the members of management and the executive officers of the Company and certain of the experts named herein are residents of (name of foreign country). As a result, it may be difficult for investors to effect service within the United States upon such directors, members of management, executive officers and experts, or to realize against them upon judgments of courts of the U.S. predicated upon civil liability under the United States Securities Act of 1933, as amended. The Company has been advised by its legal counsel, (name of legal counsel), that there is doubt as to the enforceability in (name of foreign country) in original actions or in actions for enforcement of judgments of U.S. courts of liabilities predicated solely upon such Securities Act.

It will be observed that the investor may have a problem in suing a foreign public accountant who, as an "expert," certified the financial statements appearing in the prospectus of a foreign issuer. The legal situation may be much more complicated where the certifying accountants are an international firm of accountants. In that case, the nature of the firm's legal liability would, in all probability, depend on the precise nature of the firm's partnership arrangements, which, being a legal matter, is beyond the scope of this volume.

Retention of International Accountants as Consultants or Auditors.—From what has been stated previously in this chapter, it should be apparent that foreign corporations contemplating the filing of a registration statement with the SEC may face a difficult task. They have the problems that would confront a domestic registrant plus the problems growing out of the fact that they have not done things the way they are done in the United States. They have the problem of complying with generally accepted accounting principles and standards of disclosure in the United States, or with reconciling their practices and disclosures with USA-equivalents. Their certifying accountants also have the problem of complying with auditing standards generally accepted in the United States, and with the standards of independence prescribed by the SEC. In addition, the company and its auditors are expected to be familiar with, and to comply with, the SEC's instructions for financial statements, Regulation S–X, and with all other pronouncements by the Commission bearing on accounting and auditing matters.

In these circumstances some foreign corporations have decided to employ auditors with experience in this field. For the purpose of the registration statement only, they may employ an international firm of accountants to examine and certify the company's financial statements. To the extent that the firm repeats what other auditors have done before, there is a certain amount of needless duplication. This can be kept to a reasonable minimum, however, by tailoring the new examination in the light of what was done in previous examinations. Just as an auditor will draft his audit program having in mind the work done by a company's internal auditing department, the international accounting firm may rely to some extent on the work performed by their predecessors provided the international firm is satisfied (1) that their predecessors were independent, and (2) that their work was done carefully and conscientiously.

The employment of an international firm of accountants for registration purposes may prove to be both time consuming and costly. In that event, another arrangement might be made. The foreign corporation may find it advantageous to engage an international firm of accountants or an individual with SEC experience to consult with and advise the company and its auditors in the preparation of the financial section of the registration statement. The consulting arrangement has the advantage of keeping the cost to a minimum since there is no duplication of auditing effort, and, by the same token, expedites the project. It has one disadvantage, however, namely, that the consultant's name may not appear in the registration statement or prospectus, and this might be a cause of some concern to the underwriters. The consulting procedure has been followed, however, in several cases involving foreign registrants. Consequently, the foreign corporation that is reluctant to employ new auditors to duplicate prior audits should consider this alternative and discuss it with the underwriters.[9]

Statements in Foreign Currency.—The SEC's policy with respect to the currencies in which amounts are to be set forth in the registration statements of foreign issuers is as follows:

[9] An eminent United States lawyer with considerable experience involving foreign registrants has said, "In connection with registration under the Securities Act foreign corporations have usually found it advantageous to retain an international accounting firm familiar with SEC accounting as their consultants or auditors." John R. Stevenson, "Legal Aspects of the Public Offering of Foreign Securities in the United States Market," *George Washington Law Review,* October 1959, p. 209.

In connection with registration statements filed by foreign issuers, the question arises whether money amounts may be stated only in the currency of the domicile of the registrant or whether such amounts must also be stated in U.S. dollars. It is our practice to accept the statement of such money amounts in the currency of the registrant's domicile except that, where necessary to a clear understanding, the U.S. dollar equivalent should be shown in parallel columns or otherwise, as appropriate. In all cases, however, the exchange rate in effect in New York City as of the latest practicable date should be set forth at the beginning of the prospectus in prominent (preferably bold-face) type. ("Guides for Preparation and Filing of Registration Statements.")

As far as the author has been able to determine, the SEC has not set forth the circumstances under which the U. S. dollar equivalent is "necessary to a clear understanding." In a registration statement under the 1933 Act filed in 1953 by a Dutch company (Algemene Kunstzijde Unie N. V.) the SEC permitted all the financial data to be expressed in foreign currency and required only the net income in the summary of earnings to be translated into United States currency. On the other hand, in a prospectus filed with the SEC in 1960 by an Italian company (Montecatini Societa Generale per l'Industria Mineraria e Chimica Anonima) all income statements, earnings summaries, and surplus statements were presented only in United States currency whereas the balance sheets were in Italian lire as well as United States dollars. In the 1962 registration statement of an Israeli corporation (Bank Leumi Le-Israel B. M.) all financial statements were expressed in foreign currency (Israeli pounds and pounds sterling) with no translation into United States currency.

The great majority of foreign issuers present their financial statements in two currencies, that is, in the currency of their own country, and translated into United States currency. This is the situation as far as the prospectus is concerned. The supporting schedules in Part II of the registration are usually presented in foreign currency only. In a given case if a foreign issuer contemplates filing a registration statement in which a different presentation is planned, the author would recommend that the matter be discussed with the staff of the SEC in advance of the proposed filing date.

When the dual financial presentation is followed, it is usually accompanied by a statement which typically says:

In this Prospectus certain Japanese yen amounts have been translated into United States dollars at the rate of 360 yen to the dollar. Such translations, which are printed in italics, should not be construed as representations that the Japanese yen amounts represent, or have been or could be converted into, United States dollars at that or any other rate. The official parity rate for the Japanese yen, which has prevailed since April, 1949, is 360 yen to the United States dollar or 0.277778 United States cents to the yen. On December 11, 1967, the demand buying rate for freely convertible Japanese yen in New York City was 362.19 yen to the United States dollar or 0.2761 United States cents to the yen.

Use of Forecasts in Prospectus.—A statement of the future prospects of the issuer is an important part of a prospectus prepared for use in the United Kingdom. This statement of future prospects is a responsibility of the directors of the company whose securities are offered by means of the prospectus. However, the underwriters normally request the accountants to review the future prospects and working capital position of the company and to report privately to them thereon. This represents an important difference between prospectuses prepared for use in the United Kingdom and those for use in the United States. With the exception of certain real estate companies organized to acquire and hold property primarily for investment, SEC does not permit the inclusion of anything resembling a forecast in prospectuses filed with it under the Securities Act. If such information material is intentionally or through oversight included in a registration statement as originally filed—except as indicated above—the SEC staff will insist that it be removed when the registration is amended.

Practice Under the 1933 Act as Reflected in Actual Cases.—The foregoing discussion has dealt with some of the problems faced by foreign issuers in attempting to comply with the SEC's requirements under the 1933 Act. The discussion has also been concerned with the problems faced by the Commission itself in attempting to adjust its requirements as they relate to foreign issuers in order to ease somewhat the difficulties faced by such issuers when they enter United States capital markets.

A study of representative actual cases in the eighteen year period, 1953–1970, offers the best evidence of the concessions which the SEC has made between its formal requirements on the one hand and, on the other hand, the information reasonably available to a particular foreign company. There were not many registration statements filed by foreign issuers during the 1966–1970 period mainly because the interest equalization tax on acquisitions of certain foreign securities by United States persons tended to dampen investor enthusiasm for such securities. As a consequence, some of the cases cited in the following analysis may seem dated. However, except for the AKU case, the author believes that these cases are representative of current SEC practice. The analysis which follows is limited, naturally, to the accounting and auditing aspects of the cases discussed, and does not include consideration of information of the kind which is normally presented in the narrative section of a prospectus.

THE AKU PROSPECTUS.—In a study of actual cases it seems appropriate to begin with the prospectus filed in 1953 by Algemene Kunstzijde Unie N. V. ("AKU"), a Netherlands corporation. The company's prospectus was interesting in a number of respects. It caused quite a stir in United

States accounting circles at the time and subjected the SEC to a considerable amount of adverse comment.

The prospectus contained numerous explanations in footnotes regarding the accounting principles followed by AKU and its subsidiaries, the most important ones being as follows:

1. Depreciation was based on replacement value rather than historical cost. Furthermore, depreciation was continued as long as the asset was continued in use. The summary of earnings showed separate amounts for depreciation based on cost and for the excess of replacement value over cost.

2. Inventories were at standard costs determined on the basis of estimated current replacement or reproduction costs (including general and administrative expenses, and depreciation based on replacement value).

3. With the exception of one subsidiary operated as a division of AKU, none of the subsidiaries was consolidated with the parent company. The prospectus included summaries of earnings of the principal subsidiaries and summaries of their balance sheets. (Complete financial statements were furnished for AKU and its consolidated subsidiary.)

4. Although there were significant differences in accounting for tax purposes and for financial accounting purposes, the company reflected as tax expense only the amount estimated to be payable and gave no recognition to deferred taxes and deferred credits for tax benefits.

5. All of the financial statements were presented in the currency of the respective countries in which the companies operated "because the expression of such statements in any other currency would not properly reflect the relative purchasing power of the various currencies involved and would not take into account the restrictions on the transfer of funds." Solely for the convenience of the American investor, however, a limited number of items (mainly net income) were translated from local currencies into Dutch florins and United States dollars.

For the foregoing reasons the company stated that the net income shown in the summary of earnings was not comparable with net income determined in accordance with generally accepted accounting principles in the United States.

On the other hand, a lengthy note disclosed the adjustments made to the company's previously reported figures in arriving at the amounts shown in the prospectus. Several items which the company had previously charged to earned surplus, for example, were retroactively adjusted by charging them to income or by capitalizing them and amortizing them through income. These modifications were made, it was stated, "in order to comply with American practices as to disclosure and classification which differ in some respects from those customarily followed in The Netherlands."

The financial statements made extensive disclosure of the accounting principles followed by the companies, and emphasized the fact that they deviated from accepted practice in the United States. There was no attempt, however, to estimate the effect of the deviation. It seems clear, therefore, that the financial presentation not only contravened the Commission's ASR No. 4 (see the discussion thereof beginning on page **2·6**), but, more importantly, it left the reader helpless to determine what the results might have been on a United States basis.

The prospectus contained the certificates of auditing firms in four different countries. A Dutch firm certified the consolidated statements, their opinion being based, in part, on examinations by United States, English, and German accountants with respect to the subsidiaries in their respective countries.

The United States auditors rendered a conventional report covering the American subsidiary of AKU.

The English auditors furnished a short-form report which contained a conventional scope paragraph, but, after having said "in accordance with generally accepted auditing standards," they added:

We did not make any independent physical verification of the inventory quantities, nor did we communicate with debtors asking for confirmation of the open balances shown in the books. Neither of these procedures is mandatory or customary in present day practice of independent accountants in Great Britain. We did however satisfy ourselves as to the substantial accuracy of the inventories and accounts receivable by other procedures which we considered adequate.

The English auditors did not say that they had followed "generally accepted auditing standards *except* . . ." as would have been done by a United States auditor. Instead they stated how their procedures differed from those in the United States.

The German auditors furnished a certificate the scope paragraph in which was similar to the English auditors' report. The opinion paragraph of the German report, however, ended with this clause:

. . . in conformity with German law (referred to in Notes A and G to the summarized balance sheets and in Note 5 to the summaries of earnings) and with generally accepted accounting principles applied on a consistent basis . . .

The Dutch accountants used a standard American scope paragraph and made no comment as to whether their procedures differed from those followed in the United States. Since their certificate was not in the form ordinarily used in The Netherlands, it may be assumed that their procedures with respect to inventories and receivables were comparable to those in the United States. The opinion paragraph was slightly different from a conventional one:

. . . in conformity with generally acceptable [Note that the word is not "accepted"] accounting principles in The Netherlands applied on a consistent basis . . .

One American writer noted that the Commission had permitted a registration statement to become effective which differed on two major points from what would apply in the case of a United States registrant:

. . . The Securities and Exchange Commission has permitted filing when the auditors had neither confirmed receivables nor observed inventories of important subsidiaries. Apparently the Commission is satisfied that the audit by the Netherlands accountants did include these procedures. Accounting principles substantially different from those to which we are accustomed have been permitted. The adequacy of the disclosure of the difference in principles was undoubtedly an important factor in permitting the prospectus to be issued on this basis. Nevertheless the Commission has permitted a material variation from our generally accepted principles. Is this to be interpreted as a recognition that cost-basis statements are less than adequate and a new era of current-value recognition is upon us? [10]

Another authority thought there were "weaknesses" in the SEC's decision in the AKU case. He said it was clear that the Commission had permitted the company to follow accounting procedures (particularly in accounting for fixed assets on a replacement cost basis) that would not be acceptable in a filing by an American company. He also stated that the Commission had permitted foreign accountants to omit procedures which, if omitted by American accountants, "would almost surely subject them to severe criticism." He continued:

We do not know the basis upon which the Commission concluded that it should allow the registration to become effective. However, we are inclined to believe that it may have been strongly influenced by the belief that every effort should be made to facilitate American investment abroad. Without in any way attempting to advocate either the pros or cons of the policy of facilitating such investments, we do question the propriety of accepting such deviations from American practice. . . . In the first place, it seems to us that the practices as followed by the corporation and by its foreign accountants could easily be misleading since they clearly violate those "ground rules" which, it seems to us, American investors have the right to assume have been followed in preparing the financial statements and in auditing them. Furthermore, although it is fairly easy to bring action against an American auditor if events show that he has not done a proper job, it would be almost impossible for an investor, if he believed he had been injured by relying upon the report of foreign accountants, to secure redress. Accordingly, as a minimum, it seems to us that, in the case of foreign securities being offered for sale in the United States, the SEC should require the company to prepare its statements in accordance with accounting principles generally accepted in the United States, and that it should require

---

[10] John H. Myers, quoted in "Accounting and Auditing Problems," *The Journal of Accountancy*, April 1954, p. 484.

the audits of those financial statements to be performed by United States accounting firms in accordance with auditing standards generally accepted here.[11]

THE KLM PROSPECTUS.—The adverse comment in the AKU case apparently had an effect both on the SEC and on foreign registrants, and caused them to re-examine their disclosure policies. The result of this re-examination was reflected in a registration statement of KLM Royal Dutch Airlines which became effective in May, 1957. This company—like AKU —was domiciled in The Netherlands, and the certifying accountants were the same in both cases.

KLM presented its financial statements (including the summary of earnings) in two currencies: (1) in Netherlands guilders, and (2) translated into United States dollars. Most important of all, however, was the manner in which the company reconciled its customary reporting practices as a Dutch company with accounting principles generally accepted in the United States.

In the area of depreciation accounting, KLM's policies differed significantly from what is generally accepted in the United States. Aircraft and engines were being depreciated over a five-year period on a straight-line basis to a residual value of 10 per cent. During each of the three years following such five-year period, the company charged income with an additional amount of 7.5 per cent of the cost of aircraft and engines (an aggregate of 22.5 per cent) and credited such extra depreciation to a surplus reserve entitled "extra depreciation reserve." In addition, gains on the sale of aircraft to be replaced were included in income and were offset by charges for "extra depreciation" and applicable tax. The total provision for "extra depreciation" (comprised of the aforementioned annual charge of 7.5 per cent and the gain after applicable tax on the sale of aircraft) was made because of the company's calculations that the replacement cost of aircraft would require increased amounts to maintain the same productive capacity in terms of available ton miles. (Extra depreciation was not deductible for tax purposes in The Netherlands.)

In the summary of earnings in U. S. dollars, depreciation was first shown on the basis of original cost under "operating expenses." Near the bottom of the statement, just before the provision for income taxes, was a special deduction for "extra depreciation on aircraft and engines." At the bottom of the statement, following "net earnings" and the per share amounts of earnings and dividends, a special section was appended as follows:

[11] Carman G. Blough, "Accounting and Auditing Problems," *The Journal of Accountancy,* April, 1954, p. 484. Mr. Blough was the first Chief Accountant of the SEC.

Additional statement for United States prospectus:

Net earnings adjusted to reflect depreciation of aircraft and engines on the basis of historical cost in accordance with generally accepted accounting principles in the United States (i.e., adding back "extra depreciation" shown above) would have been . . .

And net earnings per share of common stock would have been . . .

Footnotes to the summary and the financial statements explained the procedure which had been followed in the summary and in the formal financial statements.

The formal financial statements appeared later in KLM's prospectus. These included a consolidated balance sheet and a consolidated statement of reserves and surplus in both guilders and dollars, and a consolidated summary of earnings in guilders only (the summary in U. S. dollars being in the forepart of the prospectus). In the balance sheets and statements of reserves there was no adding back of the extra depreciation as had been done in the U. S. summary of earnings, presumably in recognition of the paramount importance of the operating statement and the unimportance of the matter in relation to the balance sheet. The company also stated that the adjustment to reflect depreciation on the basis of historical cost in accordance with U. S. accounting principles "has not been included in the company's published annual reports."

To clarify further just what was done in the KLM prospectus, the auditor's report, after stating that the financial statements had been prepared "in conformity with generally accepted accounting principles in The Netherlands applied on a consistent basis," included the following explanatory paragraph:

> While there are certain differences between the accounting principles followed by the company and those generally accepted in the United States of America, application of the latter, in our opinion, would not have materially affected the determination of net earnings except that "extra depreciation" on aircraft and engines would not have been deducted, as indicated in the Consolidated Summary of Earnings (in U. S. dollars). Limitation of the depreciation on aircraft and engines to the basis of historical cost in accordance with generally accepted accounting principles in the United States would have required the adjustment shown under "Additional Statement for United States Prospectus" in the Consolidated Summary of Earnings (in U. S. dollars).

The same authority who had been highly critical of the AKU prospectus, wrote that the KLM prospectus represented "quite a satisfactory solution to a difficult problem." He continued:

> . . . A company cannot ignore the accounting principles that are generally accepted in its own country and should be observed in the financial statements presented to its stockholders there, yet prospective investors (and subsequently, any security holders) in this country are entitled to know what the results

would be under our own rules. We think this has been accomplished here in a reasonable manner and we compliment those who were responsible for it.[12]

This KLM prospectus seemed to present a sensible solution to the problem of reconciling a foreign company's "official" financial statements with the needs of United States investors. Several years later—in 1962—it served as the basic pattern for the filing by another Dutch corporation, N. V. Philips Gloeilampenfabrieken.

In 1969 KLM filed another registration statement in connection with an offering of common shares. As before, KLM presented its financial statements (including the earnings summary) in two currencies: (1) in Dutch guilders, and (2) translated into United States dollars. While there were still certain differences between the accounting principles followed by KLM and those generally accepted in the United States, only one was apparently material enough to require the company to revise its customary reporting practices in the 1969 prospectus. This difference dealt with the distribution of certain profits to directors, members of management and employees as provided in the company's Articles of Association. A note to the summary of earnings appearing in the prospectus disclosed:

In calculating the net earnings of the Company shown herein for the fiscal years ended March 31, 1968 and 1969 $281,000 and $403,000, respectively, representing distributions to directors, management and personnel have been deducted. . . . The Company in its Annual Report to shareholders does not deduct such distributions in computing net income.

With this adjustment to the summary of earnings, KLM's auditors were apparently able to include the following explanatory paragraph in their report after stating that the financial statements were prepared in conformity with generally accepted accounting principles in The Netherlands:

While there are certain differences between the accounting principles followed by the Company and those generally accepted in the United States of America, application of the latter, in our opinion, would not have materially affected the determination of net earnings.

The 1969 KLM prospectus appears to present a reasonable solution to dealing with the effects of differences in accounting principles when the differences are few in number and their effects are determinable.

THE PHILIPS N. V. PROSPECTUS.—In 1962 a registration statement was filed by N. V. Gemeenschappelijk Bezit van Aandeelen Philips' Gloeilampenfabrieken (Philips N. V.), a Netherlands corporation which is the parent of Philips Lamp Works. Philips Lamp is an international manufacturing complex with headquarters in The Netherlands. The registration state-

---

[12] Carman G. Blough, "Accounting and Auditing Problems," *The Journal of Accountancy*, August, 1958, pp. 77–78.

ment was filed in connection with a rights offering to shareholders, including United States shareholders. The registration statement became effective late in May, 1962.

Philips presented its earnings summary in two currencies—in Netherlands guilders and translated into USA dollars. The summary was preceded by a headnote which stated that it had been prepared on the basis of the accounting principles customarily followed by the company and generally accepted in The Netherlands. These principles, the headnote continued, differed in a number of respects from those generally accepted in the United States, but the only differences which would have materially affected the determination of net income were those described in Note 1 following the summary.

Note 1 to the summary was a brief description of the principal areas of difference between the accounting principles employed by the company and those generally accepted in the United States:

1. Philips provided for depreciation of fixed assets on the basis of their replacement value.
2. With respect to fully depreciated fixed assets, if they were still in use, Philips continued to provide 50% of normal depreciation based on replacement value of the assets.
3. Inventories were stated on the basis of their replacement value and these amounts were used in determining cost of goods sold.
4. Gain on resale of shares of the parent company was included in income.
5. Profit-sharing bonuses to management and employees were shown as a deduction *after* net income.

The earnings summary arrived at net income on the basis of the accounting principles customarily employed by the Philips companies. From this amount was deducted the profit-sharing bonuses (Item 5 above) and the dividends on preferred stock, leaving a "balance of net income." To this balance an amount was added representing an "estimated adjustment to state the aforementioned balance of net income on basis of accounting principles generally accepted in the United States." The adjusted balance of net income approximated the balance of net income available for common stock on the basis of United States accounting principles, and these amounts (not the Dutch amounts) were also stated on a per share basis. A note to the summary explained the adjustment as follows:

Philips has attempted to estimate what adjustment, in addition to the deduction for profit sharing, would have been required if Philips had employed accounting principles generally accepted in the United States in lieu of the principles set forth above, that is, computing depreciation on the basis of historical cost, computing inventories on a cost basis, eliminating depreciation on fully depreciated assets, and eliminating the gain on sale of shares of the parent company. In the opinion of Philips, this would have required the estimated adjustments shown in the summary. There are other respects in which the accounting principles followed by Philips differ from those generally accepted in the United States, but they would not have materially affected net income.

Philips is known to be an outstanding exponent of replacement value accounting, which, however, is not generally accepted in the United States at the time of this writing. It is apparent that replacement value accounting is such an integral part of the company's accounting that restatement on a USA basis would have been an impossible task and contrary to the company's economic philosophy. Rather than restate its accounts, the company estimated the effect on its net income of the deviation from United States practice and adjusted its reported net income accordingly. The balance sheet was not adjusted; it was furnished in two currencies (Dutch and USA) on the basis of the company's customary practice.

THE COPENHAGEN TELEPHONE COMPANY PROSPECTUS.—In 1962 a registration statement filed by a foreign company furnished an interesting example of how difficult accounting problems were dealt with by the SEC to the apparent satisfaction of all concerned—that is, the company, the underwriters, the certifying accountants, and the staff of the Commission. The registrant in this case was Copenhagen Telephone Company, Inc., a company which furnishes telephone service on the Danish island of Zealand, on which Copenhagen is located, and some other islands. The registration statement covered an issue of sinking fund dollar debentures to be offered to United States investors through a group of American underwriters.

The company is a public utility operating under a concession from the Danish government. The government owned and voted 50.65 per cent of the outstanding capital stock of the company and had the right to purchase at least one-half of any capital stock which might be issued by the company. The majority of the members of the Board of Directors of the company was appointed by, and the nomination by the Board of the senior Managing Director was subject to the approval of, the government, which also supervised important activities of the company. This supervisory power was exercised principally through the Ministry of Public Works and the Public Telephone Service Supervisory Commission acting on behalf of the Ministry. The Minister of Public Works, among other things, participated in the determination of rates for telephone service and his approval was required before the company could alter the accounting regulations prescribed for the company.

In keeping with what had become a trend, the company's summary of earnings was presented in two currencies—in Danish kroner, and translated into United States dollars. The headnote to the summary called attention to a note in the financial statements regarding differences between the accounting principles employed by the company and those generally accepted in the United States. The latter note was captioned "General," and listed briefly the major areas of difference which were described in more detail in other notes to the financial statements. For example:

1. Danish tax laws contain provision for accelerated depreciation. Pursuant to this law, it is within the discretion of each company to decide the rate (with certain limitations) at which undepreciated assets are written off for tax purposes. The Company has accordingly been deducting depreciation in such amounts as to eliminate all taxable income. The Company does not provide for deferred income taxes. The Company states that, due to its construction program, "there is no likelihood that it will be necessary to pay income taxes in the foreseeable future." Further, in view of the Company's relations with the Danish Government—and especially in matters affecting rates for service—the Company believes that "flow through" accounting which it employs is appropriate in the circumstances.
2. There are other major differences between the Company's accounting for purposes of financial reporting and for tax purposes, no adjustment being made for the tax effect of the differences.
3. Subscribers' contributions to construction have been credited, in part, to property accounts and, in part, to the liability to the pension fund.
4. Depreciation is provided on property before it is placed in service.
5. A reserve fund had been set up out of earnings in prior years to meet part of capital expenditure requirements. Transfers from the fund were made in round amounts to write down the telephone plant account.
6. Debt discount is included in property accounts and written off 4% a year.
7. Debt expense is written off to income as incurred.
8. Sales of property have, in the aggregate, resulted in profits, and these accumulated gains are included in the equity section of the balance sheet.
9. The Company capitalizes interest during construction of buildings but not of other property.

There were other areas of difference, but those listed above were said to be the principal ones.

The financial statements in the company's prospectus were based upon the previously published financial statements of the company with certain revisions *in form* to achieve a presentation more customary in the United States. While certain reclassifications had been made, and in certain cases more details and explanations given, *there was no adjustment of the figures to reflect the application of accounting principles generally accepted in the United States*. The company stated:

. . . It is impossible, without unreasonable effort and expense, to state what the Company's net income would have been if the Company had followed principles of accounting generally accepted in the United States in lieu of those actually employed.

Moreover, the Company's rates for service have always been set at a level which enabled the Company to cover its costs and, in addition, to pay a fixed dividend which can exceed 7% of par value only with the approval of the govern-ment. The government has authorized the Company to pay a dividend of 8% for 1961, 1962 and 1963. In setting rates, the Company and the Board of Subscribers' Representatives have been governed by the financial state-ments customarily prepared by the Company from accounts maintained in accordance with regulations prescribed by the Minister of Public Works. The rates are appropriate to the costs and expenses shown by the prescribed ac-counting. Accordingly, the Company believes there is a proper matching of costs and revenues.

It is fundamental that the SEC does not approve or disapprove secu-rities registered with it, nor does the Commission pass upon the accuracy or adequacy of prospectuses. Without any doubt, however, the Commission and its staff must have given careful consideration to Copenhagen Tele-phone's financial statements contained in the registration statement. That the Commission in this case did not require restatement or adjustment of the company's statements to approximately a United States basis is a tribute to the Commission and its staff. It is obvious that what was appro-priate in the KLM and Philips cases was not appropriate in the Copen-hagen Telephone case. To put the company's financial statements on a USA-acceptable basis would have resulted in a meaningless conglomeration of figures having no relationship to reality. In the opinion of the author, the SEC is to be commended for not requiring the company to restate or adjust its statements and accepting in lieu thereof an explanation of the circumstances.

In 1967, the Company filed a registration statement on Form 20 for the registration under the 1934 Act of another issue of sinking fund dollar debentures. Although this issue of debentures was not being offered or sold in the United States, the company wanted to list them on a national secu-rities exchange and therefore needed to submit a registration statement both to the SEC and to the stock exchange. The financial statement treat-ment reflected in this 1967 filing was, for all practical purposes, identical to that included in the 1962 registration statement.

THE TOKIO MARINE PROSPECTUS.—In contrast to the Copenhagen Tele-phone Company case was the prospectus of the Tokio Marine and Fire In-surance Company, Limited. The company filed a registration statement in 1971 in connection with a subscription offer to holders of American De-positary Shares. The accounting and financial reporting practices of Tokio Marine are regulated by Japanese law and the reporting requirements of the Japanese Ministry of Finance.

The Japanese practices differ in a number of respects from those of American insurance companies. A note to the financial statements explained the nature of the differing practices and how they were dealt with in the prospectus:

The basic financial data and statements of Tokio Marine are presented herein to reflect the financial position and operating results on a basis comparable to American insurance companies in conformity with the Convention Annual Statement Form of the National Association of Insurance Commissioners and the requirements of Regulation S–X issued by the Securities and Exchange Commission. Japanese accounting and financial reporting practices differ from those of American insurance companies primarily as to the computation and treatment of unearned premiums, loss reserves, severance and retirement reserves, admitted assets and special reserves.

In a note to the financial statements, the company presented a reconciliation of net income and earned surplus after appropriations as reported by the company in reports to its shareholders with net income and realized gains on investments and earned surplus as reported in the prospectus. For each of the five years presented in the reconciliation, net income previously reported to shareholders was significantly increased to arrive at net income and realized gains on investments as reported in the prospectus. For example, in fiscal 1971 the net income reported to shareholders was $25,-000,000 and the net income and realized gains on investments as shown in the prospectus was $53,000,000. The principal reasons for the increase in each of the years were the net adjustments arising from computing unearned premiums, severance and retirement reserves, and loss reserves in conformity with practices used by American insurance companies. In addition, there were nine to twelve other adjustments to originally reported earnings in each of the years presented. Earned surplus after appropriations, as of March 31, 1971, was also significantly increased from the amount shown in statements to shareholders; the net increase amounted to approximately $136,000,000.

To complicate matters further, the Tokio Marine prospectus also included supplementary statements of adjusted earnings and capital stock equity. The purpose of these supplementary statements was to reconcile the net earnings and capital stock equity data prepared in conformity with accounting principles and practices followed by insurance companies with similar data prepared in conformity with generally accepted accounting principles. Such reconciliations are required in filings with the SEC where the effect of differences between generally accepted accounting principles and insurance accounting principles is material. (Regulation S–X, Rule 7–05).

The auditors for Tokio Marine furnished a report containing a conventional scope paragraph but the remainder of the report was somewhat different from a conventional one:

The financial statements have been prepared in conformity with accounting principles followed by insurance companies using the Convention Annual Statement Form of the National Association of Insurance Commissioners of the United States of America. These principles vary in some respects from generally accepted accounting principles. The differences are explained in Note 1 and the effects thereof are summarized in the supplemental statements of capital stock equity and adjusted earnings.

In our opinion, such financial statements present fairly the financial position of The Tokio Marine and Fire Insurance Company, Limited at March 31, 1971 and the related income and changes in surplus for the periods indicated in conformity with the insurance accounting principles set forth above applied on a consistent basis. Also, in our opinion, the supplemental statements of capital stock equity and adjusted earnings present fairly the capital stock equity and adjusted net income excluding realized gains and losses on investments, for the periods indicated in conformity with generally accepted accounting principles consistently applied, and the statement of changes in financial position and the summary of investments in securities other than securities of affiliates present fairly the information set forth therein.

THE PLESSEY PROSPECTUS.—In 1971 The Plessey Company Limited filed a registration statement under the 1933 Act covering American Depositary Receipts. Plessey's summary of earnings and other financial statements included in the prospectus were presented in pounds sterling and United States dollars. The reporting chartered accountants used a standard American short form report and stated that the financial statements were "in conformity with generally accepted accounting principles applied on a consistent basis." A note to the financial statements read, in part, as follows:

The property and equipment of the Company outside the United Kingdom is carried at cost. The property and equipment located in the United Kingdom was revalued as at June 30, 1964, on the following bases:

Freehold and Leasehold Property:
    Land—as valued by professional valuers
    Buildings—at cost of replacing existing buildings with similar facilities as at June 30, 1964, in accordance with valuations established by professional valuers
    Equipment—As calculated by officials of the Company giving due regard to original cost and price indices since the dates of acquisition up to June 30, 1964

As at June 30, 1964, the Company's related reserves for accumulated depreciation were also revalued as follows:

    Buildings—The accumulated depreciation at June 30, 1964, was valued at the amount required to reduce replacement cost to going-concern value as determined by valuation of professional valuers, with depreciation subsequent to June 30, 1964, to be based on 1964 replacement cost
    Equipment—Depreciation based on 1964 replacement cost

The revaluations resulted in a net increase of property and equipment of £8,588,000 ($20,611,000) which was credited, in accordance with accounting principles in the United Kingdom, to intangible assets arising from acquisitions. A portion of the net increase, £2,257,000 ($5,417,000) represented the allocations of excess costs incurred in certain acquisitions. . . .

The Company's consolidated assets at June 30, 1970 were $596,000,000 of which $136,000,000 was represented by fixed assets less depreciation. Depreciation is a significant factor in the company's results of operations.

Another note to the financial statements described the composition of a balance sheet account entitled "Intangible Assets Arising from Acquisitions" as follows:

The balance in this account as of June 30, 1970 represents the excess of the cost of the Company's investment in subsidiaries over their net assets reduced, in accordance with accounting practice in the United Kingdom, by the following credits, which would require different treatment (indicated parenthetically) to conform with generally accepted accounting principles in the United States:

	£'000	$'000
Surplus arising from revaluation of property, as explained in Note 4, not relating to any excess cost of investment in subsidiaries over book amounts at date of acquisition (surplus arising from revaluation)	6,325	15,180
Revaluation of inventories as of June 30, 1964, not relating to any excess cost of investment in subsidiaries over book amounts at date of acquisition (extraordinary credit)	512	1,229
Unrealized gain from devaluation of pound sterling in November 1967 (extraordinary credit)	1,816	4,358
Proportion attributable to the Company's interest in Plessey Incorporated of that subsidiary's increase in paid-in surplus in the year ended June 30, 1969, set off against proportion of the excess cost of investment of Plessey Incorporated in a subsidiary over book amounts of assets acquired (paid-in surplus)	876	2,102
	9,529	22,869

At June 30, 1970, Plessey's stockholders' equity aggregated $323,000,000. Net income for the year ended June 30, 1968 approximated $22,000,000; the prospectus did not include a statement of income for the year ended June 30, 1964.

This presentation and the report of the chartered accountants is an interesting contrast to what was reflected in the 1969 KLM prospectus which is discussed beginning on page 31·30. Plessey was apparently permitted to use its customary reporting practices and simply to disclose in notes to the financial statements differences between the accounting principles it followed and those generally accepted in the United States.

Registration Under 1934 Act of Foreign Securities Traded Over-the-Counter.—As discussed on page 1·6 the Securities Acts Amendments of 1964 extended to investors in the securities of many publicly held companies traded over-the-counter, the same protection which the 1934 Act previously provided only to investors in companies whose securities were listed on a national securities exchange. Section 12(g) which was added to the 1934 Act by the 1964 Amendments requires an issuer of securities traded in the over-the-counter market to register the securities if the issuer meets certain jurisdictional, asset, and stockholder tests. After registration, the issuer becomes subject to the periodic reporting, proxy rules and insider reporting and trading requirements of the 1934 Act.

The SEC recognized the difficulties that would be encountered in attempting to apply these requirements to foreign issuers. Accordingly, when it submitted the proposed Securities Acts Amendments to Congress, the SEC recommended that foreign securities traded over-the-counter be exempt from the proposed registration requirements with the understanding that the SEC could terminate the exemption if it found that a substantial public market existed for the securities of a particular issuer and that continued exemption was not in the public interest or consistent with the protection of investors.

However, in enacting the 1964 Amendments, Congress eliminated the general exemption and required that foreign securities be subject to registration in the same way as domestic securities, although the SEC could exempt foreign securities when this was in the public interest and consistent with the protection of investors. For over two years, the SEC temporarily exempted foreign securities from the registration requirements of the 1934 Act while it studied how it might best apply such requirements and elicited comments from individuals, companies and representatives of foreign governments who would either be affected by or be interested in the extent to which definitive exemptions would be granted. Following this period of study the SEC, in April, 1967, adopted definitive rules setting forth the extent to which foreign issuers would be exempt from the requirements of the 1934 Act (Release No. 34–8066, April 28, 1967). In substance, any foreign issuer, including North American and Cuban companies, which has not sought a public market in the United States for its securities through a public offering or stock exchange listing and has more than 300 shareholders resident in the United States is exempt from the registration, reporting, proxy, and insider trading requirements of the 1934 Act providing it furnishes to the SEC the information it makes public abroad pursuant to law or foreign stock exchange requirements or which it sends to its security holders. A discussion of the type of information to be furnished and the manner in which it is to be furnished appears on page **31·45**. Foreign issuers which have fewer than 300 shareholders resident in the United States are exempt from the requirements.

Certain exemptions were also made available to other categories of securities and foreign companies:

1. American Depositary Receipts (ADRs) for the securities of any foreign company are exempt from Sections 12(g) of the 1934 Act.
2. Foreign companies—including North American and Cuban companies—that are required to file reports because they have made a public offering of securities in the United States are exempt from registration under Section 12(g) of the 1934 Act. This exemption ceases if the reporting obligation is suspended. The annual and interim reports to be filed by companies in this category, except North American and Cuban companies, are discussed beginning on page **31·43**. North American and Cuban companies use annual report Form 10–K and interim report Forms 8–K and 10–Q. These forms are discussed in chapters **14** and **15**.
3. Foreign companies, except North American and Cuban companies, which have registered securities for listing on a United States stock exchange are exempt from registration under Section 12(g) of the Act for the duration of their registration of any class of securities on a national securities exchange pursuant to Section 12(b). Such companies must, however, file the annual and interim reports which are discussed beginning on page **31·43**. North American and Cuban companies in this category are required to register any additional class of equity securities under Section 12(g) if the jurisdictional tests of that section are met and the additional class is held by 300 or more United States residents. They are also required to register the class of equity securities now listed should the present listing be terminated and the criteria for 12(g) registration are met. Registration in either case will be on Form 8–A, the simplified form available for use by certain reporting companies. These companies will be required to file annual reports on Form 10–K and interim reports on Forms 8–K and 10–Q, the requirements to which these companies are now subject.

Except for the exemption arising because a company's equity securities are held by fewer than 300 persons in the United States, none of the exemptions mentioned above is available to companies which are considered to be essentially United States companies. Any company which has more than 50% of its voting securities held by United States residents and its business is principally administered in the United States or 50% of the members of its board of directors are United States residents is considered to be essentially a United States company. These companies are also subject to the proxy rules and insider reporting and trading regulations of the 1934 Act.

Registration and Listing of Foreign Issuers.—Foreign issuers desiring to register and list their securities for trading on a United States securities exchange would file a registration statement on the appropriate form together with a listing application required by the exchange. The forms promulgated by the SEC for this purpose and the conditions under which they are used are set forth below. Foreign private issuers that are required to register under Section 12(g) of the 1934 Act would use Form 20.

Form 18. This form is used to register securities of foreign governments and political subdivisions thereof.

Form 19. This form is used to register American certificates (for example, so-called American depositary receipts for foreign shares or American participation certificates in foreign bonds or notes) issued against securities of foreign issuers deposited with an American depositary (whether physically held by such depositary in America or abroad) and of the foreign securities so deposited. A registration on this form consists of two parts: Part I for the registration of American certificates; and Part II for the registration of securities of foreign issuers deposited pursuant to the deposit agreement. Part I, which requires information concerning the depositor, the depositary, and the deposit agreement, is to be signed by the depositor or depositors. Part II need be filed only if the securities deposited pursuant to the deposit agreement are not otherwise registered on the exchange on which the registration of the American certificates is sought. It requires information concerning the issuer of the securities so deposited and is to be signed by such issuer.

Form 20. This form is used to register pursuant to Sections 12(b) or 12(g) of the 1934 Act all securities, including bonds, of foreign private issuers other than certain North American and Cuban issuers.

Prior to 1967, foreign private issuers used Form 21 to register their debt securities and Form 20 to register all other types of securities. In 1967, Form 20 was revised and, as part of the revision, became the form used to register all securities of foreign private issuers other than certain North American and Cuban issuers. Form 21 was repealed but issuers who had securities registered on that form were not required to re-register. References to Form 21 may still be found in some SEC regulations even though the form itself is no longer used.

Financial Statements in Form 20.—Foreign private issuers must file as part of Form 20 the financial statements, schedules and accountant's reports which would be required if the registration statement were filed on Form 10. (See Chapter **15**.) Any material variation in accounting principles or practices from the form and content of financial statements prescribed in Regulation S–X must be disclosed and, to the extent practicable, the effect of each such variation given. Upon request of the registrant and where consistent with the protection of investors, the SEC may permit:

1. The omission of one or more of the financial statements required to be filed or the substitution therefor of appropriate statements of comparable character, or
2. *The omission of one or more generally accepted auditing standards or procedures or the substitution of other appropriate auditing standards or procedures.*

The SEC may also require the filing of other financial statements in addition to, or in substitution for, the required statements in any case where such statements are necessary or appropriate for an adequate presentation of the financial condition of any person whose financial statements are required or whose statements are otherwise necessary for the protection of investors.

Under Rule 12b–12(d) of the 1934 Act, Form 20 must be prepared in the English language and any exhibit or other paper or document filed with it which is in a foreign language must be accompanied by a translation into the English language.

Annual Reports to SEC by Foreign Private Issuers (Form 20–K). —Annual reports of all foreign private issuers of securities which have been registered under section 12 of the 1934 Act or under the 1933 Act are filed on Form 20–K. (This form is not used by certain North American and Cuban issuers.) The reports must be filed within six months after the end of the fiscal year covered by such report. The financial statements, schedules and accountant's report that are to be filed as part of the annual report on Form 20–K are the same as those that would be required if the report were filed on Form 10–K. (See the discussion of these requirements beginning on page **15·12**.) Any material variation in accounting principles or practices from the form and content of financial statements prescribed in Regulation S–X must be disclosed and, to the extent practicable, the effect of each such variation given.

Upon request of the foreign issuer and where consistent with the protection of investors, the SEC may permit:

1. The omission of one or more of the financial statements required to be filed or the substitution therefor of appropriate statements of comparable character, or
2. *The omission of one or more generally accepted auditing standards or procedures or the substitution therefor of other appropriate auditing standards or procedures.*

The SEC may also require the filing of other financial statements in addition to, or in substitution for, the required statements in any case where such statements are necessary or appropriate for adequate presentation of the financial condition of any person whose financial statements are required or whose statements are otherwise necessary for the protection of investors.

Under Rule 12b–12(d), Form 20–K must be prepared in the English language and any exhibit or other paper or document filed with it which is in a foreign language must be accompanied by a translation into the English language.

Current Reports and Quarterly Reports of Foreign Issuers (Form 6–K).—Until 1967, the great majority of foreign private issuers were not required to file current reports such as on Form 8–K. However, since 1967, foreign private issuers which have any class of securities registered under Section 12 of the 1934 Act or under the 1933 Act have been required to file current reports on Form 6–K. The report is not applicable to certain investment companies, certain North American or Cuban issuers, or issuers of American depositary receipts for securities of any foreign issuer.

In Form 6–K, foreign private issuers will furnish whatever information such issuers:

1. are required to make public in the country of their domicile or in which they are incorporated or organized pursuant to the law of that country, or
2. filed with a foreign stock exchange on which their securities are traded and which was made public by that exchange, or
3. distributed to their security holders.

The information that must be furnished is that which is significant with respect to the issuer and its subsidiaries concerning:

- financial condition or results of operations
- changes in business
- acquisitions or dispositions of assets
- changes in management or control
- granting of options or payment of other remuneration to directors or officers
- transactions with directors, officers or principal stockholders
- any other information which may be of material interest to investors

Form 6–K is to be filed promptly after the material contained in the report is made public as described in 1, 2 or 3 above. If the material contained in the report is not in the English language, it need not be accompanied by a translation into English. However, if an English translation of such material exists, it should be furnished and it need not be accompanied by the original foreign language version.

The information and documents included in Form 6–K are not deemed to be "filed" for the purpose of Section 18 of the 1934 Act or otherwise subject to the liabilities of that section.

Chapter **14** discusses the quarterly reports (Form 10–Q) which must be filed by issuers having securities registered under Section 12 of the 1934 Act or under the 1933 Act. Under Rule 13a–13 of the 1934 Act, Form 10–Q *does not have to be filed* by foreign private issuers who file reports on Form 6–K.

All Amendments on Form 8.—As in the case of domestic issuers, all amendments to registration statements and reports of foreign issuers under the 1934 Act are filed on a form designated Form 8. This form and the manner in which it is used are discussed in Chapter **15**.

Reporting by Foreign Issuers Exempt from Registration Under 1934 Act.—As discussed earlier in this chapter, certain foreign issuers who would otherwise be subject to the registration provisions of Section 12(g) of the 1934 Act can be exempted from such registration and from the annual and interim reporting requirements of the Act by furnishing the SEC with the information they make public abroad or send to their security holders. There is no special form to be used in transmitting the information to the SEC, and the issuer need not furnish an English translation of it. If, however, an English translation has been prepared by the issuer, it should be furnished, but in that case it need not be accompanied by the original foreign language version. The information should be sent to the SEC promptly after it is made public or given to security holders.

The SEC is aware that in some countries issuers are required to file many documents with government agencies which are available for public inspection. Technically, these documents would be required to be furnished under the "made public" criterion. However, the SEC is interested in receiving only information of material interest to investors and about which investors should be informed with respect to the issuer and its subsidiaries concerning:

- financial condition or results of operations
- changes in business
- acquisitions or dispositions of assets
- issuance, redemption or acquisitions of their securities
- changes in management or control
- granting of options or payment of other remuneration to directors or officers
- transactions with directors, officers or principal stockholders
- any other information about which investors ought reasonably to be informed.

Information reported to the SEC under this requirement will not be deemed to be "filed" with the Commission or otherwise subject to the liabilities of Section 18 of the 1934 Act. From time to time the SEC will issue lists of those foreign issuers which have submitted information under this requirement to alert brokers, dealers and investors that some form of information concerning foreign issuers on the list is available in the SEC's public files.

Insider Trading Rules and Foreign Issuers.—In Chapter **14** is a discussion of the reports which must be filed by officers and directors of listed companies and by persons owning more than 10 per cent of any class of any equity security listed on a national securities exchange. The reports must also be filed by officers, directors, and principal holders in respect of securities of companies traded over-the-counter which are registered under Section 12(g) of the 1934 Act. These reports are filed pursuant to Section 16(a) of the 1934 Act. As indicated on page **1·7** "short swing" profits realized by such officers, directors, and principal holders insure to, and are recoverable by, the company; this provision is in Section 16(b) of the 1934 Act.

An SEC rule exempts many foreign issuers from the provisions of Section 16. The exemption is in Rule 3a12–3 the applicable portion of which reads as follows:

(a) Securities for which the filing of registration statements on [Form] 18 [is] authorized shall be exempt from the operation of Sections . . . 16 of the Act.

(b) Securities for which the filing of registration statements on Form 20 is authorized shall be exempt from the operation of Sections . . . 16 of the Act except that this paragraph shall not apply if at the end of the last fiscal year of the issuer (i) more than 50 per cent of the outstanding voting securities of the issuer are held of record either directly or through voting trust certificates or depositary receipts by residents of the United States, and (ii) the business of such issuer is administered principally in the United States or 50 per cent or more of the members of the Board of Directors are residents of the United States. For the purpose of this paragraph, the term "resident," as applied to security holders, shall mean any person whose address appears on the records of the issuer, the voting trustee or the depositary as being located in the United States.

(c) Securities for which the filing of registration statements on Form . . . 19 is authorized shall be exempt from the operation of Sections . . . 16 of the Act if the securities deposited pursuant to the voting trust or other agreement are so exempt pursuant to paragraph (b) above.

The issuers to which Forms 18, 19, and 20 are applicable are discussed previously in this chapter. North American and Cuban companies which are exempt from the registration requirements of the 1934 Act under Rule 12g3–2 are also exempt from the provisions of Section 16.

Proxy Requirements and Foreign Issuers.—In Chapter **22** the requirements relating to solicitation of proxies are discussed, including the requirements of the SEC, the New York Stock Exchange, and the American Stock Exchange. Under SEC Rule 3a12–3 many foreign issuers are exempt from the Commission's proxy regulation. The applicable portion of Rule 3a12–3 follows:

(a) Securities for which the filing of registration statements on [Form] 18 [is] authorized shall be exempt from the operations of Sections 14 . . . of the Act.

(b) Securities for which the filing of registration statements on Form 20 is authorized shall be exempt from the operation of Section 14 . . . of the Act except that this paragraph shall not apply if at the end of the last fiscal year of the issuer (i) more than 50% of the outstanding voting securities of the issuer are held of record either directly or through voting trust certificates or depositary receipts by residents of the United States, and (ii) the business of such issuer is administered principally in the United States or 50% or more of the members of the Board of Directors are residents of the United States. For the purpose of this paragraph, the term "resident," as applied to security holders, shall mean any person whose address appears on the records of the issuer, the voting trustee or the depositary as being located in the United States.

(c) Securities for which the filing of registration statements on Form . . . 19 is authorized shall be exempt from the operation of Sections 14 . . . of the Act if the securities deposited pursuant to the voting trust or other agreement are so exempt pursuant to paragraph (b) above.

Section 14 (referred to in the foregoing rule) is the section of the 1934 Act that deals with proxies and proxy solicitations. The issuers to which Forms 18, 19, and 20 are applicable are discussed previously in this chapter.

North American and Cuban companies which are exempt from the registration requirements of the 1934 Act under Rule 12g3–2 are also exempt from the provisions of Section 14.

While the New York and American exchanges in general require listed corporations to agree to solicit proxies as a condition to listing securities on such exchanges (see Chapter **29**), this provision is ordinarily waived in the case of foreign issuers other than Canadian, although both exchanges require a listed foreign company to arrange for proxy voting by its American shareholders.

APPENDIXES

A. List of SEC Accounting Series Releases

B. Typical timetable in 1933 Act registration engagement

C. Exhibit 5 to 1971 registration statement of American Telephone and Telegraph Company showing the computation of the pro forma ratio of earnings to fixed charges

APPENDIX A. LIST OF SEC ACCOUNTING SERIES RELEASES

A·1

RELEASE
No.

92 Findings and opinion of the Commission in Rule 2(e) proceedings involving an accountant

93 Amendment of Regulation S–X by addition of Article 6C relating to employee stock purchase, savings, and similar plans

94 Commission order discontinuing Rule 2(e) proceedings against an accountant

95 Accounting for real estate transactions (including sales and leasebacks) where circumstances indicate that profits were not earned at the time the transactions were recorded

1963

96 Accounting for the "Investment Credit" provided in the Revenue Act of 1962

97 Findings and opinion of the Commission in Rule 2(e) proceedings involving an accountant

98 Maintenance of records of transactions by brokers and dealers acting as underwriters of shares of investment companies

1964

99 Rule 2(e) proceedings involving accountants dismissed due to lack of quorum of commissioners qualified to act in matter

100 Amendment of Regulation S–X by addition of Article 7A relating to life insurance companies

1965

101 SEC order reinstating the privilege of appearing and practicing before the Commission

102 Balance sheet classification of deferred income taxes arising from instalment sales

1966

103 The nature of the examination and certificate required by paragraph (a)(5) of Rule 206 (4)–2 under the Investment Advisers Act of 1940

104 Discontinuance of proceedings with respect to an accountant who may not have adhered to auditing standards, based on his resignation and agreement not to practice before the Commission

105 Rule 2(e) proceedings with respect to an accountant terminated following the accountant's withdrawal from practice and agreement not to practice before the Commission, the report, however, of the staff investigation being released by the Commission

106 Revision of Uniform System of Accounts for Mutual Service Companies and Subsidiary Service Companies

1967

107 Staff interpretation of and guide to computations under "net capital" Rule 15c3–1 under the 1934 Act

108 Discontinuance of proceedings with respect to an accountant who may not have adhered to generally accepted auditing standards and the SEC's minimum audit requirements, based on his resignation and agreement not to practice before the Commission

109 Similar to ASR No. 108

1968

110 Similar to ASR No. 108

111 Minor amendment to Regulation S–X regarding applicability thereof

112 Independence of accountants who examine a non-material segment of an international business

1969

113   Problems of investment company ownership of restricted securities—including disclosure problems

114   Amendment of Regulation S–X with respect to provision for Federal income taxes by registered investment companies

1970

115   Certification of financial statements where there is a question as to the appropriateness of the "going concern" concept

116   Extends the rationale of ASR 113 to documents other than prospectuses

117   Adoption of Article 11A amending Regulation S–X relating to content of statements of source and application of funds

118   Accounting for investment securities by registered investment companies

1971

119   Interpretation with respect to the computation of the ratio of earnings to fixed charges

120   Announcement of revision of Form N–1R (annual report under Investment Company Act) and the report of independent public accountants with respect to certain items in the form

121   Revision of exemption from certification of financial statements of banks filed under 1933 and 1934 Acts

122   Inclusion of unconsolidated subsidiaries and certain other persons in computation of ratio of earnings to fixed charges.

1972

123   Establishment of standing audit committees composed of outside directors.

124   Pro rata distributions of stock to shareholders.

125   Adoption of amendments to Regulation S–X.

126   Guides to and interpretations of accountant's independence.

APPENDIX B. TYPICAL TIMETABLE IN 1933 ACT REGISTRATION ENGAGEMENT

XYZ CORPORATION

Preliminary Timetable for Stock Offer to Stockholders with Stockholder Approval of Increased Authorized Shares at Annual Meeting (Not Including Blue-Sky Matters)

Feb. 15 Mail questionnaires to Directors and Officers (and 10 per cent stockholders, if any), covering various matters relating to proxy regulations of Securities Exchange Act.

Mar. 3 Board of Directors approves form of proxy and proxy statement for Annual Meeting, including resolution for increase in authorized capital stock.

Mar. 4 File preliminary copies of proxy material with Securities and Exchange Commission.

Mar. 14 Clearance by SEC of proxy material.

Mar. 18 Record date for voting at Annual Meeting.

Mar. 21 Mail notice of Annual Stockholders' Meeting and proxy material to stockholders. (Mail four copies to SEC and three copies to Stock Exchange.)

Apr. 15 Annual Stockholders' Meeting. Stockholders approve increase in authorized shares.

File charter amendment covering increase in authorized shares with state authorities.

Apr. 20 Meeting of Board of Directors to authorize:
1. Issuance of additional amount of stock to be offered initially through rights to stockholders. (Offering dates and price to be set at subsequent meeting.)
2. Preparation of registration statement (Form S–1) for filing with SEC.
3. Negotiation of underwriting agreement.

Advise Stock Exchange of proposed offer and issue press release.

Apr. 27 Distribute questionnaires to Directors and Officers covering matters relating to registration requirements.

May 5 File Form 8–K with SEC to report annual meeting results and to file a copy of the charter amendment.

May 11 Distribute proof of registration statement to Directors and Officers.

May 18 Meeting of Board of Directors to:
1. Approve registration statement and authorize filing with SEC.
2. Set record date for rights and expiration date of offer.
3. Approve form of subscription warrant.
4. Authorize transfer agent and registrar to issue and register additional shares.
5. Authorize listing of additional stock on Stock Exchange.

6. Execute powers of attorney for use in connection with registration statement.

May 19 Mail letter to stockholders announcing action of Directors and issue press release.

File registration statement with SEC.

File listing application with Stock Exchange with respect to common stock to be offered to stockholders.

May 31 Comment regarding registration statement received from SEC.

June 2 File amendment to registration statement to cover SEC comments and to reflect any material developments since filing on May 19.

Note: If only minor changes are involved, it may be practicable to clear them informally with the SEC staff at this time and to defer amending until the final amendment (see June 7).

Notify SEC in writing that an amendment will be filed on June 7 and that the Company desires to have the registration statement become effective after 3:30 p.m. on such date (after close of New York Stock Exchange).

Stock List Committee of Stock Exchange approves listing on official notice of issuance and subject to effectiveness of Form S–1.

June 7 Meeting of Board of Directors to:

1. Set offering price to stockholders.
2. Approve underwriting agreement.

Sign underwriting agreement.

File amendment to registration statement incorporating offering price.

Registration statement effective.

Notify Stock Exchange, transfer agent, registrar, and underwriters of effectiveness.

Print final prospectus and warrants.

June 8 When issued trading in rights begins (rights-on).

June 9 Ex-rights date.

June 14 Record date. (The Stock Exchange normally requires a full five-business-day interval between effective date of registration statement and record date to avoid necessity of using due bills and to avoid possibility that registration may not become effective as scheduled. In the case of underwritten offers the exchange recognizes that this interval may not be in conformity with the purposes and requirements of the underwriters, and therefore, not feasible.)

Mail letter to stockholders transmitting prospectus and subscription warrants. (Mail 25 copies of prospectus to SEC.)

Notify Stock Exchange of mailing of subscription warrants.

June 30 Expiration date for exercise of subscription warrants.

July 5 Advise underwriters of amount of unsubscribed stock. File supplement to prospectus with SEC setting forth subscription results and disposition to be made of unsubscribed stock or file a post-effective amendment if terms of offering differ from final prospectus.

Notify Stock Exchange of results of subscription and offering of unsubscribed stock by underwriters.

Underwriters offer unsubscribed stock. (Mail 25 copies of prospectus with supplement attached to SEC.)

July 7 Settlement with underwriters.

Aug. 2 File Form 8–K with SEC covering issuance of additional common shares.

APPENDIX C. EXHIBIT 5 TO 1971 REGISTRATION STATEMENT OF AMERICAN TELEPHONE AND TELEGRAPH COMPANY SHOWING THE COMPUTATION OF THE PRO FORMA RATIO OF EARNINGS TO FIXED CHARGES

AMERICAN TELEPHONE AND TELEGRAPH COMPANY AND ITS TELEPHONE SUBSIDIARIES—CONSOLIDATED

COMPUTATION OF PRO FORMA RATIO OF EARNINGS TO FIXED CHARGES
YEAR 1969

	Thousands of Dollars
1. *Earnings*	
(a) Income Before Interest Deductions	$2,900,741
(b) Federal Income Taxes	1,978,579
(c) Other Income Taxes	122,456
(d) Minority interests in net income of subsidiaries	64,117
(e) One-third of Total Rentals*	102,624
(f) Less: Interest of the companies consolidated in the income in excess of dividends of subsidiaries not consolidated	124,570
	$5,043,947
2. *Fixed Charges*	
(a) Total Interest Deductions	$ 702,043
Adjustments for:	
(i) *Securities being registered*	
Add: Annual charges on $500,000,000 Debentures assuming maximum cost of 7½%	37,500
(ii) *Issuance of securities during or after 1969*	
Add: Amount necessary to reflect 12 months' charges on securities issued during 1969—	
Northwestern Bell Tel. Co. $75,000,000 7% Debentures dated 1-1-69	204
Chesapeake & Potomac Tel. Co. $50,000,000 7% Debentures dated 2-1-69	477
New York Tel. Co. $150,000,000 7½% Bonds dated 3-1-69 ..	2,437
Chesapeake & Potomac Tel. Co. of W. Va. $40,000,000 7¼% Debentures dated 5-1-69	1,072
Illinois Bell Tel. Co. $150,000,000 8% Bonds dated 6-1-69 ..	5,784

* Excluding rentals charged to the companies consolidated by subsidiaries not consolidated.

	Thousands of Dollars
Southern Bell Tel. & Tel. Co. $150,000,000 8% Debentures dated 7-1-69	6,505
Bell Tel. Co. of Pennsylvania $100,000,000 8% Debentures dated 8-1-69	4,774
Pacific Northwest Bell Tel. Co. $75,000,000 7¾% Debentures dated 8-1-69	3,836
Southwestern Bell Tel. Co. $150,000,000 8¼% Debentures dated 9-1-69	8,795
Mountain States Tel. & Tel. Co. $100,000,000 8% Debentures dated 10-1-69	6,658
South Central Bell Tel. Co. $125,000,000 8½% Debentures dated 11-1-69	9,431
Pacific Tel. & Tel. Co. $150,000,000 9⅛% Debentures dated 12-1-69	12,924

Add: Annual charges on securities issued after 1969—

	Thousands of Dollars
Ohio Bell Tel. Co. $100,000,000 8¾% Debentures dated 1-1-70	8,759
Indiana Bell Tel. Co., Inc. $80,000,000 9% Debentures dated 2-1-70	7,176
Michigan Bell Tel. Co. $150,000,000 8⅝% Debentures dated 2-1-70	12,943
Chesapeake and Potomac Tel. Co. of Va. $75,000,000 8¾% Debentures dated 3-1-70	6,562
Pacific Tel. & Tel. Co. $150,000,000 8.65% Debentures dated 4-1-70	13,019
New York Tel. Co. $150,000,000 9¼% Bonds dated 5-15-70 .	13,858
American Tel. & Tel. Co. $1,569,325,800 8¾% Debentures dated 5-18-70	138,009
New Jersey Bell Tel. Co. $100,000,000 9.35% Debentures dated 6-1-70	9,374
Southern Bell Tel. & Tel. Co. $150,000,000 9.05% Debentures dated 7-1-70	13,618
Diamond State Tel. Co. $15,000,000 8¾% Debentures dated 7-1-70	1,315
Bell Tel. Co. of Pennsylvania $100,000,000 8⅝% Debentures dated 7-1-70	8,622
Southwestern Bell Tel. Co. $150,000,000 8¾% Debentures dated 8-1-70	13,144
New England Tel. & Tel. Co. $175,000,000 8⅝% Debentures dated 9-1-70	15,149
Pacific Northwest Bell Tel. Co. $100,000,000 8⅝% Debentures dated 10-1-70	8,632
Pacific Tel. & Tel. Co. $175,000,000 8¾% Debentures dated 10-1-70	15,368
Mountain States Tel. & Tel. Co. $150,000,000 9% Debentures dated 11-1-70	13,536
American Tel. & Tel. Co. $150,000,000 7.75% Notes dated 12-1-70	11,692
American Tel. & Tel. Co. $350,000,000 8.70% Debentures dated 12-1-70	30,555
South Central Bell Tel. Co. $150,000,000 8¼% Debentures dated 12-1-70	12,382
New York Tel. Co. $200,000,000 7¾% Bonds dated 12-15-70	15,474
Northwestern Bell Tel. Co. $150,000,000 7⅞% Debentures dated 1-1-71	11,841

	Thousands of Dollars
Southwestern Bell Tel. Co. $200,000,000 6⅞% Debentures dated 2-1-71	13,745
(iii) *Issuance of short-term securities after 1969*	
Add: 12 months' charges on $583,166,000 of notes payable (amount of estimated increase after 1969 to the date of receipt of proceeds from (i))	45,347
(iv) *Retirement of securities after 1969*	
Deduct: Annual charges on American Tel. & Tel. Co. $140,000,000 2¾% Debentures retired 12-1-70	3,927
Annual charges on American Tel. & Tel. Co. $200,000,000 2¾% Debentures retired 2-1-71	5,482
(v) *Presently proposed issuance of securities*	
Add: Annual charges on proposed issues assuming maximum cost of 7½% Wisconsin Tel. Co.—$90,000,000 Debentures	6,750
Pacific Tel. & Tel. Co.—$200,000,000 Debentures	15,000
New Jersey Bell Tel. Co.—$125,000,000 Debentures	9,375
Illinois Bell Tel. Co.—$200,000,000 Bonds	15,000
New England Tel. & Tel. Co.—$200,000,000 Debentures ..	15,000
Michigan Bell Tel. Co.—$150,000,000 Debentures	11,250
New York Tel. Co.—$150,000,000 Bonds	11,250
(vi) *Presently proposed retirement of securities*	
Deduct: Charges on notes payable outstanding during 1969 plus charges on notes payable from (iii) which notes payable in the aggregate were not in excess of proceeds from (i), (ii), and (v) excluding the portion of such proceeds obtained for the retirement of American Tel. & Tel. Co. maturing Debentures	126,683
Total Interest Deductions as adjusted	1,190,093
(b) One-third of Total Rentals*	102,624
(c) Dividends on preferred shares of a subsidiary consolidated held by minority interests	1,074
	$1,293,791
3. Ratio (1 ÷ 2)	3.90

* Excluding rentals charged to the companies consolidated by subsidiaries not consolidated.

APPENDIX C

AMERICAN TELEPHONE AND TELEGRAPH COMPANY
PARENT COMPANY (SEPARATELY)

COMPUTATION OF PRO FORMA RATIO OF EARNINGS TO FIXED CHARGES
YEAR 1969, CONTINUED

	Thousands of Dollars
1. *Earnings*	
(a) Income Before Interest Deductions	$1,943,932
(b) Federal Income Taxes	242,071
(c) Other Income Taxes	10,830
(d) One-third of Total Rentals*	17,223
	$2,214,056
2. *Fixed Charges*	
(a) Total Interest Deductions	$ 185,193
Adjustments for:	
(i) *Securities being registered*	
Add: Annual charges on $500,000,000 Debentures assuming maximum cost of 7½%	37,500
(ii) *Issuance of securities after 1969*	
Add: Annual charges on—	
$1,569,325,800 8¾% Debentures dated 5-18-70	138,009
$150,000,000 7.75% Notes dated 12-1-70	11,692
$350,000,000 8.70% Debentures dated 12-1-70	30,555
(iii) *Retirement of securities after 1969*	
Deduct: Annual charges on—	
$140,000,000 2¾% Debentures retired 12-1-70	3,927
$200,000,000 2¾% Debentures retired 2-1-71	5,482
Total Interest Deductions as adjusted	393,540
(b) One-third of Total Rentals*	17,223
	$ 410,763
3. Ratio (1 ÷ 2)	5.39

* Excluding rentals charged to the Company by subsidiaries.

INDEX

(Bold face numbers, followed by dot, refer to chapters; lightface
numbers following are pages)

A

Abandoned projects
Cost of, included in property, 3·25
Acceleration, 7·12, 16·5, 30·14
Accountants
Certificates (See "Certificates, Accountant's")
Change of
Responsibility of replaced auditor when his
certificate is included in 1933 Act filing,
12·16
Changes in
Reported in Form 8-K, 14·9
Consent (See "Consent, Accountants")
Disciplinary proceedings by SEC against (See
"Disciplinary Proceedings")
Displacement of small firms by big firms (See
"Displacement")
Employment and training of, 2·20
"Expertising declaration," 11·22
Failure to measure up to professional standards,
27·23
Familiarity with client's business, 5·51
Foreign (See "Foreign Accountants")
Functions under SEC statutes
Investment Company Act of 1940, 1·11
Public Utility Holding Company Act of 1935,
1·10
Securities Act of 1933, 1·5
Securities Exchange Act of 1934, 1·7
Trust Indenture Act of 1939, 1·11
Incompatible occupation, 26·53
Indemnity agreement between client and, 26·51
Independence of (See "Independence, Accoun-
tant's")
Investigation of new clients, 2·22
Liability of (See "Liability of Accountants")
No distinction between U. S. and foreign, 31·6
Opinions (See "Certificates, Accountant's")
Participation by small firms in SEC work (See
also "Displacement of Small Accounting Firms
by Big Firms"), 6·7
Practicing in corporate form, 28·4
Qualifications
Requirements of American Stock Exchange,
29·25
Requirements of Form X-17A-5, 25·40
Requirements of Regulation S-X. 26·18
Reports (See "Certificates, Accountant's")
Responsibility for detection of fraud (See
"Fraud")
Responsibility of
For financial representations, 2·18
Legal (See "Liability of Accountants")
SEC decisions involving, 26·23, 27·18
Selection of, proxy statements, 22·11
Suspension from SEC practice (See "Disciplinary
Proceedings")

Accounting changes (See also "Accounting Prin-
ciples Board, Opinion No. 20")
Letter from independent auditors regarding,
10·55, 15·23, 15·28
Pro forma financial statements, 21·22
Regulation S-X (Rule 3–07), 16·15
Reports to SEC
Form 7-Q, 15·26
Form 10-K, 10·55
Form 10-Q, 15·21
Accounting firms, size of, 2·22
Accounting practices (See also "Accounting Prin-
ciples"),
Changes in, 10·55, 15·23, 15·28, 16·15
Letter from auditors regarding changes in,
10·55, 15·23, 15·28
Summary of (Regulation S-X), 16·16
Accounting principles
Adjustments in interim figures, 10·13, 12·59,
13·9
Alternatives
Creation of, where none existed, 3·16
Elimination or reduction of, 3·3, 3·6–9, 3·16
Appraisals (See "Appraisals")
Asset write-up, 3·27
Balance sheet classification of deferred taxes on
instalment sales, 3·10
Balance sheet treatment of credit equivalent to
reduction in taxes, 3·10
Business combinations (See "Business Combi-
nations")
Cash basis accounting, 3·23, 11·3
Changes in, 10·55, 12·59, 15·23, 15·28, 16·15
Choice between conflicting, 26·7
Contingent payments based on profits, 4·22
Deferred compensation, 3·20
Departures from, accountant must justify, 24·5,
26·7
Depreciation (See "Depreciation")
Differences between SEC requirements and those
of good practice, elimination of, 3·10–20
Differences in, U. S. and abroad, 31·1–4, 31·11–
18
Direct labor, omission from inventory, 3·23
Disclosure as substitute for acceptable, 2·6
Disclosure of variations from requirements of
Regulation S-X, 31·42, 31·43
Dividends received from pre-acquisition surplus,
4·29
Generally accepted
Those having substantial authoritative sup-
port, 2·8
Good accounting practice
Judged by present-day standards or those at
time of transaction, 3·22
Goodwill, 7·10
Inadequacy of reserve for losses, 5·18
Inclusion in current assets of customers not
able to liquidate their accounts currently, 5·21